COLLINS
SPANISH
DICTIONARY

COLLINS SPANISH DICTIONARY

SPANISH·ENGLISH ENGLISH·SPANISH

Mike Gonzalez

First published in this edition 1992

© William Collins Sons & Co. Ltd. 1982

Latest reprint 1992

---

contributors
Margaret Tejerizo, John Forry,
Carmen Billinghurst, Liam Kane, Pat Feehan

editorial staff
Irene Lakhani

Printed in Great Britain

INTRODUCCIÓN

Quien desee leer y entender el inglés encontrará en este diccionario un extenso léxico moderno que abarca una amplia gama de locuciones de uso corriente. Igualmente encontrará, en su debido orden alfabético, las abreviaturas, las siglas, los nombres geográficos más conocidos y, además, las principales formas de verbo irregulares, donde se le referirá a las respectivas formas de base, hallándose allí la traducción.

Quien aspire comunicarse y expresarse en lengua extranjera, hallará aquí una clara y detallada explicación de las palabras básicas, empleándose un sistema de indicadores que le remitirán a la traducción más apta y le señalarán su correcto uso.

INTRODUCTION

The user whose aim is to read and understand Spanish will find a comprehensive and up-to-date wordlist including numerous phrases in current use. He will also find listed alphabetically the main irregular forms with a cross-reference to the basic form where a translation is given, as well as some of the most common abbreviations, acronyms and geographical names.

The user who wishes to communicate and to express himself in the foreign language will find clear and detailed treatment of all the basic words, with numerous indicators pointing to the appropriate translation, and helping him to use it correctly.

ABREVIATURAS

ABBREVIATIONS

adjetivo, locución adjetivo	**a**	adjective, adjectival phrase
abreviatura	**ab(b)r**	abbreviation
adverbio, locución adverbial	**ad**	adverb, adverbial phrase
administración, lengua administrativa	**ADMIN**	administration
agricultura	**AGR**	agriculture
América Latina	**AM**	Latin America
anatomía	**ANAT**	anatomy
arquitectura	**ARQ, ARCH**	architecture
astrología, astronomía	**ASTRO**	astrology, astronomy
el automóvil	**AUT(O)**	the motor car and motoring
aviación, viajes aéreos	**AVIAT**	flying, air travel
biología	**BIO(L)**	biology
botánica, flores	**BOT**	botany
inglés británico	**Brit**	British English
química	**CHEM**	chemistry
conjunción	**conj**	conjunction
lengua familiar	**col**	colloquial usage
comercio, finanzas, banca	**COM(M)**	commerce, finance, banking
construcción	**CONSTR**	building
compuesto	**cpd**	compound element
cocina	**CULIN**	cookery
determinante, artículo	**det**	determiner, article
economía	**ECON**	economics
electricidad, electrónica	**ELEC**	electricity, electronics
enseñanza, sistema escolar y universitario	**ESCOL**	schooling, schools and universities
especialmente	**esp**	especially
exclamación, interjección	**excl**	exclamation, interjection
femenino	**f**	feminine
lengua familiar	**fam**	colloquial usage
ferrocarril	**FERRO**	railways
uso figurado	**fig**	figurative use
fotografía	**FOTO**	photography
(verbo inglés) del cual la partícula es inseparable	**fus**	(phrasal verb) where the particle is inseparable
generalmente	**gen**	generally
geografía, geología	**GEO**	geography, geology
geometría	**GEOM**	geometry
invariable	**inv**	invariable
irregular	**irg**	irregular
lo jurídico	**JUR**	law
gramática, lingüística	**LING**	grammar, linguistics
masculino	**m**	masculine

iv

matemáticas	**MAT(H)**	mathematics
medicina	**MED**	medical term, medicine
masculino/feminino	**m/f**	masculine/feminine
lo militar, ejército	**MIL**	military matters
música	**MUS**	music
sustantivo, nombre	**n**	noun
navegación, náutica	**NAUT**	sailing, navigation
sustantivo numérico	**num**	numeral noun
complemento	**obj**	(grammatical) object
	o.s.	oneself
peyorativo	**pey, pej**	derogatory, pejorative
fotografía	**PHOT**	photography
fisiología	**PHYSIOL**	physiology
plural	**pl**	plural
política	**POL**	politics
participio de pasado	**pp**	past participle
prefijo	**pref**	prefix
preposición	**prep**	preposition
pronombre	**pron**	pronoun
psicología, psiquiatría	**PSICO, PSYCH**	psychology, psychiatry
tiempo pasado	**pt**	past tense
sustantivo no empleado en el plural	**q**	collective (uncountable) noun, not used in plural
ferrocarril	**RAIL**	railways
religión, lo eclesiástico	**REL**	religion, church service
	sb	somebody
escolar, universitario	**SCOL**	schools, universities
singular	**sg**	singular
	sth	something
sujeto	**su(b)j**	(grammatical) subject
sufijo	**suff**	suffix
tauromaquia	**TAUR**	bullfighting
técnica, tecnología	**TEC(H)**	technical term, technology
telecomunicaciones	**TELEC, TEL**	telecommunications
televisión	**TV**	television
imprenta, tipografía	**TYP**	typography, printing
inglés norteamericano	**US**	American English
verbo	**vb**	verb
verbo intransitivo	**vi**	intransitive verb
verbo pronominal	**vr**	reflexive verb
verbo transitivo	**vt**	transitive verb
zoología, animales	**ZOOL**	zoology
marca registrada	®	registered trademark
indica un equivalente cultural	≈	introduces a cultural equivalent

SPANISH PRONUNCIATION

Consonants

c	[k]	caja	c before a, o or u is pronounced as in cat
ce, ci	[θe, θi]	cero cielo	c before e or i is pronounced as in thin
ch	[tʃ]	chiste	ch is pronounced as ch in chair
d	[d, ð]	danés ciudad	at the beginning of a phrase or after l or n, d is pronounced as in English. In any other position it is pronounced like th in the
g	[g, ɤ]	gafas paga	g before a, o or u is pronounced as in gap, if at the beginning of a phrase or after n. In other positions the sound is softened
ge, gi	[xe, xi]	gente girar	g before e or i is pronounced similar to ch in Scottish loch
h		haber	h is always silent in Spanish
j	[x]	jugar	j is pronounced similar to ch in Scottish loch
ll	[ʎ]	talle	ll is pronounced like the lli in million
ñ	[ɲ]	niño	ñ is pronounced like the ni in onion
q	[k]	que	q is pronounced as k in king
r, rr	[r, rr]	quitar garra	r is always pronounced in Spanish, unlike the silent r in dancer. rr is trilled, like a Scottish r
s	[s]	quizás isla	s is usually pronounced as in pass, but before b, d, g, l, m or n it is pronounced as in rose
v	[b, ß]	vía dividir	v is pronounced something like b. At the beginning of a phrase or after m or n it is pronounced as b in boy. In any other position the sound is softened
z	[θ]	tenaz	z is pronounced as th in thin

b, f, k, l, m, n, p, t and x are pronounced as in English.

Vowels

[a]	p*a*ta	not as long as *a* in f*a*r. When followed by a consonant in the same syllable (i.e. in a closed syllable), as in am*a*nte, the *a* is short, as in b*a*t
[e]	m*e*	like *e* in th*ey*. In a closed syllable, as in g*e*nte, the *e* is short as in p*e*t
[i:]	p*i*no	as in m*ea*n or mach*i*ne
[o]	l*o*	as in l*o*cal. In a closed syllable, as in c*o*ntrol, the *o* is short as in c*o*t
[u:]	l*u*nes	as in r*u*le. It is silent after *q*, and in *gue*, *gui*, unless marked *güe*, *güi* e.g. anti*güe*dad

Diphthongs

ai, ay	b*ai*le	as *i* in r*i*de
au	*au*to	as *ou* in sh*ou*t
ei, ey	bu*ey*	as *ey* in gr*ey*
eu	d*eu*da	both elements pronounced independently [e]+[u:]
oi, oy	h*oy*	as *oy* in t*oy*

Stress

The rules of stress in Spanish are as follows:
(a)   when a word ends in a vowel or in *n* or *s*, the second last syllable is stressed: pat*a*ta, pat*a*tas, c*o*me, c*o*men
(b)   when a word ends in a consonant other than *n* or *s*, the stress falls on the last syllable: par*e*d, habl*a*r
(c)   when the rules set out in a and b are not applied, an acute accent appears over the stressed vowel: com*ú*n, geograf*í*a, ingl*é*s

In the phonetic transcription, the symbol ['] precedes the syllable on which the stress falls.

PRONUNCIACIÓN INGLESA

Vocales y diptongos

	Ejemplo inglés	Ejemplo español/explicación
ɑ:	father	Entre *a* de *padre* y *o* de *noche*
ʌ	but, come	*a* muy breve
æ	man, cat	Se mantienen los labios en la posición de *e* en *pena* y luego se pronuncia el sonido *a*
ə	father, ago	Sonido indistinto parecido a una *e* u *o* casi mudas
ə:	bird, heard	Entre *e* abierta, y *o* cerrada, sonido alargado
ɛ	get, bed	como en *perro*
ɪ	it, big	Más breve que en *si*
i:	tea, see	Como en *fino*
ɔ	hot, wash	Como en *torre*
ɔ:	saw, all	Como en *por*
u	put, book	Sonido breve, más cerrado que *burro*
u:	too, you	Sonido largo, como en *uno*
aɪ	fly, high	Como en *fraile*
au	how, house	Como en *pausa*
ɛə	there, bear	Casi como en *vea*, pero el sonido *a* se mezcla con el indistinto [ə]
eɪ	day, obey	*e* cerrada seguida por una *i* débil
ɪə	here, hear	Como en *manía*, mezclándose el sonido *a* con el indistinto [ə]
əu	go, note	[ə] seguido por una breve *u*
ɔɪ	boy, oil	Como en *voy*
uə	poor, sure	*u* bastante larga más el sonido indistinto [ə]

Consonantes

	Ejemplo inglés	Ejemplo español/explicación
d	men*d*e*d*	Como en con*d*e, an*d*ar
g	*g*o, *g*et, bi*g*	Como en *g*rande, *g*ol
dʒ	*g*in, *j*u*dg*e	Como en la *ll* andaluza y en *G*eneralitat (catalán)
ŋ	si*ng*	Como en ví*n*culo
h	*h*ouse, *h*e	Como la jota hispanoamericana
j	*y*oung, *y*es	Como en *y*a
k	*c*ome, mo*ck*	Como en *c*aña, Es*c*ocia
r	*r*ed, t*r*ead	Se pronuncia con la punta de la lengua hacia atrás y sin hacerla vibrar
s	*s*and, ye*s*	Como en ca*s*a, *s*esión
z	ro*s*e, *z*ebra	Como en de*s*de, mi*s*mo
ʃ	*sh*e, ma*ch*ine	Como en *ch*ambre (francés), ro*x*o (portugués)
tʃ	*ch*in, ri*ch*	Como en *ch*ocolate
v	*v*alley	Como en f, pero se retiran los dientes superiores vibrándolos contra el labio inferior
w	*w*ater, *wh*ich	Como en la *u* de h*u*evo, p*u*ede
ʒ	vision	Como en *j*ournal (francés)
θ	*th*ink, my*th*	Como en re*c*eta, *z*apato
ð	*th*is, *th*e	Como en la *d* de habla*d*o, verda*d*

b, p, f, m, n, l, t iguales que en español
El signo * indica que la r final escrita apenas se pronuncia en inglés británico cuando la palabra siguiente empieza con vocal. El signo ['] indica la sílaba acentuada.

ix

ESPAÑOL - INGLÉS
SPANISH - ENGLISH

A

a [a] *prep* (*a* + *el* = *al*) (*lugar*) at, in, on; (*dirección*) to; (*destino*) to, towards; (*tiempo*) at; ~ **la derecha/ izquierda** on the right/left; **al lado de** beside, at the side of; **subir** ~ **un avión/tren** to get on *or* board a plane/train; **hablar** ~ **larga distancia** to speak long distance; ~ **las cuatro** at four o'clock; *¿*~ **qué hora?** at what time?; ~ **los 30 años** at 30 years of age; **al día siguiente** the next day; ~ **eso de las cuatro** at about four o'clock; **al poco tiempo** a short time later; **al verlo yo** when I saw it; (*manera*): **hacerlo** ~ **la fuerza** to do it by force; **ir** ~ **caballo/pie** to go on horseback/foot; (*evaluación*): **poco** ~ **poco** little by little; **de dos** ~ **tres** from two to three; **ocho horas al día** eight hours a *or* per day; ~ **50 ptas el kilo** 50 pesetas a kilo; (*con verbo*): **empezó** ~ **llover** it started raining; **enseñar** ~ **leer** to teach to read; **voy** ~ **llevarlo** I am going to carry it; (*complemento de objeto*): **quiero** ~ **mis padres** (*not translated*) I love my parents; (*complemento circunstancial*): **cercano** ~ near (to); **por miedo** ~ out of fear of; (*frases elípticas*): **¡**~ **comer!** let's eat!; *¿*~ **qué viene eso?** what's the meaning of this?; ~ **ver** let's see.

abacero, a [aβa'θero, a] *nm/f* grocer.

abad, esa [a'βað, 'ðesa] *nm/f* abbot/abbess; ~**ía** *nf* abbey.

abajo [a'βaxo] *ad* (*situación*) down, below, underneath; (*en casa*) downstairs; (*dirección*) down, downwards; ~ **de** *prep* below, under; **el piso de** ~ the downstairs flat; **la parte de** ~ the lower part; **¡**~ **el gobierno!** down with the government!; **cuesta/río** ~ downhill/downstream; **de arriba** ~ from top to bottom; **el** ~ **firmante** the undersigned; **más** ~ lower *or* further down; **echar** ~ to bring down.

abalanzar [aβalan'θar] *vt* to weigh; (*equilibrar*) to balance; (*arrojar*) to hurl; ~**se** *vr*: ~**se sobre** *o* **contra** to throw o.s. at.

abandonado, a [aβando'naðo, a] *a* derelict; (*desatendido*) abandoned; (*desierto*) deserted; (*descuidado*) neglected.

abandonar [aβando'nar] *vt* (*dejar*) to leave, abandon, desert; (*descuidar*) to neglect; (*ceder, dejar de*) to give up; ~**se** *vr*: ~**se a** to abandon o.s. to.

abandono [aβan'dono] *nm* (*acto*) desertion, abandonment; (*estado*)

abandon, neglect; (*renuncia*) withdrawal, retirement; **perdió por** ~ he lost by default.

abanicar [aβani'kar] *vt* to fan; **abanico** *nm* fan; (*NAUT*) derrick.

abaratar [aβara'tar] *vt* to lower (the price of) // *vi*, ~**se** *vr* to go *or* come down in price.

abarcar [aβar'kar] *vt* to include, embrace; (*AM*) to monopolize.

abarrotar [aβarro'tar] *vt* to bar; (*NAUT*) to stow; (*fig*) to overstock.

abarrote [aβa'rrote] *nm* packing; ~**s** *nmpl* (*AM*) groceries, provisions; ~**ro, a** *nm/f* (*AM*) grocer.

abastecer [aβaste'θer] *vt* to supply; **abastecimiento** *nm* supply; (*suministrar*) supplying.

abasto [a'βasto] *nm* supply; (*abundancia*) abundance; **dar** ~ **con** to manage to finish.

abatido, a [aβa'tiðo, a] *a* dejected, downcast.

abatimiento [aβati'mjento] *nm* (*acto*) demolition; (*moral*) dejection, depression.

abatir [aβa'tir] *vt* (*muro*) to demolish; (*pájaro*) to shoot, bring down; (*fig*) to depress; (*humillar*) to humiliate // *vi* to go off course; ~**se** *vr* to be depressed; ~**se sobre** to swoop *or* pounce on.

abdicación [aβðika'θjon] *nf* abdication; **abdicar** *vi* to abdicate.

abdomen [aβ'ðomen] *nm* abdomen.

abecedario [aβeθe'ðarjo] *nm* alphabet; (*libro*) spelling book.

abedul [aβe'ðul] *nm* birch.

abeja [a'βexa] *nf* bee.

aberración [aβerra'θjon] *nf* aberration.

abertura [aβer'tura] *nf* opening, gap; (*fig*) openness.

abeto [a'βeto] *nm* fir.

abierto, a [a'βjerto, a] *pp de* **abrir** // *a* open; (*AM*) generous.

abigarrado, a [aβiɣa'rraðo, a] *a* multi-coloured.

abismar [aβis'mar] *vt* to humble, cast down; ~**se** *vr* to sink; ~**se en** (*fig*) to be plunged into.

abismo [a'βismo] *nm* abyss.

abjurar [aβxu'rar] *vt*, *vi* to abjure, forswear.

ablandar [aβlan'dar] *vt* to soften up; (*AUTO*) to run in // *vi*, ~**se** *vr* to grow softer.

ablución [aβlu'θjon] *nf* ablution.

abnegación [aβneɣa'θjon] *nf* self-denial; **abnegarse** *vr* to act unselfishly.

abobado, a [aβo'βaðo, a] a silly.
abobar [aβo'βar] vt to daze.
abocar [aβo'kar] vt to seize in one's mouth; ～**se** vr to approach.
abochornar [aβotʃor'nar] vt to embarrass; ～**se** vr to get flustered; (BOT) to wilt.
abofetear [aβofete'ar] vt to slap (in the face).
abogacía [aβoxa'θia] nf legal profession; (ejercicio) practice of the law; **abogado** nm lawyer.
abogar [aβo'xar] vi: ～ **por** to plead for; (fig) to advocate.
abolengo [aβo'lengo] nm ancestry, lineage.
abolición [aβoli'θjon] nf abolition.
abolir [aβo'lir] vt to abolish; (cancelar) to cancel.
abolladura [aβoʎa'ðura] nf dent; (chichón, choque) bump; **abollar** vt to dent; to raise a bump on.
abominación [aβomina'θjon] nf abomination.
abonado, a [aβo'naðo, a] a (deuda) paid // nm/f subscriber.
abonar [aβo'nar] vt (deuda) to settle; (terreno) to fertilize; (idea) to endorse; ～**se** vr to subscribe; **abono** nm payment; fertilizer; subscription.
abordar [aβor'ðar] vt to board; (fig) to broach.
aborigen [aβo'rixen] nm aborigine.
aborrecer [aβorre'θer] vt to hate, loathe; **aborrecible** a hateful, loathsome.
abortar [aβor'tar] vi (malparir) to have a miscarriage; (deliberadamente) to have an abortion; **hacerse** ～ to have an abortion; **aborto** nm miscarriage; abortion.
abotonar [aβoto'nar] vt to button (up), do up // vi to bud.
abovedado, a [aβoβe'ðaðo, a] a vaulted, domed.
abrasar [aβra'sar] vt to burn (up); (AGR) to dry up, parch.
abrazar [aβra'θar] vt to embrace.
abrazo [a'βraθo] nm embrace, hug; **un** ～ (en carta) with best wishes.
abrelatas [aβre'latas] nm inv tin opener.
abreviar [aβre'βjar] vt to abbreviate; (texto) to abridge; (plazo) to reduce; **abreviatura** nf abbreviation.
abrigar [aβri'xar] vt (proteger) to shelter; (suj: ropa) to keep warm; (fig) to cherish; **abrigo** nm shelter; (apoyo) support; (prenda) coat, overcoat.
abril [a'βril] nm April.
abrir [a'βrir] vt to open (up) // vi to open; ～**se** vr to open (up); (extenderse) to open out; (cielo) to clear; ～**se paso** to find or force a way through.
abrochar [aβro'tʃar] vt (vestido) to button (up); (AM) to staple; (zapato) to buckle; (atar) to lace up.
abrumar [aβru'mar] vt to overwhelm; (sobrecargar) to weigh down; (agotar) to wear out; ～ **se** vr to become foggy.

abrupto, a [a'βrupto, a] a abrupt; (empinado) steep.
absceso [aβs'θeso] nm abscess.
absolución [aβsolu'θjon] nf (REL) absolution; (JUR) pardon; (: de acusado) acquittal.
absoluto, a [aβso'luto, a] a absolute; **en** ～ ad in no way, not at all.
absolver [aβsol'βer] vt to absolve; (JUR) to pardon; (: acusado) to acquit.
absorber [aβsor'βer] vt to absorb; (embeber) to soak up.
absorción [aβsor'θjon] nf absorption.
absorto, a [aβ'sorto, a] pp de **absorber** // a absorbed, engrossed.
abstemio, a [aβs'temjo, a] a teetotal.
abstención [aβsten'θjon] nf abstention; **abstenerse** vr: **abstenerse de** to abstain or refrain from.
abstinencia [aβsti'nenθja] nf abstinence; (ayuno) fasting.
abstracción [aβstrak'θjon] nf abstraction; (despiste) absent-mindedness; ～ **hecha de** leaving aside.
abstraer [aβstra'er] vt to abstract // vi: ～ **de** to leave aside; ～**se** vr to be/become absorbed.
abstraído, a [aβstra'iðo, a] a preoccupied; (despistado) absent-minded.
absuelto [aβ'swelto] pp de **absolver.**
absurdo, a [aβ'surðo, a] a absurd.
abuelo, a [a'βwelo, a] nm/f grandfather/mother.
abulia [a'βulja] nf spinelessness, weakness.
abultado, a [aβul'taðo, a] a bulky.
abultar [aβul'tar] vt to enlarge; (aumentar) to increase; (fig) to exaggerate // vi to be bulky.
abundancia [aβun'danθja] nf abundance, plenty; **abundante** a abundant, plentiful; **abundar** vi to abound, be plentiful.
aburrido, a [aβu'rriðo, a] a (hastiado) bored; (que aburre) boring; **aburrimiento** nm boredom, tedium; **aburrir** vt to bore; **aburrirse** vr to be bored, get bored.
abusar [aβu'sar] vi to go too far; ～ **de** to abuse; **abuso** nm imposition; abuse.
abyecto, a [aβ'jekto, a] a wretched, abject.
A.C. abr de **Año de Cristo** A.D. (Anno Domini).
a/c abr de **al cuidado de** c/o (care of).
acá [a'ka] ad (lugar) here; (tiempo) now.
acabado, a [aka'βaðo, a] a finished, complete; (perfecto) perfect; (agotado) worn out; (fig) masterly // nm finish.
acabar [aka'βar] vt (llevar a su fin) to finish, complete; (llegar al final de) to finish, conclude; (perfeccionar) to complete; (consumir) to use up; (rematar) to finish off // vi to finish, end, come to an end; ～ **con** to put an end to; ～ **de llegar** to have just arrived; ～ **por** to end (up) by; ～**se** vr to finish, stop; (terminarse) to be over; (agotarse) to run out; ¡**se acabó!** that's enough!; it's all over!

academia [aka'ðemja] *nf* academy; **académico, a** *a* academic.

acaecer [akae'θer] *vi* to happen, occur; **acaecimiento** *nm* occurrence, happening.

acalorar [akalo'rar] *vt* to heat; (*fig*) to inflame; ~**se** *vr* (*fig*) to get heated.

acampar [akam'par] *vi* to camp.

acanalar [akana'lar] *vt* to groove; (*ondular*) to corrugate.

acantilado, a [akanti'laðo, a] *a* steep, sheer // *nm* cliff.

acaparar [akapa'rar] *vt* to monopolize; (*acumular*) to hoard.

acariciar [akari'θjar] *vt* to caress; (*fig*) to cherish.

acarrear [akarre'ar] *vt* to transport; (*fig*) to cause, result in; **acarreo** *nm* transport, haulage; (*precio*) carriage.

acaso [a'kaso] *ad* perhaps, maybe // *nm* chance; **por si** ~ just in case; **si** ~ in case; **al** ~ at random.

acatamiento [akata'mjento] *nm* respect; (*reverencia*) reverence; (*deferencia*) deference; **acatar** *vt* to respect; to revere; (*obedecer*) to obey.

acatarrarse [akata'rrarse] *vr* to catch a cold.

acaudalado, a [akauða'laðo, a] *a* well-off; **acaudalar** *vt* to accumulate.

acaudillar [akauði'ʎar] *vt* to lead, command.

acceder [akθe'ðer] *vi* to accede, agree.

accesible [akθe'siβle] *a* accessible.

acceso [ak'θeso] *nm* access, entry; (*camino*) access road; (MED) attack, fit.

accesorio, a [akθe'sorjo, a] *a*, *nm* accessory.

accidentado, a [akθiðen'taðo, a] *a* uneven; (*áspero*) rough; (*montañoso*) hilly; (*azaroso*) eventful // *nm/f* injured person.

accidental [akθiðen'tal] *a* accidental; **accidentarse** *vr* to have an accident.

accidente [akθi'ðente] *nm* accident; (MED) faint; ~**s** *nmpl* unevenness *sg*, roughness *sg*.

acción [ak'θjon] *nf* action; (*acto*) action, act, deed; (COM) share; (JUR) action, lawsuit; ~ **ordinaria/preferente** ordinary/preference share; **accionar** *vt* to work, operate // *vi* to gesticulate.

accionista [akθjo'nista] *nm/f* shareholder.

acebo [a'θeβo] *nm* holly; (*árbol*) holly tree.

acechanza [aθe'tʃanθa] *nf* = acecho.

acechar [aθe'tʃar] *vt* to spy on; (*aguardar*) to lie in wait for; **acecho** *nm* spying, watching; ambush.

acedía [aθe'ðia] *nf* acidity; (MED) heartburn; (*fig*) sourness.

aceitar [aθei'tar] *vt* to oil, lubricate; **aceite** *nm* oil; (*de oliva*) olive oil; **aceitera** *nf* oilcan; **aceitoso, a** *a* oily.

aceituna [aθei'tuna] *nf* olive.

acelerar [aθele'rar] *vt* to accelerate.

acento [a'θento] *nm* accent; (*acentuación*) stress; **acentuar** *vt* to accent; to stress; (*fig*) to accentuate.

acepción [aθep'θjon] *nf* meaning; (*preferencia*) preference.

acepillar [aθepi'ʎar] *vt* to brush; (*alisar*) to plane.

aceptación [aθepta'θjon] *nf* acceptance; (*aprobación*) approval; **aceptar** *vt* to accept; to approve.

acequia [a'θekja] *nf* irrigation ditch.

acera [a'θera] *nf* pavement.

acerado, a [aθe'raðo, a] *a* steel; (*afilado*) sharp; (*fig: duro*) steely; (: *mordaz*) biting.

acerbo, a [a'θerβo, a] *a* bitter; (*fig*) harsh.

acerca [a'θerka]: ~ **de** *ad* about, concerning.

acercar [aθer'kar] *vt* to bring *or* move nearer; ~**se** *vr* to approach, come near.

acero [a'θero] *nm* steel.

acérrimo, a [a'θerrimo, a] *a* out-and-out, staunch.

acertado, a [aθer'taðo, a] *a* correct; (*apropiado*) apt; (*sensato*) sensible.

acertar [aθer'tar] *vt* (*dar en: el blanco*) to hit; (*llegar a encontrar*) to get right; (*adivinar*) to guess; (*alcanzar*) to achieve // *vi* to get it right, be right; ~ **a** to manage to; ~ **con** to happen on.

acertijo [aθer'tixo] *nm* riddle, puzzle.

acervo [a'θerβo] *nm* heap; ~ **común** undivided estate.

acicalar [aθika'lar] *vt* to polish; (*adornar*) to bedeck; ~**se** *vr* to smarten o.s. up.

acicate [aθi'kate] *nm* spur.

acidez [aθi'ðeθ] *nf* acidity.

ácido, a ['aθiðo, a] *a* sour, acid // *nm* acid.

acierto [a'θjerto] *nm* success; (*buen paso*) wise move; (*solución*) solution; (*habilidad*) skill, ability.

aclamación [aklama'θjon] *nf* acclamation; (*aplausos*) applause; **aclamar** *vt* to acclaim; to applaud.

aclaración [aklara'θjon] *nf* rinsing, rinse; (*clasificación*) classification.

aclarar [akla'rar] *vt* to clarify, explain; (*ropa*) to rinse // *vi* to clear up; ~**se** *vr*: ~ **la garganta** to clear one's throat.

aclimatación [aklimata'θjon] *nf* acclimatization; **aclimatar** *vt* to acclimatize; **aclimatarse** *vr* to become acclimatized.

acobardar [akoβar'ðar] *vt* to daunt, intimidate.

acodarse [ako'ðarse] *vr*: ~ **en** to lean on.

acogedor, a [akoxe'ðor, a] *a* welcoming; (*hospitalario*) hospitable; **acoger** *vt* to welcome; (*abrigar*) to shelter; **acogerse** *vr* to take refuge; **acogida** *nf* reception; refuge.

acolchar [akol'tʃar] *vt* to pad; (*tapizar*) to upholster; (*fig*) to cushion.

acometer [akome'ter] *vt* to attack; (*emprender*) to undertake; **acometida** *nf* attack, assault.

acomodadizo, a [akomoða'ðiθo, a] *a* obliging, acquiescent.

acomodado, a [akomo'ðaðo, a] a suitable; (*precio*) moderate; (*persona*) well-to-do.

acomodador, a [akomoða'ðor, a] *nm/f* usher/ette.

acomodar [akomo'ðar] *vt* to adjust; (*alojar*) to accommodate; (*convenir*) to suit; (*reparar*) to repair; (*reconciliar*) to reconcile // *vi* to suit, be suitable; ~**se** *vr* to conform; (*instalarse*) to install o.s.; (*adaptarse*) to adapt o.s.

acomodo [ako'moðo] *nm* arrangement; (*puesto*) post.

acompañar [akompa'ɲar] *vt* to accompany; (*documentos*) to enclose.

acondicionar [akondiθjo'nar] *vt* to arrange, prepare; (*determinar*) to condition.

acongojar [akongo'xar] *vt* to distress, grieve.

aconsejar [akonse'xar] *vt* to advise, counsel; ~**se** *vr*: ~**se con** to consult.

acontecer [akonte'θer] *vi* to happen, occur; **acontecimiento** *nm* event.

acopio [a'kopjo] *nm* store, stock; (*asamblea*) gathering.

acoplamiento [akopla'mjento] *nm* coupling, joint; **acoplar** *vt* to fit, couple; (*unir*) to connect.

acorazado, a [akora'θaðo, a] a armour-plated, armoured // *nm* battleship.

acordar [akor'ðar] *vt* (*resolver*) to agree, resolve; (*recordar*) to remind; (*MUS*) to tune; ~**se** *vr* to agree; ~**se (de)** to remember; **acorde** a in agreement; (*MUS*) harmonious // *nm* chord.

acordeón [akorðe'on] *nm* accordion.

acordonado, a [akorðo'naðo, a] a cordoned-off.

acorralar [akorra'lar] *vt* to round up, corral.

acortar [akor'tar] *vt* to shorten; (*duración*) to cut short; (*cantidad*) to reduce; ~**se** *vr* to become shorter.

acosar [ako'sar] *vt* to pursue relentlessly; (*fig*) to hound, pester.

acostar [akos'tar] *vt* (*en cama*) to put to bed; (*en suelo*) to lay down; (*barco*) to bring alongside; ~**se** *vr* to go to bed; to lie down.

acostumbrar [akostum'brar] *vt*: ~ **a uno a** to accustom sb to // *vi*: ~ **a** to be used to; ~**se** *vr*: ~**se a** to get used to.

acotación [akota'θjon] *nf* marginal note; (*GEO*) elevation mark; (*de límite*) boundary mark; (*TEATRO*) stage direction.

acre ['akre] a sharp, bitter; (*fig*) biting // *nm* acre.

acrecentar [akreθen'tar] *vt* to increase, augment.

acreditar [akreði'tar] *vt* (*garantizar*) to vouch for, guarantee; (*autorizar*) to authorize; (*dar prueba de*) to prove; (*COM*: *abonar*) to credit; (*embajador*) to accredit; ~**se** *vr* to become famous.

acreedor, a [akree'ðor, a] a: ~ **a** worthy of // *nm/f* creditor.

acribillar [akriβi'ʎar] *vt*: ~ **a balazos** to riddle with bullets.

acrimonia [akri'monja], **acritud** [akri'tuð] *nf* acrimony.

acta ['akta] *nf* certificate; (*de comisión*) minutes *pl*, record; ~ **de nacimiento/matrimonial** birth/marriage certificate; ~ **notarial** affidavit.

actitud [akti'tuð] *nf* attitude; (*postura*) posture.

activar [akti'βar] *vt* to activate; (*acelerar*) to expedite.

actividad [aktiβi'ðað] *nf* activity.

activo, a [ak'tiβo, a] a active; (*vivo*) lively // *nm* assets *pl*.

acto ['akto] *nm* act, action; (*ceremonia*) ceremony; (*TEATRO*) act; **en el** ~ immediately.

actor [ak'tor] *nm* actor; (*JUR*) plaintiff.

actora [ak'tora] a: **parte** ~ prosecution; (*demandante*) plaintiff.

actriz [ak'triθ] *nf* actress.

actuación [aktwa'θjon] *nf* action; (*comportamiento*) conduct, behaviour; (*JUR*) proceedings *pl*; (*desempeño*) performance.

actual [ak'twal] a present(-day), current; ~**idad** *nf* present, present time; ~**idades** *nfpl* news *sg*; (*película, nodo*) newsreel *sg*; **en la** ~**idad** nowadays, at the present time.

actualizar [aktwali'θar] *vt* to update, modernize.

actualmente [aktwal'mente] ad now, nowadays, at present.

actuar [ak'twar] *vi* (*obrar*) to work, operate; (*actor*) to act, perform // *vt* to work, operate; ~ **de** to act as.

actuario [ak'twarjo] *nm* clerk; (*COM*) actuary.

acuarela [akwa'rela] *nf* watercolour.

acuario [a'kwarjo] *nm* aquarium; **A**~ (*ASTRO*) Aquarius.

acuático, a [a'kwatiko, a] a aquatic.

acuciar [aku'θjar] *vt* to urge on.

acuclillarse [akukli'ʎarse] *vr* to crouch down.

acudir [aku'ðir] *vi* to come along, turn up; ~ **a** to turn to; ~ **en ayuda de** to go to the aid of.

acuerdo etc vb ver **acordar** // [a'kwerðo] *nm* agreement; ¡**de** ~! agreed!; **de** ~ **con** (*persona*) in agreement with; (*acción, documento*) in accordance with.

acumulador [akumula'ðor] *nm* storage battery; **acumular** *vt* to accumulate, collect.

acuñar [aku'ɲar] *vi* (*moneda*) to coin, mint; (*poner cuñas*) to wedge.

acuoso, a [a'kwoso, a] a watery.

acurrucarse [akurru'karse] *vr* to crouch; (*ovillarse*) to curl up.

acusación [akusa'θjon] *nf* accusation; **acusar** *vt* to accuse; (*revelar*) to reveal; (*denunciar*) to denounce.

acuse [a'kuse] *nm*: ~ **de recibo**

acknowledgement of receipt.
acústico, a [a'kustiko, a] *a* acoustic // *nm* hearing aid.
achacar [atʃa'kar] *vt* to attribute.
achacoso, a [atʃa'koso, a] *a* sickly.
achaque [a'tʃake] *nm* ailment.
achicar [atʃi'kar] *vt* to reduce; (*humillar*) to humiliate; (*NAUT*) to bale out.
achicoria [atʃi'korja] *nf* chicory.
achicharrar [atʃitʃa'rrar] *vt* to scorch, burn.
adagio [a'ðaxjo] *nm* adage; (*MUS*) adagio.
adaptación [aðapta'θjon] *nf* adaptation; **adaptar** *vt* to adapt; (*acomodar*) to fit.
a. de C. *abr* = **a. de J.C.**
A. de C. *abr* = **A.C.**
adecuado, a [aðe'kwaðo, a] *a* adequate; (*apto*) suitable; (*oportuno*) appropriate; **adecuar** *vt* to adapt; to make suitable.
a. de J.C. *abr de* **antes de Jesucristo** B.C. (before Christ).
adelantado, a [aðelan'taðo, a] *a* advanced; (*reloj*) fast; **pagar por ~** to pay in advance; **adelantamiento** *nm* advance, advancement; (*AUTO*) overtaking; (*progreso*) progress.
adelantar [aðelan'tar] *vt* to move forward; (*avanzar*) to advance; (*acelerar*) to speed up // *vi*, **~se** *vr* to go forward, advance; (*AUTO*) to overtake.
adelante [aðe'lante] *ad* forward(s), onward(s), ahead // *excl* come in!; **de hoy en ~** from now on; **más ~** later on; (*más allá*) further on.
adelanto [aðe'lanto] *nm* advance; (*mejora*) improvement; (*progreso*) progress.
adelgazar [aðelxa'θar] *vt* to thin (down); (*afilar*) to taper // *vi*, **~ se** *vr* to grow thin.
ademán [aðe'man] *nm* gesture; **ademanes** *nmpl* manners; **en ~ de** as if to.
además [aðe'mas] *ad* besides; (*por otra parte*) moreover; (*también*) also; **~ de** besides, in addition to.
adentro [a'ðentro] *ad* inside, in; **mar ~** out at sea; **tierra ~** inland.
adepto, a [a'ðepto, a] *nm/f* supporter.
aderezar [aðere'θar] *vt* to prepare; (*persona, ensalada*) to dress; (*comida*) to season; **~se** *vr* to dress up; **aderezo** *nm* preparation; dressing; seasoning.
adeudar [aðeu'ðar] *vt* to owe // *vi* to become related by marriage; **~se** *vr* to run into debt.
adherirse [aðe'rirse] *vr*: **~ a** to adhere to.
adhesión [aðe'sjon] *nf* adhesion; (*fig*) adherence.
adición [aði'θjon] *nf* addition.
adicionar [aðiθjo'nar] *vt* to add.
adicto, a [a'ðikto, a] *a*: **~ a** given to; (*dedicado*) devoted to // *nm/f* supporter, follower.
adiestrar [aðjes'trar] *vt* to train, teach; (*conducir*) to guide, lead; **~se** *vr* to practise; (*enseñarse*) to train o.s.

adinerado, a [aðine'raðo, a] *a* wealthy.
adiós [a'ðjos] *excl* (*para despedirse*) goodbye!, cheerio!; (*para saludar*) hello!
aditivo [aði'tiβo] *nm* additive.
adivinanza [aðiβi'nanθa] *nf* riddle; **adivinar** *vt* to prophesy; (*conjeturar*) to guess; **adivino, a** *nm/f* fortune-teller.
adj *a abr de* **adjunto** encl. (enclosed).
adjetivo [aðxe'tiβo] *nm* adjective.
adjudicación [aðxuðika'θjon] *nf* award; **adjudicar** *vt* to award; **adjudicarse** *vr*: **adjudicarse algo** to appropriate sth.
adjuntar [aðxun'tar] *vt* to attach, enclose; **adjunto, a** *a* attached, enclosed // *nm/f* assistant.
administración [aðministra'θjon] *nf* administration; (*dirección*) management; **administrador, a** *nm/f* administrator; manager/ess.
administrar [aðminis'trar] *vt* to administer; **administrativo, a** *a a* administrative.
admirable [aðmi'raβle] *a* admirable; **admiración** *nf* admiration; (*asombro*) wonder; (*LING*) exclamation mark; **admirar** *vt* to admire; (*extrañar*) to surprise; **admirarse** *vr* to be surprised.
admisible [aðmi'siβle] *a* admissible.
admitir [aðmi'tir] *vt* to admit; (*aceptar*) to accept.
admonición [aðmoni'θjon] *nf* warning.
adobe [a'ðoβe] *nm* adobe, sun-dried brick.
adolecer [aðole'θer] *vi* to be ill, fall ill; **~ de** to suffer from.
adolescente [aðoles'θente] *nm/f* adolescent.
adonde [a'ðonðe] *conj* (to) where.
adónde [a'ðonðe] *ad* = **dónde**.
adopción [aðop'θjon] *nf* adoption.
adoptar [aðop'tar] *vt* to adopt.
adoquín [aðo'kin] *nm* paving stone.
adorar [aðo'rar] *vt* to adore.
adormecer [aðorme'θer] *vt* to put to sleep; **~se** *vr* to become sleepy, fall asleep.
adornar [aðor'nar] *vt* to adorn.
adorno [a'ðorno] *nm* adornment; (*decoración*) decoration.
adquiero *etc vb ver* **adquirir**.
adquirir [aðki'rir] *vt* to acquire, obtain.
adquisición [aðkisi'θjon] *nf* acquisition.
adrede [a'ðreðe] *ad* on purpose.
adscribir [aðskri'βir] *vt* to appoint.
aduana [a'ðwana] *nf* customs *pl*.
aduanero, a [aðwa'nero, a] *a* customs *cpd* // *nm/f* customs officer.
aducir [aðu'θir] *vt* to adduce; (*dar como prueba*) to offer as proof.
adueñarse [aðwe'ɲarse] *vr*: **~ de** to take possession of.
adulación [aðula'θjon] *nf* flattery.
adular [aðu'lar] *vt* to flatter.
adulterar [aðulte'rar] *vt* to adulterate // *vi* to commit adultery.
adulterio [aðul'terjo] *nm* adultery.
adulto, a [a'ðulto, a] *a, nm/f* adult.

adusto, a [a'ðusto, a] *a* stern; (*austero*) austere.

advenedizo, a [aðßene'ðiθo, a] *nm/f* upstart.

advenimiento [aðßeni'mjento] *nm* arrival; (*al trono*) accession.

adverbio [að'ßerßjo] *nm* adverb.

adversario, a [aðßer'sarjo, a] *nm/f* adversary.

adversidad [aðßersi'ðað] *nf* adversity; (*contratiempo*) setback.

adverso, a [að'ßerso, a] *a* adverse; (*opuesto*) opposite.

advertencia [aðßer'tenθja] *nf* warning; (*prefacio*) preface, foreword.

advertir [aðßer'tir] *vt* to notice; (*avisar*) to warn // *vi*: ~ **en** to notice.

Adviento [að'ßjento] *nm* Advent.

adyacente [aðja'θente] *a* adjacent.

aéreo, a [a'ereo, a] *a* aerial.

aerodeslizador [aeroðesliθa'ðor], **aerodeslizante** [aeroðesli'θante] *nm* hovercraft.

aeronáutica [aero'nautika] *nf* aeronautics *sg*.

aeropuerto [aero'pwerto] *nm* airport.

afabilidad [afaßili'ðað] *nf* friendliness; **afable** *a* affable.

afán [a'fan] *nm* hard work; (*deseo*) desire.

afanar [afa'nar] *vt* to harass; ~**se** *vr*: ~**se por** to strive to; **afanoso, a** *a* hard; (*trabajador*) industrious.

afear [afe'ar] *vt* to make ugly; (*mutilar*) to deface.

afección [afek'θjon] *nf* affection; (*MED*) disease.

afectación [afekta'θjon] *nf* affectation; **afectado, a** *a* affected; **afectar** *vt* to affect.

afectísimo, a [afek'tisimo, a] *a* affectionate; ~ **suyo** yours truly.

afecto, a [a'fekto, a] *a* affectionate // *nm* affection; ~ **a** fond of.

afectuoso, a [afek'twoso, a] *a* affectionate.

afeitar [afei'tar] *vt* to shave; ~**se** *vr* to shave.

afeminado, a [afemi'naðo, a] *a* effeminate.

aferrado, a [afe'rraðo, a] *a* stubborn.

aferrar [afe'rrar] *vt* to moor; (*fig*) to grasp // *vi* to moor.

afianzamiento [afjanθa'mjento] *nm* strengthening; (*garantía*) guarantee; (*COM*) security; **afianzar** *vt* to strengthen; to guarantee; to secure; **afianzarse** *vr* to become established.

afición [afi'θjon] *nf* fondness, liking; **la** ~ the fans *pl*; **pinto por** ~ I paint as a hobby; **aficionado, a** *a* keen, enthusiastic; amateur // *nm/f* enthusiast, fan; amateur.

aficionar [afiθjo'nar] *vt*: ~ **a uno a algo** to make sb like sth; ~**se** *vr*: ~**se a algo** to grow fond of sth.

afilado, a [afi'laðo, a] *a* sharp.

afilar [afi'lar] *vt* to sharpen.

afiliarse [afi'ljarse] *vr* to become affiliated to.

afín [a'fin] *a* bordering, adjacent; (*parecido*) similar; (*conexo*) related.

afinar [afi'nar] *vt* (*TEC*) to refine; (*MUS*) to tune // *vi* to play/sing in tune.

afinidad [afini'ðað] *nf* affinity; (*parentesco*) relationship; **por** ~ by marriage.

afirmación [afirma'θjon] *nf* affirmation; **afirmar** *vt* to affirm, state; (*sostener*) to strengthen; **afirmativo, a** *a* affirmative.

aflicción [aflik'θjon] *nf* affliction; (*dolor*) grief.

afligir [afli'xir] *vt* to afflict; (*apenar*) to distress; ~**se** *vr* to grieve.

aflojar [aflo'xar] *vt* to slacken; (*desatar*) to loosen, undo; (*relajar*) to relax // *vi* to drop; (*bajar*) to go down; ~**se** *vr* to relax.

afluente [aflu'ente] *a* flowing; (*elocuente*) eloquent // *nm* tributary.

afluir [aflu'ir] *vi* to flow.

afmo, a *abr de* **afectísimo(a) suyo(a)**.

afónico, a [a'foniko, a] *a* (*ronco*) hoarse; (*sin voz*) voiceless.

afortunado, a [afortu'naðo, a] *a* fortunate, lucky.

afrancesado, a [afranθe'saðo, a] *a* francophile; (*pey*) frenchified.

afrenta [a'frenta] *nf* affront, insult; (*deshonra*) dishonour, shame; **afrentar** *vt* to affront; to dishonour; **afrentarse** *vr* to be ashamed; **afrentoso, a** *a* insulting.

África ['afrika] *nf* Africa; ~ **del Sur** South Africa; **africano, a** *a*, *nm/f* African.

afrontar [afron'tar] *vt* to confront; (*poner cara a cara*) to bring face to face.

afuera [a'fwera] *ad* out, outside; ~**s** *nfpl* outskirts, suburbs.

agachar [aɤa'tʃar] *vt* to bend, bow; ~**se** *vr* to stoop, bend.

agalla [a'ɤaʎa] *nf* (*ZOOL*) gill; ~**s** *nfpl* (*MED*) tonsillitis *sg*; (*ANAT*) tonsils.

agarradera [aɤarra'ðera] *nf* (*AM*), **agarradero** [aɤarra'ðero] *nm* handle; ~**s** *npl* pull *sg*, influence *sg*.

agarrado, a [aɤa'rraðo, a] *a* mean, stingy.

agarrar [aɤa'rrar] *vt* to grasp, grab; (*AM*) to take, catch // *vi* (*planta*) to take root; ~**se** *vr* to hold on (tightly).

agarrotar [aɤarro'tar] *vt* (*llo*) to tie tightly; (*persona*) to squeeze tightly; (*reo*) to garrotte; ~**se** *vr* (*motor*) to seize up; (*MED*) to stiffen.

agasajar [aɤasa'xar] *vt* to treat well, fête; **agasajo** *nm* lavish hospitality.

agencia [a'xenθja] *nf* agency; ~ **de viajes/inmobiliaria** travel/estate agency.

agenda [a'xenda] *nf* diary.

agente [a'xente] *nm* agent; (*de policía*) policeman; ~ **femenino** policewoman.

ágil ['axil] *a* agile, nimble; **agilidad** *nf* agility, nimbleness.

agio ['axjo] *nm* speculation.

agiotista [axjo'tista] *nm* (stock)jobber; (*especulador*) speculator.

agitación [axita'θjon] *nf* shaking, waving, stirring; (*del mar*) roughness; (*fig*) agitation.

agitar [axi'tar] *vt* to wave, shake, stir; (*fig*) to stir up, excite; ~**se** *vr* to get excited.

aglomerar [axlome'rar] *vt*, ~**se** *vr* to agglomerate, crowd together.

agnóstico, a [ax'nostiko, a] *a*, *nm/f* agnostic.

agobiar [axo'ßjar] *vt* to weigh down; (*oprimir*) to oppress; (*cargar*) to burden.

agolparse [axol'parse] *vr* to crowd together.

agonía [axo'nia] *nf* agony, anguish.

agonizante [axoni'θante] *a* dying.

agonizar [axoni'θar] *vi* (*también estar agonizando*) to be dying.

agosto [a'xosto] *nm* August.

agotado, a [axo'taðo, a] *a* exhausted; (*libros*) out of print; (*acabado*) finished; (*mercancías*) sold out; **agotamiento** *nm* exhaustion.

agotar [axo'tar] *vt* to exhaust; (*consumir*) to drain; (*recursos*) to use up, deplete; ~**se** *vr* to be exhausted; (*acabarse*) to run out; (*libro*) to go out of print.

agraciar [axra'θjar] *vt* (*JUR*) to pardon; (*con premio*) to reward.

agradable [axra'ðaßle] *a* pleasing, pleasant, nice.

agradar [axra'ðar] *vt*, *vi* to please.

agradecer [axraðe'θer] *vt* to thank; (*favor etc*) to be grateful for; **agradecimiento** *nm* thanks *pl*; gratitude.

agrado [a'xraðo] *nm* affability; (*gusto*) liking.

agrandar [axran'dar] *vt* to enlarge; (*fig*) to exaggerate; ~**se** *vr* to get bigger.

agrario, a [a'xrarjo, a] *a* agrarian.

agravar [axra'ßar] *vt* to make heavier; (*irritar*) to aggravate; (*oprimir*) to oppress; ~**se** *vr* to worsen, get worse.

agraviar [axra'ßjar] *vt* to offend; (*ser injusto con*) to wrong; ~**se** *vr* to take offence; **agravio** *nm* offence; wrong; (*ofensa*) grievance.

agregado [axre'xaðo] *nm* aggregate; (*persona*) attaché.

agregar [axre'xar] *vt* to gather; (*añadir*) to add; (*persona*) to appoint.

agresión [axre'sjon] *nf* aggression; **agresivo, a** *a* aggressive.

agriar [a'xrjar] *vt* to (turn) sour; ~**se** *vr* to turn sour.

agricultor, a [axrikul'tor, a] *nm/f* farmer; **agricultura** *nf* agriculture, farming.

agridulce [axri'ðulθe] *a* bittersweet.

agrietarse [axrje'tarse] *vr* to crack; (*la piel*) to chap.

agrio, a ['axrjo, a] *a* bitter.

agronomía [axrono'mia] *nf* agronomy, agriculture.

agrupación [axrupa'θjon] *nf* group; (*acto*) grouping.

agrupar [axru'par] *vt* to group.

agua ['axwa] *nf* water; (*lluvia*) rain; (*NAUT*) wake; (*ARQ*) slope of a roof; ~**s** *nfpl* (*de piedra*) water *sg*, sparkle *sg*; (*MED*) water *sg*, urine *sg*; (*NAUT*) waters; ~**s abajo/arriba** downstream/upstream; ~ **bendita/destilada/potable** holy/distilled/drinking water; ~ **corriente** running water; ~ **de colonia** eau de cologne; ~**s jurisdiccionales** territorial waters; ~**s mayores** excrement *sg*.

aguacate [axwa'kate] *nm* avocado pear.

aguacero [axwa'θero] *nm* (heavy) shower.

aguado, a [a'xwaðo, a] *a* watery, watered down // *nf* (*AGR*) watering place; (*NAUT*) water supply; (*ARTE*) water-colour.

aguafiestas [axwa'fjestas] *nm/f inv* spoilsport.

aguafuerte [axwa'fwerte] *nf* etching.

aguamar [axwa'mar] *nm* jellyfish.

aguantable [axwan'taßle] *a* bearable; **aguantar** *vt* to bear, put up with; (*contener*) to hold; (*sostener*) to hold up // *vi* to last; **aguantarse** *vr* to restrain o.s.

aguar [a'xwar] *vt* to water down.

aguardar [axwar'ðar] *vt* to wait for.

aguardiente [axwar'ðjente] *nm* brandy.

aguarrás [axwa'rras] *nm* turpentine.

agudeza [axu'ðeθa] *nf* sharpness; (*ingenio*) wit; **agudo, a** *a* sharp; (*voz*) high-pitched, piercing; (*dolor, enfermedad*) acute.

agüero [a'xwero] *nm* omen; (*pronóstico*) prediction.

aguijar [axi'xar] *vt* to goad; (*incitar*) to urge on // *vi* to hurry along.

aguijón [axi'xon] *nm* sting; (*BOT*) spine; (*estímulo, fig*) spur; **aguijonear** *vt* = **aguijar**.

águila ['axila] *nf* eagle; (*fig*) genius.

aguileño, a [axi'leɲo, a] *a* aquiline; (*facciones*) sharp-featured.

aguinaldo [axi'naldo] *nm* Christmas box.

aguja [a'xuxa] *nf* needle; (*de reloj*) hand; (*ARQ*) spire; (*TEC*) firing-pin; ~**s** *nfpl* (*ZOOL*) ribs; (*FERRO*) points.

agujerear [axuxere'ar] *vt* to make holes in; **agujero** *nm* hole.

agujetas [axu'xetas] *nfpl* stitch *sg*; (*rigidez*) stiffness *sg*.

aguzar [axu'θar] *vt* to sharpen; (*fig*) to incite.

ahí [a'i] *ad* there; **de ~ que** so that, with the result that; ~ **llega** here he comes; **por** ~ that way; (*allá*) over there.

ahijado, a [ai'xaðo, a] *nm/f* godson/daughter.

ahínco [a'inko] *nm* earnestness.

ahitar [ai'tar] *vt* to surfeit; ~**se** *vr* to stuff o.s.

ahíto, a [a'ito, a] *a*: **estoy** ~ I have indigestion // *nm* indigestion.

ahogar [ao'xar] *vt* to drown; (*asfixiar*) to suffocate, smother; (*fuego*) to put out; ~**se** *vr* (*en el agua*) to drown; (*suicidio*) to drown o.s.; (*por asfixia*) to suffocate.

ahogo [a'oxo] *nm* shortness of breath; (*fig*) financial difficulty.

ahondar [aon'dar] *vt* to deepen, make

deeper; (*fig*) to go deeply into // *vi*: ~ **en** to go deeply into.

ahora [a'ora] *ad* now; (*poco tiempo ha*) a moment ago, just now; (*dentro de poco*) in a moment // *conj* now; ~ **voy** I'm coming; ~ **mismo** right now; ~ **bien** now then; **por** ~ for the present.

ahorcar [aor'kar] *vt* to hang; ~**se** *vr* to hang o.s.

ahorita [ao'rita] *ad* (*fam*) right now.

ahorrar [ao'rrar] *vt* (*dinero*) to save; (*esfuerzos*) to save, avoid; **ahorro** *nm* economy, saving; (*frugalidad*) thrift; **ahorros** *nmpl* savings.

ahuecar [awe'kar] *vt* to hollow (out); (*voz*) to deepen; ~**se** *vr* to give o.s. airs.

ahumar [au'mar] *vt* to smoke, cure; (*llenar de humo*) to fill with smoke // *vi* to smoke; ~**se** *vr* to fill with smoke.

ahuyentar [aujen'tar] *vt* to drive off, frighten off; (*fig*) to dispel; ~**se** *vr* to run away.

airado, a [ai'raðo, a] *a* angry; **airar** *vt* to anger; **airarse** *vr* to get angry.

aire ['aire] *nm* air; (*viento*) wind; (*corriente*) draught; (*MUS*) tune; ~**s** *nmpl*: **darse** ~**s** to give o.s. airs; **al** ~ **libre** in the open air; ~ **acondicionado** air conditioning; **airoso, a** *a* windy; draughty; (*fig*) graceful.

aislador [aisla'ðor] *nm* insulator; **aislar** *vt* to isolate; (*ELEC*) to insulate.

ajar [a'xar] *vt* to spoil; (*fig*) to abuse.

ajedrez [axe'ðreθ] *nm* chess.

ajeno, a [a'xeno, a] *a* (*que pertenece a otro*) somebody else's; (*impropio*) inappropriate; (*extraño*) alien, foreign; ~ **a** foreign to; ~ **de** free from, devoid of.

ajetreo [axe'treo] *nm* bustle.

ají [a'xi] *nm* chili, red pepper; (*salsa*) chili sauce.

ajo ['axo] *nm* garlic; ~ **porro** *o* **puerro** leek.

ajorca [a'xorka] *nf* bracelet.

ajuar [a'xwar] *nm* household furnishings *pl*; (*de novia*) trousseau; (*de niño*) layette.

ajustado, a [axus'taðo, a] *a* (*tornillo*) tight; (*cálculo*) right; (*ropa*) tight-fitting; (*DEPORTE* resultado) close.

ajustar [axus'tar] *vt* (*adaptar*) to adjust; (*encajar*) to fit; (*TEC*) to engage; (*contratar*) to hire; (*IMPRENTA*) to make up; (*apretar*) to tighten; (*concertar*) to agree (on); (*reconciliar*) to reconcile; (*cuenta*) to settle // *vi* to fit; ~**se** *vr* to come to an agreement.

ajuste [a'xuste] *nm* adjustment; (*TEC* costura) fitting; (*acuerdo*) compromise; (*de cuenta*) settlement.

al [al] = **a** + **el**, *ver* **a**.

ala ['ala] *nf* wing; (*de sombrero*) brim; (*futbolista*) winger.

alabanza [ala'ßanθa] *nf* praise.

alabar [ala'ßar] *vt* to praise; ~**se** *vr*: ~**se de** to boast of (being).

alabear [alaße'ar] *vt*, ~**se** *vr* to warp.

alacena [ala'θena] *nf* cupboard.

alacrán [ala'kran] *nm* scorpion.

alambicado, a [alambi'kaðo, a] *a* distilled; (*fig*) affected.

alambicar [alambi'kar] *vt* to distil.

alambique [alam'bike] *nm* still.

alambrado [alam'braðo] *nm* wire fence; (*red*) wire netting; **alambre** *nm* wire; **alambre de púas** barbed wire; **alambrista** *nm/f* tightrope walker.

alameda [ala'meða] *nf* (*plantío*) poplar grove; (*lugar de paseo*) avenue, tree-lined walk.

álamo ['alamo] *nm* poplar; ~ **temblón** aspen.

alano [a'lano] *nm* mastiff.

alar [a'lar] *nm* eaves *pl*.

alarde [a'larðe] *nm* (*MIL*) review; (*ostentación*) show, display; **hacer** ~ **de** to boast of.

alargar [alar'xar] *vt* to lengthen, extend; (*paso*) to hasten; (*brazo*) to stretch out; (*cuerda*) to pay out; (*conversación*) to spin out; ~**se** *vr* to get longer; ~**se en** to enlarge upon; (*pey*) to drag out.

alarido [ala'riðo] *nm* shriek.

alarma [a'larma] *nf* alarm.

alazán [ala'θan] *nm* sorrel.

alba ['alßa] *nf* dawn.

albacea [alßa'θea] *nm/f* executor/trix.

Albania [al'ßanja] *nf* Albania.

albañal [alßa'ɲal] *nm* drain, sewer.

albañil [alßa'ɲil] *nm* bricklayer; (*cantero*) mason.

albaricoque [alßari'koke] *nm* apricot.

albedrío [alße'ðrio] *nm*: **libre** ~ free will.

alberca [al'ßerka] *nf* reservoir.

albergar [alßer'xar] *vt*, ~**se** *vr* to shelter.

albergue [al'ßerxe] *nm* shelter, refuge; ~ **de juventud** youth hostel.

albóndiga [al'ßondixa] *nf* meatball.

albor [al'ßor] *nm* whiteness; (*amanecer*) dawn; ~**ada** *nf* dawn; (*diana*) reveille; ~ **ear** *vi* to dawn.

albornoz [alßor'noθ] *nm* (*de los árabes*) burnous; (*para el baño*) bathrobe.

alborotar [alßoro'tar] *vi* to make a row // *vt* to agitate, stir up; ~**se** *vr* to get excited; (*mar*) to get rough; **alboroto** *nm* row, uproar.

alborozar [alßoro'θar] *vt* to gladden; ~**se** *vr* to rejoice.

alborozo [alßo'roθo] *nm* joy.

albricias [al'ßriθjas] *nfpl* reward *sg* // *excl* good news!

álbum ['alßum] *nm* album.

albumen [al'ßumen] *nm* egg white.

alcachofa [alka'tʃofa] *nf* artichoke.

alcalde [al'kalde] *nm* mayor.

alcaldía [alkal'dia] *nf* mayoralty; (*lugar*) mayor's office.

alcance [al'kanθe] *nm* reach; (*COM*) adverse balance; (*de periódico*) stop-press (news); **de pocos** ~**s** not very clever; ~ **de última hora** late postal collection.

alcancía [alkan'θia] *nf* money box.

alcantarilla [alkanta'riʎa] *nf* (*de aguas*

cloacales) sewer; (*en la calle*) gutter.

alcanzar [alkan'θar] *vt* (*algo: con la mano, el pie*) to reach; (*alguien en el camino*) to catch up with; (*autobús*) to catch; (*suj: bala*) to hit, strike // *vi:* ~ **a hacer** to manage to do.

alcatraz [alka'traθ] *nm* gannet.

alcázar [al'kaθar] *nm* fortress; (*palacio*) royal palace; (*NAUT*) quarter-deck.

alcoba [al'koβa] *nf* bedroom.

alcohol [al'kol] *nm* alcohol; **alcohólico, a** *a* alcoholic; ~ **ismo** *nm* alcoholism.

alcornoque [alkor'noke] *nm* cork tree.

aldaba [al'daβa] *nf* (door) knocker.

aldea [al'dea] *nf* village; ~ **no, a** *a* village *cpd* // *nm/f* villager.

aleación [alea'θjon] *nf* alloy.

aleccionar [alekθjo'nar] *vt* to instruct; (*adiestrar*) to train.

alegación [aleɣa'θjon] *nf* allegation; **alegar** *vt* to allege; (*JUR*) to plead; (*AM*) to dispute, argue.

alegato [ale'ɣato] *nm* (*JUR*) allegation; (*AM*) argument.

alegoría [aleɣo'ria] *nf* allegory.

alegrar [ale'ɣrar] *vt* (*causar alegría*) to cheer (up); (*fuego*) to poke; (*fiesta*) to liven up; ~ **se** *vr* to get merry *or* tight; ~ **se de** to be glad about.

alegre [a'leɣre] *a* happy, cheerful; (*fam*) merry, tight; (*licencioso*) risqué, blue; **alegría** *nf* happiness; merriment.

alejamiento [aleχa'mjento] *nm* removal; (*distancia*) remoteness.

alejar [ale'χar] *vt* to remove; (*fig*) to estrange; ~ **se** *vr* to move away.

aleluya [ale'luja] *nm* (*canto*) hallelujah; (*Pascuas*) Easter time // *nf* Easter print.

alemán, ana [ale'man, ana] *a, nm/f* German // *nm* (*lengua*) German.

Alemania [ale'manja] *nf:* ~ **Federal/Oriental** West/East Germany.

alentado, a [alen'taðo, a] *pp de* **alentar** // *a* brave; (*orgulloso*) proud; (*fuerte*) strong.

alentador, a [alenta'ðor, a] *a* encouraging.

alentar [alen'tar] *vt* to encourage; ~ **se** *vr* to cheer up.

alerce [a'lerθe] *nm* larch.

alergia [a'lerxja] *nf* allergy.

alero [a'lero] *nm* (*de tejado*) eaves *pl*; (*de carruaje*) mudguard.

alerta [a'lerta] *a, nm* alert.

aleta [a'leta] *nf* (*de pez*) fin; (*de ave*) wing; (*de coche*) mudguard.

aletargar [aletar'ɣar] *vt* to make drowsy; (*entumecer*) to make numb; ~ **se** *vr* to grow drowsy; to become numb.

aletazo [ale'taθo] *nm* wingbeat, flap of the wing.

aletear [alete'ar] *vi* to flutter.

aleve [a'leβe] *a* treacherous.

alevosía [aleβo'sia] *nf* treachery.

alfabeto [alfa'βeto] *nm* alphabet.

alfarería [alfare'ria] *nf* pottery; (*tienda*) pottery shop; **alfarero** *nm* potter.

alférez [al'fereθ] *nm* (*MIL*) second lieutenant; (*NAUT*) ensign.

alfiler [alfi'ler] *nm* pin; (*broche*) clip; ~ **de seguridad** safety pin.

alfombra [al'fombra] *nf* carpet; (*más pequeña*) rug; **alfombrar** *vt* to carpet; **alfombrilla** *nf* rug, mat; (*MED*) German measles.

alforja [al'forxa] *nf* saddlebag.

alforza [al'forθa] *nf* pleat.

alga ['alɣa] *nf* seaweed, alga.

algarabía [alɣara'βia] *nf* (*fam*) gibberish; (*BOT*) cornflower.

algarrobo [alɣa'rroβo] *nm* carob tree.

algazara [alɣa'θara] *nf* din, uproar.

álgebra ['alxeβra] *nf* algebra.

algo ['alɣo] *pron* something; anything // *ad* somewhat, rather; **por** ~ **será** there must be some reason for it.

algodón [alɣo'ðon] *nm* cotton; (*planta*) cotton plant; (*dulce*) candy floss; ~ **hidrófilo** cotton wool.

algodonero, a [alɣoðo'nero, a] *a* cotton *cpd* // *nm/f* cotton grower // *nm* cotton plant.

alguacil [alɣwa'θil] *nm* bailiff; (*TAUR*) mounted official.

alguien ['alɣjen] *pron* someone, somebody, anybody.

alguno, a [al'ɣuno, a], **algún** [al'ɣun] *a* some, any // *pron* some; one; someone, somebody; ~ **que otro libro** some book or other; **algún día iré** I'll go one *or* some day; **sin interés** ~ without the slightest interest; ~ **que otro** an occasional one; ~ **s piensan** some (people) think.

alhaja [a'laxa] *nf* jewel; (*tesoro*) precious object, treasure; (*pey*) rogue.

aliado, a [a'ljaðo, a] *a* allied.

alianza [a'ljanθa] *nf* alliance.

aliar [a'ljar] *vt* to ally; ~ **se** *vr* to form an alliance.

alias ['aljas] *ad* alias.

alicantino, a [alikan'tino, a] *a* of *or* from Alicante.

alicates [ali'kates] *nmpl:* ~ **de uñas** nail clippers.

aliciente [ali'θjente] *nm* incentive; (*atracción*) attraction.

alienación [aljena'θjon] *nf* alienation.

aliento [a'ljento] *nm* breath; (*respiración*) breathing; **sin** ~ breathless.

aligerar [alixe'rar] *vt* to lighten; (*reducir*) to shorten; (*aliviar*) to alleviate; (*mitigar*) to ease.

alimaña [ali'maɲa] *nf* pest.

alimentación [alimenta'θjon] *nf* (*comida*) food; (*acción*) feeding; (*tienda*) grocer's (shop); **alimentar** *vt* to feed; (*nutrir*) to nourish; **alimentarse** *vr* to feed.

alimenticio, a [alimen'tiθjo, a] *a* nourishing.

alimento [ali'mento] *nm* food; (*nutrición*) nourishment; ~ **s** *nmpl* (*JUR*) alimony *sg*.

alinear [aline'ar] *vt* to align; ~ **se** *vr:* ~ **se en** to fall in with.

aliñar [ali'nar] *vt* to adorn; (*preparar*) to prepare; (*CULIN*) to season; **aliño** *nm* decoration; (*esmero*) neatness; (*CULIN*) dressing.

alisar [ali'sar] *vt* to smooth; (*pulir*) to polish.

aliso [a'liso] *nm* alder.

alistamiento [alista'mjento] *nm* recruitment; **alistar** *vt* to recruit; (*inscribir*) to enrol; **alistarse** *vr* to enlist; to enrol.

aliviar [ali'βjar] *vt* (*carga*) to lighten; (*persona*) to relieve; (*dolor*) to alleviate; ~ **se** *vr*: ~**se de** to unburden o.s. of.

alivio [a'liβjo] *nm* alleviation, relief.

aljibe [al'xiβe] *nm* cistern; (*AUTO*) oil tanker.

aljofaina [alxo'faina] *nf* = **jofaina.**

alma ['alma] *nf* soul; (*persona*) person; (*que anima*) life and soul; (*TEC*) core.

almacén [alma'θen] *nm* (*depósito*) warehouse, store; (*MIL*) magazine; (*AM*) shop; **almacenes** *nmpl* department store *sg*; **almacenaje** *nm* storage.

almacenar [almaθe'nar] *vt* to store, put in storage; (*proveerse*) to stock up (with); **almacenero** *nm* warehouseman.

almanaque [alma'nake] *nm* almanac.

almeja [al'mexa] *nf* shellfish, clam.

almendra [al'mendra] *nf* almond; **almendro** *nm* almond tree.

almiar [al'mjar] *nm* hayrick.

almíbar [al'miβar] *nm* syrup; **almibarado, a** *a* syrupy.

almidón [almi'ðon] *nm* starch; **almidonar** *vt* to starch.

almirantazgo [almiran'taθɣo] *nm* admiralty; **almirante** *nm* admiral.

almohada [almo'aða] *nf* pillow; (*funda*) pillowcase; **almohadilla** *nf* cushion; (*TEC*) pad; (*AM*) pincushion.

almoneda [almo'neða] *nf* auction; (*liquidación*) clearance sale.

almorranas [almo'rranas] *nfpl* piles, haemorrhoids.

almorzar [almor'θar] *vt*: ~ **una tortilla** to have an omelette for lunch // *vi* to (have) lunch.

almuerzo [al'mwerθo] *nm* lunch.

alnado, a [al'naðo, a] *nm/f* stepson/daughter.

alocado, a [alo'kaðo, a] *a* crazy.

alojamiento [aloxa'mjento] *nf* lodging(s) (*pl*); (*viviendas*) housing.

alojar [alo'xar] *vt* to lodge; ~**se** *vr* to lodge, stay.

alondra [a'londra] *nf* lark, skylark.

alpargata [alpar'ɣata] *nf* rope-soled sandal; (*de lona*) canvass shoe.

Alpes ['alpes] *nmpl*: **los** ~ the Alps.

alpinismo [alpi'nismo] *nm* mountaineering, climbing; **alpinista** *nm/f* mountaineer, climber.

alquería [alke'ria] *nf* farmhouse.

alquilar [alki'lar] *vt* to rent (out), let, hire (out); (*de inquilino*) to rent, hire; **se**

alquilan casas houses to let.

alquiler [alki'ler] *nm* renting, letting, hiring; (*arriendo*) rent, hire charge; **de** ~ for hire.

alquimia [al'kimja] *nf* alchemy.

alquitrán [alki'tran] *nm* tar.

alrededor [alreðe'ðor] *ad* around, about; ~**es** *nmpl* surroundings; ~ **de** *prep* around, about; **mirar a su** ~ to look (round) about one.

alta ['alta] *nf ver* **alto.**

altanería [altane'ria] *nf* haughtiness, arrogance; **altanero, a** *a* arrogant, haughty.

altar [al'tar] *nm* altar.

altavoz [alta'βoθ] *nm* loudspeaker; (*amplificador*) amplifier.

alteración [altera'θjon] *nf* alteration; (*alboroto*) disturbance; (*discusión*) quarrel; **alterar** *vt* to alter; to disturb; **alterarse** *vr* (*alimento etc*) to go bad *or* off; (*voz*) to falter; (*persona*) to get upset.

altercado [alter'kaðo] *nm* argument.

alternar [alter'nar] *vt* to alternate // *vi*, ~**se** *vr* to alternate; (*turnar*) to take turns; ~ **con** to mix with; **alternativo, a** *a* alternative; (*alterno*) alternating // *nf* alternative; (*elección*) choice; **alternativas** *nfpl* ups and downs.

alteza [al'teθa] *nf* (*tratamiento*) highness; (*altura*) height.

altibajos [alti'βaxos] *nmpl* ups and downs.

altiplanicie [altipla'niθje] *nf*, **altiplano** [alti'plano] *nm* high plateau.

altisonante [altiso'nante] *a* high-flown.

altitud [alti'tuð] *nf* altitude.

altivez [alti'βeθ] *nf* haughtiness, arrogance; **altivo, a** *a* haughty, arrogant.

alto, a ['alto, a] *a* high; (*de tamaño*) tall; (*precio, importante*) high; (*sonido*) high, sharp; (*noble*) high, lofty // *nm* halt; (*MUS*) alto; (*GEO*) hill; (*AM*) pile // *ad* (*de sitio*) high; (*de sonido*) loud, loudly // *nf* (certificate of) discharge // *excl* halt!; **tiene 2 metros de** ~ he is 2 metres tall; **en** ~**a mar** on the high seas; **en voz** ~**a** in a loud voice; **las** ~**as horas de la noche** the small hours; **en lo** ~ **de** at the top of; **pasar por** ~ to overlook; **dar de** ~**a** to discharge.

altoparlante [altopar'lante] *nm* (*AM*) loudspeaker.

altura [al'tura] *nf* height; (*NAUT*) depth; (*GEO*) latitude; **tiene 1.80 de** ~ he is 1 metre 80cm tall; **a esta** ~ **del año** at this time of the year.

alubia [a'luβja] *nf* French bean, kidney bean.

alucinación [aluθina'θjon] *nf* hallucination; **alucinar** *vi* to hallucinate // *vt* to deceive; (*fascinar*) to fascinate.

alud [a'luð] *nm* avalanche.

aludir [alu'ðir] *vi*: ~ **a** to allude to; **darse por** ~ to take the hint.

alumbrado [alum'braðo] *nm* lighting; **alumbramiento** *nm* lighting; (*MED*) childbirth, delivery.

alumbrar [alum'brar] *vt* to light (up); (*ciego*) to restore the sight of // *vi* to give birth.

aluminio [alu'minjo] *nm* aluminium.

alumno, a [a'lumno, a] *nm/f* pupil, student.

alunizar [aluni'θar] *vi* to land on the moon.

alusión [alu'sjon] *nf* allusion.

alusivo, a [alu'siβo, a] *a* allusive.

aluvión [alu'βjon] *nm* alluvium; (*fig*) flood.

alza ['alθa] *nf* rise; ~ s *nfpl* sights.

alzada [al'θaða] *nf* (*de caballos*) height; (*JUR*) appeal.

alzamiento [alθa'mjento] *nm* (*aumento*) rise, increase; (*acción*) lifting, raising; (*mejor postura*) higher bid; (*rebelión*) rising; (*COM*) fraudulent bankruptcy.

alzar [al'θar] *vt* to lift (up); (*precio, muro*) to raise; (*cuello de abrigo*) to turn up; (*AGR*) to gather in; (*IMPRENTA*) to gather; ~ se *vr* to get up, rise; (*rebelarse*) to revolt; (*COM*) to go fraudulently bankrupt; (*JUR*) appeal.

allá [a'ʎa] *ad* (*lugar*) there; (*por ahí*) over there; (*tiempo*) then; ~ **abajo** down there; **más** ~ further on; **más** ~ **de** beyond; ¡ ~ **tu!** that's your problem!

allanar [aʎa'nar] *vt* to flatten, level (out); (*igualar*) to smooth (out); (*fig*) to subdue; (*JUR*) to burgle, break into; ~ **se** *vr* to fall down; ~ **se a** to submit to, accept.

allegado, a [aʎe'ɣaðo, a] *a* near, close // *nm/f* relation.

allegar [aʎe'ɣar] *vt* to gather (together); (*añadir*) to add; ~ **se** *vr* to approach.

allí [a'ʎi] *ad* there; ~ **mismo** right there; **por** ~ over there; (*por ese camino*) that way.

ama ['ama] *nf* lady of the house; (*dueña*) owner; (*institutriz*) governess; (*madre adoptiva*) foster mother; ~ **de cría** *o* **de leche** wet-nurse; ~ **de llaves** housekeeper.

amabilidad [amaβili'ðað] *nf* kindness; (*simpatía*) niceness; **amable** *a* kind; nice.

amado, a [a'maðo, a] *nm/f* beloved, sweetheart.

amaestrar [amaes'trar] *vt* to train; (*preparar*) to coach.

amagar [ama'ɣar] *vt, vi* to threaten; **amago** *nm* threat; (*gesto*) threatening gesture; (*MED*) symptom.

amalgama [amal'ɣama] *nf* amalgam; **amalgamar** *vt* to amalgamate; (*combinar*) to combine, mix.

amamantar [amaman'tar] *vt* to suckle, nurse.

amanecer [amane'θer] *vi* to dawn // *nm* dawn; **el niño amaneció afiebrado** the child woke up with a fever.

amanerado, a [amane'raðo, a] *a* affected.

amansar [aman'sar] *vt* to tame; (*templar*) to subdue.

amante [a'mante] *a*: ~ **de** fond of // *nm/f* lover.

amapola [ama'pola] *nf* poppy.

amar [a'mar] *vt* to love.

amargado, a [amar'ɣaðo, a] *a* bitter; **amargar** *vt* to make bitter; (*fig*) to embitter; **amargarse** *vr* to get bitter.

amargo, a [a'marɣo, a] *a* bitter; **amargura** *nf* bitterness.

amarillento, a [amari'ʎento, a] *a* yellowish; (*tez*) sallow; **amarillo, a** *a, nm* yellow.

amarrar [ama'rrar] *vt* to moor; (*sujetar*) to tie up.

amartelar [amarte'lar] *vt* to make jealous; (*enamorar*) to win the heart of; ~ **se** *vr*: ~ **se de** to fall in love with.

amartillar [amarti'ʎar] *vt* = **martillar.**

amasar [ama'sar] *vt* to knead; (*mezclar*) to mix, prepare; (*MED*) to massage; (*confeccionar*) to concoct; **amasijo** *nm* kneading; mixing; (*masa*) dough; (*pasta*) paste; (*fig*) hotchpotch.

amateur ['amatur] *nm/f* amateur.

amatista [ama'tista] *nf* amethyst.

amazona [ama'θona] *nf* horsewoman; **A ~ s** *nm*: **el A ~ s** the Amazon.

ambages [am'baxes] *nmpl*: **sin** ~ in plain language.

ámbar ['ambar] *nm* amber.

ambición [ambi'θjon] *nf* ambition; **ambicionar** *vt* to aspire to; **ambicioso, a** *a* ambitious.

ambidextro, a [ambi'ðekstro, a] *a* ambidextrous.

ambiente [am'bjente] *nm* atmosphere; (*medio*) environment.

ambigüedad [ambiɣwe'ðað] *nf* ambiguity; **ambiguo, a** *a* ambiguous.

ámbito ['ambito] *nm* compass; (*campo*) field; (*límite*) boundary; (*fig*) scope.

ambos, as ['ambos, as] *apl, pron pl* both.

ambulancia [ambu'lanθja] *nf* ambulance.

ambulante [ambu'lante] *a* walking *cpd*, itinerant.

ambulatorio [ambula'torjo] *nm* national health clinic.

amedrentar [ameðren'tar] *vt* to scare.

amén [a'men] *excl* amen; ~ **de** except for.

amenaza [ame'naθa] *nf* threat; **amenazar** *vt, vi* to threaten.

amenguar [amen'ɣwar] *vt* to diminish; (*fig*) to dishonour.

amenidad [ameni'ðað] *nf* pleasantness.

ameno, a [a'meno, a] *a* pleasant.

América [a'merika] *nf* America; ~ **del Norte/del Sur** North/South America; ~ **Central/Latina** Central/Latin America; **americano, a** *a, nm/f* American // *nf* coat, jacket.

ametralladora [ametraʎa'ðora] *nf* machine gun.

amigable [ami'ɣaβle] *a* friendly.

amígdala [a'miɣðala] *nf* tonsil; **amigdalitis** *nf* tonsillitis.

amigo, a [a'miɣo, a] *a* friendly // *nm/f* friend.

amilanar [amila'nar] *vt* to scare.

aminorar [amino'rar] *vt* to diminish; (*reducir*) to reduce.

amistad [amis'taŏ] *nf* friendship; ~**es** *nfpl* friends; **amistoso, a** *a* friendly.

amnesia [am'nesja] *nf* amnesia.

amnistía [amnis'tia] *nf* amnesty.

amo ['amo] *nm* owner; (*dueño*) boss; ~ **de casa** householder.

amodorrarse [amoŏo'rrarse] *vr* to get sleepy.

amolar [amo'lar] *vt* to sharpen; (*fig*) to bore.

amoldar [amol'dar] *vt* to mould; (*adaptar*) to adapt.

amonestación [amonesta'θjon] *nf* warning; **amonestaciones** *nfpl* marriage banns; **amonestar** *vt* to warn; to publish the banns of.

amontonar [amonto'nar] *vt* to collect, pile up; ~**se** *vr* to crowd together; (*acumularse*) to pile up.

amor [a'mor] *nm* love; (*amante*) lover; **hacer el** ~ to make love; (*cortejar*) to court.

amoratado, a [amora'taŏo, a] *a* purple, blue with cold.

amordazar [amorŏa'θar] *vt* to muzzle; (*fig*) to gag.

amorío [amo'rio] *nm* (*fam*) love affair.

amoroso, a [amo'roso, a] *a* affectionate, loving.

amortajar [amorta'xar] *vt* to shroud.

amortiguador [amortigwa'ŏor] *nm* shock absorber; (*parachoques*) bumper; (*silenciador*) silencer; **amortiguar** *vt* to deaden; (*ruido*) to muffle; (*color*) to soften.

amortización [amortiθa'θjon] *nf* redemption, repayment.

amotinar [amoti'nar] *vt* to stir up, incite (to riot); ~**se** *vr* to mutiny.

amparar [ampa'rar] *vt* to protect; ~**se** *vr* to seek protection; (*abrigar*) to shelter; **amparo** *nm* help, protection.

ampliación [amplja'θjon] *nf* enlargement; (*extensión*) extension; **ampliar** *vt* to enlarge; to extend.

amplificación [amplifika'θjon] *nf* enlargement; **amplificador** *nm* amplifier; **amplificar** *vt* to amplify.

amplio, a ['ampljo, a] *a* spacious; (*de falda etc*) full; (*extenso*) extensive; (*ancho*) wide; **amplitud** *nf* spaciousness; extent; (*fig*) amplitude.

ampolla [am'poʎa] *nf* blister; (*MED*) ampoule.

amputar [ampu'tar] *vt* to cut off, amputate.

amueblar [amwe'ßlar] *vt* to furnish.

amurallar [amura'ʎar] *vt* to wall up/in.

anacronismo [anakro'nismo] *nm* anachronism.

ánade ['anaŏe] *nm* duck.

anadear [anaŏe'ar] *vi* to waddle.

anales [a'nales] *nmpl* annals.

analfabetismo [analfaße'tismo] *nm* illiteracy; **analfabeto, a** *a* illiterate.

análisis [a'nalisis] *nm* analysis.

analizar [anali'θar] *vt* to analyse.

analogía [analo'xia] *nf* analogy.

ananá(s) [ana'na(s)] *nm* pineapple.

anaquel [ana'kel] *nm* shelf.

anarquía [anar'kia] *nf* anarchy; **anarquismo** *nm* anarchism; **anarquista** *nm/f* anarchist.

anatomía [anato'mia] *nf* anatomy.

anciano, a [an'θjano, a] *a* old, aged // *nm/f* old man/woman // *nm* elder.

ancla ['ankla] *nf* anchor; ~**dero** *nm* anchorage; **anclar** *vi* to (drop) anchor.

ancho, a ['antʃo, a] *a* wide; (*falda*) full; (*fig*) liberal // *nm* width; (*FERRO*) gauge; **ponerse** ~ to get conceited; **estar a sus** ~**as** to be at one's ease.

anchoa [an'tʃoa] *nf* anchovy.

anchura [an'tʃura] *nf* width; (*extensión*) wideness; (*fig*) freedom.

andaderas [anda'ŏeras] *nfpl* baby walker *sg.*

andadura [anda'ŏura] *nf* gait, pace.

Andalucía [andalu'θia] *nf* Andalusia; **andaluz, a** *a, nm/f* Andalusian.

andamio [an'damjo], **andamiaje** [anda-'mjaxe] *nm* scaffold.

andar [an'dar] *vt* to go, cover, travel // *vi* to go, walk, travel; (*funcionar*) to go, work; (*estar*) to be // *nm* walk, gait, pace; ~**se** *vr* to go away; ~ **a pie/a caballo/en bicicleta** to go on foot/on horseback/by bicycle; ¡**anda!**, **¡andando!** go on!; (*vamos*) come on!; (*bien*) well!; **anda en los 40** he's about 40.

andariego, a [anda'rjexo, a] *a* fond of travelling.

andén [an'den] *nm* (*FERRO*) platform; (*NAUT*) quayside; (*AUTO*) hard shoulder.

Andes ['andes] *nmpl*: **los** ~ the Andes.

Andorra [an'dorra] *nf* Andorra.

andrajo [an'draxo] *nm* rag; ~**so, a** *a* ragged.

andurriales [andu'rrjales] *nmpl* out-of-the-way place *sg.*

anduve *etc vb ver* **andar**.

anécdota [a'nekŏota] *nf* anecdote, story.

anegar [ane'xar] *vt* to flood; (*ahogar*) to drown; ~**se** *vr* to drown; (*hundirse*) to sink.

anemia [a'nemja] *nf* anaemia.

anestésico [anes'tesiko] *nm* anaesthetic.

anexar [anek'sar] *vt* to annex; (*documento*) to attach; **anexo, a** *a* attached // *nm* annexe.

anfibio, a [an'fißjo, a] *a* amphibious // *nm* amphibian.

anfiteatro [anfite'atro] *nm* amphitheatre; (*TEATRO*) dress circle.

anfitrión, ona [anfi'trjon, ona] *nm/f* host.

ángel ['anxel] *nm* angel; **angélico, a**, **angélical** *a* angelic(al).

angina [an'xina] *nf* (*MED*) inflammation of the throat; ~ **de pecho** angina (pectoris).

anglicano, a [angli'kano, a] *a* a, *nm/f* Anglican.

angosto, a [an'gosto, a] *a* narrow.

angostura [angos'tura] *nf* narrowness; (*paso*) narrow passage.

anguila [an'gila] *nf* eel; ~**s** *nfpl* slipway *sg.*

ángulo ['angulo] *nm* angle; (*esquina*) corner; (*curva*) bend.

angustia [an'gustja] *nf* anguish; **angustiar** *vt* to distress, grieve.

anhelante [ane'lante] *a* eager; (*deseoso*) longing; **anhelar** *vt* to be eager for; to long for, desire // *vi* to pant, gasp; **anhelo** *nm* eagerness; desire.

anidar [ani'ðar] *vi* to nest.

anillo [a'niʎo] *nm* ring; ~ **de boda** wedding ring.

ánima ['anima] *nf* soul; **las** ~**s** the Angelus (bell) *sg.*

animación [anima'θjon] *nf* liveliness; (*vitalidad*) life; (*actividad*) bustle; **animado, a** *a* lively; (*vivaz*) animated.

animadversión [animaðβer'sjon] *nf* ill-will, antagonism.

animal [ani'mal] *a* animal; (*fig*) stupid // *nm* animal; (*fig*) fool; (*bestia*) brute.

animar [ani'mar] *vt* (*BIO*) to animate, give life to; (*fig*) to liven up, brighten up, cheer up; (*estimular*) to stimulate; ~**se** *vr* to cheer up, feel encouraged; (*decidirse*) to make up one's mind.

ánimo ['animo] *nm* soul, mind; (*valentía*) courage // *excl* cheer up!

animosidad [animosi'ðað] *nf* animosity.

animoso, a [ani'moso, a] *a* brave; (*vivo*) lively.

aniquilar [aniki'lar] *vt* to annihilate, destroy; ~**se** *vr* to be wiped out, disappear; (*empeorarse*) to deteriorate.

anís [a'nis] *nm* aniseed.

aniversario [aniβer'sarjo] *nm* anniversary.

anoche [a'notʃe] *ad* last night; **antes de** ~ the night before last.

anochecer [anotʃe'θer] *vi* to get dark // *nm* nightfall, dark.

anomalía [anoma'lia] *nf* anomaly.

anonadamiento [anonaða'mjento] *nm* annihilation; (*desaliento*) discouragement; **anonadar** *vt* to annihilate; to discourage; **anonadarse** *vr* to get discouraged.

anónimo, a [a'nonimo, a] *a* anonymous; (*COM*) limited // *nm* anonymity.

anormal [anor'mal] *a* abnormal.

anotación [anota'θjon] *nf* note.

anotar [ano'tar] *vt* to note down; (*comentar*) to annotate.

ansia ['ansja] *nf* anxiety; (*añoranza*) yearning; **ansiar** *vt* to long for.

ansiedad [ansje'ðað] *nf* anxiety.

ansioso, a [an'sjoso, a] *a* anxious; (*anhelante*) eager.

antagónico, a [anta'ɣoniko, a] *a* antagonistic; (*opuesto*) contrasting; **antagonista** *nm/f* antagonist.

antaño [an'taɲo] *ad* long ago.

Antártico [an'tartiko] *nm*: **el** ~ the Antarctic.

ante ['ante] *prep* before, in the presence of; (*encarado con*) faced with // *nm* suede, buckskin; ~ **todo** above all.

anteanoche [antea'notʃe] *ad* the night before last.

anteayer [antea'jer] *ad* the day before yesterday.

antebrazo [ante'βraθo] *nm* forearm.

antecedente [anteθe'ðente] *a* previous // *nm* antecedent; ~**s** *nmpl* record *sg*, background *sg.*

anteceder [anteθe'ðer] *vt* to precede, go before.

antecesor, a [anteθe'sor, a] *nm/f* predecessor; (*antepasado*) ancestor.

antedicho, a [ante'ðitʃo, a] *a* aforementioned.

antelación [antela'θjon] *nf*: **con** ~ in advance.

antemano [ante'mano]: **de** ~ *ad* beforehand, in advance.

antena [an'tena] *nf* antenna; (*de televisión etc*) aerial.

anteojo [ante'oxo] *nm* eyeglass; ~**s** *nmpl* spectacles, glasses.

antepasados [antepa'saðos] *nmpl* ancestors.

antepecho [ante'petʃo] *nm* guardrail, parapet; (*repisa*) ledge, sill.

anteponer [antepo'ner] *vt* to place in front; (*fig*) to prefer; ~**se** *vr*: ~**se a** to overcome.

anteproyecto [antepro'jekto] *nm* preliminary sketch; (*fig*) blueprint.

anterior [ante'rjor] *a* preceding, previous; ~**idad** *nf*: **con** ~**idad a** prior to, before.

antes ['antes] *ad* sooner; (*primero*) first; (*con prioridad*) before; (*hace tiempo*) previously, once; (*más bien*) rather // *prep*: ~ **de** before // *conj*: ~ (**de**) **que** before; ~ **bien** (but) rather; **dos días** ~ two days before *or* previously; ~ **muerto que esclavo** better dead than enslaved; **tomo el avión** ~ **que el barco** I take the plane rather than the boat; **cuanto** ~, **lo** ~ **posible** as soon as possible.

antesala [ante'sala] *nf* anteroom.

antibiótico [anti'βjotiko] *nm* antibiotic.

anticipación [antiθipa'θjon] *nf* anticipation; (*COM*) advance; **con 10 minutos de** ~ 10 minutes early; **anticipado, a** *a* (in) advance.

anticipar [antiθi'par] *vt* to anticipate; (*adelantar*) to bring forward; (*COM*) to advance; ~**se** *vr*: ~**se a su época** to be ahead of one's time.

anticipo [anti'θipo] *nm* = **anticipación.**

anticonceptivo, a [antikonθep'tiβo] *a*, *nm* contraceptive.

anticongelante [antikonxe'lante] *nm* antifreeze.

anticuado, a [anti'kwaðo, a] *a* out-of-date, old-fashioned; (*desusado*) obsolete.

anticuario [anti'kwarjo] *nm* antique dealer.

antídoto [an'tiðoto] nm antidote.
antifaz [anti'faθ] nm mask; (velo) veil.
antigualla [anti'ɣwaʎa] nf antique; (reliquia) relic.
antiguamente [antiɣwa'mente] ad formerly; (hace mucho tiempo) long ago.
antigüedad [antiɣwe'ðað] nf antiquity; (articulo) antique; (rango) seniority; **antiguo, a** a old, ancient; (que fue) former.
antílope [an'tilope] nm antelope.
antillano, a [anti'ʎano. a] a, nm/f West Indian.
Antillas [an'tiʎas] nfpl: **las** ~ the West Indies.
antipara [anti'para] nf screen.
antipatía [antipa'tia] nf antipathy, dislike; **antipático, a** a disagreeable, unpleasant.
antisemita [antise'mita] nm/f antisemite.
antítesis [an'titesis] nf antithesis.
antojadizo, a [antoxa'ðiθo, a] a capricious.
antojarse [anto'xarse] vr (desear): **se me antoja comprarlo** I have a mind to buy it; (pensar): **se me antoja que** I have a feeling that.
antojo [an'toxo] nm caprice, whim; (rosa) birthmark; (lunar) mole.
antología [antolo'xia] nf anthology.
antorcha [an'tortʃa] nf torch.
antro ['antro] nm cavern.
antropófago, a [antro'pofaxo. a] a, nm/f cannibal.
antropología [antropolo'xia] nf anthropology.
anual [a'nwal] a annual.
anualidad [anwali'ðað] nf annuity.
anuario [a'nwarjo] nm yearbook.
anublar [anu'ßlar] vt to cloud; (oscurecer) to darken; ~**se** vr to become cloudy, cloud over; (BOT) to wither.
anudar [anu'ðar] vt to knot, tie; (unir) to join; ~**se** vr to get tied up.
anulación [anula'θjon] nf annulment; (cancelación) cancellation; **anular** vt to annul; to cancel; (revocar) to revoke, repeal // nm ring finger.
anunciación [anunθja'θjon] nf announcement; **anunciar** vt to announce; (proclamar) to proclaim; (COM) to advertise.
anuncio [a'nunθjo] nm announcement; (señal) sign; (COM) advertisement; (cartel) poster.
anzuelo [an'θwelo] nm hook; (para pescar) fish hook.
añadidura [aɲaði'ðura] nf addition, extra; **por** ~ besides, in addition.
añadir [aɲa'ðir] vt to add.
añejo, a [a'ɲexo, a] a old.
añicos [a'ɲikos] nmpl: **hacer** ~ to smash, shatter.
año ['aɲo] nm year; ¡**Feliz A**~ **Nuevo!** Happy New Year!; **tener 15** ~**s** to be 15 (years old); **los** ~**s 60** the sixties; ~ **bisiesto/escolar** leap/school year.

añoranza [aɲo'ranθa] nf nostalgia; (anhelo) longing.
apacentar [apaθen'tar] vt to pasture, graze.
apacible [apa'θiβle] a gentle, mild.
apaciguar [apaθi'ɣwar] vt to pacify, calm (down).
apadrinar [apaðri'nar] vt to sponsor, support; (REL) to act as godfather to.
apagado, a [apa'xaðo, a] a out; (volcán) extinct; (cal) slaked; (color) dull; (voz) quiet, timid; (sonido) muted, muffled; (apático) listless.
apagar [apa'xar] vt to put out; (sonido) to silence, muffle; (sed) to quench; (fig) to kill.
apagón [apa'xon] nm blackout, power cut.
apalabrar [apala'ßrar] vt to agree to; (obrero) to engage.
apalear [apale'ar] vt to beat, thrash; (AGR) to winnow.
apañar [apa'ɲar] vt to pick up; (asir) to take hold of, grasp; (vestir) to dress up; (reparar) to mend, patch up; ~**se** vr to manage, get along.
aparador [apara'ðor] nm sideboard; (escaparate) shop window.
aparato [apa'rato] nm apparatus; (máquina) machine; (doméstico) appliance; (boato) ostentation; ~**so, a** a showy, ostentatious.
aparcamiento [aparka'mjento] nm car park.
aparcar [apar'kar] vt, vi to park.
aparecer [apare'θer] vi, ~**se** vr to appear.
aparejado, a [apare'xaðo, a] a fit, suitable.
aparejar [apare'xar] vt to prepare; (caballo) to saddle, harness; (NAUT) to fit out, rig out; **aparejo** nm preparation; harness, rigging; (de poleas) block and tackle.
aparentar [aparen'tar] vt to feign; (parecer) to look, seem (to be).
aparente [apa'rente] a apparent; (adecuado) suitable.
aparición [apari'θjon] nf appearance; (de libro) publication.
apariencia [apa'rjenθja] nf (outward) appearance; **en** ~ outwardly, seemingly.
apartado, a [apar'taðo, a] a separate; (lejano) remote // nm post office box; (tipográfico) paragraph.
apartamento [aparta'mento] nm apartment, flat.
apartamiento [aparta'mjento] nm separation; (aislamiento) remoteness; (AM) apartment, flat.
apartar [apar'tar] vt to separate; (quitar) to remove; (MINEROLOGÍA) to extract; ~**se** vr to separate, part; (irse) to move away, keep away; **aparte** ad (separadamente) separately; (además) besides // nm aside; (tipográfico) new paragraph.
apasionado, a [apasjo'naðo, a] a passionate; biassed, prejudiced.

apasionar [apasjo'nar] *vt* to arouse passion in; ~**se** *vr* to get excited.
apatía [apa'tia] *nf* apathy.
apático, a [a'patiko, a] *a* apathetic.
apdo *nm abr de* **apartado (de correos).**
apeadero [apea'ðero] *nm* halt, wayside station.
apearse [ape'arse] *vr* to dismount; (*bajarse*) to get down/out.
apedrear [apeðre'ar] *vt* to stone.
apegarse [ape'ɣarse] *vr*: ~**se a** to become attached to; **apego** *nm* attachment, fondness.
apelación [apela'θjon] *nf* appeal.
apelante [ape'lante] *nm/f* appellant.
apelar [ape'lar] *vi* to appeal; ~ **a** to resort to.
apellidar [apeʎi'ðar] *vt* to call, name; ~**se** *vr* to be called; **apellido** *nm* surname, name.
apenar [ape'nar] *vt* to grieve, trouble; ~**se** *vr* to grieve.
apenas [a'penas] *ad* scarcely, hardly // *conj* as soon as, no sooner.
apéndice [a'pendiθe] *nm* appendix; **apendicitis** *nf* appendicitis.
apercibir [aperθi'ßir] *vt* to prepare; (*avisar*) to warn; (*JUR*) to summon; (*AM*) to notice, see; ~**se** *vr* to get ready.
aperitivo [aperi'tißo] *nm* aperitif.
apertura [aper'tura] *nf* opening.
apesadumbrar [apesaðum'brar] *vt* to grieve, sadden; ~**se** *vr* to distress o.s.
apestar [apes'tar] *vt* to infect // *vi* to stink.
apetecer [apete'θer] *vt*: ¿**te apetece una tortilla?** do you fancy an omelette?; **apetecible** *a* desirable; (*llamativo*) attractive.
apetito [ape'tito] *nm* appetite; ~**so, a** *a* appetizing; (*fig*) tempting.
apiadarse [apja'ðarse] *vr*: ~ **de** to take pity on.
ápice ['apiθe] *nm* apex; (*fig*) whit, iota.
apio ['apjo] *nm* celery.
aplacar [apla'kar] *vt* to placate; ~**se** *vr* to calm down.
aplanamiento [aplana'mjento] *nm* smoothing, levelling.
aplanar [apla'nar] *vt* to smooth, level; (*allanar*) to roll flat, flatten.
aplastar [aplas'tar] *vt* to squash (flat); (*fig*) to crush.
aplaudir [aplau'ðir] *vt* to applaud.
aplauso [a'plauso] *nm* applause; (*fig*) approval, acclaim.
aplazamiento [aplaθa'mjento] *nm* postponement, adjournment; **aplazar** *vt* to postpone, defer.
aplicación [aplika'θjon] *nf* application; (*esfuerzo*) effort.
aplicado, a [apli'kaðo, a] *a* diligent, hard-working.
aplicar [apli'kar] *vt* (*ejecutar*) to apply; ~**se** *vr* to apply o.s.

aplomo [a'plomo] *nm* aplomb, self-assurance.
apocado, a [apo'kaðo, a] *a* timid.
apocamiento [apoka'mjento] *nm* timidity; (*depresión*) depression.
apocar [apo'kar] *vt* to reduce; ~**se** *vr* to feel small, feel humiliated.
apodar [apo'ðar] *vt* to nickname.
apoderado [apoðe'raðo] *nm* agent, representative; **apoderar** *vt* to authorize, empower; (*JUR*) to grant (a) power of attorney to; **apoderarse** *vr*: **apoderarse de** to take possession of.
apodo [a'poðo] *nm* nickname.
apogeo [apo'xeo] *nm* peak, summit.
apología [apolo'xia] *nf* eulogy; (*defensa*) defence.
apoplejía [aplple'xia] *nf* apoplexy, stroke.
aporrear [aporre'ar] *vt* to beat (up); **aporreo** *nm* beating.
aportar [apor'tar] *vt* to contribute // *vi* to reach port; ~**se** *vr* (*AM*) to arrive, come.
aposentar [aposen'tar] *vt* to lodge, put up; **aposento** *nm* lodging; (*habitación*) room.
apostar [apos'tar] *vt* to bet, stake; (*destinar*) to station, post // *vi* to bet.
apostilla [apos'tiʎa] *nf* note, comment.
apóstol [a'postol] *nm* apostle.
apóstrofe [a'postrofe] *nm* insult; (*reprimenda*) reprimand.
apóstrofo [a'postrofo] *nm* apostrophe.
apostura [apos'tura] *nf* neatness, elegance.
apoyar [apo'jar] *vt* to lean, rest; (*fig*) to support, back; ~**se** *vr*: ~**se en** to lean on; **apoyo** *nm* support, backing; (*sostén*) prop.
apreciable [apre'θjaßle] *a* considerable; (*fig*) esteemed.
apreciación [apreθja'θjon] *nf* appreciation; (*COM*) valuation; **apreciar** *vt* to evaluate, assess; (*COM*) to appreciate, value.
aprecio [a'preθjo] *nm* valuation, estimate; (*fig*) appreciation.
aprehender [apreen'der] *vt* to apprehend, seize; **aprehensión** *nf* detention, capture.
apremiante [apre'mjante] *a* urgent, pressing; **apremiar** *vt* to compel, force // *vi* to be urgent, press; **apremio** *nm* compulsion; urgency.
aprender [apren'der] *vt, vi* to learn.
aprendiz, a [apren'diθ, a] *nm/f* apprentice; (*principiante*) learner; ~**aje** *nm* apprenticeship.
aprensión [apren'sjon] *nm* apprehension, fear; (*delicadeza*) squeamishness; **aprensivo, a** *a* apprehensive; (*nervioso*) nervous, timid.
apresar [apre'sar] *vt* to seize; (*capturar*) to capture.
aprestar [apres'tar] *vt* to prepare, get ready; (*TEC*) to prime, size; ~**se** *vr* to get ready.
apresurado, a [apresu'raðo, a] *a* hurried,

hasty; **apresuramiento** nm hurry, haste.
apresurar [apresu'rar] vt to hurry, accelerate; ~**se** vr to hurry, make haste.
apretado, a [apre'taðo, a] a tight; (escritura) cramped; (difícil) difficult; (fam) stingy.
apretar [apre'tar] vt to squeeze, press; (TEC) to tighten; (presionar) to press together, pack // vi to be too tight; (insistir) to insist.
apretón [apre'ton] nm squeeze; (abrazo) hug; (aglomeración) crush; (dificultad) difficulty, jam; (carrera) dash, sprint; ~ **de manos** handshake; **apretura** nf squeeze; hug; crush; difficulty, jam; (escasez) scarcity.
aprieto [a'prjeto] nm squeeze, press; (dificultad) difficulty, jam.
aprisionar [aprisjo'nar] vt to imprison.
aprobación [aproβa'θjon] nf approval; (de examen) pass; (nota) pass mark; **aprobar** vt to approve (of); to pass // vi to pass.
apropiación [apropja'θjon] nf appropriation.
apropiado, a [apro'pjaðo, a] a appropriate.
apropiar [apro'pjar] vt to adapt, make fit; ~**se** vr: ~**se de** to appropriate.
aprovechado, a [aproβe'tʃaðo, a] a diligent, hardworking; (económico) thrifty; (pey) unscrupulous, grasping; **aprovechamiento** nm use, exploitation.
aprovechar [aproβe'tʃar] vt to use, exploit, profit from; (sacar partido de) to take advantage of // vi to progress, improve; ~**se** vr: ~**se de** to make use of, take advantage of; ¡**que aproveche!** enjoy your meal!
aproximación [aproksima'θjon] nf approximation; (cercanía) nearness; (de lotería) consolation prize; **aproximado, a** a approximate; **aproximar** vt to bring nearer; **aproximarse** vr to come near, approach.
aptitud [apti'tuð] nf aptitude; (idoneidad) suitability.
apto, a ['apto, a] a suitable.
apuesto, a [a'pwesto, a] a neat, elegant // nf bet, wager.
apuntador [apunta'ðor] nm prompter.
apuntalar [apunta'lar] vt to prop up.
apuntar [apun'tar] vt (con arma) to aim at; (con dedo) to point at or to; (anotar) to note (down); (TEATRO) to prompt; (dinero) to stake; ~**se** vr to score a point.
apunte [a'punte] nm note.
apuñalar [apuɲa'lar] vt to stab.
apurado, a [apu'raðo, a] a needy; (difícil) difficult, dangerous; (agotado) exhausted; (AM) hurried, rushed.
apurar [apu'rar] vt (purificar) to purify; (agotar) to drain; (recursos) to use up; (molestar) to annoy; ~**se** vr to worry; (AM) to hurry.
apuro [a'puro] nm (aprieto) fix, jam; (escasez) want, hardship; (aflicción) distress; (AM) haste, urgency.

aquejar [ake'xar] vt to distress, grieve; (MED) to afflict.
aquel, aquella, aquellos, as [a'kel, a'keʎa, a'keʎos, as] det that; (pl) those.
aquél, aquélla, aquéllos, as [a'kel, a'keʎa, a'keʎos, as] pron that (one); (pl) those (ones).
aquello [a'keʎo] pron that, that business.
aquí [a'ki] ad (lugar) here; (tiempo) now; ~ **arriba** up here; ~ **mismo** right here; ~ **yace** here lies; **de** ~ **a siete días** a week from now.
aquietar [akje'tar] vt to quieten (down), calm (down).
árabe ['araβe] a Arab, Arabian, Arabic // nm/f Arab // nm (lengua) Arabic.
Arabia Saudita [araβjasau'ðita] nf Saudi Arabia.
arado [a'raðo] nm plough.
aragonés, esa [arayo'nes, esa] a, nm/f Aragonese.
arancel [aran'θel] nm tariff, duty; ~ **de aduanas** customs duty.
araña [a'raɲa] nf (ZOOL) spider; (de luces) chandelier.
arañar [ara'ɲar] vt to scratch.
arañazo [ara'ɲaθo] nm scratch.
arar [a'rar] vt to plough, till.
arbitrador, a [arβitra'ðor, a] a nm/f arbiter.
arbitraje [arβi'traxe] nm arbitration.
arbitrar [arβi'trar] vt to arbitrate in; (DEPORTE) to referee // vi to arbitrate.
arbitrariedad [arβitrarje'ðað] nf arbitrariness; (acto) arbitrary act; **arbitrario, a** a arbitrary.
arbitrio [ar'βitrjo] nm free will; (JUR) adjudication, decision.
árbitro ['arβitro] nm arbitrator; (DEPORTE) referee; (TENIS) umpire.
árbol ['arβol] nm (BOT) tree; (NAUT) mast; (TEC) axle, shaft; **arbolado, a** a wooded, tree-lined // nm woodland.
arboladura [arβola'ðura] nf rigging; **arbolar** vt to hoist, raise; **arbolarse** vr to rear up.
arboleda [arβo'leða] nf grove, plantation.
arbusto [ar'βusto] nm bush, shrub.
arca ['arka] nf chest, box; (caja fuerte) strongbox.
arcada [ar'kaða] nf arcade; (de puente) arch, span; ~**s** nfpl retching sg.
arcaduz [arka'ðuθ] nm pipe, conduit.
arcaico, a [ar'kaiko, a] a archaic.
arce ['arθe] nm maple tree.
arcediano [arθe'ðjano] nm archdeacon.
arcilla [ar'θiʎa] nf clay.
arco ['arko] nm arch; (MAT) arc; (MIL, MUS) bow; ~ **iris** rainbow.
archipiélago [artʃi'pjelaxo] nm archipelago.
archivar [artʃi'βar] vt to file (away); **archivo** nm archive(s) (pl).
arder [ar'ðer] vi, vt to burn.
ardid [ar'ðið] nm ruse.

ardiente [ar'ðjente] *a* burning; (*apasionado*) ardent.
ardilla [ar'ðiʎa] *nf* squirrel.
ardor [ar'ðor] *nm* (*calor*) heat, warmth; (*fig*) ardour; ~ **de estómago** heartburn; ~**oso, a** *a* = **ardiente**.
arduo, a ['arðwo, a] *a* arduous.
área ['area] *nf* area; (*DEPORTE*) penalty area.
arena [a'rena] *nf* sand; (*de una lucha*) arena; (*MED*) stone.
arenal [are'nal] *nm* sandy ground; (*arena movediza*) quicksand.
arengar [aren'gar] *vt* to harangue.
arenisco, a [are'nisko, a] *a* sandy // *nf* sandstone; (*cascajo*) grit.
arenoso, a [are'noso, a] *a* sandy.
arenque [a'renke] *nm* herring.
arete [a'rete] *nm* earring.
argamasa [arɣa'masa] *nf* mortar, plaster; **argamasar** *vt* to mortar, plaster.
Argel [ar'xel] *n* Algiers; ~**ia** *nf* Algeria; **argelino, a** *a, nm/f* Algerian.
argentino, a [arxen'tino, a] *a* Argentinian; (*de plata*) silvery // *nm/f* Argentinian // *nf*: **A~a** Argentina.
argolla [ar'ɣoʎa] *nf* (large) ring; (*juego*) croquet.
argot [ar'ɣo] *nm* slang.
argucia [ar'ɣuθja] *nf* subtlety, sophistry.
argüir [ar'ɣwir] *vt* to deduce; (*discutir*) to argue; (*indicar*) to indicate, imply; (*censurar*) to reproach // *vi* to argue.
argumentación [arɣumenta'θjon] *nf* (line of) argument; **argumentar** *vt, vi* to argue.
argumento [arɣu'mento] *nm* argument; (*de obra*) plot.
aria ['arja] *nf* aria.
aridez [ari'ðeθ] *nf* aridity, dryness.
árido, a ['ariðo, a] *a* arid, dry; ~**s** *nmpl* dry goods.
Aries ['arjes] *nm* Aries.
ariete [a'rjete] *nm* battering ram.
ario, a [a'rjo, a] *a* Aryan.
arisco, a [a'risko, a] *a* surly; (*insociable*) unsociable.
aristócrata [aris'tokrata] *nm/f* aristocrat.
aritmética [arit'metika] *nf* arithmetic.
arma ['arma] *nf* arm; ~**s** *nfpl* arms; ~ **blanca** blade, knife; (*espada*) sword; ~ **de fuego** firearm; ~**s cortas** small arms.
armadillo [arma'ðiʎo] *nm* armadillo.
armado, a [ar'maðo, a] *a* armed; (*TEC*) reinforced // *nf* armada; (*flota*) fleet.
armadura [arma'ðura] *nf* (*MIL*) armour; (*TEC*) framework; (*ZOOL*) skeleton; (*FÍSICA*) armature.
armamento [arma'mento] *nm* armament; (*NAUT*) fitting-out.
armar [ar'mar] *vt* (*soldado*) to arm; (*máquina*) to assemble; (*navío*) to fit out; ~**la**, ~ **un lío** to start a row.
armario [ar'marjo] *nm* wardrobe.
armatoste [arma'toste] *nm* large useless object, contraption.
armazón [arma'θon] *nf* body, chassis; (*de mueble etc*) frame; (*ARQ*) skeleton.
armería [arme'ria] *nf* (*museo*) military museum; (*tienda*) gunsmith's.
armiño [ar'mino] *nm* stoat; (*piel*) ermine.
armisticio [armis'tiθjo] *nm* armistice.
armonía [armo'nia] *nf* harmony.
armónica [ar'monika] *nf* harmonica.
armonioso, a [armo'njoso, a] *a* harmonious.
arnés [ar'nes] *nm* armour; **arneses** *nmpl* harness *sg*.
aro ['aro] *nm* ring; (*tejo*) quoit; (*pendiente*) earring.
aroma [a'roma] *nm* aroma.
aromático, a [aro'matiko, a] *a* aromatic.
arpa ['arpa] *nf* harp.
arpía [ar'pia] *nf* shrew.
arpista [ar'pista] *nm/f* harpist.
arpón [ar'pon] *nm* harpoon.
arquear [arke'ar] *vt* to arch, bend; ~**se** *vr* to arch, bend; **arqueo** *nm* (*gen*) arching, curve; (*de navío*) tonnage.
arqueología [arkeolo'xia] *nf* archaeology; **arqueólogo, a** *nm/f* archaeologist.
arquero [ar'kero] *nm* archer, bowman.
arquetipo [arke'tipo] *nm* archetype.
arquitecto [arki'tekto] *nm* architect; **arquitectura** *nf* architecture.
arrabal [arra'ßal] *nm* suburb; (*AM*) slum.
arraigado, a [arrai'xaðo, a] *a* deep-rooted; (*fig*) established.
arraigar [arrai'xar] *vt* to establish // *vi*, ~**se** *vr* to take root.
arrancar [arran'kar] *vt* (*sacar*) to pull up, extract, pull out; (*separar*) to snatch (away), wrest; (*fig*) to extract // *vi* to start, pull out.
arranque [a'rranke] *nm* sudden start; (*AUTO*) start; (*fig*) fit, outburst.
arras ['arras] *nfpl* pledge *sg*, security *sg*.
arrasar [arra'sar] *vt* (*aplanar*) to level, flatten; (*destruir*) to demolish; (*llenar*) to fill up // *vi* to clear.
arrastrado, a [arras'traðo, a] *a* poor, wretched; (*AM*) servile.
arrastrar [arras'trar] *vt* to drag (along); (*fig*) to drag down, degrade; (*suj: agua, viento*) to carry away // *vi* to drag, trail on the ground; ~**se** *vr* to crawl; (*fig*) to grovel; **llevar algo arrastrado** to drag sth along.
arrastre [a'rrastre] *nm* drag, dragging; (*DEPORTE*) crawl.
arrayán [arra'jan] *nm* myrtle.
arrear [arre'ar] *vt* to drive, urge on; (*enganchar*) to harness // *vi* to hurry along; ¡**arre(a)!** get up!, gee up!
arrebatado, a [arreßa'taðo, a] *a* rash, impetuous; (*repentino*) sudden, hasty.
arrebatar [arreßa'tar] *vt* to snatch (away), seize; (*fig*) to captivate; ~**se** *vr* to get carried away, get excited.
arrebato [arre'ßato] *nm* fit of rage, fury; (*éxtasis*) rapture.
arreglado, a [arre'xlaðo, a] *a* (*ordenado*)

neat, orderly; (*moderado*) moderate, reasonable.

arreglar [arre'xlar] *vt* (*poner orden*) to tidy up; (*algo roto*) to fix, repair; (*problema*) to solve; (*MUS*) to arrange; ~**se** *vr* to reach an understanding; **arreglárselas** (*fam*) to get by, manage.

arreglo [a'rrexlo] *nm* settlement; (*orden*) order; (*acuerdo*) agreement; (*MUS*) arrangement, setting.

arremangar [arreman'gar] *vt* to roll up, turn up; ~**se** *vr* to roll up one's sleeves.

arremeter [arreme'ter] *vt* to attack, assault.

arrendador, a [arrenda'ðor, a] *nm/f* landlord/lady; (*inquilino*) tenant.

arrendamiento [arrenda'mjento] *nm* letting; (*alquilar*) hiring; (*contrato*) lease; (*alquiler*) rent; **arrendar** *vt* to let, lease; to rent; **arrendatario, a** *nm/f* tenant.

arreo [a'rreo] *nm* adornment; ~**s** *nmpl* harness *sg*, trappings.

arrepentimiento [arrepenti'mjento] *nm* regret, repentance.

arrepentirse [arrepen'tirse] *vr*: ~ **de** to regret, repent of.

arrestar [arres'tar] *vt* to arrest; (*encarcelar*) to imprison; **arresto** *nm* arrest; (*MIL*) detention; (*audacia*) boldness, daring; **arresto domiciliario** house arrest.

arriar [a'rrjar] *vt* (*velas, bandera*) to lower, strike; (*un cable*) to pay out; ~**se** *vr* to flood.

arriba [a'rriβa] *ad* (*posición*) above, overhead, on top; (*en casa*) upstairs; (*dirección*) up, upwards; ~ **de** above, higher (up) than; ~ **del todo** at the very top; **el piso de** ~ the flat upstairs; **de** ~ **abajo** from top to bottom; **calle** ~ up the street; **lo** ~ **mencionado** the aforementioned; ~ **de 20 pesetas** more than 20 pesetas; ¡~ **las manos!** hands up!

arribar [arri'βar] *vi* to put into port; (*llegar*) to arrive.

arribista [arri'βista] *nm/f* parvenu/e, upstart.

arriendo [a'rrjendo] *nm* = **arrendamiento**.

arriero [a'rrjero] *nm* muleteer.

arriesgado, a [arrjes'xaðo, a] *a* (*peligroso*) risky; (*audaz*) bold, daring; **arriesgar** *vt* to risk; (*poner en peligro*) to endanger; **arriesgarse** *vr* to take a risk.

arrimar [arri'mar] *vt* (*acercar*) to bring close; (*poner de lado*) to set aside; ~**se** *vr* to come close *or* closer; ~**se a** to lean on; **arrimo** *nm* approach; (*fig*) support.

arrinconado, a [arrinko'naðo, a] *a* forgotten, neglected; **arrinconar** *vt* to put in a corner; (*fig*) to put on one side; (*abandonar*) to push aside; **arrinconarse** *vr* to withdraw from the world.

arrodillarse [arroði'ʎarse] *vr* to kneel, kneel down.

arrogancia [arro'xanθja] *nf* arrogance; **arrogante** *a* arrogant.

arrojar [arro'xar] *vt* to throw, hurl; (*humo*) to emit, give out; (*COM*) to yield, produce; ~**se** *vr* to throw *or* hurl o.s.

arrojo [a'rroxo] *nm* daring.

arrollador, a [arroʎa'ðor, a] *a* crushing, overwhelming.

arropar [arro'par] *vt* to cover, wrap up; ~**se** *vr* to wrap o.s. up.

arrope [a'rrope] *nm* syrup.

arrostrar [arros'trar] *vt* to face (up to); ~**se** *vr* to rush into the fight.

arroyo [a'rrojo] *nm* stream; (*de la calle*) gutter.

arroz [a'rroθ] *nm* rice; ~ **con leche** rice pudding.

arruga [a'rruxa] *nf* fold; (*de cara*) wrinkle; (*de vestido*) crease; **arrugar** *vt* to fold; to wrinkle; to crease; **arrugarse** *vr* to get creased.

arruinar [arrwi'nar] *vt* to ruin, wreck; ~**se** *vr* to be ruined.

arrullar [arru'ʎar] *vi* to coo // *vt* to lull to sleep.

arsenal [arse'nal] *nm* naval dockyard; (*MIL*) arsenal.

arsénico [ar'seniko] *nm* arsenic.

arte ['arte] *nm* (*gen m en sg y siempre f en pl*) art; (*maña*) skill, guile; ~**s** *nfpl* arts.

artefacto [arte'fakto] *nm* appliance; (*ARQUEOLOGÍA*) artefact.

artejo [ar'texo] *nm* knuckle.

arteria [ar'terja] *nf* artery.

artesanía [artesa'nia] *nf* craftsmanship; (*artículos*) handicrafts *pl*; **artesano** *nm* artisan, craftsman.

ártico, a ['artiko, a] *a* Arctic // *nm*: **el Á**~ the Arctic.

articulación [artikula'θjon] *nf* articulation; (*MED, TEC*) joint; **articulado, a** *a* articulated; jointed; **articular** *vt* to articulate; to join together.

artículo [ar'tikulo] *nm* article; (*cosa*) thing, article; ~**s** *nmpl* goods.

artífice [ar'tifiθe] *nm* artist, craftsman; (*fig*) architect.

artificial [artifi'θjal] *a* artificial.

artificio [arti'fiθjo] *nm* art, skill; (*artesanía*) craftsmanship; (*astucia*) cunning; ~**so, a** a skilful, clever; cunning.

artillería [artiʎe'ria] *nf* artillery.

artillero [arti'ʎero] *nm* artilleryman, gunner.

artimaña [arti'maɲa] *nf* trap, snare; (*astucia*) cunning.

artista [ar'tista] *nm/f* (*pintor*) artist, painter; (*TEATRO*) artist, artiste; **artístico, a** *a* artistic.

artritis [ar'tritis] *nf* arthritis.

arzobispo [arθo'βispo] *nm* archbishop.

as [as] *nm* ace.

asa ['asa] *nf* handle; (*fig*) lever.

asado [a'saðo] *nm* roast (meat).

asador [asa'ðor] *nm* spit.

asalariado, a [asala'rjaðo, a] *a* paid, wage-earning // *nm/f* wage earner.

asaltabancos [asalta'bankos] *nm inv* bank robber.

asaltador, a [asalta'ðor, a], **asaltante** [asal'tante] *nm/f* assailant; **asaltar** *vt* to attack, assault; (*fig*) to assail; **asalto** *nm* attack, assault; (*DEPORTE*) round.

asamblea [asam'blea] *nf* assembly; (*reunión*) meeting.

asar [a'sar] *vt* to roast.

asbesto [as'ßesto] *nm* asbestos.

ascendencia [asθen'denθja] *nf* ancestry; (*AM*) ascendancy.

ascender [asθen'der] *vi* (*subir*) to ascend, rise; (*ser promovido*) to gain promotion // *vt* to promote; ~ **a** to amount to; **ascendiente** *nm* ascendency, influence // *nm/f* ancestor.

ascensión [asθen'sjon] *nf* ascent; **la A**~ the Ascension.

ascensionista [asθensjo'nista] *nm/f* balloonist.

ascenso [as'θenso] *nm* ascent; (*promoción*) promotion.

ascensor [asθen'sor] *nm* lift, elevator.

ascético, a [as'θetiko, a] *a* ascetic.

asco ['asko] *nm* loathing, disgust; (*cosa*) loathsome thing; **el ajo me da** ~ I hate *or* loathe garlic.

ascua ['askwa] *nf* ember.

aseado, a [ase'aðo, a] *a* clean; (*arreglado*) tidy; (*pulcro*) smart; **asear** *vt* to clean, wash; to tidy (up); (*adornar*) to adorn.

asediar [ase'ðjar] *vt* to besiege, lay siege to; (*fig*) to chase, pester; **asedio** *nm* siege; (*COM*) run.

asegurado, a [aseɤu'raðo, a] *a* insured; **asegurador, a** *nm/f* insurer; underwriter.

asegurar [aseɤu'rar] *vt* (*consolidar*) to secure, fasten; (*dar garantía de*) to guarantee; (*preservar*) to safeguard; (*afirmar, dar por cierto*) to assure, affirm; (*tranquilizar*) to reassure; (*tomar un seguro*) to insure; ~**se** *vr* to assure o.s., make sure.

asemejarse [aseme'xarse] *vr* to be alike; ~ **a** to be like, resemble.

asentado, a [asen'taðo, a] *a* established, settled.

asentar [asen'tar] *vt* (*sentar*) to seat, sit down; (*poner*) to place, establish; (*alisar*) to level, smooth down *or* out; (*anotar*) to note down; (*afirmar*) to affirm, assert; (*afinar*) to sharpen, hone // *vi* to be suitable, suit.

asentir [asen'tir] *vi* to assent, agree.

aseo [a'seo] *nm* cleanliness; ~**s** *nmpl* toilet *sg*, cloakroom *sg*.

asequible [ase'kißle] *a* attainable, available.

aserradero [aserra'ðero] *nm* sawmill; **aserrar** *vt* to saw.

aserrín [ase'rrin] *nm* sawdust.

asesinar [asesi'nar] *vt* to murder; (*POL*) to assassinate; (*fig*) to pester; **asesinato** *nm* murder; assassination.

asesino, a [ase'sino, a] *nm/f* murderer, killer; (*POL*) assassin.

asesor, a [ase'sor, a] *nm/f* adviser, consultant.

asfalto [as'falto] *nm* asphalt.

asfixia [as'fiksja] *nf* suffocation.

asfixiar [asfik'sjar] *vt*, ~**se** *vr* to asphyxiate, suffocate.

asgo *etc vb ver* **asir**.

así [a'si] *ad* (*de esta manera*) so, in this way, like this, thus; (*aunque*) although; (*tan luego como*) as soon as; ~ **que** so, therefore; ~ **como** as well as; ~ **y todo** even so; **¿no es** ~**?** isn't it?, didn't you? *etc.*

Asia ['asja] *nf* Asia; **asiático, a** *a* Asiatic, Asian.

asidero [asi'ðero] *nm* handle.

asiduidad [asiðwi'ðað] *nf* assiduousness; **asiduo, a** *a* assiduous; (*frecuente*) frequent // *nm/f* regular (customer).

asiento [a'sjento] *nm* (*mueble*) seat, chair; (*de coche, en tribunal etc*) seat; (*localidad*) seat, place; (*fundamento*) site; (*colocación*) establishment; (*depósito*) sediment; (*cordura*) good sense; ~ **delantero/trasero** front/back seat.

asignación [asixna'θjon] *nf* (*atribución*) assignment; (*reparto*) allocation; (*cita*) appointment; (*sueldo*) salary; **asignar** *vt* to assign, allocate.

asignatura [asixna'tura] *nf* subject.

asilo [a'silo] *nm* (*refugio*) asylum, refuge; (*establecimiento*) home, institution.

asimilación [asimila'θjon] *nf* assimilation.

asimilar [asimi'lar] *vt* to assimilate; ~**se** *vr*: ~**se a** to resemble; (*incorporarse*) to become assimilated to.

asimismo [asi'mismo] *ad* in the same way, likewise.

asir [a'sir] *vt* to seize, grasp.

asistencia [asis'tenθja] *nf* audience; (*MED*) attendance; (*ayuda*) assistance; **asistir** *vt* to assist // *vi* to attend, be present.

asma ['asma] *nf* asthma.

asno ['asno] *nm* donkey; (*fig*) ass.

asociación [asoθja'θjon] *nf* association; (*COM*) partnership; ~ **aduanera** customs union; **asociado, a** *a* associate // *nm/f* associate; partner.

asociar [aso'θjar] *vt* to combine.

asolear [asole'ar] *vt* to put in the sun; ~**se** *vr* to sunbathe.

asomar [aso'mar] *vt* to show, stick out // *vi* to appear; ~**se** *vr* to appear, show up; ~ **la cabeza por la ventana** to put one's head out of the window.

asombrar [asom'brar] *vt* (*causar admiración, sorpresa*) to amaze, astonish; (*asustar*) to frighten; (*dar sombra a*) to shade; ~**se** *vr* to be amazed; to be frightened; **asombro** *nm* amazement, astonishment; fright; **asombroso, a** *a* astonishing, amazing.

asomo [a'somo] *nm* hint, sign; (*apariencia*) appearance.

aspa ['aspa] *nf* (*cruz*) cross; (*de molino*) sail.

aspar [as'par] vt to reel, wind; (fig) to vex, annoy.

aspaviento [aspa'ßjento] nm exaggerated display of feeling; (fam) fuss.

aspecto [as'pekto] nm (apariencia) look, appearance; (fig) aspect.

aspereza [aspe'reθa] nf roughness; (agrura) sourness; (severidad) harshness, surliness; **áspero, a** a rough; bitter, sour; harsh.

aspersión [asper'sjon] nf sprinkling.

áspid ['aspið] nm asp.

aspiración [aspira'θjon] nf breath, inhalation; (MUS) short pause; **aspiraciones** nfpl (AM) aspirations.

aspiradora [aspira'ðora] nf vacuum cleaner.

aspirar [aspi'rar] vt to breathe in // vi: ~ a to aspire to.

aspirina [aspi'rina] nf aspirin.

asquear [aske'ar] vt to sicken // vi to be sickening; ~**se** vr to feel disgusted; **asqueroso, a** a disgusting, sickening.

asta ['asta] nf lance; (arpón) spear; (mango) shaft, handle; (ZOOL) horn; **a media ~** at half mast.

astilla [as'tiʎa] nf splinter; (pedacito) chip; ~**s** nfpl firewood sg.

astillero [asti'ʎero] nm shipyard.

astringente [astrin'xente] a, nm astringent.

astringir [astrin'xir] vt to bind.

astro ['astro] nm star.

astrología [astrolo'xia] nf astrology; **astrólogo, a** nm/f astrologer.

astronauta [astro'nauta] nm/f astronaut.

astronomía [astrono'mia] nf astronomy; **astrónomo** nm astronomer.

astucia [as'tuθja] nf astuteness; (destreza) clever trick; **astuto, a** a astute; (taimado) cunning.

asueto [a'sweto] nm holiday; (tiempo libre) time off q.

asumir [asu'mir] vt to assume.

asunción [asun'θjon] nf assumption.

asunto [a'sunto] nm (tema) matter, subject; (negocio) business.

asustar [asus'tar] vt to frighten; ~**se** vr to be/become frightened.

atacar [ata'kar] vt to attack.

atadura [ata'ðura] nf bond, tie.

atajo [a'taxo] nm short cut; (DEPORTE) tackle.

ataque [a'take] nm attack; ~ **cardíaco** heart attack.

atar [a'tar] vt to tie, tie up; ~**se** vr (fig) to be or get embarrassed.

atardecer [atarðe'θer] vi to get dark // nm evening; (crepúsculo) dusk.

atareado, a [atare'aðo, a] a busy.

atarear [atare'ar] vt to give a job to; ~**se** vr to be busy, keep busy.

atascamiento [ataska'mjento] nm = **atasco.**

atascar [atas'kar] vt to clog up; (obstruir) to jam; (fig) to hinder; ~**se** vr to stall;

(cañería) to get clogged up; **atasco** nm obstruction; (AUTO) traffic jam.

ataúd [ata'uð] nm coffin.

ataviar [ata'ßjar] vt to deck, array; ~**se** vr to dress up.

atavío [ata'ßio] nm attire, dress; ~**s** nmpl finery sg.

atemorizar [atemori'θar] vt to frighten, scare; ~**se** vr to get scared.

Atenas [a'tenas] n Athens.

atención [aten'θjon] nf attention; (bondad) kindness; (cortesía) civility // excl (be) careful!, look out!

atender [aten'der] vt to attend to, look after // vi to pay attention.

atenerse [ate'nerse] vr: ~ a to abide by, adhere to.

atentado [aten'taðo] nm crime, illegal act; (asalto) assault; (contra la vida de uno) attempt on sb's life.

atentar [aten'tar] vi: ~ a o contra to commit an outrage against.

atento, a [a'tento, a] a attentive, observant; (cortés) polite, thoughtful.

atenuación [atenwa'θjon] nf attenuation, lessening; **atenuante** a attenuating, extenuating; **atenuar** vt to attenuate; (disminuir) to lessen, minimize.

ateo, a [a'teo, a] a atheistic // nm/f atheist.

aterrador, a [aterra'ðor, a] a frightening.

aterrar [ate'rrar] vt to pull down, demolish; (AGR) to cover with earth; (espantar) to frighten; ~**se** vr to be frightened.

aterrizar [aterri'θar] vi to land.

aterrorizar [aterrori'θar] vt to terrify; (MIL, POL) to terrorize.

atesorar [ateso'rar] vt to hoard, store up.

atestar [ates'tar] vt to pack, stuff; (JUR) to attest, testify to.

atestiguar [atesti'xwar] vt to testify to, bear witness to.

atiborrar [atißo'rrar] vt to fill, stuff; ~**se** vr to stuff o.s.

ático ['atiko] nm attic.

atildar [atil'dar] vt to criticize; ~**se** vr to spruce o.s. up.

atisbar [atis'ßar] vt to spy on; (echar ojeada) to peep at.

atizar [ati'θar] vt to poke; (horno etc) to stoke; (fig) to stir up, rouse.

atlántico, a [at'lantiko, a] a Atlantic // nm: **el (océano) A~** the Atlantic (Ocean).

atlas ['atlas] nm atlas.

atleta [at'leta] nm athlete; **atlético, a** a athletic; **atletismo** nm athletics sg.

atmósfera [at'mosfera] nf atmosphere.

atolondramiento [atolondra'mjento] nm bewilderment; (insensatez) silliness.

atollar [ato'ʎar] vi, ~**se** vr to get stuck; (fig) to get into a jam.

atómico, a [a'tomiko, a] a atomic.

atomizador [atomiθa'ðor] nm atomizer.

átomo ['atomo] nm atom.

atónito, a [a'tonito, a] a astonished, amazed.

atontado, a [aton'taðo, a] a stunned; (bobo) silly, daft.

atontar [aton'tar] vt to stun; ~se vr to become bewildered.

atormentar [atormen'tar] vt to torture; (molestar) to torment; (acosar) to plague, harass.

atornillar [atorni'ʎar] vt to screw on or down.

atracar [atra'kar] vt (NAUT) to moor; (robar) to hold up, rob; (fam) to stuff (with food) // vi to moor.

atracción [atrak'θjon] nf attraction.

atraco [a'trako] nm holdup, robbery.

atractivo, a [atrak'tiβo, a] a attractive // nm attraction; (belleza) attractiveness.

atraer [atra'er] vt to attract.

atrancar [atran'kar] vt (con tranca, barra) to bar, bolt.

atrapar [atra'par] vt to trap; (fig) to take in, deceive.

atrás [a'tras] ad (movimiento) back, backwards; (lugar) behind; (tiempo) previously; **ir hacia** ~ to go back or backwards; to go to the rear; **estar** ~ to be behind or at the back.

atrasado, a [atra'saðo, a] a slow; (pago) overdue, late; (país) backward.

atrasar [atra'sar] vi to be slow; ~se vr to remain behind; (llegar tarde) to arrive late; **atraso** nm slowness; lateness, delay; (de país) backwardness; **atrasos** nmpl arrears.

atravesar [atraβe'sar] vt (cruzar) to cross (over); (traspasar) to pierce, go through; (poner al través) to lay or put across; ~se vr to come in between; (intervenir) to interfere.

atrayente [atra'jente] a attractive.

atreverse [atre'βerse] vr to dare; (insolentarse) to be insolent; **atrevido, a** a daring; insolent; **atrevimiento** nm daring; insolence.

atribuir [atriβu'ir] vt to attribute; (funciones) to confer.

atribular [atriβu'lar] vt to afflict, distress; ~se vr to grieve, be distressed.

atributo [atri'βuto] nm attribute.

atrocidad [atroθi'ðað] nf atrocity, outrage.

atropellar [atrope'ʎar] vt (derribar) to knock over, knock down; (empujar) to push (aside); (pasar por encima de) to run over, run down; (agraviar) to insult; ~se vr to act hastily; **atropello** nm accident; push; insult; (agravio) wrong; (atrocidad) outrage.

atroz [a'troθ] a atrocious, awful.

atto, a abr de **atento**.

atuendo [a'twendo] nm dress.

atún [a'tun] nm tuna, tunny.

aturdir [atur'ðir] vt to stun; (de ruido) to deafen; (fig) to dumbfound, bewilder.

audacia [au'ðaθja] nf boldness, audacity; **audaz** a bold, audacious; (descarado) cheeky, impudent.

audible [au'ðiβle] a audible.

audición [auði'θjon] nf hearing; (TEATRO) audition.

audiencia [au'ðjenθja] nf audience; (JUR) high court.

auditor [auði'tor] nm (JUR) judge-advocate; (COM) auditor.

auditorio [auði'torjo] nm audience; (sala) auditorium.

auge ['auxe] nm boom; (clímax) climax.

augurar [auxu'rar] vt to predict; (presagiar) to portend; **augurio** nm omen; **augurios** nmpl good wishes.

aula ['aula] nf classroom.

aullar [au'ʎar] vi to howl, yell.

aullido [au'ʎiðo] nm howl, yell.

aumentar [aumen'tar] vt (precios, sueldo) to raise; (producción) to increase; (con microscopio, anteojos) to magnify // vi, ~se vr to increase; (subirse) to rise; (multiplicarse) to multiply; **aumento** nm increase; rise.

aun [a'un] ad even.

aún [a'un] ad still, yet.

aunque [a'unke] conj though, although, even though, even if.

aura ['aura] nf gentle breeze; (fig) popularity.

aureola [aure'ola] nf halo.

auricular [auriku'lar] nm (dedo) little finger; (del teléfono) earpiece, receiver; ~es nmpl headphones.

ausencia [au'senθja] nf absence.

ausentarse [ausen'tarse] vr to go/stay away, absent o.s.

ausente [au'sente] a absent.

auspicios [aus'piθjos] nmpl auspices; (protección) protection sg.

austeridad [austeri'ðað] nf austerity; **austero, a** a austere.

austral [aus'tral] a southern.

Australia [aus'tralja] nf Australia; **australiano, a** a, nm/f Australian.

Austria ['austrja] nf Austria; **austríaco, a** a, nm/f Austrian.

autenticar [autenti'kar] vt to authenticate; **auténtico, a** a authentic.

auto ['auto] nm (JUR) edict, decree; (: orden) writ; (fam) car; ~s nmpl (JUR) proceedings; (: acta) court record sg.

autobiografía [autoβjoɣra'fia] nf autobiography.

autobús [auto'βus] nm bus.

autocar [auto'kar] nm coach.

autócrata [au'tokrata] nm/f autocrat.

autóctono, a [au'toktono, a] a native, indigenous.

autodefensa [autoðe'fensa] nf self-defence.

autodeterminación [autoðetermina-'θjon] nf self-determination.

autoescuela [autoes'kwela] nf driving school.

autógrafo [au'toɣrafo] nm autograph.

autómata [au'tomata] nm automaton.

automático, a [auto'matiko, a] *a* automatic.

automotor, triz [automo'tor, 'triz] *a* self-propelled // *nm* Diesel train.

automóvil [auto'moßil] *nm* (motor) car, automobile; **automovilístico, a** *a* driving *cpd*, motoring *cpd*.

autonomía [autono'mia] *nf* autonomy; **autónomo, a** *a* autonomous.

autopista [auto'pista] *nf* motorway.

autopsia [au'topsja] *nf* autopsy.

autor, a [au'tor, a] *nm/f* author.

autoridad [autori'ðað] *nf* authority; **autoritario, a** *a* authoritarian.

autorización [autoriθa'θjon] *nf* authorization; **autorizado, a** *a* authorized; (*aprobado*) approved; **autorizar** *vt* to authorize; to approve.

autorretrato [autorre'trato] *nm* self-portrait.

autoservicio [autoser'ßiθjo] *nm* self-service restaurant.

autostop [auto'stop] *nm* hitch-hiking; **hacer el** ~ to hitch-hike; ~**ista** *nm/f* hitch-hiker.

autosuficiencia [autosufi'θjenθja] *nf* self-sufficiency.

auxiliar [auksi'ljar] *vt* to help // *nm/f* assistant; **auxilio** *nm* assistance, help; **primeros auxilios** first aid *sg*.

Av *abr de* **Avenida**.

aval [a'ßal] *nm* guarantee; (*persona*) guarantor.

avalancha [aßa'lantʃa] *nf* avalanche.

avaluar [aßa'lwar] *vt* to value, appraise.

avance [a'ßanθe] *nm* advance; (*pago*) advance payment.

avanzar [aßan'θar] *vt, vi,* ~**se** *vr* to advance.

avaricia [aßa'riθja] *nf* avarice, greed; **avariento, a** *a* avaricious, greedy.

avaro, a [a'ßaro, a] *a* miserly, mean // *nm/f* miser.

avasallar [aßasa'ʎar] *vt* to subdue, subjugate; ~**se** *vr* to submit.

Avda *abr de* **Avenida**.

ave ['aße] *nf* bird; ~ **de rapiña** bird of prey.

avellana [aße'ʎana] *nf* hazelnut; **avellano** *nm* hazel tree.

avemaría [aßema'ria] *nf* Hail Mary, Ave Maria.

avena [a'ßena] *nf* oats *pl*.

avenencia [aße'nenθja] *nf* agreement; (*COM*) bargain.

avenida [aße'niða] *nf* (*calle*) avenue; (*de río*) flood, spate.

avenir [aße'nir] *vt* to reconcile; ~**se** *vr* to come to an agreement, reach a compromise.

aventajado, a [aßenta'xaðo, a] *a* outstanding; **aventajar** *vt* (*sobrepasar*) to surpass, outstrip; (*preferir*) to prefer; **aventajarse** *vr* to surpass *or* excel o.s.

aventar [aßen'tar] *vt* to fan, blow;

(*esparcir*) to scatter; (*grano*) to winnow; ~**se** *vr* to fill with air.

aventura [aßen'tura] *nf* adventure; (*casualidad*) chance; **aventurado, a** *a* risky; **aventurero, a** *a* adventurous.

avergonzar [aßerxon'θar] *vt* to shame; (*desconcertar*) to embarrass; ~**se** *vr* to be ashamed; to be embarrassed.

avería [aße'ria] *nf* damage; (*TEC*) breakdown, fault.

averiguación [aßerixwa'θjon] *nf* investigation; (*determinación*) ascertainment; **averiguar** *vt* to investigate; to find out, ascertain.

aversión [aßer'sjon] *nf* aversion, dislike.

avestruz [aßes'truθ] *nm* ostrich.

avezarse [aße'θarse] *vr*: ~**se a algo** to grow used to sth.

aviación [aßja'θjon] *nf* aviation *q*; (*fuerzas aéreas*) air force.

aviador, a [aßja'ðor, a] *nm/f* aviator, airman/woman.

avicultura [aßikul'tura] *nf* poultry farming.

avidez [aßi'ðeθ] *nf* avidity, eagerness; **ávido, a** *a* avid, eager.

avinagrado, a [aßina'xraðo, a] *a* sour, acid; **avinagrarse** *vr* to turn sour.

avío [a'ßio] *nm* preparation; ~**s** *nmpl* gear *sg*, kit *sg*.

avión [a'ßjon] *nm* aeroplane; (*ave*) martin; ~ **de reacción** jet plane.

avisar [aßi'sar] *vt* (*advertir*) to warn, notify; (*informar*) to tell; (*aconsejar*) to advise, counsel; **aviso** *nm* warning; (*noticia*) notice; (*prudencia*) caution, discretion.

avispa [a'ßispa] *nf* wasp.

avispado, a [aßis'paðo, a] *a* sharp, clever.

avispar [aßis'par] *vt* to spur (on); ~**se** *vr* to fret, worry.

avispero [aßis'pero] *nm* wasp's nest.

avispón [aßis'pon] *nm* hornet.

avistar [aßis'tar] *vt* to sight, spot; ~**se** *vr* to have an interview.

avituallar [aßitwa'ʎar] *vt* to supply with food.

avivar [aßi'ßar] *vt* to strengthen, intensify; ~**se** *vr* to revive, acquire new life.

avizorar [aßiθo'rar] *vt* to spy on.

axila [ak'sila] *nf* armpit.

axioma [ak'sjoma] *nm* axiom.

ay [ai] *excl* (*dolor*) ow!, ouch!; (*aflicción*) oh!, oh dear!; ¡~ **de mí!** poor me!; ¡~ **del que!** pity heip *or* woe betide whoever!

aya ['aja] *nf* governess; (*niñera*) children's nurse.

ayer [a'jer] *ad, nm* yesterday; **antes de** ~ the day before yesterday.

ayo ['ajo] *nm* tutor.

ayuda [a'juða] *nf* help, assistance; (*MED*) enema; (*AM*) laxative // *nm* page; **ayudante, a** *nm/f* assistant, helper; (*ESCOL*) assistant; (*MIL*) adjutant; **ayudar** *vt* to help, assist.

ayunar [aju'nar] *vi* to fast; **ayunas** *nfpl*: **estar en ayunas** (*no haber comido*) to be fasting; (*ignorante*) to be in the dark; **ayuno** *nm* fasting; ignorance.
ayuntamiento [ajunta'mjento] *nm* (*consejo*) council; (*edificio*) town hall; (*cópula*) sexual intercourse.
azabache [aθa'βatʃe] *nm* jet.
azada [a'θaða] *nf* hoe.
azafata [aθa'fata] *nf* air hostess.
azafrán [aθa'fran] *nm* saffron.
azahar [aθa'ar] *nm* orange/lemon blossom.
azar [a'θar] *nm* (*casualidad*) chance, fate; (*desgracia*) misfortune, accident; **por ~** by chance; **al ~** at random.
azarearse [aθare'arse] *vr* = **azorarse.**
azogue [a'θoxe] *nm* mercury.
azoramiento [aθora'mjento] *nm* alarm; (*confusión*) confusion.
azorar [aθo'rar] *vt* to alarm; **~se** *vr* to get alarmed.
Azores [a'θores] *nmpl*: **los ~** the Azores.
azotar [aθo'tar] *vt* to whip, beat; (*pegar*) to spank; **azote** *nm* (*látigo*) whip; (*latigazo*) lash, stroke; (*en las nalgas*) spank; (*calamidad*) calamity.
azotea [aθo'tea] *nf* terrace roof.
azteca [aθ'teka] *a, nm/f* Aztec.
azúcar [a'θukar] *nm* sugar; **azucarado, a** *a* sugary, sweet.
azucarero, a [aθuka'rero, a] *a* sugar *cpd* // *nm* sugar bowl.
azucena [aθu'θena] *nf* white lily.
azufre [a'θufre] *nm* sulphur.
azul [a'θul] *a, nm* blue.
azulejo [aθu'lexo] *nm* glazed tile.
azuzar [aθu'θar] *vt* to incite, egg on.

B

B.A. *abr de* **Buenos Aires.**
baba ['baβa] *nf* spittle, saliva; **babear** *vi* to drool, slaver.
babel [ba'βel] *nm o f* bedlam.
babero [ba'βero] *nm* bib.
babor [ba'βor] *nm* port (side).
babucha [ba'βutʃa] *nf* slipper.
bacalao [baka'lao] *nm* cod(fish).
bacía [ba'θia] *nf* basin, bowl.
bacín [ba'θin] *nm* chamber pot.
bacteria [bak'terja] *nf* bacterium, germ.
báculo ['bakulo] *nm* stick, staff.
bache ['batʃe] *nm* pothole, rut; (*fig*) bad patch.
bachillerato [batʃiʎe'rato] *nm* (*ESCOL*) school-leaving examination.
bagaje [ba'xaxe] *nm* baggage.
bagatela [baxa'tela] *nf* trinket, trifle.
bahía [ba'ia] *nf* bay.
bailar [bai'lar] *vt, vi* to dance; **~ín, ina** *nm/f* (*ballet*) dancer; **baile** *nm* dance; (*formal*) ball.
baja ['baxa] *nf ver* **bajo.**
bajada [ba'xaða] *nf* descent; (*camino*) slope; (*de aguas*) ebb.

bajamar [baxa'mar] *nf* low tide.
bajar [ba'xar] *vi* to go/come down; (*temperatura, precios*) to drop, fall; (*de coche*) to get out; (*de autobús*) to get off // *vt* (*cabeza*) to bow, bend; (*escalera*) to go/come down; (*precio, voz*) to lower; (*llevar abajo*) to take down; **~se** *vr* to bend down; to get out of; to get off; (*fig*) to humble o.s.
bajeza [ba'xeθa] *nf* baseness *q*; (*una ~*) vile deed.
bajío [ba'xio] *nm* shoal, sandbank; (*AM*) lowlands *pl*.
bajo, a ['baxo, a] *a* (*terreno*) low(-lying); (*mueble, número, precio*) low; (*piso*) ground; (*de estatura*) small, short; (*color*) pale; (*sonido*) faint, soft, low; (*voz: en tono*) deep; (*metal*) base; (*humilde*) low, humble // *ad* (*hablar*) low, quietly; (*volar*) low // *prep* under, below, underneath // *nm* (*MUS*) bass // *nf* drop, fall; (*MIL*) casualty; **~ la lluvia** in the rain; **dar de ~a** (*soldado*) to discharge; (*empleado*) to dismiss, sack.
bajón [ba'xon] *nm* (*MUS*) bassoon; (*baja*) decline, fall, drop.
bajorrelieve [baxorre'ljeße] *nm* bas-relief.
bala ['bala] *nf* bullet.
baladí [bala'ði] *a* trivial.
baladrón, ona [bala'ðron, ona] *a* boastful.
bálago ['balaxo] *nm* thatch.
balance [ba'lanθe] *nm* (*balanceo*) oscillation, rocking; (*NAUT*) roll; (*COM*) balance; (*: libro*) balance sheet; (*: cuenta general*) stocktaking; **~ar** *vt* to balance // *vi*, **~arse** *vr* to swing (to and fro); (*vacilar*) to hesitate; **balanceo** *nm* swinging.
balanza [ba'lanθa] *nf* balance, scales *pl*; **~ comercial** balance of trade; **~ de pagos** balance of payments; (*ASTRO*): **B~ = Libra.**
balar [ba'lar] *vi* to bleat.
balazo [ba'laθo] *nm* (*golpe*) shot; (*herida*) bullet wound.
balbucear [balβuθe'ar] *vi, vt* to stammer, stutter; **balbuceo** *nm* stammering, stuttering.
balbucir [balβu'θir] *vi, vt* to stammer, stutter.
balcón [bal'kon] *nm* balcony.
baldaquín [balda'kin], **baldaquino** [balda'kino] *nm* canopy.
baldar [bal'dar] *vt* to cripple.
balde ['balde] *nm* bucket, pail; **de ~** *ad* (for) free, for nothing; **en ~** *ad* in vain.
baldío, a [bal'dio, a] *a* uncultivated // *nm* waste land.
baldón [bal'don] *nm* (*injuria*) insult.
baldosa [bal'dosa] *nf* paving stone.
Baleares [bale'ares] *nfpl*: **las (Islas) ~** the Balearic Islands.
balido [ba'liðo] *nm* bleat, bleating.
balística [ba'listika] *nf* ballistics *pl*.
baliza [ba'liθa] *nf* (*AVIAT*) beacon; (*NAUT*) buoy.

balneario, a [balne'arjo, a] *a*: estación ~a bathing resort // *nm* spa, health resort.
balón [ba'lon] *nm* ball.
baloncesto [balon'θesto] *nm* basketball.
balsa ['balsa] *nf* raft; (*BOT*) balsa wood.
bálsamo ['balsamo] *nm* balsam, balm.
baluarte [ba'lwarte] *nm* bastion, bulwark.
ballena [ba'ʎena] *nf* whale.
ballesta [ba'ʎesta] *nf* crossbow; (*AUTO*) spring.
ballet [ba'le] *nm* ballet.
bambolear [bambole'ar] *vi*, ~se *vr* to swing, sway; (*silla*) to wobble; **bamboleo** *nm* swinging, swaying; wobbling.
bambú [bam'bu] *nm* bamboo.
banca ['banka] *nf* (*asiento*) bench; (*COM*) banking; ~da *nf* (*banco*) stone bench; (*TEC*) bench.
bancario, a [ban'karjo, a] *a* banking *cpd*, bank *cpd*.
bancarrota [banka'rrota] *nf* (*esp* fraudulent) bankruptcy.
banco ['banko] *nm* bench; (*ESCOL*) desk; (*COM*) bank; (*GEO*) stratum; ~ **de crédito/de ahorros** credit/ savings bank; ~ **de arena** sandbank; ~ **de hielo** iceberg.
banda ['banda] *nf* band; (*pandilla*) gang; (*NAUT*) side, edge; **la B~ Oriental** Uruguay; ~ **sonora** soundtrack.
bandada [ban'daða] *nf* (*de pájaros*) flock; (*de peces*) shoal.
bandeja [ban'dexa] *nf* tray.
bandera [ban'dera] *nf* (*de tela*) flag; (*estandarte*) banner.
banderilla [bande'riʎa] *nf* banderilla.
banderola [bande'rola] *nf* banderole, pennant.
bandidaje [bandi'ðaxe] *nm* banditry; **bandido** *nm* bandit.
bando ['bando] *nm* (*edicto*) edict, proclamation; (*facción*) faction; **los** ~**s** the banns.
bandolero [bando'lero] *nm* bandit, brigand.
banquero [ban'kero] *nm* banker.
banqueta [ban'keta] *nf* (*asiento*) bench; (*escabel*) stool.
banquete [ban'kete] *nm* banquet; (*para convivados*) formal dinner.
banquillo [ban'kiʎo] *nm* (*JUR*) dock, prisoner's bench; (*banco*) bench; (*para los pies*) footstool.
bañador [baɲa'ðor] *nm* swimming costume.
bañar [ba'ɲar] *vt* (*niño*) to bath, bathe; (*objeto*) to dip; (*de barniz*) to coat; ~se *vr* (*en el mar*) to bathe, swim; (*en la bañera*) to bath, have a bath.
bañera [ba'ɲera] *nf* bath(tub).
bañero [ba'ɲero] *nm* lifeguard.
bañista [ba'ɲista] *nm/f* bather.
baño ['baɲo] *nm* (*en bañera*) bath; (*en río*) dip, swim; (*cuarto*) bathroom; (*bañera*) bath(tub); (*capa*) coating.

baptista [bap'tista] *nm/f* baptist.
baqueta [ba'keta] *nf* (*MUS*) drumstick.
bar [bar] *nm* bar.
barahúnda [bara'unda] *nf* uproar, hubbub.
baraja [ba'raxa] *nf* pack (of cards); **barajar** *vt* (*naipes*) to shuffle; (*fig*) to jumble up.
baranda [ba'randa] *nf* rail, railing.
barandilla [baran'diʎa] *nf* rail, railing.
baratija [bara'tixa] *nf* trinket.
baratillo [bara'tiʎo] *nm* (*tienda*) junkshop; (*subasta*) bargain sale; (*conjunto de cosas*) secondhand goods *pl*.
barato, a [ba'rato, a] *a* cheap // *nm* bargain sale // *ad* cheap, cheaply; **baratura** *nf* cheapness.
baraúnda [bara'unda] *nf* = **barahúnda.**
barba ['barβa] *nf* (*ANAT*) chin; (*pelo*) beard, whiskers *pl*.
barbacoa [barβa'koa] *nf* (*parrilla*) barbecue; (*carne*) barbecued meat.
barbado, a [bar'βaðo, a] *a* bearded // *nm* seedling.
barbaridad [barβari'ðað] *nf* barbarity; (*acto*) barbarism; (*atrocidad*) outrage; **una** ~ (*fam*) a huge amount; **¡qué** ~**!** (*fam*) how awful!
barbarie [bar'βarje] *nf*, **barbarismo** [barβa'rismo] *nm* barbarism; (*crueldad*) barbarity.
bárbaro, a ['barβaro, a] *a* barbarous, cruel; (*grosero*) rough, uncouth // *nm/f* barbarian // *ad*: **lo pasamos** ~ (*fam*) we had a tremendous time; **¡qué** ~**!** (*fam*) how marvellous!; **un éxito** ~ (*fam*) a terrific success; **es un tipo** ~ (*fam*) he's a splendid chap.
barbear [barβe'ar] *vt* (*AM*) to shave.
barbecho [bar'βetʃo] *nm* fallow land.
barbero [bar'βero] *nm* barber, hairdresser.
barbilampiño [barβilam'piɲo] *a* smooth-faced; (*fig*) inexperienced.
barbilla [bar'βiʎa] *nf* chin, tip of the chin.
barbotar [barβo'tar], **barbotear** [barβote'ar] *vt, vi* to mutter, mumble.
barbudo, a [bar'βuðo, a] *a* bearded.
barca ['barka] *nf* (*small*) boat; ~ **de pesca** fishing boat; ~ **de pasaje** ferry; ~**za** *nf* barge; ~**za de desembarco** landing craft.
barcelonés, esa [barθelo'nes, esa] *a* of *or* from Barcelona.
barco ['barko] *nm* boat; (*buque*) ship; ~ **de carga** cargo boat.
bardar [bar'ðar] *vt* to thatch.
barítono [ba'ritono] *nm* baritone.
barman ['barman] *nm* barman.
Barna *abr de* **Barcelona**.
barniz [bar'niθ] *nm* varnish; (*en la loza*) glaze; (*fig*) veneer; ~ **para las uñas** nail varnish; ~**ar** *vt* to varnish; (*loza*) to glaze.
barómetro [ba'rometro] *nm* barometer.
barquero [bar'kero] *nm* boatman.
barquillo [bar'kiʎo] *nm* cone, cornet.

barra ['barra] nf bar, rod; (de un bar, café) bar; (de pan) small loaf; (palanca) lever; ~ **de carmín** o **de labios** lipstick.

barraca [ba'rraka] nf hut, cabin.

barranca [ba'rranka] nf ravine, gully; **barranco** nm ravine; (fig) difficulty.

barrena [ba'rrena] nf drill; **barrenar** vt to drill (through), bore; **barreno** nm large drill, borer.

barrer [ba'rrer] vt to sweep; (quitar) to sweep away.

barrera [ba'rrera] nf barrier.

barriada [ba'rrjaða] nf quarter, district.

barricada [barri'kaða] nf barricade.

barrido [ba'rriðo] nm, **barrida** [ba'rriða] nf sweep, sweeping.

barriga [ba'rrixa] nf belly; (panza) paunch; **barrigón, ona, barrigudo, a** a fat, potbellied.

barril [ba'rril] nm barrel, cask.

barrio ['barrjo] nm (en el pueblo) district, quarter; (fuera del pueblo) suburb.

barro ['barro] nm (lodo) mud; (objetos) earthenware; (MED) pimple.

barroco, a [ba'rroko, a] a, nm baroque.

barroso, a [ba'rroso, a] a (lodoso) muddy; (MED) pimply.

barruntar [barrun'tar] vt (conjeturar) to guess; (presentir) to suspect; **barrunto** nm guess; suspicion.

bartola [bar'tola]: **a la** ~ ad: **tirarse a la** ~ to take it easy, do nothing.

bártulos ['bartulos] nmpl things, belongings.

barullo [ba'ruʎo] nm row, uproar.

basa ['basa] nf base; (fig) basis; ~**mento** nm base, plinth.

basar [ba'sar] vt to base; ~**se** vr: ~**se en** to be based on.

basca ['baska] nf nausea.

báscula ['baskula] nf (platform) scales pl.

base ['base] nf base; **a** ~ **de** on the basis of.

básico, a ['basiko, a] a basic.

basílica [ba'silika] nf basilica.

bastante [bas'tante] a (suficiente) enough, sufficient; (no poco(s)) quite a lot of // ad (suficientemente) enough, sufficiently; (muy) quite, rather.

bastar [bas'tar] vi to be enough or sufficient; ~**se** vr to be self-sufficient; ~ **para** to be enough to; **¡basta!** (that's) enough!

bastardilla [bastar'ðiʎa] nf italics pl.

bastardo, a [bas'tarðo, a] a, nm/f bastard.

bastidor [basti'ðor] nm frame; (de coche) chassis.

basto, a ['basto, a] a coarse, rough; ~**s** nmpl (NAIPES) clubs.

bastón [bas'ton] nm (gen) stick, staff; (para el paseo) walking stick.

basura [ba'sura] nf rubbish, refuse.

basurero [basu'rero] nm (hombre) dustman; (lugar) rubbish dump; (cubo) (rubbish) bin.

bata ['bata] nf (salto de cama) dressing gown, housecoat; (de alumno etc) smock, overall.

batalla [ba'taʎa] nf battle; **de** ~ everyday, for everyday use.

batallar [bata'ʎar] vi to fight.

batallón [bata'ʎon] nm battalion.

bate ['bate] nm bat; ~**ador** nm batter, batsman.

batería [bate'ria] nf battery; (MUS) drums pl; ~ **de cocina** kitchen utensils pl.

batido, a [ba'tiðo, a] a (camino) beaten, well-trodden // nm (CULIN) batter; ~ **de leche** milk shake.

batidora [bati'ðora] nf beater, mixer.

batir [ba'tir] vt to beat, strike; (vencer) to beat, defeat; (revolver) to beat, mix; (acuñar) to strike, mint; (pelo) to comb; ~**se** vr to fight; ~ **palmas** to clap, applaud.

batuta [ba'tuta] nf baton.

baúl [ba'ul] nm trunk; (AUTO) boot.

bautismo [bau'tismo] nm baptism, christening.

bautizar [bauti'θar] vt to baptize, christen; (fam) to water down; **bautizo** nm baptism, christening.

bayo, a ['bajo, a] a bay // nf berry.

bayoneta [bajo'neta] nf bayonet.

baza ['baθa] nf trick.

bazar [ba'θar] nm bazaar.

bazofia [ba'θofja] nf left-overs pl.

beato, a [be'ato, a] a blessed; (piadoso) pious // nm/f lay brother/sister.

bebé [be'ße] nm baby.

bebedero, a [beße'ðero, a] a drinkable // nm (para animales) drinking trough; (de vasija) spout.

bebedizo, a [beße'ðiθo, a] a drinkable // nm potion.

bebedor, a [beße'ðor, a] a hard-drinking.

beber [be'ßer] vt, vi to drink.

bebida [be'ßiða] nf drink.

beca ['beka] nf grant, scholarship.

befa ['befa] nf ver **befo.**

befar [be'far] vt to scoff at.

befo, a ['befo, a] a thick-lipped // nm lip // nf: **hacer** ~**a de** to jeer, mock.

beldad [bel'dað] nf beauty.

belfo, a ['belfo, a] = **befo.**

belga ['belɣa] a, nm/f Belgian.

Bélgica ['belxika] nf Belgium.

bélico, a ['beliko, a] a warlike, martial; **belicoso, a** a (guerrero) warlike; (agresivo) aggressive, bellicose.

beligerante [belixe'rante] a belligerent.

bellaco, a [be'ʎako, a] a sly, cunning // nm villain, rogue; **bellaquería** nf (acción) dirty trick; (calidad) wickedness.

belleza [be'ʎeθa] nf beauty.

bello, a ['beʎo, a] a beautiful, lovely; ~**as artes** fine arts.

bellota [be'ʎota] nf acorn.

bemol [be'mol] nm (MUS) flat; **esto tiene** ~**es** (fam) this is a real problem.

bendecir [bende'θir] vt to bless.

bendición [bendi'θjon] nf blessing.

bendito, a [ben'dito, a] *pp de* **bendecir** // *a* holy; (*afortunado*) lucky; (*feliz*) happy; (*sencillo*) simple // *nm/f* simple soul.
benedictino, a [beneðik'tino, a] *a, nm* Benedictine.
beneficencia [benefi'θenθja] *nf* charity.
beneficiar [benefi'θjar] *vt* (*hacer bien a*) to benefit, be of benefit to; (*tierra*) to cultivate; (*mina*) to exploit; (*mineral*) to process, treat; ~**se** *vr* to benefit, profit; ~**io, a** *nm/f* beneficiary.
beneficio [bene'fiθjo] *nm* (*bien*) benefit, advantage; (*ganancia*) profit, gain; (AGR) cultivation; ~**so, a** *a* beneficial.
benéfico, a [be'nefiko, a] *a* beneficent, charitable.
beneplácito [bene'plaθito] *nm* approval, consent.
benevolencia [beneßo'lenθja] *nf* benevolence, kindness; **benévolo, a** *a* benevolent, kind.
benignidad [benixni'ðað] *nf* (*afabilidad*) kindness; (*suavidad*) mildness; **benigno, a** *a* kind; mild.
beodo, a [be'oðo, a] *a* drunk.
berenjena [beren'xena] *nf* aubergine, eggplant.
Berlín [ber'lin] *n* Berlin; **berlinés, esa** *a* of *or* from Berlin // *nm/f* Berliner.
bermejo, a [ber'mexo, a] *a* red.
Berna ['berna] *n* Berne.
berrear [berre'ar] *vi* to bellow, low.
berrido [be'rriðo] *nm* bellow, bellowing.
berrinche [be'rrintʃe] *nm* (*fam*) temper, tantrum.
berro ['berro] *nm* watercress.
berza ['berθa] *nf* cabbage.
besar [be'sar] *vt* to kiss; (*fig*) to graze; ~**se** *vr* to kiss (one another); **beso** *nm* kiss.
bestia ['bestja] *nf* beast, animal; (*fig*) idiot; ~ **de carga** beast of burden.
bestial [bes'tjal] *a* bestial; (*fam*) terrific; ~**idad** *nf* bestiality; (*fam*) stupidity.
besuquear [besuke'ar] *vt* to cover with kisses; ~**se** *vr* to kiss and cuddle.
betún [be'tun] *nm* bitumen, asphalt; (*para calzado*) shoe polish.
biberón [biße'ron] *nm* feeding bottle.
Biblia ['bißlja] *nf* Bible.
bíblico, a ['bißliko, a] *a* biblical.
bibliografía [bißljoxra'fia] *nf* bibliography.
biblioteca [bißljo'teka] *nf* library; (*mueble*) bookshelves *pl*; ~ **de consulta** reference library; ~**rio, a** *nm/f* librarian.
B.I.C. *nf abr de* **Brigada de Investigación Criminal** CID (Criminal Investigation Department); FBI (Federal Bureau of Investigation) (*US*).
bicarbonato [bikarßo'nato] *nm* bicarbonate.
bicicleta [biθi'kleta] *nf* bicycle, bike.
bicho ['bitʃo] *nm* (*animal*) small animal; (*sabandija*) bug, insect; (TAUR) bull.
bidé [bi'ðe] *nm* bidet.

bien [bjen] *nm* good; (*interés*) advantage, benefit // *ad* well; (*correctamente*) properly, right; (*oler*) nice; (*muy*) very; **más** ~ rather // *excl*: ¡(**muy**) ~! well done! // *conj*: **no** ~ **llovió, bajó la temperatura** no sooner had it rained than the temperature dropped; ~ **que** although; ~**es inmuebles/muebles** real estate *sg*/personal property *sg*; ~**es de consumo** consumer goods; ~**es raíces** real estate *sg*.
bienal [bje'nal] *a* biennial.
bienandanza [bjenan'danθa] *nf* happiness.
bienaventurado, a [bjenaßentu'raðo, a] *a* (*feliz*) happy, fortunate; (*sencillo*) simple, naïve.
bienestar [bjenes'tar] *nm* well-being.
bienhechor, a [bjene'tʃor, a] *a* beneficent.
bienvenida [bjenße'niða] *nf* welcome; **bienvenido** *excl* welcome!
biftec [bif'tek] *nm* (beef)steak.
bifurcación [bifurka'θjon] *nf* fork.
bigamia [bi'xamja] *nf* bigamy; **bígamo, a** *a* bigamous // *nm/f* bigamist.
bigote [bi'xote] *nm* moustache; **bigotudo, a** *a* moustached.
bilbaíno, a [bilßa'ino, a] *a* of *or* from Bilbao.
bilingüe [bi'lingwe] *a* bilingual.
billar [bi'ʎar] *nm* billiards *sg*; (*lugar*) billiard hall.
billete [bi'ʎete] *nm* ticket; (*de banco*) banknote; (*carta*) note; ~ **simple** single (ticket); ~ **de ida y vuelta** return (ticket); ~ **kilométrico** runabout ticket.
billetera [biʎe'tera] *nf*, **billetero** [biʎe-'tero] *nm* wallet.
billón [bi'ʎon] *nm* billion.
bimensual [bimen'swal] *a* twice monthly.
bimotor [bimo'tor] *a* twin-engined // *nm* twin-engined plane.
binóculo [bi'nokulo] *nm* pince-nez.
biografía [bjoxra'fia] *nf* biography; **biógrafo, a** *nm/f* biographer.
biología [bjolo'xia] *nf* biology; **biológico, a** *a* biological; **biólogo, a** *nm/f* biologist.
biombo ['bjombo] *nm* (folding) screen.
biopsia [bi'opsja] *nf* biopsy.
biplano [bi'plano] *nm* biplane.
birlar [bir'lar] *vt* (*derribar*) to knock down; (*matar*) to kill; (*fam*) to pinch.
bis [bis] *excl* encore! // *ad*: **viven en el 27** ~ they live at 27a.
bisabuelo, a [bisa'ßwelo, a] *nm/f* great-grandfather/mother.
bisagra [bi'saxra] *nf* hinge.
bisbisar [bisßi'sar], **bisbisear** [bisßise-'ar] *vt* to mutter, mumble.
bisexual [bisek'swal] *a* bisexual.
bisiesto [bi'sjesto] *a*: **año** ~ leap year.
bisnieto, a [bis'njeto, a] *nm/f* great-grandson/daughter.
bisonte [bi'sonte] *nm* bison.
bisoño, a [bi'soɲo, a] *a* green, inexperienced.

bistec [bis'tek], **bisté** [bis'te] *nm* steak.
bisturí [bistu'ri] *nm* scalpel.
bisutería [bisute'ria] *nf* imitation *or* costume jewellery.
bizarría [biθa'rria] *nf* (*valor*) bravery; (*generosidad*) generosity; **bizarro, a** *a* brave; generous.
bizcar [biθ'kar] *vi* to squint; **bizco, a** *a* cross-eyed.
bizcocho [biθ'kotʃo] *nm* (*CULIN*) sponge cake.
bizquear [biθke'ar] *vi* to squint.
blanco, a ['blanko, a] *a* white // *nm/f* white man/woman, white // *nm* (*color*) white; (*intervalo*) space, interval; (*en texto*) blank; (*MIL, fig*) target // *nf* (*MUS*) minim; **en** ~ blank; **noche en** ~ sleepless night; **estar sin** ~ to be broke.
blancura [blan'kura] *nf* whiteness.
blandir [blan'dir] *vt* to brandish.
blando, a ['blando, a] *a* soft; (*tierno*) tender, gentle; (*carácter*) mild; (*fam*) cowardly; **blandura** *nf* softness; tenderness; mildness.
blanquear [blanke'ar] *vt* to whiten; (*fachada*) to whitewash; (*paño*) to bleach // *vi* to turn white; **blanquecino, a** *a* whitish; **blanqueo** *nm* whitewashing; bleaching.
blanquillo, a [blan'kiʎo, a] *a* white.
blasfemar [blasfe'mar] *vi* to blaspheme, curse; **blasfemia** *nf* blasphemy.
blasón [bla'son] *nm* coat of arms; (*fig*) honour; **blasonar** *vt* to emblazon // *vi* to boast, brag.
bledo ['bleðo] *nm*: **(no) me importa un** ~ I don't care two hoots.
blindaje [blin'daxe] *nm* armour, armour-plating; **blindar** *vt* to armour, armour-plate.
bloc [blok] *nm* writing pad.
bloque ['bloke] *nm* block; (*POL*) bloc; ~ **de cilindros** cylinder block.
bloquear [bloke'ar] *vt* to blockade; **bloqueo** *nm* blockade; (*COM*) freezing, blocking.
bluejean ['bludʒin] *nm inv* jeans *pl*.
blusa ['blusa] *nf* (*de alumno*) smock; (*de mujer*) blouse.
boardilla [boar'ðiʎa] *nf* = **buhardilla.**
boato [bo'ato] *nm* show, ostentation.
bobada [bo'βaða], **bobería** [boβe'ria] *nf* foolish action/ statement.
bobina [bo'βina] *nf* (*TEC*) bobbin; (*FOTO*) spool; (*ELEC*) coil; **bobinar** *vt* to wind.
bobo, a ['boβo, a] *a* (*tonto*) daft, silly; (*cándido*) naïve // *nm* (*TEATRO*) clown, funny man, fool.
boca ['boka] *nf* mouth; (*de crustáceo*) pincer; (*de cañón*) muzzle; (*de vino*) flavour, taste; (*entrada*) mouth, entrance; ~**s** *nfpl* (*de río*) mouth *sg*; ~ **abajo/arriba** face down/up; **a** ~ **de jarro** point-blank; **se me hace la** ~ **agua** my mouth is watering.
bocacalle [boka'kaʎe] *nf* entrance to a street.

bocadillo [boka'ðiʎo] *nm* (*emparedado*) sandwich; (*comida ligera*) snack.
bocado [bo'kaðo] *nm* mouthful, bite; (*de caballo*) bridle; ~ **de Adán** Adam's apple.
bocanada [boka'naða] *nf* (*de vino*) mouthful, swallow; (*de aire*) gust, puff.
boceto [bo'θeto] *nm* sketch, outline.
bocina [bo'θina] *nf* (*MUS*) trumpet; (*AUTO*) horn; (*para hablar*) megaphone; (*para sordos*) ear trumpet.
bocha ['botʃa] *nf* bowl; ~**s** *nfpl* bowls.
bochinche [bo'tʃintʃe] *nm* (*fam*) uproar.
bochorno [bo'tʃorno] *nm* (*calor*) sultry weather; (*vergüenza*) embarrassment; ~**so, a** *a* sultry; embarrassing; (*sofocante*) stuffy.
boda ['boða] *nf* (*también* ~**s** *nfpl*) wedding, marriage; (*fiesta*) wedding reception; ~**s de plata/de oro** silver/golden wedding.
bodega [bo'ðeɣa] *nf* (*de vino*) (wine) cellar; (*depósito*) storeroom; (*de barco*) hold.
bodegón [boðe'ɣon] *nm* cheap restaurant; (*ARTE*) still life.
bofe ['bofe] *nm* (*también* ~**s** *nmpl*) lung.
bofetada [bofe'taða] *nf* slap (in the face).
bofetón [bofe'ton] *nm* punch (in the face).
boga ['boɣa] *nf* (*NAUT*) rowing; (*fig*) vogue, fashion // *nm/f* rower; **en** ~ in vogue; **bogar** *vi* (*remar*) to row; (*navegar*) to sail.
Bogotá [boɣo'ta] *n* Bogota; **bogotano, a** *a* of *or* from Bogota.
bohardilla [boar'ðiʎa] *nf* = **buhardilla.**
bohemio, a [bo'emjo, a] *a*, *nm/f* Bohemian.
boicot [boi'kot] *nm* boycott; ~**ear** *vt* to boycott; ~**eo** *nm* boycott.
boina ['boina] *nf* beret.
bola ['bola] *nf* (*gen*) ball; (*canica*) marble; (*NAIPES*) (grand) slam; (*betún*) shoe polish; ~ **de billar** billiard ball; ~ **de nieve** snowball.
bolchevique [boltʃe'βike] *nm/f* Bolshevik.
boleadoras [bolea'ðoras] *nfpl* (*AM*) bolas.
bolera [bo'lera] *nf* skittle alley.
boleta [bo'leta] *nf* (*billete*) ticket; (*permiso*) pass, permit.
boletín [bole'tin] *nm* bulletin; (*periódico*) journal, review; (*billete*) ticket; ~ **escolar** school report; ~ **de noticias** news bulletin; ~ **de pedido** application form; ~ **de precios** price list; ~ **de prensa** press release.
boleto [bo'leto] *nm* ticket.
boliche [bo'litʃe] *nm* (*bola*) jack; (*juego*) bowls *sg*; (*lugar*) bowling alley.
bolígrafo [bo'liɣrafo] *nm* ball-point pen.
bolívar [bo'liβar] *nm* monetary unit of Venezuela.
Bolivia [bo'liβja] *nf* Bolivia; **boliviano, a** *a*, *nm/f* Bolivian.
bolo ['bolo] *nm* skittle; (*píldora*) (large) pill; (**juego de**) ~**s** skittles *sg*.
bolsa ['bolsa] *nf* (*cartera*) purse; (*saco*) bag; (*ANAT*) cavity, sac; (*COM*) stock exchange; (*MINERÍA*) pocket; ~ **de agua**

caliente hot water bottle; ~ **de aire** air pocket; ~ **de papel** paper bag.

bolsillo [bol'siʎo] *nm* pocket; (*cartera*) purse; **de** ~ pocket(-size).

bolsista [bol'sista] *nm/f* stockbroker.

bolso ['bolso] *nm* (*bolsa*) bag; (*de mujer*) handbag.

bollo ['boʎo] *nm* (*pan*) roll; (*bulto*) bump, lump; (*abolladura*) dent.

bomba ['bomba] *nf* (*MIL*) bomb; (*TEC*) pump // *a* (*fam*): **noticia** ~ shattering piece of news // *ad* (*fam*): **pasarlo** ~ to have a great time; ~ **atómica/de humo/de retardo** atomic/smoke/ time bomb; ~ **de gasolina** petrol pump; ~ **de mano** grenade; ~ **lacrimógena** tear gas bomb.

bombardear [bombarðe'ar] *vt* to bombard; (*MIL*) to bomb; **bombardeo** *nm* bombardment; bombing.

bombardero [bombar'ðero] *nm* bomber.

bombear [bombe'ar] *vt* (*agua*) to pump (out *or* up); (*MIL*) to bomb; ~**se** *vr* to warp.

bombero [bom'bero] *nm* fireman.

bombilla [bom'biʎa] *nf* bulb.

bombín [bom'bin] *nm* bowler hat.

bombo ['bombo] *nm* (*MUS*) bass drum; (*TEC*) drum.

bombón [bom'bon] *nm* chocolate.

bonachón, ona [bona'tʃon, ona] *a* good-natured, easy-going.

bonaerense [bonae'rense] *a* of *or* from Buenos Aires.

bonancible [bonan'θiβle] *a* (*tiempo*) fair, calm.

bonanza [bo'nanθa] *nf* (*NAUT*) fair weather; (*fig*) bonanza; (*MINERÍA*) rich pocket *or* vein.

bondad [bon'dað] *nf* goodness, kindness; **tenga la** ~ **de** (*please*) be good enough to; ~**oso, a** *a* good, kind.

bonito, a [bo'nito, a] *a* (*lindo*) pretty; (*agradable*) nice.

bono ['bono] *nm* voucher; (*FIN*) bond.

boquear [boke'ar] *vi* to gasp.

boquerón [boke'ron] *nm* (*anchoa*) anchovy; (*agujero*) large hole.

boquete [bo'kete] *nm* gap, hole.

boquiabierto, a [bokia'βjerto, a] *a* open-mouthed (in astonishment).

boquilla [bo'kiʎa] *nf* (*para riego*) nozzle; (*para cigarro*) cigarette holder; (*MUS*) mouthpiece.

borbollar [borβo'ʎar], **borbollear** [borβoʎe'ar], **borbotar** [borβo'tar] *vi* to bubble.

borbotón [borβo'ton] *nm* bubbling.

bordado [bor'ðaðo] *nm* embroidery.

bordar [bor'ðar] *vt* to embroider.

borde ['borðe] *nm* edge, border; (*de camino etc*) side; (*en la costura*) hem; **al** ~ **de** (*fig*) on the verge *or* brink of; ~**ar** *vt* to border.

bordo ['borðo] *nm* (*NAUT*) side; **a** ~ **on** board.

Borinquén [borin'ken] *nm* Puerto Rico;

borinqueño, a *a, nm/f* Puerto Rican.

borra ['borra] *nf* (*pelusa*) fluff; (*sedimento*) sediment.

borrachera [borra'tʃera] *nf* (*ebriedad*) drunkenness; (*orgía*) spree, binge.

borracho, a [bo'rratʃo, a] *a* drunk // *nm/f* (*que bebe mucho*) drunkard, drunk; (*temporalmente*) drunk, drunk man/woman.

borrador [borra'ðor] *nm* (*escritura*) first draft, rough sketch; (*cuaderno*) scribbling pad; (*goma*) rubber, eraser.

borrajear [borraxe'ar] *vt, vi* to scribble.

borrar [bo'rrar] *vt* to erase, rub out.

borrascoso, a [borras'koso, a] *a* stormy.

borrica [bo'rrika] *nf* she-donkey; (*fig*) stupid woman; ~**da** *nf* foolish action/statement.

borrico [bo'rriko] *nm* donkey; (*fig*) stupid man.

borrón [bo'rron] *nm* (*mancha*) stain; (*proyecto*) rough draft; (*de cuadro*) sketch.

borroso, a [bo'rroso, a] *a* vague, unclear; (*escritura*) illegible.

bosque ['boske] *nm* wood, forest.

bosquejar [boske'xar] *vt* to sketch; **bosquejo** *nm* sketch.

bosta ['bosta] *nf* dung, manure.

bostezar [boste'θar] *vi* to yawn; **bostezo** *nm* yawn.

bota ['bota] *nf* (*saco*) leather wine bottle; (*calzado*) boot.

botadura [bota'ðura] *nf* launching.

botánico, a [bo'taniko, a] *nm/f* botanist // *nf* botany.

botar [bo'tar] *vt* to throw, hurl; (*NAUT*) to launch; (*fam*) to throw out // *vi* to bounce.

bote ['bote] *nm* (*salto*) bounce; (*golpe*) thrust; (*vasija*) tin, can; (*embarcación*) boat; **de** ~ **en** ~ packed, jammed full; ~ **salvavidas** lifeboat.

botella [bo'teʎa] *nf* bottle.

botica [bo'tika] *nf* chemist's (shop), pharmacy; ~**rio, a** *nm/f* chemist, pharmacist.

botija [bo'tixa] *nf* (*earthenware*) jug; **botijo** *nm* (*earthenware*) jug; (*tren*) excursion train.

botín [bo'tin] *nm* (*calzado*) half boot; (*polaina*) spat; (*MIL*) booty.

botiquín [boti'kin] *nm* (*armario*) medicine cabinet; (*portátil*) first-aid kit.

botón [bo'ton] *nm* button; (*BOT*) bud; (*de florete*) tip; ~ **de oro** buttercup.

botones [bo'tones] *nm* buttons *sg*, bellboy.

bóveda ['boβeða] *nf* (*ARQ*) vault.

boxeador [boksea'ðor] *nm* boxer.

boxeo [bok'seo] *nm* boxing.

boya ['boja] *nf* (*NAUT*) buoy; (*flotador*) float.

bozal [bo'θal] *a* (*novato*) raw, green; (*tonto*) stupid; (*salvaje*) wild // *nm* (*de caballo*) halter; (*de perro*) muzzle.

bracear [braθe'ar] *vi* (*agitar los brazos*) to wave one's arms; (*nadar*) to swim (the crawl).

bracero [bra'θero] *nm* labourer; (*en el campo*) farmhand.

bracete [bra'θete]: **de** ~ *ad* arm in arm.
braga ['braxa] *nf* (*cuerda*) sling, rope; (*de bebé*) nappy; ~**s** *nfpl* (*de mujer*) panties.
bragueta [bra'xeta] *nf* fly, flies *pl*.
braille [breil] *nm* braille.
bramar [bra'mar] *vi* to bellow, roar; **bramido** *nm* bellow, roar.
brasa ['brasa] *nf* live coal.
brasero [bra'sero] *nm* brazier.
Brasil [bra'sil] *nm*: **el** ~ Brazil; **brasileño, a** *a, nm/f* Brazilian.
bravata [bra'ßata] *nf* boast.
braveza [bra'ßeθa] *nf* (*valor*) bravery; (*ferocidad*) ferocity.
bravío, a [bra'ßio, a] *a* wild; (*feroz*) fierce.
bravo, a ['braßo, a] *a* (*valiente*) brave; (*bueno*) fine, splendid; (*feroz*) ferocious; (*salvaje*) wild // *excl* bravo!; **bravura** *nf* bravery; ferocity; (*pey*) boast.
braza ['braθa] *nf* fathom; **nadar a la** ~ to swim the breast-stroke.
brazada [bra'θaða] *nf* stroke.
brazado [bra'θaðo] *nm* armful.
brazalete [braθa'lete] *nm* (*pulsera*) bracelet; (*banda*) armband.
brazo ['braθo] *nm* arm; (*zool*) foreleg; (*bot*) limb, branch; **a** ~ **partido** hand-to-hand; **del** ~ arm in arm.
brea ['brea] *nf* pitch, tar.
brebaje [bre'ßaxe] *nm* potion.
brecha ['bretʃa] *nf* breach, gap, opening.
brega ['brexa] *nf* (*lucha*) struggle; (*trabajo*) hard work.
breve ['breße] *a* short, brief // *nf* breve; ~**dad** *nf* brevity, shortness.
brezal [bre'θal] *nm* moor(land), heath; **brezo** *nm* heather.
bribón, ona [bri'ßon, ona] *a* idle, lazy // *nm/f* (*vagabundo*) vagabond; (*pícaro*) rascal, rogue.
bricolaje [briko'laxe] *nm* do-it-yourself, DIY.
brida ['briða] *nf* bridle, rein; (*tec*) clamp; **a toda** ~ at top speed.
bridge [britʃ] *nm* bridge.
brigada [bri'xaða] *nf* (*unidad*) brigade; (*trabajadores*) squad, gang // *nm* ≈ staff-sergeant, sergeant-major.
brillante [bri'ʎante] *a* brilliant // *nm* diamond; **brillar** *vi* to shine.
brillo ['briʎo] *nm* shine; (*brillantez*) brilliance; (*fig*) splendour; **sacar** ~ **a** to polish.
brincar [brin'kar] *vi* to skip about, hop about, jump about; **está que brinca** he's hopping mad.
brinco ['brinko] *nm* hop, skip, jump.
brindar [brin'dar] *vi*: ~ **a** *o* **por** to drink (a toast) to // *vt* to offer, present.
brindis ['brindis] *nm* toast; (*taur*) (ceremony of) dedicating the bull.
brío ['brio] *nm* spirit, dash; **brioso, a** *a* spirited, dashing.
brisa ['brisa] *nf* breeze.
británico, a [bri'taniko, a] *a* British // *nm/f* Briton, British person.

brocal [bro'kal] *nm* rim.
brocha ['brotʃa] *nf* brush.
broche ['brotʃe] *nm* brooch; ~ **para papeles** (*am*) paper clip.
broma ['broma] *nf* (*bulla*) fun; (*chanza*) joke; **en** ~ in fun, as a joke; **bromear** *vi* to joke.
bromista [bro'mista] *a* fond of joking // *nm/f* joker, wag.
bronca ['bronka] *nf* row.
bronce ['bronθe] *nm* bronze; ~**ado, a** *a* bronze; (*por el sol*) tanned // *nm* (sun)tan; (*tec*) bronzing.
broncearse [bronθe'arse] *vr* to get a suntan.
bronco, a ['bronko, a] *a* (*superficie*) rough; (*manera*) rude, surly; (*voz*) harsh.
bronquitis [bron'kitis] *nf* bronchitis.
brotar [bro'tar] *vi* (*bot*) to sprout; (*aguas*) to gush (forth), flow; (*med*) to break out; **brote** *nm* (*bot*) shoot; (*med, fig*) outbreak.
bruces ['bruθes]: **de** ~ *ad*: **caer** *o* **dar de** ~ to fall headlong, fall flat; **estar de** ~ to lie face downwards.
bruja ['bruxa] *nf* witch; (*lechuza*) owl; **brujería** *nf* witchcraft.
brujo ['bruxo] *nm* wizard, magician.
brújula ['bruxula] *nf* compass.
bruma ['bruma] *nf* mist; **brumoso, a** *a* misty.
bruñido [bru'ɲiðo] *nm* polish; **bruñir** *vt* to polish.
brusco, a ['brusko, a] *a* (*súbito*) sudden; (*áspero*) brusque.
Bruselas [bru'selas] *n* Brussels.
brutal [bru'tal] *a* brutal; (*fig*) sudden; ~**idad** *nf* brutality.
bruto, a ['bruto, a] *a* (*idiota*) stupid; (*bestial*) brutish; (*peso*) gross; (*diamante etc*) raw, uncut; **en** ~ raw, unworked.
Bs.As. *abr de* **Buenos Aires.**
buba ['bußa] *nf* tumour.
bucal [bu'kal] *a*: **por vía** ~ by *or* through the mouth, orally.
bucear [buθe'ar] *vi* to dive // *vt* to explore; **buceo** *nm* diving; (*fig*) investigation.
bucle ['bukle] *nm* curl.
budismo [bu'ðismo] *nm* Buddhism.
buenamente [bwena'mente] *ad* (*fácilmente*) easily; (*voluntariamente*) willingly.
buenaventura [bwenaßen'tura] *nf* (*suerte*) good luck; (*adivinación*) fortune.
bueno, a ['bweno, a], **buen** [bwen] *a* (*amable*) kind; (*med*) well; (*guapo*) attractive; ¡~**as!** hello!; **buen día,** ~**os días** good morning!; good afternoon!; hello!; ~**as tardes** good afternoon!; good evening!; ~**as noches** good night!; ¡**buen sinvergüenza resultó!** a fine rascal he turned out to be // *excl* right!, all right!; ~, ¿**y qué?** well, so what?
buey [bwei] *nm* ox.
búfalo ['bufalo] *nm* buffalo.
bufanda [bu'fanda] *nf* scarf, muffler.
bufar [bu'far] *vi* to snort.

bufete [bu'fete] *nm* (*mesa*) desk; (*de abogado*) lawyer's office.
bufo, a ['bufo, a] *a* comic.
bufón, ona [bu'fon, ona] *a* funny // *nm* clown.
buhardilla [buar'ðiʎa] *nf* (*ventana*) skylight; (*desván*) attic.
búho ['buo] *nm* owl; (*fig*) hermit, recluse.
buhonero [buo'nero] *nm* pedlar.
buitre ['bwitre] *nm* vulture.
bujía [bu'xia] *nf* (*vela*) candle; (*ELEC*) candle (power); (*AUTO*) spark plug.
bula ['bula] *nf* (*papal*) bull.
bulbo ['bulβo] *nm* bulb.
búlgaro, a ['bulxaro, a] *a*, *nm/f* Bulgarian.
bulto ['bulto] *nm* (*paquete*) package; (*fardo*) bundle; (*tamaño*) size, bulkiness; (*MED*) swelling, lump; (*silueta*) vague shape; (*estatua*) bust, statue; **de mucho/poco** ~ important/unimportant.
bulla ['buʎa] *nf* (*ruido*) uproar; (*de gente*) crowd.
bullicio [bu'ʎiθjo] *nm* (*ruido*) uproar; (*movimiento*) bustle.
bullir [bu'ʎir] *vi* (*hervir*) to boil; (*burbujear*) to bubble; (*mover*) to move, stir.
buñuelo [bu'ɲwelo] *nm* fritter.
buque ['buke] *nm* ship, vessel.
burbuja [bur'βuxa] *nf* bubble; **burbujear** *vi* to bubble.
burdel [bur'ðel] *nm* brothel.
burdo, a ['burðo, a] *a* coarse, rough.
burgués, esa [bur'xes, esa] *a* middle-class, bourgeois; **burguesía** *nf* middle class, bourgeoisie.
burla ['burla] *nf* (*mofa*) gibe; (*broma*) joke; (*engaño*) trick.
burladero [burla'ðero] *nm* (bullfighter's) refuge.
burlador, a [burla'ðor, a] *a* mocking // *nm* (*bromista*) joker; (*libertino*) seducer.
burlar [bur'lar] *vt* (*engañar*) to deceive; (*seducir*) to seduce // *vi*, ~**se** *vr* to joke; ~**se de** to make fun of.
burlesco, a [bur'lesko, a] *a* burlesque.
burlón, ona [bur'lon, ona] *a* mocking.
burocracia [buro'kraθja] *nf* civil service; (*pey*) bureaucracy.
burócrata [bu'rokrata] *nm/f* civil servant; (*pey*) bureaucrat.
burra ['burra] *nf* (she-)donkey; (*fig*) stupid woman.
burro ['burro] *nm* donkey; (*fig*) ass, idiot.
bursátil [bur'satil] *a* stock-exchange *cpd*.
busca ['buska] *nf* search, hunt; **en** ~ **de** in search of.
buscapleitos [buska'pleitos] *nm/f inv* troublemaker.
buscar [bus'kar] *vt* to look for, search for, seek // *vi* to look, search, seek; **se busca empleado** employee wanted.
buscón, ona [bus'kon, ona] *a* thieving // *nm* petty thief // *nf* whore.
busilis [bu'silis] *nm* (*fam*) snag.
busque *etc vb ver* **buscar.**

búsqueda ['buskeða] *nf* = **busca.**
busto ['busto] *nm* bust.
butaca [bu'taka] *nf* armchair; (*de cine, teatro*) stall, seat.
butano [bu'tano] *nm* butane.
buzo ['buθo] *nm* diver.
buzón [bu'θon] *nm* letter box; (*en la calle*) pillar box.

C

c. *abr de* **capítulo.**
C. *abr de* **centígrado; compañía.**
C/ *abr de* **calle.**
c.a. *abr de* **corriente alterna.**
cabal [ka'βal] *a* (*exacto*) exact; (*correcto*) right, proper; (*acabado*) finished, complete; ~**es** *nmpl*: **estar en sus** ~**es** to be in one's right mind.
cabalgadura [kaβalxa'ðura] *nf* mount, horse.
cabalgar [kaβal'xar] *vt*, *vi* to ride.
caballa [ka'βaʎa] *nf* mackerel.
caballeresco, a [kaβaʎe'resko, a] *a* noble, chivalrous.
caballería [kaβaʎe'ria] *nf* mount; (*MIL*) cavalry.
caballeriza [kaβaʎe'riθa] *nf* stable; **caballerizo** *nm* groom, stableman.
caballero [kaβa'ʎero] *nm* rider, horseman; (*hombre galante*) gentleman; (*de la orden de caballería*) knight; (*hidalgo*) noble(man); (*señor, término de cortesía*) sir.
caballerosidad [kaβaʎerosi'ðað] *nf* chivalry.
caballo [ka'βaʎo] *nm* horse; (*AJEDREZ*) knight; (*NAIPES*) queen; ~ **de vapor** *o* **de fuerza** horsepower.
cabaña [ka'βaɲa] *nf* (*casita*) hut, cabin; (*rebaño*) flock.
cabaré, cabaret (*pl* **cabarets**) [kaβa're] *nm* cabaret.
cabás [ka'βas] *nm* satchel.
cabecear [kaβeθe'ar] *vt* to head // *vi* to nod; (*negar*) to shake one's head.
cabecera [kaβe'θera] *nf* (*gen*) head; (*de distrito*) chief town; (*IMPRENTA*) headline.
cabecilla [kaβe'θiʎa] *nm/f* ringleader; (*fig: fam*) hothead.
cabellera [kaβe'ʎera] *nf* hair; (*de cometa*) tail.
cabello [ka'βeʎo] *nm* (*también* ~**s** *nmpl*) hair *sg*; **cabelludo, a** *a* hairy.
caber [ka'βer] *vi* (*entrar*) to fit, go; (*tener lugar*) to have enough room; **caben 3 más** there's room for 3 more.
cabestrillo [kaβes'triʎo] *nm* sling.
cabestro [ka'βestro] *nm* halter.
cabeza [ka'βeθa] *nf* head; (*POL*) chief, leader; ~**da** *nf* (*golpe*) butt; (*al dormirse*) nod.
cabezudo, a [kaβe'θuðo, a] *a* bigheaded; (*fig*) pigheaded.
cabida [ka'βiða] *nf* space.
cabildo [ka'βildo] *nm* (*de iglesia*) chapter; (*POL*) town council.

cabina [ka'ßina] *nf* booth; (*de camión*) cabin.

cabizbajo, a [kaßiθ'ßaxo, a] *a* crestfallen, dejected.

cable ['kaßle] *nm* cable; ~**grama** *nm* cablegram.

cabo ['kaßo] *nm* (*de objeto*) end, extremity; (*de tiempo, proceso*) end; (*persona*) head, chief; (*MIL*) corporal; (*NAUT*) rope, cable; (*GEO*) cape; **al** ~ **de 3 días** after 3 days; **al fin y al** ~ in the end.

cabra ['kaßra] *nf* (she-)goat, nanny goat.

cabré *etc vb ver* **caber**.

cabria ['kaßrja] *nf* hoist, derrick.

cabrío, a [ka'ßrio, a] *a* goatish; **macho** ~ (he-)goat, billy goat.

cabriola [ka'ßrjola] *nf* caper.

cabritilla [kaßri'tiʎa] *nf* kid, kidskin.

cabrito [ka'ßrito] *nm* kid.

cabrón [ka'ßron] *nm* cuckold; (*fig: fam*) bastard (*fam!*).

cacahuete [kaka'wete] *nm* peanut, monkey nut.

cacao [ka'kao] *nm* cocoa; (*BOT*) cacao.

cacarear [kakare'ar] *vi* (*persona*) to boast; (*gallo*) to cackle.

cacería [kaθe'ria] *nf* hunting, shooting.

cacerola [kaθe'rola] *nf* pan, saucepan.

cacique [ka'θike] *nm* chief, local ruler; (*POL*) local boss; **caciquismo** *nm* (system of) dominance by the local boss.

caco ['kako] *nm* pickpocket.

cacto ['kakto], **cactus** ['kaktus] *nm* cactus.

cachar [ka'tʃar] *vt* to smash, break.

cacharro [ka'tʃarro] *nm* earthenware pot.

cachear [katʃe'ar] *vt* to search, frisk.

cachemira [katʃe'mira] *nf* cashmere.

cacheo [ka'tʃeo] *nm* searching, frisking.

cachimba [ka'tʃimba] *nf*, **cachimbo** [ka'tʃimbo] *nm* pipe.

cachiporra [katʃi'porra] *nf* truncheon.

cachivache [katʃi'ßatʃe] *nm* pot; (*utensilio*) utensil; (*persona*) good-for-nothing.

cacho, a ['katʃo, a] *a* bent, crooked // *nm* (small) bit.

cachondeo [katʃon'deo] *nm* (*fam*) farce, joke.

cachondo, a [ka'tʃondo, a] *a* (*ZOOL*) on heat; (*vulg*) randy, sexy; (*gracioso*) funny.

cachorro, a [ka'tʃorro, a] *nm/f* (*perro*) pup, puppy; (*león*) cub.

cada ['kaða] *a inv* each; (*antes de número*) every; ~ **día** each day, every day; ~ **uno/a** each one, every one; ~ **vez más** more and more; **uno de** ~ **diez** one out of every ten.

cadalso [ka'ðalso] *nm* scaffold.

cadáver [ka'ðaßer] *nm* (dead) body, corpse.

cadena [ka'ðena] *nf* chain; (*TV*) channel; **trabajo en** ~ assembly line work.

cadencia [ka'ðenθja] *nf* cadence, rhythm.

cadera [ka'ðera] *nf* hip.

cadete [ka'ðete] *nm* cadet.

caducar [kaðu'kar] *vi* (*permiso, ley*) to lapse, expire; (*persona*) to become senile; **caduco, a** *a* expired; (*persona*) very old.

C.A.E. *abr de* **cóbrese al entregar** COD (cash on delivery).

caer [ka'er] *vi*, ~**se** *vr* to fall (down); ~ **bien/mal** to make a good/bad impression; **el pago cae mañana** the payment is due tomorrow; ~ **en la cuenta** to catch on.

café [ka'fe] (*pl* ~**s**) *nm* (*bebida, planta*) coffee; (*lugar*) café // *a* (*color*) brown; **cafetal** *nm* coffee plantation.

cafetero, a [kafe'tero, a] *a* coffee *cpd* // *nf* coffee pot.

cáfila ['kafila] *nf* (*de personas*) group; (*de ovejas*) flock.

caída [ka'iða] *nf* (*gen*) fall; (*declive*) slope; (*disminución*) fall, drop.

caigo *etc vb ver* **caer**.

caimán [kai'man] *nm* alligator.

caimiento [kai'mjento] *nm* fall, falling.

caja ['kaxa] *nf* box; (*para reloj*) case; (*de ascensor*) shaft; (*COM*) cashbox; (*donde se hacen los pagos*) cashdesk; ~ **de ahorros** savings bank; ~ **de cambios** gearbox; ~ **fuerte**, ~ **de caudales** safe, strongbox.

cajero, a [ka'xero, a] *nm/f* cashier.

cajetilla [kaxe'tiʎa] *nf* small box; (*de cigarrillos*) packet.

cajón [ka'xon] *nm* big box; (*de mueble*) drawer.

cal [kal] *nf* lime.

cala ['kala] *nf* (*GEO*) cove, inlet; (*de barco*) hold; (*MED*) suppository.

calabaza [kala'ßaθa] *nf* (*BOT*) pumpkin.

calabozo [kala'ßoθo] *nm* prison (cell).

calamar [kala'mar] *nm* squid.

calambre [ka'lambre] *nm* cramp.

calamidad [kalami'ðað] *nf* calamity, disaster.

calamina [kala'mina] *nf* calamine.

calaña [ka'laɲa] *nf* model, pattern.

calar [ka'lar] *vt* to soak, drench; (*penetrar*) to pierce, penetrate; (*comprender*) to see through; (*vela, red*) to lower; ~**se las gafas** to stick one's glasses on.

calavera [kala'ßera] *nf* skull.

calcañar [kalka'ɲar] *nm*, **calcañal** [kalka'ɲal], **calcaño** [kal'kaɲo] *nm* heel.

calcar [kal'kar] *vt* (*reproducir*) to trace; (*imitar*) to copy.

calceta [kal'θeta] *nf* (knee-length) stocking; **hacer** ~ to knit; **calcetín** *nm* sock.

calcina [kal'θina] *nf* concrete.

calcinar [kalθi'nar] *vt* to burn, blacken.

calcio [kal'θjo] *nm* calcium.

calco ['kalko] *nm* tracing.

calcomanía [kalkoma'nia] *nm* transfer.

calculadora [kalkula'ðora] *nf* calculator; ~ **de bolsillo** pocket calculator.

calcular [kalku'lar] *vt* (*MAT*) to calculate, compute; (*suponer, creer*) to reckon, expect; **cálculo** *nm* calculation; reckoning.

caldear [kalde'ar] *vt* to warm (up), heat (up); (*los metales*) to weld.

caldera [kal'dera] *nf* boiler.

calderilla [kalde'riʎa] *nf* (*REL*) vessel for holy water; (*moneda*) small change.

caldero [kal'dero] *nm* small boiler.

calderón [kalde'ron] *nm* cauldron.

caldo ['kaldo] *nm* stock; (*consomé*) consommé; (*para la ensalada*) dressing.

calefacción [kalefak'θjon] *nf* heating.

calendario [kalen'darjo] *nm* calendar.

calentador [kalenta'ðor] *nm* heater.

calentar [kalen'tar] *vt* to heat (up); ~se *vr* to heat up, warm up; (*fig*) to get heated.

calentura [kalen'tura] *nf* (*MED*) fever, (high) temperature; **calenturiento, a** *a* feverish.

calero, a [ka'lero, a] *a* lime *cpd*.

calibrar [kali'ßrar] *vt* to gauge, measure; **calibre** *nm* (*de cañón*) calibre, bore; (*diámetro*) diameter; (*fig*) calibre.

calidad [kali'ðað] *nf* quality; **en** ~ **de** in the capacity of.

cálido, a ['kaliðo, a] *a* hot; (*fig*) warm.

caliente [ka'ljente] *a* hot; (*sin exceso*) warm; (*fig*) fiery; (*disputa*) heated.

calificación [kalifika'θjon] *nf* qualification; (*de alumno*) grade, mark.

calificado, a [kalifi'kaðo, a] *a* qualified, competent; (*trabajador*) skilled.

calificar [kalifi'kar] *vt* to qualify; (*enaltecer*) to distinguish; (*alumno*) to grade, mark; (*determinar*) to describe.

calma ['kalma] *nf* calm; (*pachorra*) slowness.

calmante [kal'mante] *nm* sedative, tranquillizer.

calmar [kal'mar] *vt* to calm, calm down // *vi* (*tempestad*) to abate; (*mente etc*) to become calm.

calmoso, a [kal'moso, a], **calmudo, a** [kal'muðo, a] *a* calm, quiet.

calofrío [kalo'frio] *nm* = **escalofrío**.

calor [ka'lor] *nm* heat; (~ *agradable*) warmth.

caloría [kalo'ria] *nf* calorie.

calorífero, a [kalo'rifero, a] *a* heat-producing, heat-giving // *nm* heating system.

calumnia [ka'lumnja] *nf* calumny, slander; **calumnioso, a** *a* slanderous.

caluroso, a [kalu'roso, a] *a* hot; (*sin exceso*) warm; (*fig*) enthusiastic.

calva ['kalßa] *nf* bald patch; (*en bosque*) clearing.

calvario [kal'ßarjo] *nm* stations *pl* of the cross.

calvicie [kal'ßiθje] *nf* baldness.

calvo, a ['kalßo, a] *a* bald; (*terreno*) bare, barren; (*tejido*) threadbare.

calza ['kalθa] *nf* wedge, chock.

calzado, a [kal'θaðo, a] *a* shod // *nm* footwear; *nf* roadway, highway.

calzador [kalθa'ðor] *nm* shoehorn.

calzar [kal'θar] *vt* to put on; (*un mueble*) to put a wedge under; ~se *vr*: ~se los zapatos to put on one's shoes; ¿qué (número) calza? what size do you wear or take?

calzón [kal'θon] *nm* (*también* **calzones** *nmpl*) shorts *pl*.

calzoncillos [kalθon'θiʎos] *nmpl* underpants.

callado, a [ka'ʎaðo, a] *a* quiet.

callar [ka'ʎar] *vt* to keep quiet about, say nothing about // *vi*, ~se *vr* to keep quiet, be silent.

calle ['kaʎe] *nf* street; (*DEPORTE*) lane; ~ **arriba/abajo** up/down the street; ~ **de un solo sentido** one-way street.

calleja [ka'ʎexa] *nf* alley, narrow street; **callejear** *vi* to wander about the streets; **callejero, a** *a* street *cpd*.

callejón [kaʎe'xon] *nm* alley, passage; ~ **sin salida** one-way street.

callejuela [kaʎe'xwela] *nf* side-street, alley.

callista [ka'ʎista] *nm/f* chiropodist.

callo ['kaʎo] *nm* callus; (*en el pie*) corn; ~s *nmpl* tripe *sg*; ~**so, a** a horny, rough.

cama ['kama] *nf* bed; (*GEO*) stratum; ~ **de matrimonio** double bed.

camada [ka'maða] *nf* litter; (*de personas*) gang, band.

camafeo [kama'feo] *nm* cameo.

camandulear [kamandule'ar] *vi* to be a hypocrite.

cámara ['kamara] *nf* (*gen*) chamber; (*habitación*) room; (*sala*) hall; (*CINE*) cine camera; (*fotográfica*) camera; ~ **de aire** inner tube.

camarada [kama'raða] *nm* comrade, companion.

camarera [kama'rera] *nf* (*en restaurante*) waitress; (*en casa, hotel*) maid.

camarero [kama'rero] *nm* waiter.

camarilla [kama'riʎa] *nf* (*clan*) clique; (*POL*) lobby.

camarín [kama'rin] *nm* dressing room.

camarón [kama'ron] *nm* shrimp.

camarote [kama'rote] *nm* cabin.

cambiable [kam'bjaßle] *a* (*variable*) changeable, variable; (*intercambiable*) interchangeable.

cambiante [kam'bjante] *a* variable // *nm* moneychanger.

cambiar [kam'bjar] *vt* (*gen*) to change; (*de moneda*) to change; (*dinero*) to exchange // *vi* (*gen*) to change; ~se *vr* (*mudarse*) to move; (*de ropa*) to change; ~(se) de... to change one's ... .

cambio ['kambjo] *nm* change; (*trueque*) exchange; (*COM*) rate of exchange; (*oficina*) (foreign) exchange office; (*dinero menudo*) small change; **en** ~ on the other hand; (*en lugar de eso*) instead; ~ **de velocidades** gear lever; ~ **de vía** points *pl*.

cambista [kam'bista] *nm* (*COM*) exchange broker; (*FERRO*) switchman.

camelar [kame'lar] vt (galantear) to flirt with; (engañar) to cajole.
camello [ka'meʎo] nm camel.
camilla [ka'miʎa] nf (cama) cot; (MED) stretcher.
caminante [kami'nante] nm/f traveller.
caminar [kami'nar] vi (marchar) to walk, go; (viajar) to travel, journey // vt (recorrer) to cover, travel.
caminata [kami'nata] nf long walk.
camino [ka'mino] nm (gen) way, road; (senda) track; **a medio** ~ halfway (there); **en el** ~ on the way, en route.
camión [ka'mjon] nm lorry, truck.
camisa [ka'misa] nf shirt; (BOT) skin; ~ **de dormir** nightdress; ~ **de fuerza** straitjacket; **camisería** nf outfitter's (shop).
camiseta [kami'seta] nf (prenda) vest; (de deportista) singlet.
camisón [kami'son] nm nightdress, nightgown.
campamento [kampa'mento] nm camp.
campana [kam'pana] nf bell; ~**da** nf peal; ~**rio** nm belfry.
campanilla [kampa'niʎa] nf (campana) small bell; (burbuja) bubble.
campaña [kam'paɲa] nf (MIL, POL) campaign; (campo) countryside.
campar [kam'par] vi to camp; (sobresalir) to excel, stand out.
campeón, ona [kampe'on, ona] nm/f champion; **campeonato** nm championship.
campesino, a [kampe'sino, a] a country cpd, rural // nm/f countryman/woman; (agricultor) farmer.
campestre [kam'pestre] a country cpd, rural.
camping ['kampin] nm camping; (lugar) campsite; **hacer** ~ to go camping.
campiña [kam'piɲa] nf countryside.
campo ['kampo] nm (fuera de la ciudad) country, countryside; (AGR, ELEC) field; (de fútbol) ground, pitch; (de golf) course; (de tenis) court; (MIL) camp.
camposanto [kampo'santo] nm cemetery.
camuflaje [kamu'flaxe] nm camouflage.
Canadá [kana'ða] nm Canada; **canadiense** a, nm/f Canadian // nf furlined jacket.
canal [ka'nal] nm canal; (GEO) channel, strait; (de televisión) channel; (de tejado) gutter; ~**izar** vt to channel.
canalón [kana'lon] nm (conducto vertical) drainpipe; (del tejado) gutter.
canalla [ka'naʎa] nf rabble, mob // nm swine, rotter.
canapé [kana'pe] (pl ~s) nm sofa, settee; (CULIN) canapé.
canario, a [ka'narjo, a] a, nm/f (native) of the Canary Isles // nm canary.
canasta [ka'nasta] nf (round) basket; **canasto** nm large basket.
cancelación [kanθela'θjon] nf cancellation.

cancelar [kanθe'lar] vt to cancel; (una deuda) to write off.
cáncer ['kanθer] nm (MED) cancer; **C**~ (ASTRO) Cancer.
canciller [kanθi'ʎer] nm chancellor.
canción [kan'θjon] nf song; ~ **de cuna** lullaby; **cancionero** nm song book.
candado [kan'daðo] nm padlock.
candela [kan'dela] nf candle.
candelero [kande'lero] nm (para vela) candlestick; (de aceite) oil lamp.
candente [kan'dente] a red-hot; (fig) burning.
candidato [kandi'ðato] nm/f candidate.
candidez [kandi'ðeθ] nf (sencillez) simplicity; (simpleza) naiveté; **cándido, a** a simple; naive.
candil [kan'dil] nm oil lamp; ~**eja** nf small oil lamp.
candor [kan'dor] nm (sinceridad) frankness; (inocencia) innocence.
canela [ka'nela] nf cinnamon.
canelón [kane'lon] nm (canal) drainpipe; (carámbano) icicle.
cangrejo [kan'grexo] nm crab.
canguro [kan'guro] nm kangaroo.
caníbal [ka'niβal] a, nm/f cannibal.
canica [ka'nika] nf marble.
canijo, a [ka'nixo, a] a frail, sickly.
canino, a [ka'nino, a] a canine // nm canine (tooth).
canjear [kanxe'ar] vt to exchange.
cano, a ['kano, a] a grey-haired, whitehaired.
canoa [ka'noa] nf canoe.
canon ['kanon] nm canon; (pensión) rent; (COM) tax.
canónigo [ka'noniɣo] nm canon.
canonizar [kanoni'θar] vt to canonize.
canoro, a [ka'noro, a] a melodious.
cansado, a [kan'saðo, a] a tired, weary; (tedioso) tedious, boring.
cansancio [kan'sanθjo] nm tiredness, fatigue.
cansar [kan'sar] vt (fatigar) to tire, tire out, weary; (aburrir) to bore; (fastidiar) to bother; ~**se** vr to tire, get tired; (aburrirse) to get bored.
cantante [kan'tante] a singing // nm/f singer.
cantar [kan'tar] vt to sing // vi (gen) to sing; (insecto) to chirp; (rechinar) to squeak // nm (acción) singing; (canción) song; (poema) poem.
cántara ['kantara] nf large pitcher.
cántaro ['kantaro] nm pitcher, jug.
cantatriz [kanta'triθ] nf singer.
cante ['kante] nm: ~ **jondo** flamenco singing.
cantera [kan'tera] nf quarry.
cantidad [kanti'ðað] nf quantity, amount.
cantilena [kanti'lena] nf = **cantinela**.
cantimplora [kantim'plora] nf (frasco) water bottle, canteen; (sifón) syphon.
cantina [kan'tina] nf canteen; (de estación) buffet; (sótano) wine cellar.

cantinela [kanti'nela] *nf* ballad, song.
canto ['kanto] *nm* (*gen*) singing; (*canción*) song; (*borde*) edge, rim; (*de un cuchillo*) back; ~ **rodado** boulder.
cantor, a [kan'tor, a] *nm/f* singer.
canturrear [kanturre'ar], **canturriar** [kantu'rrjar] *vi* to sing softly.
caña ['kaɲa] *nf* (*BOT: tallo*) stem, stalk; (*carrizo*) reed; (*de cerveza*) glass; (*ANAT: del brazo*) long bone; (: *de la pierna*) shinbone; (*MINERÍA*) gallery; ~ **de azúcar** sugar cane.
cañada [ka'ɲaða] *nf* (*entre dos montañas*) gully, ravine; (*camino*) cattle track.
caño ['kaɲo] *nm* (*tubo*) tube, pipe; (*de aguas servidas*) sewer; (*MUS*) pipe; (*NAUT*) navigation channel; (*de fuente*) jet.
cañón [ka'ɲon] *nm* tube, pipe; (*MIL*) cannon; (*de fusil*) barrel; (*GEO*) canyon, gorge.
cañonero [kaɲo'nero] *nm* gunboat.
caoba [ka'oßa] *nf* mahogany.
caos ['kaos] *nm* chaos.
cap. *abr de* **capítulo.**
capa ['kapa] *nf* cloak, cape; (*GEO*) layer, stratum; (*pretexto*) pretence.
capacidad [kapaθi'ðað] *nf* (*medida*) capacity; (*aptitud*) capacity, ability.
capacitación [kapaθita'θjon] *nf* training.
capar [ka'par] *vt* to castrate, geld.
caparazón [kapara'θon] *nm* shell.
capataz [kapa'taθ] *nm* foreman.
capaz [ka'paθ] *a* able, capable; (*amplio*) capacious, roomy.
capcioso, a [kap'θjoso, a] *a* wily, deceitful.
capellán [kape'ʎan] *nm* chaplain; (*sacerdote*) priest.
caperuza [kape'ruθa] *nf* hood; **caperucita** *nf*: **Caperucita Roja** Little Red Riding Hood.
capilla [ka'piʎa] *nf* chapel; (*capucha*) hood, cowl.
capital [kapi'tal] *a* capital // *nm* (*COM*) capital // *nf* capital; ~ **social** share capital.
capitalismo [kapita'lismo] *nm* capitalism; **capitalista** *a, nm/f* capitalist.
capitalizar [kapitali'θar] *vt* to capitalize.
capitán [kapi'tan] *nm* captain.
capitana [kapi'tana] *nf* flagship.
capitanear [kapitane'ar] *vt* to captain.
capitolio [kapi'toljo] *nm* capitol.
capitoné [kapito'ne] *nm* removal van.
capitulación [kapitula'θjon] *nf* (*rendición*) capitulation, surrender; (*acuerdo*) agreement, pact.
capitular [kapitu'lar] *vi* to come to terms, make an agreement // *a* chapter *cpd.*
capítulo [ka'pitulo] *nm* chapter; ~**s** *nmpl*: ~**s matrimoniales** marriage contract *sg.*
capó [ka'po] *nm* bonnet.
caporal [kapo'ral] *nm* chief, leader.
capota [ka'pota] *nf* (*de mujer*) bonnet; (*de coche*) hood, roof.
capote [ka'pote] *nm* (*abrigo, de militar*)

greatcoat; (*de torero*) cloak; (*NAIPES*) slam.
Capricornio [kapri'kornjo] *nm* Capricorn.
capricho [ka'pritʃo] *nm* whim, caprice; ~**so, a** *a* capricious.
cápsula ['kapsula] *nf* capsule; (*de botella*) cap.
captar [kap'tar] *vt* to win (over).
captura [kap'tura] *nf* capture; (*JUR*) arrest; **capturar** *vt* to capture; to arrest.
capucha [ka'putʃa] *nf* hood, cowl.
cara ['kara] *nf* (*ANAT*) face; (*aspecto*) appearance; (*de moneda*) face; (*de disco*) side; (*fig*) boldness; ~ **a** *ad* facing; **de** ~ opposite, facing; **dar la** ~ to face the consequences; ¿~ **o cruz?** heads or tails?
carabina [kara'ßina] *nf* carbine, rifle.
caracol [kara'kol] *nm* (*ZOOL*) snail; (*concha*) shell.
caracolear [karakole'ar] *vi* to prance about.
carácter [ka'rakter] (*pl* **caracteres**) *nm* character.
característico, a [karakte'ristiko, a] *a* characteristic // *nf* characteristic.
caracterizar [karakteri'θar] *vt* (*distinguir*) to characterize, typify; (*honrar*) to confer (a) distinction on.
caramba [ka'ramba] *excl* well!, good gracious!
carámbano [ka'rambano] *nm* icicle.
caramelo [kara'melo] *nm* (*dulce*) sweet; (*dulce de* ~) toffee; (*azúcar fundida*) caramel.
caramillo [kara'miʎo] *nm* (*flauta*) recorder; (*montón*) untidy heap; (*chisme, enredo*) bit of gossip.
carapacho [kara'patʃo] *nm* shell, carapace.
caraqueño, a [kara'keɲo, a] *a, nm/f* (*native*) of Caracas.
carátula [ka'ratula] *nf* (*careta, máscara*) mask; (*TEATRO*): **la** ~ the stage.
caravana [kara'ßana] *nf* caravan; (*fig*) group; (*sucesión de autos*) stream; (*embotellamiento*) traffic jam.
carbón [kar'ßon] *nm* coal; **papel** ~ carbon paper; **carbonero** *nm/f* coal merchant; **carbonilla** *nf* coal dust.
carbonizar [karßoni'θar] *vt* to carbonize; (*quemar*) to char.
carbono [kar'ßono] *nm* carbon.
carburador [karßura'ðor] *nm* carburettor.
carcajada [karka'xaða] *nf* (loud) laugh, guffaw.
cárcel ['karθel] *nf* prison, jail; (*TEC*) clamp; **carcelero, a** *a* prison *cpd* // *nm/f* warder.
carcomer [karko'mer] *vt* to bore into, eat into; (*fig*) to undermine; ~**se** *vr* to become worm-eaten; (*fig*) to decay.
carcomido, a [karko'miðo, a] *a* worm-eaten; (*fig*) rotten.
cardenal [karðe'nal] *nm* (*REL*) cardinal; (*equimosis*) bruise.
cárdeno, a ['karðeno, a] *a* purple; (*lívido*) livid.

cardíaco, a [kar'ðiako, a] *a* cardiac, heart *cpd.*
cardinal [karði'nal] *a* cardinal.
cardo ['karðo] *nm* thistle.
cardumen [kar'ðumen] *nm* shoal.
carear [kare'ar] *vt* to bring face to face; (*comparar*) to compare; ~**se** *vr* to come face to face, meet.
carecer [kare'θer] *vi*: ~ **de** to lack, be in need of.
carencia [ka'renθja] *nf* lack; (*escasez*) shortage; (*MED*) deficiency.
carente [ka'rente] *a*: ~ **de** lacking, devoid of.
carestía [kares'tia] *nf* (*escasez*) scarcity, shortage; (*COM*) high cost.
careta [ka'reta] *nf* mask.
carga ['karɣa] *nf* (*peso, ELEC*) load; (*de barco*) cargo, freight; (*MIL*) charge; (*obligación, responsabilidad*) duty, obligation.
cargadero [karɣa'ðero] *nm* goods platform, loading bay.
cargado, a [kar'ɣaðo, a] *a* loaded; (*ELEC*) live; (*café, te*) strong; (*el cielo*) overcast.
cargamento [karɣa'mento] *nm* (*acción*) loading; (*mercancías*) load, cargo.
cargar [kar'ɣar] *vt* (*barco, arma*) to load; (*ELEC*) to charge; (*COM: algo en cuenta*) to charge, debit; (*MIL: enemigo*) to charge // *vi* to load (up); (*inclinarse*) to lean; ~ **con** to pick up, carry away.
cargo ['karɣo] *nm* (*puesto*) post, office; (*responsabilidad*) duty, obligation; (*fig*) weight, burden; (*JUR*) charge; **hacerse ~ del gobierno** to take charge of the government.
carguero [kar'ɣero] *nm* freighter, cargo boat; (*avión*) freight plane.
caribe [ka'riße] *a, nm/f* (native) of the Caribbean.
Caribe [ka'riße] *nm*: **el** ~ the Caribbean.
caricatura [karika'tura] *nf* caricature.
caricia [ka'riθja] *nf* caress.
caridad [kari'ðað] *nf* charity.
cariño [ka'riɲo] *nm* affection, love; (*caricia*) caress; (*en carta*) love...; ~**so, a** *a* affectionate.
caritativo, a [karita'tißo, a] *a* charitable.
carmesí [karme'si] *a, nm* crimson.
carnal [kar'nal] *a* carnal; **primo** ~ first cousin.
carnaval [karna'ßal] *nm* carnival.
carne ['karne] *nf* flesh; (*CULIN*) meat; **echar** ~**s** to put on weight.
carnero [kar'nero] *nm* sheep, ram; (*carne*) mutton.
carnet [kar'ne] *nm*: ~ **de conducir** driving licence.
carnicería [karniθe'ria] *nf* butcher's (shop); (*mercado*) meat market.
carnicero, a [karni'θero, a] *a* carnivorous // *nm/f* butcher // *nm* carnivore.
carnívoro, a [kar'nißoro, a] *a* carnivorous.
carnoso, a [kar'noso, a] *a* beefy, fat.

caro, a ['karo, a] *a* dear; (*COM*) dear, expensive // *ad* dear, dearly.
carpeta [kar'peta] *nf* table cover; (*para documentos*) folder, file.
carpintería [karpinte'ria] *nf* carpentry, joinery; **carpintero** *nm* carpenter.
carraspera [karras'pera] *nf* hoarseness.
carrera [ka'rrera] *nf* (*DEPORTE*) running; (*espacio recorrido*) run; (*certamen*) race; (*trayecto*) course; (*profesión*) career; (*ESCOL*) course.
carreta [ka'rreta] *nf* wagon, cart.
carrete [ka'rrete] *nm* reel, spool; (*TEC*) coil.
carretel [karre'tel] *nm* reel, spool.
carretera [karre'tera] *nf* (main) road, highway.
carretilla [karre'tiʎa] *nf* trolley; (*AGR*) (wheel)barrow.
carril [ka'rril] *nm* furrow; (*de autopista*) lane; (*FERRO*) rail.
carrillo [ka'rriʎo] *nm* (*ANAT*) cheek; (*TEC*) pulley.
carrizo [ka'rriθo] *nm* reed.
carro ['karro] *nm* cart, wagon; (*MIL*) tank; (*AM: coche*) car.
carrocería [karroθe'ria] *nf* bodywork, coachwork.
carta ['karta] *nf* letter; (*CULIN*) menu; (*naipe*) card; (*mapa*) map; (*JUR*) document; ~ **de crédito** credit card; ~ **certificada** registered letter.
cartel [kar'tel] *nm* (*anuncio*) poster, placard; (*alfabeto*) wall chart; (*COM*) cartel.
cartera [kar'tera] *nf* (*de bolsillo*) wallet; (*de colegial, cobrador*) satchel; (*de señora*) handbag; (*para documentos*) briefcase; (*COM, POL*) portfolio.
cartero [kar'tero] *nm* postman.
cartón [kar'ton] *nm* cardboard; (*ARTE*) cartoon.
cartucho [kar'tutʃo] *nm* (*MIL*) cartridge.
casa ['kasa] *nf* house; (*hogar*) home; (*edificio*) building; (*COM*) firm, company; (*de tablero de ajedrez*) square; ~ **consistorial** town hall; ~ **de huéspedes** boarding house; ~ **de socorro** first aid post; ~ **editorial** publishing house.
casamiento [kasa'mjento] *nm* marriage, wedding.
casar [ka'sar] *vt* to marry; (*JUR*) to quash, annul // *nm* hamlet; ~**se** *vr* to marry, get married.
cascada [kas'kaða] *nf* waterfall.
cascar [kas'kar] *vt*, ~**se** *vr* to crack, split, break (open).
cáscara ['kaskara] *nf* (*de huevo, fruta seca*) shell; (*de fruta*) skin; (*de limón*) peel.
casco ['kasko] *nm* (*de bombero, soldado*) helmet; (*cráneo*) skull; (*de botella, obús*) fragment; (*BOT: de cebolla*) skin; (*tonel*) cask, barrel; (*NAUT: de barco*) hull; (*ZOOL: de caballo*) hoof; (*botella*) empty bottle.
caserío [kase'rio] *nm* hamlet; (*casa*) country house.
casero, a [ka'sero, a] *a* domestic, household *cpd* // *nm/f* (*propietario*)

landlord/lady; (*portero*) caretaker; (*COM*) house agent.
caseta [ka'seta] *nf* hut; (*para bañista*) cubicle; (*de feriantes*) stall.
casi ['kasi] *ad* almost; ~ **te caes** you almost fell.
casilla [ka'siʎa] *nf* (*casita*) hut, cabin; (*TEATRO*) box office; (*de ajedrez*) square.
casino [ka'sino] *nm* club.
caso ['kaso] *nm* case; **en ~ de...** in case of...; **el ~ es que** the fact is that; **hacer ~ a** to pay attention to; **hacer o venir al ~** to be relevant.
caspa ['kaspa] *nf* dandruff.
cassette [ka'set] *nf* cassette.
casta ['kasta] *nf* caste; (*raza*) breed; (*linaje*) lineage.
castaña [kas'taɲa] *nf* chestnut.
castaño, a [kas'taɲo, a] *a* chestnut-brown // *nm* chestnut tree.
castañuela [kasta'ɲwela] *nf* castanet.
castellano, a [kaste'ʎano, a] *a* Castilian // *nm* (*lengua*) Castilian, Spanish.
castidad [kasti'ðað] *nf* chastity, purity.
castigar [kasti'xar] *vt* to punish; (*DEPORTE*) to penalize; (*afligir*) to afflict; **castigo** *nm* punishment; (*DEPORTE*) penalty.
castillo [kas'tiʎo] *nm* castle.
castizo, a [kas'tiθo, a] *a* (*LING*) pure; (*de buena casta*) purebred, pedigree.
casto, a ['kasto, a] *a* chaste, pure.
castor [kas'tor] *nm* beaver.
castrar [kas'trar] *vt* to castrate.
casual [ka'swal] *a* fortuitous, accidental; ~**idad** *nf* chance, accident; (*combinación de circunstancias*) coincidence.
cataclismo [kata'klismo] *nm* cataclysm.
catalán, ana [kata'lan, ana] *a, nm/f* Catalan, Catalonian.
catalizador [kataliθa'ðor] *nm* catalyst.
catálogo [ka'taloxo] *nm* catalogue.
Cataluña [kata'luɲa] *nf* Catalonia.
cataplasma [kata'plasma] *nf* poultice.
catar [ka'tar] *vt* to taste, sample.
catarata [kata'rata] *nf* (*GEO*) waterfall, falls *pl*; (*MED*) cataract.
catarro [ka'tarro] *nm* catarrh; (*constipado*) cold.
catástrofe [ka'tastrofe] *nf* catastrophe.
catedral [kate'ðral] *nf* cathedral.
catedrático, a [kate'ðratiko, a] *nm/f* professor.
categoría [katexo'ria] *nf* category; (*rango*) rank, standing; (*calidad*) quality.
categórico, a [kate'xoriko, a] *a* categorical.
catolicismo [katoli'θismo] *nm* Catholicism.
católico, a [ka'toliko, a] *a, nm/f* Catholic.
catorce [ka'torθe] *num* fourteen.
caución [kau'θjon] *nf* bail; **caucionar** *vt* to prevent, guard against; (*JUR*) to bail, go bail for.
caucho ['kautʃo] *nm* rubber.
caudal [kau'ðal] *nm* (*de río*) volume, flow;

(*fortuna*) wealth; (*abundancia*) abundance; ~**oso, a** *a* (*río*) large; (*aguas*) copious; (*persona*) wealthy, rich.
caudillo [kau'ðiʎo] *nm* leader, chief.
causa ['kausa] *nf* cause; (*razón*) reason; (*JUR*) lawsuit, case; **causar** *vt* to cause.
cáustico, a ['kaustiko, a] *a* caustic.
cautela [kau'tela] *nf* caution, cautiousness; **cauteloso, a** *a* cautious, wary, careful.
cautivar [kauti'ßar] *vt* to capture; (*fig*) to captivate.
cautiverio [kauti'ßerjo] *nm*, **cautividad** [kautißi'ðað] *nf* captivity.
cautivo, a [kau'tißo, a] *a, nm/f* captive.
cauto, a ['kauto, a] *a* cautious, careful.
cavar [ka'ßar] *vt* to dig.
caverna [ka'ßerna] *nf* cave, cavern.
cavidad [kaßi'ðað] *nf* cavity.
cavilar [kaßi'lar] *vt* to ponder.
cayado [ka'jaðo] *nm* (*de pastor*) staff, crook; (*de obispo*) crozier.
cayó *etc vb ver* **caer.**
caza ['kaθa] *nf* (*gen*) hunting, shooting; (*una ~*) hunt, chase; (*animales*) game // *nm* (*AVIAT*) fighter.
cazador [kaθa'ðor] *nm* hunter.
cazar [ka'θar] *vt* to hunt; (*perseguir*) to chase; (*coger*) to catch.
cazo ['kaθo] *nm* saucepan.
cazuela [ka'θwela] *nf* pan; (*guisado*) casserole.
cebada [θe'ßaða] *nf* barley.
cebar [θe'ßar] *vt* (*animal*) to fatten (up); (*anzuelo*) to bait; (*MIL, TEC*) to prime; (*pasión*) to nourish; (*ira*) to inflame.
cebo ['θeßo] *nm* (*para animales*) feed, food; (*para peces, fig*) bait; (*de arma*) charge.
cebolla [θe'ßoʎa] *nf* onion.
cebra ['θeßra] *nf* zebra.
cecear [θeθe'ar] *vi* to lisp; **ceceo** *nm* lisp.
cedazo [θe'ðaθo] *nm* sieve.
ceder [θe'ðer] *vt* to hand over, give up, part with // *vi* (*renunciar*) to give in, yield; (*disminuir*) to diminish, decline; (*romperse*) to give way.
cedro ['θeðro] *nm* cedar.
cédula ['θeðula] *nf* certificate, document; ~ **de aduana** customs permit.
C.E.E. *nf abr de* **Comunidad Económica Europea** E.E.C. (European Economic Community).
cegar [θe'xar] *vt* to blind; (*fig: pozo*) to block up, fill up // *vi* to go blind; ~**se** *vr* to be blinded (*de by*).
ceguedad [θexe'ðað], **ceguera** [θe'xera] *nf* blindness.
ceja ['θexa] *nf* eyebrow.
cejar [θe'xar] *vi* to move back, go back; (*fig*) to back down.
cejijunto, a [θexi'xunto, a] *a* with bushy eyebrows; (*fig*) scowling.
celada [θe'laða] *nf* ambush, trap.
celador, a [θela'ðor, a] *nm/f* (*de edificio*) watchman; (*de museo etc*) attendant.
celar [θe'lar] *vt* (*vigilar*) to watch over; (*encubrir*) to conceal, hide.

celda ['θelda] nf cell.
celebración [θeleßra'θjon] nf celebration.
celebrar [θele'ßrar] vt to celebrate; (alabar) to praise // vi to be glad; ~**se** vr to occur, take place.
célebre ['θelebre] a famous; (chistoso) witty, funny.
celebridad [θeleßri'ðað] nf (gen) fame; (persona) celebrity; (festividad) celebration(s) (pl).
celeste [θe'leste] a celestial, heavenly.
celestial [θeles'tjal] a celestial, heavenly.
celibato [θeli'ßato] nm celibacy.
célibe ['θeliße] a celibate // nm/f unmarried person.
celo ['θelo] nm zeal; (REL) fervour; (pey) envy; (de animales) rut, heat; ~**s** nmpl jealousy sg.
celofán [θelo'fan] nm cellophane.
celoso, a [θe'loso, a] a (envidioso) jealous; (trabajo) zealous; (desconfiado) suspicious.
celta ['θelta] nm/f Celt.
célula ['θelula] nf cell.
cementar [θemen'tar] vt to cement.
cementerio [θemen'terjo] nm cemetery, graveyard.
cemento [θe'mento] nm cement; (hormigón) concrete.
cena ['θena] nf evening meal.
cenagal [θena'xal] nm bog, quagmire.
cenar [θe'nar] vt to have for supper // vi to dine.
cenicero [θeni'θero] nm ashtray.
cenit [θe'nit] nm zenith.
ceniza [θe'niθa] nf ash, ashes pl.
censo ['θenso] nm (empadronamiento) census; (JUR) tax; (renta) rent; (carga sobre una casa) mortgage.
censor [θen'sor] nm censor.
censura [θen'sura] nf (POL) censorship; (moral) censure, criticism.
censurar [θensu'rar] vt (idea) to censure; (cortar: película) to censor.
centella [θen'teʎa] nf spark.
centellar [θente'ʎar], **centellear** [θenteʎe'ar] vi (metal) to gleam; (estrella) to twinkle; (fig) to sparkle; **centelleo** nm gleam(ing); twinkling; sparkling.
centenar [θente'nar] nm hundred.
centenario, a [θente'narjo, a] a centenary.
centésimo, a [θen'tesimo, a] a hundredth.
centígrado, a [θen'tixraðo, a] a centigrade.
centímetro [θen'timetro] nm centimetre.
céntimo, a ['θentimo, a] a hundredth // nm cent.
centinela [θenti'nela] nm sentry, guard.
central [θen'tral] a central // nf head office; (TEC) plant; (TELEC) exchange.
centralización [θentraliθa'θjon] nf centralization.
centralizar [θentrali'θar] vt to centralize.
centrar [θen'trar] vt to centre.
céntrico, a ['θentriko, a] a centre.
centro ['θentro] nm centre.

centroamericano, a [θentroameri'kano, a] a, nm/f Central American.
ceñidor [θeɲi'ðor] nm sash.
ceñir [θe'ɲir] vt (rodear) to encircle, surround; (ajustar) to fit (tightly); (apretar) to tighten.
ceño ['θeɲo] nm frown, scowl; **fruncir el** ~ to frown, knit one's brow.
cepillar [θepi'ʎar] vt to brush; (madera) to plane (down); **cepillo** nm (gen) brush; (TEC) plane.
cera ['θera] nf wax.
cerámico, a [θe'ramiko, a] a ceramic // nf ceramics sg.
cerca ['θerka] nf fence // ad near, nearby, close; ~**s** nmpl foreground sg; ~ **de** prep near, close to.
cercanía [θerka'nia] nf nearness, closeness; ~**s** nfpl outskirts.
cercano, a [θer'kano, a] a close, near.
cercar [θer'kar] vt to fence in; (rodear) to surround.
cerciorar [θerθjo'rar] vt (informar) to inform; (asegurar) to assure; ~**se** vr (descubrir) to find out; (asegurarse) to make sure.
cerco ['θerko] nm (AGR) enclosure; (AM) fence; (MIL) siege.
cerdo ['θerðo] nm pig.
cereal [θere'al] nm cereal.
cerebro [θe'reßro] nm brain; (fig) brains pl.
ceremonia [θere'monja] nf ceremony; **ceremonial** a, nm ceremonial; **ceremonioso, a** a ceremonious; (cumplido) formal.
cereza [θe'reθa] nf cherry.
cerilla [θe'riʎa] nf (fósforo) match.
cerner [θer'ner] vt to sift, sieve; (fig) to scan, watch // vi to blossom; (lloviznar) to drizzle; ~**se** vr to hover.
cernidor [θerni'ðor] nm sieve.
cero ['θero] nm nothing, zero.
cerrado, a [θe'rraðo, a] a closed, shut; (con llave) locked; (tiempo) cloudy, overcast; (curva) sharp; (acento) thick, broad.
cerradura [θerra'ðura] nf (acción) closing; (mecanismo) lock.
cerraja [θe'rraxa] nf lock.
cerrar [θe'rrar] vt to close, shut; (paso, carretera) to close; (grifo) to turn off; (trato, cuenta, negocio) to close; ~ **con llave** to lock // vi to close, shut; (la noche) to come down; ~**se** vr to close, shut.
cerro ['θerro] nm hill.
cerrojo [θe'rroxo] nm (herramienta) bolt; (de puerta) latch.
certamen [θer'tamen] nm competition, contest.
certero, a [θer'tero, a] a accurate; (cierto) sure, certain.
certeza [θer'teθa], **certidumbre** [θerti-'ðumbre] nf certainty.
certificado [θertifi'kaðo] nm certificate.
certificar [θertifi'kar] vt (asegurar,

atestar) to certify; (*carta*) to register.
cervato [θer'βato] *nm* fawn.
cervecería [θerβeθe'ria] *nf* (*fábrica*) brewery; (*tienda*) public house.
cerveza [θer'βeθa] *nf* beer.
cesación [θesa'θjon] *nf* cessation; (*suspensión*) suspension.
cesante [θe'sante] *a* out of a job.
cesar [θe'sar] *vi* to cease, stop.
cese ['θese] *nm* (*de trabajo*) dismissal; (*de pago*) suspension.
césped ['θespeð] *nm* grass, lawn.
cesta ['θesta] *nf* basket; **cesto** *nm* (large) basket, hamper.
ch... *ver bajo la letra* CH, *después de* C.
Cía *abr de* **compañía.**
cianuro [θja'nuro] *nm* cyanide.
ciar [θjar] *vi* to go backwards.
cicatriz [θika'triθ] *nf* scar.
ciclismo [θi'klismo] *nm* cycling.
ciclo ['θiklo] *nm* cycle.
ciclón [θi'klon] *nm* cyclone.
ciego, a ['θjexo, a] *a* blind // *nm/f* blind man/woman.
cielo ['θjelo] *nm* sky; (*REL*) heaven; ¡~s! good heavens!
ciempiés [θjem'pjes] *nm* centipede.
cien [θjen] *num ver* **ciento.**
ciénaga ['θjenaxa] *nf* marsh, swamp.
ciencia ['θjenθja] *nf* science; ~-**ficción** *nf* science fiction.
cieno ['θjeno] *nm* mud, mire.
científico, a [θjen'tifiko, a] *a* scientific // *nm/f* scientist.
ciento ['θjento], **cien** *num* hundred; **pagar al 10 por** ~ to pay at 10 per cent.
cierne ['θjerne] *nm*: **en** ~ in blossom.
cierre ['θjerre] *nm* closing, shutting; (*con llave*) locking; ~ **a cremallera** zip fastener.
cierro *etc vb ver* **cerrar.**
cierto, a ['θjerto, a] *a* sure, certain; (*un tal*) a certain; (*correcto*) right, correct; ~ **hombre** a certain man; **sí, es** ~ yes, that's correct.
ciervo ['θjerβo] *nm* (*especie*) deer; (*macho*) stag.
cierzo ['θjerθo] *nm* north wind.
cifra ['θifra] *nf* number, numeral; (*cantidad*) number, quantity; (*secreta*) code; (*siglas*) abbreviation.
cifrar [θi'frar] *vt* to code, write in code; (*resumir*) to abridge.
cigarra [θi'xarra] *nf* cicada.
cigarrera [θixa'rrera] *nf* cigar case.
cigarrillo [θixa'rriʎo] *nm* cigarette.
cigarro [θi'xarro] *nm* cigarette; (*puro*) cigar.
cigüeña [θi'xweɲa] *nf* stork.
cilíndrico, a [θi'lindriko, a] *a* cylindrical.
cilindro [θi'lindro] *nm* cylinder; (*rodillo*) roller.
cima ['θima] *nf* (*de montaña*) top, peak; (*de árbol*) top; (*fig*) summit, height.
címbalo ['θimbalo] *nm* cymbal.
cimbrar [θim'brar], **cimbrear** [θimbre-

'ar] *vt* to brandish; ~**se** *vr* (*al viento*) to sway.
cimentar [θimen'tar] *vt* to lay the foundations of.
cimiento [θi'mjento] *nm* foundation.
cinc [θink] *nm* zinc.
cincel [θin'θel] *nm* chisel; ~**ar** *vt* to chisel.
cinco ['θinko] *num* five.
cincuenta [θin'kwenta] *num* fifty.
cincho ['θintʃo] *nm* sash, belt.
cine ['θine] *nm* cinema.
cinematográfico, a [θinemato'xrafiko, a] *a* cine-, film *cpd*.
cínico, a ['θiniko, a] *a* cynical // *nm/f* cynic.
cinismo [θi'nismo] *nm* cynicism.
cinta ['θinta] *nf* band, strip; (*de seda, lana, algodón*) ribbon, tape; (*película*) reel; (*de máquina de escribir*) ribbon; (*métrica*) tape measure; (*magnetofónica*) tape; (*adhesiva*) adhesive tape.
cinto ['θinto] *nm* belt, girdle.
cintura [θin'tura] *nf* waist.
cinturón [θintu'ron] *nm* belt; ~ **de seguridad** safety belt.
ciprés [θi'pres] *nm* cypress (tree).
circo ['θirko] *nm* circus.
circuito [θir'kwito] *nm* circuit.
circulación [θirkula'θjon] *nf* circulation; (*AUTO*) traffic.
circular [θirku'lar] *a*, *nf* circular // *vi*, *vt* to circulate.
círculo ['θirkulo] *nm* circle.
circuncidar [θirkunθi'dar] *vt* to circumcise; **circuncisión** *nf* circumcision; **circunciso, a** *pp de* **circuncidar** // *a* circumcised.
circundar [θirkun'dar] *vt* to surround.
circunferencia [θirkunfe'renθja] *nf* circumference.
circunlocución [θirkunloku'θjon] *nf*, **circunloquio** [θirkun'lokjo] *nm* circumlocution.
circunscribir [θirkunskri'βir] *vt* to circumscribe; ~**se** *vr* to be limited.
circunscripción [θirkunskrip'θjon] *nf* division; (*POL*) constituency.
circunspección [θirkunspek'θjon] *nf* circumspection.
circunspecto, a [θirkuns'pekto, a] *a* circumspect, cautious.
circunstancia [θirkuns'tanθja] *nf* circumstance.
circunstante [θirkuns'tante] *nm/f* onlooker, bystander.
cirio ['θirjo] *nm* (wax) candle.
ciruela [θi'rwela] *nf* plum; ~ **pasa** prune.
cirugía [θiru'xia] *nf* surgery; ~ **estética** plastic surgery.
cirujano [θiru'xano] *nm* surgeon.
cisne ['θisne] *nm* swan.
cisterna [θis'terna] *nf* cistern.
cita ['θita] *nf* appointment, engagement; (*de novios*) date; (*referencia*) quotation.
citación [θita'θjon] *nf* (*JUR*) summons *sg*; (*referencia*) quotation.

citar [θi'tar] vt (gen) to make an appointment with; (JUR) to summons; (un autor, texto) to quote.

citrón [θi'tron] nm lemon.

ciudad [θju'ðað] nf town; (capital de país etc) city; ~ano, a nm/f citizen; ~ela nf citadel, fortress.

cívico, a ['θiβiko, a] a civic.

civil [θi'βil] a civil // nm (guardia) policeman; ~idad nf civility, courtesy.

civilización [θiβiliθa'θjon] nf civilization.

civilizar [θiβili'θar] vt to civilize.

civismo [θi'βismo] nm public spirit.

cizaña [θi'θaɲa] nf discord.

clamar [kla'mar] vt to clamour for // vi to cry out, clamour.

clamor [kla'mor] nm (grito) cry, shout; (gemido) whine; (de campana) knell; (fig) clamour, protest.

clamorear [klamore'ar] vt to clamour for // vi (campana) to toll; **clamoreo** nm clamour(ing).

clandestino, a [klandes'tino, a] a clandestine; (POL) underground.

clara ['klara] nf (de huevo) white of an egg; (del día) bright interval.

claraboya [klara'βoja] nf skylight.

clarear [klare'ar] vi (el día) to dawn; (el cielo) to clear up, brighten up; ~se vr to be transparent.

claridad [klari'ðað] nf (del día) brightness; (de estilo) clarity.

clarificar [klarifi'kar] vt to clarify.

clarín [kla'rin] nm bugle.

clarinete [klari'nete] nm clarinet.

clarividencia [klariβi'ðenθja] nf clairvoyance; (fig) far-sightedness.

claro, a ['klaro, a] a (gen) clear; (luminoso) bright; (poco subido) light; (evidente) clear, evident; (ralo) sparse; (poco espeso) thin // nm (en escritura) space; (en bosque) clearing // ad clearly // excl of course!

clase ['klase] nf class; ~ alta/media/obrera upper/middle/working class.

clásico, a ['klasiko, a] a classical; (fig) classic.

clasificación [klasifika'θjon] nf classification; (DEPORTE) league.

clasificar [klasifi'kar] vt to classify.

claudicar [klauði'kar] vi to limp; (fig) to back down.

claustro ['klaustro] nm cloister.

cláusula ['klausula] nf clause.

clausura [klau'sura] nf closing, closure.

clavar [kla'βar] vt (clavo) to knock in, drive in; (cuchillo, tenedor) to stick, thrust; (mirada) to fix.

clave ['klaβe] nf key; (MUS) clef.

clavel [kla'βel] nm carnation.

clavícula [kla'βikula] nf collar bone.

clavija [kla'βixa] nf peg, dowel, pin; (ELEC) plug.

clavo ['klaβo] nm (de metal) nail; (BOT) clove; (callo) corn.

claxon ['klakson] nm horn.

clemencia [kle'menθja] nf mercy, clemency; **clemente** a merciful, clement.

cleptómano, a [klep'tomano, a] nm/f kleptomaniac.

clerical [kleri'kal] a clerical // nm clergyman.

clérigo ['klerixo] nm clergyman.

clero ['klero] nm clergy.

cliente ['kljente] nm/f client, customer.

clientela [kljen'tela] nf clientele, customers pl.

clima ['klima] nm climate.

clínica ['klinika] nf clinic; (particular) private hospital.

clip [klip] nm paper clip.

clorhídrico, a [klo'riðriko, a] a hydrochloric.

cloroformo [kloro'formo] nm chloroform.

club [klub] (pl ~s o ~es) nm club.

C.N.T. abr de **Confederación Nacional de Trabajo.**

coacción [koak'θjon] nf coercion, compulsion.

coalición [koali'θjon] nf coalition.

coartar [koar'tar] vt to limit, restrict.

cobarde [ko'βarðe] a cowardly // nm coward; **cobardía** nf cowardice.

cobertizo [koβer'tiθo] nm shelter.

cobertor [koβer'tor] nm bedspread.

cobertura [koβer'tura] nf cover.

cobija [ko'βixa] nf roof; **cobijar** vt (cubrir) to cover; (abrigar) to shelter.

cobra ['koβra] nf cobra.

cobrador [koβra'ðor] nm (de autobús) conductor; (de impuestos, gas) collector.

cobrar [ko'βrar] vt (cheque) to cash; (sueldo) to collect, draw; (objeto) to recover; (precio) to charge; (deuda) to collect // vi to draw one's pay; ~se vr to recover, get well; **cóbrese al entregar** cash on delivery (COD).

cobre ['koβre] nm copper; ~s nmpl brass instruments.

cobro ['koβro] nm recovery; (paga) payment.

cocaína [koka'ina] nf cocaine.

cocción [kok'θjon] nf cooking.

cocear [koθe'ar] vi to kick.

cocer [ko'θer] vt, vi to cook; (en agua) to boil; (en horno) to bake; ~se vr to suffer intensely.

cocido [ko'θiðo] nm stew.

cocina [ko'θina] nf kitchen; (aparato) cooker, stove; (acto) cookery; **cocinar** vt, vi to cook.

cocinero, a [koθi'nero, a] nm/f cook.

coco ['koko] nm (árbol) coconut palm; (fruto) coconut.

cocodrilo [koko'ðrilo] nm crocodile.

coche ['kotʃe] nm car, motorcar; (de tren, de caballos) coach, carriage; (fúnebre) hearse; (para niños) pram; ~ celular Black Maria, prison van.

coche-cama [kotʃekama] (pl coches-camas) nm sleeping car, sleeper.

cochera [ko'tʃera] nf garage.
cochero [ko'tʃero] nm coachman.
cochino, a [ko'tʃino, a] a filthy, dirty // nm pig.
codazo [ko'ðaθo] nm jab, poke (with the elbow).
codear [koðe'ar] vi to elbow, jostle; ~se vr: ~se con to rub shoulders with.
códice ['koðiθe] nm manuscript, codex.
codicia [ko'ðiθja] nf greed; (fig) lust; **codiciar** vt to covet; **codicioso, a** a covetous.
código ['koðiɣo] nm code; ~ civil common law.
codillo [ko'ðiʎo] nm (ZOOL) knee; (TEC) elbow (joint).
codo ['koðo] nm (ANAT, de tubo) elbow; (ZOOL) knee.
codorniz [koðor'niθ] nf quail.
coerción [koer'θjon] nf coercion.
coetáneo, a [koe'taneo, a] a contemporary.
coexistencia [koeksis'tenθja] nf coexistence; **coexistir** vi to coexist.
cofradía [kofra'ðia] nf brotherhood, fraternity.
cofre ['kofre] nm chest.
coger [ko'xer] vt (gen) to take (hold of); (objeto caído) to pick up; (frutas) to pick, harvest; (resfriado, ladrón, pelota) to catch // vi: ~ por el buen camino to take the right road; ~se vr to catch; (robar) to steal.
cogida [ko'xiða] nf gathering, harvesting; (de peces) catch.
cogote [ko'ɣote] nm back or nape of the neck.
cohabitar [koaβi'tar] vi to live together, cohabit.
cohechar [koe'tʃar] vt to bribe; **cohecho** nm (acción) bribery; (soborno) bribe.
coherente [koe'rente] a coherent.
cohesión [koe'sjon] nm cohesion.
cohete [ko'ete] nm rocket.
cohibición [koiβi'θjon] nf restraint, restriction.
cohibir [koi'ßir] vt to restrain, restrict.
coincidencia [koinθi'ðenθja] nf coincidence; (acuerdo) agreement.
coincidir [koinθi'ðir] vi (en idea) to coincide, agree; (en lugar) to coincide.
coito ['koito] nm intercourse, coitus.
cojear [koxe'ar] vi (persona) to limp, hobble; (mueble) to wobble, rock.
cojera [ko'xera] nf lameness; (andar cojo) limp.
cojín [ko'xin] nm cushion; **cojinete** nm small cushion, pad; (TEC) ball bearing.
cojo, a ['koxo, a] a (que no puede andar) lame; (manco) crippled; (mueble) shaky // nm/f lame person; cripple.
col [kol] nf cabbage; ~ de Bruselas Brussels sprouts.
cola ['kola] nf (gen) tail; (de gente) queue; (lugar) end, last place; (para pegar) glue, gum; **hacer la ~** to queue (up).

colaborador, a [kolaßora'ðor, a] nm/f collaborator.
colaborar [kolaßo'rar] vi to collaborate.
coladera [kola'ðera] nf strainer.
coladura [kola'ðura] nf (filtración) straining; (residuo) grounds pl, dregs pl.
colapso [ko'lapso] nm collapse; ~ nervioso nervous breakdown.
colar [ko'lar] vt (líquido) to strain off; (ropa) to bleach; (metal) to cast // vi to ooze, seep (through); ~se vr to slip in or past.
colateral [kolate'ral] nm collateral.
colcha ['koltʃa] nf bedspread.
colchón [kol'tʃon] nm mattress.
colear [kole'ar] vi to wag its tail.
colección [kolek'θjon] nf collection; **coleccionista** nm/f collector.
colecta [ko'lekta] nf collection.
colectar [kolek'tar] vt to collect.
colectivo, a [kolek'tißo, a] a collective, joint.
colector [kolek'tor] nm collector; (sumidero) sewer.
colega [ko'leɣa] nm/f colleague.
colegio [ko'lexjo] nm (gen) college; (escuela) (private) school; (de abogados etc) association.
colegir [kole'xir] vt (juntar, reunir) to collect, gather; (deducir) to infer, conclude.
cólera ['kolera] nf (ira) anger; (MED) cholera.
colérico, a [ko'leriko, a] a angry, furious.
coleta [ko'leta] nf pigtail.
colgadero [kolɣa'ðero] nm (gancho) hook; (percha) hanger.
colgadura [kolɣa'ðura] nf hangings pl, drapery.
colgante [kol'ɣante] a hanging // nm drop earring.
colgar [kol'ɣar] vt to hang (up); (ropa) to hang (out); (teléfono) to hang up // vi to hang.
coliflor [koli'flor] nf cauliflower.
colilla [ko'liʎa] nf fag end, butt.
colina [ko'lina] nf hill.
colindante [kolin'dante] a adjacent, neighbouring.
colindar [kolin'dar] vi to adjoin, be adjacent.
colisión [koli'sjon] nf collision; (choque) crash.
colmado, a [kol'maðo, a] a abundant, copious; (cuchara etc) heaped.
colmar [kol'mar] vt to fill to the brim; (fig) to fulfil, realize.
colmena [kol'mena] nf beehive.
colmillo [kol'miʎo] nm (diente) eye tooth; (de elefante) tusk; (de perro) fang.
colmo ['kolmo] nm height, summit.
colocación [koloka'θjon] nf placing; (empleo) job, position; (de mueble) place, position.
colocar [kolo'kar] vt to place, put,

position; (*poner en empleo*) to find a job for.
Colombia [ko'lombja] *nf* Colombia; **colombiano, a** *a, nm/f* Colombian.
colon ['kolon] *nm* colon.
colonia [ko'lonja] *nf* colony; (*de casas*) housing estate; (*agua de* ~) cologne.
colonización [koloniθa'θjon] *nf* colonization.
colonizador, a [koloniθa'ðor, a] *a* colonizing // *nm/f* colonist, settler.
colonizar [koloni'θar] *vt* to colonize.
coloquio [ko'lokjo] *nm* conversation; (*congreso*) conference.
color [ko'lor] *nm* colour.
colorado, a [kolo'raðo, a] *a* (*que tiene color*) coloured; (*rojo*) red.
colorar [kolo'rar] *vt* to colour; (*teñir*) to dye.
colorear [kolore'ar] *vt* to colour // *vi* to redden.
colorido [kolo'riðo] *nm* colouring.
colosal [kolo'sal] *a* colossal.
columbrar [kolum'brar] *vt* to glimpse, spy.
columna [ko'lumna] *nf* column; (*pilar*) pillar; (*apoyo*) support.
columpiar [kolum'pjar] *vt*, ~**se** *vr* to swing; **columpio** *nm* swing.
collar [ko'ʎar] *nm* necklace; (*de perro*) collar.
coma ['koma] *nf* comma // *nm* coma.
comadre [ko'maðre] *nf* (*partera*) midwife; (*madrina*) godmother; (*vecina*) neighbour; ~**ar** *vi* to gossip.
comandancia [koman'danθja] *nf* command.
comandante [koman'dante] *nm* commandant.
comandar [koman'dar] *vt* to command.
comarca [ko'marka] *nf* region.
comarcar [komar'kar] *vi*: ~ **con** to border on, be adjacent to.
combar [kom'bar] *vt* to bend, curve.
combate [kom'bate] *nm* fight; (*fig*) battle; **combatiente** *nm* combatant.
combatir [komba'tir] *vt* to fight, combat.
combinación [kombina'θjon] *nf* combination; (*QUÍMICA*) compound; (*bebida*) cocktail; (*plan*) scheme, setup.
combinar [kombi'nar] *vt* to combine.
combustible [kombus'tiβle] *nm* fuel.
combustión [kombus'tjon] *nf* combustion.
comedia [ko'meðja] *nf* comedy; (*TEATRO*) play, drama.
comediante [kome'ðjante] *nm/f* (comic) actor/actress.
comedido, a [kome'ðiðo, a] *a* moderate; (*cortés*) courteous.
comedirse [kome'ðirse] *vr* to behave moderately; (*ser cortés*) to be courteous.
comedor, a [kome'ðor, a] *nm/f* (*persona*) glutton // *nm* (*habitación*) dining room; (*restaurante*) restaurant; (*cantina*) canteen.

comentador, a [komenta'ðor, a] *nm/f* = **comentarista**.
comentar [komen'tar] *vt* to comment on; (*fam*) to discuss.
comentario [komen'tarjo] *nm* comment, remark; (*literario*) commentary; ~**s** *nmpl* gossip *sg*.
comentarista [komenta'rista] *nm/f* commentator.
comento [ko'mento] *nm* = **comentario**.
comenzar [komen'θar] *vt*, *vi* to begin, start, commence.
comer [ko'mer] *vt* (*gen*) to eat; (*DAMAS, AJEDREZ*) to take, capture // *vi* to eat; (*almorzar*) to have lunch; ~**se** *vr* to eat up.
comercial [komer'θjal] *a* commercial; (*relativo al negocio*) business *cpd*.
comerciante [komer'θjante] *nm/f* trader, merchant.
comerciar [komer'θjar] *vi* to trade, do business.
comercio [ko'merθjo] *nm* commerce; (*tráfico*) trade; (*negocio*) business; (*fig*) dealings *pl*.
comestible [komes'tiβle] *a* eatable, edible // *nm* foodstuff.
cometa [ko'meta] *nm* comet // *nf* kite.
cometer [kome'ter] *vt* to commit.
cometido [kome'tiðo] *nm* (*misión*) task, assignment; (*deber*) commitment.
comezón [kome'θon] *nf* itch, itching.
cómico, a ['komiko, a] *a* comic(al) // *nm/f* comedian; (*de teatro*) (comic) actor/actress.
comida [ko'miða] *nf* (*alimento*) food; (*almuerzo, cena*) meal; (*de mediodía*) lunch.
comienzo [ko'mjenθo] *nm* beginning, start.
comillas [ko'miʎas] *nfpl* inverted commas.
comisario [komi'sarjo] *nm* commissary; (*POL*) commissar.
comisión [komi'sjon] *nf* commission.
comité [komi'te] *nm* committee.
como ['komo] *ad* as; (*tal* ~) like; (*aproximadamente*) about, approximately // *conj* (*ya que, puesto que*) as, since; (*en seguida que*) as soon as; ¡~ **no!** of course!; ~ **no lo haga hoy** unless he does it today; ~ **si** as if; **es tan alto** ~ **ancho** it is as high as it is wide.
cómo ['komo] *ad* how?, why? // *excl* what?, I beg your pardon? // *nm*: **el** ~ **y el porqué** the whys and wherefores.
comodidad [komoði'ðað] *nf* comfort; **venga a su** ~ come at your convenience.
comodín [komo'ðin] *nm* joker.
cómodo, a ['komoðo, a] *a* comfortable; (*práctico, de fácil uso*) convenient.
compacto, a [kom'pakto, a] *a* compact.
compadecer [kompaðe'θer] *vt* to pity, be sorry for; ~**se** *vr*: ~**se de** to pity, be sorry for.
compadre [kom'paðre] *nm* (*padrino*) godfather; (*amigo*) friend, pal.

compañero, a [kompa'ɲero, a] *nm/f* companion; ~ **de clase** classmate.
compañía [kompa'ɲia] *nf* company.
comparación [kompara'θjon] *nf* comparison; **en ~ con** in comparison with.
comparar [kompa'rar] *vt* to compare.
comparativo, a [kompara'tiβo, a] *a* comparative.
comparecer [kompare'θer] *vi* to appear (in court).
compartimiento [komparti'mjento] *nm* division; (*distribución*) distribution; (*FERRO*) compartment.
compartir [kompar'tir] *vt* to divide (up), share (out).
compás [kom'pas] *nm* (*MUS*) beat, rhythm; (*MAT*) compasses *pl*; (*NAUT*) compass.
compasión [kompa'sjon] *nf* compassion, pity.
compasivo, a [kompa'siβo, a] *a* compassionate.
compatibilidad [kompatiβili'ðað] *nf* compatibility.
compatible [kompa'tiβle] *a* compatible.
compatriota [kompa'trjota] *nm/f* compatriot.
compeler [kompe'ler] *vt* to compel.
compendiar [kompen'djar] *vt* to summarize; (*libro*) to abridge; **compendio** *nm* summary; abridgement.
compensación [kompensa'θjon] *nf* compensation.
compensar [kompen'sar] *vt* to compensate.
competencia [kompe'tenθja] *nf* (*incumbencia*) domain, field; (*aptitud, idoneidad*) competence; (*rivalidad*) competition.
competente [kompe'tente] *a* (*persona, jurado, tribunal*) competent; (*conveniente*) fit, suitable.
competición [kompeti'θjon] *nf* competition.
competir [kompe'tir] *vi* to compete.
compilar [kompi'lar] *vt* to compile.
complacencia [kompla'θenθja] *nf* (*placer*) pleasure; (*satisfacción*) satisfaction; (*buena voluntad*) willingness.
complacer [kompla'θer] *vt* to please; ~**se** *vr* to be pleased.
complaciente [kompla'θjente] *a* kind, obliging, helpful.
complejo, a [kom'plexo, a] *a, nm* complex.
complementario, a [komplemen'tarjo, a] *a* complementary.
completar [komple'tar] *vt* to complete.
completo, a [kom'pleto, a] *a* complete; (*perfecto*) perfect; (*lleno*) full // *nm* full complement.
complicar [kompli'kar] *vt* to complicate.
cómplice ['kompliθe] *nm/f* accomplice.
complot [kom'plot] *nm* plot; (*conspiración*) conspiracy.
componenda [kompo'nenda] *nf*

compromise; (*pey*) shady deal.
componer [kompo'ner] *vt* to make up, put together; (*MUS, LITERATURA, IMPRENTA*) to compose; (*algo roto*) to mend, repair; (*adornar*) to adorn; (*arreglar*) to arrange; (*reconciliar*) to reconcile; ~**se** *vr*: ~**se de** to consist of.
comportamiento [komporta'mjento] *nm* behaviour, conduct.
comportarse [kompor'tarse] *vr* to behave.
composición [komposi'θjon] *nf* composition.
compositor, a [komposi'tor, a] *nm/f* composer.
compostura [kompos'tura] *nf* (*reparación*) mending, repair; (*arreglo*) arrangement; (*acuerdo*) agreement; (*actitud*) composure.
compra ['kompra] *nf* purchase; ~**s** *nfpl* purchases, shopping *sg*.
comprador, a [kompra'ðor, a] *nm/f* buyer, purchaser.
comprar [kom'prar] *vt* to buy, purchase.
comprender [kompren'der] *vt* to understand; (*incluir*) to comprise, include.
comprensión [kompren'sjon] *nf* understanding; (*totalidad*) comprehensiveness.
comprensivo, a [kompren'siβo, a] *a* comprehensive; (*actitud*) understanding.
compresión [kompre'sjon] *nf* compression.
comprimir [kompri'mir] *vt* to compress; (*fig*) to control.
comprobante [kompro'βante] *a* verifying, supporting // *nm* proof.
comprobar [kompro'βar] *vt* to check; (*probar*) to prove; (*TEC*) to check, test.
comprometer [komprome'ter] *vt* to compromise; (*exponer*) to endanger; ~**se** *vr* to compromise o.s.; (*involucrarse*) to get involved.
compromiso [kompro'miso] *nm* (*obligación*) obligation; (*cometido*) commitment; (*convenio*) agreement; (*dificultad*) awkward situation.
compuesto, a [kom'pwesto, a] *a*: ~ **de** composed of, made up of // *nm* compound.
compulsión [kompul'sjon] *nf* compulsion.
compunción [kompun'θjon] *nf* compunction, regret.
computador [komputa'ðor] *nm*, **computadora** [komputa'ðora] *nf* computer.
comulgar [komul'xar] *vi* to receive communion.
común [ko'mun] *a* common // *nm*: **el** ~ the community.
comunicación [komunika'θjon] *nf* communication; (*ponencia*) report.
comunicar [komuni'kar] *vt, vi,* ~**se** *vr* to communicate; **comunicativo, a** *a* communicative.
comunidad [komuni'ðað] *nf* community.
comunión [komu'njon] *nf* communion.
comunismo [komu'nismo] *nm*

communism; **comunista** *a, nm/f* communist.

con [kon] *prep* with; (*a pesar de*) in spite of; ~ **que** so, and so; ~ **apretar el botón** by pressing the button.

concebir [konθe'βir] *vt, vi* to conceive.

conceder [konθe'ðer] *vt* to concede.

concejo [kon'θexo] *nm* council.

concentración [konθentra'θjon] *nf* concentration.

concentrar [konθen'trar] *vt,* ~**se** *vr* to concentrate.

concepción [konθep'θjon] *nf* conception.

concepto [kon'θepto] *nm* concept.

concertar [konθer'tar] *vt* (*MUS*) to harmonize; (*acordar: precio*) to agree; (: *tratado*) to conclude; (*trato*) to arrange, fix up; (*combinar: esfuerzos*) to coordinate; (*reconciliar: personas*) to reconcile // *vi* to harmonize, be in tune.

concesión [konθe'sjon] *nf* concession.

conciencia [kon'θjenθja] *nf* conscience.

concienzudo, a [konθjen'θuðo, a] *a* conscientious.

concierto [kon'θjerto] *nm* concert; (*obra*) concerto.

conciliar [konθi'ljar] *vt* to reconcile.

concilio [kon'θiljo] *nm* council.

conciso, a [kon'θiso, a] *a* concise.

concluir [konklu'ir] *vt, vi,* ~**se** *vr* to conclude.

conclusión [konklu'sjon] *nf* conclusion.

concordar [konkor'ðar] *vt* to reconcile // *vi* to agree, tally; **concordia** *nf* concord, harmony.

concretar [konkre'tar] *vt* to make concrete, make more specific; ~**se** *vr* to become more definite.

concreto, a [kon'kreto, a] *a, nm* (*AM*) concrete; **en** ~ (*en resumen*) to sum up; (*específicamente*) specifically; **no hay nada en** ~ there's nothing definite.

concurrir [konku'rrir] *vi* (*juntarse: ríos*) to meet, come together; (: *personas*) to gather, meet; (*ponerse de acuerdo, coincidir*) to concur; (*competir*) to compete; (*contribuir*) to contribute.

concurso [kon'kurso] *nm* (*de público*) crowd; (*ESCOL, DEPORTE, competencia*) competition; (*coincidencia*) coincidence; (*ayuda*) help, cooperation.

concusión [konku'sjon] *nf* concussion.

concha ['kontʃa] *nf* shell.

conde ['konde] *nm* count.

condecorar [kondeko'rar] *vt* to decorate.

condena [kon'dena] *nf* sentence.

condenación [kondena'θjon] *nf* (*gen*) condemnation; (*condena*) sentence; (*REL*) damnation.

condenar [konde'nar] *vt* to condemn; (*JUR*) to convict; ~**se** *vr* (*JUR*) to confess (one's guilt); (*REL*) to be damned.

condensar [konden'sar] *vt* to condense.

condescender [kondesθen'der] *vi* to acquiesce, comply.

condición [kondi'θjon] *nf* condition;

condicionado, a *a* conditioned.

condicional [kondiθjo'nal] *a* conditional.

condimento [kondi'mento] *nm* seasoning.

condolerse [kondo'lerse] *vr* to sympathize.

conducir [kondu'θir] *vt* to take, convey; (*AUTO*) to drive // *vi* to drive; (*fig*) to lead; ~**se** *vr* to behave.

conducta [kon'dukta] *nf* conduct, behaviour.

conducto [kon'dukto] *nm* pipe, tube; (*fig*) channel.

conductor, a [konduk'tor, a] *a* leading, guiding // *nm* (*FISICA*) conductor; (*de vehículo*) driver.

conduje *etc vb ver* **conducir**.

conduzco *etc vb ver* **conducir**.

conectar [konek'tar] *vt* to connect (up), plug in.

conejo [ko'nexo] *nm* rabbit.

conexión [konek'sjon] *nf* connection.

confeccionar [konfekθjo'nar] *vt* to make (up).

confederación [konfeðera'θjon] *nf* confederation.

conferencia [konfe'renθja] *nf* conference; (*lección*) lecture; (*TELEC*) call.

conferir [konfe'rir] *vt* to award.

confesar [konfe'sar] *vt* to confess, admit.

confesión [konfe'sjon] *nf* confession.

confesionario [konfesjo'narjo] *nm* confessional.

confiado, a [kon'fjaðo, a] *a* (*crédulo*) trusting; (*presumido*) confident; (*pey*) conceited, vain.

confianza [kon'fjanθa] *nf* trust; (*aliento, confidencia*) confidence; (*familiaridad*) intimacy, familiarity; (*pey*) vanity, conceit.

confiar [kon'fjar] *vt* to entrust // *vi* to trust.

confidencia [konfi'ðenθja] *nf* confidence.

confidencial [konfiðen'θjal] *a* confidential.

confidente [konfi'ðente] *nm/f* confidant/e; (*policial*) informer.

configurar [konfiɣu'rar] *vt* to shape, form.

confín [kon'fin] *nm* limit; ~**es** *nmpl* edges.

confinar [konfi'nar] *vi* to confine; (*desterrar*) to banish.

confirmar [konfir'mar] *vt* to confirm.

confiscar [konfis'kar] *vt* to confiscate.

confitería [konfite'ria] *nf* confectionery; (*tienda*) confectioner's (shop).

confitura [konfi'tura] *nf* jam.

conflicto [kon'flikto] *nm* conflict; (*fig*) clash.

conformar [konfor'mar] *vt* to shape, fashion // *vi* to agree; ~**se** *vr* to conform; (*resignarse*) to resign o.s.

conforme [kon'forme] *a* (*gen*) alike, similar; (*de acuerdo*) agreed, in agreement; (*resignado*) resigned // *ad* as // *excl* agreed! // *nm* agreement // *prep*: ~ **a** in accordance with.

conformidad [konformi'ðað] *nf* (*semejanza*) similarity; (*acuerdo*) agreement; (*resignación*) resignation.
confortable [konfor'taßie] *a* comfortable.
confortar [konfor'tar] *vt* to comfort.
confrontar [konfron'tar] *vt* to confront; (*dos personas*) to bring face to face; (*cotejar*) to compare // *vi* to border.
confundir [konfun'dir] *vt* to blur; (*equivocar*) to mistake, confuse; (*mezclar*) to mix; (*turbar*) to confuse; ~**se** *vr* to become blurred; (*turbarse*) to get confused; (*equivocarse*) to make a mistake; (*mezclarse*) to mix.
confusión [konfu'sjon] *nf* confusion.
confuso, a [kon'fuso, a] *a* confused.
congelar [konxe'lar] *vt* to freeze; ~**se** *vr* (*sangre, grasa*) to congeal.
congeniar [konxe'njar] *vi* to get on (well).
conglomeración [konglomera'θjon] *nf* conglomeration.
congoja [kon'goxa] *nf* distress, grief.
congratular [kongratu'lar] *vt* to congratulate.
congregación [kongreʁa'θjon] *nf* congregation.
congresista [kongre'sista] *nm/f* delegate, congressman/woman.
congreso [kon'greso] *nm* congress.
conjetura [konxe'tura] *nf* guess; **conjeturar** *vt* to guess.
conjugar [konxu'ʁar] *vt* to combine, fit together; (*un verbo*) to conjugate.
conjunción [konxun'θjon] *nf* conjunction.
conjunto, a [kon'xunto, a] *a* joint, united // *nm* whole; (*MUS*) group; **en** ~ as a whole.
conmemoración [konmemora'θjon] *nf* commemoration.
conmemorar [konmemo'rar] *vt* to commemorate.
conmigo [kon'miʁo] *pron* with me; with myself.
conminar [konmi'nar] *vt* to threaten.
conmiseración [konmisera'θjon] *nf* pity, commiseration.
conmoción [konmo'θjon] *nf* shock; (*MED*) concussion; (*fig*) upheaval.
conmovedor, a [konmoße'ðor, a] *a* touching, moving; (*impresionante*) exciting.
conmover [konmo'ßer] *vt* to shake, disturb; (*fig*) to move.
conmutador [konmuta'ðor] *nm* switch.
conocedor, a [konoθe'ðor, a] *a* expert, knowledgeable // *nm/f* expert.
conocer [kono'θer] *vt* (*gen*) to know; (*por primera vez*) to meet, get to know; (*entender*) to know about; (*reconocer*) to know, recognize; ~**se** *vr* (*una persona*) to know o.s.; (*dos personas*) to (get to) know each other.
conocido, a [kono'θiðo, a] *a* (well-)known // *nm/f* acquaintance.
conocimiento [konoθi'mjento] *nm* knowledge; (*MED*) consciousness; ~**s** *nmpl*

(*personas*) acquaintances; (*ciencia*) knowledge *sg.*
conozco *etc vb ver* **conocer.**
conque ['konke] *conj* and so, so then.
conquista [kon'kista] *nf* conquest.
conquistador, a [konkista'ðor, a] *a* conquering // *nm* conqueror.
conquistar [konkis'tar] *vt* to conquer.
consagrar [konsa'ʁrar] *vt* (*REL*) to consecrate; (*fig*) to devote.
consciente [kons'θjente] *a* conscious.
consecución [konseku'θjon] *nf* acquisition; (*de fin*) attainment.
consecuencia [konse'kwenθja] *nf* consequence, outcome; (*firmeza*) consistency.
consecuente [konse'kwente] *a* consistent.
consecutivo, a [konseku'tißo, a] *a* consecutive.
conseguir [konse'ʁir] *vt* to get, obtain; (*sus fines*) to attain.
consejero, a [konse'xero, a] *nm/f* adviser, consultant; (*POL*) councillor.
consejo [kon'sexo] *nm* advice; (*POL*) council.
consenso [kon'senso] *nm* consensus.
consentimiento [konsenti'mjento] *nm* consent.
consentir [konsen'tir] *vt* (*permitir, tolerar*) to consent to; (*mimar*) to pamper, spoil; (*admitir*) to admit // *vi* to agree, consent.
conserje [kon'serxe] *nm* caretaker; (*portero*) porter.
conserva [kon'serßa] *nf* (*acción*) preserving; (*alimento*) preserved food.
conservación [konserßa'θjon] *nf* conservation; (*de alimentos, vida*) preservation.
conservador, a [konserßa'ðor, a] *a* preservative; (*POL*) conservative // *nm/f* conservative; (*de museo*) keeper.
conservar [konser'ßar] *vt* to conserve, keep; (*alimentos, vida*) to preserve; ~**se** *vr* to survive.
considerable [konsiðe'raßle] *a* considerable.
consideración [konsiðera'θjon] *nf* consideration; (*estimación*) respect.
considerado, a [konsiðe'raðo, a] *a* (*prudente, reflexivo*) considerate; (*respetado*) respected.
considerar [konsiðe'rar] *vt* to consider.
consigna [kon'siʁna] *nf* (*orden*) order, instruction; (*para equipajes*) left-luggage office.
consigo [kon'siʁo] *pron* (*m*) with him; (*f*) with her; (*Vd.*) with you; (*reflexivo*) with o.s.
consiguiente [konsi'ʁjente] *a* consequent; **por** ~ and so, therefore, consequently.
consistente [konsis'tente] *a* consistent; (*sólido*) solid, firm; (*válido*) sound.
consistir [konsis'tir] *vi*: ~ **en** (*componerse de*) to consist of; (*ser resultado de*) to be due to.
consolación [konsola'θjon] *nf* consolation.

consolar [konso'lar] vt to console.
consolidar [konsoli'ðar] vt to consolidate.
consomé [konso'me] nm consommé, clear soup.
consonante [konso'nante] a consonant, harmonious // nf consonant.
conspicuo, a [kons'pikwo, a] a conspicuous.
conspiración [konspira'θjon] nf conspiracy.
conspirador, a [konspira'ðor, a] nm/f conspirator.
conspirar [konspi'rar] vi to conspire.
constante [kons'tante] a constant,
constar [kons'tar] vi (evidenciarse) to be clear or evident; ~ de to consist of.
consternación [konsterna'θjon] nf consternation.
constipación [konstipa'θjon] nf = constipado.
constipado, a [konsti'paðo, a] a: estar ~ to have a cold // nm cold.
constitución [konstitu'θjon] nf constitution; **constitucional** a constitutional.
constituir [konstitu'ir] vt (formar, componer) to constitute, make up; (fundar, erigir, ordenar) to constitute, establish.
constitutivo, a [konstitu'tiβo, a] a constitutive, constituent.
constituyente [konstitu'jente] a constituent.
constreñir [konstre'ɲir] vt (obligar) to compel, oblige; (restringir) to restrict.
construcción [konstruk'θjon] nf construction, building.
constructor, a [konstruk'tor, a] nm/f builder.
construir [konstru'ir] vt to build, construct.
consuelo [kon'swelo] nm consolation, solace.
cónsul ['konsul] nm consul; **consulado** nm consulate.
consulta [kon'sulta] nf consultation.
consultar [konsul'tar] vt to consult.
consultorio [konsul'torjo] nm information bureau; (MED) surgery.
consumar [konsu'mar] vt to complete, carry out; (crimen) to commit; (matrimonio) to consummate.
consumición [konsumi'θjon] nf consumption; (bebida) drink; (en restaurante) meal.
consumidor, a [konsumi'ðor, a] nm/f consumer.
consumir [konsu'mir] vt to consume; ~se vr to be consumed; (persona) to waste away.
consumo [kon'sumo] nm, **consunción** [konsun'θjon] nf consumption.
contabilidad [kontaβili'ðað] nf accounting, book-keeping; (profesión) accountancy.
contacto [kon'takto] nm contact.
contado, a [kon'taðo, a] a: ~s (escasos)

numbered, scarce, few // nm: al ~ for cash.
contador [konta'ðor] nm (aparato) meter; (COM) accountant; (de café) counter.
contagiar [konta'xjar] vt (enfermedad) to pass on, transmit; (persona) to infect; ~se vr to become infected.
contagio [kon'taxjo] nm infection.
contagioso, a [konta'xjoso, a] a infectious; (fig) catching.
contaminación [kontamina'θjon] nf contamination.
contaminar [kontami'nar] vt to contaminate.
contar [kon'tar] vt (páginas, dinero) to count; (anécdota) to tell // vi to count; ~ con to rely on, count on.
contemplación [kontempla'θjon] nf contemplation.
contemplar [kontem'plar] vt to contemplate; (mirar) to look at.
contemporáneo, a [kontempo'raneo, a] a, nm/f contemporary.
contender [konten'der] vi (gen) to contend; (en un concurso) to compete.
contener [konte'ner] vt to contain, hold; (retener) to hold back, contain.
contenido, a [konte'niðo, a] a (moderado) restrained; (reprimido) suppressed // nm contents pl, content.
contentar [konten'tar] vt (satisfacer) to satisfy; (complacer) to please; ~se vr to be satisfied.
contento, a [kon'tento, a] a contented, content; (alegre) pleased; (feliz) happy // nm contentment; (felicidad) happiness.
contestación [kontesta'θjon] nf answer, reply.
contestar [kontes'tar] vt to answer, reply; (JUR) to corroborate, confirm.
contigo [kon'tixo] pron with you.
contiguo, a [kon'tixwo, a] a (de al lado) next; (vecino) adjacent, adjoining.
continental [kontinen'tal] a continental.
continente [konti'nente] a, nm continent.
contingencia [kontin'xenθja] nf contingency; (riesgo) risk; **contingente** a, nm contingent.
continuación [kontinwa'θjon] nf continuation; a ~ then, next.
continuar [konti'nwar] vt to continue, go on with // vi to continue, go on.
continuidad [kontinwi'ðað] nf continuity.
continuo, a [kon'tinwo, a] a (sin interrupción) continuous; (acción perseverante) continual.
contorno [kon'torno] nm outline; (GEO) contour; ~s nmpl neighbourhood sg, environs.
contorsión [kontor'sjon] nf contortion.
contra ['kontra] prep, ad against // nm con.
contraataque [kontraa'take] nm counter-attack.
contrabajo [kontra'βaxo] nm double bass.

contrabandista [kontraβan'dista] *nm/f* smuggler.

contrabando [kontra'βando] *nm* (*acción*) smuggling; (*mercancías*) contraband.

contracción [kontrak'θjon] *nf* contraction; (*encogimiento*) shrinkage.

contracepción [kontraθep'θjon] *nf* contraception.

contraceptivo [kontraθep'tiβo] *nm* contraceptive.

contradecir [kontraðe'θir] *vt* to contradict.

contradicción [kontraðik'θjon] *nf* contradiction.

contradictorio, a [kontraðik'torjo, a] *a* contradictory.

contraer [kontra'er] *vt* to contract; (*encoger*) to shrink; (*limitar*) to restrict; ~se *vr* to contract; to shrink; (*limitarse*) to limit o.s.

contragolpe [kontra'ɣolpe] *nm* backlash.

contrahacer [kontraa'θer] *vt* to copy, imitate; (*falsificar*) to forge.

contramaestre [kontrama'estre] *nm* foreman.

contrapelo [kontra'pelo]: **a** ~ *ad* the wrong way.

contrapesar [kontrape'sar] *vt* to counterbalance; (*fig*) to offset.

contrariar [kontra'rjar] *vt* (*oponerse*) to oppose; (*poner obstáculo*) to impede; (*enfadar*) to vex.

contrariedad [kontrarje'ðað] *nf* (*oposición*) opposition; (*obstáculo*) obstacle, setback; (*disgusto*) vexation, annoyance.

contrario, a [kon'trarjo, a] *a* contrary; (*de persona*) opposed; (*sentido, lado*) opposite // *nm/f* enemy, adversary; (*DEPORTE*) opponent; **de lo** ~ otherwise.

contrarrestar [kontrarres'tar] *vt* to counteract; (*pelota*) to return.

contrastar [kontras'tar] *vt* to resist // *vi* to contrast.

contraste [kon'traste] *nm* contrast.

contratante [kontra'tante] *nm/f* contractor.

contratar [kontra'tar] *vt* (*firmar un acuerdo para*) to contract for; (*empleados, obreros*) to hire, engage; ~se *vr* to sign on.

contratiempo [kontra'tjempo] *nm* setback.

contratista [kontra'tista] *nm/f* contractor.

contrato [kon'trato] *nm* contract.

contravención [kontraβen'θjon] *nf* contravention, violation.

contravenir [kontraβe'nir] *vi*: ~ **a** to contravene, violate.

contraventana [kontraβen'tana] *nf* shutter.

contribución [kontriβu'θjon] *nf* (*municipal etc*) tax; (*ayuda*) contribution.

contribuir [kontriβu'ir] *vt, vi* to contribute; (*COM*) to pay (in taxes).

contribuyente [kontriβu'jente] *nm/f* (*COM*) taxpayer; (*que ayuda*) contributor.

control [kon'trol] *nm* control; (*inspección*) inspection, check; ~**ar** *vt* to control; to inspect, check.

controversia [kontro'βersja] *nf* controversy.

convalecencia [konβale'θenθja] *nf* convalescence.

convalecer [konβale'θer] *vi* to convalesce, get better.

convaleciente [konβale'θjente] *a, nm/f* convalescent.

convencer [konβen'θer] *vt* to convince; (*persuadir*) to persuade.

convencimiento [konβenθi'mjento] *nm* convincing; (*persuasión*) persuasion; (*certidumbre*) conviction.

convención [konβen'θjon] *nf* convention.

convencional [konβenθjo'nal] *a* conventional.

convenido, a [konβe'niðo, a] *a* agreed.

conveniencia [konβe'njenθja] *nf* suitability; (*conformidad*) agreement; (*utilidad, provecho*) usefulness; ~**s** *nfpl* conventions; (*COM*) property *sg*.

conveniente [konβe'njente] *a* suitable; (*útil*) useful.

convenio [kon'βenjo] *nm* agreement, treaty.

convenir [konβe'nir] *vi* (*estar de acuerdo*) to agree; (*ser conveniente*) to suit, be suitable; ~se *vr* to agree.

convento [kon'βento] *nm* monastery; (*de monjas*) convent.

converger [konβer'xer], **convergir** [konβer'xir] *vi* to converge.

conversación [konβersa'θjon] *nf* conversation.

conversar [konβer'sar] *vi* to talk, converse.

conversión [konβer'sjon] *nf* conversion.

convertir [konβer'tir] *vt* to convert.

convicción [konβik'θjon] *nf* conviction.

convicto, a [kon'βikto, a] *a* convicted, found guilty; (*condenado*) condemned.

convidado, a [konβi'ðaðo, a] *nm/f* guest.

convidar [konβi'ðar] *vt* to invite.

convincente [konβin'θente] *a* convincing.

convite [kon'βite] *nm* invitation; (*banquete*) banquet.

convivencia [konβi'βenθja] *nf* coexistence, living together.

convocar [konβo'kar] *vt* to summon, call (together).

convulsión [konβul'sjon] *nf* convulsion.

conyugal [konju'ɣal] *a* conjugal.

coñac [ko'ɲak] *nm* cognac, brandy.

cooperación [koopera'θjon] *nf* cooperation.

cooperar [koope'rar] *vi* to cooperate.

cooperativo, a [koopera'tiβo, a] *a* cooperative // *nf* cooperative.

coordinación [koorðina'θjon] *nf* coordination.

coordinar [koorði'nar] *vt* to coordinate.

copa ['kopa] nf cup; (vaso) glass; (de árbol) top; (de sombrero) crown; ~s nfpl (NAIPES) ≈ hearts.

copia ['kopja] nf copy; **copiar** vt to copy.

copioso, a [ko'pjoso, a] a copious, plentiful.

copita [ko'pita] nf (small) glass; (GOLF) tee.

copla ['kopla] nf verse; (canción) (popular) song.

coqueta [ko'keta] a flirtatious, coquettish; **coquetear** vi to flirt.

coraje [ko'raxe] nm courage; (ánimo) spirit; (ira) anger.

coral [ko'ral] a choral // nf choir.

corazón [kora'θon] nm heart.

corazonada [koraθo'naða] nf impulse; (presentimiento) presentiment, hunch.

corbata [kor'ßata] nf tie.

corcovado, a [korko'ßaðo, a] a hunchbacked.

corchete [kor'tʃete] nm catch, clasp.

corcho ['kortʃo] nm cork; (PESCA) float.

cordel [kor'ðel] nm cord, line.

cordero [kor'ðero] nm lamb.

cordial [kor'ðjal] a cordial; ~**idad** nf warmth, cordiality.

cordillera [korði'ʎera] nf range, chain (of mountains).

Córdoba ['korðoßa] n Cordoba; **cordobés, esa** a of or from Cordoba.

cordón [kor'ðon] nm (cuerda) cord, string; (de zapatos) lace; (policía) cordon.

corneta [kor'neta] nf bugle.

coro ['koro] nm chorus; (conjunto de cantores) choir.

corolario [koro'larjo] nm corollary.

corona [ko'rona] nf crown; (de flores) garland; ~**ción** nf coronation; **coronar** vt to crown.

coronel [koro'nel] nm colonel.

coronilla [koro'niʎa] nf crown (of the head).

corporación [korpora'θjon] nf corporation.

corporal [korpo'ral] a corporal.

corpulento, a [korpu'lento a] a (árbol) stout; (persona) well-built.

corral [ko'rral] nm farmyard; ~**illo** nm playpen.

correa [ko'rrea] nf strap; (cinturón) belt.

corrección [korrek'θjon] nf correction; (reprensión) rebuke; **correccional** nm reformatory.

correcto, a [ko'rrekto, a] a correct; (persona) well-mannered.

corredor, a [korre'ðor, a] a running; (rápido) fast // nm (COM) agent, broker; (pasillo) corridor, passage; (DEPORTE) runner.

corregir [korre'xir] vt (error) to correct; (amonestar, reprender) to rebuke, reprimand; ~**se** vr to reform.

correo [ko'rreo] nm post, mail; (persona) courier; (cartero) postman; **C~** Post Office; ~ **aéreo** airmail.

correr [ko'rrer] vt to run; (viajar) to cover, travel; (cortinas) to draw; (cerrojo) to shoot // vi to run; (líquido) to run, flow; (moneda) to pass, be valid; ~**se** vr to slide, move; (colores) to run.

correspondencia [korrespon'denθja] nf correspondence; (FERRO) connection.

corresponder [korrespon'der] vi to correspond; (convenir) to be suitable; (pertenecer) to belong; (tocar) to concern; ~**se** vr (por escrito) to correspond; (amarse) to have mutual affection.

correspondiente [korrespon'djente] a corresponding // nm correspondent.

corrido, a [ko'rriðo, a] a (avergonzado) abashed; (fluido) fluent // nf run, dash; (de toros) bullfight; **3 noches ~as** 3 nights running; **un kilo ~** a good kilo.

corriente [ko'rrjente] a (agua) running; (fig) flowing; (dinero etc) current; (común) ordinary, normal // nf current // nm current month.

corrillo [ko'rriʎo] nm huddle; (fig) clique.

corro ['korro] nm ring, circle (of people).

corroborar [korroßo'rar] vt to corroborate.

corroer [korro'er] vt to corrode; (GEO) to erode.

corromper [korrom'per] vt (madera) to rot; (alimento) to turn bad; (fig) to corrupt.

corrosivo, a [korro'sißo, a] a corrosive.

corrupción [korrup'θjon] nf rot, decay; (fig) corruption.

corsé [kor'se] nm corset.

cortado, a [kor'taðo, a] a (con cuchillo) cut; (leche) sour; (confuso) confused; (disconcertado) embarrassed; (estilo) abrupt // nm white coffee (with just a little milk).

cortador, a [korta'ðor, a] a cutting // nf cutter, slicer.

cortadura [korta'ðura] nf cut.

cortar [kor'tar] vt to cut; (el agua) to cut off; (un pasaje) to cut out // vi to cut; ~**se** vr (turbarse) to become embarrassed; (leche) to turn, curdle; ~**se el pelo** to have one's hair cut.

corte ['korte] nm cut, cutting; (filo) edge; (de tela) piece, length; **las C~s** the Spanish Parliament.

cortedad [korte'ðað] nf shortness; (fig) bashfulness, timidity.

cortejar [korte'xar] vt to court.

cortejo [kor'texo] nm entourage; ~ **fúnebre** funeral procession.

cortés [kor'tes] a courteous, polite.

cortesía [korte'sia] nf courtesy.

corteza [kor'teθa] nf (de árbol) bark; (de pan) crust.

cortina [kor'tina] nf curtain.

corto, a ['korto, a] a (breve) short; (tímido) bashful; (poco inteligente) not very clever; ~ **de vista** short-sighted; **estar ~ de fondos** to be short of funds.

corvo, a ['korßo, a] a curved.

cosa ['kosa] nf thing; (asunto) affair; ~ **de** about; **eso es ~ mía** that's my affair.

cosecha [ko'setʃa] nf (AGR) harvest; (de vino) vintage.

cosechar [kose'tʃar] vt to harvest, gather (in).

coser [ko'ser] vt to sew.

cosmético, a [kos'metiko, a] a, nm cosmetic.

cosquillas [kos'kiʎas] nfpl: **hacer** ~ to tickle; **tener** ~ to be ticklish.

cosquilloso, a [koski'ʎoso, a] a ticklish; (fig) touchy.

costa ['kosta] nf (gasto) cost; (GEO) coast.

costado [kos'taðo] nm side.

costal [kos'tal] nm sack.

costar [kos'tar] vt (valer) to cost; (necesitar) to require, need; **me cuesta hacer** I find it hard to do.

Costa Rica [kosta'rika] nf Costa Rica; **costarricense, costarriqueño, a** a, nm/f Costa Rican.

coste ['koste] nm = **costo.**

costilla [kos'tiʎa] nf rib; (CULIN) chop.

costo ['kosto] nm cost, price; ~ **de la vida** cost of living; ~**so, a** a costly, expensive.

costra ['kostra] nf crust; (MED) scab.

costumbre [kos'tumbre] nf custom, habit.

costura [kos'tura] nf sewing, needlework; (de medias) seam.

costurera [kostu'rera] nf dressmaker.

costurero [kostu'rero] nm sewing box or case.

cotejar [kote'xar] vt to compare.

cotejo [ko'texo] nm comparison.

cotidiano, a [koti'ðjano, a] a daily, day to day.

cotización [kotiθa'θjon] nf (COM) quotation, price; (cuota) dues pl.

cotizar [koti'θar] vt (COM) to quote, price; ~**se** vr: ~**se a** to sell at, fetch.

coto ['koto] nm (terreno cercado) enclosure; (de caza) reserve.

coyote [ko'jote] nm coyote, prairie wolf.

coyuntura [kojun'tura] nf (ANAT) joint; (oportunidad) opportunity.

cráneo ['kraneo] nm skull, cranium.

cráter ['krater] nm crater.

creación [krea'θjon] nf creation.

creador, a [krea'ðor, a] a creative // nm/f creator.

crear [kre'ar] vt to create, make.

crecer [kre'θer] vi (niño) to grow; (precio) to rise; (días) to get longer; (mar) to swell.

crecido, a [kre'θiðo, a] a (persona, planta) full-grown; (cantidad) large; (fig) conceited.

creciente [kre'θjente] a (persona) growing; (cantidad) increasing; (luna) crescent // nm crescent // nf flood.

crecimiento [kreθi'mjento] nm growth; (aumento) increase.

credenciales [kreðen'θjales] nfpl credentials.

crédito ['kreðito] nm credit.

credo ['kreðo] nm creed.

crédulo, a ['kreðulo, a] a credulous.

creencia [kre'enθja] nf belief.

creer [kre'er] vt, vi to think, believe; ~**se** vr to believe o.s. (to be); ¡**ya lo creo!** I should think so!

creíble [kre'iβle] a credible, believable.

crema ['krema] nf cream; (de huevo) custard.

cremallera [krema'ʎera] nf zip (fastener).

crepúsculo [kre'puskulo] nm twilight, dusk.

crespón [kres'pon] nm crêpe.

creta ['kreta] nf chalk.

creyente [kre'jente] nm/f believer.

creyó etc vb ver **creer.**

cría ['kria] nf (de animales) rearing, breeding; (animal) baby animal; (niño) child.

criadero [kria'ðero] nm nursery; (ZOOL) breeding place.

criado, a [kri'aðo, a] a bred, reared // nm servant // nf servant, maid; **mal/bien** ~ badly/well brought up.

criador [kria'ðor] nm breeder.

crianza [kri'anθa] nf rearing, breeding; (fig) breeding.

criar [kri'ar] vt to suckle, feed; (educar) to bring up; (producir) to grow, produce; (animales) to breed.

criatura [kria'tura] nf creature; (niño) baby, (small) child.

criba ['kriβa] nf sieve; **cribar** vt to sieve.

crimen ['krimen] nm crime.

criminal [krimi'nal] a, nm/f criminal.

crin [krin] nf (también ~**es** nfpl) mane.

crisis ['krisis] nf inv crisis.

crispar [kris'par] vt (músculo) to make contract; (nervios) to set on edge.

cristal [kris'tal] nm crystal; (de ventana) glass, pane; (lente) lens; ~**ino, a** a crystalline; (fig) clear // nm lens of the eye; ~**izar** vt, vi to crystallize.

cristiandad [kristjan'daθ] nf Christianity.

cristianismo [kristja'nismo] nm Christianity.

cristiano, a [kris'tjano, a] a, nm/f Christian.

Cristo ['kristo] nm (dios) Christ; (crucifijo) crucifix.

criterio [kri'terjo] nm criterion; (juicio) judgement.

criticar [kriti'kar] vt to criticize.

crítico, a ['kritiko, a] a critical // nm critic // nf criticism.

cromo ['kromo] nm chrome.

crónico, a ['kroniko, a] a chronic // nf chronicle, account.

cronista [kro'nista] nm/f chronicler.

cruce ['kruθe] nm crossing; (de carreteras) crossroads.

crucificar [kruθifi'kar] vt to crucify.

crucifijo [kruθi'fixo] nm crucifix.

crucigrama [kruθi'ɣrama] nm crossword (puzzle).

crudo, a ['kruðo, a] a raw; (no maduro) unripe; (petróleo) crude; (rudo, cruel) cruel.

cruel [krwel] a cruel.
crueldad [krwel'ðað] nf cruelty.
crujido [kru'xiðo] nm creak.
crujir [kru'xir] vi (madera) to creak; (dedos) to crack; (dientes) to grind; (nieve, arena) to crunch.
cruz [kruθ] nf cross; (de moneda) tails sg.
cruzado, a [kru'θaðo, a] a crossed // nm crusader // nf crusade.
cruzar [kru'θar] vt to cross; ~se vr to cross; (personas) to pass each other.
cuaderno [kwa'ðerno] nm notebook; (de escuela) exercise book; (NAUT) logbook.
cuadra ['kwaðra] nf (caballeriza) stable; (gran sala) hall.
cuadrado, a [kwa'ðraðo, a] a square // nm (MAT) square; (regla) ruler.
cuadrar [kwa'ðrar] vt to square // vi: ~ con to square with, tally with; ~se vr (soldado) to stand to attention.
cuadrilla [kwa'ðriʎa] nf party, group.
cuadro ['kwaðro] nm square; (de vidrio) frame; (PINTURA) painting; (TEATRO) scene.
cuádruplo, a ['kwaðruplo, a], **cuádruple** ['kwaðruple] a quadruple.
cuajar [kwa'xar] vt to thicken; (leche) to curdle; (sangre) to congeal; (adornar) to adorn; ~se vr to curdle; to congeal; (llenarse) to fill up.
cual [kwal] ad like, as // pron: el ~ etc which; (persona: sujeto) who; (: objeto) whom // a such as; cada ~ each one; ~ más, ~ menos some more, some less; tal ~ just as it is.
cuál [kwal] pron interr which (one).
cualesquier(a) [kwales'kjer(a)] pl de cualquier(a).
cualidad [kwali'ðað] nf quality.
cualquiera [kwal'kjera], **cualquier** [kwal'kjer] a any // pron anybody, anyone; (quienquiera) whoever; en cualquier parte anywhere; ~ que sea whichever it is; (persona) whoever it is.
cuando ['kwando] ad when; (aún si) if, even if // conj (puesto que) since // prep: yo, ~ niño... when I was a child...; ~ no sea así even if it is not so; ~ más the more; ~ menos the less; ~ no if not, otherwise; de ~ en ~ from time to time.
cuándo ['kwando] ad when; ¿desde ~?, ¿de ~ acá? since when?
cuanto, a ['kwanto, a] a all that, as much as // pron all that (which), as much as; llévate todo ~ quieras take as much as you like; en ~ (en seguida que) as soon as; (ya que) since, inasmuch as; en ~ profesor as a teacher; en ~ a as for; ~ más difícil sea the more difficult it is; ~ más hace (tanto) menos avanza the more he does, the less he progresses; ~ antes as soon as possible; unos ~s libros a few books.
cuánto, a ['kwanto, a] a what a lot of; (interr: sg) how much?; (: pl) how many? // pron, ad how; (interr: sg) how much?; (: pl) how many?; ¡~a gente! what a lot of people!; ¿~ cuesta? how much does it

cost?; ¿a ~s estamos? what's the date?; Señor no sé ~s Mr. So-and-So.
cuarenta [kwa'renta] num forty.
cuarentena [kwaren'tena] nf quarantine.
cuartear [kwarte'ar] vt to quarter; (dividir) to divide up; ~se vr to crack, split.
cuartel [kwar'tel] nm (de ciudad) quarter, district; (MIL) barracks pl; ~ general headquarters pl.
cuarteto [kwar'teto] nm quartet.
cuarto, a ['kwarto, a] a fourth // nm (MAT) quarter, fourth; (habitación) room // nf (MAT) quarter, fourth; (palmo) span; ~ de baño bathroom; ~ de hora quarter (of an) hour.
cuatro ['kwatro] num four.
cuba ['kuβa] nf cask, barrel; (fig) drunkard.
Cuba ['kuβa] nf Cuba; cubano, a a, nm/f Cuban.
cúbico, a ['kuβiko, a] a cubic.
cubierto, a [ku'βjerto, a] pp de cubrir // a covered // nm cover; (en la mesa) place; ~s nmpl cutlery sg // nf cover, covering; (neumático) tyre; (NAUT) deck; a ~ de covered with or in.
cubo ['kuβo] nm cube; (de madera) bucket, tub; (TEC) drum.
cubrir [ku'βrir] vt to cover; ~se vr (cielo) to become overcast.
cucaracha [kuka'ratʃa] nf cockroach.
cuchara [ku'tʃara] nf spoon; (TEC) scoop; ~da nf spoonful; ~dita nf teaspoonful.
cucharita [kutʃa'rita] nf teaspoon.
cucharón [kutʃa'ron] nm ladle.
cuchichear [kutʃitʃe'ar] vi to whisper.
cuchilla [ku'tʃiʎa] nf (large) knife; (de arma blanca) blade.
cuchillo [ku'tʃiʎo] nm knife.
cuello ['kweʎo] nm (ANAT) neck; (de vestido, camisa) collar.
cuenca ['kwenka] nf (escudilla) hollow; (ANAT) eye socket; (GEO) bowl, deep valley.
cuenta ['kwenta] nf (cálculo) count, counting; (en café, restaurante) bill; (COM) account; (de collar) bead; (fig) account; a fin de ~s in the end; caer en la ~ to catch on; darse ~ de to realize; tener en ~ to bear in mind; echar ~s to take stock; ~ corriente/de ahorros current/ savings account.
cuento etc vb ver contar // ['kwento] nm story.
cuerdo, a ['kwerðo, a] a sane; (prudente) wise, sensible // nf rope; (hilo) string; (de reloj) spring; dar ~a a un reloj to wind up a clock.
cuerno ['kwerno] nm horn.
cuero ['kwero] nm (ZOOL) skin, hide; (TEC) leather; en ~s stark naked; ~ cabelludo scalp.
cuerpo ['kwerpo] nm body.
cuesta ['kwesta] nf slope; (en camino etc) hill; ~ arriba/abajo uphill/downhill; a ~s on one's back.
cuestión [kwes'tjon] nf matter, question,

issue; (*riña*) quarrel, dispute.
cuesto *etc vb ver* **costar.**
cueva ['kweßa] *nf* cave; (*bodega*) cellar.
cuidado [kwi'ðaðo] *nm* care, carefulness; (*preocupación*) care, worry; *excl* careful!, look out!
cuidadoso, a [kwiða'ðoso, a] *a* careful; (*preocupado*) anxious.
cuidar [kwi'ðar] *vt* (MED) to care for; (*ocuparse de*) to take care of, look after // *vi*: ~ **de** to take care of, look after; ~**se** *vr* to look after o.s.; ~**se de hacer algo** to take care not to do something.
culebra [ku'leßra] *nf* snake.
culebrear [kuleßre'ar] *vi* to wriggle along; (*río*) to meander.
culinario, a [kuli'narjo, a] *a* culinary, cooking *cpd.*
culminación [kulmina'θjon] *nf* culmination.
culo ['kulo] *nm* bottom, backside.
culpa ['kulpa] *nf* fault; (JUR) guilt; **tener la** ~ (**de**) to be to blame (for).
culpabilidad [kulpaßili'ðað] *nf* guilt.
culpable [kul'paßle] *a* guilty // *nm/f* culprit.
culpar [kul'par] *vt* to blame; (*acusar*) to accuse.
cultivador, a [kultißa'ðor, a] *nm/f* farmer // *nf* cultivator.
cultivar [kulti'ßar] *vt* to cultivate.
cultivo [kul'tißo] *nm* cultivation; (*plantas*) crop.
culto, a ['kulto, a] *a* (*cultivado*) cultivated; (*que tiene cultura*) cultured // *nm* (*homenaje*) worship; (*religión*) cult.
cultura [kul'tura] *nf* culture.
cumbre ['kumbre] *nf* summit, top.
cumpleaños [kumple'aɲos] *nm* birthday.
cumplido, a [kum'pliðo, a] *a* complete, perfect; (*abundante*) plentiful; (*cortés*) courteous // *nm* compliment; (*cortesía*) courtesy.
cumplimentar [kumplimen'tar] *vt* to congratulate.
cumplimiento [kumpli'mjento] *nm* (*de un deber*) fulfilment; (*acabamiento*) completion; (*cumplido*) compliment.
cumplir [kum'plir] *vt* (*orden*) to carry out, obey; (*promesa*) to carry out, fulfil; (*condena*) to serve; (*años*) to reach, attain // *vi*: ~ **con** (*deberes*) to carry out, fulfil; ~**se** *vr* (*plazo*) to expire.
cuna ['kuna] *nf* cradle, cot.
cuñado, a [ku'ɲaðo, a] *nm/f* brother/sister-in-law.
cuota ['kwota] *nf* (*parte proporcional*) share; (*cotización*) fee, dues *pl.*
cupe *etc vb ver* **caber.**
cura ['kura] *nf* (*curación*) cure; (*método curativo*) treatment // *nm* priest.
curación [kura'θjon] *nf* cure; (*acción*) curing.
curar [ku'rar] *vt* (*herida*) to treat, dress; (*enfermo*) to cure; (*carne, pescado*) to cure,

salt; (*cuero*) to tan // *vi*, ~**se** *vr* to get well, recover.
curiosear [kurjose'ar] *vt* to glance at, look over // *vi* to look round, wander round.
curiosidad [kurjosi'ðað] *nf* curiosity.
curioso, a [ku'rjoso, a] *a* curious // *nm/f* bystander, onlooker.
cursi ['kursi] *a* (*fam*) in bad taste, vulgar.
cursivo, a [kur'sißo, a] *a* italic // *nf* italics *pl.*
curso ['kurso] *nm* course; **en** ~ (*año*) current; (*proceso*) going on, under way.
curvo, a ['kurßo, a] *a* (*gen*) curved; (*torcido*) bent // *nf* (*gen*) curve, bend.
custodia [kus'toðja] *nf* care, safekeeping, custody.
custodiar [kusto'ðjar] *vt* (*guardar*) to keep, take care of; (*vigilar*) to guard, watch over.
custodio [kus'toðjo] *nm* guardian, keeper.
cutis ['kutis] *nm* skin, complexion.
cuyo, a ['kujo, a] *pron* (*de quien*) whose, of whom; (*de que*) of which.

CH

chabacano, a [tʃaßa'kano, a] *a* vulgar, coarse.
chacal [tʃa'kal] *nm* jackal.
chacota [tʃa'kota] *nf* fun (and games).
chal [tʃal] *nm* shawl.
chalán [tʃa'lan] *nm* (*pey*) shady dealer.
chaleco [tʃa'leko] *nm* waistcoat, vest (US); ~ **salvavidas** life jacket.
chalupa [tʃa'lupa] *nf* launch, boat.
champán [tʃam'pan] *nm*, **champaña** [tʃam'paɲa] *nm* champagne.
champiñón [tʃampi'ɲon] *nm* mushroom.
champú [tʃam'pu] *nm* shampoo.
chamuscar [tʃamus'kar] *vt* to scorch, sear, singe.
chantaje [tʃan'taxe] *nm* blackmail.
chapa ['tʃapa] *nf* (*de metal*) plate, sheet; (*de madera*) board, panel.
chaparrón [tʃapa'rron] *nm* downpour, cloudburst.
chapotear [tʃapote'ar] *vt* to sponge down // *vi* (*fam*) to splash about.
chapucero, a [tʃapu'θero, a] *a* rough, crude // *nm/f* bungler.
chapurrar [tʃapu'rrar], **chapurrear** [tʃapurre'ar] *vt* (*idioma*) to speak badly; (*bebidas*) to mix.
chapuzar [tʃapu'θar] *vi* to duck.
chaqueta [tʃa'keta] *nf* jacket.
charca ['tʃarka] *nf* pond, pool.
charco ['tʃarko] *nm* pool, puddle.
charla ['tʃarla] *nf* talk, chat; (*conferencia*) lecture.
charlar [tʃar'lar] *vi* to talk, chat.
charlatán, ana [tʃarla'tan, ana] *nm/f* chatterbox; (*embaidor*) trickster; (*curandero*) charlatan.
charol [tʃa'rol] *nm* varnish; (*cuero*) patent leather.

chascarrillo [tʃaska'rriʎo] *nm* (*fam*) funny story.

chasco ['tʃasko] *nm* (*broma*) trick, joke; (*desengaño*) disappointment.

chasquear [tʃaske'ar] *vt* (*engañar*) to disappoint; (*bromear*) to play a trick on; (*látigo*) to crack; (*lengua*) to click.

chasquido [tʃas'kiðo] *nm* (*de lengua*) click; (*de látigo*) crack.

chato, a ['tʃato, a] *a* flat // *excl* hey handsome/beautiful!

chaval, a [tʃa'βal, a] *nm/f* lad/girl.

checo(e)slovaco, a [tʃeko(e)slo'βako, a] *a*, *nm/f* Czech, Czechoslovak.

Checo(e)slovaquia [tʃeko(e)slo'βakja] *nf* Czechoslovakia.

cheque ['tʃeke] *nm* cheque.

chequeo [tʃe'keo] *nm* (*MED*) check-up; (*AUTO*) service.

chequera [tʃe'kera] *nf* cheque-book.

chico, a ['tʃiko, a] *a* small, little // *nm/f* (*niño, niña*) child; (*muchacho, muchacha*) boy/girl.

chicharrón [tʃitʃa'rron] *nm* crackling.

chichón [tʃi'tʃon] *nm* bump, hump.

chiflado, a [tʃi'flaðo, a] *a* daft, barmy.

chiflar [tʃi'flar] *vt* to hiss, boo; ～**se** *vr*: ～**se por** to be/go crazy about.

chile ['tʃile] *nm* chilli, red pepper.

Chile ['tʃile] *nm* Chile; **chileno, a** *a*, *nm/f* Chilean.

chillar [tʃi'ʎar] *vi* (*persona*) to yell, scream; (*animal salvaje*) to howl; (*cerdo*) to squeal; (*puerta*) to creak.

chillido [tʃi'ʎiðo] *nm* (*de persona*) yell, scream; (*de animal*) howl; (*de frenos*) screech(ing).

chillón, ona [tʃi'ʎon, ona] *a* (*niño*) noisy; (*color*) loud, gaudy.

chimenea [tʃime'nea] *nf* chimney; (*hogar*) fireplace.

China ['tʃina] *nf*: **la** ～ China.

chinche ['tʃintʃe] *nf* bug; (*TEC*) drawing pin // *nm/f* nuisance, pest.

chino, a ['tʃino, a] *a*, *nm/f* Chinese // *nm* (*lengua*) Chinese.

Chipre ['tʃipre] *nf* Cyprus; **chipriota, chipriote** *a*, *nm/f* Cypriot.

chiquito, a [tʃi'kito, a] *a* very small, tiny // *nm/f* kid.

chirle ['tʃirle] *a* watery, wishy-washy.

chirriar [tʃi'rrjar] *vi* (*goznes*) to creak, squeak; (*pájaros*) to chirp, sing.

chirrido [tʃi'rriðo] *nm* creak(ing), squeak(ing); (*de pájaro*) chirp(ing).

chis [tʃis] *excl* sh!

chisme ['tʃisme] *nm* (*habladurías*) piece of gossip; (*fam*: *objeto*) thing, thingummyjig.

chismoso, a [tʃis'moso, a] *a* gossiping // *nm/f* gossip.

chispa ['tʃispa] *nf* spark; (*fig*) sparkle; (*ingenio*) wit; (*fam*) drunkenness.

chispeante [tʃispe'ante] *a* sparkling, scintillating.

chispear [tʃispe'ar] *vi* to spark; (*lloviznar*) to drizzle.

chisporrotear [tʃisporrote'ar] *vi* (*fuego*) to throw out sparks; (*leña*) to crackle; (*aceite*) to hiss, splutter.

chiste ['tʃiste] *nm* joke, funny story.

chistoso, a [tʃis'toso, a] *a* (*gracioso*) funny, amusing; (*bromista*) witty.

chivo, a ['tʃiβo, a] *nm/f* (billy/nanny-)goat.

chocante [tʃo'kante] *a* startling; (*extraño*) odd; (*ofensivo*) shocking; (*antipático*) annoying.

chocar [tʃo'kar] *vi* (*coches, trenes*) to collide, crash // *vt* to shock; (*sorprender*) to startle; ～ **con** to collide with; (*fig*) to run into *or* up against; ¡**chócala!** put it there!

chocolate [tʃoko'late] *a*, *nm* chocolate.

chochear [tʃotʃe'ar] *vi* to dodder, be senile.

chocho, a ['tʃotʃo, a] *a* doddering, senile; (*fig*) soft, doting.

chollo ['tʃoʎo] *nm* (*fam*) bargain, snip.

choque ['tʃoke] *nm* (*impacto*) impact; (*golpe*) jolt; (*AUTO*) crash; (*ELEC, MED*) shock; (*MIL*) clash; (*fig*) conflict.

chorizo [tʃo'riθo] *nm* hard pork sausage, salami.

chorrear [tʃorre'ar] *vi* to gush, spout (out); (*gotear*) to drip, trickle.

chorro ['tʃorro] *nm* jet; (*fig*) stream.

choza ['tʃoθa] *nf* hut, shack.

chuleta [tʃu'leta] *nf* chop, cutlet.

chulo ['tʃulo] *nm* (*pícaro*) rascal; (*fam*: *joven lindo*) dandy.

chupado, a [tʃu'paðo, a] *a* (*delgado*) skinny, gaunt; (*ajustado*) tight.

chupar [tʃu'par] *vt* to suck; (*absorber*) to absorb; ～**se** *vr* to grow thin.

churro, a ['tʃurro, a] *a* coarse // *nm* fritter.

chuscada [tʃus'kaða] *nf* funny remark, joke.

chusco, a ['tʃusko, a] *a* funny; (*persona*) coarse but amusing.

chusma ['tʃusma] *nf* rabble, mob.

D

D. *abr de* **Don.**

Da. *abr de* **Doña.**

dactilógrafo, a [dakti'loɤrafo, a] *nm/f* typist.

dádiva ['daðiβa] *nf* (*donación*) donation; (*regalo*) gift.

dado, a ['daðo, a] *pp de* **dar** // *nm* die; ～**s** *nmpl* dice; ～ **que** *conj* given that.

dador, a [da'ðor, a] *nm/f* (*gen*) giver.

dama ['dama] *nf* (*gen*) lady; (*AJEDREZ*) queen; ～**s** *nfpl* draughts.

damasco [da'masko] *nm* (*tela*) damask.

damnificar [damnifi'kar] *vt* (*gen*) to harm; (*persona*) to injure.

danés, esa [da'nes, esa] *a* Danish // *nm/f* Dane.

danzar [dan'θar] *vt*, *vi* to dance.

dañar [da'ɲar] *vt* (*objeto*) to damage;

(*persona*) to hurt; ~**se** *vr* to get hurt.

dañino, a [da'ɲino, a] *a* harmful.

daño ['daɲo] *nm* (*a un objeto*) damage; (*a una persona*) harm, injury; ~**s y perjuicios** (*JUR*) damages; **hacer** ~ **a** to damage; to harm, injure.

dar [dar] *vt* (*gen*) to give; (*TEATRO*) to perform, put on; (*película*) to show; (*intereses*) to yield; (*naipes*) to deal; (*la hora*): ~ **las 3** to strike 3 // *vi*: ~ **a** to look out on(to), overlook; ~ **con** (*persona etc*) to meet, run into; (*idea*) to hit on; ~ **contra** to knock against, bang into; ~ **de cabeza** to fall on one's head; ~ **en** (*objeto*) to strike, hit; (*broma*) to catch on to; ~ **de sí** to give, stretch; ~**se** *vr* (*pasar*) to happen; (*presentarse*) to occur; ~**se a** to be given to; ~**se por** to consider o.s.; **dárselas de** to pose as; ~ **de comer/beber a uno** to give sb sth to eat/drink; **da lo mismo** *o* **qué más da** it's all the same; ~ **en el blanco** to hit the mark; **me da pena** it saddens me; ~**se prisa** to hurry (up).

dardo ['darðo] *nm* dart.

dársena ['darsena] *nf* dock.

datar [da'tar] *vi*: ~ **de** to date from.

dátil ['datil] *nm* date.

dato ['dato] *nm* fact, piece of information.

d. de J. C. *abr de* **después de Jesucristo** A.D. (Anno Domini).

de [de] *prep* of; from; **libro** ~ **cocina** cookery book; **el hombre** ~ **largos cabellos** the man with long hair; **guantes** ~ **cuero** leather gloves; **fue a Londres** ~ **profesor** he went to London as a teacher; **una** ~ **dos** one or the other; ~ **mañana** in the morning; **vestido** ~ **negro** dressed in black; **más/menos** ~ more/less than; ~ **cabeza** on one's head; ~ **cara a** facing.

deambular [deambu'lar] *vi* to stroll, wander.

debajo [de'βaxo] *ad* underneath; ~ **de** below, under; **por** ~ **de** beneath.

debate [de'βate] *nm* debate; **debatir** *vt* to debate.

deber [de'βer] *nm* duty // *vt* to owe // *vi*: **debe (de)** it must, it should; **debo hacerlo** I must do it; **debe de ir** he should go; ~**se** *vr*: ~**se a** to be owing *or* due to.

debido, a [de'βiðo, a] *a* proper, just; ~ **a** due to, because of.

débil ['deβil] *a* (*persona, carácter*) weak; (*luz*) dim; **debilidad** *nf* weakness; dimness; **debilidad senil** senility.

debilitar [deβili'tar] *vt* to weaken; ~**se** *vr* to grow weak.

débito ['deβito] *nm* debit.

década ['dekaða] *nf* decade.

decadencia [deka'ðenθja] *nf* decadence.

decaer [deka'er] *vi* (*declinar*) to decline; (*debilitarse*) to weaken.

decaimiento [dekai'mjento] *nm* (*inclinación*) decline; (*desaliento*) (*ánimo*)ragement; (*MED: empeoramiento*) (*empeoram*)ning; (: *estado débil*) weakness.

decano, a [de'kano, a] *nm/f* dean.

decapitar [dekapi'tar] *vt* to behead.

decena [de'θena] *nf*: **una** ~ ten (or so).

decencia [de'θenθja] *nf* (*modestia*) modesty; (*honestidad*) respectability.

decente [de'θente] *a* (*correcto*) seemly, proper; (*honesto*) respectable.

decepción [deθep'θjon] *nf* disappointment; **decepcionar** *vt* to disappoint.

decidir [deθi'ðir] *vt* (*persuadir*) to convince, persuade; (*resolver*) to decide // *vi* to decide; ~**se** *vr*: ~**se a** to make up one's mind to.

décimo, a ['deθimo, a] *a* tenth // *nm* tenth.

decir [de'θir] *vt* (*expresar*) to say; (*contar*) to tell; (*hablar*) to speak // *nm* saying; ~**se** *vr*: **se dice que** it is said that; ~ **para/entre sí** to say to o.s.; **querer** ~ to mean.

decisión [deθi'sjon] *nf* (*resolución*) decision; (*firmeza*) decisiveness.

decisivo, a [deθi'siβo, a] *a* decisive.

declamar [dekla'mar] *vt, vi* to declaim.

declaración [deklara'θjon] *nf* (*manifestación*) statement; (*explicación*) explanation; **declarar** *vt* to declare, state; to explain // *vi* to declare; (*JUR*) to testify; **declararse** *vr* to propose.

declinar [dekli'nar] *vt* (*gen*) to decline; (*JUR*) to reject // *vi* (*el día*) to draw to a close; (*salud*) to deteriorate.

declive [de'kliβe] *nm* (*cuesta*) slope; (*inclinación*) incline.

decolorarse [dekolo'rarse] *vr* to become discoloured.

decoración [dekora'θjon] *nf* decoration.

decorado [deko'raðo] *nm* scenery, set.

decorar [deko'rar] *vt* to decorate; **decorativo, a** *a* ornamental, decorative.

decoro [de'koro] *nm* (*respeto*) respect; (*dignidad*) decency; (*recato*) decorum, propriety; ~**so, a** *a* (*decente*) decent; (*modesto*) modest; (*digno*) proper.

decrecer [dekre'θer] *vi* to decrease, diminish.

decrépito, a [de'krepito, a] *a* decrepit.

decretar [dekre'tar] *vt* to decree; **decreto** *nm* decree.

dedal [de'ðal] *nm* thimble.

dedicación [deðika'θjon] *nf* dedication; **dedicar** *vt* (*libro*) to dedicate; (*tiempo, dinero*) to devote; (*palabras: decir, consagrar*) to dedicate, devote; **dedicatoria** *nf* (*de libro*) dedication.

dedo ['deðo] *nm* finger; ~ (**del pie**) toe; ~ **pulgar** thumb; ~ **índice** index finger; ~ **mayor** *o* **cordial** middle finger; ~ **anular** ring finger; ~ **meñique** little finger.

deducción [deðuk'θjon] *nf* deduction.

deducir [deðu'θir] *vt* (*concluir*) to deduce, infer; (*COM*) to deduct.

defecto [de'fekto] *nm* defect, flaw; (*ELEC*) fault; **defectuoso, a** *a* defective, faulty.

defender [defen'der] *vt* to defend.

defensa [de'fensa] *nf* defence; (*DEPORTE*)

back; **defensivo, a** a defensive // nf: **a la defensiva** on the defensive.

defensor, a [defen'sor, a] a defending // nm/f (abogado) defending counsel; (protector) protector.

deficiencia [defi'θjenθja] nf deficiency; **deficiente** a (defectuoso) defective; (imperfecto) deficient, wanting.

déficit ['defiθit] nm deficit.

definición [defini'θjon] nf definition.

definir [defi'nir] vt (determinar) to determine, establish; (decidir) to define; (aclarar) to clarify; **definitivo, a** a definitive; **en definitiva** definitively.

deformación [deforma'θjon] nf (alteración) deformation; (distorsión) distortion.

deformar [defor'mar] vt (gen) to deform; ~**se** vr to become deformed; **deforme** a (informe) deformed; (feo) ugly; (mal hecho) misshapen.

defraudar [defrau'ðar] vt (decepcionar) to disappoint; (estafar) to cheat, defraud; (engañar) to deceive.

defunción [defun'θjon] nf decease, demise.

degeneración [dexenera'θjon] nf (de las células) degeneration; (moral) degeneracy; **degenerar** vi to degenerate.

degollar [dexo'ʎar] vt (animal) to slaughter; (decapitar) to behead, decapitate.

degradar [dexra'ðar] vt to debase, degrade; ~**se** vr to demean o.s.

degüello [de'xweʎo] nm: **entrar a** ~ **to** slaughter, put to the sword.

degustación [dexusta'θjon] nf sampling, tasting.

deidad [dei'ðað] nf deity, divinity.

deificar [deifi'kar] vt (persona) to deify.

dejación [dexa'θjon] nf (abandono) abandonment.

dejadez [dexa'ðeθ] nf (negligencia) neglect; (descuido) untidiness, carelessness; **dejado, a** a (negligente) careless; (indolente) lazy.

dejar [de'xar] vt (gen) to leave; (permitir) to allow, let; (abandonar) to abandon, forsake; (beneficios) to produce, yield // vi: ~ **de** (parar) to stop; (no hacer) to fail to; ~ **a un lado** to leave or set aside.

dejo ['dexo] nm (LING) accent; (sabor fuerte) tang; (sabor que queda) aftertaste.

del [del] = **de + el**, ver **de**.

delantal [delan'tal] nm apron.

delante [de'lante] ad in front; (enfrente) opposite; (adelante) ahead; ~ **de** in front of, before.

delantero, a [delan'tero, a] a front // nm (DEPORTE) forward // nf (de vestido, casa) front part; (DEPORTE) forward line; **llevar la** ~**a a uno** to be ahead of sb.

delatar [dela'tar] vt to inform on or against, betray; **delator, a** nm/f informer.

delegación [dexa'θjon] nf delegation; (COM) office, branch; ~ **de policía** police station; ~ **municipal** local government

office; **delegado, a** nm/f delegate; (COM) agent; **delegar** vt to delegate.

deleitar [delei'tar] vt to delight; ~**se** vr: ~**se con** o **en** to delight in, take pleasure in; **deleite** nm delight, pleasure.

deletrear [deletre'ar] vi to spell (out); (fig) to interpret, decipher; **deletreo** nm spelling; interpretation, decipherment.

deleznable [deleθ'naβle] a inv (frágil) fragile; (resbaloso) slippery; (fugaz) fleeting.

delfín [del'fin] nm dolphin.

delgadez [delxa'ðeθ] nf thinness, slimness; **delgado, a** a (gen) thin; (persona) slim, thin; (tierra) poor; (tela etc) light, delicate.

deliberación [deliβera'θjon] nf deliberation; **deliberar** vt to debate, discuss.

delicadeza [delika'ðeθa] nf (gen) delicacy; (refinamiento, sutileza) refinement.

delicado, a [deli'kaðo, a] a (gen) delicate; (sensible) sensitive; (quisquilloso) touchy.

delicia [de'liθja] nf delight.

delicioso, a [deli'θjoso, a] a (gracioso) delightful, agreeable; (placentero) pleasant; (exquisito) delicious.

delincuencia [delin'kwenθja] nf delinquency; **delincuente** nm/f delinquent, criminal.

delinquir [delin'kir] vi to commit an offence.

delirante [deli'rante] a delirious; **delirar** vi to be delirious, rave.

delirio [de'lirjo] nm (MED) delirium; (palabras insensatas) wanderings pl, ravings pl.

delito [de'lito] nm (infracción) offence; (crimen) crime; ~ **político/común** political/common crime.

demagogo [dema'xoxo] nm demagogue.

demanda [de'manda] nf (pedido, COM) demand; (petición) request; (JUR) action, lawsuit; **demandante** nm/f claimant.

demandar [deman'dar] vt (gen) to demand; (JUR) to sue.

demarcación [demarka'θjon] nf (de terreno) demarcation; **demarcar** vt to demarcate.

demás [de'mas] a: **los** ~ **niños** the other children, the remaining children // pron: **los/las** ~ the others, the rest (of them); **lo** ~ the rest (of it) // ad besides.

demasía [dema'sia] nf (exceso) excess, surplus; (atrevimiento) boldness; (insolencia) outrage; **comer en** ~ to eat to excess.

demasiado, a [dema'sjaðo, a] a too, too much; ~**s** too many // ad too, too much; **¡es** ~**!** it's too much!

demencia [de'menθja] nf (locura) madness; **demente** nm/f lunatic // a mad, insane.

democracia [demo'kraθja] nf democracy.

demócrata [de'mokrata] nm/f democrat; **democrático, a** a democratic.

demoler [demo'ler] vt to demolish; **demolición** nf demolition.

demonio [de'monjo] nm devil, demon; ¡~s! hell!, confound it!; ¿cómo ~s? how the hell?

demora [de'mora] nf delay; **demorar** vt (retardar) to delay, hold back; (dilatar) to hold up // vi to linger, stay on.

demostración [demostra'θjon] nf (de teorema) demonstration; (de afecto) show, display.

demostrar [demos'trar] vt (probar) to prove; (mostrar) to show; (manifestar) to demonstrate; **demostrativo, a** a demonstrative.

denegar [dene'xar] vt (rechazar) to refuse; (JUR) to reject.

denigrar [deni'xrar] vt (desacreditar, infamar) to denigrate; (injuriar) to insult.

denominación [denomina'θjon] nf (nombramiento) designation; (clase) denomination.

denotar [deno'tar] vt (indicar) to indicate; (significar) to denote.

densidad [densi'ðað] nf (FÍSICA) density; (fig) thickness.

denso, a ['denso, a] a (apretado) solid; (espeso, pastoso) thick; (fig) heavy.

dentadura [denta'ðura] nf (set of) teeth pl; ~ postiza false teeth pl.

dentera [den'tera] nf (sensación desagradable) the shivers pl, the shudders pl; (envidia) envy, jealousy; (deseo) desire.

dentista [den'tista] nm/f dentist.

dentro ['dentro] ad inside // prep: ~ de in, inside, within; **vayamos a** ~ let's go inside; **mirar por** ~ to look inside; ~ de **tres meses** within three months.

denuedo [de'nweðo] nm boldness, daring.

denuncia [de'nunθja] nf (delación) denunciation; (acusación) accusation; (de accidente) report; **denunciar** vt to report; (delatar) to inform on or against.

departamento [departa'mento] nm (sección administrativa) department, section; (de caja, tren) compartment; (AM: piso) apartment, flat.

dependencia [depen'denθja] nf dependence; (POL) dependency; (COM) office, section.

depender [depen'der] vi: ~ de to depend on.

dependienta [depen'djenta] nf saleswoman, shop assistant; **dependiente** a dependent // nm salesman.

deplorable [deplo'raßle] a deplorable; **deplorar** vt to deplore.

deponer [depo'ner] vt to lay down // vi (JUR) to give evidence; (declarar) to testify.

deportar [depor'tar] vt to deport.

deporte [de'porte] nm sport; **deportista** a sp...ts cpd // nm/f sportsman/woman.

...itante [deposi'tante], **deposi-...**, **a** [deposita'ðor, a] nm/f depositor.

...ar [deposi'tar] vt (dinero) to ...(mercaderías) to put away, store;

(AM: persona) to confide; ~se vr to settle; ~io, a nm/f trustee.

depósito [de'posito] nm (gen) deposit; (de mercaderías) warehouse, store; (de agua, gasolina etc) tank; ~ de equipajes cloakroom.

depravar [depra'ßar] vt to deprave; ~se vr to become depraved.

depreciar [depre'θjar] vt to depreciate, reduce the value of; ~se vr to depreciate, lose value.

depredación [depreða'θjon] nf (saqueo, pillaje) pillage; (malversación) depredation.

depresión [depre'sjon] nf depression.

deprimido, a [depri'miðo, a] a depressed.

deprimir [depri'mir] vt to depress; ~se vr (persona) to become depressed.

depuración [depura'θjon] nf purification; (POL) purge; **depurar** vt to purify; (purgar) to purge.

derecha [de'retʃa] nf right(-hand) side; (POL) right.

derechamente [deretʃa'mente] ad (dirección) straight.

derecho, a [de'retʃo, a] a right, right-hand // nm (privilegio) right; (lado) right(-hand) side; (leyes) law // ad straight, directly; ~s nmpl (de aduana) duty sg; (de autor) royalties; **tener** ~ **a** to have a right to.

deriva [de'rißa] nf: **ir** o **estar a la** ~ to drift, be adrift.

derivación [derißa'θjon] nf derivation.

derivar [deri'ßar] vt (gen) to derive; (desviar) to drift; ~se vr to derive, be derived; to drift.

derramamiento [derrama'mjento] nm (de sangre) shedding; (dispersión) spilling.

derramar [derra'mar] vt to spill; (echar) to pour out; (dispersar) to scatter; ~se vr to pour out; ~ lágrimas to weep.

derrame [de'rrame] nm (de líquido) spilling; (de sangre) shedding; (de tubo etc) overflow; (perdida) loss, leakage; (MED) discharge; (declive) slope.

derredor [derre'ðor] ad: **al** o **en** ~ de around, about.

derretido, a [derre'tiðo, a] a melted, molten.

derretir [derre'tir] vt (gen) to melt; (nieve) to thaw; (fig) to squander; ~se vr to melt.

derribar [derri'ßar] vt to knock down; (construcción) to demolish; (persona, gobierno, político) to bring down; ~se vr to fall down.

derrocar [derro'kar] vt (despeñar) to demolish, knock down; (gobierno) to bring down, overthrow.

derrochar [derro'tʃar] vt to squander; **derroche** nm (despilfarro) waste squandering.

derrota [de'rrota] nf (camino, vereda) road, route; (NAUT) course; (MIL) defea rout; (fig) disaster; **derrotar** vt (gen) t defeat; (destruir) to ruin; **derrotero** n (rumbo) course.

derrumbar [derrum'bar] *vt* to throw down; ~**se** *vr* (*despeñarse*) to collapse; (*precipitarse*) to throw o.s. down.
desabotonar [desaßoto'nar] *vt* to unbutton, undo // *vi* to open out; ~**se** *vr* to come undone.
desabrido, a [desa'ßriðo, a] *a* (*insípido, soso*) insipid, tasteless; (*persona*) rude, surly; (*respuesta*) sharp.
desabrochar [desaßro'tʃar] *vt* (*botones, broches*) to undo, unfasten; (*fig*) to expose; ~**se** *vr* to confide, unburden o.s.
desacato [desa'kato] *nm* (*falta de respeto*) disrespect; (*irreverencia*) insulting behaviour; (*JUR*) contempt.
desacertado, a [desaθer'taðo, a] *a* (*equivocado*) mistaken; (*inoportuno*) unwise.
desacertar [desaθer'tar] *vi* (*errar*) to be mistaken; (*desatinar*) to act unwisely.
desacierto [desa'θjerto] *nm* mistake, error.
desacomodar [desakomo'ðar] *vt* (*molestar*) to put out, inconvenience; **desacomodo** *nm* (*incomodidad*) inconvenience; (*molestia*) trouble.
desaconsejado, a [desakonse'xaðo, a] *a* ill-advised; **desaconsejar** *vt* to dissuade, advise against.
desacordarse [desakor'ðarse] *vr* (*MUS*) to get out of tune; **desacorde** *a inv* discordant.
desacreditar [desakreði'tar] *vt* (*desprestigiar*) to discredit, bring into disrepute; (*denigrar*) to run down.
desacuerdo [desa'kwerðo] *nm* (*conflicto*) discord, disagreement; (*error*) error, blunder.
desafecto, a [deːa'fekto, a] *a* (*opuesto*) disaffected // *nm* (*hostilidad*) disaffection.
desafiar [desa'fjar] *vt* (*retar*) to challenge; (*enfrentarse a*) to defy.
desafilar [desafi'lar] *vt* to blunt; ~**se** *vr* to become blunt.
desafinado, a [desafi'naðo] *a*: **estar** ~ to be out of tune; **desafinarse** *vr* (*MUS*) to go out of tune.
desafío [desa'fio] *nm* (*reto*) challenge; (*combate*) duel; (*resistencia*) defiance; (*competencia*) competition.
desafortunado, a [desafortu'naðo, a] *a* (*desgraciado*) unfortunate, unlucky.
desagradable [desaɣra'ðaßle] *a* (*fastidioso, enojoso*) unpleasant; (*irritante*) disagreeable.
desagradar [desaɣra'ðar] *vi* (*disgustar*) to displease; (*molestar*) to bother; **desagradecido, a** *a* ungrateful.
desagrado [desa'ɣraðo] *nm* (*disgusto*) displeasure; (*contrariedad*) dissatisfaction.
desagraviar [desaɣra'ßjar] *vt* to make amends to; **desagravio** *nm* (*recompensa*) amends; (: *en efectivo*) compensation.
desaguadero [desaɣwa'ðero] *nm* drain.
desagüe [des'aɣwe] *nm* (*de un líquido*) drainage; (*cañería*) drainpipe.

desaguisado, a [desaxi'saðo, a] *a* illegal // *nm* outrage.
desahogado, a [desao'xaðo, a] *a* (*descarado*) brazen, impudent; (*holgado*) comfortable; (*espacioso*) roomy.
desahogar [desao'xar] *vt* (*consolar*) to console; (*aliviar*) to ease, relieve; (*ira*) to vent; ~**se** *vr* (*distenderse*) to take it easy; (*desfogarse*) to let off steam.
desahogo [desa'oxo] *nm* (*alivio*) relief; (*comodidad*) comfort, ease; (*descaro*) impudence.
desahuciar [desau'θjar] *vt* (*enfermo*) to give up hope for; (*inquilino*) to evict; **desahucio** *nm* eviction.
desairado, a [desai'raðo, a] *a* (*menospreciado*) disregarded; (*desgarbado*) shabby.
desairar [desai'rar] *vt* (*menospreciar*) to slight, snub; (*ultrajar*) to dishonour.
desaire [des'aire] *nm* (*afrenta*) rebuff; (*menosprecio*) slight; (*falta de garbo*) unattractiveness, lack of charm.
desajustar [desaxus'tar] *vt* (*desarreglar*) to disarrange; (*desconcertar*) to throw off balance; ~**se** *vr* to get out of order; (*cintura*) to loosen.
desajuste [desa'xuste] *nm* (*de máquina*) disorder; (*situación*) imbalance.
desalentador, a [desalenta'ðor, a] *a* disheartening; **desalentar** *vt* (*desanimar*) to discourage; **desalentar a uno** to make sb breathless.
desaliento [desa'ljento] *nm* discouragement.
desalinear [desaline'ar] *vt* to throw out of the straight; ~**se** *vr* to go off the straight.
desaliño [desa'liɲo] *nm* (*negligencia*) slovenliness.
desalmado, a [desal'maðo, a] *a* (*cruel*) cruel, heartless.
desalojamiento [desaloxa'mjento] *nm* ousting; (*cambio de residencia*) removal; (: *forzado*) eviction.
desalojar [desalo'xar] *vt* (*expulsar, echar*) to eject; (*abandonar*) to abandon, evacuate // *vi* to move out.
desamarrar [desama'rrar] *vt* to untie; (*NAUT*) to cast off.
desamor [desa'mor] *nm* (*frialdad*) indifference; (*odio*) dislike; (*enemistad*) enmity.
desamparado, a [desampa'raðo, a] *a* (*persona*) helpless; (*lugar: expuesto*) exposed; (*desierto*) deserted.
desamparar [desampa'rar] *vt* (*abandonar*) to desert, abandon; (*JUR*) to leave defenceless; (*barco*) to abandon.
desandar [desan'dar] *vt*: ~ **lo andado** o **el camino** to retrace one's steps.
desanimado, a [desani'maðo, a] *a* (*persona*) downhearted; (*espectáculo, fiesta*) dull; **desanimar** *vt* (*desalentar*) to discourage; (*deprimir*) to depress.
desapacible [desapa'θißle] *a* (*gen*) unpleasant; (*carácter*) disagreeable; (*voz*) harsh.

desaparecer [desapare'θer] vt (gen) to hide // vi (gen) to disappear; (el sol, la luz) to vanish; **desaparición** nf disappearance.

desapego [desa'peɤo] nm (frialdad) coolness; (distancia) detachment.

desapercibido, a [desaperθi'ßiðo, a] a (desprevenido) unprepared; **pasar ~** to go unnoticed.

desaplicación [desaplika'θjon] nf (negligencia) slackness; (ocio) laziness; **desaplicado, a** a slack; lazy.

desaprensivo, a [desapren'sißo, a] a unscrupulous.

desaprobar [desapro'ßar] vt (reprobar) to disapprove of; (condenar) to condemn; (no consentir) to reject.

desaprovechado, a [desaproße'tʃaðo, a] a (improductivo) unproductive; (atrasado) backward; **desaprovechar** vt to waste.

desarmar [desar'mar] vt (MIL, fig) to disarm; (TEC) to take apart, dismantle; **desarme** nm disarmament.

desarraigar [desarrai'ɤar] vt to uproot; **desarraigo** nm uprooting.

desarreglado, a [desarre'ɤlaðo, a] a (TEC) out of order; (desordenado) disorderly, untidy.

desarreglar [desarre'ɤlar] vt (desordenar) to disarrange; (mecánica) to put out of order; (trastocar) to upset, disturb.

desarreglo [desa'rreɤlo] nm (de casa, persona) untidiness; (desorden) disorder.

desarrollar [desarro'ʎar] vt (gen) to develop; (extender) to unfold; **~se** vr to develop; (extenderse) to open (out); (film) to develop; **desarrollo** nm development.

desarticular [desartiku'lar] vt (hueso) to put out; (objeto) to take apart; (fig) to break up.

desaseo [desa'seo] nm (suciedad) slovenliness; (desarreglo) untidiness.

desasir [desa'sir] vt to loosen; **~se** vr to extricate o.s.; **~se de** to let go, give up.

desasosegar [desasose'ɤar] vt (inquietar) to disturb; (afligir) to make uneasy; **~se** vr to become uneasy.

desasosiego [desaso'sjeɤo] nm (intranquilidad) uneasiness; (aflicción) restlessness; (ansiedad) anxiety.

desastrado, a [desas'traðo, a] a (desaliñado) shabby; (sucio) dirty; (desgraciado, adverso) wretched.

desastre [de'sastre] nm disaster; **desastroso, a** a disastrous.

desatado, a [desa'taðo, a] a (desligado) untied; (violento) violent, wild.

desatar [desa'tar] vt (nudo) to untie; (paquete) to undo; (separar) to detach; **~se** vr (zapatos) to come untied; (tormenta) to break.

desatender [desaten'der] vt (no prestar atención a) to disregard; (abandonar) to neglect; (invitado) to slight.

desatento, a [desa'tento, a] a (distraído) inattentive; (descortés) discourteous.

desatinado, a [desati'naðo, a] a (disparatado) wild, reckless; (absurdo) foolish, silly; **desatinar** vi (desvariar) to behave foolishly; **desatino** nm (idiotez) foolishness, folly; (error) blunder.

desautorizado, a [desautori'θaðo, a] a unauthorized; **desautorizar** vt (oficial) to deprive of authority; (informe) to deny.

desavenencia [desaße'nenθja] nf (desacuerdo) disagreement; (discrepancia) rift, quarrel.

desaventajado, a [desaßenta'xaðo, a] a (inferior) inferior; (poco ventajoso) disadvantageous.

desayunar [desaju'nar] vi to have breakfast // vt to have for breakfast; **desayuno** nm breakfast.

desazón [desa'θon] nf (insipidez) tastelessness; (angustia) anxiety; (fig) annoyance.

desazonar [desaθo'nar] vt to make tasteless; (fig) to annoy, upset; **~se** vr (enojarse) to be annoyed; (preocuparse) to worry, be anxious; (MED) to be off colour.

desbandarse [desßan'darse] vr (MIL) to disband; (fig) to flee in disorder.

desbarajuste [desßara'xuste] nm confusion, disorder.

desbaratar [desßara'tar] vt (deshacer, destruir) to ruin; (malgastar) to squander; (mecánica) to take apart.

desbordar [desßor'ðar] vt (sobrepasar) to go beyond; (exceder) to exceed // vi, **~se** vr (río) to overflow; (entusiasmo) to erupt; (persona) to express one's feelings freely.

descabalgar [deskaßal'ɤar] vi to dismount.

descabellado, a [deskaße'ʎaðo, a] a (disparatado) wild, crazy; (insensato) ridiculous.

descabellar [deskaße'ʎar] vt to ruffle; (TAUR: toro) to give the coup de grace to.

descabezar [deskaße'θar] vt (persona) to behead; (árbol) to lop; **~se** vr (AGR) to shed the grain; (fig) to rack one's brains.

descafeinado [deskafei'naðo] nm decaffeinated coffee.

descalabro [deska'laßro] nm blow; (desgracia) misfortune.

descalzar [deskal'θar] vt (zapato) to take off; **descalzo, a** a barefoot(ed); (fig) destitute.

descaminado, a [deskami'naðo, a] a (equivocado) on the wrong road; (fig) misguided.

descaminar [deskami'nar] vt (alguien) to misdirect; (: fig) to lead astray; **~se** vr (en la ruta) to go the wrong way; (fig) to go astray.

descansado, a [deskan'saðo, a] a (gen) rested; (que tranquiliza) restful; **descansar** vt (gen) to rest // vi to rest, have a rest; (echarse) to lie down.

descanso [des'kanso] nm (reposo) rest; (alivio) relief; (pausa) break; (DEPORTE) interval, half time.

descarado, a [deska'raðo, a] a (sin

vergüenza) shameless; (*insolente*) cheeky;
descararse *vr* to be insolent or cheeky.
descarga [des'karxa] *nf* (ARQ, ELEC, MIL)
discharge; (NAUT) unloading.
descargadero [deskarxa'ðero] *nm* wharf.
descargar [deskar'xar] *vt* to unload;
(*golpe*) to let fly; ~**se** *vr* to unburden o.s.;
descargo *nm* unloading; (COM) receipt;
(JUR) evidence.
descarnado, a [deskar'naðo, a] *a*
scrawny; (*fig*) bare.
descaro [des'karo] *nm* (*atrevimiento*)
shamelessness, nerve; (*insolencia*) cheek.
descarriar [deska'rrjar] *vt* (*descaminar*)
to misdirect; (*fig*) to lead astray; ~**se** *vr*
(*perderse*) to lose one's way; (*separarse*) to
stray; (*pervertirse*) to err, go astray.
descarrilamiento [deskarrila'mjento]
nm (*de tren*) derailment.
descartar [deskar'tar] *vt* (*rechazar*) to
reject; (*poner a un lado*) to set aside;
(*eliminar*) to rule out; ~**se** *vr* (NAIPES) to
discard; ~**se de** to shirk; **descartado, a** *a*
rejected; set aside, eliminated.
descendencia [desθen'denθja] *nf* (*origen*)
origin, descent; (*hijos*) offspring.
descender [desθen'der] *vt* (*bajar:
escalera*) to go down; (: *equipajes*) to take
down // *vi* to descend; (*temperatura, nivel*)
to fall, drop; ~ **de** to be descended from.
descendiente [desθen'djente] *nm/f*
descendant.
descenso [des'θenso] *nm* descent; (*de
temperatura*) drop.
descifrar [desθi'frar] *vt* to decipher.
descolgar [deskol'xar] *vt* (*bajar*) to take
down; (*teléfono*) to pick up; ~**se** *vr* to let
o.s. down.
descolorir [deskolo'rir], **descolorar**
[deskolo'rar] *vt* = **decolorar.**
descomedido, a [deskome'ðiðo, a] *a*
(*descortés*) rude; (*excesivo*) excessive.
descompaginar [deskompaxi'nar] *vt*
(*desordenar*) to disarrange, mess up.
descompasado, a [deskompa'saðo, a] *a*
(*sin proporción*) out of all proportion; (*excesivo*) excessive.
descomponer [deskompo'ner] *vt*
(*desordenar*) to disarrange, disturb; (TEC)
to put out of order; (*dividir*) to break down
(into parts); (*fig*) to provoke; ~**se** *vr*
(*corromperse*) to rot, decompose; (*el
tiempo*) to change (for the worse); (TEC) to
break down; (*irritarse*) to lose one's
temper.
descomposición [deskomposi'θjon] *nf*
(*gen*) breakdown; (*de fruta etc*)
decomposition.
descompostura [deskompos'tura] *nf*
(TEC) breakdown; (*desorganización*)
disorganization; (*desorden*) untidiness.
descompuesto, a [deskom'pwesto, a] *a*
(*corrompido*) decomposed; (*roto*) broken;
(*descarado*) brazen; (*furioso*) angry.
desconcertado, a [deskonθer'taðo, a] *a*
disconcerted, bewildered.
desconcertar [deskonθer'tar] *vt*

(*confundir*) to baffle; (*incomodar*) to upset,
put out; (TEC) to put out of order; (ANAT) to
dislocate; ~**se** *vr* (*turbarse*) to be upset.
desconcierto [deskon'θjerto] *nm* (*gen*)
disorder; (*daño*) damage; (*desorientación*)
uncertainty; (*inquietud*) uneasiness.
desconectar [deskonek'tar] *vt* to
disconnect.
desconfianza [deskon'fjanθa] *nf* distrust;
desconfiar *vi* to be distrustful;
desconfiar de to distrust, suspect.
desconocer [deskono'θer] *vt* (*alguien*) to
ignore; (*ignorar*) not to know, be ignorant
of; (*no recordar*) to fail to remember; (*no
aceptar*) to deny; (*repudiar*) to disown.
desconocimiento [deskonoθi'mjento] *nm*
(*falta de conocimientos*) ignorance;
(*repudio*) disregard; (*ingratitud*)
ingratitude.
desconsiderado, a [deskonsiðe'raðo, a] *a*
(*descuidado*) inconsiderate; (*insensible*)
thoughtless.
desconsolar [deskonso'lar] *vt* to distress;
~**se** *vr* to despair.
desconsuelo [deskon'swelo] *nm* (*tristeza*)
distress; (*desesperación*) despair.
descontar [deskon'tar] *vt* (*deducir*) to
take away, deduct; (*rebajar*) to discount;
(*predecir, dar por cierto*) to take for
granted.
descontento, a [deskon'tento, a] *a*
dissatisfied // *nm* dissatisfaction,
discontent.
descorazonar [deskoraθo'nar] *vt* to
discourage, dishearten.
descorchar [deskor'tʃar] *vt* to uncork.
descortés [deskor'tes] *a* (*mal educado*)
discourteous; (*grosero*) rude.
descoser [desko'ser] *vt* to unstitch; ~**se**
vr to come apart (at the seams).
descosido, a [desko'siðo, a] *a* (*costura*)
unstitched; (*indiscreto*) indiscreet; (*desordenado*) disjointed.
descoyuntar [deskojun'tar] *vt* (ANAT) to
dislocate.
descrédito [des'kreðito] *nm* discredit.
descreído, a [deskre'iðo, a] *a* (*incrédulo*)
incredulous; (*falto de fe*) unbelieving.
describir [deskri'ßir] *vt* to describe.
descripción [deskrip'θjon] *nf* description.
descrito [des'krito] *pp de* **describir.**
descuajar [deskwa'xar] *vt* (*disolver*) to
melt; (*planta*) to pull out by the roots.
descubierto, a [desku'ßjerto, a] *pp de*
descubrir // *a* uncovered, bare; (*persona*)
bareheaded; **al** ~ in the open.
descubrimiento [deskußri'mjento] *nm*
(*hallazgo*) discovery; (*revelación*)
revelation.
descubrir [desku'ßrir] *vt* to discover, find;
(*inaugurar*) to unveil; (*vislumbrar*) to
detect; (*revelar*) to reveal, show; (*quitar la
tapa*) to uncover; ~**se** *vr* to reveal o.s.;
(*quitarse sombrero*) to take off one's hat;
(*confesar*) to confess.
descuento [des'kwento] *nm* discount; ~
jubilatorio retirement pension.

descuidado, a [deskwi'ðaðo, a] *a* (*sin cuidado*) careless; (*desordenado*) untidy; (*olvidadizo*) forgetful; (*dejado*) neglected; (*desprevenido*) unprepared.

descuidar [deskwi'ðar] *vt* (*dejar*) to neglect; (*olvidar*) to overlook // *vi*, ~**se** *vr* (*distraerse*) to be careless; (*estar desaliñado*) to let o.s. go; (*desprevenirse*) to drop one's guard; ¡**descuida!** don't worry!; **descuido** *nm* (*dejadez*) carelessness; (*olvido*) negligence.

desde ['desðe] *ad* from; ~ **que** *conj* since; ~ **lejos** from afar; ~ **ahora en adelante** from now onwards; ~ **hace 3 días** for 3 days now; ~ **luego** of course.

desdecirse [desðe'θirse] *vr* (*de promesa*) to go back on one's word.

desdén [des'ðen] *nm* scorn.

desdeñar [desðe'ɲar] *vt* (*despreciar*) to scorn.

desdicha [des'ðitʃa] *nf* (*desgracia*) misfortune; (*infelicidad*) unhappiness; **desdichado, a** *a* (*sin suerte*) unlucky; (*infeliz*) unhappy.

desdoblar [desðo'ßlar] *vt* (*extender*) to spread out; (*desplegar*) to unfold; (*separar en dos*) to split.

desear [dese'ar] *vt* to want, desire, wish for.

desecar [dese'kar] *vt*, ~**se** *vr* to dry up.

desechar [dese'tʃar] *vt* (*basura*) to throw out *or* away; (*ideas*) to reject, discard; **desechos** *nmpl* rubbish *sg*, waste *sg*.

desembalar [desemba'lar] *vt* to unpack.

desembarazado, a [desembara'θaðo, a] *a* (*libre*) clear, free; (*desenvuelto*) free and easy.

desembarazar [desembara'θar] *vt* (*desocupar*) to clear; (*desenredar*) to free; ~**se** *vr*: ~**se de** to free o.s. of, get rid of.

desembarcar [desembar'kar] *vt*, *vi*, ~**se** *vr* to land.

desembocadura [desemboka'ðura] *nf* (*de río*) mouth; (*de calle*) opening.

desembocar [desembo'kar] *vi* to flow into; (*fig*) to result in.

desembolso [desem'bolso] *nm* payment; ~**s** *nmpl* expenses; ~ **inicial** deposit, down payment.

desemejante [deseme'xante] *a* dissimilar, unlike; **desemejanza** *nf* dissimilarity.

desempeñar [desempe'ɲar] *vt* (*cargo*) to hold; (*papel*) to perform; (*lo empeñado*) to redeem; ~**se** *vr* to get out of debt; ~ **un papel** (*fig*) to play (a role).

desempeño [desem'peɲo] *nm* redeeming; (*de cargo*) occupation; (*TEATRO*, *fig*) performance.

desempleado, a [desemple'aðo, a] *nm/f* unemployed person; **desempleo** *nm* unemployment.

desencadenar [desenkaðe'nar] *vt* to unchain; (*ira*) to unleash; ~**se** *vr* to break loose; (*tormenta*) to burst.

desencajar [desenka'xar] *vt* (*hueso*) to put out of joint; (*mandíbula*) to dislocate;

(*mecanismo*, *pieza*) to disconnect, disengage.

desencanto [desen'kanto] *nm* disillusionment.

desenfadado, a [desenfa'ðaðo, a] *a* (*desenvuelto*) uninhibited; (*descarado*) forward; **desenfado** *nm* (*libertad*) freedom; (*comportamiento*) free and easy manner; (*descaro*) forwardness.

desenfrenado, a [desenfre'naðo, a] *a* (*descontrolado*) uncontrolled; (*inmoderado*) unbridled; **desenfreno** *nm* (*vicio*) wildness; (*de las pasiones*) lack of self-control.

desengañar [desenga'ɲar] *vt* to disillusion; ~**se** *vr* to become disillusioned; **desengaño** *nm* disillusionment; (*decepción*) disappointment.

desenlace [desen'laθe] *nm* outcome.

desenmarañar [desenmara'ɲar] *vt* (*desenredar*) to disentangle; (*fig*) to unravel.

desenredar [desenre'ðar] *vt* to resolve; (*intriga*) to unravel; ~**se** *vr* to extricate o.s.

desentenderse [desenten'derse] *vr*: ~ **de** to pretend to be ignorant about; (*apartarse*) to have nothing to do with.

desenterrar [desente'rrar] *vt* to exhume; (*tesoro*, *fig*) to unearth, dig up.

desentrañar [desentra'ɲar] *vt* to disembowel; (*misterio*) to unravel.

desentumecer [desentume'θer] *vt* (*pierna etc*) to stretch; (*DEPORTE*) to loosen up.

desenvoltura [desenßol'tura] *nf* (*libertad*, *gracia*) ease; (*descaro*) free and easy manner; (*desvergüenza*) forwardness.

desenvolver [desenßol'ßer] *vt* (*paquete*) to unwrap; (*madeja*) to disentangle; (*fig*) to develop; ~**se** *vr* (*desarrollarse*) to unfold, develop; (*arreglárselas*) to extricate o.s.

deseo [de'seo] *nm* desire, wish; ~**so, a** *a*: **estar** ~**so de** to be anxious to.

desequilibrado, a [desekili'ßraðo, a] *a* unbalanced.

desertar [deser'tar] *vi* to desert.

desesperación [desespera'θjon] *nf* (*impaciencia*) desperation; (*irritación*) fury. despair;

desesperar [desespe'rar] *vt* to drive to despair; (*exasperar*) to drive to distraction // *vi*: ~ **de** to despair of; ~**se** *vr* to despair, lose hope.

desestimar [desesti'mar] *vt* (*menospreciar*) to have a low opinion of; (*rechazar*) to reject.

desfachatez [desfatʃa'teθ] *nf* (*insolencia*) impudence; (*descaro*) cheek.

desfalco [des'falko] *nm* embezzlement.

desfallecer [desfaʎe'θer] *vi* (*perder las fuerzas*) to become weak; (*desvanecerse*) to faint.

desfavorable [desfaßo'raßle] *a* unfavourable.

desfigurar [desfiɣu'rar] vt (cara) to disfigure; (cuerpo) to deform.

desfilar [desfi'lar] vi to parade; **desfile** nm procession.

desgaire [des'ɣaire] nm (desaliño, desgano) slovenliness; (menosprecio) disdain.

desgajar [desɣa'xar] vt (arrancar) to tear off; (romper) to break off; ~**se** vr to come off.

desgana [des'ɣana] nf (falta de apetito) loss of appetite; (renuencia) unwillingness; **desganarse** vr to lose one's appetite; (cansarse) to become bored.

desgarrar [desɣa'rrar] vt to tear (up); (fig) to shatter; **desgarro** nm (muscular) tear; (aflicción) grief; (descaro) impudence.

desgastar [desɣas'tar] vt (deteriorar) to wear away or down; (estropear) to spoil; ~**se** vr to get worn out; **desgaste** nm wear (and tear); (MED) weakening, decline.

desgracia [des'ɣraθja] nf misfortune; (accidente) accident; (vergüenza) disgrace; (contratiempo) setback; **por** ~ unfortunately.

desgraciado, a [desɣra'θjaðo, a] a (infortunado) unlucky, unfortunate; (miserable) wretched; (infeliz) miserable; (feo) ugly; (desagradable) unpleasant.

desgreñado, a [desɣre'ɲaðo, a] a dishevelled.

deshacer [desa'θer] vt (casa) to break up; (dañar) to damage; (TEC) to take apart; (enemigo) to defeat; (diluir) to melt; (contrato) to break; (intriga) to solve; ~**se** vr (disolverse) to melt; (despedazarse) to come apart or undone; ~**se de** to get rid of; ~**se en lágrimas** to burst into tears.

deshecho, a [des'etʃo, a] a undone.

deshelar [dese'lar] vt (cañería) to thaw; (heladera) to defrost.

desheredar [desere'ðar] vt to disinherit.

deshielo [des'jelo] nm (de cañería) thaw; (de heladera) defrosting.

deshilar [desi'lar] vt (tela) to unravel.

deshonesto, a [deso'nesto, a] a indecent.

deshonra [des'onra] nf (deshonor) dishonour; (vergüenza) shame; **deshonrar** vt to dishonour; (insultar) to insult.

deshora [des'ora]: **a** ~ ad at the wrong time.

desierto, a [de'sjerto, a] a (casa, calle, negocio) deserted // nm desert.

designar [desiɣ'nar] vt (nombrar) to designate; (indicar) to fix.

designio [de'siɣnjo] nm (proyecto) plan; (destino) fate.

desigual [desi'ɣwal] a (terreno) uneven; (lucha etc) unequal.

desilusión [desilu'sjon] nf disappointment, disillusionment; **desilusionar** vt to disappoint; **desilusionarse** vr to become disillusioned.

desinfectar [desinfek'tar] vt to disinfect.

desinflar [desin'flar] vt to deflate.

desintegración [desinteɣra'θjon] nf disintegration.

desinterés [desinte'res] nm (objetividad) disinterestedness; (altruismo) unselfishness.

desistir [desis'tir] vi (renunciar) to stop, desist.

desleal [desle'al] a (infiel) disloyal; ~**tad** nf disloyalty.

deslenguado, a [deslen'gwaðo, a] a (grosero) foul-mouthed.

desligar [desli'ɣar] vt (desatar) to untie, undo; (separar) to separate; ~**se** vr (dos personas) to break up, separate; (de un compromiso) to extricate o.s.

desliz [des'liθ] nm (de coche) skid; (de persona) slip, slide; (fig) lapse; ~**ar** vt to slip, slide; ~**arse** vr (escurrirse: persona) to slip, slide; (coche) to skid; (aguas mansas) to flow gently; (error) to slip in.

deslucido, a [deslu'θiðo, a] a (gen) dull; (torpe) awkward, graceless; (marchitado) tarnished.

deslumbrar [deslum'brar] vt to dazzle.

desmán [des'man] nm (exceso) outrage; (abuso de poder) abuse.

desmandarse [desman'darse] vr (abusarse) to behave badly; (excederse) to get out of hand; (caballo) to bolt.

desmantelar [desmante'lar] vt (deshacer) to dismantle; (casa) to strip.

desmayado, a [desma'jaðo, a] a (sin sentido) unconscious; (carácter) dull; (débil) faint, weak.

desmayar [desma'jar] vi to lose heart; ~**se** vr (MED) to faint; **desmayo** nm (desvanecimiento) faint; (sin conciencia) unconsciousness; (depresión) dejection.

desmedido, a [desme'ðiðo, a] a excessive; **desmedirse** vr to go too far, forget o.s.

desmejorar [desmexo'rar] vt (dañar) to impair, spoil; (MED) to weaken.

desmembrar [desmem'brar] vt (MED) to dismember; (fig) to separate.

desmentir [desmen'tir] vt (contradecir) to contradict; (refutar) to deny // vi: ~ **de** to refute; ~**se** vr to contradict o.s.

desmenuzar [desmenu'θar] vt (deshacer) to crumble; (examinar) to examine closely.

desmerecer [desmere'θer] vt to be unworthy of // vi (deteriorarse) to deteriorate.

desmesurado, a [desmesu'raðo, a] a disproportionate.

desmontar [desmon'tar] vt (deshacer) to dismantle; (tierra) to level // vi to dismount.

desmoralizar [desmorali'θar] vt to demoralize.

desmoronar [desmoro'nar] vt to wear away, erode; ~**se** vr (edificio, dique) to fall into disrepair; (sociedad) to decay; (economía) to decline.

desnivel [desni'βel] nm (de terreno) unevenness; **paso a** ~ (AUTO) flyover.

desnudar [desnu'ðar] vt (desvestir) to

undress; (*despojar*) to strip; ~**se** *vr* (*desvestirse*) to get undressed; **desnudo, a** *a* naked // *nm/f* nude; **desnudo de** devoid *or* bereft of.

desobedecer [desoβeðe'θer] *vt, vi* to disobey; **desobediencia** *nf* disobedience.

desocupación [desokupa'θjon] *nf* (*ocio*) leisure; (*desempleo*) unemployment; **desocupado, a** *a* at leisure; unemployed; (*deshabitado*) empty, vacant; **desocupar** *vt* to vacate.

desodorante [desoðo'rante] *nm* deodorant.

desolación [desola'θjon] *nf* (*lugar*) desolation; (*fig*) grief; **desolar** *vt* to ruin, lay waste; **desolarse** *vr* to grieve.

desorden [des'orðen] *nm* confusion; (*político*) disorder.

desorganizar [desorɣani'θar] *vt* (*desordenar*) to disorganize; (*deshacer*) to disrupt.

desorientar [desorjen'tar] *vt* (*extraviar*) to mislead; (*confundir, desconcertar*) to confuse; ~**se** *vr* (*perderse*) to lose one's way.

despabilado, a [despaβi'laðo, a] *a* (*despierto*) wide-awake; (*fig*) alert, sharp.

despabilar [despaβi'lar] *vt* (*vela*) to snuff; (*el ingenio*) to sharpen; (*fortuna, negocio*) to squander // *vi*, ~**se** *vr* to wake up.

despacio [des'paθjo] *ad* slowly.

despachar [despa't∫ar] *vt* (*negocio*) to do, complete; (*enviar*) to send, dispatch; (*vender*) to sell, deal in; (*billete*) to issue; (*mandar ir*) to send away.

despacho [des'pat∫o] *nm* (*oficina*) office; (*de paquetes*) dispatch; (*venta*) sale; (*comunicación*) message; (*eficacia*) efficiency; (*rapidez*) promptness.

desparramar [desparra'mar] *vt* (*esparcir*) to scatter; (*noticia*) to spread; (*dinero, fortuna*) to squander; (*líquido*) to spill.

despavorido, a [despaβo'riðo, a] *a* terrified.

despectivo, a [despek'tiβo, a] *a* (*despreciativo*) derogatory; (*LING*) pejorative.

despecho [des'pet∫o] *nm* spite; **a** ~ **de** in spite of.

despedazar [despeða'θar] *vt* to tear to pieces.

despedida [despe'ðiða] *nf* (*adios*) farewell; (*de obrero*) sacking.

despedir [despe'ðir] *vt* (*visita*) to see off, show out; (*licenciar: empleado*) to discharge; (*inquilino*) to evict; (*objeto*) to hurl; (*flecha*) to fire; (*olor etc*) to give out *or* off; ~**se** *vr*: ~ **se de** to say goodbye to.

despegar [despe'ɣar] *vt* to unstick // *vi* to take off; ~**se** *vr* to come loose, come unstuck; **despegue** *nm* detachment.

despegue [des'peɣe] *nm* takeoff.

despeinado, a [despei'naðo, a] *a* dishevelled, unkempt.

despejado, a [despe'xaðo, a] *a* (*lugar*) clear, free; (*cielo*) cloudless, clear; (*persona*) wide-awake.

despejar [despe'xar] *vt* (*gen*) to clear; (*misterio*) to clarify, clear up // *vi* (*el tiempo*) to clear; ~**se** *vr* (*tiempo, cielo*) to clear (up); (*misterio*) to become clearer; (*persona*) to relax.

despejo [des'pexo] *nm* (*de casa, calle etc*) brightness; (*desenvoltura*) self-confidence; (*talento, ingenio*) alertness.

despensa [des'pensa] *nf* larder.

despeñadero [despeɲa'ðero] *nm* (*GEO*) cliff, precipice.

desperdicio [desper'ðiθjo] *nm* (*despilfarro*) squandering; (*residuo*) waste.

desperezarse [despere'θarse] *vr* to stretch (o.s.).

desperfecto [desper'fekto] *nm* (*deterioro*) slight damage; (*defecto*) flaw, imperfection.

despertador [desperta'ðor] *nm* alarm clock.

despertar [desper'tar] *vt* (*persona*) to wake up; (*vocación*) to awaken; (*recuerdos*) to revive; (*apetito*) to arouse // *vi*, ~**se** *vr* to awaken, wake up // *nm* awakening.

despido [des'piðo] *nm* dismissal, sacking.

despierto *etc vb ver* **despertar**.

despierto, a [des'pjerto, a] *a* awake; (*fig*) sharp, alert.

despilfarro [despil'farro] *nm* (*derroche*) squandering; (*lujo desmedido*) extravagance.

despistar [despis'tar] *vt* to throw off the track *or* scent; (*fig*) to mislead, confuse; ~**se** *vr* to take the wrong road; (*fig*) to become confused.

desplazamiento [despɣaθa'mjento] *nm* displacement; ~ **de tierras** landslip.

desplegar [desple'ɣar] *vt* (*tela, papel*) to unfold, open out; (*bandera*) to unfurl.

despoblar [despo'βlar] *vt* (*de gente*) to depopulate.

despojar [despo'xar] *vt* (*alguien: de sus bienes*) to divest of, deprive of; (*casa*) to strip, leave bare; (*alguien: de su cargo*) to strip of; **despojo** *nm* (*acto*) plundering; (*objetos*) plunder, loot; **despojos** *nmpl* waste *sg*; (*rocas, ladrillos*) debris *sg*.

desposado, a [despo'saðo, a] *a*, *nm/f* newly-wed.

desposeer [despose'er] *vt* (*despojar*) to dispossess.

déspota ['despota] *nm* despot.

despreciar [despre'θjar] *vt* (*desdeñar*) to despise, scorn; (*afrentar*) to slight; **desprecio** *nm* scorn, contempt; slight.

desprender [despren'der] *vt* (*separar*) to separate; (*desatar*) to unfasten; (*olor*) to give off; ~**se** *vr* (*botón: caerse*) to fall off; (: *abrirse*) to unfasten; (*olor, perfume*) to be given off; ~**se de** to follow from; **se desprende que** it transpires that.

desprendimiento [desprendi'mjento] *nm* (*gen*) loosening; (*de botón que se cae*) detachment; (*de botón que se abre*)

unfastening; *(generosidad)* disinterestedness; *(indiferencia)* detachment; *(de gas)* release; *(de tierra, rocas)* landslide.

despreocupado, a [despreoku'paðo, a] *a* *(sin preocupación)* unworried, nonchalant; *(desprejuiciado)* impartial; *(negligente)* careless; **despreocuparse** *vr* to be carefree; **despreocuparse de** to have no interest in.

desprevenido, a [despreβe'niðo, a] *a (no preparado)* unprepared, unready.

desproporción [despropor'θjon] *nf* disproportion, lack of proportion.

después [des'pwes] *ad* afterwards, later; *(próximo paso)* next; ~ **de comer** after lunch; **un año** ~ a year later; ~ **se debatió el tema** next the matter was discussed; ~ **de corregido el texto** after the text had been corrected; ~ **de todo** after all.

desquite [des'kite] *nm (satisfacción)* satisfaction; *(venganza)* revenge.

destacar [desta'kar] *vt* to emphasize, point up; *(MIL)* to detach, detail // *vi,* ~**se** *vr (resaltarse)* to stand out; *(persona)* to be outstanding *or* exceptional.

destajo [des'taxo] *nm:* **trabajar a** ~ to do piecework.

destapar [desta'par] *vt (gen)* to open; *(cacerola)* to take the lid off, uncover; ~**se** *vr (revelarse)* to reveal one's true character.

destartalado, a [destarta'laðo, a] *a (desordenado)* untidy; *(ruinoso)* tumbledown.

destello [des'teʎo] *nm (de estrella)* twinkle; *(de faro)* signal light.

destemplado, a [destem'plaðo, a] *a (MUS)* out of tune; *(voz)* harsh; *(MED)* out of sorts, indisposed.

desteñir [deste'nir] *vt* to fade // *vi,* ~**se** *vr (color)* to fade; **esta tela no destiñe** this fabric will not run.

desterrar [deste'rrar] *vt (exilar)* to exile; *(fig)* to banish, dismiss.

destierro [des'tjerro] *nm* exile.

destilación [destila'θjon] *nf* distillation; **destilar** *vt* to distil; **destilería** *nf* distillery.

destinar [desti'nar] *vt* to destine; *(funcionario)* to appoint, assign; *(fondos)* to set aside *(a for);* ~**se** *vr* to be destined.

destinatario, a [destina'tarjo, a] *nm/f* addressee.

destino [des'tino] *nm (suerte)* destiny; *(de viajero)* destination; *(función)* use.

destituir [destitu'ir] *vt* to dismiss.

destornillador [destorniʎa'ðor] *nm* screwdriver; **destornillar** *vt,* **destornillarse** *vr (tornillo)* to unscrew.

destreza [des'treθa] *nf (habilidad)* skill; *(maña)* dexterity; *(facilidad)* handiness.

destrozar [destro'θar] *vt (romper)* to smash, break (up); *(estropear)* to ruin; *(deshacer)* to shatter; *(el corazón)* to break.

destrozo [des'troθo] *nm (acción)*

destruction; *(desastre)* smashing; ~**s** *nmpl (pedazos)* pieces; *(daños)* havoc *sg.*

destrucción [destruk'θjon] *nf* destruction.

destruir [destru'ir] *vt* to destroy.

desunir [desu'nir] *vt* to separate; *(TEC)* to disconnect; *(fig)* to cause a quarrel *or* rift between.

desusado, a [desu'saðo, a] *a (anticuado)* obsolete.

desvalido, a [desβa'liðo, a] *a (desprotegido)* destitute; *(POL)* underprivileged; *(sin fuerzas)* helpless.

desván [des'βan] *nm* attic.

desvanecer [desβane'θer] *vt (disipar)* to dispel; *(borrar)* to blur; ~**se** *vr (humo)* to vanish, disappear; *(color)* to fade; *(recuerdo)* to fade away.

desvanecimiento [desβaneθi'mjento] *nm (desaparición)* disappearance; *(de colores)* fading; *(evaporación)* evaporation; *(MED)* fainting fit.

desvariar [desβa'rjar] *vi (enfermo)* to be delirious; **desvarío** *nm* delirium.

desvelar [desβe'lar] *vt* to keep awake; ~**se** *vr* to stay awake; *(fig)* to be vigilant *or* watchful; **desvelo** *nm* lack of sleep; *(insomnio)* sleeplessness; *(fig)* vigilance.

desventaja [desβen'taxa] *nf* disadvantage.

desventura [desβen'tura] *nf* misfortune.

desvergonzado, a [desβerɣon'θaðo, a] *a* shameless.

desvergüenza [desβer'ɣwenθa] *nf (descaro)* shamelessness; *(insolencia)* impudence; *(mala conducta)* effrontery.

desviación [desβja'θjon] *nf* deviation.

desviar [des'βjar] *vt* to turn aside; *(río)* to alter the course of; *(navío)* to divert, reroute; *(conversación)* to sidetrack; ~**se** *vr (apartarse del camino)* / to turn aside, deviate; *(: barco)* to go off course.

desvío [des'βio] *nm (desviación)* detour, diversion; *(fig)* indifference.

desvirtuar [desβir'twar] *vt,* ~**se** *vr* to spoil.

desvivirse [desβi'βirse] *vr:* ~ **por** to long for, crave for.

detallar [deta'ʎar] *vt* to detail; *(COM)* to sell retail.

detalle [de'taʎe] *nm* detail; *(fig)* gesture, token; **al** ~ in detail.

detallista [deta'ʎista] *nm/f* retailer.

detener [dete'ner] *vt (tren, persona)* to stop; *(JUR)* to arrest; *(objeto)* to keep; ~**se** *vr* to stop; *(demorarse):* ~**se en** to delay over, linger over.

detenido, a [dete'niðo, a] *a (preso)* arrested, under arrest; *(minucioso)* detailed; *(tímido)* timid // *nm/f* person under arrest, prisoner.

detergente [deter'xente] *nm* detergent.

deteriorar [deterjo'rar] *vt* to spoil, damage; ~**se** *vr* to deteriorate; *(relaciones)* to become damaged; **deterioro** *nm* deterioration.

determinación [determina'θjon] *nf (empeño)* determination; *(decisión)* decision; **determinar** vt (plazo) to fix; (precio) to settle; **determinarse** vr to decide.

detestar [detes'tar] vt to detest.

detonar [deto'nar] vi to detonate.

detrás [de'tras] ad behind; (atrás) at the back; ~ **de** behind.

detrimento [detri'mento] nm harm, damage; **en** ~ **de** to the detriment of.

deuda ['deuða] nf (condición) indebtedness, debt; (cantidad) debt.

deudor, a [deu'ðor, a] a: **saldo** ~ debit balance // nm/f debtor.

devaluación [deßalwa'θjon] nf devaluation.

devastar [deßas'tar] vt (destruir) to devastate.

devoción [deßo'θjon] nf devotion.

devolución [deßolu'θjon] nf devolution; (reenvío) return, sending back; (reembolso) repayment.

devolver [deßol'ßer] vt (gen) to return; (carta al correo) to send back; (com) to repay, refund; (visita, la palabra) to return.

devorar [deßo'rar] vt to devour.

devoto, a [de'ßoto, a] a devout // nm/f admirer.

di vb ver **dar; decir.**

día ['dia] nm day; ¿**qué** ~ **es?** what's the date?; **estar/poner al** ~ to be/keep up to date; **el** ~ **de hoy/de mañana** today/tomorrow; **al** ~ **siguiente** on the following day; **vivir al** ~ to live from hand to mouth; **de** ~ by day, in daylight; **en pleno** ~ in full daylight.

diablo ['djaßlo] nm devil; **diablura** nf prank; **diabluras** nfpl mischief sg.

diabólico, a [dja'ßoliko, a] a diabolical.

diafragma [dja'fraxma] nm diaphragm.

diagnosis [djax'nosis] nf, **diagnóstico** [djax'nostiko] nm diagnosis.

dialecto [dja'lekto] nm dialect.

diálogo ['djaloxo] nm dialogue.

diamante [dja'mante] nm diamond.

diapositiva [djaposi'tißa] nf (foto) slide, transparency.

diario, a ['djarjo, a] a daily // nm newspaper.

diarrea [dja'rrea] nf diarrhoea.

dibujar [dißu'xar] vt to draw, sketch; **dibujo** nm drawing; **dibujos animados** cartoons.

diccionario [dikθjo'narjo] nm dictionary.

dice etc vb ver **decir.**

diciembre [di'θjembre] nm December.

dictado [dik'taðo] nm dictation.

dictador [dikta'ðor] nm dictator; **dictadura** nf dictatorship.

dictamen [dik'tamen] nm (opinión) opinion; (juicio) judgment.

dicho, a ['ditʃo, a] pp de **decir** // a: **en** ~**s países** in the aforementioned countries // nm saying // nf happiness.

diente ['djente] nm (anat, tec) tooth; (zool) fang; (: de elefante) tusk; (de ajo) clove; **da** ~ **con** ~ his teeth are

chattering; **hablar entre** ~**s** to mutter, mumble.

dieron vb ver **dar.**

diesel ['disel] a: **motor** ~ diesel engine.

dieta ['djeta] nf diet.

diez [djeθ] num ten.

diferencia [dife'renθja] nf difference; **diferenciar** vt to differentiate between // vi to differ; **diferenciarse** vr to differ, be different; (distinguirse) to distinguish o.s.

diferente [dife'rente] a different.

difícil [di'fiθil] a difficult.

dificultad [difikul'taθ] nf difficulty; (problema) trouble.

dificultar [difikul'tar] vt (complicar) to complicate, make difficult; (estorbar) to obstruct.

difundir [difun'dir] vt (esparcir) to spread, diffuse; (divulgar) to divulge; ~**se** vr to spread (out).

difunto, a [di'funto, a] a dead, deceased // nm/f deceased (person).

digerir [dixe'rir] vt to digest; (fig) to absorb.

digital [dixi'tal] a digital.

dignarse [dix'narse] vr to deign to.

dignidad [dixni'ðaθ] nf dignity; (honra) honour.

digno, a ['dixno, a] a worthy.

digo etc vb ver **decir.**

dije etc vb ver **decir.**

dilatación [dilata'θjon] nf (expansión) dilation.

dilatado, a [dila'taðo, a] a dilated; (ancho) widened; (largo) long drawn-out; (extenso) extensive.

dilatar [dila'tar] vt (cuerpo) to dilate; (prolongar) to stretch; (en el tiempo) to prolong.

dilema [di'lema] nm dilemma.

diligencia [dili'xenθja] nf diligence; (ocupación) errand, job; ~**s** nfpl (jur) formalities; **diligente** a diligent.

diluir [dilu'ir] vt to dilute.

diluvio [di'lußjo] nm deluge, flood.

dimensión [dimen'sjon] nf dimension.

diminuto, a [dimi'nuto, a] a tiny.

dimitir [dimi'tir] vi to resign.

dimos vb ver **dar.**

Dinamarca [dina'marka] nf Denmark; **dinamarqués, esa** a Danish // nm/f Dane.

dinámico, a [di'namiko, a] a dynamic.

dinamita [dina'mita] nf dynamite.

dínamo ['dinamo] nf dynamo.

dineral [dine'ral] nm large sum of money, fortune.

dinero [di'nero] nm money; ~ **efectivo** cash, ready cash.

dio vb ver **dar.**

dios [djos] nm god.

diosa ['djosa] nf goddess.

diplomacia [diplo'maθja] nf diplomacy; (fig) tact; **diplomático, a** a diplomatic // nm/f diplomat.

diputado, a [dipu'taðo, a] *nm/f* delegate; (*Cortes*) deputy.
diré *etc vb ver* **decir.**
dirección [direk'θjon] *nf* direction; (*señas*) address; (*AUTO*) steering; (*gerencia*) management; (*POL*) leadership; ~ **única** *o* **obligatoria** *o* **prohibida** one-way.
directo, a [di'rekto, a] *a* direct; **transmitir en** ~ to broadcast live.
director, a [direk'tor, a] *a* leading // *nm/f* director; ~ **de cine/de escena** producer/stage manager.
dirigir [diri'xir] *vt* to direct; (*carta*) to address; (*obra de teatro, film*) to produce, direct; (*coche, barco*) to steer; (*avión*) to fly; (*MUS*) to conduct; (*comercio*) to manage; ~**se** *vr*: ~**se a** to go towards, make one's way towards; (*fig*) to speak to.
discernir [disθer'nir] *vt* (*distinguir, discriminar*) to discern.
disciplina [disθi'plina] *nf* discipline; **disciplinar** *vt* to discipline.
discípulo, a [dis'θipulo, a] *nm/f* disciple.
disco ['disko] *nm* disc; (*DEPORTE*) discus; (*TELEC*) dial; (*AUTO*) signal; (*fam*) boring affair; ~ **de larga duración/de duración extendida** long-playing record (L.P.)/extended play record (E.P.); ~ **de freno** brake disc.
discordia [dis'korðja] *nf* discord.
discoteca [disko'teka] *nf* discotheque.
discreción [diskre'θjon] *nf* discretion; (*reserva*) prudence; (*secreto) secrecy;* **comer a** ~ to eat as much as one wishes; **discrecional** *a* (*facultativo*) discretionary.
discrepancia [diskre'panθja] *nf* (*diferencia*) discrepancy; (*desacuerdo*) disagreement.
discreto, a [dis'kreto, a] *a* (*diplomático*) discreet; (*sensato*) sensible; (*listo*) shrewd; (*reservado*) quiet; (*sobrio*) sober; (*retraído*) unobtrusive; (*razonable*) reasonable.
discriminación [diskrimina'θjon] *nf* discrimination.
disculpa [dis'kulpa] *nf* excuse; (*pedir perdón*) apology; **disculpar** *vt* to excuse, pardon; **disculparse** *vr* to excuse o.s.; to apologize.
discurrir [disku'rrir] *vt* to invent // *vi* (*pensar, reflexionar*) to think, meditate; (*recorrer*) to roam, wander; (*el tiempo*) to pass, flow by.
discurso [dis'kurso] *nm* speech; (*razonamiento*) reasoning power.
discutir [disku'tir] *vt* (*debatir*) to discuss; (*pelear*) to argue about; (*contradecir*) to contradict.
diseminar [disemi'nar] *vt* to disseminate, spread.
diseño [di'seɲo] *nm* (*dibujo*) design.
disfraz [dis'fraθ] *nm* (*máscara*) disguise; (*excusa*) pretext; ~**ar** *vt* to disguise; ~**arse** *vr*: ~**arse de** to disguise o.s. as.
disfrutar [disfru'tar] *vt* to enjoy // *vi* to enjoy o.s.; ~ **de** to enjoy, possess.
disgustar [disxus'tar] *vt* (*no gustar*) to displease; (*contrariar, enojar*) to annoy,

upset; ~**se** *vr* to be annoyed; (*dos personas*) to fall out.
disgusto [dis'xusto] *nm* (*repugnancia*) disgust; (*contrariedad*) annoyance; (*tristeza*) grief; (*riña*) quarrel; (*avería*) misfortune.
disidente [disi'ðente] *nm* dissident.
disimular [disimu'lar] *vt* (*ocultar*) to hide, conceal; (*perdonar*) to excuse // *vi* to dissemble.
disipar [disi'par] *vt* to dispel; (*fortuna*) to squander; ~**se** *vr* (*nubes*) to vanish; (*indisciplinarse*) to dissipate.
disminución [disminu'θjon] *nf* diminution.
disminuir [disminu'ir] *vt* (*acortar*) to decrease; (*achicar*) to diminish; (*estrechar*) to lessen.
disoluto, a [diso'luto, a] *a* dissolute.
disolver [disol'βer] *vt* (*gen*) to dissolve; ~**se** *vr* to be dissolved.
disparar [dispa'rar] *vt, vi* to shoot, fire.
disparate [dispa'rate] *nm* (*tontería*) foolish remark; (*error*) blunder.
disparo [dis'paro] *nm* shot.
dispensar [dispen'sar] *vt* to dispense; (*disculpar*) to excuse.
dispersar [disper'sar] *vt* to disperse; ~**se** *vr* to scatter.
disponer [dispo'ner] *vt* (*arreglar*) to arrange; (*ordenar*) to put in order; (*preparar*) to prepare, get ready // *vi*: ~ **de** to have, own; ~**se** *vr*: ~**se para** to prepare to, prepare for.
disponible [dispo'niβle] *a* available.
disposición [disposi'θjon] *nf* arrangement, disposition; (*aptitud*) aptitude; **a la** ~ **de** at the disposal of.
dispuesto, a [dis'pwesto, a] *pp de* **disponer** // *a* (*arreglado*) arranged; (*preparado*) disposed.
disputar [dispu'tar] *vt* (*discutir*) to dispute, question; (*contender*) to contend for // *vi* to argue.
distanciar [distan'θjar] *vt* to space out; ~**se** *vr* to become estranged.
distante [dis'tante] *a* distant.
diste, disteis *vb ver* **dar.**
distinción [distin'θjon] *nf* (*gen*) distinction; (*claridad*) clarity; (*elegancia*) elegance; (*honor*) honour.
distinguir [distin'gir] *vt* to distinguish; (*escoger*) to single out; ~**se** *vr* to be distinguished.
distinto, a [dis'tinto, a] *a* different; (*claro*) clear.
distracción [distrak'θjon] *nf* (*pasatiempo*) hobby, pastime; (*olvido*) absent-mindedness, distraction.
distraer [distra'er] *vt* (*entretener*) to entertain; (*divertir*) to amuse; (*fondos*) to embezzle; ~**se** *vr* (*entretenerse*) to amuse o.s.; (*perder la concentración*) to allow one's attention to wander.
distraído, a [distra'iðo, a] *a* (*gen*) absent-minded; (*entretenido*) amusing.
distribuir [distriβu'ir] *vt* to distribute.

distrito [dis'trito] nm (sector, territorio) region; (barrio) district.
disturbio [dis'turβjo] nm disturbance.
disuadir [diswa'ðir] vt to dissuade.
disuelto [di'swelto] pp de **disolver.**
divagar [diβa'xar] vi (desviarse) to digress; (errar) to wander.
diván [di'βan] nm divan.
divergencia [diβer'xenθja] nf divergence.
diversidad [diβersi'ðað] nf diversity, variety.
diversificar [diβersifi'kar] vt to diversify.
diversión [diβer'sjon] nf (gen) entertainment; (actividad) hobby, pastime.
diverso, a [di'βerso, a] a diverse; ~s sundry.
divertir [diβer'tir] vt (entretener, recrear) to amuse, entertain; (apartar, distraer) to divert; ~se vr (pasarlo bien) to have a good time; (distraerse) to amuse o.s.
dividir [diβi'ðir] vt (gen) to divide; (separar) to separate; (distribuir) to distribute, share out.
divino, a [di'βino, a] a divine.
divisa [di'βisa] nf (emblema, moneda) emblem, badge; ~s nfpl currency sg.
división [diβi'sjon] nf (gen) division; (de partido) split; (de país) partition; (LING) hyphen; (divergencia) divergence.
divorciar [diβor'θjar] vt to divorce; ~se vr to get divorced; **divorcio** nm divorce.
divulgar [diβul'xar] vt (desparramar) to spread; (hacer circular) to divulge, circulate; ~se vr to leak out.
doblar [do'βlar] vt (gen) to double; (papel) to fold; (caño) to bend; (la esquina) to turn, go round; (film) to dub // vi to turn; (campana) to toll; ~se vr (plegarse) to fold (up), crease; (encorvarse) to bend; ~se de risa/dolor to be doubled up with laughter/pain.
doble ['doβle] a (gen) double; (de dos aspectos) dual; (fig) two-faced // nm double; (campana) toll(ing); ~s nmpl (DEPORTE) doubles sg // nm/f (TEATRO) double, stand-in; con ~ sentido with a double meaning.
doblegar [doβle'xar] vt to fold, crease; ~se vr to yield.
doce ['doθe] num twelve.
docena [do'θena] nf dozen.
dócil ['doθil] a (pasivo) docile; (obediente) obedient.
doctor, a [dok'tor, a] nm/f doctor.
doctrina [dok'trina] nf doctrine, teaching.
documentación [dokumenta'θjon] nf documentation, papers pl.
documento [doku'mento] nm (certificado) document.
dólar ['dolar] nm dollar.
doler [do'ler] vt, vi to hurt; (fig) to grieve; ~se vr (de su situación) to grieve, feel sorry; (de las desgracias ajenas) to sympathize; me duele el brazo my arm hurts.
dolor [do'lor] nm pain; (fig) grief, sorrow.

domar [do'mar], **domesticar** [domesti'kar] vt to tame.
domicilio [domi'θiljo] nm home; ~ particular private residence; ~ social head office.
dominante [domi'nante] a dominant; (person) domineering.
dominar [domi'nar] vt (gen) to dominate; (idiomas etc) to have a command of // vi to dominate, prevail; ~se vr to control o.s.
domingo [do'mingo] nm Sunday.
dominio [do'minjo] nm (tierras) domain; (autoridad) power, authority; (de las pasiones) grip, hold; (de varios idiomas) command.
don [don] nm (talento) gift; ~ Juan Gómez Mr Juan Gomez or Juan Gomez Esq.
donaire [do'naire] nm charm.
doncella [don'θeʎa] nf (criada) maid; (muchacha) girl.
donde ['donde] ad where // prep: el coche está allí ~ el farol the car is over there by the lamppost or where the lamppost is; por ~ through which; en ~ where, in which.
dónde ['donde] ad interr where?; ¿a ~ vas? where are you going (to)?; ¿de ~ vienes? where have you come from?; ¿por ~? where?, whereabouts?
dondequiera [donde'kjera] ad anywhere; por ~ everywhere, all over the place // conj: ~ que wherever.
doña ['dona] nf título de mujer que no se traduce.
dorado, a [do'raðo, a] a (color) golden; (TEC) gilt.
dormir [dor'mir] vt: ~ la siesta por la tarde to have an afternoon nap // vi to sleep; ~se vr to go to sleep.
dormitar [dormi'tar] vi to doze.
dormitorio [dormi'torjo] nm bedroom; ~ común dormitory.
dos [dos] num two.
dosis ['dosis] nf inv dose, dosage.
dotado, a [do'taðo, a] a gifted; ~ de endowed with.
dotar [do'tar] vt to endow; dote nf dowry; dotes nfpl gifts.
doy vb ver **dar.**
drama ['drama] nm drama.
dramaturgo [drama'turxo] nm dramatist, playwright.
droga ['droxa] nf drug.
drogadicto, a [droxa'ðikto, a] nm/f drug addict.
ducha ['dutʃa] nf (baño) shower; (MED) douche; **ducharse** vr to take a shower.
duda ['duða] nf doubt.
dudoso, a [du'ðoso, a] a (incierto) hesitant; (sospechoso) doubtful.
duelo ['dwelo] nm (combate) duel; (luto) mourning.
duende ['dwende] nm imp, goblin.
dueño, a ['dweno, a] nm/f (propietario)

owner; (*de casa*) landlord/lady; (*empresario*) employer.
duermo *etc vb ver* **dormir**.
dulce ['dulθe] *a* sweet // *ad* gently, softly // *nm* sweet.
dulzura [dul'θura] *nf* sweetness; (*ternura*) gentleness.
duplicar [dupli'kar] *vt* (*hacer el doble de*) to duplicate; ~**se** *vr* to double.
duque ['duke] *nm* duke.
duquesa [du'kesa] *nf* duchess.
duración [dura'θjon] *nf* duration.
duradero, a [dura'ðero, a] *a* lasting.
durante [du'rante] *ad* during.
durar [du'rar] *vi* (*permanecer*) to last; (*recuerdo*) to remain.
dureza [du'reθa] *nf* (*calidad*) hardness.
durmí *etc vb ver* **dormir**.
durmiente [dur'mjente] *nm/f* sleeper.
duro, a ['duro, a] *a* (*gen*) hard; (*carácter*) tough // *ad* hard // *nm* (*moneda*) five peseta coin/note.

E

e [e] *conj* and.
E *abr de* **este**.
ebanista [eβa'nista] *nm* cabinetmaker.
ébano ['eβano] *nm* ebony.
ebrio, a ['eβrjo, a] *a* drunk.
ebullición [eβuʎi'θjon] *nf* boiling; (*fig*) ferment.
eclesiástico, a [ekle'sjastiko, a] *a* ecclesiastical.
eclipse [e'klipse] *nm* eclipse.
eco ['eko] *nm* echo; **tener** ~ to catch on.
ecología [ekolo'xia] *nf* ecology.
economato [ekono'mato] *nm* cooperative store.
economía [ekono'mia] *nf* (*sistema*) economy; (*cualidad*) thrift.
económico, a [eko'nomiko, a] *a* (*barato*) cheap, economical; (*persona*) thrifty; (*COM: plan*) financial; (: *situación*) economic.
economista [ekono'mista] *nm/f* economist.
ecuador [ekwa'ðor] *nm* equator; **el E**~ Ecuador.
ecuánime [e'kwanime] *a* (*carácter*) level-headed; (*estado*) calm.
ecuestre [e'kwestre] *a* equestrian.
echar [e'tʃar] *vt* to throw; (*agua, vino*) to pour (out); (*empleado: despedir*) to fire, sack; (*bigotes*) to grow; (*hojas*) to sprout; (*cartas*) to post; (*humo*) to emit, give out // *vi*: ~ **a correr/llorar** to break into a run/burst into tears; ~**se** *vr* to lie down; ~ **llave a** to lock (up); ~ **abajo** (*gobierno*) to overthrow; (*edificio*) to demolish; ~ **mano a** to lay hands on.
edad [e'ðað] *nf* age; ¿**qué** ~ **tienes?** how old are you?; **tiene ocho años de** ~ he is eight (years old); **de** ~ **mediana/avanzada** middle-aged/ advanced in years; **la E**~ **Media** the Middle Ages.

edición [eði'θjon] *nf* (*acto*) publication; (*ejemplar*) edition.
edicto [e'ðikto] *nm* edict, proclamation.
edificio [eði'fiθjo] *nm* building; (*fig*) edifice, structure.
editar [eði'tar] *vt* (*publicar*) to publish; (*preparar textos*) to edit.
editor, a [eði'tor, a] *nm/f* (*que publica*) publisher; (*de periódico etc*) editor // *a*: **casa** ~**a** publishing house; ~**ial** *a* editorial // *nm* leading article, editorial; **casa** ~**ial** publishing house.
educación [eðuka'θjon] *nf* education; (*crianza*) upbringing; (*modales*) (good) manners *pl*.
educar [eðu'kar] *vt* to educate; (*criar*) to bring up; (*voz*) to train.
EE. UU. *nmpl abr de* **Estados Unidos** USA (United States of America).
efectivo, a [efek'tiβo, a] *a* effective; (*real*) actual, real // *nm*: **pagar en** ~ to pay (in) cash; **hacer** ~ **un cheque** to cash a cheque.
efecto [e'fekto] *nm* effect, result; ~**s** *nmpl* goods; (*COM*) assets; **en** ~ in fact; (*respuesta*) exactly, indeed.
efectuar [efek'twar] *vt* to carry out; (*viaje*) to make.
eficacia [efi'kaθja] *nf* (*de persona*) efficiency; (*de medicamento*) effectiveness.
eficaz [efi'kaθ] *a* (*persona*) efficient; (*acción*) effective.
egipcio, a [e'xipθjo, a] *a, nm/f* Egyptian.
Egipto [e'xipto] *nm* Egypt.
egoísmo [eɣo'ismo] *nm* egoism.
egoísta [eɣo'ista] *a* egoistical, selfish // *nm/f* egoist.
egregio, a [e'ɣrexjo, a] *a* eminent, distinguished.
Eire ['eire] *nm* Eire.
ej. *abr de* **ejemplo**.
eje ['exe] *nm* (*GEO, MAT*) axis; (*de rueda*) axle; (*de máquina*) shaft, spindle; **la idea** ~ the central idea.
ejecución [exeku'θjon] *nf* (*gen*) execution; (*cumplimiento*) fulfilment; (*actuación*) performance; (*JUR: embargo de deudor*) attachment, distraint.
ejecutar [exeku'tar] *vt* (*gen*) to execute, carry out; (*matar*) to execute; (*cumplir*) to fulfil; (*MUS*) to perform; (*JUR: embargar*) to attach, distrain (on).
ejecutivo, a [exeku'tiβo, a] *a* executive; **el poder** ~ the Executive (Power).
ejemplar [exem'plar] *a* exemplary // *nm* example; (*ZOOL*) specimen; (*de libro*) copy; (*de periódico*) number, issue.
ejemplo [e'xemplo] *nm* example; **por** ~ for example.
ejercer [exer'θer] *vt* to exercise; (*influencia*) to exert; (*un oficio*) to practise // *vi* (*practicar*) to practise (*de* as); (*tener oficio*) to hold office.
ejercicio [exer'θiθjo] *nm* exercise; (*período*) tenure; ~ **comercial** financial year.
ejército [e'xerθito] *nm* army; **entrar en**

el ~ to join the army, join up.
el [el] *det* the.
él [el] *pron* (*persona*) he; (*cosa*) it; (*después de prep: persona*) him; (: *cosa*) it.
elaborar [elaβo'rar] *vt* to elaborate; (*hacer*) to make; (*preparar*) to prepare; (*trabajar*) to work; (*calcular*) to work out.
elasticidad [elastiθi'ðað] *nf* elasticity; **elástico, a** *a* elastic; (*flexible*) flexible // *nm* elastic.
elección [elek'θjon] *nf* election; (*selección*) choice, selection.
electorado [elekto'raðo] *nm* electorate, voters *pl.*
electricidad [elektriθi'ðað] *nf* electricity.
electricista [elektri'θista] *nm/f* electrician.
eléctrico, a [e'lektriko, a] *a* electric // *nm* electric train.
electrizar [elektri'θar] *vt* to electrify.
electro... [elektro] *pref* electro...; ~**cardiógrafo** *nm* electrocardiograph; ~**cución** *nf* electrocution; ~**cutar** *vt* to electrocute; ~**chapado, a** *a* electroplated; **electrodo** *nm* electrode; ~**domésticos** *nmpl* (electrical) household appliances; ~**imán** *nm* electromagnet; ~**magnético, a** *a* electromagnetic; ~**motor** *nm* electric motor.
electrónico, a [elek'troniko, a] *a* electronic // *nf* electronics *sg.*
electrotecnia [elektro'teknja] *nf* electrical engineering; **electrotécnico, a** *nm/f* electrical engineer.
electrotermo [elektro'termo] *nm* immersion heater.
elefante [ele'fante] *nm* elephant; ~ **marino** elephant seal.
elegancia [ele'ɣanθja] *nf* (*gracia*) elegance, grace; (*estilo*) stylishness; **elegante** *a* elegant, graceful; stylish, fashionable.
elegía [ele'xia] *nf* elegy.
elegir [ele'xir] *vt* (*escoger*) to choose, select; (*optar*) to opt for; (*presidente*) to elect.
elemental [elemen'tal] *a* (*claro, obvio*) elementary; (*fundamental*) elemental, fundamental.
elemento [ele'mento] *nm* element; (*fig*) ingredient; ~**s** *nmpl* elements, rudiments.
elevación [eleβa'θjon] *nf* elevation; (*acto*) raising, lifting; (*de precios*) rise; (*GEO etc*) height, altitude; (*de persona*) loftiness; (*pey*) conceit, pride.
elevar [ele'βar] *vt* to raise, lift (up); (*precio*) to put up; ~**se** *vr* (*edificio*) to rise; (*precios*) to go up; (*transportarse, enajenarse*) to get carried away; (*engreírse*) to become conceited.
eliminar [elimi'nar] *vt* to eliminate, remove.
eliminatoria [elimina'torja] *nf* heat, preliminary (round).
elite [e'lite] *nf* elite.
elocuencia [elo'kwenθja] *nf* eloquence.
elogiar [elo'xjar] *vt* to praise, eulogize;

elogio *nm* praise; (*tributo*) tribute.
eludir [elu'ðir] *vt* (*evitar*) to avoid, evade; (*escapar*) to escape, elude.
ella ['eʎa] *pron* (*persona*) she; (*cosa*) it; (*después de prep: persona*) her; (: *cosa*) it.
ellas ['eʎas] *pron* (*personas y cosas*) they; (*después de prep*) them.
ello ['eʎo] *pron* it.
ellos ['eʎos] *pron* they; (*después de prep*) them.
emanar [ema'nar] *vi*: ~ **de** to emanate from, come from; (*derivar de*) to originate in.
emancipar [emanθi'par] *vt* to emancipate; ~**se** *vr* to become emancipated, free o.s.
embadurnar [embaður'nar] *vt* to smear.
embajada [emba'xaða] *nf* embassy; (*mensaje*) message, errand.
embajador, a [embaxa'ðor, a] *nm/f* ambassador/ambassadress.
embalar [emba'lar] *vt* (*envolver*) to parcel, wrap (up); (*envasar*) to package // *vi* to sprint.
embarazada [embara'θaða] *a* pregnant // *nf* pregnant woman.
embarazar [embara'θar] *vt* to obstruct, hamper; (*a una mujer*) to make pregnant; ~**se** *vr* (*aturdirse*) to become embarrassed; (*confundirse*) to get into a muddle; (*mujer*) to become pregnant.
embarazo [emba'raθo] *nm* (*de mujer*) pregnancy; (*impedimento*) obstacle, obstruction; (*timidez*) embarrassment.
embarcación [embarka'θjon] *nf* (*barco*) boat, craft; (*acto*) embarkation.
embarcadero [embarka'ðero] *nm* pier, landing stage.
embarcar [embar'kar] *vt* (*cargamento*) to ship, stow; (*persona*) to embark, put on board; ~**se** *vr* to embark, go on board.
embargar [embar'ɣar] *vt* (*impedir*) to impede, hinder; (*JUR*) to seize, impound.
embarque [em'barke] *nm* shipment, loading.
embaular [embau'lar] *vt* to pack (into a trunk); (*fig*) to stuff o.s. with.
embebecerse [embeβe'θerse] *vr* (*extasiarse*) to be lost in wonder, be amazed.
embeber [embe'βer] *vt* (*absorber*) to absorb, soak up; (*empapar*) to saturate // *vi* to shrink; ~**se** *vr*: ~**se en la lectura** to be engrossed or absorbed in a book.
embellecer [embeʎe'θer] *vt* to embellish, beautify.
embestida [embes'tiða] *nf* attack, onslaught; (*carga*) charge; **embestir** *vt* to attack, assault; to charge, attack // *vi* to attack.
emblema [em'blema] *nm* emblem.
embobado, a [embo'βaðo, a] *a* (*atontado*) stunned, bewildered.
embocadura [emboka'ðura] *nf* narrow entrance; (*de río*) mouth; (*MUS*) mouthpiece.
émbolo ['embolo] *nm* (*AUTO*) piston.

embolsar [embol'sar] *vt* to pocket, put in one's pocket.

emborrachar [emborra'tʃar] *vt* to intoxicate, make drunk; ~**se** *vr* to get drunk.

emboscada [embos'kaða] *nf* (*celada*) ambush.

embotar [embo'tar] *vt* to blunt, dull; ~**se** *vr* (*adormecerse*) to go numb.

embotellar [embote'ʎar] *vt* to bottle; ~**se** *vr* (*circulación*) to get into a jam.

embozar [embo'θar] *vt* to muffle (up).

embragar [embra'xar] *vi* to let in the clutch.

embrague [em'braxe] *nm* (*también* **pedal de** ~) clutch.

embravecer [embraβe'θer] *vt* to enrage, infuriate; ~**se** *vr* to become furious; (*el mar*) to get rough; (*tormenta*) to rage.

embriagado, a [embrja'xaðo, a] *a* (*emborrachado*) intoxicated, drunk.

embriagar [embrja'xar] *vt* (*emborrachar*) to intoxicate, make drunk; (*alegrar*) to delight; ~**se** *vr* (*emborracharse*) to get drunk.

embriaguez [embrja'xeθ] *nf* (*borrachera*) drunkenness; (*fig*) rapture, delight.

embrollar [embro'ʎar] *vt* (*el asunto*) to confuse, complicate; (*persona*) to involve, embroil; ~**se** *vr* (*confundirse*) to get into a muddle *or* mess; ~**se con uno** to get into an argument with sb.

embrollo [em'broʎo] *nm* (*enredo*) muddle, confusion; (*aprieto*) fix, jam; (*pey: engaño*) fraud; (: *trampa*) trick.

embromar [embro'mar] *vt* (*burlarse de*) to tease, make fun of.

embrutecer [embrute'θer] *vt* (*brutalizar*) to brutalize; (*depravar*) to deprave; (*atontar*) to stupefy; ~**se** *vr* to become brutal; to become depraved.

embudo [em'buðo] *nm* funnel; (*fig*: *engaño*) fraud; (: *trampa*) trick.

embuste [em'buste] *nm* trick; (*impostura*) imposture; (*mentira*) lie; (*hum*) fib; ~**ro, a** *a* lying, deceitful // *nm/f* (*tramposo*) cheat; (*impostor*) impostor; (*mentiroso*) liar; (*hum*) fibber.

embutido [embu'tiðo] *nm* (*CULIN*) sausage; (*TEC*) inlay.

embutir [embu'tir] *vt* (*TEC*) to inlay; (*llenar*) to pack tight, cram, stuff.

emergencia [emer'xenθja] *nf* emergency; (*surgimiento*) emergence.

emerger [emer'xer] *vi* to emerge, appear.

emigración [emixra'θjon] *nf* (*éxodo*) migration; (*destierro*) emigration.

emigrar [emi'xrar] *vi* (*pájaros*) to migrate; (*personas*) to emigrate.

eminencia [emi'nenθja] *nf* eminence; **eminente** *a* eminent, distinguished; (*GEO*) high.

emisario [emi'sarjo] *nm* emissary.

emisión [emi'sjon] *nf* (*acto*) emission; (*COM etc*) issue; (*RADIO, TV*: *acto*) broadcasting; (: *programa*) broadcast, programme.

emisora [emi'sora] *nf* (*de onda corta*) shortwave radio station; (*aparato*) broadcasting station.

emitir [emi'tir] *vt* (*olor etc*) to emit, give off; (*moneda etc*) to issue; (*opinión*) to express; (*RADIO*) to broadcast.

emoción [emo'θjon] *nf* emotion; (*excitación*) excitement; (*turbación*) worry, anxiety.

emocionante [emoθjo'nante] *a* (*excitante*) exciting, thrilling; (*conmovedor*) moving, touching; (*impresionante*) striking, impressive.

emocionar [emoθjo'nar] *vt* (*excitar*) to excite, thrill; (*conmover*) to move, touch; (*impresionar*) to impress.

empacho [em'patʃo] *nm* (*MED*) indigestion; (*fig*) embarrassment.

empalagoso, a [empala'xoso, a] *a* cloying; (*fig*) tiresome.

empalmar [empal'mar] *vt* to join, connect // *vi* (*dos caminos*) to meet, join; **empalme** *nm* joint, connection; junction; (*de trenes*) connection.

empanada [empa'naða] *nf* pie, patty.

empantanarse [empanta'narse] *vr* to get swamped; (*fig*) to get bogged down.

empañar [empa'nar] *vt* (*niño*) to swaddle, wrap up; ~**se** *vr* (*nublarse*) to get misty, steam up.

empapar [empa'par] *vt* (*mojar*) to soak, saturate; (*absorber*) to soak up, absorb; ~**se** *vr*: ~**se de** to soak up.

empapelar [empape'lar] *vt* (*paredes*) to paper; (*envolver con papel*) to wrap (up) in paper.

empaquetar [empake'tar] *vt* to pack, parcel up.

empastar [empas'tar] *vt* (*embadurnar*) to paste; (*diente*) to fill.

empatar [empa'tar] *vi* to draw, tie; **empate** *nm* draw, tie.

empedernido, a [empeðer'niðo, a] *a* hard, heartless; (*fijado*) hardened, inveterate.

empedernir [empeðer'nir] *vt* to harden.

empedrado, a [empe'ðraðo, a] *a* paved // *nm* paving; **empedrar** *vt* to pave.

empeñado, a [empe'ɲaðo, a] *a* (*objeto*) pawned; (*persona*) determined.

empeñar [empe'ɲar] *vt* (*objeto*) to pawn, pledge; (*persona*) to compel; ~**se** *vr* (*obligarse*) to bind o.s., pledge o.s.; (*endeudarse*) to get into debt; ~**se en** to be set on, be determined to.

empeño [em'peɲo] *nm* (*cosa prendada*) pledge; (*determinación*, *insistencia*) determination, insistence; **banco de** ~**s** pawnshop.

empeorar [empeo'rar] *vt* to make worse, worsen // *vi* to get worse, deteriorate.

empequeñecer [empekeɲe'θer] *vt* to dwarf; (*fig*) to belittle.

emperador [empera'ðor] *nm* emperor.

emperatriz [empera'triθ] *nf* empress.

empezar [empe'θar] *vt, vi* to begin, start.

empiezo *etc vb ver* **empezar.**

empinar [empi'nar] *vt* to raise (up) // *vi* (*fam*) to drink, booze (*fam*); ~**se** *vr* (*persona*) to stand on tiptoe; (*animal*) to rear up; (*camino*) to climb steeply; (*edificio*) to tower.

empírico, a [em'piriko, a] *a* empirical.

emplasto [em'plasto], **emplaste** [em-'plaste] *nm* (*MED*) plaster; (: *cataplasma*) poultice; (*componenda*) compromise.

emplazamiento [emplaθa'mjento] *nm* site, location; (*JUR*) summons *sg*.

emplazar [empla'θar] *vt* (*ubicar*) to site, place, locate; (*JUR*) to summons; (*convocar*) to summon.

empleado, a [emple'aðo, a] *nm/f* (*gen*) employee; (*de banco etc*) clerk.

emplear [emple'ar] *vt* (*usar*) to use, employ; (*dar trabajo a*) to employ; ~**se** *vr* (*conseguir trabajo*) to be employed; (*ocuparse*) to occupy o.s.

empleo [em'pleo] *nm* (*puesto*) job; (*puestos: colectivamente*) employment; (*uso*) use, employment.

empobrecer [empoßre'θer] *vt* to impoverish; ~**se** *vr* to become poor *or* impoverished; **empobrecimiento** *nm* impoverishment.

emporio [em'porjo] *nm* emporium, trading centre; (*gran almacén*) department store.

emprender [empren'der] *vt* (*empezar*) to begin, embark on; (*acometer*) to tackle, take on.

empreñar [empre'ɲar] *vt* to make pregnant; ~**se** *vr* to become pregnant.

empresa [em'presa] *nf* enterprise.

empréstito [em'prestito] *nm* (public) loan.

empujar [empu'xar] *vt* to push, shove; **empuje** *nm* thrust; (*presión*) pressure; (*fig*) vigour, drive.

empujón [empu'xon] *nm* push, shove.

empuñar [empu'ɲar] *vt* (*asir*) to grasp, take (firm) hold of.

emular [emu'lar] *vt* to emulate; (*rivalizar*) to rival.

émulo, a ['emulo, a] *nm/f* rival, competitor.

en [en] *prep* (*gen*) in; (*sobre*) on, upon; **meter** ~ **el bolsillo** to put in *or* into one's pocket; (*lugar*): **vivir** ~ **Toledo** to live in Toledo; (*casa*): **casa** at home; (*tiempo*): **lo terminó** ~ **6 días** he finished it in 6 days; ~ **el mes de enero** in the month of January; ~ **aquel momento/aquella época** at that moment/that time; ~ **aquel día/aquella ocasión** on that day/that occasion; ~ **serio** seriously; ~ **fin** well, well then; **ir de puerta** ~ **puerta** to go from door to door; ~ **tren** by train.

enajenación [enaxena'θjon] *nf*, **enajenamiento** [enaxena'mjento] *nm* alienation; (*fig: distracción*) absent-mindedness; (: *embelesamiento*) rapture, trance; (*extrañamiento*) estrangement.

enajenar [enaxe'nar] *vt* to alienate; (*fig*)

to carry away; ~**se** *vr* (*de un bien*) to deprive o.s.; (*amigos*) to become estranged, fall out.

enamorado, a [enamo'raðo, a] *a* in love; **enamorar** *vt* to inspire love; **enamorarse** *vr* to fall in love.

enano, a [e'nano, a] *a* tiny // *nm/f* dwarf.

enardecer [enarðe'θer] *vt* (*pasiones*) to fire, inflame; (*persona*) to fill with enthusiasm; (: *llenar de ira*) to fill with anger; ~**se** *vr* to get excited; (*entusiasmarse*) to get enthusiastic (*por about*); (*de cólera*) to blaze.

encabezamiento [enkaßeθa'mjento] *nm* (*de carta*) heading; (*de periódico*) headline; (*preámbulo*) foreword, preface; (*registro*) roll, register.

encabezar [enkaße'θar] *vt* (*manifestación*) to lead, head; (*lista*) to be at the top of; (*carta*) to put a heading to; (*libro*) to entitle; (*empadronar*) to register.

encadenar [enkaðe'nar] *vt* to chain (together); (*poner grilletes a*) to shackle.

encajar [enka'xar] *vt* (*ajustar*) to fit (into); (*golpe*) to give, deal; (*entrometer*) to insert // *vi* to fit (well); (*fig: corresponder a*) to match; ~**se** *vr* to intrude; ~**se en un sillón** to squeeze into a chair.

encaje [en'kaxe] *nm* (*labor*) lace; (*inserción*) insertion; (*ajuste*) fitting.

encajonar [enkaxo'nar] *vt* to box (up), put in a box.

encaminar [enkami'nar] *vt* to direct, send; ~**se** *vr*: ~**se a** to set out for.

encandilar [enkandi'lar] *vt* to dazzle; (*fuego*) to poke.

encantador, a [enkanta'ðor, a] *a* charming, lovely // *nm/f* magician, enchanter/tress.

encantar [enkan'tar] *vt* to charm, delight; (*hechizar*) to bewitch, cast a spell on; **encanto** *nm* (*magia*) spell, charm; (*fig*) charm, delight.

encarcelar [enkarθe'lar] *vt* to imprison, jail.

encarecer [enkare'θer] *vt* to put up the price of; (*pedir*) tc recommend, urge // *vi*, ~**se** *vr* to get dearer.

encarecimiento [enkareθi'mjento] *nm* price increase; (*pedido insistente*) urging.

encargado, a [enkar'xaðo, a] *a* in charge // *nm/f* agent, representative; (*responsable*) person in charge; ~ **de negocios** chargé d'affaires.

encargar [enkar'xar] *vt* to entrust; (*recomendar*) to urge, recommend; ~**se** *vr*: ~**se de** to look after, take charge of.

encargo [en'karxo] *nm* (*pedido*) assignment, job; (*responsabilidad*) responsibility; (*recomendación*) recommendation; (*COM*) order.

encarnación [enkarna'θjon] *nf* incarnation, embodiment.

encarrilar [enkarri'lar] *vt* to correct, put on the right track; (*tren*) to put back on the rails.

encausar [enkau'sar] *vt* to prosecute, sue.

encauzar [enkau'θar] *vt* to channel.
enceguecer [enθeхe'θer] *vt* to blind // *vi*,
~**se** *vr* to go blind.
encendedor [enθende'dor] *nm* lighter.
encender [enθen'der] *vt* (*con fuego*) to
light; (*incendiar*) to set fire to; (*luz, radio*)
to put on, switch on; (*inflarse*) to inflame;
~**se** *vr* to catch fire; (*excitarse*) to get
excited; (*de cólera*) to flare up; (*el rostro*)
to blush.
encendido [enθen'diðo] *nm* ignition.
encerrar [enθe'rrar] *vt* (*confinar*) to shut
in, shut up; (*comprender, incluir*) to
include, contain.
encía [en'θia] *nf* gum.
encierro [en'θjerro] *nm* shutting in,
shutting up; (*calabozo*) prison.
encima [en'θima] *ad* (*sobre*) above, over;
(*además*) besides; ~ **de** (*en*) on, on top of;
(*sobre*) above, over; (*además de*) besides,
on top of; **por** ~ **de** over; **¿llevas dinero**
~? have you any money on you?; **se me**
vino ~ it got on top of me.
encinta [en'θinta] *a* pregnant.
enclavar [enkla'ßar] *vt* (*clavar*) to nail;
(*atravesar*) to pierce; (*sitio*) to set; (*fig:
fam*) to swindle.
encoger [enko'xer] *vt* (*gen*) to shrink,
contract; (*fig: asustar*) to scare; (:
desanimar) to discourage; ~**se** *vr* to
shrink, contract; (*fig*) to cringe; ~**se de**
hombros to shrug one's shoulders.
encojar [enko'xar] *vt* to lame; (*tullir*) to
cripple; ~**se** *vr* to go lame; to become
crippled.
encolar [enko'lar] *vt* (*engomar*) to glue,
paste; (*pegar*) to stick down.
encolerizar [enkoleri'θar] *vt* to anger,
provoke; ~**se** *vr* to get angry.
encomendar [enkomen'dar] *vt* to entrust,
commend; ~**se** *vr*: ~**se a** to put one's
trust in.
encomiar [enko'mjar] *vt* to praise, pay
tribute to.
encomienda [enko'mjenda] *nf* (*encargo*)
charge, commission; (*precio*) price;
(*elogio*) tribute; ~ **postal** (*AM*) parcel
post.
encomio [en'komjo] *nm* praise, tribute.
enconado, a [enko'naðo, a] *a* (*MED*)
inflamed; (: *dolorido*) sore; (*fig*) angry.
enconar [enko'nar] *vt* (*MED*) to inflame;
(*fig*) to anger, irritate; ~**se** *vr* (*MED*) to
become inflamed; (*fig*) to get angry or
irritated.
encono [en'kono] *nm* (*rencor*) rancour,
spite; (*odio*) ill-feeling.
encontrado, a [enkon'traðo, a] *a*
(*contrario*) contrary, conflicting; (*hostil*)
hostile.
encontrar [enkon'trar] *vt* (*hallar*) to find;
(*inesperadamente*) to meet, run into; ~**se**
vr to meet (each other); (*situarse*) to be
(situated; (*entrar en conflicto*) to crash,
collide; ~**se con** to meet (with); ~**se**
bien de salud to feel well.
encorvar [enkor'ßar] *vt* to curve;

(*inclinar*) to bend (down); ~**se** *vr* to bend
down, bend over, stoop.
encrespar [enkres'par] *vt* (*cabellos*) to
curl; (*agua*) to ripple; (*fig*) to anger,
irritate; ~**se** *vr* (*el mar*) to get rough;
(*fig*) to get annoyed, irritated.
encrucijada [enkruθi'xaða] *nf* crossroads
sg; (*empalme*) junction.
encuadernación [enkwaðerna'θjon] *nf*
binding.
encuadernador, a [enkwaðerna'ðor, a]
nm/f bookbinder.
encuadrar [enkwa'ðrar] *vt* (*retrato*) to
frame; (*ajustar*) to fit, insert; (*encerrar*) to
contain.
encubrir [enku'ßrir] *vt* (*ocultar*) to hide,
conceal; (*criminal*) to harbour, shelter.
encuentro etc *vb ver* **encontrar** // [en-
'kwentro] *nm* (*de personas*) meeting; (*de
trenes*) collision, crash; (*DEPORTE*) match,
game; (*MIL*) encounter.
encuesta [en'kwesta] *nf* inquiry,
investigation; ~ **judicial** post mortem.
encumbrado, a [enkum'braðo, a] *a*
(*edificio*) lofty, towering; (*persona*)
eminent, distinguished.
encumbrar [enkum'brar] *vt* (*edificio*) to
raise; (*elevar*) to elevate; (*persona*) to
exalt; ~**se** *vr* to rise, tower; (*fig*) to
become conceited.
encharcado, a [entʃar'kaðo, a] *a* still;
(*estancado*) stagnant.
enchufar [entʃu'far] *vt* (*ELEC*) to plug in;
(*TEC*) to connect, fit together; **enchufe** *nm*
(*ELEC. clavija*) plug; (: *toma*) plug, socket;
(*de dos tubos*) joint, connection; (*fam:
influencia*) contact, connection; (: *puesto*)
cushy job.
endemoniado, a [endemo'njaðo, a] *a*
possessed (of the devil); (*endiabolado*)
devilish; (*furioso*) furious, wild.
endentar [enden'tar] *vt, vi* to engage,
mesh.
enderezar [endere'θar] *vt* (*poner derecho*)
to straighten (out); (: *verticalmente*) to set
upright; (*carta*) to address; (*fig*) to
straighten *or* sort out; (*dirigir*) to direct;
~**se** *vr* (*persona sentado*) to stand up; (*fig*)
to correct one's ways.
endeudarse [endeu'ðarse] *vr* to get into
debt.
endiablado, a [endja'ßlaðo, a] *a* devilish,
diabolical; (*hum*) mischievous; (*fig*)
furious, angry.
endomingarse [endomin'garse] *vr* to
dress up, put on one's best clothes.
endosar [endo'sar] *vt* (*cheque etc*) to
endorse.
endulzar [endul'θar] *vt* to sweeten; (*fig*) to
soften.
endurecer [endure'θer] *vt* to harden; (*fig*)
to harden, toughen; ~**se** *vr* to harden,
grow hard.
endurecido, a [endure'θiðo, a] *a* (*duro*)
hard; (*fig*) hardy, tough; **estar** ~ **a algo**
to be hardened *or* used to sth.
endurecimiento [endureθi'mjento] *nm*

(*acto*) hardening; (*tenacidad*) toughness; (*crueldad*) cruelty; (*insensibilidad*) callousness.

enemigo, a [ene'mixo, a] *a* enemy, hostile // *nm/f* enemy // *nf* enmity, hostility.

enemistad [enemis'tað] *nf* enmity.

enemistar [enemis'tar] *vt* to make enemies of, cause a rift between; ~**se** *vr* to become enemies; (*amigos*) to fall out.

energía [ener'xia] *nf* (*vigor*) energy, drive; (*TEC, ELEC*) energy, power.

enérgico, a [e'nerxiko, a] *a* (*gen*) energetic; (*voz, modales*) forceful.

enero [e'nero] *nm* January.

enfadar [enfa'ðar] *vt* to anger, annoy; ~**se** *vr* to get angry or annoyed.

enfado [en'faðo] *nm* (*enojo*) anger, annoyance; (*disgusto*) trouble, bother; ~**so, a** *a* annoying; (*aburrido*) tedious.

énfasis ['enfasis] *nm* emphasis, stress.

enfático, a [en'fatiko, a] *a* emphatic; (*afectado*) pompous.

enfermar [enfer'mar] *vt* to make ill // *vi* to fall ill, be taken ill.

enfermedad [enferme'ðað] *nf* illness; ~ **venérea** venereal disease.

enfermería [enferme'ria] *nf* infirmary; (*de colegio etc*) sick bay.

enfermero, a [enfer'mero, a] *nm/f* male nurse/nurse.

enfermizo, a [enfer'miθo, a] *a* (*persona*) sickly, unhealthy; (*lugar*) unhealthy.

enfermo, a [en'fermo, a] *a* ill, sick // *nm/f* invalid, sick person; (*en hospital*) patient.

enflaquecer [enflake'θer] *vt* (*adelgazar*) to make thin; (*debilitar*) to weaken; ~**se** *vr* (*adelgazarse*) to become thin, lose weight; (*debilitarse*) to grow weak; (*fig*) to lose heart.

enfocar [enfo'kar] *vt* (*foto etc*) to focus; (*problema etc*) to approach, look at.

enfoque [en'foke] *nm* focus.

enfrentar [enfren'tar] *vt* (*peligro*) to face (up to), confront; (*oponer, carear*) to put face to face; ~**se** *vr* (*dos personas*) to face or confront each other; (*dos equipos*) to meet; ~**se a** *o* **con** to face up to, confront.

enfrente [en'frente] *ad* opposite; ~ **de** *prep* opposite, facing; **la casa de** ~ the house opposite, the house across the street.

enfriamiento [enfria'mjento] *nm* chilling, refrigeration; (*MED*) cold, chill.

enfriar [enfri'ar] *vt* (*alimentos*) to cool, chill; (*algo caliente*) to cool down; (*habitación*) to air, freshen; ~**se** *vr* to cool down; (*MED*) to catch a chill; (*amistad*) to cool.

enfurecer [enfure'θer] *vt* to enrage, madden; ~**se** *vr* to become furious, fly into a rage; (*mar*) to get rough.

engalanar [engala'nar] *vt* (*adornar*) to adorn; (*ciudad*) to decorate; ~**se** *vr* to get dressed up.

enganchar [engan'tʃar] *vt* (*gen*) to hook; (*ropa*) to hang up; (*dos vagones*) to hitch up; (*TEC*) to couple, connect; (*MIL*) to recruit; (*fig: fam: persona*) to rope into; ~**se** *vr* (*MIL*) to enlist, join up.

enganche [en'gantʃe] *nm* hook; (*TEC*) coupling, connection; (*acto*) hooking (up); (: *ropa*) hanging up; (*MIL*) recruitment, enlistment.

engañar [enga'ɲar] *vt* to deceive; (*trampear*) to cheat, swindle; ~**se** *vr* (*equivocarse*) to be wrong; (*disimular la verdad*) to deceive or kid o.s.

engaño [en'gaɲo] *nm* deceit; (*trampa*) trick, swindle; (*error*) mistake, misunderstanding; (*ilusión*) delusion; ~**so, a** *a* (*tramposo*) crooked; (*mentiroso*) dishonest, deceitful; (*aspecto*) deceptive; (*consejo*) misleading, wrong.

engarzar [engar'θar] *vt* (*joya*) to set, mount; (*fig*) to link, connect.

engatusar [engatu'sar] *vt* (*fam*) to coax.

engendrar [enxen'drar] *vt* to breed; (*procrear*) to beget; (*fig*) to cause, produce; **engendro** *nm* (*BIO*) foetus; (*fig*) monstrosity; (*idea*) brainchild.

engolfarse [engol'farse] *vr*: ~ **en** to bury o.s. in, become deeply involved in.

engomar [engo'mar] *vt* to gum, glue, stick.

engordar [engor'ðar] *vt* to fatten // *vi* to get fat, put on weight.

engranaje [engra'naxe] *nm* gear.

engranar [engra'nar] *vt* to put into gear // *vi* to interlock.

engrandecer [engrande'θer] *vt* to enlarge, magnify; (*alabar*) to praise, speak highly of; (*exagerar*) to exaggerate.

engrasar [engra'sar] *vt* (*TEC: poner grasa*) to grease; (: *lubricar*) to lubricate, oil; (*manchar*) to make greasy; (*animal*) to fatten.

engreído, a [engre'iðo, a] *a* vain, conceited; **engreírse** *vr* to become conceited.

engrosar [engro'sar] *vt* (*ensanchar*) to enlarge; (*aumentar*) to increase; (*hinchar*) to swell // *vi* to get fat; ~**se** *vr* to increase; to swell.

enhebrar [ene'ßrar] *vt* to thread.

enhorabuena [enora'ßwena] *nf* congratulations *pl* // *ad* well and good.

enigma [e'nixma] *nm* enigma; (*problema*) puzzle; (*misterio*) mystery.

enjabonar [enxaßo'nar] *vt* to soap; (*fam: adular*) to soft-soap; (: *regañar*) to scold.

enjambre [en'xamßre] *nm* swarm.

enjaular [enxau'lar] *vt* to put in a cage; (*fam*) to jail, lock up.

enjuagar [enxwa'xar] *vt* (*ropa*) to rinse (out).

enjugar [enxu'xar] *vt* to wipe (off); (*lágrimas*) to dry; (*déficit*) to wipe out.

enjuiciar [enxwi'θjar] *vt* (*JUR: procesar*) to prosecute, try; (*fig*) to judge.

enjuto, a [en'xuto, a] *a* dry, dried up; (*fig*) lean, skinny.

enlace [en'laθe] *nm* link, connection; (*relación*) relationship; (*casamiento*) marriage; (*de carretera, trenes*) connection; **agente**

de ~ broker; ~ **sindical** shop steward.
enlazar [enla'θar] *vt* (*atar*) to tie; (*conectar*) to link, connect; (*AM*) to lasso; ~**se** *vr* (*novios*) to get married; (*dos familias*) to become related by marriage; (*conectarse*) to link (up), be linked.
enlodar [enlo'δar], **enlodazar** [enloδa-'θar] *vt* to muddy, cover in mud; (*fig:* *manchar*) to stain; (: *rebajar*) to debase.
enloquecer [enloke'θer] *vt* to drive mad // *vi,* ~**se** *vr* to go mad.
enlutar [enlu'tar] *vt* to dress in mourning; ~**se** *vr* to go into mourning.
enmarañar [enmara'ɲar] *vt* (*enredar*) to tangle (up), entangle; (*complicar*) to complicate; (*confundir*) to confuse; ~**se** *vr* (*enredarse*) to become entangled; (*confundirse*) to get confused; (*nublarse*) to cloud over.
enmascarar [enmaska'rar] *vt* to mask; ~**se** *vr* to put on a mask; ~**se de** to masquerade as.
enmendar [enmen'dar] *vt* to emend, correct; (*constitución etc*) to amend; (*compensar*) to make good; (*comportamiento*) to reform; ~**se** *vr* to reform, mend one's ways; **enmienda** *nf* correction; amendment; reform; (*compensación*) compensation, indemnity.
enmohecerse [enmoe'θerse] *vr* (*metal*) to rust, go rusty; (*muro, plantas*) to get mouldy.
enmudecer [enmuδe'θer] *vt* to silence // *vi,* ~**se** *vr* (*perder el habla*) to go silent; (*guardar silencio*) to keep quiet.
ennegrecer [enneɣre'θer] *vt* (*poner* *negro*) to blacken; (*oscurecer*) to darken; ~**se** *vr* to turn black; (*oscurecerse*) to get dark.
ennoblecer [ennoβle'θer] *vt* to ennoble; (*fig*) to embellish, adorn.
enojadizo, a [enoxa'δiθo, a] *a* irritable, short-tempered.
enojar [eno'xar] *vt* (*encolerizar*) to anger; (*disgustar*) to annoy, upset; ~**se** *vr* to get angry; to get annoyed.
enojo [e'noxo] *nm* (*cólera*) anger; (*disgusto*) annoyance; ~**s** *nmpl* trials, problems; ~**so, a** *a* annoying.
enorgullecerse [enorɣuʎe'θerse] *vr* to be proud; ~ **de** to pride o.s. on, be proud of.
enorme [e'norme] *a* enormous, huge; (*fig*) monstrous; **enormidad** *nf* hugeness, immensity; (*despropósito*) absurdity, piece of nonsense; (*perversidad*) monstrosity.
enraizar [enrai'θar] *vi* to take root.
enredadera [enreδa'δera] *nf* (*BOT*) creeper, climbing plant.
enredar [enre'δar] *vt* (*ovillo*) to tangle (up), entangle; (*peces*) to net; (*situación*) to complicate, confuse; (*meter cizaña*) to sow discord among *or* between; (*implicar*) to embroil, implicate; ~**se** *vr* to get entangled, get tangled (up); (*situación*) to get complicated; (*persona*) to get embroiled; (*AM: fam*) to meddle.
enredo [en'reδo] *nm* (*maraña*) tangle;

(*confusión*) mix-up, confusion; (*intriga*) intrigue.
enrevesado, a [enreβe'saδo, a] *a* unruly, uncontrollable; (*enredado*) complicated, involved.
enriquecer [enrike'θer] *vt* to make rich, enrich; ~**se** *vr* to get rich.
enrojecer [enroxe'θer] *vt* to redden // *vi,* ~**se** *vr* (*metal*) to become red hot; (*persona*) to blush.
enrollar [enro'ʎar] *vt* to roll (up), wind (up).
enroscar [enros'kar] *vt* (*torcer, doblar*) to coil (round), wind; (*tornillo, rosca*) to screw in; ~**se** *vr* to coil, wind.
ensalada [ensa'laδa] *nf* salad; **ensaladilla** *nf* Russian salad.
ensalzar [ensal'θar] *vt* (*alabar*) to praise, extol; (*exaltar*) to exalt.
ensambladura [ensambla'δura] *nf,* **ensamblaje** [ensam'blaxe] *nm* assembly; (*TEC*) joint; **ensamblar** *vt* to assemble.
ensanchar [ensan'tʃar] *vt* (*hacer más ancho*) to widen; (*agrandar*) to enlarge, expand; ~**se** *vr* to get wider, expand; (*pey*) to give o.s. airs; **ensanche** *nm* (*de* *vestido, calle*) widening; (*de negocio*) expansion.
ensangrentar [ensangren'tar] *vt* to stain with blood; ~**se** *vr* (*fig*) to get angry.
ensañar [ensa'ɲar] *vt* to enrage; ~**se** *vr:* ~**se con** to delight in tormenting.
ensartar [ensar'tar] *vt* (*gen*) to string (together); (*aguja*) to thread.
ensayar [ensa'jar] *vt* to test, try (out); (*TEATRO*) to rehearse.
ensayista [ensa'jista] *nm/f* essayist.
ensayo [en'sajo] *nm* test, trial; (*QUÍMICA*) experiment; (*TEATRO*) rehearsal; (*DEPORTE*) try; (*obra literaria*) essay.
ensenada [ense'naδa] *nf* inlet, cove.
enseñanza [ense'ɲanθa] *nf* (*educación*) education; (*acción*) teaching; (*doctrina*) teaching, doctrine.
enseñar [ense'ɲar] *vt* (*educar*) to teach; (*instruir*) to teach, instruct; (*mostrar, señalar*) to show.
enseres [en'seres] *nmpl* goods and chattels, things.
ensimismarse [ensimis'marse] *vr* (*abstraerse*) to become lost in thought; (*estar absorto*) to be lost in thought; (*AM*) to become conceited.
ensoberbecerse [ensoβerβe'θerse] *vr* to become proud; (*hacerse arrogante*) to become arrogant; (*mar*) to get rough.
ensordecer [ensorδe'θer] *vt* to deafen // *vi* to go deaf.
ensortijar [ensorti'xar] *vt,* ~**se** *vr* (*cabellos*) to curl.
ensuciar [ensu'θjar] *vt* (*manchar*) to dirty, soil; (*fig*) to defile; ~**se** *vr* (*mancharse*) to get dirty; (*fig*) to dirty/wet o.s.
ensueño [en'sweɲo] *nm* (*sueño*) dream, fantasy; (*ilusión*) illusion; (*soñando* *despierto*) reverie.
entablado [enta'βlaδo] *nm* (*piso*)

floorboards pl; (armazón) boarding.

entablar [enta'ßlar] vt (recubrir) to board (up); (AJEDREZ, DAMAS) to set up; (conversación) to strike up; (JUR) to file // vi to draw.

entallar [enta'ʎar] vt (piedra) to sculpt; (madera) to carve; (grabar) to engrave; (traje) to tailor // vi: **el traje entalla bien** the suit fits well.

entender [enten'der] vt (comprender) to understand; (darse cuenta) to realize; (creer, pensar) to think, believe; (querer decir) to mean // vi: ~ **de** to know all about; ~ **en** to deal with, have to do with; ~**se** vr (comprenderse) to be understood; (ponerse de acuerdo) to understand one another, have an understanding; (aliarse) to agree, reach an agreement; (fam) to have an affair; **me entiendo con la mecánica** I'm (quite) good at mechanics.

entendido, a [enten'diðo, a] a (comprendido) understood; (hábil) skilled; (inteligente) knowledgeable // nm/f (experto) expert; (docto) knowledgeable person // excl agreed!; **entendimiento** nm (comprensión) understanding; (facultad intelectual) the mind, intellect; (juicio) judgement.

enterado, a [ente'raðo, a] a well-informed; **estar** ~ **de** to know about, be aware of.

enteramente [entera'mente] ad entirely, completely.

enterar [ente'rar] vt (informar) to inform, tell; ~**se** vr to find out, get to know.

entereza [ente'reθa] nf (totalidad) entirety; (fig: energía) strength of mind; (honradez) integrity; (severidad) strictness, severity.

enternecer [enterne'θer] vt (ablandar) to soften; (apiadar) to touch, move; ~**se** vr to be touched, be moved.

entero, a [en'tero, a] a (total) whole, entire; (fig: recto) honest; (: firme) firm, resolute // nm (COM: punto) point; (AM: pago) payment.

enterrador [enterra'ðor] nm gravedigger.

enterrar [ente'rrar] vt to bury.

entibiar [enti'ßjar] vt to cool; (fig) to cool (down).

entidad [enti'ðað] nf (empresa) firm, company; (organismo) body; (sociedad) society; (FILOSOFÍA) entity.

entiendo etc vb ver **entender.**

entierro [en'tjerro] nm (acción) burial; (funeral) funeral.

entomología [entomolo'xia] nf entomology.

entonación [entona'θjon] nf (LING) intonation; (fig) conceit.

entonado, a [ento'naðo, a] a (MUS) in tune; (fig) conceited.

entonar [ento'nar] vt (canción) to intone; (colores) to tone; (MED) to tone up // vi to be in tune; ~**se** vr (engreírse) to give o.s. airs.

entonces [en'tonθes] ad then, at that time;

desde ~ since then; **en aquel** ~ at that time; **(pues)** ~ and so.

entornar [entor'nar] vt (puerta, ventana) to half close, leave ajar; (los ojos) to screw up.

entorpecer [entorpe'θer] vt (adormecer los sentidos) to dull, benumb; (impedir) to obstruct, hinder; (: tránsito) to slow down, delay; **entorpecimiento** nm numbness; slowing-down, delay; (letargia) lethargy.

entrado, a [en'traðo, a] a: ~ **en años** elderly; **una vez** ~ **el verano** in the summer(time), when summer comes // nf (acción) entry, access; (sitio) entrance, way in; (COM) receipts pl, takings pl; (CULIN) entree; (DEPORTE) innings sg; (TEATRO) house, audience; (para el cine etc) ticket; (COM): ~**as y salidas** income and expenditure; (TEC): ~**a de aire** air intake or inlet.

entrante [en'trante] a next, coming // nm inlet; **ser** ~ **en una casa** to have the run of a house.

entraña [en'traɲa] nf (fig: centro) heart, core; (raíz) root; ~**s** nfpl (ANAT) entrails; **entrañable** a close, intimate.

entrar [en'trar] vt (introducir) to bring in // vi (meterse) to go/come in, enter; (comenzar): ~ **diciendo** to begin by saying; **no me entra** I can't get the hang of it; **el año que entra** next year.

entre ['entre] prep (dos) between; (más de dos) among(st); **pensaba** ~ **mí** I thought to myself.

entreabrir [entrea'ßrir] vt to half-open, open halfway.

entrecejo [entre'θexo] nm: **fruncir el** ~ to frown.

entredicho [entre'ðitʃo] nm prohibition, ban; (JUR) injunction.

entrega [en'trexa] nf (de mercancías) delivery; (rendición) surrender; **novela por** ~**s** serial, novel in instalments.

entregar [entre'xar] vt (dar) to hand (over), deliver; (ceder) to give up; ~**se** vr (rendirse) to surrender, give in, submit; (dedicarse) to devote o.s.

entrelazar [entrela'θar] vt to entwine.

entremés [entre'mes] nm (CULIN) side-dish; **entremeses** nmpl hors d'œuvres.

entremeter [entreme'ter] vt to insert, put in; ~**se** vr to meddle, interfere; **entremetido, a** a a meddling, interfering.

entremezclar [entremeθ'klar] vt, ~**se** vr to intermingle.

entrenador [entrena'ðor] nm trainer, coach; **entrenarse** vr to train.

entreoír [entreo'ir] vt to half hear.

entresacar [entresa'kar] vt to pick out, select.

entresuelo [entre'swelo] nm (sótano) basement.

entretanto [entre'tanto] ad meanwhile, meantime; **en el** ~ in the meantime.

entretejer [entrete'xer] vt to interweave.

entretener [entrete'ner] vt (divertir) to entertain, amuse; (detener) to hold up,

delay; (*cuidar*) to maintain; ~**se** *vr*
(*divertirse*) to amuse o.s.; (*retrasarse*) to
delay, linger; **entretenido, a** *a*
entertaining, amusing; **entretenimiento**
nm entertainment, amusement; (*cuidado*)
upkeep, maintenance.

entrever [entre'ßer] *vt* to glimpse, catch
a glimpse of.

entreverar [entreße'rar] *vt* to mix (up).

entrevista [entre'ßista] *nf* interview;
entrevistar *vt* to interview;
entrevistarse *vr* to have an interview.

entristecer [entriste'θer] *vt* to sadden,
grieve; ~**se** *vr* to grow sad.

entrometer [entrome'ter] *etc* =
entremeter *etc.*

entroncar [entron'kar] *vi* to be connected
or related.

entronque [en'tronke] *nm* connection,
link.

entuerto [en'twerto] *nm* wrong, injustice.

entumecer [entume'θer] *vt* to numb,
benumb; ~**se** *vr* (*por el frío*) to go *or*
become numb; **entumecido, a** *a* numb,
stiff.

enturbiar [entur'ßjar] *vt* (*el agua*) to
disturb, make cloudy; (*fig*) to fog, confuse;
~**se** *vr* (*oscurecerse*) to become cloudy;
(*fig*) to get confused, become obscure.

entusiasmar [entusjas'mar] *vt* to excite,
fill with enthusiasm; (*gustar mucho*) to
delight; ~**se** *vr*: ~**se con** *o* **por** to get
enthusiastic *or* excited about.

entusiasmo [entu'sjasmo] *nm*
enthusiasm; (*deleite*) delight; (*excitación*)
excitement.

entusiasta [entu'sjasta] *a* enthusiastic //
nm/f enthusiast.

enumerar [enume'rar] *vt* to enumerate.

enunciación [enunθja'θjon] *nf*,
enunciado [enun'θjaðo] *nm* enunciation;
(*declaración*) declaration, statement;
enunciar *vt* to enunciate; to declare,
state.

envainar [enßai'nar] *vt* to sheathe.

envalentonar [enßalento'nar] *vt* to give
courage to; ~**se** *vr* to take courage,
become bolder; (*pey: jactarse*) to boast,
brag.

envanecer [enßane'θer] *vt* to make
conceited; ~**se** *vr* to grow vain *or*
conceited.

envasar [enßa'sar] *vt* (*empaquetar*) to
pack, wrap; (*enfrascar*) to bottle; (*enlatar*)
to tin; (*embolsar*) to pocket // *vi* (*fig: fam:
vino*) to knock back; **envase** *nm* packing,
wrapping; bottling; tinning, canning;
pocketing; (*recipiente*) container;
(*paquete*) package; (*botella*) bottle; (*lata*)
tin, can.

envejecer [enßexe'θer] *vt* to make old,
age // *vi*, ~**se** *vr* (*volverse viejo*) to grow
old; (*fig*) to become old-fashioned.

envenenar [enßene'nar] *vt* to poison; (*fig*)
to embitter.

envergadura [enßerɣa'ðura] *nf* (*fig*)
scope, compass.

envés [en'ßes] *nm* (*de tela*) back, wrong
side.

enviar [en'ßjar] *vt* to send.

envidia [en'ßiðja] *nf* (*deseo ferviente*)
envy; (*celos*) jealousy; **envidiar** *vt*
(*desear*) to envy; (*tener celos de*) to be
jealous of.

envilecer [enßile'θer] *vt* to debase,
degrade; ~**se** *vr* to lower o.s.

envío [en'ßio] *nm* (*acción*) sending; (*de
mercancías*) consignment; (*COM*)
remittance.

enviudar [enßju'ðar] *vi* to be widowed.

envoltura [enßol'tura] *nf* (*cobertura*)
cover; (*embalaje*) wrapper, wrapping; (*funda*) case.

envolver [enßol'ßer] *vt* to wrap (up);
(*cubrir*) to cover; (*enemigo*) to surround;
(*implicar*) to involve, implicate; ~**se** *vr*
(*cubrirse*) to wrap o.s. up; (*implicarse*) to
become involved.

envuelto [en'ßwelto] *pp de* **envolver.**

enzarzar [enθar'θar] *vt* (*fig*) to involve (in
a dispute).

épico, a ['epiko, a] *a* epic // *nf* epic.

epidemia [epi'ðemja] *nf* epidemic;
epidémico, a *a* epidemic.

epifanía [epifa'nia] *nf* Epiphany.

epilepsia [epi'lepsja] *nf* epilepsy.

epílogo [e'piloxo] *nm* epilogue.

episodio [epi'soðjo] *nm* episode.

epístola [e'pistola] *nf* epistle; (*fam*) letter.

epitafio [epi'tafjo] *nm* epitaph.

época ['epoka] *nf* period, time; (*HISTORIA*)
age, epoch; **hacer** ~ to be epoch-making.

equidad [eki'ðað] *nf* equity.

equilibrar [ekili'ßrar] *vt* to balance;
equilibrio *nm* balance, equilibrium; **equi-
librista** *nm/f* (*funámbulo*) tightrope
walker; (*acróbata*) acrobat.

equipaje [eki'paxe] *nm* luggage; (*equipo*)
equipment, kit; (*NAUT: tripulación*) crew;
~ **de mano** hand luggage.

equipar [eki'par] *vt* (*proveer*) to equip.

equipararse [ekipa'rarse] *vr*: ~ **con** to
be on a level with.

equipo [e'kipo] *nm* (*materiales*)
equipment; (*grupo*) team; (: *de obreros*)
shift.

equis ['ekis] *nf* (the letter) X.

equitación [ekita'θjon] *nf* (*acto*) riding;
(*arte*) horsemanship.

equitativo, a [ekita'tißo, a] *a* equitable,
fair.

equivalente [ekißa'lente] *a*, *nm*
equivalent; **equivaler** *vi* to be equivalent
or equal.

equivocación [ekißoka'θjon] *nf* mistake,
error; **equivocarse** *vr* to be wrong, make
a mistake; **equivocarse de camino** to
take the wrong road; **equívoco, a** *a* (*dudoso*) suspect; (*ambiguo*) ambiguous // *nm*
ambiguity; (*juego de palabras*) play on
words.

era *vb ver* **ser** // ['era] *nf* era, age.

erais *vb ver* **ser.**

éramos vb ver **ser.**
eran vb ver **ser.**
erario [e'rarjo] nm exchequer, treasury.
eras vb ver **ser.**
eres vb ver **ser.**
erguir [er'xir] vt to raise, lift; (poner derecho) to straighten; ~**se** vr to straighten up; (fig) to swell with pride.
erigir [eri'xir] vt to erect, build; ~**se** vr: ~**se en** to set o.s. up as.
erizado, a [eri'θaðo, a] a bristly.
erizarse [eri'θarse] vr to stand on end.
erizo [e'riθo] nm hedgehog; (~ de mar) sea-urchin.
ermitaño, a [ermi'taɲo, a] nm/f hermit.
erótico, a [e'rotiko, a] a erotic; **erotismo** nm eroticism.
erradicar [erraði'kar] vt to eradicate.
errado, a [e'rraðo, a] a mistaken, wrong.
errante [e'rrante] a wandering, errant.
errar [e'rrar] vi (vagar) to wander, roam; (equivocarse) to err, make a mistake // vt: ~ **el camino** to take the wrong road; ~ **el tiro** to miss.
erróneo, a [e'rroneo, a] a (equivocado) wrong, mistaken; (falso) false, untrue.
error [e'rror] nm error, mistake; ~ **de imprenta** misprint.
eructar [eruk'tar] vt to belch.
erudición [eruði'θjon] nf erudition, learning.
erudito, a [eru'ðito, a] a erudite, learned.
erupción [erup'θjon] nf eruption; (MED) rash.
es vb ver **ser.**
esa, esas det ver **ese.**
ésa, ésas pron ver **ése.**
esbelto, a [es'ßelto, a] a slim, slender.
esbozo [es'ßoθo] nm sketch, outline.
escabeche [eska'ßetʃe] nm brine; (de aceitunas etc) pickle; **pescado en** ~ pickled fish.
escabel [eska'ßel] nm (low) stool.
escabroso, a [eska'ßroso, a] a (accidentado) rough, uneven; (fig) tough, difficult; (: atrevido) risqué.
escabullirse [eskaßu'ʎirse] vr to slip away; (irse) to clear out.
escala [es'kala] nf (proporción, mus) scale; (de mano) ladder; (AVIAT) stopover; **hacer** ~ **en** to stop or call in at; ~ **de colores** range of colours.
escalafón [eskala'fon] nm (escala de salarios) salary scale, wage scale; (lista etc) list; (registro) register.
escalar [eska'lar] vt (montaña etc) to climb, scale; (casa) to burgle, break into.
escalera [eska'lera] nf stairs pl, staircase; (escala) ladder; (NAIPES) run; ~ **mecánica** escalator; ~ **de caracol** spiral staircase.
escalinata [eskali'nata] nf outside staircase.
escalofrío [eskalo'frio] nm chill; ~**s** nmpl (fig) shivers; **escalofriante** a chilling.

escalón [eska'lon] nm step, stair; (de escalera) rung.
escama [es'kama] nf (de pez, serpiente) scale; (de jabón) flake; (fig) resentment.
escamado, a [eska'maðo, a] a wary, cautious.
escamotar [eskamo'tar], **escamotear** [eskamote'ar] vt (quitar) to lift, swipe (fam); (hacer desaparecer) to make disappear.
escampar [eskam'par] vb impersonal to stop raining; (del cielo) to clear (up).
escandalizar [eskandali'θar] vt to scandalize, shock; ~**se** vr to be shocked; (ofenderse) to be offended.
escándalo [es'kandalo] nm scandal; (alboroto, tumulto) row, uproar; **escandaloso, a** a scandalous, shocking.
escandinavo, a [eskandi'naßo, a] a, nm/f Scandinavian.
escaño [es'kaɲo] nm bench; (POL) seat.
escapar [eska'par] vi (gen) to escape, run away; (DEPORTE) to break away; ~**se** vr to escape, get away; (gas) to leak (out).
escaparate [eskapa'rate] nm shop window; (AM) wardrobe.
escape [es'kape] nm (de gas) leak; (de motor) exhaust; (de persona) escape.
escarabajo [eskara'ßaxo] nm beetle; ~**s** nmpl (fam) scribble sg.
escaramuza [eskara'muθa] nf skirmish; (fig) brush.
escarbar [eskar'ßar] vt (gallina) to scratch; (dientes) to pick; (orejas) to clean; (fig) to inquire into, investigate.
escarcha [es'kartʃa] nf frost.
escarlata [eskar'lata] a inv scarlet; **escarlatina** nf scarlet fever.
escarmentar [eskarmen'tar] vt to punish severely // vi to learn one's lesson; **escarmiento** nm (ejemplo) lesson, example; (castigo) punishment.
escarnecer [eskarne'θer] vt to mock, ridicule; **escarnio, escarnecimiento** nm mockery; (injuria) insult.
escarpado, a [eskar'paðo, a] a (abrupto) sheer; (inclinado) steep; (accidentado) craggy.
escasear [eskase'ar] vt to skimp (on) // vi to be scarce.
escasez [eska'seθ] nf (falta) shortage, scarcity; (pobreza) poverty; (mezquindad) meanness.
escaso, a [es'kaso, a] a (poco) scarce; (raro) rare; (ralo) thin, sparse; (limitado) limited.
escatimar [eskati'mar] vt (limitar) to skimp (on); (reducir) to curtail, cut down.
escena [es'θena] nf scene.
escenario [esθe'narjo] nm (TEATRO) stage; (CINE) set; (fig) scene.
escepticismo [esθepti'θismo] nm scepticism; **escéptico, a** a sceptical // nm/f sceptic.
esclarecer [esklare'θer] vt (iluminar) to light up, illuminate; (misterio, problema) to shed light on; (ennoblecer) to ennoble.

esclavitud [eskla'βi'tuð] *nf* slavery.
esclavizar [esklaβi'θar] *vt* to enslave.
esclavo, a [es'klaβo, a] *nm/f* slave.
escoba [es'koβa] *nf* broom.
escocer [esko'θer] *vt* to annoy // *vi* to burn, sting; ~**se** *vr* to chafe, get chafed.
escocés, esa [esko'θes, esa] *a* Scottish // *nm/f* Scotsman/woman, Scot.
Escocia [es'koθja] *nf* Scotland.
escoger [esko'xer] *vt* to choose, pick, select; **escogido, a** *a* chosen, selected; (*calidad*) choice, select; **escogimiento** *nm* choice.
escolar [esko'lar] *a* school *cpd* // *nm/f* schoolboy/girl, pupil.
escolta [es'kolta] *nf* escort; **escoltar** *vt* to escort.
escombro [es'kombro] *nm* mackerel; ~**s** *nmpl* (*basura*) rubbish *sg*; (*restos*) debris *sg*.
esconder [eskon'der] *vt* to hide, conceal; ~**se** *vr* to hide; **escondite** *nm* hiding place; (*juego*) hide-and-seek.
escondrijo [eskon'drixo] *nm* hiding-place, hideout.
escopeta [esko'peta] *nf* shotgun.
escoplo [es'koplo] *nm* chisel.
Escorpio [es'korpjo] *nm* Scorpio.
escorpión [eskor'pjon] *nm* scorpion.
escote [es'kote] *nm* (*de vestido*) low neck; (*parte*) share; **pagar a** ~ to share the expenses.
escotillón [eskoti'ʎon] *nm* trapdoor.
escozor [esko'θor] *nm* (*dolor*) sting(ing); (*fig*) grief, heartache.
escribano, a [eskri'βano, a], **escribiente** [eskri'βjente] *nm/f* clerk.
escribir [eskri'βir] *vt, vi* to write; ~ **a máquina** to type; ¿**cómo se escribe?** how do you spell it?
escrito, a [es'krito, a] *pp de* **escribir** // *nm* (*documento*) document; (*manuscrito*) text, manuscript; **por** ~ in writing.
escritor, a [eskri'tor, a] *nm/f* writer.
escritorio [eskri'torjo] *nm* desk; (*oficina*) office.
escritura [eskri'tura] *nf* (*acción*) writing; (*caligrafía*) (hand)writing; (*JUR*: *documento*) deed.
escrúpulo [es'krupulo] *nm* scruple; (*minuciosidad*) scrupulousness; **escrupuloso, a** *a* scrupulous.
escrutar [eskru'tar] *vt* to scrutinize, examine; (*votos*) to count.
escrutinio [eskru'tinjo] *nm* (*examen atento*) scrutiny; (*recuento de votos*) poll; (*resultado de elección*) voting, ballot.
escuadra [es'kwaðra] *nf* (*MIL etc*) squad; (*NAUT*) squadron; (*de coches etc*) fleet; **escuadrilla** *nf* (*de aviones*) squadron; (*AM: de obreros*) gang.
escuadrón [eska'ðron] *nm* squadron.
escuálido, a [es'kwaliðo, a] *a* (*flaco, macilento*) pale, wan; (*sucio*) squalid.
escuchar [esku'tʃar] *vt* to listen to // *vi* to listen.

escudilla [esku'ðiʎa] *nf* bowl, basin.
escudo [es'kuðo] *nm* shield.
escudriñar [eskuðri'ɲar] *vt* (*examinar*) to investigate, examine closely; (*mirar de lejos*) to scan.
escuela [es'kwela] *nf* school.
escueto, a [es'kweto, a] *a* plain, unadorned.
esculpir [eskul'pir] *vt* to sculpt; (*grabar*) to engrave; (*tallar*) to carve; **escultor, a** *nm/f* sculptor/tress; **escultura** *nf* sculpture.
escupidora [eskupi'ðora], **escupidera** [eskupi'ðera] *nf* spittoon; (*orinal*) bedpan.
escupir [esku'pir] *vt, vi* to spit (out).
escurridero [eskurri'ðero] *nm* draining-board.
escurridizo, a [eskurri'ðiθo, a] *a* slippery.
escurrir [esku'rrir] *vt* (*ropa*) to wring out; (*verduras*) to strain; (*platos*) to drain // *vi* (*los líquidos*) to drip; (*resbalarse*) to slip, slide; ~**se** *vr* (*gotear*) to drip; (*secarse*) to drain; (*resbalarse*) to slip, slide; (*escaparse*) to slip away.
ese, esa, esos, esas ['ese, 'esa, 'esos, 'esas] *det* (*sg*) that; (*pl*) those.
ése, ésa, ésos, ésas ['ese, 'esa, 'esos, 'esas] *pron* (*sg*) that (one); (*pl*) those (ones); ~... **éste**... the former... the latter...; ¡**no me vengas con** ~**as** don't give me any more of that nonsense.
esencia [e'senθja] *nf* essence; **esencial** *a* essential.
esfera [es'fera] *nf* sphere; (*de reloj*) face; **esférico, a** *a* spherical.
esforzado, a [esfor'θaðo, a] *a* (*enérgico*) energetic, vigorous; (*valiente*) brave.
esforzar [esfor'θar] *vt* (*fortalecer*) to strengthen; (*alentar*) to encourage; ~**se** *vr* to exert o.s., make an effort.
esfuerzo [es'fwerθo] *nm* effort; (*TEC*) stress; (*valor*) courage, spirit.
esfumarse [esfu'marse] *vr* to fade away.
esgrima [es'ɣrima] *nf* fencing.
esguince [es'ɣinθe] *nm* (*MED*) sprain; (*ademán*) swerve, dodge; (*ceño*) scowl, frown.
eslabón [esla'βon] *nm* link; **eslabonar** *vt* to link, connect.
esmaltar [esmal'tar] *vt* to enamel; (*las uñas*) to paint, varnish; **esmalte** *nm* enamel; **esmalte de uñas** nail varnish, nail polish.
esmerado, a [esme'raðo, a] *a* careful, neat.
esmeralda [esme'ralda] *nf* emerald.
esmerarse [esme'rarse] *vr* (*aplicarse*) to take great pains, exercise great care; (*brillar*) to shine, do well.
esmero [es'mero] *nm* (great) care.
esnob [es'nob] *a inv* (*persona*) snobbish; (*coche etc*) posh // *nm/f* snob; ~**ismo** *nm* snobbery.
eso ['eso] *pron* that, that thing *or* matter; ~ **de su coche** all that about his car; ~ **de ir al cine** all that about going to the cinema, the idea of going to the cinema; **a** ~ **de las cinco** at about five o'clock; **en**

~ thereupon, at that point; ~ **es** that's it; ~ **sí que es vida!** now this is really living!; **por** ~ **te lo dije** that's why I told you.

esos ['esos] *det ver* **ese.**

ésos ['esos] *pron ver* **ése.**

espabilar [espaßi'lar] *vt* (*vela*) to snuff; ~**se** *vr* (*despertarse*) to wake up; (*animarse*) to liven up, look lively.

espacial [espa'θjal] *a inv* (*del espacio*) space *cpd.*

espaciar [espa'θjar] *vt* to space (out); (*divulgar*) to spread; ~**se** *vr*: ~**se en un tema** to enlarge on a subject.

espacio [es'paθjo] *nm* space; (MUS) interval; (*emisión*) (short) programme; spot; **el** ~ space; ~**so, a** *a* spacious, roomy; (*lento*) slow.

espada [es'paða] *nf* sword; ~**s** *nfpl* (NAIPES) spades.

espaguetis [espa'xetis] *nmpl* spaghetti *sg.*

espalda [es'palda] *nf* (*gen*) back; ~**s** *nfpl* (*hombros*) shoulders; **a** ~**s de uno** behind sb's back; **cargado de** ~**s** round-shouldered; **tenderse de** ~**s** to lie (down) on one's back; **volver la** ~ **a alguien** to give sb the cold shoulder.

espaldar [espal'dar] *nm* (*de asiento*) back.

espaldilla [espal'ðiʎa] *nf* shoulder-blade.

espantadizo, a [espanta'ðiθo, a] *a* timid, easily frightened.

espantajo [espan'taxo] *nm*, **espantapájaros** [espanta'paxaros] *nmpl* scarecrow *sg.*

espantar [espan'tar] *vt* (*asustar*) to frighten, scare; (*ahuyentar*) to frighten off; (*asombrar*) to horrify, appal; ~**se** *vr* to get frightened *or* scared; to be appalled.

espanto [es'panto] *nm* (*susto*) fright; (*terror*) terror; (*fantasma*) ghost; (*asombro*) astonishment; ~**so, a** *a* frightening; terrifying; astonishing.

España [es'paɲa] *nf* Spain; **español, a** *a* Spanish // *nm/f* Spaniard // *nm* (*lengua*) Spanish.

esparadrapo [espara'ðrapo] *nm* sticking plaster.

esparcido, a [espar'θiðo, a] *a* scattered; (*fig*) jolly, cheerful.

esparcimiento [esparθi'mjento] *nm* (*de líquido*) spilling; (*dispersión*) spreading; (*derramamiento*) scattering; (*fig*) cheerfulness.

esparcir [espar'θir] *vt* to spread; (*derramar*) to scatter; (*líquido*) to spill; ~**se** *vr* to spread (out); to scatter; to spill; (*divertirse*) to enjoy o.s.

espárrago [es'parraxo] *nm* asparagus.

espasmo [es'pasmo] *nm* spasm.

especia [es'peθja] *nf* spice.

especial [espe'θjal] *a* special; ~**idad** *nf* speciality.

especie [es'peθje] *nf* (BIO) species; (*clase*) kind, sort; (*asunto*) matter; (*comentario*) remark, comment; **en** ~ in kind.

especificar [espeθifi'kar] *vt* to specify; **específico, a** *a* specific.

espécimen [es'peθimen] (*pl* **especímenes**) *nm* specimen.

especioso, a [espe'θjoso, a] *a* (*perfecto*) perfect; (*fig*) deceitful.

espectáculo [espek'takulo] *nm* (*gen*) spectacle; (TEATRO *etc*) show.

espectador, a [espekta'ðor, a] *nm/f* spectator.

espectro [es'pektro] *nm* ghost; (*fig*) spectre.

especular [espeku'lar] *vt, vi* to speculate; **especulativo, a** *a* speculative.

espejismo [espe'xismo] *nm* mirage.

espejo [es'pexo] *nm* mirror; (*fig*) model; ~ **de retrovisión** rear-view mirror.

espeluznante [espeluθ'nante] *a inv* horrifying, hair-raising.

espera [es'pera] *nf* (*pausa, intervalo*) wait, period of waiting; (JUR: *plazo*) respite; **en** ~ **de** waiting for; (*con expectativa*) expecting.

esperanza [espe'ranθa] *nf* (*confianza*) hope; (*expectativa*) expectation; (*perspectiva*) prospect; **esperanzar** *vt* to give hope to.

esperar [espe'rar] *vt* (*aguardar*) to wait for; (*tener expectativa de*) to expect; (*desear*) to hope for // *vi* to wait; to expect; to hope.

esperma [es'perma] *nf* sperm.

espesar [espe'sar] *vt* to thicken; ~**se** *vr* to thicken, get thicker.

espeso, a [es'peso, a] *a* thick; **espesor** *nm* thickness.

espetar [espe'tar] *vt* (*pollo*) to put on a spit *or* skewer; (*pregunta*) to pop; (*dar: reto, sermón*) to give.

espetón [espe'ton] *nm* (*asador*) spit, skewer; (*aguja*) large pin; (*empujón*) jab, poke.

espía [es'pia] *nm/f* spy; **espiar** *vt* (*observar*) to spy on; (*acechar*) to watch out for.

espina [es'pina] *nf* thorn; (*de madera, astilla*) splinter; (*de pez*) bone; ~ **dorsal** spine.

espinaca [espi'naka] *nf* spinach.

espinar [espi'nar] *vt* (*herir*) to prick; (*fig*) to sting, hurt.

espinazo [espi'naθo] *nm* spine, backbone.

espino [es'pino] *nm* hawthorn.

espinoso, a [espi'noso, a] *a* (*planta*) thorny, prickly; (*fig*) bony.

espionaje [espjo'naxe] *nm* spying, espionage.

espiral [espi'ral] *a, nf* spiral.

espirar [espi'rar] *vt* to breathe out, exhale.

espiritista [espiri'tista] *a, nm/f* spiritualist.

espíritu [es'piritu] *nm* spirit; **espiritual** *a* spiritual.

espita [es'pita] *nf* tap; (*fig: fam*) drunkard.

esplendidez [esplendi'ðeθ] *nf* (*abundancia*) lavishness; (*magnificencia*) splendour.

esplendor [esplen'dor] *nm* splendour.

espolear [espole'ar] *vt* to spur on.

espolvorear [espolßore'ar] *vt* (*echar polvos*) to dust; (*esparcir*) to dust, sprinkle.

esponja [es'ponxa] *nf* sponge; (*fig*) sponger.

esponjarse [espon'xarse] *vr* (*fam*: *hincharse*) to swell with pride; (: *de salud*) to glow with health.

esponjoso, a [espon'xoso, a] *a* spongy, porous.

espontaneidad [espontanei'ðað] *nf* spontaneity; **espontáneo, a** *a* spontaneous.

esposa [es'posa] *nf* wife; ~s *nfpl* handcuffs; **esposar** *vt* to handcuff.

esposo [es'poso] *nm* husband.

espuela [es'pwela] *nf* spur.

espuma [es'puma] *nf* foam; (*de cerveza*) froth, head; (*de jabón*) lather; **espumoso, a** *a* frothy, foamy; (*vino*) sparkling.

esqueleto [eske'leto] *nm* skeleton.

esquema [es'kema] *nm* (*diagrama*) diagram; (*dibujo*) plan; (*plan*) scheme; (*FILOSOFIA*) schema.

esquí [es'ki] (*pl* **esquís**) *nm* (*objeto*) ski; (*deporte*) skiing.

esquilar [eski'lar] *vt* to shear.

esquilmar [eskil'mar] *vt* (*cosechar*) to harvest; (*empobrecer: suelo*) to exhaust; (*fig*) to skin.

esquimal [eski'mal] *a, nm/f* Eskimo.

esquina [es'kina] *nf* corner.

esquirol [eski'rol] *nm* (*fam*) blackleg.

esquivar [eski'ßar] *vt* to avoid; (*evadir*) to dodge, elude; ~se *vr* to withdraw.

esquivez [eski'ßeθ] *nf* (*altanería*) aloofness; (*desdeño*) scorn, disdain; **esquivo, a** *a* (*altanero*) aloof; (*desdeñoso*) scornful, disdainful.

esta ['esta] *det ver* **este**.

ésta ['esta] *pron ver* **éste**.

está *vb ver* **estar**.

estabilidad [estaßili'ðað] *nf* stability; **estable** *a* stable.

establecer [estaßle'θer] *vt* to establish; ~se *vr* to establish o.s.; (*echar raíces*) to settle; **establecimiento** *nm* establishment.

estaca [es'taka] *nf* stake, post; (*para tiendas*) peg.

estacada [esta'kaða] *nf* (*cerca*) fence, fencing; (*palenque*) stockade.

estación [esta'θjon] *nf* station; (*del año*) season; ~ **de autobuses** bus station.

estacionamiento [estaθjona'mjento] *nm* (*AUTO*) parking; (*MIL*) stationing; (*colocación*) placing.

estacionar [estaθjo'nar] *vt* (*AUTO*) to park; (*MIL*) to station; (*colocar*) to place; ~**io, a** *a* stationary; (*COM: mercado*) slack.

estadio [es'taðjo] *nm* (*fase*) stage, phase; (*DEPORTE*) stadium.

estadista [esta'ðista] *nm* (*POL*) statesman; (*ESTADÍSTICA*) statistician.

estadística [esta'ðistika] *nf* (*una* ~) figure, statistic; (*ciencia*) statistics *sg*.

estado [es'taðo] *nm* (*POL*: *condición*) state; (*social*) status; ~ **de las cuentas** statement of accounts; ~ **mayor** staff; **E~s Unidos** (**EE. UU.**) United States (USA).

estafa [es'tafa] *nf* swindle, trick; **estafar** *vt* to swindle, defraud.

estafeta [esta'feta] *nf* (*correo*) post; (*oficina de correos*) post office; ~ **diplomática** diplomatic bag.

estallar [esta'ʎar] *vi* to burst; (*explotar*) to explode; (*epidemia, rebelión*) to break out; ~ **en llanto** to burst into tears; **estallido** *nm* explosion; (*fig*) outbreak.

estampa [es'tampa] *nf* (*imagen*) image; (*impresión, imprenta*) print, engraving; (*imagen, figura: de persona*) appearance; (*fig: huella*) footprint.

estampado, a [estam'paðo, a] *a* printed // *nm* (*impresión: acción*) printing; (: *efecto*) print; (*marca*) stamping.

estampar [estam'par] *vt* (*imprimir*) to print; (*marcar*) to stamp; (*metal*) to engrave; (*poner sello en*) to stamp; (*fig*) to stamp, imprint.

estampida [estam'piða] *nf* stampede; (*estampido*) bang, report.

estampido [estam'piðo] *nm* bang, report.

estampilla [estam'piʎa] *nf* stamp.

están *vb ver* **estar**.

estancar [estan'kar] *vt* (*aguas*) to hold up, hold back; (*COM*) to monopolize; (*fig*) to block, hold up; ~se *vr* to stagnate.

estancia [es'tanθja] *nf* (*permanencia*) stay; (*sala*) living-room; (*AM*) farm, ranch; **estanciero** *nm* farmer, rancher.

estanco, a [es'tanko, a] *a* watertight // *nm* (*monopolio*) state monopoly; (*tienda*) tobacconist's (shop).

estandarizar [estandari'θar] *vt* to standardize.

estandarte [estan'darte] *nm* banner, standard.

estanque [es'tanke] *nm* (*lago*) pool, pond; (*AGR*) reservoir.

estanquero, a [estan'kero, a], **estanquillero, a** [estanki'ʎero, a] *nm/f* tobacconist.

estante [es'tante] *nm* (*armario*) rack, stand; (*biblioteca*) bookcase; (*anaquel*) shelf; (*AM*) prop; **estantería** *nf* shelving, shelves *pl*.

estantigua [estan'tiɣwa] *nf* (*fantasma*) apparition.

estaño [es'taɲo] *nm* tin.

estar [es'tar] *vi* (*gen*) to be; (*en casa*) to be in; (*ubicarse*) to be found; (*presente*) to be present; **estamos a 2 de mayo** it is the 2nd May; **¿cómo está Ud?** how are you?; ~ **enfermo** to be ill; ~ **viejo/joven** (*parecerse*) to seem old/young; (*seguido de una preposición*): **¿a cuánto estamos de Madrid?** how far are we from Madrid?; ~ **de fiesta** *o* **vacaciones** to be on holiday; **las uvas están a 5 pesetas** grapes are at 5 pesetas; **María no está** Maria isn't in; ~ **por** (: *moción*) to be in favour of; (: *persona*) to support, back; **está por hacer** it remains to be done; **¿estamos?** are we agreed?

estas ['estas] *det ver* **este**.

éstas ['estas] *pron ver* **éste**.

estás *vb ver* **estar**.

estatal [esta'tal] *a inv* state *cpd*.

estático, a [es'tatiko, a] *a* static.

estatificar [estatifi'kar] *vt* to nationalize.

estatua [es'tatwa] *nf* statue.

estatuir [estatu'ir] *vt* (*establecer*) to establish; (*determinar*) to prove.

estatura [esta'tura] *nf* stature, height.

estatuto [esta'tuto] *nm* (*JUR*) statute; (*de ciudad*) bye-law; (*de comité*) rule.

este ['este] *nm* east.

este, esta, estos, estas ['este, 'esta, 'estos, 'estas] *det* (*sg*) this; (*pl*) these.

éste, ésta, éstos, éstas ['este, 'esta, 'estos, 'estas] *pron* (*sg*) this (one); (*pl*) these (ones); ~... **ése**... the latter... the former... .

esté *etc vb ver* **estar**.

estela [es'tela] *nf* wake, wash; (*fig*) trail.

estenografía [estenoxra'fia] *nf* shorthand, stenography.

estepa [es'tepa] *nf* (*GEO*) steppe.

estera [es'tera] *nf* mat(ting).

estereo... [estereo] *pref* stereo...; ~**fónico, a** *a* stereophonic; ~**tipar** *vt* to stereotype; ~**tipo** *nm* stereotype.

estéril [es'teril] *a* sterile, barren; (*fig*) vain, futile.

esterlina [ester'lina] *a*. **libra** ~ pound sterling.

estético, a [es'tetiko, a] *a* aesthetic // *nf* aesthetics *sg*.

estiércol [es'tjerkol] *nm* dung, manure.

estigma [es'tixma] *nm* stigma.

estilar [esti'lar] *vi*, ~**se** *vr* to be in fashion, be used, be worn.

estilo [es'tilo] *nm* style; (*TEC*) stylus; (*DEPORTE*) stroke; **algo por el** ~ something of the sort.

estima [es'tima] *nf* esteem, respect.

estimación [estima'θjon] *nf* (*evaluación*) estimation; (*aprecio, afecto*) esteem, regard.

estimar [esti'mar] *vt* (*evaluar*) to estimate; (*valorar*) to value; (*apreciar*) to esteem, respect; (*pensar, considerar*) to think, reckon; **¡se estima!** thanks very much!

estimulante [estimu'lante] *a* stimulating // *nm* stimulant; **estimular** *vt* to stimulate; (*excitar*) to excite; (*animar*) to encourage; **estímulo** *nm* stimulus; (*ánimo*) encouragement.

estío [es'tio] *nm* summer.

estipulación [estipula'θjon] *nf* stipulation, condition; **estipular** *vt* to stipulate.

estirado, a [esti'raðo, a] *a* (*tenso*) (stretched *or* drawn) tight; (*fig*) stiff, pompous.

estirar [esti'rar] *vt* to stretch; (*conversa-*

ción, presupuesto) to stretch out; ~**se** *vr* to stretch.

estirón [esti'ron] *nm* pull, tug; (*crecimiento*) spurt, sudden growth; **dar un** ~ to shoot up.

estirpe [es'tirpe] *nf* stock, lineage.

estival [esti'ßal] *a* summer *cpd*.

esto ['esto] *pron* this, this thing *or* matter; ~ **de la boda** this business about the wedding.

estofa [es'tofa] *nf* (*tela*) quilting; (*calidad, clase*) quality, class.

estofado, a [esto'faðo, a] *a* (*CULIN*) stewed; (*bordado*) quilted // *nm* stew.

estofar [esto'far] *vt* (*bordar*) to quilt; (*CULIN*) to stew.

estoico, a [es'toiko, a] *a* (*FILOSOFÍA*) stoic(al); (*fig*) cold, indifferent.

estólido, a [es'toliðo, a] *a* stupid.

estómago [es'tomaxo] *nm* stomach; **tener** ~ to be thick-skinned.

estorbar [estor'ßar] *vt* to hinder, obstruct; (*fig*) to bother, disturb // *vi* to be in the way; **estorbo** *nm* (*molestia*) bother, nuisance; (*obstáculo*) hindrance, obstacle.

estornudar [estornu'ðar] *vi* to sneeze.

estos ['estos] *det ver* **este**.

éstos ['estos] *pron ver* **éste**.

estoy *vb ver* **estar**.

estrafalario, a [estrafa'larjo, a] *a* odd, eccentric; (*desarreglado*) slovenly, sloppy.

estragar [estra'xar] *vt* to deprave, corrupt; (*deteriorar*) to ruin; **estrago** *nm* ruin, destruction; **hacer estragos en** to wreak havoc among.

estragón [estra'xon] *nm* (*CULIN*) tarragon.

estrangul [estran'gul] *nm* mouthpiece.

estrangulación [estrangula'θjon] *nf* strangulation.

estrangulador, a [estrangula'ðor, a] *nm/f* strangler // *nm* (*TEC*) throttle; (*AUTO*) choke.

estrangulamiento [estrangula'mjento] *nm* (*AUTO*) bottleneck.

estrangular [estrangu'lar] *vt* (*persona*) to strangle; (*MED*) to strangulate.

estraperlo [estra'perlo] *nm* black market.

estratagema [estrata'xema] *nf* (*MIL*) stratagem; (*astucia*) cunning.

estrategia [estra'texja] *nf* strategy; **estratégico, a** *a* strategic.

estratificar [estratifi'kar] *vt* to stratify.

estrato [es'trato] *nm* stratum, layer.

estrechar [estre'tʃar] *vt* (*reducir*) to narrow; (*vestido*) to take in; (*persona*) to hug, embrace; ~**se** *vr* (*reducirse*) to narrow, grow narrow; (*apretarse*) to embrace; (*reducir los gastos*) to economize; ~ **la mano** to shake hands; ~ **amistad con alguien** to become very friendly with sb.

estrechez [estre'tʃeθ] *nf* narrowness; (*de ropa*) tightness; (*intimidad*) intimacy; (*COM*) want *or* shortage of money; **estrecheces** *nfpl* financial difficulties; ~ **de conciencia** small-mindedness; ~ **de miras** narrow-mindedness.

estrecho, a [es'tretʃo, a] a narrow; (*apretado*) tight; (*íntimo*) close, intimate; (*miserable*) mean // nm strait.

estregar [estre'xar] vt (*sobar*) to rub (hard); (*rascar*) to scrape.

estrella [es'treʎa] nf star; ~ **de mar** starfish.

estrellar [estre'ʎar] vt (*hacer añicos*) to smash (to pieces); (*huevos*) to fry; ~**se** vr to smash; (*chocarse*) to crash; (*fracasar*) to be smashed to pieces.

estremecer [estreme'θer] vt to shake; ~**se** vr to shake, tremble; **estremecimiento** nm (*conmoción*) tremor; (*sobresalto*) shock; (*temblor*) trembling, shaking.

estrenar [estre'nar] vt (*vestido*) to wear for the first time; (*casa*) to move into; (*película, obra de teatro*) to present for the first time; ~**se** vr (*persona*) to make one's début; **estreno** nm (*primer uso*) first use; (*en un empleo*) début, first appearance; (*CINE etc*) première.

estreñir [estre'ɲir] vt to constipate; ~**se** vr to become constipated.

estrépito [es'trepito] nm noise, racket; (*fig*) fuss; **estrepitoso, a** a noisy; (*fiesta*) rowdy, boisterous.

estría [es'tria] nf groove.

estribar [estri'βar] vi: ~ **en** to rest on, be supported by.

estribo [es'triβo] nm (*de jinete*) stirrup; (*de coche, tren*) step; (*de puente*) support; (*fig*) basis, foundation; (*GEO*) spur.

estribor [estri'βor] nm starboard.

estricnina [estrik'nina] nf strychnine.

estricto, a [es'trikto, a] a (*riguroso*) strict; (*severo*) severe.

estro ['estro] nm inspiration.

estropajo [estro'paxo] nm scourer.

estropear [estrope'ar] vt (*arruinar*) to spoil; (*dañar*) to damage; (*lisiar*) to maim; (*tullir*) to cripple; ~**se** vr (*objeto*) to get damaged; (*persona*) to be crippled.

estructura [estruk'tura] nf structure.

estruendo [es'trwendo] nm (*ruido*) racket, din; (*fig: alboroto*) uproar, turmoil; (*pompa*) pomp.

estrujar [estru'xar] vt (*apretar*) to squeeze; (*aplastar*) to crush; (*magullar*) to bruise; (*fig*) to drain, bleed.

estuario [es'twarjo] nm estuary.

estuche [es'tutʃe] nm box, case.

estudiante [estu'ðjante] nm/f student; **estudiantil** a inv student cpd.

estudiantina [estuðjan'tina] nf student music group.

estudiar [estu'ðjar] vt to study.

estudio [es'tuðjo] nm study; (*CINE, ARTE, RADIO*) studio; ~**s** nmpl studies; (*erudición*) learning sg; ~**so, a** a studious.

estufa [es'tufa] nf heater, fire.

estulticia [estul'tiθja] nf foolishness.

estupefacto, a [estupe'fakto, a] a speechless, thunderstruck.

estupendo, a [estu'pendo, a] a wonderful, terrific; (*fam*) great; ¡~! that's great!, fantastic!

estupidez [estupi'ðeθ] nf (*torpeza*) stupidity; (*tontería*) piece of nonsense.

estúpido, a [es'tupiðo, a] a stupid, silly.

estupor [estu'por] nm stupor; (*fig*) astonishment, amazement.

estupro [es'tupro] nm rape.

estuve etc vb ver **estar.**

etapa [e'tapa] nf stage; (*DEPORTE*) leg; (*parada*) stopping place; (*fig*) stage, phase.

eternidad [eterni'ðað] nf eternity; **eterno, a** a eternal, everlasting.

ético, a ['etiko, a] a ethical // nf ethics pl.

etíope [e'tiope] a, nm/f Ethiopian.

Etiopía [etjo'pia] nf Ethiopia.

etiqueta [eti'keta] nf (*modales*) etiquette; (*papel*) label, tag.

eucalipto [euka'lipto] nm eucalyptus.

Eucaristía [eukaris'tia] nf Eucharist.

eufemismo [eufe'mismo] nm euphemism.

euforia [eu'forja] nf euphoria.

eugenesia [euxe'nesja] nf, **eugenismo** [euxe'nismo] nm eugenics sg.

eunuco [eu'nuko] nm eunuch.

Europa [eu'ropa] nf Europe; **europeo, a** a, nm/f European.

éuscaro, a ['euskaro, a] a Basque // nm (*lengua*) Basque.

Euskadi [eus'kaði] nm the Basque Provinces pl.

eutanasia [euta'nasja] nf euthanasia.

evacuación [eβakwa'θjon] nf evacuation; **evacuar** vt to evacuate.

evadir [eβa'ðir] vt to evade, avoid; ~**se** vr to escape.

evaluar [eβa'lwar] vt to evaluate.

evangélico, a [eβan'xeliko, a] a evangelic(al).

evangelio [eβan'xeljo] nm gospel.

evaporación [eβapora'θjon] nf evaporation.

evaporar [eβapo'rar] vt to evaporate; ~**se** vr to vanish.

evasión [eβa'sjon] nf escape, flight; (*fig*) evasion.

evasivo, a [eβa'siβo, a] a evasive, non-committal.

evento [e'βento] nm unforeseen event; (*eventualidad*) eventuality; **a cualquier** ~ in any event.

eventual [eβen'twal] a possible, conditional (upon circumstances); (*trabajador*) casual, temporary.

evidencia [eβi'ðenθja] nf (*certidumbre*) evidence, proof; **evidenciar** vt (*hacer patente*) to make evident; (*probar*) to prove, show; **evidenciarse** vr to be evident.

evidente [eβi'ðente] a obvious, clear, evident.

evitar [eβi'tar] vt (*evadir*) to avoid; (*impedir*) to prevent.

evocar [eβo'kar] vt to evoke, call forth.

evolución [eβolu'θjon] nf (*desarrollo*) evolution, development; (*cambio*) change;

(MIL) manoeuvre; **evolucionar** vi to evolve; (MIL, AVIAT) to manoeuvre.

ex [eks] a ex-; **el ~ ministro** the former minister, the ex-minister.

exacerbar [eksaθer'ßar] vt to irritate, annoy; (agravar) to aggravate.

exactitud [eksakti'tuð] nf exactness; (precisión) accuracy; (puntualidad) punctuality; **exacto, a** a exact; accurate; punctual; ¡**exacto!** exactly!

exageración [eksaxera'θjon] nf exaggeration; **exagerar** vt, vi to exaggerate.

exaltado, a [eksal'taðo, a] a (apasionado) over-excited, worked-up; (exagerado) extreme; (excitado) elated.

exaltar [eksal'tar] vt to exalt, glorify; ~**se** vr (excitarse) to get excited or worked-up; (arrebatarse) to get carried away.

examen [ek'samen] nm examination.

examinar [eksami'nar] vt to examine; ~**se** vr to be examined, sit an examination.

exangüe [ek'sangwe] a (desangrado) bloodless; (sin fuerzas) weak.

exasperar [eksaspe'rar] vt to exasperate; ~**se** vr to get exasperated, lose patience.

Exca. abr de **Excelencia.**

excedente [eksθe'ðente] a, nm excess, surplus.

exceder [eksθe'ðer] vt to exceed, surpass; ~**se** vr (extralimitarse) to go too far; (sobrepasarse) to excel o.s.

excelencia [eksθe'lenθja] nf excellence; **E~** Excellency; **excelente** a excellent.

excelso, a [eks'θelso, a] a lofty, sublime.

excentricidad [eksθentriθi'ðað] nf eccentricity; **excéntrico, a** a, nm/f eccentric.

excepción [eksθep'θjon] nf exception; **excepcional** a exceptional.

excepto [eks'θepto] ad excepting, except (for).

exceptuar [eksθep'twar] vt to except, exclude.

excesivo, a [eksθe'sißo, a] a excessive.

exceso [eks'θeso] nm (gen) excess; (COM) surplus.

excitación [eksθita'θjon] nf (sensación) excitement; (acción) excitation.

excitado, a [eksθi'taðo, a] a excited; (emociones) aroused; **excitar** vt to excite; (incitar) to urge; **excitarse** vr to get excited.

exclamación [eksklama'θjon] nf exclamation; **exclamar** vi to exclaim.

excluir [eksklu'ir] vt to exclude; (dejar fuera) to shut out; (descartar) to reject; **exclusión** nf exclusion; (descarte) rejection; **con exclusión de** excluding.

exclusiva [eksklu'sißa], **exclusividad** [eksklusißi'ðað] nf exclusiveness; (PRENSA) exclusive; (COM) sole right or agency.

exclusivo, a [eksklu'sißo, a] a exclusive; (único) sole.

Excmo. abr de **excelentísmo.**

excomulgar [ekskomul'var] vt (REL) to

excommunicate; (excluir) to ban, banish.

excomunión [ekskomu'njon] nf excommunication.

excoriar [eksko'rjar] vt to flay, skin.

excursión [ekskur'sjon] nf excursion, outing; **excursionismo** nm sightseeing.

excusa [eks'kusa] nf excuse; (disculpa) apology.

excusado, a [eksku'saðo, a] a unnecessary; (disculpado) excused, forgiven // nm lavatory, toilet.

excusar [eksku'sar] vt to excuse; (evitar) to avoid; (impedir) to prevent; ~**se** vr (rehusarse) to decline a request; (disculparse) to apologize.

execrar [ekse'krar] vt to loathe.

exención [eksen'θjon] nf exemption.

exento, a [ek'sento, a] pp de **eximir** // a exempt; ~ **de derechos** tax-free.

exequias [ek'sekjas] nfpl funeral rites, obsequies.

exhalación [eksala'θjon] nf (del aire) exhalation; (vapor) fumes pl, vapour; (rayo) shooting star.

exhalar [eksa'lar] vt to exhale, breathe out; (olor etc) to give off; (suspiro) to breathe, heave.

exhausto, a [ek'sausto, a] a exhausted.

exhibición [eksißi'θjon] nf exhibition; display, show.

exhibir [eksi'ßir] vt to exhibit, display, show.

exhortación [eksorta'θjon] nf exhortation; **exhortar** vt: **exhortar a** to exhort to.

exigencia [eksi'xenθja] nf demand, requirement; **exigente** a demanding.

exigir [eksi'xir] vt (gen) to demand, require; (pago) to exact.

exilio [ek'siljo] nm exile.

eximio, a [ek'simjo, a] a (excelente) choice, select; (eminente) distinguished, eminent.

eximir [eksi'mir] vt to exempt.

existencia [eksis'tenθja] nf existence; ~**s** nfpl stock(s) (pl).

existir [eksis'tir] vi to exist, be.

éxito ['eksito] nm (resultado) result, outcome; (triunfo) success; **tener ~** to be successful.

exonerar [eksone'rar] vt to exonerate; ~ **de una obligación** to free from an obligation.

exorcizar [eksorθi'θar] vt to exorcize.

exótico, a [ek'sotiko, a] a exotic.

expandir [ekspan'dir] vt to expand.

expansión [ekspan'sjon] nf expansion.

expatriarse [ekspa'trjarse] vr to emigrate; (POL) to go into exile.

expectativa [ekspekta'tißa] nf (espera) expectation; (perspectiva) prospect.

expedición [ekspeði'θjon] nf (excursión) expedition; (envío) shipment; (rapidez) speed.

expediente [ekspe'ðjente] nm expedient; (JUR: procedimento) action, proceedings pl; (: papeles) dossier, file, record.

expedir [ekspe'ðir] vt (despachar) to send, forward; (libreta cívica, pasaporte) to issue; (fig) to deal with.

expedito, a [ekspe'ðito, a] a (libre) clear, free; (pronto) prompt, speedy.

expendedor, a [ekspende'ðor, a] nm/f (vendedor) dealer; (aparato) (vending) machine; ~ **de cigarrillos** cigarette machine.

expendeduría [ekspendedu'ria] nf shop; (estanco) tobacconist's (shop).

expensas [eks'pensas] nfpl expenses; a ~ **de** at the expense of.

experiencia [ekspe'rjenθja] nf experience; (científica) experiment.

experimentado, a [eksperimen'taðo, a] a experienced.

experimentar [eksperimen'tar] vt (en laboratorio) to experiment with; (probar) to test, try out; (notar, observar) to experience; (sufrir) to suffer; **experimento** nm experiment.

experto, a [eks'perto, a] a (práctico) expert; (diestro) skilled, experienced // nm/f expert.

expiar [ekspi'ar] vt to atone for.

expirar [ekspi'rar] vi to expire.

explayar [ekspla'jar] vt to extend, expand; ~**se** vr to extend, spread; ~**se con uno** to confide in sb.

explicación [eksplika'θjon] nf explanation; **explicar** vt to explain; **explicarse** vr to explain (o.s.).

explícito, a [eks'pliθito, a] a explicit.

explorador, a [eksplora'ðor, a] nm/f (pionero) explorer; (MIL) scout // nm (MED) probe; (TEC) (radar) scanner; **los E~es** the Scouts.

explorar [eksplo'rar] vt to explore; (MED) to probe; (radar) to scan.

explosión [eksplo'sjon] nf explosion; **explosivo, a** a explosive.

explotación [eksplota'θjon] nf exploitation; (de planta etc) running, operation; **explotar** vt to exploit; to run, operate // vi to explode.

exponer [ekspo'ner] vt to expose; (cuadro) to display; (vida) to risk; (idea) to explain; ~**se** vr to expose o.s., leave o.s. open.

exportación [eksporta'θjon] nf (acción) export; (mercancías) exports pl; **exportar** vt to export.

exposición [eksposi'θjon] nf (gen) exposure; (de arte) show, exhibition; (petición) petition; (explicación) explanation; (narración) account, statement.

exposímetro [ekspo'simetro] nm (FOTO) exposure meter.

exprés [eks'pres] nm (AM) express (train).

expresar [ekspre'sar] vt to express; **expresión** nf expression; **expresiones** nfpl regards.

expreso, a [eks'preso, a] pp de **expresar** // a (claro) specific, clear; (rápido) fast // nm: **mandar por** ~ to send by express (delivery).

exprimir [ekspri'mir] vt (fruta) to squeeze (out); (ropa) to wring out; (fig) to express emphatically.

expropiar [ekspro'pjar] vt to expropriate.

expuesto, a [eks'pwesto, a] a exposed; (cuadro etc) on show, on display.

expugnar [ekspuɣ'nar] vt to take by storm.

expulsar [ekspul'sar] vt (echar) to eject; (arrojar) to throw out; (expeler) to expel; (desalojar) to drive out; (despedir) to sack, fire; (a un futbolista) to send off; **expulsión** nf expulsion; sending-off.

expurgar [ekspur'ɣar] vt to expurgate.

exquisito, a [ekski'sito, a] a exquisite; (agradable) delightful.

éxtasis ['ekstasis] nm ecstasy.

extender [eksten'der] vt (gen) to extend; (los brazos) to stretch out, hold out; (mapa) to spread (out), open (out); (mantequilla) to spread; (certificado) to issue; (cheque, recibo) to make out; (documento) to draw up; ~**se** vr (gen) to extend; (en el suelo) to stretch out; (epidemia) to spread; **extendido, a** a (abierto) spread out, open; (brazos) outstretched; (prevaleciente) widespread; **extensión** nf (de país) expanse, stretch; (de libro) extent; (de tiempo) length, duration; (AM) extension; **en toda la extensión de la palabra** in every sense of the word; **extenso, a** a extensive; (prevaleciente) widespread.

extenuar [ekste'nwar] vi (agotar) to exhaust; (debilitar) to weaken.

exterior [ekste'rjor] a inv (de fuera) external; (afuera) outside, exterior; (apariencia) outward; (comercio) foreign // nm (gen) exterior, outside; (aspecto) outward appearance; (DEPORTE) wing(er); **el** ~ foreign parts pl; **al** ~ outwardly, on the surface.

exterminar [ekstermi'nar] vt to exterminate; **exterminio** nm extermination.

externo, a [eks'terno, a] a (exterior) external, outside; (superficial) outward // nm/f day pupil.

extinguir [ekstin'gir] vt (fuego) to extinguish, put out; (raza, población) to wipe out; ~**se** vr (fuego) to go out; (BIO) to die out, become extinct.

extinto, a [eks'tinto, a] a extinct.

extintor [ekstin'tor] nm (fire) extinguisher.

extra ['ekstra] a, nm/f extra // nm extra; (bono) bonus.

extracción [ekstrak'θjon] nf extraction; (en lotería) draw.

extracto [eks'trakto] nm extract.

extraer [ekstra'er] vt to extract, take out.

extralimitarse [ekstralimi'tarse] vr to go too far.

extranjero, a [ekstran'xero, a] a foreign // nm/f foreigner // nm foreign lands pl; **en el** ~ abroad.

extrañar [ekstra'nar] vt (desterrar) to exile; (sorprender) to find strange or odd;

(*AM*) to miss; **~se** *vr* (*sorprenderse*) to be amazed, be surprised; (*distanciarse*) to become estranged, grow apart.

extrañeza [ekstra'ɲeθa] *nf* (*rareza*) strangeness, oddness; (*asombro*) amazement, surprise.

extraño, a [eks'traɲo, a] *a* (*extranjero*) foreign; (*raro, sorprendente*) strange, odd.

extraordinario, a [ekstraorði'narjo, a] *a* extraordinary; (*edición, número*) special // *nm* (*plato*) special dish; (*de periódico*) special edition; **horas ~as** overtime *sg*.

extravagancia [ekstraßa'xanθja] *nf* extravagance; **extravagante** *a* extravagant; (*extraño*) strange, odd; (*excéntrico*) eccentric; (*estrafalario*) outlandish.

extraviado, a [ekstra'ßjaðo, a] *a* lost, missing.

extraviar [ekstra'ßjar] *vt* (*desviar*) to mislead; (*perder*) to lose, misplace; **~se** *vr* to lose one's way, get lost.

extravío [ekstra'ßio] *nm* loss; (*fig*) deviation.

extremar [ekstre'mar] *vt* to carry to extremes; **~se** *vr* to do one's utmost, make every effort.

extremaunción [ekstremaun'θjon] *nf* extreme unction.

extremeño, a [ekstre'meɲo, a] *a, nm/f* Extremaduran.

extremidad [ekstremi'ðað] *nf* (*punta*) extremity; (*fila*) edge; **~es** *nfpl* (*ANAT*) extremities.

extremo, a [eks'tremo, a] *a* extreme; (*último*) last // *nm* end; (*límite, grado sumo*) extreme; **en último ~** as a last resort; **~ derecho/izquierdo** outside-right/ outside-left.

extrínseco, a [eks'trinseko, a] *a* extrinsic.

extrovertido, a [ekstroßer'tiðo, a] *a, nm/f* extrovert.

exuberancia [eksuße'ranθja] *nf* exuberance; **exuberante** *a* exuberant; (*fig*) luxuriant, lush.

exvoto [eks'ßoto] *nm* votive offering.

eyacular [ejaku'lar] *vt, vi* to ejaculate.

F

f.a.b. *abr de* **franco a bordo** f.o.b. (free on board).

fábrica ['faßrika] *nf* factory; **marca de ~** trademark; **precio de ~** factory price.

fabricación [faßrika'θjon] *nf* (*manufactura*) manufacture; (*producción*) production; **de ~ casera** home-made; **~ en serie** mass production.

fabricante [faßri'kante] *nm/f* manufacturer.

fabricar [faßri'kar] *vt* (*hacer*) to manufacture, make; (*construir*) to build; (*elaborar*) to fabricate, devise.

fabril [fa'ßril] *a*: **industria ~** manufacturing industry.

fábula ['faßula] *nf* (*cuento*) fable; (*chisme*) rumour.

facción [fak'θjon] *nf* (*POL*) faction; (*del rostro*) feature.

fácil ['faθil] *a* (*simple*) easy; (*probable*) likely.

facilidad [faθili'ðað] *nf* (*capacidad*) ease; (*sencillez*) simplicity; (*de palabra*) fluency; **~es** *nfpl* facilities.

facilitar [faθili'tar] *vt* (*hacer fácil*) to make easy; (*proporcionar*) to provide; (*hacer posible*) to arrange; (*hacer más fácil*) to facilitate.

fácilmente ['faθilmente] *ad* easily.

factible [fak'tißle] *a* feasible.

factor [fak'tor] *nm* factor.

factura [fak'tura] *nf* (*cuenta*) bill; (*hechura*) manufacture; **facturar** *vt* (*COM*) to invoice, charge for.

facultad [fakul'tað] *nf* (*aptitud, ESCOL etc*) faculty; (*poder*) power.

facha ['fatʃa] *nf* (*fam: aspecto*) look; (: *desagradable*) unpleasant sight.

fachada [fa'tʃaða] *nf* (*ARQ*) façade, front.

faena [fa'ena] *nf* (*trabajo*) work; (*quehacer*) task, job; **~s de la casa** housework *sg*.

fagot [fa'got] *nm* (*MUS*) bassoon.

faisán [fai'san] *nm* pheasant.

faja ['faxa] *nf* (*para la cintura*) sash; (*de mujer*) corset; (*de tierra*) strip; (*venda*) bandage.

falange [fa'lanxe] *nf* (*POL*) Falange.

falda ['falda] *nf* (*prenda de vestir*) skirt.

falibilidad [falißili'ðað] *nf* fallibility.

fálico, a ['faliko, a] *a* phallic.

falo ['falo] *nm* phallus.

falsedad [false'ðað] *nf* (*hipocresía*) falseness; (*mentira*) falsehood.

falsificar [falsifi'kar] *vt* (*firma etc*) to forge; (*voto etc*) to rig; (*moneda*) to counterfeit.

falso, a ['falso, a] *a* (*gen*) false; (*erróneo*) mistaken; (*moneda etc*) fake; **en ~** falsely.

falta ['falta] *nf* (*defecto*) fault, flaw; (*privación*) lack, want; (*ausencia*) absence; (*carencia*) shortage; (*equivocación*) mistake; (*DEPORTE*) foul; **hacer ~** to be missing *or* lacking.

faltar [fal'tar] *vi* (*escasear*) to be lacking, be wanting; (*ausentarse*) to be absent, be missing; (*fallar: mecanismo*) to go wrong, break down; **faltan 2 horas para llegar** there are 2 hours to go till arrival; **~ el respeto a alguien** to be disrespectful to sb; **echar a ~ a alguien** to miss sb; **¡no faltaba más!** that's the last straw!

falto, a ['falto, a] *a* (*desposeído*) deficient, lacking; (*necesitado*) poor, wretched.

falla ['faʎa] *nf* (*defecto*) fault, flaw; (*fracaso*) failure.

fallar [fa'ʎar] *vt* (*JUR*) to pronounce sentence on // *vi* (*memoria*) to fail; (*motor*) to miss.

fallecer [faʎe'θer] *vi* to pass away, die; **fallecimiento** *nm* decease, demise.

fallo ['faʎo] *nm* (*JUR*) verdict, ruling; (*fracaso*) failure.

fama ['fama] *nf* (*renombre*) fame; (*reputación*) reputation.
familia [fa'milja] *nf* family.
familiar [fami'ljar] *a* (*relativo a la familia*) family *cpd*; (*conocido, informal*) familiar // *nm* relative; ~**idad** *nf* (*gen*) familiarity; (*informalidad*) homeliness; ~**izarse** *vr* to familiarize o.s. with.
famoso, a [fa'moso, a] *a* (*renombrado*) famous; (*fam: fabuloso*) great.
fanático, a [fa'natiko, a] *a* fanatical // *nm/f* (*gen*) fanatic; (*CINE etc*) fan; (*de deportes*) supporter; **fanatismo** *nm* fanaticism.
fanfarrón, ona [fanfa'rron, ona] *a* boastful; (*pey*) showy.
fango ['fango] *nm* mud; ~**so, a** *a* muddy.
fantasía [fanta'sia] *nf* fantasy, imagination; (*fam*) conceit, vanity; **joyas de** ~ imitation jewellery *sg*.
fantasma [fan'tasma] *nm* (*espectro*) ghost, apparition.
fantástico, a [fan'tastiko, a] *a* fantastic.
farmacéutico, a [farma'θeutiko, a] *a* pharmaceutical // *nm/f* chemist, pharmacist.
farmacia [far'maθja] *nf* chemist's (shop), pharmacy; ~ **de turno** all-night chemist.
faro ['faro] *nm* (*NAUT: torre*) lighthouse; (*AUTO*) headlamp; ~**s laterales** sidelights; ~**s traseros** rear lights.
farol [fa'rol] *nm* (*luz*) lantern, lamp; (*de calle*) streetlamp.
farsa ['farsa] *nf* (*gen*) farce.
farsante [far'sante] *nm/f* fraud, fake.
fascinar [fasθi'nar] *vt* (*deslumbrar*) to fascinate.
fascismo [fas'θismo] *nm* fascism; **fascista** *a, nm/f* fascist.
fase ['fase] *nf* phase.
fastidiar [fasti'ðjar] *vt* (*disgustar*) to annoy, bother; (*estropear*) to spoil; (*aburrir*) to bore; ~**se** *vr* (*dañarse*) to harm o.s.; (*disgustarse*) to get annoyed *or* cross.
fastidio [fas'tiðjo] *nm* (*disgusto*) annoyance; (*tedio*) boredom; ~**so, a** *a* (*molesto*) annoying; (*aburrido*) tedious.
fatal [fa'tal] *a* (*gen*) fatal; (*inevitable*) unavoidable; (*desgraciado*) ill-fated; (*fam: malo, pésimo*) awful; ~**idad** *nf* (*destino*) fate; (*mala suerte*) misfortune.
fatiga [fa'tixa] *nf* (*cansancio*) fatigue, weariness; **fatigar** *vt* to tire, weary; **fatigarse** *vr* to get tired; **fatigoso, a** *a* (*cansador*) tiring; (*aburrido*) tiresome.
fatuo, a ['fatwo, a] *a* (*vano*) fatuous; (*presuntuoso*) conceited.
fauces ['fauθes] *nfpl* jaws, mouth *sg*.
favor [fa'ßor] *nm* favour; **entrada de** ~ complimentary ticket; **haga el** ~ **de...** would you be so good as to..., kindly...; **por** ~ please; ~**able** *a* favourable.
favorecer [faßore'θer] *vt* (*gen*) to favour; (*vestido etc*) to become, flatter; **este peinado le favorece** this hairstyle suits her.

favorito, a [faßo'rito, a] *a, nm/f* favourite.
faz [faθ] *nf*: **la** ~ **de la tierra** the face of the earth.
fe [fe] *nf* (*REL*) faith; (*confianza*) belief; (*documento*) certificate; (*lealtad*) fidelity, loyalty; **prestar** ~ **a** to believe, credit; **actuar con buena/mala** ~ to act in good/bad faith; **dar** ~ **de** to bear witness to.
fealdad [feal'dað] *nf* ugliness.
febrero [fe'ßrero] *nm* February.
febril [fe'ßril] *a* feverish.
fecundar [fekun'dar] *vt* (*generar*) to fertilize, make fertile; **fecundo, a** *a* (*fértil*) fertile; (*prolífico*) prolific; (*fructífero*) fruitful; (*abundante*) abundant; (*productivo*) productive.
fecha ['fetʃa] *nf* date; **en** ~ **próxima** soon; **hasta la** ~ to date, so far; **poner** ~ to date; **con** ~ **adelantada** post-dated.
federación [federa'θjon] *nf* federation.
federal [feðe'ral] *a* federal; ~**ismo** *nm* federalism.
felicidad [feliθi'ðað] *nf* (*satisfacción, contento*) happiness; (*suerte feliz*) (good) luck; ~**es** *nfpl* best wishes, congratulations.
felicitación [feliθita'θjon] *nf* congratulation; **felicitar** *vt* to congratulate.
feligrés, esa [feli'xres, esa] *nm/f* parishioner.
feliz [fe'liθ] *a* (*contento*) happy; (*afortunado*) lucky.
felonía [felo'nia] *nf* felony, crime.
felpudo [fel'puðo] *nm* doormat.
femenino, a [feme'nino, a] *a, nm* feminine.
feminista [femi'nista] *nf* feminist.
fénix ['feniks] *nm* (*ave*) phoenix.
fenómeno [fe'nomeno] *nm* phenomenon; (*fig*) freak, accident // *a inv* great // *excl* smashing!, marvellous!
feo, a ['feo, a] *a* (*gen*) ugly; (*desagradable*) bad, nasty.
féretro ['feretro] *nm* (*ataúd*) coffin; (*sarcófago*) bier.
feria ['ferja] *nf* (*gen*) fair; (*AM*) village market; (*día de asueto*) holiday, rest day.
fermentar [fermen'tar] *vi* to ferment.
ferocidad [feroθi'ðað] *nf* fierceness, ferocity.
feroz [fe'roθ] *a* (*cruel*) cruel; (*salvaje*) fierce.
férreo, a ['ferreo, a] *a* iron.
ferretería [ferrete'ria], **ferrería** [ferre'ria] *nf* (*trastes*) ironmongery; (*tienda*) ironmonger's (shop); hardware store.
ferrocarril [ferroka'rril] *nm* railway; ~ **de cremallera** rack railway.
fértil ['fertil] *a* (*productivo*) fertile; (*rico*) rich; **fertilidad** *nf* (*gen*) fertility; (*productividad*) fruitfulness; **fertilizar** *vt* to fertilize.
fervor [fer'ßor] *nm* fervour; ~**oso, a** *a* fervent.
festejar [feste'xar] *vt* (*agasajar*) to

entertain lavishly; (*galantear*) to court; (*su cumpleaños*) to celebrate; **festejo** *nm* (*diversión*) entertainment; (*galanteo*) courtship; (*fiesta*) celebration.
festividad [festiβi'ðað] *nf* festivity.
festivo, a [fes'tiβo, a] *a* (*de fiesta*) festive; (*fig*) witty; (*CINE, LITERATURA*) humorous.
fétido, a ['fetiðo, a] *a* (*hediondo*) foul-smelling; (*podrido*) rotten.
fiado [fi'aðo] *nm*: **comprar al** ~ to buy on credit.
fiador, a [fia'ðor, a] *nm/f* (*JUR*) surety, guarantor; (*COM*) backer // *nm* (*de arma*) safety catch; (*cerrojo*) tumbler; **salir** ~ **por alguien** to go bail for sb.
fiambre ['fjambre] *nm* cold meat.
fianza ['fjanθa] *nf* surety; (*JUR*): **libertad bajo** ~ release on bail.
fiar [fi'ar] *vt* (*salir garante de*) to guarantee; (*vender a crédito*) to sell on credit // *vi* to trust; ~**se** *vr* to trust (in), rely on; ~**se de uno** to rely on sb.
fiasco ['fjasko] *nm* fiasco.
fibra ['fiβra] *nf* fibre.
ficción [fik'θjon] *nf* fiction.
ficticio, a [fik'tiθjo, a] *a* (*imaginario*) fictitious; (*falso*) fabricated.
ficha ['fitʃa] *nf* (*en juegos*) token, counter; (*tarjeta*) (index) card; (*ELEC*) plug; **fichar** *vt* (*archivar*) to file, index; **estar fichado** to have a record; **fichero** *nm* card index.
fidelidad [fiðeli'ðað] *nf* (*lealtad*) fidelity, loyalty; **alta** ~ high fidelity, hi-fi.
fideos [fi'ðeos] *nmpl* noodles.
fiebre ['fjeβre] *nf* (*MED*) fever; (*fig*) feverish excitement; ~ **amarilla/del heno** yellow/hay fever; ~ **palúdica** malaria; **tener** ~ to have a temperature.
fiel [fjel] *a* (*leal*) faithful, loyal; (*fiable*) reliable; (*exacto*) accurate, exact // *nm* inspector; (*aguja*) needle, pointer; **los** ~**es** the faithful.
fieltro ['fjeltro] *nm* felt.
fiereza [fje'reθa] *nf* (*bravura*) fierceness; (*fealdad*) ugliness.
fiero, a ['fjero, a] *a* (*cruel*) cruel; (*feroz*) fierce; (*duro*) harsh // *nf* (*animal feroz*) wild animal or beast.
fiesta ['fjesta] *nf* party; (*de pueblo*) festival; ~**s** *nfpl* (*caricias*) endearments; (*vacaciones*) holiday *sg*; (*broma*) jokes; (*juerga*) fun and games; (*REL*): ~ **de guardar** day of obligation.
figura [fi'ɣura] *nf* (*gen*) figure; (*forma, imagen*) shape, form; (*cara*) face; (*TEATRO*) marionette; (*NAIPES*) face card.
figurar [fiɣu'rar] *vt* (*representar*) to represent; (*fingir*) to figure // *vi* to figure; ~**se** *vr* (*imaginarse*) to imagine; (*suponer*) to suppose.
fijar [fi'xar] *vt* (*gen*) to fix; (*estampilla*) to affix, stick (on); (*fig*) to settle (on), decide; ~ **con hilos** to sew on; ~**se** *vr*: ~**se en** to notice.
fijo, a ['fixo, a] *a* (*gen*) fixed; (*firme*) firm; (*permanente*) permanent // *ad*: **mirar** ~ to stare.

fila ['fila] *nf* row; (*cola, columna*) queue; (*cadena*) line; **ponerse en** ~ to line up, get into line.
filántropo [fi'lantropo] *nm* philanthropist.
filatelia [fila'telja] *nf* philately.
filete [fi'lete] *nm* (*carne*) steak; (*pescado*) fillet.
filial [fi'ljal] *a* filial // *nf* subsidiary.
Filipinas [fili'pinas] *nfpl*: **las** ~ the Philippines.
filmar [fil'mar] *vt* to film, shoot.
filo ['filo] *nm* (*gen*) edge; **sacar** ~ **a** to sharpen; **al** ~ **del mediodía** at about midday; **de doble** ~ double-edged.
filosofía [filoso'fia] *nf* philosophy; **filósofo** *nm* philosopher.
filtrar [fil'trar] *vt, vi* to filter, strain; ~**se** *vr* to filter; (*fig*) to dwindle; **filtro** *nm* (*TEC, utensilio*) filter; (*CULIN*) strainer.
fin [fin] *nm* (*gen*) end; (*objetivo*) aim, purpose; **al** ~ **y al cabo** when all's said and done; **a** ~ **de** in order to; **por** ~ finally; **en** ~ in short; ~ **de semana** weekend; ~**al** *a* final // *nm* end, conclusion // *nf* final; ~**alista** *nm/f* finalist; ~**alizar** *vt* to end, finish // *vi*, ~**alizarse** *vr* to end, come to an end.
financiar [finan'θjar] *vt* to finance; **financiero, a** *a* financial.
finca ['finka] *nf* country estate; (*casa*) country house.
fingir [fin'xir] *vt* (*simular*) to simulate; (*pretextar*) to sham, fake // *vi* (*aparentar*) to pretend, feign; ~**se** *vr* to pretend to be.
finlandés, esa [finlan'des, esa] *a* Finnish // *nm/f* Finn // *nm* (*lengua*) Finnish.
Finlandia [fin'landja] *nf* Finland.
fino, a ['fino, a] *a* (*gen*) fine; (*delgado*) slender; (*puro*) pure; (*de buenas maneras*) polite, refined; (*inteligente*) shrewd.
firma ['firma] *nf* signature; (*COM*) firm, company; **firmar** *vt* to sign.
firme ['firme] *a* (*gen*) firm; (*estable*) stable; (*sólido*) solid; (*compacto*) compact; (*constante*) steady; (*decidido*) resolute // *nm* road (surface); ~**mente** *ad* firmly; ~**za** *nf* firmness; (*constancia*) steadiness; (*solidez*) solidity.
fiscal [fis'kal] *a* fiscal // *nm* Public Prosecutor.
fisgar [fis'ɣar] *vt* to pry into; (*pescar*) to spear, harpoon.
físico, a ['fisiko, a] *a* physical // *nm* physique // *nm/f* physicist // *nf* physics *sg*.
flaco, a ['flako, a] *a* (*muy delgado*) skinny, lean; (*débil*) weak, feeble.
flagrante [fla'ɣrante] *a* flagrant.
flamante [fla'mante] *a* brilliant; (*nuevo*) brand-new.
flamenco, a [fla'menko, a] *a* (*de Flandes*) Flemish; (*agitanado*) gipsy // *nm* (*canto y baile*) flamenco.
flan [flan] *nm* creme caramel.
flaqueza [fla'keθa] *nf* (*delgadez*) leanness; (*fig*) weakness.
flash [flaʃ] *nm* (*FOTO*) flash.
flauta ['flauta] *nf* flute.

fleco ['fleko] nm fringe.
flecha ['fletʃa] nf arrow.
flema ['flema] nm phlegm.
flequillo [fle'kiʎo] nm (pelo) fringe.
flete ['flete] nm (carga) freight; (alquiler) charter; (precio) freightage.
flexible [flek'siβle] a flexible.
flojo, a ['floxo, a] a (gen) loose; (sin fuerzas) limp; (débil) weak.
flor [flor] nf flower; (piropo) compliment; **a ~ de** on the surface of; **~ecer** vi (BOT) to flower; (fig) to flourish; **~eciente** a (BOT) in flower, flowering; (fig) thriving.
flota ['flota] nf fleet.
flotar [flo'tar] vi (gen) to float; (colgar) to hang; **flote** nm: **a flote** afloat; **sacar a flote** (fig) to get back on one's feet.
fluctuar [fluk'twar] vi (oscilar) to fluctuate; (vacilar) to waver.
fluidez [flui'ðeθ] nf fluidity; (fig) fluency.
flúido, a ['fluiðo, a] a, nm fluid.
fluir [flu'ir] vi to flow.
flujo ['fluxo] nm flow; **~ y reflujo** ebb and flow; **~ de sangre** (MED) loss of blood.
foca ['foka] nf seal.
foco ['foko] nm focus; (ELEC) floodlight.
fogón [fo'ɤon] nm (de cocina) stove.
fogoso, a [fo'ɤoso, a] a spirited.
follaje [fo'ʎaxe] nm foliage.
folleto [fo'ʎeto] nm pamphlet.
fomentar [fomen'tar] vt (MED) to foment; **fomento** nm (MED) fomentation; (promoción) promotion; **Ministerio de Fomento** Ministry of Public Works.
fonda ['fonda] nf inn; (restaurante) buffet.
fondo ['fondo] nm (de mar) bottom; (cuarto) back; (ARTE etc) background; (reserva) fund; **~s** nmpl (COM) funds, resources; **una investigación a ~** a thorough investigation; **en el ~** at bottom, deep down.
fontanería [fontane'ria] nf plumbing; **fontanero** nm plumber.
forastero, a [foras'tero, a] a (extraño) alien, strange // nm/f stranger.
forcejear [forθexe'ar] vi (luchar) to struggle; (esforzarse) to make violent efforts.
forjar [for'xar] vt to forge.
forma ['forma] nf (figura) form, shape; (molde) mould, pattern; (MED) fitness; (método) way, means; **las ~s** the conventions.
formación [forma'θjon] nf (gen) formation; (educación) education.
formal [for'mal] a (gen) formal; (fig: persona) serious; **~idad** nf formality; seriousness.
formar [for'mar] vt (componer) to form, shape; (constituir) to make up, constitute; (ESCOL) to train, educate; **~se** vr (cobrar forma) to form, take form; (hacer línea) to form up; (desarrollarse) to develop.
formidable [formi'ðaβle] a (temible) formidable; (asombroso) tremendous.
formulario [formu'larjo] nm form.

fornido, a [for'niðo, a] a strapping, well-built.
foro ['foro] nm (gen) forum; (JUR) court.
forrar [fo'rrar] vt (abrigo) to line; (libro) to cover; **forro** nm (de cuaderno) cover; (costura) lining; (de sillón) upholstery; **forro de freno** brake lining.
fortalecer [fortale'θer] vt to strengthen.
fortaleza [forta'leθa] nf (gen) strength; (determinación) resolution.
fortuito, a [for'twito, a] a accidental.
fortuna [for'tuna] nf (suerte) fortune, (good) luck; (riqueza, caudal) fortune, wealth.
forzar [for'θar] vt (puerta) to force (open); (casa) to break into; (compeler) to compel.
forzoso, a [for'θoso, a] a necessary.
fosa ['fosa] nf (sepultura) grave; (en tierra) pit; (MED) cavity.
fósforo ['fosforo] nm (metaloide) phosphorus; (AM) match.
foso ['foso] nm ditch; (TEATRO) pit; (AUTO): **~ de reconocimiento** inspection pit.
foto ['foto] nf photo, snap(shot); **~copia** nf photocopy; **~copiador** nm photocopier; **~copiar** vt to photocopy.
fotografía [fotoɤra'fia] nf (gen) photography; (una ~) photograph; **fotografiar** vt to photograph.
fotógrafo, a [fo'toɤrafo, a] nm/f photographer.
fracaso [fra'kaso] nm (desgracia, revés) failure; **fracasar** vi (gen) to fail.
fracción [frak'θjon] nf fraction; (POL) faction; **fraccionar** vt to divide, break up.
fractura [frak'tura] nf fracture, break.
fragancia [fra'xanðja] nf (olor) fragrance; (perfume) perfume.
frágil ['fraxil] a (débil) fragile; (quebradizo) breakable; **fragilidad** nf fragility; (de persona) frailty.
fragmento [fraɤ'mento] nm (pedazo) fragment.
fragor [fra'ɤor] nm (ruido intenso) din; (de gente) uproar.
fragua ['fraɤwa] nf forge; **fraguar** vt to forge; (fig) to concoct // vi to harden.
fraile ['fraile] nm (REL) friar; (: monje) monk.
frambuesa [fram'bwesa] nf raspberry.
francés, esa [fran'θes, esa] a French // nm/f Frenchman/woman // nm (lengua) French.
Francia ['franθja] nf France.
franco, a ['franko, a] a (leal, abierto) frank, open; (generoso, liberal) generous, liberal; (COM: exento) free // nm franc.
francotirador, a [frankotira'ðor, a] nm/f sniper.
franela [fra'nela] nf flannel.
franja ['franxa] nf fringe.
franquear [franke'ar] vt (camino) to clear; (carta, paquete postal) to frank, stamp; (obstáculo) to overcome; **~se** vr (ceder) to give way; (confiarse a alguien) to unburden o.s.

franqueo [fran'keo] nm postage.

franqueza [fran'keθa] nf (candor) frankness; (generosidad) generosity.

frasco ['frasko] nm bottle; (al vacío) (vacuum) flask.

frase ['frase] nf sentence; ~ **hecha** set phrase.

fraude ['frauðe] nm (cualidad) dishonesty; (acto) fraud; **fraudulento, a** a fraudulent.

frecuencia [fre'kwenθja] nf frequency; **con** ~ frequently, often.

fregador [freʃa'ðor] nm sink.

fregar [fre'ʃar] vt (frotar) to scrub; (platos) to wash (up); (AM) to annoy.

freír [fre'ir] vt to fry.

frenar [fre'nar] vt to brake; (fig) to check.

frenesí [frene'si] nm frenzy; **frenético, a** a frantic.

freno ['freno] nm (TEC, AUTO) brake; (de cabalgadura) bit; (fig) check.

frente ['frente] nm (ARQ, POL) front; (de objeto) front part // nf forehead, brow; **en** ~ **de** in front of; (en situación opuesta de) opposite; **chocar de** ~ to crash head-on; **hacer** ~ **a** to face up to.

fresa ['fresa] nf strawberry.

fresco, a ['fresko, a] a (nuevo) fresh; (frío) cool // nm (aire) fresh air; (ARTE) fresco; (fam) shameless person; (persona insolente) impudent person // nf cool part of the day; **tomar el** ~ to get some fresh air; **frescura** nf freshness; (descaro) cheek, nerve; (calma) calmness.

frialdad [frial'dað] nf (gen) coldness; (indiferencia) indifference.

fricción [frik'θjon] nf (gen) friction; (acto) rub(bing); (MED) massage.

frigidez [frixi'ðeθ] nf frigidity.

frigorífico [friʃo'rifiko] nm refrigerator.

frijol [fri'xol] nm kidney bean.

frío, a ['frio, a] a cold // nm cold(ness).

frito, a ['frito, a] a fried; **me trae** ~ **ese hombre** I'm sick and tired of that man.

frívolo, a ['friβolo, a] a frivolous.

frontera [fron'tera] nf frontier; **fronterizo, a** a frontier cpd; (contiguo) bordering.

frontón [fron'ton] nm (DEPORTE) pelota court.

frotar [fro'tar] vt to rub; ~**se** vr: ~**se las manos** to rub one's hands.

fructífero, a [fruk'tifero, a] a fruitful.

frugal [fru'ʃal] a frugal.

fruncir [frun'θir] vt to pucker; (costura) to pleat; ~ **el ceño** to knit one's brow.

frustrar [frus'trar] vt to frustrate.

fruta ['fruta] nf fruit; **frutería** nf fruit shop.

fue vb ver **ser, ir.**

fuego ['fweʃo] nm (gen) fire; (MED) rash; **a** ~ **lento** on a low flame or gas; **¿tienes** ~? have you a light?

fuente ['fwente] nf (de una plaza) fountain; (manantial, fig) spring; (origen) source; (plato) large dish.

fuera etc vb ver **ser, ir** // ['fwera] ad out(side); (en otra parte) away; (excepto, salvo) except, save // prep: ~ **de** outside; (fig) besides; ~ **de sí** beside o.s.

fuerte ['fwerte] a (gen) strong; (golpe) hard; (ruido) loud; (comida) rich; (lluvia) heavy; (dolor) intense // ad strongly; hard; loud(ly).

fuerza ['fwerθa] nf (fortaleza) strength; (TEC, ELEC) power; (coacción) force; (MIL) forces pl; **a** ~ **de** by dint of; **cobrar** ~**s** to recover one's strength; **tener** ~**s para** to have the strength to; **a la** ~, **por** ~ forcibly, by force.

fuga ['fuʃa] nf (huida) flight, escape; (de gas) leak; **fugarse** vr to flee, escape; **fugaz** a fleeting; **fugitivo, a** a, nm/f fugitive.

fui vb ver **ser, ir.**

fulano, a [fu'lano, a] nm/f so-and-so, what's-his-name.

fulgor [ful'ʃor] nm brilliance.

fumar [fu'mar] vt, vi to smoke; ~**se** vr (disipar) to squander; ~ **en pipa** to smoke a pipe.

funámbulo, a [fu'nambulo, a] nm/f tightrope-walker.

función [fun'θjon] nf function; (de puesto) duties pl; (espectáculo) show; **entrar en funciones** to take up one's duties; **funcionar** vi (gen) to function; (máquina) to work.

funcionario, a [funθjo'narjo, a] nm/f official; (público) civil servant.

funda ['funda] nf (gen) cover; (de almohada) pillowcase.

fundación [funda'θjon] nf foundation.

fundamental [fundamen'tal] a fundamental, basic.

fundamentar [fundamen'tar] vt (poner base) to lay the foundations of; (establecer) to found; (fig) to base; **fundamento** nm (base) foundation.

fundar [fun'dar] vt to found; (dotar de fondos) to endow; ~**se** vr: ~**se en** to be founded on.

fundición [fundi'θjon] nf fusing; (fábrica) foundry.

fundir [fun'dir] vt (gen) to fuse; (metal) to smelt, melt down; (COM) to merge; (estatua) to cast; ~**se** vr (sólido) to merge, blend; (unirse) to fuse together.

fúnebre ['funeβre] a funeral cpd, funereal.

funeral [fune'ral] nm funeral.

furgón [fur'ʃon] nm wagon.

furia ['furja] nf (ira) fury; (violencia) violence; **furibundo, a** a furious; **furioso, a** a (iracundo) furious; (violento) violent; **furor** nm (cólera) rage.

furtivo, a [fur'tiβo, a] a furtive.

furúnculo [fu'runkulo] nm (MED) boil.

fusible [fu'siβle] nm fuse.

fusil [fu'sil] nm rifle; ~**ar** vt to shoot.

fusión [fu'sjon] nf (gen) melting; (unión) fusion; (COM) merger.

fútbol ['futβol] nm football; **futbolín** nm table football; **futbolista** nm footballer.

fútil ['futil] a trifling; **futilidad, futileza** nf triviality.
futuro, a [fu'turo, a] a, nm future.

G

gabacho, a [ga'ßatʃo, a] a Pyrenean; (fam) frenchified // nm/f Pyrenean villager.
gabán [ga'ßan] nm overcoat.
gabardina [gaßar'ðina] nf raincoat, gabardine.
gabinete [gaßi'nete] nm (POL) cabinet; (estudio) study; (de abogados etc) office.
gaceta [ga'θeta] nf gazette; **gacetilla** nf (en periódico) news in brief; (de personalidades) gossip column.
gacha ['gatʃa] nf mush; ~s nfpl porridge sg.
gafas ['gafas] nfpl glasses; ~ **oscuras** dark glasses.
gaita ['gaita] nf flute; (~ gallega) bagpipes pl.
gajes ['gaxes] nmpl (salario) pay; **los ~ del oficio** occupational hazards.
gajo ['gaxo] nm (gen) bunch; (de árbol) bough; (de naranja) segment.
gala ['gala] nf full dress; (fig: lo mejor) cream, flower; ~s nfpl finery sg; **estar de ~** to be in one's best clothes; **hacer ~ de** to display, show off.
galán [ga'lan] nm lover, gallant; (hombre atractivo) ladies' man; (TEATRO): **primer ~** leading man.
galano, a [ga'lano, a] a (elegante) elegant; (bien vestido) smart.
galante [ga'lante] a gallant; **galantear** vt (hacer la corte a) to court, woo; **galanteo** nm (coqueteo) flirting; (de pretendiente) wooing; **galantería** nf (caballerosidad) gallantry; (cumplido) politeness; (comentario) compliment.
galaxia [ga'laksja] nf galaxy.
galera [ga'lera] nf (nave) galley; (carro) wagon; (MED) hospital ward; (IMPRENTA) galley.
galería [gale'ria] nf (gen) gallery; (balcón) veranda(h); (de casa) corridor.
Gales ['gales] nm Wales; **galés, esa** a Welsh // nm/f Welshman/woman // nm (lengua) Welsh.
galgo, a ['galɣo, a] nm/f greyhound.
galimatías [galima'tias] nmpl (lenguaje) gibberish sg, nonsense sg.
galón [ga'lon] nm (MIL) stripe; (medida) gallon.
galopar [galo'par] vi to gallop; **galope** nm gallop.
galvanizar [galßani'θar] vt to galvanize.
gallardía [gaʎar'ðia] nf (galantería) dash; (valor) bravery; (elegancia) elegance.
gallego, a [ga'ʎeɣo, a] a, nm/f Galician.
galleta [ga'ʎeta] nf biscuit.
gallina [ga'ʎina] nf hen // nm (fam) coward; ~ **ciega** blind man's buff.
gallo ['gaʎo] nm cock, rooster.

gama ['gama] nf (MUS) scale; (fig) range.
gamba ['gamba] nf prawn.
gamberro, a [gam'berro, a] nm/f hooligan, lout.
gamuza [ga'muθa] nf chamois.
gana ['gana] nf (deseo) desire, wish; (apetito) appetite; (voluntad) will; (añoranza) longing; **de buena ~** willingly; **de mala ~** reluctantly; **me da la ~ de** I feel like, I want to; **tener ~s de** to feel like.
ganadería [ganaðe'ria] nf (ganado) livestock; (ganado vacuno) cattle pl; (cría, comercio) cattle raising.
ganado [ga'naðo] nm livestock; ~ **lanar** sheep pl; ~ **vacuno** cattle pl; ~ **porcino** pigs pl.
ganador, a [gana'ðor, a] a winning // nm/f winner.
ganancia [ga'nanθja] nf (lo ganado) gain; (aumento) increase; (beneficio) profit; ~s nfpl (ingresos) earnings; (beneficios) profit sg, winnings.
ganapán [gana'pan] nm (obrero casual) odd-job man; (individuo tosco) lout.
ganar [ga'nar] vt (obtener) to get, obtain; (sacar ventaja) to gain; (COM) to earn; (DEPORTE, premio) to win; (derrotar a) to beat; (alcanzar) to reach // vi (DEPORTE) to win; ~**se** vr: ~**se la vida** to earn one's living.
gancho ['gantʃo] nm (gen) hook; (colgador) hanger.
gandul, a [gan'dul, a] a, nm/f good-for-nothing.
ganga ['ganga] nf (cosa buena y barata) bargain; (buena situación) cushy job.
gangrena [gan'grena] nf gangrene.
gansada [gan'saða] nf (fam) stupid thing to do.
ganso, a ['ganso, a] nm/f (ZOOL) gander/goose; (fam) idiot.
ganzúa [gan'θua] nf skeleton key // nm/f burglar.
gañán [ga'ɲan] nm farmhand, farm labourer.
garabato [gara'ßato] nm (gancho) hook; (garfio) grappling iron; (escritura) scrawl, scribble; (fam) sex appeal.
garaje [ga'raxe] nm garage.
garante [ga'rante] a responsible // nm/f guarantor.
garantía [garan'tia] nf guarantee.
garantizar [garanti'θar], **garantir** [garan'tir] vt (hacerse responsable de) to vouch for; (asegurar) to guarantee.
garbanzo [gar'ßanθo] nm chickpea.
garbo ['garßo] nm grace, elegance; ~**so, a** a graceful, elegant.
garfa ['garfa] nf claw.
garfio ['garfjo] nm grappling iron.
garganta [gar'xanta] nf (interna) throat; (externa, de botella) neck; **gargantilla** nf necklace.
gárgara ['garɣara] nf gargle, gargling.
gárgola ['garɣola] nf gargoyle.

garita [ga'rita] *nf* cabin, hut; (MIL) sentry box; (*de camión*) cab.

garra ['garra] *nf* (*de gato*, TEC) claw; (*de ave*) talon; (*fam*) hand, paw (*fam*).

garrafa [ga'rrafa] *nf* carafe, decanter.

garrido, a [ga'rriðo, a] *a* handsome.

garrote [ga'rrote] *nm* (*palo*) stick; (*porra*) cudgel; (*suplicio*) garrotte; (MED) tourniquet.

garrulería [garrule'ria] *nf* chatter.

gárrulo, a ['garrulo, a] *a* (*charlatán*) talkative; (*ave*) twittering; (*arroyo*) murmuring.

garzo, a ['garθo, a] *a* blue // *nf* heron.

gas [gas] *nm* gas.

gasa ['gasa] *nf* gauze.

gaseoso, a [gase'oso, a] *a* gassy, fizzy // *nf* lemonade, fizzy drink; (*fam*) pop.

gasolina [gaso'lina] *nf* petrol, gas(oline) (US); **gasolinera** *nf* petrol station.

gasómetro [ga'sometro] *nm* gasometer.

gastado, a [gas'taðo, a] *a* (*rendido*) spent; (*raído*) worn, threadbare; (*usado: frase etc*) trite.

gastar [gas'tar] *vt* (*dinero, tiempo*) to spend; (*fuerzas*) to use up; (*desperdiciar*) to waste; (*llevar*) to wear; ~**se** *vr* to wear out; (*estropearse*) to waste; ~ **bromas** to crack jokes.

gasto ['gasto] *nm* (*desembolso*) expenditure, spending; (*consumo, uso*) use; ~**s** *nmpl* (*desembolsos*) expenses; (*cargos*) charges, costs.

gatear [gate'ar] *vi* (*andar a gatas*) to go on all fours; (*trepar*) to climb // *vt* to scratch.

gatillo [ga'tiʎo] *nm* (*de arma de fuego*) trigger; (*de dentista*) forceps.

gato, a ['gato, a] *nm/f* cat // *nm* (TEC) jack; **andar a** ~**as** to go on all fours.

gatuno, a [ga'tuno, a] *a* feline.

gaucho ['gautʃo] *nm* gaucho.

gaveta [ga'ßeta] *nf* drawer.

gavilla [ga'ßiʎa] *nf* sheaf.

gaviota [ga'ßjota] *nf* seagull.

gay [ge] *a* gay, homosexual.

gayo, a ['gajo, a] *a* gay, merry.

gazapera [gaθa'pera] *nf* (*conejera*) rabbit warren; (*de gente*) den of thieves; **gazapo** *nm* young rabbit; (*fam*) sly fellow.

gazmoño, a [gaθ'moɲo, a], **gazmoñero, a** [gaθmo'ɲero, a] *a* *nm/f* prude; (*pretencioso*) prig; (*hipócrita*) hypocrite.

gazpacho [gaθ'patʃo] *nm* gazpacho, cold vegetable soup.

gelatina [xela'tina] *nf* (*plato*) jelly; (*polvos etc*) gelatine.

gema ['xema] *nf* gem.

gemelo, a [xe'melo, a] *a, nm/f* twin; ~**s** *nmpl* (*de camisa*) cufflinks; **G**~**s** (ASTRO) Gemini *sg*; ~**s de campo** field glasses.

gemido [xe'miðo] *nm* (*quejido*) moan, groan; (*aullido*) howl.

gemir [xe'mir] *vi* (*quejarse*) to moan, groan; (*aullar*) to howl.

genealogía [xenealo'xia] *nf* genealogy.

generación [xenera'θjon] *nf* generation.

generador [xenera'ðor] *nm* generator.

general [xene'ral] *a* general // *nm* general; **por lo** *o* **en** ~ in general; ~**idad** *nf* generality; **G**~**itat** *nf* Catalan parliament; ~**ización** *nf* generalization; ~**izar** *vt* to generalize; ~**izarse** *vr* to become generalised, spread; ~**mente** *ad* generally.

generar [xene'rar] *vt* to generate.

genérico, a [xe'neriko, a] *a* generic.

género ['xenero] *nm* (*clase*) kind, sort; (*tipo*) type; (BIO) genus; (LING) gender; (COM) material; ~ **humano** human race.

generosidad [xenerosi'ðað] *nf* generosity; **generoso, a** *a* generous.

genial [xe'njal] *a* inspired; (*idea*) brilliant; (*afable*) genial.

genio ['xenjo] *nm* (*carácter*) nature, disposition; (*humor*) temper; (*facultad creadora*) genius; **de mal** ~ bad-tempered.

gente ['xente] *nf* (*personas*) people *pl*; (*raza*) race; (*nación*) nation; (*parientes*) relatives *pl*.

gentil [xen'til] *a* (*elegante*) graceful; (*encantador*) charming; ~**eza** *nf* grace; charm; (*cortesía*) courtesy.

gentío [xen'tio] *nm* crowd, throng.

genuflexión [xenuflek'sjon] *nf* genuflexion.

genuino, a [xe'nwino, a] *a* genuine.

geografía [xeoɣra'fia] *nf* geography.

geología [xeolo'xia] *nf* geology.

geometría [xeome'tria] *nf* geometry.

gerencia [xe'renθja] *nf* management; **gerente** *nm* (*supervisor*) manager; (*jefe*) director.

germen ['xermen] *nm* germ.

germinar [xermi'nar] *vi* to germinate.

gesticulación [xestikula'θjon] *nf* (*ademán*) gesticulation; (*mueca*) grimace.

gestión [xes'tjon] *nf* management; (*diligencia, acción*) negotiation; (*esfuerzo*) effort; **gestionar** *vt* (*lograr*) to try to arrange; (*llevar*) to manage; (*discutir*) to negotiate.

gesto ['xesto] *nm* (*mueca*) grimace; (*ademán*) gesture.

gestoría [xesto'ria] *nf* estate agent's.

Gibraltar [xißral'tar] *nm* Gibraltar.

gigante [xi'ßante] *a, nm/f* giant.

gilipollas [xili'poʎas] *excl* (*fam*) bastard! (*fam*).

gimnasia [xim'nasja] *nf* gymnastics *pl*; **gimnasio** *nm* gymnasium; **gimnásta** *nm/f* gymnast.

gimotear [ximote'ar] *vi* to whine, whimper.

ginebra [xi'neßra] *nf* gin.

ginecólogo, a [xine'koloɣo, a] *nm/f* gynecologist.

gira ['xira] *nf* tour, trip.

girar [xi'rar] *vt* (*dar la vuelta*) to turn (around); (*: rápidamente*) to spin; (COM: *cheque*) to draw; (*comerciar: letra de cambio*) to issue // *vi* to turn (round); (*rápido*) to spin; (COM) to draw.

girasol [xira'sol] *nm* sunflower.

giratorio, a [xira'torjo, a] *a* (*gen*) revolving; (*puente*) swing.

giro ['xiro] *nm* (*movimiento*) turn, revolution; (*LING*) expression; (*COM*) draft; ~ **bancario/postal** money/ postal order.

gitano, a [xi'tano, a] *a, nm/f* gypsy.

glacial [gla'θjal] *a* icy, freezing.

glándula ['glandula] *nf* gland.

globo ['gloβo] *nm* (*esfera*) globe, sphere; (*aerostato, juguete*) balloon.

gloria ['glorja] *nf* glory; **gloriarse** *vr* to boast.

glorieta [glo'rjeta] *nf* (*de jardín*) bower, arbour; (*plazoleta*) roundabout.

glorificar [glorifi'kar] *vt* (*enaltecer*) to glorify, praise; ~**se** *vr*: ~**se de** to boast of.

glorioso, a [glo'rjoso, a] *a* glorious.

glosa ['glosa] *nf* comment; **glosar** *vt* (*comentar*) to comment on; (*fig*) to criticize.

glosario [glo'sarjo] *nm* glossary.

glotón, ona [glo'ton, ona] *a* gluttonous, greedy; **glotonería** *nf* gluttony, greed.

gobernación   [goβerna'θjon]   *nf* government, governing; **gobernador, a** *a* governing // *nm* governor; **gobernante** *a* governing.

gobernar [goβer'nar] *vt* (*dirigir*) to guide, direct; (*regir*) to rule, govern // *vi* to govern; (*NAUT*) to steer.

gobierno   [go'βjerno]   *nm*   (*POL*) government; (*dirección*) guidance, direction; (*NAUT*) steering.

goce ['goθe] *nm* enjoyment.

gol [gol] *nm* goal.

gola ['gola] *nf* gullet; (*garganta*) throat.

golf [golf] *nm* golf.

golfa ['golfa] *nf* (*fam*) tart, whore.

golfo ['golfo] *nm* (*GEO*) gulf; (*fam*: *niño*) urchin; (*gamberro*) lout.

golondrina [golon'drina] *nf* swallow.

golosina [golo'sina] *nf* (*gen*) titbit; (*dulce*) sweet; **goloso, a** *a* sweet-toothed.

golpe ['golpe] *nm* (*gen*) blow; (*de puño*) punch; (*de mano*) smack; (*de corazón*) beat; (*de remo*) stroke; (*fig: choque*) clash; **no dar** ~ to be bone idle; **de un** ~ with one blow; **de** ~ suddenly; ~ **de estado** coup d'état; **golpear** *vt, vi* to strike, knock; (*asestar*) to beat; (*de puño*) to punch; (*golpetear*) to tap.

goma ['goma] *nf* (*caucho*) rubber; (*elástico*) elastic; ~ **espuma** foam rubber; ~ **de pegar** gum, glue.

gomita [go'mita] *nf* elastic band.

góndola ['gondola] *nf* (*barco*) gondola; (*de tren*) goods wagon.

gordo, a [gorðo, a] *a* (*gen*) fat; (*persona*) plump; (*tela*) coarse; (*fam*) enormous; **el premio** ~ (*en lotería*) first prize; **gordura** *nf* fat; (*corpulencia*) fatness, stoutness.

gorgojo [gor'xoxo] *nm* (*insecto*) grub; (*fam*) runt.

gorila [go'rila] *nm* gorilla.

gorjear [gorxe'ar] *vi* to twitter, chirp; **gorjeo** *nm* twittering, chirping.

gorra ['gorra] *nf* (*gen*) cap; (*de niño*) bonnet; (*militar*) bearskin // *nm* scrounger.

gorrión [go'rrjon] *nm* sparrow.

gorro ['gorro] *nm* (*gen*) cap; (*de niño, mujer*) bonnet.

gorrón [go'rron] *nm* pebble.

gota ['gota] *nf* (*gen*) drop; (*de sudor*) bead; (*MED*) gout; **gotear** *vi* to drip; (*lloviznar*) to drizzle; **gotera** *nf* leak.

gótico, a ['gotiko, a] *a* Gothic.

gozar [go'θar] *vi* to enjoy o.s.; ~ **de** (*disfrutar*) to enjoy; (*poseer*) to possess.

gozne ['goθne] *nm* hinge.

gozo ['goθo] *nm* (*alegría*) joy; (*placer*) pleasure; ~**so, a** *a* joyous, joyful.

grabación [graβa'θjon] *nf* recording.

grabado [gra'βaðo] *nm* print, engraving; **grabador** *nm* engraver.

grabadora [graβa'ðora] *nf* tape-recorder.

grabar [gra'βar] *vt* to engrave; (*discos, cintas*) to record.

gracejo [gra'θexo] *nm* (*humor*) wit, humour; (*elegancia*) grace.

gracia ['graθja] *nf* (*encanto*) grace, gracefulness; (*chiste*) joke; (*humor*) humour, wit; ¡~**s!** thanks!; ¡**muchas** ~**s!** thanks very much!; ~**s a** thanks to; **tener** ~ to be funny; (*ser divertido*) to be enjoyable; **no me hace** ~ I am not keen; **gracioso, a** *a* (*divertido*) funny, amusing; (*cómico*) comical // *nm* (*TEATRO*) comic character.

grada ['graða] *nf* (*de escalera*) step; (*de anfiteatro*) tier, row.

gradación [graða'θjon] *nf* gradation.

gradería [graðe'ria] *nf* (*gradas*) (flight of) steps *pl*; (*de anfiteatro*) tiers *pl*, rows *pl*; ~ **cubierta** covered stand.

grado ['graðo] *nm* degree; (*de aceite, vino*) grade; (*grada*) step; (*MIL*) rank; **de buen** ~ willingly.

graduación [graðwa'θjon] *nf* (*del alcohol*) proof, strength; (*ESCOL*) graduation.

gradual [gra'ðwal] *a* gradual.

graduar [gra'ðwar] *vt* (*gen*) to graduate; (*clasificar*) to grade; (*MIL*) to commission; ~**se** *vr* to graduate.

gráfico, a ['grafiko, a] *a* graphic // *nm* diagram // *nf* graph.

grajo ['graxo] *nm* rook.

Gral *abr de* **General.**

gramática [gra'matika] *nf* grammar.

gramo ['gramo] *nm* gramme.

gran [gran] *a ver* **grande.**

grana ['grana] *nf* (*BOT*) seedling; (*ZOOL*) cochineal; (*color, tela*) scarlet.

Granada [gra'naða] *n* Granada.

granada [gra'naða] *nf* pomegranate; (*MIL*) grenade; **granadina** *nf* grenadine.

granadino, a [grana'ðino, a] *a* of Granada // *nm/f* native *or* inhabitant of Granada.

granado, a [gra'naðo, a] *a* choice, select // *nm* pomegranate tree.
granar [gra'nar] *vi* to seed.
granate [gra'nate] *nm* garnet.
Gran Bretaña [granbre'taɲa] *nf* Great Britain.
grande ['grande], **gran** [gran] *a* (*de tamaño*) big, large; (*alto*) tall; (*distinguido*) great; (*impresionante*) grand // *nm* grandee; **grandeza** *nf* greatness.
grandioso, a [gran'djoso, a] *a* magnificent, grand.
grandor [gran'dor] *nm* size.
granel [gra'nel]: **a ~ ad** in abundance; (*COM*) in bulk.
granero [gra'nero] *nm* granary, barn.
granito [gra'nito] *nm* (*AGR*) small grain; (*roca*) granite; (*MED*) pimple.
granizado [grani'θaðo] *nm* iced drink; **granizar** *vi* to hail; **granizo** *nm* hail.
granja ['granxa] *nf* (*gen*) farm; (*lechería*) dairy; (*café*) milk bar.
granjear [granxe'ar] *vt* (*cobrar*) to earn; (*ganar*) to win; (*avanzar*) to gain; **granjería** *nf* (*COM*) profit; (*AGR*) farming.
grano ['grano] *nm* grain; (*semilla*) seed; (*baya*) berry; (*MED*) pimple; **~s** *nmpl* cereals.
granoso, a [gra'noso, a] *a* granulated.
granuja [gra'nuxa] *nf* grape seed // *nm* rogue; (*golfillo*) urchin.
grapa ['grapa] *nf* staple; (*TEC*) clamp.
grasa ['grasa] *nf* (*gen*) grease; (*de cocina*) fat, lard; (*sebo*) suet; (*mugre*) filth; (*escoria*) dross; **grasiento, a** *a* greasy; (*de aceite*) oily.
gratificación [gratifika'θjon] *nf* (*propina*) tip; (*bono*) bonus; (*recompensa*) reward; **gratificar** *vt* to tip; to reward.
gratis ['gratis] *ad* free.
gratitud [grati'tuð] *nf* gratitude.
grato, a ['grato, a] *a* (*agradable*) pleasant, agreeable; (*bienvenido*) welcome.
gratuito, a [gra'twito, a] *a* (*gratis*) free; (*sin razón*) gratuitous.
gravamen [gra'βamen] *nm* (*carga*) burden; (*impuesto*) tax.
gravar [gra'βar] *vt* to burden.
grave ['graβe] *a* heavy; (*serio*) grave, serious; **~dad** *nf* gravity.
grávido, a ['graβiðo, a] *a* (*preñada*) pregnant; (*lleno, cargado*) full.
gravitación [graβita'θjon] *nf* gravitation; **gravitar** *vi* to gravitate; **gravitar sobre** to rest on.
gravoso, a [gra'βoso, a] *a* (*pesado*) burdensome; (*costoso*) costly.
graznar [graθ'nar] *vi* (*cuervo*) to squawk; (*pato*) to quack; (*hablar ronco*) to croak; **graznido** *nm* squawk; croak.
Grecia ['greθja] *nf* Greece.
greguería [greɣe'ria] *nf* hubbub.
gremio ['gremjo] *nm* (*sindicato*) trade union; (*asociación*) professional association.
greña ['greɲa] *nf* (*cabellos*) shock of hair;

(*maraña*) tangle; **greñudo, a** *a* (*persona*) dishevelled; (*hair*) tangled.
gresca ['greska] *nf* uproar.
grey [grei] *nf* flock.
griego, a ['grjeɣo, a] *a, nm/f* Greek.
grieta ['grjeta] *nf* crack; **grietarse** *vr* = agrietarse.
grifo, a ['grifo, a] *a* curly, kinky // *nm* tap.
grillo ['griʎo] *nm* (*ZOOL*) cricket; (*BOT*) shoot; **~s** *nmpl* shackles, irons.
gripe ['gripe] *nf* flu, influenza.
gris [gris] *a* (*color*) grey.
grita ['grita] *nf* uproar; **gritar** *vt, vi* to shout, yell; **grito** *nm* shout, yell; (*de horror*) scream; **a grito pelado** at the top of one's voice.
grosella [gro'seʎa] *nf* (red)currant; **~ negra** blackcurrant.
grosería [grose'ria] *nf* (*actitud*) rudeness; (*comentario*) vulgar comment; **grosero, a** *a* (*poco cortés*) rude; (*ordinario*) vulgar, crude.
grosor [gro'sor] *nm* thickness.
grotesco, a [gro'tesko, a] *a* grotesque.
grúa ['grua] *nf* (*TEC*) crane; (*de petróleo*) derrick.
grueso, a ['grweso, a] *a* thick; (*voluminoso*) stout // *nm* bulk // *nf* gross; **el ~ de** the bulk of.
grulla ['gruʎa] *nf* crane.
gruñido [gru'ɲiðo] *nm* grunt; (*fig*) grumble; **gruñir** *vi* (*animal*) to growl; (*fam*) to grumble.
grupa ['grupa] *nf* (*ZOOL*) rump.
grupo ['grupo] *nm* group; (*TEC*) unit, set.
gruta ['gruta] *nf* grotto.
guadamecí [gwaðame'θi], **guadamecil** [gwaðame'θil] *nm* embossed leather.
guadaña [gwa'ðaɲa] *nf* scythe; **guadañar** *vt* to scythe, mow.
guano ['gwano] *nm* (*AM*) guano.
guante ['gwante] *nm* glove.
guapo, a ['gwapo, a] *a* good-looking, attractive; (*hombre*) handsome; (*elegante*) smart // *nm* lover, gallant.
guarda ['gwarða] *nm* guard, keeper // *nf* guarding; (*custodia*) custody; **~bosque** *nm* gamekeeper; **~costas** *nm inv* coastguard vessel; **~dor, a** *a* protective // *nm/f* guardian, protector; **~espaldas** *nm/f inv* bodyguard; **~polvo** *nm* dust cover; (*de niño*) smock; (*para el trabajo*) overalls *pl*; **guardar** *vt* (*gen*) to keep; (*vigilar*) to guard, watch over; (*dinero: ahorrar*) to save, put by; **guardarse** *vr* (*preservarse*) to protect o.s.; (*evitar*) to avoid; **guardarropa** *nm* (*armario*) wardrobe; (*en establecimiento público*) cloakroom.
guardería [gwarðe'ria] *nf* (children's) nursery.
guardia ['gwarðja] *nf* (*MIL*) guard; (*cuidado*) care, custody // *nm* guard; (*policía*) policeman; **estar de ~** to be on guard; **montar ~** to mount guard; **G~ Civil** Civil Guard; **G~ Nacional** police; **~ urbano** traffic policeman.

guardián, ana [gwar'ðjan, ana] nm/f (gen) guardian, keeper; (sereno) watchman.

guardilla [gwar'ðiʎa] nf attic.

guarecer [gware'θer] vt (proteger) to ·protect; (abrigar) to shelter; ~se vr to take refuge.

guarida [gwa'riða] nf (de animal) den, lair; (refugio) refuge.

guarismo [gwa'rismo] nm figure, number.

guarnecer [gwarne'θer] vt (equipar) to provide; (adornar) to adorn; (TEC) to reinforce; **guarnición** nf (de vestimenta) trimming; (de piedra) mount; (CULIN) garnish; (arneses) harness; (MIL) garrison.

guarro, a ['gwarro, a] nm/f pig.

guasa ['gwasa] nf joke; **guasón, ona** a witty; (bromista) joking // nm/f wit; joker.

Guatemala [gwate'mala] nf Guatemala.

gubernativo, a [guβerna'tiβo, a] a governmental.

guedeja [ge'ðexa] nf long hair; (de león) mane.

guerra ['gerra] nf war; (pelea) struggle; ~ fría cold war; **dar** ~ to annoy; **guerrear** vi to wage war; **guerrero, a** a fighting; (carácter) warlike // nm/f warrior.

guerrilla [ge'rriʎa] nf guerrilla warfare; (tropas) guerrilla band or group.

guía ['gia] nm/f guide // nf (libro) guidebook; ~ **de ferrocarriles** railway timetable; ~ **de teléfonos** telephone directory; **guiar** vt to guide, direct; (AUT) to steer; **guiarse** vr: **guiarse por** to be guided by.

guija ['gixa] nf, **guijarro** [gi'xarro] nm pebble; (camino) cobblestone.

guijo ['gixo] nm gravel; (de playa) shingle.

guillotina [giʎo'tina] nf guillotine.

guinda ['ginda] nf morello cherry.

guindar [gin'dar] vt to hoist.

guindilla [gin'diʎa] nf Guinea pepper.

guiñapo [gi'ɲapo] nm (harapo) rag; (persona) reprobate, rogue.

guiñar [gi'ɲar] vi to wink; (parpadear) to blink.

guión [gi'on] nm (conductor) leader; (LING) hyphen, dash; (CINE) script; **guionista** nm/f scriptwriter.

guirnalda [gir'nalda] nf garland.

guisa ['gisa] nf: **a** ~ **de** as, like, in the way of.

guisado [gi'saðo] nm stew.

guisante [gi'sante] nm pea; ~ **de olor** sweet pea.

guisar [gi'sar] vt, vi to cook; **guiso** nm cooked dish.

guita ['gita] nf twine.

guitarra [gi'tarra] nf guitar.

gula ['gula] nf gluttony, greed.

gusano [gu'sano] nm maggot; (lombriz) earthworm; ~ **de luz** glow-worm; ~ **de seda** silk-worm.

gustar [gus'tar] vt to taste, sample // vi to please, be pleasing; ~ **de algo** to like or

enjoy sth; **me gustan las uvas** I like grapes.

gusto ['gusto] nm (sentido, sabor) taste; (placer) pleasure; **tiene** ~ **a menta** it tastes of mint; **tener buen** ~ to have good taste; **sentirse a** ~ to feel at ease; **mucho** ~ **en conocerle** pleased to meet you; **el** ~ **es mío** the pleasure is mine; **con** ~ willingly, gladly; ~**so, a** a (sabroso) tasty; (agradable) pleasant.

gutural [gutu'ral] a guttural.

H

ha vb ver **haber**.

haba ['aβa] nf bean.

Habana [a'βana] nf: **la** ~ Havana.

habano [a'βano] nm Havana cigar.

haber [a'βer] vb auxiliar to have; **de** ~ **lo sabido** if I had known (it); ~ **de** to have to // vb impersonal: **hay** there is/are; **hay que** it is necessary to, one must; **¿qué hay?** how's it going?; **no hay de qué** don't mention it // nm (ingreso) income; (COM. crédito) credit; ~**es** nmpl assets.

habichuela [aβi'tʃwela] nf kidney bean.

hábil ['aβil] a (listo) clever, smart; (capaz) fit, capable; (experto) expert; **día** ~ working day; **habilidad** nf (gen) skill, ability; (inteligencia) cleverness.

habilitación [aβilita'θjon] nf qualification; (colocación de muebles) fitting out; (financiamiento) financing.

habilitar [aβili'tar] vt (capacitar) to enable; (dar instrumentos) to equip; (financiar) to finance.

hábilmente [aβil'mente] ad skilfully, expertly.

habitación [aβita'θjon] nf (cuarto) room; (casa) dwelling, abode; (BIO: morada) habitat; ~ **sencilla** o **particular** single room; ~ **doble** o **matrimonial** double room.

habitante [aβi'tante] nm/f inhabitant.

habitar [aβi'tar] vt (residir en) to inhabit; (ocupar) to occupy // vi to live.

hábito ['aβito] nm habit; **habitual** a habitual.

habituar [aβi'twar] vt to accustom; ~**se** vr: ~**se a** to get used to.

habla ['aβla] nf (capacidad de hablar) speech; (idioma) language; (dialecto) dialect; **perder el** ~ to become speechless; **de** ~ **francesa** French-speaking; **estar al** ~ to be in contact; **¡González al** ~! Gonzalez speaking!

hablador, a [aβla'ðor, a] a talkative // nm/f chatterbox.

habladuría [aβlaðu'ria] nf rumour; (sarcasmo) sarcastic comment; ~**s** nfpl gossip sg.

hablar [a'βlar] vt to speak, talk // vi to speak; ~**se** vr to speak to each other; ~ **con** to speak to; ~ **de** to speak of or about; **'se habla inglés'** 'English spoken here'.

hablilla [a'βliʎa] nf story, rumour.

habré *etc vb ver* **haber.**

hacedero, a [aθe'ðero, a] *a* feasible.

hacedor, a [aθe'ðor, a] *nm/f* maker.

hacendoso, a [aθen'doso, a] *a* industrious.

hacer [a'θer] *vt* (*gen*) to make; (*crear*) to create; (*TEC*) to manufacture; (*preparar*) to prepare; (*ejecutar*) to do, execute; (*obligar*) to force, compel // *vi* (*comportarse*) to act, behave; (*disimular*) to pretend; (*importar*) to be important, matter; (*convenir, ser apto*) to be suitable; ~se *vr* (*fabricarse*) to be made, be done; (*volverse*) to become; (*acostumbrarse a*) to get used to; ~ **la maleta** to pack; ~ **una pregunta** to ask a question; ~ **una visita** to visit; ~ **bien/mal** to act rightly/wrongly; **hace frío/calor** it's cold/hot; **hace dos años** two years ago; **hace poco** a little while ago; ~ **el malo** (*TEATRO*) to play (the part of) the villain; ¿**qué** ~? what is to be done?; ~ **como que** *o* **como si** to act as though *or* as if; ~ **de** to act as; **me hice un traje** I had a suit made; ~**se el sordo** to turn a deaf ear; ~**se viejo** to grow old; ~**se con algo** to get hold of sth; ~**se a un lado** to stand aside.

hacia ['aθja] *prep* (*en dirección de*) towards; (*cerca de*) near; ~ **arriba/abajo** up(wards)/down(wards); ~ **mediodía** about noon.

hacienda [a'θjenda] *nf* (*propiedad*) property; (*estancia*) farm, ranch; (*AM*) plantation; ~ **pública** public finance; (**Ministerio de**) **H**~ Treasury, Exchequer.

hacina [a'θina] *nf* pile, stack.

hacha ['atʃa] *nf* axe; (*antorcha*) torch.

hache ['atʃe] *nf* (the letter) H.

hada ['aða] *nf* fairy.

hago *etc vb ver* **hacer.**

Haití [ai'ti] *nm* Haiti.

halagar [ala'xar] *vt* (*mostrar afecto*) to show affection to; (*lisonjear*) to flatter.

halago [a'laxo] *nm* pleasure, delight; (*atractivo*) attraction; (*adulación*) flattery; **halagüeño, a** *a* pleasing; attractive; flattering.

halcón [al'kon] *nm* falcon, hawk.

hálito ['alito] *nm* breath.

hallar [a'ʎar] *vt* (*gen*) to find; (*descubrir*) to discover; (*toparse con*) to run up against; ~**se** *vr* to be (situated); **hallazgo** *nm* discovery; (*cosa*) find.

hamaca [a'maka] *nf* hammock; ~ **plegable** deckchair.

hambre ['ambre] *nf* hunger; (*carencia*) famine; (*fig*) longing; **tener** ~ to be hungry; ~**ar** *vi, vt* to starve; **hambriento, a** *a* hungry, starving.

hamburguesa [ambur'xesa] *nf* hamburger.

hampa ['ampa] *nf* underworld; **hampón** *nm* tough.

han *vb ver* **haber.**

haragán, ana [ara'xan, ana] *a, nm/f* good-for-nothing; **haraganear** *vi* to idle, loaf about.

harapiento, a [ara'pjento, a] *a* tattered, in rags; **harapo** *nm* rag.

haré *etc vb ver* **hacer.**

harina [a'rina] *nf* flour; (*polvo*) powder; **harinero, a** *nm/f* flour merchant; **harinoso, a** *a* floury.

hartar [ar'tar] *vt* to satiate, glut; (*fig*) to tire, sicken; ~**se** *vr* (*de comida*) to fill o.s., gorge o.s.; (*cansarse*) to get fed up (de with); **hartazgo** *nm* surfeit, glut; **harto, a** *a* (*lleno*) full; (*cansado*) fed up // *ad* (*bastante*) enough; (*muy*) very; **estar harto de** to be fed up with; **hartura** *nf* (*exceso*) surfeit; (*abundancia*) abundance; (*satisfacción*) satisfaction.

has *vb ver* **haber.**

hasta ['asta] *ad* even // *prep* (*alcanzando a*) as far as, up/down to; (*de tiempo: a tal hora*) till, until; (*antes de*) before // *conj* ~ **que** until; ~ **luego/la vista** see you soon.

hastiar [as'tjar] *vt* (*gen*) to weary; (*aburrir*) to bore; (*asquear*) to disgust; ~**se** *vr*: ~**se de** to get fed up with; **hastío** *nm* weariness; boredom; disgust.

hato ['ato], **hatillo** [a'tiʎo] *nm* belongings *pl*, kit; (*víveres*) provisions *pl*; (*banda*) gang, group; (*montón*) bundle, heap.

hay *vb ver* **haber.**

Haya ['aja] *nf*: **la** ~ The Hague.

haya *etc vb ver* **haber** // ['aja] *nf* beech tree; **hayal, hayedo** *nm* beech grove.

haz [aθ] *vb ver* **hacer** // *nm* bundle, bunch; (*rayo: de luz*) beam.

hazaña [a'θaɲa] *nf* feat, exploit.

hazmerreír [aθmerre'ir] *nm* laughing stock.

he *vb ver* **haber.**

hebilla [e'ßiʎa] *nf* buckle, clasp.

hebra ['eßra] *nf* thread; (*BOT: fibra*) fibre, grain; **tabaco de** ~ loose tobacco.

hebreo, a [e'ßreo, a] *a, nm/f* Hebrew // *nm* (*lengua*) Hebrew.

hectárea [ek'tarea] *nf* hectare.

hechizar [etʃi'θar] *vt* to cast a spell on, bewitch.

hechizo, a [e'tʃiθo, a] *a* (*gen*) false, artificial; (*removible*) detachable // *nm* witchcraft, magic; (*acto de magía*) spell, charm.

hecho, a ['etʃo, a] *pp de* **hacer** // *a* complete; (*maduro*) mature; (*costura*) ready-to-wear // *nm* deed, act; (*dato*) fact; (*cuestión*) matter; (*suceso*) event // *excl* agreed!, done!; ¡**bien** ~! well done!; **de** ~ in fact, as a matter of fact.

hechura [e'tʃura] *nf* making, creation; (*producto*) product; (*forma*) form, shape; (*de persona*) build; (*TEC*) craftsmanship; ~**s** *nfpl* (*COSTURA*) cost of making up *sg*.

heder [e'ðer] *vi* to stink, smell; (*fig*) to be unbearable.

hediondez [eðjon'deθ] *nf* stench, stink; (*cosa*) stinking thing; **hediondo, a** *a* stinking; (*insoportable*) repulsive, unbearable.

hedor [e'ðor] *nm* stench.

helado, a [e'laðo, a] *a* frozen; (*glacial*) icy; (*fig*) chilly, cold // *nm* ice-cream // *nf* frost.

helar [e'lar] *vt* to freeze, ice (up); (*dejar atónito*) to amaze; (*desalentar*) to discourage // *vi*, ~**se** *vr* to freeze.

hélice ['eliθe] *nf* spiral; (*TEC*) propeller.

helicóptero [eli'koptero] *nm* helicopter.

hembra ['embra] *nf* (*BOT, ZOOL*) female; (*mujer*) woman; (*TEC*) nut.

hemorragia [emo'rraxja] *nf* haemorrhage.

hemorroides [emo'rroiðes] *nfpl* haemorrhoids.

hemos *vb ver* **haber.**

henchir [en'tʃir] *vt* to fill, stuff; ~**se** *vr* (*llenarse de comida*) to stuff o.s. (with food); (*inflarse*) to swell (up).

hender [en'der] *vt* to cleave, split; **hendidura** *nf* crack, split; (*GEO*) fissure.

heno ['eno] *nm* hay.

herbicida [erβi'θiða] *nm* weed-killer.

heredad [ere'ðað] *nf* landed property; (*granja*) farm.

heredar [ere'ðar] *vt* to inherit; **heredero, a** *nm/f* heir/heiress.

hereje [e'rexe] *nm/f* heretic; **herejía** *nf* heresy.

herencia [e'renθja] *nf* inheritance.

herido, a [e'riðo, a] *a* injured, wounded // *nm/f* casualty // *nf* wound, injury; (*insulto*) insult.

herir [e'rir] *vt* to wound, injure; (*fig*) to offend.

hermanar [erma'nar] *vt* to match; (*unir*) to join.

hermandad [erman'dað] *nf* brotherhood.

hermano, a [er'mano, a] *nm/f* brother/sister; ~ **gemelo** twin brother; ~ **político** brother-in-law; ~**a política** sister-in-law.

hermético, a [er'metiko, a] *a* hermetic; (*fig*) watertight.

hermoso, a [er'moso, a] *a* beautiful, lovely; (*estupendo*) splendid; (*guapo*) handsome; **hermosura** *nf* beauty.

héroe ['eroe] *nm* hero; **heroico, a** *a* heroic.

heroína [ero'ina] *nf* (*mujer*) heroine; (*droga*) heroin.

heroísmo [ero'ismo] *nm* heroism.

herrador [erra'ðor] *nm* blacksmith; **herradura** *nf*: **curva en herradura** hairpin bend.

herramienta [erra'mjenta] *nf* tool; (*conjunto*) set of tools.

herrería [erre'ria] *nf* smithy; (*TEC*) forge; **herrero** *nm* blacksmith.

herrumbre [e'rrumbre] *nf* rust.

hervidero [erβi'ðero] *nm* (*burbujeo*) boiling, seething; (*fuente*) hot spring.

hervir [er'βir] *vi* (*gen*) to boil; (*burbujear*) to bubble; (*fig*): ~ **de** to teem with; ~ **a**

fuego lento to simmer; **hervor** *nm* boiling; (*fig*) ardour, fervour.

heterogéneo, a [etero'xeneo, a] *a* heterogeneous.

heterosexual [eterosek'swal] *a* heterosexual.

hice *etc vb ver* **hacer.**

hidráulico, a [i'ðrauliko, a] *a* hydraulic // *nf* hydraulics *sg.*

hidro... [iðro] *pref* hydro..., water-...; ~**ala** *nf* hovercraft; ~**avión** *nm* seaplane; ~**eléctrico, a** a hydroelectric; ~**fobia** *nf* hydrophobia, rabies; **hidrófugo, a** *a* damp-proof; **hidrógeno** *nm* hydrogen.

hiedra ['jeðra] *nf* ivy.

hiel [jel] *nf* gall, bile; (*fig*) bitterness.

hiela *etc vb ver* **helar.**

hielo ['jelo] *nm* (*gen*) ice; (*escarza*) frost; (*fig*) coldness, reserve.

hiena ['jena] *nf* hyena.

hierba ['jerβa] *nf* (*BOT*) grass; (*MED*) herb; **mala** ~ weed; (*fig*) evil influence; ~**buena** *nf* mint.

hierro ['jerro] *nm* (*metal*) iron; (*objeto*) iron object; (*herramienta*) tool; ~ **acanalado** corrugated iron; ~ **colado** *o* **fundido** cast iron.

hígado ['ixaðo] *nm* liver.

higiene [i'xjene] *nf* hygiene; **higiénico, a** *a* hygienic.

higo ['ixo] *nm* fig; ~ **paso** *o* **seco** dried fig; **higuera** *nf* fig tree.

hijastro, a [i'xastro, a] *nm/f* stepson/daughter.

hijo, a ['ixo, a] *nm/f* son/daughter, child; ~**s** *nmpl* children, sons and daughters; ~ **de papá/mamá** daddy's/mummy's boy; ~ **de puta** bastard, son of a bitch.

hilado, a [i'laðo, a] *a* spun // *nm* yarn.

hilandero, a [ilan'dero, a] *nm/f* spinner.

hilar [i'lar] *vt* to spin; ~ **delgado** to split hairs.

hilera [i'lera] *nf* row, file.

hilo ['ilo] *nm* (*gen*) thread; (*BOT*) fibre; (*metal*) wire; (*de agua*) trickle, thin stream; (*de luz*) beam, ray.

hilvanar [ilβa'nar] *vt* to tack; (*fig*) to do hurriedly.

Himalayas [ima'lajas] *nfpl*: **las** ~ the Himalayas.

himno ['imno] *nm* hymn; ~ **nacional** national anthem.

hincapié [inka'pje] *nm*: **hacer** ~ **en** to emphasize.

hincar [in'kar] *vt* to drive (in), thrust (in); ~**se** *vr*: ~**se de rodillas** to kneel down.

hinchado, a [in'tʃaðo, a] *a* (*gen*) swollen; (*persona*) pompous.

hinchar [in'tʃar] *vt* (*gen*) to swell; (*inflar*) to blow up, inflate; (*fig*) to exaggerate; ~**se** *vr* (*inflarse*) to swell up; (*fam*: *llenarse*) to stuff o.s.; **hinchazón** *nf* (*MED*) swelling; (*altivez*) arrogance.

hinojo [i'noxo] *nm* fennel.

hipar [i'par] *vi* to hiccup; (*perro*) to pant.

hipnotismo [ipno'tismo] *nm* hypnotism; **hipnotizar** *vt* to hypnotize.

hipo ['ipo] *nm* hiccups *pl.*

hipocresía [ipokre'sia] *nf* hypocrisy; **hipócrita** *a* hypocritical // *nm/f* hypocrite.

hipódromo [i'poðromo] *nm* racetrack.

hipopótamo [ipo'potamo] *nm* hippopotamus.

hipoteca [ipo'teka] *nf* mortgage.

hipótesis [i'potesis] *nf* hypothesis.

hiriente [i'rjente] *a* offensive, cutting.

hirsuto, a [ir'suto, a] *a* hairy; (*fig*) rough.

hispánico, a [is'paniko, a] *a* Hispanic.

hispano, a [is'pano, a] *a* Hispanic, Spanish, Hispano-; **H~américa** *nf* Spanish *or* Latin America; **~americano, a** *a, nm/f* Spanish *or* Latin American.

histeria [is'terja] *nf* hysteria.

historia [is'torja] *nf* (*gen*) history; (*cuento*) story, tale; **~s** *nfpl* (*chismes*) gossip *sg*; **dejarse de ~s** to come to the point; **pasar a la ~** to go down in history; **~dor, a** *nm/f* historian; **historiar** *vt* to chronicle, write the history of; **histórico, a** *a* historical; (*fig*) historic.

historieta [isto'rjeta] *nf* tale, anecdote; (*dibujos*) strip cartoon.

hito ['ito] *nm* (*gen*) landmark; (*objetivo*) goal, target.

hizo *vb ver* **hacer.**

hocico [o'θiko] *nm* snout; (*fig*) grimace; **caer** *o* **dar de ~s** to fall on one's face.

hockey ['xoki] *nm* hockey; **~ sobre patines** *o* **hielo** ice hockey.

hogar [o'xar] *nm* fireplace, hearth; (*casa*) home; (*vida familiar*) home life; **~eño, a** *a* home; (*persona*) home-loving.

hoguera [o'xera] *nf* (*gen*) bonfire; (*llamas*) blaze.

hoja ['oxa] *nf* (*gen*) leaf; (*de flor*) petal; (*de papel*) sheet; (*página*) page; **~ de afeitar** razor blade; **~ de estaño** tinfoil.

hojalata [oxa'lata] *nf* tin(plate).

hojear [oxe'ar] *vt* to leaf through, turn the pages of.

hola ['ola] *excl* hello!

Holanda [o'landa] *nf* Holland; **holandés, esa** *a* Dutch // *nm/f* Dutchman/woman // *nm* (*lengua*) Dutch.

holgado, a [ol'xaðo, a] *a* loose, baggy; (*libre*) free; (*desempleado*) idle; (*rico*) well-to-do.

holganza [ol'xanθa] *nf* (*ocio*) leisure; (*pereza*) idleness; (*diversión*) amusement.

holgar [ol'xar] *vi* (*descansar*) to rest; (*sobrar*) to be superfluous; **~se** *vr* to enjoy o.s.; **huelga decir que** it goes without saying that.

holgazán, ana [olxa'θan, ana] *a* idle, lazy // *nm/f* loafer.

holgura [ol'xura] *nf* looseness, bagginess; (*TEC*) play, free movement; (*vida*) comfortable living, luxury.

holiar [o'ʎar] *vt* to tread (on), trample.

hollín [o'ʎin] *nm* soot.

hombradía [ombra'ðia] *nf* manliness.

hombre ['ombre] *nm* (*gen*) man(kind); (*uno*) man // *excl* (*claro*) of course!; (*para énfasis*) man, old boy; (*sorpresa*) you don't say!; **~ de negocios** businessman; **~-rana** frogman; **~ de pro** *o* **de provecho** honest man.

hombrera [om'brera] *nf* shoulder strap.

hombro ['ombro] *nm* shoulder.

hombruno, a [om'bruno, a] *a* mannish.

homenaje [ome'naxe] *nm* (*gen*) homage; (*lealtad*) allegiance; (*tributo*) tribute.

homicida [omi'θiða] *a* homicidal // *nm/f* murderer; **homicidio** *nm* murder, homicide.

homosexual [omosek'swal] *a, nm/f* homosexual.

hondo, a ['ondo, a] *a* deep; (*profundo*) low // *nm* depth(s) (*pl*); bottom; **~nada** *nf* hollow, depression; (*cañón*) ravine; (*GEO*) lowland; **hondura** *nf* depth, profundity.

Honduras [on'duras] *nf* Honduras.

hondureño, a [ondu'reɲo, a] *a, nm/f* Honduran.

honestidad [onesti'ðað] *nf* purity, chastity; (*decencia*) decency; **honesto, a** *a* chaste; decent, honest; (*justo*) just.

hongo ['ongo] *nm* (*BOT: gen*) fungus; (: *comestible*) mushroom; (: *venenoso*) toadstool.

honor [o'nor] *nm* (*gen*) honour; (*gloria*) glory; **en ~ a la verdad** to be fair; **~able** a honourable.

honorario, a [ono'rarjo, a] *a* honorary; **~s** *nmpl* fees.

honra ['onra] *nf* (*gen*) honour; (*nombre*) reputation; **~dez** *nf* honesty; (*de persona*) integrity; **~do, a** a honest, upright.

honrar [on'rar] *vt* to honour; **~se** *vr*: **~se con algo/de hacer algo** to be honoured by/to do sth.

honroso, a [on'roso, a] *a* (*honrado*) honourable; (*respetado*) respectable.

hora ['ora] *nf* (*gen*) time; (*específica*) hour; **¿qué ~ es?** what time is it?; **¿a qué ~?** at what time?; **media ~** half an hour; **a la ~ de recreo** at playtime; **a primera ~** first thing (in the morning); **a última ~** at the last moment; **en las altas ~s** in the small hours; **¡a buena ~!** it's high time!; **dar la ~** to strike the hour; **~s de oficina/de trabajo** office/working hours; **~s de visita** visiting times; **~s extras** *o* **extraordinarias** overtime *sg*; **~s punta** rush hours.

horadar [ora'ðar] *vt* to drill, bore.

horario, a [o'rarjo, a] *a* hourly, hour *cpd* // *nm* timetable.

horca ['orka] *nf* gallows *sg.*

horcajadas [orka'xaðas]: **a ~** *ad* astride.

horda ['orða] *nf* horde.

horizontal [oriθon'tal] *a* horizontal; **horizonte** *nm* horizon.

horma ['orma] *nf* mould.

hormiga [or'mixa] *nf* ant; **~s** *nfpl* (*MED*) pins and needles.

hormigón [ormi'xon] *nm* concrete; **~**

hormigueo

armado/pretensado reinforced/pre-stressed concrete.

hormigueo [ormi'ɣeo] nm (comezón) itch; (fig) uneasiness; (amontonamiento) swarming.

hormona [or'mona] nf hormone.

hornillo [or'niʎo] nm small furnace; (cocina) portable stove.

horno ['orno] nm (CULIN) oven; (TEC) furnace; **alto** ~ blast furnace.

horóscopo [o'roskopo] nm horoscope.

horquilla [or'kiʎa] nf hairpin; (AGR) pitchfork.

horrendo, a [o'rrendo, a] a horrendous, frightful.

horrible [o'rriβle] a horrible, dreadful.

horripilante [orripi'lante] a hair-raising; (espeluznante) creepy.

horripilar [orripi'lar] vt: ~ **a uno** to horrify sb; ~**se** vr to be horrified.

horror [o'rror] nm horror, dread; (atrocidad) atrocity; ¡**qué** ~! (fam) oh, my God!; ~**izar** vt to horrify, frighten; ~**izarse** vr to be horrified; ~**oso, a** a horrifying, ghastly.

hortaliza [orta'liθa] nf vegetable.

hortelano, a [orte'lano, a] nm/f (market) gardener.

hosco, a ['osko, a] a dark; (triste, ceñudo) sullen, gloomy.

hospedar [ospe'ðar] vt to put up, lodge; ~**se** vr to stay, lodge.

hospital [ospi'tal] nm hospital.

hospitalario, a [ospita'larjo, a] a hospitable; **hospitalidad** nf hospitality.

hosquedad [oske'ðað] nf sullenness.

hostal [os'tal] nm small hotel.

hostelero, a [oste'lero, a] nm/f innkeeper, landlord/lady.

hostería [oste'ria] nf hostelry.

hostia ['ostja] nf host, consecrated wafer; (fam: golpe) whack, punch // excl: ¡~s! damn it!

hostigar [osti'ɣar] vt to whip; (fig) to harass, pester.

hostil [os'til] a hostile; ~**idad** nf hostility.

hotel [o'tel] nm hotel; ~**ero, a** a hotel cpd // nm/f hotelier.

hoy [oi] ad (este día) today; (el ahora) now(adays) // nm present time; ~ **(en) día** now(adays).

hoya ['oja] nf pit; (sepulcro) grave; (GEO) valley.

hoyo ['ojo] nm hole, pit; **hoyuelo** nm dimple.

hoz [oθ] nf sickle.

hube etc vb ver **haber**.

hucha ['utʃa] nf money box; (fig) nest egg.

hueco, a ['weko, a] a (vacío) hollow, empty; (blanco: papel) blank; (resonante) booming // nm hollow, cavity.

huelga etc vb ver **holgar** // ['welɣa] nf strike; **declararse en** ~ to go on strike, come out on strike; ~ **de brazos caídos/de hambre** sit-down/hunger strike; ~ **patronal** lockout.

huelgo etc vb ver **holgar** // ['welɣo] nm breath; (espacio) room, space.

huelguista [wel'ɣista] nm/f striker.

huelo etc vb ver **oler**.

huella ['weʎa] nf (acto de pisar, pisada) tread(ing); (marca del paso) footprint, footstep; (: de animal, máquina) track; ~ **digital** fingerprint; ~ **del sonido** sound track.

huérfano, a ['werfano, a] a orphan(ed) // nm/f orphan.

huerta ['werta] nf market garden; (área de regadío) irrigated region.

huerto ['werto] nm orchard.

hueso ['weso] nm (ANAT) bone; (de fruta) stone.

huésped, a ['wespeð, a] nm/f (invitado) guest; (habitante) resident; (anfitrión) host.

huesudo, a [we'suðo, a] a bony, big-boned.

huevo ['weβo] nm egg; ~ **en cáscara/escalfado/estrellado** o **frito/pasado por agua** boiled/poached/fried/soft-boiled egg; ~**s revueltos** scrambled eggs.

huida [u'iða] nf escape, flight.

huidizo, a [ui'ðiθo, a] a (tímido) shy; (pasajero) fleeting.

huir [u'ir] vt (escapar) to flee, escape (from); (evadir) to avoid; ~**se** vr (escaparse) to escape; (el tiempo) to fly.

hule ['ule] nm (goma) rubber; (encerado) oilskin.

humanidad [umani'ðað] nf (los hombres) man(kind); (cualidad) humanity.

humanizar [umani'θar] vt to humanize.

humano, a [u'mano, a] a (gen) human; (humanitario) humane // nm human; **ser** ~ human being.

humareda [uma'reða] nf cloud of smoke.

humear [ume'ar] vi to smoke.

humedad [ume'ðað] nf (del clima) humidity; (de pared etc) dampness; **a prueba de** ~ damp-proof; **humedecer** vt to moisten, wet; **humedecerse** vr to get wet.

húmedo, a ['umeðo, a] a (mojado) damp, wet; (tiempo etc) humid.

humildad [umil'dað] nf humility, humbleness; **humilde** a humble, modest; (pequeño: voz) small.

humillación [umiʎa'θjon] nf humiliation; **humillante** a humiliating; **humillar** vt to humiliate; **humillarse** vr to humble o.s., grovel.

humo ['umo] nm (de fuego) smoke; (gas nocivo) fumes pl; ~**s** nmpl (fig) conceit sg.

humor [u'mor] nm (disposición) mood, temper; (lo que divierte) humour; **de buen/mal** ~ in a good/bad mood; ~**ada** nf witticism; ~**ismo** nm humour; ~**ista** nm/f humorist; ~**ístico, a** a funny, humorous.

hundido, a [un'diðo, a] a (de mejillas) sunken; (de ojos) deep-set.

hundimiento [undi'mjento] nm (gen) sinking; (colapso) collapse.

hundir [un'dir] vt to sink; (edificio, plan) to

ruin, destroy; ~ se *vr* to sink, collapse.
húngaro, a ['ungaro, a] *a, nm/f*
Hungarian.
Hungría [un'gria] *nf* Hungary.
huracán [ura'kan] *nm* hurricane.
huraño, a [u'raño, a] *a* shy; (*antisocial*)
unsociable.
hurgar [ur'xar] *vt* to poke, jab; (*remover*)
to stir (up).
hurgonear [urxone'ar] *vt* to poke.
hurón, ona [u'ron, ona] *a* unsociable //
nm (*zool*) ferret; (*persona tímida*) shy
person; (*persona arisca*) unsociable person.
hurtadillas [urta'ðiʎas]: **a** ~ *ad*
stealthily, on the sly.
hurtar [ur'tar] *vt* to steal; ~ se *vr* to hide,
withdraw; **hurto** *nm* theft, stealing.
husmear [usme'ar] *vt* (*oler*) to sniff out,
scent; (*fam*) to pry into // *vi* to smell bad;
husmo *nm* strong smell.
huyo *etc vb ver* **huir.**

I

iba *etc vb ver* **ir.**
ibérico, a [i'ßeriko, a] *a* Iberian.
iberoamericano, a [ißeroameri'kano, a]
a, nm/f Spanish American.
íbice ['ißiθe] *nm* ibex.
ibicenco, a [ißi'θenko, a] *a* Ibizan.
Ibiza [i'ßiθa] *nf* Ibiza.
ibón [i'ßon] *nm* lake, tarn.
iceberg ['aisßerx] *nm* iceberg.
ícono ['ikono] *nm* ikon, icon.
iconoclasta [ikono'klasta] *a* iconoclastic
// *nm/f* iconoclast.
ictericia [ikte'riθja] *nf* jaundice.
ida ['iða] *nf* going, departure; ~ **y vuelta**
round trip, return.
ideal [iðe'al] *a, nm* ideal; ~ **ista** *nm/f*
idealist; ~ **izar** *vt* to idealize.
idear [iðe'ar] *vt* to think up; (*aparato*) to
invent; (*viaje*) to plan.
ídem ['iðem] *pron* ditto.
idéntico, a [i'ðentiko, a] *a* identical.
identidad [iðenti'ðað] *nf* identity; **carné**
de ~ identity card.
identificación [iðentifika'θjon] *nf*
identification; **identificar** *vt* to identify;
identificarse *vr:* **identificarse con** to
identify o.s. with.
ideología [iðeolo'xia] *nf* ideology;
ideológico, a *a* ideological.
idioma [i'ðjoma] *nm* (*gen*) language; (*giro*)
idiom.
idiota [i'ðjota] *a* idiotic // *nm/f* idiot;
idiotez *nf* idiocy.
idólatra [i'ðolatra] *nm/f* idolater/tress;
idolatría *nf* idolatry.
ídolo ['iðolo] *nm* idol.
idóneo, a [i'ðoneo, a] *a* (*apto*) fit; (*conveniente*) suitable.
iglesia [i'xlesja] *nf* church.
ignición [ixni'θjon] *nf* ignition.

ignominia [ixno'minja] *nf* ignominy;
ignominioso, a *a* ignominious.
ignorado, a [ixno'raðo, a] *a* unknown;
(*dato*) obscure.
ignorancia [ixno'ranθja] *nf* ignorance;
ignorante *a* ignorant, uninformed // *nm/f*
ignoramus.
ignorar [ixno'rar] *vt* not to know, be
ignorant of.
ignoto, a [ix'noto, a] *a* unknown.
igual [i'xwal] *a* (*gen*) equal; (*similar*) like,
similar; (*mismo*) (the) same; (*constante*)
constant; (*temperatura*) even // *nm/f*
equal; **al** ~ **que** *prep, conj* like, just like.
igualada [ixwa'laða] *nf* equaliser.
igualar [ixwa'lar] *vt* (*gen*) to equalize,
make equal; (*allanar, nivelar*) to level (off),
even (out); ~ **se** *vr* (*platos de balanza*) to
balance out; (*equivaler*) to be equal.
igualdad [ixwal'dað] *nf* equality;
(*similaridad*) sameness; (*uniformidad*)
evenness, uniformity.
igualmente [ixwal'mente] *ad* equally;
(*también*) also, likewise // *excl* the same
to you.
ikurriña [iku'rriña] *nf* Basque flag.
ilegal [ile'xal] *a* illegal.
ilegítimo, a [ile'xitimo, a] *a* illegitimate.
ileso, a [i'leso, a] *a* unhurt.
ilícito, a [i'liθito, a] *a* illicit.
ilimitado, a [ilimi'taðo, a] *a* unlimited.
ilógico, a [i'loxiko, a] *a* illogical.
iluminación [ilumina'θjon] *nf* (*gen*)
illumination; (*alumbrado*) lighting.
iluminar [ilumi'nar] *vt* to illuminate, light
(up); (*fig*) to enlighten.
ilusión [ilu'sjon] *nf* illusion; (*quimera*)
delusion; (*esperanza*) hope; **ilusionado, a**
a excited.
ilusionista [ilusjo'nista] *nm/f* conjurer.
iluso, a [i'luso, a] *a* easily deceived.
ilusorio, a [ilu'sorjo, a] *a* (*de ilusión*)
illusory, deceptive; (*esperanza*) vain.
ilustración [ilustra'θjon] *nf* illustration;
(*saber*) learning, erudition; **la I** ~ the Enlightenment; **ilustrado, a** *a* illustrated;
learned.
ilustrar [ilus'trar] *vt* (*gen*) to illustrate;
(*instruir*) to instruct; (*explicar*) to explain,
make clear; ~ **se** *vr* to acquire
knowledge.
ilustre [i'lustre] *a* famous, illustrious.
imagen [i'maxen] *nf* (*gen*) image; (*dibujo*)
picture; (*semejanza*) likeness.
imaginación [imaxina'θjon] *nf*
imagination.
imaginar [imaxi'nar] *vt* (*gen*) to imagine;
(*idear*) to think up; (*suponer*) to suppose;
~ **se** *vr* to imagine; ~ **io, a** *a* imaginary;
imaginativa, a *a* imaginative.
imán [i'man] *nm* magnet.
imbécil [im'beθil] *nm/f* imbecile, idiot;
imbecilidad *nf* imbecility.
imbuir [imbu'ir] *vi* to imbue.
imitación [imita'θjon] *nf* imitation; **imitar**

vt to imitate; (*parodiar, remedar*) to mimic, ape.

impaciencia [impa'θjenθja] *nf* impatience; **impaciente** *a* impatient; (*nervioso*) anxious.

impacto [im'pakto] *nm* impact.

impar [im'par] *a* odd.

imparcial [impar'θjal] *a* impartial, fair; ~ **idad** *nf* impartiality, fairness.

impartir [impar'tir] *vt* to impart, give.

impasible [impa'siβle] *a* impassive.

impavidez [impaβi'ðeθ] *nf* fearlessness, intrepidness; **impávido, a** *a* fearless, intrepid.

impecable [impe'kaβle] *a* impeccable.

impedimento [impeði'mento] *nm* impediment, obstacle.

impedir [impe'ðir] *vt* (*obstruir*) to impede, obstruct; (*estorbar*) to prevent.

impeler [impe'ler] *vt* to drive, propel; (*fig*) to impel.

impenetrabilidad [impenetraβili'ðað] *nf* impenetrability; **impenetrable** *a* impenetrable; (*fig*) incomprehensible.

impenitente [impeni'tente] *a* unrepentant.

impensado, a [impen'saðo, a] *a* unexpected.

imperar [impe'rar] *vi* (*reinar*) to rule, reign; (*fig*) to prevail, reign; (*precio*) to be current.

imperativo, a [impera'tiβo, a] *a* (*persona*) imperious; (*urgente, LING*) imperative.

imperceptible [imperθep'tiβle] *a* imperceptible.

imperdible [imper'ðiβle] *nm* safety pin.

imperdonable [imperðo'naβle] *a* unforgivable, inexcusable.

imperfección [imperfek'θjon] *nf* imperfection.

imperfecto, a [imper'fekto, a] *a* imperfect.

imperial [impe'rjal] *a* imperial; ~ **ismo** *nm* imperialism.

impericia [impe'riθja] *nf* (*torpeza*) unskilfulness; (*inexperiencia*) inexperience.

imperio [im'perjo] *nm* empire; (*reino, dominación*) rule, authority; (*fig*) pride, haughtiness; ~ **so, a** *a* imperious; (*urgente*) urgent; (*imperativo*) imperative.

impermeable [imperme'aβle] *a* impermeable; (*a prueba de agua*) waterproof // *nm* raincoat.

impersonal [imperso'nal] *a* impersonal.

impertérrito, a [imper'territo, a] *a* undaunted.

impertinencia [imperti'nenθja] *nf* (*inoportunidad*) irrelevant; (*insolencia*) impertinence; **impertinente** *a* irrelevant; impertinent.

imperturbable [impertur'βaβle] *a* imperturbable.

ímpetu ['impetu] *nm* (*impulso*) impetus, impulse; (*impetuosidad*) impetuosity; (*violencia*) violence.

impetuosidad [impetwosi'ðað] *nf* impetuousness; (*violencia*) violence; **impetuoso, a** *a* impetuous; (*persona*) headstrong; (*río*) rushing, violent; (*acto*) hasty.

impío, a [im'pio, a] *a* impious, ungodly.

implacable [impla'kaβle] *a* implacable.

implicar [impli'kar] *vt* (*gen*) to implicate, involve; (*entrañar*) to imply.

implícito, a [im'pliθito, a] *a* (*tácito*) implicit; (*sobreentendido*) implied.

implorar [implo'rar] *vt* to beg, implore.

imponente [impo'nente] *a* (*impresionante*) impressive, imposing; (*solemne*) grand // *nm/f* investor.

imponer [impo'ner] *vt* (*gen*) to impose; (*informar*) to inform, instruct; (*exigir*) to exact, command; (*COM*) to invest; ~ **se** *vr* to assert o.s.; (*prevalecer*) to prevail.

impopular [impopu'lar] *a* unpopular.

importación [importa'θjon] *nf* (*acto*) importing; (*objetos*) imports *pl*.

importancia [impor'tanθja] *nf* importance; (*valor*) value, significance; (*extensión*) size, magnitude; **importante** *a* important; valuable, significant.

importar [impor'tar] *vt* (*del extranjero*) to import; (*valer*) to amount to, be worth // *vi* to be important, matter; **me importa el rábano** I don't give a damn; **no importa** it doesn't matter.

importe [im'porte] *nm* (*total*) amount; (*valor*) value.

importunar [importu'nar] *vt* to bother, pester.

importuno, a [impor'tuno, a] *a* (*inoportuno, molesto*) inopportune; (*indiscreto*) troublesome.

imposibilidad [imposiβili'ðað] *nf* impossibility; **imposibilitar** *vt* to make impossible, prevent; (*incapacitar*) to disable, cripple.

imposible [impo'siβle] *a* (*gen*) impossible; (*insoportable*) unbearable, intolerable.

imposición [imposi'θjon] *nf* imposition; (*COM*) tax; (*enganche*) deposit.

impostor, a [impos'tor, a] *nm/f* impostor; **impostura** *nf* fraud, imposture.

impotencia [impo'tenθja] *nf* impotence; **impotente** *a* impotent, powerless.

impracticable [imprakti'kaβle] *a* (*irrealizable*) impracticable; (*intransitable*) impassable.

imprecar [impre'kar] *vi* to curse.

impregnar [impreɣ'nar] *vt* to impregnate; ~ **se** *vr* to become impregnated.

imprenta [im'prenta] *nf* (*gen*) printing; (*aparato*) press; (*casa*) printer's; (*letra*) print.

imprescindible [impresθin'diβle] *a* essential, indispensable.

impresión [impre'sjon] *nf* (*gen*) impression; (*IMPRENTA*) printing; (*edición*) edition; (*FOTO*) print; (*marca*) imprint; ~ **digital** fingerprint.

impresionable [impresjo'naβle] *a*

impresionante [impresjo'nante] *a* impressive; (*tremendo*) tremendous; (*maravilloso*) great, marvellous.

impresionar [impresjo'nar] *vt* (*conmover*) to move; (*afectar*) to impress, strike; (*película fotográfica*) to expose; ~**se** *vr* to be impressed; (*conmoverse*) to be moved.

impreso, a [im'preso, a] *pp de* **imprimir** // *a* printed // *nm* printed paper/book *etc.*

impresor [impre'sor] *nm* printer.

imprevisto, a [impre'βisto, a] *a* (*gen*) unforeseen; (*inesperado*) unexpected.

imprimir [impri'mir] *vt* to imprint, impress, stamp; (*textos*) to print.

improbabilidad [improβaβili'ðað] *nf* (*sin seguridad*) improbability; (*inverosimilitud*) unlikelihood; **improbable** *a* improbable; unlikely.

improcedente [improθe'ðente] *a* (*inconveniente*) unsuitable; (*inadecuado*) inappropriate.

improductivo, a [improðuk'tiβo, a] *a* unproductive.

improperio [impro'perjo] *nm* insult, taunt.

impropiedad [impropje'ðað] *nf* impropriety (of language).

impropio, a [im'propjo, a] *a* improper.

impróvido, a [im'proβiðo, a] *a* improvident.

improvisación [improβisa'θjon] *nf* improvisation; **improvisado, a** *a* improvised; **improvisar** *vt* to improvise.

improviso, a [impro'βiso, a], **improvisto, a** [impro'βisto, a] *a* unexpected, unforeseen; **de** ~ unexpectedly, suddenly.

imprudencia [impru'ðenθja] *nf* imprudence; (*indiscreción*) indiscretion; (*descuido*) carelessness; **imprudente** *a* imprudent; indiscreet; (*irreflexivo*) unwise.

impúdico, a [im'puðiko, a] *a* shameless, immodest; (*lujurioso*) lecherous, lewd.

impudor [impu'ðor] *nm* shamelessness, immodesty; (*lujuria*) lechery, lewdness.

impuesto, a [im'pwesto, a] *a* imposed; (*informado*) informed // *nm* tax.

impugnar [impux'nar] *vt* to oppose, contest; (*refutar*) to refute, impugn.

impulsar [impul'sar] *vt* = **impeler.**

impulsión [impul'sjon] *nf* (*TEC*) propulsion; (*fig*) impulse.

impulso [im'pulso] *nm* impulse; (*fuerza, empuje*) thrust, drive; (*rapto*) urge, impulse.

impune [im'pune] *a* unpunished; **impunidad** *nf* impunity.

impureza [impu'reθa] *nf* impurity; (*fig*) lewdness; **impuro, a** *a* impure; lewd.

imputación [imputa'θjon] *nf* imputation.

imputar [impu'tar] *vt* (*atribuir*) to attribute to; (*cargar*) to impute to.

inacabable [inaka'βaβle] *a* (*infinito*) endless; (*interminable*) interminable.

inaccesible [inakθe'siβle] *a* inaccessible.

inacción [inak'θjon] *nf* (*gen*) inaction; (*desocupación*) inactivity; (*ocio*) idleness.

inaceptable [inaθep'taβle] *a* inacceptable.

inactividad [inaktiβi'ðað] *nf* inactivity; (*pereza*) laziness, idleness; (*COM*) dullness; **inactivo, a** *a* inactive.

inadaptación [inaðapta'θjon] *nf* maladjustment.

inadecuado, a [inaðe'kwaðo, a] *a* (*insuficiente*) inadequate; (*inapto*) unsuitable.

inadmisible [inaðmi'siβle] *a* inadmissible.

inadvertencia [inaðβer'tenθja] *nf* oversight.

inadvertido, a [inaðβer'tiðo, a] *a* (*distraído*) inattentive; (*no visto*) unnoticed; (*descuidado*) careless.

inagotable [inaxo'taβle] *a* inexhaustible.

inaguantable [inaɣwan'taβle] *a* unbearable.

inalterable [inalte'raβle] *a* immutable, unchangeable; (*permanente*) permanent.

inanición [inani'θjon] *nf* starvation.

inanimado, a [inani'maðo, a] *a* inanimate.

inapto, a [in'apto, a] *a* unsuited.

inaudito, a [inau'ðito, a] *a* unheard-of.

inauguración [inauɣura'θjon] *nf* inauguration; (*de exposición*) opening; **inaugurar** *vt* to inaugurate; to open.

I.N.B. *abr de* **Instituto Nacional de Bachillerato** ≈ secondary school.

inca ['inka] *nm/f* Inca; ~**ico, a** *a* Inca.

incalculable [inkalku'laβle] *a* incalculable.

incandescente [inkandes'θente] *a* incandescent.

incansable [inkan'saβle] *a* tireless, untiring.

incapacidad [inkapaθi'ðað] *nf* incapacity; (*incompetencia*) incompetence; ~ **física/mental** physical/mental incapacity *or* disability.

incapacitar [inkapaθi'tar] *vt* (*inhabilitar*) to incapacitate, render unfit; (*descalificar*) to disqualify.

incapaz [inka'paθ] *a* incapable.

incautación [inkauta'θjon] *nf* confiscation; **incautarse** *vr*: **incautarse de** to seize, confiscate.

incauto, a [in'kauto, a] *a* (*imprudente*) incautious, unwary.

incendiar [inθen'djar] *vt* to set on fire; (*fig*) to inflame; ~**se** *vr* to catch fire; ~**io, a** *a* incendiary; (*fig*) inflammatory.

incendio [in'θendjo] *nm* fire.

incentivo [inθen'tiβo] *nm* incentive.

incertidumbre [inθerti'ðumbre] *nf* (*inseguridad*) uncertainty; (*duda*) doubt.

incesante [inθe'sante], **incesable** [inθe'saβle] *a* incessant.

incesto [in'θesto] *nm* incest.

incidencia [inθi'ðenθja] *nf* (*accidente*) incident; (MAT) incidence.

incidente [inθi'ðente] *a* incidental // *nm* incident.

incidir [inθi'ðir] *vi* (*influir*) to influence; (*afectar*) to affect; ~ **en un error** to fall into error.

incienso [in'θjenso] *nm* incense.

incierto, a [in'θjerto, a] *a* uncertain.

incineración [inθinera'θjon] *nf* incineration; (*de cadáveres*) cremation; **incinerar** *vt* to burn; to cremate.

incipiente [inθi'pjente] *a* incipient.

incisión [inθi'sjon] *nf* incision.

incisivo, a [inθi'siβo, a] *a* sharp, cutting; (*fig*) incisive.

incitación [inθita'θjon] *nf* incitement.

incitante [inθi'tante] *a* (*estimulante*) exciting; (*provocativo*) provocative; **incitar** *vt* to incite, rouse.

incivil [inθi'βil] *a* rude, uncivil.

inclemencia [inkle'menθja] *nf* (*severidad*) harshness, severity; (*del tiempo*) inclemency; **inclemente** *a* harsh, severe; inclement.

inclinación [inklina'θjon] *nf* (*gen*) inclination; (*de tierras*) slope, incline; (*de cabeza*) nod, bow; (*fig*) leaning, bent.

inclinar [inkli'nar] *vt* to incline; (*cabeza*) to nod, bow; (*tierras*) to slope; (*persuadir*) to persuade; ~**se** *vr* to bow; (*encorvarse*) to stoop; ~**se a** to take after, resemble; ~**se ante** to bow down to; **me inclino a pensar que** I'm inclined to think that.

ínclito, a ['inklito, a] *a* illustrious, renowned.

incluir [inklu'ir] *vt* to include; (*incorporar*) to incorporate; (*meter*) to enclose.

inclusive [inklu'siβe] *ad* inclusive // *prep* including.

incluso, a [in'kluso, a] *a* included // *ad* inclusively; (*hasta*) even.

incógnito, a [in'koɣnito, a] *a* unknown // *nm*: **de** ~ incognito // *nf* unknown factor.

incoherente [inkoe'rente] *a* incoherent.

incoloro, a [inko'loro, a] *a* colourless.

incólume [in'kolume] *a* (*gen*) safe; (*indemne*) unhurt, unharmed.

incomodar [inkomo'ðar] *vt* to inconvenience; (*molestar*) to bother, trouble; (*fastidiar*) to annoy; ~**se** *vr* to put o.s. out; (*fastidiarse*) to get annoyed.

incomodidad [inkomoði'ðað] *nf* inconvenience; (*fastidio, enojo*) annoyance; (*de vivienda*) discomfort.

incómodo, a [in'komoðo, a] *a* (*inconfortable*) uncomfortable; (*molesto*) annoying; (*inconveniente*) inconvenient.

incomparable [inkompa'raβle] *a* incomparable.

incompatible [inkompa'tiβle] *a* incompatible.

incompetencia [inkompe'tenθja] *nf* incompetence; **incompetente** *a* incompetent.

incompleto, a [inkom'pleto, a] *a* incomplete, unfinished.

incomprensible [inkompren'siβle] *a* incomprehensible.

incomunicado, a [inkomuni'kaðo, a] *a* (*aislado*) cut off, isolated; (*confinado*) in solitary confinement.

inconcebible [inkonθe'βiβle] *a* inconceivable.

inconcluso, a [inkon'kluso, a] *a* (*inacabado*) unfinished; (*incompleto*) incomplete.

incondicional [inkondiθjo'nal] *a* unconditional; (*apoyo*) wholehearted; (*partidario*) staunch.

inconexo, a [inko'nekso, a] *a* (*gen*) unconnected; (*desunido*) disconnected.

inconfundible [inkonfun'diβle] *a* unmistakable.

incongruente [inkon'ɣrwente] *a* incongruous.

inconmensurable [inkonmensu'raβle] *a* immeasurable, vast.

inconsciencia [inkons'θjenθja] *nf* unconsciousness; (*fig*) thoughtlessness; **inconsciente** *a* unconscious; thoughtless.

inconsecuencia [inkonse'kwenθja] *nf* inconsistency; **inconsecuente** *a* inconsistent.

inconsiderado, a [inkonsiðe'raðo, a] *a* inconsiderate.

inconsistente [inkonsis'tente] *a* weak; (*tela*) flimsy.

inconstancia [inkon'stanθja] *nf* (*inconsecuencia, veleidad*) inconstancy; (*inestabilidad*) unsteadiness; **inconstante** *a* inconstant.

incontestable [inkontes'taβle] *a* unanswerable; (*innegable*) undeniable.

incontinencia [inkonti'nenθja] *nf* incontinence; **incontinente** *a* incontinent.

inconveniencia [inkonβe'njenθja] *nf* unsuitability, inappropriateness; (*incorrección*) impoliteness; **inconveniente** *a* unsuitable; impolite // *nm* obstacle; (*desventaja*) disadvantage.

incorporación [inkorpora'θjon] *nf* incorporation; (*del cuerpo*) sitting/standing up; **incorporar** *vt* to incorporate; **incorporarse** *vr* to sit up/stand up.

incorrección [inkorrek'θjon] *nf* (*gen*) incorrectness, inaccuracy; (*descortesía*) bad-mannered behaviour; **incorrecto, a** *a* (*gen*) incorrect, wrong; (*facciones*) irregular, odd; (*comportamiento*) bad-mannered.

incorregible [inkorre'xiβle] *a* incorrigible.

incorruptible [inkorrup'tiβle] *a* incorruptible; ~ **a la intemperie** rustproof.

incredulidad [inkreðuli'ðað] *nf* incredulity; (*escepticismo*) scepticism; **incrédulo, a** *a* incredulous, unbelieving; sceptical.

increíble [inkre'iβle] *a* incredible.

incremento [inkre'mento] *nm* increment; (*aumento*) rise, increase.

increpar [inkre'par] *vt* to reprimand.

incruento, a [in'krwento, a] a bloodless.
incrustar [inkrus'tar] vt to incrust;
(piedras: en joya) to inlay.
incubar [inku'ßar] vt to incubate; (fig) to
hatch.
inculcar [inkul'kar] vt to inculcate.
inculpar [inkul'par] vt (acusar) to accuse;
(achacar, atribuir) to charge, blame.
inculto, a [in'kulto, a] a (persona)
uneducated, uncultured; (terreno)
uncultivated // nm/f ignoramus.
incumplimiento [inkumpli'mjento] nm
non-fulfilment; ~ de contrato breach of
contract.
incurrir [inku'rrir] vi: ~ en to incur;
(crimen) to commit; ~ en un error to
fall into error.
indagación [indaxa'θjon] nf investigation;
(búsqueda) search; (JUR) inquest; **indagar**
vt to investigate; to search; (averiguar) to
ascertain.
indecente [inde'θente] a indecent,
improper; (lascivo) obscene.
indecible [inde'θißle] a unspeakable;
(indescriptible) indescribable.
indeciso, a [inde'θiso, a] a (por decidir)
undecided; (vacilante) hesitant; (resultado)
indecisive.
indefectible [indefek'tißle] a unfailing.
indefenso, a [inde'fenso, a] a defenceless.
indefinido, a [indefi'niðo, a] a indefinite;
(vago) vague, undefined.
indeleble [inde'leßle] a indelible.
indemnizar [indemni'θar] vt to
indemnify; (compensar) to compensate.
independencia [indepen'denθja] nf
independence.
independiente [indepen'djente] a (libre)
independent; (autónomo) self-sufficient.
indeterminado, a [indetermi'naðo, a] a
indefinite; (desconocido) indeterminate.
India ['indja] nf: la ~ India.
indicación [indika'θjon] nf indication;
(señal) sign; (sugerencia) suggestion, hint;
(de termómetro) reading.
indicador [indika'ðor] nm indicator; (TEC)
gauge, meter.
indicar [indi'kar] vt (mostrar) to indicate,
show; (termómetro etc) to read, register;
(señalar) to point to.
índice ['indiθe] nm index; (catálogo)
catalogue; (ANAT) index finger, forefinger;
(de cuadrante) pointer, needle; (de reloj)
hand.
indicio [in'diθjo] nm indication, sign;
(huella) trace; (pesquisa) clue.
indiferencia [indife'renθja] nf
indifference; (apatía) apathy; **indiferente**
a indifferent.
indígena [in'dixena] a indigenous, native;
(aborigen) aboriginal // nm/f native;
aborigine.
indigencia [indi'xenθja] nf poverty, need.
indigestión [indixes'tjon] nf indigestion.
indigesto, a [indi'xesto, a] a undigested;
(indigestible) indigestible; (fig) turgid.

indignación [indixna'θjon] nf indignation;
indignado, a a indignant.
indignar [indix'nar] vt to anger, make
indignant; ~se vr: ~se de o por to get
indignant about.
indignidad [indixni'ðað] nf (insulto)
indignity, insult; (ruindad) vile act;
indigno, a a (despreciable) low,
contemptible; (inmerecido) unworthy.
indio, a ['indjo, a] a, nm/f Indian.
indirecta [indi'rekta] nf insinuation,
innuendo; (sugerencia) hint.
indirecto, a [indi'rekto, a] a indirect.
indiscreción [indiskre'θjon] nf
(imprudencia) indiscretion; (irreflexión)
tactlessness; (acto) gaffe, tactless act.
indiscreto, a [indis'kreto, a] a indiscreet.
indiscutible [indisku'tißle] a disputable,
unquestionable.
indispensable [indispen'saßle] a
indispensable.
indisponer [indispo'ner] vt to spoil, upset;
(salud) to make ill; ~se vr to fall ill; ~se
con uno to fall out with sb.
indisposición [indisposi'θjon] nf
indisposition.
indistinto, a [indis'tinto, a] a indistinct;
(vago) vague.
individual [indißi'ðwal] a individual;
(habitación) single // nm (DEPORTE) singles
sg.
individuo, a [indi'ßiðwo, a] a individual //
nm individual; (miembro, socio) member,
fellow.
indiviso, a [indi'ßiso, a] a undivided.
índole ['indole] nf (naturaleza) nature;
(clase) sort, kind.
indolencia [indo'lenθja] nf indolence,
laziness.
indomable [indo'maßle] a indomitable;
(animal) untameable; (fig) unmanageable.
indómito, a [in'domito, a] a indomitable.
inducir [indu'θir] vt to induce; (inferir) to
infer; (persuadir) to persuade.
indudable [indu'ðaßle] a undoubted;
(incuestionable) unquestionable.
indulgencia [indul'xenθja] nf indulgence.
indultar [indul'tar] vt (perdonar) to
pardon, reprieve; (librar de pago) to
exempt; **indulto** nm pardon; exemption.
industria [in'dustrja] nf industry;
(habilidad) skill; **industrial** a industrial //
nm industrialist.
industrioso, a [indus'trjoso, a] a
industrious.
inédito, a [in'eðito, a] a (libro)
unpublished; (nuevo) unheard-of.
inefable [ine'faßle] a ineffable,
indescribable.
ineficaz [inefi'kaθ] a (inútil) ineffective;
(ineficiente) inefficient.
ineludible [inelu'ðißle] a inescapable,
unavoidable.
ineptitud [inepti'tuð] nf ineptitude,
incompetence; **inepto, a** a inept,
incompetent.

inequívoco, a [ine'kiβoko, a] *a* unequivocal; (*inconfundible*) unmistakable.

inercia [in'erθja] *nf* inertia; (*fig*) passivity.

inerme [in'erme] *a* (*sin armas*) unarmed; (*indefenso*) defenceless.

inerte [in'erte] *a* inert; (*fig*) passive.

inesperado, a [inespe'raðo, a] *a* unexpected, unforeseen.

inestable [ines'taβle] *a* unstable.

inevitable [ineβi'taβle] *a* inevitable.

inexactitud [ineksakti'tuð] *nf* inaccuracy; **inexacto, a** *a* inaccurate; (*falso*) untrue.

infamar [infa'mar] *vt* to dishonour; (*calumniar*) to defame, slander.

infame [in'fame] *a* infamous // *nm/f* vile person; **infamia** *nf* infamy; (*deshonra*) disgrace.

infancia [in'fanθja] *nf* infancy, childhood.

infante [in'fante] *nm* (*niño*) infant, child; (*hijo del rey*) prince.

infantería [infante'ria] *nf* infantry.

infantil [infan'til] *a* (*pueril, aniñado*) infantile; (*cándido*) childlike; (*literatura*) children's.

infarto [in'farto] *nm* heart attack.

infatigable [infati'βaβle] *a* tireless, untiring.

infausto, a [in'fausto, a] *a* unlucky.

infección [infek'θjon] *nf* infection; **infeccioso, a** *a* infectious.

infectar [infek'tar] *vt* to infect; ~**se** *vr* to become infected.

infelicidad [infeliθi'ðað] *nf* unhappiness.

infeliz [infe'liθ] *a* unhappy, wretched // *nm/f* wretch.

inferior [infe'rjor] *a* inferior; (*situación*) lower // *nm/f* inferior, subordinate.

inferir [infe'rir] *vt* (*deducir*) to infer, deduce; (*causar*) to cause.

infestar [infes'tar] *vt* (*infectar*) to infect; (*apestar*) to infest; (*fig*) to harass.

inficionar [infiθjo'nar] *vt* to infect; (*fig*) to corrupt.

infidelidad [infiðeli'ðað] *nf* (*gen*) infidelity, unfaithfulness; (*REL*) lack of faith.

infiel [in'fjel] *a* unfaithful, disloyal; (*falso*) inaccurate // *nm/f* infidel, unbeliever.

infierno [in'fjerno] *nm* hell.

ínfimo, a ['infimo, a] *a* vile, mean.

infinidad [infini'ðað] *nf* infinity; (*abundancia*) great quantity.

infinito, a [infi'nito, a] *a, nm* infinite.

inflación [infla'θjon] *nf* (*hinchazón*) swelling; (*monetaria*) inflation; (*fig*) conceit; **inflacionario, a** *a* inflationary.

inflamar [infla'mar] *vt* to set on fire; (*MED*) to inflame; ~**se** *vr* to catch fire; (*fig*) to become inflamed.

inflar [in'flar] *vt* (*hinchar*) to inflate, blow up; (*fig*) to exaggerate; ~**se** *vr* to swell (up); (*fig*) to get conceited.

inflexible [inflek'siβle] *a* inflexible; (*irrompible*) unbending; (*fig*) strict.

infligir [infli'xir] *vt* to inflict.

influencia [influ'enθja] *nf* influence; **influenciar** *vt* to influence.

influir [influ'ir] *vt* to influence.

influjo [in'fluxo] *nm* influence.

influyente [influ'jente] *a* influential.

información [informa'θjon] *nf* information; (*noticias*) news *sg*; (*JUR*) inquiry.

informal [infor'mal] *a* (*gen*) irregular, incorrect; (*persona*) unreliable; (*poco serio*) frivolous; (*trabajo*) disorganized; (*comportamiento*) unconventional.

informalidad [informali'ðað] *nf* (*impuntualidad*) unpunctuality; (*incorrección*) bad manners *pl*; (*ligereza*) frivolity.

informante [infor'mante] *nm/f* informant.

informar [infor'mar] *vt* (*gen*) to inform; (*revelar*) to reveal, make known // *vi* (*JUR*) to plead; (*denunciar*) to inform; (*dar cuenta de*) to report on; ~**se** *vr* to find out; ~**se de** to inquire into.

informe [in'forme] *a* shapeless // *nm* report.

infortunio [infor'tunjo] *nm* misfortune.

infracción [infrak'θjon] *nf* infraction, infringement; (*transgresión*) transgression.

infranqueable [infranke'aβle] *a* impassable; (*impracticable*) insurmountable.

infringir [infrin'xir] *vt* to infringe, contravene.

infructuoso, a [infruk'twoso, a] *a* fruitless, unsuccessful.

infundado, a [infun'daðo, a] *a* groundless, unfounded.

infundir [infun'dir] *vt* to infuse, instil.

ingeniar [inxe'njar] *vt* to think up, devise; ~**se** *vr*: ~**se para** to manage to.

ingeniería [inxenje'ria] *nf* engineering; **ingeniero, a** *nm/f* engineer; **ingeniero agrónomo/de sonido** agronomist/sound engineer.

ingenio [in'xenjo] *nm* (*talento*) talent; (*agudeza*) wit; (*habilidad*) ingenuity, inventiveness; (*TEC*): ~ **azucarero** sugar refinery.

ingenioso, a [inxe'njoso, a] *a* ingenious, clever; (*divertido*) witty.

ingénito, a [in'xenito, a] *a* innate.

ingenuidad [inxenwi'ðað] *nf* ingenuousness; (*candor*) candour; **ingenuo, a** *a* ingenuous.

ingerencia [inxe'renθja] *nf* = **injerencia.**

ingerir [inxe'rir] *vt* to ingest; (*tragar*) to swallow; (*consumir*) to consume.

Inglaterra [ingla'terra] *nf* England.

ingle ['ingle] *nf* groin.

inglés, esa [in'gles, esa] *a* English // *nm/f* Englishman/woman // *nm* (*lengua*) English.

ingratitud [ingrati'tuð] *nf* ingratitude; **ingrato, a** *a* (*gen*) ungrateful; (*desagradable*) unpleasant.

ingrediente [ingre'ðjente] *nm* ingredient.

ingresar [ingre'sar] vt (dinero) to deposit // vi to come in; ~ **en un club** to join a club; ~ **en el hospital** to go into hospital.

ingreso [in'greso] nm (entrada) entry; (: en hospital etc) admission; (de dinero) income, takings pl.

inhábil [in'aβil] a unskilful, clumsy; **día** ~ non-working day.

inhabitable [inaβi'taβle] a uninhabitable.

inherente [ine'rente] a inherent.

inhibir [ini'βir] vt to inhibit; (REL) to restrain.

inhospitalario, a [inospita'larjo, a] a inhospitable.

inhumano, a [inu'mano, a] a inhuman.

I. N. I. ['ini] nm abr de **Instituto Nacional de Industria** = National Enterprise Board.

inicial [ini'θjal] a, nf initial.

iniciar [ini'θjar] vt (persona) to initiate; (estudios) to begin, commence; (conversación) to start up.

iniciativa [iniθja'tiβa] nf initiative; **la** ~ **privada** private enterprise.

inicuo, a [in'ikwo, a] a iniquitous.

ininterrumpido, a [ininterrum'piðo, a] a uninterrupted.

injerencia [inxe'renθja] nf interference.

injertar [inxer'tar] vt to graft; (inyectar) to inject; **injerto** nm graft.

injuria [in'xurja] nf (agravio, ofensa) offence; (insulto) insult; (daño) harm; **injuriar** vt to insult; to harm; **injurioso, a** a offensive; insulting; harmful.

injusticia [inxus'tiθja] nf injustice.

injusto, a [in'xusto, a] a unjust, unfair.

inmadurez [inmaðu're θ] nf immaturity.

inmarcesible [inmarθe'siβle], **inmarchitable** [inmartʃi'taβle] a imperishable.

inmediaciones [inmeðja'θjones] nfpl neighbourhood sg, environs.

inmediato, a [inme'ðjato, a] a immediate; (contiguo) adjoining; (rápido) prompt; (próximo) close, next; **de** ~ immediately.

inmejorable [inmexo'raβle] a unsurpassable; (precio) unbeatable.

inmenso, a [in'menso, a] a immense, huge.

inmerecido [inmere'θiðo, a] a undeserved.

inmigración [inmixra'θjon] nf immigration.

inmiscuirse [inmisku'irse] vr to interfere, meddle.

inmobiliario, a [inmoβi'ljarjo, a] a real-estate cpd // nf estate agency.

inmoderado, a [inmoðe'raðo, a] a immoderate, excessive.

inmolar [inmo'lar] vt to immolate, sacrifice.

inmoral [inmo'ral] a immoral.

inmortal [inmor'tal] a immortal; ~**izar** vt to immortalize.

inmotivado, a [inmoti'βaðo, a] a motiveless.

inmóvil [in'moβil] a immobile;

(inamovible) immovable; (invariable) unchanging; (parado) still, stationary.

inmueble [in'mweβle] nm property.

inmundicia [inmun'diθja] nf filth; **inmundo, a** a filthy.

inmunidad [inmuni'ðað] nf immunity.

inmutar [inmu'tar] vt to alter; ~**se** vr to turn pale.

innato, a [in'nato, a] a innate.

innecesario, a [inneθe'sarjo, a] a unnecessary.

innoble [in'noβle] a ignoble.

innocuo, a [in'nokwo, a] a innocuous.

innovación [innoβa'θjon] nf innovation; **innovar** vt to introduce.

inocencia [ino'θenθja] nf innocence.

inocentada [inoθen'taða] nf practical joke.

inocente [ino'θente] a (ingenuo) naive, simple; (inculpable) innocent // nm/f simpleton.

inodoro [ino'ðoro] nm toilet, lavatory.

inofensivo, a [inofen'siβo, a] a inoffensive.

inolvidable [inolβi'ðaβle] a unforgettable.

inoperante [inope'rante] a unworkable.

inopinado, a [inopi'naðo, a] a unexpected.

inoportuno, a [inopor'tuno, a] a untimely; (molesto) inconvenient.

inoxidable [inoksi'ðaβle] a: **acero** ~ stainless steel.

inquebrantable [inkeβran'taβle] a unbreakable.

inquietar [inkje'tar] vt to worry, trouble, disturb; ~**se** vr to worry, get upset; **inquieto, a** a anxious, worried; **inquietud** nf anxiety, worry.

inquilino, a [inki'lino, a] nm/f tenant.

inquirir [inki'rir] vt to enquire into, investigate.

insaciable [insa'θjaβle] a insatiable.

insalubre [insa'luβre] a unhealthy.

inscribir [inskri'βir] vt to inscribe; (lista) to list; (censo) to register; ~**se** vr to register; (ESCOL etc) to enrol.

inscripción [inskrip'θjon] nf inscription; (ESCOL etc) enrolment; (censo) registration.

insecto [in'sekto] nm insect.

inseguridad [insexuri'ðað] nf insecurity.

inseguro, a [inse'xuro, a] a insecure; (inconstante) unsteady; (incierto) uncertain.

insensato, a [insen'sato, a] a foolish, stupid.

insensibilidad [insensiβili'ðað] nf (gen) insensitivity; (dureza de corazón) callousness.

insensible [insen'siβle] a (gen) insensitive; (duro) callous; (movimiento) imperceptible; (sin sentido) numb.

insertar [inser'tar] vt to insert.

inservible [inser'βiβle] a useless.

insidioso, a [insi'ðjoso, a] a insidious.

insignia [in'sixnja] nf (señal distintivo)

badge; (*estandarte*) flag; (*condecoración*) decoration.
insignificante [insixnifi'kante] a insignificant.
insinuar [insi'nwar] vt to insinuate, imply; ~**se** vr: ~**se con uno** to ingratiate o.s. with sb.
insípido, a [in'sipiðo, a] a insipid.
insistencia [insis'tenθja] nf (*obstinación*) insistence; (*porfía*) persistence.
insistir [insis'tir] vi to insist; ~ **en algo** to stress sth.
insolación [insola'θjon] nf (MED) sunstroke.
insolencia [inso'lenθja] nf insolence; **insolente** a insolent.
insólito, a [in'solito, a] a unusual.
insoluble [inso'luβle] a insoluble.
insolvencia [insol'βenθja] nf insolvency.
insomnio [in'somnjo] nm insomnia.
insondable [inson'daβle] a bottomless.
insoportable [insopor'taβle] a unbearable.
inspección [inspek'θjon] nf inspection, check; **inspeccionar** vt (*examinar*) to inspect, examine; (*controlar*) to check.
inspector, a [inspek'tor, a] nm/f inspector.
inspiración [inspira'θjon] nf inspiration; **inspirar** vt to inspire; (MED) to inhale; **inspirarse** vr: **inspirarse en** to be inspired by.
instalar [insta'lar] vt (*establecer*) to instal; (*erguir*) to set up, erect; ~**se** vr to establish o.s.
instancia [ins'tanθja] nf (JUR) petition; (*ruego*) request; **en última** ~ in the last resort.
instantáneo, a [instan'taneo, a] a instant, instantaneous // nf snap(shot).
instante [ins'tante] nm instant, moment.
instar [ins'tar] vt to press, urge // vi to be pressing or urgent.
instigar [insti'xar] vt to instigate.
instinto [ins'tinto] nm instinct; **por** ~ instinctively.
institución [institu'θjon] nf institution, establishment.
instituir [institu'ir] vt to establish; (*fundar*) to found; **instituto** nm (*gen*) institute; (*escuela*) high school.
instrucción [instruk'θjon] nf instruction.
instructivo, a [instruk'tiβo, a] a instructive.
instruir [instru'ir] vt (*gen*) to instruct; (*enseñar*) to teach, educate; (MIL, DEPORTE) to train.
instrumento [instru'mento] nm (*gen*) instrument; (*herramienta*) tool, implement.
insubordinarse [insuβorði'narse] vr to rebel.
insuficiencia [insufi'θjenθja] nf (*carencia*) lack; (*inadecuación*) inadequacy; **insuficiente** a (*gen*) insufficient; (*incompetente*) incompetent; (*nota*) inadequate.
insufrible [insu'friβle] a insufferable.

insular [insu'lar] a insular.
insulsez [insul'seθ] nf (*insipidez*) insipidity; (*fig*) dullness.
insultar [insul'tar] vt to insult; **insulto** nm insult.
insuperable [insupe'raβle] a (*excelente*) unsurpassable; (*arduo*) insurmountable.
insurgente [insur'xente] a, nm/f insurgent.
insurrección [insurrek'θjon] nf insurrection, rebellion.
intacto, a [in'takto, a] a intact.
intachable [inta'tʃaβle] a irreproachable.
integral [inte'xral] a: **pan** ~ wholemeal bread.
integrar [inte'xrar] vt to make up, compose; (COM) to repay; (MAT) to integrate.
integridad [intexri'ðað] nf wholeness; (*carácter*) integrity; **íntegro, a** a whole, entire; (*honrado*) honest.
intelectual [intelek'twal] a, nm/f intellectual.
inteligencia [inteli'xenθja] nf intelligence; (*ingenio*) ability; **inteligente** a intelligent.
intemperancia [intempe'ranθja] nf excess, intemperance.
intemperie [intem'perje] nf bad weather; **a la** ~ outdoors, in the open air.
intempestivo, a [intempes'tiβo, a] a untimely.
intención [inten'θjon] nf (*gen*) intention; (*propósito*) purpose; **con segundas intenciones** maliciously; **de primera** ~ provisionally; **con** ~ deliberately.
intencionado, a [intenθjo'naðo, a] a deliberate; **bien/mal** ~ well-meaning/ill-disposed.
intendencia [inten'denθja] nf management, administration.
intenso, a [in'tenso, a] a intense; (*impresión*) vivid; (*sentimiento*) profound, deep.
intentar [inten'tar] vt (*tratar*) to try, attempt; **intento** nm (*intención*) intention, purpose; (*tentativa*) attempt.
intercalar [interka'lar] vt to insert.
intercambio [inter'kambjo] nm exchange, swap.
interceder [interθe'ðer] vi to intercede.
intercesión [interθe'sjon] nf intercession.
interés [inte'res] nm (*gen*) interest; (*parte*) share, part; (*pey*) self-interest; **intereses creados** vested interests.
interesado, a [intere'saðo, a] a interested; (*prejuiciado*) prejudiced; (*pey*) mercenary, self-seeking.
interesar [intere'sar] vt, vi to interest, be of interest to; ~**se** vr: ~**se en** o **por** to take an interest in.
interferir [interfe'rir] vt to interfere with; (TELEC) to jam // vi to interfere.
interior [inte'rjor] a inner, inside; (COM) domestic, internal // nm interior, inside; (*fig*) soul, mind; **Ministerio del I**~ Home Office.

interjección [interxek'θjon] *nf* interjection.

interlocutor, a [interloku'tor] *nm/f* speaker.

intermediario, a [interme'ðjarjo, a] *nm/f* intermediary // *nm* middleman.

intermedio, a [inter'meðjo, a] *a* intermediate // *nm* interval.

interminable [intermi'naβle] *a* endless.

intermitente [intermi'tente] *a* intermittent // *nm* indicator.

internacional [internaθjo'nal] *a* international.

internar [inter'nar] *vt* to intern; (*loco*) to commit; ~se *vr* (*en un hospital*) to go into hospital; (*penetrar*) to penetrate.

interno, a [in'terno, a] *a* internal, interior; (*POL etc*) domestic // *nm/f* (*alumno*) boarder.

interpelar [interpe'lar] *vt* (*rogar*) to implore; (*hablar*) to speak to.

interponer [interpo'ner] *vt* to interpose, put in; ~se *vr* to intervene.

interposición [interposi'θjon] *nf* insertion.

interpretación [interpreta'θjon] *nf* interpretation; **interpretar** *vt* to interpret; **interprete** *nm/f* interpreter; (*traductor*) translator; (*músico, TEATRO*) performer, artist(e).

interrogación [interroxa'θjon] *nf* interrogation; (*LING*) question mark; **interrogar** *vt* to interrogate, question.

interrumpir [interrum'pir] *vt* to interrupt; (*ELEC*) to switch off, cut off.

interrupción [interrup'θjon] *nf* interruption.

interruptor [interrup'tor] *nm* (*ELEC*) switch.

intersección [intersek'θjon] *nf* intersection.

interurbano, a [interur'βano, a] *a*: **llamada** ~a trunk call.

intervalo [inter'βalo] *nm* interval; (*descanso*) break; **a** ~s at intervals, every now and then.

intervenir [interβe'nir] *vt* (*controlar*) to control, supervise; (*MED*) to operate on // *vi* (*participar*) to take part, participate; (*mediar*) to intervene.

interventor, a [interβen'tor, a] *nm/f* inspector; (*COM*) auditor.

interviú [inter'βju] *nf* interview.

intestino, a [intes'tino, a] *a* internal; (*doméstico*) domestic // *nm* intestine.

intimar [inti'mar] *vt* to intimate, announce // *vi* to become friendly.

intimidad [intimi'ðað] *nf* intimacy; (*confianza*) confidence; (*familiaridad*) familiarity; (*vida privada*) private life; (*soledad*) privacy.

íntimo, a ['intimo, a] *a* intimate.

intolerable [intole'raβle] *a* intolerable, unbearable.

intransitable [intransi'taβle] *a* impassable.

intrepidez [intrepi'ðeθ] *nf* courage, bravery; **intrépido, a** *a* intrepid.

intriga [in'triɣa] *nf* intrigue; (*plan*) plot; **intrigar** *vt, vi* to intrigue.

intrincado, a [intrin'kaðo, a] *a* intricate.

intrínseco, a [in'trinseko, a] *a* intrinsic.

introducción [introðuk'θjon] *nf* introduction.

introducir [introðu'θir] *vt* (*gen*) to introduce; (*hacer penetrar*) to insert.

intruso, a [in'truso, a] *a* intrusive // *nm/f* intruder.

intuición [intwi'θjon] *nf* intuition.

inundación [inunda'θjon] *nf* flood(ing); **inundar** *vt* to flood; (*fig*) to swamp, inundate.

inusitado, a [inusi'taðo, a] *a* unusual.

inútil [in'util] *a* useless; (*esfuerzo*) vain, fruitless; **inutilidad** *nf* uselessness.

inutilizar [inutili'θar] *vt* to make useless, render useless; ~se *vr* to become useless.

invadir [inβa'ðir] *vt* to invade.

inválido, a [in'βaliðo, a] *a* invalid // *nm/f* invalid.

invariable [inβa'rjaβle] *a* invariable.

invasión [inβa'sjon] *nf* invasion.

invasor, a [inβa'sor, a] *a* invading // *nm/f* invader.

invención [inβen'θjon] *nf* invention.

inventar [inβen'tar] *vt* to invent.

inventario [inβen'tarjo] *nm* inventory.

inventiva [inβen'tiβa] *nf* inventiveness.

inventor, a [inβen'tor, a] *nm/f* inventor.

inverosímil [inβero'simil] *a* implausible; (*improbable*) unlikely, improbable.

inversión [inβer'sjon] *nf* (*COM*) investment; (*AUTO*) reversing; **inversionista** *nm/f* investor.

inverso, a [in'βerso, a] *a* inverse, opposite; **en el orden** ~ in reverse order; **a la** ~a inversely, the other way round.

invertir [inβer'tir] *vt* (*COM*) to invest; (*volcar*) to turn upside down; (*tiempo etc*) to spend; (*AUTO*) to reverse.

investigación [inβestiɣa'θjon] *nf* investigation; (*estudio*) research; **investigar** *vt* to investigate; (*estudiar*) to do research into.

inveterado, a [inβete'raðo, a] *a* inveterate, confirmed.

invicto, a [in'βikto, a] *a* unconquered.

invierno [in'βjerno] *nm* winter.

invitar [inβi'tar] *vt* to invite; (*incitar*) to entice; (*pagar*) to buy, pay for.

invocar [inβo'kar] *vt* to invoke, call on.

inyección [injek'θjon] *nf* injection.

inyectar [injek'tar] *vt* to inject.

ir [ir] *vi* (*gen*) to go; (*viajar*) to travel; (*ropa*) to suit; ~ **caminando** to walk; ~ **en coche/bicicleta/caballo/a pie** to drive/cycle/ride/walk; ¡**voy**! I'm coming!; ~ **de viaje** to travel, go away; **voy para viejo** I'm getting on (in years); ~ **por/a por algo** to go for/go and get sth; ¡**qué va**! (*no diga*) you don't say!; (: ¡*no*!) no way!, rubbish!; ¡**vamos**! come on!; **vaya susto que me has dado** what a fright

you gave me; **~se** *vr* to go away, leave; (*mano etc*) to slip; ¡**vete!** go away!
ira ['ira] *nf* anger, rage.
iracundo, a [ira'kundo, a] *a* irascible; (*colérico*) irate.
Irán [i'ran] *nm* Iran; **iranés, esa, iraní** *a, nm/f* Iranian.
iris ['iris] *nm* (*arco* ~) rainbow; (ANAT) iris.
Irlanda [ir'landa] *nf* Ireland; **irlandés, esa** *a* Irish // *nm/f* Irishman/woman.
ironía [iro'nia] *nf* irony; **irónico, a** *a* ironic(al).
irreal [irre'al] *a* unreal.
irreflexión [irreflek'sjon] *nf* thoughtlessness.
irremediable [irreme'ðjaßle] *a* incurable, hopeless.
irresoluto, a [irreso'luto, a] *a* irresolute, hesitant.
irrespetuoso, a [irrespe'twoso, a] *a* disrespectful.
irresponsable [irrespon'saßle] *a* irresponsible.
irrigar [irri'γar] *vt* to irrigate.
irrisorio, a [irri'sorjo, a] *a* derisory, ridiculous.
irritar [irri'tar] *vt* to irritate, annoy.
irrupción [irrup'θjon] *nf* irruption; (*invasión*) invasion.
isla ['isla] *nf* island.
islandés, esa [islan'des, esa] *a* Icelandic // *nm/f* Icelander.
Islandia [is'landja] *nf* Iceland.
isleño, a [is'leɲo, a] *a* island *cpd* // *nm/f* islander.
Israel [isra'el] *nm* Israel; **israelí** *a, nm/f* Israeli.
istmo ['istmo] *nm* isthmus.
Italia [i'talja] *nf* Italy; **italiano, a** *a, nm/f* Italian.
itinerario [itine'rarjo] *nm* itinerary, route.
izar [i'θar] *vt* to hoist.
izquierdista [iθkjer'ðista] *nm/f* left-winger, leftist.
izquierdo, a [iθ'kjerðo, a] *a* left // *nf* left; **a la** ~**a** on the left.

J

jabalí [xaßa'li] *nm* wild boar.
jabalina [xaßa'lina] *nf* javelin.
jabón [xa'ßon] *nm* soap; **jabonar** *vt* to soap.
jaca ['xaka] *nf* pony.
jacinto [xa'θinto] *nm* hyacinth.
jactancia [xak'tanθja] *nf* boasting, boastfulness.
jactarse [xak'tarse] *vr* to boast, brag.
jadeante [xaðe'ante] *a* panting, gasping; **jadear** *vi* to pant, gasp for breath; **jadeo** *nm* panting, gasping.
jaez [xa'eθ] *nm* (*de caballerías*) harness; (*clase*) kind, sort.
jaguar [xa'γwar] *nm* jaguar.

jalar [xa'lar] *vt* to pull, haul.
jalbegue [xal'ßeγe] *nm* (*pintura*) whitewash; (*fig*) make-up.
jalea [xa'lea] *nf* jelly.
jaleo [xa'leo] *nm* racket, uproar; (*baile*) Andalusian popular dance; **estar de** ~ to be having a good time; **armar un** ~ to kick up a din.
Jamaica [xa'maika] *nf* Jamaica.
jamás [xa'mas] *ad* never; (*sin negación*) ever.
jamón [xa'mon] *nm* ham.
Japón [xa'pon] *nm*: **el** ~ Japan; **japonés, esa** *a, nm/f* Japanese.
jaque ['xake] *nm* cheque; (*fam*) bully; ~ **mate** checkmate.
jaqueca [xa'keka] *nf* (severe) headache, migraine.
jarabe [xa'raße] *nm* syrup.
jarcia ['xarθja] *nf* (NAUT) ropes *pl*, rigging; (*para pescar*) (fishing) tackle; (*confusión, revoltijo*) jumble, mess.
jardín [xar'ðin] *nm* garden; **jardinería** *nf* gardening; **jardinero, a** *nm/f* gardener.
jarra ['xarra] *nf* jar.
jarro ['xarro] *nm* jug.
jaula ['xaula] *nf* cage.
jauría [xau'ria] *nf* pack of hounds.
J. C. *abr de* **Jesucristo.**
jefatura [xefa'tura] *nf*: ~ **de policía** police headquarters *sg*.
jefe ['xefe] *nm* (*gen*) chief, head; (*patrón*) boss; ~ **de camareros** head waiter; ~ **de cocina** chef; ~ **de estación** stationmaster; ~ **de estado** head of state; ~ **supremo** commander-in-chief; **ser el** ~ (*fig*) to be the boss.
jengibre [xen'xißre] *nm* ginger.
jeque ['xeke] *nm* sheik.
jerarquía [xerar'kia] *nf* (*orden*) hierarchy; (*rango*) rank; **jerárquico, a** *a* hierarchic(al).
jerez [xe'reθ] *nm* sherry.
jerga ['xerγa] *nf* (*tela*) coarse cloth; (*lenguaje*) jargon, slang.
jerigonza [xeri'γonθa] *nf* (*jerga*) jargon, slang; (*galimatías*) nonsense, gibberish.
jeringa [xe'ringa] *nf* syringe; (AM) annoyance, bother; ~ **de engrase** grease gun; **jeringar** *vt* to syringe; (*inyectar*) to inject; (AM) to annoy, bother.
jeroglífico [xero'γlifiko] *nm* hieroglyphic.
jersé, jersey (*pl* **jerseys**) [xer'sei] *nm* jersey, pullover, jumper.
Jerusalén [xerusa'len] *n* Jerusalem.
Jesucristo [xesu'kristo] *n* Jesus Christ.
jesuita [xe'swita] *a, nm* Jesuit.
Jesús [xe'sus] *nm* Jesus; ¡~! good heavens!; (*al estornudar*) bless you!
jícara ['xikara] *nf* small cup.
jifero, a [xi'fero, a] *a* (*fam*) filthy // *nm* butcher's knife; (*matarife*) butcher, slaughterer.
jinete [xi'nete] *nm* (horse)rider.
jipijapa [xipi'xapa] *nm* (AM) straw hat.

jira ['xira] *nf* (*de tela*) strip; (*excursión*) picnic.

jirafa [xi'rafa] *nf* giraffe.

jirón [xi'ron] *nm* rag, shred.

jocosidad [xokosi'ðað] *nf* humour; (*chiste*) joke.

jocoso, a [xo'koso, a] *a* humorous, jocular.

jofaina [xo'faina] *nf* washbasin.

jornada [xor'naða] *nf* day's journey; (*camino o viaje entero*) journey; (*día de trabajo*) working day; (*fig*) lifetime.

jornal [xor'nal] *nm* (day's) wage; ~**ero** *nm* (day) labourer.

joroba [xo'roßa] *nf* hump, hunched back; (*fam*) nuisance; ~**do, a** *a* hunchbacked // *nm/f* hunchback.

jota ['xota] *nf* letter J; (*danza*) Aragonese dance; (*fam*) iota; **no saber** ~ to have no idea.

joven ['xoßen] *a* young // *nm* young man, youth // *nf* young woman, girl.

jovial [xo'ßjal] *a* cheerful, jovial; ~**idad** *nf* cheerfulness, joviality.

joya ['xoja] *nf* jewel, gem; (*fig: persona*) gem; **joyería** *nf* (*joyas*) jewellery; (*tienda*) jeweller's (shop); **joyero** *nm* (*persona*) jeweller; (*caja*) jewel case.

juanete [xwa'nete] *nm* bunion.

jubilación [xußila'θjon] *nf* (*retiro*) retirement; (*alegría*) jubilation.

jubilar [xußi'lar] *vt* to pension off, retire; (*fam*) to discard // *vi* to rejoice; ~**se** *vr* to retire.

jubileo [xußi'leo] *nm* (*indulgencia*) jubilee; (*fam*) comings and goings *pl.*

júbilo ['xußilo] *nm* joy, jubilation, rejoicing; ~**so, a** *a* jubilant.

judaísmo [xuða'ismo] *nm* Judaism.

judía [xu'ðia] *nf* Jewess; (*CULIN*) bean.

judicatura [xuðika'tura] *nf* (*cargo de juez*) office of judge; (*magistratura*) judicature.

judicial [xuði'θjal] *a* judicial.

judío, a [xu'ðio, a] *a* Jewish // *nm/f* Jew/ess.

juego *etc vb ver* **jugar** // ['xweɣo] *nm* (*gen*) play; (*pasatiempo, partido*) game; (*en casino*) gambling; (*conjunto*) set; **fuera de** ~ (*persona*) offside; (*pelota*) out of play.

juerga ['xwerɣa] *nf* good time; (*fiesta*) party; **ir de** ~ to go out on a spree.

jueves ['xweßes] *nm inv* Thursday.

juez [xweθ] *nm* judge; ~ **de línea** linesman; ~ **de salida** starter.

jugada [xu'ɣaða] *nf* play; **buena** ~ good move/shot/stroke *etc.*

jugador, a [xuɣa'ðor, a] *nm/f* player; (*en casino*) gambler.

jugar [xu'ɣar] *vt, vi* to play; (*en casino*) to gamble; ~**se** *vr* to gamble (away).

juglar [xu'ɣlar] *nm* minstrel.

jugo ['xuɣo] *nm* (*BOT*) juice; (*fig*) essence, substance; ~**so, a** *a* juicy; (*fig*) substantial, important.

juguete [xu'ɣete] *nm* toy; (*TEATRO*) sketch; ~**ar** *vi* to play; ~**ría** *nf* toyshop.

juguetón, ona [xuɣe'ton, ona] *a* playful.

juicio ['xwiθjo] *nm* judgement; (*sana razón*) sanity, reason; (*opinión*) opinion; **estar fuera de** ~ to be out of one's mind; ~**so, a** *a* wise, sensible.

julio ['xuljo] *nm* July.

jumento, a [xu'mento, a] *nm/f* donkey.

junco ['xunko] *nm* rush, reed.

jungla ['xungla] *nf* jungle.

junio ['xunjo] *nm* June.

junta ['xunta] *nf ver* **junto**.

juntamente [xunta'mente] *ad* (*conjuntamente*) together; (*al mismo tiempo*) together, at the same time.

juntar [xun'tar] *vt* to join, unite; (*maquinaria*) to assemble, put together; (*dinero*) to collect; (*puerta*) to half-close, leave ajar; ~**se** *vr* to join, meet; (*reunirse: personas*) to meet, assemble; (*arrimarse*) to approach, draw closer; (*vivir juntos*) to live together; ~ **se con uno** to join sb.

junto, a ['xunto, a] *a* (*unido*) joined, united; (*anexo*) near, close; (*continuo, próximo*) next, adjacent // *ad*: **todo** ~ all at once // *nf* (*asamblea*) meeting, assembly; (*comité, consejo*) board, council, committee; (*articulación*) joint; ~ **a** near (to), next to; ~**s** together.

juntura [xun'tura] *nf* (*punto de unión*) join, junction; (*articulación*) joint.

jurado [xu'raðo] *nm* (*JUR*) juror; (*: conjunto de* ~**s**) jury; (*de concurso*) panel (of judges); (*: individuo*) member of a panel.

juramentar [xuramen'tar] *vt* to swear in, administer the oath to; ~**se** *vr* to be sworn in, take the oath.

juramento [xura'mento] *nm* oath; (*maldición*) oath, curse; **prestar** ~ to take the oath; **tomar** ~ **a** to swear in, administer the oath to.

jurar [xu'rar] *vt, vi* to swear; ~ **en falso** to commit perjury; **jurárselas a uno** to have it in for sb.

jurídico, a [xu'riðiko, a] *a* legal.

jurisdicción [xurisðik'θjon] *nf* (*poder, autoridad*) jurisdiction; (*territorio*) district.

jurisprudencia [xurispru'ðenθja] *nf* jurisprudence.

jurista [xu'rista] *nm/f* jurist.

justamente [xusta'mente] *ad* justly, fairly; (*precisamente*) just, precisely, exactly.

justicia [xus'tiθja] *nf* justice; (*equidad*) fairness, justice; **justiciero, a** *a* just, righteous.

justificación [xustifika'θjon] *nf* justification; **justificar** *vt* to justify.

justo, a ['xusto, a] *a* (*equitativo*) just, fair, right; (*preciso*) exact, correct; (*ajustado*) tight // *ad* (*precisamente*) exactly, precisely.

juvenil [xuße'nil] *a* youthful.

juventud [xußen'tuð] *nf* (*adolescencia*) youth; (*jóvenes*) young people *pl.*

juzgado [xuθ'ɣaðo] *nm* tribunal; (*JUR*) court.

juzgar [xuθ'ɣar] *vt* to judge; **a** ~ **por...** to judge by..., judging by... .

K

kg *abr de* **kilogramo.**
kilo ['kilo] *nm* kilo // *pref:* ~**gramo** *nm* kilogramme; ~**litro** *nm* kilolitre; ~**metraje** *nm* distance in kilometres; **kilómetro** *nm* kilometre; ~**vatio** *nm* kilowatt.
kiosco ['kjosko] *nm* = **quiosco.**
km *abr de* **kilómetro.**
kv *abr de* **kilovatio.**

L

l *abr de* **litro.**
la [la] *det* the // *pron* her; (*Ud.*) you; (*cosa*) it // *nm* (*MUS*) la; ~ **del sombrero rojo** the girl in the red hat.
laberinto [laβe'rinto] *nm* labyrinth.
labia ['laβja] *nf* fluency; (*pey*) glibness.
labial [la'βjal] *a* labial; **lectura** ~ lip-reading.
labio ['laβjo] *nm* lip.
labor [la'βor] *nf* labour; (*AGR*) farm work; (*tarea*) job, task; (*costura*) needlework; ~**able** *a* workable; **día** ~**able** working day; ~**ar** *vi* to work; ~**eo** *nm* (*AGR*) cultivation; (*de minas*) working; ~**ioso, a** *a* (*persona*) hard-working; (*trabajo*) tough; ~**ista** *a*: **Partido L**~**ista** Labour Party.
labrado, a [la'βraðo, a] *a* worked; (*cincelado*) carved; (*metal*) wrought // *nm* (*AGR*) cultivated field.
labrador, a [laβra'ðor, a] *a* farming // *nm/f* farmer.
labrantío, a [laβran'tio, a] *a* arable.
labranza [la'βranθa] *nf* (*AGR*) cultivation.
labrar [la'βrar] *vt* (*gen*) to work; (*madera etc*) to carve; (*fig*) to cause.
labriego, a [la'βrjexo, a] *nm/f* peasant.
laca ['laka] *nf* lacquer.
lacayo [la'kajo] *nm* lackey.
lacerar [laθe'rar] *vt* to lacerate.
lacio, a ['laθjo, a] *a* (*pelo*) lank; (*movimento*) limp; (*BOT*) withered.
lacónico, a [la'koniko, a] *a* laconic.
lacrar [la'krar] *vt* (*MED*) to injure the health of; (*dañar*) to harm; (*cerrar*) to seal (with sealing wax); ~**se** *vr* to harm o.s.; **lacre** *nm* sealing wax.
lacrimoso, a [lakri'moso, a] *a* tearful.
lactar [lak'tar] *vt, vi* to suckle.
ladear [laðe'ar] *vt* to tip, tilt; (*ciudad, colina*) to skirt // *vi* to tilt; ~**se** *vr* to lean.
ladera [la'ðera] *nf* slope.
ladino, a [la'ðino, a] *a* cunning.
lado ['laðo] *nm* (*gen*) side; (*fig*) protection; (*MIL*) flank; **al** ~ **de** beside; **poner de** ~ to put on its side; **poner a un** ~ to put aside; **por todos** ~**s** on all sides, all round.
ladrar [la'ðrar] *vi* to bark; **ladrido** *nm* bark, barking.
ladrillo [la'ðriʎo] *nm* (*gen*) brick; (*azulejo*) tile; (*color*) brick red.

ladrón, ona [la'ðron, ona] *nm/f* thief.
lagar [la'xar] *nm* (wine/oil) press.
lagarto [la'xarto] *nm* (*ZOOL*) lizard; (*fig: fam*) sharp customer; ~ **de Indias** alligator.
lago ['laxo] *nm* lake.
lágrima ['laxrima] *nf* tear; **lagrimar** *vi* to weep.
laguna [la'xuna] *nf* (*lago*) lagoon; (*hueco*) gap.
laico, a ['laiko, a] *a* lay.
lamentable [lamen'taβle] *a* lamentable, regrettable; (*miserable*) pitiful.
lamentar [lamen'tar] *vt* (*sentir*) to regret; (*deplorar*) to lament; ~**se** *vr* to lament; **lamento** *nm* lament.
lamer [la'mer] *vt* to lick.
lámina ['lamina] *nf* (*plancha delgada*) sheet; (*para estampar, estampa*) plate; **laminar** *vt* (*en libro*) to laminate.
lámpara ['lampara] *nf* lamp; ~ **de alcohol/gas** spirit/gas lamp; ~ **de bolsillo** torch; ~ **de pie** standard lamp.
lampiño [lam'piɲo] *a* clean-shaven.
lana ['lana] *nf* wool.
lance ['lanθe] *nm* (*golpe*) stroke; (*suceso*) event, incident; (*riña*) quarrel; (*tirada*) throw; **libros de** ~ second-hand books.
lancha ['lantʃa] *nf* launch; ~ **automóvil** motorboat; ~ **de pesca** fishing boat; ~ **salvavidas/torpedera** lifeboat/torpedo boat; **lanchero** *nm* boatman.
lanero, a [la'nero, a] *a* woollen.
langosta [lan'gosta] *nf* (*insecto*) locust; (*crustáceo*) lobster; (*fig*) plague; **langostín, langostino** *nm* prawn.
languidecer [langiðe'θer] *vi* to languish; **languidez** *nf* languour; **lánguido, a** *a* (*gen*) languid; (*sin energía*) listless.
lanilla [la'niʎa] *nf* nap.
lanudo, a [la'nuðo, a] *a* woolly.
lanza ['lanθa] *nf* (*arma*) lance, spear; (*de vagón*) pole.
lanzadera [lanθa'ðera] *nf* shuttle.
lanzamiento [lanθa'mjento] *nm* (*gen*) throwing; (*NAUT, COM*) launch, launching; ~ **de pesos** putting the shot.
lanzar [lan'θar] *vt* (*gen*) to throw; (*DEPORTE*) to bowl; (*NAUT, COM*) to launch; (*JUR*) to evict; (*MED*) to vomit; ~**se** *vr* to throw o.s.
laña ['laɲa] *nf* clamp.
lapa ['lapa] *nf* limpet.
lapicero [lapi'θero] *nm* propelling pencil.
lápida ['lapiða] *nf* stone; ~ **mortuoria** headstone; ~ **conmemorativa** memorial stone; **lapidar** *vt* to stone; **lapidario, a** *a, nm* lapidary.
lápiz ['lapiθ] *nm* pencil; ~ **de color** coloured pencil; ~ **de labios** lipstick.
lapón, ona [la'pon, ona] *nm/f* Laplander, Lapp.
lapso ['lapso] *nm* (*de tiempo*) interval; (*error*) error.
largar [lar'xar] *vt* (*soltar*) to release; (*aflojar*) to loosen; (*lanzar*) to launch;

(*fam*) to let fly; (*pelota*) to throw; (*velas*) to unfurl; (*AM*) to throw; ~**se** *vr* (*fam*) to beat it; (*NAUT*) to set sail; ~**se a** (*AM*) to start to.

largo, a ['larxo, a] *a* (*longitud*) long; (*tiempo*) lengthy; (*persona*: *alta*) tall; (*fig*) generous // *nm* length; (*MUS*) largo // *ad* widely; **dos años** ~**s** two long years; **tiene 9 metros de** ~ it is 9 metres long; **a lo** ~ **de** along.

largueza [lar'veθa] *nf* generosity.
lárice ['lariθe] *nm* larch.
laringe [la'rinxe] *nf* larynx; **laringitis** *nf* laryngitis.
larva ['larβa] *nf* larva.
las [las] *det* the // *pron* them; ~ **que cantan** the ones/women/girls who sing.
lascivo, a [las'θiβo, a] *a* lewd.
láser ['laser] *nm* laser.
lasitud [lasi'tuð] *nf* lassitude, weariness.
lástima ['lastima] *nf* (*pena*) pity; (*queja*) complaint; **dar** ~ to be pitiful; **es** ~ **que** it's a pity that; **¡qué** ~**!** what a pity!; **ella está hecha una** ~ she looks pitiful.
lastimar [lasti'mar] *vt* (*herir*) to wound; (*ofender*) to offend; (*compadecer*) to pity; ~**se** *vr* to hurt o.s.; ~**se de** to feel sorry for; **lastimero, a, lastimoso, a** *a* pitiful, pathetic.
lastre ['lastre] *nm* (*TEC, NAUT*) ballast; (*fig*) dead weight.
lata ['lata] *nf* (*metal*) tin; (*caja*) tin, can; (*fam*) nuisance; **hoja de** ~ tin(plate); **en** ~ tinned; **dar (la)** ~ to be a nuisance.
latente [la'tente] *a* latent.
lateral [late'ral] *a* side, lateral // *nm* (*TEATRO*) wings.
latido [la'tiðo] *nm* (*del corazón*) beat; (*de perro*) yelp.
latifundio [lati'fundjo] *nm* large estate; **latifundista** *nm/f* owner of a large estate.
latigazo [lati'xaθo] *nm* (*golpe*) lash; (*sonido*) crack; (*fig: regaño*) sharp reproof; (*fam*: *bebida*) swig.
látigo ['latixo] *nm* whip.
latín [la'tin] *nm* Latin.
latino, a [la'tino, a] *a* Latin; ~**americano, a** *a*, *nm/f* Latin-American.
latir [la'tir] *vi* (*corazón, pulso*) to beat; (*perro*) to yelp.
latitud [lati'tuð] *nf* (*GEO*) latitude; (*fig*) breadth.
lato, a ['lato, a] *a* broad.
latón [la'ton] *nm* brass.
latoso, a [la'toso, a] *a* (*cansado*) annoying; (*aburrido*) boring.
latrocinio [latro'θinjo] *nm* robbery.
laúd [la'uð] *nm* lute.
laudo ['lauðo] *nm* (*JUR*) decision.
laureado, a [laure'aðo, a] *a* honoured // *nm* laureate.
laurel [lau'rel] *nm* (*BOT*) laurel; (*CULIN*) bay.
lava ['laβa] *nf* lava.
lavabo [la'βaβo] *nm* washbasin.
lavadero [laβa'ðero] *nm* laundry.

lavado [la'βaðo] *nm* washing; (*de ropa*) laundry; (*ARTE*) wash; ~ **de cerebro** brainwashing; ~ **en seco** dry cleaning.
lavadora [laβa'ðora] *nf* washing machine.
lavamanos [laβa'manos] *nm inv* wash-basin.
lavandería [laβande'ria] *nf* laundry; ~ **automática** launderette.
lavaplatos [laβa'platos] *nm o f inv* dish-washer.
lavar [la'βar] *vt* to wash; (*borrar*) to wipe away; ~**se** *vr* to wash o.s.; ~**se las manos** to wash one's hands; ~ **y marcar** (*pelo*) to shampoo and set; ~ **en seco** to dry clean.
lavavajillas [laβaβa'xiʎas] *nm inv* dish-washer.
laxante [lak'sante] *nm* laxative.
laya ['laja] *nf* spade; **de la misma** ~ (*fig*) of the same sort.
lazada [la'θaða] *nf* bow.
lazo ['laθo] *nm* knot; (*lazada*) bow; (*para animales*) lasso; (*trampa*) snare; (*de camino*) hairpin bend; (*vínculo*) tie.
lb(s) *abr de* **libra(s)**.
le [le] *pron* (*directo*) him; (: *usted*) you; (*indirecto*) to him; (: *usted*) to you.
leal [le'al] *a* loyal; ~**tad** *nf* loyalty.
lebrel [le'βrel] *nm* greyhound.
lección [lek'θjon] *nf* lesson.
lector, a [lek'tor, a] *nm/f* reader.
lectura [lek'tura] *nf* reading.
leche ['letʃe] *nf* milk; **tener mala** ~ to be nasty; ~ **condensada/en polvo** condensed/powdered milk; ~ **desnatada** skimmed milk; ~ **de magnesia** milk of magnesia; ~**ra** *nf* (*vendedora*) milkmaid; (*para hervir*) milk pan; (*para servir*) milkjug; (*AM*) cow; ~**ría** *nf* dairy.
lecho ['letʃo] *nm* (*cama*) bed; (*de río*) bottom; (*GEO*) layer.
lechón [le'tʃon] *nm* sucking pig.
lechoso, a [le'tʃoso, a] *a* milky.
lechuga [le'tʃuxa] *nf* lettuce.
lechuza [le'tʃuθa] *nf* owl.
leer [le'er] *vt* to read.
legación [lexa'θjon] *nf* legation.
legado [le'xaðo] *nm* (*don*) bequest; (*herencia*) legacy; (*enviado*) legate.
legajo [le'xaxo] *nm* file.
legal [le'xal] *a* (*gen*) legal; (*persona*) trust-worthy; ~**idad** *nf* legality; ~**izar** *vt* to legalize; (*documento*) to authenticate.
légamo ['lexamo] *nm* (*cieno*) mud, ooze.
legar [le'xar] *vt* to bequeath, leave; **legatario, a** *nm/f* legatee.
legión [le'xjon] *nf* legion; **legionario, a** *a* legionary // *nm* legionnaire.
legislación [lexisla'θjon] *nf* legislation; **legislar** *vt* to legislate.
legitimar [lexiti'mar] *vt* to legitimize; **legítimo, a** *a* (*genuino*) authentic; (*legal*) legitimate.
lego, a ['lexo, a] *a* (*REL*) secular; (*ignorante*) ignorant // *nm* layman.
legua ['lexwa] *nf* league.

leguleyo [lexu'lejo] *nm* (*pey*) petty lawyer.

legumbre [le'xumbre] *nf* vegetable.

leído, a [le'iðo, a] *a* well-read.

lejanía [lexa'nia] *nf* distance; **lejano, a** *a* far-off; (*en el tiempo*) distant; (*fig*) remote.

lejía [le'xia] *nf* bleach.

lejos ['lexos] *ad* far, far away; **a lo** ~ in the distance; **de** *o* **desde** ~ from afar; ~ **de** *prep* far from.

lelo, a ['lelo, a] *a* silly; (*fig*) open-mouthed // *nm/f* idiot.

lema ['lema] *nm* motto; (*POL*) slogan.

lencería [lenθe'ria] *nf* drapery.

lengua ['lengwa] *nf* tongue; ~ **moderna** modern language; **morderse la** ~ to hold one's tongue.

lenguado [len'gwaðo] *nm* sole.

lenguaje [len'gwaxe] *nm* language.

lenguaraz [lengwa'raθ] *a* talkative; (*pey*) foul-mouthed.

lengüeta [len'gweta] *nf* (*ANAT*) epiglottis; (*de balanza, zapatos, MUS*) tongue; (*herramienta*) needle.

lenidad [leni'ðað] *nf* lenience.

lente ['lente] *nm* o f lens; (*lupa*) magnifying glass; ~s *npl* glasses; ~s **de contacto** contact lenses.

lenteja [len'texa] *nf* lentil; **lentejuela** *nf* sequin.

lentitud [lenti'tuð] *nf* slowness; **con** ~ slowly.

lento, a ['lento, a] *a* slow.

leña ['leɲa] *nf* firewood; ~**dor, a**, ~**tero, a** *nm/f* woodcutter.

leño ['leɲo] *nm* (*trozo de árbol*) log; (*madera*) timber; (*fig*) blockhead.

Leo ['leo] *nm* Leo.

león [le'on] *nm* lion; (*AM*) puma; ~ **marino** sea lion; **leonino, a** *a* leonine.

leontina [leon'tina] *nf* watch chain.

leopardo [leo'parðo] *nm* leopard.

lepra ['lepra] *nf* leprosy; **leproso, a** *nm/f* leper.

lerdo, a ['lerðo, a] *a* (*lento*) slow; (*patoso*) clumsy.

les [les] *pron* (*directo*) them; (: *ustedes*) you; (*indirecto*) to them; (: *ustedes*) to you.

lesbiana [les'βjana] *a, nf* lesbian.

lesión [le'sjon] *nf* (*daño*) lesion; (*fig*) injury; **lesionado, a** *a* injured // *nm/f* injured person.

letal [le'tal] *a* lethal.

letanía [leta'nia] *nf* litany.

letargo [le'tarxo] *nm* (*MED*) lethargy.

letra ['letra] *nf* letter; (*escritura*) handwriting; (*MUS*) lyrics *pl*; ~ **de cambio** bill of exchange; ~ **de imprenta** print; ~**do, a** *a* learned; (*fam*) pedantic // *nm* lawyer; **letrero** *nm* (*cartel*) sign; (*etiqueta*) label.

leva ['leβa] *nf* (*NAUT*) weighing anchor; (*MIL*) levy; (*TEC*) lever.

levadizo [leβa'ðiθo] *a*: **puente** ~ drawbridge.

levadura [leβa'ðura] *nf* (*para el pan*) yeast; (*de la cerveza*) brewer's yeast.

levantamiento [leβanta'mjento] *nm* raising, lifting; (*rebelión*) revolt, rising; ~ **de pesos** weight-lifting.

levantar [leβan'tar] *vt* (*gen*) to raise; (*del suelo*) to pick up; (*hacia arriba*) to lift (up); (*plan*) to make, draw up; (*mesa*) to clear away; (*campamento*) to strike; (*fig*) to cheer up, hearten; ~**se** *vr* to get up; (*enderezarse*) to straighten up; (*rebelarse*) to rebel; ~ **el ánimo** to cheer up.

levante [le'βante] *nm* east coast; **el L**~ the Near East, the Levant.

levar [le'βar] *vi* to weigh anchor; ~**se** *vr* to set sail.

leve ['leβe] *a* light; (*fig*) trivial; ~**dad** *nf* lightness.

levita [le'βita] *nf* frock coat.

léxico ['leksiko] *nm* lexicon, dictionary.

ley [lei] *nf* (*gen*) law; (*fig*) loyalty; (*metal*) standard.

leyenda [le'jenda] *nf* legend.

leyó *etc vb ver* **leer.**

liar [li'ar] *vt* to tie (up); (*unir*) to bind; (*envolver*) to wrap (up); (*enredar*) to confuse; (*cigarrillo*) to roll; ~**se** *vr* (*fam*) to get involved; ~**se a palos** to get involved in a fight.

Líbano ['liβano] *nm*: **el** ~ the Lebanon.

libar [li'βar] *vt* to suck.

libelo [li'βelo] *nm* satire, lampoon; (*JUR*) petition.

libélula [li'βelula] *nf* dragonfly.

liberación [liβera'θjon] *nf* liberation; (*de la cárcel*) release.

liberal [liβe'ral] *a, nm/f* liberal; ~**idad** *nf* liberality; (*lujo*) lavishness.

liberar [liβe'rar] *vt* to liberate.

libertad [liβer'tað] *nf* liberty; (*soltura*) freedom; ~ **de culto/de prensa/de comercio** freedom of worship/the press/of trade; ~ **condicional** probation; ~ **bajo palabra** parole; ~ **bajo fianza** bail.

libertar [liβer'tar] *vt* (*preso*) to set free; (*de una obligación*) to release; (*eximir*) to exempt.

libertino, a [liβer'tino, a] *a* loose-living // *nm/f* libertine.

libra ['liβra] *nf* pound; **L**~ (*ASTRO*) Libra; ~ **esterlina** pound sterling.

librador, a [liβra'ðor, a] *nm/f* drawer.

libramiento [liβra'mjento] *nm* rescue; (*COM*) delivery.

libranza [li'βranθa] *nf* (*COM*) draft; (*de letra de cambio*) bill of exchange.

librar [li'βrar] *vt* (*de peligro*) to save; (*batalla*) to wage, fight; (*de impuestos*) to exempt; (*secreto*) to reveal; (*mercancías*) to draw; (*cheque*) to make out; (*JUR*) to exempt // *vi* to give birth; ~**se** *vr*: ~**se de** to escape from, free o.s. from.

libre ['liβre] *a* (*gen*) free; (*lugar*) unoccupied; (*asiento*) vacant; (*de impuestos*) tax-free; (*de deudas*) free of debts; (*pey*) outspoken; **tiro** ~ free kick; **los 100 metros** ~ the 100 metres freestyle (race); **al aire** ~ in the open air.

librería [liβre'ria] *nf* (*biblioteca*) library; (*comercio*) bookshop; **librero, a** *nm/f* bookseller.

libreta [li'βreta] *nf* notebook; ~ **de ahorros** savings book; ~ **de banco** bank book.

libro ['liβro] *nm* book; ~ **en rústica/en pasta** *o* **encuadernado** paperback/hardback; ~ **de bolsillo** paperback; ~ **de caja** cashbook; ~ **de cheques** cheque book; ~ **de inventario** stock-list; ~ **de pedidos** order book; ~ **de texto** textbook.

Lic. *abr de* **licenciado, a.**

licencia [li'θenθja] *nf* (*gen*) licence; (*permiso*) permission; ~ **por enfermedad/con goce de sueldo** sick leave/paid leave; ~ **de caza/de conductor** game/driving licence; ~ **de derecho/de letras** law/arts degree; ~**do, a** *a* licensed // *nm/f* graduate; **licenciar** *vt* (*empleado*) to dismiss; (*permitir*) to permit, allow; (*soldado*) to discharge; (*estudiante*) to confer a degree upon; **licenciarse** *vr*: **licenciarse en letras** to graduate in arts.

licencioso, a [liθen'θjoso, a] *a* licentious.

liceo [li'θeo] *nm* (high) school.

licitador [liθita'ðor] *nm* bidder; (*AM*) auctioneer; **licitar** *vt* to bid for; (*AM*) to sell by auction.

lícito, a ['liθito, a] *a* (*legal*) lawful; (*justo*) fair, just; (*permisible*) permissible.

licor [li'kor] *nm* spirits *pl*; (*preparado*) liqueur.

licuadora [likwa'ðora] *nf* food-mixer, liquidizer; **licuar** *vt* to liquidize.

lid [lið] *nf* combat; (*fig*) controversy.

líder ['liðer] *nm/f* leader; **liderato** *nm* leadership.

lidia ['liðja] *nf* bullfight; **toros de** ~ fighting bulls; **lidiar** *vt*, *vi* to fight.

liebre ['ljeβre] *nf* hare.

lienzo ['ljenθo] *nm* linen; (*ARTE*) canvas; (*pañuelo*) handkerchief; (*ARQ*) wall.

liga ['liɣa] *nf* (*de medias*) garter, suspender; (*confederación*) league; (*venda*) band; (*aleación*) alloy; (*BOT*) mistletoe.

ligadura [liɣa'ðura] *nf* bond, tie; (*MED*, *MUS*) ligature.

ligamento [liɣa'mento] *nm* (*ANAT*) ligament; (*atadura*) tie; (*unión*) bond.

ligar [li'ɣar] *vt* (*atar*) to tie; (*unir*) to join; (*MED*) to bind up; (*MUS*) to slur; (*metales*) to alloy // *vi* to mix, blend; (*fam*) to pick up; (*entenderse*) to get on (well); ~**se** *vr* to commit o.s.

ligereza [liɣe'reθa] *nf* lightness; (*rapidez*) swiftness; (*agilidad*) agility; (*superficialidad*) flippancy.

ligero, a [li'xero, a] *a* (*de peso*) light; (*tela*) thin; (*rápido*) swift, quick; (*ágil*) agile, nimble; (*de importancia*) slight; (*de carácter*) flippant, superficial // *ad*: **a la** ~**a** superficially.

lija ['lixa] *nf* (*ZOOL*) dogfish; (**papel de**) ~ sandpaper.

lila ['lila] *nf* lilac // *nm* (*fam*) twit.

lima ['lima] *nf* file; (*BOT*) lime; ~ **de carpintero** file; ~ **de uñas** nail-file; **limar** *vt* to file.

limitación [limita'θjon] *nf* limitation, limit.

limitar [limi'tar] *vt* to limit; (*reducir*) to reduce, cut down // *vi*: ~ **con** to border on; ~**se** *vr*: ~**se a** to limit o.s. to.

límite ['limite] *nm* (*gen*) limit; (*fin*) end; (*frontera*) border; ~ **de velocidad** speed limit.

limítrofe [li'mitrofe] *a* bordering, neighbouring.

limón [li'mon] *nm* lemon // *a*: **amarillo** ~ lemon-yellow; **limonada** *nf* lemonade; **limonero** *nm* lemon tree.

limosna [li'mosna] *nf* alms *pl*; **vivir de** ~ to live on charity.

limpiabotas [limpja'βotas] *nm inv* bootblack, shoeshine boy/girl.

limpiaparabrisas [limpjapara'βrisas] *nm inv* windscreen wiper.

limpiar [lim'pjar] *vt* (*gen*) to clean; (*con trapo*) to wipe; (*quitar*) to wipe away; (*zapatos*) to shine, polish; (*fig*) to clean up.

limpieza [lim'pjeθa] *nf* (*estado*) cleanliness; (*acto*) cleaning; (: *de las calles*) cleansing; (: *de zapatos*) polishing; (*habilidad*) skill; (*fig*) clean-up; (*pureza*) purity; (*MIL*): **operación de** ~ mopping-up operation; ~ **en seco** dry cleaning.

limpio, a ['limpjo, a] *a* clean; (*moralmente*) pure; (*COM*) clear, net; (*fam*) honest // *ad*: **jugar** ~ to play fair // *nm*: **pasar en** ~ to make a fair copy.

linaje [li'naxe] *nm* lineage, family; **linajudo, a** *a* highborn.

linaza [li'naθa] *nf* linseed; **aceite de** ~ linseed oil.

lince ['linθe] *nm* lynx.

linchar [lin'tʃar] *vt* to lynch.

lindante [lin'dante] *a* adjoining; ~ **con** bordering on.

lindar [lin'dar] *vi* to adjoin; ~ **con** to border on; **linde** *nm o f* boundary; **lindero, a** *a* adjoining // *nm* boundary.

lindo, a ['lindo, a] *a* pretty, lovely // *ad* (*AM*): **nos divertimos de lo** ~ we had a marvellous time; **canta muy** ~ he/she sings beautifully.

línea ['linea] *nf* (*gen*) line; ~ **aérea** airline; ~ **delantera** (*DEPORTE*) forward line; ~ **de meta** goal line; (*de carrera*) finishing line; ~ **de saque** service line, base line; ~ **recta** straight line.

lingüista [lin'gwista] *nm/f* linguist.

linimento [lini'mento] *nm* liniment.

lino ['lino] *nm* linen; (*BOT*) flax.

linóleo [li'noleo] *nm* lino, linoleum.

linterna [lin'terna] *nf* lantern, lamp; ~ **eléctrica** *o* **a pilas** torch.

lío ['lio] *nm* bundle; (*fam*) fuss; (*desorden*) muddle, mess; **armar un** ~ to make a fuss.

liquidación [likiða'θjon] *nf* liquidation; **venta de** ~ clearance sale.

liquidar [liki'ðar] *vt* (*licuar*) to liquidize; (*eliminar*) to liquidate; (*mercaderías*) to sell off; (*pagar*) to pay off; (*terminar*) to wind up; (*AM*) to ruin; ~**se** *vr* to liquefy.

líquido, a [a ['likiðo, a] *a* liquid; (*ganancia*) net; (*AM*) accurate // *nm* liquid; ~ **imponible** net taxable income.

lira ['lira] *nf* (*MUS*) lyre; (*moneda*) lira.

lirio ['lirjo] *nm* (*BOT*) iris.

Lisboa [lis'ßoa] *n* Lisbon.

lisiado, a [li'sjaðo, a] *a* injured // *nm/f* cripple.

lisiar [li'sjar] *vt* to maim; ~**se** *vr* to injure o.s.

liso, a ['liso, a] *a* (*terreno*) flat; (*cabello*) straight; (*superficie*) even; (*tela*) smooth.

lisonja [li'sonxa] *nf* flattery; **lisonjear** *vt* to flatter; (*fig*) to please; **lisonjero, a** *a* (*gen*) flattering; (*agradable*) gratifying, pleasing // *nm/f* flatterer.

lista ['lista] *nf* (*gen*) list; (*de alumnos*) school register; (*de libros*) catalogue; (*de correos*) poste restante; (*de platos*) menu; (*de precios*) price list; **pasar** ~ to call the roll; ~ **de espera** waiting list; **tela a** ~**s** striped material.

listado, a [lis'taðo, a] *a* striped.

listo, a ['listo, a] *a* (*perspicaz*) smart, clever; (*preparado*) ready.

listón [lis'ton] *nm* (*tela*) ribbon; (*de madera, metal*) strip.

litera [li'tera] *nf* (*en barco, tren*) berth; (*en dormitorio*) bunk, bunk bed.

literato, a [lite'rato, a] *a* literary // *nm/f* writer.

literatura [litera'tura] *nf* literature.

litigar [liti'xar] *vt* to fight // *vi* (*JUR*) to go to law; (*fig*) to dispute, argue.

litigio [li'tixjo] *nm* (*JUR*) lawsuit; (*fig*): **en** ~ **con** in dispute with.

litografía [litoxra'fia] *nf* lithography; (*una* ~) lithograph.

litoral [lito'ral] *a* coastal // *nm* coast, seaboard.

litro ['litro] *nm* litre.

liviano, a [li'ßjano, a] *a* (*persona*) fickle; (*cosa, objeto*) trivial.

lívido, a ['lißiðo, a] *a* livid; (*AM*) pale.

ll... ver bajo la letra LL, después de L.

lo [lo] *det neuter def art*; ~ **bueno** the good // *pron* (*persona*) him; (*cosa*) it.

loa ['loa] *nf* praise; **loable** *a* praiseworthy; **loar** *vt* to praise.

lobato [lo'ßato] *nm* wolf cub.

lobo ['loßo] *nm* wolf; ~ **de mar** sea dog; ~ **marino** seal.

lóbrego, a ['loßrexo, a] *a* dark; (*fig*) gloomy.

lóbulo ['loßulo] *nm* lobe.

locación [loca'θjon] *nf* lease.

local [lo'kal] *a* local // *nm* place, site; (*oficinas*) premises *pl*; ~**idad** *nf* (*barrio*) locality; (*lugar*) location; (*TEATRO*) seat, ticket; ~**izar** *vt* (*ubicar*) to locate, find; (*restringir*) to localize; (*situar*) to place.

loco, a ['loko, a] *a* mad // *nm/f* lunatic, mad person.

locomoción [lokomo'θjon] *nf* locomotion.

locomotora [lokomo'tora] *nf* engine.

locuaz [lo'kwaθ] *a* loquacious.

locución [loku'θjon] *nf* expression.

locura [lo'kura] *nf* madness; (*acto*) crazy act.

lodo ['loðo] *nm* mud; ~**s** *nmpl* (*MED*) mudbath *sg*.

lógico, a ['loxiko, a] *a* logical // *nf* logic.

logística [lo'xistika] *nf* logistics *pl*.

lograr [lo'xrar] *vt* to achieve; (*obtener*) to get, obtain; ~ **hacer** to manage to do; ~ **que uno venga** to manage to get sb to come.

logro ['loxro] *nm* achievement, success; **prestar a** ~ to lend at a high rate of interest.

loma ['loma] *nf* hillock.

lombriz [lom'briθ] *nf* worm; ~ **solitaria** tapeworm.

lomo ['lomo] *nm* (*de animal*) back; (*de cerdo*) pork loin; (*de vaca*) rib steak; (*de libro*) spine.

lona ['lona] *nf* canvas.

Londres ['londres] *n* London.

longaniza [longa'niθa] *nf* pork sausage.

longitud [lonxi'tuð] *nf* length; (*GEO*) longitude; **tener 3 metros de** ~ to be 3 metres long; ~ **de onda** wavelength.

lonja ['lonxa] *nf* slice; (*de jamón*) rasher; ~ **de pescado** fish market.

lontananza [lonta'nanθa] *nf* background.

loor [lo'or] *nm* praise.

loro ['loro] *nm* parrot.

los [los] *det* the // *pron* them; (*ustedes*) you; **mis libros y** ~ **de Ud** my books and yours.

losa ['losa] *nf* stone; ~ **sepulcral** gravestone.

lote ['lote] *nm* portion; (*COM*) lot.

lotería [lote'ria] *nf* lottery; (*juego*) lotto.

loza ['loθa] *nf* crockery.

lozanía [loθa'nia] *nf* (*lujo*) luxuriance; (*orgullo*) pride; **lozano, a** *a* luxuriant; (*animado*) lively; (*altanero*) haughty.

lubricante [lußri'kante] *nm* lubricant; **lubricar** *vt* to lubricate.

lucero [lu'θero] *nm* (*ASTRO*) bright star; (*fig*) brilliance.

lucidez [luθi'ðeθ] *nf* lucidity; **lúcido, a** *a* lucid.

luciente [lu'θjente] *a* shining.

luciérnaga [lu'θjernaxa] *nf* glow-worm.

lucimiento [luθi'mjento] *nm* (*brillo*) brilliance; (*éxito*) success.

lucir [lu'θir] *vt* to illuminate, light (up); (*fig*) to show off // *vi* (*brillar*) to shine; (*tener éxito*) to be successful; ~**se** *vr* to dress up.

lucrarse [lu'krarse] *vr* to enrich o.s.

lucro ['lukro] *nm* profit, gain.

luctuoso, a [luk'twoso, a] *a* mournful.

lucha ['lutʃa] *nf* fight, struggle; ~ **de**

clases class struggle; ~ **libre** wrestling; **luchar** vi to fight.

ludibrio [lu'ðiβrjo] nm mockery.

luego ['lweҳo] ad (después) next; (más tarde) later, afterwards; (pronto) soon; **desde** ~ of course; **tan** ~ **como** as soon as.

lugar [lu'ҳar] nm place; (sitio) spot; **en** ~ **de** instead of; **hacer** ~ to make room; **fuera de** ~ out of place; **tener** ~ to take place; ~ **común** commonplace.

lugareño, a [luҳa'reɲo, a] a village cpd // nm/f villager.

lúgubre ['luҳuβre] a mournful.

lujo ['luҳo] nm luxury; (fig) profusion, abundance; ~**so, a** a luxurious.

lujuria [lu'xurja] nf lust; (fig) lewdness.

lumbre ['lumbre] nf (gen) light.

lumbrera [lum'brera] nf luminary; (en techo) skylight; (de barco) vent, port.

luminoso, a [lumi'noso, a] a luminous, shining.

luna ['luna] nf moon; (de un espejo) glass; (de gafas) lens; (fig) crescent; ~ **llena/nueva** full/new moon; **estar con** ~ to have one's head in the clouds.

lunar [lu'nar] a lunar // nm (ANAT) mole; **tela a** ~**es** spotted material.

lunes ['lunes] nm inv Monday.

luneta [lu'neta] nf lens.

lupa ['lupa] nf magnifying glass.

lustrar [lus'trar] vt (mueble) to polish; (zapatos) to shine; **lustre** nm polish; (fig) lustre; **dar lustre a** to polish; **lustroso, a** a shining.

luterano, a [lute'rano, a] a Lutheran.

luto ['luto] nm mourning; (congoja) grief, sorrow; ~**s** nmpl mourning clothes; **llevar el** o **vestirse de** ~ to be in mourning.

Luxemburgo [luksem'burҳo] nm Luxembourg.

luz [luθ] (pl **luces**) nf light; **dar a** ~ **un niño** to give birth to a child; **sacar a** ~ to bring to light; (ELEC): **dar** ~ to switch on the light; **prender/apagar la** ~ to put the light on/off; **a todas luces** by any reckoning; **hacer la** ~ **sobre** to shed light on; **tener pocas luces** to be dim or stupid; ~ **roja/verde** red/green light; (AUTO): ~ **de costado** sidelight; ~ **de freno** brake light; ~ **del relámpago** flashlight; **luces de tráfico** traffic lights; **traje de luces** bullfighter's costume.

LL

llaga ['ʎaҳa] nf wound.

llama ['ʎama] nf flame; (ZOOL) llama.

llamada [ʎa'maða] nf call; ~ **al orden** call to order; **toque de** ~ (MIL) call-up; ~ **a pie de página** reference note.

llamamiento [ʎama'mjento] nm call.

llamar [ʎa'mar] vt to call; (atención) to attract // vi (por teléfono) to telephone; (a la puerta) to knock/ring; (por señas) to beckon; (MIL) to call up; ~**se** vr to be

called, be named; ¿**cómo se llama Usted?** what's your name?

llamarada [ʎama'raða] nf (llamas) blaze; (rubor) flush; (fig) flare-up.

llamativo, a [ʎama'tiβo, a] a showy; (color) loud.

llamear [ʎame'ar] vi to blaze.

llaneza [ʎa'neθa] nf (gen) simplicity; (honestidad) straightforwardness, frankness.

llano, a ['ʎano, a] a (superficie) flat; (persona) straightforward; (estilo) clear // nm plain, flat ground.

llanta ['ʎanta] nf (wheel) rim; (AM): ~ **de goma** tyre.

llanto ['ʎanto] nm weeping.

llanura [ʎa'nura] nf plain.

llave ['ʎaβe] nf key; (del agua) tap; (MECÁNICA) spanner; (de la luz) switch; (MUS) key; ~ **inglesa** monkey wrench; ~ **de contacto** (AUTO) ignition key; **echar** ~ **a** to lock up; ~**ro** nm keyring; **llavín** nm latchkey.

llegada [ʎe'ҳaða] nf arrival.

llegar [ʎe'ҳar] vi to arrive; (alcanzar) to reach; (bastar) to be enough; ~**se** vr: ~**se a** to approach; ~ **a** to manage to, succeed in; ~ **a ser** to become; ~ **a las manos de** to come into the hands of.

llenar [ʎe'nar] vt (gen) to fill; (espacio) to cover; (formulario) to fill in or up; (deber) to fulfil; (fig) to heap.

lleno, a ['ʎeno, a] a full, filled; (repleto) full up // nm (abundancia) abundance; (ASTRO) full moon; (TEATRO) full house; **dar de** ~ **contra un muro** to hit a wall head-on.

llevadero, a [ʎeβa'ðero, a] a bearable, tolerable.

llevar [ʎe'βar] vt (gen) to take; (ropa) to wear; (cargar) to carry; (quitar) to take away; (conducir a alguien) to drive; (cargar hacia) to transport; (traer: dinero) to carry; (conducir) to lead; (MAT) to carry; ~**se** vr to carry off, take away; **llevamos dos días aquí** we have been here for two days; **él me lleva 2 años** he's 2 years older than me; (COM): ~ **los libros** to keep the books; ~**se bien** to get on well (together).

llorar [ʎo'rar] vt, vi to weep; ~ **de risa** to cry with laughter.

lloriquear [ʎorike'ar] vi to snivel, whimper.

lloro ['ʎoro] nm weeping; **llorón, ona** a tearful // nm/f cry-baby; ~**so, a** a (gen) weeping, tearful; (triste) sad, sorrowful.

llover [ʎo'βer] vi to rain; ~**se** vr (techo) to leak.

llovizna [ʎo'βiθna] nf drizzle; **lloviznar** vi to drizzle.

llueve etc vb ver **llover.**

lluvia ['ʎuβja] nf rain; ~ **radioactiva** radioactive fallout; **lluvioso, a** a rainy.

M

m *abr de* **metro; minuto.**

macarrones [maka'rrones] *nmpl* macaroni *sg.*

macerar [maθe'rar] *vt* to macerate; *(fig)* to mortify; ~**se** *vr* to mortify o.s.

maceta [ma'θeta] *nf (de flores)* pot of flowers; *(para plantas)* flowerpot; *(mazo pequeño)* mallet.

macilento, a [maθi'lento, a] *a* wan; *(ojeroso)* haggard.

macis ['maθis] *nf* mace.

macizo, a [ma'θiθo, a] *a* massive; *(puerta)* solid // *nm* mass, chunk; *(de edificios)* block; *(AUTO)* solid tyre.

mácula ['makula] *nf* stain, blemish; *(ANAT)* blind spot.

machacar [matʃa'kar] *vt* to crush, pound // *vi* to go on, keep on.

machamartillo [matʃamar'tiʎo]: **a** ~ *ad:* **cumplir a** ~ to carry out a task to the letter; **eran cristianos a** ~ they were totally convinced Christians.

machete [ma'tʃete] *nm* (*AM*) machete, (large) knife.

macho ['matʃo] *a* male; *(fig)* virile // *nm* male; *(fig)* he-man.

machucar [matʃu'kar] *vt* to pound.

madeja [ma'ðexa] *nf (de lana)* skein, hank; *(de pelo)* mop.

madera [ma'ðera] *nf* wood; *(fig)* nature, character; **una** ~ a piece of wood.

madero [ma'ðero] *nm* beam; *(fig)* ship.

madrastra [ma'ðrastra] *nf* stepmother.

madre ['maðre] *a* mother *cpd*; *(AM)* tremendous // *nf* mother; *(ANAT)* womb; *(AGR)* main channel; *(de vino etc)* dregs *pl*; *(de río)* bed; ~ **política/soltera** mother-in-law/unmarried mother.

madreperla [maðre'perla] *nf* mother-of-pearl.

madreselva [maðre'selßa] *nf* honeysuckle.

madriguera [maðri'ɤera] *nf* burrow.

madrileño, a [maðri'leɲo, a] *a* of *or* from Madrid // *nm/f* native of Madrid.

madrina [ma'ðrina] *nf (protectora)* godmother; *(ARQ)* prop, shore; *(TEC)* brace; ~ **de boda** bridesmaid.

madrugada [maðru'xaða] *nf* early morning; *(alba)* dawn, daybreak; **madrugador, a** *a* early-rising; **madrugar** *vi* to get up early; *(fig)* to get ahead.

madurar [maðu'rar] *vt, vi (fruta)* to ripen; *(fig)* to mature; **madurez** *nf* ripeness; maturity; **maduro, a** *a* ripe; mature.

maestra [ma'estra] *nf ver* **maestro.**

maestría [maes'tria] *nf* mastery; *(habilidad)* skill, expertise.

maestro, a [ma'estro, a] *a* masterly; *(perito)* skilled, expert; *(principal)* main; *(educado)* trained // *nm/f* master/mistress; *(que enseña)* teacher // *nm (autoridad)* authority; *(MUS)* maestro;

(AM) skilled workman; **obra** ~**a** masterpiece; ~ **albañil** master mason.

magia ['maxja] *nf* magic; **mágico, a** *a* magic(al) // *nm/f* magician.

magisterio [maxis'terjo] *nm (enseñanza)* teaching; *(profesión)* teaching profession; *(maestros)* teachers *pl.*

magistrado [maxis'traðo] *nm* magistrate.

magistral [maxis'tral] *a* magisterial; *(fig)* masterly.

magnánimo, a [max'nanimo, a] *a* magnanimous.

magnate [max'nate] *nm* magnate, tycoon.

magnético, a [max'netiko, a] *a* magnetic; **magnetizar** *vt* to magnetize.

magnetofón [maxneto'fon], **magnetófono** [maxne'tofono] *nm* tape recorder; **magnetofónico, a** *a:* **cinta magnetofónica** recording tape.

magnífico, a [max'nifiko, a] *a* splendid, magnificent, wonderful.

magnitud [maxni'tuð] *nf* magnitude.

mago, a ['maxo, a] *nm/f* magician; **los Reyes M**~**s** the Magi, the Three Wise Men.

magro, a ['maxro, a] *a (persona)* thin, lean; *(carne)* lean.

magullar [maxu'ʎar] *vt (amoratar)* to bruise; *(dañar)* to damage; *(fam: golpear)* to bash, beat.

mahometano, a [maome'tano, a] *a* Mohammedan.

maíz [ma'iθ] *nm* maize, sweet corn.

majada [ma'xaða] *nf (abrigo)* sheepfold; *(abono)* dung.

majadero, a [maxa'ðero, a] *a* silly, stupid // *nm (TEC)* pestle; *(canilla)* bobbin.

majar [ma'xar] *vt* to crush, grind; *(fig)* to bother, pester.

majestad [maxes'taθ] *nf* majesty; **majestuoso, a** *a* majestic.

majo, a ['maxo, a] *a (guapo)* nice; *(guapo)* attractive, good-looking; *(lujoso)* smart.

mal [mal] *ad* badly; *(equivocadamente)* wrongly; *(con dificultad)* with difficulty // *a* = **malo** // *nm* evil; *(desgracia)* misfortune; *(daño)* harm, hurt; *(MED)* illness; **¡menos** ~**!** just as well!; ~ **que bien** rightly or wrongly.

malabarismo [malaßa'rismo] *nm* juggling; **malabarista** *nm/f* juggler.

malaconsejado, a [malakonse'xaðo, a] *a* ill-advised.

malagueño, a [mala'ɤeɲo, a] *a* of *or* from Málaga.

malaria [ma'larja] *nf* malaria.

malbaratar [malßara'tar] *vt (malgastar)* to squander; *(malvender)* to sell off cheap.

malcontento, a [malkon'tento, a] *a* discontented.

malcriado, a [mal'krjaðo, a] *a (grosero)* rude, bad-mannered; *(consentido)* spoiled.

maldad [mal'daθ] *nf* evil, wickedness.

maldecir [malde'θir] *vt* to curse // *vi:* ~ **de** to speak ill of.

maldición [maldi'θjon] *nf* curse.

maldito, a [mal'dito, a] *pp de* **maldecir** // *a* (*condenado*) damned; (*perverso*) wicked // *nf*: **soltar la ～a** to talk too much.

maleante [male'ante] *a* wicked // *nm/f* malefactor; **malear** *vt* to spoil; (*fig*) to corrupt.

malecón [male'kon] *nm* pier, jetty.

maledicencia [maleði'θenθja] *nf* slander, scandal.

maleficiar [malefi'θjar] *vt* to harm, damage; (*hechizar*) to bewitch; **maleficio** *nm* curse, spell.

malestar [males'tar] *nm* (*gen*) discomfort; (*fig*) uneasiness; (*POL*) unrest.

maleta [ma'leta] *nf* case, suitcase; (*AUTO*) boot; **maletín** *nm* small case, bag.

malevolencia [maleßo'lenθja] *nf* malice, spite; **malévolo, a** *a* malicious, spiteful.

maleza [ma'leθa] *nf* (*hierbas malas*) weeds *pl*; (*arbustos*) thicket.

malgastar [malɣas'tar] *vt* (*tiempo, dinero*) to waste; (*salud*) to ruin.

malhechor, a [male'tʃor, a] *nm/f* malefactor; (*criminal*) criminal.

malicia [ma'liθja] *nf* (*maldad*) wickedness; (*astucia*) slyness, guile; (*mala intención*) malice, spite; (*carácter travieso*) mischievousness; **～s** *nfpl* suspicions; **malicioso, a** *a* wicked, evil; sly, crafty; malicious, spiteful; mischievous.

malignidad [maliɣni'ðað] *nf* (*MED*) malignancy; (*malicia*) malice.

maligno, a [ma'liɣno, a] *a* evil; (*malévolo*) malicious; (*MED*) malignant.

malo, a ['malo, a] *a* bad; (*falso*) false // *nm/f* villain // *nf* spell of bad luck; **estar ～** to be ill; **estar de ～as** to be in a bad mood.

malograr [malo'ɣrar] *vt* to spoil; (*plan*) to upset; (*tiempo, ocasión*) to waste; **～se** *vr* (*plan etc*) to fail, come to grief; (*persona*) to die before one's time; **malogro** *nm* (*fracaso*) failure; (*pérdida*) waste; (*muerte*) early death.

malparado, a [malpa'raðo, a] *a*: **salir ～** to come off badly.

malparir [malpa'rir] *vi* to have a miscarriage.

malquistar [malkis'tar] *vt* to estrange, cause a rift with/between.

malsano, a [mal'sano, a] *a* unhealthy.

Malta ['malta] *nf* Malta.

maltratar [maltra'tar] *vt* to ill-treat; **maltrato** *nm* ill-treatment; (*ofensa*) abuse, insults *pl*.

maltrecho, a [mal'tretʃo, a] *a* battered, damaged.

malvado, a [mal'ßaðo, a] *a* evil, villainous.

malvavisco [malßa'ßisko] *nm* marshmallow.

malversar [malßer'sar] *vt* to embezzle, misappropriate.

Malvinas [mal'ßinas]: **Islas ～** *nfpl* Falkland Islands.

malla ['maʎa] *nf* mesh; (*de baño*) bathing costume; **～s** *nfpl* tights; **～ de alambre**

wire mesh; **hacer ～** to knit.

Mallorca [ma'ʎorka] *nf* Majorca.

mama ['mama] *nf* (*de animal*) teat; (*de persona*) breast.

mamá [ma'ma] (*pl* **～s**) *nf* (*fam*) mum, mummy.

mamar [ma'mar] *vt* (*pecho*) to suck; (*fig*) to absorb, assimilate // *vi* to suck.

mamarracho [mama'rratʃo] *nm* sight, mess.

mampara [mam'para] *nf* (*entre habitaciones*) partition; (*biombo*) screen.

mampostería [mamposte'ria] *nf* masonry.

mampuesto [mam'pwesto] *nm* (*piedra*) rough stone; (*muro*) wall, parapet; **de ～** spare, emergency.

mamut [ma'mut] *nm* mammoth.

manada [ma'naða] *nf* (*rebaño*) herd; (*de ovejas*) flock; (*de lobos*) pack.

manantial [manan'tjal] *nm* spring; (*fuente*) fountain; (*fig*) source.

manar [ma'nar] *vt* to run with, flow with // *vi* to run, flow; (*abundar*) to abound.

mancebo [man'θeßo] *nm* (*joven*) young man; (*soltero*) bachelor; (*dependiente*) assistant.

mancilla [man'θiʎa] *nf* stain, blemish.

manco, a ['manko, a] *a* one-armed, one-handed; (*fig*) defective, faulty.

mancomún [manko'mun]: **de ～** *ad* jointly, together; **mancomunar** *vt* to unite, bring together; (*recursos*) to pool; (*JUR*) to make jointly responsible; **mancomunarse** *vr* to unite, merge; **mancomunidad** *nf* union, association; (*POL*) commonwealth; (*JUR*) joint responsibility.

mancha ['mantʃa] *nf* stain, mark; (*boceto*) sketch, outline; **manchar** *vt* (*gen*) to stain, mark; (*ensuciar*) to soil, dirty.

manchego, a [man'tʃeɣo, a] *a* of *or* from La Mancha.

mandadero [manda'ðero] *nm* messenger; (*niño*) errand boy.

mandado [man'daðo] *nm* (*orden*) order; (*comisión*) commission, errand.

mandamiento [manda'mjento] *nm* (*orden*) order, command; (*REL*) commandment; **～ judicial** warrant.

mandar [man'dar] *vt* (*ordenar*) to order; (*dirigir*) to lead, command; (*enviar*) to send; (*pedir*) to order, ask for // *vi* to be in charge; (*pey*) to be bossy; **～se** *vr* (*MED*) to get about by o.s.; **¿mande?** pardon?; **～ hacer un traje** to have a suit made; **～se cambiar** to go away, leave.

mandarín [manda'rin] *nm* mandarin // *nf* tangerine, mandarin.

mandatario, a [manda'tarjo, a] *nm/f* (*representante*) agent; (*AM*) leader.

mandato [man'dato] *nm* (*orden*) order; (*POL*) term of office; (: *territorio*) mandate; **～ judicial** (*search*) warrant.

mandíbula [man'dißula] *nf* jaw.

mandil [man'dil] *nm* (*delantal*) apron; (*vestido*) pinafore dress.

mando ['mando] nm (MIL) command; (de país) rule; (el primer lugar) lead; (POL) term of office; (TEC) control; ~ **a la izquierda** left-hand drive; ~ **remoto** remote control.

mandolina [mando'lina] nf mandolin(e).

mandón, ona [man'don, ona] a bossy, domineering.

manea [ma'nea] nf hobble.

manejable [mane'xaβle] a manageable.

manejar [mane'xar] vt (gen) to manage; (máquina) to work, operate; (idioma, caballo etc) to handle; (casa) to run, manage; (AM) to drive; ~**se** vr (comportarse) to act, behave; (arreglárselas) to manage; (MED) to get about unaided; **manejo** nm management; handling; running; driving; (facilidad de trato) ease, confidence; **manejos** nmpl intrigues.

manera [ma'nera] nf way, manner, fashion; ~**s** nfpl manners; ~ **de ser** way of life; (aire) manner; **de ninguna** ~ no way, by no means; **de otra** ~ otherwise; **de todas** ~**s** at any rate; **no hay** ~ **de persuadirle** there's no way of convincing him.

manga ['manga] nf (de camisa) sleeve; (de riego) hose; (tromba) downpour; (filtro) filter; (NAUT) beam.

mangana [man'gana] nf lasso.

mango ['mango] nm handle; (BOT) mango.

mangonear [mangone'ar] vt to manage, boss about // vi (meterse) to meddle, interfere; (ser mandón) to boss people about.

manguera [man'gera] nf (de riego) hose; (tubo) pipe.

maní [ma'ni] nm (AM) peanut.

manía [ma'nia] nf (MED) mania; (capricho) rage, craze; (disgusto) dislike; (malicia) spite; **maníaco, a** a maniac(al) // nm/f maniac.

maniatar [manja'tar] vt to tie the hands of.

maniático, a [ma'njatiko, a] a maniac(al) // nm/f maniac.

manicomio [mani'komjo] nm asylum, mental hospital.

manifestación [manifesta'θjon] nf (declaración) statement, declaration; (demostración) show, manifestation; (POL) demonstration.

manifestar [manifes'tar] vt to show, manifest; (declarar) to state, declare; **manifiesto, a** a clear, manifest // nm manifesto.

manija [ma'nixa] nf handle.

manilla [ma'niʎa] nf: ~**s de hierro** handcuffs.

maniobra [ma'njoβra] nf manœuvring; (maneja) handling; (fig) manœuvre; (estratagema) stratagem; ~**s** nfpl manœuvres; **maniobrar** vt to manœuvre; (manejar) to handle.

manipulación [manipula'θjon] nf manipulation; **manipular** vt to

manipulate; (manejar) to handle.

maniquí [mani'ki] nm dummy // nf model.

manirroto, a [mani'rroto, a] a lavish, extravagant // nm/f spendthrift.

manivela [mani'βela] nf crank.

manjar [man'xar] nm (tasty) dish; ~ **blanco** blancmange.

mano ['mano] nf hand; (ZOOL) foot, paw; (de pintura) coat; (serie) lot, series; a ~ by hand; **a la** ~ on hand, within reach; a ~ **derecha/izquierda** on the right(-hand side)/left(-hand side); **de primera** ~ (at) first hand; **de segunda** ~ (at) second hand; **robo a** ~ **armada** armed robbery; ~ **de obra** labour, manpower; **estrechar la** ~ **a uno** to shake sb's hand.

manojo [ma'noxo] nm handful, bunch; ~ **de llaves** bunch of keys.

manoseado, a [manose'aðo, a] a well-worn; **manosear** vt (tocar) to handle, touch; (desordenar) to mess up, rumple; (insistir en) to overwork; (AM) to caress, fondle.

manotazo [mano'taθo] nm slap, smack.

mansalva [man'salβa]: **a** ~ ad without risk, without any danger.

mansedumbre [manse'ðumbre] nf gentleness, meekness.

mansión [man'sjon] nf mansion.

manso, a ['manso, a] a gentle, mild, meek; (animal) tame.

manta ['manta] nf blanket; (abrigo) shawl.

manteca [man'teka] nf fat; ~ **de cacahuete/cacao** peanut/cocoa butter; ~ **de cerdo** lard.

mantecado [mante'kaðo] nm ice-cream.

mantel [man'tel] nm tablecloth.

mantener [mante'ner] vt (gen) to support, maintain; (alimentar) to sustain; (conservar) to keep; (TEC) to maintain, service; ~**se** vr (seguir de pie) to be still standing; (no ceder) to hold one's ground; (subsistir) to sustain o.s., keep going; **mantenimiento** nm maintenance; sustenance; (sustento) support.

mantequera [mante'kera] nf (para hacer) churn; (para servir) butter dish.

mantequilla [mante'kiʎa] nf butter.

mantilla [man'tiʎa] nf mantilla; ~**s** nfpl baby clothes.

manto ['manto] nm (capa) cloak; (chal) shawl; (de ceremonia) robe, gown.

mantón [man'ton] nm shawl.

manual [ma'nwal] a manual // nm manual, handbook.

manufactura [manufak'tura] nf manufacture; (fábrica) factory.

manuscrito, a [manus'krito, a] a hand-written // nm manuscript.

manutención [manuten'θjon] nf maintenance; (sustento) support.

manzana [man'θana] nf apple; (ARQ) block.

manzanilla [manθa'niʎa] nf (planta) camomile; (infusión) camomile tea; (vino) manzanilla.

manzano [man'θano] nm apple tree.

maña ['maɲa] nf (gen) skill, dexterity; (pey) guile; (costumbre) habit; (una ~-) trick, knack.

mañana [ma'ɲana] ad tomorrow // nm future // nf morning; **de** o **por la** ~ in the morning; **¡hasta ~!** see you tomorrow!; ~ **por la** ~ tomorrow morning; **mañanero, a** a early-rising.

mañoso, a [ma'ɲoso, a] a (hábil) skilful; (astuto) smart, clever.

mapa ['mapa] nm map.

maque ['make] nm lacquer.

maqueta [ma'keta] nf (scale) model.

maquillaje [maki'ʎaxe] nm make-up; (acto) making up; **maquillar** vt to make up; **maquillarse** vr to put on (some) make-up.

máquina ['makina] nf machine; (de tren) locomotive, engine; (cámara) camera; (fig) machinery; (: proyecto) plan, project; **escrito a** ~ typewritten; ~ **de afeitar** (safety) razor; ~ **de escribir** typewriter; ~ **de coser/lavar** sewing/washing machine.

maquinación [makina'θjon] nf machination, scheme, plot.

maquinal [maki'nal] a (fig) mechanical, automatic.

maquinaria [maki'narja] nf (máquinas) machinery; (mecanismo) mechanism, works pl.

maquinista [maki'nista] nm (de tren) engine driver; (TEC) operator; (NAUT) engineer.

mar [mar] nm o f sea; (marea) tide; ~ **adentro** o **afuera** out at sea; **en alta** ~ on the high seas; **la** ~ **de** (fam) lots of; **el M**~ **Negro/Báltico** the Black/Baltic Sea.

maraña [ma'raɲa] nf (maleza) thicket; (confusión) tangle.

maravilla [mara'βiʎa] nf marvel, wonder; (BOT) marigold; **maravillar** vt to astonish, amaze; **maravillarse** vr to be astonished, be amazed; **maravilloso, a** a wonderful, marvellous.

marca ['marka] nf (gen) mark; (sello) stamp; (COM) make, brand; **de** ~ excellent, outstanding; ~ **de fábrica** trademark.

marcado, a [mar'kaðo, a] a marked, strong.

marcar [mar'kar] vt (gen) to mark; (número de teléfono) to dial; (gol) to score; (números) to record, keep a tally of; (el pelo) to set; (fig) to indicate, point to // vi (DEPORTE) to score; (TELEC) to dial; ~**se** vr (NAUT) to take one's bearings; (fig) to make one's mark, stand out.

marcial [mar'θjal] a martial, military.

marciano, a [mar'θjano, a] a Martian.

marco ['marko] nm frame; (DEPORTE) goal-posts pl; (moneda) mark; (fig) framework; ~ **de chimenea** mantelpiece.

marcha ['martʃa] nf march; (TEC) running, working; (AUTO) gear; (velocidad) speed;

(fig) progress; (dirección) course; **poner en** ~ to put into gear; **dar** ~ **atrás** to reverse, put into reverse; **estar en** ~ to be under way, be in motion.

marchante, a [mar'tʃante, a] nm/f dealer, merchant; (AM: cliente) client, customer; (: buhonero) pedlar.

marchar [mar'tʃar] vi to go; (funcionar) to work, go; ~**se** vr to go (away), leave.

marchitar [martʃi'tar] vt to wither, dry up; ~**se** vr (BOT) to wither; (fig) to go into a decline; **marchito, a** a withered, faded; (fig) in decline.

marea [ma'rea] nf tide; (llovizna) drizzle.

marear [mare'ar] vt (NAUT) to sail, navigate; (fig) to annoy, upset; (MED): ~ **a uno** to make sb feel sick; ~**se** vr (tener náuseas) to feel/be sick; (desvanecerse) to feel faint; (aturdirse) to feel dizzy; (fam: emborracharse) to get a bit drunk.

maremoto [mare'moto] nm tidal wave.

mareo [ma'reo] nm (náusea) sick feeling; (aturdimiento) dizziness; (fam: lata) nuisance.

marfil [mar'fil] nm ivory.

margarina [marɣa'rina] nf margarine.

margarita [marɣa'rita] nf (BOT) daisy; (perla) pearl.

margen ['marxen] nm (borde) edge, border; (fig) margin, space // nf bank; **dar** ~ **para** to give an opportunity for; **mantenerse al** ~ to keep out (of things).

marica [ma'rika] nm magpie; (fam) sissy.

maricón [mari'kon] nm (fam) queer (fam).

marido [ma'riðo] nm husband.

marijuana [mari'xwana] nf marijuana, cannabis.

marina [ma'rina] nf navy; ~ **mercante** merchant navy.

marinero, a [mari'nero, a] a sea cpd; (barco) seaworthy // nm sailor, seaman.

marino, a [ma'rino, a] a sea cpd, marine // nm sailor.

marioneta [marjo'neta] nf puppet.

mariposa [mari'posa] nf butterfly.

mariscos [ma'riskos] nmpl shellfish, seafood sg.

marisma [ma'risma] nf marsh, swamp.

marítimo, a [ma'ritimo, a] a sea cpd, maritime.

marmita [mar'mita] nf pot.

mármol ['marmol] nm marble; **marmóreo, a** a marble.

marqués, esa [mar'kes, esa] nm/f marquis/marchioness.

marrar [ma'rrar] vi to miss.

marrón [ma'rron] a brown.

marroquí [marro'ki] a Moroccan // nm Morocco (leather).

Marruecos [ma'rrwekos] nm Morocco.

Marsellas [mar'seʎas] n Marseille.

martes ['martes] nm inv Tuesday.

martillar [marti'ʎar] vt to hammer.

martillo [mar'tiʎo] nm hammer; ~

neumático pneumatic drill; ~ **de orejas** claw-hammer.

mártir ['martir] nm/f martyr; **martirio** nm martyrdom; (fig) torture, torment.

marxismo [mark'sismo] nm Marxism; **marxista** nm/f Marxist.

marzo ['marθo] nm March.

mas [mas] conj but.

más [mas] a, ad more; (superlativo) most // conj and, plus; **es** ~ **de medianoche** it's after midnight; **el libro** ~ **leído del año** the most-read book of the year; ¡**qué perro** ~ **feo!** what an ugly dog!; ~ **de,** ~ **de lo que,** ~ **que** more than; ~ **bien** rather; ~ **o menos** more or less.

masa ['masa] nf (mezcla) dough; (volumen) volume, mass; (FÍSICA) mass; (ELEC) earth; **en** ~ **en masse; las** ~**s** the masses.

masacre [ma'sakre] nm massacre.

masaje [ma'saxe] nm massage.

mascar [mas'kar] vt to chew; (fig) to mumble, mutter.

máscara ['maskara] nf (gen) mask // nm/f masked person; **mascarada** nf masquerade.

masculino, a [masku'lino, a] a masculine; (BIO) male.

mascullar [masku'ʎar] vt to mumble, mutter.

masilla [ma'siʎa] nf putty.

masivo, a [ma'siβo, a] a (enorme) massive; (en masa) mass, en masse.

masón [ma'son] nm (free)mason.

masoquista [maso'kista] nm/f masochist.

masticar [masti'kar] vt to chew; (fig) to ponder.

mástil ['mastil] nm (de navío) mast; (de guitarra) neck; (sostén) post, support.

mastín [mas'tin] nm mastiff; ~ **danés** Great Dane.

masturbación [masturβa'θjon] nf masturbation; **masturbarse** vr to masturbate.

mata ['mata] nf bush, shrub; (de hierbas) tuft; (campo) field; (AM) clump (of trees).

matadero [mata'ðero] nm slaughterhouse, abattoir.

matador, a [mata'ðor, a] a killing // nm/f killer // nm (TAUR) matador, bullfighter.

matanza [ma'tanθa] nf (de personas) killing; (de animales) slaughter(ing).

matar [ma'tar] vt, vi to kill; ~**se** vr (suicidarse) to kill o.s., commit suicide; (por otro) to be killed; ~ **el hambre** to stave off hunger.

mate ['mate] a (sin brillo: color) dull // nm (en ajedrez) (check)mate; (AM: hierba) maté; (: vasija) gourd.

matemáticas [mate'matikas] nfpl mathematics; **matemático, a** a mathematical // nm/f mathematician.

materia [ma'terja] nf (gen) matter; (TEC) material; **en** ~ **de** on the subject of; ~ **prima** raw material; **material** a material; (dolor) physical // nm material; (TEC) equipment; **materialismo** nm

materialism; **materialista** a materialist(ic); **materialmente** ad materially; (fig) absolutely.

maternal [mater'nal] a motherly, maternal.

maternidad [materni'ðað] nf motherhood, maternity; **materno, a** a motherly, maternal; (lengua) mother cpd.

matinal [mati'nal] a morning cpd.

matiz [ma'tiθ] nm shade; ~**ar** vt (dar tonos de) to tinge, tint; (variar) to vary; (ARTE) to blend.

matón [ma'ton] nm bully.

matorral [mato'rral] nm thicket.

matraca [ma'traka] nf rattle.

matrícula [ma'trikula] nf (registro) register; (AUTO) registration number; (: placa) licence plate; **matricular** vt to register, enrol.

matrimonial [matrimo'njal] a matrimonial.

matrimonio [matri'monjo] nm (boda) wedding; (pareja) (married) couple; (unión) marriage.

matriz [ma'triθ] nf womb; (TEC) mould; **casa** ~ (COM) head office.

matrona [ma'trona] nf (persona de edad) matron; (partera) midwife.

matute [ma'tute] nm contraband.

maullar [mau'ʎar] vi to mew, miaow.

mausoleo [mauso'leo] nm mausoleum.

maxilar [maksi'lar] nm jaw(bone).

máxima ['maksima] ver **máximo.**

máxime ['maksime] ad especially.

máximo, a ['maksimo, a] a maximum; (más alto) highest; (más grande) greatest // nm maximum // nf maxim.

mayo ['majo] nm May.

mayonesa [majo'nesa] nf mayonnaise.

mayor [ma'jor] a (gen) main, chief; (adulto) adult; (de edad avanzada) elderly; (MUS) major; (comparativo: de tamaño) bigger; (: de edad) older; (superlativo: de tamaño) biggest; (: de edad) oldest // nm chief, boss; **al por** ~ wholesale; ~ **de edad** adult; ~**es** nmpl ancestors.

mayoral [majo'ral] nm foreman.

mayordomo [major'ðomo] nm (criado) butler; (de hotel) steward.

mayoría [majo'ria] nf majority, greater part.

mayorista [majo'rista] nm/f wholesaler.

mayúsculo, a [ma'juskulo, a] a (fig) big, tremendous // nf capital (letter).

mazapán [maθa'pan] nm marzipan.

mazo ['maθo] nm (martillo) mallet; (de flores) bunch; (fig) bore; (DEPORTE) bat; (palo) club.

me [me] pron (directo) me; (indirecto) (to) me; (reflexivo) (to) myself; ¡**démelo!** give it to me!

mecánico, a [me'kaniko, a] a mechanical // nm/f mechanic // nf (estudio) mechanics sg; (mecanismo) mechanism.

mecanismo [meka'nismo] nm mechanism; (marcha) gear.

mecanografía [mekanoʃra'fia] *nf* typewriting; **mecanógrafo, a** *nm/f* typist.

mecedor, a [meθe'ðor, a] *a* rocking // *nm* (*columpio*) swing // *nf* rocking chair.

mecer [me'θer] *vt* (*cuna*) to rock; (*líquido*) to stir; ~**se** *vr* to rock; (*ramo*) to sway.

mechero [me'tʃero] *nm* (cigarette) lighter.

mechón [me'tʃon] *nm* (*gen*) tuft; (*manojo*) bundle; (*de pelo*) lock.

medalla [me'ðaʎa] *nf* medal.

media ['meðja] *nf ver* **medio.**

mediado, a [me'ðjaðo, a] *a* half-full; (*trabajo*) half-complete; **a** ~**s de** in the middle of, halfway through.

mediano, a [me'ðjano, a] *a* (*regular*) medium, average; (*mediocre*) mediocre; (*indiferente*) indifferent.

medianoche [meðja'notʃe] *nf* midnight.

mediante [me'ðjante] *ad* by (means of), through.

mediar [me'ðjar] *vi* (*llegar a la mitad*) to get to the middle, get halfway; (*estar en medio*) to be in the middle; (*interceder*) to mediate, intervene.

medicación [meðika'θjon] *nf* medication, treatment.

medicamento [meðika'mento] *nm* medicine, drug.

medicina [meði'θina] *nf* medicine.

medición [meði'θjon] *nf* measurement.

médico, a ['meðiko, a] *a* medical // *nm/f* doctor.

medida [me'ðiða] *nf* (*gen*) measure; (*medición*) measurement; (*prudencia*) moderation, prudence; **en cierta/gran** ~ up to a point/to a great extent; **un traje a la** ~ made-to-measure suit; ~ **de cuello** collar size; **a** ~ **de** in proportion to; (*de acuerdo con*) in keeping with.

medio, a ['meðjo, a] *a* half (a); (*punto*) mid, middle; (*promedio*) average // *ad* half // *nm* (*centro*) middle, centre; (*promedio*) average; (DEPORTE) half-back; (*método*) means, way; (*ambiente*) environment // *nf* (*prenda de vestir*) stocking; (*promedio*) average; ~**s** *nmpl* means, resources; ~ **litro** half a litre; **las tres y** ~**a** half past three; **M**~ **Oriente** Middle East; **a** ~ **terminar** half finished; **pagar a** ~**as** to share the cost; **hacer** ~ **a** to knit.

mediocre [me'ðjokre] *a* middling, average; (*pey*) mediocre.

mediodía [meðjo'ðia] *nm* midday, noon.

medir [me'ðir] *vt* (*gen*) to measure; (*pesar*) to weigh up // *vi* to measure.

meditar [meði'tar] *vt* to ponder, think over, meditate (on); (*planear*) to think out.

mediterráneo, a [meðite'rraneo, a] *a* Mediterranean // *nm*: **el M**~ the Mediterranean.

medroso, a [me'ðroso, a] *a* fearful, timid.

medusa [me'ðusa] *nf* jellyfish.

megáfono [me'ɣafono] *nm* megaphone.

megalómano, a [meɣa'lomano, a] *nm/f* megalomaniac.

mejicano, a [mexi'kano, a] *a*, *nm/f* Mexican.

Méjico ['mexiko] *nm* Mexico.

mejilla [me'xiʎa] *nf* cheek.

mejor [me'xor] *a*, *ad* (*comparativo*) better; (*superlativo*) best; **a lo** ~ probably; (*quizá*) maybe; ~ **dicho** rather; **tanto** ~ so much the better.

mejora [me'xora] *nf* improvement; **mejorar** *vt* to improve, make better // *vi*, **mejorarse** *vr* to improve, get better.

melancólico, a [melan'koliko, a] *a* (*triste*) sad, melancholy; (*soñador*) dreamy.

melena [me'lena] *nf* (*de persona*) long hair; (*del león*) mane.

melocotón [meloko'ton] *nm* peach.

melodía [melo'ðia] *nf* melody; (*aire*) tune.

melodrama [melo'ðrama] *nm* melodrama; **melodramático, a** *a* melodramatic.

melón [me'lon] *nm* melon.

meloso, a [me'loso, a] *a* honeyed, sweet.

mellizo, a [me'ʎiθo, a] *a*, *nm/f* twin.

membrete [mem'brete] *nm* letterhead.

memorable [memo'raβle] *a* memorable.

memorándum [memo'randum] *nm* (*libro*) notebook; (*comunicación*) memorandum.

memoria [me'morja] *nf* (*gen*) memory; (*informe*) report; ~**s** *nfpl* (*de autor*) memoirs.

mencionar [menθjo'nar] *vt* to mention.

mendigar [mendi'ɣar] *vt* to beg (for).

mendigo, a [men'diɣo, a] *nm/f* beggar.

mendrugo [men'druɣo] *nm* crust.

menear [mene'ar] *vt* to move; (*fig*) to handle; ~**se** *vr* to shake; (*balancearse*) to sway; (*moverse*) to move; (*fig*) to get a move on.

menester [menes'ter] *nm* (*necesidad*) necessity; (*ocupación*) job; ~**es** *nmpl* (*deberes*) duties; (*instrumentos*) tackle *sg*, tools; **es** ~ it is necessary.

mengua ['mengwa] *nf* (*disminución*) decrease; (*falta*) lack; (*pobreza*) poverty; (*fig*) discredit; ~**do, a** *a* cowardly, timid; (*cicatero*) mean.

menguante [men'gwante] *a* decreasing, diminishing; **menguar** *vt* to lessen, diminish; (*fig*) to discredit // *vi* to diminish, decrease; (*fig*) to decline.

menopausia [meno'pausja] *nf* menopause.

menor [me'nor] *a* (*más pequeño*: comparativo) smaller; (: superlativo) smallest; (*más joven*: comparativo) younger; (: superlativo) youngest; (MUS) minor // *nm/f* (*joven*) young person, juvenile; **no tengo la** ~ **idea** I haven't the slightest idea; **al por** ~ retail; ~ **de edad** person under age.

menos ['menos] *a* (*comparativo*: *sg*) less; (: *pl*) fewer; (*superlativo*: *sg*) least; (: *pl*) fewest // *ad* (*comparativo*) less; (*superlativo*) least // *conj* except // *nm* (MAT) minus; **es lo** ~ **que puedo hacer**

it's the least I can do; **lo** ~ **posible** as little as possible; **a** ~ **que** unless; **te echo de** ~ I miss you; **al** o **por lo** ~ at least.

menoscabar [menoska'ßar] vt (estropear) to damage, harm; (acortar) to lessen, reduce; (fig) to discredit.

menospreciar [menospre'θjar] vt to underrate, undervalue; (despreciar) to scorn, despise; **menosprecio** nm underrating, undervaluation; scorn, contempt.

mensaje [men'saxe] nm message; ~**ro, a** nm/f messenger.

menstruar [mens'trwar] vi to menstruate; **menstruo** nm menstruation, period.

mensual [men'swal] a monthly; **100 ptas** ~**es** 100 ptas. a month.

menta ['menta] nf mint.

mental [men'tal] a mental.

mentar [men'tar] vt to mention, name.

mente ['mente] nf mind.

mentecato, a [mente'kato, a] a silly, stupid // nm/f fool, idiot.

mentir [men'tir] vi to lie; ~**a** nf (una ~a) lie; (acto) lying; (invención) fiction; **parece** ~**a que...** it seems incredible that..., I can't believe that...; ~**oso, a** a lying; (texto) full of errors // nm/f liar.

mentís [men'tis] nm: **dar el** ~ **a** to deny.

menú [me'nu] nm menu.

menudeo [menu'ðeo] nm: **vender al** ~ to sell retail.

menudo, a [me'nuðo, a] a (pequeño) small, tiny; (sin importancia) petty, insignificant; (exacto) exact, meticulous; **¡**~ **negocio!** (fam) some deal!; **a** ~ **often**, frequently; **por** ~ in detail.

meñique [me'ɲike] nm little finger.

meollo [me'oʎo] nm (gen) marrow; (fig) core.

mercadería [merkaðe'ria] nf commodity; ~**s** nfpl goods, merchandise sg.

mercado [mer'kaðo] nm market; **M**~ **Común** Common Market.

mercadotecnia [merkaðo'teknja] nf marketing.

mercancía [merkan'θia] nf commodity; ~**s** nfpl goods, merchandise sg.

mercantil [merkan'til] a mercantile, commercial.

mercenario, a [merθe'narjo, a] a, nm mercenary.

mercurio [mer'kurjo] nm mercury.

merecer [mere'θer] vt to deserve, merit // vi to be deserving, be worthy; **merece la pena** it's worthwhile; **merecido, a** a (well) deserved; **llevar su merecido** to get one's deserts.

merendar [meren'dar] vt to have for tea // vi to have tea; (en el campo) to have a picnic.

merengue [me'renge] nm meringue.

merienda [me'rjenda] nf (light) tea, afternoon snack; (de campo) picnic.

mérito ['merito] nm merit; (valor) worth, value.

merluza [mer'luθa] nf hake.

merma ['merma] nf decrease; (pérdida) wastage; **mermar** vt to reduce, lessen // vi, **mermarse** vr to decrease, dwindle; (fig) to waste away.

mermelada [merme'laða] nf jam.

mero, a ['mero, a] a mere.

mes [mes] nm month; (salario) month's pay.

mesa ['mesa] nf table; (de trabajo) desk; (GEO) plateau; (ARQ) landing; ~ **directiva** board; **poner/quitar la** ~ to lay/clear the table.

meseta [me'seta] nf (GEO) meseta, tableland; (ARQ) landing.

mesón [me'son] nm olde-worlde bar.

mestizo, a [mes'tiθo, a] a half-caste, of mixed race; (ZOOL) crossbred // nm/f half-caste, half-breed.

mesura [me'sura] nf (moderación) moderation, restraint; (dignidad) dignity, calm; (cortesía) courtesy.

meta ['meta] nf goal; (de carrera) finish.

metáfora [me'tafora] nf metaphor.

metal [me'tal] nm (materia) metal; (MUS) brass; (fig) quality; **metálico, a** a metallic; (de metal) metal // nm cash.

metalurgia [meta'lurxja] nf metallurgy.

meteoro [mete'oro] nm meteor.

meter [me'ter] vt (colocar) to put, place; (introducir) to put in, insert; (añadir) to add; (involucrar) to involve; (causar) to make, cause; ~**se** vr: ~**se en** to go into, enter; (fig) to interfere in, meddle in; ~**se a** to start; ~**se a escritor** to become a writer; ~**se con alguien** to provoke sb, pick a quarrel with sb.

meticuloso, a [metiku'loso, a] a meticulous, thorough.

metódico, a [me'toðiko, a] a methodical.

metodismo [meto'ðismo] nm Methodism.

método ['metoðo] nm method.

metralleta [metra'ʎeta] nf submachine gun.

métrico, a ['metriko, a] a metric.

metro ['metro] nm metre; (tren) underground, subway.

México ['meksiko] nm Mexico.

mezcla ['meθkla] nf mixture; (ARQ) mortar; **mezclar** vt to mix (up); (naipes) to shuffle; **mezclarse** vr to mix, mingle; **mezclarse en** to get mixed up in, get involved in.

mezquino, a [meθ'kino, a] a (cicatero) mean; (pobre) miserable.

mezquita [meθ'kita] nf mosque.

mi [mi] det my.

mí [mi] pron me; myself.

miaja ['mjaxa] nf crumb.

microbús [mikro'ßus] nm minibus.

micrófono [mi'krofono] nm microphone.

microlentillas [mikrolen'tiʎas] nfpl contact lenses.

microscopio [mikro'skopjo] nm microscope.

miedo ['mjeðo] nm fear; (nerviosismo) apprehension, nervousness; **tener** ~ to

be afraid; **de** ~ wonderful, marvellous; **hace un frío de** ~ (fam) it's terribly cold; ~**so, a** a fearful, timid.
miel [mjel] nf honey.
miembro ['mjembro] nm limb; (socio) member; ~ **viril** penis.
mientes ['mjentes] nfpl: **no parar** ~ **en** to pay no attention to; **traer a las** ~ to recall.
mientras ['mjentras] conj while; (duración) as long as // ad meanwhile; ~ **tanto** meanwhile; ~ **más tiene, más quiere** the more he has, the more he wants.
miércoles ['mjerkoles] nm inv Wednesday.
mierda ['mjerða] nf (fam) shit.
miga ['miɣa] nf crumb; (fig) essence; **hacer buenas** ~**s** (fam) to get on well.
migración [miɣra'θjon] nf migration.
mil [mil] num thousand; **dos** ~ **libras** two thousand pounds.
milagro [mi'laɣro] nm miracle; ~**so, a** a miraculous.
mili ['mili] nf: **hacer la** ~ (fam) to do one's military service.
milicia [mi'liθja] nf (MIL) militia; (: arte) art of war; (servicio militar) military service.
milímetro [mi'limetro] nm millimetre.
militante [mili'tante] a militant.
militar [mili'tar] a (del ejército) military; (guerrero) warlike // nm/f soldier // vi to serve in the army; (fig) to be a member of a party.
milla ['miʎa] nf mile.
millar [mi'ʎar] nm thousand.
millón [mi'ʎon] num million; **millonario, a** nm/f millionaire.
mimar [mi'mar] vt (gen) to spoil, pamper; (al poderoso) to flatter.
mimbre ['mimbre] nm wicker.
mímica ['mimika] nf (para comunicarse) sign language; (imitación) mimicry.
mimo ['mimo] nm (caricia) affectionate caress; (de niño) spoiling; (TEATRO) mime.
mina ['mina] nf mine; **minar** vt to mine; (fig) to undermine.
mineral [mine'ral] a mineral // nm (GEO) mineral; (mena) ore.
minero, a [mi'nero, a] a mining // nm/f miner.
miniatura [minja'tura] a inv, nf miniature.
minifalda [mini'falda] nf miniskirt.
mínimo, a ['minimo, a] a, nm minimum.
ministerio [minis'terjo] nm Ministry; **M~ de Hacienda/del Exterior** Treasury/Foreign Office.
ministro [mi'nistro] nm minister.
minorar [mino'rar] vt to reduce.
minoría [mino'ria] nf minority.
minucioso, a [minu'θjoso, a] a thorough, meticulous; (prolijo) very detailed.
minúsculo, a [mi'nuskulo, a] a tiny, minute // nf small letter.
minuta [mi'nuta] nf (de comida) menu;

(borrador) rough draft; (apunte) note.
minutero [minu'tero] nm minute hand.
minuto [mi'nuto] nm minute.
mío, a ['mio, a] pron: **el** ~ mine; **un amigo** ~ a friend of mine; **lo** ~ what is mine.
miope [mi'ope] a short-sighted.
mira ['mira] nf (de arma) sight(s) (pl); (fig) aim, intention; **estar a la** ~ to be on the look-out, keep watch; ~**da** nf look, glance; (expresión) look, expression; **echar una** ~**da a** to glance at; ~**do, a** a (sensato) sensible; (considerado) considerate; **bien/mal** ~**do** well/not well thought of.
mirador [mira'ðor] nm viewpoint, vantage point.
mirar [mi'rar] vt to look at; (observar) to watch; (considerar) to consider, think over; (vigilar, cuidar) to watch, look after // vi to look; (ARQ) to face; ~**se** vr (dos personas) to look at each other; ~ **bien/mal** to think highly of/have a poor opinion of; ~**se al espejo** to look at o.s. in the mirror.
mirlo ['mirlo] nm blackbird.
misa ['misa] nf mass.
miserable [mise'raβle] a (avaro) mean, stingy; (nimio) miserable, paltry; (lugar) squalid; (fam) vile, despicable // nm/f (indigente) wretch, poor person; (perverso) rotter.
miseria [mi'serja] nf misery; (pobreza) poverty; (tacañería) meanness, stinginess; (condiciones) squalor; **una** ~ a pittance.
misericordia [miseri'korðja] nf (compasión) compassion, pity; (piedad) mercy.
misil [mi'sil] nm missile.
misión [mi'sjon] nf mission; **misionero, a** nm/f missionary.
mismo, a ['mismo, a] a (semejante) same; (después de pronombre) -self; (para énfasis) very; **el** ~ **traje** the same suit; **en ese** ~ **momento** at that very moment; **vino el** ~ **Ministro** the minister himself came; **yo** ~ **lo vi** I saw it myself; **lo** ~ the same (thing); **da lo** ~ it's all the same; **quedamos en las** ~**as** we're no further forward // ad: **aquí/hoy** ~ right here/this very day; **ahora** ~ right now // conj: **lo** ~ **que** just like, just as; **por lo** ~ for the same reason.
misterio [mis'terjo] nm (gen) mystery; (lo secreto) secrecy.
mitad [mi'tað] nf (medio) half; (centro) middle; **a** ~ **de precio** (at) half-price; **en o a** ~ **del camino** halfway along the road; **cortar por la** ~ to cut through the middle.
mitin ['mitin] nm meeting.
mito ['mito] nm myth.
mixto, a ['miksto, a] a mixed.
mobiliario [moβi'ljarjo] nm furniture.
mocedad [moθe'ðað] nf youth.
moción [mo'θjon] nf motion.
mochila [mo'tʃila] nf rucksack.

moda ['moða] *nf* (*gen*) fashion; (*estilo*) style: **de** *o* **a la** ~ in fashion, fashionable; **pasado** *o* **fuera de** ~ out of fashion.
modales [mo'ðales] *nmpl* manners.
modalidad [moðali'ðað] *nf* kind, variety.
modelar [moðe'lar] *vt* to model.
modelo [mo'ðelo] *a inv, nm/f* model.
moderado, a [moðe'raðo, a] *a* moderate.
moderar [moðe'rar] *vt* to moderate; (*violencia*) to restrain, control; (*velocidad*) to reduce; ~**se** *vr* to restrain o.s., control o.s.
modernizar [moðerni'θar] *vt* to modernize.
moderno, a [mo'ðerno, a] *a* modern; (*actual*) present-day.
modestia [mo'ðestja] *nf* modesty; **modesto, a** *a* modest.
módico, a ['moðiko, a] *a* moderate, reasonable.
modificar [moðifi'kar] *vt* to modify.
modista [mo'ðista] *nm/f* dressmaker.
modo ['moðo] *nm* (*manera, forma*) way, manner; (*MUS*) mode; ~**s** *nmpl* manners; **de ningún** ~ in no way; **de todos** ~**s** at any rate; ~ **de empleo** directions *pl* (for use).
modorra [mo'ðorra] *nf* drowsiness.
modular [moðu'lar] *vt* to modulate.
mofa ['mofa] *nf* mockery, ridicule; **hacer** ~ **de** to mock; **mofar** *vi* to mock, scoff; **mofarse** *vr*: **mofarse de** to mock, scoff at.
mohino, a [mo'ino, a] *a* (*triste*) gloomy, depressed; (*enojado*) sulky.
moho ['moo] *nm* (*BOT*) mould; (*oxidación*) rust; ~**so, a** *a* mouldy; rusty.
mojar [mo'xar] *vt* to wet; (*humedecer*) to damp(en), moisten; (*calar*) to soak // *vi*: ~ **en** to get involved in; ~**se** *vr* to get wet.
mojón [mo'xon] *nm* (*en un camino*) signpost; (*montón*) heap, pile.
molde ['molde] *nm* mould; (*de costura*) pattern; (*fig*) model; **el vestido le está de** ~ the dress is just right for her; ~**ar** *vt* to mould.
mole ['mole] *nf* mass, bulk.
moledora [mole'ðora] *nf* grinder, mill.
moler [mo'ler] *vt* to grind, crush; (*cansar*) to tire out, exhaust; (*irritar*) to annoy.
molestar [moles'tar] *vt* (*gen*) to bother; (*fastidiar*) to annoy; (*incomodar*) to inconvenience, put out // *vi* to be a nuisance; ~**se** *vr* to bother; (*incomodarse*) to go to trouble; (*ofenderse*) to take offence.
molestia [mo'lestja] *nf* (*gen*) bother, trouble; (*incomodidad*) inconvenience; (*MED*) discomfort; **es una** ~ it's a nuisance; **molesto, a** *a* (*que causa molestia*) annoying; (*incómodo*) inconvenient; (*inquieto*) uncomfortable, ill at ease; (*enfadado*) annoyed.
molinillo [moli'niʎo] *nm*: ~ **de café/carne** coffee grinder/mincer.

molino [mo'lino] *nm* (*edificio*) mill; (*máquina*) grinder.
momentáneo, a [momen'taneo, a] *a* momentary.
momento [mo'mento] *nm* (*gen*) moment; (*TEC*) momentum; **de** ~ at the moment, for the moment.
momia ['momja] *nf* mummy.
monarca [mo'narka] *nm/f* monarch, ruler; **monarquía** *nf* monarchy; **monarquista** *nm/f* royalist, monarchist.
monasterio [monas'terjo] *nm* monastery.
mondar [mon'dar] *vt* (*limpiar*) to clean; (*podar*) to prune, trim; (*pelar*) to peel; ~**se** *vr*: ~**se los dientes** to pick one's teeth.
moneda [mo'neða] *nf* (*tipo de dinero*) currency, money; (*pieza*) coin; **una** ~ **de 5p** a 5p piece; **monedero** *nm* purse; **monetario, a** *a* monetary, financial.
monja ['monxa] *nf* nun.
monje ['monxe] *nm* monk.
mono, a ['mono, a] *a* (*bonito*) lovely, pretty; (*gracioso*) nice, charming // *nm/f* monkey, ape // *nm* (*overoles*) overalls *pl*.
monopolio [mono'poljo] *nm* monopoly; **monopolizar** *vt* to monopolize.
monoriel [mono'riel] *nm* monorail.
monotonía [monoto'nia] *nf* (*sonido*) monotone; (*fig*) monotony.
monótono, a [mo'notono, a] *a* monotonous.
monstruo ['monstrwo] *nm* monster // *a* fantastic; ~**so, a** *a* monstrous.
monta ['monta] *nf* total, sum; **de poca** ~ unimportant, of little account.
montaje [mon'taxe] *nm* assembly; (*ARQ*) erection; (*TEATRO*) décor; (*CINE*) montage.
montaña [mon'taɲa] *nf* (*monte*) mountain; (*sierra*) mountains *pl*, mountainous area; (*AM*) forest; ~ **rusa** roller coaster; **montañés, esa** *a* mountain *cpd* // *nm/f* highlander; (*de Santander*) native of the Santander region.
montar [mon'tar] *vt* (*subir a*) to mount, get on; (*caballo etc*) to ride; (*TEC*) to assemble, put together; (*ARQ*) to erect; (*negocio*) to set up; (*arma*) to cock; (*colocar*) to lift on to // *vi* to mount, get on; (*sobresalir*) to overlap; ~ **a** to amount to, come to; ~ **en cólera** to get angry.
montaraz [monta'raθ] *a* mountain *cpd*, highland *cpd*; (*salvaje*) wild, untamed; (*pey*) uncivilized.
monte ['monte] *nm* (*montaña*) mountain; (*bosque*) woodland; (*área sin cultivar*) wild area, wild country; ~ **de Piedad** pawnshop; ~ **alto** forest; ~ **bajo** scrub(land).
monto ['monto] *nm* total, amount.
montón [mon'ton] *nm* heap, pile; (*fig*): **un** ~ **de** heaps of, lots of.
monumento [monu'mento] *nm* monument.
monzón [mon'θon] *nm* monsoon.
moña ['moɲa] *nf* hair ribbon.
moño ['moɲo] *nm* bun.

morado, a [mo'raðo, a] a purple; (*violado*) violet // nm bruise // nf (*casa*) dwelling, abode; (*período*) stay.

moral [mo'ral] a moral // nf (*ética*) ethics; (*moralidad*) morals pl, morality; (*ánimo*) morale.

moraleja [mora'lexa] nf moral.

moralizar [morali'θar] vt to moralize.

morboso, a [mor'ßoso, a] a morbid.

morcilla [mor'θiʎa] nf blood sausage, black pudding.

mordaz [mor'ðaθ] a biting, scathing.

mordaza [mor'ðaθa] nf (*para la boca*) gag; (*TEC*) clamp.

morder [mor'ðer] vt to bite; (*mordisquear*) to nibble; (*consumir*) to eat away, eat into; **mordisco** nm bite.

moreno, a [mo'reno, a] a (*color*) (dark) brown; (*de tez*) dark; (*de pelo* ~) dark-haired; (*negro*) Negro.

moretón [more'ton] nm (*fam*) bruise.

morfina [mor'fina] nf morphine.

moribundo, a [mori'ßundo, a] a dying.

morir [mo'rir] vi (*gen*) to die; (*fuego*) to die down; (*luz*) to go out; ~**se** vr (*gen*) to die; (*pierna etc*) to go to sleep, go numb; (*fig*) to be dying; **fue muerto en un accidente** he was killed in an accident; ~**se por algo** to be dying for sth.

morisco, a [mo'risko, a], **moro, a** ['moro, a] a Moorish // nm/f Moor.

morral [mo'rral] nm haversack.

morsa ['morsa] nf walrus.

mortaja [mor'taxa] nf shroud; (*TEC*) mortise; (*AM*) cigarette paper.

mortal [mor'tal] a mortal; (*golpe*) deadly; ~**idad, mortandad** nf mortality.

mortero [mor'tero] nm mortar.

mortífero, a [mor'tifero, a] a deadly, lethal.

mortificar [mortifi'kar] vt (*MED*) to damage, affect seriously; (*fig*) to mortify; ~**se** vr to be (very) embarrassed.

mosca ['moska] nf fly.

Moscú [mos'ku] n Moscow.

mosquitero [moski'tero] nm mosquito net.

mosquito [mos'kito] nm mosquito.

mostaza [mos'taθa] nf mustard.

mostrador [mostra'ðor] nm (*de tienda*) counter; (*de café*) bar; (*de reloj*) face, dial.

mostrar [mos'trar] vt (*gen*) to show; (*exhibir*) to display, exhibit; (*explicar*) to explain; ~**se** vr: ~**se amable** to be kind, to prove to be kind; **no se muestra muy inteligente** he doesn't seem (to be) very intelligent.

mostrenco, a [mos'trenko, a] a ownerless, unclaimed; (*perro*) stray; (*persona*) homeless; (*fam*) dense, slow.

mota ['mota] nf speck, tiny piece; (*en diseño*) dot.

mote ['mote] nm (*apodo*) nickname; (*sentencia*) motto.

motín [mo'tin] nm (*del pueblo*) revolt, rising; (*del ejército*) mutiny.

motivar [moti'ßar] vt (*causar*) to cause, motivate; (*explicar*) to explain, justify; **motivo, a** a motive // nm motive, reason.

moto ['moto] nf, **motocicleta** [motoθi-'kleta] nf motorbike.

motoniveladora [motonißela'ðora] nf bulldozer.

motor [mo'tor] nm motor, engine; ~ **a chorro** o **de reacción/de explosión** jet engine/internal combustion engine.

motora [mo'tora] nf, **motorbote** [motor-'ßote] nm motorboat.

motosierra [moto'sjerra] nf mechanical saw.

movedizo, a [moße'ðiθo, a] a easily moved, movable; (*inseguro*) unsteady; (*fig*) unsettled, changeable; (*persona*) fickle.

mover [mo'ßer] vt (*gen*) to move; (*cabeza*) to shake; (*accionar*) to drive; (*fig*) to cause, provoke; ~**se** vr to move; (*fig*) to get a move on.

móvil ['moßil] a mobile; (*pieza de máquina*) moving; (*mueble*) movable // nm motive; **movilidad** nf mobility; **movilizar** vt to mobilize.

movimiento [moßi'mjento] nm (*gen*) movement; (*TEC*) motion; (*actividad*) activity; **el M**~ the Falangist Movement.

mozo, a ['moθo, a] a (*joven*) young; (*soltero*) single, unmarried // nm/f (*joven*) youth, lad/girl; (*criado*) servant // nm (*camarero*) waiter.

muchacho, a [mu'tʃatʃo, a] nm/f (*niño*) boy/girl; (*criado*) servant/servant or maid.

muchedumbre [mutʃe'ðumbre] nf crowd.

mucho, a ['mutʃo, a] a (*sg*) a lot of; (*gen en frase negativa o interrogativa*) much; (*pl*) many, a lot of, lots of // ad (*en cantidad*) a lot, a great deal, much; (*del tiempo*) long; (*muy*) very // pron: **tengo** ~ **que hacer** I have a lot to do; ~**s dicen que** a lot of people say that; **ni** ~ **menos** far from it.

mudanza [mu'ðanθa] nf (*cambio*) change; (*de casa*) move; ~**s** nfpl (*fig*) moodiness sg.

mudar [mu'ðar] vt to change; (*ZOOL*) to shed // vi to change; ~**se** vr (*la ropa*) to change; (*de casa*) to move (house).

mudo, a ['muðo, a] a dumb; (*callado, CINE*) silent.

mueble ['mweßle] nm piece of furniture; ~**s** nmpl furniture sg; ~**ría** nf furniture shop.

mueca ['mweka] nf face, grimace; **hacer** ~**s a** to make faces at.

muela ['mwela] nf (*diente*) tooth; (: *de atrás*) molar.

muelle ['mweʎe] a (*blando*) soft; (*elástico*) springy; (*fig*) soft, easy // nm spring; (*NAUT*) wharf; (*malecón*) jetty.

muero etc vb ver **morir**.

muerte ['mwerte] nf death; (*homicidio*) murder; **dar** ~ **a** to kill.

muerto, a [a 'mwerto, a] pp de **morir** // a dead; (*color*) dull // nm/f dead man/woman; (*difunto*) deceased;

(*cadáver*) corpse; **estar** ~ **de cansancio** to be dead tired.

muestra ['mwestra] *nf* (*señal*) indication, sign; (*demostración*) demonstration; (*prueba*) proof; (*estadística*) sample; (*modelo*) model, pattern; (*testimonio*) token; **muestreo** *nm* sample, sampling.

muestro *etc vb ver* **mostrar.**

muevo *etc vb ver* **mover.**

mugir [mu'xir] *vi* (*vaca*) to moo; (*persona*) to roar, howl.

mugre ['muxre] *nf* dirt, filth; **mugriento, a** *a* dirty, filthy.

mujer [mu'xer] *nf* (*de sexo femenino*) woman; (*esposa*) wife; ~**iego** *nm* womaniser.

mula ['mula] *nf* mule.

muladar [mula'ðar] *nm* dungheap, dung-hill.

muleta [mu'leta] *nf* (*para andar*) crutch; (*TAUR*) stick with red cape attached; (*fig*) prop, support.

multa ['multa] *nf* fine; **multar** *vt* to fine.

multicopista [multiko'pista] *nm* duplicator.

múltiple ['multiple] *a* multiple; (*pl*) many, numerous.

multiplicar [multipli'kar] *vt* (*MAT*) to multiply; (*fig*) to increase; ~**se** *vr* (*BIO*) to multiply; (*fig*) to attend to a lot of things at one time.

multitud [multi'tuð] *nf* (*gentío, muchedumbre*) crowd; ~ **de** lots of.

mullido, a [mu'ʎiðo, a] *a* (*cama*) soft; (*hierba*) soft, springy // *nm* stuffing, filling.

mundano, a [mun'dano, a] *a* worldly; (*de moda*) fashionable.

mundial [mun'djal] *a* world-wide, universal; (*guerra, récord*) world *cpd*.

mundo ['mundo] *nm* world; **todo el** ~ everybody; **tener** ~ to be experienced, know one's way around.

munición [muni'θjon] *nf* (*MIL*) stores *pl*, supplies *pl*; (*de arma*) ammunition.

municipio [muni'θipjo] *nm* (*municipalidad*) town council, corporation; (*comuna*) town, municipality.

muñeca [mu'ɲeka] *nf* (*ANAT*) wrist; (*juguete*) doll; (*maniquí*) dummy.

muñeco [mu'ɲeko] *nm* (*figura*) figure; (*marioneta*) puppet; (*maniquí*) dummy; (*fig*) puppet, pawn.

muralla [mu'raʎa] *nf* (*city*) wall(s) (*pl*).

murciélago [mur'θjelaxo] *nm* bat.

murmullo [mur'muʎo] *nm* murmur(ing); (*cuchicheo*) whispering; (*de arroyo*) murmur, rippling.

murmuración [murmura'θjon] *nf* gossip; **murmurar** *vi* to murmur, whisper; (*criticar*) to criticize; (*cotillear*) to gossip.

muro ['muro] *nm* wall.

muscular [musku'lar] *a* muscular.

músculo ['muskulo] *nm* muscle.

museo [mu'seo] *nm* museum.

musgo ['musxo] *nm* moss.

músico, a ['musiko, a] *a* musical // *nm/f* musician // *nf* music.

musitar [musi'tar] *vt, vi* to mutter, mumble.

muslo ['muslo] *nm* thigh.

mustio, a ['mustjo, a] *a* (*persona*) depressed, gloomy; (*planta*) faded, withered.

musulmán, ana [musul'man, ana] *nm/f* Moslem.

mutación [muta'θjon] *nf* (*BIO*) mutation; (*cambio*) (sudden) change.

mutilar [muti'lar] *vt* to mutilate; (*a una persona*) to maim.

mutuamente [mutwa'mente] *ad* mutually; **mutuo, a** *a* mutual.

muy [mwi] *ad* very; (*demasiado*) too; **M**~ **Señor mío** Dear Sir; ~ **de noche** very late at night; **eso es** ~ **de él** that's just like him.

N

N *abr de* **norte.**

n/ *abr de* **nuestro, a.**

nabo ['naβo] *nm* turnip; (*raíz*) root.

nácar ['nakar] *nm* mother-of-pearl.

nacer [na'θer] *vi* to be born; (*de huevo*) to hatch; (*vegetal*) to sprout; (*río*) to rise; ~ **al amor** to awaken to love; **nació una sospecha en su mente** a suspicion formed in her mind; **nacido, a** *a* born; **recién nacido** newborn; **naciente** *a* new, emerging; (*sol*) rising; **nacimiento** *nm* birth; (*fig*) birth, origin; (*de Navidad*) Nativity; (*linaje*) descent, family; (*de río*) source.

nación [na'θjon] *nf* nation; **nacional** *a* national; **nacionalismo** *nm* nationalism; **nacionalista** *nm/f* nationalist; **nacionalizar** *vt* to nationalize; **nacionalizarse** *vr* to become naturalized.

nada ['naða] *pron* nothing // *ad* not at all, in no way; **no decir** ~ to say nothing, not to say anything; **de** ~ don't mention it.

nadaderas [naða'ðeras] *nfpl* waterwings.

nadador, a [naða'ðor, a] *nm/f* swimmer.

nadar [na'ðar] *vi* to swim.

nadie ['naðje] *pron* nobody, no-one; ~ **habló** nobody spoke; **no había** ~ there was nobody there, there wasn't anybody there.

nado ['naðo]: **a** ~ *ad*: **pasar a** ~ to swim across.

naipe ['naipe] *nm* playing card; ~**s** *nmpl* cards.

nalgas ['nalxas] *nfpl* buttocks.

nana ['nana] *nf* (*fam: abuela*) grandma (*fam*), granny (*fam*); (: *canción*) lullaby.

naranja [na'ranxa] *a, nf* orange; **media** ~ (*fam*) better half (*fam*); ~**do, a** *a* orange // *nf* orangeade; **naranjo** *nm* orange tree.

narciso [nar'θiso] *nm* narcissus.

narcótico, a [nar'kotiko, a] *a, nm* narcotic; **narcotizar** *vt* to drug.

nardo ['narðo] *nm* lily.

narigón, ona [nari'ɣon, ona], **narigudo, a** [nari'ɣuðo, a] *a* big-nosed.

nariz [na'riθ] *nf* nose; **narices** *nfpl* nostrils; **en las narices de uno** under one's (very) nose.

narración [narra'θjon] *nf* narration; **narrador, a** *nm/f* narrator.

narrar [na'rrar] *vt* to narrate, recount; **narrativa** *nf* narrative, story.

nata ['nata] *nf* cream.

natación [nata'θjon] *nf* swimming.

natal [na'tal] *a:* **ciudad** ~ home town; ~**icio** *nm* birthday; ~**idad** *nf* birth rate.

natillas [na'tiʎas] *nfpl* custard *sg*.

natividad [natiβi'ðað] *nf* nativity.

nativo, a [na'tiβo, a] *a* native; (*innato*) innate, natural // *nm/f* native.

nato, a ['nato, a] *a* born; **un músico** ~ a born musician.

natural [natu'ral] *a* natural; (*fruta etc*) fresh // *nm/f* native // *nm* nature; ~**eza** *nf* nature; (*género*) nature, kind; ~**eza muerta** still life; ~**idad** *nf* naturalness; ~**ización** *nf* naturalization; ~**izarse** *vr* to become naturalized; (*aclimatarse*) to become acclimatized; ~**mente** *ad* naturally.

naufragar [naufra'ɣar] *vi* to sink; **naufragio** *nm* shipwreck; **náufrago, a** *nm/f* castaway, shipwrecked person.

náusea ['nausea] *nf* nausea; **me da** ~ it makes me feel sick; **nauseabundo, a** *a* nauseating, sickening.

náutico, a ['nautiko, a] *a* nautical.

nava ['naβa] *nf* (*GEO*) level plain.

navaja [na'βaxa] *nf* (*cortaplumas*) clasp knife, penknife; (*de barbero, peluquero*) razor.

navarro, a [na'βarro, a] *a* Navarrese.

nave ['naβe] *nf* (*barco*) ship, vessel; (*ARQ*) nave; ~ **espacial** spaceship.

navegación [naβeɣa'θjon] *nf* navigation; (*viaje*) sea journey; ~ **aérea** air traffic; ~ **costera** coastal shipping; **navegante** *nm/f* navigator; **navegar** *vi* (*barco*) to sail; (*avión*) to fly // *vt* to sail; to fly; (*dirigir el rumbo*) to navigate.

navidad [naβi'ðað] *nf* Christmas; **navideño, a** *a* Christmas *cpd*.

navío [na'βio] *nm* ship.

nazi ['naθi] *a, nm/f* Nazi.

neblina [ne'βlina] *nf* mist.

nebuloso, a [neβu'loso, a] *a* foggy; (*calinoso*) misty; (*cielo*) cloudy; (*indefinido*) nebulous, vague // *nf* nebula.

necedad [neθe'ðað] *nf* foolishness; (*una* ~) foolish act.

necesario, a [neθe'sarjo, a] *a* necessary.

neceser [neθe'ser] *nm* vanity case; (*bolsa*) holdall; ~ **de viaje** travelling case.

necesidad [neθesi'ðað] *nf* need; (*lo inevitable*) necessity; (*miseria*) poverty, need; **en caso de** ~ in case of need *or* emergency; **hacer sus** ~**es** to relieve o.s.

necesitado, a [neθesi'taðo, a] *a* needy, poor; ~ **de** in need of.

necesitar [neθesi'tar] *vt* to need, require // *vi:* ~ **de** to have need of.

necio, a ['neθjo, a] *a* foolish.

necrología [nekrolo'xia] *nf* obituary.

necrópolis [ne'kropolis] *nf* cemetery.

nectarina [nekta'rina] *nf* nectarine.

nefando, a [ne'fando, a] *a* unspeakable.

nefasto, a [ne'fasto, a] *a* ill-fated, unlucky.

negación [neɣa'θjon] *nf* negation; (*rechazo*) refusal, denial.

negar [ne'ɣar] *vt* (*renegar, rechazar*) to refuse; (*prohibir*) to refuse, deny; (*desmentir*) to deny; ~**se** *vr:* ~**se a** to refuse to.

negativo, a [neɣa'tiβo, a] *a, nm* negative // *nf* (*gen*) negative; (*rechazo*) refusal, denial.

negligencia [neɣli'xenθja] *nf* negligence; **negligente** *a* negligent.

negociable [neɣo'θjaβle] *a* (*COM*) negotiable.

negociado [neɣo'θjaðo] *nm* department, section.

negociante [neɣo'θjante] *nm/f* businessman/woman; (*comerciante*) merchant.

negociar [neɣo'θjar] *vt, vi* to negotiate; ~ **en** to deal in, trade in.

negocio [ne'ɣoθjo] *nm* (*COM*) business; (*asunto*) affair, business; (*operación comercial*) deal, transaction; (*AM*) firm; (*lugar*) place of business; **los** ~**s** business *sg*; **hacer** ~ to do business.

negro, a ['neɣro, a] *a* black; (*suerte*) awful // *nm* black // *nm/f* Negro/Negress, black // *nf* (*MUS*) crotchet; **negrura** *nf* blackness.

nene, a ['nene, a] *nm/f* baby, small child; (*fam*) dear.

nenúfar [ne'nufar] *nm* water lily.

neologismo [neolo'xismo] *nm* neologism.

neoyorquino, a [neojor'kino, a] *a* (of) New York.

nepotismo [nepo'tismo] *nm* nepotism.

nervio ['nerβjo] *nm* (*ANAT*) nerve; (: *tendón*) tendon; (*fig*) vigour; ~**sidad** *nf* nervousness, nerves *pl*; ~**so, a, nervudo, a** *a* nervous.

neto, a ['neto, a] *a* clear; (*verdad etc*) pure; (*limpio*) clean; (*COM*) net.

neumático, a [neu'matiko, a] *a* pneumatic // *nm* tyre; ~ **de recambio** spare tyre.

neuralgia [neu'ralxja] *nf* neuralgia.

neurastenia [neuras'tenja] *nf* nervous exhaustion.

neuritis [neu'ritis] *nf* neuritis.

neurólogo, a [neu'roloɣo, a] *nm/f* neurologist.

neurosis [neu'rosis] *nf inv* neurosis.

neutral [neu'tral] *a* neutral; ~**izar** *vt* to neutralize; (*contrarrestar*) to counteract.

neutro, a ['neutro, a] *a* (*BIO*) neuter, sexless; (*LING*) neuter.

neutrón [neu'tron] *nm* neutron; **bomba de neutrones** neutron bomb.

nevada [ne'ßaða] *nf* snowstorm; (*caída de nieve*) snowfall.

nevar [ne'ßar] *vi* to snow; **nevasca** *nf* snowstorm.

nevera [ne'ßera] *nf* refrigerator, icebox.

nevisca [ne'ßiska] *nf* flurry of snow; (*aguanieve*) sleet; **neviscar** *vi* to snow lightly; to sleet.

ni [ni] *conj* nor, neither; (~ *siquiera*) not ... even; ~ **que** not even if; ~ **blanco** ~ **negro** neither white nor black.

Nicaragua [nika'raɣwa] *nf* Nicaragua; **nicaragüense** *a, nm/f* Nicaraguan.

nicotina [niko'tina] *nf* nicotine.

nicho ['nitʃo] *nm* niche.

nido ['niðo] *nm* nest; (*fig*) hiding place; (*lugar predilecto*) haunt.

niebla ['njeßla] *nf* fog; (*neblina*) mist.

niego *etc vb ver* **negar**.

nieto, a ['njeto, a] *nm/f* grandson/daughter; ~**s** *nmpl* grandchildren.

nieva *etc vb ver* **nevar**.

nieve ['njeße] *nf* snow.

nigromancia [niɣro'manθja] *nf* necromancy, black magic.

nihilismo [nii'lismo] *nm* nihilism.

Nilo ['nilo] *nm*: **el** ~ the Nile.

nimbo ['nimbo] *nm* (*aureola*) halo; (*nube*) nimbus.

nimiedad [nimje'ðað] *nf* smallmindedness; (*prolijidad*) long-windedness; (*trivialidad*) triviality.

nimio, a ['nimjo, a] *a* (*insignificante*) trivial, insignificant; (*escrupuloso*) fussy, overparticular.

ninfa ['ninfa] *nf* nymph.

ninfómana [nin'fomana] *nf* nymphomaniac.

ninguno, a [nin'guno, a], **ningún** [nin-'gun] *a no* // *pron* (*nadie*) nobody; (*ni uno*) none, not one; (*ni uno ni otro*) neither; **de** ~**a manera** by no means, not at all.

niña ['nina] *nf ver* **niño**.

niñera [ni'nera] *nf* nursemaid, nanny; **niñería** *nf* childish act.

niñez [ni'neθ] *nf* childhood; (*infancia*) infancy.

niño, a ['nino, a] *a* (*joven*) young; (*inmaduro*) immature // *nm* (*chico*) boy, child // *nf* (*chica*) girl, child; (ANAT) pupil.

nipón, ona [ni'pon, ona] *a, nm/f* Japanese.

níquel ['nikel] *nm* nickel; **niquelar** *vt* (TEC) to nickel-plate.

nitidez [niti'ðeθ] *nf* (*claridad*) clarity; (: *de atmósfera*) brightness; (: *de imagen*) sharpness; **nítido, a** *a* clear; sharp.

nitrato [ni'trato] *nm* nitrate.

nitrógeno [ni'troxeno] *nm* nitrogen.

nitroglicerina [nitroɣliθe'rina] *nf* nitroglycerine.

nivel [ni'ßel] *nm* (GEO) level; (*norma*) level, standard; (*altura*) height; ~ **de aceite** oil level; ~ **de aire** spirit level; ~ **de vida** standard of living; ~**ar** *vt*

(*terreno*) to level out; (*equilibrar: mueble*) to even up; (COM) to balance.

NN. UU. *nfpl abr de* **Naciones Unidas** U.N. *sg* (United Nations).

no [no] *ad* no; not; (*con verbo*) not // *excl* no!; ~ **tengo nada** I don't have anything, I have nothing; ~ **es el mío** it's not mine; **ahora** ~ not now; ¿~ **lo sabes?** don't you know?; ~ **mucho** not much; ~ **bien termine, lo entregaré** as soon as I finish I'll hand it over; ¡**a que** ~ **lo sabes!** I bet you don't know!; ¡**cuándo** o **cómo** ~! of course!; **los países** ~ **alineados** the non-aligned countries; **el** ~ **conformismo** non-conformism; **la** ~ **intervención** non-intervention.

NO *abr de* **noroeste**.

no. *abr de* **número**.

noble ['noßle] *a, nm/f* noble; ~**za** *nf* nobility.

noción [no'θjon] *nf* notion.

nocivo, a [no'θißo, a] *a* harmful.

noctambulismo [noktamßu'lismo] *nm* sleepwalking; **noctámbulo, a** *nm/f* sleepwalker.

nocturno, a [nok'turno, a] *a* (*de la noche*) nocturnal, night *cpd*; (*de la tarde*) evening *cpd* // *nm* nocturne.

noche ['notʃe] *nf* night, night-time; (*la tarde*) evening; (*fig*) darkness; **de** ~, **por la** ~ at night.

nochebuena [notʃe'ßwena] *nf* Christmas Eve.

nochevieja [notʃe'ßjexa] *nf* New Year's Eve.

nodriza [no'ðriθa] *nf* wet nurse.

nogal [no'ɣal] *nm* walnut tree.

nómada ['nomaða] *a* nomadic // *nm/f* nomad.

nombradía [nombra'ðia] *nf* fame.

nombramiento [nombra'mjento] *nm* naming; (*a un empleo*) appointment.

nombrar [nom'brar] *vt* (*designar*) to name; (*mencionar*) to mention; (*dar puesto a*) to appoint.

nombre [nombre] *nm* name; (*sustantivo*) noun; (*fama*) renown; ~ **y apellidos** name in full; ~ **común/propio** common/proper noun; ~ **de pila/de soltera** Christian/maiden name.

nomenclatura [nomenkla'tura] *nf* nomenclature.

nomeolvides [nomeol'ßiðes] *nm inv* forget-me-not.

nómina ['nomina] *nf* (*lista*) list; (COM) payroll.

nominal [nomi'nal] *a* nominal.

nominativo, a [nomina'tißo, a] *a* (COM): **cheque** ~ **a X** cheque made out to X.

non [non] *a* odd, uneven // *nm* odd number.

nonada [no'naða] *nf* trifle.

nono, a ['nono, a] *a* ninth.

nordeste [nor'ðeste] *a* north-east, north-eastern, north-easterly // *nm* north-east.

nórdico, a ['norðiko, a] *a* (*del norte*) northern, northerly; (*escandinavo*) Nordic.

noria ['norja] *nf* (AGR) waterwheel; (*de carnaval*) big wheel.

normal [nor'mal] *a* (*corriente*) normal; (*habitual*) usual, natural; **(gasolina)** ~ two-star petrol; **~idad** *nf* normality; **restablecer la ~idad** to restore order; **~izar** *vt* (*reglamentar*) to normalize; (TEC) to standardize; **~izarse** *vr* to return to normal.

normando, a [nor'mando, a] *a, nm/f* Norman.

noroeste [noro'este] *a* north-west, north-western, north-westerly // *nm* north-west.

norte ['norte] *a* north, northern, northerly // *nm* north; (*fig*) guide.

norteamericano, a [norteameri'kano, a] *a, nm/f* (North) American.

noruego, a [no'rweɣo, a] *a, nm/f* Norwegian; **N~a** *nf* Norway.

nos [nos] *pron* (*directo*) us; (*indirecto*) us; to us; for us; from us; (*reflexivo*) (to) ourselves; (*recíproco*) (to) each other; **~ levantamos a las 7** we get up at 7.

nosotros [no'sotros] *pron* (*sujeto*) we; (*después de prep*) us.

nostalgia [nos'talxja] *nf* nostalgia.

nota ['nota] *nf* note; (ESCOL) mark.

notabilidad [notaßili'ðað] *nf* (*persona*) notable.

notable [no'taßle] *a, nm/f* notable.

notación [nota'θjon] *nf* (*nota*) note; (MAT, MUS) notation.

notar [no'tar] *vt* (*advertir*) to notice, note; (*anotar, asentar*) to note (down); (*censurar*) to criticize; **~se** *vr* to be obvious.

notarial [nota'rjal] *a*: **acta ~** affidavit.

notario [no'tarjo] *nm* notary.

noticia [no'tiθja] *nf* (*información*) piece of news; **las ~s** the news *sg*; **tener ~s de alguien** to hear from sb.

noticiar [noti'θjar] *vt* to notify; **~io** *nm* (CINE) newsreel; (TV) news bulletin; **noticioso, a** *a* well-informed.

notificación [notifika'θjon] *nf* notification; **notificar** *vt* to notify, inform.

notoriedad [notorje'ðað] *nf* fame, renown; **notorio, a** *a* (*público*) well-known; (*evidente*) obvious.

novato, a [no'ßato, a] *a* inexperienced // *nm/f* beginner.

novecientos [noße'θjentos] *num* nine hundred.

novedad [noße'ðað] *nf* (*calidad de nuevo*) newness; (*noticia*) piece of news; (*cambio*) change, (new) development.

novedoso, a [noße'ðoso, a] *a* novel.

novel [no'ßel] *a* new; (*inexperto*) inexperienced // *nm/f* beginner.

novela [no'ßela] *nf* novel.

novelero, a [noße'lero, a] *a* highly imaginative; (*voluble*) fickle; (*chismoso*) gossipy.

novelesco, a [noße'lesko, a] *a* fictional; (*romántico*) romantic; (*fantástico*) fantastic.

noveno, a [no'ßeno, a] *a* ninth.

noventa [no'ßenta] *num* ninety.

novia ['noßja] *nf ver* **novio.**

noviazgo [no'ßjaθɣo] *nm* engagement.

novicio, a [no'ßiθjo, a] *nm/f* novice.

noviembre [no'ßjembre] *nm* November.

novilla [no'ßiʎa] *nf* heifer; **~da** *nf* (TAUR) *bullfight with young bulls*; **novillero** *nm* novice bullfighter; **novillo** *nm* young bull; **hacer novillos** (*fam*) to play truant.

novio, a ['noßjo, a] *nm/f* boyfriend/girlfriend; (*prometido*) fiancé/fiancée; (*recién casado*) bridegroom/bride; **los ~s** the newly-weds.

N. S. *abr de* **Nuestro Señor.**

nubarrón [nußa'rron] *nm* storm cloud.

nube ['nuße] *nf* cloud.

nublado, a [nu'ßlaðo, a] *a* cloudy // *nm* storm cloud; **nublar** *vt* (*oscurecer*) to darken; (*confundir*) to cloud; **nublarse** *vr* to grow dark.

nuca ['nuka] *nf* nape of the neck.

nuclear [nukle'ar] *a* nuclear.

núcleo ['nukleo] *nm* (*centro*) core; (FÍSICA) nucleus.

nudillo [nu'ðiʎo] *nm* knuckle.

nudo ['nuðo] *nm* (*gen*) knot; (*unión*) bond; (*de problema*) crux; (*de comunicaciones*) centre; **~so, a** *a* knotty.

nuera ['nwera] *nf* daughter-in-law.

nuestro, a ['nwestro, a] *det* our // *pron* ours; **~ padre** our father; **un amigo ~** a friend of ours; **es el ~** it's ours.

nueva ['nweßa] *nf ver* **nuevo.**

nuevamente [nweßa'mente] *ad* (*otra vez*) again; (*de nuevo*) anew.

nueve ['nweße] *num* nine.

nuevo, a ['nweßo, a] *a* (*gen*) new // *nf* piece of news; **de ~** again; **N~a York** *n* New York; **N~a Zelandia** *nf* New Zealand.

nuez [nweθ] (*pl* **nueces**) *nf* (*fruto*) nut; (*del nogal*) walnut; **~ de Adán** Adam's apple; **~ moscada** nutmeg.

nulidad [nuli'ðað] *nf* (*incapacidad*) incompetence; (*abolición*) nullity.

nulo, a ['nulo, a] *a* (*inepto, torpe*) useless; (*inválido*) (null and) void; (DEPORTE) drawn, tied.

núm. *abr de* **número.**

numen ['numen] *nm* inspiration.

numeración [numera'θjon] *nf* (*cifras*) numbers *pl*; (*arábiga, romana etc*) numerals *pl.*

numeral [nume'ral] *nm* numeral.

numerar [nume'rar] *vt* to number.

numerario [nume'rarjo] *nm* hard cash.

numérico, a [nu'meriko, a] *a* numerical.

número ['numero] *nm* (*gen*) number; (*tamaño: de zapato*) size; (*ejemplar: de diario*) number, issue; **sin ~** numberless, unnumbered; **~ de matrícula/telefónico** registration/telephone number; **~ atrasado** back number.

numeroso, a [nume'roso, a] *a* numerous.

nunca ['nunka] *ad* (*jamás*) never; **~ lo pensé** I never thought it; **no vino ~** he

never came; ~ más never again.
nuncio ['nunθjo] nm (REL) nuncio.
nupcias ['nupθjas] nfpl wedding sg,
nuptials.
nutria ['nutrja] nf otter.
nutrición [nutri'θjon] nf nutrition.
nutrido, a [nu'triðo, a] a (alimentado)
nourished; (fig: grande) large; (abundante)
abundant.
nutrir [nu'trir] vt (alimentar) to nourish;
(dar de comer) to feed; (alentar) to
encourage; (esperanzas) to cherish;
nutritivo, a a nourishing, nutritious.
nylon [ni'lon] nm nylon.

Ñ

ñame ['ɲame] nm yam.
ñaque ['ɲake] nm junk.
ñato, a ['ɲato, a] a (AM) snub-nosed.
ñoñería [ɲoɲe'ria], **ñoñez** [ɲo'ɲeθ] nf
insipidness.
ñoño, a ['ɲoɲo, a] a (AM: tonto) silly, stupid;
(soso) insipid; (persona) spineless.

O

o [o] conj or.
O abr de **oeste**.
o/ abr de **orden**.
oasis [o'asis] nm oasis.
obcecar [oβθe'kar] vt to blind.
obedecer [oβeðe'θer] vt to obey;
obediencia nf obedience; **obediente** a
obedient.
obertura [oβer'tura] nf overture.
obesidad [oβesi'ðað] nf obesity; **obeso, a** a
obese.
obispo [o'βispo] nm bishop.
objeción [oβxe'θjon] nf objection; **objetar**
vt, vi to object.
objetivo, a [oβxe'tiβo, a] a, nm objective.
objeto [oβ'xeto] nm (cosa) object; (fin)
aim.
oblicuo, a [o'βlikwo, a] a oblique; (mirada)
sidelong.
obligación [oβlixa'θjon] nf obligation;
(COM) bond.
obligar [oβli'xar] vt to force; ~se vr to
bind o.s.; **obligatorio, a** a compulsory,
obligatory.
oboe [o'βoe] nm oboe.
obra ['oβra] nf (gen) work; (hechura) piece
of work; (ARQ) construction, building;
(TEATRO) play; ~ **maestra** masterpiece;
(Ministerio de) O~s Públicas Ministry
of Public Works; **en** ~ **de** in about; **por**
~ **de** thanks to (the efforts of); **obrar** vt
to work; (tener efecto) to have an effect on
// vi to act, behave; (tener efecto) to have
an effect; **la carta obra en su poder** the
letter is in his/her possession; **obrero, a** a
working, labour cpd; **clase obrera**
working class // nm/f (gen) worker; (sin
oficio) labourer.

obscenidad [oβsθeni'ðað] nf obscenity;
obsceno, a a obscene.
obscu... = oscu... .
obsequiar [oβse'kjar] vt (ofrecer) to
present with; (agasajar) to make a fuss of,
lavish attention on; **obsequio** nm (regalo)
gift; (cortesía) courtesy, attention;
obsequioso, a a attentive.
observación [oβserβa'θjon] nf
observation; (reflexión) remark.
observancia [oβser'βanθja] nf
observance.
observar [oβser'βar] vt to observe;
(anotar) to notice; ~se vr to keep to,
observe.
obsesión [oβse'sjon] nf obsession;
obsesionar vt to obsess.
obstaculizar [oβstakuli'θar] vt (dificultar)
to hinder; (impedir) to stand in the way of.
obstáculo [oβ'stakulo] nm (gen) obstacle;
(impedimento) hindrance, drawback.
obstante [oβ'stante]: **no** ~ ad
nevertheless // prep in spite of.
obstar [oβ'star] vi: ~ **a** to hinder.
obstetricia [oβste'triθja] nf obstetrics sg;
obstétrico, a a obstetric // nm/f
obstetrician.
obstinado, a [oβsti'naðo, a] a (gen)
obstinate; (terco) stubborn.
obstinarse [oβsti'narse] vr to be
obstinate; ~ **en** to persist in.
obstrucción [oβstruk'θjon] nf obstruction;
obstruir vt to obstruct.
obtener [oβte'ner] vt (conseguir) to
obtain; (ganar) to gain.
obtuso, a [oβ'tuso, a] a (filo) blunt; (MAT,
fig) obtuse.
obviar [oβ'βjar] vt to clear away // vi to
stand in the way.
obvio, a ['oββjo, a] a obvious.
ocasión [oka'sjon] nf (oportunidad)
opportunity, chance; (momento) occasion,
time; (causa) cause; **de** ~ secondhand;
ocasionar vt to cause.
ocaso [o'kaso] nm (oeste) west; (fig)
decline.
occidente [okθi'ðente] nm west.
océano [o'θeano] nm ocean; **el** ~ **Índico**
the Indian Ocean.
O.C.E.D. nf abr de **Organización de
Cooperación Económica y Desarrollo**
OECD (Organization for Economic
Cooperation and Development).
ocio ['oθjo] nm (tiempo) leisure; (pey)
idleness; ~**s** nmpl pastime sg; ~**sidad** nf
idleness; ~**so, a** a (inactivo) idle; (inútil)
useless.
octanaje [okta'naxe] nm: **de alto** ~ high
octane; **octano** nm octane.
octavín [okta'βin] nm piccolo.
octavo, a [ok'taβo, a] a eighth.
octogenario, a [oktoxe'narjo, a] a
octogenarian.
octubre [ok'tuβre] nm October.
ocular [oku'lar] a ocular, eye cpd; **testigo**
~ eyewitness.

oculista [oku'lista] *nm/f* oculist.

ocultar [okul'tar] *vt* (*esconder*) to hide; (*callar*) to withhold; **oculto, a** *a* hidden; (*fig*) secret.

ocupación [okupa'θjon] *nf* occupation.

ocupado, a [oku'paðo, a] *a* (*persona*) busy; (*sitio*) occupied; (*teléfono*) engaged; **ocupar** *vt* (*gen*) to occupy; **ocuparse** *vr*: **ocuparse con** *o* **de** *o* **en** (*gen*) to concern o.s. with; (*cuidar*) to look after.

ocurrencia [oku'rrenθja] *nf* (*ocasión*) occurrence; (*agudeza*) witticism.

ocurrir [oku'rrir] *vi* to happen; ~**se** *vr*: **se me ocurre que...** it occurs to me that... .

ochenta [o'tʃenta] *num* eighty.

ocho ['otʃo] *num* eight.

odiar [o'ðjar] *vt* to hate; **odio** *nm* (*gen*) hate, hatred; (*disgusto*) dislike; **odioso, a** *a* (*gen*) hateful; (*malo*) nasty.

O.E.A. *nf abr de* **Organización de Estados Americanos** O.A.S. (Organization of American States).

oeste [o'este] *nm* west; **una película del** ~ a western.

ofender [ofen'der] *vt* (*agraviar*) to offend; (*ser ofensivo a*) to be offensive to; ~**se** *vr* to take offence; **ofensa** *nf* offence; **ofensivo, a** *a* (*insultante*) insulting; (*MIL*) offensive // *nf* offensive.

oferta [o'ferta] *nf* offer; (*propuesta*) proposal; **la** ~ **y la demanda** supply and demand; **artículos en** ~ goods on offer.

oficial [ofi'θjal] *a* official // *nm* official; (*MIL*) officer.

oficina [ofi'θina] *nf* office; **oficinista** *nm/f* clerk.

oficio [o'fiθjo] *nm* (*profesión*) profession; (*puesto*) post; (*REL*) service; **ser del** ~ to be an old hand; **tener mucho** ~ to have a lot of experience; ~ **de difuntos** funeral service; **de** ~ officially.

oficiosidad [ofiθjosi'ðað] *nf* helpfulness; (*pey*) officiousness.

oficioso, a [ofi'θjoso, a] *a* (*diligente*) attentive; (*pey*) officious; (*no oficial*) unofficial, informal.

ofrecer [ofre'θer] *vt* (*dar*) to offer; (*proponer*) to propose; ~**se** *vr* (*persona*) to offer o.s., volunteer; (*situación*) to present itself; **¿qué se le ofrece?, ¿se le ofrece algo?** what can I do for you?, can I get you anything?

ofrecimiento [ofreθi'mjento] *nm* offer, offering.

ofrendar [ofren'dar] *vt* to offer, contribute.

oftálmico, a [of'talmiko, a] *a* ophthalmic.

ofuscación [ofuska'θjon] *nf*, **ofuscamiento** [ofuska'mjento] *nm* (*fig*) bewilderment; **ofuscar** *vt* (*confundir*) to bewilder; (*enceguecer*) to dazzle, blind.

oída [o'iða] *nf* hearing; **de** ~**s** by hearsay.

oído [o'iðo] *nm* ear; (*sentido*) hearing.

oigo *etc vb ver* **oír**.

oír [o'ir] *vt* (*gen*) to hear; (*atender a*) to listen to; **¡oiga!** listen!; ~ **misa** to attend mass.

O.I.T. *nf abr de* **Organización Internacional del Trabajo** I.L.O. (International Labour Organization).

ojal [o'xal] *nm* buttonhole.

ojalá [oxa'la] *excl* if only it were so!, some hope(s)! // *conj* if only...!, would that...!; ~ **que venga hoy** I hope he comes today.

ojeada [oxe'aða] *nf* glance; **ojear** *vt* (*mirar fijo*) to stare at; (*examinar*) to eye; (*mirar de reojo*) to glance at.

ojera [o'xera] *nf*: **tener** ~**s** to have rings or circles under the eyes.

ojeriza [oxe'riθa] *nf* ill-will.

ojeroso, a [oxe'roso, a] *a* haggard.

ojete [o'xete] *nm* eye(let).

ojo ['oxo] *nm* eye; (*de puente*) span; (*de cerradura*) keyhole // *excl* careful!; **tener** ~ **para** to have an eye for; ~ **de buey** porthole.

ola ['ola] *nf* wave.

oié [o'le] *excl* bravo!, olé!

oleada [ole'aða] *nf* big wave, swell; (*fig*) surge.

oleaje [ole'axe] *nm* swell.

óleo ['oleo] *nm* oil; **oleoducto** *nm* (oil) pipeline.

oler [o'ler] *vt* (*gen*) to smell; (*husmear*) to pry into; (*fig*) to sniff out // *vi*: ~ **a** to smell of.

olfatear [olfate'ar] *vt* to smell; (*fig*) to sniff out; (*husmear*) to pry into; **olfato** *nm* sense of smell.

oliente [o'ljente] *a* smelling; **bien/mal** ~ sweet-/foul-smelling.

oligarquía [olixar'kia] *nf* oligarchy.

olimpíada [olim'piaða] *nf*: **las O**~**s** the Olympics.

oliva [o'liβa] *nf* (*aceituna*) olive; (*árbol*) olive tree; **aceite de** ~ olive oil; **olivo** *nm* olive tree.

olmo ['olmo] *nm* elm (tree).

olor [o'lor] *nm* smell; ~**oso, a** *a* scented.

olvidadizo, a [olβiða'ðiθo, a] *a* (*desmemoriado*) forgetful; (*distraído*) absent-minded.

olvidar [olβi'ðar] *vt* to forget; (*omitir*) to omit; ~**se** *vr* to forget o.s.; **se me olvidó** I forgot.

olvido [ol'βiðo] *nm* oblivion.

olla ['oʎa] *nf* pan; (*comida*) stew; ~ **a presión** *o* **autopresión** pressure cooker; ~ **podrida** Spanish stew.

ombligo [om'blixo] *nm* navel.

ominoso, a [omi'noso, a] *a* ominous.

omisión [omi'sjon] *nf* (*abstención*) omission; (*descuido*) neglect.

omiso, a [o'miso, a] *a*: **hacer caso** ~ **de** to ignore, pass over.

omitir [omi'tir] *vt* to omit.

omnipotente [omnipo'tente] *a* omnipotent.

omnívoro, a [om'niβoro, a] *a* omnivorous.

omóplato [o'moplato] *nm* shoulder blade.

O.M.S. *nf abr de* **Organización Mundial**

de la Salud W.H.O. (World Health Organization).

once ['onθe] num eleven; las ~ (fam) elevenses.

onda ['onda] nf wave; ~ corta/larga/media short/long/ medium wave; ~s acústicas/ hertzianas acoustic/Hertzian waves; ondear vt to wave // vi to wave; (tener ondas) to be wavy; (pelo) to flow; (agua) to ripple; ondearse vr to swing, sway.

ondulación [ondula'θjon] nf undulation; ondulado, a a wavy // nm wave; ondulante a undulating; (cartón, chapa) corrugated.

ondular [ondu'lar] vt (el pelo) to wave // vi, ~se vr to undulate.

oneroso, a [one'roso, a] a onerous.

ONU nf abr de Organización de las Naciones Unidas UNO (United Nations Organization).

O.P. nfpl abr de Obras Públicas Public Works.

opaco, a [o'pako, a] a opaque; (fig) dull.

opalescente [opales'θente] a opalescent.

ópalo ['opalo] nm opal.

opción [op'θjon] nf (gen) option; (derecho) right, option.

ópera ['opera] nf opera; ~ bufa o cómica comic opera.

operación [opera'θjon] nf (gen) operation; (COM) transaction, deal.

operador, a [opera'ðor, a] nm/f operator; (en cine) projectionist; (de cine) camera operator.

operante [ope'rante] a operating.

operar [ope'rar] vt (producir) to produce, bring about; (MED) to operate on // vi (COM) to operate, deal; ~se vr to occur; (MED) to have an operation.

opereta [ope'reta] nf operetta.

opinar [opi'nar] vt (estimar) to think // vi (enjuiciar) to give one's opinion; opinión nf (creencia) belief; (criterio) opinion.

opio ['opjo] nm opium.

oponente [opo'nente] nm/f opponent.

oponer [opo'ner] vt (resistencia) to put up, offer; (negativa) to raise; ~se vr (objetar) to object; (estar frente a frente) to be opposed; (dos personas) to oppose each other; ~ A a B to set A against B; me opongo a pensar que... I refuse to believe or think that... .

oportunidad [oportuni'ðað] nf (ocasión) opportunity; (posibilidad) chance.

oportunismo [oportu'nismo] nm opportunism; oportunista nm/f opportunist.

oportuno, a [opor'tuno, a] a (apto) appropriate, suitable; (en su tiempo) opportune; (conveniente) convenient; en el momento ~ at the right moment.

oposición [oposi'θjon] nf opposition; oposiciones nfpl public examinations.

opositor, a [oposi'tor, a] nm/f (adversario) opponent; (concurrente) competitor.

opresión [opre'sjon] nf oppression;

opresivo, a [opre'siβo] a oppressive; opresor, a nm/f oppressor.

oprimir [opri'mir] vt to squeeze; (fig) to oppress.

oprobio [o'proβjo] nm (infamia) ignominy; (descrédito) shame.

optar [op'tar] vi (elegir) to choose; ~ a o por to opt for.

óptico, a ['optiko, a] a optic(al) // nm/f optician.

optimismo [opti'mismo] nm optimism; optimista nm/f optimist.

óptimo, a ['optimo, a] a (bueno) very good; (el mejor) very best.

opuesto, a [o'pwesto, a] a (contrario) opposite; (antagónico) opposing.

opugnar [opux'nar] vt to attack.

opulencia [opu'lenθja] nf opulence; opulento, a a opulent.

oquedad [oke'ðað] nf (fig) void.

ora ['ora] ad: ~ tú ~ yo now you, now me.

oración [ora'θjon] nf (discurso) speech; (REL) prayer; (LING) sentence.

oráculo [o'rakulo] nm oracle.

orador, a [ora'ðor, a] nm/f (predicador) preacher; (conferenciante) speaker.

oral [o'ral] a oral.

orangután [orangu'tan] nm orang-utan.

orar [o'rar] vi (REL) to pray; (hablar) to make a speech.

oratoria [ora'torja] nf oratory.

órbita ['orβita] nf orbit.

orden ['orðen] nm (gen) order // nf (gen) order; ~ del día agenda; de primer ~ first-rate; en ~ de prioridad in order of priority.

ordenado, a [orðe'naðo, a] a (metódico) methodical; (arreglado) orderly.

ordenador [orðena'ðor] nm computer.

ordenanza [orðe'nanθa] nf ordinance.

ordenar [orðe'nar] vt (mandar) to order; (poner orden) to put in order, arrange; ~se vr (REL) to be ordained.

ordeñadora [orðeɲa'ðora] nf milking machine.

ordeñar [orðe'ɲar] vt to milk.

ordinario, a [orði'narjo, a] a (común) ordinary, usual; (bajo) vulgar, common.

orégano [o'rexano] nm oregano.

oreja [o'rexa] nf ear; (de zapatos) tongue; (MECÁNICA) lug, flange.

orfandad [orfan'dað] nf orphanhood.

orfebrería [orfeβre'ria] nf gold/silver work.

organillo [orxa'niʎo] nm barrel organ.

organismo [orxa'nismo] nm (BIO) organism; (POL) organization.

organista [orxa'nista] nm/f organist.

organización [orxaniθa'θjon] nf organization; organizar vt to organize.

órgano ['orxano] nm organ.

orgasmo [or'xasmo] nm orgasm.

orgía [or'xia] nf orgy.

orgullo [or'xuʎo] nm (altanería) pride; (autorespeto) self-respect; orgulloso, a a (*gen*) proud; (*altanero*) haughty.

orientación [orjenta'θjon] *nf* (*posición*) position; (*dirección*) direction; (*entrenamiento*) training.

orientar [orjen'tar] *vt* (*situar*) to orientate; (*señalar*) to point; (*dirigir*) to direct; (*informar*) to guide; ~**se** *vr* to get one's bearings; (*decidirse*) to decide on a course of action.

oriente [o'rjente] *nm* east; **Cercano/Medio/Lejano O**~ Near/Middle/Far East.

origen [o'rixen] *nm* (*germen*) origin; (*nacimiento*) lineage, birth.

original [orixi'nal] *a* (*nuevo*) original; (*extraño*) odd, strange; ~**idad** *nf* originality.

originar [orixi'nar] *vt* to originate; ~**se** *vr* to originate; ~**io, a** *a* (*nativo*) native; (*primordial*) original.

orilla [o'riʎa] *nf* (*borde*) border; (*de río*) bank; (*de bosque, tela*) edge; (*de taza etc*) rim, lip; (*de calle*) pavement; **orillar** *vt* (*bordear*) to skirt, go round; (*resolver*) to wind up; (*tocar: asunto*) to touch briefly on.

orín [o'rin] *nm* rust.

orina [o'rina] *nf* urine; **orinal** *nm* (chamber) pot; **orinar** *vi* to urinate; **orinarse** *vr* to wet o.s.; **orines** *nmpl* urine *sg*.

oriundo, a [o'rjundo, a] *a*: ~ **de** native of.

orlar [or'lar] *vt* (*adornar*) to adorn, decorate; (*encuadrar*) to frame.

ornamentar [ornamen'tar] *vt* (*adornar, ataviar*) to adorn; (*revestir*) to bedeck.

ornamento [orna'mento] *nm* ornament.

ornar [or'nar] *vt* to adorn.

oro ['oro] *nm* gold; ~**s** *nmpl* (*NAIPES*) hearts.

oropel [oro'pel] *nm* tinsel.

orozuz [oro'θuθ] *nm* liquorice.

orquesta [or'kesta] *nf* orchestra; ~ **de cámara/sinfónica** chamber/symphony orchestra.

orquídea [or'kiðea] *nf* orchid.

ortiga [or'tixa] *nf* nettle.

ortodoxo, a [orto'ðokso, a] *a* orthodox.

ortografía [ortoxra'fia] *nf* spelling.

ortopedia [orto'peðja] *nf* orthopaedics *sg*.

oruga [o'ruxa] *nf* caterpillar; (*BOT*) rocket.

orzuelo [or'θwelo] *nm* (*MED*) stye.

os [os] *pron* (*gen*) you; (*a vosotros*) to you.

osa ['osa] *nf* (she-)bear; **O**~ **Mayor/Menor** Great/Little Bear.

osadía [osa'ðia] *nf* daring.

osar [o'sar] *vi* to dare.

oscilación [osθila'θjon] *nf* (*movimiento*) oscillation; (*fluctuación*) fluctuation; (*vacilación*) hesitation; (*columpio*) swinging, movement to and fro; **oscilar** *vi* to oscillate; to fluctuate; to hesitate.

ósculo ['oskulo] *nm* kiss.

oscurecer [oskure'θer] *vt* to darken // *vi* to grow dark; ~**se** *vr* to grow *or* get dark.

oscuridad [oskuri'ðað] *nf* obscurity; (*tinieblas*) darkness.

oscuro, a [os'kuro, a] *a* dark; (*fig*) obscure; **a** ~**as** in the dark.

óseo, a ['oseo, a] *a* bony.

oso ['oso] *nm* bear; ~ **de peluche** teddy bear; ~ **hormiguero** anteater.

ostensible [osten'siβle] *a* obvious.

ostentación [ostenta'θjon] *nf* (*gen*) ostentation; (*acto*) display; **ostentar** *vt* (*gen*) to show; (*pey*) to flaunt, show off; (*poseer*) to have, possess; **ostentoso, a** *a* ostentatious, showy.

osteópata [oste'opata] *nm/f* osteopath.

ostra ['ostra] *nf* oyster.

ostracismo [ostra'θismo] *nm* ostracism.

osuno, a [o'suno, a] *a* bear-like.

OTAN ['otan] *nf* abr de **Organización del Tratado del Atlántico Norte** NATO (North Atlantic Treaty Organization).

otear [ote'ar] *vt* to observe; (*fig*) to look into.

otitis [o'titis] *nf* earache.

otoñal [oto'ɲal] *a* autumnal.

otoño [o'toɲo] *nm* autumn.

otorgamiento [otorxa'mjento] *nm* conferring, granting; (*JUR*) execution.

otorgar [otor'xar] *vt* (*conceder*) to concede; (*dar*) to grant.

otro, a ['otro, a] *a* (*sg*) another; (*pl*) other // *pron* another one; ~**s** others; ~**a cosa** something else; **de** ~**a manera** otherwise; **en** ~ **tiempo** formerly, once; **ni uno ni** ~ neither one nor the other; ~ **tanto** the same again.

ovación [oβa'θjon] *nf* ovation.

oval [o'βal], **ovalado, a** [oβa'laðo, a] *a* oval; **óvalo** *nm* oval.

oveja [o'βexa] *nf* sheep; **ovejuno, a** *a* sheep *cpd*.

overol [oβe'rol] *nm* overalls *pl*.

ovillar [oβi'ʎar] *vt* to wind (into a ball); ~**se** *vr* to curl up into a ball.

OVNI ['oβni] *nm* abr de **objeto volante no identificado** UFO (unidentified flying object).

ovulación [oβula'θjon] *nf* ovulation; **óvulo** *nm* ovum.

oxidación [oksiða'θjon] *nf* rusting; **oxidar** *vt* to rust; **oxidarse** *vr* to become rusty.

óxido ['oksiðo] *nm* oxide.

oxigenado, a [oksixe'naðo, a] *a* (*QUÍMICA*) oxygenated; (*pelo*) bleached // *nm* peroxide.

oxígeno [ok'sixeno] *nm* oxygen.

oyente [o'jente] *nm/f* listener, hearer.

oyes, oyó *etc vb ver* **oír.**

P

P *abr de* **padre.**

pabellón [paβe'ʎon] *nm* bell tent; (*ARQ*) pavilion; (*de hospital etc*) block, section; (*bandera*) flag.

pábilo ['paβilo] *nm* wick.

pacer [pa'θer] *vi* to graze // *vt* to graze on.

paciencia [pa'θjenθja] *nf* patience.

paciente [pa'θjente] *a, nm/f* patient.

pacificación [paθifika'θjon] *nf* pacification; **pacificar** *vt* to pacify; (*tranquilizar*) to calm.

pacífico, a [pa'θifiko, a] *a* (*persona*) peace-loving; (*existencia*) pacific; **el** (**océano**) **P~** the Pacific (Ocean).

pacifismo [paθi'fismo] *nm* pacifism; **pacifista** *nm/f* pacifist.

pactar [pak'tar] *vt* to agree to, agree on // *vi* to come to an agreement.

pacto ['pakto] *nm* (*tratado*) pact; (*acuerdo*) agreement.

padecer [paðe'θer] *vt* (*sufrir*) to suffer; (*soportar*) to endure, put up with; (*ser víctima de*) to be a victim of; **padecimiento** *nm* suffering.

padrastro [pa'ðrastro] *nm* stepfather.

padre ['paðre] *nm* father // *a* (*fam*): **un éxito** ~ a tremendous success; ~**s** *nmpl* parents.

padrino [pa'ðrino] *nm* (*REL*) godfather; (*fig*) sponsor, patron; ~**s** *nmpl* godparents; ~ **de boda** best man.

padrón [pa'ðron] *nm* (*censo*) census, roll; (*de socios*) register; (*TEC*) pattern.

paella [pa'eʎa] *nf* paella, *dish of rice with meat, shellfish etc.*

paga ['paɣa] *nf* (*dinero pagado*) payment; (*sueldo*) pay, wages *pl.*

pagadero, a [paɣa'ðero, a] *a* payable; ~ **a la entrega/a plazos** payable on delivery/in instalments.

pagador, a [paɣa'ðor, a] *nm/f* (*quien paga*) payer; (*cajero*) cashier.

pagano, a [pa'ɣano, a] *a, nm/f* pagan, heathen.

pagar [pa'ɣar] *vt* (*gen*) to pay; (*las compras, crimen*) to pay for; (*fig: favor*) to repay // *vi* to pay; ~ **al contado/a plazos** to pay (in) cash/in instalments; ~**se** *vr*: ~**se con algo** to be content with sth; ~**se de sí mismo** to be conceited.

pagaré [paɣa're] *nm* I.O.U.

página ['paxina] *nf* page.

pago ['paɣo] *nm* (*dinero*) payment; (*fig*) return; (*barrio*) district; (*AM*) home region, home area; **estar** ~ to be even *or* quits; ~ **anticipado/a cuenta/a la entrega/en especie** advance payment/payment on account/cash on delivery/payment in kind.

país [pa'is] *nm* (*gen*) country; (*región*) land; (*paisaje*) landscape; **los P~es Bajos** the Low Countries; **el P~ Vasco** the Basque Country; **paisaje** *nm* countryside, scenery.

paisano, a [pai'sano, a] *a* of the same country // *nm/f* (*compatriota*) fellow countryman/woman; (*campesino*) peasant; **vestir de** ~ (*soldado*) to be in civvies (*fam*); (*guardia*) to be in plain clothes.

paja ['paxa] *nf* straw; (*fig*) trash, rubbish.

pájara ['paxara] *nf* hen bird; (*cometa*) kite; (*mujer*) thief.

pájaro ['paxaro] *nm* bird.

pajita [pa'xita] *nf* (drinking) straw.

pala ['pala] *nf* (*de mango largo*) spade; (*de mango corto*) shovel; (*raqueta etc*) bat; (: *de tenis*) racquet; (*CULIN*) slice; ~ **matamoscas** fly swat.

palabra [pa'laβra] *nf* (*gen*) word; (*facultad*) (power of) speech; (*derecho de hablar*) right to speak; **palabrota** *nf* swearword.

palacio [pa'laθjo] *nm* palace; (*mansión*) mansion, large house; ~ **de justicia** courthouse; ~ **municipal** town/city hall.

paladar [pala'ðar] *nm* (*gen*) palate; **paladear** *vt* to taste.

palanca [pa'lanka] *nf* lever; (*fig*) pull, influence.

palangana [palan'gana] *nf* washbasin.

palco ['palko] *nm* box.

palenque [pa'lenke] *nm* (*cerca*) stockade, fence; (*área*) arena, enclosure; (*de gallos*) pit.

Palestina [pales'tina] *nf* Palestine.

paliar [pa'ljar] *vt* (*mitigar*) to mitigate; (*disfrazar*) to conceal; **paliativo** *nm* palliative.

palidecer [paliðe'θer] *vi* to turn pale; **palidez** *nf* paleness; **pálido, a** *a* pale.

palillo [pa'liʎo] *nm* small stick; (*para dientes*) toothpick.

paliza [pa'liθa] *nf* beating, thrashing.

palizada [pali'θaða] *nf* fence; (*lugar cercado*) enclosure.

palma ['palma] *nf* (*ANAT*) palm; (*árbol*) palm tree; **batir** *o* **dar** ~**s** to clap, applaud; ~**da** *nf* slap; ~**s** *nfpl* clapping *sg*, applause *sg.*

palmear [palme'ar] *vi* to clap.

palmo ['palmo] *nm* (*medida*) span; (*fig*) small amount; ~ **a** ~ inch by inch.

palmotear [palmote'ar] *vi* to clap, applaud; **palmoteo** *nm* clapping, applause; (*palmada*) slap.

palo ['palo] *nm* stick; (*poste*) post, pole; (*mango*) handle, shaft; (*golpe*) blow, hit; (*de golf*) club; (*de béisbol*) bat; (*NAUT*) mast; (*NAIPES*) suit; ~ **de tienda** tent pole.

paloma [pa'loma] *nf* dove, pigeon.

palomilla [palo'miʎa] *nf* moth; (*TEC: tuerca*) wing nut; (: *hierro*) angle iron.

palomitas [palo'mitas] *nfpl* popcorn *sg.*

palpar [pal'par] *vt* to touch, feel; (*acariciar*) to caress, fondle; (*caminar a tientas*) to grope one's way along; (*fig*) to appreciate, understand; ~ **a uno** to frisk sb.

palpitación [palpita'θjon] *nf* palpitation; **palpitante** *a* palpitating; (*fig*) burning; **palpitar** *vi* to palpitate; (*latir*) to beat.

palúdico, a [pa'luðiko, a] *a* marshy.

paludismo [palu'ðismo] *nm* malaria.

pampa ['pampa] *nf* (*AM*) pampa(s), prairie.

pan [pan] *nm* (*en general*) bread; (*una barra*) loaf; (*trigo*) wheat; **de** ~ **llevar** arable; ~ **integral** wholemeal bread; ~ **molido** breadcrumbs *pl.*

pana ['pana] *nf* corduroy.

panadería [panaðe'ria] *nf* baker's (shop); **panadero, a** *nm/f* baker.

Panamá [pana'ma] *nm* Panama; **panameño, a** *a* Panamanian.
pancarta [pan'karta] *nf* placard, banner.
panda ['panda] *nf* panda.
pandereta [pande'reta] *nf* tambourine.
pandilla [pan'diʎa] *nf* set, group; (*de criminales*) gang; (*pey*) clique.
pando, a ['pando, a] *a* sagging.
panel [pa'nel] *nm* panel.
pánico ['paniko] *nm* panic.
panorama [pano'rama] *nm* panorama; (*vista*) view.
pantalones [panta'lones] *nmpl* trousers.
pantalla [pan'taʎa] *nf* (*de cine*) screen; (*cubre-luz*) lampshade.
pantano [pan'tano] *nm* (*ciénaga*) marsh, swamp; (*depósito: de agua*) reservoir; (*fig*) jam, fix, difficulty.
pantera [pan'tera] *nf* panther.
pantimedias [panti'meðjas] *nfpl* tights.
pantomima [panto'mima] *nf* pantomime.
pantorrilla [panto'rriʎa] *nf* calf (of the leg).
pantufla [pan'tufla] *nf* slipper.
panza ['panθa] *nf* belly, paunch; **panzudo, a, panzón, ona** *a* fat, potbellied.
pañal [pa'ɲal] *nm* nappy; ~**es** *nmpl* (*fig*) early stages, infancy *sg*.
pañería [paɲe'ria] *nf* drapery; **pañero, a** *nm/f* draper.
paño ['paɲo] *nm* (*tela*) cloth; (*pedazo de tela*) (piece of) cloth; (*trapo*) duster, rag; ~ **higiénico** sanitary towel; ~**s menores** underclothes.
pañuelo [pa'ɲwelo] *nm* handkerchief, hanky (*fam*); (*para la cabeza*) (head)scarf.
papa ['papa] *nf* (*AM*) potato // *nm*: **el P**~ the Pope.
papá [pa'pa] (*pl* ~**s**) *nm* (*fam*) dad, daddy.
papagayo [papa'ʁajo] *nm* parrot.
papamoscas [papa'moskas] *nm inv* fly-catcher.
papanatas [papa'natas] *nm inv* (*fam*) sucker, simpleton.
papar [pa'par] *vt* to swallow, gulp (down).
paparrucha [papa'rrutʃa] *nf* (*tontería*) piece of nonsense; (*engaño*) hoax.
papaya [pa'paja] *nf* papaya.
papel [pa'pel] *nm* (*en general*) paper; (*hoja de papel*) sheet of paper; (*TEATRO*) part, role; ~ **de calcar/carbón/de cartas** tracing paper/carbon paper/stationery; ~ **de envolver/de empapelar** brown paper, wrapping paper/wallpaper; ~ **de estaño/higiénico** tinfoil/toilet paper; ~ **de lija** sandpaper; ~ **moneda** paper money; ~ **secante** blotting paper.
papeleo [pape'leo] *nm* red tape.
papelera [pape'lera] *nf* (*cesto*) wastepaper basket; (*escritorio*) desk.
papelería [papele'ria] *nf* (*papeles*) mass of papers; (*tienda*) stationer's (shop).
papeleta [pape'leta] *nf* (*pedazo de papel*) slip *or* bit of paper; (*tarjeta de archivo*) index card; (*POL*) ballot paper; (*ESCOL*) report.

paperas [pa'peras] *nfpl* mumps.
paquete [pa'kete] *nm* (*caja*) packet; (*bulto*) parcel; (*AM, fam*) nuisance, bore.
par [par] *a* (*igual*) like, equal; (*MAT*) even // *nm* equal; (*de guantes*) pair; (*de veces*) couple; (*dignidad*) peer; (*GOLF, COM*) par; **abrir de** ~ **en** ~ to open wide.
para ['para] *prep* (*gen*) for; **no es** ~ **comer** it's not for eating; **decir** ~ **sí** to say to o.s.; ¿~ **qué lo quieres?** what do you want it for?; **se casaron** ~ **separarse otra vez** they married only to separate again; **lo tendré** ~ **mañana** I'll have it for tomorrow; **ir** ~ **casa** to go home, head for home; ~ **profesor es muy estúpido** he's very stupid for a teacher; ¿**quién es usted** ~ **gritar así?** who are you to shout like that?; **tengo bastante** ~ **vivir** I have enough to live on; **estoy** ~ **cantar** I'm about to sing.
parabién [para'βjen] *nm* congratulations *pl*.
parábola [pa'raβola] *nf* parable; (*MAT*) parabola.
parabrisas [para'βrisas] *nm inv* windscreen.
paracaídas [paraka'iðas] *nm inv* parachute; **paracaidista** *nm/f* parachutist; (*MIL*) paratrooper.
parachoques [para'tʃokes] *nm inv* bumper; (*en auto*) shock absorber.
parada [pa'raða] *nf ver* **parado**.
paradero [para'ðero] *nm* stopping-place; (*situación*) whereabouts; (*fin*) end.
parado, a [pa'raðo, a] *a* (*persona*) motionless, standing still; (*fábrica*) closed, at a standstill; (*coche*) stopped; (*AM*) standing (up); (*sin empleo*) unemployed, idle; (*confuso*) confused // *nf* (*gen*) stop; (*acto*) stopping; (*de industria*) shutdown, stoppage; (*de pagos*) suspension; (*lugar*) stopping-place; (*apuesta*) bet; ~**a de autobús** bus stop.
paradoja [para'ðoxa] *nf* paradox.
parador [para'ðor] *nm* (*luxury*) hotel.
paráfrasis [pa'rafrasis] *nm inv* paraphrase.
paragolpes [para'ʁolpes] *nm inv* bumper.
paraguas [pa'raʁwas] *nm inv* umbrella.
Paraguay [para'ʁwai] *nm*: **el** ~ Paraguay.
paraíso [para'iso] *nm* paradise, heaven.
paraje [pa'raxe] *nm* place, spot.
paralelo, a [para'lelo, a] *a* parallel.
parálisis [pa'ralisis] *nf* paralysis; **paralítico, a** *a, nm/f* paralytic; **paralizar** *vt* to paralyse; **paralizarse** *vr* to become paralysed; (*fig*) to come to a standstill.
paramilitar [paramili'tar] *a* para-military.
páramo ['paramo] *nm* bleak plateau.
parangón [paran'gon] *nm*: **sin** ~ incomparable.
paranoico, a [para'noiko, a] *nm/f* paranoiac.
parapléjico, a [para'plexiko, a] *a, nm/f* paraplegic.

parar [pa'rar] *vt* to stop; (*golpe*) to ward off // *vi* to stop; ~**se** *vr* to stop; (AM) to stand up; **ha parado de llover** it has stopped raining; **van a ~ en la comisaria** they're going to end up in the police station; ~**se en** to pay attention to.

parásito, a [pa'rasito, a] *nm/f* parasite.

parasol [para'sol] *nm* parasol, sunshade.

parcela [par'θela] *nf* plot, piece of ground.

parcial [par'θjal] *a* (*pago*) part-; (*eclipse*) partial; (*juez*) prejudiced, biased; ~**idad** *nf* (*prejuicio*) prejudice, bias; (*partido, facción*) party, faction.

parco, a ['parko, a] *a* (*frugal*) frugal; (*mezquino*) mean; (*moderado*) moderate.

parche ['partʃe] *nm* (MED) sticking plaster; (*gen*) patch.

parear [pare'ar] *vt* (*juntar, hacer par*) to match, put together; (*calcetines*) to put into pairs; (BIO) to mate, pair.

parecer [pare'θer] *nm* (*opinión*) opinion, view; (*aspecto*) looks *pl* // *vi* (*tener apariencia*) to seem, look; (*asemejarse*) to look like, seem like; (*aparecer, llegar*) to appear; ~**se** *vr* to look alike, resemble each other; ~**se a** to look like, resemble; **según o a lo que parece** evidently, apparently; **me parece que** I think (that), it seems to me that; **parecido, a** *a* similar // *nm* similarity, likeness, resemblance; **bien parecido** good-looking, nice-looking.

pared [pa'reð] *nf* wall.

parejo, a [pa'rexo, a] *a* (*igual*) equal; (*liso*) smooth, even // *nf* (*dos*) pair; (: *de personas*) couple; (*el otro: de un par*) other one (of a pair); (: *persona*) partner.

parentela [paren'tela] *nf* relations *pl*.

parentesco [paren'tesko] *nm* relationship.

paréntesis [pa'rentesis] *nm inv* parenthesis; (*digresión*) digression; (*en escrito*) bracket.

parezco *etc vb ver* **parecer.**

pariente, a [pa'rjente, a] *nm/f* relative, relation.

parihuela [pari'wela] *nf* stretcher.

parir [pa'rir] *vt* to give birth to // *vi* (*mujer*) to give birth, have a baby.

París [pa'ris] *n* Paris.

parlamentar [parlamen'tar] *vi* (*hablar*) to talk, converse; (*negociar*) to parley.

parlamentario, a [parlamen'tarjo, a] *a* parliamentary // *nm/f* member of parliament.

parlamento [parla'mento] *nm* (POL) parliament; (*conversación*) parley.

parlanchín, ina [parlan'tʃin, ina] *a* loose-tongued, indiscreet // *nm/f* chatterbox.

parlar [par'lar] *vi* to chatter (away), talk (a lot); (*chismear*) to gossip; **parlero, a** *a* talkative; gossipy; (*pájaro*) singing.

paro ['paro] *nm* (*huelga*) stoppage (of work), strike; (*desempleo*) unemployment; **subsidio de ~** unemployment benefit; **hay ~ en la industria** work in the industry is at a standstill.

parodia [pa'roðja] *nf* parody; **parodiar** *vt* to parody.

parpadear [parpaðe'ar] *vi* (*los ojos*) to blink; (*luz*) to flicker.

párpado ['parpaðo] *nm* eyelid.

parque ['parke] *nm* (*lugar verde*) park; (*depósito*) depot; ~ **de atracciones/de estacionamiento/zoológico** fairground/car park/zoo.

parquímetro [par'kimetro] *nm* parking meter.

párrafo ['parrafo] *nm* paragraph; **echar un ~** (*fam*) to have a chat.

parranda [pa'rranda] *nf* (*fam*) spree, binge.

parrilla [pa'rriʎa] *nf* (CULIN) grill; (*de coche*) grille; (**carne de**) ~ barbecue; ~**da** *nf* barbecue.

párroco ['parroko] *nm* parish priest.

parroquia [pa'rrokja] *nf* parish; (*iglesia*) parish church; (COM) clientele, customers *pl*; ~**no, a** *nm/f* parishioner; client, customer.

parte ['parte] *nm* message; (*informe*) report // *nf* (*gen*) part; (*lado, cara*) side; (*de reparto*) share; (JUR) party; **en alguna ~ de Europa** somewhere in Europe; **en cualquier ~** anywhere; **en gran ~** to a large extent; **la mayor ~ de los españoles** most Spaniards; **de algún tiempo a esta ~** for some time past; **de ~ de alguien** on sb's behalf; **por ~ de** on the part of; **yo por mi ~** I for my part; **por otra ~** on the other hand; **dar ~ to** inform; **tomar ~** to take part.

partera [par'tera] *nf* midwife.

partición [parti'θjon] *nf* division, sharing-out; (POL) partition.

participación [partiθipa'θjon] *nf* (*acto*) participation, taking part; (*parte, COM*) share; (*de lotería*) small prize; (*aviso*) notice, notification.

participante [partiθi'pante] *nm/f* participant; **participar** *vt* to notify, inform // *vi* to take part, participate; (*compartir*) to share.

partícipe [par'tiθipe] *nm/f* participant.

particular [partiku'lar] *a* (*especial*) particular, special; (*individual, personal*) private, personal // *nm* (*punto, asunto*) particular, point; (*individuo*) individual; **tiene coche ~** he has a car of his own; ~**izar** *vt* to distinguish; (*especificar*) to specify; (*detallar*) to give details about.

partida [par'tiða] *nf* (*salida*) departure; (COM) entry, item; (*juego*) game; (*apuesta*) bet; (*grupo, bando*) band, group; **mala ~** dirty trick; ~ **de nacimiento/matrimonio/defunción** birth/marriage/death certificate.

partidario, a [parti'ðarjo, a] *a* partisan // *nm/f* (DEPORTE) supporter; (POL) partisan.

partido [par'tiðo] *nm* (POL) party; (*encuentro*) game, match; (*apoyo*) support; (*equipo*) team; **sacar ~ de** to profit from, benefit from; **tomar ~** to take sides.

partir [par'tir] *vt* (*dividir*) to split, divide;

(*compartir*, *distribuir*) to share (out), distribute; (*romper*) to break open, split open; (*rebanada*) to cut (off) // *vi* (*tomar camino*) to set off, set out; (*comenzar*) to start (off *or* out); ~**se** *vr* to crack *or* split *or* break (in two *etc*); **a** ~ **de** (starting) from.

parto ['parto] *nm* birth; (*fig*) product, creation; **estar de** ~ to be in labour.

parvulario [parβu'larjo] *nm* nursery school, kindergarten.

pasa ['pasa] *nf* raisin; ~ **de Corinto/de Esmirna** currant/sultana.

pasada [pa'saða] *nf ver* **pasado.**

pasadizo [pasa'ðiθo] *nm* (*pasillo*) passage, corridor; (*callejuela*) alley.

pasado, a [pa'saðo, a] *a* past; (*malo*: *comida*, *fruta*) bad; (*muy cocido*) overdone; (*anticuado*) out of date // *nm* past // *nf* passing, passage; (*acción de pulir*) rub, polish; ~**s** *nmpl* ancestors; ~ **mañana** the day after tomorrow; **el mes** ~ last month; **de** ~**a** in passing, incidentally; **una mala** ~**a** a dirty trick.

pasador [pasa'ðor] *nm* (*gen*) bolt; (*de pelo*) pin, grip; ~**es** *nmpl* cufflinks.

pasaje [pa'saxe] *nm* (*gen*) passage; (*pago de viaje*) fare; (*los pasajeros*) passengers *pl*; (*pasillo*) passageway.

pasajero, a [pasa'xero, a] *a* passing; (*calle*) busy // *nm/f* passenger; (*viajero*) traveller.

pasamanos [pasa'manos] *nm* rail, handrail; (*de escalera*) banister.

pasaporte [pasa'porte] *nm* passport.

pasar [pa'sar] *vt* (*gen*) to pass; (*tiempo*) to spend; (*durezas*) to suffer, endure; (*noticia*) to give, pass on; (*río*) to cross; (*barrera*) to pass through; (*falta*) to overlook, tolerate; (*contrincante*) to surpass, do better than; (*coche*) to overtake; (*enfermedad*) to give, infect with // *vi* (*gen*) to pass; (*terminarse*) to be over; (*ocurrir*) to happen; ~**se** *vr* (*flores*) to fade; (*comida*) to go bad, go off; (*fig*) to overdo it, go too far; ~ **de** to go beyond, exceed; **¡pase!** come in!; ~**se al enemigo** to go over to the enemy; **se me pasó** I forgot; **no se le pasa nada** nothing escapes him, he misses nothing; **pase lo que pase** come what may.

pasarela [pasa'rela] *nf* footbridge; (*en barco*) gangway.

pasatiempo [pasa'tjempo] *nm* pastime; (*distracción*) amusement.

Pascua ['paskwa] *nf*: ~ (**de Resurrección**) Easter; ~ **de Navidad** Christmas; ~**s** *nfpl* Christmas time; **¡felices** ~**s!** Merry Christmas.

pase ['pase] *nm* pass.

pasear [pase'ar] *vt* to take for a walk; (*exhibir*) to parade, show off // *vi*, ~**se** *vr* to walk, go for a walk; (*holgazanear*) to idle, loaf about; ~ **en coche** to go for a drive; **paseo** *nm* (*avenida*) avenue; (*distancia corta*) short walk; **dar un paseo** to go for a walk.

pasillo [pa'siλo] *nm* passage, corridor.

pasión [pa'sjon] *nf* passion.

pasivo, a [pa'siβo, a] *a* passive; (*inactivo*) inactive // *nm* (*com*) liabilities *pl*, debts *pl*.

pasmar [pas'mar] *vt* (*asombrar*) to amaze, astonish; (*enfriar*) to chill (to the bone); **pasmo** *nm* amazement, astonishment; chill; (*fig*) wonder, marvel; **pasmoso, a** *a* amazing, astonishing.

paso, a ['paso, a] *a* dried // *nm* (*gen*) step; (*modo de andar*) walk; (*huella*) footprint; (*rapidez*) speed, pace, rate; (*camino accesible*) way through, passage; (*cruce*) crossing; (*pasaje*) passing, passage; (*GEO*) pass; (*estrecho*) strait; **a ese** ~ (*fig*) at that rate; **salir al** ~ **de** *o* **a** to waylay; **estar de** ~ to be passing through; ~ **elevado** flyover; **prohibido el** ~ no entry; **ceda el** ~ give way.

pasta ['pasta] *nf* (*gen*) paste; (*CULIN: masa*) dough; (: *de bizcochos etc*) pastry; (*cartón*) cardboard; (*fam*) money, dough (*fam*); ~**s** *nfpl* (*bizcochos*) pastries, small cakes; (*fideos, espaguetis etc*) noodles, spaghetti *sg etc*; ~ **de dientes** *o* **dentífrica** toothpaste; ~ **de madera** wood pulp.

pastar [pas'tar], **pastear** [paste'ar] *vt*, *vi* to graze.

pastel [pas'tel] *nm* (*dulce*) cake; (*de carne*) pie; (*pintura*) pastel; ~**ería** *nf* cake shop, pastry shop.

pasteurizado, a [pasteuri'θaðo, a] *a* pasteurized.

pastilla [pas'tiλa] *nf* (*de jabón, chocolate*) cake, bar; (*píldora*) tablet, pill.

pasto ['pasto] *nm* (*hierba*) grass; (*lugar*) pasture, field.

pastor, a [pas'tor, a] *nm/f* shepherd/ess // *nm* clergyman, pastor.

pata ['pata] *nf* (*pierna*) leg; (*pie*) foot; (*de muebles*) leg; ~**s arriba** upside down; **meter la** ~ to put one's foot in it; (*TEC*): ~ **de cabra** crowbar; **tener buena/mala** ~ to be lucky/unlucky; ~**da** *nf* stamp; (*puntapié*) kick.

patalear [patale'ar] *vi* to stamp one's feet.

patata [pa'tata] *nf* potato; ~**s fritas** *o* **a la española** chips, French fries; ~**s inglesas** crisps.

patear [pate'ar] *vt* (*pisar*) to stamp on, trample (on); (*pegar con el pie*) to kick // *vi* to stamp (with rage), stamp one's foot.

patente [pa'tente] *a* obvious, evident; (*com*) patent // *nf* patent; **patentizar** *vt* to show, reveal, make evident.

paternal [pater'nal] *a* fatherly, paternal; **paterno, a** *a* paternal.

patético, a [pa'tetiko, a] *a* pathetic, moving.

patillas [pa'tiλas] *nfpl* sideburns.

patín [pa'tin] *nm* skate; (*de tobogán*) runner; **patinaje** *nm* skating; **patinar** *vi* to skate; (*resbalarse*) to skid, slip; (*fam*) to slip up, blunder.

patio ['patjo] *nm* (*de casa*) patio, courtyard; ~ **de recreo** playground.

pato ['pato] *nm* duck; **pagar el** ~ (*fam*) to take the blame, carry the can.

patológico, a [pato'loxiko, a] a pathological.

patraña [pa'traɲa] nf story, fib.

patria ['patrja] nf native land, mother country.

patrimonio [patri'monjo] nm inheritance; (fig) heritage.

patriota [pa'trjota] nm/f patriot; **patriotismo** nm patriotism.

patrocinar [patroθi'nar] vt to sponsor; (apoyar) to back, support; **patrocinio** nm sponsorship; backing, support.

patrón, ona [pa'tron, ona] nm/f (jefe) boss, chief, master/mistress; (propietario) landlord/lady; (REL) patron saint // nm (TEC, costura) pattern; **patronal** a: **la clase patronal** management; **patronato** nm sponsorship; (acto) patronage; (COM) employers' association.

patrulla [pa'truʎa] nf patrol.

pausa ['pausa] nf pause; (intervalo) break; (interrupción) interruption.

pausado, a [pau'saðo, a] a slow, deliberate.

pauta ['pauta] nf line, guide line.

pavo ['paβo] nm turkey; ~ **real** peacock.

pavor [pa'βor] nm dread, terror.

payaso, a [pa'jaso, a] nm/f clown.

paz [paθ] nf peace; (tranquilidad) peacefulness, tranquillity; **hacer las paces** to make peace; (fig) to make up.

P.C.E. abr de **Partido Comunista Español.**

peaje [pe'axe] nm toll.

peatón [pea'ton] nm pedestrian.

peca ['peka] nf freckle.

pecado [pe'kaðo] nm sin; **pecador, a** a sinful // nm/f sinner.

pecaminoso, a [pekami'noso, a] a sinful.

pecar [pe'kar] vi (REL) to sin; (fig): **peca de generoso** he is too generous.

peculiar [peku'ljar] a special, peculiar; (característico) typical, characteristic; ~**idad** nf peculiarity; special feature, characteristic.

pecho ['petʃo] nm (ANAT) chest; (de mujer) breast(s) (pl), bosom; (corazón) heart, breast; (valor) courage, spirit; **dar el ~ a** to breast-feed; **tomar algo a ~** to take sth to heart.

pechuga [pe'tʃuxa] nf breast (of chicken etc).

pedal [pe'ðal] nm pedal; ~**ear** vi to pedal.

pedante [pe'ðante] a pedantic // nm/f pedant; ~**ría** nf pedantry.

pedazo [pe'ðaθo] nm piece, bit; **hacerse** ~**s** to fall to pieces; (romperse) to smash, shatter.

pedernal [peðer'nal] nm flint.

pediatra [pe'ðjatra] nm/f pediatrician.

pedicuro, a [peði'kuro, a] nm/f chiropodist.

pedido [pe'ðiðo] nm (COM: mandado) order; (petición) request.

pedir [pe'ðir] vt to ask for, request; (comida, COM: mandar) to order; (exigir: precio) to ask; (necesitar) to need, demand, require // vi to ask; **me pidió que cerrara la puerta** he asked me to shut the door; ¿**cuánto piden por el coche?** how much are they asking for the car?

pegadizo, a [pexa'ðiθo, a] a sticky; (MED) infectious // nm/f sponger, hanger-on (fam).

pegajoso, a [pexa'xoso, a] a sticky, adhesive; (MED) infectious.

pegamento [pexa'mento] nm gum, sticky stuff.

pegar [pe'xar] vt (papel, sellos) to stick (on); (cartel) to post, stick up; (coser) to sew (on); (unir: partes) to join, fix together; (MED) to give, infect with; (dar: golpe) to give, deal // vi (adherirse) to stick, adhere; (prender: fuego) to catch; (ir juntos: colores) to match, go together; (golpear) to hit; (quemar: el sol) to strike hot, burn (fig); ~**se** vr (gen) to stick; (dos personas) to hit each other, fight; (fam): ~ **un grito** to let out a yell; ~ **un salto** to jump (with fright); ~ **en** to touch; ~**se un tiro** to shoot o.s.

peinado [pei'naðo] nm (en peluquería) hairdo; (estilo) hair style.

peinador, a [peina'ðor, a] nm/f hairdresser.

peinar [pei'nar] vt to comb; (hacer estilo) to style; ~**se** vr to comb one's hair.

peine ['peine] nm comb; ~**ta** nf ornamental comb.

Pekín [pe'kin] n Pekin(g).

pelado, a [pe'laðo, a] a (cabeza) shorn; (fruta) peeled; (campo, fig) bare // nm bare patch; (fig) wretch, poor devil.

pelaje [pe'laxe] nm (ZOOL) fur, coat; (fig) appearance.

pelambre [pe'lambre] nm (pelo largo) long hair, mop; (piel de animal cortado) fur; (: de oveja) fleece; (parte sin piel) bare patch.

pelar [pe'lar] vt (cortar el pelo a) to cut the hair of; (quitar la piel: animal) to skin; ~**se** vr (la piel) to peel off; (persona) to lose one's hair; **voy a** ~**me** I'm going to get my hair cut.

peldaño [pel'daɲo] nm step.

pelea [pe'lea] nf (lucha) fight; (discusión) quarrel, row; **pelear** vi to fight; **pelearse** vr to fight; (reñirse) to fall out, quarrel.

peletería [pelete'ria] nf furrier's, fur shop.

pelicano [peli'kano], **pelícano** [pe'likano] nm pelican.

pelicorto, a [peli'korto, a] a short-haired.

película [pe'likula] nf film; (cobertura ligera) thin covering; (FOTO: rollo) roll or reel of film.

peligro [pe'lixro] nm danger; (riesgo) risk; **correr** ~ **de** to be in danger of; ~**so, a** a dangerous; risky.

pelirrojo, a [peli'roxo, a] a red-haired, red-headed.

pelo ['pelo] nm (cabellos) hair; (de barba, bigote) whisker; (de animal: pellejo) fur, coat; (de perro etc) hair, coat; al ~ just right; venir al ~ to be exactly what one needs; un hombre de ~ en pecho a brave man; por los ~s by the skin of one's teeth; no tener ~s en la lengua to be outspoken, not mince words; tomar el ~ a uno to pull sb's leg.

pelón, ona [pe'lon, ona] a hairless, bald; (fig) broke, skint (fam).

pelota [pe'lota] nf ball; (fam: cabeza) nut (fam); en ~ stark naked; ~ vasca pelota.

pelotón [pelo'ton] nm (pelota) big ball; (muchedumbre) crowd; (MIL) squad, detachment.

peluca [pe'luka] nf wig.

peluche [pe'lutʃe] nm felt.

peludo, a [pe'luðo, a] a hairy, shaggy.

peluquería [peluke'ria] nf hairdresser's; (para hombres) barber's (shop); peluquero, a nm/f hairdresser; barber.

pelleja [pe'ʎexa] nf skin, hide; (fam) whore.

pellejo [pe'ʎexo] nm (de animal) skin, hide; (de fruta) skin, peel.

pellizcar [peʎiθ'kar] vt to pinch, nip.

pena ['pena] nf (congoja) grief, sadness; (ansia) anxiety; (remordimiento) regret; (dificultad) trouble; (dolor) pain; merecer o valer la ~ to be worthwhile; a duras ~s with great difficulty; ~ de muerte death penalty; ~ pecuniaria fine; ¡qué ~! what a shame!

penal [pe'nal] a penal // nm (cárcel) prison; (FÚTBOL) penalty.

penalidad [penali'ðað] nf (problema, dificultad) trouble, hardship; (JUR) penalty, punishment.

penar [pe'nar] vt to penalize; (castigar) to punish // vi to suffer; ~se vr to grieve, mourn.

pender [pen'der] vi (colgar) to hang; (JUR) to be pending.

pendiente [pen'djente] a (colgante) hanging; (por resolver) pending, unsettled // nm earring // nf hill, slope.

pene ['pene] nm penis.

penetración [penetra'θjon] nf (acto) penetration; (agudeza) sharpness, insight.

penetrante [pene'trante] a (herida) deep; (persona, arma) sharp; (sonido) penetrating, piercing; (mirada) searching; (viento, ironía) biting.

penetrar [pene'trar] vt to penetrate, pierce; (entender) to grasp // vi to penetrate, go in; (líquido) to soak in; (emoción) to pierce.

penicilina [peniθi'lina] nf penicillin.

península [pe'ninsula] nf peninsula; peninsular a peninsular.

penitencia [peni'tenθja] nf (remordimiento) penitence; (castigo) penance; penitencial a penitential; ~ría nf prison, penitentiary.

penoso, a [pe'noso, a] a (afligido) painful, distressing; (trabajoso) laborious, difficult.

pensador, a [pensa'ðor, a] nm/f thinker.

pensamiento [pensa'mjento] nm (gen) thought; (mente) mind; (idea) idea; (intento) intention.

pensar [pen'sar] vt to think; (considerar) to think over, think out; (proponerse) to intend, plan, propose; (imaginarse) to think up, invent // vi to think; ~ en to aim at, aspire to; pensativo, a a thoughtful, pensive.

pensión [pen'sjon] nf (casa) boarding house, guest house; (dinero) pension; (cama y comida) board and lodging; (beca) scholarship; pensionista nm/f (jubilado) (old-age) pensioner; (quien vive en pensión) lodger.

penúltimo, a [pe'nultimo, a] a penultimate, second last.

penumbra [pe'numbra] nf half-light, semi-darkness.

penuria [pe'nurja] nf shortage, want.

peña ['peɲa] nf (roca) rock; (cuesta) cliff, crag; (grupo) group, circle.

peñascal [peɲas'kal] nm rocky place; peñasco nm large rock, boulder.

peñón [pe'ɲon] nm mass of rock; el P~ the Rock of Gibraltar.

peón [pe'on] nm labourer; (AM) farm labourer, farmhand; (eje) spindle, shaft, axle; (AJEDREZ) pawn.

peor [pe'or] a (comparativo) worse; (superlativo) worst // ad worse; worst; de mal en ~ from bad to worse.

pepino [pe'pino] nm cucumber; (no) me importa un ~ I don't care two hoots.

pepita [pe'pita] nf (BOT) pip; (MINERÍA) nugget.

pequeñez [peke'ɲeθ] nf smallness, littleness; (infancia) infancy; (trivialidad) trifle, triviality.

pequeño, a [pe'keɲo, a] a small, little.

pera ['pera] nf pear; peral nm pear tree.

percance [per'kanθe] nm setback, misfortune.

percatarse [perka'tarse] vr: ~ de to notice, take note of.

percepción [perθep'θjon] nf (vista) perception; (idea) notion, idea; (colecta de fondos) collection.

perceptible [perθep'tiβle] a perceptible, noticeable; (COM) payable, receivable.

percibir [perθi'βir] vt to perceive, notice; (COM) to earn, receive, get.

percusión [perku'sjon] nf percussion.

percha ['pertʃa] nf (poste) pole, support; (ganchos) coat stand; (colgador) coat hanger; (de ave) perch.

perdedor, a [perðe'ðor, a] a (que pierde) losing; (olvidadizo) forgetful // nm/f loser.

perder [per'ðer] vt (gen) to lose; (tiempo, palabras) to waste; (oportunidad) to lose, miss; (tren) to miss // vi to lose; ~se vr (extraviarse) to get lost; (desaparecer) to disappear, be lost to view; (arruinarse) to be ruined; (hundirse) to sink; echar a ~ (comida) to spoil, ruin; (oportunidad) to waste.

perdición [perði'θjon] nf perdition, ruin.

pérdida ['perðiða] *nf* (*gen*) loss; (*de tiempo*) waste; ~s *nfpl* (*COM*) losses.

perdido, a [per'ðiðo, a] *a* lost; (*incorregible*) incorrigible; ~**so, a** *a* (*que pierde*) losing; (*fácilmente* ~) easily lost.

perdiz [per'ðiθ] *nf* partridge.

perdón [per'ðon] *nm* (*disculpa*) pardon, forgiveness; (*clemencia*) mercy; ¡~! sorry!, I beg your pardon!; **perdonar** *vt* to pardon, forgive; (*la vida*) to spare; (*excusar*) to exempt, excuse.

perdurable [perðu'raßle] *a* lasting; (*eterno*) everlasting; **perdurar** *vi* (*resistir*) to last, endure; (*seguir existiendo*) to stand, still exist.

perecer [pere'θer] *vi* (*morir*) to perish, die; (*objeto*) to shatter.

peregrinación [pereɣrina'θjon] *nf* long tour, travels *pl*; (*REL*) pilgrimage; **peregrino, a** *a* travelling; (*nuevo*) newly-introduced // *nm/f* pilgrim.

perejil [pere'xil] *nm* parsley.

perenne [pe'renne] *a* everlasting, perennial.

perentorio, a [peren'torjo, a] *a* (*urgente*) urgent, peremptory; (*fijo*) set, fixed.

pereza [pe'reθa] *nf* (*flojera*) laziness; (*lentitud*) sloth, slowness; **perezoso, a** *a* lazy; slow, sluggish.

perfección [perfek'θjon] *nf* perfection; (*acto*) completion; **perfeccionar** *vt* to perfect; (*acabar*) to complete, finish.

perfecto, a [per'fekto, a] *a* perfect; (*terminado*) complete, finished.

perfidia [per'fiðja] *nf* perfidy, treachery.

perfil [per'fil] *nm* (*parte lateral*) profile; (*silueta*) silhouette, outline; (*ARQ*) (cross) section; ~**es** *nmpl* features; (*fig*) social graces; ~**ado, a** *a* (*bien formado*) well-shaped; (*largo: cara*) long; ~**ar** *vt* (*trazar*) to outline; (*dar carácter a*) to shape, give character to.

perforación [perfora'θjon] *nf* perforation; (*con taladro*) drilling; **perforadora** *nf* drill.

perforar [perfo'rar] *vt* to perforate; (*agujero*) to drill, bore; (*papel*) to punch a hole in // *vi* to drill, bore.

perfumado, a [perfu'maðo, a] *a* scented, perfumed.

perfume [per'fume] *nm* perfume, scent.

pericia [pe'riθja] *nf* skill, expertise.

periferia [peri'ferja] *nf* periphery; (*de ciudad*) outskirts *pl*.

perímetro [pe'rimetro] *nm* perimeter.

periódico, a [pe'rjoðiko, a] *a* periodic(al) // *nm* newspaper; **periodismo** *nm* journalism; **periodista** *nm/f* journalist.

periodo [pe'rjoðo], **período** [pe'rioðo] *nm* period.

perito, a [pe'rito, a] *a* (*experto*) expert; (*diestro*) skilled, skilful // *nm/f* expert; skilled worker; (*técnico*) technician.

perjudicar [perxuði'kar] *vt* (*gen*) to damage, harm; **ese vestido le perjudica** that dress doesn't suit her; **perjudicial** *a* damaging, harmful; (*en detrimento*) detri-

mental; **perjuicio** *nm* damage, harm; (*pérdidas*) financial loss.

perjurar [perxu'rar] *vi* to commit perjury.

perla ['perla] *nf* pearl; **me viene de** ~ it suits me fine.

permanecer [permane'θer] *vi* (*quedarse*) to stay, remain; (*seguir*) to continue to be.

permanencia [perma'nenθja] *nf* (*duración*) permanence; (*estancia*) stay.

permanente [perma'nente] *a* (*que queda*) permanent; (*constante*) constant // *nf* perm.

permisible [permi'sißle] *a* permissible, allowable.

permiso [per'miso] *nm* permission; (*licencia*) permit, licence; **con** ~ excuse me; **estar de** ~ (*MIL*) to be on leave; ~ **de conducir** *o* **conductor** driving licence.

permitir [permi'tir] *vt* to permit, allow.

pernicioso, a [perni'θjoso, a] *a* (*maligno*, *MED*) pernicious; (*persona*) wicked.

pernio ['pernjo] *nm* hinge.

perno ['perno] *nm* bolt.

pero ['pero] *conj* but; (*aún*) yet // *nm* (*defecto*) flaw, defect; (*reparo*) objection.

perorar [pero'rar] *vi* to make a speech.

perpendicular [perpendiku'lar] *a* perpendicular; **el camino es** ~ **al río** the road is at right angles to the river.

perpetrar [perpe'trar] *vt* to perpetrate.

perpetuamente [perpetwa'mente] *ad* perpetually; **perpetuar** *vt* to perpetuate; **perpetuo, a** *a* perpetual.

perplejo, a [per'plexo, a] *a* perplexed, bewildered.

perra ['perra] *nf* bitch; (*fam*) mania, crazy idea.

perrera [pe'rrera] *nf* kennel.

perrillo [pe'rriʎo] *nm* puppy.

perro ['perro] *nm* dog; ~ **caliente** hot dog.

persa ['persa] *a*, *nm/f* Persian.

persecución [perseku'θjon] *nf* pursuit, hunt, chase; (*REL*, *POL*) persecution.

perseguir [perse'ɣir] *vt* to pursue, hunt; (*cortejar*) to chase after; (*molestar*) to pester, annoy; (*REL*, *POL*) to persecute.

perseverante [perseße'rante] *a* persevering, persistent; **perseverar** *vi* to persevere, persist; **perseverar en** to persevere in, persist with.

persiana [per'sjana] *nf* (Venetian) blind.

persignarse [persiɣ'narse] *vr* to cross o.s.

persistente [persis'tente] *a* persistant; **persistir** *vi* to persist.

persona [per'sona] *nf* person; **10** ~**s** 10 people.

personaje [perso'naxe] *nm* important person, celebrity; (*TEATRO*) character.

personal [perso'nal] *a* (*particular*) personal; (*para una persona*) single, for one person // *nm* personnel, staff; ~**idad** *nf* personality.

personarse [perso'narse] *vr* to appear in person.

personificar [personifi'kar] *vt* to personify.

perspectiva [perspek'tiβa] *nf* perspective; (*vista*, *panorama*) view, panorama; (*posibilidad futura*) outlook, prospect.

perspicacia [perspi'kaθja] *nf* keensightedness; (*fig*) discernment, perspicacity.

perspicaz [perspi'kaθ] *a* (*agudo: de la vista*) keen; (*fig*) shrewd.

persuadir [perswa'ðir] *vt* (*gen*) to persuade; (*convencer*) to convince; ~**se** *vr* to become convinced; **persuasión** *nf* (*acto*) persuasion; (*estado de mente*) conviction; **persuasivo, a** *a* persuasive; convincing.

pertenecer [pertene'θer] *vi* to belong; (*fig*) to concern; **pertenencia** *nf* ownership; **pertenencias** *nfpl* possessions, property *sg*; **perteneciente** *a*: **perteneciente a** belonging to.

pertinaz [perti'naθ] *a* (*persistente*) persistent; (*terco*) obstinate.

pertinente [perti'nente] *a* relevant, pertinent; (*apropiado*) appropriate; ~ **a** concerning, relevant to.

perturbación [perturβa'θjon] *nf* (*POL*) disturbance; (*MED*) upset, disturbance.

perturbado, a [pertur'βaðo, a] *a* mentally unbalanced.

perturbador, a [perturβa'ðor, a] *a* (*que perturba*) perturbing, disturbing; (*subversivo*) subversive.

perturbar [pertur'βar] *vt* (*el orden*) to disturb; (*MED*) to upset, disturb; (*mentalmente*) to perturb.

Perú [pe'ru] *nm*: **el** ~ Peru; **peruano, a** *a*, *nm/f* Peruvian.

perversión [perβer'sjon] *nf* perversion; **perverso, a** *a* perverse; (*depravado*) depraved; **pervertido, a** *a* perverted // *nm/f* pervert; **pervertir** *vt* to pervert, corrupt; (*distorsionar*) to distort.

pesa ['pesa] *nf* weight; (*DEPORTE*) shot.

pesadez [pesa'ðeθ] *nf* (*calidad de pesado*) heaviness; (*lentitud*) slowness; (*aburrimiento*) tediousness.

pesadilla [pesa'ðiʎa] *nf* nightmare, bad dream.

pesado, a [pe'saðo, a] *a* (*gen*) heavy; (*lento*) slow; (*difícil, duro*) tough, hard; (*aburrido*) tedious, boring; (*bochornoso*) sultry.

pesadumbre [pesa'ðumbre] *nf* grief, sorrow.

pésame ['pesame] *nm* expression of condolence, message of sympathy.

pesar [pe'sar] *vt* to weigh // *vi* to weigh; (*ser pesado*) to weigh a lot, be heavy; (*fig: opinión*) to carry weight // *nm* (*sentimiento*) regret; (*pena*) grief, sorrow; **a** ~ **de** *o* **pese a (que)** in spite of, despite.

pesario [pe'sarjo] *nm* pessary.

pesca ['peska] *nf* (*acto*) fishing; (*cantidad de pescado*) catch; **ir de** ~ to go fishing.

pescadería [peskaðe'ria] *nf* fish shop.

pescado [pes'kaðo] *nm* fish.

pescador, a [peska'ðor, a] *nm/f* fisherman/woman.

pescar [pes'kar] *vt* (*coger*) to catch; (*tratar de coger*) to fish for; (*conseguir: trabajo*) to manage to get // *vi* to fish, go fishing; **viene a** ~ **un marido** she's come to get a husband.

pescuezo [pes'kweθo] *nm* neck.

pesebre [pe'seβre] *nm* manger.

peseta [pe'seta] *nf* peseta.

pesimista [pesi'mista] *a* pessimistic // *nm/f* pessimist.

pésimo, a ['pesimo, a] *a* abominable, vile.

peso ['peso] *nm* weight; (*balanza*) scales *pl*; (*moneda*) peso; ~ **bruto/neto** gross/net weight; **vender a** ~ to sell by weight.

pesquero, a [pes'kero, a] *a* fishing *cpd*.

pesquisa [pes'kisa] *nf* inquiry, investigation.

pestaña [pes'taɲa] *nf* (*ANAT*) eyelash; (*borde*) rim; **pestañear, pestañar** *vi* to blink.

peste ['peste] *nf* (*gen*) plague; (*mal olor*) stink, stench.

pesticida [pesti'θiða] *nm* pesticide.

pestilencia [pesti'lenθja] *nf* (*plaga*) pestilence, plague; (*mal olor*) stink, stench.

pétalo ['petalo] *nm* petal.

petardista [petar'ðista] *nm/f* (*tramposo*) cheat; (*rompehuelgas*) blackleg.

petición [peti'θjon] *nf* (*pedido*) request, plea; (*memorial*) petition; (*JUR*) plea.

petrificar [petrifi'kar] *vt* to petrify.

petróleo [pe'troleo] *nm* oil, petroleum; **petrolero, a** *a* petroleum *cpd* // *nm* (*COM*) oil man; (*extremista*) extremist, revolutionary; (*buque*) (oil) tanker.

peyorativo, a [pejora'tiβo, a] *a* pejorative.

pez [peθ] *nm* fish.

pezón [pe'θon] *nm* teat, nipple; (*MECÁNICA*) nipple, lubrication point.

piadoso, a [pja'ðoso, a] *a* (*devoto*) pious, devout; (*misericordioso*) kind, merciful.

pianista [pja'nista] *nm/f* pianist.

piano ['pjano] *nm* piano.

piar [pi'ar] *vi* to cheep.

picadillo [pika'ðiʎo] *nm* mince, minced meat.

picado, a [pi'kaðo, a] *a* pricked, punctured; (*mar*) choppy; (*diente*) bad; (*tabaco*) cut; (*enfadado*) cross // *nf* prick; (*de abeja*) sting; (*de mosquito*) bite.

picador [pika'ðor] *nm* (*TAUR*) picador; (*entrenador de caballos*) horse trainer; (*minero*) faceworker.

picadura [pika'ðura] *nf* (*diente*) bad tooth; (*pinchazo*) puncture; (*de abeja*) sting; (*de mosquito*) bite; (*tabaco picado*) cut tobacco.

picante [pi'kante] *a* hot; (*comentario*) racy, spicy.

picar [pi'kar] *vt* (*agujerear, perforar*) to prick, puncture; (*abeja*) to sting; (*mosquito, serpiente*) to bite; (*incitar*) to incite, goad; (*dañar, irritar*) to annoy, bother; (*quemar:*

lengua) to burn, sting // *vi* (*pez*) to bite, take the bait; (*el sol*) to burn, scorch; (*abeja*, MED) to sting; (*mosquito*) to bite; ~**se** *vr* (*decaer*) to decay; (*agriarse*) to turn sour, go off; (*ofenderse*) to take offence; ~ **en** (*fig*) to dabble in.

picardía [pikar'ðia] *nf* villainy; (*astucia*) slyness, craftiness; (*una* ~) dirty trick; (*palabra*) rude/bad word *or* expression.

pícaro, a ['pikaro, a] *a* (*malicioso*) villainous; (*travieso*) mischievous // *nm* (*ladrón*) crook; (*astuto*) sly sort; (*sinvergüenza*) rascal, scoundrel.

pico ['piko] *nm* (*de ave*) beak; (*punto agudo*) peak, sharp point; (TEC) pick, pickaxe; (GEO) peak, summit; **y** ~ and a bit.

picotear [pikote'ar] *vt* to peck // *vi* to nibble, pick; (*fam*) to chatter; ~**se** *vr* to squabble.

picudo, a [pi'kuðo, a] *a* pointed, with a point.

pichón [pi'tʃon] *nm* young pigeon.

pido, pidió *etc vb ver* **pedir.**

pie [pje] (*pl* ~**s**) *nm* (*gen*) foot; (*fig: motivo*) motive, basis; (: *fundamento*) foothold; **ir a** ~ to go on foot, walk; **estar de** ~ to be standing (up); **ponerse de** ~ to stand up; **al** ~ **de la letra** (*citar*) literally, verbatim; (*copiar*) exactly, word for word; **en** ~ **de guerra** on a war footing; **dar** ~ **a** to give cause for.

piedad [pje'ðað] *nf* (*lástima*) pity, compassion; (*clemencia*) mercy; (*devoción*) piety, devotion.

piedra ['pjeðra] *nf* stone; (*roca*) rock; (*de mechero*) flint; (METEOROLOGÍA) hailstone.

piel [pjel] *nf* (ANAT) skin; (ZOOL) skin, hide; (*de oso*) fur; (*cuero*) leather; (BOT) skin, peel; ~ **de ante** *o* **de Suecia** suede.

pienso *etc vb ver* **pensar.**

pierdo *etc vb ver* **perder.**

pierna ['pjerna] *nf* leg.

pieza ['pjeθa] *nf* piece; (*habitación*) room; ~ **de recambio** *o* **repuesto** spare (part).

pigmeo, a [piɣ'meo, a] *a, nm/f* pigmy.

pijama [pi'xama] *nm* pyjamas *pl.*

pila ['pila] *nf* (ELEC) battery; (*montón*) heap, pile; (*fuente*) sink.

píldora ['pildora] *nf* pill; **la** ~ **(anticonceptiva)** the pill.

pileta [pi'leta] *nf* basin, bowl; (AM) swimming pool.

pilón [pi'lon] *nm* pillar, post; (ELEC) pylon.

piloto [pi'loto] *nm* pilot; (*de aparato*) rear light, tail light; (AUTO) driver.

pillaje [pi'ʎaxe] *nm* pillage, plunder.

pillar [pi'ʎar] *vt* (*saquear*) to pillage, plunder; (*fam: coger*) to catch; (: *agarrar*) to grasp, seize; (: *entender*) to grasp, catch on to.

pillo, a ['piʎo, a] *a* villainous; (*astuto*) sly, crafty // *nm/f* rascal, rogue, scoundrel.

pimentón [pimen'ton] *nm* (*polvo*) paprika; (*pimiento*) red pepper.

pimienta [pi'mjenta] *nf* pepper.

pimiento [pi'mjento] *nm* pepper, pimiento.

pinacoteca [pinako'teka] *nf* art gallery.

pinar [pi'nar] *nm* pinewood.

pincel [pin'θel] *nm* paintbrush.

pinchar [pin'tʃar] *vt* (*perforar*) to prick, pierce; (*neumático*) to puncture; (*incitar*) to prod; (*herir*) to wound.

pinchazo [pin'tʃaθo] *nm* (*perforación*) prick; (*de llanta*) puncture; (*fig*) prod.

pinchitos [pin'tʃitos] *nmpl* bar snacks.

pingüino [pin'gwino] *nm* penguin.

pino ['pino] *nm* pine (tree); **en** ~ upright, vertical.

pinta ['pinta] *nf* spot; (*medida*) spot, drop; (*aspecto*) appearance, look(s) (*pl*); ~**do, a** a spotted; (*de muchos colores*) colourful.

pintar [pin'tar] *vt* to paint // *vi* to paint; (*fam*) to count, be important; ~**se** *vr* to put on make-up.

pintor, a [pin'tor, a] *nm/f* painter.

pintoresco, a [pinto'resko, a] *a* picturesque.

pintura [pin'tura] *nf* painting; ~ **a la acuarela** watercolour; ~ **al óleo** oil painting; ~ **rupestre** cave painting.

pinza ['pinθa] *nf* (ZOOL) claw; (*para colgar ropa*) clothes peg; (TEC) pincers *pl*; ~**s** *nfpl* (*para depilar*) tweezers *pl.*

piña ['piɲa] *nf* (*fruto del pino*) pine cone; (*fruta*) pineapple; (*fig*) group.

pío, a ['pio, a] *a* (*devoto*) pious, devout; (*misericordioso*) merciful // *nm* cheep, chirp.

piojo ['pjoxo] *nm* louse.

pionero, a [pjo'nero, a] *a* pioneering // *nm/f* pioneer.

pipa ['pipa] *nf* pipe; (BOT) edible sunflower seed.

pipí [pi'pi] *nm* (*fam*): **hacer** ~ to have a wee(wee).

pique ['pike] *nm* (*resentimiento*) pique, resentment; (*rivalidad*) rivalry, competition; **irse a** ~ to sink; (*familia*) to be ruined.

piquera [pi'kera] *nf* hole, vent.

piqueta [pi'keta] *nf* pick(axe).

piquete [pi'kete] *nm* (*herida*) prick, jab; (*agujerito*) small hole; (MIL) squad, party; (*de obreros*) picket.

piragua [pi'raɣwa] *nf* canoe; **piragüismo** *nm* (DEPORTE) canoeing.

pirámide [pi'ramiðe] *nf* pyramid.

pirata [pi'rata] *a, nm* pirate.

Pirineo(s) [piri'neo(s)] *nm(pl)* Pyrenees *pl.*

piropo [pi'ropo] *nm* compliment, (piece of) flattery.

pisada [pi'saða] *nf* (*paso*) footstep; (*huella*) footprint.

pisar [pi'sar] *vt* (*caminar sobre*) to walk on, tread on; (*apretar con el pie*) to press; (*fig*) to trample on, walk all over // *vi* to tread, step, walk.

piscina [pis'θina] *nf* swimming pool; (*para peces*) fishpond.

Piscis ['pisθis] *nm* Pisces.
piso ['piso] *nm* (*suelo, de edificio*) floor; (*apartamento*) flat, apartment.
pisotear [pisote'ar] *vt* to trample (on *or* underfoot).
pista ['pista] *nf* track, trail; (*indicio*) clue; ~ de aterrizaje runway; ~ de baile dance floor; ~ de tenis tennis court; ~ de hielo ice rink.
pistola [pis'tola] *nf* pistol; (*TEC*) spray-gun; **pistolero, a** *nm/f* gunman, gangster // *nf* holster.
pistón [pis'ton] *nm* (*TEC*) piston; (*MUS*) key.
pitar [pi'tar] *vt* (*hacer sonar*) to blow; (*rechiflar*) to whistle at, boo // *vi* to whistle; (*AUTO*) to sound *or* toot one's horn; (*AM*) to smoke.
pitillo [pi'tiʎo] *nm* cigarette.
pito ['pito] *nm* whistle; (*de coche*) horn.
pitón [pi'ton] *nm* (*ZOOL*) python; (*protuberancia*) bump, lump; (*de jarro*) spout.
pitonisa [pito'nisa] *nf* fortune-teller.
pizarra [pi'θarra] *nf* (*piedra*) slate; (*encerado*) blackboard.
pizca ['piθka] *nf* pinch, spot; (*fig*) spot, speck, trace; **ni ~ not a bit.**
placa ['plaka] *nf* plate; ~ de matrícula number plate.
placentero, a [plaθen'tero, a] *a* pleasant, agreeable.
placer [pla'θer] *nm* pleasure // *vt* to please.
plácido, a ['plaθiðo, a] *a* placid.
plaga ['plaɣa] *nf* pest; (*MED*) plague; (*abundancia*) abundance; **plagar** *vt* to infest, plague; (*llenar*) to fill.
plagio ['plaxjo] *nm* plagiarism.
plan [plan] *nm* (*esquema, proyecto*) plan; (*idea, intento*) idea, intention; **tener ~** (*fam*) to have a date; **tener un ~** (*fam*) to have an affair; **en ~ económico** (*fam*) on the cheap; **vamos en ~ de turismo** we're going as tourists; **si te pones en ese ~...** if that's your attitude... .
plana ['plana] *nf ver* **plano.**
plancha ['plantʃa] *nf* (*para planchar*) iron; (*rótulo*) plate, sheet; (*NAUT*) gangway; ~ do *nm* ironing; **planchar** *vt* to iron // *vi* to do the ironing.
planeador [planea'ðor] *nm* glider; ~ a *nf* bulldozer.
planear [plane'ar] *vt* to plan // *vi* to glide.
planeta [pla'neta] *nm* planet.
planicie [pla'niθje] *nf* plain.
planificación [planifika'θjon] *nf* planning; ~ familiar family planning.
plano, a ['plano, a] *a* flat, level, even // *nm* (*MAT, TEC, AVIAT*) plane; (*FOTO*) shot; (*ARQ*) plan; (*GEO*) map; (*de ciudad*) map, street plan // *nf* sheet (of paper), page; (*TEC*) trowel; **primer ~** close-up; **caer de ~** to fall flat; **en primera ~a** on the front page; ~a **mayor** staff.
planta ['planta] *nf* (*BOT, TEC*) plant; (*ANAT*) sole of the foot, foot; ~ **baja** ground floor.

plantación [planta'θjon] *nf* (*AGR*) plantation; (*acto*) planting.
plantar [plan'tar] *vt* (*BOT*) to plant; (*levantar*) to erect, set up; ~**se** *vr* to stand firm; ~ **a uno en la calle** to chuck sb out; **dejar plantado a uno** (*fam*) to stand sb up.
plantear [plante'ar] *vt* (*problema*) to pose; (*dificultad*) to raise; (*planificar*) to plan; (*institución*) to set up, establish; (*reforma*) to implant.
plantilla [plan'tiʎa] *nf* (*de zapato*) insole; (*de media*) sole; (*personal*) personnel; **ser de ~** to be on the staff.
plantío [plan'tio] *nm* (*acto*) planting; (*lugar*) plot, bed, patch.
plantón [plan'ton] *nm* (*MIL*) guard, sentry; (*fam*) long wait; **dar (un) ~ a uno** to stand sb up.
plañidero, a [plaɲi'ðero, a] *a* mournful, plaintive.
plañir [pla'ɲir] *vi* to mourn.
plasmar [plas'mar] *vt* (*dar forma*) to mould, shape; (*representar*) to represent // *vi*: ~ **en** to take the form of.
plasticina [plasti'θina] *nf* plasticine.
plástico, a ['plastiko, a] *a* plastic // *nf* (art of) sculpture, modelling // *nm* plastic.
plata ['plata] *nf* (*metal*) silver; (*cosas hechas de plata*) silverware; (*AM*) money; **hablar en ~** to speak bluntly *or* frankly.
plataforma [plata'forma] *nf* platform; ~ de lanzamiento/perforación launch(ing) pad/drilling rig.
plátano ['platano] *nm* (*fruta*) banana; (*árbol*) banana tree.
platea [pla'tea] *nf* (*TEATRO*) pit.
plateado, a [plate'aðo, a] *a* silver; (*TEC*) silver-plated.
platería [plate'ria] *nf* silversmith's.
plática ['platika] *nf* talk, chat; **platicar** *vi* to talk, chat.
platillo [pla'tiʎo] *nm* saucer; ~**s** *nmpl* cymbals; ~ **volador** *o* **volante** flying saucer.
platino [pla'tino] *nm* platinum; ~**s** *nmpl* (*AUTO*) contact points.
plato ['plato] *nm* plate, dish; (*parte de comida*) course; (*guiso*) dish.
playa ['plaja] *nf* beach; (*lugar veraniego*) seaside resort; (*costa*) seaside; ~ de **estacionamiento** (*AM*) car park.
playera [pla'jera] *nf* T-shirt.
plaza ['plaθa] *nf* square; (*mercado*) market(place); (*sitio*) room, space; (*en vehículo*) seat, place; (*colocación*) post, job.
plazco *etc vb ver* **placer.**
plazo ['plaθo] *nm* (*lapso de tiempo*) time, period, term; (*fecha de vencimiento*) expiry date; (*pago parcial*) instalment; **a corto/largo ~** short-/long-term; **comprar a ~s** to buy on hire purchase, pay for in instalments.
plazoleta [plaθo'leta], **plazuela** [pla'θwela] *nf* small square.
pleamar [plea'mar] *nf* high tide.
plebe ['pleβe] *nf*: **la ~** the common

people *pl*, the masses *pl*; (*pey*) the plebs *pl*; ~**yo**, a *a* plebeian; (*pey*) coarse, common.

plebiscito [pleßis'θito] *nm* plebiscite.

plegable [ple'xaßle], **plegadizo, a** [plexa'θiθo, a] *a* pliable; (*silla*) folding.

plegar [ple'xar] *vt* (*doblar*) to fold, bend; (*COSTURA*) to pleat; ~**se** *vr* to yield, submit.

pleito ['pleito] *nm* (*JUR*) lawsuit, case; (*fig*) dispute, feud.

plenilunio [pleni'lunjo] *nm* full moon.

plenitud [pleni'tuð] *nf* plenitude, fullness; (*abundancia*) abundance.

pleno, a ['pleno, a] *a* (*gen*) full; (*completo*) complete // *nm* plenum; **en ~ día** in broad daylight; **en ~ verano** at the height of summer; **en ~a cara** full in the face.

pleuresía [pleure'sia] *nf* pleurisy.

plexiglás [pleksi'xlas] *nm* perspex.

pliego ['pljexo] *nm* (*hoja*) sheet (of paper); (*carta*) sealed letter/document; ~ **de condiciones** details *pl*, specifications *pl*.

pliegue ['pljexe] *nm* fold, crease; (*de vestido*) pleat.

plisado [pli'saðo] *nm* pleating; ~ **de acordeón** accordion pleats *pl*.

plomero [plo'mero] *nm* plumber.

plomo ['plomo] *nm* (*metal*) lead; (*ELEC*) fuse.

pluma ['pluma] *nf* (*gen*) feather; (*para escribir*) pen.

plural [plu'ral] *a* plural; ~**idad** *nf* plurality; **una ~idad de votos** a majority of votes.

plus [plus] *nm* bonus.

plutocracia [pluto'kraθja] *nf* plutocracy.

población [poßla'θjon] *nf* population; (*pueblo, ciudad*) town, city; **poblado, a** *a* inhabited // *nm* (*aldea*) village; (*pueblo*) (small) town; **densamente poblado** densely populated.

poblador, a [poßla'ðor, a] *nm/f* settler, colonist; (*fundador*) founder.

poblar [po'ßlar] *vt* (*colonizar*) to colonize; (*fundar*) to found; (*habitar*) to inhabit.

pobre ['poßre] *a* poor // *nm/f* poor person; ¡~! poor thing!; ~**za** *nf* poverty.

pocilga [po'θilxa] *nf* pigsty.

poción [po'θjon], **pócima** ['poθima] *nf* potion.

poco, a ['poko, a] *a* little; ~**s** few // *ad* (*no mucho*) little, not much // *nm*: **un ~** a little, a bit; **tener a uno en** ~ to think little *or* not think much of sb; **por** ~ almost, nearly; ~ **a** ~ little by little, gradually; **dentro de** ~ (+ *presente o futuro*) shortly; (+ *pasado*) soon after; **hace** ~ a short time ago, not long ago.

podar [po'ðar] *vt* to prune.

podenco [po'ðenko] *nm* hound.

poder [po'ðer] *vi* can; (*sujeto: persona*) to be able to, can; (*permiso*) can, may; (*posibilidad, hipótesis*) may // *nm* (*gen*) power; (*autoridad*) authority; **puede que sea así** it may be, maybe; ¿**se puede?** may I come in?; ¿**puedes con eso?** can

you manage that?; **a más no** ~ to the utmost; **no ~ menos de hacer algo** not to be able to help doing sth; **no ~ más** to have had enough; ~**ío** *nm* power; (*autoridad*) authority; ~**oso, a** a powerful.

podrido, a [po'ðriðo, a] *a* rotten, bad; (*fig*) rotten, corrupt.

podrir [po'ðrir] = **pudrir**.

poema [po'ema] *nm* poem.

poesía [poe'sia] *nf* poetry.

poeta [po'eta] *nm* poet; **poético, a** a poetic(al).

póker ['poker] *nm* poker.

polaco, a [po'lako, a] *a* Polish // *nm/f* Pole.

polar [po'lar] *a* polar; ~**idad** *nf* polarity; ~**izarse** *vr* to polarize.

polea [po'lea] *nf* pulley.

polémica [po'lemika] *nf* (*gen*) polemics *sg*; (*una* ~) controversy.

policía [poli'θia] *nm/f* policeman/woman // *nf* police; ~**co, a** a police *cpd*; **novela** ~**ca** detective story.

poligamia [poli'xamja] *nf* polygamy.

polilla [po'liʎa] *nf* moth.

polio ['poljo] *nf* polio.

politécnico [poli'tekniko] *nm* polytechnic.

politene [poli'tene], **politeno** [poli'teno] *nm* polythene.

político, a [po'litiko, a] *a* political; (*discreto*) tactful; (*de familia*) in-law // *nm/f* politician // *nf* politics *sg*; (*económica, agraria*) policy; **padre** ~ father-in-law; **politicastro** *nm* (*pey*) politician, politico.

póliza ['poliθa] *nf* insurance policy.

polo ['polo] *nm* (*GEO, ELEC*) pole; (*helado*) iced lolly; (*DEPORTE*) polo; (*suéter*) polo-neck; ~ **Norte/Sur** North/South Pole.

Polonia [po'lonja] *nf* Poland.

poltrona [pol'trona] *nf* reclining chair, easy chair.

polución [polu'θjon] *nf* pollution.

polvera [pol'ßera] *nf* powder compact, vanity case.

polvo ['polßo] *nm* dust; (*QUÍMICA, CULIN, MED*) powder; ~**s** *nmpl* powder *sg*; ~ **de talco** talcum powder; **estar hecho** ~ to be worn out *or* exhausted.

pólvora ['polßora] *nf* gunpowder; (*fuegos artificiales*) fireworks *pl*.

polvoriento, a [polßo'rjento, a] *a* (*superficie*) dusty; (*sustancia*) powdery.

pollería [poʎe'ria] *nf* poulterer's (shop).

pollo ['poʎo] *nm* chicken.

pomada [po'maða] *nf* pomade.

pomelo [po'melo] *nm* grapefruit.

pómez ['pomeθ] *nf*: **piedra** ~ pumice stone.

pompa ['pompa] *nf* (*burbuja*) bubble; (*bomba*) pump; (*esplendor*) pomp, splendour; **pomposo, a** a splendid, magnificent; (*pey*) pompous.

pómulo ['pomulo] *nm* cheekbone.

pon [pon] *vb ver* **poner**.

ponche ['pontfe] *nm* punch.

poncho ['pontʃo] *nm* (AM) poncho, cape.

ponderado, a [ponde'raðo, a] *a* calm, steady, balanced.

ponderar [ponde'rar] *vt* (*considerar*) to weigh up, consider; (*elogiar*) to praise highly, speak in praise of.

pondré *etc vb ver* **poner.**

poner [po'ner] *vt* (*gen*) to put; (*colocar*) to place, set; (*ropa*) to put on; (*problema, la mesa*) to set; (*telegrama*) to send; (TELEC) to connect; (*radio, TV*) to switch on, turn on; (*tienda*) to open, set up; (*nombre*) to give; (*añadir*) to add; (TEATRO, CINE) to put on; (+ *adjetivo*) to make, turn; (*suponer*) to suppose // *vi* (*ave*) to lay (eggs); ~**se** *vr* to put *or* place o.s.; (*ropa*) to put on; (+ *adjetivo*) to turn, get, become; (*el sol*) to set; **póngame con el Señor X** get me Mr X, put me through to Mr X; ~**se de zapatero** to take a job as a shoemaker; ~**se a bien con uno** to get on good terms with sb; ~**se con uno** to quarrel with sb; ~**se rojo** to blush; ~**se a** to begin to.

pongo *etc vb ver* **poner.**

pontificado [pontifi'kaðo] *nm* papacy, pontificate; **pontífice** *nm* pope, pontiff.

pontón [pon'ton] *nm* pontoon.

ponzoña [pon'θoɲa] *nf* poison, venom; **ponzoñoso, a** *a* poisonous, venomous.

popa ['popa] *nf* stern.

popular [popu'lar] *a* popular; (*del pueblo*) of the people; ~**idad** *nf* popularity; ~**izarse** *vr* to become popular.

poquedad [poke'ðað] *nf* (*escasez*) scantiness; (*una* ~) small thing, trifle; (*fig*) timidity.

por [por] *prep* (*con el fin de*) in order to; (*a favor de, hacia*) for; (*a causa de*) out of, because of, from; (*según*) according to; (*por agencia de*) by; (*a cambio de*) for, in exchange for; (*en lugar de*) instead of, in place of; (*durante*) for; **10** ~ **10 son 100** 10 times 10 are 100; **será** ~ **poco tiempo** it won't be for long; ~ **correo/avión** by post/plane; ~ **centenares** by the hundred; (**el**) **10** ~ **ciento** 10 per cent; ~ **orden** in order; **ir a Bilbao** ~ **Santander** to go to Bilbao via Santander; **pasar** ~ **Madrid** to pass through Madrid; **camina** ~ **la izquierda** walk on the left; ~ **todo el país** throughout the country; **entra** ~ **delante/detrás** come/go in by the front/back (door); ~ **la calle** along the street; ~ **la mañana** in the morning; ~ **la noche** at night; **£2** ~ **hora** £2 an hour; ~ **allí** over there; **está** ~ **el norte** it's somewhere in the north; ~ **mucho que quisiera, no puedo** much as I would like to, I can't; ~**que** because; **¿**~ **qué?** why?; ~ **(lo) tanto** so, therefore; ~ **cierto** (*seguro*) certainly; (*a propósito*) by the way; ~ **ejemplo** for example; ~ **favor** please; ~ **fuera/dentro** outside/inside; ~ **si (acaso)** just in case; ~ **sí mismo** *o* **sólo** by o.s.

porcelana [porθe'lana] *nf* porcelain; (*china*) china.

porcentaje [porθen'taxe] *nm* percentage.

porción [por'θjon] *nf* (*parte*) portion, share; (*cantidad*) quantity, amount.

pordiosear [porðjose'ar] *vi* to beg; **pordiosero, a** *nm/f* beggar.

porfía [por'fia] *nf* persistence; (*terquedad*) obstinacy; **porfiado, a** *a* persistent; obstinate; **porfiar** *vi* to persist, insist; (*disputar*) to argue stubbornly.

pormenor [porme'nor] *nm* detail, particular.

pornografía [pornoɣra'fia] *nf* pornography.

poro ['poro] *nm* pore; ~**so, a** *a* porous.

porque ['porke] *conj* (*a causa de*) because; (*ya que*) since; (*con el fin de*) so that, in order that.

porqué [por'ke] *nm* reason, cause.

porquería [porke'ria] *nf* (*suciedad*) filth, muck, dirt; (*acción*) dirty trick; (*objeto*) small thing, trifle; (*fig*) rubbish.

porro, a ['porro, a] *a* (*fam*) stupid // *nf* (*arma*) stick, club; (TEC) large hammer; (*fam*) bore.

porrón, ona [po'rron, ona] *a* slow, stupid // *nm* glass wine jar with a long spout.

portada [por'taða] *nf* (*entrada*) porch, doorway; (*de revista*) cover.

portador, a [porta'ðor, a] *nm/f* carrier, bearer.

portaequipajes [portaeki'paxes] *nm inv* boot; (*arriba del coche*) luggage rack.

portal [por'tal] *nm* (*entrada*) vestibule, hall; (*portada*) porch, doorway; (*puerta de entrada*) main door; (*de ciudad*) gate; (DEPORTE) goal.

portaligas [porta'liɣas] *nm inv* suspender belt.

portamaletas [portama'letas] *nm inv* boot.

portamonedas [portamo'neðas] *nm inv* purse.

portarse [por'tarse] *vr* to behave, conduct o.s.

portátil [por'tatil] *a* portable.

portaviones [porta'βjones] *nm inv* aircraft carrier.

portavoz [porta'βoθ] *nm* (*megáfono*) megaphone, loudhailer; (*vocero*) spokesman/woman.

portazo [por'taθo] *nm*: **dar un** ~ to slam the door.

porte ['porte] *nm* (COM) transport; (*precio*) transport charges *pl*; (*comportamiento*) conduct, behaviour.

portento [por'tento] *nm* marvel, wonder; ~**so, a** *a* marvellous, extraordinary.

porteño, a [por'teɲo, a] *a* of *or* from Buenos Aires.

portería [porte'ria] *nf* (*oficina*) porter's office; (*gol*) goal.

portero, a [por'tero, a] *nm/f* porter; (*conserje*) caretaker; (*ujier*) doorman // *nm* goalkeeper.

pórtico ['portiko] *nm* (*patio*) portico, porch; (*fig*) gateway; (*arcada*) arcade.
portilla [por'tiʎa] *nf* porthole.
portillo [por'tiʎo] *nm* (*abertura*) gap, opening; (*GEO*) narrow pass.
portorriqueño, a [portorri'keɲo, a] *a* Puerto Rican.
Portugal [portu'ɣal] *nm* Portugal; **portugués, esa** *a, nm/f* Portuguese.
porvenir [porβe'nir] *nm* future.
pos [pos] *prep:* **en ~ de** after, in pursuit of.
posada [po'saða] *nf* (*refugio*) shelter, lodging; (*mesón*) guest house; **dar ~ a** to give shelter to, take in.
posaderas [posa'ðeras] *nfpl* backside *sg*, buttocks.
posar [po'sar] *vt* (*en el suelo*) to lay down, put down; (*la mano*) to place, put gently // *vi* to sit, pose; **~se** *vr* to settle; (*pájaro*) to perch ; (*avión*) to land, come down.
posdata [pos'ðata] *nf* postscript.
pose ['pose] *nf* pose.
poseedor, a [posee'ðor, a] *nm/f* owner, possessor; (*de récord, puesto*) holder.
poseer [pose'er] *vt* to have, possess, own; (*ventaja*) to enjoy; (*récord, puesto*) to hold; **poseído, a** *a* possessed; **posesión** *nf* possession; **posesionarse** *vr:* **posesionarse de** to take possession of, take over; **posesivo, a** *a* possessive.
posibilidad [posiβili'ðað] *nf* possibility; (*oportunidad*) chance; **posibilitar** *vt* to make possible, permit; (*hacer factible*) to make feasible.
posible [po'siβle] *a* possible; (*factible*) feasible; **de ser ~** if possible; **en lo ~** as far as possible.
posición [posi'θjon] *nf* (*gen*) position; (*rango social*) status.
positivo, a [posi'tiβo, a] *a* positive // *nf* (*FOTO*) print.
poso ['poso] *nm* sediment.
posponer [pospo'ner] *vt* to put behind/below; (*AM*) to postpone.
posta ['posta] *nf* (*de caballos*) relay, team; (*pedazo*) slice // *nm* courier.
postal [pos'tal] *a* postal // *nf* postcard.
poste ['poste] *nm* (*de telégrafos*) post, pole; (*columna*) pillar; **dar ~ a uno** (*fam*) to keep sb hanging about.
postergar [poster'ɣar] *vt* (*AM: posponer*) to postpone, delay.
posteridad [posteri'ðað] *nf* posterity.
posterior [poste'rjor] *a* back, rear; (*siguiente*) following, subsequent; (*más tarde*) later; **~idad** *nf:* **con ~idad** later, subsequently.
postizo, a [pos'tiθo, a] *a* false, artificial // *nm* hairpiece.
postor, a [pos'tor, a] *nm/f* bidder.
postrado, a [pos'traðo, a] *a* prostrate; **postrar** *vt* (*derribar*) to cast down, overthrow; (*humillar*) to humble; (*MED*) to weaken, exhaust.
postre ['postre] *nm* sweet, dessert.
postremo, a [pos'tremo, a], **postrer,**

ero, a [pos'trer, ero, a] *a* (*último*) last; (*que viene detrás*) rear.
postulado [postu'laðo] *nm* postulate; **postular** *vt* (*empleo*) to apply for; (*pedir*) to seek, demand; (*proponer*) to postulate.
póstumo, a ['postumo, a] *a* posthumous.
postura [pos'tura] *nf* (*del cuerpo*) posture, position; (*fig*) attitude, position.
potable [po'taβle] *a* drinkable.
potaje [po'taxe] *nm* stew; **~s** *nmpl* mixed vegetables.
pote ['pote] *nm* pot, jar.
potencia [po'tenθja] *nf* power.
potencial [poten'θjal] *a, nm* potential.
potente [po'tente] *a* powerful.
pozo ['poθo] *nm* well; (*de río*) deep pool; (*de mina*) shaft.
práctica ['praktika] *nf ver* **práctico.**
practicable [prakti'kaβle] *a* practicable; (*camino*) passable, usable.
practicante [prakti'kante] *nm/f* (*MED: ayudante de doctor*) medical assistant; (: *enfermero*) male nurse; (*quien practica algo*) practitioner // *a* practising.
practicar [prakti'kar] *vt* to practise; (*deporte*) to go in for, play; (*realizar*) to carry out, perform.
práctico, a ['praktiko, a] *a* (*gen*) practical; (*conveniente*) handy; (*instruído: persona*) skilled, expert // *nf* practice; (*método*) method; (*arte, capacidad*) skill; **en la ~a** in practice.
pradera [pra'ðera] *nf* meadow; (*de Canadá*) prairie.
prado ['praðo] *nm* (*campo*) meadow, field; (*pastizal*) pasture.
Praga ['praɣa] *n* Prague.
pragmático, a [praɣ'matiko, a] *a* pragmatic.
preámbulo [pre'ambulo] *nm* preamble, introduction.
precario, a [pre'karjo, a] *a* precarious.
precaución [prekau'θjon] *nf* (*medida preventiva*) preventive measure, precaution; (*prudencia*) caution, wariness.
precaver [preka'βer] *vt* to guard against; (*impedir*) to forestall; **~se** *vr:* **~se de** *o* **contra algo** to (be on one's) guard against sth; **precavido, a** *a* cautious, wary.
precedencia [preθe'ðenθja] *nf* precedence; (*prioridad*) priority; (*superioridad*) greater importance, superiority; **precedente** *a* preceding; (*anterior*) former // *nm* precedent; **preceder** *vt, vi* to precede, go/come before.
precepto [pre'θepto] *nm* precept.
preciado, a [pre'θjaðo, a] *a* (*estimado*) esteemed, valuable; (*vanidoso*) presumptuous; **preciar** *vt* to esteem, value; **preciarse** *vr* to boast; **preciarse de** to pride o.s. on, boast of being.
precio ['preθjo] *nm* (*de mercado*) price; (*costo*) cost; (*valor*) value, worth; (*de viaje*) fare; **~ al contado/de coste/de**

oportunidad cash/cost/bargain price; ~ **tope** top price.

preciosidad [preθjosi'ðað] *nf* (*valor*) (high) value, (great) worth; (*encanto*) charm; (*cosa bonita*) beautiful thing; **es una** ~ it's lovely, it's really beautiful; **precioso, a** *a* precious; (*de mucho valor*) valuable; (*fam*) lovely, beautiful.

precipicio [preθi'piθjo] *nm* cliff, precipice; (*fig*) abyss.

precipitación [preθipita'θjon] *nf* haste; (*lluvia*) rainfall.

precipitado, a [preθipi'taðo, a] *a* hasty, rash; (*salida*) hasty, sudden.

precipitar [preθipi'tar] *vt* (*arrojar*) to hurl down, throw; (*apresurar*) to hasten; (*acelerar*) to speed up, accelerate; ~**se** *vr* to throw o.s.; (*apresurarse*) to rush; (*actuar sin pensar*) to act rashly.

precipitoso, a [preθipi'toso, a] *a* (*escarpado*) steep, sheer; (*a la carrera, imprudente*) hasty, rash.

precisamente [preθisa'mente] *ad* precisely; (*justo*) precisely, exactly, just.

precisar [preθi'sar] *vt* (*necesitar*) to need, require; (*fijar*) to determine exactly, fix; (*especificar*) to specify // *vi* to be necessary.

precisión [preθi'sjon] *nf* (*exactitud*) precision; (*necesidad*) need, necessity.

preciso, a [pre'θiso, a] *a* (*exacto*) precise; (*necesario*) necessary, essential.

preconcebido, a [prekonθe'βiðo, a] *a* preconceived.

preconizar [prekoni'θar] *vt* (*aconsejar*) to advise; (*prever*) to foresee.

precoz [pre'koθ] *a* (*persona*) precocious; (*calvicie*) premature.

precursor, a [prekur'sor, a] *nm/f* precursor.

predecir [preðe'θir] *vt* to predict, foretell, forecast.

predestinado, a [preðesti'naðo, a] *a* predestined.

predeterminar [preðetermi'nar] *vt* to predetermine.

prédica ['preðika] *nf* sermon; **predicador, a** *nm/f* preacher; **predicar** *vt, vi* to preach.

predicción [preðik'θjon] *nf* prediction.

predilecto, a [preði'lekto, a] *a* favourite.

predio ['preðjo] *nm* property, estate.

predisponer [preðispo'ner] *vt* to predispose; (*pey*) to prejudice; **predisposición** *nf* predisposition, inclination; prejudice, bias.

predominante [preðomi'nante] *a* predominant.

predominar [preðomi'nar] *vt* to dominate // *vi* to predominate; (*prevalecer*) to prevail; **predominio** *nm* predominance, prevalence.

prefabricado, a [prefaβri'kaðo, a] *a* prefabricated.

prefacio [pre'faθjo] *nm* preface.

preferencia [prefe'renθja] *nf* preference; **de** ~ preferably, for preference;

preferible *a* preferable; **preferir** *vt* to prefer.

prefigurar [prefixu'rar] *vt* to foreshadow, prefigure.

pregonar [prexo'nar] *vt* to proclaim, announce.

pregunta [pre'xunta] *nf* question; **hacer una** ~ to ask *or* put a question.

preguntar [prexun'tar] *vt* to ask; (*cuestionar*) to question // *vi* to ask; ~**se** *vr* to wonder; ~ **por alguien** to ask for sb; **preguntón, ona** *a* inquisitive.

prehistórico, a [preis'toriko, a] *a* prehistoric.

prejuicio [pre'xwiθjo] *nm* prejudgement; (*preconcepción*) preconception; (*pey*) prejudice, bias.

prelación [prela'θjon] *nf* priority.

preliminar [prelimi'nar] *a* preliminary.

preludio [pre'luðjo] *nm* prelude.

prematuro, a [prema'turo, a] *a* premature.

premeditación [premeðita'θjon] *nf* premeditation; **premeditar** *vt* to premeditate.

premiar [pre'mjar] *vt* to reward; (*en un concurso*) to give a prize to; **premio** *nm* reward; prize; (*COM*) premium.

premonición [premoni'θjon] *nf* premonition.

premura [pre'mura] *nf* (*aprieto*) pressure; (*prisa*) haste, urgency.

prenatal [prena'tal] *a* antenatal, prenatal.

prenda ['prenda] *nf* (*ropa*) garment, article of clothing; (*garantía*) pledge; ~**s** *nfpl* talents, gifts.

prendar [pren'dar] *vt* to captivate, enchant; ~**se de uno** to fall in love with sb.

prendedor [prende'ðor] *nm* brooch.

prender [pren'der] *vt* (*captar*) to catch, capture; (*detener*) to arrest; (*coser*) to pin, attach; (*sujetar*) to fasten // *vi* to catch; (*arraigar*) to take root; ~**se** *vr* (*encenderse*) to catch fire; (*engalanarse*) to dress up.

prensa ['prensa] *nf* press; **la P~** the press; **prensar** *vt* to press.

preñado, a [pre'ɲaðo, a] *a* (*mujer*) pregnant; ~ **de** pregnant with, full of; **preñez** *nf* pregnancy.

preocupación [preokupa'θjon] *nf* worry, concern; (*ansiedad*) anxiety; **preocupado, a** *a* worried, concerned; anxious.

preocupar [preoku'par] *vt* to worry; ~**se** *vr* to worry; ~**se de algo** (*hacerse cargo*) to worry about sth, take care of sth.

preparación [prepara'θjon] *nf* (*acto*) preparation; (*estado*) preparedness, readiness; (*entrenamiento*) training; **preparado, a** *a* (*dispuesto*) prepared; (*CULIN*) ready (to serve) // *nm* preparation.

preparador, a [prepara'ðor, a] *nm/f* trainer.

preparar [prepa'rar] *vt* (*disponer*) to prepare, get ready; (*TEC: tratar*) to prepare, process, treat; (entrenar) to teach, train; ~se vr: ~se a o para to prepare to or for, get ready to or for; **preparativo, a** a preparatory, preliminary; **preparativos** nmpl preparations; **preparatorio, a** a preparatory.

prerrogativa [prerroxa'tiβa] nf prerogative, privilege.

presa ['presa] nf (captura) capture, seizure; (cosa apresada) catch; (víctima) victim; (de animal) prey; (de agua) dam.

presbítero [pres'βitero] nm priest.

prescindible [presθin'diβle] a dispensable.

prescindir [presθin'dir] vi: ~ de (privarse de) to do without, go without; (descartar) to dispense with.

prescribir [preskri'βir] vt to prescribe; **prescripción** nf prescription.

presencia [pre'senθja] nf presence; **presencial** a: **testigo presencial** eyewitness; **presenciar** vt to be present at; (asistir a) to attend; (ver) to see, witness.

presentación [presenta'θjon] nf presentation; (introducción) introduction.

presentador, a [presenta'ðor, a] nm/f compère.

presentar [presen'tar] vt to present; (ofrecer) to offer; (mostrar) to show, display; (a una persona) to introduce; ~se vr (llegar inesperadamente) to appear, turn up; (ofrecerse: como candidato) to run, stand; (aparecer) to show, appear; (solicitar empleo) to apply.

presente [pre'sente] a present // nm present; **hacer** ~ to state, declare; **tener** ~ to remember, bear in mind.

presentimiento [presenti'mjento] nm premonition, presentiment; **presentir** vt to have a premonition of.

preservación [preserβa'θjon] nf protection, preservation; **preservar** vt to protect, preserve; **preservativo** nm sheath, condom.

presidencia [presi'ðenθja] nf presidency; (de comité) chairmanship; **presidente** nm/f president; chairman/woman.

presidiario [presi'ðjarjo] nm convict; **presidio** nm (penitenciaría) prison, penitentiary; (trabajo forzoso) hard labour; (MIL) garrison.

presidir [presi'ðir] vt (dirigir) to preside at, preside over; (: comité) to take the chair at; (dominar) to dominate, rule // vi to preside; to take the chair.

presión [pre'sjon] nf pressure; **presionar** vt to press; (fig) to press, put pressure on // vi: **presionar para o por** to press for.

preso, a ['preso, a] nm/f prisoner; **tomar** o **llevar** ~ **a uno** to arrest sb, take sb prisoner.

prestado, a [pres'taðo, a] a on loan; **pedir** ~ to borrow.

prestamista [presta'mista] nm/f moneylender.

préstamo ['prestamo] nm loan.

prestar [pres'tar] vt to lend, loan; (atención) to pay; (ayuda) to give // vi to give, stretch.

prestatario, a [presta'tarjo, a] nm/f borrower.

presteza [pres'teθa] nf speed, promptness.

prestigio [pres'tixjo] nm prestige; ~**so, a** a (honorable) prestigious; (famoso, renombrado) renowned, famous.

presto, a ['presto, a] a (rápido) quick, prompt; (dispuesto) ready // ad at once, right away.

presumir [presu'mir] vt to presume // vi (tener aires) to be conceited; **según cabe** ~ as may be presumed, presumably; **presunción** nf presumption; **presunto, a** a (supuesto) supposed, presumed; (así llamado) so-called; **presuntuoso, a** a a conceited, presumptuous.

presuponer [presupo'ner] vt to presuppose.

presupuesto [presu'pwesto] nm (FINANZAS) budget; (estimación: de costo) estimate.

presuroso, a [presu'roso, a] a (rápido) quick, speedy; (que tiene prisa) hasty.

pretencioso, a [preten'θjoso, a] a pretentious.

pretender [preten'der] vt (intentar) to try to, seek to; (reivindicar) to claim; (buscar) to seek, try for; (cortejar) to woo, court; ~ **que** to expect that; **pretendiente** nm/f (candidato) candidate, applicant; (amante) suitor; **pretensión** nf (aspiración) aspiration; (reivindicación) claim; (orgullo) pretension.

pretexto [pre'teksto] nm pretext; (excusa) excuse.

prevalecer [preβale'θer] vi to prevail; **prevaleciente** a prevailing, prevalent.

prevalerse [preβa'lerse] vr: ~ **de** to avail o.s. of.

prevención [preβen'θjon] nf (preparación) preparation; (estado) preparedness, readiness; (el evitar) prevention; (previsión) foresight, forethought; (prejuicio) bias, prejudice; (precaución) precaution.

prevenido, a [preβe'niðo, a] a prepared, ready; (cauteloso) cautious.

prevenir [preβe'nir] vt (impedir) to prevent; (prever) to foresee, anticipate; (predisponer) to prejudice, bias; (avisar) to warn; (preparar) to prepare, get ready; ~**se** vr to get ready, prepare; ~**se contra** vr to take precautions against; **preventivo, a** a preventive, precautionary.

prever [pre'βer] vt to foresee.

previo, a ['preβjo, a] a (anterior) previous; (preliminar) preliminary // prep: ~ **acuerdo de los otros** subject to the agreement of the others.

previsión [preβi'sjon] nf (perspicacia) foresight; (predicción) forecast; ~ **social** social security.

prieto, a ['prjeto, a] a (oscuro) dark; (fig) mean; (comprimido) tight, compressed.

prima ['prima] *nf ver* **primo.**
primacía [prima'θia] *nf* primacy.
primario, a [pri'marjo, a] *a* primary.
primavera [prima'ßera] *nf (temporada)* spring; *(período)* springtime.
primer, primero, a [pri'mer, pri'mero, a] *a* first; *(fig)* prime // *ad* first; *(más bien)* sooner, rather // *nf (AUTO)* first gear; *(FERRO)* first class; **de ~a** *(fam)* first-class, first-rate; **~a plana** front page.
primitivo, a [primi'tißo, a] *a* primitive; *(original)* original.
primo, a ['primo, a] *nm/f* cousin; *(fam)* fool, dupe // *nf (COM)* bonus; **~ hermano** first cousin; **materias ~as** raw materials.
primogénito, a [primo'xenito, a] *a* first-born.
primordial [primor'ðjal] *a* basic, fundamental.
primoroso, a [primo'roso, a] *a* exquisite, delicate.
princesa [prin'θesa] *nf* princess.
principal [prinθi'pal] *a* principal, main // *nm (jefe)* chief, principal.
príncipe ['prinθipe] *nm* prince.
principiante [prinθi'pjante] *nm/f* beginner; **principiar** *vt* to begin.
principio [prin'θipjo] *nm (comienzo)* beginning, start; *(origen)* origin; *(primera etapa)* rudiment, basic idea; *(moral)* principle; **a ~s de** at the beginning of; **tener** *o* **tomar en ~** to start from, be based on.
pringue ['pringe] *nm (grasa)* grease, fat, dripping; *(mancha)* grease stain.
prioridad [priori'ðað] *nf* priority.
prisa ['prisa] *nf (apresuramiento)* hurry, haste; *(rapidez)* speed; *(urgencia)* (sense of) urgency; **a** *o* **de ~** quickly; **correr ~** to be urgent; **darse ~** to hurry up; **estar de** *o* **tener ~** to be in a hurry.
prisión [pri'sjon] *nf (cárcel)* prison; *(período de cárcel)* imprisonment; **prisionero, a** *nm/f* prisoner.
prismáticos [pris'matikos] *nmpl* binoculars.
privación [prißa'θjon] *nf* deprivation; *(falta)* want, privation.
privado, a [pri'ßaðo, a] *a* private.
privar [pri'ßar] *vt* to deprive; *(prohibir)* to forbid // *vi (gozar de favor)* to be in favour; *(prevalecer)* to prevail; **privativo, a** *a* exclusive.
privilegiado, a [prißile'xjaðo, a] *a* privileged; *(memoria)* very good; **privilegiar** *vt* to grant a privilege to; *(favorecer)* to favour.
privilegio [prißi'lexjo] *nm* privilege; *(concesión)* concession; **~ de invención** patent.
pro [pro] *nm* *o* *f* profit, advantage // *prep*: **asociación ~ ciegos** association for the blind // *pref*: **~ soviético/americano** pro-Soviet/American; **en ~ de** on behalf of, for; **los ~s y los contras** the pros and cons.

probabilidad [proßaßili'ðað] *nf* probability, likelihood; *(oportunidad, posibilidad)* chance, prospect; **probable** *a* probable, likely.
probanza [pro'ßanθa] *nf* proof, evidence.
probar [pro'ßar] *vt (demostrar)* to prove; *(someter a prueba)* to test, try out; *(ropa)* to try on; *(comida)* to taste // *vi* to try; **~se un traje** to try on a suit.
probeta [pro'ßeta] *nf* test tube.
problema [pro'ßlema] *nm* problem.
procaz [pro'kaθ] *a* insolent, impudent.
procedente [proθe'ðente] *a (razonable)* reasonable; *(conforme a derecho)* proper, fitting; **~ de** coming from, originating in.
proceder [proθe'ðer] *vi (avanzar)* to proceed; *(actuar)* to act; *(ser correcto)* to be right (and proper), be fitting // *nm (acción)* course of action; *(comportamiento)* behaviour, conduct; **procedimiento** *nm* procedure; *(proceso)* process; *(método)* means, method.
procesado, a [proθe'saðo, a] *nm/f* accused (person); **procesar** *vt* to try, put on trial.
procesión [proθe'sjon] *nf* procession.
proceso [pro'θeso] *nm* process; *(JUR)* trial; *(lapso)* course (of time).
proclama [pro'klama] *nf (acto)* proclamation; *(cartel)* poster; **proclamar** *vt* to proclaim.
procreación [prokrea'θjon] *nf* procreation; **procrear** *vt, vi* to procreate.
procurador, a [prokura'ðor, a] *nm/f* attorney.
procurar [proku'rar] *vt (intentar)* to try, endeavour; *(conseguir)* to get, obtain; *(asegurar)* to secure; *(producir)* to produce.
prodigio [pro'ðixjo] *nm* prodigy; *(milagro)* wonder, marvel; **~so, a** *a* prodigious, marvellous.
pródigo, a ['proðiɣo, a] *a*: **hijo ~** prodigal son.
producción [proðuk'θjon] *nf* production; *(suma de productos)* output; *(producto)* product; **~ en serie** mass production.
producir [proðu'θir] *vt* to produce; *(generar)* to cause, bring about; **~se** *vr (gen)* to come about, happen; *(hacerse)* to be produced, be made; *(estallar)* to break out.
productividad [proðuktißi'ðað] *nf* productivity; **productivo, a** *a* productive; *(provechoso)* profitable.
producto [pro'ðukto] *nm* product; *(producción)* production.
productor, a [proðuk'tor, a] *a* productive, producing // *nm/f* producer.
proeza [pro'eθa] *nf* exploit, feat.
profanar [profa'nar] *vt* to desecrate, profane; **profano, a** *a* profane // *nm/f* layman/woman.
profecía [profe'θia] *nf* prophecy.
proferir [profe'rir] *vt (palabra, sonido)* to utter; *(injuria)* to hurl, let fly.
profesar [profe'sar] *vt (declarar)* to profess; *(practicar)* to practise.

profesión [profe'sjon] *nf* profession; **profesional** *a* professional.

profesor, a [profe'sor, a] *nm/f* teacher; ~**ado** *nm* teaching profession.

profeta [pro'feta] *nm/f* prophet; **profetizar** *vt, vi* to prophesy.

prófugo, a ['profuxo, a] *nm/f* fugitive; (*desertor*) deserter.

profundidad [profundi'ðað] *nf* depth; **profundizar** *vt* (*fig*) to go deeply into; **profundo, a** *a* deep; (*misterio, pensador*) profound.

progenie [pro'xenje] *nf* offspring.

progenitor [proxeni'tor] *nm* ancestor; ~**es** *nmpl* (*fam*) parents.

programa [pro'xrama] *nm* programme; ~**ción** *nf* programming; ~**dor, a** *nm/f* programmer; **programar** *vt* to programme.

progresar [proxre'sar] *vi* to progress, make progress; **progresista** *a, nm/f* progressive; **progresivo, a** *a* progressive; (*gradual*) gradual; (*continuo*) continuous; **progreso** *nm* progress.

prohibición [proißi'θjon] *nf* prohibition, ban; **prohibir** *vt* to prohibit, ban, forbid; **se prohibe fumar** no smoking.

prohijar [proi'xar] *vt* to adopt.

prójimo, a ['proximo, a] *nm/f* fellow man, neighbour.

proletariado [proleta'rjaðo] *nm* proletariat; **proletario, a** *a, nm/f* proletarian.

proliferación [prolifera'θjon] *nf* proliferation; **proliferar** *vi* to proliferate; **prolífico, a** *a* prolific.

prolijo, a [pro'lixo, a] *a* long-winded, tedious.

prólogo ['proloxo] *nm* prologue.

prolongación [prolonga'θjon] *nf* extension; **prolongado, a** *a* (*largo*) long; (*alargado*) lengthy; **prolongar** *vt* (*gen*) to extend; (*en el tiempo*) to prolong; (*calle, tubo*) to make longer, extend.

promedio [pro'meðjo] *nm* average; (*de distancia*) middle, mid-point.

promesa [pro'mesa] *nf* promise.

prometer [prome'ter] *vt* to promise // *vi* to show promise; ~**se** *vr* (*dos personas*) to get engaged; **prometido, a** *a* promised; engaged // *nm/f* fiancé/fiancée.

prominente [promi'nente] *a* prominent.

promiscuo, a [pro'miskwo, a] *a* (*mezclado*) mixed(-up), in disorder; (*ambiguo*) ambiguous.

promoción [promo'θjon] *nf* promotion.

promotor [promo'tor] *nm* promoter; (*instigador*) instigator.

promover [promo'ßer] *vt* to promote; (*causar*) to cause; (*instigar*) to instigate, stir up.

promulgar [promul'xar] *vt* to promulgate; (*fig*) to proclaim.

pronosticar [pronosti'kar] *vt* to predict, foretell, forecast; **pronóstico** *nm* prediction, forecast.

prontitud [pronti'tuð] *nf* speed, quickness;

(*de ingenio*) quickness, sharpness.

pronto, a ['pronto, a] *a* (*rápido*) prompt, quick; (*preparado*) ready; (*astuto*) quick, sharp // *ad* quickly, promptly; (*en seguida*) at once, right away; (*dentro de poco*) soon; (*temprano*) early // *nm*: **tener** ~**s de enojo** to be quick-tempered; **al** ~ at first; **de** ~ suddenly; **por lo** ~ meanwhile, for the present.

pronunciación [pronunθja'θjon] *nf* pronunciation; **pronunciar** *vt* to pronounce; (*discurso*) to make, deliver; **pronunciarse** *vr* to revolt, rise, rebel; (*declararse*) to declare o.s.

propagación [propaxa'θjon] *nf* propagation.

propaganda [propa'xanda] *nf* (*política*) propaganda; (*comercial*) advertising.

propagar [propa'xar] *vt* to propagate.

propensión [propen'sjon] *nf* inclination, propensity; **propenso, a** *a* inclined to; **ser propenso a** to be inclined to, have a tendency to.

propiamente [propja'mente] *ad* properly; (*realmente*) really, exactly.

propicio, a [pro'piθjo, a] *a* favourable, propitious.

propiedad [propje'ðað] *nf* (*gen*) property; (*posesión*) possession, ownership; ~ **industrial** patent rights *pl*; ~ **literaria** copyright; ~ **particular** private property.

propietario, a [propje'tarjo, a] *nm/f* owner, proprietor.

propina [pro'pina] *nf* tip.

propio, a ['propjo, a] *a* own, of one's own; (*característico*) characteristic, typical; (*conveniente*) proper; (*mismo*) selfsame, very; **el** ~ **ministro** the minister himself; **¿tienes casa** ~**a?** have you a house of your own?

proponer [propo'ner] *vt* to propose, put forward; (*problema*) to pose; ~**se** *vr* to propose, plan, intend.

proporción [propor'θjon] *nf* proportion; (*MAT*) ratio; (*oportunidad*) chance, opportunity; **proporciones** *nfpl* dimensions; (*fig*) size *sg*; **proporcionado, a** *a* proportionate; (*regular*) medium, middling; (*justo*) just right; **proporcionar** *vt* (*dar*) to give, supply, provide; (*adaptar*) to adjust, adapt.

proposición [proposi'θjon] *nf* proposition; (*propuesta*) proposal.

propósito [pro'posito] *nm* purpose; (*intento*) aim, intention // *a*: **a** ~ appropriate, suitable // *ad*: **a** ~ by the way, incidentally; **a** ~ **de** about, with regard to; **de** ~ on purpose, deliberately.

propuesta [pro'pwesta] *nf* proposal.

propulsar [propul'sar] *vt* to drive, propel; (*fig*) to promote, encourage; **propulsión** *nf* propulsion; **propulsión a chorro** *o* **por reacción** jet propulsion.

prórroga ['prorroxa] *nf* (*gen*) extension; (*JUR*) stay; (*COM*) deferment; **prorrogar** *vt* (*período*) to extend; (*decisión*) to defer, postpone.

prorrumpir [prorrum'pir] *vi* to burst forth, break out.

prosa ['prosa] *nf* prose.

proscribir [proskri'ßir] *vt* to prohibit, ban; (*desterrar*) to exile, banish; (*partido*) to proscribe; **proscripción** *nf* prohibition, ban; banishment; proscription.

prosecución [proseku'θjon] *nf* continuation; (*persecución*) pursuit.

proseguir [prose'xir] *vt* to continue, carry on, proceed with // *vi* to continue, go on.

prospección [prospek'θjon] *nf* exploration; (*del petróleo, del oro*) prospecting.

prospecto [pros'pekto] *nm* prospectus.

prosperar [prospe'rar] *vi* to prosper, thrive, flourish; **prosperidad** *nf* prosperity; (*éxito*) success; **próspero, a** *a* prosperous, thriving, flourishing; (*que tiene éxito*) successful.

prostíbulo [pros'tißulo] *nm* brothel.

prostitución [prostitu'θjon] *nf* prostitution; **prostituir** *vt* to prostitute; **prostituirse** *vr* to prostitute o.s., become a prostitute; **prostituta** *nf* prostitute.

protagonista [protaxo'nista] *nm/f* protagonist.

protección [protek'θjon] *nf* protection.

protector, a [protek'tor, a] *a* protective, protecting // *nm/f* protector.

proteger [prote'xer] *vt* to protect; **protegido, a** *nm/f* protégé/ protégée.

proteína [prote'ina] *nf* protein.

protesta [pro'testa] *nf* protest; (*declaración*) protestation.

protestante [protes'tante] *a* Protestant.

protestar [protes'tar] *vt* to protest, declare; (*fe*) to protest // *vi* to protest.

protocolo [proto'kolo] *nm* protocol.

prototipo [proto'tipo] *nm* prototype.

provecho [pro'ßetʃo] *nm* advantage, benefit; (*FINANZAS*) profit; ¡**buen** ~! bon appétit!; **en** ~ **de** to the benefit of; **sacar** ~ **de** to benefit from, profit by.

proveer [proße'er] *vt* to provide, supply; (*preparar*) to provide, get ready; (*vacante*) to fill; (*negocio*) to transact, dispatch // *vi*: ~ **a** to provide for.

provenir [proße'nir] *vi*: ~ **de** to come from, stem from.

proverbio [pro'ßerßjo] *nm* proverb.

providencia [proßi'ðenθja] *nf* providence; (*previsión*) foresight; ~**s** *nfpl* measures, steps.

provincia [pro'ßinθja] *nf* province; ~**no, a** *a* provincial; (*del campo*) country *cpd*.

provisión [proßi'sjon] *nf* provision; (*abastecimiento*) provision, supply; (*medida*) measure, step.

provisional [proßisjo'nal] *a* provisional.

provocación [proßoka'θjon] *nf* provocation; **provocar** *vt* to provoke; (*alentar*) to tempt, invite; (*causar*) to bring about, lead to; (*promover*) to promote;

(*estimular*) to rouse, stir, stimulate; **provocativo, a** *a* provocative.

próximamente [proksima'mente] *ad* shortly, soon.

proximidad [proksimi'ðað] *nf* closeness, proximity; **próximo, a** *a* near, close; (*vecino*) neighbouring; (*el que viene*) next.

proyectar [projek'tar] *vt* (*objeto*) to hurl, throw; (*luz*) to cast, shed; (*CINE*) to screen, show; (*planear*) to plan.

proyectil [projek'til] *nm* projectile, missile; (*MIL*) missile.

proyecto [pro'jekto] *nm* plan; (*estimación de costo*) detailed estimate.

proyector [projek'tor] *nm* (*CINE*) projector; (*MIL*) searchlight; (*de teatro*) spotlight.

prudencia [pru'ðenθja] *nf* (*sabiduría*) wisdom, prudence; (*cautela*) care; **prudente** *a* sensible, wise, prudent; (*conductor*) careful.

prueba ['prweßa] *nf* proof; (*ensayo*) test, trial; (*saboreo*) testing, sampling; (*de ropa*) fitting; ~**s** *nfpl* trials; **a** ~ on trial; **a** ~ **de** proof against; **a** ~ **de agua/fuego** waterproof/fireproof; **sala de** ~**s** fitting room; **someter a** ~ to put to the test.

prurito [pru'rito] *nm* itch; (*de bebé*) nappy rash.

psico... [siko] *pref* psycho...; ~**análisis** *nm* psychoanalysis; ~**logía** *nf* psychology; ~**lógico, a** *a* psychological; **psicólogo, a** *nm/f* psychologist; **psicópata** *nm/f* psychopath; ~**sis** *nf inv* psychosis.

psiquiatra [si'kjatra] *nm/f* psychiatrist; **psiquiátrico, a** *a* psychiatric.

psíquico, a ['sikiko, a] *a* psychic(al).

PSOE *abr de* **Partido Socialista Obrero Español.**

púa ['pua] *nf* sharp point; (*para guitarra*) plectrum; **alambre de** ~ barbed wire.

pubertad [pußer'tað] *nf* puberty.

publicación [pußlika'θjon] *nf* publication; **publicar** *vt* (*editar*) to publish; (*hacer público*) to publicize; (*vulgarizar*) to make public, divulge.

publicidad [pußliθi'ðað] *nf* publicity; (*COM*) advertising; **publicitario, a** *a* publicity *cpd*; advertising *cpd*.

público, a ['pußliko, a] *a* public // *nm* public; (*TEATRO etc*) audience.

puchero [pu'tʃero] *nm* stew; **hacer** ~**s** to pout.

pude *etc vb ver* **poder.**

púdico, a ['puðiko, a] *a* modest.

pudiera *etc vb ver* **poder.**

pudor [pu'ðor] *nm* modesty.

pudrir [pu'ðrir] *vt* to rot; (*fam*) to upset, annoy; ~**se** *vr* to rot, decay.

pueblo ['pweßlo] *nm* people; (*nación*) nation; (*aldea*) village.

puedo *etc vb ver* **poder.**

puente ['pwente] *nm* (*gen*) bridge; ~ **aéreo** airlift; ~ **colgante** suspension bridge; **hacer el** ~ (*fam*) to take an extra day off work between 2 public holidays.

puerco, a ['pwerko, a] *nm/f* pig/sow // *a*

(sucio) dirty, filthy; (*obsceno*) disgusting; ~ **de mar** porpoise; ~ **marino** dolphin.

pueril [pwe'ril] a childish.

puerro ['pwerro] nm leek.

puerta ['pwerta] nf door; (*de jardín*) gate; (*portal*) doorway; (*fig*) gateway; (*gol*) goal; **a ~ cerrada** behind closed doors; ~ **giratoria** swing door, revolving door.

puertaventana [pwertaßen'tana] nf shutter.

puerto ['pwerto] nm port; (*paso*) pass; (*fig*) haven, refuge.

Puerto Rico [pwerto'riko] nm Puerto Rico; **puertorriqueño, a** a Puerto Rican.

pues [pwes] ad (*entonces*) then; (¡*entonces*!) well, well then; (*así que*) so // conj (*ya que*) since; ¡ ~! (*sí*) yes!, certainly!

puesto, a ['pwesto, a] pp de **poner** // a dressed // nm (*lugar, posición*) place; (*trabajo*) post, job; (*COM*) stall // conj: ~ **que** since, as // nf (*apuesta*) bet, stake; ~**a en marcha** starting; ~**a del sol** sunset.

púgil ['puxil] nm boxer.

pugna ['puxna] nf battle, conflict; ~**cidad** nf pugnacity, aggressiveness; **pugnar** vi (*luchar*) to struggle, fight; (*pelear*) to fight.

pulcro, a ['pulkro, a] a neat, tidy; (*bello*) exquisite.

pulga ['pulxa] nf flea.

pulgada [pul'xaða] nf inch.

pulgar [pul'xar] nm thumb.

pulir [pu'lir], **pulimentar** [pulimen'tar] vt to polish; (*alisar*) to smooth; (*fig*) to polish up, touch up.

pulmón [pul'mon] nm lung; **pulmonía** nf pneumonia.

pulpa ['pulpa] nf pulp; (*de fruta*) flesh, soft part.

púlpito ['pulpito] nm pulpit.

pulpo ['pulpo] nm octopus.

pulsación [pulsa'θjon] nf beat, pulsation; (*ANAT*) throb(bing).

pulsador [pulsa'ðor] nm button, push button.

pulsar [pul'sar] vt (*tecla*) to touch, tap; (*MUS*) to play; (*botón*) to press, push // vi to pulsate; (*latir*) to beat, throb; (*MED*): ~ **a uno** to take sb's pulse.

pulsera [pul'sera] nf bracelet.

pulso ['pulso] nm (*ANAT*) pulse; (: *muñeca*) wrist; (*fuerza*) strength; (*firmeza*) steadiness, steady hand; (*tacto*) tact, good sense.

pulverizador [pulßeriθa'ðor] nm spray, spray gun; **pulverizar** vt to pulverize; (*líquido*) to spray.

pulla ['puʎa] nf cutting remark; (*expresión grosera*) obscene remark.

pungir [pun'xir] vt to puncture, prick, pierce; (*fig*) to cause suffering to.

punición [puni'θjon] nf punishment; **punitivo, a** a punitive.

punta ['punta] nf point, tip; (*extremidad*) end; (*fig*) touch, trace; **horas ~s** peak hours, rush hours; **sacar ~ a** to sharpen; **estar de ~** to be edgy.

puntada [pun'taða] nf (*COSTURA*) stitch; (*fam*) hint; **no ha dado ~** he hasn't done a stroke.

puntal [pun'tal] nm prop, support.

puntapié [punta'pje] nm kick.

puntear [punte'ar] vt (*marcar*) to tick, mark; (*coser*) to stitch (up).

puntería [punte'ria] nf (*de arma*) aim, aiming; (*destreza*) marksmanship.

puntiagudo, a [puntja'xuðo, a] a sharp, pointed.

puntilla [pun'tiʎa] nf (*de pluma*) point, nib; **(andar) de ~s** (to walk) on tiptoe.

punto ['punto] nm (*gen*) point; (*señal diminuta*) spot, dot; (*lugar*) spot, place; (*momento*) point, moment; **a ~** ready; **estar a ~ de** to be on the point of or about to; **en ~** on the dot; ~ **de arranque** starting point; ~ **muerto** dead centre; (*AUTO*) neutral (gear); ~ **y coma** semicolon; ~ **de interrogación** question mark.

puntuación [puntwa'θjon] nf punctuation; (*puntos: en examen*) mark(s) (*pl*); (: *DEPORTE*) score.

puntual [pun'twal] a (*a tiempo*) punctual; (*exacto*) exact, accurate; (*seguro*) reliable; ~**idad** nf punctuality; exactness, accuracy; reliability; ~**izar** vt to fix, specify; (*en la memoria*) to fix in one's mind/memory.

punzante [pun'θante] a (*dolor*) shooting, sharp; (*herramienta*) sharp; **punzar** vt to prick, pierce // vi to shoot, stab.

puñado [pu'ɲaðo] nm handful.

puñal [pu'ɲal] nm dagger; ~**ada** nf stab; ~**ada de misericordia** coup de grâce.

puñetazo [puɲe'taθo] nm punch.

puño ['puɲo] nm (*ANAT*) fist; (*cantidad*) fistful, handful; (*COSTURA*) cuff; (*de herramienta*) handle.

pupila [pu'pila] nf pupil.

pupitre [pu'pitre] nm desk.

puré [pu're] nm puree; (*sopa*) (thick) soup; ~ **de patatas** mashed potatoes.

pureza [pu'reθa] nf purity.

purga ['purxa] nf purge; **purgante** a, nm purgative; **purgar** vt to purge.

purgatorio [purxa'torjo] nm purgatory.

purificar [purifi'kar] vt to purify; (*refinar*) to refine.

puritano, a [puri'tano, a] a (*actitud*) puritanical; (*iglesia, tradición*) puritan // nm/f puritan.

puro, a ['puro, a] a pure; (*cielo*) clear; (*verdad*) simple, plain // ad: **de ~ cansado** out of sheer tiredness // nm cigar.

púrpura ['purpura] nf purple; **purpúreo, a** a purple.

puse, pusiera etc vb ver **poner.**

pústula ['pustula] nf pimple, sore.

puta ['puta] nf whore, prostitute.

putrefacción [putrefak'θjon] nf rotting, putrefaction.

pútrido, a ['putriðo, a] a rotten.

Q

q.e.p.d. *abr de* **que en paz descanse.**
q.e.s.m. *abr de* **que estrecha su mano.**
que [ke] *pron (sujeto)* who, that; (: *cosa*) which, that; (*complemento*) whom, that; (: *cosa*) which, that // *conj* that; **el momento en ~ llegó** the moment he arrived; **lo ~ digo** what I say; **dar ~ hablar** to give cause to talk, cause talk; **le ruego ~ se calle** I'm asking you to keep quiet; **te digo ~ sí** I'm telling you, I assure you; **yo ~ tú** if I were you.
qué [ke] *a* what?, which? // *pron* what?; **¡~ divertido!** how funny!; **¿~ edad tiene Ud?** how old are you?; **¿de ~ me hablas?** what are you saying to me?; **¿~ tal?** how are you?, how are things?; **¿~ hay (de nuevo)?** what's new?
quebrada [ke'ßraða] *nf ver* **quebrado.**
quebradizo, a [keßra'ðiθo, a] *a* fragile; (*persona*) frail.
quebrado, a [ke'ßraðo, a] *a* (*roto*) broken; (*pálido*) pale; (*COM*) bankrupt // *nm/f* bankrupt // *nf* ravine.
quebradura [keßra'ðura] *nf* (*fisura*) fissure; (*GEO*) gorge; (*MED*) rupture.
quebrantadura [keßranta'ðura] *nf*, **quebrantamiento** [keßranta'mjento] *nm* (*acto*) breaking; (*estado*) exhaustion.
quebrantar [keßran'tar] *vt* (*romper*) to break; (*infringir*) to violate, transgress; **~se** *vr* (*persona*) to fail in health; (*deshacerse*) to break.
quebranto [ke'ßranto] *nm* damage, harm; (*decaimiento*) exhaustion; (*debilidad*) weakness; (*dolor*) grief, pain.
quebrar [ke'ßrar] *vt* to break, smash; (*interrumpir*) to interrupt // *vi* to go bankrupt; **~se** *vr* to break, get broken; (*MED*) to be ruptured.
quedar [ke'ðar] *vi* (*permanecer*) to stay; (*seguir siendo*) to remain; (*encontrarse*) to be; (*restar*) to remain, be left; **~se** *vr* to remain, stay (behind); **~se con** to keep; **~ en** (*acordar*) to agree on/to; (*acabar siendo*) to end up as; **~ por hacer** to be still to be done; **~ ciego/mudo** to be left blind/dumb; **no te queda bien ese vestido** that dress doesn't suit you; **quedamos a las seis** we agreed to meet at six.
quedo, a ['keðo, a] *a* still // *ad* softly, gently.
quehacer [kea'θer] *nm* task, job; (*doméstico*) chore.
queja ['kexa] *nf* complaint; **quejarse** *vr* (*enfermo*) to moan, groan; (*protestar*) to complain; **quejido** *nm* moan; **quejoso, a** *a* complaining.
quemado, a [ke'maðo, a] *a* burnt.
quemadura [kema'ðura] *nf* burn, scald.
quemar [ke'mar] *vt* to burn; (*fig*) to burn up, squander // *vi* to be burning hot; **~se** *vr* to burn (up); (*del sol*) to get sunburnt.

quemarropa [kema'rropa]: **a ~** *ad* point-blank.
quemazón [kema'θon] *nf* burn; (*calor*) intense heat; (*sensación*) itch.
quepo *etc vb ver* **caber.**
querella [ke're/a] *nf* (*JUR*) charge; (*disputa*) dispute.
querer [ke'rer] *vt* (*desear*) to want, wish; (*amar a*) to love; **~ hacer algo** to want to do sth; **querido, a** *a* dear // *nm/f* darling // *nf* mistress.
quesería [kese'ria] *nf* dairy, cheese factory.
queso ['keso] *nm* cheese; **~ crema** cream cheese; **~ helado** ice-cream brick.
quicio ['kiθjo] *nm* hinge; **sacar a uno de ~** to get on sb's nerves.
quiebra ['kjeßra] *nf* break, split; (*COM*) bankruptcy; (*ECON*) slump.
quiebro ['kjeßro] *nm* (*del cuerpo*) swerve.
quien [kjen] *pron* who; **hay ~ piensa que** there are those who think that; **no hay ~ lo haga** no-one will do it.
quién [kjen] *pron* who, whom; **¿~ es?** who's there?
quienquiera [kjen'kjera] (*pl* **quienesquiera**) *pron* whoever.
quiero *etc vb ver* **querer.**
quieto, a ['kjeto, a] *a* still; (*carácter*) placid; **quietud** *nf* stillness.
quijada [ki'xaða] *nf* jaw, jawbone.
quilate [ki'late] *nm* carat.
quimera [ki'mera] *nf* chimera; **quimérico, a** *a* fantastic.
químico, a ['kimiko, a] *a* chemical // *nm/f* chemist // *nf* chemistry.
quincalla [kin'ka/a] *nf* hardware, ironmongery.
quince ['kinθe] *num* fifteen; **~na** *nf* fortnight; (*pago*) fortnightly pay; **~nal** *a* fortnightly.
quiniela [ki'njela] *nf* pools coupon; **~s** *nfpl* football pools.
quinientos [ki'njentos] *num* five hundred.
quinina [ki'nina] *nf* quinine.
quinqui ['kinki] *nm* gangster.
quinto, a ['kinto, a] *a* fifth // *nf* country house; (*MIL*) call-up, draft.
quiosco ['kjosko] *nm* (*de música*) bandstand; (*de periódicos*) news stand.
quirúrgico, a [ki'rurxiko, a] *a* surgical.
quise, quisiera *etc vb ver* **querer.**
quisquilloso, a [kiski'/oso, a] *a* touchy; (*fam*) pernickety.
quiste ['kiste] *nm* cyst.
quita ['kita] *nf* remission of debt; **de ~ y pon** detachable.
quitaesmalte [kitaes'malte] *nm* nail-polish remover.
quitamanchas [kita'mantʃas] *nm inv* stain remover.
quitar [ki'tar] *vt* to remove, take away; (*ropa*) to take off; (*dolor*) to kill, stop; **¡quita de ahí!** get away!; **~se** *vr* to

withdraw; **se quitó el sombrero** he took off his hat.
quitasol [kita'sol] *nm* sunshade.
quite ['kite] *nm* (*esgrima*) parry; (*evasión*) dodge.
quizá(s) [ki'θa(s)] *ad* perhaps, maybe.

R

rábano ['raβano] *nm* radish; **me importa un ~** I don't give a damn.
rabia ['raβja] *nf* (*MED*) rabies; (*fig*) fury, rage; **rabiar** *vi* to have rabies; to rage, be furious; **rabiar por algo** to be dying for *or* long for sth.
rabieta [ra'βjeta] *nf* tantrum, fit of temper.
rabino [ra'βino] *nm* rabbi.
rabioso, a [ra'βjoso, a] *a* rabid; (*fig*) furious.
rabo ['raβo] *nm* tail.
racial [ra'θjal] *a* racial, race *cpd*.
racimo [ra'θimo] *nm* bunch.
raciocinio [raθjo'θinjo] *nm* reason.
ración [ra'θjon] *nf* portion; **raciones** *nfpl* rations.
racional [raθjo'nal] *a* (*razonable*) reasonable; (*lógico*) rational; **~izar** *vt* to rationalize.
racionar [raθjo'nar] *vt* to ration (out).
racismo [ra'θismo] *nm* racialism, racism; **racista** *a, nm/f* racist.
racha ['ratʃa] *nf* gust of wind.
radar [ra'ðar] *nm* radar.
radiador [raðja'ðor] *nm* radiator.
radiante [ra'ðjante] *a* radiant.
radical [raði'kal] *a, nm/f* radical.
radicar [raði'kar] *vi* to take root; **~ en** to lie *or* consist in; **~se** *vr* to establish o.s., put down (one's) roots.
radio ['raðjo] *nf* radio; (*aparato*) radio (set) // *nm* (*MAT*) radius; (*QUIMICA*) radium; **~activo, a** *a* radioactive; **~difusión** *nf* broadcasting; **~emisora** *nf* transmitter, radio station; **~escucha** *nm/f* listener; **~grafia** *nf* X-ray; **~grafiar** *vt* to X-ray; **~terapia** *nf* radiotherapy; **radioyente** *nm/f* listener.
raer [ra'er] *vt* to scrape (off).
ráfaga ['rafaɣa] *nf* gust; (*de luz*) flash; (*de tiros*) burst.
raído, a [ra'iðo, a] *a* (*ropa*) threadbare; (*persona*) shameless.
raigambre [rai'ɣambre] *nf* (*BOT*) roots *pl*; (*fig*) tradition.
raíz [ra'iθ] (*pl* **raíces**) *nf* root; **~ cuadrada** square root; **a ~ de** as a result of.
raja ['raxa] *nf* (*de melón etc*) slice; (*grieta*) crack; **rajar** *vt* to split; (*fam*) to slash; (*fruta etc*) to slice; **rajarse** *vr* to split, crack; (*AM*) to quit.
rajatabla [raxa'taβla]: **a ~** *ad* (*estrictamente*) strictly, to the letter; (*cueste lo que cueste*) at all costs.
ralo, a ['ralo, a] *a* thin, sparse.

rallado, a [ra'ʎaðo, a] *a* grated; **rallador** *nm* grater; **rallar** *vt* to grate.
rama ['rama] *nf* branch; **~da** *nf*, **~je** *nm* branches *pl*, foliage; **ramal** *nm* (*de cuerda*) strand; (*FERRO*) branch line; (*AUTO*) branch (road).
rambla ['rambla] *nf* (*de agua*) stream; (*avenida*) avenue.
ramera [ra'mera] *nf* whore.
ramificación [ramifika'θjon] *nf* ramification; **ramificarse** *vr* to branch out.
ramillete [rami'ʎete] *nm* bouquet; (*fig*) select group.
ramo ['ramo] *nm* branch; (*COM*) department, section.
rampa ['rampa] *nf* (*MED*) cramp; (*plano*) ramp.
ramplón, ona [ram'plon, ona] *a* uncouth, coarse.
rana ['rana] *nf* frog; **~ toro** bullfrog; **salto de ~** leapfrog.
rancio, a ['ranθjo, a] *a* rancid; (*vino*) aged, mellow; (*fig*) ancient.
rancho ['rantʃo] *nm* grub (*fam*); (*AM*) farm.
rango ['rango] *nm* rank, standing.
ranura [ra'nura] *nf* groove; (*de teléfono*) slot.
rapacidad [rapaθi'ðað] *nf* rapacity.
rapar [ra'par] *vt* to shave; (*los cabellos*) to crop; (*fam*) to pinch, nick (*fam*).
rapaz [ra'paθ] *a* (*ladrón*) thieving; (*ZOOL*) predatory.
rapaz, a [ra'paθ, a] *nm/f* young boy/girl.
rape ['rape] *nm* quick shave; **al ~** cropped.
rapé [ra'pe] *nm* snuff.
rapidez [rapi'ðeθ] *nf* speed, rapidity; **rápido, a** *a* rapid, fast, quick // *ad* quickly // *nm* (*tren*) express; **rápidos** *nmpl* rapids.
rapiña [ra'piɲa] *nm* robbery; **ave de ~** bird of prey.
raptar [rap'tar] *vt* to kidnap; **rapto** *nm* kidnapping; (*impulso*) sudden impulse; (*éxtasis*) ecstasy, rapture.
raqueta [ra'keta] *nf* racquet.
raquítico, a [ra'kitiko, a] *a* stunted; (*fig*) poor, inadequate; **raquitismo** *nm* rickets *sg*.
rareza [ra'reθa] *nf* rarity; (*fig*) eccentricity.
raro, a ['raro, a] *a* (*poco común*) rare; (*extraño*) odd, strange; (*excepcional*) remarkable.
ras [ras] *nm*: **a ~ de** level with; **a ~ de tierra** at ground level.
rasar [ra'sar] *vt* (*igualar*) to level; (*frotar*) to graze.
rascacielos [raska'θjelos] *nm inv* skyscraper.
rascar [ras'kar] *vt* (*con las uñas*) to scratch; (*raspar*) to scrape; **~se** *vr* to scratch (o.s.).
rasgadura [rasɣa'ðura] *nf* tear, rip; **rasgar** *vt* to tear, rip (up).
rasgo ['rasɣo] *nm* stroke; **~s** *nmpl*

features, characteristics; **a grandes ~s** in outline, broadly.

rasguñar [rasˣuˈɲar] *vt* to scratch; **rasguño** *nm* scratch.

raso, a [ˈraso, a] *a* (*liso*) flat, level; (*a baja altura*) very low // *nm* satin; **cielo ~** clear sky; **soldado ~** private.

raspador [raspaˈðor] *nm* scraper.

raspadura [raspaˈðura] *nf* scrape; (*marca*) scratch; **~s** *nfpl* scrapings; **raspar** *vt* to scrape; (*arañar*) to scratch; (*limar*) to file.

rastra [ˈrastra] *nf* (*huella*) track; (*AGR*) rake; **a ~s** by dragging; (*fig*) unwillingly; **pescar a la ~** to trawl.

rastreador [rastreaˈðor] *nm* tracker; (*NAUT*) trawler; **~ de minas** minesweeper; **rastrear** *vt* to track; (*laguna, río*) to dredge, drag.

rastrero, a [rasˈtrero, a] *a* creeping; (*vestido*) trailing; (*fig*) despicable, mean.

rastrillar [rastriˈʎar] *vt* to rake; **rastrillo** *nm* rake.

rastro [ˈrastro] *nm* (*AGR*) rake; (*pista*) track, trail; (*curso*) course; (*vestigio*) trace; (*matadero*) slaughterhouse; **el R~** the Madrid fleamarket.

rastrojo [rasˈtroxo] *nm* stubble.

rasurador [rasuraˈðor] *nm*, **rasuradora** [rasuraˈðora] *nf* electric shaver; **rasurarse** *vr* to shave.

rata [ˈrata] *nf* rat.

ratear [rateˈar] *vt* (*robar*) to steal; (*distribuir*) to share out.

ratería [rateˈria] *nf* petty theft.

ratero, a [raˈtero, a] *a* light-fingered // *nm/f* pickpocket.

ratificar [ratifiˈkar] *vt* to ratify.

rato [ˈrato] *nm* while, short time; **a ~s** at times; **hay para ~** there's still a long way to go; **pasar el ~** to kill time; **pasar un buen/mal ~** to have a good/rough time.

ratón [raˈton] *nm* mouse; **ratonera** *nf* mousetrap.

raudal [rauˈðal] *nm* torrent; **a ~es** in abundance.

raya [ˈraja] *nf* line; (*marca*) scratch; (*en tela*) stripe; (*de pelo*) parting; (*límite*) boundary; **tener a ~** to keep in check; **rayar** *vt* to line; to scratch; (*talón*) to cross; (*subrayar*) to underline // *vi*: **rayar en o con** to border on.

rayo [ˈrajo] *nm* (*del sol*) ray, beam; (*de luz*) shaft; (*en una tormenta*) lightning, flash of lightning; **~s X** X-rays.

rayón [raˈjon] *nm* rayon.

raza [ˈraθa] *nf* race; **~ humana** human race.

razón [raˈθon] *nf* (*gen*) reason; (*justicia*) right, justice; (*razonamiento*) reasoning; (*motivo*) course; (*MAT*) ratio; **a ~ de 10 cada día** at the rate of 10 a day; '**~: ...**' "inquiries to ..."; **en ~ de** with regard to; **dar ~ a uno** to agree that sb is right; **tener ~** to be right; **~ directa/inversa** direct/inverse proportion; **~ de ser**

raison d'être; **razonable** *a* reasonable; (*justo, moderado*) fair; **razonamiento** *nm* (*juicio*) judgement; (*argumento*) reasoning; **razonar** *vt* to reason, argue; (*cuenta*) to itemize // *vi* to reason, argue.

reabastecer [reaβasteˈθer] *vt* to refuel.

reabrir [reaˈβrir] *vt* to reopen.

reacción [reakˈθjon] *nf* reaction; **avión a ~** jet plane; **~ en cadena** chain reaction; **reaccionar** *vi* to react; **reaccionario, a** *a* reactionary.

reacio, a [reˈaθjo, a] *a* stubborn.

reactor [reakˈtor] *nm* reactor.

readaptación [reaðaptaˈθjon] *nf*: **~ profesional** industrial retraining.

reafirmar [reafirˈmar] *vt* to reaffirm.

reagrupar [reaˣruˈpar] *vt* to regroup.

reajuste [reaˈxuste] *nm* readjustment.

real [reˈal] *a* real; (*del rey, fig*) royal.

realce [reˈalθe] *nm* (*TEC*) embossing; (*lustre, fig*) splendour; (*ARTE*) highlight; **poner de ~** to emphasize.

realidad [realiˈðað] *nf* reality, fact; (*verdad*) truth.

realista [reaˈlista] *nm/f* realist.

realización [realiθaˈθjon] *nf* fulfilment; (*COM*) sale, selling-up.

realizador, a [realiθaˈðor, a] *nm/f* (*TV etc*) producer.

realizar [realiˈθar] *vt* (*objetivo*) to achieve; (*plan*) to carry out; (*viaje*) to make, undertake; (*COM*) to sell up; **~se** *vr* to come about, come true.

realmente [realˈmente] *ad* really, actually.

realzar [realˈθar] *vt* (*TEC*) to raise; (*embellecer*) to enhance; (*acentuar*) to highlight.

reanimar [reaniˈmar] *vt* to revive; (*alentar*) to encourage; **~se** *vr* to revive.

reanudar [reanuˈðar] *vt* (*renovar*) to renew; (*retomar*) to resume.

reaparición [reapariˈθjon] *nf* reappearance.

rearme [reˈarme] *nm* rearmament.

reata [reˈata] *nf* rope, rein; **de ~** in single file.

rebaja [reˈβaxa] *nf* (*COM*) reduction; (*menoscabo*) lessening; **rebajar** *vt* (*bajar*) to lower; (*reducir*) to reduce; (*disminuir*) to lessen; (*humillar*) to humble.

rebanada [reβaˈnaða] *nf* slice.

rebaño [reˈβaɲo] *nm* herd; (*de ovejas*) flock.

rebasar [reβaˈsar] *vt* (*también ~ de*) to exceed; (*AUTO*) to overtake.

rebatir [reβaˈtir] *vt* to refute; (*descontar*) to deduct.

rebato [reˈβato] *nm* alarm; (*ataque*) surprise attack.

rebelarse [reβeˈlarse] *vr* to rebel, revolt.

rebelde [reˈβelde] *a* rebellious; (*indócil*) unruly // *nm/f* rebel; **rebeldía** *nf* rebelliousness; (*desobediencia*) disobedience; **rebelión** *nf* rebellion.

reblandecer [reβlandeˈθer] *vt* to soften.

rebosante [reβo'sante] a overflowing; **rebosar** vi to overflow; (abundar) to abound, be plentiful.

rebotar [reβo'tar] vt to bounce; (rechazar) to repel; ~se vr (pelota) to rebound; (bala) to ricochet; **rebote** nm rebound; **de rebote** on the rebound.

rebozar [reβo'θar] vt to wrap up; (CULIN) to fry in batter; **rebozo** nm muffler; (AM) shawl; **decir algo sin rebozo** to call a spade a spade.

rebuscado, a [reβus'kaðo, a] a affected.

rebuscar [reβus'kar] vt to search carefully; (objeto) to search for carefully.

rebuznar [reβuθ'nar] vi to bray.

recabar [reka'βar] vt to manage to get.

recado [re'kaðo] nm errand; (mensaje) message; **tomar un** ~ (TELEC) to take a message.

recaer [reka'er] vi to relapse; ~ **en** to fall to or on; **recaída** nf relapse.

recalcar [rekal'kar] vt (fig) to stress, emphasize.

recalcitrante [rekalθi'trante] a recalcitrant.

recalcitrar [rekalθi'trar] vi (echarse atrás) to step back; (resistir) to resist, be stubborn.

recalentar [rekalen'tar] vt (volver a calentar) to reheat; (demasiado) to overheat.

recambio [re'kambjo] nm spare; (de pluma) refill.

recapacitar [rekapaθi'tar] vt to think over // vi to reflect.

recargado, a [rekar'xaðo, a] a overloaded; **recargar** vt to overload; (batería) to recharge; **recargar los precios** to increase prices; **recargo** nm surcharge; (aumento) increase.

recatado, a [reka'taðo, a] a modest, demure; (prudente) cautious.

recatar [reka'tar] vt to hide; ~se vr to hide o.s.

recato [re'kato] nm modesty, demureness; (cautela) caution.

recaudación [rekauða'θjon] nf collection; (suma) takings pl; (en deporte) gate; **recaudador** nm tax collector.

recelar [reθe'lar] vt: ~ **que** (sospechar) to suspect that; (temer) to fear that // vi, ~se vr: ~(se) **de** to distrust; **recelo** nm distrust, suspicion; **receloso, a** a distrustful, suspicious.

recepción [reθep'θjon] nf reception; **recepcionista** nm/f receptionist.

receptáculo [reθep'takulo] nm receptacle.

receptivo, a [reθep'tiβo, a] a receptive.

receptor, a [reθep'tor, a] nm/f recipient // nm receiver.

recesión [reθe'sjon] nf recession.

receta [re'θeta] nf (CULIN) recipe; (MED) prescription.

recibidor, a [reθiβi'ðor, a] nm/f receiver, recipient.

recibimiento [reθiβi'mjento] nm

(recepción) reception; (acogida) welcome.

recibir [reθi'βir] vt (gen) to receive; (dar la bienvenida) to welcome // vi to entertain; ~se vr: ~se **de** to qualify as; **recibo** nm receipt.

reciedumbre [reθje'ðumbre] nf strength; (vigor) vigour.

recién [re'θjen] ad recently, newly; **el** ~ **llegado** the newcomer; **el** ~ **nacido** the newborn child.

reciente [re'θjente] a a recent; (fresco) fresh.

recinto [re'θinto] nm (gen) enclosure; (área) area, place.

recio, a ['reθjo, a] a strong, tough; (voz) loud; (tiempo) harsh // ad hard; loud(ly).

recipiente [reθi'pjente] nm receptacle.

reciprocidad [reθiproθi'ðað] nf reciprocity; **recíproco, a** a reciprocal.

recital [reθi'tal] nm (MUS) recital; (LITERATURA) reading; **recitar** vt to recite.

reclamación [reklama'θjon] nf claim, demand; (queja) complaint.

reclamar [rekla'mar] vt to claim, demand // vi: ~ **contra** to complain about; ~ **en justicia** to take to court; **reclamo** nm (anuncio) advertisement; (tentación) attraction.

reclinar [rekli'nar] vt to recline, lean; ~se vr to lean back.

recluir [reklu'ir] vt to intern, confine.

reclusión [reklu'sjon] nf (prisión) prison; (refugio) seclusion; ~ **perpetua** life imprisonment.

recluta [re'kluta] nm/f recruit // nf recruitment.

reclutamiento [rekluta'mjento] nm recruitment.

recobrar [reko'βrar] vt (recuperar) to recover; (rescatar) to get back; ~se vr to recover.

recodo [re'koðo] nm (de río, camino) bend.

recogedor, a [rekoxe'ðor, a] nm/f picker, harvester.

recoger [reko'xer] vt (gen) to collect; (AGR) to harvest; (levantar) to pick up; (juntar) to gather; (pasar a buscar) to come for, fetch; (dar asilo) to give shelter to; (faldas) to gather up; (pelo) to put up; ~se vr (retirarse) to retire; **recogido, a** a (lugar) quiet, secluded; (persona) modest, retiring; (pequeño) small // nf (del correo) collection; (AGR) harvest.

recolección [rekolek'θjon] nf (de las mieses) harvesting; (colecta) collection.

recomendación [rekomenda'θjon] nf (sugerencia) suggestion, recommendation; (elogio) praise; **recomendar** vt to suggest, recommend; to praise; (confiar) to entrust.

recompensa [rekom'pensa] nf reward, recompense; **recompensar** vt to reward, recompense; (por pérdidas) to compensate.

recomponer [rekompo'ner] vt to mend; ~se vr (fam) to doll up.

reconciliación [rekonθilja'θjon] nf reconciliation; **reconciliar** vt to reconcile; **reconciliarse** vr to become reconciled.

reconfortar [rekonfor'tar] vt to comfort; ~se vr. ~se con to fortify o.s. with.

reconocer [rekono'θer] vt to recognize; (registrar) to search; (MED) to examine; **reconocido, a** a recognized; (agradecido) grateful; **reconocimiento** nm recognition; search; examination; gratitude; (confesión) admission.

reconquista [rekon'kista] nf reconquest.

reconstituyente [rekonstitu'jente] nm tonic.

reconstruir [rekonstru'ir] vt to reconstruct.

recopilación [rekopila'θjon] nf (sumario) summary; (compendio) compilation; **recopilar** vt to compile.

récord ['rekorð] a inv, nm record.

recordar [rekor'ðar] vt (acordarse de) to remember; (acordar a otro) to remind // vi to remember.

recorrer [reko'rrer] vt (país) to cross, travel through; (distancia) to cover; (repasar) to go over, look over; **recorrido** nm run, journey; **tren de largo recorrido** main-line train.

recortado, a [rekor'taðo, a] a uneven, irregular.

recortar [rekor'tar] vt to cut out; **recorte** nm (acción) cutting; (de prensa) cutting, clipping; (de telas, chapas) trimming.

recostado, a [rekos'taðo, a] a leaning; **estar** ~ to be lying down.

recostar [rekos'tar] vt to lean; ~se vr to lie down.

recoveco [reko'ßeko] nm bend; (en casa) cubby hole.

recreación [rekrea'θjon] nf recreation; (TEATRO, CINE) interval, intermission.

recrear [rekre'ar] vt (entretener) to entertain; (volver a crear) to recreate; **recreativo, a** a recreational; **recreo** nm recreation; (ESCOL) break, playtime.

recriminar [rekrimi'nar] vt to reproach // vi to recriminate; ~se vr to reproach each other.

recrudecer [rekruðe'θer] vt, vi, ~se vr to worsen.

recrudecimiento [rekruðeθi'mjento] nm, **recrudescencia** [rekruðes'θenθja] nf upsurge.

recta ['rekta] nf ver recto.

rectángulo, a [rek'tangulo, a] a rectangular // nm rectangle.

rectificar [rektifi'kar] vt to rectify; (volverse recto) to straighten // vi to correct o.s.

rectitud [rekti'tuð] nf (exactitud) correctness; (fig) rectitude.

recto, a ['rekto, a] a straight; (persona) honest, upright // nm rectum // nf straight line.

rector, a [rek'tor, a] a governing.

recua ['rekwa] nf mule train.

recuento [re'kwento] nm inventory; **hacer el** ~ **de** to count or reckon up.

recuerdo [re'kwerðo] nm souvenir; ~s nmpl memories; ¡~s a tu madre! give my regards to your mother.

recular [reku'lar] vi to fall back; (fig) to back down.

recuperable [rekupe'raßle] a recoverable; **recuperación** nf recovery.

recuperar [rekupe'rar] vt to recover; (tiempo) to make up; ~se vr to recuperate.

recurrir [reku'rrir] vi (JUR) to appeal; ~ a to resort to; (persona) to turn to; **recurso** nm resort; (medios) means pl, resources pl; (JUR) appeal.

recusar [reku'sar] vt to reject, refuse.

rechazo [re'tʃaθo] nm (retroceso) recoil; (rebote) rebound; (negación) rebuff.

rechazar [retʃa'θar] vt to repel, drive back; (idea) to reject; (oferta) to turn down.

rechifla [re'tʃifla] nf hissing, booing; (fig) derision; **rechiflar** vt to hiss, boo; **rechiflarse** vr to take things as a joke.

rechinar [retʃi'nar] vi to creak; (gruñir) to grumble; (dientes) to grind.

rechoncho, a [re'tʃontʃo, a] a (fam) chubby, thickset.

red [reð] nf net, mesh; (de ferrocarriles etc) network; (trampa) trap.

redacción [reðak'θjon] nf editing; (oficina) newspaper office; (personal) editorial staff.

redactar [reðak'tar] vt to draw up, draft; (periódico) to edit.

redada [re'ðaða] nf: ~ **policíaca** police raid, round-up.

rededor [reðe'ðor] nm: **al** o **en** ~ around, round about.

redención [reðen'θjon] nf redemption; **redentor, a** a redeeming.

redescubrir [reðesku'ßrir] vt to rediscover.

redicho, a [re'ðitʃo, a] a affected, stilted.

redil [re'ðil] nm sheepfold.

redimir [reði'mir] vt to redeem.

rédito ['reðito] nm interest, yield.

redoblar [reðo'ßlar] vt to redouble; (plegar) to fold back // vi (tambor) to play a roll on the drums.

redomado, a [reðo'maðo, a] a sly, crafty.

redonda [re'ðonda] nf ver **redondo**.

redondear [reðonde'ar] vt to round, round off; ~se vr to become wealthy.

redondel [reðon'del] nm (círculo) circle; (TAUR) bullring, arena.

redondo, a [re'ðondo, a] a (circular) round; (directo) straight; (completo) complete // nf: **a la** ~**a** around, round about.

reducción [reðuk'θjon] nf reduction; (MED) setting.

reducido, a [reðu'θiðo, a] a reduced; (limitado) limited; (pequeño) small; **reducir** vt to reduce; to limit; (MED) to set a bone; **reducirse** vr to diminish.

redundancia [reðun'danθja] *nf* redundancy.

reembolsar [reembol'sar] *vt* to reimburse; (*depósito*) to refund; **reembolso** *nm* reimbursement; refund.

reemplazar [reempla'θar] *vt* to replace; **reemplazo** *nm* replacement; **de reemplazo** (*MIL*) reserve.

refacción [refak'θjon] *nf* (*AM*) repair(s) (*pl*).

refajo [re'faxo] *nm* (*enagua*) flannel underskir'; (*falda*) short skirt.

referenc.a [refe'renθja] *nf* reference; (*informe*) :eport; **con ~ a** with reference to.

referente [refe'rente] *a*: **~ a** concerning, relating to.

referir [refe'rir] *vt* (*contar*) to tell, recount; (*relacionar*) to refer, relate; **~se** *vr*: **~se a** to refer to.

refilón [refi'lon]: **de ~** *ad* obliquely, aslant.

refinado, a [refi'naðo, a] *a* refined; **refinamiento** *nm* refinement; **refinar** *vt* to refine; (*fig*) to perfect, polish.

reflejar [refle'xar] *vt* (*gen*) to reflect; **reflejo, a** *a* reflected; (*movimiento*) reflex // *nm* reflection; (*ANAT*) reflex.

reflexión [reflek'sjon] *nf* reflection; **reflexionar** *vt* to reflect on // *vi* to reflect; (*detenerse*) to pause (to think).

reflexivo, a [reflek'siβo, a] *a* thoughtful; (*LING, fig*) reflexive.

reflujo [re'fluxo] *nm* ebb.

refocilar [refoθi'lar] *vt* to cheer up.

reforma [re'forma] *nf* reform; (*ARQ etc*) repair; **~ agraria** agrarian reform.

reformar [refor'mar] *vt* (*modificar*) to change, alter; (*formar de nuevo*) to reform; (*ARQ*) to repair; **~se** *vr* to mend one's ways.

reformatorio [reforma'torjo] *nm* reformatory.

reforzar [refor'θar] *vt* (*gen*) to strengthen; (*ARQ*) to reinforce; (*fig*) to encourage.

refractario, a [refrak'tarjo, a] *a* stubborn; (*TEC*) heat-resistant.

refrán [re'fran] *nm* proverb, saying.

refregar [refre'xar] *vt* to scrub.

refrenar [refre'nar] *vt* to check, restrain.

refrendar [refren'dar] *vt* (*firma*) to endorse, countersign; (*pasaporte*) to stamp; (*ley*) to approve.

refrescar [refres'kar] *vt* (*gen*) to refresh // *vi* to cool down; **~se** *vr* to get cooler; (*tomar aire fresco*) to go out for a breath of fresh air.

refresco [re'fresko] *nm* soft drink, cool drink; "**~s**" "refreshments".

refriega [re'frjeɣa] *nf* scuffle, brawl.

refrigeración [refrixera'θjon] *nf* refrigeration; (*de casa*) air-conditioning; **refrigerador** *nm* refrigerator; **refrigerar** *vt* to refrigerate; to air-condition.

refuerzo [re'fwerθo] *nm* reinforcement; (*TEC*) support.

refugiado, a [refu'xjaðo, a] *nm/f* refugee; **refugiarse** *vr* to take refuge, shelter; **refugio** *nm* refuge; (*protección*) shelter.

refulgencia [reful'xenθja] *nf* brilliance; **refulgir** *vi* to shine, be dazzling.

refundición [refundi'θjon] *nf* recasting, revision; **refundir** *vt* to recast.

refunfuñar [refunfu'ɲar] *vi* to grunt, growl; (*quejarse*) to grumble.

refutación [refuta'θjon] *nf* refutation; **refutar** *vt* to refute.

regadera [reɣa'ðera] *nf* watering can.

regadío [reɣa'ðio] *nm* irrigated land.

regalado, a [reɣa'laðo, a] *a* comfortable, luxurious; (*gratis*) free, for nothing; (*pey*) soft.

regalar [reɣa'lar] *vt* (*dar*) to give, present; (*entregar*) to give away; (*mimar*) to pamper, make a fuss of.

regalía [reɣa'lia] *nf* privilege, prerogative; (*COM*) bonus; (*de autor*) royalty.

regaliz [reɣa'liθ] *nm*, **regaliza** [reɣa'liθa] *nf* liquorice.

regalo [re'ɣalo] *nm* (*obsequio*) gift, present; (*gusto*) pleasure; (*comodidad*) comfort.

regalón, ona [reɣa'lon, ona] *a* spoiled, pampered.

regañadientes [reɣaɲa'ðjentes]: **a ~** *ad* reluctantly.

regañar [reɣa'ɲar] *vt* to scold // *vi* to grumble; **regaño** *nm* scolding, telling-off; (*queja*) grumble; **regañón, ona** *a* grumbling; (*mujer*) nagging.

regar [re'ɣar] *vt* to water, irrigate; (*fig*) to scatter, sprinkle.

regatear [reɣate'ar] *vt* to bargain over; (*guardar*) to be mean with // *vi* to bargain, haggle; (*DEPORTE*) to dribble; **regateo** *nm* bargaining; dribbling; (*del cuerpo*) swerve, dodge.

regazo [re'ɣaθo] *nm* lap.

regeneración [rexenera'θjon] *nf* regeneration; **regenerar** *vt* to regenerate.

regentar [rexen'tar] *vt* to direct, manage; **regente** *nm* manager; (*POL*) regent.

régimen ['reximen] (*pl* **regímenes**) *nm* regime; (*MED*) diet.

regimiento [rexi'mjento] *nm* regiment; (*organización*) administration.

regio, a ['rexjo, a] *a* royal, regal; (*fig: suntuoso*) splendid.

región [re'xjon] *nf* region; **regionalista** *nm/f* regionalist.

regir [re'xir] *vt* to govern, rule; (*dirigir*) to manage, run // *vi* to apply, be in force.

registrador [rexistra'ðor] *nm* registrar, recorder.

registrar [rexis'trar] *vt* (*buscar en cajón*) to look through, search; (*inspeccionar*) to inspect; (*anotar*) to register, record; **~se** *vr* to register; (*ocurrir*) to happen.

registro [re'xistro] *nm* registration; (*MUS, libro*) register; (*inspección*) inspection, search; ~ **civil** registry office.

regla ['rexla] *nf* (*ley*) rule, regulation; (*de medir*) ruler, rule; **la** ~ (*MED*) periods *pl*; **salir de** ~ to step out of line.

reglamentación [rexlamenta'θjon] *nf* (*acto*) regulation; (*lista*) rules *pl*; **reglamentar** *vt* to regulate; **reglamentario**, **a** a statutory; **reglamento** *nm* rules *pl*, regulations *pl*.

reglar [re'xlar] *vt* (*papel*) to rule; (*actos*) to regulate.

regocijado, a [rexoθi'xaðo, a] a merry; **regocijar** *vt* to cheer up, gladden; **regocijarse** *vr* to have a good time, make merry; (*alegrarse*) to rejoice; **regocijo** *nm* joy, happiness.

regodearse [rexoðe'arse] *vr* to be glad, be delighted; **regodeo** *nm* delight.

regresar [rexre'sar] *vi* to come/go back, return; **regresivo, a** a backward; (*fig*) regressive; **regreso** *nm* return.

reguero [re'xero] *nm* irrigation ditch.

regulador [rexula'ðor] *nm* (*gen*) regulator; (*de radio etc*) knob, control.

regular [rexu'lar] a (*gen*) regular; (*normal*) normal, usual; (*común*) ordinary; (*organizado*) regular, orderly; (*mediano*) average; (*fam*) not bad, so-so // ad so-so, alright // *vt* (*controlar*) to control, regulate; (*TEC*) to adjust; **por lo** ~ as a rule; ~**idad** *nf* regularity; ~**izar** *vt* to regularize.

regusto [re'xusto] *nm* aftertaste.

rehabilitación [reaβilita'θjon] *nf* rehabilitation; (*ARQ*) restoration; **rehabilitar** *vt* to rehabilitate; to restore; (*reintegrar*) to reinstate.

rehacer [rea'θer] *vt* (*reparar*) to mend, repair; (*volver a hacer*) to redo, repeat; ~**se** *vr* (*MED*) to recover; (*dominarse*) to pull o.s. together.

rehén [re'en] *nm* hostage.

rehilete [rei'lete] *nm* (*dardo*) dart; (*DEPORTE*) badminton, shuttlecock.

rehuir [reu'ir] *vt* to avoid, shun.

rehusar [reu'sar] *vt, vi* to refuse.

reina ['reina] *nf* queen; ~**do** *nm* reign; **reinante** a (*fig*) prevailing; **reinar** *vi* to reign.

reincidir [reinθi'ðir] *vi* to relapse.

reincorporarse [reinkorpo'rarse] *vr:* ~ **a** to rejoin.

reino ['reino] *nm* kingdom; **el R** ~ **Unido** the United Kingdom.

reintegrar [reinte'xrar] *vt* (*reconstituir*) to reconstruct; (*persona*) to reinstate; (*dinero*) to return, pay back; ~**se** *vr:* ~**se a** to return to.

reír [re'ir] *vi*, ~**se** *vr* to laugh; ~**se de** to laugh at.

reiterar [reite'rar] *vt* to reiterate.

reivindicación [reiβindika'θjon] *nf* (*demanda*) claim, demand; (*justificación*) vindication; **reivindicar** *vt* to claim; (*restaurar*) to restore.

reja ['rexa] *nf* (*de ventana*) grille, bars *pl*;

(*en la calle*) grating; (*del arado*) ploughshare.

rejilla [re'xiʎa] *nf* (*de ventana*) grille; (*de silla*) wickerwork; (*de ventilación*) vent; (*de coche*) luggage rack.

rejoneador [rexonea'ðor] *nm* mounted bullfighter.

rejuvenecer [rexuβene'θer] *vt, vi* to rejuvenate; ~**se** *vr* to be rejuvenated.

relación [rela'θjon] *nf* relation, relationship; (*MAT*) ratio; (*informe*) report; **relaciones públicas** public relations; **con** ~ **a** *o* **en** ~ **con** in relation to; **relacionar** *vt* to relate, connect; **relacionarse** *vr* to be connected, be linked.

relajación [relaxa'θjon] *nf* relaxation; **relajado, a** a (*disoluto*) loose; (*cómodo*) relaxed; (*MED*) ruptured; **relajar** *vt*, **relajarse** *vr* to relax.

relamer [rela'mer] *vt* to lick (repeatedly); ~**se** *vr* to lick one's lips.

relamido, a [rela'miðo, a] a (*pulcro*) overdressed; (*afectado*) affected.

relámpago [re'lampaxo] *nm* flash of lightning; **visita/huelga** ~ lightning visit/strike; **relampaguear** *vi* to flash.

relatar [rela'tar] *vt* to tell, relate.

relativo, a [rela'tiβo, a] a relative; **en lo** ~ **a** concerning.

relato [re'lato] *nm* (*narración*) story, tale; (*informe*) report.

relegar [rele'xar] *vt* to relegate.

relevante [rele'βante] a eminent, outstanding.

relevar [rele'βar] *vt* (*sustituir*) to relieve; ~**se** *vr* to relay; ~ **a uno de un cargo** to relieve sb of his post.

relevo [re'leβo] *nm* relief; **carrera de** ~**s** relay race.

relieve [re'ljeβe] *nm* (*ARTE, TEC*) relief; (*fig*) prominence, importance; ~**s** *nmpl* left-overs; **bajo** ~ bas-relief.

religión [reli'xjon] *nf* religion; **religiosidad** *nf* religiosity; **religioso, a** a religious // *nm/f* monk/nun // *nm* cleric.

relinchar [relin'tʃar] *vi* to neigh; **relincho** *nm* neigh; (*acto*) neighing.

reliquia [re'likja] *nf* relic; ~ **de familia** family heirloom.

reloj [re'lo(x)] *nm* watch; (*de iglesia etc*) clock; ~ **de pulsera** wristwatch; ~**ero, a** *nm/f* **despertador** alarm clock; watchmaker; clockmaker.

reluciente [relu'θjente] a brilliant, shining; **relucir** *vi* to shine; (*fig*) to excel.

relumbrante [relum'brante] a dazzling; **relumbrar** *vi* to dazzle, shine brilliantly.

rellano [re'ʎano] *nm* (*ARQ*) landing.

rellenar [reʎe'nar] *vt* (*llenar*) to fill up; (*CULIN*) to stuff; (*COSTURA*) to pad; **relleno, a** a full up; stuffed // *nm* stuffing; (*de tapicería*) padding.

remachar [rema'tʃar] *vt* to rivet; (*fig*) to hammer home, drive home; **remache** *nm* rivet.

remanente [rema'nente] *nm* remainder;

(COM) balance; (de producto) surplus.
remanso [re'manso] nm pool; (fig) quiet place.
remar [re'mar] vi to row.
rematado, a [rema'taðo, a] a complete, utter.
rematar [rema'tar] vt to finish off; (COM) to sell off cheap // vi to end, finish off.
remate [re'mate] nm end, finish; (punta) tip; (DEPORTE) shot; (ARQ) top; (COM) auction sale; **de** o **para** ~ to crown it all.
remedar [reme'ðar] vt to imitate.
remediar [reme'ðjar] vt (gen) to remedy; (subsanar) to make good, repair; (ayudar) to help; (evitar) to avoid.
remedio [re'meðjo] nm remedy; (alivio) relief, help; (JUR) recourse, remedy; **poner** ~ **a** to correct, stop; **no tener más** ~ to have no alternative; **¡qué** ~! there's no choice; **sin** ~ hopeless, incurable.
remedo [re'meðo] nm imitation; (pey) parody.
remendar [remen'dar] vt to repair; (con parche) to patch.
remesa [re'mesa] nf remittance; (COM) shipment; **remesar** vt to remit, send.
remiendo [re'mjendo] nm (gen) mend; (con parche) patch; (cosido) darn.
remilgado, a [remil'ɣaðo, a] a prim; (afectado) affected; **remilgo** nm primness; affectation.
reminiscencia [reminis'θenθja] nf reminiscence.
remisión [remi'sjon] nf (acto) sending, shipment.
remiso, a [re'miso, a] a remiss.
remitir [remi'tir] vt to remit, send; (perdonar) to pardon; (posponer) to postpone // vi to slacken; (en carta): **remite:** X sender: X; **remitente** nm/f sender.
remo ['remo] nm (de barco) oar; (deporte) rowing.
remoción [remo'θjon] nf removal.
remojar [remo'xar] vt to steep, soak; (galleta etc) to dip.
remojo [re'moxo] nm: **dejar la ropa a** ~ to leave clothes to soak.
remolacha [remo'latʃa] nf beet, beetroot.
remolcador [remolka'ðor] nm (NAUT) tug; (AUTO) breakdown lorry.
remolinar [remoli'nar] vi to whirl, eddy; **remolino** nm (gen) eddy; (de agua) whirlpool; (de viento) whirlwind; (de gente) throng.
remolque [re'molke] nm tow, towing; (cuerda) towrope; **llevar a** ~ to tow.
remontar [remon'tar] vt to mend; ~**se** vr to soar; ~**se a** (COM) to amount to; ~ **el vuelo** to soar.
rémora ['remora] nf hindrance.
remorder [remor'ðer] vt to distress, disturb; ~**se** vr to suffer remorse; ~**se la conciencia** to have a troubled conscience; **remordimiento** nm remorse.
remoto, a [re'moto, a] a remote.

remover [remo'ßer] vt to stir; (tierra) to turn over; (objetos) to move around; (quitar) to remove.
remozar [remo'θar] vt to rejuvenate; ~**se** vr to be rejuvenated, look younger.
remuneración [remunera'θjon] nf remuneration; **remunerar** vt to remunerate; (premiar) to reward.
renacer [rena'θer] vi to be reborn; (fig) to revive; **renacimiento** nm rebirth; **el Renacimiento** the Renaissance.
renal [re'nal] a renal, kidney cpd.
rencilla [ren'θiʎa] nf quarrel.
rencor [ren'kor] nm rancour, bitterness; ~**oso, a** a spiteful.
rendición [rendi'θjon] nf surrender.
rendido, a [ren'diðo, a] a (sumiso) submissive; (cansado) worn-out.
rendimiento [rendi'mjento] nm (MIL) surrender; (producción) output; (agotamiento) exhaustion; (TEC, COM) efficiency.
rendir [ren'dir] vt (vencer) to defeat; (producir) to produce; (dar beneficio) to yield; (agotar) to exhaust; (dominar) to dominate // vi to pay; ~**se** vr (someterse) to surrender; (cansarse) to wear o.s. out; ~ **homenaje** o **culto a** to pay homage to.
renegado, a [rene'ɣaðo, a] a, nm/f renegade.
renegar [rene'ɣar] vi (renunciar) to renounce; (blasfemar) to blaspheme; (fam) to curse; (quejarse) to complain.
RENFE nf abr de **Red Nacional de los Ferrocarriles Españoles.**
renglón [ren'glon] nm (línea) line; (COM) item, article; **a** ~ **seguido** immediately after.
reniego [re'njeɣo] nm curse, oath; (queja) grumble, complaint.
renombrado, a [renom'braðo, a] a renowned; **renombre** nm renown.
renovación [renoßa'θjon] nf (de contrato) renewal; (ARQ) renovation; **renovar** vt to renew; to renovate.
renta ['renta] nf (ingresos) income; (beneficio) profit; (alquiler) rent; ~ **vitalicia** annuity; **rentable** a profitable; **rentar** vt to produce, yield.
rentero, a [ren'tero, a] nm/f tenant farmer.
rentista [ren'tista] nm/f stockholder.
renuencia [re'nwenθja] nf reluctance; **renuente** a inv reluctant.
renuncia [re'nunθja] nf (gen) resignation.
renunciar [renun'θjar] vt to renounce // vi to resign; ~ **a hacer algo** to give up doing sth.
reñido, a [re'niðo, a] a (batalla) bitter, hard-fought; **estar** ~ **con uno** to be on bad terms with sb.
reñir [re'nir] vt (regañar) to scold // vi (estar peleado) to quarrel, fall out; (combatir) to fight.
reo ['reo] nm/f culprit, offender; ~ **de muerte** prisoner condemned to death.
reojo [re'oxo]: **de** ~ ad out of the corner of one's eye; (fig) askance.

reorganizar [reorɣani'θar] *vt* to reorganize.

reorientar [reorjen'tar] *vt* to reorientate; (*reajustar*) to readjust.

reparación [repara'θjon] *nf* (*acto*) mending, repairing; (*TEC*) repair; (*fig*) amends, reparation; **reparar** *vt* to repair; to make amends for; (*suerte*) to retrieve; (*observar*) to observe // *vi*: **reparar en** (*darse cuenta de*) to notice; (*poner atención en*) to pay attention to.

reparo [re'paro] *nm* (*reparación*) repair; (*advertencia*) observation; (*duda*) doubt; (*dificultad*) difficulty; (*resguardo*) defence.

reparón, ona [repa'ron, ona] *a* carping.

repartición [reparti'θjon] *nf* distribution; (*división*) division; **repartidor, a** *nm/f* distributor.

repartir [repar'tir] *vt* to distribute, share out; (*correo*) to deliver; **reparto** *nm* distribution; delivery; (*TEATRO, CINE*) cast.

repasar [repa'sar] *vt* (*sitio*) to pass by again; (*lección*) to revise; (*MECÁNICA*) to check; **repaso** *nm* revision; overhaul, checkup; (*de ropa*) mending.

repatriar [repa'trjar] *vt* to repatriate.

repecho [re'petʃo] *nm* steep incline; **a ~** uphill.

repelente [repe'lente] *a* repellent, repulsive; **repeler** *vt* to repel.

repensar [repen'sar] *vt* to reconsider.

repente [re'pente] *nm*: **de ~** suddenly; **un ~ de ira** a fit of anger.

repentino, a [repen'tino, a] *a* sudden.

repercusión [reperku'sjon] *nf* repercussion.

repercutir [reperku'tir] *vi* to rebound; (*sonido*) to echo; **~se** *vr* to reverberate; **~ en** to have repercussions on.

repertorio [reper'torjo] *nm* list; (*TEATRO*) repertoire.

repetición [repeti'θjon] *nf* repetition; **repetir** *vt* to repeat; (*plato*) to have a second helping // *vi* to repeat; **repetirse** *vr* (*volver sobre tema*) to repeat o.s.; (*sabor*) to come back.

repicar [repi'kar] *vt* (*desmenuzar*) to chop up finely; (*campanas*) to ring; **~se** *vr* to boast.

repique [re'pike] *nm* pealing, ringing; **~teo** *nm* pealing; (*de tambor*) drumming.

repisa [re'pisa] *nf* ledge, shelf; **~ de chimenea** mantelpiece.

repito *etc vb ver* **repetir.**

replegar [reple'ɣar] *vt* to fold over; **~se** *vr* to fall back, retreat.

repleto, a [re'pleto, a] *a* replete, full up.

réplica ['replika] *nf* answer; (*ARTE*) replica.

replicar [repli'kar] *vi* to answer; (*objetar*) to argue, answer back.

repliegue [re'pljeɣe] *nm* (*MIL*) withdrawal.

repoblación [repoβla'θjon] *nf* repopulation; (*de río*) restocking; **~ forestal** reafforestation; **repoblar** *vt* to repopulate; to reafforest.

repollo [re'poʎo] *nm* cabbage.

reponer [repo'ner] *vt* to replace, put back; (*TEATRO*) to revive; **~se** *vr* to recover; **~ que** to reply that.

reportaje [repor'taxe] *nm* report, article.

reposacabezas [reposaka'ßeθas] *nm inv* headrest.

reposado, a [repo'saðo, a] *a* (*descansado*) restful; (*tranquilo*) calm; **reposar** *vi* to rest, repose.

reposición [reposi'θjon] *nf* replacement; (*CINE*) remake.

repositorio [reposi'torjo] *nm* repository.

reposo [re'poso] *nm* rest.

repostar [repos'tar] *vt* to replenish; (*AUTO*) to fill up (with petrol).

repostería [reposte'ria] *nf* confectioner's (shop); (*depósito*) pantry, larder; **repostero, a** *nm/f* confectioner.

reprender [repren'der] *vt* to reprimand; **reprensión** *nf* rebuke, reprimand.

represa [re'presa] *nf* dam; (*lago artificial*) lake, pool.

represalia [repre'salja] *nf* reprisal.

representación [representa'θjon] *nf* representation; (*TEATRO*) performance; **representante** *nm/f* representative; performer.

representar [represen'tar] *vt* to represent; (*TEATRO*) to play; (*edad*) to look; **~se** *vr* to imagine; **representativo, a** *a* representative.

represión [repre'sjon] *nf* repression.

reprimir [repri'mir] *vt* to repress.

reprobar [repro'ßar] *vt* to censure, reprove.

réprobo, a ['reproßo, a] *nm/f* reprobate.

reprochar [repro'tʃar] *vt* to reproach; **reproche** *nm* reproach.

reproducción [reproðuk'θjon] *nf* reproduction.

reproducir [reproðu'θir] *vt* to reproduce; **~se** *vr* to breed; (*situación*) to recur.

reptil [rep'til] *nm* reptile.

república [re'puβlika] *nf* republic; **republicano, a** *a, nm/f* republican.

repudiar [repu'ðjar] *vt* to repudiate; (*fe*) to renounce; **repudio** *nm* repudiation.

repuesto [re'pwesto] *nm* (*pieza de recambio*) spare (part); (*abastecimiento*) supply; **rueda de ~** spare wheel.

repugnancia [repuɣ'nanθja] *nf* repugnance; **repugnante** *a* repugnant, repulsive.

repugnar [repuɣ'nar] *vt* to disgust // *vi*, **~se** *vr* (*contradecirse*) to conflict; (*dar asco*) to be disgusting.

repujar [repu'xar] *vt* to emboss.

repulgar [repul'ɣar] *vt* to hem.

repulido, a [repu'liðo, a] *a* (*gen*) polished; (*persona*) dressed up, dolled up.

repulsa [re'pulsa] *nf* rebuff; (*fig*) reprimand.

repulsión [repul'sjon] *nf* repulsion, aversion; **repulsivo, a** *a* repulsive.

reputación [reputa'θjon] *nf* reputation.

reputar [repu'tar] *vt* to consider, deem.
requemado, a [reke'maðo, a] *a* (*quemado*) scorched; (*bronceado*) tanned.
requerimiento [rekeri'mjento] *nm* request; (*JUR*) summons.
requerir [reke'rir] *vt* (*rogar*) to ask, request; (*exigir*) to require; (*llamar*) to send for, summon.
requesón [reke'son] *nm* cottage cheese.
requete... [re'kete] *pref* extremely.
réquiem ['rekjem] *nm* requiem.
requisa [re'kisa] *nf* (*inspección*) survey, inspection; (*MIL*) requisition.
requisito [reki'sito] *nm* requirement, requisite.
res [res] *nf* beast, head of cattle.
resabio [re'saßjo] *nm* (*maña*) vice, bad habit; (*dejo*) aftertaste.
resaca [re'saka] *nf* (*en el mar*) undertow, undercurrent; (*fig*) backlash; (*fam*) hangover.
resalado, a [resa'laðo, a] *a* (*fam*) lively.
resaltar [resal'tar] *vi* to project, stick out; (*persona*) to stand out, be conspicuous.
resarcimiento [resarθi'mjento] *nm* compensation; **resarcir** *vt* to compensate; **resarcirse** *vr* to make up for.
resbaladero [resßala'ðero] *nm* (*gen*) slippery place; (*en parque infantil*) slide.
resbaladizo, a [resßala'ðiθo, a] *a* slippery.
resbalar [resßa'lar] *vi*, ~se *vr* to slip, slide; (*fig*) to slip (up).
rescatar [reska'tar] *vt* (*heridos*) to save, rescue; (*objeto*) to get back, recover; (*cautivos*) to ransom.
rescate [res'kate] *nm* rescue, recovery; **pagar un** ~ to pay a ransom.
rescindir [resθin'dir] *vt* to rescind.
rescisión [resθi'sjon] *nf* cancellation.
rescoldo [res'koldo] *nm* embers *pl*; (*fig*) scruple.
resecar [rese'kar] *vt* to dry thoroughly; (*MED*) to remove; ~se *vr* to dry up.
reseco, a [re'seko, a] *a* very dry; (*fig*) skinny.
resentido, a [resen'tiðo, a] *a* resentful; **resentimiento** *nm* resentment, bitterness.
resentirse [resen'tirse] *vr* (*debilitarse: persona*) to suffer; ~ **con** to resent; ~ **de** (*consecuencias*) to feel the effects of.
reseña [re'seɲa] *nf* (*cuenta*) account; (*informe*) report; (*LITERATURA*) review; **reseñar** *vt* to describe; to review.
reserva [re'serßa] *nf* (*gen*) reserve; (*reservación*) reservation; **a** ~ **de** except for; **con toda** ~ in strictest confidence.
reservado, a [reser'ßaðo, a] *a* reserved; (*retraído*) cold, distant // *nm* private room.
reservar [reser'ßar] *vt* (*guardar*) to keep; (*habitación, entrada*) to reserve; (*callar*) to keep to o.s.; ~se *vr* to save o.s.
resfriado [resfri'aðo] *nm* cold; **resfriarse** *vr* to cool; (*MED*) to catch (a) cold.
resguardar [resɣwar'ðar] *vt* to protect,

shield; ~se *vr*: ~se de to guard against;
resguardo *nm* defence; (*custodia*) protection; (*garantía*) guarantee; (*vale*) voucher.
residencia [resi'ðenθja] *nf* residence.
residente [resi'ðente] *a, nm/f* resident.
residir [resi'ðir] *vi* to reside, live; ~ **en** to reside in, lie in.
residuo [re'siðwo] *nm* residue.
resignación [resiɣna'θjon] *nf* resignation; **resignar** *vt* to resign; **resignarse** *vr*: **resignarse a** *o* **con** to resign o.s. to, be resigned to.
resistencia [resis'tenθja] *nf* (*dureza*) endurance, strength; (*oposición, eléctrica*) resistance; **resistente** *a* strong, hardy, resistant.
resistir [resis'tir] *vt* (*soportar*) to bear; (*oponerse a*) to resist, oppose; (*aguantar*) to put up with // *vi* to resist; (*aguantar*) to last, endure; ~se *vr*: ~se a to refuse to, resist.
resma ['resma] *nf* ream.
resol [re'sol] *nm* glare of the sun.
resolución [resolu'θjon] *nf* (*gen*) resolution; (*decisión*) decision; **resoluto, a** *a* resolute.
resolver [resol'ßer] *vt* to resolve; (*solucionar*) to solve, resolve; (*decidir*) to decide, settle; ~se *vr* to make up one's mind.
resollar [reso'ʎar] *vi* to breathe noisily, wheeze.
resonancia [reso'nanθja] *nf* (*del sonido*) resonance; (*repercusión*) repercussion; **resonante** *a* resonant, resounding; (*fig*) tremendous; **resonar** *vi* to ring, echo.
resoplar [reso'plar] *vi* to snort; **resoplido** *nm* heavy breathing.
resorte [re'sorte] *nm* (*pieza*) spring; (*elasticidad*) elasticity; (*fig*) lever.
respaldar [respal'dar] *vt* to endorse; (*fig*) to back (up), support; ~se *vr* to lean back; ~se **con** *o* **en** to take one's stand on; **respaldo** *nm* (*de cama*) headboard; (*de sillón*) back; (*fig*) support, backing.
respectivo, a [respek'tißo, a] *a* respective; **en lo** ~ **a** with regard to.
respecto [res'pekto] *nm*: **al** ~ on this matter; **con** ~ **a**, ~ **de** with regard to, in relation to.
respetable [respe'taßle] *a* respectable; **respetar** *vt* to respect; **respeto** *nm* respect; (*acatamiento*) deference; **respetos** *nmpl* respects; **respetuoso, a** *a* respectful.
respingar [respin'gar] *vi* to shy; **respingo** *nm* start, jump; (*fig*) gesture of disgust.
respiración [respira'θjon] *nf* breathing; (*MED*) respiration; (*ventilación*) ventilation; **respirar** *vi* to breathe; (*inhalar*) to inhale; **respiratorio, a** *a* respiratory; **respiro** *nm* breathing; (*fig*) respite.
resplandecer [resplande'θer] *vi* to shine; **resplandeciente** *a* resplendent, shining;

resplandor *nm* brilliance, brightness; (*del fuego*) blaze.

responder [respon'der] *vt* to answer ¡/ *vi* to answer; (*fig*) to respond; (*pey*) to answer back; ~ **de** o **por** to answer for.

responsabilidad [responsaβili'ðað] *nf* responsibility; **responsable** *a* responsible.

respuesta [res'pwesta] *nf* answer, reply.

resquebrajar [reskeβra'xar] *vt*, ~**se** *vr* to crack, split.

resquemor [reske'mor] *nm* resentment.

resquicio [res'kiθjo] *nm* chink; (*hendedura*) crack.

restablecer [restaβle'θer] *vt* to re-establish, restore; ~**se** *vr* to recover.

restallar [resta'ʎar] *vi* to crack.

restante [res'tante] *a* remaining; **lo** ~ the remainder.

restar [res'tar] *vt* (*MAT*) to subtract; (*fig*) to take away // *vi* to remain, be left.

restauración [restaura'θjon] *nf* restoration.

restaurán [restau'ran], **restaurante** [restau'rante] *nm* restaurant.

restaurar [restau'rar] *vt* to restore.

restitución [restitu'θjon] *nf* return, restitution.

restituir [restitu'ir] *vt* (*devolver*) to return, give back; (*rehabilitar*) to restore; ~**se** *vr*: ~**se a** to rejoin.

resto ['resto] *nm* (*residuo*) rest, remainder; (*apuesta*) stake; ~**s** *nmpl* remains.

restregar [restre'xar] *vt* to scrub, rub.

restricción [restrik'θjon] *nf* restriction.

restrictivo, a [restrik'tiβo, a] *a* restrictive.

restringir [restrin'xir] *vt* to restrict, limit.

resucitar [resuθi'tar] *vt*, *vi* to resuscitate, revive.

resuelto, a [re'swelto, a] *pp de* **resolver** // *a* resolute, determined.

resuello [re'sweʎo] *nm* breath.

resultado [resul'taðo] *nm* (*conclusión*) outcome; (*consecuencia*) result, consequence; **resultante** *a* resulting, resultant.

resultar [resul'tar] *vi* (*llegar a ser*) to turn out to be; (*salir bien*) to turn out well; (*COM*) to amount to; ~ **de** to stem from; **me resulta difícil hacerlo** it's difficult for me to do it.

resumen [re'sumen] *nm* summary, résumé; **en** ~ in short.

resumir [resu'mir] *vt* to sum up; (*cortar*) to abridge, cut down.

retablo [re'taβlo] *nm* altarpiece.

retaguardia [reta'xwarðja] *nf* rearguard.

retahíla [reta'ila] *nf* series, string.

retal [re'tal] *nm* remnant.

retama [re'tama] *nf* (*AM*) broom.

retar [re'tar] *vt* (*gen*) to challenge; (*desafiar*) to defy, dare.

retardar [retar'ðar] *vt* (*demorar*) to delay; (*hacer más lento*) to slow down; (*retener*) to hold back; **retardo** *nm* delay.

retazo [re'taθo] *nm* snippet.

rete... ['rete] *pref* very, extremely.

retén [re'ten] *nm* (*TEC*) catch; (*reserva*) store, reserve.

retener [rete'ner] *vt* (*guardar*) to retain, keep; (*intereses*) to withhold.

retina [re'tina] *nf* retina.

retintín [retin'tin] *nm* jangle.

retirada [reti'raða] *nf* (*MIL*, *refugio*) retreat; (*de dinero*) withdrawal; (*de embajador*) recall; **retirado, a** *a* (*distante*) remote; (*tranquilo*) quiet; (*jubilado*) retired.

retirar [reti'rar] *vt* to withdraw; (*quitar*) to remove; (*jubilar*) to retire, pension off; ~**se** *vr* to retreat, withdraw; to retire; (*acostarse*) to retire, go to bed; **retiro** *nm* retreat; retirement; (*pago*) pension.

reto ['reto] *nm* dare, challenge.

retocar [reto'kar] *vt* (*fotografía*) to touch up, retouch.

retoño [re'toɲo] *nm* sprout, shoot; (*fig*) offspring, child.

retoque [re'toke] *nm* retouching; (*MED*) symptom.

retorcer [retor'θer] *vt* (*gen*) to twist; (*manos, lavado*) to wring; ~**se** *vr* to become twisted; (*mover el cuerpo*) to writhe.

retorcimiento [retorθi'mjento] *nm* twist, twisting; (*fig*) deviousness.

retórica [re'torika] *nf* rhetoric; (*fig*) affectedness.

retornar [retor'nar] *vt* to return, give back // *vi* to return, go/come back; **retorno** *nm* return.

retortijón [retorti'xon] *nm* twist, twisting.

retozar [reto'θar] *vi* (*juguetear*) to frolic, romp; (*saltar*) to gambol; **retozón, ona** *a* playful.

retracción [retrak'θjon], **retractación** [retrakta'θjon] *nf* retraction.

retractar [retrak'tar] *vt* to retract; ~**se** *vr* to retract; **me retracto** I take that back.

retraer [retra'er] *vt* to dissuade; ~**se** *vr* to retreat, withdraw; **retraído, a** *a* shy, retiring; **retraimiento** *nm* (*gen*) retirement; (*timidez*) shyness; (*lugar*) retreat.

retransmisión [retransmi'sjon] *nf* repeat (broadcast); **retransmitir** *vt* (*mensaje*) to relay; (*TV etc*) to retransmit; (: *en vivo*) to broadcast live.

retrasado, a [retra'saðo, a] *a* late; (*MED*) mentally retarded; (*país etc*) backward, underdeveloped; **retrasar** *vt* (*demorar*) to postpone, put off; (*retardar*) to slow down // *vi*, **retrasarse** *vr* (*atrasarse*) to be late; (*reloj*) to be slow; (*producción*) to fall (away); (*quedarse atrás*) to lag behind.

retraso [re'traso] *nm* (*demora*) delay; (*lentitud*) slowness; (*tardanza*) lateness; (*atraso*) backwardness; **llegar con** ~ to arrive late; ~ **mental** mental deficiency.

retratar [retra'tar] *vt* (*ARTE*) to paint the portrait of; (*fotografiar*) to photograph; (*fig*) to depict; ~**se** *vr* to have one's portrait painted; to have one's photograph taken; **retrato** nm portrait; (fig) likeness; **retrato-robot** nm identikit picture.

retreta [re'treta] nf retreat.

retrete [re'trete] nm toilet, lavatory.

retribución [retriβu'θjon] nf (recompensa) reward; (pago) pay, payment; **retribuir** vt to reward; to pay.

retro... [retro] pref retro... .

retroactivo, a [retroak'tiβo, a] a retroactive, retrospective.

retroceder [retroθe'ðer] vi (echarse atrás) to move back(wards); (tropas) to fall back, retreat; (arma de fuego) to recoil; (fig) to back down.

retroceso [retro'θeso] nm backward movement; (MIL) withdrawal, retreat; (MED) relapse; (fig) backing down.

retrógrado, a [re'troɣraðo, a] a (atrasado) retrograde; (POL) reactionary.

retropropulsión [retropropul'sjon] nf jet propulsion.

retrospectivo, a [retrospek'tiβo, a] a retrospective.

retrovisor [retroβi'sor] nm driving or rear-view mirror.

retumbante [retum'bante] a resounding; **retumbar** vi to echo, resound.

reuma ['reuma] nm rheumatism; **reumático, a** a rheumatic; **reumatismo** nm rheumatism.

reunificar [reunifi'kar] vt to reunify.

reunión [reu'njon] nf (asamblea) meeting; (fiesta) party; (reencuentro) reunion.

reunir [reu'nir] vt (juntar) to reunite, join; (recoger) to gather; (personas) to assemble; (cualidades) to combine; ~se vr to meet, gather.

revalidar [reβali'ðar] vt to confirm, ratify.

revalorar [reβalo'rar] vt to revalue, reassess.

revancha [re'βantʃa] nf revenge.

revelación [reβela'θjon] nf revelation.

revelado [reβe'laðo] nm developing.

revelar [reβe'lar] vt to reveal; (FOTO) to develop.

revendedor, a [reβende'ðor, a] nm/f retailer; (pey) ticket tout.

reventar [reβen'tar] vt to burst, explode; (fam: plan) to ruin // vi, ~se vr (estallar) to burst, explode; (fam: morirse) to kick the bucket (fam); ~ **por** to be bursting to.

reventón [reβen'ton] nm burst, explosion; (AUTO) blow-out, puncture.

reverberación [reβerβera'θjon] nf reverberation; **reverberar** vi to reverberate; **reverbero** nm reverberation.

reverdecer [reβerðe'θer] vi (fig) to revive, come to life again.

reverencia [reβe'renθja] nf reverence; **reverenciar** vt to revere.

reverendo, a [reβe'renðo, a] a reverend; **reverente** a reverent.

reversión [reβer'sjon] nf reversion.

reverso [re'βerso] nm back, wrong side; (de moneda) reverse.

revertir [reβer'tir] vi to revert.

revés [re'βes] nm back, wrong side; (fig) reverse, setback; (DEPORTE) backhand; **hacer al** ~ to do sth the wrong way round; **volver algo al** ~ to turn sth round; (ropa) to turn sth inside out.

revestir [reβes'tir] vt to put on; (cubrir) to cover, coat; ~ **con** o **de** to invest with.

revisar [reβi'sar] vt (examinar) to check; (rever) to revise; **revisión** nf revision.

revisor, a [reβi'sor, a] nm/f inspector; (FERRO) ticket collector.

revista [re'βista] nf magazine, review; (TEATRO) revue; (inspección) inspection; **pasar** ~ **a** to review, inspect.

revivir [reβi'βir] vi to revive.

revocación [reβoka'θjon] nf repeal; **revocar** vt to revoke.

revolcar [reβol'kar] vt to knock down, send flying; ~se vr to roll about.

revolotear [reβolote'ar] vi to flutter; **revoloteo** nm fluttering.

revoltijo [reβol'tixo] nm mess, jumble.

revoltoso, a [reβol'toso, a] a (travieso) naughty, unruly; (rebelde) rebellious.

revolución [reβolu'θjon] nf revolution; **revolucionar** vt to revolutionize; **revolucionario, a** a a, nm/f revolutionary.

revólver [re'βolβer] nm revolver.

revolver [reβol'βer] vt (desordenar) to disturb, mess up; (mover) to move about; (poner al revés) to turn over; (investigar) to look through; (adentrarse en) to go into; (POL) to stir up; (hacer paquete) to wrap up // vi: ~ **en** to go through, rummage (about) in; ~se vr to turn round; (por dolor) to writhe; (volver contra) to turn on or against.

revuelco [re'βwelko] nm fall, tumble.

revuelo [re'βwelo] nm fluttering; (fig) commotion.

revuelto, a [re'βwelto, a] pp de **revolver** // a (mezclado) mixed-up; (huevos) scrambled; (descontento) discontented; (travieso) mischievous // nf (motín) revolt; (conmoción) commotion.

revulsivo [reβul'siβo] nm enema.

rey [rei] nm king.

reyerta [re'jerta] nf quarrel, brawl.

rezagado, a [reθa'ɣaðo, a] nm/f straggler.

rezagar [reθa'ɣar] vt (dejar atrás) to leave behind; (retrasar) to delay, postpone.

rezar [re'θar] vi to pray; ~ **con** (fam) to concern, have to do with; **rezo** nm prayer.

rezongar [reθon'gar] vi to grumble.

rezumar [reθu'mar] vt to ooze // vi to leak; ~se vr to leak out.

ría ['ria] nf estuary.

riada [ri'aða] nf flood.

ribera [ri'βera] nf (de río) bank; (: área) riverside; (del mar) shore.

ribete [ri'βete] nm (de vestido) border; (fig) addition; ~ar vt to edge, border.

rico, a ['riko, a] a (gen) rich; (adinerado)

wealthy; (*lujoso*) luxurious; (*comida*) tasty, delicious // *nm/f* rich person.

rictus ['riktus] *nm* (*mueca*) sneer, grin.

ridiculez [riðiku'leθ] *nf* absurdity; **ridiculizar** *vt* to ridicule.

ridículo, a [ri'ðikulo, a] *a* ridiculous; **hacer el** ~ to make o.s. ridiculous; **poner a uno en** ~ to ridicule sb.

riego ['rjeʂo] *nm* (*aspersión*) watering; (*irrigación*) irrigation.

riel [rjel] *nm* rail.

rienda ['rjenda] *nf* rein; **dar** ~ **suelta a** to give free rein to.

riente ['rjente] *a* laughing.

riesgo ['rjesʂo] *nm* risk; **correr el** ~ **de** to run the risk of.

rifa ['rifa] *nf* (*lotería*) raffle; (*disputa*) quarrel; **rifar** *vt* to raffle // *vi* to quarrel; **rifarse** *vr*: **rifarse algo** to fight over sth.

rifle ['rifle] *nm* rifle.

rigidez [rixi'ðeθ] *nf* rigidity, stiffness; (*fig*) strictness; **rígido, a** *a* rigid, stiff; strict, inflexible.

rigor [ri'ʂor] *nm* strictness, rigour; (*inclemencia*) harshness; **de** ~ de rigueur, essential; **riguroso, a** *a* rigorous; harsh; (*severo*) severe.

rimar [ri'mar] *vi* to rhyme.

rimbombante [rimbom'bante] *a* resounding; (*fig*) pompous.

rincón [rin'kon] *nm* (inside) corner.

rinoceronte [rinoθe'ronte] *nm* rhinoceros.

riña ['riɲa] *nf* (*disputa*) argument; (*pelea*) brawl.

riñón [ri'ɲon] *nm* (*gen*) kidney; **tener riñones** to have guts.

río *etc vb ver* **reír** // ['rio] *nm* river; (*fig*) torrent, stream; ~ **abajo/arriba** downstream/upstream.

rioplatense [riopla'tense] *a* of the River Plate region.

ripio ['ripjo] *nm* (*residuo*) refuse, waste; (*cascotes*) rubble, debris.

riqueza [ri'keθa] *nf* wealth, riches *pl*; (*cualidad*) richness.

risa ['risa] *nf* (*una* ~) laugh; (*gen*) laughter.

risco ['risko] *nm* crag, cliff; ~**so, a** *a* steep.

risible [ri'siβle] *a* (*ridículo*) ludicrous; (*jocoso*) laughable.

risotada [riso'taða] *nf* guffaw.

ristra ['ristra] *nf* string.

risueño, a [ri'sweɲo, a] *a* (*sonriente*) smiling; (*contento*) cheerful.

ritmo ['ritmo] *nm* rhythm; **a** ~ **lento** slowly; **trabajar a** ~ **lento** to go slow.

rito ['rito] *nm* rite.

ritual [ri'twal] *a, nm* ritual.

rival [ri'βal] *a, nm/f* rival; ~**idad** *nf* rivalry; ~**izar** *vi*: ~**izar con** to rival, vie with.

rizado, a [ri'θaðo, a] *a* curly // *nm* curls *pl*; **rizar** *vt* to curl; **rizarse** *vr* (*el pelo*) to

curl; (*el mar*) to ripple; **rizo** *nm* curl; ripple.

RNE *nf abr de* **Radio Nacional de España.**

robar [ro'βar] *vt* to rob; (*objeto*) to steal; (*casa etc*) to break into; (*NAIPES*) to draw.

roble ['roβle] *nm* oak; ~**do,** ~**dal** *nm* oakwood.

roblón [ro'βlon] *nm* rivet.

robo ['roβo] *nm* robbery, theft; ~ **relámpago** smash-and-grab raid.

robot [ro'βo(t)] *nm* robot.

robustecer [roβuste'θer] *vt* to strengthen.

robusto, a [ro'βusto, a] *a* robust, strong.

roca ['roka] *nf* rock.

rocalla [ro'kaʎa] *nf* pebbles *pl*.

roce ['roθe] *nm* (*caricia*) brush; (*TEC*) friction; (*en la piel*) graze; **tener** ~ **con** to be in close contact with.

rociada [ro'θjaða] *nf* (*aspersión*) sprinkling; (*fig*) hail, shower; **rociar** *vt* to spray.

rocín [ro'θin] *nm* nag, hack.

rocío [ro'θio] *nm* dew.

rocoso, a [ro'koso, a] *a* rocky.

rodado, a [ro'ðaðo, a] *a* (*con ruedas*) wheeled; (*redondo*) round // *nf* rut.

rodaja [ro'ðaxa] *nf* (*raja*) slice; (*rueda*) small wheel.

rodaje [ro'ðaxe] *nm* (*TEC*) wheels *pl*, set of wheels; (*CINE*) shooting, filming; (*AUTO*): **en** ~ running in.

rodar [ro'ðar] *vt* (*vehículo*) to wheel; (*escalera*) to roll down; (*viajar por*) to travel (over) // *vi* to roll; (*coche*) to go, run; (*CINE*) to shoot, film.

rodear [roðe'ar] *vt* to surround // *vi* to go round; ~**se** *vr*: ~**se de amigos** to surround o.s. with friends.

rodeo [ro'ðeo] *nm* (*ruta indirecta*) detour; (*evasión*) evasion; (*AM*) rodeo; **hablar sin** ~**s** to come to the point, speak plainly.

rodilla [ro'ðiʎa] *nf* knee; **de** ~**s** kneeling.

rodillo [ro'ðiʎo] *nm* roller; (*CULIN*) rolling-pin; ~ **apisonador** *o* **de vapor** steamroller.

rododendro [roðo'ðendro] *nm* rhododendron.

roedor, a [roe'ðor, a] *a* gnawing // *nm* rodent.

roer [ro'er] *vt* (*masticar*) to gnaw; (*corroer, fig*) to corrode.

rogar [ro'ʂar] *vt, vi* (*pedir*) to ask for; (*suplicar*) to beg, plead; **se ruega no fumar** please do not smoke.

rojete [ro'xete] *nm* rouge.

rojizo, a [ro'xiθo, a] *a* reddish.

rojo, a ['roxo, a] *a, nm* red; **al** ~ **vivo** red-hot; ~ **de labios** lipstick.

rol [rol] *nm* list, roll; (*AM: papel*) role.

rollizo, a [ro'ʎiθo, a] *a* (*objeto*) cylindrical; (*persona*) plump.

rollo ['roʎo] *nm* (*gen*) roll; (*de cuerda*) coil; (*madera*) log; (*fam*) bore; ¡**qué** ~! what a carry-on!

Roma ['roma] *n* Rome.

romance [ro'manθe] *nm* Romance language; (*LITERATURA*) ballad; **hablar en** ~ to speak plainly.
romántico, a [ro'mantiko, a] *a* romantic.
romería [rome'ria] *nf* (*REL*) pilgrimage; (*excursión*) trip, outing.
romero, a [ro'mero, a] *nm/f* pilgrim // *nm* rosemary.
romo, a ['romo, a] *a* blunt; (*fig*) dull.
rompecabezas [rompeka'βeθas] *nm inv* riddle, puzzle; (*juego*) jigsaw.
rompehuelgas [rompe'welɣas] *nm inv* strikebreaker, blackleg.
rompeolas [rompe'olas] *nm inv* breakwater.
romper [rom'per] *vt* (*gen*) to break; (*hacer pedazos*) to smash; (*papel etc*) to tear, rip // *vi* (*olas*) to break; (*sol, diente*) to break through; ~ **un contrato** to break a contract; ~ **a** to start (suddenly) to; ~ **en llanto** to burst into tears; ~ **con uno** to fall out with sb.
rompimiento [rompi'mjento] *nm* breaking; (*fig*) break; (*quiebra*) crack; ~ **de hostilidades** outbreak of hostilities.
ron [ron] *nm* rum.
roncar [ron'kar] *vi* to snore.
ronco, a ['ronko, a] *a* (*sin voz*) hoarse; (*áspero*) raucous.
roncha ['rontʃa] *nf* weal; (*contusión*) bruise.
ronda ['ronda] *nf* (*gen*) round; (*patrulla*) patrol; **rondar** *vt* to patrol // *vi* to patrol; (*fig*) to prowl round.
rondón [ron'don]: **de** ~ *ad* unexpectedly.
ronquear [ronke'ar] *vi* to be hoarse; **ronquedad** *nf* hoarseness.
ronquido [ron'kiðo] *nm* snore, snoring.
ronronear [ronrone'ar] *vi* to purr; **ronroneo** *nm* purr.
ronzal [ron'θal] *nm* halter.
roña ['roɲa] *nf* scab; (*mugre*) crust (of dirt).
roñoso, a [ro'ɲoso, a] *a* (*mugriento*) filthy; (*inútil*) useless; (*tacaño*) mean.
ropa ['ropa] *nf* clothes *pl*, clothing; ~ **blanca** linen; ~ **de cama** bed linen; ~ **interior** underwear; ~**je** *nm* gown, robes *pl*; ~**vejero, a** *nm/f* second-hand clothes dealer.
ropero [ro'pero] *nm* linen cupboard; (*guardarropa*) wardrobe.
roque ['roke] *nm* rook, castle.
roquedal [roke'ðal] *nm* rocky place.
rosa ['rosa] *a inv* pink // *nf* rose; (*ANAT*) red birthmark; ~ **de los vientos** the compass; ~**s** *nfpl* popcorn *sg*.
rosado, a [ro'saðo, a], **rosáceo, a** [ro-'saθeo, a] *a* pink // *nm* rosé.
rosal [ro'sal] *nm* rosebush.
rosario [ro'sarjo] *nm* (*REL*) rosary; **rezar el** ~ to say the rosary.
rosca ['roska] *nf* (*de tornillo*) thread; (*de humo*) coil, spiral; (*pan, postre*) ring-shaped roll/pastry.
rosetón [rose'ton] *nm* rosette; (*ARQ*) rose

window; (*AUTO*) cloverleaf (junction).
rostro ['rostro] *nm* (*cara*) face.
rotación [rota'θjon] *nf* rotation; ~ **de cultivos** crop rotation.
rotativo, a [rota'tiβo, a] *a* rotary.
roto, a ['roto, a] *pp de* **romper** // *a* broken; (*disipado*) debauched.
rótula ['rotula] *nf* kneecap; (*TEC*) ball-and-socket joint.
rotular [rotu'lar] *vt* (*titular, encabezar*) to head, entitle; (*etiquetar*) to label; **rótulo** *nm* heading, title; label.
rotundo, a [ro'tundo, a] *a* round; (*enfático*) emphatic.
rotura [ro'tura] *nf* (*rompimiento*) breaking; (*quiebra*) crack; (*MED*) fracture.
roturar [rotu'rar] *vt* to plough.
rozado, a [ro'θaðo, a] *a* worn.
rozadura [roθa'ðura] *nf* abrasion, graze.
rozar [ro'θar] *vt* (*frotar*) to rub; (*arañar*) to scratch; (*arrugar*) to crumple; (*AGR*) to graze; (*tocar ligeramente*) to shave, touch lightly; ~**se** *vr* to rub (together); (*trabarse*) to trip over one's own feet; ~ **con** (*fam*) to rub shoulders with.
roznar [roθ'nar] *vi* to bray.
rte *abr de* **remite, remitente** sender.
rubí [ru'βi] *nm* ruby.
rubicundo, a [ruβi'kundo, a] *a* ruddy; (*de salud*) rosy with health.
rubio, a ['ruβjo, a] *a* fair-haired // *nm/f* blond/blonde; **tabaco** ~ Virginia tobacco.
rubor [ru'βor] *nm* (*timidez*) bashfulness; (*sonrojo*) blush; ~**izarse** *vr* to blush; ~**oso, a** *a* blushing.
rúbrica ['ruβrika] *nf* title, heading; (*de la firma*) flourish; **rubricar** *vt* (*firmar*) to sign with a flourish; (*concluir*) to sign and seal.
rucio, a ['ruθjo, a] *a* grey.
rudeza [ru'ðeθa] *nf* (*tosquedad*) coarseness; (*sencillez*) simplicity.
rudimento [ruði'mento] *nm* rudiment.
rudo, a ['ruðo, a] *a* (*sin pulir*) unpolished; (*tosco*) coarse; (*violento*) violent; (*vulgar*) common; (*estúpido*) stupid.
rueda ['rweða] *nf* (*gen*) wheel; (*círculo*) ring, circle; (*rodaja*) slice, round; ~ **delantera/trasera/de repuesto** front/back/spare wheel; ~ **de prensa** press conference.
ruedo ['rweðo] *nm* (*contorno*) edge, border; (*de vestido*) hem; (*círculo*) circle; (*TAUR*) arena, bullring.
ruego *etc vb ver* **rogar** // ['rweɣo] *nm* request.
rufián [ru'fjan] *nm* scoundrel.
rugby ['ruɣβi] *nm* rugby.
rugido [ru'xiðo] *nm* roar; **rugir** *vi* to roar.
rugoso, a [ru'xoso, a] *a* (*arrugado*) wrinkled; (*áspero*) rough; (*desigual*) ridged.
ruibarbo [rui'βarβo] *nm* rhubarb.
ruido ['rwiðo] *nm* (*gen*) noise; (*sonido*) sound; (*alboroto*) racket, row; (*escándalo*)

commotion, rumpus; ~**so, a** *a* noisy, loud; (*fig*) sensational.
ruin [ru'in] *a* contemptible, mean.
ruina ['rwina] *nf* (*gen*) ruin; (*colapso*) collapse; (*de persona*) ruin, downfall; (*de imperio*) decline.
ruindad [rwin'dað] *nf* lowness, meanness; (*acto*) low *or* mean act.
ruinoso, a [rui'noso, a] *a* ruinous; (*destartalado*) dilapidated, tumbledown; (*COM*) disastrous.
ruiseñor [rwise'ɲor] *nm* nightingale.
rula ['rula], **ruleta** [ru'leta] *nf* roulette.
Rumania [ru'manja] *nf* Rumania.
rumba ['rumba] *nf* rumba.
rumbo ['rumbo] *nm* (*ruta*) route, direction; (*ángulo de dirección*) course, bearing; (*fig*) course of events.
rumboso, a [rum'boso, a] *a* generous.
rumiante [ru'mjante] *nm* ruminant.
ruminar [rumi'nar] *vt* to chew; (*fig*) to chew over // *vi* to chew the cud.
rumor [ru'mor] *nm* (*ruido sordo*) low sound; (*murmuración*) murmur, buzz; ~**earse** *vr*: **se** ~**ea que** it is rumoured that; ~**eo** *nm* murmur.
rupestre [ru'pestre] *a* rock *cpd*.
ruptura [rup'tura] *nf* (*MED*) fracture; (*fig*) rupture.
rural [ru'ral] *a* rural.
Rusia ['rusja] *nf* Russia; **ruso, a** *a, nm/f* Russian.
rústico, a ['rustiko, a] *a* rustic; (*ordinario*) coarse, uncouth // *nm/f* yokel // *nf*: **libro en** ~ **a** paperback.
ruta ['ruta] *nf* route.
rutina [ru'tina] *nf* routine; ~**rio, a** *a* routine.

S

S *abr de* **santo, a; sur.**
s. *abr de* **siglo; siguiente.**
sábado ['saβaðo] *nm* Saturday.
sábana ['saβana] *nf* sheet.
sabandija [saβan'dixa] *nf* bug, insect.
sabañón [saβa'ɲon] *nm* chilblain.
sabelotodo [saβelo'toðo] *nm/f inv* know-all.
saber [sa'ßer] *vt* to know; (*llegar a conocer*) to find out, learn; (*tener capacidad de*) to know how to // *vi*: ~ **a** to taste of, taste like // *nm* knowledge, learning; **a** ~ namely; ¿**sabes nadar?** can you swim?; ¿**sabes ir?** do you know the way?
sabiduría [saβiðu'ria] *nf* (*conocimientos*) wisdom; (*instrucción*) knowledge, learning.
sabiendas [sa'βjendas]: **a** ~ *ad* knowingly.
sabio, a ['saβjo,a] *a* (*docto*) learned; (*prudente*) wise, sensible.
sabor [sa'ßor] *nm* taste, flavour; ~**ear** *vt* to savour, relish; (*dar* ~ *a*) to flavour.
sabotaje [saβo'taxe] *nm* sabotage; **sabotear** *vt* to sabotage.
sabré *etc vb ver* **saber.**

sabroso, a [sa'ßroso, a] *a* tasty; (*fig: fam*) racy, salty.
sacacorchos [saka'kortʃos] *nm inv* corkscrew.
sacapuntas [saka'puntas] *nm inv* pencil sharpener.
sacar [sa'kar] *vt* (*gen*) to take out; (*fig*) to get (out); (*quitar*) to remove, get out; (*hacer salir*) to bring out; (*conclusión*) to draw; (*novela etc*) to publish, bring out; (*ropa*) to take off; (*obra*) to make; (*FOTO*) to take; (*premio*) to receive; (*entradas*) to get; ~ **adelante** to bring up; ~ **a alguien a bailar** to get sb up to dance; ~ **apuntes** to take notes; ~ **la cara por alguien** to stick up for sb; ~ **la lengua** to stick out one's tongue.
sacarina [saka'rina] *nf* saccharin(e).
sacerdote [saθer'ðote] *nm* priest.
saco ['sako] *nm* (*gen*) bag; (*grande*) sack; (*su contenido*) bagful; (*AM*) jacket; ~ **de dormir** sleeping bag.
sacramento [sakra'mento] *nm* sacrament.
sacrificar [sakrifi'kar] *vt* to sacrifice; **sacrificio** *nm* sacrifice.
sacrilegio [sakri'lexjo] *nm* sacrilege; **sacrílego, a** *a* sacrilegious.
sacristía [sakris'tia] *nf* sacristy.
sacro, a ['sakro, a] *a* sacred.
sacudida [saku'ðiða] *nf* (*zarandeada*) shake, shaking; (*sacudimiento*) jolt, bump; ~ **eléctrica** electric shock; **sacudir** *vt* to shake; (*golpear*) to hit.
sádico, a ['saðiko, a] *a* sadistic; **sadismo** *nm* sadism.
saeta [sa'eta] *nf* (*flecha*) arrow; (*de reloj*) hand; (*brújula*) magnetic needle.
sagacidad [saɣaθi'ðað] *nf* shrewdness, cleverness; **sagaz** *a* shrewd, clever; (*astuto*) astute.
sagrado, a [sa'ɣraðo, a] *a* sacred, holy // *nm* sanctuary, asylum.
Sáhara ['saara] *nm*: **el** ~ the Sahara (desert).
sahumar [sau'mar] *vt* to fumigate.
sal [sal] *vb ver* **salir** // *nf* salt; ~ **de la Higuera** Epsom salts.
sala ['sala] *nf* (*cuarto grande*) large room; (~ *de estar*) living room; (*TEATRO*) house, auditorium; (*de hospital*) ward; ~ **de apelación** court; ~ **de espera** waiting room.
salado, a [sa'laðo, a] *a* salty; (*fig*) witty, amusing; **agua** ~**a** salt water; **salar** *vt* to salt, add salt to.
salario [sa'larjo] *nm* wage, pay.
salchicha [sal'tʃitʃa] *nf* pork sausage; **salchichón** *nm* (*salami-type*) sausage.
saldar [sal'dar] *vt* to pay; (*vender*) to sell off; (*fig*) to settle, resolve; **saldo** *nm* (*pago*) settlement; (*de una cuenta*) balance; (*lo restante*) remnant(s) (*pl*), remainder.
saldré *etc vb ver* **salir.**
salero [sa'lero] *nm* salt cellar.
salgo *etc vb ver* **salir.**

salida [sa'liða] *nf* exit, way out, (*acto*) leaving, going out; (*de tren*, AVIAT) departure; (TEC) output, production; (*fig*) way out; (COM) opening; (GEO, *válvula*) outlet; (*de gas, aire*) escape, leak; **calle sin** ~ cul-de-sac; ~ **de emergencia** emergency exit.

saliente [sa'ljente] *a* (ARQ) projecting; (*que se retira*) outgoing, retiring; (*el sol*) rising; (*fig*) outstanding.

salir [sa'lir] *vi* (*gen*) to come/go out; (*resultar*) to turn out; (*partir*) to leave, depart; (*aparecer*) to appear; (*sobresalir*) to project, jut out; ~**se** *vr* (*vasija*) to leak; (*animal*) to escape, get out; ~ **con** to go out with; ~ **a la superficie** to come to the surface; ~ **caro/barato** to work out expensive/cheap.

saliva [sa'liβa] *nf* saliva.

salmantino, a [salman'tino, a] *a* of Salamanca.

salmo ['salmo] *nm* psalm.

salmón [sal'mon] *nm* salmon.

salmuera [sal'mwera] *nf* pickle, brine.

salón [sa'lon] *nm* (*de casa*) living-room, lounge; (*muebles*) lounge suite; ~ **de belleza** beauty parlour; ~ **de pintura** art gallery; ~ **de baile** dance hall.

salpicadero [salpika'ðero] *nm* dashboard.

salpicar [salpi'kar] *vt* (*rociar*) to sprinkle, spatter; (*esparcir*) to scatter.

salsa ['salsa] *nf* sauce; (*con carne asada*) gravy; (*fig*) spice.

saltamontes [salta'montes] *nm inv* grasshopper.

saltar [sal'tar] *vt* to jump (over), leap (over); (*dejar de lado*) to skip, miss out // *vi* to jump, leap; (*pelota*) to bounce; (*al aire*) to fly up; (*quebrarse*) to break; (*al agua*) to dive; (*fig*) to explode, blow up.

saltear [salte'ar] *vt* (*robar*) to rob (in a holdup); (*asaltar*) to assault, attack; (CULIN) to sauté.

saltimbanqui [saltim'banki] *nm/f* acrobat.

salto ['salto] *nm* jump, leap; (*al agua*) dive; (DEPORTE) jump; ~ **de agua** waterfall.

saltón, ona [sal'ton, ona] *a* (*ojos*) bulging, popping; (*dientes*) protruding.

salubre [sa'luβre] *a* healthy, salubrious.

salud [sa'luð] *nf* health; ¡(**a su**) ~! good health!; ~**able** *a* (*de buena* ~) healthy; (*provechoso*) good, beneficial.

saludar [salu'ðar] *vt* to greet; (MIL) to salute; **saludo** *nm* greeting; **saludos** (*en carta*) best wishes, regards, greetings.

salvación [salβa'θjon] *nf* (*gen*) salvation; (*rescate*) rescue.

salvaguardar [salβaɣwar'ðar] *vt* to safeguard.

salvaje [sal'βaxe] *a* wild; (*tribú*) savage; **salvajismo** *nm*, **salvajez** *nf* savagery.

salvar [sal'βar] *vt* (*rescatar*) to save, rescue; (*resolver*) to overcome, resolve; (*cubrir distancias*) to cover, travel; (*hacer excepción*) to except, exclude; (*un barco*) to salvage.

salvavidas [salβa'βiðas] *nm inv* lifebelt // *a*: **bote/chaleco/cinturón** ~ lifeboat/jacket/belt.

salvia ['salβja] *nf* sage.

salvo, a ['salβo, a] *a* safe // *ad* except (for), save; **a** ~ out of danger; ~ **que** unless; ~ **conducto** *nm* safe-conduct.

san [san] *a* saint; ~ **Juan** St. John.

sanar [sa'nar] *vt* (*herida*) to heal; (*persona*) to cure // *vi* (*persona*) to get well, recover; (*herida*) to heal.

sanatorio [sana'torjo] *nm* sanatorium.

sanción [san'θjon] *nf* sanction; **sancionar** *vt* to sanction.

sandalia [san'dalja] *nf* sandal.

sandía [san'dia] *nf* watermelon.

sandwich ['sandwitʃ] *nm* sandwich.

saneamiento [sanea'mjento] *nm* sanitation; (*de la tierra*) drainage; (*indemnización*) compensation; (*fig*) remedy; **sanear** *vt* to drain; to compensate; to remedy, repair; (*garantizar*) to guarantee; (*asegurar*) to insure.

sangrar [san'grar] *vt, vi* to bleed; **sangre** *nf* blood.

sangría [san'gria] *nf* sangria, *sweetened drink of red wine with fruit*.

sangriento, a [san'grjento, a] *a* (*herido*) bleeding; (*batalla*) bloody.

sanguinario, a [sangi'narjo, a] *a* bloodthirsty.

sanguíneo, a [san'gineo, a] *a* blood *cpd*.

sanidad [sani'ðað] *nf* sanitation; (*calidad de sano*) health, healthiness; ~ **pública** public health.

sanitario, a [sani'tarjo, a] *a* sanitary; (*de la salud*) health *cpd*.

sano, a ['sano, a] *a* healthy; (*sin daños*) sound; (*comida*) good; (*entero*) whole, intact; ~ **y salvo** safe and sound.

santidad [santi'ðað] *nf* holiness, sanctity; **santificar** *vt* to sanctify, make holy.

santiguar [santi'ɣwar] *vt* (*fig*) to slap, hit; ~**se** *vr* to make the sign of the cross.

santo, a ['santo, a] *a* holy; (*fig*) wonderful, miraculous // *nm/f* saint // *nm* saint's day; ~ **y seña** password.

santuario [san'twarjo] *nm* sanctuary, shrine.

saña ['saɲa] *nf* rage, fury.

sapo ['sapo] *nm* toad.

saque ['sake] *nm* (TENIS) service, serve; (FÚTBOL) throw-in; ~ **de esquina** corner (kick).

saquear [sake'ar] *vt* (MIL) to sack; (*robar*) to loot, plunder; (*fig*) to ransack; **saqueo** *nm* sacking; looting, plundering; ransacking.

sarampión [saram'pjon] *nm* measles *sg*.

sarcasmo [sar'kasmo] *nm* sarcasm; **sarcástico, a** *a* sarcastic.

sardina [sar'ðina] *nf* sardine.

sardónico, a [sar'ðoniko, a] *a* sardonic; (*irónico*) ironical, sarcastic.

sargento [sar'xento] *nm* sergeant.

sarna ['sarna] nf itch; (*MED*) scabies.
sartén [sar'ten] nf frying pan.
sastre ['sastre] nm tailor; ~**ría** nf (*arte*) tailoring; (*tienda*) tailor's (shop).
satélite [sa'telite] nm satellite.
sátira ['satira] nf satire.
satisfacción [satisfak'θjon] nf satisfaction; **satisfacer** vt to satisfy; (*gastos*) to meet; (*pérdida*) to make good; **satisfacerse** vr to satisfy o.s., be satisfied; (*vengarse*) to take revenge; **satisfecho, a** a satisfied; (*contento*) content(ed), happy; (*vanidoso*) self-satisfied, smug.
saturar [satu'rar] vt to saturate.
sauce ['sauθe] nm willow; ~ **llorón** weeping willow.
sauna ['sauna] nf sauna.
savia ['saβja] nf sap.
saxofón [sakso'fon], **saxófono** [sak-'sofono] nm saxophone.
sayo ['sajo] nm smock.
sazonado, a [saθo'naðo, a] a (*fruta*) ripe; (*CULIN*) flavoured, seasoned; **sazonar** vt to ripen; to flavour, season.
se [se] pron reflexivo oneself; (*sg: m*) himself; (: *f*) herself; (: *de una cosa*) itself; (: *de Ud*) yourself; (*pl*) themselves; (: *de Uds*) yourselves; (*de uno*) oneself; ~ **mira en el espejo** he looks at himself in the mirror; (*recíproco*) each other, one another; ~ **ayudan** they help each other; ~ **miraron (el uno al otro)** they looked at one another; (*uso impersonal*): ~ **compró hace 3 años** it was bought 3 years ago; **en esa parte** ~ **habla francés** in that area French is spoken or people speak French; (*dativo*): ~ **lo daré** I'll give it to him/her/you; **él** ~ **ha comprado un sombrero** he has bought himself a hat.
SE abr de **sudeste.**
sé vb ver **saber, ser.**
sea etc vb ver **ser.**
sebo ['seβo] nm fat, grease.
seca ['seka] nf ver **seco.**
secador [seka'ðor] nm: ~ **de cabello** o **para el pelo** hair-dryer.
secadora [seka'ðora] nf wringer; ~ **centrífuga** spin-dryer.
secar [se'kar] vt to dry; ~**se** vr to dry (off); (*río, planta*) to dry up.
sección [sek'θjon] nf section.
seco, a ['seko, a] a dry; (*carácter*) cold; (*respuesta*) sharp, curt; (*coñac*) straight // nf drought; **vivir a pan** ~ to live by bread alone; **habrá pan a** ~ as there will be just bread; **decir algo a** ~ **as** to say sth curtly; **parar en** ~ to stop dead.
secretaría [sekreta'ria] nf secretariat; **secretario, a** nm/f secretary.
secreto, a [se'kreto, a] a secret; (*persona*) secretive // nm secret; (*calidad*) secrecy.
secta ['sekta] nf sect; ~**rio, a** a sectarian.
sector [sek'tor] nm sector.
secuela [se'kwela] nf consequence.
secuestrar [sekwes'trar] vt to kidnap; (*bienes*) to seize, confiscate; **secuestro**

nm kidnapping; seizure, confiscation.
secular [seku'lar] a secular.
secundar [sekun'dar] vt to second, support.
secundario, a [sekun'darjo, a] a secondary.
sed [seð] nf thirst; **tener** ~ to be thirsty.
seda ['seða] nf silk.
sedal [se'ðal] nm fishing line.
sedante [se'ðante], **sedativo** [seða'tiβo] nm sedative.
sede ['seðe] nf (*de gobierno*) seat; (*de compañía*) headquarters pl; **Santa S**~ Holy See.
sediento, a [se'ðjento, a] a thirsty.
sedimentar [seðimen'tar] vt to deposit; ~**se** vr to settle; **sedimento** nm sediment.
seducción [seðuk'θjon] nf seduction; **seducir** vt to seduce; (*sobornar*) to bribe; (*cautivar*) to charm, fascinate; **seductor, a** a seductive; charming, fascinating; (*engañoso*) deceptive, misleading // nm/f seducer.
segadora-trilladora [seɣa'ðora triʎa-'ðora] nf combine harvester.
seglar [se'ɣlar] a secular, lay.
segregación [seɣreɣa'θjon] nf segregation; ~ **racial** racial segregation; **segregar** vt to segregate, separate.
seguido, a [se'ɣiðo, a] a (*continuo*) continuous, unbroken; (*recto*) straight; ~**s** consecutive, successive // ad (*directo*) straight (on); (*después*) after // nf: **en** ~**a** at once, right away; **5 días** ~**s** 5 days running, 5 days in a row.
seguimiento [seɣi'mjento] nm chase, pursuit; (*continuación*) continuation.
seguir [se'ɣir] vt (*gen*) to follow; (*venir después*) to follow on, come after; (*proseguir*) to continue; (*perseguir*) to chase, pursue // vi (*gen*) to follow; (*continuar*) to continue, carry or go on; ~**se** vr to follow; **sigo sin comprender** I still don't understand; **sigue lloviendo** it's still raining.
según [se'ɣun] prep according to // ad according to circumstances; ~ **y conforme** it all depends; ~ **esté el tiempo** depending on the weather.
segundo, a [se'ɣundo, a] a second // nm second // nf second meaning; **de** ~**a mano** second hand.
segur [se'ɣur] nf (*hacha*) axe; (*hoz*) sickle.
seguramente [seɣura'mente] ad surely; (*con certeza*) for sure, with certainty.
seguridad [seɣuri'ðað] nf (*gen*) safety; (*del estado, de casa etc*) security; (*certidumbre*) certainty; (*confianza*) confidence; (*estabilidad*) stability; ~ **social** social security.
seguro, a [se'ɣuro, a] a (*cierto*) sure, certain; (*fiel*) trustworthy; (*libre del peligro*) safe; (*bien defendido, firme*) secure // ad for sure, certainly // nm (*COM*) insurance; ~ **contra terceros/a todo riesgo** third party/comprehensive insurance; ~**s sociales** social security sg.

seis [seis] *num* six.

seismo ['seismo] *nm* tremor, earthquake.

selección [selek'θjon] *nf* selection; **seleccionar** *vt* to pick, choose, select; **selecto, a** *a* select, choice; (*escogido*) selected.

selva ['selßa] *nf* (*bosque*) forest, woods *pl*; (*jungla*) jungle.

sello ['seλo] *nm* stamp; (*medicinal*) capsule, pill.

semáforo [se'maforo] *nm* (AUTO) traffic lights *pl*; (FERRO) signal.

semana [se'mana] *nf* week; **entre** ~ during the week; **semanal, semanario, a** *a* weekly.

semblante [sem'blante] *nm* face; (*fig*) face, appearance.

sembrar [sem'brar] *vt* to sow; (*objetos*) to sprinkle, scatter about; (*noticias*) to spread.

semejante [seme'xante] *a* (*parecido*) similar; ~**s** alike, similar // *nm* fellow man, fellow creature; **no he dicho cosa** ~ I have not said any such thing; **semejanza** *nf* similarity, resemblance.

semejar [seme'xar] *vi* to seem like, resemble; ~**se** *vr* to look alike, be similar.

semen ['semen] *nm* semen; ~**tal** *nm* stud.

semestral [semes'tral] *a* half-yearly, bi-annual.

semicírculo [semi'θirkulo] *nm* semicircle.

semiconsciente [semikons'θjente] *a* semiconscious.

semilla [se'miλa] *nf* seed.

seminario [semi'narjo] *nm* (REL) seminary; (*en universidad*) seminar.

sémola ['semola] *nf* semolina.

sempiterno, a [sempi'terno, a] *a* everlasting // *a* evergreen.

Sena ['sena] *nm*: **el** ~ the (river) Seine.

senado [se'naðo] *nm* senate; **senador, a** *nm/f* senator.

sencillez [senθi'λeθ] *nf* (*gen*) simplicity; (*naturalidad*) naturalness; **sencillo, a** *a* simple; natural, unaffected.

senda ['senda] *nf*, **sendero** [sen'dero] *nm* path, track.

sendos, as ['sendos, as] *apl*: **les dio** ~ **golpes** he hit both of them.

senil [se'nil] *a* senile.

seno ['seno] *nm* (ANAT) bosom, bust; (*fig*) bosom; (*vacío*) hollow; ~**s** breasts.

sensación [sensa'θjon] *nf* (*gen*) sensation; (*sentido*) sense; (*sentimiento*) feeling.

sensato, a [sen'sato, a] *a* sensible.

sensible [sen'sible] *a* sensitive; (*apreciable*) perceptible, appreciable; (*pérdida*) considerable.

sensitivo, a [sensi'tiβo, a], **sensorio, a** [sen'sorjo, a], **sensorial** [senso'rjal] *a* sensory.

sensual [sen'swal] *a* sensual.

sentado, a [sen'taðo, a] *a* (*establecido*) settled; (*carácter*) sensible; **estar** ~ to sit, be sitting (down) // *nf* sitting; **dar por** ~ to take for granted, assume.

sentar [sen'tar] *vt* to sit, seat; (*fig*) to establish // *vi* (*vestido*) to suit; (*alimento*): ~ **bien/mal a** to agree/disagree with; ~**se** *vr* (*persona*) to sit, sit down; (*el tiempo*) to settle (down); (*los depósitos*) to settle.

sentencia [sen'tenθja] *nf* (*máxima*) maxim, saying; (JUR) sentence; **sentenciar** *vt* to sentence // *vi* to give one's opinion.

sentido, a [sen'tiðo, a] *a* (*pérdida*) regrettable; (*carácter*) sensitive // *nm* (*gen*) sense; (*sentimiento*) feeling; (*significado*) sense, meaning; (*dirección*) direction; **mi más** ~ **pésame** my deepest sympathy; ~ **del humor** sense of humour; ~ **único** one-way (street).

sentimental [sentimen'tal] *a* sentimental; **vida** ~ love life.

sentimiento [senti'mjento] *nm* (*emoción*) feeling, emotion; (*sentido*) sense; (*pesar*) regret, sorrow.

sentir [sen'tir] *vt* (*gen*) to feel; (*percibir*) to perceive, sense; (*lamentar*) to regret, be sorry for // *vi* (*tener la sensación*) to feel; (*lamentarse*) to feel sorry // *nm* opinion, judgement; ~**se bien/mal** to feel well/ill; **lo siento** I'm sorry.

seña ['seɲa] *nf* sign; (MIL) password; ~**s** *nfpl* address *sg*; ~**s personales** personal details.

señal [se'ɲal] *nf* (*gen*) sign; (*síntoma*) symptom; (FERRO, TELEC) signal; (*marca*) mark; (COM) deposit; **en** ~ **de** as a token of, as a sign of; ~**ar** *vt* to mark; (*indicar*) to point out, indicate; (*fijar*) to fix, settle; ~**arse** *vr* to make one's mark.

señor [se'ɲor] *nm* (*hombre*) man; (*caballero*) gentleman; (*dueño*) owner, master; (*trato: antes de nombre propio*) Mr; (: *directo*) sir; **muy** ~ **mío** Dear Sir; **el** ~ **alcalde/presidente** the mayor/president.

señora [se'ɲora] *nf* (*dama*) lady; (*trato*) Mrs; (*tratamiento de cortesía*) madam; (*fam*) wife; **Nuestra S**~ Our Lady.

señorita [seɲo'rita] *nf* (*gen*) Miss; (*mujer joven*) young lady.

señuelo [se'ɲwelo] *nm* decoy.

sepa *etc vb ver* **saber.**

separación [separa'θjon] *nf* separation; (*división*) division; (*distancia*) gap, distance.

separar [sepa'rar] *vt* to separate; (*dividir*) to divide; ~**se** *vr* (*parte*) to come away; (*partes*) to come apart; (*persona*) to leave, go away; (*matrimonio*) to separate; **separatismo** *nm* separatism.

sepia ['sepja] *nf* cuttlefish.

séptico, a ['septiko, a] *a* septic.

septiembre [sep'tjembre] *nm* September.

séptimo, a ['septimo, a] *a, num* seventh.

sepultar [sepul'tar] *vt* to bury; **sepultura** *nf* (*acto*) burial; (*tumba*) grave, tomb; **sepulturero, a** *nm/f* gravedigger.

sequedad [seke'ðað] *nf* dryness; (*fig*) brusqueness, curtness.

sequía [se'kia] *nf* drought.
séquito ['sekito] *nm* followers *pl*, retinue.
ser [ser] *vi* (*gen*) to be; (*devenir*) to become // *nm* being; ~ **de** (*origen*) to be from, come from; (*hecho de*) to be (made) of; (*pertenecer a*) to belong to; **es la una** it is one o'clock; **es de esperar que** it is to be hoped that; **era de ver** it was worth seeing, you should have seen it; **a no** ~ **que** unless; **de no** ~ **así** if it were not so, were it not so; **o sea** that is to say; **sea como sea** be that as it may.
serenarse [sere'narse] *vr* to calm down.
sereno, a [se'reno, a] *a* (*persona*) calm, unruffled; (*el tiempo*) fine, settled; (*ambiente*) calm, peaceful // *nm* night watchman.
serie ['serje] *nf* series; (*cadena*) sequence, succession; **fuera de** ~ out of order; **fabricación en** ~ mass production.
seriedad [serje'ðað] *nf* seriousness; (*formalidad*) reliability; (*de crisis*) gravity, seriousness; **serio, a** *a* serious; reliable, dependable; grave, serious; **en serio** *ad* seriously.
sermón [ser'mon] *nm* (REL) sermon.
serpentear [serpente'ar] *vi* to wriggle; (*fig*) to wind, snake.
serpentina [serpen'tina] *nf* streamer.
serpiente [ser'pjente] *nf* snake; ~ **boa** boa constrictor; ~ **pitón** python; ~ **de cascabel** rattlesnake.
serranía [serra'nia] *nf* mountainous area; **serrano, a** *a* highland *cpd*, hill *cpd* // *nm/f* highlander.
serrar [se'rrar] *vt* = **aserrar.**
serrín [se'rrin] *nm* = **aserrín.**
serrucho [se'rrutʃo] *nm* saw.
servicio [ser'βiθjo] *nm* service; ~**s** toilet(s).
servidor, a [serβi'ðor, a] *nm/f* servant; **su seguro** ~ **(s.s.s.)** yours faithfully; **servidumbre** *nf* (*sujeción*) servitude; (*criados*) servants *pl*, staff.
servil [ser'βil] *a* servile.
servilleta [serβi'ʎeta] *nf* serviette, napkin.
servir [ser'βir] *vt* to serve // *vi* to serve; (*tener utilidad*) to be of use, be useful; ~**se** *vr* to serve *or* help o.s.; ~**se de algo** to make use of sth, use sth; **sírvase pasar** please come in.
sesenta [se'senta] *num* sixty.
sesgado, a [ses'ɣaðo, a] *a* slanted, slanting; **sesgo** *nm* slant; (*fig*) slant, twist.
sesión [se'sjon] *nf* (POL) session, sitting; (CINE) showing.
seso ['seso] *nm* brain; **sesudo, a** *a* sensible, wise.
seta ['seta] *nf* mushroom.
setenta [se'tenta] *num* seventy.
seudo... ['seuðo] *pref* pseudo... .
seudónimo [seu'ðonimo] *nm* pseudonym.
severidad [seβeri'ðað] *nf* severity; **severo, a** *a* severe.
Sevilla [se'βiʎa] *n* Seville.

sexo ['sekso] *nm* sex.
sexto, a ['seksto, a] *a, nm* sixth.
sexual [sek'swal] *a* sexual; **vida** ~ **sex** life.
si [si] *conj* if; **me pregunto** ~... I wonder if *or* whether... .
sí [si] *ad* yes // *nm* consent (*gen*) oneself; (*sg: m*) himself; (: *f*) herself; (: *de cosa*) itself; (*de usted*) yourself; (*pl*) themselves; (*de ustedes*) yourselves; (*recíproco*) each other; **él no quiere pero yo** ~ he doesn't want to but I do; **ella** ~ **vendrá** she will certainly come, she is sure to come; **claro que** ~ of course; **creo que** ~ I think so.
siderúrgico, a [siðe'rurxico, a] *a* iron and steel *cpd* // *nf*: **la** ~**a** the iron and steel industry.
sidra ['siðra] *nf* cider.
siembra ['sjembra] *nf* sowing.
siempre ['sjempre] *ad* (*gen*) always; (*todo el tiempo*) all the time; ~ **que** *conj* (*cada vez*) whenever; (*dado que*) provided that; **para** ~ for ever.
sien [sjen] *nf* temple.
siento *etc vb ver* **sentar, sentir.**
sierra ['sjerra] *nf* (TEC) saw; (*cadena de montañas*) mountain range.
siervo, a ['sjerβo, a] *nm/f* slave.
siesta ['sjesta] *nf* siesta, nap.
siete ['sjete] *num* seven.
sífilis ['sifilis] *nf* syphilis.
sifón [si'fon] *nm* syphon; **whisky con** ~ whisky and soda.
sigla ['siɣla] *nf* symbol.
siglo ['siɣlo] *nm* century; (*fig*) age.
significación [siɣnifika'θjon] *nf* significance.
significado [siɣnifi'kaðo] *nm* significance; (*de palabra*) meaning.
significar [siɣnifi'kar] *vt* to mean, signify; (*notificar*) to make known, express; ~**se** *vr* to become known, make a name for o.s.; **significativo, a** *a* significant.
signo ['siɣno] *nm* sign; ~ **de admiración** *o* **exclamación** exclamation mark; ~ **de interrogación** question mark.
sigo *etc vb ver* **seguir.**
siguiente [si'ɣjente] *a* next, following.
siguió *etc vb ver* **seguir.**
sílaba ['silaβa] *nf* syllable.
silbar [sil'βar] *vt, vi* to whistle; **silbato** *nm* whistle; **silbido** *nm* whistle, whistling.
silenciador [silenθja'ðor] *nm* silencer.
silenciar [silen'θjar] *vt* (*persona*) to silence; (*escándalo*) to hush up; **silencio** *nm* silence, quiet; **silencioso, a** *a* silent, quiet.
silicio [si'liθjo] *nm* silicon.
silueta [si'lweta] *nf* silhouette; (*de edificio*) outline; (*figura*) figure.
silvestre [sil'βestre] *a* rustic, rural; (*salvaje*) wild.
silla ['siʎa] *nf* (*asiento*) chair; (*de jinete*) saddle.

sillón [si'ʎon] *nm* armchair, easy chair; ~ **de ruedas** wheelchair.

simbólico, a [sim'boliko, a] *a* symbolic(al); **símbolo** *nm* symbol.

simetría [sime'tria] *nf* symmetry.

simiente [si'mjente] *nf* seed.

similar [simi'lar] *a* similar.

simio ['simjo] *nm* ape.

simpatía [simpa'tia] *nf* liking; (*afecto*) affection; (*amabilidad*) kindness; (*solidaridad*) mutual support, solidarity; **simpático, a** *a* nice, pleasant; kind; **simpatizante** *nm/f* sympathiser; **simpatizar** *vi*: **simpatizar con** to get on well with.

simple ['simple] *a* (*gen*) simple; (*elemental*) simple, easy; (*mero*) mere; (*puro*) pure, sheer // *nm/f* simpleton; ~**za** *nf* simpleness; (*necedad*) silly thing; **simplicidad** *nf* simplicity; **simplificar** *vt* to simplify.

simular [simu'lar] *vt* to simulate.

simultáneo, a [simul'taneo, a] *a* simultaneous.

sin [sin] *prep* without; **la ropa está** ~ **lavar** the clothes are unwashed; ~ **que** *conj* without; ~ **embargo** however, still.

sinagoga [sina'xoxa] *nf* synagogue.

sinceridad [sinθeri'ðað] *nf* sincerity; **sincero, a** *a* sincere.

sincronizar [sinkroni'θar] *vt* to synchronize.

sindical [sindi'kal] *a* union *cpd*, trade-union *cpd*; ~**ista** *nm/f* trade-unionist; **sindicato** *nm* (*de trabajadores*) trade(s) union; (*de negociantes*) syndicate.

sinfín [sin'fin] *nm*: **un** ~ **de** a great many, no end of.

sinfonía [sinfo'nia] *nf* symphony.

singular [singu'lar] *a* singular; (*fig*) outstanding, exceptional; (*pey*) peculiar, odd; ~**idad** *nf* singularity, peculiarity; ~**izar** *vt* to single out; ~**izarse** *vr* to distinguish o.s., stand out.

siniestro, a [si'njestro, a] *a* left; (*fig*) sinister.

sinnúmero [sin'numero] *nm* = **sinfín**.

sino ['sino] *nm* fate, destiny // *conj* (*pero*) but; (*salvo*) except, save.

sinónimo [si'nonimo] *nm* synonym.

sinrazón [sinra'θon] *nf* wrong, injustice.

síntesis ['sintesis] *nf* synthesis; **sintético, a** *a* synthetic; **sintetizar** *vt* to synthesize.

sintió *vb ver* **sentir**.

síntoma ['sintoma] *nm* symptom.

sinvergüenza [sinβer'ɣwenθa] *nm/f* shameless person.

sionismo [sjo'nismo] *nm* Zionism.

siquiera [si'kjera] *conj* even if, even though // *ad* at least; **ni** ~ not even.

sirena [si'rena] *nf* siren.

sirviente, a [sir'βjente, a] *nm/f* servant.

sirvo *etc vb ver* **servir**.

sisear [sise'ar] *vt*, *vi* to hiss.

sismógrafo [sis'moxrafo] *nm* seismograph.

sistema [sis'tema] *nm* system; (*método*) method; **sistemático, a** *a* systematic.

sitiar [si'tjar] *vt* to beseige, lay seige to.

sitio ['sitjo] *nm* (*lugar*) place; (*espacio*) room, space; (*MIL*) siege.

situación [sitwa'θjon] *nf* situation, position; (*estatus*) position, standing.

situar [si'twar] *vt* to place, put; (*edificio*) to locate, situate.

slip [slip] *nm* pants *pl*, briefs *pl*.

smoking ['smokin] (*pl* ~**s**) *nm* dinner jacket.

so [so] *prep* under.

SO *abr de* **sudoeste**.

sobaco [so'βako] *nm* armpit.

soberanía [soβera'nia] *nf* sovereignty; **soberano, a** *a* sovereign; (*fig*) supreme // *nm/f* sovereign.

soberbio [so'βerβjo, a] *a* (*orgulloso*) proud; (*altivo*) haughty, arrogant; (*fig*) magnificent, superb // *nf* pride; haughtiness, arrogance; magnificence; (*cólera*) anger.

sobornar [soβor'nar] *vt* to bribe; **soborno** *nm* bribe.

sobra ['soβra] *nf* excess, surplus; ~**s** *nfpl* left-overs, scraps; **de** ~ surplus, extra; **tengo de** ~ I've more than enough; ~**do, a** (*de* ~) more than enough; (*excesivo*) excessive // *ad* too, exceedingly; **sobrante** *a* remaining, extra // *nm* surplus, remainder; **sobrar** *vt* to exceed, surpass // *vi* (*tener de más*) to be more than enough; (*quedar*) to remain, be left (over).

sobre ['soβre] *prep* (*gen*) on; (*encima*) on (top of); (*por encima de, arriba de*) over, above; (*más que*) more than; (*además*) in addition to, besides; (*alrededor de, tratando de*) about // *nm* envelope.

sobrecama [soβre'kama] *nf* bedspread.

sobrecargar [soβrekar'xar] *vt* (*camión*) to overload; (*COM*) to surcharge.

sobrehumano, a [soβreu'mano, a] *a* superhuman.

sobrellevar [soβreʎe'βar] *vt* (*fig*) to bear, endure.

sobremarcha [soβre'martʃa] *nf* (*AUTO*) overdrive.

sobrenatural [soβrenatu'ral] *a* supernatural.

sobrepasar [soβrepa'sar] *vt* to exceed, surpass.

sobreponer [soβrepo'ner] *vt* (*poner encima*) to put on top; (*añadir*) to add; ~**se** *vr*: ~**se a** to win through, pull through.

sobreprecio [soβre'preθjo] *nm* surcharge.

sobresaliente [soβresa'ljente] *a* projecting; (*fig*) outstanding, excellent; **sobresalir** *vi* to project, jut out; to stand out, excel.

sobresaltar [soβresal'tar] *vt* (*asustar*) to scare, frighten; (*sobrecoger*) to startle; **sobresalto** *nm* (*movimiento*) start; (*susto*) scare; (*turbación*) sudden shock; **de sobresalto** suddenly.

sobrescrito [soβres'krito] *nm* address.
sobretodo [soβre'toðo] *nm* overcoat.
sobreviviente [soβreβi'βjente] *a* surviving // *nm/f* survivor; **sobrevivir** *vi* to survive.
sobriedad [soβrje'ðað] *nf* sobriety, soberness; (*moderación*) moderation, restraint.
sobrino, a [so'βrino, a] *nm/f* nephew/niece.
sobrio, a ['soβrjo, a] *a* sober; (*moderado*) moderate, restrained.
socarrón, ona [soka'rron, ona] *a* (*sarcástico*) sarcastic, ironic(al); (*astuto*) crafty, cunning.
sociable [so'θjaβle] *a* (*persona*) sociable, friendly; (*animal*) social.
social [so'θjal] *a* social; (*COM*) company *cpd.*
socialdemócrata [soθjalde'mokrata] *nm/f* social democrat.
socialista [soθja'lista] *a, nm/f* socialist.
socializar [soθjali'θar] *vt* to socialize.
sociedad [soθje'ðað] *nf* (*gen*) society; (*COM*) company; ~ **anónima (SA)** limited company.
socio, a ['soθjo, a] *nm/f* (*miembro*) member; (*COM*) partner; ~ **comandatario** sleeping partner.
sociología [soθjolo'xia] *nf* sociology.
socorrer [soko'rrer] *vt* to help; **socorro** *nm* (*ayuda*) help, aid; (*MIL*) relief; ¡**socorro!** help!
soda ['soða] *nf* (*sosa*) soda; (*bebida*) soda water.
sofá [so'fa] (*pl* ~**s**) *nm* sofa, settee; ~-**cama** *nm* studio couch.
sofisticación [sofistika'θjon] *nf* sophistication.
sofocar [sofo'kar] *vt* to suffocate; (*apagar*) to smother, put out; ~**se** *vr* to suffocate; (*fig*) to blush, feel embarrassed; **sofoco** *nm* suffocation; embarrassment.
soga ['soɣa] *nf* rope.
sois *vb ver* **ser.**
sojuzgar [soxuθ'ɣar] *vt* to subdue, rule despotically.
sol [sol] *nm* sun; (*luz*) sunshine, sunlight; **hace** ~ it is sunny.
solamente [sola'mente] *ad* only, just.
solapa [so'lapa] *nf* (*de ropa*) lapel; (*de libro*) jacket.
solar [so'lar] *a* solar, sun *cpd.*
solaz [so'laθ] *nm* recreation, relaxation; (*alivio*) solace; ~**ar** *vt* (*divertir*) to amuse; (*aliviar*) to console.
soldada [sol'daða] *nf* pay.
soldado [sol'daðo] *nm* soldier.
soldador [solda'ðor] *nm* soldering iron; (*persona*) welder; **soldar** *vt* to solder, weld; (*unir*) to join, unite.
soledad [sole'ðað] *nf* solitude; (*estado infeliz*) loneliness; (*nostalgia*) grieving, mourning.
solemne [so'lemne] *a* solemn; **solemnidad** *nf* solemnity.

soler [so'ler] *vi* to be in the habit of, be accustomed to.
solfa ['solfa] *nf*, **solfeo** [sol'feo] *nm* solfa; (*conjunto de signos*) musical notation.
solicitación [soliθita'θjon] *nf* request; (*de votos*) canvassing; **solicitar** *vt* (*permiso*) to ask for, seek; (*puesto*) to apply for; (*votos*) to canvass; (*atención*) to attract; (*persona*) to pursue, chase after.
solícito, a [so'liθito, a] *a* (*diligente*) diligent; (*cuidadoso*) careful; **solicitud** *nf* (*calidad*) great care; (*petición*) request; (*memorial*) petition; (*a un puesto*) application.
solidaridad [soliðari'ðað] *nf* solidarity; **solidario, a** *a* (*participación*) joint, common; (*compromiso*) mutually binding.
solidez [soli'ðeθ] *nf* solidity; **sólido, a** *a* solid.
soliloquio [soli'lokjo] *nm* soliloquy, monologue.
solista [so'lista] *nm/f* soloist.
solitario, a [soli'tarjo, a] *a* lonely, solitary // *nm/f* recluse; (*en la sociedad*) loner // *nm* solitaire.
soliviar [soli'βjar] *vt* to lift.
solo, a ['solo, a] *a* (*único*) single, sole; (*sin compañía*) alone; (*solitario*) lonely; **hay una** ~**a dificultad** there is just one difficulty; **a** ~**as** alone, by o.s.
sólo ['solo] *ad* only, just.
solomillo [solo'miʎo] *nm* sirloin.
soltar [sol'tar] *vt* (*dejar ir*) to let go of; (*desprender*) to unfasten, loosen; (*librar*) to release, set free; (*estornudo, risa*) to let out.
soltero, a [sol'tero, a] *a* single, unmarried // *nm* bachelor // *nf* single woman, spinster.
soltura [sol'tura] *nf* looseness, slackness; (*de los miembros*) agility, ease of movement; (*en el hablar*) fluency, ease; (*MED*) diarrhoea.
soluble [so'luβle] *a* (*QUÍMICA*) soluble; (*problema*) solvable.
solución [solu'θjon] *nf* solution; **solucionar** *vt* (*problema*) to solve; (*asunto*) to settle.
solventar [solβen'tar] *vt* (*pagar*) to settle, pay; (*resolver*) to resolve.
sollozar [soʎo'θar] *vi* to sob; **sollozo** *nm* sob.
sombra ['sombra] *nf* shadow; (*como protección*) shade; ~**s** *nfpl* darkness *sg*; **tener buena/mala** ~ to be lucky/unlucky.
sombreador [sombrea'ðor] *nm*: ~ **de ojos** eyeshadow.
sombrero [som'brero] *nm* hat.
sombrilla [som'briʎa] *nf* parasol, sunshade.
sombrío, a [som'brio, a] *a* (*oscuro*) dark; (*sombreado*) shaded; (*fig*) sombre, sad; (*persona*) gloomy.
somero, a [so'mero, a] *a* superficial.
someter [some'ter] *vt* (*país*) to conquer; (*persona*) to subject to one's will; (*informe*) to present, submit; ~**se** *vr* to give in,

yield, submit; ~ **a** to subject to.
somnambulismo [somnambu'lismo] *nm*
sleepwalking; **somnámbulo, a** *nm/f*
sleepwalker.
somnífero [som'nifero] *nm* sleeping pill.
somos *vb ver* **ser.**
son [son] *vb ver* **ser** // *nm* sound; **en ~ de
broma** as a joke.
sonar [so'nar] *vt* to ring // *vi* to sound;
(*hacer ruido*) to make a noise;
(*pronunciarse*) to be sounded, be
pronounced; (*ser conocido*) to sound
familiar; (*campana*) to ring; (*reloj*) to
strike, chime; ~**se** *vr*: ~**se** (**las narices**)
to blow one's nose; **me suena ese
nombre** that name rings a bell.
sonda ['sonda] *nf* (*NAUT*) sounding; (*TEC*)
bore, drill; (*MED*) probe; **sondear** *vt* to
sound; to bore (into), drill; to probe, sound;
(*fig*) to sound out; **sondeo** *nm* sounding;
boring, drilling; (*fig*) poll, enquiry.
sónico, a ['soniko, a] *a* sonic, sound *cpd.*
sonido [so'niðo] *nm* sound.
sonoro, a [so'noro, a] *a* sonorous;
(*resonante*) loud, resonant.
sonreír [sonre'ir] *vi*, ~**se** *vr* to smile;
sonriente *a* smiling; **sonrisa** *nf* smile.
sonrojo [son'roxo] *nm* blush.
soñador, a [sopa'ðor, a] *nm/f* dreamer;
soñar *vt*, *vi* to dream; **soñar con** to
dream about, dream of.
soñoliento, a [sopo'ljento, a] *a* sleepy,
drowsy.
sopa ['sopa] *nf* soup.
soplador [sopla'ðor] *nm* fan, ventilator.
soplar [so'plar] *vt* (*polvo*) to blow away,
blow off; (*inflar*) to blow up; (*vela*) to blow
out // *vi* to blow; ~**se** *vr* (*fam*: *ufanarse*)
to get conceited; **soplo** *nm* blow, puff; (*de
viento*) puff, gust.
soporífero [sopo'rifero] *nm* sleeping pill.
soportable [sopor'taßle] *a* bearable;
soportar *vt* to bear, carry; (*fig*) to bear,
put up with; **soporte** *nm* support; (*fig*)
pillar, support.
soprano [so'prano] *nf* soprano.
sorber [sor'ßer] *vt* (*chupar*) to sip;
(*inhalar*) to inhale; (*tragar*) to swallow
(up); (*absorber*) to soak up, absorb.
sorbete [sor'ßete] *nm* iced fruit drink.
sorbo ['sorßo] *nm* (*trago*) gulp, swallow;
(*chupada*) sip.
sordera [sor'ðera] *nf* deafness.
sórdido, a ['sorðiðo, a] *a* dirty, squalid;
(*palabra*) nasty, dirty; (*fig*) mean.
sordo, a ['sorðo, a] *a* (*persona*) deaf;
(*máquina*) quiet // *nm/f* deaf person; a
~**as** on the quiet; ~**mudo, a** *a* deaf and
dumb.
sorprendente [sorpren'dente] *a*
surprising; **sorprender** *vt* to surprise;
sorpresa *nf* surprise.
sortear [sorte'ar] *vt* to draw lots for;
(*objeto*) to raffle; (*dificultad*) to avoid;
sorteo *nm* drawing lots; raffle.
sosegado, a [sose'xaðo, a] *a* quiet, calm;
sosegar *vt* to quieten, calm; (*el ánimo*) to

reassure // *vi* to rest; **sosiego** *nm*
quiet(ness), calm(ness).
soslayo [sos'lajo]: **al** *o* **de** ~ *ad* obliquely,
sideways.
soso, a ['soso, a] *a* (*CULIN*) tasteless; (*fig*)
dull, uninteresting.
sospecha [sos'petʃa] *nf* suspicion;
sospechar *vt* to suspect; **sospechoso, a** *a*
suspicious; (*testimonio, opinión*) suspect //
nm/f suspect.
sostén [sos'ten] *nm* (*apoyo*) support;
(*prenda femenina*) bra, brassière;
(*alimentación*) sustenance, food.
sostener [soste'ner] *vt* to support;
(*mantener*) to keep up, maintain;
(*alimentar*) to sustain, keep going; ~**se** *vr*
to support o.s.; (*seguir*) to continue,
remain; **sostenido, a** a continuous,
sustained; (*prolongado*) prolonged.
sótano ['sotano] *nm* basement.
soterrar [sote'rrar] *vt* to bury.
soviético, a [so'ßjetiko, a] *a* Soviet.
soy *vb ver* **ser.**
sport [sport] *nm* sport.
Sr *abr de* **Señor.**
Sra *abr de* **Señora.**
S.R.C. *abr de* **se ruega contestación**
R.S.V.P.
Sta *abr de* **Santa; Señorita.**
status ['status] *nm inv* status.
Sto *abr de* **Santo.**
su [su] *pron* (*de él*) his; (*de ella*) her; (*de una
cosa*) its; (*de ellos, ellas*) their; (*de usted,
ustedes*) your.
suave ['swaße] *a* gentle; (*superficie*)
smooth; (*trabajo*) easy; (*música, voz*) soft,
sweet; **suavidad** *nf* gentleness;
smoothness; softness, sweetness; **suavizar**
vt to soften; (*quitar la aspereza*) to smooth
(out).
subalimentado, a [sußalimen'taðo, a] *a*
undernourished.
subasta [su'ßasta] *nf* auction; **subastar** *vt*
to auction (off).
subconsciencia [sußkons'θjenθja] *nf*
subconscious; **subconsciente** *a*
subconscious.
subdesarrollado, a [sußðesarro'ʎaðo, a]
a underdeveloped; **subdesarrollo** *nm*
underdevelopment.
súbdito, a ['sußðito, a] *nm/f* subject.
subdividir [sußðißi'ðir] *vt* to subdivide.
subestimar [sußesti'mar] *vt* to
underestimate, underrate; (*propiedad*) to
undervalue.
subexpuesto, a [sußeks'pwesto, a] *a*
underexposed.
subido, a [su'ßiðo, a] *a* (*color*) bright,
strong; (*precio*) high // *nf* (*gen*) ascent,
climb; (*de precio*) rise, increase; (*camino*)
way up; (*pendiente*) slope, hill.
subir [su'ßir] *vt* (*objeto*) to raise, lift up;
(*cuesta, calle*) to go up; (*montaña*) to climb;
(*precio*) to raise, put up // *vi* to go/come
up; (*a un coche*) to get in; (*a un autobús*) to
get on; (*precio*) to rise, go up; (*río*) to rise;
~**se** *vr* to get up, climb.

súbito, a ['suβito, a] a (*repentino*) sudden; (*imprevisto*) unexpected; (*precipitado*) hasty, rash // *ad*: **(de)** ~ suddenly.
sublevación [suβleβa'θjon] *nf* revolt, rising.
sublime [su'βlime] a sublime.
submarino, a [suβma'rino, a] a underwater // *nm* submarine.
subordinado, a [suβorði'naðo, a] a, *nm/f* subordinate.
subrayar [suβra'jar] *vt* to underline.
subrepticio, a [suβrep'tiθjo, a] a surreptitious.
subsanar [suβsa'nar] *vt* (*reparar*) to make good; (*perdonar*) to excuse; (*sobreponerse a*) to overcome.
subscribir [suβskri'βir] *vt* = **suscribir**.
subsidiario, a [suβsi'ðjarjo, a] a subsidiary.
subsidio [suβ'siðjo] *nm* (*ayuda*) aid, financial help; (*subvención*) subsidy, grant; (*de enfermedad, paro etc*) benefit.
subsistencia [suβsis'tenθja] *nf* subsistence; **subsistir** *vi* (*gen*) to subsist; (*vivir*) to live; (*sobrevivir*) to survive, endure.
subterráneo, a [suβte'rraneo, a] a underground, subterranean // *nm* underpass, underground passage.
suburbano, a [suβur'βano, a] a suburban.
suburbio [su'βurβjo] *nm* (*barrio*) slum quarter; (*afueras*) suburbs *pl*.
subvencionar [suββenθjo'nar] *vt* to subsidize.
subversión [suββer'sjon] *nf* subversion; **subversivo, a** a subversive.
subyugar [suβju'xar] *vt* (*país*) to subjugate, subdue; (*enemigo*) to overpower; (*voluntad*) to dominate.
suceder [suθe'ðer] *vt, vi* to happen; (*seguir*) to succeed, follow; **lo que sucede es que...** the fact is that...; **sucesión** *nf* succession; (*serie*) sequence, series.
sucesivamente [suθesiβa'mente] *ad*: **y así** ~ and so on.
sucesivo, a [suθe'siβo, a] a successive, following; **en lo** ~ in future, from now on.
suceso [su'θeso] *nm* (*hecho*) event, happening; (*incidente*) incident; (*resultado*) outcome.
suciedad [suθje'ðað] *nf* (*estado*) dirtiness; (*mugre*) dirt, filth.
sucinto, a [su'θinto, a] a succinct, concise.
sucio, a ['suθjo, a] a dirty.
suculento, a [suku'lento, a] a succulent.
sucumbir [sukum'bir] *vi* to succumb.
sucursal [sukur'sal] *nf* branch (office).
sudamericano, a [suðameri'kano, a] a South American.
sudar [su'ðar] *vt, vi* to sweat.
sudeste [su'ðeste] *nm* south-east; **sudoeste** *nm* south-west.
sudor [su'ðor] *nm* sweat; ~**oso, a**, **sudoso, a**, ~**iento, a** a sweaty, sweating.
Suecia ['sweθja] *nf* Sweden; **sueco, a** a Swedish // *nm/f* Swede.

suegro, a ['swexro, a] *nm/f* father-/mother-in-law.
suela ['swela] *nf* sole.
sueldo ['sweldo] *nm* pay, wage(s) (*pl*); **el** ~ **mínimo** the minimum wage.
suele *etc vb ver* **soler**.
suelo ['swelo] *nm* (*tierra*) ground; (*de casa*) floor.
suelto, a ['swelto, a] a loose; (*libre*) free; (*separado*) detached, individual; (*ágil*) quick, agile; (*corriente*) fluent, flowing // *nm* (loose) change, small change.
sueño *etc vb ver* **soñar** // ['sweɲo] *nm* sleep; (*somnolencia*) sleepiness, drowsiness; (*lo soñado, fig*) dream; **tener** ~ to be sleepy.
suero ['swero] *nm* serum.
suerte ['swerte] *nf* (*fortuna*) luck; (*azar*) chance; (*destino*) fate, destiny; (*condición*) lot; (*género*) sort, kind; **tener** ~ to be lucky; **de otra** ~ otherwise, if not; **de** ~ **que** so that, in such a way that.
suéter ['sweter] *nm* sweater.
suficiente [sufi'θjente] a enough, sufficient; (*capaz*) capable.
sufragio [su'fraxjo] *nm* (*voto*) vote; (*derecho de voto*) suffrage; (*ayuda*) help, aid.
sufrimiento [sufri'mjento] *nm* (*dolor*) suffering; (*paciencia*) patience; (*tolerancia*) tolerance.
sufrir [su'frir] *vt* (*padecer*) to suffer; (*soportar*) to bear, stand, put up with; (*apoyar*) to hold up, support // *vi* to suffer.
sugerencia [suxe'renθja] *nf* suggestion; **sugerir** *vt* to suggest; (*sutilmente*) to hint.
sugestión [suxes'tjon] *nf* suggestion; (*sutil*) hint; **sugestionar** *vt* to influence.
sugestivo, a [suxes'tiβo, a] a stimulating; (*fascinante*) fascinating.
suicida [sui'θiða] a suicidal // *nm/f* suicidal person; (*muerto*) suicide, person who has committed suicide; **suicidio** *nm* suicide.
Suiza ['swiθa] *nf* Switzerland; **suizo, a** a a, *nm/f* Swiss.
sujeción [suxe'θjon] *nf* subjection.
sujetador [suxeta'ðor] *nm* fastener, clip; (*de papeles*) paper clip.
sujetar [suxe'tar] *vt* (*fijar*) to fasten; (*detener*) to hold down; (*fig*) to subject, subjugate; ~**se** *vr* to subject o.s.; **sujeto, a** a fastened, secure // *nm* subject; (*individuo*) individual; **sujeto a** subject to.
suma ['suma] *nf* (*cantidad*) total, sum; (*de dinero*) sum; (*acto*) adding (up), addition; (*resumen*) summary; (*esencia*) essence; **en** ~ in short; ~**dora** *nf* adding machine.
sumamente [suma'mente] *ad* extremely, exceedingly.
sumar [su'mar] *vt* to add (up); (*reunir*) to collect, gather; (*abreviar*) to summarize, sum up // *vi* to add up.
sumario, a [su'marjo, a] a brief, concise // *nm* summary.
sumergir [sumer'xir] *vt* to submerge; (*hundir*) to sink; (*bañar*) to immerse, dip;

sumersión *nf* submersion; (*fig*) absorption.

sumidero [sumi'ðero] *nm* drain; (*TEC*) sump.

suministrador, a [suministra'ðor, a] *nm/f* supplier; **suministrar** *vt* to supply, provide; **suministro** *nm* supply; (*acto*) supplying, providing.

sumir [su'mir] *vt* to sink, submerge; (*fig*) to plunge.

sumisión [sumi'sjon] *nf* (*acto*) submission; (*calidad*) submissiveness, docility; **sumiso, a** *a* submissive, docile.

sumo, a ['sumo, a] *a* great, extreme; (*mayor*) highest, supreme.

supe *etc vb ver* **saber.**

super... [super] *pref* super..., over... // *nm* high-grade fuel.

superar [supe'rar] *vt* (*sobreponerse a*) to overcome; (*rebasar*) to surpass, do better than; (*pasar*) to go beyond; ~**se** *vr* to excel o.s.

superávit [supe'raßit] *nm* surplus.

supercarburante [superkarßu'rante] *nm* high-grade fuel.

superestructura [superestruk'tura] *nf* superstructure.

superficial [superfi'θjal] *a* superficial; (*medida*) surface *cpd*, of the surface.

superficie [super'fiθje] *nf* surface; (*área*) area.

superfluo, a [su'perflwo, a] *a* superfluous.

superintendente [superinten'dente] *nm/f* supervisor, superintendent.

superior [supe'rjor] *a* (*piso, clase*) upper; (*temperatura, número, nivel*) higher; (*mejor: calidad, producto*) superior, better // *nm/f* superior; ~**idad** *nf* superiority.

supermercado [supermer'kaðo] *nm* supermarket.

supersónico, a [super'soniko, a] *a* supersonic.

superstición [supersti'θjon] *nf* superstition; **supersticioso, a** *a* superstitious.

supervisor, a [superßi'sor, a] *nm/f* supervisor.

supervivencia [superßi'ßenθja] *nf* survival.

supiera *etc vb ver* **saber.**

suplementario, a [suplemen'tarjo, a] *a* supplementary; **suplemento** *nm* supplement.

suplente [su'plente] *a, nm/f* substitute.

súplica ['suplika] *nf* request; (*REL*) supplication.

suplicante [supli'kante] *nm/f* applicant.

suplicar [supli'kar] *vt* (*cosa*) to beg (for), plead for; (*persona*) to beg, plead with.

suplicio [su'pliθjo] *nm* torture.

suplir [su'plir] *vt* (*compensar*) to make good, make up for; (*reemplazar*) to replace, substitute // *vi*: ~ **a** *o* **por** to take the place of, substitute for.

suponer [supo'ner] *vt* to suppose // *vi* to have authority; **suposición** *nf* supposition; (*autoridad*) authority.

supremacía [suprema'θia] *nf* supremacy.

supremo, a [su'premo, a] *a* supreme.

supresión [supre'sjon] *nf* suppression; (*de derecho*) abolition; (*de dificultad*) removal; (*de palabra*) deletion; (*de restricción*) cancellation, lifting.

suprimir [supri'mir] *vt* to suppress; (*derecho, costumbre*) to abolish; (*dificultad*) to remove; (*palabra*) to delete; (*restricción*) to cancel, lift.

supuesto, a [su'pwesto, a] *a* (*hipotético*) supposed; (*falso*) false // *nm* assumption, hypothesis; ~ **que** *conj* since; **por** ~ of course.

sur [sur] *nm* south.

surcar [sur'kar] *vt* to plough, furrow; (*superficie*) to cut, score; **surco** *nm* groove; (*AGR*) furrow.

surgir [sur'xir] *vi* to arise, emerge; (*dificultad*) to come up, crop up.

surtido, a [sur'tiðo, a] *a* mixed, assorted // *nm* (*gen*) selection, assortment; (*abastecimiento*) supply, stock.

surtir [sur'tir] *vt* to supply, provide // *vi* to spout, spurt.

susceptible [susθep'tißle] *a* susceptible; (*sensible*) sensitive; ~ **de** capable of.

suscitar [susθi'tar] *vt* to cause, provoke; (*interés*) to arouse.

suscribir [suskri'ßir] *vt* (*firmar*) to sign; (*respaldar*) to subscribe to; endorse; ~**se** *vr* to subscribe; **suscripción** *nf* subscription.

suspender [suspen'der] *vt* (*objeto*) to hang (up), suspend; (*trabajo*) to stop, suspend; (*a estudiante*) to fail; **suspensión** *nf* suspension; (*fig*) stoppage, suspension.

suspenso, a [sus'penso, a] *a* hanging, suspended; (*estudiante*) failed; (*admirado*) astonished, amazed // *nm*: **quedar** *o* **estar en** ~ to be pending.

suspicacia [suspi'kaθja] *nf* suspicion, mistrust; **suspicaz** *a* suspicious, distrustful.

suspirar [suspi'rar] *vi* to sigh; **suspiro** *nm* sigh.

sustancia [sus'tanθja] *nf* substance.

sustentar [susten'tar] *vt* (*alimentar*) to sustain, nourish; (*objeto*) to hold up, support; (*idea, teoría*) to maintain, uphold; (*fig*) to sustain, keep going; **sustento** *nm* support; (*alimento*) sustenance, food.

sustituir [sustitu'ir] *vt* to substitute, replace; **sustituto, a** *nm/f* substitute, replacement.

susto ['susto] *nm* fright, scare.

sustraer [sustra'er] *vt* to remove, take away; (*MAT*) to subtract; ~**se** *vr* (*evitar*) to avoid; (*retirarse*) to withdraw.

susurrar [susu'rrar] *vi* to whisper; **susurro** *nm* whisper.

sutil [su'til] *a* subtle; (*tenue*) thin; ~**eza** *nf* subtlety; thinness.

suyo, a ['sujo, a] *a* (*con artículo o después del verbo ser: de él*) his; (: *de ella*) hers; (: *de ellos, ellas*) theirs; (: *de Ud, Uds*) yours; (*después de un nombre: de él*) of his; (: *de* *ella*) of hers; (: *de ellos, ellas*) of theirs; (: *de Ud, Uds*) of yours.

T

t *abr de* **tonelada.**

taba ['taβa] *nf* (ANAT) ankle bone; (*juego*) jacks *sg.*

tabaco [ta'βako] *nm* tobacco; (*fam*) cigarettes *pl.*

taberna [ta'βerna] *nf* bar; **tabernero, a** *nm/f* (*encargado*) publican; (*camarero*) barman.

tabique [ta'βike] *nm* (*pared*) thin wall; (*para dividir*) partition.

tabla ['taβla] *nf* (*de madera*) plank; (*estante*) shelf; (*de anuncios*) board; (*lista, catálogo*) list; (*mostrador*) counter; (*de vestido*) pleat; (ARTE) panel; ~s (TAUR, TEATRO) boards; **hacer** ~s to draw; ~**do** *nm* (*plataforma*) platform; (*suelo*) plank floor; (TEATRO) stage.

tablero [ta'βlero] *nm* (*de madera*) plank, board; (*pizarra*) blackboard; (*de ajedrez, damas*) board; (AUTO) dashboard.

tablilla [ta'βliʎa] *nf* small board; (MED) splint.

tablón [ta'βlon] *nm* (*de suelo*) plank; (*de techo*) beam; (*de anuncios*) notice board.

tabú [ta'βu] *nm* taboo.

tabular [taβu'lar] *vt* to tabulate.

taburete [taβu'rete] *nm* stool.

tacaño, a [ta'kaɲo, a] *a* (*avaro*) mean; (*astuto*) crafty.

tácito, a ['taθito, a] *a* tacit.

taciturno, a [taθi'turno, a] *a* (*callado*) silent; (*malhumorado*) sullen.

taco ['tako] *nm* (BILLAR) cue; (*libro de billetes*) book; (*manojo de billetes*) wad; (AM) heel; (*tarugo*) peg; (*fam: bocado*) snack; (: *palabrota*) swear word; (: *trago de vino*) swig.

tacón [ta'kon] *nm* heel; **de** ~ **alto** high heeled; **taconeo** *nm* (heel) stamping.

táctico, a ['taktiko, a] *a* tactical // *nf* tactics *pl.*

tacto ['takto] *nm* touch; (*acción*) touching.

tacha ['tatʃa] *nf* flaw; (TEC) stud; **poner** ~ **a** to find fault with; **tachar** *vt* (*borrar*) to cross out; (*corregir*) to correct; (*criticar*) to criticize; **tachar de** to accuse of.

tafetán [tafe'tan] *nm* taffeta; **tafetanes** *nmpl* (*fam*) frills; ~ **adhesivo** *o* **inglés** sticking plaster.

tafilete [tafi'lete] *nm* morocco leather.

tahona [ta'ona] *nf* (*panadería*) bakery; (*molino*) flourmill.

tahur [ta'ur] *nm* gambler; (*pey*) cheat.

taimado, a [tai'maðo, a] *a* (*astuto*) sly; (*resentido*) sullen.

taja ['taxa] *nf* (*corte*) cut; (*repartición*) division; ~**da** *nf* slice; ~**dera** *nf* (*instrumento*) chopper; (*madera*) chopping block; **tajante** *a* sharp.

tajar [ta'xar] *vt* to cut; **tajo** *nm* (*corte*) cut; (*filo*) cutting edge; (GEO) cleft.

tal [tal] *a* such; ~ **vez** perhaps // *pron* (*persona*) someone, such a one; (*cosa*) something, such a thing; ~ **como** such as; ~ **para cual** tit for tat; (*dos iguales*) two of a kind // *ad*: ~ **como** (*igual*) just as; ~ **cual** (*como es*) just as it is; ~ **el padre, cual el hijo** like father, like son; **¿qué** ~? how are things?; **¿qué** ~ **te gusta?** how do you like it? // *conj*: **con** ~ **de que** provided that.

talabartero [talaβar'tero] *nm* saddler.

taladrar [tala'ðrar] *vt* to drill; **taladro** *nm* (*gen*) drill; (*hoyo*) drill hole; **taladro neumático** pneumatic drill.

talante [ta'lante] *nm* (*humor*) mood; (*voluntad*) will, willingness.

talar [ta'lar] *vt* to fell, cut down; (*fig*) to devastate.

talco ['talko] *nm* (*polvos*) talcum powder; (MINEROLOGÍA) talc.

talego [ta'leɣo] *nm*, **talega** [ta'leɣa] *nf* sack.

talento [ta'lento] *nm* talent; (*capacidad*) ability; (*don*) gift.

talidomida [taliðo'miða] *nm* thalidomide.

talismán [talis'man] *nm* talisman.

talmente [tal'mente] *ad* (*de esta forma*) in such a way; (*hasta tal punto*) to such an extent; (*exactamente*) exactly.

talón [ta'lon] *nm* (*gen*) heel; (COM) counterfoil.

talonario [talo'narjo] *nm* (*de cheques*) chequebook; (*de billetes*) book of tickets; (*de recibos*) receipt book.

talud [ta'luð] *nm* slope.

talla ['taʎa] *nf* (*estatura, fig, MED*) height, stature; (*palo*) measuring rod; (ARTE) carving.

tallado, a [ta'ʎaðo, a] *a* carved // *nm* carving; **tallar** *vt* (*trabajar*) to work, carve; (*grabar*) to engrave; (*medir*) to measure; (*repartir*) to deal // *vi* to deal.

tallarín [taʎa'rin] *nm* noodle.

talle ['taʎe] *nm* (ANAT) waist; (*medida*) size; (*física*) build; (: *de mujer*) figure; (*fig*) appearance.

taller [ta'ʎer] *nm* (TEC) workshop; (*de artista*) studio.

tallo ['taʎo] *nm* (*de planta*) stem; (*de hierba*) blade; (*brote*) shoot; (*col*) cabbage; (CULIN) candied peel.

tamaño, a [ta'maɲo, a] *a* such a (big/small) // *nm* size; **de** ~ **natural** full-size.

tamarindo [tama'rindo] *nm* tamarind.

tambalearse [tambale'arse] *vr* (*persona*) to stagger; (*vehículo*) to sway.

también [tam'bjen] *ad* (*igualmente*) also, too, as well; (*además*) besides.

tambor [tam'bor] *nm* drum; (ANAT) eardrum; ~ **del freno** brake drum.

tamiz [ta'miθ] *nm* sieve; ~**ar** *vt* to sieve.

tamo ['tamo] *nm* fluff.

tampoco [tam'poko] *ad* nor, neither; **yo** ~ **lo compré** I didn't buy it either.

tampón [tam'pon] *nm* plug; (MED) tampon.

tan [tan] *ad* so; ~ **es así que** so much so that.

tanda ['tanda] *nf* (*gen*) series; (*juego*) set; (*turno*) shift; (*grupo*) gang.

tangente [tan'xente] *nf* tangent.

Tánger ['tanxer] *n* Tangier(s).

tangible [tan'xiβle] *a* tangible.

tanque ['tanke] *nm* (*gen*) tank; (*AUTO, NAUT*) tanker.

tantear [tante'ar] *vt* (*calcular*) to reckon (up); (*medir*) to take the measure of; (*probar*) to test, try out; (*tomar la medida: persona*) to take the measurements of; (*considerar*) to weigh up // *vi* (*DEPORTE*) to score; **tanteo** *nm* (*cálculo*) (rough) calculation; (*prueba*) test, trial; (*DEPORTE*) scoring; (*adivinanzas*) guesswork; **al tanteo** by trial and error.

tanto, a ['tanto, a] *a* (*cantidad*) so much, as much; ~**s** so many, as many; **20 y ~s** 20-odd // *ad* (*cantidad*) so much, as much; (*tiempo*) so long, as long; ~ **tú como yo** both you and I; ~ **como eso** it's not as bad as that; ~ **más ... cuanto que** it's all the more ... because; ~ **mejor/peor** so much the better/the worse; ~ **si viene como si va** whether he comes or whether he goes; ~ **es así que** so much so that; **por** *o* **por lo** ~ therefore; **me he vuelto ronco de** *o* **con** ~ **hablar** I have become hoarse with so much talking // *conj*: **con** ~ **que** provided (that); **en** ~ **que** while; **hasta** ~ (**que**) until such time as // *nm* (*suma*) certain amount; (*proporción*) so much; (*punto*) point; (*gol*) goal; **al** ~ up to date; **un** ~ **perezoso** somewhat lazy; **al** ~ **de que** because of the fact that // *pron*: **cada uno paga** ~ each one pays so much; **a** ~**s de agosto** on such and such a day in August.

tapar [ta'par] *vt* (*cubrir*) to cover; (*envolver*) to wrap *or* cover up; (*la vista*) to obstruct; (*persona, falta*) to conceal; (*AM*) to fill; ~**se** *vr* to wrap o.s. up.

taparrabo [tapa'rraβo] *nm* (*bañador*) (bathing *or* swimming) trunks *pl*.

tapete [ta'pete] *nm* table cover.

tapia ['tapja] *nf* (garden) wall; **tapiar** *vt* to wall in.

tapicería [tapiθe'ria] *nf* tapestry; (*para muebles*) upholstery; (*tienda*) upholsterer's (shop); **tapiz** *nm* (*alfombra*) carpet; (*tela tejida*) tapestry; **tapizar** *vt* (*pared*) to wallpaper; (*suelo*) to carpet; (*muebles*) to upholster.

tapón [ta'pon] *nm* (*corcho*) stopper; (*TEC*) plug; (*MED*) tampon; ~ **de rosca** *o* **de tuerca** screw-top.

taquigrafía [takixra'fia] *nf* shorthand; **taquígrafo, a** *nm/f* shorthand writer.

taquilla [ta'kiʎa] *nf* (*donde se compra*) booking office; (*suma recogida*) takings *pl*; **taquillero, a** *a*: **función taquillera** box office success // *nm/f* ticket clerk.

taquímetro [ta'kimetro] *nm* speedometer; (*de control*) tachymeter.

tara ['tara] *nf* (*defecto*) defect; (*COM*) tare.

tarántula [ta'rantula] *nf* tarantula.

tararear [tarare'ar] *vi* to hum.

tardanza [tar'ðanθa] *nf* (*demora*) delay; (*lentitud*) slowness.

tardar [tar'ðar] *vi* (*tomar tiempo*) to take a long time; (*llegar tarde*) to be late; (*demorar*) to delay; ¿**tarda mucho el tren?** does the train take long?; **a más** ~ at the latest; **no tardes en venir** come soon, come before long.

tarde ['tarðe] *ad* (*hora*) late; (*después de tiempo*) too late // *nf* (*de día*) afternoon; (*al anochecer*) evening; **de** ~ **en** ~ from time to time; ¡**buenas** ~**s!** (*de día*) good afternoon!; (*de noche*) good evening!; **a** *o* **por la** ~ in the afternoon; in the evening.

tardío, a [tar'ðio, a] *a* (*retrasado*) late; (*lento*) slow (to arrive).

tardo, a ['tarðo, a] *a* (*lento*) slow; (*torpe*) dull.

tarea [ta'rea] *nf* task; (*ESCOL*) homework; ~ **de ocasión** chore.

tarifa [ta'rifa] *nf* (*lista de precios*) price list; (*COM*) tariff; ~ **completa** all-in cost.

tarima [ta'rima] *nf* (*plataforma*) platform; (*taburete*) stool; (*litera*) bunk.

tarjeta [tar'xeta] *nf* card; ~ **postal/de crédito/de Navidad** postcard/credit card/Christmas card.

tarro ['tarro] *nm* jar, pot.

tarta ['tarta] *nf* (*pastel*) cake; (*torta*) tart.

tartamudear [tartamuðe'ar] *vi* to stammer; **tartamudo, a** *a* stammering // *nm/f* stammerer.

tartana [tar'tana] *nf* (*barco*) dinghy.

tartárico, a [tar'tariko, a] *a*: **ácido** ~ tartaric acid.

tártaro ['tartaro] *a, nm* Tartar.

tasa ['tasa] *nf* (*precio*) (fixed) price, rate; (*valoración*) valuation; (*medida, norma*) measure, standard; ~ **de interés** rate of interest; ~**ción** *nf* (*gen*) valuation; (*de oro etc*) appraisal; ~**dor** *nm* valuer.

tasajo [ta'saxo] *nm* dried beef.

tasar [ta'sar] *vt* (*arreglar el precio*) to fix a price for; (*valorar*) to value, assess; (*limitar*) to limit.

tasca ['taska] *nf* (*fam*) pub.

tatarabuelo [tatara'βwelo] *nm* great-great-grandfather.

tatuaje [ta'twaxe] *nm* (*dibujo*) tattoo; (*acto*) tattooing; **tatuar** *vt* to tattoo.

taumaturgo [tauma'turxo] *nm* miracle-worker.

taurino, a [tau'rino, a] *a* bullfighting *cpd*.

Tauro ['tauro] *nm* Taurus.

tauromaquia [tauro'makja] *nf* tauromachy.

tautología [tautolo'xia] *nf* tautology.

taxi ['taksi] *nm* taxi.

taxidermia [taksi'ðermja] *nf* taxidermy.

taxista [tak'sista] *nm/f* taxi driver.

taza ['taθa] *nf* cup; (*de retrete*) bowl; ~ **para café** coffee cup; **tazón** *nm* (~ *grande*) large cup; (*escudilla*) basin.

te [te] *pron* (*complemento de objeto*) you; (*complemento indirecto*) (to) you; (*reflexivo*) (to) yourself; ¿~ **duele**

mucho el brazo? does your arm hurt a lot?; ~ **equivocas** you're wrong; **¡cálma**~! calm yourself!

té [te] *nm* tea.

tea ['tea] *nf* torch.

teatral [tea'tral] *a* theatre *cpd*; (*fig*) theatrical; **teatro** *nm* (*gen*) theatre; (*LITERATURA*) plays *pl*, drama.

tebeo [te'ßeo] *nm* children's comic.

tecla ['tekla] *nf* key; ~**do** *nm* keyboard; **teclear** *vi* to strum; (*fam*) to drum; **tecleo** *nm* (*MUS; sonido*) strumming; (*forma de tocar*) fingering; (*fam*) drumming.

técnico, a ['tekniko, a] *a* technical // *nm* technician; (*experto*) expert // *nf* (*procedimientos*) technique; (*arte, oficio*) craft.

tecnócrata [tek'nokrata] *nm/f* technocrat.

tecnología [teknolo'xia] *nf* technology; **tecnológico, a** *a* technological; **tecnólogo** *nm* technologist.

techo ['tetʃo] *nm* (*externo*) roof; (*interno*) ceiling; **techumbre** *nf* roof.

tedio ['teðjo] *nm* (*aburrimiento*) boredom; (*apatía*) apathy; (*fastidio*) depression; ~**so, a** *a* boring; (*cansado*) wearisome, tedious.

teja ['texa] *nf* (*azulejo*) tile; (*BOT*) lime (tree); ~**do** *nm* (*tiled*) roof.

tejanos [te'xanos] *nmpl* jeans.

tejemaneje [texema'nexe] *nm* (*bullicio*) bustle; (*lío*) fuss; (*aspaviento*) to-do; (*intriga*) intrigue.

tejer [te'xer] *vt* to weave; (*AM*) to knit; (*fig*) to fabricate; **tejido** *nm* fabric; (*telaraña*) web; (*estofa, tela*) (knitted) material; (*ANAT*) tissue; (*textura*) texture.

tel, teléf *abr de* **teléfono.**

tela ['tela] *nf* (*material*) material; (*telaraña*) web; (*de fruta, en líquido*) skin; (*del ojo*) film; **telar** *nm* (*máquina*) loom; (*de teatro*) gridiron; **telares** *nmpl* textile mill *sg*.

telaraña [tela'raɲa] *nf* cobweb.

tele ['tele] *nf* (*fam*) TV.

tele... [tele] *pref* tele...; ~**comunicación** *nf* telecommunication; ~**control** *nm* remote control; ~**diario** *nm* television news; ~**difusión** *nf* (television) broadcast; ~**dirigido, a** *a* remote-controlled; ~**férico** *nm* (*tren*) cable-railway; (*de esquí*) ski-lift; ~**fonear** *vi* to telephone; ~**fónico, a** *a* telephone *cpd*; ~**fonista** *nm/f* telephonist; **teléfono** *nm* telephone; ~**foto** *nf* telephoto; ~**grafía** *nf* telegraphy; **telégrafo** *nm* telegraph; (*fam: persona*) telegraph boy; ~**grama** *nm* telegram; ~**impresor** *nm* teleprinter; **telémetro** *nm* rangefinder; ~**objetivo** *nm* telephoto lens; ~**pático, a** *a* telepathic; ~**scópico, a** *a* telescopic; ~**scopio** *nm* telescope; ~**silla** *nf* chairlift; ~**spectador, a** *nm/f* viewer; ~**squí** *nm* ski-lift; ~**tipista** *nm/f* teletypist; ~**tipo** *nm* teletype; ~**vidente** *nm/f* viewer; ~**visar** *vt* to televise;

~**visión** *nf* television; ~**visión en colores** colour television; ~**visor** *nm* television set.

telex [te'leks] *nm* telex.

telón [te'lon] *nm* curtain; ~ **de boca/seguridad** front/safety curtain; ~ **de acero** (*POL*) iron curtain; ~ **de fondo** backcloth, background.

tema ['tema] *nm* (*asunto*) subject, topic; (*MUS*) theme // *nf* (*obsesión*) obsession; (*manía*) ill-will; **tener** ~ **a uno** to have a grudge against sb; **temático, a** *a* thematic.

tembladera [tembla'ðera] *nf* shaking; (*AM*) quagmire.

temblar [tem'blar] *vi* to shake, tremble; (*de frío*) to shiver; **tembleque** *a* shaking // *nm* = **tembladera; temblón, ona** *a* shaking; **temblor** *nm* trembling; (*AM: de tierra*) earthquake; **tembloroso, a** *a* trembling.

temer [te'mer] *vt* to fear // *vi* to be afraid; **temo que llegue tarde** I am afraid he may be late.

temerario, a [teme'rarjo, a] *a* (*descuidado*) reckless; (*arbitrario*) hasty; **temeridad** *nf* (*imprudencia*) rashness; (*audacia*) boldness.

temeroso, a [teme'roso, a] *a* (*miedoso*) fearful; (*que inspira temor*) frightful.

temible [te'mißle] *a* fearsome.

temor [te'mor] *nm* (*miedo*) fear; (*duda*) suspicion.

témpano ['tempano] *nm* (*MUS*) kettledrum; ~ **de hielo** ice-flow; ~ **de tocino** flitch of bacon.

temperamento [tempera'mento] *nm* temperament.

temperatura [tempera'tura] *nf* temperature.

temperie [tem'perje] *nf* state of the weather.

tempestad [tempes'taծ] *nf* storm; **tempestuoso, a** *a* stormy.

templado, a [tem'plaծo, a] *a* (*moderado*) moderate; (: *en el comer*) frugal; (: *en el beber*) abstemious; (*agua*) lukewarm; (*clima*) mild; (*MUS*) well-tuned; **templanza** *nf* moderation; abstemiousness; mildness.

templar [tem'plar] *vt* (*moderar*) to moderate; (*furia*) to restrain; (*calor*) to reduce; (*solución*) to dilute; (*afinar*) to tune (up); (*acero*) to temper; (*tuerca*) to tighten up // *vi* to moderate; ~**se** *vr* to be restrained; **temple** *nm* (*humor*) mood; (*ajuste*) tempering; (*afinación*) tuning; (*clima*) temperature; (*pintura*) tempera.

templete [tem'plete] *nm* bandstand.

templo ['templo] *nm* (*iglesia*) church; (*pagano etc*) temple.

temporada [tempo'raծa] *nf* time, period; (*estación*) season.

temporal [tempo'ral] *a* (*no permanente*) temporary; (*REL*) temporal // *nm* storm.

tempranero, a [tempra'nero, a] *a* (*BOT*) early; (*persona*) early-rising.

temprano, a [tem'prano, a] *a* early;

(*demasiado pronto*) too soon, too early.

ten *vb ver* **tener.**

tenacidad [tenaθi'ðað] *nf* (*gen*) tenacity; (*dureza*) toughness; (*terquedad*) stubbornness.

tenacillas [tena'θiʎas] *nfpl* (*gen*) tongs; (*para el pelo*) curling tongs; (*MED*) forceps.

tenaz [te'naθ] *a* (*material*) tough; (*persona*) tenacious; (*pegajoso*) sticky; (*terco*) stubborn.

tenaza(s) [te'naθa(s)] *nf*(*pl*) (*MED*) forceps; (*TEC*) pliers; (*ZOOL*) pincers.

tendal [ten'dal] *nm* awning.

tendedero [tende'ðero] *nm* (*para ropa*) drying-place; (*cuerda*) clothes line.

tendencia [ten'denθja] *nf* tendency; (*proceso*) trend; **tener ~ a** to tend or have a tendency to; **tendencioso, a** *a* tendentious.

tender [ten'der] *vt* (*extender*) to spread out; (*colgar*) to hang out; (*vía férrea, cable*) to lay; (*cuerda*) to stretch // *vi* to tend; **~se** *vr* to lie down; (*fig: dejarse llevar*) to let o.s. go; (: *dejar ir*) to let things go; **~ la cama/la mesa** (*AM*) to make the bed/lay the table.

ténder ['tender] *nm* tender.

tenderete [tende'rete] *nm* (*puesto*) stall; (*carretilla*) barrow; (*exposición*) display of goods; (*jaleo*) mess.

tendero, a [ten'dero, a] *nm/f* shopkeeper.

tendido, a [ten'diðo, a] *a* (*acostado*) lying down, flat; (*colgado*) hanging // *nm* (*ropa*) washing; (*TAUR*) front rows of seats; (*colocación*) laying; (*ARQ: enyesado*) coat of plaster; **a galope ~** flat out.

tendón [ten'don] *nm* tendon.

tendré *etc vb ver* **tener.**

tenducho [ten'dutʃo] *nm* small dirty shop.

tenebroso, a [tene'ßroso, a] *a* (*oscuro*) dark; (*fig*) gloomy; (*siniestro*) sinister.

tenedor [tene'ðor] *nm* (*CULIN*) fork; (*poseedor*) holder; **~ de libros** book-keeper.

teneduría [teneðu'ria] *nf* keeping; **~ de libros** book-keeping.

tenencia [te'nenθja] *nf* (*de casa*) tenancy; (*de oficio*) tenure; (*de propiedad*) possession.

tener [te'ner] *vt* (*poseer*) to have; (*en la mano*) to hold; (*caja*) to hold, contain; (*considerar*) to consider; **~ suerte** to be lucky; **~ permiso** to have permission; **tiene 10 años** he is 10 years old; **¿cuántos años tienes?** how old are you?; **~ sed/hambre/frío/calor** to be thirsty/hungry/cold/hot; **~ ganas (de)** to want (to); **~ celos** to be jealous; **~ cuidado** to be careful; **~ razón** to be right; **~ un metro de ancho/de largo** to be one metre wide/long; **~ a bien** to see fit to; **~ en cuenta** to bear in mind, take into account; **~ a menos** to consider it beneath o.s.; **~ a uno en más (estima)** to think all the more of sb; **~ a uno por...** to think sb...; **~ por seguro** to be sure; **~ presente** to remember, bear in mind; **~**

que (*obligación*) to have to; **tiene que ser así** it has to be this way; **nos tiene preparada una sorpresa** he has prepared a surprise for us; **¿qué tiene?** what's the matter with him?; **¿ésas tenemos?** what's all this?; **tiene un mes de muerto** he has been dead for a month; **~se** *vr* (*erguirse*) to stand; (*apoyarse*) to lean (on); (*fig*) to control o.s.; (*considerarse*) to consider o.s.

tenería [tene'ria] *nf* tannery.

tengo *etc vb ver* **tener.**

tenia ['tenja] *nf* tapeworm.

teniente [te'njente] *nm* (*rango*) lieutenant; (*ayudante*) deputy.

tenis ['tenis] *nm* tennis; **~ta** *nm/f* tennis player.

tenor [te'nor] *nm* (*tono*) tone; (*sentido*) meaning; (*MUS*) tenor; **a ~ de** on the lines of.

tensar [ten'sar] *vt* to tauten; (*arco*) to draw.

tensión [ten'sjon] *nf* (*gen*) tension; (*TEC*) stress; (*MED*): **~ arterial** blood pressure; **tener la ~ alta** to have high blood pressure; **tenso, a** *a* tense.

tentación [tenta'θjon] *nf* temptation.

tentáculo [ten'takulo] *nm* tentacle.

tentador, a [tenta'ðor, a] *a* tempting // *nm/f* tempter/temptress.

tentar [ten'tar] *vt* (*tocar*) to touch, feel; (*seducir*) to tempt; (*atraer*) to attract; (*probar*) to try (out); (*lanzarse a*) to venture; (*MED*) to probe; **tentativa** *nf* attempt; **tentativa de asesinato** attempted murder.

tentempié [tentem'pje] *nm* (*fam*) snack.

tenue ['tenwe] *a* (*delgado*) thin, slender; (*alambre*) fine; (*insustancial*) tenuous; (*sonido*) faint; (*neblina*) light; (*lazo, vínculo*) slight; **tenuidad** *nf* thinness; fineness; (*ligereza*) lightness; (*sencillez*) simplicity.

teñir [te'ɲir] *vt* to dye; (*fig*) to tinge; **~se** *vr* to dye; **~se el pelo** to dye one's hair.

teología [teolo'xia] *nf* theology.

teorema [teo'rema] *nm* theorem.

teoría [teo'ria] *nf* theory; **en ~** in theory; **teóricamente** *ad* theoretically; **teórico, a** *a* theoretic(al) // *nm/f* theoretician, theorist; **teorizar** *vi* to theorize.

terapéutico, a [tera'peutiko, a] *a* therapeutic.

terapia [te'rapja] *nf* therapy; **~ laboral** occupational therapy.

tercer [ter'θer] *a ver* **tercero.**

tercería [terθe'ria] *nf* (*mediación*) mediation; (*arbitraje*) arbitration.

tercero, tercer, a [ter'θero, ter'θer, a] *a* third // *nm* (*árbitro*) mediator; (*JUR*) third party.

terceto [ter'θeto] *nm* trio.

terciado, a [ter'θjaðo, a] *a* slanting; **azúcar ~** brown sugar.

terciar [ter'θjar] *vt* (*MAT*) to divide into three; (*inclinarse*) to slope; (*llevar*) to wear (across the shoulder) // *vi* (*participar*) to take part; (*hacer de árbitro*) to mediate;

~**se** *vr* to come up; ~**io, a** *a* tertiary.
tercio ['terθjo] *nm* third.
terciopelo [terθjo'pelo] *nm* velvet.
terco, a ['terko, a] *a* obstinate; (*material*) tough.
tergiversación [terxiβersa'θjon] *nf* (*deformación*) distortion; (*evasivas*) prevarication; **tergiversar** *vt* to distort // *vi* to prevaricate.
termas ['termas] *nfpl* hot springs.
terminación [termina'θjon] *nf* (*final*) end; (*conclusión*) conclusion, ending; **terminal** *a, nm, nf* terminal; **terminante** *a* (*final*) final, definitive; (*tajante*) categorical; **terminar** *vt* (*completar*) to complete, finish; (*concluir*) to end // *vi* (*llegar a su fin*) to end; (*parar*) to stop; (*acabar*) to finish; **terminarse** *vr* to come to an end; **término** *nm* end, conclusion; (*parada*) terminus; (*límite*) boundary; **término medio** average; (*fig*) middle way; **en último término** (*a fin de cuentas*) in the last analysis; (*como último recurso*) as a last resort; **en términos de** in terms of.
terminología [terminolo'xia] *nf* terminology.
termodinámico, a [termoði'namiko, a] *a* thermodynamic.
termómetro [ter'mometro] *nm* thermometer.
termonuclear [termonukle'ar] *a* thermonuclear.
termo(s) ['termo(s)] *nm* thermos.
termostato [termo'stato] *nm* thermostat.
ternero, a [ter'nero, a] *nm/f* (*animal*) calf // *nf* (*carne*) veal.
terneza [ter'neθa] *nf* tenderness.
terno ['terno] *nm* (*traje*) three-piece suit; (*conjunto*) set of three.
ternura [ter'nura] *nf* (*trato*) tenderness; (*palabra*) endearment; (*cariño*) fondness.
terquedad [terke'ðað] *nf* obstinacy; (*dureza*) harshness.
terrado [te'rraðo] *nm* terrace.
terraplén [terra'plen] *nm* (*AGR*) terrace; (*FERRO*) embankment; (*MIL*) rampart; (*cuesta*) slope.
terrateniente [terrate'njente] *nm* landowner.
terraza [te'rraθa] *nf* (*balcón*) balcony; (*techo*) flat roof; (*AGR*) terrace.
terremoto [terre'moto] *nm* earthquake.
terrenal [terre'nal] *a* earthly.
terreno [te'rreno] *nm* (*tierra*) land; (*parcela*) plot; (*suelo*) soil; (*fig*) field; **un** ~ a piece of land.
terrero, a [te'rrero, a] *a* (*de la tierra*) earthy; (*vuelo*) low; (*fig*) humble.
terrestre [te'rrestre] *a* terrestrial; (*ruta*) land *cpd*.
terrible [te'rriβle] *a* (*espantoso*) terrible; (*aterrador*) dreadful; (*tremendo*) awful.
territorio [terri'torjo] *nm* territory.
terrón [te'rron] *nm* (*de azúcar*) lump; (*de tierra*) clod, lump; **terrones** *nmpl* land *sg*.

terror [te'rror] *nm* terror; ~**ífico, a** *a* terrifying; ~**ista** *a, nm/f* terrorist.
terroso, a [te'rroso, a] *a* earthy.
terruño [te'rruɲo] *nm* (*pedazo*) clod; (*parcela*) plot; (*fig*) native soil.
terso, a ['terso, a] *a* (*liso*) smooth; (*pulido*) polished; (*fig: estilo*) flowing; **tersura** *nf* smoothness; (*brillo*) shine.
tertulia [ter'tulja] *nf* (*reunión informal*) social gathering; (*grupo*) group, circle; (*sala*) clubroom.
tesar [te'sar] *vt* to tighten up.
tesis ['tesis] *nf inv* thesis.
tesón [te'son] *nm* (*firmeza*) firmness; (*tenacidad*) tenacity.
tesorero, a [teso'rero, a] *nm/f* treasurer; **tesoro** *nm* (*gen*) treasure; (*FIN, POL*) treasury.
testaferro [testa'ferro] *nm* figurehead.
testamentaría [testamenta'ria] *nf* execution of a will.
testamentario, a [testamen'tarjo, a] *a* testamentary // *nm/f* executor/executrix; **testamento** *nm* will; **testar** *vi* to make a will.
testarudo, a [testa'ruðo, a] *a* stubborn.
testero, a [tes'tero, a] *nm/f* (*gen*) front // *nm* (*ARQ*) front wall.
testes ['testes] *nmpl* testes.
testículo [tes'tikulo] *nm* testicle.
testificar [testifi'kar] *vt* to testify; (*fig*) to attest // *vi* to give evidence.
testigo [tes'tixo] *nm/f* witness; ~ **de cargo/descargo** witness for the prosecution/defence; ~ **ocular** eye witness.
testimoniar [testimo'njar] *vt* to testify to; (*fig*) to show; **testimonio** *nm* testimony.
teta ['teta] *nf* (*de biberón*) teat; (*ANAT*) nipple; (*fam*) breast.
tétanos ['tetanos] *nm* tetanus.
tetera [te'tera] *nf* teapot.
tetilla [te'tiʎa] *nf* (*ANAT*) nipple; (*de biberón*) teat.
tétrico, a ['tetriko, a] *a* gloomy, dismal.
textil [teks'til] *a* textile; ~**es** *nmpl* textiles.
texto ['teksto] *nm* text; **textual** *a* textual.
textura [teks'tura] *nf* (*de tejido*) texture; (*de mineral*) structure.
tez [teθ] *nf* (*cutis*) complexion; (*color*) colouring.
ti [ti] *pron* you; (*reflexivo*) yourself.
tía ['tia] *nf* (*pariente*) aunt; (*mujer cualquiera*) girl, bird (*col*); (*fam: pej: vieja*) old bag; (: *prostituta*) whore.
tibia ['tiβja] *nf* tibia.
tibieza [ti'βjeθa] *nf* (*temperatura*) tepidness; (*fig*) coolness; **tibio, a** *a* lukewarm.
tiburón [tiβu'ron] *nm* shark.
tic [tik] *nm* (*ruido*) click; (*de reloj*) tick; (*MED*): ~ **nervioso** nervous tic.
tictac [tik'tak] *nm* (*de reloj*) tick tock.
tiempo ['tjempo] *nm* (*gen*) time; (*época, período*) age, period; (*METEOROLOGÍA*) weather; (*LING*) tense; (*edad*) age; (*de

juego) half; **a** ~ in time; **a un** *o* **al mismo** ~ at the same time; **al poco** ~ very soon (after); **de** ~ **en** ~ from time to time; **hace buen/mal** ~ the weather is fine/bad; **estar a** ~ to be in time; **hace** ~ some time ago; **hacer** ~ to while away the time; **motor de 2** ~**s** two-stroke engine.

tienda ['tjenda] *nf* (*gen*) shop; (*más grande*) store; (NAUT) awning; ~ **de campaña** tent.

tienes *etc vb ver* **tener.**

tienta ['tjenta] *nf* (MED) probe; (*fig*) tact; **andar a** ~**s** to grope one's way along.

tiento ['tjento] *nm* (*tacto*) touch; (*precaución*) wariness; (*pulso*) steady hand; (ZOOL) feeler; (*de ciego*) blind man's stick.

tierno, a ['tjerno, a] *a* (*blando, dulce*) tender; (*fresco*) fresh.

tierra ['tjerra] *nf* earth; (*suelo*) soil; (*mundo*) world; (*país*) country, land; ~ **adentro** inland.

tieso, a ['tjeso, a] *a* (*rígido*) rigid; (*duro*) stiff; (*fig: testarudo*) stubborn; (*fam: orgulloso*) conceited // *ad* strongly.

tiesto ['tjesto] *nm* flowerpot; (*pedazo*) piece of pottery.

tiesura [tje'sura] *nf* rigidity; (*fig*) stubbornness; (*fam*) conceit.

tifo ['tifo] *nm* typhus.

tifoidea [tifoi'ðea] *nf* typhoid.

tifón [ti'fon] *nm* (*huracán*) typhoon; (*de mar*) tidal wave.

tifus ['tifus] *nm* typhus.

tigre ['tiɤre] *nm* tiger.

tijera [ti'xera] *nf* (AM) scissors *pl*; (ZOOL) claw; (*persona*) gossip; **de** ~ folding; ~**s** *nfpl* scissors; (*para plantas*) shears; **tijeretear** *vt* to snip // *vi* (*fig*) to meddle.

tildar [til'dar] *vt*: ~ **de** to brand as.

tilde ['tilde] *nf* (*defecto*) defect; (*trivialidad*) triviality; (TIPOGRAFÍA) tilde.

tilín [ti'lin] *nm* tinkle.

tilo ['tilo] *nm* lime tree.

timar [ti'mar] *vt* (*robar*) to steal; (*estafar*) to swindle; ~**se** *vr* (*fam*) to make eyes (*con uno* at sb).

timbal [tim'bal] *nm* small drum.

timbrar [tim'brar] *vt* to stamp.

timbre ['timbre] *nm* (*sello*) stamp; (*campanilla*) bell; (*tono*) timbre; (COM) stamp duty.

timidez [timi'ðeθ] *nf* shyness; **tímido, a** *a* shy.

timo ['timo] *nm* swindle.

timón [ti'mon] *nm* helm, rudder; **timonel** *nm* helmsman.

tímpano ['timpano] *nm* (ANAT) eardrum; (MUS) small drum.

tina ['tina] *nf* tub; (*baño*) bathtub; **tinaja** *nf* large jar.

tinglado [tin'glaðo] *nm* (*cobertizo*) shed; (*fig: truco*) trick; (*intriga*) intrigue.

tinieblas [ti'njeβlas] *nfpl* (*gen*) darkness *sg*; (*sombras*) shadows.

tino ['tino] *nm* (*habilidad*) skill; (MIL) marksmanship; (*juicio*) insight; (*moderación*) moderation.

tinta ['tinta] *nf* ink; (TEC) dye; (ARTE) colour.

tinte ['tinte] *nm* (*acto*) dyeing; (*carácter*) tinge; (*barniz*) veneer.

tinterillo [tinte'riʎo] *nm* penpusher.

tintero [tin'tero] *nm* inkwell.

tintinear [tintine'ar] *vt* to tinkle.

tinto, a ['tinto, a] *a* (*teñido*) dyed; (*manchado*) stained // *nm* red wine.

tintorera [tinto'rera] *nf* shark.

tintorería [tintore'ria] *nf* dry cleaner's.

tintura [tin'tura] *nf* (*acto*) dyeing; (QUÍMICA) dye; (*farmacéutico*) tincture.

tío ['tio] *nm* (*pariente*) uncle; (*fam: viejo*) old fellow; (: *individuo*) bloke, chap.

tiovivo [tio'βiβo] *nm* roundabout.

típico, a ['tipiko, a] *a* typical.

tiple ['tiple] *nm* soprano (voice) // *nf* soprano.

tipo ['tipo] *nm* (*clase*) type, kind; (*norma*) norm; (*patrón*) pattern; (*hombre*) fellow; (ANAT) build; (: *de mujer*) figure; (IMPRENTA) type; ~ **bancario/de descuento/de interés/de cambio** bank/discount/interest/exchange rate.

tipografía [tipoxra'fia] *nf* (*tipo*) printing; (*lugar*) printing press; **tipográfico, a** *a* printing; **tipógrafo, a** *nm/f* printer.

tiquismiquis [tikis'mikis] *nm* fussy person // *nmpl* (*querellas*) squabbling *sg*; (*escrúpulos*) silly scruples.

tira ['tira] *nf* strip; (*fig*) abundance; ~ **y afloja** give and take.

tirabuzón [tiraβu'θon] *nm* corkscrew.

tirado, a [ti'raðo, a] *a* (*barato*) dirt-cheap; (*fam: fácil*) very easy // *nf* (*acto*) cast, throw; (*distancia*) distance; (*serie*) series; (TIPOGRAFÍA) printing, edition; **de una** ~**a** at one go.

tirador [tira'ðor] *nm* (*mango*) handle; (ELEC) flex.

tiranía [tira'nia] *nf* tyranny; **tirano, a** *a* tyrannical // *nm/f* tyrant.

tirante [ti'rante] *a* (*cuerda*) tight, taut; (*relaciones*) strained // *nm* (ARQ) brace; (TEC) stay; (*correa*) shoulder strap; ~**s** *nmpl* braces; **tirantez** *nf* tightness; (*fig*) tension.

tirar [ti'rar] *vt* (*aventar*) to throw; (*dejar caer*) to drop; (*volcar*) to upset; (*derribar*) to knock down *or* over; (*jalar*) to pull; (*desechar*) to throw out *or* away; (*disipar*) to squander; (*imprimir*) to print; (*dar: golpe*) to deal // *vi* (*disparar*) to shoot; (*jalar*) to pull; (*fig*) to draw; (*fam: andar*) to go; (*tender a, buscar realizar*) to tend to; (DEPORTE) to shoot; ~**se** *vr* to throw o.s.; (*fig*) to cheapen o.s.; ~ **abajo** to bring down, destroy; **tira más a su padre** he takes more after his father; **ir tirando** to manage; **a todo** ~ at the most.

tirita [ti'rita] *nf* (sticking) plaster.

tiritar [tiri'tar] *vi* to shiver.

tiro ['tiro] *nm* (*lanzamiento*) throw;

(*disparo*) shot; (*disparar*) shooting; (DEPORTE) drive; (*alcance*) range; (*de escalera*) flight (of stairs); (*golpe*) blow; (*engaño*) hoax; ~ **al blanco** target practice; **caballo de** ~ cart-horse; **andar de** ~**s largos** to be all dressed up; **al** ~ (AM) at once.

tirón [ti'ron] *nm* (*sacudida*) pull, tug; **de un** ~ in one go.

tirotear [tirote'ar] *vt* to shoot at; ~**se** *vr* to exchange shots; **tiroteo** *nm* exchange of shots, shooting.

tísico, a ['tisiko, a] *a* consumptive.

títere ['titere] *nm* puppet.

titilar [titi'lar] *vi* (*luz, estrella*) to twinkle; (*parpado*) to flutter.

titiritero, a [titiri'tero, a] *nm/f* puppeteer.

titubeante [tituβe'ante] *a* (*inestable*) shaky, tottering; (*farfullante*) stammering; (*dudoso*) hesitant; **titubear** *vi* to stagger; (*fig*) to hesitate; **titubeo** *nm* staggering; stammering; hesitation.

titulado, a [titu'laðo, a] *a* (*libro*) entitled; (*persona*) titled; **titular** *a* titular // *nm/f* occupant // *nm* headline // *vt* to title; **titularse** *vr* to be entitled; **título** *nm* (*gen*) title; (*de diario*) headline; (*certificado*) professional qualification; (*universitario*) university degree; (*fig*) right; **a título de** in the capacity of.

tiza ['tiθa] *nf* chalk.

tizna ['tiθna] *nf* grime; **tiznar** *vt* to blacken; (*fig*) to tarnish.

tizón [ti'θon], **tizo** ['tiθo] *nm* brand; (*fig*) stain.

toalla [to'aʎa] *nf* towel.

tobillo [to'βiʎo] *nm* ankle.

tobogán [toβo'ɣan] *nm* toboggan; (*montaña rusa*) switchback; (*resbaladilla*) chute, slide.

toca ['toka] *nf* headdress.

tocadiscos [toka'ðiskos] *nm inv* record player.

tocado, a [to'kaðo, a] *a* rotten; (*fam*) touched // *nm* headdress.

tocador [toka'ðor] *nm* (*mueble*) dressing table; (*cuarto*) boudoir; (*neceser*) toilet case; (*fam*) ladies' toilet.

tocante [to'kante]: ~ **a** *prep* with regard to.

tocar [to'kar] *vt* to touch; (MUS) to play; (*topar con*) to run into, strike; (*referirse a*) to allude to; (*padecer*) to suffer; (*el pelo*) to do // *vi* (*a la puerta*) to knock (on or at the door); (*ser de turno*) to fall to, be the turn of; (*ser hora*) to be due; (*barco, avión*) to call at; (*atañer*) to concern; ~**se** *vr* (*cubrirse la cabeza*) to cover one's head; (*tener contacto*) to touch (each other); **por lo que a mí me toca** as far as I am concerned; **esto toca en la locura** this verges on madness.

tocayo, a [to'kajo, a] *nm/f* namesake.

tocino [to'θino] *nm* bacon.

todavía [toða'βia] *ad* (*aun*) still; (*aún*) yet; ~ **más** yet more; ~ **no** not yet.

todo, a ['toðo, a] *a* all; (*cada*) every;

(*entero*) whole; (*sentido negativo*): **en** ~ **el día lo he visto** I haven't seen him all day; ~**as las semanas**/~**s los martes** every week/Tuesday // *ad* all, completely // *nm* everything // *pron*: ~**s**/~**as** everyone; **a** ~**a velocidad** at full speed; **estaba** ~ **ojos** he was all eyes; **puede ser** ~ **lo honesto que quiera** he can be as honest as he likes; **ante** ~ above all; **en un** ~ as a whole; **corriendo y** ~, **no llegaron a tiempo** even though they ran, they still didn't arrive in time; **con** ~ still, even so; **del** ~ completely.

todopoderoso, a [toðopoðe'roso, a] *a* all powerful; (REL) almighty.

toga ['toɣa] *nf* toga; (ESCOL) gown.

Tokio ['tokjo] *n* Tokyo.

toldo ['toldo] *nm* (*para el sol*) sunshade; (*tienda*) marquee; (*fig*) pride.

tole ['tole] *nm* (*fam*) commotion.

tolerable [tole'raβle] *a* tolerable; **tolerancia** *nf* tolerance; **tolerar** *vt* to tolerate; (*resistir*) to endure.

toma ['toma] *nf* (*gen*) taking; (MED) dose.

tomar [to'mar] *vt* (*gen*) to take; (*aspecto*) to take on; (*beber*) to drink // *vi* to take; (AM) to drink; ~**se** *vr* to take; ~**se por** to consider o.s. to be; ~ **a bien/a mal** to take well/badly; ~ **en serio** to take seriously; ~ **el pelo a alguien** to pull sb's leg; ~**la con uno** to pick a quarrel with sb.

tomate [to'mate] *nm* tomato; ~**ra** *nf* tomato plant.

tomillo [to'miʎo] *nm* thyme.

tomo ['tomo] *nm* (*libro*) volume; (*tamaño*) size; (*fig*) importance.

ton [ton] *abr de* **tonelada** // *nm*: **sin** ~ **ni son** without rhyme or reason.

tonada [to'naða] *nf* tune.

tonalidad [tonali'ðað] *nf* tone.

tonel [to'nel] *nm* barrel.

tonelada [tone'laða] *nf* ton; **tonelaje** *nm* tonnage.

tonelero [tone'lero] *nm* cooper.

tónico, a ['toniko, a] *a* tonic // *nm* (MED) tonic // *nf* (MUS) tonic; (*fig*) keynote.

tonificar [tonifi'kar] *vt* to tone up.

tonillo [to'niʎo] *nm* monotonous voice.

tono ['tono] *nm* tone; **fuera de** ~ inappropriate; **darse** ~ to put on airs.

tontería [tonte'ria] *nf* (*estupidez*) foolishness; (*una* ~) stupid remark; ~**s** *nfpl* rubbish *sg*, nonsense *sg*.

tonto, a ['tonto, a] *a* stupid; (*sentimental*) silly // *nm/f* fool; (*payaso*) clown.

topacio [to'paθjo] *nm* topaz.

topar [to'par] *vt* (*tropezar*) to bump into; (*encontrar*) to find, come across; (ZOOL) to butt // *vi*: ~ **contra** *o* **en** to run into; ~ **con** to run up against; **el problema topa en eso** that's where the problem lies.

tope ['tope] *a* maximum // *nm* (*fin*) end; (*límite*) limit; (*riña*) quarrel; (FERRO) buffer; (AUTO) bumper; **al** ~ end to end.

tópico, a ['topiko, a] *a* topical // *nm* platitude.

topo ['topo] *nm* (*ZOOL*) mole; (*fig*) blunderer.
topografía [topoʁra'fia] *nf* topography; **topógrafo, a** *nm/f* topographer.
toque ['toke] *nm* touch; (*MUS*) beat; (*de campana*) peal; (*fig*) crux; **dar un ~ a** to test; **~ de queda** curfew; **~tear** *vt* to handle.
toquilla [to'kiʎa] *nf* (*bufanda*) headscarf; (*chal*) shawl.
torbellino [torbe'ʎino] *nm* whirlwind; (*fig*) whirl.
torcedura [torθe'ðura] *nf* twist; (*MED*) sprain.
torcer [tor'θer] *vt* to twist; (*la esquina*) to turn; (*MED*) to sprain; (*cuerda*) to plait; (*ropa, manos*) to wring; (*persona*) to corrupt // *vi* (*desviar*) to turn off; (*pelota*) to spin; **~se** *vr* (*ladearse*) to bend; (*desviarse*) to go astray; (*fracasar*) to go wrong; **torcido, a** *a* twisted; (*fig*) crooked // *nm* curl.
tordo, a ['torðo, a] *a* dappled // *nm* thrush.
torear [tore'ar] *vt* (*fig*: *evadir*) to avoid; (*jugar con*) to tease // *vi* to fight bulls; **toreo** *nm* bullfighting; **torero, a** *nm/f* bullfighter.
tormenta [tor'menta] *nf* storm; (*fig*: *confusión*) turmoil; (*desgracia*) misfortune.
tormento [tor'mento] *nm* torture; (*fig*) anguish.
tornar [tor'nar] *vt* (*devolver*) to return, give back; (*transformar*) to transform // *vi* to go back; **~se** *vr* (*ponerse*) to become; (*volver*) to return.
tornasol [torna'sol] *nm* (*BOT*) sunflower; **papel de ~** litmus paper; **~ado, a** *a* (*brillante*) iridescent; (*reluciente*) shimmering.
torneo [tor'neo] *nm* tournament.
tornero, a [tor'nero, a] *nm/f* machinist.
tornillo [tor'niʎo] *nm* screw.
torniquete [torni'kete] *nm* (*puerta*) turnstile; (*MED*) tourniquet.
torno ['torno] *nm* (*TEC*) winch; (*tambor*) drum; **en ~ (a)** round, about.
toro ['toro] *nm* bull; (*fam*) he-man; **los ~s** bullfighting.
toronja [to'ronxa] *nf* grapefruit.
torpe ['torpe] *a* (*poco hábil*) clumsy, awkward; (*necio*) dim; (*lento*) slow; (*indecente*) crude; (*no honrado*) dishonest.
torpedo [tor'peðo] *nm* torpedo.
torpeza [tor'peθa] *nf* (*falta de agilidad*) clumsiness; (*lentitud*) slowness; (*rigidez*) stiffness; (*error*) mistake; (*crudeza*) obscenity.
torre ['torre] *nf* tower; (*de petróleo*) derrick.
torrente [to'rrente] *nm* torrent.
tórrido, a ['torriðo, a] *a* torrid.
torrija [to'rrixa] *nf* fried bread; **~s** French toast *sg*.
torsión [tor'sjon] *nf* twisting.
torso ['torso] *nm* torso.
torta ['torta] *nf* cake; (*fam*) slap.

tortícolis [tor'tikolis] *nm* stiff neck.
tortilla [tor'tiʎa] *nf* omelette; (*AM*) maize pancake; **~ francesa/española** plain/potato omelette.
tórtola ['tortola] *nf* turtledove.
tortuga [tor'tuxa] *nf* tortoise.
tortuoso, a [tor'twoso, a] *a* winding.
tortura [tor'tura] *nf* torture; **torturar** *vt* to torture.
tos [tos] *nf* cough; **~ ferina** whooping cough.
tosco, a ['tosko, a] *a* coarse.
toser [to'ser] *vi* to cough.
tostado, a [tos'taðo, a] *a* toasted; (*por el sol*) dark brown; (*piel*) tanned // *nf* tan; **tostador** *nm* toaster; **tostar** *vt* to toast; (*café*) to roast; (*al sol*) to tan; **tostarse** *vr* to get brown.
total [to'tal] *a* total // *ad* in short; (*al fin y al cabo*) when all is said and done // *nm* total; **~ que** to cut a long story short.
totalidad [totali'ðað] *nf* whole.
totalitario, a [totali'tarjo, a] *a* totalitarian.
tóxico, a ['toksiko, a] *a* toxic // *nm* poison.
tozudo, a [to'θuðo, a] *a* obstinate.
traba ['traβa] *nf* bond, tie; (*cadena*) fetter.
trabajador, a [traβaxa'ðor, a] *nm/f* worker // *a* hard-working.
trabajar [traβa'xar] *vt* to work; (*arar*) to till; (*empeñarse en*) to work at; (*empujar*: *persona*) to push; (*convencer*) to persuade // *vi* to work; (*esforzarse*) to strive; **trabajo** *nm* work; (*tarea*) task; (*POL*) labour; (*fig*) effort; **tomarse el trabajo de** to take the trouble to; **trabajo por turno/a destajo** shift work/ piecework; **trabajoso, a** *a* hard; (*MED*) pale.
trabalenguas [traβa'lengwas] *nm inv* tongue twister.
trabar [tra'βar] *vt* (*juntar*) to join, unite; (*atar*) to tie down, fetter; (*agarrar*) to seize; (*amistad*) to strike up; **~se** *vr* to become entangled; (*reñir*) to squabble; **trabazón** *nf* (*TEC*) joining, assembly; (*fig*) bond, link.
trabucar [traβu'kar] *vt* (*confundir*) to confuse, mix up; (*palabras*) to misplace.
tracción [trak'θjon] *nf* traction; **~ delantera/trasera** front-wheel/rear-wheel drive.
tractor [trak'tor] *nm* tractor.
tradición [traði'θjon] *nf* tradition; **tradicional** *a* traditional.
traducción [traðuk'θjon] *nf* translation; **traducir** *vt* to translate; **traductor, a** *nm/f* translator.
traer [tra'er] *vt* (*gen*) to bring; (*llevar*) to carry; (*ropa*) to wear; (*imán*) to draw; (*incluir*) to carry; (*fig*) to cause; **~se** *vr*: **~se algo** to be up to sth; **~se bien/mal** to dress well/badly.
traficar [trafi'kar] *vi* to trade.
tráfico ['trafiko] *nm* (*COM*) trade; (*AUTO*) traffic.
tragaluz [traxa'luθ] *nm* skylight.
tragamonedas [traxamo'neðas] *nm inv*,

tragaperras [traχa'perras] *nm inv* slot machine.

tragar [tra'χar] *vt* to swallow; (*devorar*) to devour, bolt down; ~**se** *vr* to swallow.

tragedia [tra'xeðja] *nf* tragedy; **trágico, a** *a* tragic.

trago ['traχo] *nm* (*líquido*) drink; (*comido de golpe*) gulp; (*fam*: *de bebida*) swig; (*desgracia*) blow.

traición [trai'θjon] *nf* treachery; (*JUR*) treason; (*una* ~) act of treachery; **traicionar** *vt* to betray; **traidor, a, traicionero, a** *a* treacherous // *nm/f* traitor.

traigo *etc vb ver* **traer.**

traje ['traxe] *vb ver* **traer** // *nm* (*gen*) dress; (*de hombre*) suit; (*vestimenta típica*) costume; (*fig*) garb; ~ **de baño** swimsuit; ~ **de luces** bullfighter's costume.

trajera *etc vb ver* **traer.**

trajín [tra'xin] *nm* haulage; (*fam*: *movimiento*) bustle; **trajines** *nmpl* goings-on; **trajinar** *vt* (*llevar*) to carry, transport // *vi* (*moverse*) to bustle about; (*viajar*) to travel around.

trama ['trama] *nf* (*fig*) link; (: *intriga*) plot; (*de tejido*) weft; **tramar** *vt* to plot; (*TEC*) to weave.

tramitar [trami'tar] *vt* (*asunto*) to transact; (*negociar*) to negotiate; (*manejar*) to handle; **trámite** *nm* (*paso*) step; (*JUR*) transaction; **trámites** *nmpl* (*burocracia*) paperwork *sg*, procedures; (*JUR*) proceedings.

tramo ['tramo] *nm* (*de tierra*) plot; (*de escalera*) flight; (*de vía*) section.

tramoya [tra'moja] *nf* (*TEATRO*) piece of stage machinery; (*fig*) trick; **tramoyista** *nm/f* scene shifter; (*fig*) trickster.

trampa ['trampa] *nf* (*gen*) trap; (*en el suelo*) trapdoor; (*prestidigitación*) conjuring trick; (*engaño*) trick; (*fam*) fiddle; (*de pantalón*) fly; **trampear** *vt, vi* to cheat; **trampista** *nm/f* = **tramposo.**

trampolín [trampo'lin] *nm* trampoline; (*de piscina etc*) diving board.

tramposo, a [tram'poso, a] *a* crooked, cheating // *nm/f* crook, cheat.

tranca ['tranka] *nf* (*palo*) stick; (*viga*) beam; (*de puerta, ventana*) bar; **trancar** *vt* to bar // *vi* to stride along.

trance ['tranθe] *nm* (*momento difícil*) difficult moment; (*situación crítica*) critical situation; (*estado hipnotizado*) trance.

tranco ['tranko] *nm* stride.

tranquilidad [trankili'ðað] *nf* (*calma*) calmness, stillness; (*paz*) peacefulness; **tranquilizar** *vt* (*calmar*) to calm (down); (*asegurar*) to reassure; **tranquilo, a** *a* (*calmado*) calm; (*apacible*) peaceful; (*mar*) calm; (*mente*) untroubled.

transacción [transak'θjon] *nf* transaction.

transar [tran'sar] *vt* = **transigir.**

transbordador [transβorða'ðor] *nm* ferry.

transbordar [transβor'ðar] *vt* to transfer; ~**se** *vr* to change; **transbordo** *nm*

transfer; **hacer transbordo** to change (trains).

transcurrir [transku'rrir] *vi* (*tiempo*) to pass; (*hecho*) to turn out.

transcurso [trans'kurso] *nm*: ~ **del tiempo** lapse (of time).

transeúnte [transe'unte] *a* transient // *nm/f* passer-by.

transferencia [transfe'renθja] *nf* transference; (*COM*) transfer; **transferir** *vt* to transfer; (*de tiempo*) to postpone.

transfigurar [transfiχu'rar] *vt* to transfigure.

transformador [transforma'ðor] *nm* transformer.

transformar [transfor'mar] *vt* to transform; (*convertirse*) to convert.

tránsfuga ['transfuχa] *nm/f* (*MIL*) deserter; (*POL*) turncoat.

transgresión [transχre'sjon] *nf* transgression.

transición [transi'θjon] *nf* transition.

transido, a [tran'siðo, a] *a* overcome.

transigir [transi'xir] *vi* to compromise, make concessions.

transistor [transis'tor] *nm* transistor.

transitar [transi'tar] *vi* to go (from place to place); **tránsito** *nm* transit; (*AUTO*) traffic; (*parada*) stop; **transitorio, a** *a* transitory.

transmisión [transmi'sjon] *nf* (*TEC*) transmission; (*transferencia*) transfer; ~ **en directo/exterior** live/outside broadcast; **transmitir** *vt* (*gen*) to transmit; (*RADIO, TV*) to broadcast.

transparencia [transpa'renθja] *nf* transparency; (*claridad*) clearness, clarity; (*foto*) slide; **transparentar** *vt* to reveal // *vi* to be transparent; **transparente** *a* transparent; clear; (*ligero*) diaphanous // *nm* curtain.

transpirar [transpi'rar] *vi* to perspire; (*fig*) to transpire.

transponer [transpo'ner] *vt* to transpose; (*cambiar de sitio*) to change the place of // *vi* (*desaparecer*) to disappear; (*ir más allá*) to go beyond; ~**se** *vr* to change places; (*ocultarse*) to hide; (*sol*) to go down.

transportación [transporta'θjon] *nf* transportation; **transportar** *vt* to transport; (*llevar*) to carry; **transporte** *nm* transport; (*COM*) haulage.

tranvía [tran'βia] *nm* tram.

trapecio [tra'peθjo] *nm* trapeze; **trapecista** *nm/f* trapeze artist.

trapero, a [tra'pero, a] *nm/f* ragman.

trapicheos [trapi'tʃeos] *nmpl* (*fam*) schemes, fiddles.

trapisonda [trapi'sonda] *nf* (*jaleo*) row; (*estafa*) swindle.

trapo ['trapo] *nm* (*tela*) rag; (*de cocina*) cloth.

traqueteo [trake'teo] *nm* (*crujido*) crack; (*golpeteo*) rattling.

tras [tras] *prep* (*detrás*) behind; (*después*) after; ~ **de** besides.

trascendencia [trasθen'denθja] *nf*

(*importancia*) importance; (*filosofía*) transcendence; **trascendental** *a* important; transcendental; **trascender** *vi* (*oler*) to smell; (*evocar*) to evoke, suggest; (*noticias*) to come out; (*suceso*) to have a wide effect; **trascender a** to smack of.

trasegar [trase'ɣar] *vt* (*moverse*) to move about; (*vino*) to decant.

trasero, a [tra'sero, a] *a* back // *nm* (*ANAT*) bottom; ~s *nmpl* ancestors.

trasfondo [tras'fondo] *nm* background.

trasgredir [trasɣre'ðir] *vt* to contravene.

trashumante [trasu'mante] *a* migrating.

trasladar [trasla'ðar] *vt* (*gen*) to move; (*persona*) to transfer; (*postergar*) to postpone; (*copiar*) to copy; (*interpretar*) to interpret; **traslado** *nm* (*gen*) move; (*mudanza*) move, removal; (*copia*) copy.

traslucir [traslu'θir] *vt* to show; ~**se** *vr* to be translucent; (*fig*) to be revealed.

trasluz [tras'luθ] *nm* reflected light; **al** ~ against *or* up to the light.

trasnochar [trasno'tʃar] *vi* (*acostarse tarde*) to stay up late; (*no dormir*) to have a sleepless night; (*pasar la noche*) to stay the night.

traspasar [traspa'sar] *vt* (*bala*) to pierce, go through; (*propiedad*) to sell, transfer; (*calle*) to cross over; (*límites*) to go beyond; (*ley*) to break; **traspaso** *nm* transfer; (*fig*) anguish.

traspié [tras'pje] *nm* (*caída*) stumble; (*tropezón*) trip; (*fig*) blunder.

trasplantar [trasplan'tar] *vt* to transplant.

traste ['traste] *nm* (*MUS*) fret; **dar al** ~ **con algo** to ruin sth.

trastienda [tras'tjenda] *nf* backshop; **obtener algo por la** ~ to get sth by underhand means.

trasto ['trasto] *nm* (*mueble*) piece of furniture; (*tarro viejo*) old pot; (*pey: cosa*) piece of junk; (: *persona*) dead loss; ~s *nmpl* (*TEATRO*) scenery *sg*.

trastornado, a [trastor'naðo, a] *a* (*loco*) mad; (*agitado*) crazy; **trastornar** *vt* to overturn, upset; (*fig: ideas*) to confuse; (: *nervios*) to shatter; (: *persona*) to drive crazy; **trastornarse** *vr* (*plan*) to fall through; **trastorno** *nm* (*acto*) overturning; (*confusión*) confusion.

trasunto [tra'sunto] *nm* copy.

tratable [tra'taβle] *a* friendly.

tratado [tra'taðo] *nm* (*POL*) treaty; (*COM*) agreement.

tratamiento [trata'mjento] *nm* treatment.

tratar [tra'tar] *vt* (*ocuparse de*) to treat; (*manejar, TEC*) to handle; (*MED*) to treat; (*dirigirse a: persona*) to address // *vi*: ~ **de** (*hablar sobre*) to deal with, be about; (*intentar*) to try to; ~ **con** (*COM*) to trade in; (*negociar*) to negotiate with; (*tener contactos*) to have dealings with; ~**se** *vr* to treat each other; **trato** *nm* dealings *pl*; (*relaciones*) relationship; (*comportamiento*)

manner; (*COM*) agreement; (*título*) (form of) address.

trauma ['trauma] *nm* trauma.

través [tra'ßes] *nm* (*fig*) reverse; **al** ~ *ad* across, crossways; **a** ~ **de** *prep* across; (*sobre*) over; (*por*) through.

travesaño [traße'saɲo] *nm* (*ARQ*) crossbeam; (*DEPORTE*) crossbar.

travesía [traße'sia] *nf* (*calle*) cross-street; (*NAUT*) crossing.

travesura [traße'sura] *nf* (*broma*) prank; (*ingenio*) wit; **travieso, a** *a* (*niño*) naughty; (*adulto*) restless; (*ingenioso*) witty // *nf* crossing; (*ARQ*) crossbeam.

trayecto [tra'jekto] *nm* (*ruta*) road, way; (*viaje*) journey; (*tramo*) stretch; (*curso*) course; ~**ria** *nf* trajectory; (*fig*) path.

traza ['traßa] *nf* (*ARQ*) plan, design; (*aspecto*) looks *pl*; (*señal*) sign; (*engaño*) trick; (*habilidad*) skill; ~**do, a** *a*: **bien** ~**do** shapely, well-formed // *nm* (*ARQ*) plan, design; (*fig*) outline; **trazar** *vt* (*ARQ*) to plan; (*ARTE*) to sketch; (*fig*) to trace; (*plan*) to follow; **trazo** *nm* (*línea*) line; (*bosquejo*) sketch.

trébol ['treßol] *nm* (*BOT*) clover.

trece ['treθe] *num* thirteen.

trecho ['tretʃo] *nm* (*distancia*) distance; (*de tiempo*) while; (*fam*) piece; **de** ~ **en** ~ at intervals.

tregua ['treɣwa] *nf* (*MIL*) truce; (*fig*) lull.

treinta ['treinta] *num* thirty.

tremendo, a [tre'mendo, a] *a* (*terrible*) terrible; (*imponente: cosa*) imposing; (*fam: fabuloso*) tremendous; (*divertido*) entertaining.

trémulo, a ['tremulo, a] *a* quivering.

tren [tren] *nm* train; ~ **de aterrizaje** undercarriage.

trenza ['trenθa] *nf* (*de pelo*) plait; **trenzar** *vt* (*el pelo*) to plait // *vi* (*en baile*) to weave in and out; **trenzarse** *vr* (*AM*) to become involved with.

trepadora [trepa'ðora] *nf* (*BOT*) climber; **trepar** *vt, vi* to climb; (*TEC*) to drill.

trepidación [trepiða'θjon] *nf* shaking, vibration; **trepidar** *vi* to shake, vibrate.

tres [tres] *num* three.

tresillo [tre'siʎo] *nm* three-piece suite; (*MUS*) triplet.

treta ['treta] *nf* (*COM etc*) gimmick; (*fig*) trick.

triángulo ['trjangulo] *nm* triangle.

tribu ['trißu] *nf* tribe.

tribuna [tri'ßuna] *nf* (*plataforma*) platform; (*DEPORTE*) stand; (*fig*) public speaking.

tribunal [trißu'nal] *nm* (*juicio*) court; (*comisión, fig*) tribunal.

tributar [trißu'tar] *vt* to pay; (*las gracias*) to give; (*cariño*) to show; **tributo** *nm* (*COM*) tax.

trigal [tri'ɣal] *nm* wheat field; **trigo** *nm* wheat; **trigos** *nmpl* wheat field(s) (*pl*).

trigueño, a [tri'ɣeɲo, a] *a* (*pelo*) corn-coloured; (*piel*) olive-skinned.

trillado, a [tri'ʎaðo, a] *a* threshed; (*fig*)

trite, hackneyed; **trilladora** nf threshing machine; **trillar** vt (fig) to frequent; (AGR) to thresh.

trimestral [trimes'tral] a quarterly; (ESCOL) termly; **trimestre** nm (ESCOL) term.

trincar [trin'kar] vt (atar) to tie up; (NAUT) to lash; (agarrar) to pinion.

trinchar [trin'tʃar] vt to carve.

trinchera [trin'tʃera] nf (fosa) trench; (para vía) cutting; (impermeable) trench-coat.

trineo [tri'neo] nm sledge.

trinidad [trini'ðað] nf trio; (REL): **la T~** the Trinity.

trino ['trino] nm trill.

trinquete [trin'kete] nm (TEC) pawl; (NAUT) foremast.

tripa ['tripa] nf (ANAT) intestine; (fam) insides pl.

triple ['triple] a triple.

triplicado [tripli'kaðo] a: **por ~** in triplicate.

tripulación [tripula'θjon] nf crew; **tripulante** nm/f crewman/woman; **tripular** vt (barco) to man; (AUTO) to drive.

triquiñuela [triki'ɲwela] nf trick.

tris [tris] nm crack; **en un ~** in an instant.

triste ['triste] a (afligido) sad; (sombrío) melancholy, gloomy; (desolado) desolate; (lamentable) sorry, miserable; (viejo) old; **~za** nf (aflicción) sadness; (melancolía) melancholy.

triturar [tritu'rar] vt (moler) to grind; (mascar) to chew.

triunfar [trjun'far] vi (tener éxito) to triumph; (ganar) to win; **triunfo** nm triumph.

trivial [tri'βjal] a trivial; **~izar** vt to minimize, play down.

triza ['triθa] nf bit, piece; **hacer ~s** to smash to bits; **trizar** vt to smash to bits.

trocar [tro'kar] vt (COM) to exchange; (dinero, de lugar) to change; (palabras) to exchange; (confundir) to confuse; (vomitar) to vomit.

trocha ['trotʃa] nf (sendero) by-path; (atajo) short cut.

troche ['trotʃe]: **a ~ y moche** ad helter-skelter, pell-mell.

trofeo [tro'feo] nm (premio) trophy; (éxito) success.

troj(e) ['trox(e)] nf granary.

tromba ['tromba] nf whirlwind.

trombón [trom'bon] nm trombone.

trombosis [trom'bosis] nf thrombosis.

trompa ['trompa] nf horn; (trompo) humming top; (hocico) snout; (fam): **cogerse una ~** to get tight.

trompeta [trom'peta] nf trumpet; (clarín) bugle.

trompo ['trompo] nm spinning top.

trompón [trom'pon] nm bump.

tronado, a [tro'naðo, a] a broken-down.

tronar [tro'nar] vt (AM) to shoot // vi to thunder; (fig) to rage; (fam) to go broke.

tronco ['tronko] nm (de árbol, ANAT) trunk; (de planta) stem.

tronchar [tron'tʃar] vt (árbol) to chop down; (fig: vida) to cut short; (esperanza) to shatter; (persona) to tire out; **~se** vr to fall down.

tronera [tro'nera] nf (MIL) loophole; (ARQ) small window.

trono ['trono] nm throne.

tropa ['tropa] nf (MIL) troop; (soldados) soldiers pl; (gentío) mob.

tropel [tro'pel] nm (muchedumbre) crowd; (prisa) rush; (montón) throng.

tropelía [trope'lia] nm outrage.

tropezar [trope'θar] vi to trip, stumble; (fig) to slip up; **~ con** (encontrar) to run into; (topar con) to bump into; (reñir) to fall out with; **tropezón** nm trip; (fig) blunder.

tropical [tropi'kal] a tropical; **trópico** nm tropic.

tropiezo [tro'pjeθo] nm (error) slip, blunder; (desgracia) misfortune; (obstáculo) snag; (discusión) quarrel.

trotamundos [trota'mundos] nm inv globetrotter.

trotar [tro'tar] vi to trot; **trote** nm trot; (fam) travelling; **de mucho trote** hard-wearing.

trozo ['troθo] nm bit, piece.

truco ['truko] nm (habilidad) knack; (engaño) trick; **~s** nmpl billiards sg.

trucha ['trutʃa] nf (pez) trout; (TEC) crane.

trueno ['trweno] nm (gen) thunder; (estampido) boom; (de arma) bang.

trueque ['trweke] nm exchange; (COM) barter.

trufa ['trufa] nf (BOT) truffle; (fig: fam) fib.

truhán, ana [tru'an, ana] nm/f rogue.

truncado, a [trun'kaðo, a] a truncated; **truncar** vt (cortar) to truncate; (la vida etc) to cut short; (el desarrollo) to stunt.

tu [tu] a your.

tú [tu] pron you.

tubérculo [tu'βerkulo] nm (BOT) tuber.

tuberculosis [tuβerku'losis] nf tuberculosis.

tubería [tuβe'ria] nf pipes pl; (conducto) pipeline; **tubo** nm tube, pipe; **tubo de ensayo** test-tube; **tubo de escape** exhaust (pipe).

tuerca ['twerka] nf nut.

tuerto, a ['twerto, a] a (torcido) twisted; (ciego) blind in one eye // nm one-eyed person; (ofensa) wrong; **a ~as** upside-down.

tuétano ['twetano] nm (gen) marrow; (BOT) pith.

tufo ['tufo] nm vapour; (fig: pey) stench.

tul [tul] nm tulle.

tulipán [tuli'pan] nm tulip.

tullido, a [tu'ʎiðo, a] a crippled; (cansado) exhausted.

tumba ['tumba] nf (sepultura) tomb; (sacudida) shake; (voltereta) somersault.

tumbar [tum'bar] *vt* to knock down; (*doblar*) to knock over; (*fam: suj: olor*) to overpower // *vi* to fall down; ~**se** *vr* (*echarse*) to lie down; (*extenderse*) to stretch out.

tumbo ['tumbo] *nm* (*caída*) fall; (*de vehículo*) jolt; (*momento crítico*) critical moment.

tumido, a [tu'miðo, a] *a* swollen.

tumor [tu'mor] *nm* tumour.

tumulto [tu'multo] *nm* turmoil.

tuna ['tuna] *nf ver* **tuno.**

tunante [tu'nante] *a* rascally.

tunda ['tunda] *nf* (*de tela*) shearing; (*golpeo*) beating; **tundir** *vt* (*tela*) to shear; (*hierba*) to mow; (*fig*) to exhaust; (*fam: golpear*) to beat.

túnel ['tunel] *nm* tunnel.

Túnez ['tuneθ] *nm* Tunisia; (*ciudad*) Tunis.

tuno, a ['tuno, a] *nm/f* (*fam*) rogue // *nf* (*BOT*) prickly pear; (*MUS*) student music group.

tuntún [tun'tun]: **al** ~ *ad* thoughtlessly.

tupido, a [tu'piðo, a] *a* (*denso*) dense; (*fig*) dim; (*tela*) close-woven.

turba ['turßa] *nf* crowd.

turbación [turßa'θjon] *nf* (*molestia*) disturbance; (*preocupación*) worry; **turbado, a** *a* (*molesto*) disturbed; (*preocupado*) worried; **turbar** *vt* (*molestar*) to disturb; (*incomodar*) to upset; **turbarse** *vr* to be disturbed.

turbina [tur'ßina] *nf* turbine.

turbio, a ['turßjo, a] *a* cloudy; (*lenguaje*) confused // *ad* indistinctly.

turbión [tur'ßjon] *nf* (*fig*) shower.

turbohélice [turßo'eliθe] *nm* turboprop.

turbulencia [turßu'lenθja] *nf* turbulence; (*fig*) restlessness; **turbulento, a** *a* turbulent; (*fig: intranquilo*) restless; (: *ruidoso*) noisy.

turco, a ['turko, a] *a* Turkish.

turismo [tu'rismo] *nm* tourism; (*coche*) saloon car; **turista** *nm/f* tourist; **turístico, a** *a* tourist *cpd*.

turnar [tur'nar] *vi,* ~**se** *vr* to take (it in) turns; **turno** *nm* (*INDUSTRIA*) shift; (*oportunidad, orden de prioridad*) opportunity; (*DEPORTE etc*) turn.

turquesa [tur'kesa] *nf* turquoise.

Turquía [tur'kia] *nf* Turkey.

turrón [tu'rron] *nm* (*dulce*) nougat; (*fam*) sinecure.

tutear [tute'ar] *vt* to address as familiar 'tú'; ~**se** *vr* to be on familiar terms.

tutela [tu'tela] *nf* (*legal*) guardianship; (*instrucción*) guidance; **tutelar** *a* tutelary // *vt* to protect.

tutor, a [tu'tor, a] *nm/f* (*legal*) guardian; (*ESCOL*) tutor.

tuve, tuviera *etc vb ver* **tener.**

tuyo, a ['tujo, a] *a* yours, of yours // *pron* yours; **los** ~**s** (*fam*) your relations, your family.

TVE *nf abr de* **Televisión Española.**

U

u [u] *conj* or.

ubérrimo, a [u'ßerrimo, a] *a* very rich, fertile.

ubicar [ußi'kar] *vt* (*AM*) to place, situate; (: *fig*) to install in a post; ~**se** *vr* to lie, be located.

ubicuo, a [u'ßikwo, a] *a* ubiquitous.

ubre ['ußre] *nf* udder.

U.C.D. *abr de* **Unión del Centro Democrático.**

Ud(s) *abr de* **usted(es).**

ufanarse [ufa'narse] *vr* to boast; ~ **de** to pride o.s. on; **ufano, a** *a* (*arrogante*) arrogant; (*presumido*) conceited.

U.G.T. *abr de* **Unión General de Trabajadores.**

ujier [u'xjer] *nm* usher; (*portero*) doorkeeper.

úlcera ['ulθera] *nf* ulcer; **ulcerar** *vt* to make sore; **ulcerarse** *vr* to ulcerate.

ulterior [ulte'rjor] *a* (*más allá*) farther, further; (*subsecuente, siguiente*) subsequent; ~**mente** *ad* later, subsequently.

últimamente [ultima'mente] *ad* (*recientemente*) lately, recently; (*finalmente*) finally; (*como último recurso*) as a last resort.

ultimar [ulti'mar] *vt* to finish; (*finalizar*) to finalize; (*AM: rematar*) to finish off.

último, a ['ultimo, a] *a* last; (*más reciente*) latest, most recent; (*más bajo*) bottom; (*más alto*) top; (*fig*) final, extreme; **en las** ~**as** on one's last legs; **por** ~ finally.

ultra ['ultra] *a* ultra // *nm/f* extreme rightwinger.

ultrajar [ultra'xar] *vt* (*escandalizar*) to outrage; (*insultar*) to insult, abuse; **ultraje** *nm* outrage; insult.

ultramar [ultra'mar] *nm*: **de** *o* **en** ~ abroad, overseas; ~**ino, a** *a* overseas, foreign; ~**inos** *nmpl* groceries; **tienda de** ~**inos** grocer's (shop).

ultranza [ul'tranθa]: **a** ~ *ad* to the death; (*a todo trance*) at all costs; (*completo*) outright.

ultrasónico, a [ultra'soniko, a] *a* ultrasonic.

ulular [ulu'lar] *vi* to howl; (*búho*) to hoot.

umbral [um'bral] *nm* (*gen*) threshold.

umbroso, a [um'broso, a], **umbrío, a** [um'brio, a] *a* shady.

un, una [un, 'una] *det* a // *num* one; *ver* **uno.**

unánime [u'nanime] *a* unanimous; **unanimidad** *nf* unanimity.

unción [un'θjon] *nf* anointing; **extrema** ~ Extreme Unction.

undécimo, a [un'deθimo, a] *a* eleventh.

undular [undu'lar] *vi ver* **ondular.**

ungir [un'xir] *vt* to rub with ointment; (*REL*) to anoint.

ungüento [un'gwento] *nm* ointment; (*fig*) salve, balm.

únicamente ['unikamente] *ad* solely; (*solamente*) only; **único, a** *a* only; (*solo*) sole, single; (*sin par*) unique.

unidad [uni'ðað] *nf* unity; (*TEC*) unit.

unido, a [u'niðo, a] *a* joined, linked; (*fig*) united.

unificar [unifi'kar] *vt* to unite, unify.

uniformar [unifor'mar] *vt* to make uniform, level up; (*persona*) to put into uniform; **uniforme** *a* uniform, equal; (*superficie*) even // *nm* uniform; **uniformidad** *nf* uniformity; (*llaneza*) levelness, evenness.

unilateral [unilate'ral] *a* unilateral.

unión [u'njon] *nf* (*gen*) union; (*acto*) uniting, joining; (*calidad*) unity; (*TEC*) joint; (*fig*) closeness, togetherness; **la U~ Soviética** the Soviet Union.

unir [u'nir] *vt* (*juntar*) to join, unite; (*atar*) to tie, fasten; (*combinar*) to combine // *vi* to mix well; **~se** *vr* to join together, unite; (*empresas*) to merge.

unísono [u'nisono] *nm*: **al ~** in unison.

universal [uniβer'sal] *a* universal; (*mundial*) world *cpd*.

universidad [uniβersi'ðað] *nf* university.

universo [uni'βerso] *nm* universe.

uno ['uno] *num*, *det* one // *pron* one; (*alguien*) someone, somebody; **~s** some, a few; **~ a ~, ~ por ~** one by one; **cada ~** each *or* every one; **estar en ~** to be at one; **~ que otro** some, a few; **~s y otros** all of them; **~ y otro** both.

untar [un'tar] *vt* (*gen*) to rub; (*engrasar*) to grease, oil; (*MED*) to rub with ointment; (*fig*) to bribe; **~se** *vr* to be crooked; **unto** *nm* animal fat; (*MED*) ointment; (*fam*) slush fund.

uña ['uɲa] *nf* (*ANAT*) nail; (*garra*) claw; (*casco*) hoof; (*arrancaclavos*) claw.

uranio [u'ranjo] *nm* uranium.

urbanidad [urβani'ðað] *nf* courtesy, politeness.

urbanismo [urβa'nismo] *nm* town planning.

urbanización [urβaniθa'θjon] *nf* housing scheme.

urbano, a [ur'βano, a] *a* (*de ciudad*) urban; (*cortés*) courteous, polite.

urbe ['urβe] *nf* large city.

urdimbre [ur'ðimbre] *nf* (*de tejido*) warp; (*intriga*) intrigue; **urdir** *vt* to warp; (*fig*) to plot, contrive.

urgencia [ur'xenθja] *nf* urgency; (*prisa*) haste, rush; **servicios de ~** emergency services; **urgente** *a* urgent; (*insistente*) insistent; **urgir** *vi* to be urgent.

urinario, a [uri'narjo, a] *a* urinary // *nm* urinal.

urna ['urna] *nf* urn; (*POL*) ballot box.

urraca [u'rraka] *nf* magpie.

URSS *nf*: **la ~** the USSR.

Uruguay [uru'ɣwai] *nm*: **el ~** Uruguay; **uruguayo, a** *a, nm/f* Uruguayan.

usado, a [u'saðo, a] *a* (*gen*) used; (*ropa etc*) worn.

usanza [u'sanθa] *nf* custom, usage.

usar [u'sar] *vt* to use; (*ropa*) to wear; (*tener costumbre*) to be in the habit of; **~se** *vr* to be used; **uso** *nm* use; wear; (*costumbre*) usage, custom; (*moda*) fashion; **al uso** in keeping with custom; **al uso de** in the style of.

usted [us'teð] *pron* you.

usual [u'swal] *a* usual.

usuario, a [usu'arjo, a] *nm/f* user.

usura [u'sura] *nf* usury; **usurero, a** *nm/f* usurer.

usurpar [usur'par] *vt* to usurp.

utensilio [uten'siljo] *nm* tool; (*CULIN*) utensil.

útero ['utero] *nm* uterus, womb.

útil ['util] *a* useful // *nm* tool; **utilidad** *nf* usefulness; (*COM*) profit; **utilizar** *vt* to use, utilize.

utopía [uto'pia] *nf* Utopia; **utópico, a** *a* Utopian.

uva ['uβa] *nf* grape.

V

v *abr de* **voltio.**

va *vb ver* **ir.**

vaca ['baka] *nf* (*animal*) cow; (*carne*) beef; (*cuero*) cowhide.

vacaciones [baka'θjones] *nfpl* holidays.

vacante [ba'kante] *a* vacant, empty // *nf* vacancy.

vacar [ba'kar] *vi* to fall vacant; **~ a o en** to devote o.s. to.

vaciado, a [ba'θjaðo, a] *a* (*hecho en molde*) cast in a mould; (*hueco*) hollow // *nm* cast.

vaciar [ba'θjar] *vt* to empty out; (*ahuecar*) to hollow out; (*moldear*) to cast // *vi* (*río*) to flow (*en* into); **~se** *vr* to empty; (*fig*) to blab, spill the beans.

vaciedad [baθje'ðað] *nf* emptiness.

vacilación [baθila'θjon] *nf* hesitation; **vacilante** *a* unsteady; (*habla*) faltering; (*fig*) hesitant; **vacilar** *vi* to be unsteady; to falter; to hesitate, waver; (*persona*) to stagger, stumble; (*memoria*) to fail.

vacío, a [ba'θio, a] *a* empty; (*puesto*) vacant; (*desocupado*) idle; (*vano*) vain // *nm* emptiness; (*FISICA*) vacuum; (*un ~*) (empty) space.

vacuna [ba'kuna] *nf* vaccine; **vacunar** *vt* to vaccinate.

vacuno, a [ba'kuno, a] *a* bovine.

vacuo, a ['bakwo, a] *a* empty.

vadear [baðe'ar] *vt* (*río*) to ford; (*problema*) to overcome; (*persona*) to sound out; **vado** *nm* ford; (*solución*) solution; (*descanso*) respite.

vagabundo, a [baɣa'βundo, a] *a* wandering; (*pey*) vagrant // *nm* tramp.

vagamente [baɣa'mente] *ad* vaguely.

vagancia [ba'ɣanθja] *nf* vagrancy; **vagar** *vi* (*gen*) to wander; (*no hacer nada*) to idle // *nm* leisure.

vagido [ba'xiðo] *nm* wail.

vagina [ba'xina] *nf* vagina.

vago, a ['baxo, a] *a* vague; (*perezoso*) lazy; (*ambulante*) wandering // *nm/f* (*vagabundo*). tramp; (*flojo*) lazybones *sg*, idler.

vagón [ba'xon] *nm* (*de pasajeros*) carriage; (*de mercancías*) wagon.

vaguedad [baxe'ðað] *nf* vagueness.

vaho ['bao] *nm* (*vapor*) vapour, steam; (*olor*) smell; (*respiración*) breath.

vaina ['baina] *nf* sheath.

vainilla [bai'niʌa] *nf* vanilla.

vais *vb ver* **ir**.

vaivén [bai'ßen] *nm* to-and-fro movement; (*de tránsito*) coming and going; **vaivenes** *nmpl* (*fig*) ups and downs.

vajilla [ba'xiʌa] *nf* crockery, dishes *pl.*

val, valdré *etc vb ver* **valer**.

vale ['bale] *nm* voucher; (*recibo*) receipt; (*pagaré*) I.O.U.

valedero, a [bale'ðero, a] *a* valid.

valenciano, a [balen'θjano, a] *a* Valencian.

valentía [balen'tia] *nf* courage, bravery; (*pey*) boastfulness; (*acción*) heroic deed; **valentón, ona** *a* blustering.

valer [ba'ler] *vt* to aid, protect; (*MAT*) to equal // *vi* to be worth; (*costar*) to cost; (*ser útil*) to be useful; (*ser válido*) to be valid; ~**se** *vr* to defend o.s.; ~**se de** to make use of, take advantage of // *nm* worth, value; ~ **la pena** to be worthwhile; ¿**vale?** O. K.?

valgo *etc vb ver* **valer**.

validar [bali'ðar] *vt* to validate; **validez** *nf* validity; **válido, a** *a* valid.

valiente [ba'ljente] *a* brave, valiant; (*pey*) boastful // *nm* hero.

valija [ba'lixa] *nf* case; (*mochila*) satchel.

valioso, a [ba'ljoso, a] *a* valuable; (*rico*) wealthy.

valor [ba'lor] *nm* value, worth; (*precio*) price; (*valentía*) valour, courage; (*importancia*) importance; ~**es** *nmpl* (*COM*) securities; ~**ación** *nf* valuation; ~**ar** *vt* to value.

vals [bals] *nm* waltz.

válvula ['balßula] *nf* valve.

valla ['baʌa] *nf* fence; (*DEPORTE*) hurdle; (*fig*) barrier; **vallar** *vt* to fence in.

valle ['baʌe] *nm* valley, vale.

vamos *vb ver* **ir**.

vampiro, resa [bam'piro, i'resa] *nm/f* vampire.

van *vb ver* **ir**.

vanagloriarse [banaxlo'rjarse] *vr* to boast.

vándalo, a ['bandalo, a] *nm/f* vandal; **vandalismo** *nm* vandalism.

vanguardia [ban'gwardja] *nf* vanguard; (*ARTE*) avant-garde.

vanidad [bani'ðað] *nf* vanity; (*irrealidad*) unreality; **vanidoso, a** *a* vain, conceited.

vano, a ['bano, a] *a* (*irreal*) unreal; (*irracional*) unreasonable; (*inútil*) useless;

(*persona*) vain, conceited; (*frívolo*) frivolous.

vapor [ba'por] *nm* vapour; (*vaho*) steam; (*neblina*) mist; ~**es** *nmpl* (*MED*) hysterics; **al** ~ (*CULIN*) steamed; ~**izar** *vt* to vaporize; ~**oso, a** *a* vaporous; (*vahoso*) steamy.

vaquero, a [ba'kero, a] *a* cattle *cpd* // *nm* cowboy; ~**s** *nmpl* jeans.

vara ['bara] *nf* stick, wand; (*TEC*) rod.

varear [bare'ar] *vt* to hit, beat.

variable [ba'rjaßle] *a*, *nf* variable; **variación** *nf* variation; **variar** *vt* to vary; (*modificar*) to modify; (*cambiar de posición*) to switch around // *vi* to vary; **variedad** *nf* variety.

varilla [ba'riʌa] *nf* stick; (*BOT*) twig; (*TEC*) rod; (*de rueda*) spoke.

vario, a ['barjo, a] *a* (*variado*) varied; (*multicolor*) motley; (*cambiable*) changeable; ~**s** various, several.

varón [ba'ron] *nm* male, man; **varonil** *a* manly.

Varsovia [bar'soßja] *n* Warsaw.

vas *vb ver* **ir**.

vascongado, a [baskon'xaðo, a], **vascuence** [bas'kwenθe], **vasco, a** ['basko, a] *a* Basque; **las Vascongadas** the Basque Country.

vaselina [base'lina] *nf* vaseline.

vasija [ba'sixa] *nf* container, vessel.

vaso ['baso] *nm* glass, tumbler; (*ANAT*) vessel.

vástago ['bastaxo] *nm* (*BOT*) shoot; (*TEC*) rod; (*fig*) offspring.

vasto, a ['basto, a] *a* vast, huge.

Vaticano [bati'kano] *nm*: **el** ~ the Vatican.

vaticinio [bati'θinjo] *nm* prophecy.

vatio ['batjo] *nm* (*ELEC*) watt.

vaya *etc vb ver* **ir**.

Vd(s) *abr de* **usted(es)**.

ve *vb ver* **ir, ver**.

vecindad [beθin'dað] *nf*, **vecindario** [beθin'darjo] *nm* neighbourhood; (*habitantes*) residents *pl*; **vecino, a** *a* neighbouring // *nm/f* neighbour; (*residente*) resident.

veda ['beða] *nf* prohibition.

vedado [be'ðaðo] *nm* preserve.

vedar [be'ðar] *vt* (*prohibir*) to ban, prohibit; (*impedir*) to stop, prevent.

vegetación [bexeta'θjon] *nf* vegetation.

vegetal [bexe'tal] *a*, *nm* vegetable.

vehemencia [bee'menθja] *nf* (*insistencia*) vehemence; (*pasión*) passion; (*fervor*) fervour; (*violencia*) violence; **vehemente** *a* vehement; passionate; fervent.

vehículo [be'ikulo] *nm* vehicle; (*MED*) carrier.

veía *etc vb ver* **ver**.

veinte ['beinte] *num* twenty.

vejación [bexa'θjon] *nf* vexation; (*humillación*) humiliation.

vejamen [be'xamen] *nm* satire.

vejar [be'xar] vt (*irritar*) to annoy, vex; (*humillar*) to humiliate.

vejez [be'xeθ] nf old age.

vejiga [be'xiɣa] nf (ANAT) bladder.

vela ['bela] nf (*de cera*) candle; (NAUT) sail; (*insomnio*) sleeplessness; (*vigilia*) vigil; (MIL) sentry duty; (*fam*) snot; **estar a dos ~s** (*fam*) to be skint (*fam*).

velado, a [be'laðo, a] a veiled; (*sonido*) muffled; (FOTO) blurred // nf soirée.

velador [bela'ðor] nm watchman; (*candelero*) candlestick.

velar [be'lar] vt (*hacer guardia*) to keep watch over; (*cubrir*) to veil // vi to stay awake; ~ **por** to watch over, look after.

veleidad [belei'ðað] nf (*ligereza*) fickleness; (*capricho*) whim.

velero [be'lero] nm (NAUT) sailing ship; (AVIAT) glider.

veleta [be'leta] nf weather vane.

velo ['belo] nm veil.

velocidad [beloθi'ðað] nf speed; (TEC, AUTO) gear.

velocímetro [belo'θimetro] nm speedometer.

velódromo [be'loðromo] nm cycle track.

veloz [be'loθ] a fast.

vello ['beʎo] nm down, fuzz; **vellón** nm fleece; ~**so, a** a fuzzy; **velludo, a** a shaggy // nm plush, velvet.

ven vb ver **venir**.

vena ['bena] nf vein.

venablo [be'naβlo] nm javelin.

venado [be'naðo] nm deer.

venal [be'nal] a (ANAT) venous; (*pey*) venal; ~**idad** nf venality.

vencedor, a [benθe'ðor, a] a victorious // nm/f victor, winner.

vencer [ben'θer] vt (*dominar*) to defeat, beat; (*derrotar*) to vanquish; (*superar, controlar*) to overcome, master // vi (*triunfar*) to win (through), triumph; (*plazo*) to expire; **vencido, a** a (*derrotado*) defeated, beaten; (COM) due // ad: **pagar vencido** to pay in arrears; **vencimiento** nm collapse; (COM) maturity.

venda ['benda] nf bandage; ~**je** nm bandage, dressing; **vendar** vt to bandage; **vendar los ojos** to blindfold.

vendaval [benda'βal] nm (*viento*) gale; (*huracán*) hurricane.

vendedor, a [bende'ðor, a] nm/f seller.

vender [ben'der] vt to sell; ~ **al contado/al por mayor/al por menor** to sell for cash/wholesale/retail.

vendimia [ben'dimja] nf grape harvest.

vendré etc vb ver **venir**.

veneno [be'neno] nm poison, venom; ~**so, a** a poisonous.

venerable [bene'raβle] a venerable; **veneración** nf veneration; **venerar** vt (*reconocer*) to venerate; (*adorar*) to worship.

venéreo, a [be'nereo, a] a venereal.

venero [be'nero] nm (*veta*) seam, lode; (*fuente*) spring.

venezolano, a [beneθo'lano, a] a Venezuelan.

Venezuela [bene'θwela] nf Venezuela.

venganza [ben'ganθa] nf vengeance, revenge; **vengar** vt to avenge; **vengarse** vr to take revenge; **vengativo, a** a (*persona*) vindictive.

vengo etc vb ver **venir**.

venia ['benja] nf (*perdón*) pardon; (*permiso*) consent.

venial [be'njal] a venial.

venida [be'niða] nf (*llegada*) arrival; (*regreso*) return; (*fig*) rashness.

venidero, a [beni'ðero, a] a coming, future.

venir [be'nir] vi to come; (*llegar*) to arrive; (*fig*) to stem from; (*ocurrir*) to happen; ~ **bien/mal** to be suitable/unsuitable; **el año que viene** next year; ~**se abajo** to collapse.

venta ['benta] nf (COM) sale; ~ **a plazos** hire purchase; ~ **al contado/al por mayor/al por menor** o **al detalle** cash sale/ wholesale/retail; ~ **de liquidación** clearance sale.

ventaja [ben'taxa] nf advantage; **ventajoso, a** a advantageous.

ventana [ben'tana] nf window; ~ **de guillotina/salediza** sash/bay window; **ventanilla** nf (*de taquilla*) window (*of booking office etc*).

ventear [bente'ar] vt (*ropa*) to hang out to dry; (*oler*) to sniff // vi (*investigar*) to investigate; (*soplar*) to blow; ~**se** vr (*romperse*) to crack; (ANAT) to break wind.

ventilación [bentila'θjon] nf ventilation; (*corriente*) draught; **ventilar** vt to ventilate; (*a secar*) to put out to dry; (*fig*) to air, discuss.

ventisca [ben'tiska] nf, **ventisquero** [bentis'kero] nm blizzard; (*nieve amontonada*) snowdrift.

ventosear [bentose'ar] vi to break wind.

ventoso, a [ben'toso, a] a windy.

ventrílocuo, a [ben'trilokwo, a] nm/f ventriloquist; **ventriloquia** nf ventriloquism.

ventura [ben'tura] nf (*felicidad*) happiness; (*buena suerte*) luck; (*destino*) fortune; **a la (buena)** ~ at random; **venturoso, a** a happy; (*afortunado*) lucky, fortunate.

veo etc vb ver **ver**.

ver [ber] vt, vi to see; (*mirar*) to look at, watch; (*investigar*) to look into; ~**se** vr (*encontrarse*) to meet; (*dejarse* ~) to be seen; (*hallarse: en un apuro*) to find o.s., be // nm looks pl, appearance; **a** ~ let's see; **dejarse** ~ to become apparent; **no tener nada que** ~ **con** to have nothing to do with; **a mi modo de** ~ as I see it.

vera ['bera] nf edge, verge; (*de río*) bank.

veracidad [beraθi'ðað] nf truthfulness.

veranear [berane'ar] vi to spend the summer; **veraneo** nm summer holiday; **veraniego, a** a summer cpd; **verano** nm summer.

veras ['beras] *nfpl* truth *sg*; **de** ~ really, truly.

veraz [be'raθ] *a* truthful.

verbal [ber'βal] *a* verbal.

verbena [ber'βena] *nf* street party.

verbigracia [berβi'xraθja] *ad* for example.

verbo ['berβo] *nm* verb; ~**so, a** *a* verbose.

verdad [ber'ðað] *nf* (*lo verídico*) truth; (*fiabilidad*) reliability // *ad* really; **de** ~ *a* real, proper; **a decir** ~ to tell the truth; ~**ero, a** *a* (*veraz*) true, truthful; (*fiable*) reliable; (*fig*) real.

verde ['berðe] *a* green; (*sucio*) blue, dirty // *nm* green; **viejo** ~ dirty old man; ~**ar**, ~**cer** *vi* to turn green; **verdor** *nm* (*lo* ~) greenness; (*BOT*) verdure; (*fig*) youthful vigour.

verdugo [ber'ðuxo] *nm* executioner; (*BOT*) shoot; (*cardenal*) weal.

verdulero, a [berðu'lero, a] *nm/f* greengrocer.

verdura [ber'ðura] *nf* greenness; ~**s** *nfpl* (*CULIN*) greens.

vereda [be'reða] *nf* path.

veredicto [bere'ðikto] *nm* verdict.

vergonzoso, a [berxon'θoso, a] *a* shameful; (*tímido*) timid, bashful.

vergüenza [ber'xwenθa] *nf* shame, sense of shame; (*timidez*) bashfulness; (*pudor*) modesty.

verídico, a [be'riðiko, a] *a* true, truthful.

verificar [berifi'kar] *vt* to check; (*corroborar*) to verify; (*llevar a cabo*) to carry out; ~**se** *vr* to occur, happen.

verja ['berxa] *nf* grating.

vermut [ber'mut] *nm* vermouth.

verosímil [bero'simil] *a* likely, probable; (*relato*) credible.

verruga [be'rruxa] *nf* wart.

versado, a [ber'saðo, a] *a*: ~ **en** versed in.

versar [ber'sar] *vi* to go round, turn.

versátil [ber'satil] *a* versatile.

versión [ber'sjon] *nf* version; (*traducción*) translation.

verso ['berso] *nm* (*gen*) verse; **un** ~ a line of poetry.

vértebra ['berteβra] *nf* vertebra.

verter [ber'ter] *vt* (*vaciar*) to empty, pour (out); (*tirar*) to dump // *vi* to flow.

vertical [berti'kal] *a* vertical.

vértice ['bertiθe] *nm* vertex, apex.

vertiente [ber'tjente] *nf* slope.

vertiginoso, a [bertixi'noso, a] *a* giddy, dizzy; **vértigo** *nm* vertigo; (*mareo*) dizziness.

vesícula [be'sikula] *nf* blister.

vespertino, a [besper'tino, a] *a* evening *cpd*.

vestíbulo [bes'tiβulo] *nm* hall; (*de teatro*) foyer.

vestido [bes'tiðo] *nm* (*ropa*) clothes *pl*, clothing; (*de mujer*) dress, frock.

vestigio [bes'tixjo] *nm* (*trazo*) trace; (*señal*) sign; ~**s** *nmpl* remains.

vestimenta [besti'menta] *nf* clothing.

vestir [bes'tir] *vt* (*poner: ropa*) to put on; (*llevar: ropa*) to wear; (*cubrir*) to clothe, cover; (*pagar: la ropa*) to pay for the clothing of; (*sastre*) to make clothes for // *vi* (*ponerse: ropa*) to dress; (*verse bien*) to look good; ~**se** *vr* to get dressed, dress o.s.

vestuario [bes'twarjo] *nm* clothes *pl*, wardrobe; (*TEATRO*) dressing room; (*DEPORTE*) changing room.

veta ['beta] *nf* (*vena*) vein, seam; (*raya*) streak; (*de madera*) grain.

vetar [be'tar] *vt* to veto.

veterano, a [bete'rano, a] *a, nm* veteran.

veterinario, a [beteri'narjo, a] *nm/f* vet(erinary surgeon) // *nf* veterinary science.

veto ['beto] *nm* veto.

vetusto, a [be'tusto, a] *a* ancient.

vez [beθ] *nf* time; (*turno*) turn; **a la** ~ **que** at the same time as; **a su** ~ in its turn; **cada** ~ **más/menos** more and more/less and less; **una** ~ once; **de una** ~ in one go; **de una** ~ **para siempre** once and for all; **en** ~ **de** instead of; **a veces** sometimes; **una y otra** ~ repeatedly; **de** ~ **en cuando** from time to time; **7 veces 9** 7 times 9; **hacer las veces de** to stand in for; **tal** ~ perhaps.

v. g., v. gr. *abr de* **verbigracia.**

vía ['bia] *nf* track, route; (*FERRO*) line; (*fig*) way; (*ANAT*) passage, tube // *prep* via, by way of; **por** ~ **judicial** by legal means; **por** ~ **oficial** through official channels; **por** ~ **de** by way of; **en** ~**s de** in the process of; ~ **aérea** airway.

viaducto [bja'ðukto] *nm* viaduct.

viajante [bja'xante] *nm* commercial traveller.

viajar [bja'xar] *vi* to travel; **viaje** *nm* journey; (*gira*) tour; (*NAUT*) voyage; **estar de viaje** to be on a journey; **viaje de ida y vuelta** round trip; **viaje de novios** honeymoon; **viajero, a** *a* travelling; (*ZOOL*) migratory // *nm/f* (*quien viaja*) traveller; (*pasajero*) passenger.

vial [bjal] *a* road *cpd*, traffic *cpd*.

víbora ['biβora] *nf* viper.

vibración [biβra'θjon] *nf* vibration; **vibrador** *nm* vibrator; **vibrante** *a* vibrant; **vibrar** *vt*, *vi* to vibrate.

vicario [bi'karjo] *nm* curate.

vicepresidente [biθepresi'ðente] *nm/f* vice president.

viciado, a [bi'θjaðo, a] *a* (*corrompido*) corrupt; (*contaminado*) foul, contaminated; **viciar** (*pervertir*) to pervert; (*adulterar*) to adulterate; (*falsificar*) to falsify; (*JUR*) to nullify; (*estropear*) to spoil; (*sentido*) to twist; **viciarse** *vr* to become corrupted.

vicio ['biθjo] *nm* (*libertinaje*) vice; (*mala costumbre*) bad habit; (*mimo*) spoiling; (*alabeo*) warp, warping; ~**so, a** *a* (*muy malo*) vicious; (*corrompido*) depraved; (*mimado*) spoiled // *nm/f* depraved person.

vicisitud [biθisi'tuð] *nf* vicissitude.

víctima ['biktima] nf victim.
victoria [bik'torja] nf victory; **victorioso, a** a victorious.
vicuña [bi'kuɲa] nf vicuna.
vid [bið] nf vine.
vida ['biða] nf (gen) life; (duración) lifetime; **de por** ~ for life; **en la/mi** ~ never; **estar con** ~ to be still alive; **ganarse la** ~ to earn one's living.
vidriero, a [bi'ðrjero, a] nm/f glazier // nf (ventana) stained-glass window; (puerta) glass door.
vidrio ['biðrjo] nm glass; ~**so, a** a glassy; (frágil) fragile, brittle; (resbaladizo) slippery.
viejo, a ['bjexo, a] a old // nm/f old man/woman.
vienes etc vb ver **venir.**
vienés, esa [bje'nes, esa] a Viennese.
viento ['bjento] nm wind; (olfato) scent.
vientre ['bjentre] nm belly; (matriz) womb; ~**s** nmpl bowels.
viernes ['bjernes] nm inv Friday.
Vietnam [bjet'nam] nm: **el** ~ Vietnam; **vietnamita** a Vietnamese.
viga ['bixa] nf beam, rafter.
vigencia [bi'xenθja] nf validity; **estar en** ~ to be in force; **vigente** a valid, in force; (imperante) prevailing.
vigésimo, a [bi'xesimo, a] a twentieth.
vigía [bi'xia] nm look-out // nf (atalaya) watchtower; (acción) watching.
vigilancia [bixi'lanθja] nf vigilance; **vigilar** vt to watch over // vi (gen) to be vigilant; (hacer guardia) to keep watch.
vigilia [vi'xilja] nf wakefulness, being awake; (REL) fast; **comer de** ~ to fast.
vigor [bi'xor] nm vigour, vitality; **en** ~ in force; **entrar/poner en** ~ to take/put into effect; ~**oso, a** a vigorous.
vil [bil] a vile, low; ~**eza** nf vileness; (acto) base deed.
vilipendiar [bilipen'djar] vt to vilify, revile.
vilo ['bilo]: **en** ~ ad in the air, suspended.
villa ['biʎa] nf (pueblo) small town; (municipalidad) municipality.
villorrio [bi'ʎorrjo] nm one-horse town, dump (fam).
vinagre [bi'naxre] nm vinegar.
vinculación [binkula'θjon] nf (lazo) link, bond; (acción) linking; **vincular** vt to link, bind; **vínculo** nm link, bond.
vindicar [bindi'kar] vt to vindicate; (vengar) to avenge; (JUR) to claim.
vine etc vb ver **venir.**
vinicultura [binikul'tura] nf wine growing.
viniera etc vb ver **venir.**
vino ['bino] nm wine.
viña ['biɲa] nf, **viñedo** [bi'ɲeðo] nm vineyard.
violación [bjola'θjon] nf violation; ~ (**sexual**) rape; **violar** vt to violate; to rape.
violencia [bjo'lenθja] nf (fuerza) violence,

force; (embarazo) embarrassment; (acto injusto) unjust act; **violentar** vt to force; (casa) to break into; (agredir) to assault; (violar) to violate; **violento, a** a violent; (furioso) furious; (situación) embarrassing; (acto) forced, unnatural; (difícil) awkward.
violeta [bjo'leta] nf violet.
violín [bjo'lin] nm violin.
violón [bjo'lon] nm double bass.
viraje [bi'raxe] nm turn; (de vehículo) swerve; (de carretera) bend; (fig) change of direction; **virar** vt, vi to change direction.
virgen ['birxen] a, nf virgin.
Virgo ['birxo] nm Virgo.
viril [bi'ril] a virile; ~**idad** nf virility.
virtualmente [birtwal'mente] ad virtually.
virtud [bir'tuð] nf virtue; **virtuoso, a** a virtuous // nm/f virtuoso.
viruela [bi'rwela] nf smallpox; ~**s** nfpl pockmarks; ~**s locas** chickenpox.
virulento, a [biru'lento, a] a virulent.
virus ['birus] nm virus.
visado [bi'saðo] nm visa.
viscoso, a [bis'koso, a] a viscous.
visera [bi'sera] nf visor.
visibilidad [bisiβili'ðað] nf visibility; **visible** a visible; (fig) obvious.
visión [bi'sjon] nf (ANAT) vision, (eye)sight; (fantasía) vision, fantasy; (panorama) view; **visionario, a** a (que preve) visionary; (alucinado) deluded // nm/f visionary; (chalado) lunatic.
visita [bi'sita] nf call, visit; (persona) visitor; **visitar** vt to visit, call on; (inspeccionar) to inspect.
vislumbrar [bislum'brar] vt to glimpse, catch a glimpse of; **vislumbre** nf glimpse; (centelleo) gleam; (idea vaga) glimmer.
viso ['biso] nm (del metal) glint, gleam; (de tela) sheen; (aspecto) appearance.
visón [bi'son] nm mink.
visor [bi'sor] nm (FOTO) viewfinder.
víspera ['bispera] nf eve, day before.
vista ['bista] nf sight, vision; (capacidad de ver) (eye)sight; (mirada) look(s) (pl) // nm customs officer; **a primera** ~ at first glance; **hacer la** ~ **gorda** to turn a blind eye; **volver la** ~ to look back; **está a la** ~ **que** it's obvious that; **en** ~ **de** in view of; **en** ~ **de que** in view of the fact that; **¡hasta la** ~! so long!, see you!; **con** ~**s a** with a view to; ~**zo** nm glance; **dar** o **echar un** ~**zo a** to glance at.
visto etc vb ver **vestir.**
visto, a ['bisto, a] pp de ver // ~ seen; (considerado) considered // nm: ~ **bueno** approval; '~ **bueno**' approved; **por lo** ~ evidently; **está** ~ **que** it's clear that; **está bien/mal** ~ it's acceptable/unacceptable; ~ **que** conj since, considering that.
vistoso, a [bis'toso, a] a colourful; (alegre) gay; (pey) gaudy.
vital [bi'tal] a life cpd, living cpd; (fig) vital; (persona) lively, vivacious; ~**icio, a** a for life.

vitamina [bita'mina] *nf* vitamin.
viticultor, a [bitikul'tor, a] *nm/f* vine grower; **viticultura** *nf* vine growing.
vitorear [bitore'ar] *vt* to cheer, acclaim.
vítreo, a ['bitreo, a] *a* vitreous.
vitrina [bi'trina] *nf* glass case.
vituperar [bitupe'rar] *vt* to condemn; **vituperio** *nm* (*condena*) condemnation; (*censura*) censure; (*insulto*) insult.
viudo, a ['bjuðo, a] *nm/f* widower/widow; **viudez** *nf* widowhood.
vivacidad [biβaθi'ðað] *nf* (*vigor*) vigour; (*vida*) vivacity.
vivaracho, a [biβa'ratʃo, a] *a* jaunty, lively; (*ojos*) bright, twinkling.
vivaz [bi'βaθ] *a* (*que dura*) enduring; (*vigoroso*) vigorous; (*vivo*) lively.
víveres ['biβeres] *nmpl* provisions.
viveza [bi'βeθa] *nf* liveliness; (*agudeza*) sharpness.
vivienda [bi'βjenda] *nf* (*alojamiento*) housing; (*morada*) dwelling.
viviente [bi'βjente] *a* living.
vivificar [biβifi'kar] *vt* to give life to.
vivir [bi'βir] *vt*, *vi* to live // *nm* life, living.
vivo, a ['biβo, a] *a* living, live, alive; (*fig*) vivid; (*astuto*) smart, clever; **llegar a lo ~** to cut to the quick.
vocablo [bo'kaβlo] *nm* (*palabra*) word; (*término*) term.
vocabulario [bokaβu'larjo] *nm* vocabulary.
vocación [boka'θjon] *nf* vocation.
vocal [bo'kal] *a* vocal // *nf* vowel; **~izar** *vt* to vocalize.
vocear [boθe'ar] *vt* (*para vender*) to cry; (*aclamar*) to acclaim; (*fig*) to proclaim // *vi* to yell; **vocerío** *nm*, **vocería** *nf* shouting.
vocero [bo'θero] *nm/f* spokesman/woman.
vociferar [boθife'rar] *vt* to shout; (*jactarse*) to proclaim boastfully // *vi* to yell.
vocinglero, a [boθin'glero, a] *a* vociferous; (*gárrulo*) garrulous; (*fig*) blatant.
vodka ['boðka] *nf* vodka.
vol *abr de* **volumen.**
volador, a [bola'ðor, a] *a* flying.
volante [bo'lante] *a* flying // *nm* (*de máquina, coche*) steering wheel; (*de reloj*) balance.
volar [bo'lar] *vt* (*demolir*) to blow up, demolish // *vi* to fly.
volátil [bo'latil] *a* volatile; (*fig*) changeable.
volcán [bol'kan] *nm* volcano; **~ico, a** *a* volcanic.
volcar [bol'kar] *vt* to upset, overturn; (*tumbar, derribar*) to knock over; (*vaciar*) to empty out // *vi* to overturn; **~se** *vr* to tip over.
volibol [boli'βol] *nm* volleyball.
volición [boli'θjon] *nf* volition.
voltaje [bol'taxe] *nm* voltage.
volteador, a [boltea'ðor, a] *nm/f* acrobat.

voltear [bolte'ar] *vt* to turn over; (*volcar*) to turn upside down; (*doblar*) to peal // *vi* to roll over.
voltio ['boltjo] *nm* volt.
voluble [bo'luβle] *a* fickle.
volumen [bo'lumen] *nm* volume; **voluminoso, a** *a* voluminous; (*enorme*) massive.
voluntad [bolun'tað] *nf* will, willpower; (*deseo*) desire, wish; (*afecto*) fondness.
voluntario, a [bolun'tarjo, a] *a* voluntary // *nm/f* volunteer.
voluntarioso, a [bolunta'rjoso, a] *a* headstrong.
voluptuoso, a [bolup'twoso, a] *a* voluptuous.
volver [bol'βer] *vt* (*gen*) to turn; (*dar vuelta*) to turn (over); (*voltear*) to turn round, turn upside down; (*poner al revés*) to turn inside out; (*devolver*) to return; (*transformar*) to change, transform // *vi* to return, go/come back; **~se** *vr* to turn round; (*llegar a ser*) to become; **~ la espalda** to turn one's back; **~ bien por mal** to return good for evil; **~ a hacer** to do again; **~ en sí** to come to; **~se loco** to go mad.
vomitar [bomi'tar] *vt*, *vi* to vomit; **vómito** *nm* (*acto*) vomiting; (*resultado*) vomit.
voraz [bo'raθ] *a* voracious; (*fig*) fierce.
vórtice ['bortiθe] *nm* whirlpool; (*de aire*) whirlwind.
vosotros [bo'sotros] *pron* you.
votación [bota'θjon] *nf* (*acto*) voting; (*voto*) vote; **votar** *vi* to vote; **voto** *nm* vote; (*promesa*) vow; (*maldición*) oath, curse; **votos** (good) wishes.
voy *vb ver* **ir.**
voz [boθ] *nf* voice; (*grito*) shout; (*chisme*) rumour; (*LING*) word; **dar voces** to shout, yell; **a media ~** in a low voice; **a ~ en cuello** *o* **en grito** at the top of one's voice; **de viva ~** verbally; **en ~ alta** aloud; **~ de mando** command.
vuelco ['bwelko] *nm* spill, overturning; (*fig*) collapse.
vuelo ['bwelo] *vb ver* **voler** // *nm* flight; (*encaje*) lace, frill; (*fig*) importance; **coger al ~** to catch in flight.
vuelta ['bwelta] *nf* (*gen*) turn; (*curva*) bend, curve; (*regreso*) return; (*revolución*) revolution; (*paseo*) stroll; (*circuito*) lap; (*de papel, tela*) reverse; (*cambio*) change; **V~ de Francia** Tour de France; **~ cerrada** hairpin bend; **a la ~** on one's return; **a ~ de correo** by return of post; **dar ~s** to turn, revolve; **dar ~ a una idea** to turn over an idea (in one's head); **estar de ~** (*fam*) to be back; **dar una ~** to go for a walk.
vuelto *pp de* **volver.**
vuelvo *etc vb ver* **volver.**
vuestro, a ['bwestro, a] *a* your; **un amigo ~** a friend of yours // *pron*: **el ~/la ~/los ~s/las ~as** yours.
vulgar [bul'xar] *a* (*ordinario*) vulgar; (*común*) common; **~idad** *nf* commonness; (*acto*) vulgarity; (*expresión*) coarse

expression; ~**idades** *nfpl* banalities;
~**izar** *vt* to popularize.
vulgo ['bulxo] *nm* common people.
vulnerable [bulne'raßle] *a* vulnerable.
vulnerar [bulne'rar] *vt* to harm, damage.
vulpino, a [bul'pino, a] *a* vulpine; (*fig*) foxy.

W

wáter ['bater] *nm* lavatory.
wátman ['watman] *a inv* (*fam*) cool.
whisky ['wiski] *nm* whisky.

X

xenofobia [kseno'foßja] *nf* xenophobia.
xilófono [ksi'lofono] *nm* xylophone.

Y

y [i] *conj* and.
ya [ja] *ad* (*gen*) already; (*ahora*) now; (*en seguida*) at once; (*pronto*) soon // *excl* all right! // *conj* (*ahora que*) now that; ~ **lo sé** I know; ~ **dice que sí,** ~ **dice que no** first he says yes, then he says no; ~ **que** since.
yacer [ja'θer] *vi* to lie.
yacimiento [jaθi'mjento] *nm* bed, deposit.
yanqui ['janki] *a* Yankee.
yate ['jate] *nm* yacht.
yazco *etc vb ver* **yacer.**
yedra ['jeðra] *nf* ivy.
yegua ['jexwa] *nf* mare.
yema ['jema] *nf* (*del huevo*) yoke; (*BOT*) leaf bud; (*fig*) best part; ~ **del dedo** fingertip.
yergo *etc vb ver* **erguir.**
yermo, a ['jermo, a] *a* uninhabited // *nm* waste land.
yerno ['jerno] *nm* son-in-law.
yerro *etc vb ver* **errar.**
yerto, a ['jerto, a] *a* stiff.
yesca ['jeska] *nf* tinder.
yeso ['jeso] *nm* (*GEO*) gypsum; (*ARQ*) plaster.
yodo ['joðo] *nm* iodine.
yugo ['juxo] *nm* yoke.
Yugoslavia [juxos'laßja] *nf* Yugoslavia.
yugular [juxu'lar] *a* jugular.
yunque ['junke] *nm* anvil.
yunta ['junta] *nf* yoke; **yuntero** *nm* ploughman.
yute ['jute] *nm* jute.
yuxtaponer [jukstapo'ner] *vt* to juxtapose; **yuxtaposición** *nf* juxtaposition.

Z

zafar [θa'far] *vt* (*soltar*) to untie; (*superficie*) to clear; ~**se** *vr* (*escaparse*) to escape; (*ocultarse*) to hide o.s. away; (*TEC*) to slip off.
zafio, a ['θafjo, a] *a* coarse.

zafiro [θa'firo] *nm* sapphire.
zaga ['θaxa] *nf* rear; **a la** ~ behind, in the rear.
zagal, a [θa'xal, a] *nm/f* boy/girl, lad/lass.
zaguán [θa'xwan] *nm* hallway.
zahareño, a [θaa'reɲo, a] *a* (*salvaje*) wild; (*arisco*) unsociable.
zaherir [θae'rir] *vt* (*criticar*) to criticize; (*fig: herir*) to wound.
zahorí [θao'ri] *nm* clairvoyant.
zaino, a ['θaino, a] *a* (*color de caballo*) chestnut; (*pérfido*) treacherous; (*animal*) vicious.
zalameria [θala'merja] *nf* flattery; **zalamero, a** *a* flattering; (*relamido*) suave.
zamarra [θa'marra] *nf* (*piel*) sheepskin; (*saco*) sheepskin jacket.
zambra ['θambra] *nf* gypsy dance.
zambullirse [θambu'ʎirse] *vr* to dive; (*ocultarse*) to hide o.s.
zampar [θam'par] *vt* (*esconder*) to hide *or* put away (hurriedly); (*comer*) to gobble; (*arrojar*) to hurl // *vi* to eat voraciously; ~**se** *vr* (*chocar*) to bump; (*fig*) to gatecrash.
zanahoria [θana'orja] *nf* carrot.
zancada [θan'kaða] *nf* stride.
zancadilla [θanka'ðiʎa] *nf* trip; (*fig*) stratagem.
zancajo [θan'kaxo] *nm* (*ANAT*) heel; (*fig*) dwarf.
zanco ['θanko] *nm* stilt.
zancudo, a [θan'kuðo, a] *a* long-legged // *nm* (*AM*) mosquito.
zángano [θ'angano] *nm* drone.
zanja ['θanxa] *nf* (*fosa*) ditch; (*tumba*) grave; **zanjar** *vt* (*fosa*) to ditch, trench; (*problema*) to surmount; (*conflicto*) to resolve.
zapapico [θapa'piko] *nm* pick, pickaxe.
zapata [θa'pata] *nf* half-boot; (*MECÁNICA*) shoe.
zapatear [θapate'ar] *vt* (*tocar*) to tap with one's foot; (*patear*) to kick; (*fam*) to ill-treat // *vi* to tap with one's feet.
zapatería [θapate'ria] *nf* (*oficio*) shoemaking; (*tienda*) shoe-shop; (*fábrica*) shoe factory; **zapatero, a** *nm/f* shoemaker.
zapatilla [θapa'tiʎa] *nf* slipper.
zapato [θa'pato] *nm* shoe.
zarabanda [θara'ßanda] *nf* saraband; (*fig*) whirl.
zaranda [θa'randa] *nf* sieve; **zarandear** *vt* to sieve; (*fam*) to shake vigorously.
zarcillo [θar'θiʎo] *nm* earring.
zarpa ['θarpa] *nf* (*garra*) claw.
zarpar [θar'par] *vi* to weigh anchor.
zarza ['θarθa] *nf* (*BOT*) bramble; **zarzal** *nm* (*matorral*) bramble patch.
zarzamora [θarθa'mora] *nf* blackberry.
zarzuela [θar'θwela] *nf* Spanish light opera.
zigzag [θix'θax] *a* zigzag; **zigzaguear** *vi* to zigzag.

zinc [θink] *nm* zinc.

zócalo ['θokalo] *nm* (ARQ) plinth, base.

zona ['θona] *nf* zone; ~ **fronteriza** border area.

zoología [θoolo'xia] *nf* zoology; **zoológico, a** *a* zoological // *nm* zoo; **zoólogo, a** *nm/f* zoologist.

zopilote [θopi'lote] *nm* (AM) buzzard.

zoquete [θo'kete] *nm* (*madera*) block; (*pan*) crust; (*fam*) blockhead.

zorro, a ['θorro, a] *a* crafty // *nm/f* fox/vixen.

zozobra [θo'θoβra] *nf* (*fig*) anxiety; **zozobrar** *vi* (*hundirse*) to capsize; (*fig*) to fail.

zueco ['θweko] *nm* clog.

zumbar [θum'bar] *vt* (*burlar*) to tease; (*golpear*) to hit // *vi* to buzz; (*fam*) to be very close; ~**se** *vr*: ~**se de** to tease; **zumbido** *nm* buzzing; (*fam*) punch.

zumo ['θumo] *nm* juice; (*ganancia*) profit.

zurcir [θur'θir] *vt* (*coser*) to darn; (*fig*) to put together.

zurdo, a ['θurðo, a] *a* (*mano*) left; (*persona*) left-handed.

zurrar [θu'rrar] *vt* (TEC) to dress; (*fam*: *pegar duro*) to wallop; (: *aplastar*) to flatten; (: *criticar*) to criticize harshly.

zurriago [θu'rrjaɣo] *nm* whip, lash.

zurrón [θu'rron] *nm* pouch.

zutano, a [θu'tano, a] *nm/f* so-and-so.

ENGLISH - SPANISH
INGLÉS - ESPAÑOL

A

a, an [eɪ, ə, æn, ən, n] *det* un(a); **3 a day/week** 3 por día/semana; **10 km an hour** 10 km por hora.

A.A. *n abbr of* **Automobile Association; Alcoholics Anonymous.**

aback [ə'bæk] *ad*: **to be taken** ~ quedar desconcertado.

abandon [ə'bændən] *vt* abandonar; (*renounce*) renunciar a // *n* abandono; (*wild behaviour*) desenfreno.

abashed [ə'bæʃt] *a* avergonzado, confuso.

abate [ə'beɪt] *vi* moderarse; (*lessen*) disminuir; (*calm down*) calmarse.

abattoir ['æbətwɑː*] *n* matadero.

abbey ['æbɪ] *n* monasterio.

abbot ['æbət] *n* abad *m*.

abbreviate [ə'briːvɪeɪt] *vt* abreviar; **abbreviation** [-'eɪʃən] *n* (*short form*) abreviatura; (*act*) abreviación *f*.

abdicate ['æbdɪkeɪt] *vt, vi* abdicar; **abdication** [-'keɪʃən] *n* abdicación *f*.

abdomen ['æbdəmən] *n* abdomen *m*.

abduct [æb'dʌkt] *vt* raptar, secuestrar; ~**ion** [-'dʌkʃən] *n* rapto, secuestro.

aberration [æbə'reɪʃən] *n* aberración *f*.

abet [ə'bet] *vt* (*incite*) incitar; (*aid*) ser cómplice de.

abeyance [ə'beɪəns] *n*: **in** ~ (*law*) en desuso; (*matter*) en suspenso.

abhor [əb'hɔː*] *vt* aborrecer, abominar (de); ~**rent** *a* aborrecible, detestable.

abide [ə'baɪd], *pt, pp* **abode** *or* **abided** *vt* aguantar, soportar; **to** ~ **by** *vt fus* atenerse a.

ability [ə'bɪlɪtɪ] *n* habilidad *f*, capacidad *f*; (*talent*) talento.

ablaze [ə'bleɪz] *a* en llamas, ardiendo.

able ['eɪbl] *a* capaz; (*skilled*) hábil; **to be** ~ **to do sth** poder hacer algo; ~**-bodied** *a* sano; **ably** *ad* hábilmente.

abnormal [æb'nɔːmǝl] *a* anormal; ~**ity** [-'mælɪtɪ] *n* anormalidad *f*.

aboard [ə'bɔːd] *ad* a bordo // *prep* a bordo de.

abode [ə'bəud] *pt, pp of* **abide** // *n* domicilio.

abolish [ə'bɔlɪʃ] *vt* suprimir, abolir; **abolition** [æbəu'lɪʃən] *n* supresión *f*, abolición *f*.

abominable [ə'bɔmɪnəbl] *a* abominable.

aborigine [æbə'rɪdʒɪnɪ] *n* aborigen *m*.

abort [ə'bɔːt] *vt* abortar; ~**ion** [ə'bɔːʃən] *n* aborto (provocado); **to have an** ~**ion** abortarse, hacerse abortar; ~**ive** *a* fracasado.

abound [ə'baund] *vi* abundar.

about [ə'baut] *prep* (*subject*) acerca de, sobre; (*place*) alrededor de, por // *ad* casi, más o menos, a eso de; **to walk** ~ **the town** andar por la ciudad; **it takes** ~ **10 hours** es cosa de 10 horas más o menos; **at** ~ **2 o'clock** a eso de las 2; **to be** ~ **to** estar a punto de; **what** *or* **how** ~ **doing this?** ¿qué tal si hacemos esto?; ~ **turn** *n* media vuelta.

above [ə'bʌv] *ad* encima, por encima, arriba // *prep* encima de; **mentioned** ~ susodicho; ~ **all** sobre todo; ~ **board** *a* legítimo.

abrasion [ə'breɪʒən] *n* (*on skin*) abrasión *f*; **abrasive** [ə'breɪzɪv] *a* abrasivo.

abreast [ə'brest] *ad* de frente; **to keep** ~ **of** mantenerse al corriente de.

abridge [ə'brɪdʒ] *vt* abreviar.

abroad [ə'brɔːd] *ad* (*to be*) en el extranjero; (*to go*) al extranjero.

abrupt [ə'brʌpt] *a* (*sudden*) brusco; (*gruff*) áspero.

abscess ['æbsɪs] *n* absceso.

abscond [əb'skɔnd] *vi* fugarse.

absence ['æbsəns] *n* ausencia.

absent ['æbsənt] *a* ausente; ~**ee** [-'tiː] *n* ausente *m/f*; ~**eeism** [-'tiːɪzəm] *n* absentismo; ~**-minded** *a* distraído.

absolute ['æbsəluːt] *a* absoluto; ~**ly** [-'luːtlɪ] *ad* absolutamente.

absolve [əb'zɔlv] *vt*: **to** ~ **sb (from)** absolver a alguien (de).

absorb [əb'zɔːb] *vt* absorber; **to be** ~**ed in a book** estar absorto en un libro; ~**ent** *a* absorbente; ~**ing** *a* absorbente.

abstain [əb'steɪn] *vi*: **to** ~ **(from)** abstenerse (de).

abstention [əb'stɛnʃən] *n* abstención *f*.

abstinence ['æbstɪnəns] *n* abstinencia.

abstract ['æbstrækt] *a* abstracto.

absurd [əb'sɔːd] *a* absurdo; ~**ity** *n* absurdo.

abundance [ə'bʌndəns] *n* abundancia; **abundant** [-dənt] *a* abundante.

abuse [ə'bjuːs] *n* (*insults*) improperios *mpl*, injurias *fpl*; (*misuse*) abuso // *vt* [ə'bjuːz] (*ill-treat*) maltratar; (*take advantage of*) abusar de; **abusive** *a* ofensivo.

abysmal [ə'bɪzmǝl] *a* abismal; (*ignorance etc*) profundo.

abyss [ə'bɪs] *n* abismo.

academic [ækə'dɛmɪk] *a* académico, universitario; (*pej: issue*) puramente teórico.

academy [ə'kædəmɪ] *n* (*learned body*) academia; (*school*) instituto, colegio.

accede [æk'siːd] *vi*: **to** ~ **to** (*request*) consentir en; (*throne*) subir a.

accelerate [æk'sɛləreɪt] vt acelerar // vi
acelerarse; **acceleration** [-'reɪʃən] n
aceleración f; **accelerator** n acelerador
m.

accent ['æksɛnt] n acento.

accept [ək'sɛpt] vt aceptar; (approve)
aprobar; (permit) admitir; ~**able** a
aceptable; admisible; ~**ance** n
aceptación f; aprobación f.

access ['æksɛs] n acceso; **to have** ~ **to**
tener libre acceso a; ~**ible** [-'sɛsəbl] a
accesible.

accessory [æk'sɛsərɪ] n accesorio; **toilet
accessories** npl artículos mpl de tocador.

accident ['æksɪdənt] n accidente m;
(chance) casualidad f; **by** ~
(unintentionally) sin querer; (by
coincidence) por casualidad; ~**al** [-'dɛntl]
a accidental, fortuito; ~**ally** [-'dɛntəlɪ] ad
sin querer; por casualidad; ~-**prone** a
con tendencia a sufrir/causar accidentes.

acclaim [ə'kleɪm] vt aclamar, aplaudir //
n aclamación f, aplausos mpl.

acclimatize [ə'klaɪmətaɪz] vt: **to become**
~**d** aclimatarse.

accommodate [ə'kɔmədeɪt] vt alojar,
hospedar; (reconcile) componer; (oblige,
help) complacer; (adapt): **to** ~ **one's
plans to** acomodar sus proyectos a;
accommodating a servicial, complaciente.

accommodation [əkɔmə'deɪʃən] n
alojamiento; (space) sitio.

accompaniment [ə'kʌmpənɪmənt] n
acompañamiento; **accompany** [-nɪ] vt
acompañar.

accomplice [ə'kʌmplɪs] n cómplice m/f.

accomplish [ə'kʌmplɪʃ] vt (finish) acabar,
alcanzar; (achieve) realizar, llevar a cabo;
~**ed** a experto, hábil; ~**ment** n (ending)
conclusión f; (bringing about) realización f;
(skill) talento.

accord [ə'kɔ:d] n acuerdo // vt concordar;
of his own ~ espontáneamente; ~**ance**
n: **in** ~**ance with** de acuerdo con; ~**ing
to** prep según; (in accordance with)
conforme a; ~**ingly** ad (thus) por
consiguiente.

accordion [ə'kɔ:dɪən] n acordeón m.

accost [ə'kɔst] vt abordar, dirigirse a.

account [ə'kaunt] n (COMM) cuenta,
factura; (report) informe m; **of little** ~
de poca importancia; **on** ~ a cuenta; **on
no** ~ de ninguna manera, bajo ningún
concepto; **on** ~ **of** a causa de, por motivo
de; **to take into** ~, **take** ~ **of** tomar o
tener en cuenta; **to** ~ **for** vt (answer for)
responder de; (explain) dar cuenta o razón
de; ~**able** a responsable.

accountancy [ə'kauntənsɪ] n contabilidad
f; **accountant** [-tənt] n contador/a m/f.

accumulate [ə'kju:mjuleɪt] vt acumular
// vi acumularse; **accumulation** [-'leɪʃən]
n acumulación f.

accuracy ['ækjurəsɪ] n exactitud f,
precisión f; **accurate** [-rɪt] a (number)
exacto; (answer) acertado; (shot) certero.

accusation [ækju'zeɪʃən] n acusación f;
accuse [ə'kju:z] vt acusar; (blame) echar
la culpa a; **accused** [ə'kju:zd] n acusado/a.

accustom [ə'kʌstəm] vt acostumbrar;
~**ed** a: ~**ed to** acostumbrado a.

ace [eɪs] n as m.

ache [eɪk] n dolor m // vi doler; **my head**
~**s** me duele la cabeza.

achieve [ə'tʃi:v] vt (reach) alcanzar;
(realize) llevar a cabo; (victory, success)
lograr, conseguir; ~**ment** n (completion)
realización f; (success) éxito.

acid ['æsɪd] a ácido; (bitter) agrio // n
ácido; ~**ity** [ə'sɪdɪtɪ] n acidez f; (MED)
acedía.

acknowledge [ək'nɔlɪdʒ] vt (letter)
acusar recibo de; (fact) reconocer;
~**ment** n acuse m de recibo;
reconocimiento.

acne ['æknɪ] n acné m.

acorn ['eɪkɔ:n] n bellota.

acoustic [ə'ku:stɪk] a acústico; ~**s** n, npl
acústica sg.

acquaint [ə'kweɪnt] vt: **to** ~ **sb with sth**
(warn) avisar a uno de algo; (inform)
poner a uno al corriente de algo; **to be**
~**ed with** (person) conocer; (fact) estar
al corriente de; ~**ance** n conocimiento;
(person) conocido/a.

acquiesce [ækwɪ'ɛs] vi: **to** ~ **in** consentir
en, conformarse con.

acquire [ə'kwaɪə*] vt adquirir; (achieve)
conseguir; **acquisition** [ækwɪ'zɪʃən] n
adquisición f; **acquisitive** [ə'kwɪzɪtɪv] a
codicioso.

acquit [ə'kwɪt] vt absolver, exculpar; **to** ~
o.s. well defenderse, salir con éxito; ~**tal**
n absolución f, exculpación f.

acre ['eɪkə*] n acre m.

acrimonious [ækrɪ'məunɪəs] a (remark)
mordaz; (argument) reñido.

acrobat ['ækrəbæt] n acróbata m/f; ~**ics**
[ækrəu'bætɪks] n, npl acrobacia sg.

across [ə'krɔs] prep (on the other side of) al
otro lado de, del otro lado de; (crosswise) a
través de // ad de un lado a otro, de una
parte a otra; a través, al través; **to
run/swim** ~ atravesar corriendo/na-
dando; ~ **from** enfrente de.

act [ækt] n acto, acción f; (THEATRE) acto;
(in music-hall etc) número; (LAW) decreto,
ley f // vi (machine) funcionar, marchar;
(person) actuar, comportarse; (THEATRE)
actuar, trabajar; (pretend) fingir; (take
action) obrar // vt (part) hacer el papel
de, representar; **to** ~ **as** actuar o hacer
de; ~**ing** a suplente // n: **to do some**
~**ing** ser actor/actriz.

action ['ækʃən] n acción f, acto; (MIL)
acción f, batalla; (LAW) proceso, demanda;
to take ~ tomar medidas.

activate ['æktɪveɪt] vt (mechanism)
activar.

active ['æktɪv] a activo, enérgico;
(volcano) en actividad; **activity** [-'tɪvɪtɪ] n
actividad f.

actor ['æktə*] n actor m; **actress** [-trɪs] n actriz f.
actual ['æktjuəl] a verdadero, real; ~ly ad realmente, en realidad.
acupuncture ['ækjupʌŋktʃə*] n acupuntura.
acute [ə'kju:t] a (gen) agudo.
ad [æd] n abbr of **advertisement**.
A.D. ad abbr of **Anno Domini** A.C. (año de Cristo).
Adam ['ædəm] n Adán; ~'s **apple** n nuez f de la garganta.
adamant ['ædəmənt] a firme, inflexible.
adapt [ə'dæpt] vt adaptar; (reconcile) acomodar // vi: **to ~ (to)** adaptarse (a), ajustarse (a); ~**able** a (device) adaptable; (person) que se adapta; ~**ation** [ædæp-'teɪʃən] n adaptación f; ~**er** n (ELEC) adaptador m.
add [æd] vt añadir, agregar; (figures: also: ~ **up**) sumar // vi: **to ~ to** (increase) aumentar, acrecentar; **it doesn't ~ up** no tiene sentido.
adder ['ædə*] n víbora.
addict ['ædɪkt] n (enthusiast) entusiasta m/f; (to drugs etc) adicto/a; ~**ed** [ə'dɪktɪd] a: **to be ~ed to** ser aficionado de; ser adicto a; **addiction** [ə'dɪkʃən] n (enthusiasm) afición f; (dependence) hábito morboso.
adding machine ['ædɪŋməʃi:n] n calculadora.
addition [ə'dɪʃən] n (adding up) adición f; (thing added) añadidura, añadido; **in ~** además, por añadidura; **in ~ to** además de; ~**al** a adicional.
additive ['ædɪtɪv] n aditivo.
address [ə'drɛs] n dirección f, señas fpl; (speech) discurso // vt (letter) dirigir; (speak to) dirigirse a, dirigir la palabra a; ~**ee** [ædrɛ'si:] n destinatario/a.
adenoids ['ædɪnɔɪdz] npl vegetaciones fpl adenoideas.
adept ['ædɛpt] a: ~ **at** experto o hábil en.
adequate ['ædɪkwɪt] a (apt) adecuado; (enough) suficiente.
adhere [əd'hɪə*] vi: **to ~ to** pegarse a; (fig: abide by) observar; (: hold to) adherirse a; **adherent** n partidario/a.
adhesive [əd'hi:zɪv] a, n adhesivo.
adjacent [ə'dʒeɪsənt] a: ~ **to** contiguo a, inmediato a.
adjective ['ædʒɛktɪv] n adjetivo.
adjoining [ə'dʒɔɪnɪŋ] a contiguo, vecino.
adjourn [ə'dʒɜ:n] vt aplazar; (session) suspender, levantar // vi suspenderse.
adjudicate [ə'dʒu:dɪkeɪt] vi sentenciar; **adjudicator** n juez m, árbitro.
adjust [ə'dʒʌst] vt (change) modificar; (arrange) arreglar; (machine) ajustar // vi: **to ~ (to)** adaptarse (a); ~**able** a ajustable; ~**ment** n modificación f; arreglo; (of prices, wages) ajuste m.
adjutant ['ædʒətənt] n ayudante m.
ad-lib [æd'lɪb] vt, vi improvisar; **ad lib** ad a voluntad, a discreción.
administer [əd'mɪnɪstə*] vt proporcionar;

(justice) administrar; **administration** [-'treɪʃən] n administración f; (government) gobierno; **administrative** [-trətɪv] a administrativo; **administrator** [-treɪtə*] n administrador/a m/f.
admirable ['ædmərəbl] a admirable.
admiral ['ædmərəl] n almirante m; **A~ty** n Ministerio de Marina, Almirantazgo.
admiration [ædmə'reɪʃən] n admiración f.
admire [əd'maɪə*] vt admirar; **admirer** n admirador/a m/f; (suitor) pretendiente m.
admission [əd'mɪʃən] n (entry) entrada; (enrolment) ingreso; (confession) confesión f.
admit [əd'mɪt] vt dejar entrar, dar entrada a; (permit) admitir; (acknowledge) reconocer; (accept) aceptar; **to ~ to** confesarse culpable de; ~**tance** n entrada; ~**tedly** ad de acuerdo que.
admonish [əd'mɔnɪʃ] vt amonestar; (advise) aconsejar.
ado [ə'du:] n: **without (any) more ~** sin más (ni más).
adolescence [ædəu'lɛsns] n adolescencia; **adolescent** [-'lɛsnt] a, n adolescente m/f.
adopt [ə'dɔpt] vt adoptar; ~**ion** [ə'dɔpʃən] n adopción f; ~**ed** a adoptivo.
adore [ə'dɔ:*] vt adorar.
adorn [ə'dɔ:n] vt adornar.
adrenalin [ə'drɛnəlɪn] n adrenalina.
Adriatic [eɪdrɪ'ætɪk] n: **the ~ (Sea)** el (Mar) Adriático.
adrift [ə'drɪft] ad a la deriva; **to come ~** desprenderse.
adult ['ædʌlt] n (gen) adulto.
adulterate [ə'dʌltəreɪt] vt adulterar.
adultery [ə'dʌltərɪ] n adulterio.
advance [əd'vɑ:ns] n (gen) adelanto, progreso; (money) anticipo, préstamo; (MIL) avance m // vt avanzar, adelantar; anticipar, prestar // vi avanzar, adelantarse; **in ~** por adelantado; ~**d** a avanzado; (SCOL: studies) adelantado; ~**d in years** entrado en años; ~**ment** n progreso; (in rank) ascenso.
advantage [əd'vɑ:ntɪdʒ] n (also TENNIS) ventaja; **to take ~ of** (use) aprovecharse de; (gain by) sacar partido de; ~**ous** [ædvən'teɪdʒəs] a ventajoso, provechoso.
advent ['ædvənt] n advenimiento; **A~** Adviento.
adventure [əd'vɛntʃə*] n aventura; **adventurous** [-tʃərəs] a aventurero.
adverb ['ædvə:b] n adverbio.
adversary ['ædvəsərɪ] n adversario, contrario.
adverse ['ædvə:s] a adverso, contrario; ~ **to** adverso a.
adversity [əd'və:sɪtɪ] n infortunio.
advert ['ædvə:t] n abbr of **advertisement**.
advertise ['ædvətaɪz] vi hacer propaganda; (in newspaper etc) poner un anuncio // vt anunciar; ~**ment** [əd-'və:tɪsmənt] n (COMM) anuncio; **advertising** n publicidad f, propaganda; anuncios mpl.

advice [əd'vaɪs] *n* consejo, consejos *mpl*; (*notification*) aviso; **to take legal** ~ consultar a un abogado.
advisable [əd'vaɪzəbl] *a* aconsejable, conveniente.
advise [əd'vaɪz] *vt* aconsejar; (*inform*) avisar; **adviser** *n* consejero; (*business adviser*) asesor *m*; **advisory** *a* consultivo.
advocate ['ædvəkeɪt] *vt* (*argue for*) abogar por; (*give support to*) ser partidario de // *n* [-kɪt] abogado.
aerial ['ɛərɪəl] *n* antena // *a* aéreo.
aeroplane ['ɛərəpleɪn] *n* avión *m*.
aerosol ['ɛərəsɔl] *n* aerosol *m*.
aesthetic [iːs'θɛtɪk] *a* estético.
afar [ə'fɑ:*] *ad*: **from** ~ desde lejos.
affable ['æfəbl] *a* afable.
affair [ə'fɛə*] *n* asunto; (*also*: **love** ~) aventura *o* relación *f* (amorosa).
affect [ə'fɛkt] *vt* afectar, influir en; (*move*) conmover; ~**ation** [æfɛk'teɪʃən] *n* afectación *f*; ~**ed** *a* afectado.
affection [ə'fɛkʃən] *n* afecto, cariño; ~**ate** *a* afectuoso, cariñoso.
affiliated [ə'fɪlɪeɪtɪd] *a* afiliado.
affinity [ə'fɪnɪtɪ] *n* afinidad *f*.
affirmation [æfə'meɪʃən] *n* afirmación *f*.
affirmative [ə'fɔ:mətɪv] *a* afirmativo.
affix [ə'fɪks] *vt* (*signature*) poner, añadir; (*stamp*) pegar.
afflict [ə'flɪkt] *vt* afligir; ~**ion** [ə'flɪkʃən] *n* enfermedad *f*, aflicción *f*.
affluence ['æfluəns] *n* opulencia, riqueza; **affluent** [-ənt] *a* opulento, acaudalado.
afford [ə'fɔ:d] *vt* (*provide*) dar, proporcionar; **can we** ~ **it?** ¿tenemos bastante dinero para comprarlo?
affront [ə'frʌnt] *n* afrenta, ofensa.
afield [ə'fiːld] *ad*: **far** ~ muy lejos.
afloat [ə'fləut] *ad* (*floating*) a flote; (*at sea*) en el mar.
afoot [ə'fut] *ad*: **there is something** ~ algo se está tramando.
aforesaid [ə'fɔ:sɛd] *a* susodicho.
afraid [ə'freɪd] *a*: **to be** ~ **of** (*person*) tener miedo a; (*thing*) tener miedo de; **to be** ~ **to** tener miedo de, temer; **I am** ~ **that** me temo que.
afresh [ə'frɛʃ] *ad* de nuevo, otra vez.
Africa ['æfrɪkə] *n* África; ~**n** *a*, *n* africano/a.
aft [ɑːft] *ad* (*to be*) en popa; (*to go*) a popa.
after ['ɑːftə*] *prep* (*time*) después de; (*place, order*) detrás de, tras // *ad* después // *conj* después (de) que; **what/who are you** ~? ¿qué/a quién busca Usted?; **to ask** ~ **sb** preguntar por alguien; ~ **all** después de todo, al fin y al cabo; ~ **you!** ¡pase Usted!; ~**birth** *n* secundinas *fpl*; ~**-effects** *npl* consecuencias *fpl*, efectos *mpl*; ~**life** *n* vida futura; ~**math** *n* consecuencias *fpl*, resultados *mpl*; ~**noon** *n* tarde *f*; ~**-shave** (**lotion**) *n* loción *f* para después del afeitado; ~**thought** *n* ocurrencia (tardía); ~**wards** *ad* después, más tarde.

again [ə'gɛn] *ad* otra vez, de nuevo; **to do sth** ~ volver a hacer algo; ~ **and** ~ una y otra vez; **now and** ~ de vez en cuando.
against [ə'gɛnst] *prep* (*opposed*) contra, en contra de; (*close to*) contra, junto a.
age [eɪdʒ] *n* (*gen*) edad *f*; (*old* ~) vejez *f*; (*period*) época // *vi* envejecer(se) // *vt* envejecer; **to come of** ~ llegar a la mayoría de edad; **it's been** ~**s since** hace muchísimo tiempo que; ~**d** *a* ['eɪdʒɪd] viejo, anciano // *a* [eɪdʒd]: ~**d 10** de 10 años de edad; ~ **group** *n*: **to be in the same** ~ **group** tener la misma edad; ~**less** *a* (*eternal*) eterno; (*ever young*) siempre joven; ~ **limit** *n* edad mínima/máxima.
agency ['eɪdʒənsɪ] *n* agencia; **through** *or* **by the** ~ **of** por medio de.
agenda [ə'dʒɛndə] *n* orden *m* del día.
agent ['eɪdʒənt] *n* (*gen*) agente *m/f*; (*representative*) representante *m/f*, delegado/a.
aggravate ['ægrəveɪt] *vt* agravar; (*annoy*) irritar, exasperar; **aggravation** [-'veɪʃən] *n* agravación *f*.
aggregate ['ægrɪgeɪt] *n* (*whole*) conjunto; (*collection*) agregado.
aggression [ə'grɛʃən] *n* agresión *f*; **aggressive** [ə'grɛsɪv] *a* agresivo; (*zealous*) enérgico.
aggrieved [ə'griːvd] *a* ofendido, agraviado.
aghast [ə'gɑːst] *a* horrorizado; **to be** ~ pasmarse.
agile ['ædʒaɪl] *a* ágil.
agitate ['ædʒɪteɪt] *vt* (*shake*) agitar; (*trouble*) inquietar; **to** ~ **for** hacer campaña pro *o* en favor de; **agitator** *n* agitador/a *m/f*.
ago [ə'gəu] *ad*: **2 days** ~ hace 2 días; **not long** ~ hace poco; **how long** ~? ¿hace cuánto tiempo?
agog [ə'gɔg] *a* (*anxious*) ansiado; (*excited*) emocionado.
agonizing ['ægənaɪzɪŋ] *a* (*pain*) atroz, agudo; (*suspense*) angustioso.
agony ['ægənɪ] *n* (*pain*) dolor *m* agudo; (*distress*) angustia; **to be in** ~ sufrir atrozmente.
agree [ə'griː] *vt* (*price*) acordar, quedar en // *vi* (*statements etc*) coincidir, concordar; **to** ~ (**with**) (*person*) estar de acuerdo (con), ponerse de acuerdo (con); **to** ~ **to do** aceptar hacer; **to** ~ **to sth** consentir en algo; **to** ~ **that** (*admit*) estar de acuerdo en que; **garlic doesn't** ~ **with me** el ajo no me sienta bien; ~**able** *a* agradable; (*person*) simpático; (*willing*) de acuerdo, conforme; ~**d** *a* (*time, place*) convenido; ~**ment** *n* acuerdo; (*COMM*) contrato; **in** ~**ment** de acuerdo, conforme.
agricultural [ægrɪ'kʌltʃərəl] *a* agrícola; **agriculture** ['ægrɪkʌltʃə*] *n* agricultura.
aground [ə'graund] *ad*: **to run** ~ encallar, embarrancar.
ahead [ə'hɛd] *ad* delante; ~ **of** delante de;

(*fig*: *schedule etc*) antes de; ~ **of time** antes de la hora; **to be** ~ **of sb** (*fig*) llevar la ventaja a alguien; **go right** *or* **straight** ~ ¡siga adelante!

aid [eid] *n* ayuda, auxilio // *vt* ayudar, auxiliar; **in** ~ **of** a beneficio de; **to** ~ **and abet** (*LAW*) ser cómplice de.

aide [eid] *n* (*person*) edecán *m*.

ailment ['eilmənt] *n* enfermedad *f*, achaque *m*.

aim [eim] *vt* (*gun, camera*) apuntar; (*missile, remark*) dirigir; (*blow*) asestar // *vi* (*also*: **take** ~) apuntar // *n* puntería; (*objective*) propósito, meta; **to** ~ **at** (*objective*) aspirar a, pretender; **to** ~ **to do** tener la intención de hacer; ~**less** sin propósito, sin objeto; ~**lessly** *ad* a la ventura, a la deriva.

air [ɛɔ*] *n* aire *m*; (*appearance*) aspecto // *vt* ventilar; (*grievances, ideas*) airear // *cpd* (*currents, attack etc*) aéreo, aeronáutico; ~**borne** *a* (*in the air*) en el aire; (*MIL*) aerotransportado; ~**-conditioned** *a* con aire acondicionado; ~ **conditioning** *n* aire acondicionado; ~**craft** *n*, *pl inv* avión *m*; ~**craft carrier** *n* portaaviones *m inv*; **A**~ **Force** *n* Fuerzas Aéreas *fpl*, aviación *f*; ~**gun** *n* escopeta de aire comprimido; ~ **hostess** *n* azafata; ~ **letter** *n* carta aérea; ~**lift** *n* puente *m* aéreo; ~**line** *n* línea aérea; ~**liner** *n* avión *m* de pasajeros; ~**lock** *n* esclusa de aire; ~**mail** *n*: **by** ~**mail** por avión; ~**port** *n* aeropuerto; ~ **raid** *n* ataque *m* aéreo; ~**sick** *a*: **to be** ~**sick** marearse (en un avión); ~**strip** *n* pista de aterrizaje; ~**tight** *a* hermético; ~**y** *a* (*room*) bien ventilado; (*manners*) ligero.

aisle [ail] *n* (*of church*) nave *f*; (*of theatre*) pasillo.

ajar [ə'dʒɑ:*] *a* entreabierto.

akin [ə'kin] *a*: ~ **to** relacionado con.

alarm [ə'lɑ:m] *n* alarma; (*anxiety*) inquietud *f* // *vt* asustar, inquietar; ~ **clock** *n* despertador *m*.

Albania [æl'beiniə] *n* Albania.

album ['ælbəm] *n* álbum *m*; (*L.P.*) elepé *m*.

alcohol ['ælkəhɔl] *n* alcohol *m*; ~**ic** [-'hɔlik] *a*, *n* alcohólico/a; ~**ism** *n* alcoholismo.

alcove ['ælkəuv] *n* nicho, hueco.

alderman ['ɔːldəmən] *n*, *pl* **-men** concejal *m*.

ale [eil] *n* cerveza.

alert [ə'lɔːt] *a* alerta; (*sharp*) despierto, despabilado // *n* alerta *m*, alarma // *vt* poner sobre aviso; **to be on the** ~ estar alerta *o* sobre aviso.

algebra ['ældʒibrə] *n* álgebra.

Algeria [æl'dʒiəriə] *n* Argelia; ~**n** *a*, *n* argelino/a.

alias ['eiliəs] *ad* alias, por otro nombre // *n* alias *m*.

alibi ['ælibai] *n* coartada.

alien ['eiliən] *n* extranjero/a // *a*: ~ **to** distinto de, ajeno a; ~**ate** *vt* enajenar, alejar; ~**ation** [-'neiʃən] *n* enajenación *f*.

alight [ə'lait] *a* ardiendo, quemando // *vi* apearse, bajar.

align [ə'lain] *vt* alinear; ~**ment** *n* alineación *f*.

alike [ə'laik] *a* semejantes, iguales // *ad* igualmente, del mismo modo; **to look** ~ parecerse.

alimony ['æliməni] *n* (*payment*) alimentos *mpl*.

alive [ə'laiv] *a* (*gen*) vivo; (*lively*) activo, enérgico.

alkali ['ælkəlai] *n* álcali *m*.

all [ɔːl] *a* todo; (*pl*) todos(as) // *pron* todo; (*pl*) todos(as) // *ad* completamente, del todo; ~ **alone** completamente solo; **at** ~ en absoluto, del todo; ~ **the time/his life** todo el tiempo/toda su vida; ~ **five** todos los cinco; ~ **of them** todos (ellos); ~ **of us went** fuimos todos; **not as hard as** ~ **that** no tan difícil; ~ **in** ~ con todo, así y todo.

allay [ə'lei] *vt* (*fears*) aquietar; (*pain*) aliviar.

allegation [æli'geiʃən] *n* aseveración *f*, alegación *f*.

allege [ə'ledʒ] *vt* afirmar, pretender.

allegiance [ə'liːdʒəns] *n* lealtad *f*.

allegory ['æligɔri] *n* alegoría.

allergic [ə'lɔːdʒik] *a*: ~ **to** alérgico a; **allergy** ['ælədʒi] *n* alergia.

alleviate [ə'liːvieit] *vt* aliviar, mitigar.

alley ['æli] *n* (*street*) callejuela; (*in garden*) paseo.

alliance [ə'laiəns] *n* alianza *f*; **allied** ['ælaid] *a* aliado; (*related*) relacionado.

alligator ['æligeitə*] *n* caimán *m*.

all-in ['ɔːlin] *a* (*also ad*: *charge*) todo incluido; ~ **wrestling** *n* lucha libre.

alliteration [əlitə'reiʃən] *n* aliteración *f*.

all-night ['ɔːl'nait] *a* (*café*) abierto toda la noche; (*party*) que dura toda la noche.

allocate ['æləkeit] *vt* (*share out*) repartir, distribuir; (*devote*) asignar; **allocation** [-'keiʃən] *n* (*of money*) ración *f*, cuota; (*distribution*) reparto.

allot [ə'lɔt] *vt* asignar; ~**ment** *n* ración *f*, porción *f*; (*garden*) parcela.

all-out ['ɔːlaut] *a* (*effort etc*) máximo; **all out** *ad* con todas sus fuerzas; (*speed*) a máxima velocidad.

allow [ə'lau] *vt* (*practice, behaviour*) permitir, dejar; (*sum to spend etc*) pagar, dar; (*a claim*) admitir; (*sum, time estimated*) dar, conceder; (*concede*): **to** ~ **that** reconocer que; **to** ~ **sb to do** permitir a alguien hacer; **to** ~ **for** *vt fus* tener en cuenta, tomar en consideración; ~**ance** *n* (*gen*) concesión *f*; (*payment*) subvención *f*, pensión *f*; (*discount*) descuento, rebaja; **family** ~**ance** subsidio familiar; **to make** ~**ances for** ser indulgente con; tener en cuenta.

alloy ['ælɔi] *n* (*mix*) mezcla.

all: ~ **right** *ad* (*well*) bien; (*correct*) correcto; (*as answer*) ¡conforme!, ¡está bien!; ~**-round** *a* (*gen*) completo; (*view*) amplio; (*person*) que hace de todo;

~-**time** a (record) de todos los tiempos.
allude [ə'luːd] vi: **to** ~ **to** aludir a.
alluring [ə'ljuərɪŋ] a seductor(a), atractivo.
allusion [ə'luːʒən] n referencia, alusión f.
ally ['ælaɪ] n aliado/a // vr [ə'laɪ]: **to** ~ o.s. **with** aliarse con.
almighty [ɔːl'maɪtɪ] a todopoderoso, omnipotente.
almond ['ɑːmənd] n (fruit) almendra; (tree) almendro.
almost ['ɔːlməust] ad casi, por poco.
alms [ɑːmz] npl limosna sg.
aloft [ə'lɔft] ad arriba, en alto.
alone [ə'ləun] a solo // ad sólo, solamente; **to leave sb** ~ dejar a uno solo o en paz; **to leave sth** ~ no tocar algo, dejar algo sin tocar; **let** ~ sin hablar de.
along [ə'lɔŋ] prep a lo largo de, por // ad: **is he coming** ~ **with us?** ¿nos acompaña?; **he was limping** ~ iba cojeando; ~ **with** junto con, además de; ~**side** prep junto a, al lado de // ad (NAUT) al costado.
aloof [ə'luːf] a reservado // ad: **to stand** ~ mantenerse a distancia.
aloud [ə'laud] ad en voz alta.
alphabet ['ælfəbɛt] n alfabeto; ~**ical** [-'bɛtɪkəl] a alfabético.
alpine ['ælpaɪn] a alpino, alpestre.
Alps [ælps] npl: **the** ~ los Alpes.
already [ɔːl'rɛdɪ] ad ya.
alright ['ɔːl'raɪt] ad = **all right.**
also ['ɔːlsəu] ad también, además.
altar ['ɔltə*] n altar m.
alter ['ɔltə*] vt cambiar, modificar // vi cambiarse, mudarse; (worsen) alterarse; ~**ation** [ɔltə'reɪʃən] n cambio, modificación f; alteración f.
alternate [ɔl'tɔːnɪt] a alterno, alternativo // vi ['ɔltɔːneɪt] alternarse; **on** ~ **days** un día sí y otro no; ~**ly** ad alternativamente, por turno; **alternating** [-'neɪtɪŋ] a (current) alterno.
alternative [ɔl'tɔːnətɪv] a alternativo // n alternativa; ~**ly** ad: ~**ly one could...** por otra parte se podría... .
alternator ['ɔltɔːneɪtə*] n (AUT) alternador m.
although [ɔːl'ðəu] conj aunque; (given that) si bien.
altitude ['æltɪtjuːd] n altitud f, altura.
alto ['æltəu] n (female) contralto f; (male) alto.
altogether [ɔːltə'gɛðə*] ad enteramente, del todo; (on the whole, in all) en total, en conjunto.
aluminium [ælju'mɪnɪəm], **aluminum** [ə'luːmɪnəm] (US) n aluminio.
always ['ɔːlweɪz] ad siempre.
am [æm] vb see **be.**
a.m. ad abbr of **ante meridiem** de la mañana, antes de mediodía.
amalgamate [ə'mælgəmeɪt] vi amalgamarse, unirse // vt amalgamar,

unir; **amalgamation** [-'meɪʃən] n (COMM) amalgamación f, unión f.
amass [ə'mæs] vt amontonar, acumular.
amateur ['æmətə*] n aficionado/a, amateur m/f.
amaze [ə'meɪz] vt asombrar, pasmar; ~**ment** n asombro, sorpresa.
Amazon ['æməzən] n (GEO) Amazonas m.
ambassador [æm'bæsədə*] n embajador m.
amber ['æmbə*] n ámbar m; **at** ~ (AUT) en el amarillo.
ambidextrous [æmbɪ'dɛkstrəs] a ambidextro.
ambiguity [æmbɪ'gjuɪtɪ] n ambigüedad f; (of meaning) doble sentido; **ambiguous** [-'bɪgjuəs] a ambiguo.
ambition [æm'bɪʃən] n ambición f; **ambitious** [-ʃəs] a ambicioso; (plan) grandioso.
ambivalent [æm'bɪvələnt] a ambivalente; (pej) equívoco.
amble ['æmbl] vi (gen: ~ **along**) deambular, andar sin prisa.
ambulance ['æmbjuləns] n ambulancia.
ambush ['æmbuʃ] n emboscada // vt tender una emboscada a; (fig) coger por sorpresa.
amenable [ə'miːnəbl] a: ~ **to** (advice etc) sensible a.
amend [ə'mɛnd] vt (law, text) enmendar; (habits) corregir, mejorar; **to make** ~**s** compensar, dar satisfacción por; ~**ment** n enmienda.
amenities [ə'miːnɪtɪz] npl conveniencias fpl, comodidades fpl.
America [ə'mɛrɪkə] n Estados Unidos mpl; ~**n** a, n norteamericano/a.
amiable ['eɪmɪəbl] a (kind) amable, simpático; (hearty) bonachón(ona).
amicable ['æmɪkəbl] a amistoso, amigable.
amid(st) [ə'mɪd(st)] prep entre, en medio de.
amiss [ə'mɪs] ad: **to take sth** ~ tomar algo a mal.
ammonia [ə'məunɪə] n amoníaco.
ammunition [æmju'nɪʃən] n municiones fpl.
amnesia [æm'niːzɪə] n amnesia.
amnesty ['æmnɪstɪ] n amnistía.
amok [ə'mɔk] ad: **to run** ~ enloquecerse, desbocarse.
among(st) [ə'mʌŋ(st)] prep entre, en medio de.
amoral [æ'mɔrəl] a amoral.
amorous ['æmərəs] a amoroso; (in love) enamorado.
amount [ə'maunt] n (gen) cantidad f; (of bill etc) suma, importe m // vi: **to** ~ **to** (reach) alcanzar; (total) sumar; (be same as) equivaler a, significar.
amp(ère) ['æmp(εə*)] n amperio.
amphibian [æm'fɪbɪən] n anfibio; **amphibious** [-bɪəs] a anfibio.
amphitheatre ['æmfɪθɪətə*] n anfiteatro.

ample ['æmpl] a (spacious) amplio, ancho; (abundant) abundante; (enough) bastante, suficiente.

amplifier ['æmplɪfaɪə*] n amplificador m.

amplify ['æmplɪfaɪ] vt amplificar, aumentar; (explain) explicar.

amputate ['æmpjuteɪt] vt amputar.

amuck [ə'mʌk] ad = **amok.**

amuse [ə'mjuːz] vt divertir; (distract) distraer, entretener; ~ment n diversión f; (pastime) pasatiempo; (laughter) risa.

an [æn, ən, n] det see **a.**

anaemia [ə'niːmɪə] n anemia; **anaemic** [-mɪk] a anémico; (fig) soso, insípido.

anaesthetic [ænɪs'θetɪk] n anestesia; **anaesthetist** [æ'niːsθɪtɪst] n anestesista m/f.

analgesic [ænæl'dʒiːsɪk] a, n analgésico.

analogy [ə'nælədʒɪ] n análogo.

analyse ['ænəlaɪz] vt analizar; **analysis** [ə'næləsɪs], pl -ses [-siːz] n análisis m inv; **analyst** [-lɪst] n (US) analista m/f; **analytic(al)** [-'lɪtɪk(əl)] a analítico.

anarchist ['ænəkɪst] a, n anarquista m/f; **anarchy** [-kɪ] n anarquía, desorden m.

anatomy [ə'nætəmɪ] n anatomía.

ancestor ['ænsɪstə*] n antepasado; **ancestry** [-trɪ] n ascendencia, abolengo.

anchor ['æŋkə*] n ancla, áncora // vi anclar // vt (fig) sujetar, asegurar; **to weigh** ~ levar anclas; ~age n ancladero.

anchovy ['æntʃəvɪ] n anchoa.

ancient ['eɪnʃənt] a antiguo.

and [ænd] conj y; (before i, hi) e; ~ **so on** etcétera, y así sucesivamente; **try** ~ **come** procure o intente venir; **better** ~ **better** cada vez mejor.

Andes ['ændiːz] npl: **the** ~ los Andes.

anecdote ['ænɪkdəut] n anécdota.

anew [ə'njuː] ad de nuevo, otra vez.

angel ['eɪndʒəl] n ángel m.

anger ['æŋgə*] n cólera, ira // vt enojar, provocar.

angina [æn'dʒaɪnə] n angina (de pecho).

angle ['æŋgl] n ángulo; **from their** ~ desde su punto de vista.

angler ['æŋglə*] n pescador/a m/f (de caña).

Anglican ['æŋglɪkən] a, n anglicano/a.

angling ['æŋglɪŋ] n pesca con caña.

Anglo- [æŋgləu] pref anglo... .

angrily ['æŋgrɪlɪ] ad con enojo, airadamente.

angry ['æŋgrɪ] a enfadado, enojado; **to be** ~ **with sb/at sth** estar enfadado con alguien/por algo; **to get** ~ enfadarse, enojarse.

anguish ['æŋgwɪʃ] n (physical) dolor m agudo; (mental) angustia.

angular ['æŋgjulə*] a (shape) angular; (features) anguloso.

animal ['ænɪməl] n animal m, bestia; (insect) bicho // a animal.

animate ['ænɪmeɪt] vt (enliven) animar;

(encourage) estimular, alentar; ~**d** a vivo, animado.

animosity [ænɪ'mɔsɪtɪ] n animosidad f, rencor m.

aniseed ['ænɪsiːd] n anís m.

ankle ['æŋkl] n tobillo m.

annex ['ænɛks] n (also: **annexe**) (edificio) anexo, dependencia // vt [æ'nɛks] (territory) anexar; (document) adjuntar.

annihilate [ə'naɪəleɪt] vt aniquilar.

anniversary [ænɪ'vɔːsərɪ] n aniversario.

annotate ['ænəuteɪt] vt anotar, comentar.

announce [ə'nauns] vt comunicar, anunciar; ~**ment** n anuncio, aviso, declaración f; **announcer** n (RADIO, TV) locutor/a m/f.

annoy [ə'nɔɪ] vt molestar, fastidiar, irritar; **don't get** ~**ed!** ¡no se enfade!; ~**ance** n enojo; (thing) molestia; ~**ing** a molesto, fastidioso; (person) pesado.

annual ['ænjuəl] a anual // n (BOT) anual m; (book) anuario; ~**ly** ad anualmente, cada año.

annuity [ə'njuːɪtɪ] n renta o pensión f vitalicia.

annul [ə'nʌl] vt anular, cancelar; (law) revocar; ~**ment** n anulación f, cancelación f.

annum ['ænəm] n see **per.**

anoint [ə'nɔɪnt] vt untar.

anomaly [ə'nɔməlɪ] n anomalía.

anonymity [ænə'nɪmɪtɪ] n anonimato; **anonymous** [ə'nɔnɪməs] a anónimo.

anorak ['ænəræk] n anorak m.

anorexia [ænə'rɛksɪə] n (MED) anorexia.

another [ə'nʌðə*] a: ~ **book** (one more) otro libro; (a different one) un libro distinto // pron otro; see also **one.**

answer ['ɑːnsə*] n contestación f, respuesta; (to problem) solución f // vi contestar, responder // vt (reply to) contestar a, responder a; (problem) resolver; **to** ~ **the phone** contestar el teléfono; **in** ~ **to your letter** contestando o en contestación a su carta; **to** ~ **the bell** o **the door** acudir a la puerta; **to** ~ **back** vi replicar, ser respondón(ona); **to** ~ **for** vt fus responder de o por; **to** ~ **to** vt fus (description) corresponder a; (needs) satisfacer; ~**able** a: ~**able to sb for sth** responsable ante uno de algo.

ant [ænt] n hormiga.

antacid [ænt'æsɪd] a antiácido.

antagonist [æn'tægənɪst] n antagonista m/f, adversario/a; ~**ic** [-'nɪstɪk] a antagónico, (opposed) contrario, opuesto; **antagonize** [-naɪz] vt enemistarse con.

Antarctic [ænt'ɑːktɪk] n: **the** ~ el Antártico // a n Antártida.

antelope ['æntɪləup] n antílope m.

antenatal ['æntɪ'neɪtl] a antenatal, prenatal; ~ **clinic** n clínica prenatal.

antenna [æn'tɛnə], pl ~**e** [-niː] n antena.

anthem ['ænθəm] n: **national** ~ himno nacional.

anthology [æn'θɔlədʒɪ] n antología.

anthropologist [ænθrə'pɔlədʒɪst] n antropólogo; anthropology [-dʒɪ] n antropología.

anti... [ænti] pref anti...; ~-aircraft a antiaéreo.

antibiotic [æntɪbaɪ'ɔtɪk] a, n antibiótico.

anticipate [æn'tɪsɪpeɪt] vt (foresee) prever; (expect) esperar, contar con; (forestall) anticiparse a, adelantarse a; (look forward to) prometerse; anticipation [-'peɪʃən] n previsión f; esperanza; anticipación f, prevención f.

anticlimax [æntɪ'klaɪmæks] n decepción f.

anticlockwise [æntɪ'klɔkwaɪz] ad en dirección contraria a la de las agujas del reloj.

antics ['æntɪks] npl payasadas fpl; (of child) travesuras fpl.

anticyclone [æntɪ'saɪkləun] n anticiclón m.

antidote ['æntɪdəut] n antídoto.

antifreeze ['æntɪfriːz] n anticongelante m, solución f anticongelante.

antihistamine [æntɪ'hɪstəmiːn] n antihistamínico.

antiquated ['æntɪkweɪtɪd] a anticuado.

antique [æn'tiːk] n antigüedad f, antigualla // a antiguo, anticuado; ~ dealer n anticuario; ~ shop n tienda de antigüedades.

antiquity [æn'tɪkwɪtɪ] n antigüedad f.

antiseptic [æntɪ'sɛptɪk] a, n antiséptico.

antisocial [æntɪ'səuʃəl] a antisocial.

antlers ['æntləz] npl cuernas fpl.

anus ['eɪnəs] n ano.

anvil ['ænvɪl] n yunque m.

anxiety [æŋ'zaɪətɪ] n (worry) inquietud f; (eagerness) ansia, anhelo; (MED) ansiedad f.

anxious ['æŋkʃəs] a (worried) inquieto; (keen) deseoso; ~ly ad con inquietud, de manera angustiada.

any ['ɛnɪ] a (in negative and interrogative sentences = some) algún, alguno, alguna; (negative sense) ningún, ninguno, ninguna; (no matter which) cualquier(a); (each and every) todo; I haven't ~ money/books no tengo dinero/libros; have you ~ butter/children? ¿tiene mantequilla/hijos?; at ~ moment en cualquier momento; in ~ case de todas formas, de todas maneras; at ~ rate de todas formas, sea como sea // pron alguno; ninguno; (anybody) cualquiera; (in negative and interrogative sentences): I haven't ~ no tengo ninguno; have you got ~? ¿tiene algunos?; can ~ of you sing? ¿alguno de Ustedes sabe cantar? // ad (in negative sentences) nada; (in interrogative and conditional constructions) algo; I can't hear him ~ more no le oigo más; do you want ~ more soup? ¿quiere más sopa?; ~body pron cualquiera, cualquier persona; (in interrogative sentences) alguien; (in negative sentences): I don't see ~body no veo a nadie; ~how ad de todos modos, de todas maneras;

(carelessly) de cualquier manera; ~one = ~body; ~thing pron (see ~body) algo, cualquier cosa; algo; (in negative sentences) nada; (everything) todo; ~time ad (at any moment) en cualquier momento, de un momento a otro; (whenever) no importa cuándo, cuando quiera; ~way ad de todas maneras; de cualquier modo; ~where ad (see ~body) dondequiera; en algún sitio; (negative sense) en ningún sitio; (everywhere) en or por todas partes; I don't see him ~where no le veo en ningún sitio.

apart [ə'pɑːt] ad aparte, separadamente; 10 miles ~ separados por 10 millas; ~ from prep aparte de.

apartheid [ə'pɑːteɪt] n apartheid m.

apartment [ə'pɑːtmənt] n (US) piso, apartamento; (room) cuarto.

apathetic [æpə'θɛtɪk] a apático, indiferente; apathy ['æpəθɪ] n apatía, indiferencia.

ape [eɪp] n mono // vt imitar, remedar.

aperitif [ə'pɛrɪtɪv] n aperitivo.

aperture ['æpətʃuə*] n rendija, resquicio; (PHOT) abertura.

apex ['eɪpɛks] n ápice m; (fig) cumbre f.

aphrodisiac [æfrəu'dɪzɪæk] a, n afrodisíaco.

apiece [ə'piːs] ad cada uno.

apologetic [əpɔlə'dʒɛtɪk] a (tone, letter) lleno de disculpas.

apologize [ə'pɔlədʒaɪz] vi: to ~ (for sth to sb) disculparse (con alguien de algo); apology [-dʒɪ] n disculpa, excusa.

apostle [ə'pɔsl] n apóstol m/f.

apostrophe [ə'pɔstrəfɪ] n apóstrofe m.

appal [ə'pɔːl] vt horrorizar, espantar; ~ling a espantoso; (awful) pésimo.

apparatus [æpə'reɪtəs] n aparato.

apparent [ə'pærənt] a aparente; (obvious) manifiesto, claro; ~ly ad por lo visto, al parecer.

apparition [æpə'rɪʃən] n aparición f; (ghost) fantasma m.

appeal [ə'piːl] vi (LAW) apelar // n (LAW) apelación f; (request) llamamiento; (plea) súplica, ruego; (charm) atractivo, encanto; to ~ for suplicar, reclamar; to ~ to (subj: person) rogar a, suplicar a; (subj: thing) atraer, interesar; to ~ to sb for mercy rogarle misericordia a alguien; it doesn't ~ to me no me atrae, no me llama la atención; ~ing a (nice) atrayente, atractivo; (touching) conmovedor(a), emocionante.

appear [ə'pɪə*] vi aparecer, presentarse; (LAW) comparecer; (publication) salir (a luz), publicarse; (seem) parecer; it would ~ that parecería que; ~ance n aparición f; (look, aspect) apariencia, aspecto.

appease [ə'piːz] vt (pacify) apaciguar; (satisfy) satisfacer, saciar.

appendicitis [əpɛndɪ'saɪtɪs] n apendicitis f.

appendix [ə'pɛndɪks], pl -dices [-dɪsiːz] n apéndice m.

appetite ['æpɪtaɪt] n apetito; (fig) deseo, anhelo.
appetizing ['æpɪtaɪzɪŋ] a apetitoso.
applaud [ə'plɔːd] vt, vi aplaudir; **applause** [-ɔːz] n aplausos mpl.
apple ['æpl] n manzana; ~ **tree** n manzano.
appliance [ə'plaɪəns] n aparato.
applicable [ə'plɪkəbl] a aplicable, pertinente.
applicant ['æplɪkənt] n candidato/a, solicitante m/f.
application [æplɪ'keɪʃən] n aplicación f; (for a job, a grant etc) solicitud f, petición f; ~ **form** n formulario.
apply [ə'plaɪ] vt: to ~ (to) aplicar (a); (fig) emplear (para) // vi: to ~ to (ask) presentarse a, ser candidato a; (be suitable for) ser aplicable a; (be relevant to) tener que ver con; to ~ for (permit, grant, job) solicitar; to ~ the brakes aplicar los frenos; to ~ o.s. to aplicarse a, dedicarse a.
appoint [ə'pɔɪnt] vt (to post) nombrar; (date, place) fijar, señalar; ~ment n (engagement) cita; (date) compromiso; (act) nombramiento; (post) puesto.
apportion [ə'pɔːʃən] vt repartir, distribuir; (blame) dar.
appraisal [ə'preɪzl] n tasación f, valoración f.
appreciable [ə'priːʃəbl] a sensible.
appreciate [ə'priːʃɪeɪt] vt (like) apreciar, tener en mucho; (be grateful for) agradecer; (assess) valorar, apreciar; (be aware of) comprender, percibir // vi (COMM) aumentar(se) en valor, subir; **appreciation** [-'eɪʃən] n aprecio; reconocimiento, agradecimiento; aumento en valor.
appreciative [ə'priːʃɪətɪv] a (person) agradecido; (comment) elogioso.
apprehend [æprɪ'hɛnd] vt percibir, comprender; (arrest) detener.
apprehension [æprɪ'hɛnʃən] n (fear) recelo, aprensión f; **apprehensive** [-'hɛnsɪv] a aprensivo.
apprentice [ə'prɛntɪs] n aprendiz/a m/f; ~**ship** n aprendizaje m.
approach [ə'prəʊtʃ] vi acercarse // vt acercarse a; (be approximate) aproximarse a; (ask, apply to) dirigirse a // n acercamiento; aproximación f; (access) acceso; (proposal) proposición f; ~**able** a (person) abordable; (place) accesible.
appropriate [ə'prəʊprɪeɪt] vt (take) apropiarse; (allot): to ~ sth for destinar algo a // a [-rɪɪt] (apt) apropiado, conveniente; (relevant) competente.
approval [ə'pruːvəl] n aprobación f, visto bueno; on ~ (COMM) a prueba.
approve [ə'pruːv] vt aprobar; ~**d school** n correccional m.
approximate [ə'prɔksɪmɪt] a aproximado // vt [-meɪt] aproximarse a, acercarse a;

approximation [-'meɪʃən] n aproximación f.
apricot ['eɪprɪkɔt] n albaricoque m.
April ['eɪprəl] n abril m; ~ **Fool's Day** n Día m de los Inocentes.
apron ['eɪprən] n delantal m.
apt [æpt] a (suitable) acertado, oportuno; (appropriate) conveniente; (likely): ~ to do con tendencia a hacer.
aptitude ['æptɪtjuːd] n aptitud f, capacidad f.
aqualung ['ækwəlʌŋ] n aparato de buceo autónomo.
aquarium [ə'kwɛərɪəm] n acuario.
Aquarius [ə'kwɛərɪəs] n Acuario.
aquatic [ə'kwætɪk] a acuático.
aqueduct ['ækwɪdʌkt] n acueducto.
Arab ['ærəb] n árabe m/f.
Arabia [ə'reɪbɪə] n Arabia; ~**n** a árabe.
Arabic ['ærəbɪk] n árabe m.
arable ['ærəbl] a cultivable.
arbitrary ['ɑːbɪtrərɪ] a arbitrario.
arbitrate ['ɑːbɪtreɪt] vi arbitrar; **arbitration** [-'treɪʃən] n arbitraje m; **arbitrator** n juez m árbitro.
arc [ɑːk] n arco.
arcade [ɑː'keɪd] n arcada; (round a square) soportales mpl; (passage with shops) galería, pasaje m.
arch [ɑːtʃ] n arco; (vault) bóveda; (of foot) empeine m // vt arquear.
archaeologist [ɑːkɪ'ɔlədʒɪst] n arqueólogo; **archaeology** [-dʒɪ] n arqueología.
archaic [ɑː'keɪɪk] a arcaico.
archbishop [ɑːtʃ'bɪʃəp] n arzobispo.
arch-enemy ['ɑːtʃ'ɛnɪmɪ] n enemigo jurado.
archer ['ɑːtʃə*] n arquero; ~**y** n tiro con arco.
archetype ['ɑːkɪtaɪp] n arquetipo.
archipelago [ɑːkɪ'pɛlɪgəʊ] n archipiélago.
architect ['ɑːkɪtɛkt] n arquitecto; ~**ural** [-'tɛktʃərəl] a arquitectónico; ~**ure** n arquitectura.
archives ['ɑːkaɪvz] npl archivo sg.
archway ['ɑːtʃweɪ] n arco, arcada.
Arctic ['ɑːktɪk] a ártico // n: the ~ el Ártico.
ardent ['ɑːdənt] a (passionate) ardiente, apasionado; (fervent) fervoroso; **ardour** ['ɑːdə*] n ardor m; fervor m.
arduous ['ɑːdjuəs] a (gen) arduo; (journey) penoso.
are [ɑː*] vb see **be**.
area ['ɛərɪə] n (gen) área f; (MATH etc) superficie f, extensión f; (zone) región f, zona.
arena [ə'riːnə] n arena; (of circus) pista; (for bullfight) plaza, ruedo.
aren't [ɑːnt] = **are not**.
Argentina [ɑːdʒən'tiːnə] n Argentina; **Argentinian** [-'tɪnɪən] a, n argentino/a.
argue ['ɑːgjuː] vi (quarrel) discutir; (reason) argüir, discurrir; to ~ that sostener que; **argument** n (reasons)

argumento; (*quarrel*) discusión f; (*debate*) debate m, disputa; **argumentative** [-mɛntɔtɪv] a discutidor(a).
aria ['ɑːrɪə] n (*MUS*) aria.
arid ['ærɪd] a árido.
Aries ['ɛɔrɪz] n Aries m.
arise [ə'raɪz], pt **arose**, pp **arisen** [ə'rɪzn] vi (*rise up*) levantarse, alzarse; (*emerge*) surgir, presentarse; **to** ~ **from** resultar de.
aristocracy [ærɪs'tɔkrɔsɪ] n aristocracia; **aristocrat** ['ærɪstɔkræt] n aristócrata m/f.
arithmetic [ə'rɪθmɔtɪk] n aritmética.
ark [ɑːk] n: **Noah's A** ~ Arca de Noé.
arm [ɑːm] n (*ANAT*) brazo; (*weapon*, *MIL*: *branch*) arma // vt armar; ~**s** npl (*weapons*) armas fpl; (*HERALDRY*) escudo sg; ~**s race** carrera de armamentos; ~ **in** ~ cogidos del brazo; ~**band** n brazalete m; ~**chair** n sillón m; ~**ed** a armado; ~**ed robbery** n robo a mano armada; ~**ful** n brazado, brazada.
armistice ['ɑːmɪstɪs] n armisticio.
armour ['ɑːmɔ*] n armadura; ~**ed car** n coche m blindado; ~**y** n armería, arsenal m.
armpit ['ɑːmpɪt] n sobaco, axila.
army ['ɑːmɪ] n ejército.
aroma [ə'rɔumə] n aroma m, fragancia; ~**tic** [ærə'mætɪk] a aromático, fragante.
arose [ə'rɔuz] pt of **arise**.
around [ə'raund] ad alrededor; (*in the area*) a la redonda // prep alrededor de, en torno de; (*fig*: *about*) alrededor de.
arouse [ə'rauz] vt despertar.
arrange [ə'reɪndʒ] vt arreglar, ordenar; (*programme*) organizar; ~**ment** n arreglo; (*agreement*) acuerdo; ~**ments** npl (*plans*) planes mpl, medidas fpl; (*preparations*) preparativos mpl.
arrears [ə'rɪɔz] npl atrasos mpl; **to be in** ~ **with one's rent** atrasarse en el arriendo.
arrest [ə'rɛst] vt detener; (*sb's attention*) llamar // n detención f; **under** ~ detenido.
arrival [ə'raɪvɔl] n llegada; **new** ~ recién llegado.
arrive [ə'raɪv] vi llegar.
arrogance ['ærɔgɔns] n arrogancia; **arrogant** [-gɔnt] a arrogante.
arrow ['ærɔu] n flecha.
arsenal ['ɑːsɪnl] n arsenal m.
arsenic ['ɑːsnɪk] n arsénico.
arson ['ɑːsn] n delito de incendiar.
art [ɑːt] n arte m; (*craft*) artes fpl y oficios mpl; (*skill*) destreza; (*technique*) técnica; **A**~**s** npl (*SCOL*) Letras fpl; ~ **gallery** n museo de bellas artes; (*small and private*) galería de arte.
artery ['ɑːtɔrɪ] n (*MED*) arteria; (*fig*) vía principal.
arthritis [ɑː'θraɪtɪs] n artritis f.
artichoke ['ɑːtɪtʃɔuk] n alcachofa; **Jerusalem** ~ aguaturma.
article ['ɑːtɪkl] n artículo, objeto, cosa; (*in*

newspaper) artículo; (*LAW*: *training*): ~**s** npl contrato sg de aprendizaje.
articulate [ɑː'tɪkjulɪt] a claro o distinto en el hablar // vt [-leɪt] articular; ~**d lorry** n camión m articulado.
artificial [ɑːtɪ'fɪʃəl] a artificial; (*teeth etc*) postizo; ~ **respiration** n respiración f artificial.
artillery [ɑː'tɪlɔrɪ] n artillería.
artisan ['ɑːtɪzæn] n artesano.
artist ['ɑːtɪst] n artista m/f; (*MUS*) intérprete m/f; ~**ic** [ɑː'tɪstɪk] a artístico; ~**ry** n arte m, habilidad f artística.
artless ['ɑːtlɪs] a (*innocent*) natural, sencillo; (*clumsy*) desmañado.
as [æz, ɔz] conj (*cause*) como, ya que; (*time*: *moment*) como, cuando; (: *duration*) mientras; (*manner*) como, lo mismo que, tal como; (*in the capacity of*) como; ~ **big** ~ tan grande como; **twice** ~ **big** ~ dos veces más grande que; ~ **she said** como ella dijo; ~ **if** or **though** como si; ~ **for** or **to** **that** en cuanto a eso, en lo que a eso se refiere; ~ or **so long** ~ conj mientras (que); ~ **much/many** ~ tanto(s)... como; ~ **soon** ~ conj tan pronto como; ~ **such** ad como tal; ~ **well** ad también, además; ~ **well** ~ conj así como; *see also* **such**.
asbestos [æz'bɛstɔs] n asbesto, amianto.
ascend [ə'sɛnd] vt subir; ~**ancy** n ascendiente m, dominio.
ascent [ə'sɛnt] n subida; (*slope*) cuesta, pendiente m; (*promotion*) ascenso.
ascertain [æsɔ'teɪn] vt averiguar, determinar.
ascetic [ə'sɛtɪk] a ascético.
ascribe [ə'skraɪb] vt: **to** ~ **sth to** atribuir algo a.
ash [æʃ] n ceniza; (*tree*) fresno.
ashamed [ə'feɪmd] a avergonzado; **to be** ~ **of** avergonzarse de.
ashen ['æʃn] a ceniciento, pálido.
ashore [ə'ʃɔ*] ad en tierra.
ashtray ['æʃtreɪ] n cenicero.
Asia ['eɪʃə] n Asia; ~**n,** ~**tic** [eɪsɪ'ætɪk] a, n asiático/a.
aside [ə'saɪd] ad aparte, a un lado.
ask [ɑːsk] vt (*question*) preguntar; (*demand*) pedir; (*invite*) invitar; **to** ~ **sb sth/to do sth** preguntar algo a alguien/pedir a alguien que haga algo; **to** ~ **sb about sth** preguntar algo a alguien; **to** ~ **(sb) a question** hacer una pregunta (a alguien); **to** ~ **sb out to dinner** invitar a comer a uno; **to** ~ **for** vt fus pedir.
askance [ə'skɑːns] ad: **to look** ~ **at sb** mirar con recelo a uno.
askew [ə'skjuː] ad sesgado, ladeado, oblicuamente.
asleep [ə'sliːp] a dormido; **to fall** ~ dormirse, quedarse dormido.
asparagus [əs'pærɔgɔs] n espárragos mpl.
aspect ['æspɛkt] n aspecto, apariencia; (*direction in which a building etc faces*) orientación f.

aspersions [əsˈpɔːʃənz] npl: **to cast ~ on** difamar a, calumniar a.

asphalt [ˈæsfælt] n asfalto; (place) pista asfaltada.

asphyxiate [æsˈfɪksɪeɪt] vt asfixiar // vi asfixiarse; **asphyxiation** [-ˈeɪʃən] n asfixia.

aspiration [æspəˈreɪʃən] n (fig) anhelo, deseo, ambición f.

aspire [əsˈpaɪə*] vi: **to ~ to** aspirar a, ambicionar.

aspirin [ˈæsprɪn] n aspirina.

ass [æs] n asno, burro; (col) imbécil m.

assailant [əˈseɪlənt] n asaltador/a m/f, agresor/a m/f.

assassin [əˈsæsɪn] n asesino; **~ate** vt asesinar; **~ation** [-ˈneɪʃən] n asesinato.

assault [əˈsɔːlt] n (gen: attack) asalto, ataque m // vt asaltar, atacar; (sexually) violar.

assemble [əˈsɛmbl] vt reunir, juntar; (TECH) montar // vi reunirse, juntarse.

assembly [əˈsɛmblɪ] n (meeting) reunión f, asamblea; (people) concurrencia; (construction) montaje m; **~ line** n línea de producción.

assent [əˈsɛnt] n asentimiento, aprobación f // vi consentir, asentir.

assert [əˈsɜːt] vt afirmar; (claim etc) hacer valer; **~ion** [əˈsɔːʃən] n afirmación f.

assess [əˈsɛs] vt valorar, calcular; (tax, damages) fijar; (property etc: for tax) gravar; **~ment** n valoración f; gravamen m; **~or** n asesor/a m/f; (of tax) tasador/a m/f.

asset [ˈæsɛt] n posesión f; (quality) ventaja sg; **~s** npl (funds) activo sg, fondos mpl.

assiduous [əˈsɪdjuəs] a asiduo.

assign [əˈsaɪn] vt (date) fijar; (task) asignar; (resources) destinar; (property) traspasar; **~ment** n asignación f; (task) tarea.

assimilate [əˈsɪmɪleɪt] vt asimilar.

assist [əˈsɪst] vt ayudar; (progress etc) fomentar; **~ance** n ayuda, auxilio; (welfare) subsidio; **~ant** n ayudante m/f, auxiliar m/f; (also: **shop ~ant**) dependiente/a m/f.

assizes [əˈsaɪzɪz] npl sesión f de un tribunal.

associate [əˈsəʊʃɪt] a asociado // n asociado, colega m; (in crime) cómplice m/f; (member) miembro // (vb: [-ʃeɪt]) vt asociar, relacionar // vi: **to ~ with sb** tratar con alguien.

association [əsəʊsɪˈeɪʃən] n asociación f; (COMM) sociedad f.

assorted [əˈsɔːtɪd] a surtido, variado.

assortment [əˈsɔːtmənt] n surtido.

assume [əˈsjuːm] vt (suppose) suponer, dar por sentado; (responsibilities etc) asumir; (attitude, name) adoptar, tomar.

assumption [əˈsʌmpʃən] n (supposition) suposición f, presunción f; (act) asunción f.

assurance [əˈʃuərəns] n garantía, promesa; (confidence) confianza, aplomo; (certainty) certeza; (insurance) seguro.

assure [əˈʃuə*] vt asegurar.

asterisk [ˈæstərɪsk] n asterisco.

astern [əˈstɜːn] ad a popa, por la popa.

asteroid [ˈæstərɔɪd] n asteroide m.

asthma [ˈæsmə] n asma; **~tic** [æsˈmætɪk] a, n asmático/a.

astonish [əˈstɒnɪʃ] vt asombrar, pasmar; **~ment** n asombro, sorpresa.

astound [əˈstaʊnd] vt asombrar, pasmar.

astray [əˈstreɪ] ad: **to go ~** extraviarse; **to lead ~** llevar por mal camino.

astride [əˈstraɪd] ad a horcajadas // prep a caballo o horcajadas sobre.

astrologer [əsˈtrɒlədʒə*] n astrólogo; **astrology** [-dʒɪ] n astrología.

astronaut [ˈæstrənɔːt] n astronauta m/f.

astronomer [əsˈtrɒnəmə*] n astrónomo; **astronomical** [æstrəˈnɒmɪkəl] a astronómico; (fig) tremendo, enorme; **astronomy** [-mɪ] n astronomía.

astute [əsˈtjuːt] a astuto.

asunder [əˈsʌndə*] ad: **to tear ~** romper en dos, hacer pedazos.

asylum [əˈsaɪləm] n (refuge) asilo; (hospital) manicomio.

at [æt] prep en, a; **~ the top** en la cumbre; **~ 4 o'clock** a las cuatro; **~ £1 a kilo** a libra el kilo; **~ night** de noche, por la noche; **~ a stroke** de un golpe; **two ~ a time** de dos en dos; **~ times** a veces.

ate [eɪt] pt of **eat**.

atheist [ˈeɪθɪɪst] n ateo/a.

Athens [ˈæθɪnz] n Atenas f.

athlete [ˈæθliːt] n atleta m/f.

athletic [æθˈlɛtɪk] a atlético; **~s** n atletismo.

Atlantic [ətˈlæntɪk] n: **the ~ (Ocean)** el (Océano) Atlántico.

atlas [ˈætləs] n atlas m.

atmosphere [ˈætməsfɪə*] n atmósfera; (fig) ambiente m.

atom [ˈætəm] n átomo; **~ic** [əˈtɒmɪk] a atómico; **~(ic) bomb** n bomba atómica; **~izer** [ˈætəmaɪzə*] n atomizador m.

atone [əˈtəʊn] vi: **to ~ for** expiar.

atrocious [əˈtrəʊʃəs] a (very bad) atroz; (fig) horrible, infame.

atrocity [əˈtrɒsɪtɪ] n atrocidad f.

attach [əˈtætʃ] vt (gen) sujetar, pegar; (document, letter) adjuntar; **to be ~ed to sb/sth** (to like) tener cariño a alguien/algo.

attaché [əˈtæʃeɪ] n agregado; **~ case** n maletín m.

attachment [əˈtætʃmənt] n (tool) accesorio; (love): **~ (to)** cariño (a).

attack [əˈtæk] vt (MIL) atacar; (criminal) agredir, asaltar; (task etc) emprender // n ataque m, asalto; (on sb's life) atentado; **heart ~** ataque al corazón o cardíaco; **~er** n agresor/a m/f, asaltante m/f.

attain [əˈteɪn] vt (also: **~ to**) alcanzar; (achieve) lograr, conseguir; **~ments** npl dotes fpl, talento sg.

attempt [əˈtɛmpt] n tentativa, intento; (attack) atentado // vt intentar, tratar de.

attend [ə'tɛnd] *vt* asistir a; (*patient*) atender; **to ~ to** *vt fus* (*needs, affairs etc*) ocuparse de; (*speech etc*) prestar atención a; (*customer*) atender a; **~ance** *n* asistencia, presencia; (*people present*) concurrencia; **~ant** *n* sirviente/a *m/f*, mozo/a; (*THEATRE*) acomodador/a *m/f* // *a* concomitante.

attention [ə'tɛnʃən] *n* atención *f* // *excl* (*MIL*) ¡firme(s)!; **for the ~ of...** (*ADMIN*) atención... .

attentive [ə'tɛntɪv] *a* atento; (*polite*) cortés.

attest [ə'tɛst] *vi*: **to ~ to** dar fe de.

attic ['ætɪk] *n* desván *m*, ático.

attitude ['ætɪtjuːd] *n* (*gen*) actitud *f*; (*disposition*) disposición *f*.

attorney [ə'tɜːnɪ] *n* (*lawyer*) abogado; (*having proxy*) apoderado; **A~ General** *n* (*Brit*) fiscal *m* de la corona; (*US*) procurador *m* general.

attract [ə'trækt] *vt* atraer; (*attention*) llamar; **attraction** [ə'trækʃən] *n* (*gen pl*) encantos *mpl*; (*amusements*) diversiones *fpl*; (*PHYSICS*) atracción *f*; (*fig: towards sth*) atractivo; **~ive** *a* atractivo; (*interesting*) atrayente; (*pretty*) guapo, mono.

attribute ['ætrɪbjuːt] *n* atributo // *vt* [ə'trɪbjuːt]: **to ~ sth to** atribuir *o* achacar algo a.

aubergine ['əʊbəʒiːn] *n* berenjena.

auburn ['ɔːbən] *a* castaño rojizo.

auction ['ɔːkʃən] *n* (*also*: **sale by ~**) subasta // *vt* subastar; **~eer** [-'nɪə*] *n* subastador/a *m/f*.

audacious [ɔː'deɪʃəs] *a* audaz, atrevido; (*pej*) descarado; **audacity** [ɔː'dæsɪtɪ] *n* audacia, atrevimiento; (*pej*) descaro.

audible ['ɔːdɪbl] *a* audible, que se puede oír.

audience ['ɔːdɪəns] *n* auditorio, público; (*interview*) audiencia.

audio-visual [ɔːdɪəʊ'vɪzjuəl] *a* audiovisual.

audit ['ɔːdɪt] *vt* revisar, intervenir.

audition [ɔː'dɪʃən] *n* audición *f*.

auditor ['ɔːdɪtə*] *n* interventor/a *m/f*, censor/a *m/f* de cuentas.

auditorium [ɔːdɪ'tɔːrɪəm] *n* auditorio.

augment [ɔːg'mɛnt] *vt* aumentar // *vi* aumentarse.

augur ['ɔːgə*] *vi*: **it ~s well** es de buen agüero.

August ['ɔːgəst] *n* agosto.

aunt [ɑːnt] *n* tía; **~ie, ~y** *n diminutive of* **aunt**.

au pair ['əʊ'pɛə*] *n* (*also*: **~ girl**) au pair *f*.

aura ['ɔːrə] *n* emanación *f*; (*atmosphere*) ambiente *m*.

auspices ['ɔːspɪsɪz] *npl*: **under the ~ of** bajo los auspicios de.

auspicious [ɔːs'pɪʃəs] *a* propicio, de buen augurio.

austere [ɔs'tɪə*] *a* austero; (*manner*) adusto; **austerity** [ɔs'stɛrətɪ] *n* austeridad *f*.

Australia [ɔs'treɪlɪə] *n* Australia; **~n** *a, n* australiano/a.

Austria ['ɔstrɪə] *n* Austria; **~n** *a, n* austríaco/a.

authentic [ɔː'θɛntɪk] *a* auténtico.

author ['ɔːθə] *n* autor/a *m/f*.

authoritarian [ɔːθɔrɪ'tɛərɪən] *a* autoritario.

authoritative [ɔː'θɔrɪtətɪv] *a* autorizado; (*manner*) autoritario.

authority [ɔː'θɔrɪtɪ] *n* autoridad *f*; **the authorities** *npl* las autoridades.

authorize ['ɔːθəraɪz] *vt* autorizar.

auto ['ɔːtəʊ] *n* (*US*) coche *m*, automóvil *m*.

autobiography [ɔːtəbaɪ'ɔgrəfɪ] *n* autobiografía.

autocratic [ɔːtə'krætɪk] *a* autocrático.

autograph ['ɔːtəgrɑːf] *n* autógrafo // *vt* firmar; (*photo etc*) dedicar.

automatic [ɔːtə'mætɪk] *a* automático // *n* (*gun*) pistola automática.

automation [ɔːtə'meɪʃən] *n* automatización *f*.

automaton [ɔː'tɔmətən] *pl* **-mata** [-tə] *n* autómata *m/f*.

automobile ['ɔːtəməbiːl] *n* (*US*) coche *m*, automóvil *m*.

autonomous [ɔː'tɔnəməs] *a* autónomo.

autopsy ['ɔːtɔpsɪ] *n* autopsia.

autumn ['ɔːtəm] *n* otoño.

auxiliary [ɔːg'zɪlɪərɪ] *a* auxiliar.

Av. *abbr of* **avenue.**

avail [ə'veɪl] *vt*: **to ~ o.s. of** aprovechar(se) de, valerse de // *n*: **to no ~** en vano, sin resultado.

availability [əveɪlə'bɪlɪtɪ] *n* disponibilidad *f*.

available [ə'veɪləbl] *a* disponible; (*usable*) asequible.

avalanche ['ævəlɑːnʃ] *n* alud *m*, avalancha.

avant-garde ['ævãŋ'gɑːd] *a* de vanguardia.

avaricious [ævə'rɪʃəs] *a* avaro, avariento.

Ave. *abbr of* **avenue.**

avenge [ə'vɛndʒ] *vt* vengar.

avenue ['ævənjuː] *n* avenida; (*path*) camino.

average ['ævərɪdʒ] *n* promedio, término medio // *a* (*mean*) medio, de término medio; (*ordinary*) regular, corriente // *vt* calcular el promedio de, prorratear; **on ~** por regla general; **to ~ out** *vi*: **to ~ out at** resultar por promedio, ser por regla general.

averse [ə'vɜːs] *a*: **to be ~ to sth/doing** sentir aversión *o* antipatía por algo/por hacer; **aversion** [ə'vɜːʃən] *n* aversión *f*, repugnancia.

avert [ə'vɜːt] *vt* prevenir; (*blow*) desviar; (*one's eyes*) apartar.

aviary ['eɪvɪərɪ] *n* pajarera, avería.

aviation [eɪvɪ'eɪʃən] *n* aviación *f*.

avid ['ævɪd] *a* ávido, ansioso.

avocado [ævə'kɑːdəʊ] *n* (*also*: **~ pear**) aguacate *m*.

avoid [ə'vɔɪd] *vt* evitar, eludir; **~able** *a*

evitable, eludible; ~ance n el evitar, evitación f.

await [ə'weɪt] vt esperar, aguardar.

awake [ə'weɪk] a despierto // (vb: pt awoke, pp awoken or awaked) vt despertar // vi despertarse; ~ning n el despertar.

award [ə'wɔːd] n (prize) premio, condecoración f; (LAW) fallo, sentencia; (act) concesión f // vt (prize) otorgar, conceder; (LAW: damages) adjudicar, decretar.

aware [ə'wɛə*] a consciente; (awake) despierto; (informed) enterado; to become ~ of darse cuenta de, enterarse de; ~ness n conciencia, conocimiento.

awash [ə'wɔʃ] a inundado.

away [ə'weɪ] ad (gen) fuera; (far ~) lejos; two kilometres ~ a dos kilómetros de distancia; two hours ~ by car a dos horas en coche; the holiday was two weeks ~ faltaba dos semanas para las vacaciones; ~ from lejos de, fuera de; he's ~ for a week estará ausente una semana; to take ~ vt llevar(se); to work/pedal ~ seguir trabajando/pedaleando; to fade ~ desvanecerse; (sound) apagarse; ~ match n (SPORT) partido de fuera.

awe [ɔː] n pavor m, respeto, temor m reverencial; ~-inspiring, ~some a imponente, pasmoso; ~struck a pasmado.

awful ['ɔːfəl] a tremendo, terrible, pasmoso; ~ly ad (very) terriblemente.

awhile [ə'waɪl] ad durante un rato, un rato, algún tiempo.

awkward ['ɔːkwəd] a (clumsy) desmañado, torpe; (shape) incómodo; (problem) difícil; (embarrassing) delicado, desagradable.

awning ['ɔːnɪŋ] n (of shop) toldo; (of window etc) marquesina.

awoke [ə'wəuk], awoken [-kən] pt, pp of awake.

awry [ə'raɪ] ad: to be ~ estar de través o al sesgo; to go ~ salir mal, fracasar.

axe, ax (US) [æks] n hacha // vt (employee) despedir; (project etc) parar, cortar; (jobs) reducir.

axiom ['æksɪəm] n axioma m.

axis ['æksɪs], pl axes [-siːz] n eje m.

axle ['æksl] n eje, árbol m.

ay(e) [aɪ] excl (yes) sí; the ayes npl los que votan a favor.

Aztec ['æztɛk] n azteca m/f.

B

B.A. abbr of Bachelor of Arts licenciado en letras.

babble ['bæbl] vi barbullar.

baboon [bə'buːn] n mandril m.

baby ['beɪbɪ] n nene/a m/f; ~ carriage n (US) cochecito; ~ish a infantil; ~-sit vi hacer de canguro; ~-sitter n canguro m/f.

bachelor ['bætʃələ*] n soltero.

back [bæk] n (of person) espalda; (of animal) lomo; (of hand) dorso; (of house, car, train) parte f de atrás; (of chair) respaldo; (of page) reverso; (FOOTBALL) defensa m // vt (candidate: also: ~ up) respaldar, apoyar; (horse: at races) apostar a; (car) dar marcha atrás a o con // vi (car etc) dar marcha atrás // a (in compounds) tras; ~ seats/wheels (AUT) asientos mpl/ruedas fpl de atrás; ~ payments pagos mpl con efecto retroactivo; ~ rent renta atrasada // ad (not forward) (hacia) atrás; (returned): he's ~ está de vuelta, ha vuelto; he ran ~ retrocedió corriendo; (restitution): throw the ball ~ devuelve la pelota; can I have it ~? ¿me lo devuelve?; (again): he called ~ llamó de nuevo; to ~ down vi echarse atrás; to ~ out vi (of promise) volverse atrás.

back: ~ache n dolor m de espalda; ~bencher n miembro del parlamento sin portafolio; ~biting n murmuración f; ~bone n columna vertebral; ~-cloth n telón m de foro; ~-date vt (letter) poner fecha atrasada a; ~dated pay rise alza de sueldo con efecto retroactivo; ~er n partidario; (COMM) promotor m; ~fire vi (AUT) petardear; (plans) fallar, salir al revés; ~gammon n backgammon m; ~ground n fondo; (of events) antecedentes mpl; (basic knowledge) bases fpl; (experience) conocimientos mpl, educación f; family ~ground origen m, antecedentes mpl; ~hand n (TENNIS: also: ~hand stroke) revés m; ~handed a (fig) ambiguo, equívoco; ~hander n (bribe) soborno; ~ing n (fig) apoyo, respaldo; ~lash n reacción f, resaca; ~log n: ~log of work atrasos mpl; ~number n (of magazine etc) número atrasado; ~ pay n pago atrasado; ~side n (col) trasero, culo; ~stage ad entre bastidores; ~stroke n braza de espaldas; ~ward a (movement) hacia atrás; (person, country) atrasado; (shy) tímido; ~wards ad (move, go) hacia atrás; (read a list) al revés; (fall) de espaldas; ~water n (fig) lugar m atrasado o apartado; ~yard n traspatio.

bacon ['beɪkən] n tocino.

bacteria [bæk'tɪərɪə] npl bacteria sg.

bad [bæd] a malo; (serious) grave; (meat, food) podrido, pasado; to go ~ echarse a perder.

badge [bædʒ] n insignia; (of policeman) chapa, placa.

badger ['bædʒə*] n tejón m.

badly ['bædlɪ] ad (work, dress etc) mal; ~ wounded gravemente herido; he needs it ~ le hace gran falta; to be ~ off (for money) andar mal de dinero.

badminton ['bædmɪntən] n badminton m.

bad-tempered ['bæd'tɛmpəd] a de mal genio o carácter; (temporary) de mal humor.

baffle ['bæfl] vt (puzzle) desconcertar, confundir.

bag [bæg] n bolsa, saco; (handbag) bolso; (satchel) mochila; (case) maleta; (of hunter) caza // vt (col: take) coger, pescar; ~**ful** n saco (lleno); ~**gage** n equipaje m; ~**gy** a que hace bolsas; ~**pipes** npl gaita sg.

bail [beıl] n fianza, caución f // vt (prisoner: gen: **give** ~ **to**) poner en libertad bajo fianza; (boat: also: ~ **out**) achicar; **to** ~ **sb out** obtener la libertad de uno bajo fianza; see also **bale.**

bailiff ['beılıf] n alguacil m.

bait [beıt] n cebo // vt cebar, poner el cebo en.

bake [beık] vt cocer (al horno) // vi (cook) cocerse; (be hot) hacer un calor terrible; ~**d beans** npl judías fpl en salsa de tomate; **baker** n panadero; ~**ry** n (for bread) panadería; (for cakes) pastelería; **baking** n (act) cocción f; (batch) hornada; **baking powder** n polvos mpl de levadura.

balaclava [bælə'kla:və] n (also: ~ **helmet**) pasamontañas m inv.

balance ['bæləns] n equilibrio; (COMM. sum) balance m; (remainder) resto; (scales) balanza // vt equilibrar; (budget) nivelar; (account) saldar; (compensate) contrapesar; ~ **of trade/payments** balanza de comercio/pagos; ~**d** a (personality, diet) equilibrado; ~ **sheet** n balance m.

balcony ['bælkənı] n (open) balcón m; (closed) galería.

bald [bɔ:ld] a calvo; ~**ness** n calvicie f.

bale [beıl] n (AGR) paca, fardo; **to** ~ **out** (of a plane) lanzarse en paracaídas; **to** ~ **sb out of a difficulty** sacar a uno de un problema.

baleful ['beılful] a (look) triste; (sinister) funesto, siniestro.

ball [bɔ:l] n bola; (football) balón m; (for tennis, golf) pelota; (dance) baile m.

ballad ['bæləd] n balada, romance m.

ballast ['bæləst] n lastre m.

ballerina [bælə'ri:nə] n bailarina.

ballet ['bæleı] n ballet m, baile m; ~ **dancer** n bailarín/ina m/f.

balloon [bə'lu:n] n globo; ~**ist** n ascensionista m/f.

ballot ['bælət] n votación f; ~ **box** n urna (electoral); ~ **paper** n papeleta.

ball-point pen ['bɔ:lpɔınt'-] n bolígrafo.

ballroom ['bɔ:lrum] n salón m de baile.

balmy ['ba:mı] a (breeze, air) suave, fragante; (col) = **barmy.**

Baltic ['bɔ:ltık] n: **the** ~ (**Sea**) el (Mar) Báltico.

balustrade ['bæləstreıd] n barandilla.

bamboo [bæm'bu:] n bambú m.

ban [bæn] n prohibición f, proscripción f // vt prohibir, proscribir; (exclude) excluir.

banal [bə'na:l] a banal, vulgar.

banana [bə'na:nə] n plátano.

band [bænd] n (group) banda; (gang) pandilla; (strip) faja, tira; (at a dance) orquesta; (MIL) banda; **to** ~ **together** vi juntarse, asociarse.

bandage ['bændıdʒ] n venda, vendaje m // vt vendar.

bandit ['bændıt] n bandido; **one-armed** ~ máquina tragaperras.

bandstand ['bændstænd] n quiosco.

bandwagon ['bændwægən] n: **to jump on the** ~ (fig) seguir la corriente o la moda.

bandy ['bændı] vt (jokes, insults) cambiar.

bandy-legged ['bændı'lɛgd] a estevado.

bang [bæŋ] n estallido; (of door) portazo; (blow) golpe m // vt hacer estallar; (door) cerrar de golpe // vi estallar.

banger ['bæŋə*] n (car: gen: **old** ~) chatarra.

bangle ['bæŋgl] n ajorca.

banish ['bænıʃ] vt desterrar.

banister(s) ['bænıstə(z)] n(pl) pasamanos m inv.

banjo ['bændʒəu], pl ~**es** or ~**s** n banjo.

bank [bæŋk] n (COMM) banco; (of river, lake) ribera, orilla; (of earth) terraplén m // vi (AVIAT) ladearse; **to** ~ **on** vt fus contar con; **to** ~ **with** tener la cuenta con; ~ **account** n cuenta de banco; ~**er** n banquero; **B**~ **holiday** n día m festivo; ~**ing** n banca; ~**note** n billete m de banco; ~ **rate** n tipo de interés bancario.

bankrupt ['bæŋkrʌpt] n quebrado/a // a quebrado, insolvente; **to go** ~ quebrar; **to be** ~ estar en quiebra; ~**cy** n quiebra; (fraudulent) bancarrota.

banner ['bænə*] n bandera; (in demonstration) pancarta.

banns [bænz] npl amonestaciones fpl.

banquet ['bæŋkwıt] n banquete m.

baptism ['bæptızəm] n bautismo.

baptize [bæp'taız] vt bautizar.

bar [ba:*] n barra; (of window etc) tranca; (of soap) pastilla; (fig: hindrance) obstáculo; (prohibition) proscripción f; (pub) bar m; (counter: in pub) mostrador m; (MUS) barra // vt (road) obstruir; (window) atrancar; (person) excluir; (activity) prohibir; **behind** ~**s** en la cárcel; **the B**~ (LAW) (profession) la abogacía; (people) el cuerpo de abogados; ~ **none** sin excepción.

barbaric [ba:'bærık] a bárbaro.

barbarous ['ba:bərəs] a bárbaro.

barbecue ['ba:bıkju:] n barbacoa.

barbed wire ['ba:bd-] n alambre m de púas.

barber ['ba:bə*] n peluquero, barbero.

barbiturate [ba:'bıtjurıt] n barbitúrico.

bare [bɛə*] a desnudo; (head) descubierto // vt desnudar; **to** ~ **one's teeth** enseñar los dientes; ~**back** ad sin montura; ~**faced** a descarado; ~**foot** a, ad descalzo; ~**ly** ad apenas.

bargain ['ba:gın] n pacto, negocio; (good buy) ganga // vi negociar; (haggle) regatear; **into the** ~ además, por añadidura.

barge [ba:dʒ] n barcaza; **to** ~ **in** vi

irrumpir, entrar sin permiso; **to ~ into** vt fus dar contra.
baritone ['bærɪtɔun] n barítono.
bark [baːk] n (of tree) corteza; (of dog) ladrido // vi ladrar.
barley ['baːlɪ] n cebada.
barmaid ['baːmeɪd] n camarera.
barman ['baːmɔn] n camarero, barman m.
barmy ['baːmɪ] a (col) chiflado, lelo.
barn [baːn] n granero.
barnacle ['baːnɔkl] n percebe m.
barometer [bɔ'rɔmɪtɔ*] n barómetro.
baron ['bærɔn] n barón m; **~ess** n baronesa.
barracks ['bærɔks] npl cuartel m.
barrage ['bæraːʒ] n (MIL) descarga, bombardeo; (dam) presa.
barrel ['bærɔl] n tonel m, barril m; (of gun) cañón m.
barren ['bærɔn] a estéril, árido.
barricade [bærɪ'keɪd] n barricada // vt levantar barricadas.
barrier ['bærɪɔ*] n barrera.
barring ['baːrɪŋ] prep excepto, salvo.
barrister ['bærɪstɔ*] n abogado m/f.
barrow ['bærɔu] n (cart) carretilla (de mano).
bartender ['baːtɛndɔ*] n (US) camarero, barman m.
barter ['baːtɔ*] vt: **to ~ sth for sth** trocar algo por algo.
base [beɪs] n base f // vt: **to ~ sth on** basar o fundar algo en // a bajo, infame; **~ball** n béisbol m; **~ment** n sótano.
bash [bæʃ] vt (col) golpear.
bashful ['bæʃful] a tímido, vergonzoso.
bashing ['bæʃɪŋ] n (col) tunda.
basic ['beɪsɪk] a básico; **~ally** ad fundamentalmente, en el fondo.
basil ['bæzl] n albahaca.
basin ['beɪsn] n (vessel) cuenco, tazón m; (GEO) cuenca; (also: **wash~**) palangana, jofaina.
basis ['beɪsɪs], pl **-ses** [-siːz] n base f.
bask [baːsk] vi: **to ~ in the sun** tomar el sol.
basket ['baːskɪt] n cesta, cesto; (with handle) canasta; **~ball** n baloncesto; **~work** n cestería.
Basque [bæsk] a, n vasco/a; **~ Country** Euskadi m, País m Vasco.
bass [beɪs] n (MUS) contrabajo.
bassoon [bɔ'suːn] n bajón m.
bastard ['baːstɔd] n bastardo.
baste [beɪst] vt (CULIN) pringar.
bastion ['bæstɪɔn] n baluarte m.
bat [bæt] n (ZOOL) murciélago; (for ball games) palo; (for cricket, baseball) bate m; (for table tennis) raqueta; **he didn't ~ an eyelid** ni pestañeó.
batch [bætʃ] n (of bread) hornada; (of papers) colección f, lote m.
bated ['beɪtɪd] a: **with ~ breath** sin respiración.
bath [baːθ ó baːðz] n (~ tub) baño, bañera; (also: **~s** pl) baño, piscina // vt bañar; **to**

have a ~ bañarse, tomar un baño; **~chair** n silla de ruedas.
bathe [beɪð] vi bañarse // vt bañar; **bather** n bañista m/f.
bathing ['beɪðɪŋ] n el bañarse; **~ cap** n gorro de baño; **~ costume** n traje m de baño; **~ trunks** npl bañador m.
bath: **~mat** n estera de baño; **~room** n (cuarto de) baño; **~s** npl piscina sg; **~ towel** n toalla de baño.
baton ['bætɔn] n (MUS) batuta.
battalion [bɔ'tælɪɔn] n batallón m.
batter ['bætɔ*] vt apalear, azotar // n batido; **~ed** a (hat, pan) estropeado.
battery ['bætɔrɪ] n batería; (of torch) pila.
battle ['bætl] n batalla; (fig) lucha // vi luchar; **~field** n campo m de batalla; **~ments** npl almenas fpl; **~ship** n acorazado.
bawdy ['bɔːdɪ] a indecente; (joke) verde.
bawl [bɔːl] vi chillar, gritar.
bay [beɪ] n (GEO) bahía; (BOT) laurel m // vi aullar; **to hold sb at ~** mantener a alguien a raya.
bayonet ['beɪɔnɪt] n bayoneta.
bay window ['beɪ-] n ventana salediza.
bazaar [bɔ'zaː*] n bazar m.
bazooka [bɔ'zuːkɔ] n bazuca.
b. & b., B. & B. abbr of bed and breakfast cama y desayuno.
BBC n abbr of British Broadcasting Corporation.
B.C. ad abbr of before Christ a. de J.C. (antes de Jesucristo).
be [biː], pt **was, were**, pp **been** vi (of state) ser; (of place, temporary condition) estar; **I am English** soy inglés; **I am tired** estoy cansado; **how are you?** ¿cómo está Usted?; **who is it?** ¿quién es?; **it is raining** está lloviendo; **I am warm** tengo calor; **it is cold** hace frío; **how much is it?** ¿cuánto es o cuesta?; **he is four (years old)** tiene cuatro años; **2 and 2 are 4** dos más dos son cuatro; **where have you been?** ¿dónde has estado?, ¿de dónde vienes?
beach [biːtʃ] n playa // vt varar.
beacon ['biːkɔn] n (lighthouse) faro; (marker) guía.
bead [biːd] n cuenta, abalorio; (of sweat) gota.
beak [biːk] n pico.
beaker ['biːkɔ*] n jarra.
beam [biːm] n (ARCH) viga, travesaño; (of light) rayo, haz m de luz // vi brillar; (smile) sonreír; **~ing** a (sun, smile) radiante.
bean [biːn] n judía; **runner/broad ~** habichuela/haba; **coffee ~** grano de café.
bear [bɛɔ*] n oso // (vb: pt **bore**, pp **borne**) vt (weight etc) llevar; (cost) pagar; (responsibility) tener; (endure) soportar, aguantar; (stand up to) resistir a; (children) parir // vi: **to ~ right/left** torcer a la derecha/izquierda; **~able** a soportable.
beard [bɪɔd] n barba; **~ed** a barbado.

bearing ['bɛərɪŋ] *n* porte *m*, comportamiento; (*connection*) relación *f*; (**ball**) ~s *npl* cojinetes *mpl* a bolas; **to take a** ~ marcarse; **to find one's** ~s orientarse.

beast [bi:st] *n* bestia; (*col*) bruto, salvaje *m*; ~**ly** *a* bestial; (*awful*) horrible.

beat [bi:t] *n* (*of heart*) latido; (*MUS*) ritmo, compás *m*; (*of policeman*) ronda // (*vb: pt* **beat,** *pp* **beaten**) *vt* (*hit*) golpear; (*eggs*) batir; (*defeat*) vencer, derrotar; (*better*) sobrepasar; (*drum*) tocar; (*rhythm*) marcar // *vi* (*heart*) latir; **to** ~ **about the bush** ir por rodeos; **to** ~ **it** largarse; **to** ~ **off** *vt* rechazar; **to** ~ **up** *vt* (*col*: *person*) dar una paliza a; ~**er** *n* (*for eggs, cream*) batidora; ~**ing** *n* golpeo.

beautiful ['bju:tɪful] *a* hermoso, bello; ~**ly** *ad* maravillosamente; **beautify** [-faɪ] *vt* embellecer.

beauty ['bju:tɪ] *n* belleza, hermosura; (*person*) belleza; ~ **salon** *n* salón *m* de belleza; ~ **spot** *n* lunar *m* postizo; (*TOURISM*) lugar *m* de excepcional belleza.

beaver ['bi:və*] *n* castor *m*.

becalmed [bɪ'kɑ:md] *a* encalmado.

became [bɪ'keɪm] *pt of* **become.**

because [bɪ'kɔz] *conj* porque; ~ **of** *prep* debido a, a causa de.

beck [bɛk] *n*: **to be at the** ~ **and call of** estar a disposición de.

beckon ['bɛkən] *vt* (*also*: ~ **to**) llamar con señas.

become [bɪ'kʌm] (*irg: like* **come**) *vt* (*suit*) favorecer, sentar a // *vi* (+ *noun*) hacerse, llegar a ser; (+ *adj*) ponerse, volverse; **to** ~ **fat** engordarse.

becoming [bɪ'kʌmɪŋ] *a* (*behaviour*) decoroso; (*clothes*) favorecedor(a).

bed [bɛd] *n* cama; (*of flowers*) macizo; (*of coal, clay*) capa; **to go to** ~ acostarse; **single/double** ~ cama individual/matrimonial; ~**clothes** *npl* ropa *sg* de cama; ~**ding** *n* ropa de cama.

bedlam ['bɛdləm] *n* confusión *f.*

bedraggled [bɪ'drægld] *a* mojado, ensuciado.

bed: ~**ridden** *a* postrado (en cama); ~**room** *n* dormitorio, alcoba; ~**side** *n*: **at sb's** ~**side** a la cabecera de alguien; ~**sit(ter)** *n* apartamento; ~**spread** *n* sobrecama *m*, colcha.

bee [bi:] *n* abeja.

beech [bi:tʃ] *n* haya.

beef [bi:f] *n* carne *f* de vaca; **roast** ~ rosbif *m.*

bee: ~**hive** *n* colmena; ~**line** *n*: **to make a** ~**line for** ir derecho a.

been [bi:n] *pp of* **be.**

beer [bɪə*] *n* cerveza.

beetle ['bi:tl] *n* escarabajo.

beetroot ['bi:tru:t] *n* remolacha.

before [bɪ'fɔ:*] *prep* (*of time*) antes de; (*of space*) delante de // *conj* antes (de) que // *ad* (*time*) antes, anteriormente; (*space*) delante, adelante; **the week** ~ la semana

anterior; **I've never seen it** ~ no lo he visto nunca.

befriend [bɪ'frɛnd] *vt* ofrecer amistad a, ayudar.

beg [bɛg] *vi* pedir, rogar; (*as beggar*) pedir limosna // *vt* pedir, rogar; (*entreat*) suplicar.

began [bɪ'gæn] *pt of* **begin.**

beggar ['bɛgə*] *n* mendigo.

begin [bɪ'gɪn] *pt* **began,** *pp* **begun** *vt, vi* empezar, comenzar; ~**ner** *n* principiante *m/f*; ~**ning** *n* principio, comienzo.

begrudge [bɪ'grʌdʒ] *vt*: **to** ~ **sb sth** tenerle envidia a alguien por algo.

begun [bɪ'gʌn] *pp of* **begin.**

behalf [bɪ'hɑ:f] *n*: **on** ~ **of** en nombre de, por.

behave [bɪ'heɪv] *vi* (*person*) portarse, comportarse; (*thing*) funcionar; (*well: also:* ~ **o.s.**) portarse bien; **behaviour, behavior** (*US*) *n* comportamiento, conducta.

behind [bɪ'haɪnd] *prep* detrás de // *ad* detrás, por detrás, atrás // *n* trasero; ~ **time** atrasado.

behold [bɪ'həʊld] (*irg: like* **hold**) *vt* contemplar.

beige [beɪʒ] *a* beige.

being ['bi:ɪŋ] *n* ser *m*; **to come into** ~ nacer, aparecer.

belated [bɪ'leɪtɪd] *a* atrasado, tardío.

belch [bɛltʃ] *vi* eructar // *vt* (*gen*: ~ **out**: *smoke etc*) arrojar.

belfry ['bɛlfrɪ] *n* campanario.

Belgian ['bɛldʒən] *a, n* belga *m/f.*

Belgium ['bɛldʒəm] *n* Bélgica.

belie [bɪ'laɪ] *vt* desmentir, contradecir.

belief [bɪ'li:f] *n* (*opinion*) opinión *f*; (*trust, faith*) fe *f*; (*acceptance as true*) creencia.

believable [bɪ'li:vəbl] *a* creíble.

believe [bɪ'li:v] *vt, vi* creer; **believer** *n* creyente *m/f*, fiel *m/f*; (*POL*) partidario/a.

belittle [bɪ'lɪtl] *vt* minimizar, despreciar.

bell [bɛl] *n* campana; (*small*) campanilla; (*on door*) timbre *m*; (*animal's*) cencerro; (*on toy etc*) cascabel *m.*

belligerent [bɪ'lɪdʒərənt] *a* (*at war*) beligerante; (*fig*) agresivo.

bellow ['bɛləʊ] *vi* bramar; (*person*) rugir // *vt* (*orders*) gritar, vociferar.

bellows ['bɛləʊz] *npl* fuelle *m.*

belly ['bɛlɪ] *n* barriga, panza.

belong [bɪ'lɔŋ] *vi*: **to** ~ **to** pertenecer a; (*club etc*) ser socio de; ~**ings** *npl* pertenencias *fpl.*

beloved [bɪ'lʌvɪd] *a, n* querido/a, amado/a.

below [bɪ'ləʊ] *prep* bajo, debajo de // *ad* abajo, (por) debajo; **see** ~ véase más abajo.

belt [bɛlt] *n* cinturón *m*; (*MED*) faja; (*TECH*) correa, cinta // *vt* (*thrash*) golpear con correa.

bench [bɛntʃ] *n* banco; **the B**~ (*LAW*) tribunal *m*; (*people*) judicatura.

bend [bɛnd], *pt, pp* **bent** *vt* doblar, inclinar;

(*leg, arm*) torcer // *vi* doblarse, inclinarse // *n* (*in road*) recodo, vuelta; (*in pipe, river*) ángulo, curva; **to** ~ **down** *vi* inclinar, doblar; **to** ~ **over** *vi* inclinarse.
beneath [bɪ'niːθ] *prep* bajo, debajo de; (*unworthy of*) indigno de // *ad* abajo, (por) debajo.
benefactor ['bɛnɪfæktə*] *n* bienhechor *m*.
beneficial [bɛnɪ'fɪʃəl] *a* provechoso, beneficioso.
benefit ['bɛnɪfɪt] *n* beneficio, provecho; (*profit*) utilidad *f*; (*money*) subsidio // *vt* beneficiar, aprovechar // *vi*: **he'll** ~ **from it** le sacará provecho.
Benelux ['bɛnɪlʌks] *n* Benelux *m*.
benevolent [bɪ'nɛvələnt] *a* benévolo.
bent [bɛnt] *pt, pp* of **bend** // *n* inclinación *f* // *a*: **to be** ~ **on** estar empeñado en.
bequeath [bɪ'kwiːð] *vt* legar.
bequest [bɪ'kwɛst] *n* legado.
bereaved [bɪ'riːvd] *n*: **the** ~ los afligidos *mpl*; **bereavement** [-'riːvmənt] *n* aflicción *f*.
beret ['bɛreɪ] *n* boina.
berry ['bɛrɪ] *n* baya.
berserk [bə'sɜːk] *a*: **to go** ~ perder los estribos.
berth [bɜːθ] *n* (*bed*) litera; (*cabin*) camarote *m*; (*for ship*) amarradero // *vi* atracar, amarrar.
beseech [bɪ'siːtʃ], *pt, pp* **besought** [-'sɔːt] *vt* suplicar.
beset [bɪ'sɛt], *pt, pp* **beset** *vt* rodear; (*person*) acosar.
beside [bɪ'saɪd] *prep* junto a, al lado de; **to be** ~ **o.s. (with anger)** estar fuera de sí.
besides [bɪ'saɪdz] *ad* además // *prep* (*as well as*) además de; (*except*) fuera de, excepto.
besiege [bɪ'siːdʒ] *vt* (*town*) sitiar; (*fig*) asediar.
best [bɛst] *a* (el/la) mejor // *ad* (lo) mejor; **the** ~ **part of** (*quantity*) la mayor parte de; **at** ~ en el mejor de los casos; **to make the** ~ **of sth** sacar el mejor partido de algo; **to the** ~ **of my knowledge** que yo sepa; **to the** ~ **of my ability** como mejor puedo; ~ **man** *n* padrino de boda.
bestow [bɪ'stəu] *vt* otorgar; (*affection*) ofrecer.
bestseller ['bɛst'sɛlə*] *n* éxito de librería, bestseller *m*.
bet [bɛt] *n* apuesta // *vt, vi, pt, pp* **bet** or **betted** apostar, jugar.
betray [bɪ'treɪ] *vt* traicionar; (*denounce*) delatar; ~**al** *n* traición *f*.
better ['bɛtə*] *a* mejor // *ad* mejor // *vt* mejorar; (*go above*) superar // *n*: **to get the** ~ **of** quedar por encima de alguien; **you had** ~ **do it** más vale que lo haga; **he thought** ~ **of it** cambió de parecer; **to get** ~ mejorar(se); (*MED*) reponerse; ~ **off** *a* más acomodado.
betting ['bɛtɪŋ] *n* juego, el apostar; ~ **shop** *n* agencia de apuestas.

between [bɪ'twiːn] *prep* entre // *ad* en medio.
beverage ['bɛvərɪdʒ] *n* bebida.
bevy ['bɛvɪ] *n*: **a** ~ **of** una bandada de.
beware [bɪ'wɛə*] *vi*: **to** ~ **(of)** precaverse de, tener cuidado con // *excl* ¡cuidado!
bewildered [bɪ'wɪldəd] *a* aturdido, perplejo.
bewitching [bɪ'wɪtʃɪŋ] *a* hechicero, encantador(a).
beyond [bɪ'jɔnd] *prep* (*in space*) más allá de; (*exceeding*) además de, fuera de; (*above*) superior a // *ad* más allá, más lejos; ~ **doubt** fuera de toda duda; ~ **repair** irreparable.
bias ['baɪəs] *n* (*prejudice*) prejuicio, pasión *f*; (*preference*) predisposición *f*; ~**(s)ed** *a* (*against*) con prejuicios; (*towards*) partidario.
bib [bɪb] *n* babero.
Bible ['baɪbl] *n* Biblia.
bibliography [bɪblɪ'ɔgrəfɪ] *n* bibliografía.
bicker ['bɪkə*] *vi* reñir.
bicycle ['baɪsɪkl] *n* bicicleta.
bid [bɪd] *n* (*at auction*) oferta, postura; (*attempt*) tentativa, conato // (*vb*: *pt* **bade** [bæd] *or* **bid**, *pp* **bidden** ['bɪdn] *or* **bid**) *vi* hacer una oferta // *vt* mandar, ordenar; **to** ~ **sb good day** dar a uno los buenos días; ~**der** *n*: **the highest** ~**der** el mejor postor; ~**ding** *n* (*at auction*) ofertas *fpl*; (*order*) orden *f*, mandato.
bide [baɪd] *vt*: **to** ~ **one's time** esperar el momento adecuado.
bidet ['biːdeɪ] *n* bidet *m*.
bier [bɪə*] *n* féretro.
big [bɪg] *a* grande.
bigamy ['bɪgəmɪ] *n* bigamia.
bigheaded ['bɪg'hɛdɪd] *a* engreído.
bigot ['bɪgət] *n* fanático, intolerante *m/f*; ~**ed** *a* fanático, intolerante; ~**ry** *n* fanatismo, intolerancia.
bike [baɪk] *n* bici *f*.
bikini [bɪ'kiːnɪ] *n* bikini *m*.
bile [baɪl] *n* bilis *f*.
bilingual [baɪ'lɪŋgwəl] *a* bilingüe.
bill [bɪl] *n* (*account*) cuenta; (*invoice*) factura; (*POL*) proyecto de ley; (*US: banknote*) billete *m*; (*of bird*) pico; **stick no** ~**s** prohibido fijar carteles.
billet ['bɪlɪt] *n* alojamiento.
billfold ['bɪlfəuld] *n* (*US*) cartera.
billiards ['bɪlɪədz] *n* billar *m*.
billion ['bɪlɪən] *n* (*Brit*) billón *m*; (*US*) mil millones.
billy goat ['bɪlɪ-] *n* macho cabrío.
bin [bɪn] *n* (*gen*) cubo; **bread/litter** ~ nasa/papelera.
bind [baɪnd], *pt, pp* **bound** *vt* atar, liar; (*wound*) vendar; (*book*) encuadernar; (*oblige*) obligar; ~**ing** *a* (*contract*) obligatorio.
binge [bɪndʒ] *n* borrachera, juerga.
bingo ['bɪŋgəu] *n* bingo *m*.
binoculars [bɪ'nɔkjuləz] *npl* gemelos *mpl*, prismáticos *mpl*.

bio... [baɪə] *pref:* ~**chemistry** *n* bioquímica; ~**graphy** [baɪˈɔgrəfi] *n* biografía; ~**logical** *a* biológico; ~**logy** [baɪˈɔlədʒi] *n* biología.

birch [bəːtʃ] *n* abedul *m*; (*cane*) vara.

bird [bəːd] *n* ave *f*, pájaro; (*col: girl*) chica; ~**cage** *n* jaula; ~**'s eye view** *n* vista de pájaro; ~ **watcher** *n* ornitólogo.

birth [bəːθ] *n* nacimiento; (MED) parto; **to give** ~ **to** parir, dar a luz; ~ **certificate** *n* partida de nacimiento; ~ **control** *n* control *m* de natalidad; (*methods*) métodos *mpl* anticonceptivos; ~**day** *n* cumpleaños *m*; ~**place** *n* lugar *m* de nacimiento; ~**rate** *n* (tasa de) natalidad *f.*

biscuit [ˈbɪskɪt] *n* galleta.

bisect [baɪˈsɛkt] *vt* bisecar.

bishop [ˈbɪʃəp] *n* obispo.

bit [bɪt] *pt of* **bite** // *n* trozo, pedazo, pedacito; (*of horse*) freno, bocado; **a** ~ **of** un poco de; **a** ~ **mad** algo loco; ~ **by** ~ poco a poco.

bitch [bɪtʃ] *n* (*dog*) perra.

bite [baɪt], *pt* **bit**, *pp* **bitten** *vt, vi* morder; (*insect etc*) picar // *n* mordedura; (*insect* ~) picadura; (*mouthful*) bocado; **let's have a** ~ **(to eat)** comamos algo.

biting [ˈbaɪtɪŋ] *a* penetrante, cortante; (*sharp*) mordaz.

bitten [ˈbɪtn] *pp of* **bite.**

bitter [ˈbɪtə*] *a* amargo; (*wind, criticism*) cortante, penetrante; (*battle*) encarnizado // *n* (*beer*) cerveza clara; ~**ness** *n* amargura; (*anger*) rencor *m.*

bizarre [bɪˈzɑː*] *a* raro, estrafalario.

blab [blæb] *vi* chismear, soplar // *vt* (*also:* ~ **out**) revelar, contar.

black [blæk] *a* (*colour*) negro; (*dark*) oscuro // *n* negro; (*colour*) color *m* negro // *vt* (*shoes*) lustrar; (INDUSTRY) boicotear; **to give sb a** ~ **eye** darle a uno una bofetada (en el ojo); ~ **and blue** *a* amoratado; ~**berry** *n* zarzamora; ~**bird** *n* mirlo; ~**board** *n* pizarra; ~**currant** *n* grosella negra; ~**en** *vt* ennegrecer; (*fig*) denigrar; ~**leg** *n* esquirol *m*, rompehuelgas *m inv*; ~**list** *n* lista negra; ~**mail** *n* chantaje *m* // *vt* chantajear; ~**mailer** *n* chantajista *m/f*; ~ **market** *n* mercado negro; ~**out** *n* apagón *m*; (*fainting*) desmayo, pérdida de conocimiento; ~**smith** *n* herrero.

bladder [ˈblædə*] *n* vejiga.

blade [bleɪd] *n* hoja; (*cutting edge*) filo; **a** ~ **of grass** una brizna de hierba.

blame [bleɪm] *n* culpa // *vt:* **to** ~ **sb for sth** echar a uno la culpa de algo; **to be to** ~ tener la culpa de; ~**less** *a* (*person*) inocente.

bland [blænd] *a* suave; (*taste*) soso.

blank [blæŋk] *a* en blanco; (*shot*) sin bala; (*look*) sin expresión // *n* blanco, espacio en blanco; cartucho sin bala *o* de fogueo.

blanket [ˈblæŋkɪt] *n* manta // *vt* envolver.

blare [blɛə*] *vi* (*brass band, horns, radio*) resonar.

blasé [ˈblɑːzeɪ] *a* hastiado.

blasphemy [ˈblæsfɪmɪ] *n* blasfemia.

blast [blɑːst] *n* (*of wind*) ráfaga, soplo; (*of whistle*) toque *m*; (*of explosive*) carga explosiva; (*force*) choque *m* // *vt* (*blow up*) volar; (*blow open*) abrir con carga explosiva; ~**-off** *n* (SPACE) lanzamiento.

blatant [ˈbleɪtənt] *a* descarado.

blaze [bleɪz] *n* (*fire*) fuego; (*flames*) llamarada; (*fig*) arranque *m* // *vi* (*fire*) arder en llamas; (*fig*) brillar // *vt:* **to** ~ **a trail** (*fig*) abrir (un) camino.

blazer [ˈbleɪzə*] *n* chaqueta ligera.

bleach [bliːtʃ] *n* (*also:* **household** ~) lejía // *vt* (*linen*) blanquear; ~**ed** *a* (*hair*) decolorado.

bleak [bliːk] *a* (*countryside*) desierto; (*prospect*) poco prometedor(a).

bleary-eyed [ˈblɪərɪˈaɪd] *a* de ojos legañosos.

bleat [bliːt] *vi* balar.

bleed [bliːd], *pt, pp* **bled** [blɛd] *vt, vi* sangrar.

blemish [ˈblɛmɪʃ] *n* mancha, tacha.

blend [blɛnd] *n* mezcla // *vt* mezclar // *vi* (*colours etc*) combinarse, mezclarse.

bless [blɛs], *pt, pp* **blessed** *or* **blest** [blɛst] *vt* bendecir; ~**ing** *n* bendición *f*; (*advantage*) beneficio, ventaja.

blew [bluː] *pt of* **blow.**

blight [blaɪt] *vt* (*hopes etc*) frustrar, arruinar.

blimey [ˈblaɪmɪ] *excl* (*col*) ¡caray!

blind [blaɪnd] *a* ciego // *n* (*for window*) persiana // *vt* cegar; (*dazzle*) deslumbrar; ~ **alley** *n* callejón *m* sin salida; ~ **corner** *n* esquina escondida; ~**fold** *n* venda // *a, ad* con los ojos vendados // *vt* vendar los ojos a; ~**ly** *ad* a ciegas, ciegamente; ~**ness** *n* ceguera; ~ **spot** *n* mácula.

blink [blɪŋk] *vi* parpadear, pestañear; (*light*) oscilar; ~**ers** *npl* anteojeras *fpl.*

blinking [ˈblɪŋkɪŋ] *a* (*col*): **this** ~... este condenado... .

bliss [blɪs] *n* felicidad *f*; (*fig*) éxtasis *m.*

blister [ˈblɪstə*] *n* (*on skin*) ampolla // *vi* (*paint*) ampollarse; ~**ing** *a* (*heat*) abrasador(a).

blithe [blaɪð] *a* alegre.

blithering [ˈblɪðərɪŋ] *a* (*col*): **this** ~ **idiot** este tonto perdido.

blitz [blɪts] *n* bombardeo aéreo.

blizzard [ˈblɪzəd] *n* ventisca.

bloated [ˈbləʊtɪd] *a* hinchado.

blob [blɔb] *n* (*drop*) gota; (*stain, spot*) mancha.

block [blɔk] *n* bloque *m*; (*in pipes*) obstáculo; (*of buildings*) manzana // *vt* (*gen*) obstruir, cerrar; (*progress*) estorbar; ~**ade** [-ˈkeɪd] *n* bloqueo // *vt* bloquear; ~**age** *n* estorbo, obstrucción *f*; ~ **of flats** *n* bloque *m* de pisos; ~ **letters** *npl* letras *fpl* de molde.

bloke [bləʊk] *n* (*col*) tipo, tío.

blond(e) [blɔnd] *a, n* rubio/a.

blood [blʌd] *n* sangre *f*; ~ **donor** *n*

donador/a *m/f* de sangre; ~ **group** *n* grupo sanguíneo; ~ **hound** *n* sabueso; ~ **pressure** *n* presión *f* sanguínea; ~ **shed** *n* matanza; ~ **shot** *a* inyectado en sangre; ~ **stained** *a* manchado de sangre; ~ **stream** *n* corriente *f* sanguínea; ~ **thirsty** *a* sanguinario; ~ **transfusion** *n* transfusión *f* de sangre; ~**y** *a* sangriento; (*col!*): **this** ~**y...** este condenado/puñetero...; ~**y strong/ good** (*col!*) terriblemente fuerte/ bueno; ~**y- minded** *a* (*col*) malintencionado.

bloom [blu:m] *n* floración *f*; (*fig*) perfección *f*, plenitud *f* // *vi* florecer; ~**ing** *a* (*col*): **this** ~**ing...** este condenado... .

blossom ['blɔsəm] *n* flor *f* // *vi* florecer; (*fig*) desarrollarse.

blot [blɔt] *n* borrón *m* // *vt* secar; (*ink*) manchar; **to** ~ **out** *vt* (*view*) oscurecer, hacer desaparecer.

blotchy ['blɔtʃi] *a* (*complexion*) enrojecido, lleno de manchas.

blotting paper ['blɔtiŋ-] *n* papel *m* secante.

blouse [blauz] *n* blusa.

blow [bləu] *n* golpe *m* // (*vb*: *pt* **blew,** *pp* **blown** [bləun]) *vi* soplar // *vt* (*glass*) soplar; (*fuse*) quemar; (*instrument*) tocar; **to** ~ **one's nose** sonarse; **to** ~ **away** *vt* llevarse, arrancar; **to** ~ **down** *vt* derribar; **to** ~ **off** *vt* arrebatar; **to** ~ **out** *vi* apagarse; **to** ~ **over** *vi* pasar, quedar olvidado; **to** ~ **up** *vi* estallar // *vt* volar; (*tyre*) inflar; (*PHOT*) ampliar; ~**lamp** *n* soplete *m*, lámpara de soldar; ~**-out** *n* (*of tyre*) pinchazo.

blubber ['blʌbə*] *n* grasa de ballena // *vi* (*pej*) lloriquear.

blue [blu:] *a* azul; ~ **film/joke** film/chiste verde; **to have the** ~**s** estar melancólico; ~**bell** *n* campanilla, campánula azul; ~**bottle** *n* moscarda, mosca azul; ~ **jeans** *npl* bluejean *m inv*, vaqueros *mpl*; ~**print** *n* (*fig*) anteproyecto.

bluff [blʌf] *vi* hacer un bluff, farolear // *n* bluff *m*, farol *m*.

blunder ['blʌndə*] *n* error *m* garrafal, metedura de pata // *vi* cometer un error, meter la pata.

blunt [blʌnt] *a* embotado, desafilado; (*person*) franco, directo // *vt* embotar, desafilar; ~**ness** *n* (*of person*) franqueza, brusquedad *f*.

blur [blə:*] *n* aspecto borroso // *vt* hacer borroso, desdibujar.

blurt [blə:t] ~ **out** *vt* (*say*) descolgarse con, dejar escapar.

blush [blʌʃ] *vi* ruborizarse, ponerse colorado // *n* rubor *m*.

blustering ['blʌstəriŋ] *a* (*person*) fanfarrón(ona).

blustery ['blʌstəri] *a* (*weather*) tempestuoso, tormentoso.

board [bɔ:d] *n* tabla, tablero; (*on wall*) tablón *m*; (*for chess etc*) tablero; (*commit- tee*) junta, consejo; (*in firm*) mesa *o* junta

directiva // *vt* (*ship*) embarcarse en; (*train*) subir a; **full** ~ pensión *f* completa; **to go by the** ~ (*fig*) ser abandonado/olvidado; **to** ~ **up** *vt* (*door*) entablar, enmaderar; ~ **and lodging** *n* pensión *f*; ~**er** *n* huésped/a *m/f*; (*SCOL*) interno; ~**ing house** *n* casa de huéspedes; ~**ing school** *n* internado; ~ **room** *n* sala de juntas.

boast [bəust] *vi* jactarse, presumir // *vt* ostentar // *n* alarde *m*, baladronada; ~**ful** *a* presumido, jactancioso.

boat [bəut] *n* barco, buque *m*; (*small*) barca, bote *m*; ~**er** *n* (*hat*) sombrero de paja; ~**ing** *n* canotaje *m*; ~**man** *n* barquero; ~**swain** ['bəusn] *n* contramaestre *m*.

bob [bɔb] *vi* (*boat, cork on water: also:* ~ **up and down**) menearse, balancearse; **to** ~ **up** *vi* aparecer, levantarse // *n* (*col*) = **shilling.**

bobbin ['bɔbin] *n* (*of sewing machine*) carrete *m*, bobina.

bobby ['bɔbi] *n* (*col*) poli *m/f*.

bobsleigh ['bɔbslei] *n* bob *m*.

bodice ['bɔdis] *n* corpiño.

bodily ['bɔdili] *a* corpóreo, corporal // *ad* (*in person*) en persona; (*lift*) en peso.

body ['bɔdi] *n* cuerpo; (*corpse*) cadáver *m*; (*of car*) caja, carrocería; (*fig: society*) conjunto; (*fig: quantity*) parte *f* principal; **in a** ~ en bloque, en conjunto; ~**guard** *n* guardaespaldas *m inv*; ~**work** *n* carrocería.

bog [bɔg] *n* pantano, ciénaga // *vt*: **to get** ~**ged down** (*fig*) empantanarse, atascarse.

boggle ['bɔgl] *vi*: **the mind** ~**s** le deja boquiabierto a uno.

bogus ['bəugəs] *a* falso, fraudulento; (*person*) fingido.

boil [bɔil] *vt* cocer; (*eggs*) pasar por agua // *vi* hervir // *n* (*MED*) furúnculo, divieso; **to come to the** ~ comenzar a hervir; **to** ~ **down** *vi* (*fig*) reducirse a; ~**er** *n* caldera; ~**er suit** *n* mono; ~**ing point** *n* punto de ebullición *f*.

boisterous ['bɔistərəs] *a* (*noisy*) bullicioso; (*excitable*) exuberante; (*crowd*) tumultuoso.

bold [bəuld] *a* (*brave*) valiente, audaz; (*excessively*) atrevido; (*pej*) descarado; (*outline, colour*) fuerte; ~**ness** *n* valor *m*, audacia; (*cheek*) descaro.

Bolivia [bə'liviə] *n* Bolivia.

bollard ['bɔləd] *n* (*AUT*) poste *m*.

bolster ['bəulstə*] *n* travesero, cabezal *m*; **to** ~ **up** *vt* reforzar; (*fig*) alentar.

bolt [bəult] *n* (*lock*) cerrojo; (*with nut*) perno, tornillo // *vt* (*door*) echar el cerrojo a; (*food*) engullir // *vi* fugarse; (*horse*) desbocarse.

bomb [bɔm] *n* bomba // *vt* bombardear; ~**ard** [-'ba:d] *vt* bombardear; (*fig*) asediar; ~**ardment** [-'ba:dmənt] *n* bombardeo.

bombastic [bɔm'bæstɪk] a rimbombante; (*person*) farolero.
bomb: ~ **disposal** n desmontaje m de explosivos; ~**er** n (*AVIAT*) bombardero; ~**shell** n obús m, granada; (*fig*) bomba.
bona fide ['bəunə'faɪdɪ] a genuino, auténtico.
bond [bɔnd] n (*binding promise*) fianza; (*FINANCE*) bono; (*link*) vínculo, lazo.
bondage [bɔndɪdʒ] n esclavitud f.
bone [bəun] n hueso; (*of fish*) espina // vt deshuesar; quitar las espinas a; ~-**dry** a completamente seco; ~ **idle** a gandul.
bonfire ['bɔnfaɪə*] n hoguera, fogata.
bonnet ['bɔnɪt] n gorra; (*Brit: of car*) capó m.
bonus ['bəunəs] n sobrepaga, prima.
bony ['bəunɪ] a (*arm, face, MED: tissue*) huesudo; (*meat*) lleno de huesos; (*fish*) lleno de espinas.
boo [bu:] vt abuchear, rechiflar.
booby trap ['bu:bɪ-] n trampa explosiva.
book [buk] n libro; (*notebook*) libreta; (*of stamps etc*) librito; (*COMM*): ~**s** las cuentas, el balance // vt (*ticket*) sacar; (*seat, room*) reservar; (*driver*) fichar; ~**case** n librería, estante m para libros; ~**ing office** n (*RAIL*) despacho de billetes; (*THEATRE*) taquilla; ~**-keeping** n teneduría de libros; ~**let** n folleto; ~**maker** n corredor m de apuestas; ~**seller** n librero; ~**shop** n librería; ~**stall** n quiosco de libros.
boom [bu:m] n (*noise*) trueno, estampido; (*in prices etc*) alza rápida; (*ECON*) boom m, prosperidad f repentina.
boomerang ['bu:məræŋ] n bumerang m.
boon [bu:n] n favor m, beneficio.
boost [bu:st] n estímulo, empuje m // vt estimular, empujar; ~**er** n (*MED*) reinyección f.
boot [bu:t] n bota; (*Brit: of car*) maleta, maletero // vt dar un puntapié a; **to** ~ (*in addition*) además, por añadidura.
booth [bu:ð] n (*at fair*) barraca; (*telephone* ~, *voting* ~) cabina.
booty ['bu:tɪ] n botín m.
booze [bu:z] (*col*) n bebida, trago // vi emborracharse.
border ['bɔ:də*] n borde m, margen m, orilla; (*of a country*) frontera // a fronterizo; **the B**~**s** región fronteriza entre Escocia e Inglaterra; **to** ~ **on** vt fus lindar con; (*fig*) rayar en; ~**line** n (*fig*) frontera.
bore [bɔ:*] pt of **bear** // vt (*hole*) taladrar, agujerear; (*person*) aburrir // n (*person*) pelmazo, pesado; (*of gun*) calibre m; ~**dom** n aburrimiento.
boring ['bɔ:rɪŋ] a aburrido.
born [bɔ:n] a: **to be** ~ nacer; **I was** ~ **in 1960** nací en 1960.
borne [bɔ:n] pp of **bear**.
borough ['bʌrə] n municipio.
borrow ['bɔrəu] vt: **to** ~ **sth (from sb)** pedir algo prestado a alguien.
borstal ['bɔ:stl] n reformatorio (de menores).

bosom ['buzəm] n pecho; (*fig*) seno; ~ **friend** n amigo del alma o íntimo.
boss [bɔs] n jefe m; (*employer*) patrón/ona m/f; (*political etc*) cacique m // vt regentar, dar órdenes a; ~**y** a mandón(ona).
bosun ['bəusn] n contramaestre m.
botanist ['bɔtənɪst] n botanista m/f; **botany** [-nɪ] n botánica.
botch [bɔtʃ] vt (*also:* ~ **up**) arruinar, estropear.
both [bəuθ] a, pron ambos(as), los dos; ~ **of us went, we** ~ **went** fuimos los dos, ambos fuimos // ad: ~ **A and B** tanto A como B.
bother ['bɔðə*] vt (*worry*) preocupar; (*disturb*) molestar, fastidiar // vi (*gen:* ~ **o.s.**) molestarse; **to** ~ **doing** tomarse la molestia de hacer // n: **what a** ~! ¡qué lata!
bottle ['bɔtl] n botella; (*small*) frasco; (*baby's*) biberón m // vt embotellar; to ~ **up** vt embotellar, contener; ~**neck** n embotellamiento; ~**-opener** n destapador m, abrebotellas m inv.
bottom ['bɔtəm] n (*of box, sea*) fondo; (*buttocks*) trasero, culo; (*of page, list*) pie m // a (*low*) inferior, más bajo; (*last*) último; ~**less** a sin fondo, insondable.
bough [bau] n rama.
bought [bɔ:t] pt, pp of **buy**.
boulder ['bəuldə*] n canto rodado.
bounce [bauns] vi (*ball*) (re)botar; (*cheque*) ser rechazado o incobrable // vt hacer (re)botar // n (*rebound*) (re)bote m.
bound [baund] pt, pp of **bind** // n (*leap*) salto; (*gen pl: limit*) límite m // vi (*leap*) saltar // a: ~ **by** (*limited by*) rodeado de, confinado con; **to be** ~ **to do sth** (*obliged*) tener el deber de hacer algo; (*likely*) estar seguro de hacer algo; **out of** ~**s** prohibido el paso; ~ **for** con destino a.
boundary ['baundrɪ] n límite m, lindero.
boundless ['baundlɪs] a ilimitado.
bouquet ['bukeɪ] n (*of flowers*) ramo; (*of wine*) aroma m.
bout [baut] n (*of malaria etc*) ataque m; (*BOXING etc*) combate m, encuentro.
bow [bəu] n (*knot*) lazo; (*weapon, MUS*) arco // n [bau] (*of the head*) reverencia; (*NAUT*) proa // vi [bau] inclinarse, hacer una reverencia; (*yield*): **to** ~ **to** or **before** ceder ante, someterse a.
bowels [bauəlz] npl intestinos mpl, vientre m.
bowl [bəul] n tazón m, cuenco; (*for washing*) palangana, jofaina; (*ball*) bola // vi (*CRICKET*) arrojar la pelota; ~**s** n juego de las bochas, bolos mpl.
bow-legged ['bəulɛgɪd] a estevado.
bowler ['bəulə*] n (*CRICKET*) lanzador m (de la pelota); (*also:* ~ **hat**) hongo, bombín m.
bowling ['bəulɪŋ] n (*game*) bochas fpl, bolos mpl; ~ **alley** n bolera; ~ **green** n pista para bochas.

bow tie ['bəu-] *n* corbata de lazo.
box [bɔks] *n* (*also*: **cardboard ~**) caja, cajón *m*; (*for jewels*) estuche *m*; (*for money*) cofre *m*; (*THEATRE*) palco // *vt* encajonar // *vi* (*SPORT*) boxear; **~er** *n* (*person*) boxeador *m*; (*dog*) boxer *m*; **~ing** *n* (*SPORT*) boxeo; **B~ing Day** *n* Día de San Esteban, 26 de diciembre; **~ing gloves** *npl* guantes *mpl* de boxeo; **~ing ring** *n* ring *m*, cuadrilátero; **~ office** *n* taquilla; **~room** *n* trastero.
boy [bɔi] *n* (*young*) niño; (*older*) muchacho; (*servant*) criado.
boycott ['bɔikɔt] *n* boicot *m* // *vt* boicotear.
boyfriend ['bɔifrɛnd] *n* novio.
boyish ['bɔiiʃ] *a* muchachil.
B.R. *abbr of* **British Rail.**
bra [brɑː] *n* sostén *m*.
brace [breis] *n* refuerzo, abrazadera; (*on teeth*) aparato; (*tool*) berbiquí *m* // *vt* asegurar, reforzar; **~s** *npl* tirantes *mpl*; **to ~ o.s.** (*fig*) fortalecer el ánimo.
bracelet ['breislit] *n* pulsera, brazalete *m*.
bracing ['breisiŋ] *a* vigorizante, tónico.
bracken ['brækən] *n* helecho.
bracket ['brækit] *n* (*TECH*) soporte *m*, puntal *m*; (*group*) clase *f*, categoría; (*also*: **brace ~**) soporte *m*, abrazadera; (*also*: **round ~**) paréntesis *m inv*; (*gen*: **square ~**) corchete *m* // *vt* (*group*) agrupar.
brag [bræg] *vi* jactarse.
braid [breid] *n* (*trimming*) galón *m*; (*of hair*) trenza.
Braille [breil] *n* Braille *m*.
brain [brein] *n* cerebro; **~s** *npl* sesos *mpl*; **~child** *n* parto del ingenio; **~wash** *vt* lavar el cerebro a; **~wave** *n* idea luminosa; **~y** *a* muy listo *o* inteligente.
braise [breiz] *vt* cocer a fuego lento.
brake [breik] *n* (*on vehicle*) freno // *vt, vi* frenar; **~ drum** *n* tambor *m* de freno; **~ fluid** *n* líquido para freno.
bramble ['bræmbl] *n* zarza.
branch [brɑːntʃ] *n* rama; (*fig*) ramo; (*road*) ramal *m*; (*COMM*) sucursal *f* // *vi* (*also*: **~ out**) ramificarse; (: *fig*) extenderse.
brand [brænd] *n* marca; (*iron*) hierro de marcar // *vt* (*cattle*) marcar con hierro candente.
brandish ['brændiʃ] *vt* blandir.
brand-new ['brænd'njuː] *a* flamente, completamente nuevo.
brandy ['brændi] *n* coñac *m*, brandy *m*.
brash [bræʃ] *a* (*rough*) tosco; (*cheeky*) descarado.
brass [brɑːs] *n* latón *m*; **~ band** *n* banda de metal.
brassière ['bræsiə*] *n* sostén *m*.
brat [bræt] *n* (*pej*) mocoso.
bravado [brə'vɑːdəu] *n* baladronada.
brave [breiv] *a* valiente, valeroso // *n* valiente *m* // *vt* (*challenge*) desafiar; (*resist*) aguantar; **~ry** *n* valor *m*, valentía.
brawl [brɔːl] *n* pendencia, reyerta // *vi* pelearse.

brawn [brɔːn] *n* fuerza; (*meat*) carne *f* en gelatina; **~y** *a* fornido, musculoso.
bray [brei] *n* rebuzno // *vi* rebuznar.
brazen ['breizn] *a* descarado, cínico // *vt*: **to ~ it out** defenderse con descaro.
brazier ['breiziə*] *n* brasero.
Brazil [brə'zil] *n* (el) Brasil; **~ian** *a, n* brasileño/a.
breach [briːtʃ] *vt* abrir brecha en // *n* (*gap*) brecha; (*breaking*): **~ of contract** infracción *f* de contrato; **~ of the peace** perturbación *f* del órden público.
bread [brɛd] *n* pan *m*; **~ and butter** *n* pan *m* con mantequilla; (*fig*) pan (de cada día) // *a* común y corriente; **~crumbs** *npl* migajas *fpl*; (*CULIN*) pan molido.
breadth [brɛtθ] *n* anchura; (*fig*) amplitud *f*.
breadwinner ['brɛdwinə*] *n* sostén *m* de la familia.
break [breik] *pt* **broke**, *pp* **broken** *vt* (*gen*) romper; (*promise*) faltar a; (*fall*) amortiguar; (*journey*) interrumpir; (*law*) violar, infringir; (*record*) batir; (*news*) comunicar // *vi* romperse, quebrarse; (*storm*) estallar // *n* (*gap*) abertura; (*crack*) grieta; (*fracture*) fractura; (*breakdown*) ruptura, rompimiento; (*rest*) descanso; (*time*) intérvalo; (: *at school*) (período de) recreo; (*chance*) oportunidad *f*; (*escape*) evasión *f*, fuga; **to ~ down** *vt* (*figures, data*) analizar, descomponer; (*undermine*) acabar con // *vi* estropearse; (*MED*) sufrir un colapso; (*AUT*) averiarse; (*person*) romper a llorar; **to ~ even** *vi* salir sin ganar ni perder; **to ~ free** *or* **loose** *vi* abrirse paso; **to ~ in** *vt* (*horse etc*) domar // *vi* (*burglar*) forzar una entrada; **to ~ into** *vt fus* (*house*) forzar; **to ~ off** *vi* (*speaker*) pararse, detenerse; (*branch*) partir; **to ~ open** *vt* (*door etc*) abrir por la fuerza, forzar; **to ~ out** *vi* estallar; **to ~ out in spots** salir a uno granos; **to ~ up** *vi* romperse // *vt* romper, intervenir en; **~able** *a* quebradizo; **~age** *n* rotura; **~down** *n* (*AUT*) avería; (*in communications*) interrupción *f*; (*MED*: *also*: **nervous ~down**) colapso, crisis *f* nerviosa; **~down lorry** *n* grúa, camión *m* grúa; **~er** *n* rompiente *m*, ola grande.
breakfast ['brɛkfəst] *n* desayuno.
break: **~through** *n* ruptura; (*fig*) avance *m*, adelanto; **~water** *n* rompeolas *m inv*.
breast [brɛst] *n* (*of woman*) pecho, seno; (*chest*) pecho; (*of bird*) pechuga; **~-stroke** *n* braza de pecho.
breath [brɛθ] *n* aliento, respiración *f*; **out of ~** sin aliento, sofocado; **~alyser** *n* prueba de alcohol por el aliento.
breathe [briːð] *vt, vi* respirar; (*noisily*) resollar; **breather** *n* respiro.
breath: **~less** *a* sin aliento, jadeante; **~taking** *a* imponente, pasmoso.
breed [briːd] *pt, pp* **bred** [brɛd] *vt* criar, engendrar // *vi* reproducirse, procrear // *n* raza, casta; **~er** *n* (*person*) criador/a *m/f*; **~ing** *n* (*of person*) educación *f*.

breeze [bri:z] n brisa.
breezy ['bri:zɪ] a de mucho viento, ventoso; (person) despreocupado.
brevity ['brɛvɪtɪ] n brevedad f.
brew [bru:] vt (tea) hacer; (beer) elaborar // vi hacerse, prepararse; (fig) amenazar; ~er n cervecero; ~ery n fábrica de cerveza.
bribe [braɪb] n soborno // vt sobornar, cohechar; ~ry n soborno, cohecho.
brick [brɪk] n ladrillo; ~layer n albañil m; ~works n ladrillar m.
bridal ['braɪdl] a nupcial.
bride [braɪd] n novia; ~groom n novio; **bridesmaid** n dama de honor.
bridge [brɪdʒ] n puente m; (NAUT) puente m de mando; (of nose) caballete m; (CARDS) bridge m // vt (river) tender un puente sobre; ~head n cabeza de puente.
bridle ['braɪdl] n brida, freno // vt poner la brida a; (fig) reprimir, refrenar; ~ path n camino de herradura.
brief [bri:f] a breve, corto // n (LAW) escrito // vt (inform) informar; (instruct) dar órdenes a; ~s npl (for men) calzoncillos mpl; (for women) bragas fpl; ~case n cartera; ~ing n (PRESS) informe m.
brigade [brɪ'geɪd] n (MIL) brigada.
brigadier [brɪgə'dɪə*] n general m de brigada.
bright [braɪt] a claro, luminoso; (weather) de sol; (person: clever) listo, inteligente; (: lively) alegre, animado; (colour) vivo; ~en vt (room) hacer más alegre // vi (weather) despejarse; (person: gen: ~en up) animarse, alegrarse.
brilliance ['brɪljəns] n brillo, brillantez f; **brilliant** [-ənt] a brillante; (clever) genial.
brim [brɪm] n borde m; (of hat) ala; ~ful a lleno hasta el borde; (fig) rebosante (de).
brine [braɪn] n (CULIN) salmuera.
bring [brɪŋ], pt, pp **brought** vt (thing) traer; (person) conducir; to ~ about vt ocasionar, producir; to ~ back vt volver a traer; (return) devolver; to ~ down vt bajar; (price) rebajar; to ~ forward vt adelantar; to ~ in vt (harvest) recoger; to ~ off vt (task, plan) lograr, conseguir; to ~ out vt (object) sacar; to ~ round vt (unconscious person) hacer volver en sí; (convince) convencer, ganar; to ~ up vt (person) educar, criar; (carry up) subir; (question) sacar a colación.
brink [brɪŋk] n borde m.
brisk [brɪsk] a enérgico, vigoroso; (speedy) rápido; (trade) activo.
brisket ['brɪskɪt] n carne f de vaca para asar.
bristle ['brɪsl] n cerda // vi erizarse.
Britain ['brɪtən] n Gran Bretaña.
British ['brɪtɪʃ] a británico; the ~ npl los británicos; the ~ Isles npl las Islas Británicas.
Briton ['brɪtən] n británico/a.
brittle ['brɪtl] a quebradizo, frágil.
broach [brəʊtʃ] vt (subject) abordar.

broad [brɔ:d] a ancho, amplio; (accent) cerrado; in ~ daylight en pleno día; ~cast n emisión f // (vb: pt, pp ~cast) vt (RADIO) emitir; (TV) transmitir // vi hablar o tocar por la radio; ~casting n radiodifusión f, difusión f; ~en vt ensanchar // vi ensancharse; ~ly ad en general; ~-minded a tolerante, liberal.
brochure ['brəʊʃjuə*] n folleto.
broke [brəʊk] pt of break // a (col) pelado, sin blanca.
broken ['brəʊkən] pp of break // a: ~ leg pierna rota; in ~ English en un inglés imperfecto; ~-hearted con el corazón partido.
broker ['brəʊkə*] n agente m/f, bolsista m/f.
bronchitis [brɔŋ'kaɪtɪs] n bronquitis f.
bronze [brɔnz] n bronce m.
brooch [brəʊtʃ] n prendedor m.
brood [bru:d] n camada, cría; (children) progenie f; (: pej) prole f // vi (hen) empollar; (obsessively) darle vueltas (a).
brook [bruk] n arroyo.
broom [brum] n escoba; (BOT) retama; ~stick n palo de escoba.
Bros. abbr of Brothers.
broth [brɔθ] n caldo.
brothel ['brɔθl] n burdel m.
brother ['brʌðə*] n hermano; ~-in-law n cuñado.
brought [brɔ:t] pt, pp of bring.
brow [brau] n ceja; (forehead) frente m; (of hill) cumbre f.
brown [braun] a moreno; (hair) castaño; (tanned) bronceado // n (colour) color m moreno o pardo // vt poner moreno; (tan) broncear; (CULIN) dorar; ~ie n niña Girl Guide.
browse [brauz] vi (among books) hojear libros.
bruise [bru:z] n cardenal m, contusión f // vt magullar.
brunette [bru:'nɛt] n morena.
brunt [brʌnt] n: the ~ of lo más fuerte de, lo peor de.
brush [brʌʃ] n cepillo; (large) escoba; (for painting, shaving etc) brocha; (artist's) pincel m; (BOT) maleza; (quarrel) escaramuza, encuentro // vt cepillar; (gen: ~ past, ~ against) rozar al pasar; to ~ aside vt rechazar, no hacer caso a; to ~ up vt (knowledge) repasar, refrescar; ~wood n (bushes) maleza; (sticks) leña.
brusque [bru:sk] a brusco, áspero.
Brussels ['brʌslz] n Bruselas; ~ sprout n colecilla de Bruselas.
brutal ['bru:tl] a brutal; ~ity [-'tælɪtɪ] n brutalidad f.
brute [bru:t] n bruto; (person) bestia.
B.Sc. abbr of Bachelor of Science licenciado en ciencias.
bubble ['bʌbl] n burbuja, ampolla // vi burbujear, borbotar; ~ gum n chicle m de globo.
buck [bʌk] n macho; (US: col) dólar m // vi

corcovear; **to pass the** ~ (**to sb**) echar (a uno) el muerto; **to** ~ **up** vi (cheer up) animarse, cobrar ánimo.

bucket ['bʌkɪt] n cubo, balde m.

buckle ['bʌkl] n hebilla // vt abrochar con hebilla // vi torcerse, combarse.

bud [bʌd] n brote m, yema; (of flower) capullo // vi brotar, echar brotes; (fig) florecer.

Buddhism ['budɪzm] n Budismo.

budding ['bʌdɪŋ] a en ciernes, en embrión.

buddy ['bʌdɪ] n (US) compañero, compinche m.

budge [bʌdʒ] vt mover; (fig) hacer ceder // vi moverse.

budgerigar ['bʌdʒərɪgɑ:*] n periquito.

budget ['bʌdʒɪt] n presupuesto.

budgie ['bʌdʒɪ] n = **budgerigar.**

buff [bʌf] a (colour) color m de ante // n (enthusiast) entusiasta m/f.

buffalo ['bʌfələu], pl ~ or ~es n búfalo.

buffer ['bʌfə*] n amortiguador m.

buffet ['bufeɪ] n (bar) bar m, cafetería; (food) buffet m // vt ['bʌfɪt] (strike) abofetear; (wind etc) golpear; ~ **car** n coche-comedor m.

buffoon [bə'fu:n] n bufón m.

bug [bʌg] n (insect) chinche m; (: gen) bicho, sabandija; (: fig: germ) microbio, bacilo; (spy device) micrófono oculto; (tap) intervención f; (machine for tapping) aparato de intervención // vt (fam) fastidiar; (spy on) poner micrófono oculto en.

bugle ['bju:gl] n corneta, clarín m.

build [bɪld] n (of person) talle m, tipo // vt, pt, pp **built** construir, edificar; ~**er** n constructor m; (contractor) contratista m/f; ~**ing** n (act of) construcción f; (habitation, offices) edificio; ~**ing society** n sociedad f inmobiliaria, cooperativa de construcciones; **to** ~ **up** vt (MED) fortalecer; (stocks) acumular.

built [bɪlt] pt, pp of **build** // a: ~-**in** (cupboard) empotrado; (device) interior, incorporado; ~-**up** (area) urbanizado.

bulb [bʌlb] n (BOT) bulbo; (ELEC) bombilla.

Bulgaria [bʌl'gɛərɪə] n Bulgaria; ~**n** a, n búlgaro/a.

bulge [bʌldʒ] n bombeo, pandeo // vi bombearse, pandearse; (pocket etc) hacer bulto.

bulk [bʌlk] n (mass) bulto, volumen m; (major part) grueso; **in** ~ (COMM) a granel; **the** ~ **of** la mayor parte de; ~**head** n mamparo; ~**y** a voluminoso, abultado.

bull [bul] n toro; ~**dog** n dogo.

bulldozer ['buldəuzə*] n aplanadora, motoniveladora.

bullet ['bulɪt] n bala; ~**proof** a a prueba de balas; ~ **wound** n balazo.

bulletin ['bulɪtɪn] n anuncio, parte m.

bullfight ['bulfaɪt] n corrida de toros; ~**er** n torero; ~**ing** n los toros mpl, el toreo; (art of ~ing) tauromaquia.

bullion ['buljən] n oro o plata en barras.

bullock ['bulək] n novillo.

bull's-eye ['bulzaɪ] n centro del blanco.

bully ['bulɪ] n valentón m, matón m // vt intimidar, tiranizar.

bum [bʌm] n (col: backside) culo, trasero; (tramp) vagabundo.

bumblebee ['bʌmblbi:] n (ZOOL) abejorro.

bump [bʌmp] n (blow) tope m, choque m; (jolt) sacudida; (on road etc, on head) bollo, abolladura // vt (strike) chocar contra, topetar // vi dar sacudidas; **to** ~ **into** vt fus chocar contra, tropezar con; (person) topar; ~**er** n (Brit) parachoques m inv // a: ~**er crop/harvest** cosecha abundante.

bumpy ['bʌmpɪ] a (road) lleno de baches; (journey) zarandeado.

bun [bʌn] n bollo; (of hair) moño.

bunch [bʌntʃ] n (of flowers) ramo; (of keys) manojo; (of bananas) piña; (of people) grupo; (pej) pandilla.

bundle ['bʌndl] n (gen) bulto, fardo; (of sticks) haz f; (of papers) legajo // vt (also: ~ **up**) atar, envolver; (put): **to** ~ **sth/sb into** meter algo/a alguien precipitadamente en.

bung [bʌŋ] n tapón m, bitoque m // vt (throw: gen: ~ **into**) arrojar.

bungalow ['bʌŋgələu] n bungalow m, chalé m.

bungle ['bʌŋgl] vt chapucear.

bunion ['bʌnjən] n juanete m.

bunk [bʌŋk] n tonterías fpl; ~ **beds** npl literas fpl.

bunker ['bʌŋkə*] n (coal store) carbonera; (MIL) refugio; (GOLF) bunker m.

bunny ['bʌnɪ] n (also: ~ **rabbit**) conejito.

bunting ['bʌntɪŋ] n empavesada, banderas fpl.

buoy [bɔɪ] n boya; **to** ~ **up** vt mantener a flote; (fig) animar; ~**ant** a boyante.

burden ['bə:dn] n carga // vt cargar.

bureau [bjuə'rəu], pl ~**x** [-z] n (furniture) escritorio, buró m; (office) oficina, agencia.

bureaucracy [bjuə'rɔkrəsɪ] n burocracia; **bureaucrat** ['bjuərəkræt] n burócrata m/f.

burglar ['bə:glə*] n ladrón/ona m/f; ~ **alarm** n alarma f de ladrones; ~**y** n robo con allanamiento, robo de una casa; **burgle** ['bə:gl] vt robar (con allanamiento).

burial ['berɪəl] n entierro; ~ **ground** n cementerio.

burlesque [bə'lesk] n parodia.

burly ['bə:lɪ] a fornido, membrudo.

Burma ['bə:mə] n Birmania.

burn [bə:n], pt, pp **burned** or **burnt** vt quemar; (house) incendiar // vi quemarse, arder; incendiarse; (sting) escocer // n quemadura; **to** ~ **down** vt incendiar; ~**er** n (gas) quemador m, fuego; ~**ing** a ardiente.

burp [bə:p] (col) n eructo // vi eructar.

burrow ['bʌrəu] n madriguera // vt hacer una madriguera.

bursar ['bɔːsə*] n tesorero; (student) becario; ~**y** n beca.

burst [bɔːst], pt, pp **burst** vt (balloon, pipe) reventar; (banks etc) romper // vi reventarse; romperse; (tyre) pincharse; (bomb) estallar // n (gen) reventón m; (explosion) estallido; (shots) ráfaga de tiros; **a** ~ **of energy** una explosión f de energía; **to** ~ **into flames** estallar en llamas; **to** ~ **into laughter** soltar la carcajada; **to** ~ **into tears** deshacerse en lágrimas; **to be** ~**ing with** reventar por o de; **to** ~ **into** vt fus (room etc) irrumpir en; **to** ~ **open** vi abrirse de golpe.

bury ['bɛrɪ] vt enterrar; (body) enterrar, sepultar.

bus [bʌs] n autobús m.

bush [buʃ] n arbusto; (scrub land) monte m; **to beat about the** ~ ir por rodeos; ~**y** a (thick) espeso, poblado.

busily ['bɪzɪlɪ] ad atareadamente, afanosamente.

business ['bɪznɪs] n (matter) negocio; (trading) comercio, negocios mpl; (firm) empresa, casa; (occupation) oficio; (affair) asunto; **it's my** ~ **to...** me toca o corresponde...; **it's none of my** ~ yo no tengo nada que ver; **he means** ~ habla en serio; ~**like** a formal, metódico; ~**man** n hombre m de negocios.

bus-stop ['bʌsstɔp] n parada de autobús.

bust [bʌst] n (ANAT) pecho // a (broken) roto, estropeado; **to go** ~ quebrarse.

bustle ['bʌsl] n bullicio, movimiento // vi menearse, apresurarse; **bustling** a (town) animado, bullicioso.

busy ['bɪzɪ] a ocupado, atareado; (shop, street) concurrido, animado // vr: **to** ~ **o.s. with** ocuparse en; ~**body** n entrometido.

but [bʌt] conj pero // prep excepto, menos; **nothing** ~ nada más que; ~ **for** a no ser por, si no fuera por; **all** ~ **finished** casi terminado.

butane ['bjuːteɪn] n butano.

butcher ['butʃə*] n carnicero // vt hacer una carnicería con; (cattle etc for meat) matar; ~'**s (shop)** n carnicería.

butler ['bʌtlə*] n mayordomo.

butt [bʌt] n (cask) tonel m; (for rain) tina; (thick end) cabo, extremo; (of gun) culata; (of cigarette) colilla; (fig: target) blanco // vt dar cabezadas contra, topetar.

butter ['bʌtə*] n mantequilla // vt untar con mantequilla; ~ **bean** n judía blanca; ~**cup** n ranúnculo.

butterfly ['bʌtəflaɪ] n mariposa.

buttocks ['bʌtəks] npl nalgas fpl.

button ['bʌtn] n botón m // vt abotonar, abrochar // vi abrocharse; ~**hole** n ojal m; (flower) flor f que se lleva en el ojal // vt obligar a escuchar.

buttress ['bʌtrɪs] n contrafuerte m; (fig) apoyo, sostén m.

buxom ['bʌksəm] a (baby) rollizo; (woman) frescachona.

buy [baɪ], pt, pp **bought** vt comprar // n compra; **to** ~ **sb sth/sth from sb** comprar algo para alguien/comprarle algo a alguien; ~**er** n comprador/a m/f.

buzz [bʌz] n zumbido; (col: phone call) llamada (por teléfono) // vi zumbar.

buzzard ['bʌzəd] n águila ratonera.

buzzer ['bʌzə*] n zumbador m, vibrador m.

by [baɪ] prep por; (beside) junto a, cerca de; (according to) según, de acuerdo con; (before): ~ **4 o'clock** para las cuatro // ad see **pass**, **go** etc; ~ **bus/car** en autobús/coche; **paid** ~ **the hour** pagado por horas; ~ **night/day** de noche/día; (all) ~ **oneself** (completamente) solo; ~ **the way** a propósito, por cierto; ~ **and large** en general; ~ **and** ~ luego, más tarde.

bye(-bye) ['baɪ('baɪ)] excl adiós, hasta luego.

by(e)-law ['baɪlɔː] n ordenanza municipal.

by-election ['baɪɪlɛkʃən] n elección f parcial.

bygone ['baɪgɔn] a pasado, del pasado // n: **let** ~**s be** ~**s** lo pasado, pasado está.

bypass ['baɪpɑːs] n carretera de circunvalación // vt evitar.

by-product ['baɪprɔdʌkt] n subproducto, derivado.

bystander ['baɪstændə*] n espectador/a m/f.

byword ['baɪwɔːd] n: **to be a** ~ **for** ser conocidísimo por.

C

C. abbr of **centigrade.**

C.A. abbr of **chartered accountant.**

cab [kæb] n taxi m; (of truck) cabina.

cabaret ['kæbəreɪ] n cabaret m.

cabbage ['kæbɪdʒ] n col m, berza.

cabin ['kæbɪn] n cabaña; (on ship) camarote m; ~ **cruiser** n yate m de motor.

cabinet ['kæbɪnɪt] n (POL) consejo de ministros; (furniture) armario; (also: display ~) vitrina; ~-**maker** n ebanista m.

cable ['keɪbl] n cable m // vt cablegrafiar; ~-**car** n coche m de teleférico, tren m aéreo.

cackle ['kækl] vi cacarear.

cactus ['kæktəs], pl -**ti** [-taɪ] n cacto.

caddie ['kædɪ] n cadi m.

cadet [kə'dɛt] n (MIL) cadete m.

cadge [kædʒ] vt gorronear; **cadger** n gorrón/ona m/f.

Caesarean (section) [siː'zɛərɪən] n cesárea.

café ['kæfeɪ], **cafeteria** [kæfɪ'tɪərɪə] n café m.

caffein(e) ['kæfiːn] n cafeína.

cage [keɪdʒ] n jaula // vt enjaular.

cagey ['keɪdʒɪ] a (col) cauteloso, reservado.

Cairo ['kaɪərəu] n el Cairo.

cajole [kə'dʒəul] vt engatusar.
cake [keɪk] n (large) pastel m; (small) pasta, bizcocho; (of soap) pastilla; ~**d with** cubierto de.
calamitous [kə'læmɪtəs] a calamitoso; **calamity** [-ɪtɪ] n calamidad f.
calcium ['kælsɪəm] n calcio.
calculate ['kælkjuleɪt] vt calcular; **calculating** a (clever) astuto; (devious) calculador(a); **calculation** [-'leɪʃən] n cálculo, cómputo; **calculator** n calculadora.
calculus ['kælkjuləs] n cálculo.
calendar ['kæləndə*] n calendario; ~ **month/year** mes m/año civil.
calf [kɑːf], pl **calves** n (of cow) ternero, becerro; (of other animals) cría; (also: ~**skin**) piel m de becerro; (ANAT) pantorrilla.
calibre, caliber (US) ['kælɪbə*] n calibre m.
call [kɔːl] vt (gen, also TEL) llamar // vi (shout) llamar; (telephone) llamar por teléfono; (visit: also: ~ **in**, ~ **round**) hacer una visita // n (shout, TEL) llamada; (of bird) canto; (appeal) llamamiento; **to ~ for** vt fus (demand) pedir, exigir; (fetch) venir por; **to ~ off** vt suspender; (cancel) cancelar; **to ~ on** vt fus (visit) visitar; (turn to) acudir a; **to ~ out** vi gritar, dar voces; **to ~ up** vt (MIL) llamar al servicio militar; ~**box** n cabina telefónica; ~**er** n visita m/f; (TEL) usuario; ~ **girl** n prostituta; ~**ing** n vocación f, profesión f.
callous ['kæləs] a insensible, cruel.
calm [kɑːm] n calma, tranquilidad f // vt calmar, tranquilizar // a (gen) tranquilo; (sea) liso, en calma; ~**ly** ad tranquilamente, con calma; ~**ness** n calma; **to ~ down** vi calmarse, tranquilizarse // vt calmar, tranquilizar.
calorie ['kælərɪ] n caloría.
calve [kɑːv] vi parir.
calves [kɑːvz] pl of **calf.**
camber ['kæmbə*] n (of road) combadura, comba.
Cambodia [kæm'bəudjə] n Camboya.
came [keɪm] pt of **come.**
camel ['kæməl] n camello.
cameo ['kæmɪəu] n camafeo.
camera ['kæmərə] n máquina fotográfica; (CINEMA, TV) cámara; **in ~** en secreto; ~**man** n cámaraman m, cámara m/f.
camouflage ['kæməflɑːʒ] n camuflaje m // vt camuflar.
camp [kæmp] n campo, campamento // vi acampar // a afectado, afeminado.
campaign [kæm'peɪn] n (MIL, POL etc) campaña // vi hacer campaña.
camp: ~**bed** n cama de campaña; ~**er** n campista m/f; (vehicle) caravana; ~**ing** n camping m; **to go** ~**ing** hacer camping; ~**site** n camping m.
campus ['kæmpəs] n ciudad f universitaria.
can [kæn] auxiliary vb (gen) poder; (know

how to) saber; **I ~ swim** sé nadar // n (of oil, water) lata, bote m // vt enlatar; (preserve) conservar en lata.
Canada ['kænədə] n el Canadá; **Canadian** [kə'neɪdɪən] a, n canadiense m/f.
canal [kə'næl] n canal m.
canary [kə'nɛərɪ] n canario; **C~ Islands** npl las (Islas) Canarias fpl.
cancel ['kænsəl] vt cancelar; (train) suprimir; (appointment) anular; (cross out) tachar, borrar; ~**lation** [-'leɪʃən] n cancelación f; supresión f.
cancer ['kænsə*] n cáncer m; **C~** (ASTRO) Cáncer m.
candid ['kændɪd] a franco, abierto.
candidate ['kændɪdeɪt] n candidato.
candle ['kændl] n vela; (in church) cirio; ~**stick** n (also: ~ **holder**) (single) candelero; (low) palmatoria; (bigger, ornate) candelabro.
candour ['kændə*] n franqueza.
candy ['kændɪ] n azúcar m cande; (US) dulce m, caramelo.
cane [keɪn] n (BOT) caña; (stick) vara, palmeta // vt (SCOL) castigar (con palmeta).
canine ['kænaɪn] a canino.
canister ['kænɪstə*] n bote m, lata.
cannabis ['kænəbɪs] n cáñamo, marijuana.
canned [kænd] a en lata, de lata.
cannibal ['kænɪbəl] n caníbal m/f; ~**ism** n canibalismo.
cannon ['kænən], pl ~ or ~**s** n cañón m; ~**ball** n bala (de cañón).
cannot ['kænɔt] = **can not.**
canny ['kænɪ] a astuto.
canoe [kə'nuː] n canoa; (SPORT) piragua; ~**ing** n (SPORT) piragüismo; ~**ist** n piragüista m/f.
canon ['kænən] n (clergyman) canónigo; (standard) canon m.
canonize ['kænənaɪz] vt canonizar.
can opener ['kænəupnə*] n abrelatas m inv.
canopy ['kænəpɪ] n dosel m, toldo; (ARCH) baldaquín m.
can't [kænt] = **can not.**
cantankerous [kæn'tæŋkərəs] a arisco, malhumorado.
canteen [kæn'tiːn] n cantina; (bottle) cantimplora; (of cutlery) juego (de cubiertos).
canter ['kæntə*] n medio galope // vi ir a medio galope.
canvas ['kænvəs] n (gen) lona; (painting) lienzo; (NAUT) velas fpl; **under ~** (camping) bajo lona.
canvass ['kænvəs] vt (POL) solicitar votos de.
canyon ['kænjən] n cañón m.
cap [kæp] n gorra; (of pen) capuchón m; (of bottle) tapa, cápsula; (MED) diafragma m // vt coronar, poner remate a; (outdo) superar; (FOOTBALL) seleccionar (para el equipo nacional).

capability [keɪpə'bɪlɪtɪ] n capacidad f; **capable** ['keɪpəbl] a capaz.

capacity [kə'pæsɪtɪ] n capacidad f; (position) calidad f.

cape [keɪp] n capa; (GEO) cabo.

caper ['keɪpə*] n (CULIN: gen: ~s) alcaparra; (prank) travesura.

capital ['kæpɪtl] n (also: ~ city) capital f; (money) capital m; (also: ~ letter) mayúscula; ~ism n capitalismo; ~ist a, n capitalista m/f; ~ punishment n pena de muerte.

capitulate [kə'pɪtjuleɪt] vi capitular, rendirse; **capitulation** [-'leɪʃən] n capitulación f, rendición f.

capricious [kə'prɪʃəs] a caprichoso.

Capricorn ['kæprɪkɔ:n] n Capricornio.

capsize [kæp'saɪz] vt volcar, hacer zozobrar // vi volcarse, zozobrar.

capstan ['kæpstən] n cabrestante m.

capsule ['kæpsju:l] n cápsula.

captain ['kæptɪn] n capitán m // vt capitanear, ser el capitán de.

caption ['kæpʃən] n (heading) título; (to picture) leyenda.

captivate ['kæptɪveɪt] vt cautivar, encantar.

captive ['kæptɪv] a, n cautivo/a; **captivity** [-'tɪvɪtɪ] n cautiverio.

capture ['kæptʃə*] vt prender, apresar; (place) tomar; (attention) captar, llamar // n apresamiento; toma; (thing taken) presa.

car [ka:*] n coche m, automóvil m; (RAIL) vagón m.

carafe [kə'ræf] n garrafa.

caramel ['kærəməl] n caramelo.

carat ['kærət] n quilate m.

caravan ['kærəvæn] n caravana, rulota; (of camels) caravana.

caraway ['kærəweɪ] n: ~ seed carvi m.

carbohydrate [ka:bəu'haɪdreɪt] n hidrato de carbono; (food) fécula.

carbon ['ka:bən] n carbono; ~ copy n copia al carbón; ~ paper n papel m carbón.

carburettor [ka:bju'retə*] n carburador m.

carcass ['ka:kəs] n cadáver m de animal.

card [ka:d] n carta, naipe m; (visiting ~, post~ etc) tarjeta; ~board n cartón m, cartulina; ~ game n juego de naipes.

cardiac ['ka:dɪæk] a cardíaco.

cardigan ['ka:dɪgən] n rebeca.

cardinal ['ka:dɪnl] a cardinal // n cardenal m.

card index n fichero.

care [kɛə*] n (gen) cuidado; (worry) inquietud f, solicitud f; (charge) cargo, custodia // vi: to ~ about preocuparse de, tener interés en; **in sb's** ~ a cargo de alguien; **to take** ~ **to** cuidarse o tener cuidado de; **to take** ~ **of** vt cuidar; **to** ~ **for** vt fus cuidar a; (like) querer; **I don't** ~ no me importa.

career [kə'rɪə*] n carrera // vi (also: ~

along) correr a toda velocidad.

carefree ['kɛəfri:] a despreocupado.

careful ['kɛəful] a cuidadoso; (cautious) cauteloso; **(be)** ~! ¡tenga cuidado!; ~ly ad con cuidado, cuidadosamente.

careless ['kɛəlɪs] a descuidado; (heedless) poco atento; ~ly ad sin cuidado, a la ligera; ~ness n descuido, falta de atención.

caress [kə'rɛs] n caricia // vt acariciar.

caretaker ['kɛəteɪkə*] n portero, conserje m/f.

car-ferry ['ka:fɛrɪ] n transbordador m para coches.

cargo ['ka:gəu], pl ~es n cargamento, carga.

Caribbean [kærɪ'bi:ən] n: the ~ (Sea) el Caribe.

caricature ['kærɪkətjuə*] n caricatura.

carnal ['ka:nl] a carnal.

carnation [ka:'neɪʃən] n clavel m.

carnival ['ka:nɪvəl] n fiesta, feria, carnaval m.

carnivore ['ka:nɪvɔ:*] n carnívoro.

carol ['kærəl] n: **(Christmas)** ~ villancico.

carp [ka:p] n (fish) carpa; **to** ~ **at** vt fus quejarse de.

car park n aparcamiento, parking m.

carpenter ['ka:pɪntə*] n carpintero; **carpentry** [-trɪ] n carpintería.

carpet ['ka:pɪt] n alfombra // vt alfombrar; ~ **slippers** npl zapatillas fpl.

carriage ['kærɪdʒ] n coche m; (RAIL) vagón m; (for goods) transporte m; (bearing) porte m; ~**way** n (part of road) carretera; **dual** ~**way** n carretera de doble calzada.

carrier ['kærɪə*] n trajinista m/f; (company) empresa de transportes; ~ **bag** n bolsa (de papel).

carrot ['kærət] n zanahoria.

carry ['kærɪ] vt (gen) llevar; (transport) transportar; (a motion, bill) aprobar; (involve: responsibilities etc) entrañar, implicar // vi (sound) oírse; **to** ~ **on** vi (continue) seguir (adelante), continuar; (fam: complain) quejarse, protestar // vt proseguir, continuar; **to** ~ **out** vt (orders) cumplir; (investigation) llevar a cabo, realizar.

cart [ka:t] n carro, carreta // vt acarrear, llevar (en carro).

cartilage ['ka:tɪlɪdʒ] n cartílago.

cartographer [ka:'tɔgrəfə*] n cartógrafo.

carton ['ka:tən] n (box) caja (de cartón); (of yogurt) pote m.

cartoon [ka:'tu:n] n (PRESS) caricatura; (comic strip) tira cómica; (film) dibujos mpl animados; ~**ist** n caricaturista m/f; dibujante m/f.

cartridge ['ka:trɪdʒ] n cartucho.

carve [ka:v] vt (meat) trinchar; (wood, stone) cincelar, esculpir; (on tree) grabar; **to** ~ **up** dividir, repartir; **carving** n (in wood etc) escultura, (obra de) talla; **carving knife** n trinchante m.

car wash n lavado de coches.
cascade [kæs'keɪd] n salto de agua, cascada; (fig) chorro // vi caer a chorros o en forma de cascada.
case [keɪs] n (container) caja; (MED) caso; (for jewels etc) estuche m; (LAW) causa, proceso; (also: **suit** ~) maleta; **in** ~ **(of)** en caso de (que), por si; **in any** ~ en todo caso; **just in** ~ por si acaso; **to make a good** ~ tener buenos argumentos.
cash [kæʃ] n (dinero en) efectivo, dinero contante // vt cobrar, hacer efectivo; **to pay (in)** ~ pagar al contado; ~ **on delivery** cóbrese al entregar; ~**book** n libro de caja; ~**desk** n caja.
cashew [kæ'ʃuː] n (also: ~ **nut**) anacardo.
cashier [kæ'ʃɪə*] n cajero.
cashmere [kæʃ'mɪə*] n casimir m, cachemira.
cash register n caja.
casing ['keɪsɪŋ] n envoltura; (of boiler etc) revestimiento.
casino [kə'siːnəu] n casino.
cask [kɑːsk] n tonel m, barril m.
casket ['kɑːskɪt] n cofre m, estuche m; (US: coffin) ataúd m.
casserole ['kæsərəul] n cacerola; (food) cazuela.
cassette [kæ'sɛt] n cassette m; ~ **player** n tocacassettes m inv.
cassock ['kæsək] n sotana.
cast [kɑːst], pt, pp **cast** vt (throw) echar, arrojar, lanzar; (skin) mudar, perder; (metal) fundir; (THEATRE) hacer el reparto de // vi (FISHING) lanzar // n (THEATRE) reparto; (mould) forma, molde m; (also: **plaster** ~) vaciado; **to** ~ **away** vt desechar; **to** ~ **down** vt derribar; **to** ~ **loose** soltar; **to** ~ **one's vote** dar el voto; **to** ~ **off** vi (NAUT) desamarrar.
castanets [kæstə'nɛts] npl castañuelas fpl.
castaway ['kɑːstəwəɪ] n náufrago.
caste [kɑːst] n casta.
casting vote ['kɑːstɪŋ-] n voto decisivo.
cast iron n hierro fundido.
castle ['kɑːsl] n castillo; (CHESS) torre f.
castor ['kɑːstə*] n (wheel) ruedecilla; ~ **oil** n aceite m de ricino; ~ **sugar** n azúcar m extrafino.
castrate [kæs'treɪt] vt castrar.
casual ['kæʒjul] a (by chance) fortuito; (irregular: work etc) eventual, temporero; (unconcerned) despreocupado; (informal: clothes) de sport; ~**ly** ad por casualidad; de manera despreocupada.
casualty ['kæʒjultɪ] n víctima m/f, herido; (dead) muerto; (MIL) baja; **casualties** npl pérdidas fpl.
cat [kæt] n gato.
Catalan ['kætələn] a, n Catalán/ana m/f.
catalogue, catalog (US) ['kætələg] n catálogo // vt catalogar.
Catalonia [kætə'ləunɪə] n Cataluña.
catalyst ['kætəlɪst] n catalizador m.
catapult ['kætəpʌlt] n tirador m.

cataract ['kætərækt] n (also MED) catarata.
catarrh [kə'tɑː*] n catarro.
catastrophe [kə'tæstrəfɪ] n catástrofe m; **catastrophic** [kætə'strɔfɪk] a catastrófico.
catch [kætʃ], pt, pp **caught** vt (gen) coger; (arrest) detener; (grasp) asir; (breath) suspender; (person: by surprise) sorprender; (attract: attention) ganar; (MED) contagiarse de, coger; (also: ~ **up**) alcanzar // vi (fire) encenderse; (in branches etc) enredarse // n (fish etc) pesca; (act of catching) cogida; (trick) trampa; (of lock) pestillo, cerradura; **to** ~ **on** vi (understand) caer en la cuenta; (grow popular) hacerse popular; **to** ~ **sight of** divisar; **to** ~ **up** vi (fig) ponerse al día.
catch: ~**ing** a (MED) contagioso; ~**ment area** n zona de captación; ~ **phrase** n lema m, slogan m; ~**y** a (tune) pegadizo.
catechism ['kætɪkɪzəm] n (REL) catequismo.
categoric(al) [kætɪ'gɔrɪk(əl)] a categórico, terminante.
categorize ['kætɪgəraɪz] vt clasificar; **category** [-rɪ] n categoría, clase f.
cater ['keɪtə*] vi: **to** ~ **for** abastecer a; (needs) atender a; (consumers) proveer a; ~**er** n abastecedor m, proveedor m; ~**ing** n servicio de comidas; (trade) abastecimiento.
caterpillar ['kætəpɪlə*] n oruga, gusano; ~ **track** n rodado de oruga.
cathedral [kə'θiːdrəl] n catedral f.
catholic ['kæθəlɪk] a católico; **C**~ a, n (REL) católico/a.
cattle ['kætl] npl ganado sg.
catty ['kætɪ] a malicioso, rencoroso.
Caucasus ['kɔːkəsəs] n Cáucaso.
caught [kɔːt] pt, pp of **catch.**
cauliflower ['kɔlɪflauə*] n coliflor f.
cause [kɔːz] n causa, motivo, razón f // vt causar; (provoke) provocar.
causeway ['kɔːzweɪ] n (road) carretera elevada; (embankment) terraplén m.
caustic ['kɔːstɪk] a cáustico; (fig) mordaz.
caution ['kɔːʃən] n cautela, prudencia; (warning) advertencia, amonestación f // vt amonestar.
cautious ['kɔːʃəs] a cauteloso, prudente, precavido; ~**ly** ad con cautela; ~**ness** n cautela.
cavalier [kævə'lɪə*] a arrogante, desdeñoso.
cavalry ['kævəlrɪ] n caballería.
cave [keɪv] n cueva, caverna; **to** ~ **in** vi (roof etc) derrumbarse, hundirse; ~**man** n cavernícola m/f, troglodita m/f.
cavern ['kævən] n caverna.
caviar(e) ['kævɪɑː*] n caviar m.
cavity ['kævɪtɪ] n hueco, cavidad f.
cavort [kə'vɔːt] vi dar cabriolas.
caw [kɔː] vi graznar.
CBI n abbr of **Confederation of British Industries.**

cc *abbr of* **cubic centimetres; carbon copy.**
cease [si:s] *vt, vi* cesar; ~**fire** *n* cese *m* de hostilidades o fuego; ~**less** *a* incesante; ~**lessly** *ad* sin cesar.
cedar ['si:də*] *n* cedro.
cede [si:d] *vt* ceder.
ceiling ['si:lɪŋ] *n* techo; (*fig*) límite *m*.
celebrate ['sɛlɪbreɪt] *vt* celebrar; (*marriage*) solemnizar // *vi* divertirse; ~**d** *a* célebre; **celebration** [-'breɪʃən] *n* fiesta, celebración *f*.
celebrity [sɪ'lɛbrɪtɪ] *n* celebridad *f*.
celery ['sɛlərɪ] *n* apio.
celestial [sɪ'lɛstɪəl] *a* (*of sky*) celeste; (*divine*) celestial.
celibacy ['sɛlɪbəsɪ] *n* celibato.
cell [sɛl] *n* celda; (*BIOL*) célula; (*ELEC*) elemento.
cellar ['sɛlə*] *n* sótano; (*for wine*) bodega.
'cello ['tʃɛləu] *n* violoncelo.
cellophane ['sɛləfeɪn] *n* celofán *m*.
cellular ['sɛljulə*] *a* celular.
cellulose ['sɛljuləus] *n* celulosa.
Celt [kɛlt, sɛlt] *a, n* celta *m/f*; ~**ic** *a* celta.
cement [sə'mɛnt] *n* cemento // *vt* cementar; (*fig*) cimentar, fortalecer.
cemetery ['sɛmɪtrɪ] *n* cementerio.
cenotaph ['sɛnətɑ:f] *n* cenotafio.
censor ['sɛnsə*] *n* censor // *vt* (*cut*) tachar, suprimir; ~**ship** *n* censura.
censure ['sɛnʃə*] *vt* censurar.
census ['sɛnsəs] *n* censo.
cent [sɛnt] *n* (*US: coin*) centavo, céntimo; *see also* **per.**
centenary [sɛn'ti:nərɪ] *n* centenario.
centi... [sɛntɪ] *pref:* ~**grade** *a* centígrado; ~**litre** *n* centilitro; ~**metre** *n* centímetro; ~**pede** *n* ciempiés *m*.
central ['sɛntrəl] *a* central; (*of town*) céntrico; **C**~ **American** *a* centroamericano; ~ **heating** *n* calefacción *f* central; ~**ize** *vt* centralizar.
centre ['sɛntə*] *n* centro; ~- **forward** *n* (*SPORT*) delantero centro; ~-**half** *n* (*SPORT*) medio centro.
century ['sɛntjurɪ] *n* siglo; **20th** ~ siglo veinte.
ceramic [sɪ'ræmɪk] *a* cerámico; ~**s** *n* cerámica.
cereal ['si:rɪəl] *n* cereal *m*.
ceremony ['sɛrɪmənɪ] *n* ceremonia.
certain ['sɔ:tən] *a* (*gen*) seguro; (*correct*) cierto; (*person*) seguro; (*a particular*) cierto; **for** ~ a ciencia cierta; ~**ly** *ad* desde luego, por cierto; ~**ty** *n* certeza, certidumbre *f*, seguridad *f*.
certificate [sə'tɪfɪkɪt] *n* certificado.
certify ['sɔ:tɪfaɪ] *vt* certificar.
cervix ['sɔ:vɪks] *n* cerviz *f*.
cessation [sə'seɪʃən] *n* cesación *f*, suspensión *f*.
cf. *abbr* = **compare** cfr.
chafe [tʃeɪf] *vt* (*rub*) rozar; (*wear*) desgastar; (*irritate*) irritar.
chaffinch ['tʃæfɪntʃ] *n* pinzón *m* vulgar.

chagrin ['ʃægrɪn] *n* disgusto, desazón *f*.
chain [tʃeɪn] *n* (*gen*) cadena // *vt* (*also:* ~ up) encadenar; ~ **reaction** *n* reacción *f* en cadena; ~ **store** *n* tienda de una cadena.
chair [tʃɛə*] *n* silla; (*armchair*) sillón *m*; (*of university*) cátedra // *vt* (*meeting*) presidir; ~**lift** *n* telesilla; ~**man** *n* presidente *m*.
chalet ['ʃæleɪ] *n* chalet *m*.
chalice ['tʃælɪs] *n* cáliz *m*.
chalk [tʃɔ:k] *n* (*GEO*) creta; (*for writing*) tiza.
challenge ['tʃælɪndʒ] *n* desafío, reto // *vt* desafiar, retar; (*statement, right*) poner en duda, cuestionar; **to** ~ **sb to do sth** retar a uno a que haga algo; **challenger** *n* (*SPORT*) contrincante *m/f*; **challenging** *a* desafiante; (*tone*) de desafío.
chamber ['tʃeɪmbə*] *n* cámara, sala; ~ **of commerce** cámara de comercio; ~**maid** *n* camarera; ~ **music** *n* música de cámara.
chamois ['ʃæmwɑ:] *n* gamuza.
champagne [ʃæm'peɪn] *n* champaña *m*, champán *m*.
champion ['tʃæmpɪən] *n* campeón/ona *m/f*; ~**ship** *n* campeonato.
chance [tʃɑ:ns] *n* (*luck*) casualidad *f*, suerte *f*; (*fate*) azar *m*; (*opportunity*) ocasión *f*, oportunidad *f*; (*likelihood*) posibilidad *f*; (*risk*) riesgo // *vt* arriesgar, probar // *a* fortuito, casual; **to** ~ **it** aventurarse, arriesgarse; **to take a** ~ arriesgarse; **by** ~ por casualidad.
chancel ['tʃɑ:nsəl] *n* coro y presbiterio.
chancellor ['tʃɑ:nsələ*] *n* canciller *m*; **C**~ **of the Exchequer** *n* Ministro de Hacienda.
chandelier [ʃændə'lɪə*] *n* araña (de luces).
change [tʃeɪndʒ] *vt* (*gen*) cambiar; (*replace*) reemplazar; (*gear, clothes, house*) cambiar de, mudar de; (*exchange*) trocar; (*transform*) transformar // *vi* (*gen*) cambiar(se), mudar; (*trains*) hacer transbordo; **to** ~ **into** transformarse en // *n* cambio, modificación *f*, transformación *f*; (*coins*) moneda suelta, suelto; (*money returned*) vuelta; **for a** ~ para variar; ~**able** *a* (*weather*) cambiable, mudable; ~**less** *a* inmutable; ~**over** *n* (*to new system*) cambio.
changing ['tʃeɪndʒɪŋ] *a* cambiante; ~ **room** *n* vestuario.
channel ['tʃænl] *n* (*TV*) canal *m*; (*of river*) cauce *m*; (*of sea*) estrecho; (*groove, fig: medium*) conducto, medio // *vt* canalizar, encauzar; **the (English) C**~ el Canal (de la Mancha); **the C**~ **Islands** las Islas Normandas *fpl*.
chant [tʃɑ:nt] *n* canto // *vt* cantar; (*fig*) recitar en tono monótono.
chaos ['keɪɔs] *n* caos *m*; **chaotic** [keɪ'ɔtɪk] *a* caótico, desordenado.
chap [tʃæp] *n* (*col: man*) tío, tipo // *vi* (*skin*) agrietarse.

chapel ['tʃæpəl] n capilla.
chaperon ['ʃæpərəun] n carabina.
chaplain ['tʃæplɪn] n capellán m.
chapter ['tʃæptə*] n capítulo.
char [tʃɑ:*] vt (burn) carbonizar, chamuscar // n = **charlady**.
character ['kærɪktə*] n carácter m, naturaleza, índole f, calidad f; (in novel, film) personaje m; (role) papel m; ~**istic** [-'rɪstɪk] a característico // n característica; ~**ize** vt caracterizar.
charade [ʃə'rɑ:d] n charada.
charcoal ['tʃɑ:kəul] n carbón m vegetal; (ART) carboncillo.
charge [tʃɑ:dʒ] n carga; (LAW) cargo, acusación f; (cost) precio, coste m; (responsibility) cargo; (task) encargo // vt (LAW) acusar (with de); (gun, battery, MIL: enemy) cargar; (price) pedir; (customer) cobrar; (sb with task) encargar // vi cargar, precipitarse; (make pay) cobrar; ~**s** npl: **bank** ~**s** suplemento cobrado por el banco; **free of** ~ gratis; **to reverse the** ~**s** (TEL) poner una conferencia por cobrar; **to take** ~ **of** hacerse cargo de, encargarse de; **to be in** ~ **of** estar a cargo de o encargado de; **how much do you** ~? ¿cuánto cobra Usted?; **to** ~ **an expense (up) to sb's account** cargar algo a cuenta de alguien.
charitable ['tʃærɪtəbl] a caritativo.
charity ['tʃærɪtɪ] n (gen) caridad f; (sympathy) compasión f; (organization) sociedad f benéfica.
charlady ['tʃɑ:leɪdɪ] n mujer f de la limpieza.
charm [tʃɑ:m] n encanto, atractivo; (spell) hechizo; (object) amuleto // vt encantar; hechizar; ~**ing** a encantador(a), simpático.
chart [tʃɑ:t] n cuadro; (graph) gráfica; (map) carta de navegación // vt (course) trazar.
charter ['tʃɑ:tə*] vt (plane) alquilar; (ship) fletar // n (document) carta; ~**ed accountant** n perito contable; ~ **flight** n vuelo charter.
charwoman ['tʃɑ:wumən] n = **charlady**.
chase [tʃeɪs] vt (follow) perseguir; (hunt) cazar // n persecución f; caza; **to** ~ **after** correr tras.
chasm ['kæzəm] n abismo.
chassis ['ʃæsɪ] n chasis m.
chaste [tʃeɪst] a casto; **chastity** ['tʃæstɪtɪ] n castidad f.
chat [tʃæt] vi (also: **have a** ~) charlar // n charla.
chatter ['tʃætə*] vi (person) charlar; (teeth) castañetear // n (of birds) parloteo; (of people) charla, cháchara; ~**box** n parlanchín/ina m/f.
chatty ['tʃætɪ] a (style) familiar; (person) hablador(a), locuaz.
chauffeur ['ʃəufə*] n chófer m.
cheap [tʃi:p] a barato; (trick) malo; (poor quality) barato, de poca calidad // ad barato; ~**en** vt rebajar el precio,

abaratar; **to** ~**en o.s.** rebajarse; ~**ly** ad barato, a bajo precio.
cheat [tʃi:t] vi hacer trampa // vt defraudar, timar // n trampa, fraude m; (person) tramposo; ~**ing** n trampa, fraude m.
check [tʃek] vt (examine) controlar; (facts) comprobar; (count) contar; (halt) parar, detener; (restrain) refrenar, restringir // n (inspection) control m, inspección f; (curb) freno; (bill) nota, cuenta; (obstacle) impedimento, estorbo; (token) ficha; (pattern: gen pl) cuadro; **to** ~ **in** vi (in hotel, airport) registrarse // vt (luggage) facturar; **to** ~ **out** vi (of hotel) pagar la cuenta y marcharse; **to** ~ **up** vi: **to** ~ **up on sth** comprobar algo; **to** ~ **up on sb** investigar a una persona; ~**mate** n jaque m mate; ~**out** n caja; ~**point** n (punto de) control m; ~**up** n (MED) reconocimiento general; (of machine) repaso.
cheek [tʃi:k] n mejilla; (impudence) descaro; ~**bone** n pómulo; ~**y** a fresco, descarado.
cheer [tʃɪə*] vt vitorear, aplaudir; (gladden) alegrar, animar // vi aplaudir, gritar con entusiasmo // n grito (de entusiasmo); ~**s** npl aplausos mpl; ~**s!** ¡salud!; **to** ~ **up** vi animarse, cobrar ánimos // vt alegrar, animar; ~**ful** a alegre; ~**fulness** n alegría; **cheerio** excl ¡hasta luego!; ~**less** a triste, sombrío.
cheese [tʃi:z] n queso.
chef [ʃef] n jefe/a m/f de cocina.
chemical ['kemɪkəl] a químico // n elemento químico.
chemist ['kemɪst] n farmacéutico; (scientist) químico; ~**ry** n química; ~'**s (shop)** n farmacia.
cheque [tʃek] n cheque m; ~**book** n libro de cheques, chequera.
chequered ['tʃekəd] a (fig) variado, accidentado.
cherish ['tʃerɪʃ] vt (love) querer, apreciar; (protect) cuidar; (hope etc) abrigar.
cherry ['tʃerɪ] n cereza.
chess [tʃes] n ajedrez m; ~**board** n tablero (de ajedrez); ~**man** n pieza, trebejo.
chest [tʃest] n (ANAT) pecho; (box) cofre m, cajón m; ~ **of drawers** n cómoda.
chestnut ['tʃesnʌt] n castaña; ~ **(tree)** n castaño.
chew [tʃu:] vt mascar, masticar; ~**ing gum** n chicle m.
chic [ʃi:k] a elegante.
chick [tʃɪk] n pollito, polluelo; (fam) chica.
chicken ['tʃɪkɪn] n gallina, pollo; (food) pollo; ~**pox** n varicela.
chickpea ['tʃɪkpi:] n garbanzo.
chicory ['tʃɪkərɪ] n (for coffee) achicoria; (salad) escarola.
chief [tʃi:f] n jefe/a m/f // a principal; ~**ly** ad principalmente.
chiffon ['ʃɪfɔn] n gasa.
chilblain ['tʃɪlbleɪn] n sabañón m.

child

circulate

child [tʃaɪld], pl ~**ren** ['tʃɪldrən] n niño/a; (offspring) hijo/a; ~**birth** n parto; ~**hood** n niñez f, infancia; ~**ish** a pueril, aniñado; ~**like** a como (de) niño; ~ **minder** n cuidadora de niños.
Chile ['tʃɪlɪ] n Chile m; ~**an** a, n chileno/a.
chill [tʃɪl] n frío; (MED) escalofrío, resfriado // vt enfriar; (CULIN) congelar; ~**y** a frío.
chime [tʃaɪm] n (peal) repique m, campanada // vi repicar, sonar.
chimney ['tʃɪmnɪ] n chimenea; ~ **sweep** n deshollinador m.
chimpanzee [tʃɪmpæn'ziː] n chimpancé m.
chin [tʃɪn] n barba, barbilla.
china ['tʃaɪnə] n porcelana; (gen) loza.
China ['tʃaɪnə] n China; **Chinese** [tʃaɪ'niːz] a chino // n chino/a; (LING) el chino.
chink [tʃɪŋk] n (opening) grieta, hendedura; (noise) tintineo.
chip [tʃɪp] n (gen pl: CULIN) patata frita; (of wood) astilla; (of glass, stone) lasca; (at poker) ficha // vt (cup, plate) astillar; to ~ **in** vi interrumpir; (contribute) compartir los gastos.
chiropodist [kɪ'rɔpədɪst] n pedicuro.
chirp [tʃəːp] vi gorjear, piar; (cricket) chirriar.
chisel ['tʃɪzl] n (for wood) formón m; (for stone) cincel m.
chit [tʃɪt] n nota.
chitchat ['tʃɪttʃæt] n chismes mpl, habladurías fpl.
chivalrous ['ʃɪvəlrəs] a caballeroso; **chivalry** [-rɪ] n caballerosidad f.
chives [tʃaɪvz] npl cebollino sg.
chlorine ['klɔːriːn] n cloro.
chock [tʃɔk]: ~**-a-block**, ~**-full** a de bote en bote, atestado.
chocolate ['tʃɔklɪt] n chocolate m.
choice [tʃɔɪs] n elección f, selección f; (preference) preferencia // a selecto, elegido.
choir ['kwaɪə*] n coro; ~**boy** n corista m.
choke [tʃəuk] vi sofocarse; (on food) atragantarse // vt ahogar, sofocar; (block) obstruir // n (AUT) estrangulador m; **choker** n (necklace) gargantilla.
cholera ['kɔlərə] n cólera m.
choose [tʃuːz], pt **chose**, pp **chosen** vt escoger, elegir; (team) seleccionar.
chop [tʃɔp] vt (wood) cortar, tajar; (CULIN: also: ~ **up**) desmenuzar; (meat) picar // n golpe m cortante; (CULIN) chuleta; ~**s** npl (jaws) boca sg, labios mpl; ~**py** a (sea) picado, agitado; ~**sticks** npl palillos mpl.
choral ['kɔːrəl] a coral.
chord [kɔːd] n (MUS) acorde m.
chore [tʃɔː*] n faena, tarea; (routine task) trabajo rutinario.
choreographer [kɔrɪ'ɔgrəfə*] n coreógrafo.
chorister ['kɔrɪstə*] n corista m/f.
chortle ['tʃɔːtl] vi reír entre dientes.
chorus ['kɔːrəs] n coro; (repeated part of song) estribillo.

chose [tʃəuz], **chosen** ['tʃəuzn] pt, pp of **choose**.
Christ [kraɪst] n Cristo.
christen ['krɪsn] vt bautizar; ~**ing** n bautizo.
Christian ['krɪstɪən] a, n cristiano/a; ~**ity** [-'ænɪtɪ] n cristianismo; ~ **name** n nombre m de pila.
Christmas ['krɪsməs] n Navidad f; **Merry** ~! ¡Felices Pascuas!; ~ **Eve** n Nochebuena.
chrome [krəum], **chromium** ['krəumɪəm] n cromo.
chromosome ['krəuməsəum] n cromosoma m.
chronic ['krɔnɪk] a crónico.
chronicle ['krɔnɪkl] n crónica.
chronological [krɔnə'lɔdʒɪkəl] a cronológico.
chrysanthemum [krɪ'sænθəməm] n crisantemo.
chubby ['tʃʌbɪ] a rechoncho.
chuck [tʃʌk] vt lanzar, arrojar; to ~ **out** vt echar (fuera), tirar; to ~ (**up**) vt abandonar.
chuckle ['tʃʌkl] vi reírse entre dientes.
chug [tʃʌg] vi resoplar; to ~ **along** vi (fig) ir tirando.
chum [tʃʌm] n compinche m, compañero.
chunk [tʃʌŋk] n pedazo, trozo.
church [tʃəːtʃ] n iglesia; ~**yard** n campo santo.
churlish ['tʃəːlɪʃ] a grosero, hosco.
churn [tʃəːn] n (for butter) mantequera; (for milk) lechera // vt revolver, agitar.
chute [ʃuːt] n (also: **rubbish** ~) vertedero; (children's slide) tobogán m.
chutney ['tʃʌtnɪ] n salsa picante.
CID n abbr of **Criminal Investigation Department** B.I.C. (Brigada de Investigación Criminal).
cider ['saɪdə*] n sidra.
cigar [sɪ'gɑː*] n puro.
cigarette [sɪgə'rɛt] n cigarrillo; (fam) pitillo; ~ **case** n pitillera; ~ **end** n colilla; ~ **holder** n boquilla.
Cinderella [sɪndə'rɛlə] n la Cenicienta.
cinders ['sɪndəz] npl cenizas fpl.
cine [sɪnɪ]: ~**-camera** n cámara cinematográfica; ~**-film** n película cinematográfica.
cinema ['sɪnəmə] n cine m.
cinnamon ['sɪnəmən] n canela.
cipher ['saɪfə*] n cifra.
circle ['səːkl] n círculo; (in cinema) anfiteatro // vi dar vueltas // vt (surround) rodear, cercar; (move round) dar la vuelta a.
circuit ['səːkɪt] n circuito; (tour) gira; (track) pista; (lap) vuelta; ~**ous** [səː'kjuɪtəs] a tortuoso, indirecto.
circular ['səːkjulə*] a circular // n circular f.
circulate ['səːkjuleɪt] vi circular // vt poner en circulación, hacer circular;

circulation [-'leɪʃən] n circulación f; (of newspaper) tirada.
circumcise ['sɔːkəmsaɪz] vt circuncidar.
circumference [sɔ'kʌmfərəns] n circunferencia.
circumspect ['sɔːkəmspɛkt] a circunspecto, prudente.
circumstances ['sɔːkəmstənsɪz] npl circunstancias fpl; (financial condition) situación f económica.
circus ['sɔːkəs] n circo; (roundabout) glorieta.
cistern ['sɪstən] n tanque m, depósito; (in toilet) cisterna.
cite [saɪt] vt citar.
citizen ['sɪtɪzn] n (POL) ciudadano/a; (resident) vecino/a, habitante m/f; ~ship n ciudadanía.
citrus fruit ['sɪtrəs-] n agrios mpl.
city ['sɪtɪ] n ciudad f; the C~ centro financiero de Londres.
civic ['sɪvɪk] a cívico, municipal.
civil ['sɪvɪl] a civil; (polite) atento, cortés; (defence) pasivo; (well-bred) educado; ~ engineer n ingeniero civil; C~ Service administración f pública; ~ian [sɪ'vɪlɪən] a civil, de paisano // n civil m/f, paisano.
civilization [sɪvɪlaɪ'zeɪʃən] n civilización f.
civilized ['sɪvɪlaɪzd] a civilizado.
claim [kleɪm] vt exigir, reclamar; (rights etc) reivindicar; (assert) pretender // vi (for insurance) reclamar // n reclamación f; (LAW) demanda; (pretension) pretensión f; ~ant n (ADMIN, LAW) demandante m/f.
clairvoyant [klɛə'vɔɪənt] n clarividente m/f.
clam [klæm] n almeja.
clamber ['klæmbə*] vi subir gateando, trepar.
clammy ['klæmɪ] a (cold) frío y húmedo; (sticky) pegajoso.
clamp [klæmp] n abrazadera, grapa // vt afianzar (con abrazadera); to ~ down on vt fus suprimir, restringir.
clan [klæn] n clan m.
clang [klæŋ] n sonido metálico // vi sonar, hacer estruendo.
clap [klæp] vi aplaudir // vt (hands) batir; (put) poner // n (of hands) palmada; (of thunder) estampido (de trueno); ~ping n aplausos mpl.
claret ['klærət] n clarete m.
clarification [klærɪfɪ'keɪʃən] n aclaración f; **clarify** ['klærɪfaɪ] vt aclarar.
clarinet [klærɪ'nɛt] n clarinete m.
clarity ['klærɪtɪ] n claridad f.
clash [klæʃ] n estruendo; (fig) choque m // vi (meet) encontrarse; (battle) chocar; (disagree) estar en desacuerdo.
clasp [klɑːsp] n broche m; (on jewels) cierre m // vt abrochar; (hand) apretar, estrechar; (embrace) abrazar.
class [klɑːs] n (gen) clase f // a clasista, de clase // vt clasificar.
classic ['klæsɪk] a clásico // n (work) obra clásica; ~al a clásico.

classification [klæsɪfɪ'keɪʃən] n clasificación f; **classify** ['klæsɪfaɪ] vt clasificar.
class: ~mate n compañero de clase; ~room n aula.
clatter ['klætə*] n ruido, estruendo; (of hooves) trápala // vi hacer ruido o estruendo.
clause [klɔːz] n cláusula; (LING) oración f.
claustrophobia [klɔːstrə'fəubɪə] n claustrofobia.
claw [klɔː] n (of cat) uña; (of bird of prey) garra; (of lobster) pinza; (TECH) garfio // vt: to ~ at arañar; (tear) desgarrar.
clay [kleɪ] n arcilla.
clean [kliːn] a limpio; (clear) neto, bien definido // vt limpiar; to ~ out vt limpiar; to ~ up vt limpiar, asear; ~-cut a (person) de buen parecer; (clear) nítido; ~er n (person) asistenta; ~ing n (gen) limpieza; (clothes) limpieza en seco; ~liness ['klɛnlɪnɪs] n limpieza; ~-shaven a sin barba, lampiño.
cleanse [klɛnz] vt limpiar; **cleanser** n agente m de limpieza; (for face) desmaquillador m; **cleansing department** n departamento de limpieza.
clear [klɪə*] a claro; (road, way) limpio, libre; (complete) completo // vt (space) despejar, limpiar; (LAW: suspect) absolver; (obstacle) salvar, saltar por encima de; (debt) liquidar // vi (gen) aclararse; (fog etc) despejarse // ad: ~ of a distancia de; to ~ up vt limpiar; (mystery) aclarar, resolver; ~ance n (removal) despeje m; (permission) acreditación f; ~-cut a bien definido, nítido; ~ing n (in wood) claro; ~ing bank n cámara de compensación; ~ly ad claramente; ~way n (Brit) carretera donde no se puede aparcar.
cleaver ['kliːvə] n cuchilla (de carnicero).
clef [klɛf] n (MUS) clave f.
clemency ['klɛmənsɪ] n clemencia.
clench [klɛntʃ] vt apretar, cerrar.
clergy ['klɔːdʒɪ] n clero; ~man n clérigo.
clerical ['klɛrɪkəl] a oficinista; (REL) clerical.
clerk [klɑːk, (US) klɔːrk] n empleado, oficinista m/f.
clever ['klɛvə*] a (mentally) inteligente, listo; (deft, crafty) hábil; (device, arrangement) ingenioso.
cliché ['kliːʃeɪ] n cliché m, frase f hecha.
click [klɪk] vt (tongue) chasquear; (heels) taconear.
client ['klaɪənt] n cliente m/f; ~ele [kliːɑːn'tɛl] n clientela.
cliff [klɪf] n acantilado.
climate ['klaɪmɪt] n clima m; (fig) ambiente m.
climax ['klaɪmæks] n colmo, punto culminante; (sexual) clímax m.
climb [klaɪm] vi subir, trepar // vt (stairs) subir; (tree) trepar a; (hill) escalar // n subida; ~er n alpinista m/f, montañista m/f; ~ing n alpinismo.

clinch [klɪntʃ] vt (deal) cerrar; (argument) remachar.

cling [klɪŋ], pt, pp **clung** [klʌŋ] vi: **to ~ to** pegarse a, quedar pegado a; (of clothes) ajustarse a.

clinic ['klɪnɪk] n clínica; **~al** a clínico.

clink [klɪŋk] vi tintinar.

clip [klɪp] n (for hair) prendido; (also: **paper ~**) sujetapapeles m inv; (clamp) grapa // vt (cut) cortar; (shorten) acortar; (clamp) sujetar; **~pers** npl (for gardening) tijeras fpl; (for hair) maquinilla sg; (for nails) cortauñas m inv; **~ping** n recorte m.

clique [kli:k] n camarilla, pandilla.

cloak [kləuk] n capa, manto // vt (fig) encubrir, disimular; **~room** n guardarropa; (in station) consigna; (WC) lavabo, aseos mpl.

clock [klɔk] n reloj m; (in taxi) taxímetro; (fam) cara; **~wise** ad en el sentido de las agujas del reloj; **~work** n aparato de relojería // a de cuerda.

clog [klɔg] n zueco, chanclo // vt atascar // vi atascarse.

cloister ['klɔɪstə*] n claustro.

close a, ad and derivatives [kləus] a cercano, próximo; (print, weave) tupido, compacto; (friend) íntimo; (connection) estrecho; (examination) detallado, minucioso; (weather) bochornoso; (atmosphere) sofocante; (room) mal ventilado // ad cerca // vb and derivatives [kləuz] vt (shut) cerrar; (end) concluir, terminar // vi (shop etc) cerrarse; (end) concluirse, terminarse // n (end) fin m, final m, conclusión f; **to ~ down** vi cerrarse definitivamente; **to ~ up** vi (crowd) arrimarse; **~d** a (shop etc) cerrado; **~d shop** n acuerdo de emplear sólo trabajadores sindicados; **~ly** ad (exactly) fielmente; (carefully) atentamente.

closet ['klɔzɪt] n (cupboard) armario; (wc) lavabo.

close-up ['kləusʌp] n primer plano.

closure ['kləuʒə*] n (close-down) cierre m, clausura; (end) fin m.

clot [klɔt] n (gen: **blood ~**) embolia; (fam: idiot) imbécil m/f // vi (blood) cuajarse, coagularse.

cloth [klɔθ] n (material) tela, paño; (rag) trapo.

clothe [kləuð] vt vestir; (fig) revestir; **~s** npl ropa sg; **~s brush** n cepillo (para la ropa); **~s line** n cuerda (para tender la ropa); **~s peg** n pinza; **clothing** n = **clothes.**

cloud [klaud] n nube f; (storm~) nubarrón m; **~burst** n chaparrón m; **~y** a nublado, nubloso; (liquid) turbio.

clout [klaut] vt dar un tortazo a.

clove [kləuv] n clavo; **~ of garlic** diente m de ajo.

clover ['kləuvə*] n trébol m.

clown [klaun] n payaso // vi (also: **~ about, ~ around**) hacer el payaso.

club [klʌb] n (society) club m; (weapon)

porra, cachiporra; (also: **golf ~**) palo // vt aporrear // vi: **to ~ together** hacer una colecta; **~s** npl (CARDS) tréboles mpl; **~house** n sala de reunión.

cluck [klʌk] vi cloquear.

clue [klu:] n pista; (in crosswords) indicación f; **I haven't a ~** no tengo idea.

clump [klʌmp] n (of trees) grupo.

clumsy ['klʌmzɪ] a (person) torpe, desmañado; (movement) pesado.

cluster ['klʌstə*] n grupo; (BOT) racimo // vi agruparse, apiñarse.

clutch [klʌtʃ] n (grip, grasp) apretón m, agarro; (AUT) embrague m; (pedal) pedal m de embrague // vt sujetar, empuñar.

clutter ['klʌtə*] vt atestar, llenar desordenadamente.

Co. abbr of county; company.

c/o abbr of care of c/a (en casa de), a/c (a cuidado de).

coach [kəutʃ] n (bus) autocar m; (horse-drawn) coche m; (of train) vagón m, coche m; (SPORT) entrenador m, instructor m // vt (SPORT) entrenar; (student) preparar, enseñar.

coagulate [kəu'æɡjuleɪt] vi coagularse.

coal [kəul] n carbón m; **~ face** n frente m de carbón; **~field** n yacimiento de carbón.

coalition [kəuə'lɪʃən] n coalición f.

coal: ~man, ~ merchant n carbonero; **~mine** n mina de carbón.

coarse [kɔ:s] a basto, burdo; (vulgar) grosero, ordinario.

coast [kəust] n costa, litoral m // vi (AUT) ir en punto muerto; **~al** a costero, costanero; **~er** n buque m costero, barco de cabotaje; **~guard** n guardacostas m inv; **~line** n litoral m.

coat [kəut] n (jacket) chaqueta; (overcoat) abrigo; (of animal) pelo, lana; (of paint) mano f, capa // vt cubrir, revestir; **~ of arms** n escudo de armas; **~ hanger** n percha; **~ing** n capa, baño.

coax [kəuks] vt engatusar.

cob [kɔb] n see **corn.**

cobbler ['kɔblə] n zapatero remendón.

cobbles ['kɔblz], **cobblestones** ['kɔblstəunz] npl guijarros mpl.

cobra ['kəubrə] n cobra.

cobweb ['kɔbwɛb] n telaraña.

cocaine [kə'keɪn] n cocaína.

cock [kɔk] n (rooster) gallo; (male bird) macho // vt (gun) amartillar; **~atoo** n cacatúa; **~erel** n gallito.

cockle ['kɔkl] n berberecho.

cockney ['kɔknɪ] n habitante m/f de ciertos barrios bajos de Londres.

cockpit ['kɔkpɪt] n (in aircraft) carlinga, cabina.

cockroach ['kɔkrəutʃ] n cucaracha.

cocktail ['kɔkteɪl] n combinado, coctel m; **~ cabinet** n mueble-bar m; **~ party** n coctel m, cóctel m.

cocoa ['kəukəu] n cacao; (drink) chocolate m.

coconut ['kəukənʌt] n coco.
cocoon [kə'ku:n] n capullo.
cod [kɔd] n bacalao.
code [kəud] n código; (cipher) clave f;
codify vt codificar.
coerce [kəu'ə:s] vt forzar, obligar;
coercion [-'ə:ʃən] n coacción f.
coexistence ['kəuɪg'zɪstəns] n
coexistencia.
coffee ['kɔfɪ] n café m; ~ **bean** n grano de
café; ~ **grounds** npl heces fpl de café;
~**pot** n cafetera.
coffin ['kɔfɪn] n ataúd m.
cog [kɔg] n diente m; ~**wheel** n rueda
dentada.
cognac ['kɔnjæk] n coñac m.
coherent [kəu'hɪərənt] a coherente.
coil [kɔɪl] n rollo; (rope) adujada; (ELEC)
bobina, carrete m; (contraceptive) espiral f
// vi enrollarse, arrollarse.
coin [kɔɪn] n moneda // vt (word) inventar,
idear; ~**age** n moneda; ~**-box** n caja
recaudadora.
coincide [kəuɪn'saɪd] vi coincidir; (agree)
estar de acuerdo; **coincidence** [kəu-
'ɪnsɪdəns] n casualidad f.
coke [kəuk] n (coal) coque m.
Coke ® [kəuk] n (drink) Coca-Cola f.
colander ['kɔləndə*] n colador m,
escurridor m.
cold [kəuld] a frío // n frío; (MED) resfriado;
it's ~ hace frío; **to be** ~ tener frío; **to
catch** ~ resfriarse, acatarrarse; **to
~-shoulder** tratar con frialdad; ~**ly** a
fríamente; ~ **sore** n herpes m labial.
coleslaw ['kəulslɔ:] n ensalada de col.
colic ['kɔlɪk] n cólico.
collaborate [kə'læbəreɪt] vi colaborar;
collaboration [-'reɪʃən] n colaboración f.
collage [kɔ'lɑ:ʒ] n collage m.
collapse [kə'læps] vi (gen) hundirse,
derrumbarse; (MED) sufrir colapso // n
(gen) hundimiento; (MED) colapso;
collapsible a plegable.
collar ['kɔlə*] n (of coat, shirt) cuello;
~**bone** n clavícula.
collate [kɔ'leɪt] vt cotejar.
colleague ['kɔli:g] n colega m/f.
collect [kə'lɛkt] vt reunir; (as a hobby)
coleccionar; (call and pick up) recoger;
(wages) cobrar; (debts) recaudar;
(donations, subscriptions) colectar // vi
reunirse; coleccionar; ~**ion** [kə'lɛkʃən] n
colección f; cobro; (of people) grupo; (of
donations) recaudación f; (of post)
recogida.
collective [kə'lɛktɪv] a colectivo.
collector [kə'lɛktə*] n coleccionista m/f;
(of taxes etc) recaudador m.
college ['kɔlɪdʒ] n colegio.
collide [kə'laɪd] vi chocar.
collie ['kɔlɪ] n perro pastor.
collision [kə'lɪʒən] n choque m.
colloquial [kə'ləukwɪəl] a familiar,
coloquial.

colon ['kəulən] n (sign) dos puntos; (MED)
colón m.
colonel ['kə:nl] n coronel m.
colonial [kə'ləunɪəl] a colonial.
colonize ['kɔlənaɪz] vt colonizar.
colony ['kɔlənɪ] n colonia.
colossal [kə'lɔsl] a colosal.
colour, color (US) ['kʌlə*] n color m // vt
color(e)ar; (with crayons) pintar; (dye)
teñir // vi (blush) sonrojarse; ~**s** npl (of
party, club) colores mpl; ~**-blind** a
daltoniano; ~**ed** a de color; (photo) a
colores; ~**eds** npl gente f de color; ~
film n película en colores; ~**ful** a lleno de
color; (personality) animado; ~**ing** n
colorido; ~**less** a incoloro, sin color; ~
scheme n combinación f de colores; ~
television n televisión f en color(es).
colt [kəult] n potro.
column ['kɔləm] n columna; ~**ist**
['kɔləmnɪst] n columnista m/f.
coma ['kəumə] n coma m.
comb [kəum] n peine m; (ornamental)
peineta // vt (hair) peinar; (area)
registrar.
combat ['kɔmbæt] n combate m // vt
combatir.
combination [kɔmbɪ'neɪʃən] n (gen)
combinación f.
combine [kəm'baɪn] vt combinar;
(qualities) reunir // vi combinarse // n
['kɔmbaɪn] (ECON) asociación f; (pej)
monopolio; ~ (**harvester**) n
cosechadora.
combustion [kəm'bʌstʃən] n combustión f.
come [kʌm], pt **came**, pp **come** vi venir;
to ~ **about** vi suceder, ocurrir; **to** ~
across vt fus (person) topar; (thing) dar
con; **to** ~ **away** vi marcharse; **to** ~ **back**
vi volver; **to** ~ **by** vt fus (acquire)
conseguir; **to** ~ **down** vi bajar; (plane)
aterrizar; (crash) estrellarse; (buildings)
desplomarse; **to** ~ **forward** vi
presentarse; **to** ~ **in** vi entrar; (train)
llegar; (fashion) ponerse de moda; **to** ~ **in
for** vt fus (criticism etc) merecer; **to** ~
into vt fus (money) heredar; **to** ~ **off** vi
(button) soltarse, desprenderse; (attempt)
tener lugar; **to** ~ **on** vi (pupil, undertaking)
crecer, desarrollarse // vt (find)
encontrar; ~ **on!** ¡vamos!; **to** ~ **out** vi
salir, aparecer; (be revealed) salir a luz; **to**
~ **out for/against** declararse
por/contra; **to** ~ **to** vi volver en sí; (total)
sumar; **to** ~ **up** vi subir; (sun) salir;
(problem) surgir; **to** ~ **up against** vt fus
(resistance, difficulties) tropezar con; **to** ~
up with vt fus (idea) sugerir, proponer; **to**
~ **upon** vt fus dar o topar con; ~**back** n
(THEATRE) reaparición f.
comedian [kə'mi:dɪən] n cómico;
comedienne [-'ɛn] n cómica.
comedown ['kʌmdaun] n (fam) revés m,
bajón m.
comedy ['kɔmɪdɪ] n comedia.
comet ['kɔmɪt] n cometa m.
comfort ['kʌmfət] n comodidad f, confort

m; (*well-being*) bienestar m; (*solace*) consuelo; (*relief*) alivio // vt consolar; aliviar; ~**able** a cómodo.

comic ['kɔmɪk] a (*also*: ~**al**) cómico // n (*magazine*) tebeo; ~ **strip** n tira cómica.

coming ['kʌmɪŋ] n venida, llegada // a que viene; ~**(s) and going(s)** n(*pl*) ir y venir m, ajetreo.

comma ['kɔmə] n coma.

command [kə'mɑ:nd] n orden f, mandato; (*MIL*: *authority*) mando; (*mastery*) dominio // vt (*troops*) mandar; (*give orders to*) mandar, ordenar; (*dispose of*) disponer de; (*deserve*) merecer; ~**eer** [kɔmən'dɪə*] vt requisar; ~**er** n (*MIL*) comandante m/f, jefe/a m/f.

commando [kə'mɑ:ndəu] n comando.

commemorate [kə'mɛməreɪt] vt conmemorar; **commemoration** [-'reɪʃən] n conmemoración f; **commemorative** [-rətɪv] a conmemorativo.

commence [kə'mɛns] vt, vi comenzar, empezar.

commend [kə'mɛnd] vt (*praise*) elogiar, alabar; (*recommend*) recomendar; (*entrust*) encomendar; ~**ation** [kɔmɛn-'deɪʃən] n elogio, encomio; recomendación f.

commensurate [kə'mɛnʃərɪt] a equivalente (*with* a).

comment ['kɔmɛnt] n comentario // vi hacer comentarios; ~**ary** ['kɔməntərɪ] n comentario; ~**ator** ['kɔmənteɪtə*] n comentador m.

commerce ['kɔmə:s] n comercio.

commercial [kə'mə:ʃəl] a comercial // n (*TV*) anuncio (comercial); ~ **break** n emisión f publicitaria; ~**ize** vt comercializar.

commiserate [kə'mɪzəreɪt] vi: **to** ~ **with** compadecerse de, condolerse de.

commission [kə'mɪʃən] n (*fee*) comisión f; (*act*) perpetración f // vt (*MIL*) nombrar; (*work of art*) encargar; **out of** ~ inutilizado; ~**aire** [kəmɪʃə'nɛə*] n portero; ~**er** n comisario; (*POLICE*) jefe/a m/f de policía.

commit [kə'mɪt] vt (*act*) cometer; (*to sb's care*) entregar; **to** ~ **o.s. (to do)** comprometerse (a hacer); **to** ~ **suicide** suicidarse; ~**ment** n compromiso.

committee [kə'mɪtɪ] n comité m.

commodity [kə'mɔdɪtɪ] n mercancía.

common ['kɔmən] a (*gen*) común; (*pej*) ordinario // n campo común; **the C**~**s** npl (la Cámara de) los Comunes; **in** ~ en común; ~**er** n plebeyo; ~ **law** n ley f consuetudinaria; ~**ly** ad comúnmente; **C**~ **Market** n Mercado Común; ~**place** a vulgar, trivial; ~**room** n salón m común; ~ **sense** n sentido común; **the C**~**wealth** n la Mancomunidad.

commotion [kə'məuʃən] n tumulto, confusión f.

communal ['kɔmju:nl] a comunal.

commune ['kɔmju:n] n (*group*) comuna //

vi [kə'mju:n]: **to** ~ **with** comulgar o conversar con.

communicate [kə'mju:nɪkeɪt] vt comunicar // vi: **to** ~ **(with)** comunicarse (con).

communication [kəmju:nɪ'keɪʃən] n comunicación f; ~ **cord** n timbre m de alarma.

communion [kə'mju:nɪən] n (*also*: **Holy C**~) comunión f.

communiqué [kə'mju:nɪkeɪ] n comunicado, parte m.

communism ['kɔmjunɪzəm] n comunismo; **communist** a, n comunista m/f.

community [kə'mju:nɪtɪ] n comunidad f; (*large group*) colectividad f; (*locals*) vecindario; ~ **centre** n centro social.

commute [kə'mju:t] vi viajar a diario // vt conmutar; **commuter** n persona que viaja a menudo.

compact [kəm'pækt] a compacto; (*style*) conciso; (*packed*) apretado // n ['kɔmpækt] (*pact*) pacto; (*for powder*) polvera.

companion [kəm'pænɪən] n compañero; ~**ship** n compañerismo.

company ['kʌmpənɪ] n (*gen*) compañía; (*COMM*) sociedad f, compañía; **to keep sb** ~ acompañar a uno; **limited** ~ sociedad f anónima.

comparable ['kɔmpərəbl] a comparable.

comparative [kəm'pærətɪv] a relativo.

compare [kəm'pɛə*] vt comparar; (*set side by side*) cotejar // vi: **to** ~ **(with)** compararse (con); **comparison** [-'pærɪsn] n comparación f; cotejo; **in comparison (with)** en comparación (con).

compartment [kəm'pɑ:tmənt] n (*also RAIL*) departamento.

compass ['kʌmpəs] n brújula; ~**es** npl compás m.

compassion [kəm'pæʃən] n compasión f; ~**ate** a compasivo.

compatible [kəm'pætɪbl] a compatible.

compel [kəm'pɛl] vt obligar; ~**ling** a (*fig*: *argument*) convincente.

compendium [kəm'pɛndɪəm] n compendio.

compensate ['kɔmpənseɪt] vt compensar // vi: **to** ~ **for** compensar; **compensation** [-'seɪʃən] n (*for loss*) indemnización f.

compère ['kɔmpɛə*] n presentador m.

compete [kəm'pi:t] vi (*take part*) tomar parte, concurrir; (*vie with*) competir, hacer competencia.

competence ['kɔmpɪtəns] n capacidad f, aptitud f; **competent** [-ənt] a competente, capaz.

competition [kɔmpɪ'tɪʃən] n (*contest*) concurso; (*ECON*) competencia; (*rivalry*) competencia.

competitive [kəm'petɪtɪv] a (*ECON*) competitivo; (*spirit*) competidor(a), de competencia.

competitor [kəm'petɪtə*] n (*rival*)

competidor/a *m/f*; (*participant*) concursante *m/f*.
compile [kəm'paıl] *vt* recopilar, compilar.
complacency [kəm'pleısnsı] *n* satisfacción *f* de sí mismo; **complacent** [-sənt] *a* complacido.
complain [kəm'pleın] *vi* (*gen*) quejarse; ~**t** *n* (*gen*) queja; (*JUR*) demanda, querella; (*MED*) enfermedad *f*.
complement ['komplımənt] *n* complemento; (*esp ship's crew*) dotación *f*; ~**ary** [komplı'mɛntərı] *a* complementario.
complete [kəm'pli:t] *a* (*full*) completo; (*finished*) acabado // *vt* (*fulfil*) completar; (*finish*) acabar; (*a form*) llenar; ~**ly** *ad* completamente; **completion** *n* (*gen*) conclusión *f*, terminación *f*; (*of contract etc*) realización *f*.
complex ['komplɛks] *a* complejo // *n* (*gen*) complejo.
complexion [kəm'plɛkʃən] *n* (*of face*) tez *f*, cutis *m*; (*fig*) aspecto.
complexity [kəm'plɛksıtı] *n* complejidad *f*.
compliance [kəm'plaıəns] *n* (*submission*) sumisión *f*; (*agreement*) conformidad *f*; **in** ~ **with** de acuerdo con; **compliant** [-ənt] *a* sumiso; conforme.
complicate ['komplıkeıt] *vt* complicar; ~**d** *a* complicado; **complication** [-'keıʃən] *n* complicación *f*.
compliment ['komplımənt] (*formal*) cumplido; (*lovers'*) piropo; ~**s** *npl* saludos *mpl*; **to pay sb a** ~ (*amorously*) piropear, echar piropos a alguien; ~**ary** [-'mɛntərı] *a* lisonjero; (*free*) de favor.
comply [kəm'plaı] *vi*: **to** ~ **with** cumplir con.
component [kəm'pəunənt] *a* componente // *n* (*TECH*) pieza.
compose [kəm'pəuz] *vt* componer; **to be** ~**d of** componerse de, constar de; **to** ~ **o.s.** tranquilizarse; ~**d** *a* sosegado; **composer** *n* (*MUS*) compositor *m*.
composite ['kompəzıt] *a* compuesto.
composition [kompə'zıʃən] *n* composición *f*.
compost ['kompost] *n* abono compuesto.
composure [kəm'pəuʒə*] *n* serenidad *f*, calma.
compound ['kompaund] *n* (*CHEM, LING*) compuesto; (*enclosure*) recinto // *a* (*gen*) compuesto; (*fracture*) complicado.
comprehend [komprı'hɛnd] *vt* comprender; **comprehension** [-'hɛnʃən] *n* comprensión *f*.
comprehensive [komprı'hɛnsıv] *a* (*broad*) extenso; (*general*) de conjunto; (*INSURANCE*) contra todo riesgo; ~ (**school**) *n* integrado.
compress [kəm'prɛs] *vt* comprimir // *n* ['komprɛs] (*MED*) compresa; ~**ion** [-'prɛʃən] *n* compresión *f*.
comprise [kəm'praız] *vt* (*also*: **be** ~**d of**) comprender, constar de.
compromise ['komprəmaız] *n*

(*agreement*) componenda, arreglo; (*midpoint*) término medio // *vt* comprometer // *vi* transigir.
compulsion [kəm'pʌlʃən] *n* obligación *f*.
compulsive [kəm'pʌlsıv] *a* compulsivo; (*PSYCH*) empedernido.
compulsory [kəm'pʌlsərı] *a* obligatorio.
computer [kəm'pju:tə*] *n* ordenador *m*, computador *m*, computadora; ~**ize** *vt* computerizar; ~ **programmer** *n* programador/a *m/f*; ~ **programming** *n* programación *f*; ~ **science** *n* ciencia de computadoras.
comrade ['komrıd] *n* camarada *m/f*; ~**ship** *n* camaradería, compañerismo.
con [kon] *vt* estafar // *n* estafa.
concave ['kon'keıv] *a* cóncavo.
conceal [kən'si:l] *vt* ocultar.
concede [kən'si:d] *vt* conceder // *vi* ceder, darse por vencido.
conceit [kən'si:t] *n* presunción *f*; ~**ed** *a* presumido.
conceivable [kən'si:vəbl] *a* concebible.
conceive [kən'si:v] *vt, vi* concebir.
concentrate ['konsəntreıt] *vi* concentrarse // *vt* concentrar.
concentration [konsən'treıʃən] *n* concentración *f*; ~ **camp** *n* campo de concentración.
concept ['konsɛpt] *n* concepto.
conception [kən'sɛpʃən] *n* (*idea*) concepto, idea; (*BIOL*) concepción *f*.
concern [kən'sə:n] *n* (*matter*) asunto; (*COMM*) empresa; (*anxiety*) preocupación *f* // *vt* tener que ver con; **to be** ~**ed** (**about**) interesarse (por), preocuparse (por); ~**ing** *prep* sobre, acerca de.
concert ['konsət] *n* concierto; ~ **hall** *n* sala de conciertos.
concertina [konsə'ti:nə] *n* concertina.
concerto [kən'tʃə:təu] *n* concierto.
concession [kən'sɛʃən] *n* concesión *f*; **tax** ~ privilegió fiscal.
conciliation [kənsılı'eıʃən] *n* conciliación *f*; **conciliatory** [-'sılıətrı] *a* conciliador(a).
concise [kən'saıs] *a* conciso.
conclude [kən'klu:d] *vt* (*finish*) concluir; (*treaty etc*) firmar; (*agreement*) llegar a; (*decide*) llegar a la conclusión de; **conclusion** [-'klu:ʒən] *n* conclusión *f*; **conclusive** [-'klu:sıv] *a* decisivo, concluyente.
concoct [kən'kokt] *vt* (*gen*) confeccionar; (*plot*) tramar.
concrete ['konkri:t] *n* hormigón *m* // *a* concreto.
concur [kən'kə:*] *vi* estar de acuerdo, asentir.
concurrently [kən'kʌrntlı] *ad* al mismo tiempo.
concussion [kən'kʌʃən] *n* conmoción *f* cerebral.
condemn [kən'dɛm] *vt* condenar; ~**ation** [kondɛm'neıʃən] *n* (*gen*) condenación *f*; (*blame*) censura.

condensation [kɔndɛn'seɪʃən] n condensación f.

condense [kən'dɛns] vi condensarse // vt condensar, abreviar; ~d milk n leche f condensada.

condescend [kɔndɪ'sɛnd] vi condescender, dignarse; ~ing a condescendiente.

condition [kən'dɪʃən] n condición f // vt condicionar; on ~ that a condición (de) que.

condolences [kən'dəʊlənsɪz] npl pésame m.

condone [kən'dəʊn] vt condonar.

conducive [kən'djuːsɪv] a: ~ to conducente a.

conduct ['kɔndʌkt] n conducta, comportamiento // vt [kən'dʌkt] (lead) conducir; (manage) llevar, dirigir; (MUS) dirigir // vi (MUS) llevar la batuta; to ~ o.s. comportarse; ~or n (of orchestra) director m; (on bus) cobrador m; (ELEC) conductor m; ~ress n (on bus) cobradora.

cone [kəʊn] n cono; (for ice-cream) barquillo.

confectioner [kən'fɛkʃənə*] n pastelero; ~'s (shop) n pastelería; (sweet shop) confitería; ~y n (cakes) pasteles mpl; (sweets) dulces mpl.

confederation [kənfɛdə'reɪʃən] n confederación f.

confer [kən'fɜː*] vt otorgar (on a) // vi conferenciar.

conference ['kɔnfərns] n (meeting) congreso.

confess [kən'fɛs] vt confesar // vi confesarse; ~ion [-'fɛʃən] n confesión f; ~ional [-'fɛʃənl] n confesionario; ~or n confesor m.

confetti [kən'fɛtɪ] n confeti m.

confide [kən'faɪd] vi: to ~ in confiar en, fiarse de.

confidence ['kɔnfɪdns] n (gen) confianza; (secret) confidencia; ~ trick n timo; **confident** a seguro de sí mismo; **confidential** [kɔnfɪ'dɛnʃəl] a confidencial; (secretary) de confianza.

confine [kən'faɪn] vt (limit) limitar; (shut up) encerrar; ~d a (space) reducido; ~ment n (prison) prisión f; (enclosure) encierro; (MED) parto, sobreparto; ~s ['kɔnfaɪnz] npl confines mpl.

confirm [kən'fɜːm] vt confirmar; ~ation [kɔnfə'meɪʃən] n confirmación f; ~ed a empedernido.

confiscate ['kɔnfɪskeɪt] vt confiscar; **confiscation** [-'keɪʃən] n incautación f.

conflict ['kɔnflɪkt] n conflicto // vi [kən-'flɪkt] (opinions) chocar; ~ing a contrario.

conform [kən'fɔːm] vi conformarse; to ~ to ajustarse a, cuadrar con; ~ist n conformista m/f.

confound [kən'faʊnd] vt confundir; ~ed a condenado.

confront [kən'frʌnt] vt (problems) encararse con; (enemy, danger)

enfrentarse con; ~ation [kɔnfrən'teɪʃən] n enfrentamiento.

confuse [kən'fjuːz] vt (perplex) aturdir, desconcertar; (mix up) confundir; ~d a confuso; (person) perplejo, despistado; **confusing** a confuso; **confusion** [-'fjuːʒən] n confusión f.

congeal [kən'dʒiːl] vi (freeze) congelarse; (coagulate) coagularse.

congenial [kən'dʒiːnɪəl] a simpático, agradable.

congenital [kən'dʒɛnɪtl] a congénito.

congested [kən'dʒɛstɪd] a (gen) lleno; (area) superpoblado; **congestion** [-'dʒɛstʃən] n congestión f.

conglomeration [kənɡlɔmə'reɪʃən] n conglomeración f.

congratulate [kən'ɡrætjuleɪt] vt felicitar; **congratulations** [-'leɪʃənz] npl felicidades fpl.

congregate ['kɔŋɡrɪɡeɪt] vi congregarse; **congregation** [-'ɡeɪʃən] n (in church) fieles mpl; (assembly) reunión f.

congress ['kɔŋɡrɛs] n congreso; ~man n (US) diputado.

conical ['kɔnɪkl] a cónico.

conifer ['kɔnɪfə*] n conífera; ~ous [kə'nɪfərəs] a (forest) conífero.

conjecture [kən'dʒɛktʃə*] n conjetura.

conjugal ['kɔndʒuɡl] a conyugal.

conjugate ['kɔndʒuɡeɪt] vt conjugar.

conjunction [kən'dʒʌŋkʃən] n conjunción f.

conjure ['kʌndʒə*] vi hacer juegos de manos; to ~ up vt (ghost, spirit) hacer aparecer; (memories) evocar; **conjurer** n ilusionista m/f; **conjuring trick** n ilusionismo, juego de manos.

conk [kɔŋk]: ~ out vi (col) estropearse.

con man ['kɔn-] n timador m.

connect [kə'nɛkt] vt juntar, unir; (ELEC) conectar; (fig) relacionar, asociar // vi: to ~ with (train) enlazar con; ~ion [-ʃən] n juntura, conexión f; (ELEC) conexión f; (RAIL) correspondencia; (TEL) comunicación f; (fig) relación f.

connive [kə'naɪv] vi: to ~ at hacer la vista gorda a.

connoisseur [kɔnɪ'sə*] n experto, entendido.

connotation [kɔnə'teɪʃən] n connotación f.

conquer ['kɔŋkə*] vt (gen) conquistar; (enemy) vencer; (feelings) dominar; ~or n conquistador m.

conquest ['kɔŋkwɛst] n conquista.

cons [kɔnz] npl see **pro**.

conscience ['kɔnʃəns] n conciencia.

conscientious [kɔnʃɪ'ɛnʃəs] a concienzudo; (objection) de conciencia.

conscious ['kɔnʃəs] a consciente; ~ness n conciencia; (MED) conocimiento.

conscript ['kɔnskrɪpt] n recluta m/f; ~ion [kən'skrɪpʃən] n servicio militar (obligatorio).

consecrate ['kɔnsɪkreɪt] vt consagrar.

consecutive [kən'sɛkjutɪv] a sucesivo, seguido.

consensus [kən'sɛnsəs] n consenso.

consent [kən'sɛnt] n consentimiento // vi: **to ~ to** consentir en.

consequence ['kɔnsɪkwəns] n consecuencia.

consequently ['kɔnsɪkwəntlɪ] ad por consiguiente.

conservation [kɔnsə'veɪʃən] n conservación f.

conservative [kən'sɔːvətɪv] a conservador(a); (cautious) cauteloso; **C~** a, n conservador/a m/f.

conservatory [kən'sɔːvətrɪ] n (greenhouse) invernadero.

conserve [kən'sɔːv] vt conservar // n conserva.

consider [kən'sɪdə*] vt (gen) considerar; (take into account) tomar en cuenta; (study) estudiar, examinar; **~able** a considerable; (sum) importante.

considerate [kən'sɪdərɪt] a considerado; **consideration** [-'reɪʃən] n consideración f; (reward) retribución f.

considering [kən'sɪdərɪŋ] prep en consideración a.

consign [kən'saɪn] vt consignar; **~ment** n envío.

consist [kən'sɪst] vi: **to ~ of** consistir en.

consistency [kən'sɪstənsɪ] n (of person etc) consecuencia; (thickness) consistencia.

consistent [kən'sɪstənt] a (person) consecuente; (even) constante.

consolation [kɔnsə'leɪʃən] n consuelo.

console [kən'səul] vt consolar // n ['kɔnsəul] consola.

consolidate [kən'sɔlɪdeɪt] vt consolidar.

consommé [kən'sɔmeɪ] n consomé m, caldo.

consonant ['kɔnsənənt] n consonante f.

consortium [kən'sɔːtɪəm] n consorcio.

conspicuous [kən'spɪkjuəs] a (visible) visible; (garish etc) llamativo; (outstanding) notable.

conspiracy [kən'spɪrəsɪ] n conjura, complot m.

conspire [kən'spaɪə*] vi conspirar.

constable ['kʌnstəbl] n policía m/f; **chief ~** jefe m de policía.

constabulary [kən'stæbjulərɪ] n policía.

constant ['kɔnstənt] a (gen) constante; (loyal) leal, fiel.

constellation [kɔnstə'leɪʃən] n constelación f.

consternation [kɔnstə'neɪʃən] n consternación f.

constipated ['kɔnstɪpeɪtəd] a estreñido.

constituency [kən'stɪtjuənsɪ] n (POL) distrito electoral; **constituent** [-ənt] n (POL) elector/a m/f; (part) componente m.

constitute ['kɔnstɪtjuːt] vt constituir.

constitution [kɔnstɪ'tjuːʃən] n constitución f; **~al** a constitucional.

constrain [kən'streɪn] vt obligar; **~ed** a:

to feel ~ed to... sentirse en la necesidad de...; **~t** n (force) fuerza; (confinement) encierro; (shyness) reserva.

constrict [kən'strɪkt] vt apretar, estrechar.

construct [kən'strʌkt] vt construir; **~ion** [-ʃən] n construcción f; **~ive** a constructivo.

construe [kən'struː] vt interpretar.

consul ['kɔnsl] n cónsul m/f; **~ate** ['kɔnsjulɪt] n consulado.

consult [kən'sʌlt] vt, vi consultar; **~ant** n (MED) especialista m/f; (other specialist) asesor m; **~ation** [kɔnsəl'teɪʃən] n consulta; **~ing room** n consultorio.

consume [kən'sjuːm] vt (eat) comerse; (drink) beberse; (fire etc, COMM) consumir; **consumer** n consumidor/a m/f; **consumer goods** npl bienes mpl de consumo; **consumer society** n sociedad f de consumo.

consummate ['kɔnsʌmeɪt] vt consumar.

consumption [kən'sʌmpʃən] n consumo.

cont. abbr of **continued.**

contact ['kɔntækt] n contacto; (pej) enchufe m // vt ponerse en contacto con; **he has good ~s** tiene buenas relaciones; **~ lenses** npl lentes fpl de contacto, microlentillas fpl.

contagious [kən'teɪdʒəs] a contagioso.

contain [kən'teɪn] vt contener; **to ~ o.s.** contenerse; **~er** n recipiente m; (for shipping etc) contenedor m.

contaminate [kən'tæmɪneɪt] vt contaminar; **contamination** [-'neɪʃən] n contaminación f.

cont'd abbr of **continued.**

contemplate ['kɔntəmpleɪt] vt (gen) contemplar; (expect) contar con; (intend) · pensar; **contemplation** [-'pleɪʃən] n contemplación f.

contemporary [kən'tɛmpərərɪ] a, n contemporáneo/a.

contempt [kən'tɛmpt] n desprecio; **~ible** a despreciable; **~uous** a despectivo, desdeñoso.

contend [kən'tɛnd] vt (argue) afirmar // vi (struggle) luchar; **~er** n contendiente m/f.

content [kən'tɛnt] a (happy) contento; (satisfied) satisfecho // vt contentar; satisfacer // n ['kɔntɛnt] contento; satisfacción f; **~s** npl contenido sg; **~ed** a contento; satisfecho.

contention [kən'tɛnʃən] n contienda; (argument) argumento.

contentment [kən'tɛntmənt] n contento.

contest ['kɔntɛst] n contienda; (competition) concurso // vt [kən'tɛst] (dispute) impugnar; (legal case) defender; (POL) ser candidato en; **~ant** [kən'tɛstənt] n concursante m/f; (in fight) contendiente m/f.

context ['kɔntɛkst] n contexto.

continent ['kɔntɪnənt] n continente m; **the C~** el continente europeo; **~al** [-'nɛntl] a continental.

contingency [kən'tındʒənsı] *n* contingencia; **contingent** [-ənt] *n* contingente *m*.

continual [kən'tınjuəl] *a* continuo; ~**ly** *ad* constantemente.

continuation [kəntınju'eıʃən] *n* prolongación *f*; (*after interruption*) continuación *f*.

continue [kən'tınjuː] *vi* seguir, continuar // *vt* seguir, continuar; (*start again*) proseguir.

continuity [kontı'njuıtı] *n* continuidad *f*.

continuous [kən'tınjuəs] *a* continuo.

contort [kən'tɔːt] *vt* retorcer; ~**ion** [-'tɔːʃən] *n* contorsión *f*; ~**ionist** [-'tɔːʃənıst] *n* contorsionista *m/f*.

contour ['kontuə*] *n* contorno; (*also:* ~ **line**) curva de nivel.

contraband ['kontrəbænd] *n* contrabando.

contraception [kontrə'sɛpʃən] *n* contracepción *f*; **contraceptive** [-'sɛptıv] *a*, *n* anticonceptivo.

contract ['kontrækt] *n* contrato // (*vb:* [kən'trækt]) *vi* (*COMM*): **to ~ to do sth** comprometerse por contrato a hacer algo; (*become smaller*) contraerse, encogerse // *vt* contraer; ~**ion** [-ʃən] *n* contracción *f*; ~**or** *n* contratista *m/f*.

contradict [kontrə'dıkt] *vt* (*deny*) desmentir; (*be contrary to*) contradecir; ~**ion** [-ʃən] *n* contradicción *f*.

contralto [kən'træltəu] *n* contralto.

contraption [kən'træpʃən] *n* (*pej*) armatoste *m*.

contrary ['kontrərı] *a*, *n* contrario.

contrast ['kontrɑːst] *n* contraste *m* // *vt* [kən'trɑːst] comparar; ~**ing** *a* opuesto.

contravene [kontrə'viːn] *vt* oponerse a; (*law*) contravenir.

contribute [kən'trıbjuːt] *vi* contribuir // *vt*: **to ~ to** (*gen*) contribuir a; (*newspaper*) escribir para; **contribution** [kontrı'bjuːʃən] *n* (*money*) aportación *f*; (*to debate*) intervención *f*; (*to journal*) colaboración *f*; **contributor** *n* (*to newspaper*) colaborador *m*.

contrive [kən'traıv] *vt* (*invent*) idear; (*carry out*) efectuar; (*plot*) tramar // *vi*: **to ~ to do** lograr hacer.

control [kən'trəul] *vt* (*gen*) controlar; (*traffic etc*) dirigir; (*machinery*) regular; (*temper*) dominar // *n* (*command*) control *m*; (*of car*) conducción *f*; (*check*) freno; ~**s** *npl* mando *sg*; ~ **panel** *n* tablero de instrumentos; ~ **room** *n* sala de mando; ~ **tower** *n* (*AVIAT*) torre *f* de control.

controversial [kontrə'vəːʃl] *a* discutible; **controversy** ['kontrəvəːsı] *n* controversia.

convalesce [konvə'lɛs] *vi* convalecer; **convalescence** *n* convalecencia; **convalescent** *a*, *n* convaleciente *m/f*.

convector [kən'vɛktə*] *n* (*heater*) calentador *m* de convección.

convene [kən'viːn] *vt* convocar // *vi* reunirse.

convenience [kən'viːnıəns] *n* (*comfort*) comodidad *f*; (*advantage*) ventaja; **at your** ~ cuando le sea conveniente; **public** ~ aseos públicos *mpl*; **convenient** [-ənt] *a* cómodo; (*useful*) útil; (*place*) accesible; (*time*) oportuno, conveniente.

convent ['konvənt] *n* convento; ~ **school** *n* colegio de monjas.

convention [kən'vɛnʃən] *n* convención *f*; (*meeting*) asamblea; ~**al** *a* convencional.

converge [kən'vəːdʒ] *vi* converger.

conversant [kən'vəːsnt] *a*: **to be ~ with** ser enterado de.

conversation [konvə'seıʃən] *n* conversación *f*; ~**al** *a* (*familiar*) familiar; (*talkative*) locuaz.

converse ['konvəːs] *n* inversa // *vi* [kən'vəːs] conversar; ~**ly** [-'vəːslı] *ad* a la inversa.

conversion [kən'vəːʃən] *n* conversión *f*; ~ **table** *n* tabla de conversión.

convert [kən'vəːt] *vt* (*REL, COMM*) convertir; (*alter*) transformar // *n* ['konvəːt] converso/a; ~**ible** *a* convertible // *n* descapotable *m*.

convex ['kon'vɛks] *a* convexo.

convey [kən'veı] *vt* (*gen*) llevar; (*thanks*) comunicar; (*idea*) expresar; ~**or belt** *n* cinta transportadora.

convict [kən'vıkt] *vt* (*gen*) condenar; (*sentence*) declarar culpable // *n* ['konvıkt] presidiario; ~**ion** [-ʃən] *n* condena; (*belief*) creencia, convicción *f*.

convince [kən'vıns] *vt* convencer; **convincing** *a* convincente.

convoy ['konvɔı] *n* convoy *m*.

convulse [kən'vʌls] *vt* convulsionar; (*laughter*) hacer morir de la risa; **convulsion** [-'vʌlʃən] *n* convulsión *f*; (*laughter*) paroxismo.

coo [kuː] *vi* arrullar.

cook [kuk] *vt* (*gen*) cocinar; (*stew etc*) guisar; (*meal*) preparar // *vi* cocer; (*person*) cocinar // *n* cocinero; ~**er** *n* cocina; ~**ery** *n* (*dishes*) cocina; (*art*) arte *m* de cocinar; ~**ery book** *n* libro de cocina; ~**ie** *n* (*US*) bizcocho; ~**ing** *n* cocina.

cool [kuːl] *a* fresco; (*not hot*) tibio; (*not afraid*) tranquilo; (*unfriendly*) frío // *vt* enfriar // *vi* enfriarse; ~**ness** *n* frescura; tranquilidad *f*; (*hostility*) frialdad *f*; (*indifference*) falta de entusiasmo.

coop [kuːp] *n* gallinero // *vt*: **to ~ up** (*fig*) encerrar.

co-op ['kəuɔp] *n* abbr of **Cooperative** (**Society**).

cooperate [kəu'ɔpəreıt] *vi* cooperar, colaborar; **cooperation** [-'reıʃən] *n* cooperación *f*, colaboración *f*; **cooperative** [-rətıv] *a* cooperativo // *n* cooperativa.

coordinate [kəu'ɔːdıneıt] *vt* coordinar; **coordination** [-'neıʃən] *n* coordinación *f*.

cop [kop] *n* (*col*) poli *m*.

cope [kəup] *vi*: **to ~ with** poder con; (*problem*) hacer frente a.

co-pilot ['kəu'paılət] *n* copiloto.

copious ['kəupıəs] *a* copioso, abundante.

copper ['kɔpə*] n (metal) cobre m; (col: policeman) poli m; ~s npl monedas fpl de poco valor.
coppice ['kɔpɪs], **copse** [kɔps] n bosquecillo.
copulate ['kɔpjuleɪt] vi copularse; **copulation** [-'leɪʃən] n cópula.
copy ['kɔpɪ] n copia; (of book etc) ejemplar m; (of writing) original m // vt copiar; ~right n derechos mpl de autor.
coral ['kɔrəl] n coral m; ~ reef n arrecife m (de coral).
cord [kɔːd] n cuerda; (ELEC) cordón m; (fabric) pana.
cordial ['kɔːdɪəl] a afectuoso // n cordial m.
cordon ['kɔːdn] n cordón m; to ~ off vt acordonar.
corduroy ['kɔːdərɔɪ] n pana.
core [kɔː*] n (gen) centro, núcleo; (of fruit) corazón m // vt quitar el corazón de.
coriander [kɔrɪ'ændə*] n culantro.
cork [kɔːk] n corcho; (tree) alcornoque m; ~screw n sacacorchos m inv.
cormorant ['kɔːmərnt] n cormorán m grande.
corn [kɔːn] n (wheat) trigo; (US: maize) maíz m; (cereals) granos mpl; (on foot) callo; ~ on the cob (CULIN) maíz en la mazorca.
corned beef ['kɔːnd-] n carne f de vaca acecinada.
corner ['kɔːnə*] n (gen) ángulo; (outside) esquina; (inside) rincón m; (in road) curva; (FOOTBALL) córner m // vt (trap) arrinconar; (COMM) acaparar // vi (in car) tomar una curva; ~stone n piedra angular.
cornet ['kɔːnɪt] n (MUS) corneta; (of ice-cream) barquillo.
cornflour ['kɔːnflauə*] n harina de maíz.
Cornwall ['kɔːnwəl] n Cornualles m.
corny ['kɔːnɪ] a (col) viejo, gastado.
corollary [kə'rɔlərɪ] n corolario.
coronary ['kɔrənərɪ] n: ~ (thrombosis) trombosis f coronaria.
coronation [kɔrə'neɪʃən] n coronación f.
coroner ['kɔrənə*] n juez m de primera instancia.
coronet ['kɔrənɪt] n corona.
corporal ['kɔːpərl] n cabo // a corporal.
corporate ['kɔːpərɪt] a corporativo.
corporation [kɔːpə'reɪʃən] n (of town) ayuntamiento; (COMM) corporación f.
corps [kɔː*], pl **corps** [kɔːz] n cuerpo.
corpse [kɔːps] n cadáver m.
corpuscle ['kɔːpʌsl] n corpúsculo.
corral [kə'rɑːl] n corral m.
correct [kə'rɛkt] a (accurate) justo, exacto; (proper) correcto // vt corregir; (exam) calificar; ~ion [-ʃən] n rectificación f; (erasure) tachadura.
correlate ['kɔrɪleɪt] vt correlacionar.
correspond [kɔrɪs'pɔnd] vi (write) escribirse; (be equal to) corresponder; ~ence n correspondencia; ~ence

course n curso por correspondencia; ~ent n corresponsal m/f; ~ing a correspondiente.
corridor ['kɔrɪdɔː*] n pasillo.
corroborate [kə'rɔbəreɪt] vt corroborar.
corrode [kə'rəud] vt corroer // vi corroerse; **corrosion** [-'rəuʒən] n corrosión f.
corrugated ['kɔrəgeɪtɪd] a ondulado; ~ iron n chapa ondulada.
corrupt [kə'rʌpt] a corrompido; (person) venal // vt corromper; (bribe) sobornar; ~ion [-ʃən] n corrupción f.
corset ['kɔːsɪt] n faja.
Corsica ['kɔːsɪkə] n Córcega.
cortège [kɔː'teːʒ] n cortejo, desfile m.
cortisone ['kɔːtɪzəun] n cortisona.
cosh [kɔʃ] n cachiporra.
cosiness ['kəuzɪnɪs] n comodidad f; (atmosphere) lo holgado.
cos lettuce [kɔs-] n lechuga cos.
cosmetic [kɔz'mɛtɪk] n cosmético.
cosmic ['kɔzmɪk] a cósmico.
cosmonaut ['kɔzmənɔːt] n cosmonauta m/f.
cosmopolitan [kɔzmə'pɔlɪtn] a cosmopolita.
cosmos ['kɔzmɔs] n cosmos m.
cost [kɔst] n (gen) coste m, costo; (price) precio; ~s npl costes mpl // vi, pt, pp cost costar, valer // vt preparar el presupuesto de; at the ~ of a costa de; how much does it ~? ¿cuánto cuesta?
co-star ['kəustɑː*] n colega m/f de reparto.
Costa Rican ['kɔstə'riːkən] a costarriqueño.
costly ['kɔstlɪ] a (expensive) costoso; (valuable) suntuoso.
cost price n precio de coste.
costume ['kɔstjuːm] n traje m; (also: swimming ~) traje de baño.
cosy ['kəuzɪ] a cómodo; (atmosphere) acogedor(a); (life) holgado.
cot [kɔt] n (child's) cuna.
cottage ['kɔtɪdʒ] n casita de campo; (rustic) barraca; ~ cheese n requesón m.
cotton ['kɔtn] n algodón m; (thread) hilo; to ~ on to vt (col) caer en la cuenta de; ~ wool n algodón m (hidrófilo).
couch [kautʃ] n sofá m.
cough [kɔf] vi toser // n tos f; to ~ up vt escupir; ~ drop n pastilla para la tos.
could [kud] pt of can; ~n't = could not.
council ['kaunsl] n consejo; **city** or **town** ~ consejo municipal; ~ estate n polígono de renta limitada; ~ house n vivienda de renta limitada; ~lor n concejal m/f.
counsel ['kaunsl] n (advice) consejo; (lawyer) abogado // vt aconsejar; ~lor n consejero.
count [kaunt] vt (gen) contar; (include) incluir // vi contar // n (gen) cuenta; (of votes) escrutinio; (nobleman) conde m; (sum) total m, suma; to ~ on vt fus contar con; that doesn't ~! ¡eso no vale!;

~**down** n cuenta hacia atrás.

counter ['kauntɔ*] n (in shop) mostrador m; (in games) ficha // (in shop) mostrador m; (blow) parar; (attack) contestar a // ad: ~ to contrario a; ~**act** vt contrarrestar; ~**attack** n contrataque m // vi contratacar; ~**balance** n contrapeso; ~-**espionage** n contraespionaje m.

counterfeit ['kauntɔfɪt] n moneda falsa // vt falsificar // a falso, falsificado.

counterfoil ['kauntɔfɔil] n talón m.

counterpart ['kauntɔpɑ:t] n (of person) colega m/f.

counter-revolution [kauntɔrɛvɔ'lu:ʃɔn] n contrarrevolución f.

countersign ['kauntɔsaɪn] vt refrendar.

countess ['kauntɪs] n condesa.

countless ['kauntlɪs] a incontable.

country ['kʌntrɪ] n país m; (native land) patria; (as opposed to town) campo; (region) región f, tierra; ~ **dancing** n baile m regional; ~ **house** n quinta, finca; ~**side** n campo.

county ['kauntɪ] n condado; ~ **town** n cabeza de partido.

coup [ku:], pl ~**s** [-z] n golpe m; ~ **d'état/de grâce** golpe de estado/de gracia.

coupé ['ku:peɪ] n cupé m.

couple ['kʌpl] n (of things) par m; (of people) pareja; (married ~) matrimonio // vt (ideas, names) unir, juntar; (machinery) acoplar; a ~ of un par de.

coupling ['kʌplɪŋ] n (RAIL) enganche m.

coupon ['ku:pɔn] n cupón m; (pools ~) boleto.

courage ['kʌrɪdʒ] n valor m, valentía; ~**ous** [kɔ'reɪdʒɔs] a valiente.

courier ['kurɪɔ*] n estafeta; (diplomatic) correo; (for tourists) agente m/f de turismo.

course [kɔ:s] n (direction) dirección f; (of river, ESCOL) curso; (of ship) rumbo, derrota; (of bullet) trayectoria; (fig) proceder m; (GOLF) campo; (part of meal) plato; **of** ~ ad desde luego, naturalmente; **of** ~! ¡claro!; **in due** ~ en el momento oportuno.

court [kɔ:t] n (royal) corte m; (LAW) tribunal m, juzgado; (TENNIS) pista, cancha // vt (woman) cortejar, hacer la corte a; (danger etc) buscar; **to take to** ~ demandar.

courteous ['kɔ:tɪɔs] a cortés.

courtesan [kɔ:tɪ'zæn] n cortesana.

courtesy ['kɔ:tɔsɪ] n cortesía; **by** ~ **of** con permiso de.

court-house ['kɔ:thaus] n (US) palacio de justicia.

courtier ['kɔ:tɪɔ*] n cortesano.

court: ~-**martial**, pl ~**s-martial** n consejo de guerra // vt someter a consejo de guerra; ~**room** n sala de justicia; ~**yard** n patio.

cousin ['kʌzn] n primo/a; **first** ~ primo carnal.

cove [kɔuv] n cala, ensenada.

covenant ['kʌvɔnɔnt] n convenio.

cover ['kʌvɔ*] vt (gen) cubrir; (with lid) tapar; (chairs etc) revestir; (distance) recorrer; (include) abarcar; (protect) abrigar; (journalist) investigar; (issues) tratar // n (gen) cubierta; (lid) tapa; (for chair etc) funda; (for bed) cobertor m; (envelope) sobre m; (for book) forro; (of magazine) portada; (shelter) abrigo; (insurance) cobertura; **under** ~ (indoors) bajo techo; **under** ~ **of** al abrigo de; (fig) so capa de; **to** ~ **up for sb** encubrir a uno; ~**age** n alcance m; ~ **charge** n precio del cubierto; ~**ing** n cubierta, envoltura; ~**ing letter** n carta explicatoria.

covet ['kʌvɪt] vt codiciar.

cow [kau] n vaca // vt intimidar.

coward ['kauɔd] n cobarde m/f; ~**ice** [-ɪs] n cobardía; ~**ly** a cobarde.

cowboy ['kaubɔɪ] n vaquero.

cower ['kauɔ*] vi encogerse (de miedo).

cowshed ['kauʃed] n establo.

coxswain ['kɔksn] n (abbr: **cox**) timonel m/f.

coy [kɔɪ] a tímido.

coyote [kɔɪ'ɔutɪ] n coyote m.

crab [kræb] n cangrejo; ~ **apple** n manzana silvestre.

crack [kræk] n grieta; (noise) crujido; (: of whip) chasquido; (fam) chiste m // vt agrietar, romper; (nut) cascar; (safe) forzar; (whip etc) chasquear; (knuckles) crujir; (joke) contar // a (expert) experto; **to** ~ **up** vi (MED) sufrir un colapso nervioso; ~**er** n (biscuit) cracker m; (Christmas cracker) sorpresa.

crackle ['krækl] vi crepitar; **crackling** n (of fire) crepitación f; (of leaves etc) crujido; (of pork) chicharrón m.

cradle ['kreidl] n cuna.

craft [krɑ:ft] n (skill) arte m; (trade) oficio; (cunning) astucia; (boat) barco.

craftsman ['krɑ:ftsmɔn] n artesano; ~**ship** n artesanía.

crafty ['krɑ:ftɪ] a astuto.

crag [kræg] n peñasco; ~**gy** a escarpado.

cram [kræm] vt (fill) llenar, henchir; ~**med** a atestado.

cramp [kræmp] n (MED) calambre m; (TECH) grapa // vt (limit) restringir; (annoy) estorbar; ~**ed** a apretado, estrecho.

crampon ['kræmpɔn] n crampón m.

cranberry ['krænbɔrɪ] n arándano agrio.

crane [kreɪn] n (TECH) grúa; (bird) grulla.

crank [kræŋk] n manivela; (person) chiflado; ~**shaft** n eje m del cigüeñal.

cranky ['kræŋkɪ] a (eccentric) maniático; (bad-tempered) irritable.

cranny ['krænɪ] n see **nook**.

crash [kræʃ] n (noise) estruendo; (of cars etc) choque m; (of plane) accidente m de avión; (COMM) quiebra // vt (plane) estrellar // vi (plane) estrellarse; (two cars) chocar; (fall noisily) caer con estrépito; ~ **course** n curso acelerado; ~

helmet *n* casco (protector); ~ **landing** *n* aterrizaje *m* forzoso.
crate [kreɪt] *n* cajón *m* de embalaje; (*fam*) armatoste *m*.
crater ['kreɪtə*] *n* cráter *m*.
cravat(e) [krə'væt] *n* pañuelo.
crave [kreɪv] *vt*: **to** ~ **for** ansiar, anhelar; **craving** *n* (*of pregnant woman*) antojo.
crawl [krɔːl] *vi* (*gen*) arrastrarse; (*child*) andar a gatas, gatear; (*vehicle*) avanzar a paso de tortuga // *n* (*swimming*) crol *m*.
crayfish ['kreɪfɪʃ] *n*, *pl inv* langostino.
crayon ['kreɪən] *n* pastel *m*, lápiz *m* de color.
craze [kreɪz] *n* manía; (*fashion*) moda.
crazy ['kreɪzɪ] *a* (*person*) loco; (*idea*) disparatado.
creak [kriːk] *vi* chirriar, rechinar; (*door etc*) crujir.
cream [kriːm] *n* (*of milk*) nata; (*gen*) crema; (*fig*) flor y nata // *a* (*colour*) color *m* (de) crema; ~ **cake** *n* pastel *m* de nata; ~ **cheese** *n* queso de nata; ~**y** *a* cremoso.
crease [kriːs] *n* (*fold*) pliegue *m*; (*in trousers*) raya; (*wrinkle*) arruga // *vt* (*fold*) doblar, plegar; (*wrinkle*) arrugar // *vi* (*wrinkle up*) arrugarse.
create [kriːˈeɪt] *vt* crear; **creation** [-ʃən] *n* creación *f*; **creative** *a* creador(a); **creator** *n* creador *m*.
creature ['kriːtʃə*] *n* (*animal*) animal *m*, bicho; (*living thing*) criatura.
crèche, creche [krɛʃ] *n* guardería infantil.
credentials [krɪˈdɛnʃlz] *npl* credenciales *fpl*.
credibility [krɛdɪˈbɪlɪtɪ] *n* credibilidad *f*.
credible ['krɛdɪbl] *a* creíble.
credit ['krɛdɪt] *n* (*gen*) crédito; (*merit*) honor *m*, mérito // *vt* (*comm*) abonar; (*believe*) creer, prestar fe a // a crediticio; ~**s** *npl* (*cinema*) fichas técnicas; ~**able** *a* estimable, digno de elogio; ~ **card** *n* tarjeta de crédito; ~**or** *n* acreedor *m*.
credulity [krɪˈdjuːlɪtɪ] *n* credulidad *f*.
creed [kriːd] *n* credo.
creek [kriːk] *n* cala, ensenada; (*US*) riachuelo.
creep [kriːp], *pt*, *pp* **crept** *vi* (*animal*) deslizarse; (*gen*) arrastrarse; (*plant*) trepar; ~**er** *n* enredadera; ~**y** *a* (*frightening*) horripilante.
cremate [krɪˈmeɪt] *vt* incinerar; **cremation** [-ʃən] *n* incineración *f*.
crematorium [krɛməˈtɔːrɪəm], *pl* **-ria** [-rɪə] *n* (*horno*) crematorio.
creosote ['krɪəsəʊt] *n* creosota.
crêpe [kreɪp] *n* (*fabric*) crespón *m*; (*rubber*) crepé *m*; ~ **bandage** *n* venda de crepé.
crept [krɛpt] *pt*, *pp of* **creep**.
crescent ['krɛsnt] *n* media luna; (*street*) calle *f* en semicírculo.
cress [krɛs] *n* mastuerzo.
crest [krɛst] *n* (*of bird*) cresta; (*of hill*)

cima, cumbre *f*; (*of helmet*) cimera; (*of coat of arms*) blasón *m*; ~**fallen** *a* alicaído.
Crete [kriːt] *n* Creta.
crevasse [krɪˈvæs] *n* grieta.
crevice ['krɛvɪs] *n* grieta, hendedura.
crew [kruː] *n* (*of ship etc*) tripulación *f*; (*gang*) banda; (*mil*) dotación *f*; ~**-cut** *n* corte *m* al rape; ~**-neck** *n* cuello plano.
crib [krɪb] *n* pesebre *m* // *vt* (*col*) plagiar.
crick [krɪk] *n* (*in neck*) tortícolis *m*.
cricket ['krɪkɪt] *n* (*insect*) grillo; (*game*) críquet *m*.
crime [kraɪm] *n* crimen *m*; (*less serious*) delito; **criminal** ['krɪmɪnl] *n* criminal *m*, delincuente *m* // *a* criminal, delictivo; (*law*) penal; **the Criminal Investigation Department (CID)** Brigada de Investigación Criminal (B.I.C.).
crimson ['krɪmzn] *a* carmesí.
cringe [krɪndʒ] *vi* agacharse, encogerse.
crinkle ['krɪŋkl] *vt* arrugar.
cripple ['krɪpl] *n* lisiado, mutilado // *vt* lisiar, tullir.
crisis ['kraɪsɪs], *pl* **-ses** [-siːz] *n* crisis *f*.
crisp [krɪsp] *a* fresco; (*cooked*) tostado; (*hair*) crespo; (*manner*) seco; ~**s** *npl* papas fritas *fpl*.
criss-cross ['krɪskrɔs] *a* entrelazado.
criterion [kraɪˈtɪərɪən], *pl* **-ria** [-rɪə] *n* criterio.
critic ['krɪtɪk] *n* (*gen*) criticón/ona *m/f*; (*paper*) crítico; ~**al** *a* (*gen*) crítico; (*illness*) grave; ~**ally** *ad* (*ill*) gravemente; ~**ism** ['krɪtɪsɪzm] *n* crítica; ~**ize** ['krɪtɪsaɪz] *vt* criticar.
croak [krəʊk] *vi* (*frog*) croar; (*raven*) graznar // *n* graznido.
crochet ['krəʊʃeɪ] *n* ganchillo.
crockery ['krɔkərɪ] *n* loza, vajilla.
crocodile ['krɔkədaɪl] *n* cocodrilo.
crocus ['krəʊkəs] *n* azafrán *m*.
croft [krɔft] *n* granja pequeña; ~**er** *n* pequeño granjero.
croissant ['krwasã] *n* croissant *m*, medialuna.
crone [krəʊn] *n* bruja.
crony ['krəʊnɪ] *n* compinche *m/f*.
crook [kruk] *n* (*fam*) maleante *m/f*; (*of shepherd*) cayado; (*of arm*) pliegue *m*; ~**ed** ['krukɪd] *a* torcido; (*path*) tortuoso; (*action*) poco limpio.
crop [krɔp] *n* (*species*) cultivo; (*quantity*) cosecha // *vt* cortar, recortar; **to** ~ **up** *vi* surgir, presentarse.
croquet ['krəʊkeɪ] *n* croquet *m*.
croquette [krəˈkɛt] *n* croqueta.
cross [krɔs] *n* cruz *f* // *vt* (*street etc*) cruzar, atravesar // *a* de mal humor, malhumorado; **to** ~ **o.s.** santiguarse; **to** ~ **out** *vt* tachar; **to** ~ **over** *vi* cruzar; ~**bar** *n* travesaño; (*sport*) larguero; ~**country (race)** *n* carrera a campo traviesa, cross *m*; ~**-examination** *n* repregunta, interrogatorio; ~**-examine** *vt* repreguntar; ~**-eyed** *a* bizco; ~**ing** *n*

(*road*) cruce *m*; (*rail*) paso a nivel; (*seapassage*) travesía; (*also*: **pedestrian ~ing**) paso para peatones; **~ purposes** *npl*: **to be at ~ purposes** malentenderse uno a otro; **~-reference** *n* contrarreferencia; **~roads** *n* cruce *m*, encrucijada; **~ section** *n* corte *m* transversal; (*of population*) sección *f* representativa; **~wind** *n* viento de costado; **~word** *n* crucigrama *m*.

crotch [krɔtʃ] *n* (*of garment*) entrepierna.

crotchet ['krɔtʃɪt] *n* (*MUS*) negra.

crotchety ['krɔtʃɪtɪ] *a* (*person*) arisco.

crouch [krautʃ] *vi* agacharse, acurrucarse.

croupier ['kru:pɪə] *n* crupier *m/f.*

crow [krəu] *n* (*bird*) cuervo; (*of cock*) canto, cacareo // *vi* (*cock*) cantar, cacarear.

crowbar ['krəubɑ:*] *n* palanca.

crowd [kraud] *n* muchedumbre *f*; (*SPORT*) público; (*unruly*) tropel *m*; (*common herd*) vulgo // *vt* (*gather*) amontonar; (*fill*) llenar // *vi* (*gather*) reunirse; (*pile up*) amontonarse; **~ed** *a* (*full*) atestado; (*wellattended*) concurrido.

crown [kraun] *n* corona; (*of head*) coronilla; (*of hat*) copa; (*of hill*) cumbre *f* // *vt* coronar; **~ jewels** *npl* joyas *fpl* reales; **~ prince** *n* príncipe *m* heredero.

crucial ['kru:ʃl] *a* decisivo.

crucifix ['kru:sɪfɪks] *n* crucifijo; **~ion** [-'fɪkʃən] *n* crucifixión *f*; **crucify** [-faɪ] *vt* crucificar.

crude [kru:d] *a* (*materials*) bruto; (*fig*: *basic*) tosco; (: *vulgar*) ordinario; **~ (oil)** *n* aceite *m* crudo.

cruel ['kruəl] *a* cruel; **~ty** *n* crueldad *f.*

cruet ['kru:ɪt] angarillas *fpl.*

cruise [kru:z] *n* crucero, viaje *m* por mar // *vi* (*ship*) hacer un crucero; (*car*) circular lentamente; **cruiser** *n* crucero.

crumb [krʌm] *n* miga, migaja.

crumble ['krʌmbl] *vt* desmenuzar // *vi* (*gen*) desmenuzarse; (*building*) desmoronarse; **crumbly** *a* desmenuzable.

crumpet ['krʌmpɪt] *n* bollo blando.

crumple ['krʌmpl] *vt* (*paper*) estrujar; (*material*) arrugar.

crunch [krʌntʃ] *vt* (*food etc*) mascar; (*underfoot*) hacer crujir // *n* (*fig*) crisis *f*; **~y** *a* crujiente.

crusade [kru:'seɪd] *n* cruzada.

crush [krʌʃ] *n* (*people*) agolpamiento; (*crowd*) aglomeración *f*; (*drink*): **lemon ~** limonada // *vt* (*gen*) aplastar; (*paper*) estrujar; (*cloth*) arrugar; (*fruit*) exprimir; **~ing** *a* aplastante; (*burden*) agobiador(a).

crust [krʌst] *n* corteza; (*MED*) costra.

crutch [krʌtʃ] *n* muleta.

crux [krʌks] *n* lo esencial.

cry [kraɪ] *vi* llorar; (*shout*) gritar // *n* grito.

crypt [krɪpt] *n* cripta.

cryptic ['krɪptɪk] *a* enigmático, secreto.

crystal ['krɪstl] *n* cristal *m*; **~-clear** *a* transparente, claro como el agua; **crystallize** *vt* cristalizar // *vi* cristalizarse.

cub [kʌb] *n* cachorro.

Cuba ['kju:bə] *n* Cuba; **~n** *a*, *n* cubano/a.

cubbyhole ['kʌbɪhəul] *n* chiribitil *m.*

cube [kju:b] *n* cubo; (*of sugar*) terrón *m* // *vt* (*MATH*) cubicar; **~ root** *n* raíz *f* cúbica; **cubic** *a* cúbico.

cubicle ['kju:bɪkl] *n* (*at pool*) caseta; (*for bed*) camarilla.

cuckoo ['kuku:] *n* cuco; **~ clock** *n* reloj *m* de cuclillo.

cucumber ['kju:kʌmbə*] *n* pepino.

cuddle ['kʌdl] *vt* abrazar amorosamente // *vi* abrazarse; **cuddly** *a* mimoso.

cue [kju:] *n* (*snooker*) taco; (*THEATRE etc*) entrada, apunte *m.*

cuff [kʌf] *n* (*of shirt, coat etc*) puño; (*blow*) bofetada; **off the ~** *ad* de improviso; **~links** *npl* gemelos *mpl.*

cuisine [kwɪ'zi:n] *n* cocina.

cul-de-sac ['kʌldəsæk] *n* callejón *m* sin salida.

culinary ['kʌlɪnərɪ] *a* culinario.

cull [kʌl] *vt* (*flowers*) coger; (*select*) entresacar.

culminate ['kʌlmɪneɪt] *vi*: **to ~ in** terminar en; **culmination** [-'neɪʃən] *n* culminación *f*, colmo.

culpable ['kʌlpəbl] *a* culpable.

culprit ['kʌlprɪt] *n* (*persona*) culpable, delincuente *m/f.*

cult [kʌlt] *n* culto.

cultivate ['kʌltɪveɪt] *vt* (*also fig*) cultivar; **cultivation** [-'veɪʃən] *n* cultivo; (*fig*) cultura.

cultural ['kʌltʃərəl] *a* cultural.

culture ['kʌltʃə*] *n* (*also fig*) cultura; **~d** *a* culto.

cumbersome ['kʌmbəsəm] *a* molesto, incómodo.

cumulative ['kju:mjulətɪv] *a* cumulativo.

cunning ['kʌnɪŋ] *n* astucia // *a* astuto.

cup [kʌp] *n* taza; (*prize, event*) copa.

cupboard ['kʌbəd] *n* armario; (*on wall*) alacena.

Cupid ['kju:pɪd] *n* Cupido.

cupola ['kju:pələ] *n* cúpula.

cup-tie ['kʌptaɪ] *n* partido de copa.

cur [kə:] *n* perro de mala raza; (*person*) canalla *m/f.*

curable ['kjuərəbl] *a* curable.

curate ['kjuərɪt] *n* cura *m.*

curator [kjuə'reɪtə*] *n* director *m.*

curb [kə:b] *vt* refrenar // *n* freno.

curdle ['kə:dl] *vi* cuajarse.

curds [kə:dz] *npl* requesón *m.*

cure [kjuə*] *vt* curar // *n* cura, curación *f.*

curfew ['kə:fju:] *n* toque *m* de queda.

curio ['kjuərɪəu] *n* curiosidad *f.*

curiosity [kjuərɪ'ɔsɪtɪ] *n* curiosidad *f*; **curious** ['kjuərɪəs] *a* curioso.

curl [kə:l] *n* rizo, bucle *m* // *vt* (*hair*) rizar; (*paper*) arrollar; (*lip*) fruncir // *vi* rizarse; arrollarse; **to ~ up** *vi* arrollarse; (*person*) hacer un ovillo; (*fam*) morirse de risa; **~er** *n* bigudí *m*, chincho; **~y** *a* rizado.

currant ['kʌrnt] *n* pasa; (*black, red*) grosella.
currency ['kʌrnsı] *n* moneda.
current ['kʌrnt] *n* corriente *f* // *a* corriente, actual; ~ **account** *n* cuenta corriente; ~ **affairs** *npl* actualidades *fpl*; ~**ly** *ad* actualmente.
curriculum [kə'rɪkjuləm], *pl* ~**s** *or* -**la** [-lə] *n* plan *m* de estudios; ~ **vitae** *n* currículum *m*.
curry ['kʌrı] *n* curry *m* // *vt*: **to** ~ **favour with** buscar favores con; ~ **powder** *n* polvos *mpl* de curry.
curse [kəːs] *vi* echar pestes // *vt* maldecir, echar pestes de // *n* maldición *f*; (*swearword*) palabrota.
cursory ['kəːsərı] *a* rápido, superficial.
curt [kəːt] *a* corto, seco.
curtail [kəː'teɪl] *vt* (*visit etc*) acortar; (*expenses etc*) restringir.
curtain ['kəːtn] *n* cortina; (*THEATRE*) telón *m*; ~ **ring** *n* anilla.
curts(e)y ['kəːtsı] *n* reverencia // *vi* hacer una reverencia.
curve [kəːv] *n* curva // *vt* encorvar, torcer // *vi* encorvarse, torcerse; (*road*) hacer (una) curva.
cushion ['kuʃən] *n* cojín *m*; (*SNOOKER*) banda // *vt* (*seat*) acolchar; (*shock*) amortiguar.
custard ['kʌstəd] *n* (*for pouring*) natilla.
custodian [kʌs'təudıən] *n* custodio.
custody ['kʌstədı] *n* custodia; **to take into** ~ detener.
custom ['kʌstəm] *n* costumbre *f*; (*COMM*) clientela; ~**ary** *a* acostumbrado.
customer ['kʌstəmə*] *n* cliente *m/f*.
custom-made ['kʌstəm'meɪd] *a* hecho a la medida.
customs ['kʌstəmz] *npl* aduana *sg*; ~ **duty** *n* derechos *mpl* de aduana; ~ **officer** *n* aduanero.
cut [kʌt], *pt, pp* **cut** *vt* cortar; (*price*) rebajar; (*record*) grabar; (*reduce*) reducir // *vi* cortar; (*intersect*) cruzarse // *n* (*gen*) corte *m*; (*in skin*) cortadura; (*with sword*) tajo; (*of knife*) cuchillada; (*in salary etc*) rebaja; (*of meat*) tajada; **power** ~ apagón *m*; **to** ~ **a tooth** salirle a uno un diente; **to** ~ **down** *vt* (*tree*) derribar; (*reduce*) reducir; **to** ~ **off** *vt* (*gen*) cortar; (*retreat*) impedir; (*troops*) cercar; **to** ~ **out** *vt* (*shape*) recortar; (*delete*) suprimir; **to** ~ **through** *vi* abrirse camino; ~**back** *n* reducción *f*.
cute [kjuːt] *a* lindo; (*shrewd*) listo.
cuticle ['kjuːtɪkl] *n* cutícula.
cutlery ['kʌtlərı] *n* cubiertos *mpl*.
cutlet ['kʌtlɪt] *n* chuleta.
cut: ~**out** *n* recortable *m*; ~**-price** *a* a precio reducido; ~**throat** *n* asesino // *a* intenso.
cutting ['kʌtıŋ] *a* (*gen*) cortante; (*remark*) mordaz // *n* (*PRESS*) recorte *m*; (*RAIL*) desmonte *m*.
cwt *abbr of* **hundredweight(s)**.
cyanide ['saɪənaɪd] *n* cianuro.

cyclamen ['sɪkləmən] *n* ciclamen *m*.
cycle ['saɪkl] *n* ciclo; (*bicycle*) bicicleta // *vi* ir en bicicleta; **cycling** *n* ciclismo; **cyclist** *n* ciclista *m/f*.
cyclone ['saɪkləun] *n* ciclón *m*.
cygnet ['sɪgnɪt] *n* pollo de cisne.
cylinder ['sɪlɪndə*] *n* cilindro; ~ **block** *n* bloque *m* de cilindros; ~ **capacity** *n* cilindrada; ~ **head** *n* culata de cilindro; ~**-head gasket** *n* junta de culata.
cymbals ['sɪmblz] *npl* platillos *mpl*.
cynic ['sɪnɪk] *n* cínico; ~**al** *a* cínico; ~**ism** ['sɪnɪsɪzəm] *n* cinismo.
cypress ['saɪprɪs] *n* ciprés *m*.
Cypriot ['sɪprɪət] *a, n* chipriota *m/f*.
Cyprus ['saɪprəs] *n* Chipre *f*.
cyst [sɪst] *n* quiste *m*; ~**itis** *n* cistitis *f*.
czar [zɑː*] *n* zar *m*.
Czech [tʃɛk] *a, n* checo/a.
Czechoslovakia [tʃɛkəslə'vækıə] *n* Checoslovaquia.

D

dab [dæb] *vt* (*eyes, wound*) tocar (ligeramente); (*paint, cream*) mojar ligeramente // *n* (*of paint*) brochazo; (*of liquid*) gota; (*amount*) pequeña cantidad *f*.
dabble ['dæbl] *vi*: **to** ~ **in** interesarse por.
dad [dæd], **daddy** ['dædı] *n* papá *m*; **daddy-long-legs** *n* típula.
daffodil ['dæfədɪl] *n* narciso trompón.
daft [dɑːft] *a* estúpido, tonto.
dagger ['dægə*] *n* puñal *m*, daga; **to look** ~**s at sb** apuñalar a alguien con la mirada.
daily ['deɪlı] *a* diario, cotidiano // *n* (*paper*) diario; (*domestic help*) asistenta // *ad* a diario, cada día.
dainty ['deɪntı] *a* delicado; (*tasteful*) elegante, primoroso.
dairy ['dɛərı] *n* (*shop*) lechería; (*on farm*) vaquería // *a* lechero; ~ **farm** *n* granja; ~ **produce** *n* productos *mpl* lácteos.
daisy ['deɪzı] *n* margarita.
dale [deɪl] *n* valle *m*.
dam [dæm] *n* presa // *vt* represar.
damage ['dæmɪdʒ] *n* daño, perjuicio; (*to machine*) avería // *vt* dañar, perjudicar; averiar; ~**s** *npl* (*LAW*) daños y perjuicios.
damn [dæm] *vt* condenar; (*curse*) maldecir // *n* (*col*): **I don't give a** ~ me trae sin cuidado // *a* (*col*) maldito; ~ **(it)!** ¡mecachis!; ~**ing** *a* (*evidence*) irrecusable.
damp [dæmp] *a* húmedo, mojado // *n* humedad *f* // *vt* (*also*: ~**en**) (*cloth, rag*) mojar; (*enthusiasm etc*) desalentar; ~**ness** *n* humedad *f*.
damson ['dæmzən] *n* ciruela damascena.
dance [dɑːns] *n* baile *m* // *vi* bailar; ~ **hall** *n* salón *m* de baile; **dancer** *n* bailador/a *m/f*; (*professional*) bailarín/ina *m/f*; **dancing** *n* baile *m*.
dandelion ['dændɪlaɪən] *n* diente *m* de león.

dandruff ['dændrəf] n caspa.
Dane [deɪn] n danés/esa m/f.
danger ['deɪndʒə*] n peligro; (risk) riesgo; ~! (on sign) ¡peligro de muerte!; to be in ~ of correr riesgo de; ~ous a peligroso; ~ously ad peligrosamente.
dangle ['dæŋgl] vt colgar // vi pender, estar colgado.
Danish ['deɪnɪʃ] a, n danés/esa m/f.
dare [dɛə*] vt: to ~ sb to do desafiar a uno a hacer algo // vi: to ~ (to) do sth atreverse a hacer algo; ~devil n temerario, atrevido; **daring** a atrevido, osado // n atrevimiento, osadía.
dark [dɑːk] a (gen) oscuro; (hair, complexion) moreno; (cheerless) triste, sombrío; (fig) secreto, escondido // n (gen) oscuridad f; (night) tinieblas fpl; to be left in the ~ about (fig) quedar sin saber nada de; after ~ después del anochecer; ~en vt oscurecer; (colour) hacer más oscuro // vi oscurecerse; (sky) anublarse; ~ glasses npl gafas fpl oscuras; ~ness n oscuridad f, tinieblas fpl; ~ room n cuarto oscuro.
darling ['dɑːlɪŋ] a, n querido/a.
darn [dɑːn] vt zurcir.
dart [dɑːt] n dardo; (in game) rehilete m; (in sewing) sisa // vi precipitarse; to ~ away/along irse/seguir precipitado; ~board n blanco; ~s n juego de rehiletes.
dash [dæʃ] n (sign) guión m; (: long) raya; (rush) carrera // vt (break) romper, estrellar; (hopes) defraudar // vi precipitarse, ir de prisa; to ~ away or off vi marcharse apresuradamente; ~board n tablero de instrumentos; ~ing a gallardo.
data ['deɪtə] npl datos mpl; ~ processing n procesamiento de datos.
date [deɪt] n (day) fecha; (with friend) cita; (fruit) dátil m; (tree) palmera // vt fichar; citar; to ~ ad hasta la fecha; out of ~ fuera de moda; up to ~ moderno, al día; ~d a anticuado.
daub [dɔːb] vt manchar.
daughter ['dɔːtə*] n hija; ~-in-law n nuera, hija política.
daunting ['dɔːntɪŋ] a desalentador(a).
dawdle ['dɔːdl] vi (waste time) perder el tiempo; (go slow) andar muy despacio.
dawn [dɔːn] n alba, amanecer m // vi (day) amanecer; (fig): it ~ed on him that... cayó en la cuenta de que... .
day [deɪ] n día m; (working ~) jornada; the ~ before el día anterior; the following ~ el día siguiente; by ~ de día; ~break n amanecer m; ~dream n ensueño // vi soñar despierto; ~light n luz f (del día); ~time n día m // a de día.
daze [deɪz] vt (stun) aturdir // n: in a ~ aturdido.
dazzle ['dæzl] vt deslumbrar; **dazzling** a deslumbrante.
dead [dɛd] a (gen) muerto; (deceased) difunto; (telephone) cortado; (ELEC) sin

corriente // ad (gen) totalmente; (exactly) justo; ~ tired muerto de cansancio; to stop ~ parar en seco; the ~ los muertos; ~en vt (blow, sound) amortiguar; (make numb) calmar, aliviar; ~ end n callejón m sin salida; ~ heat n (SPORT) empate m; ~line n fecha o hora tope; ~lock n punto muerto; ~ly a mortal, fatal; ~pan a sin expresión.
deaf [dɛf] a sordo; ~-aid n audífono; ~en vt ensordecer; ~ening a ensordecedor(a); ~ness n sordera; ~-mute n sordomudo/a.
deal [diːl] n (agreement) pacto, convenio; (business) negocio, trato; (CARDS) reparto // vt, pt, pp dealt [dɛlt] (gen) dar; a great ~ (of) bastante, mucho; to ~ in tratar en, comerciar en; to ~ with vt fus (people) tratar con; (problem) ocuparse de; (subject) tratar de; (punish) castigar; ~er n comerciante m, tratante m; (CARDS) mano f; ~ings npl transacciones fpl; (relations) relaciones fpl.
dear [dɪə*] a querido; (expensive) caro // n: my ~ mi querido/a // excl: ~ me! ¡Dios mío!; D~ Sir/Madam (in letter) Muy Señor Mío, estimado Señor/estimada Señora; ~ly ad (love) tiernamente; (pay) caro.
death [dɛθ] n muerte f; ~bed n lecho de muerte; ~ certificate n partida de defunción; ~ duties npl (Brit) derechos mpl de herencia; ~ly a mortal; (silence) profundo; ~ penalty n pena de muerte; ~ rate n mortalidad f.
debar [dɪ'bɑː*] vt (exclude) excluir.
debase [dɪ'beɪs] vt degradar.
debate [dɪ'beɪt] n debate m // vt discutir.
debauchery [dɪ'bɔːtʃərɪ] n libertinaje m.
debit ['dɛbɪt] n debe m // vt: to ~ a sum to sb or to sb's account cargar una suma en cuenta a alguien.
debris ['dɛbriː] n escombros mpl.
debt [dɛt] n deuda; to be in ~ tener deudas; ~or n deudor/a m/f.
début ['deɪbjuː] n presentación f.
decade ['dɛkeɪd] n decenio.
decadence ['dɛkədəns] n decadencia.
decay [dɪ'keɪ] n decadencia; (of building) desmoronamiento; (fig) deterioro; (rotting) pudrición f; (of tooth) caries f // vi (rot) pudrirse; (fig) decaer.
deceased [dɪ'siːst] a difunto.
deceit [dɪ'siːt] n engaño; ~ful a engañoso.
deceive [dɪ'siːv] vt engañar.
decelerate [diː'sɛləreɪt] vt moderar la marcha de // vi decelerar.
December [dɪ'sɛmbə*] n diciembre m.
decency ['diːsənsɪ] n decencia.
decent ['diːsənt] a (proper) decente; (person) amable, bueno.
decentralize [diː'sɛntrəlaɪz] vt descentralizar.
deception [dɪ'sɛpʃən] n engaño; **deceptive** [-tɪv] a engañoso.
decibel ['dɛsɪbɛl] n decibel(io) m.
decide [dɪ'saɪd] vt (person) decidir;

(*question, argument*) resolver // *vi* decidir;
to ~ on sth decidir por algo; **~d** *a*
(*resolute*) decidido; (*clear, definite*)
indudable; **~dly** [-dɪdlɪ] *ad* decididamente.
deciduous [dɪ'sɪdjuəs] *a* de hoja caduca.
decimal ['dɛsɪməl] *a* decimal // *n* decimal
f; **~ point** *n* coma de decimales.
decimate ['dɛsɪmeɪt] *vt* diezmar.
decipher [dɪ'saɪfə*] *vt* descifrar.
decision [dɪ'sɪʒən] *n* decisión *f*.
decisive [dɪ'saɪsɪv] *a* decisivo; (*conclusive*)
terminante; (*manner*) tajante.
deck [dɛk] *n* (*NAUT*) cubierta; (*of bus*) piso;
(*of cards*) baraja; **~chair** *n* tumbona,
hamaca.
declaration [dɛklə'reɪʃən] *n* declaración *f*;
declare [dɪ'klɛə*] *vt* (*gen*) declarar.
decline [dɪ'klaɪn] *n* decaimiento,
decadencia; (*lessening*) disminución *f* // *vt*
rehusar // *vi* decaer; disminuir; (*fall*)
bajar.
declutch ['di:'klʌtʃ] *vi* desembragar.
decode [di:'kəud] *vt* descifrar.
decompose [di:kəm'pəuz] *vi*
descomponerse; **decomposition**
[di:kɔmpə'zɪʃən] *n* descomposición *f*.
decontaminate [di:kən'tæmɪneɪt] *vt*
descontaminar.
décor ['deɪkɔ:*] *n* decoración *f*; (*THEATRE*)
decorado.
decorate ['dɛkəreɪt] *vt* adornar, decorar;
(*paint*) pintar; (*paper*) empapelar;
decoration [-'reɪʃən] *n* adorno; (*act*)
decoración *f*; (*medal*) condecoración *f*;
decorator *n* (*painter*) pintor *m*.
decoy ['di:kɔɪ] *n* señuelo.
decrease ['di:kri:s] *n* disminución *f* // (*vb*:
[di:'kri:s]) *vt* disminuir, reducir // *vi*
reducirse.
decree [dɪ'kri:] *n* decreto; **~ nisi** *n* orden
f provisional de divorcio.
decrepit [dɪ'krɛpɪt] *a* decrépito.
dedicate ['dɛdɪkeɪt] *vt* dedicar;
dedication [-'keɪʃən] *n* (*devotion*)
dedicación *f*; (*in book*) dedicatoria.
deduce [dɪ'dju:s] *vt* deducir.
deduct [dɪ'dʌkt] *vt* restar; (*from wage etc*)
descontar; **~ion** [dɪ'dʌkʃən] *n* descuento;
(*conclusion*) deducción *f*, conclusión *f*.
deed [di:d] *n* hecho, acto; (*feat*) hazaña;
(*LAW*) escritura.
deem [di:m] *vt* juzgar.
deep [di:p] *a* (*gen*) profundo; (*voice*) bajo;
(*breath*) profundo, a pleno pulmón;
(*person*) insondable // *ad*: **the spectators
stood 20 ~** los espectadores se formaron
de 20 en fondo; **to be 4 metres ~** tener 4
metros de profundo; **~en** *vt* ahondar,
profundizar // *vi* (*darkness*) intensificarse;
~-freeze *n* congeladora; **~-fry** *vt* freír
en aceite abundante; **~-sea diving** *n*
buceo de altura; **~-seated** *a* (*beliefs*)
(profundamente) arraigado; **~-set** *a*
(*eyes*) hundido.
deer [dɪə*] *n*, *pl inv* ciervo; **~skin** *n*
gamuza, piel *f* de ciervo.
deface [dɪ'feɪs] *vt* desfigurar, mutilar.

defamation [dɛfə'meɪʃən] *n* difamación *f*.
default [dɪ'fɔ:lt] *vi* no pagar; (*SPORT*) dejar
de presentarse // *n*: **by ~** (*LAW*) en
rebeldía; (*SPORT*) por no presentarse el
adversario; **~er** *n* (*in debt*) moroso/a.
defeat [dɪ'fi:t] *n* derrota // *vt* derrotar,
vencer; (*fig*: *efforts*) frustrar; **~ist** *a*, *n*
derrotista *m/f*.
defect ['di:fɛkt] *n* defecto // *vi* [dɪ'fɛkt]
desertar; **~ive** [dɪ'fɛktɪv] *a* (*gen*)
defectuoso; (*person*) anormal.
defence [dɪ'fɛns] *n* defensa; **~less** *a*
indefenso.
defend [dɪ'fɛnd] *vt* defender; **~ant** *n*
acusado/a; (*in civil case*) demandado/a;
~er *n* defensor *m*.
defensive [dɪ'fɛnsɪv] *a* defensivo; **on the
~** a la defensiva.
defer [dɪ'fɔ:*] *vt* (*postpone*) aplazar; **to ~
to** diferir a; **~ence** ['dɛfərəns] *n*
deferencia, respeto.
defiance [dɪ'faɪəns] *n* desafío; **in ~ of** en
contra de; **defiant** [-ənt] *a* (*insolent*)
insolente; (*challenging*) retador(a).
deficiency [dɪ'fɪʃənsɪ] *n* (*lack*) falta;
(*defect*) defecto; **deficient** [-ənt] *a*
(*lacking*) insuficiente; (*incomplete*)
incompleto; (*defective*) defectuoso;
(*mentally*) anormal; **deficient in** falto de.
deficit ['dɛfɪsɪt] *n* déficit *m*.
defile [dɪ'faɪl] *vt* manchar, deshonrar.
define [dɪ'faɪn] *vt* definir.
definite ['dɛfɪnɪt] *a* (*fixed*) determinado;
(*clear, obvious*) claro, categórico; **he was
~ about it** no dejó lugar a dudas (sobre
ello); **~ly** *ad* claramente.
definition [dɛfɪ'nɪʃən] *n* definición *f*.
definitive [dɪ'fɪnɪtɪv] *a* definitivo.
deflate [di:'fleɪt] *vt* (*gen*) desinflar;
(*person*) quitar los humos a.
deflect [dɪ'flɛkt] *vt* desviar.
deform [dɪ'fɔ:m] *vt* deformar; **~ed** *a*
deformado; **~ity** *n* deformación *f*.
defraud [dɪ'frɔ:d] *vt* estafar; **to ~ sb of**
sth estafar algo a uno.
defrost [di:'frɔst] *vt* (*fridge*) deshelar,
descongelar.
deft [dɛft] *a* diestro, hábil.
defunct [dɪ'fʌŋkt] *a* difunto.
defuse [di:'fju:z] *vt* quitar el fusible a.
defy [dɪ'faɪ] *vt* (*resist*) oponerse
resueltamente a; (*challenge*) desafiar;
(*order*) contravenir.
degenerate [dɪ'dʒɛnəreɪt] *vi* degenerar //
a [dɪ'dʒɛnərɪt] degenerado.
degradation [dɛgrə'deɪʃən] *n* degradación
f; **degrading** [dɪ'greɪdɪŋ] *a* degradante.
degree [dɪ'gri:] *n* grado; (*SCOL*) título; **~ in
maths** licencia en matemáticas.
dehydrated [di:haɪ'dreɪtɪd] *a*
deshidratado; (*milk*) en polvo.
de-ice [di:'aɪs] *vt* (*windscreen*) deshelar.
deign [deɪn] *vi*: **to ~ to do** dignarse
hacer.
deity ['di:ɪtɪ] *n* deidad *f*, divinidad *f*.
dejected [dɪ'dʒɛktɪd] *a* abatido,

desanimado; (*face*) cariacontecido; **dejection** [-ʃən] *n* abatimiento.
delay [dɪˈleɪ] *vt* demorar, aplazar; (*person*) entretener; (*trains*) retrasar // *vi* tardar // *n* (*gen*) dilación *f*; (*a* ~) demora, retraso; **without** ~ en seguida, sin tardar.
delegate [ˈdɛlɪgɪt] *n* delegado/a // *vt* [ˈdɛlɪgeɪt] delegar; **delegation** [-ˈgeɪʃən] *n* delegación *f*.
delete [dɪˈliːt] *vt* suprimir, tachar.
deliberate [dɪˈlɪbərɪt] *a* (*intentional*) intencionado; (*slow*) pausado, lento // *vi* [dɪˈlɪbəreɪt] deliberar; ~**ly** *ad* (*on purpose*) a propósito; (*slowly*) pausadamente.
delicacy [ˈdɛlɪkəsɪ] *n* delicadeza; (*choice food*) golosina.
delicate [ˈdɛlɪkɪt] *a* (*gen*) delicado; (*fragile*) frágil; (*skilled*) fino.
delicatessen [dɛlɪkəˈtɛsn] *n* tienda especializada en comida exótica.
delicious [dɪˈlɪʃəs] *a* delicioso, rico.
delight [dɪˈlaɪt] *n* (*feeling*) placer *m*, deleite *m*; (*object*) encanto, delicia // *vt* encantar, deleitar; **to take** ~ **in** deleitarse con; ~**ful** *a* encantador(a), delicioso.
delinquency [dɪˈlɪŋkwənsɪ] *n* delincuencia; **delinquent** [-ənt] *a*, *n* delincuente *m/f*.
delirious [dɪˈlɪrɪəs] *a* delirante; **delirium** [-ɪəm] *n* delirio.
deliver [dɪˈlɪvə*] *vt* (*distribute*) repartir; (*hand over*) entregar; (*message*) comunicar; (*speech*) pronunciar; (*blow*) lanzar, dar; (*MED*): **to be** ~**ed** dar a luz; ~**y** *n* reparto; entrega; (*distribution*) distribución *f*; (*of speaker*) modo de expresarse; (*MED*) parto, alumbramiento; (*saving*) liberación *f*; **to take** ~**y of** recibir.
delta [ˈdɛltə] *n* delta *m*.
delude [dɪˈluːd] *vt* engañar.
deluge [ˈdɛljuːdʒ] *n* diluvio // *vt* inundar.
delusion [dɪˈluːʒən] *n* ilusión *f*, engaño.
de luxe [dəˈlʌks] *a* de lujo.
delve [dɛlv] *vi*: **to** ~ **into** ahondar en.
demand [dɪˈmɑːnd] *vt* (*gen*) exigir; (*rights*) reclamar // *n* (*gen*) exigencia; (*claim*) reclamación *f*; (*ECON*) demanda; **to be in** ~ ser muy solicitado; **on** ~ a solicitud; ~**ing** *a* (*boss*) exigente; (*work*) absorbente.
demarcation [diːmɑːˈkeɪʃən] *n* demarcación *f*.
demean [dɪˈmiːn] *vt*: **to** ~ **o.s.** rebajarse.
demeanour [dɪˈmiːnə*] *n* porte *m*, conducta.
demented [dɪˈmɛntɪd] *a* demente.
demister [diːˈmɪstə*] *n* (*AUT*) de(s)fumador *m* de vapores.
democracy [dɪˈmɒkrəsɪ] *n* democracia; **democrat** [ˈdɛməkræt] *n* demócrata *m/f*; **democratic** [dɛməˈkrætɪk] *a* democrático.
demolish [dɪˈmɒlɪʃ] *vt* derribar, demoler; **demolition** [dɛməˈlɪʃən] *n* derribo, demolición *f*.
demonstrate [ˈdɛmənstreɪt] *vt* demostrar

// *vi* manifestarse; **demonstration** [-ˈstreɪʃən] *n* (*POL*) manifestación *f*; (*proof*) prueba, demostración *f*; **demonstrator** *n* (*POL*) manifestante *m/f*.
demoralize [dɪˈmɒrəlaɪz] *vt* desmoralizar.
demote [dɪˈməut] *vt* degradar.
demure [dɪˈmjuə*] *a* recatado.
den [dɛn] *n* (*of animal*) guarida; (*study*) estudio.
denial [dɪˈnaɪəl] *n* (*refusal*) negativa; (*of report etc*) desmentimiento; **self-**~ abnegación *f*.
denim [ˈdɛnɪm] *n* dril *m*; ~**s** *npl* vaqueros *mpl*.
Denmark [ˈdɛnmɑːk] *n* Dinamarca.
denomination [dɪnɒmɪˈneɪʃən] *n* valor *m*; (*REL*) confesión *f*.
denominator [dɪˈnɒmɪneɪtə*] *n* denominador *m*.
denote [dɪˈnəut] *vt* indicar, significar.
denounce [dɪˈnauns] *vt* denunciar.
dense [dɛns] *a* (*thick*) espeso; (: *foliage etc*) tupido; (*stupid*) torpe, duro de mollera; ~**ly** *ad*: ~**ly populated** con gran densidad de población.
density [ˈdɛnsɪtɪ] *n* densidad *f*.
dent [dɛnt] *n* abolladura // *vt* (*also:* **make a** ~ **in**) abollar.
dental [ˈdɛntl] *a* dental; ~ **surgeon** *n* odontólogo.
dentist [ˈdɛntɪst] *n* dentista *m/f*; ~**ry** *n* odontología.
dentures [ˈdɛntʃəz] *npl* dentadura *sg* (postiza).
deny [dɪˈnaɪ] *vt* (*gen*) negar; (*charge*) rechazar; (*report*) desmentir; **to** ~ **o.s.** privarse (de).
deodorant [diːˈəudərənt] *n* desodorante *m*.
depart [dɪˈpɑːt] *vi* irse, marcharse; (*train*) salir; **to** ~ **from** (*fig: differ from*) apartarse de.
department [dɪˈpɑːtmənt] *n* (*COMM*) sección *f*; (*SCOL*) ramo; (*POL*) ministerio; ~ **store** *n* gran almacén *m*.
departure [dɪˈpɑːtʃə*] *n* partida, ida; (*of train*) salida; **a new** ~ un nuevo rumbo.
depend [dɪˈpɛnd] *vi*: **to** ~ **on** depender de; (*rely on*) contar con; **it** ~**s** ¡depende!, ¡según!; ~**able** *a* (*person*) formal, serio; ~**ence** *n* dependencia; ~**ant**, ~**ent** *n* dependiente *m/f*.
depict [dɪˈpɪkt] *vt* (*in picture*) pintar; (*describe*) representar.
depleted [dɪˈpliːtɪd] *a* reducido.
deplorable [dɪˈplɔːrəbl] *a* lamentable, deplorable; **deplore** [dɪˈplɔː*] *vt* lamentar, deplorar.
deploy [dɪˈplɔɪ] *vt* desplegar.
depopulation [diːpɒpjuˈleɪʃən] *n* despoblación *f*.
deport [dɪˈpɔːt] *vt* deportar; ~**ation** [-ˈteɪʃən] *n* deportación *f*; ~**ment** *n* comportamiento.
depose [dɪˈpəuz] *vt* deponer.
deposit [dɪˈpɒzɪt] *n* (*gen*) depósito; (*CHEM*) sedimento; (*of ore, oil*) yacimiento // *vt*

(gen) depositar; ~ **account** n cuenta de ahorros; ~**or** n cuentacorrentista m/f.

depot ['dɛpəʊ] n (storehouse) depósito; (for vehicles) parque m.

depraved [dɪ'preɪvd] a depravado, vicioso; **depravity** [-'prævɪtɪ] n depravación f, vicio.

depreciate [dɪ'pri:ʃɪeɪt] vi depreciarse, perder valor; **depreciation** [-'eɪʃən] n depreciacion f.

depress [dɪ'prɛs] vt deprimir; (press down) presionar; ~**ed** a deprimido; ~**ing** a deprimente; ~**ion** [dɪ'prɛʃən] n depresión f.

deprivation [dɛprɪ'veɪʃən] n privación f; (loss) pérdida.

deprive [dɪ'praɪv] vt: **to** ~ **sb of** privar a alguien de; ~**d** a pobre.

depth [dɛpθ] n (gen) profundidad f; (of room etc) fondo; **in the** ~**s of** en lo más hondo de.

deputation [dɛpju'teɪʃən] n delegación f.

deputize ['dɛpjutaɪz] vi: **to** ~ **for sb** sustituir por uno.

deputy ['dɛpjutɪ] a: ~ **head** subdirector/a m/f // n sustituto/a, suplente m; (POL) diputado; (agent) representante m.

derail [dɪ'reɪl] vt: **to be** ~**ed** descarrilarse; ~**ment** n descarrilamiento.

deranged [dɪ'reɪndʒd] a (person) vuelto loco, trastornado (mentalmente).

derelict ['dɛrɪlɪkt] a abandonado.

deride [dɪ'raɪd] vt ridiculizar, mofarse de; **derision** [-'rɪʒən] n irrisión f, mofas fpl.

derivative [dɪ'rɪvətɪv] n derivado // a derivado; (work) poco original.

derive [dɪ'raɪv] vt derivar // vi: **to** ~ **from** derivarse de.

dermatitis [dɔ:mə'taɪtɪs] n dermatitis f; **dermatology** [-'tɔlədʒɪ] n dermatología.

derogatory [dɪ'rɔgətərɪ] a despectivo.

derrick ['dɛrɪk] n torre f de perforación.

descend [dɪ'sɛnd] vt, vi descender, bajar; **to** ~ **from** descender de; ~**ant** n descendiente m/f.

descent [dɪ'sɛnt] n descenso; (GEO) pendiente m, declive m; (origin) descendencia.

describe [dɪs'kraɪb] vt describir; **description** [-'krɪpʃən] n descripción f; (sort) clase f, género; **descriptive** [-'krɪptɪv] a descriptivo.

desecrate ['dɛsɪkreɪt] vt profanar.

desert ['dɛzət] n desierto // (vb: [dɪ'zɔ:t]) vt abandonar, desamparar // vi (MIL) desertar; ~**er** n desertor m; ~**ion** [dɪ'zɔ:ʃən] n deserción f.

deserve [dɪ'zɔ:v] vt merecer, ser digno de; **deserving** a (person) digno; (action, cause) meritorio.

design [dɪ'zaɪn] n (sketch) bosquejo; (layout, shape) diseño; (pattern) dibujo; (intention) propósito, intención f // vt (gen) diseñar; (plan) proyectar.

designate ['dɛzɪgneɪt] vt (point to) señalar; (appoint) nombrar; (destine)

designar // a ['dɛzɪgnɪt] designado; **designation** [-'neɪʃən] n (appointment) nombramiento; (name) denominación f.

designer [dɪ'zaɪnə*] n (ART) dibujante m; (TECH) diseñador m; (fashion ~) modista m/f.

desirable [dɪ'zaɪərəbl] a (proper) deseable; (attractive) atractivo.

desire [dɪ'zaɪə*] n deseo // vt desear.

desk [dɛsk] n (in office) escritorio; (for pupil) pupitre m; (in hotel, at airport) recepción f.

desolate ['dɛsəlɪt] a (place) desierto; (person) afligido; **desolation** [-'leɪʃən] n (of place) desolación f; (of person) aflicción f.

despair [dɪs'pɛə*] n desesperación f // vi: **to** ~ **of** desesperarse de.

despatch [dɪs'pætʃ] n, vt = **dispatch**.

desperate ['dɛspərɪt] a desesperado; (fugitive) peligroso; ~**ly** ad desesperadamente; (very) terriblemente, gravemente.

desperation [dɛspə'reɪʃən] n desesperación f; **in** ~ desesperado.

despicable [dɪs'pɪkəbl] a vil, despreciable.

despise [dɪs'paɪz] vt despreciar.

despite [dɪs'paɪt] prep a pesar de, pese a.

despondent [dɪs'pɔndənt] a deprimido, abatido.

dessert [dɪ'zɔ:t] n postre m; ~**spoon** n cuchara (de postre).

destination [dɛstɪ'neɪʃən] n destino.

destiny ['dɛstɪnɪ] n destino.

destitute ['dɛstɪtju:t] a desamparado, indigente.

destroy [dɪs'trɔɪ] vt (gen) destruir; (finish) acabar con; ~**er** n (NAUT) destructor m.

destruction [dɪs'trʌkʃən] n destrucción f; (fig) ruina; **destructive** [-tɪv] a destructivo, destructor(a).

detach [dɪ'tætʃ] vt separar; (unstick) despegar; ~**able** a separable; (TECH) desmontable; ~**ed** a (attitude) objetivo, imparcial; (house) independiente, solo; ~**ment** n (gen) separación f; (MIL) destacamento; (fig) objetividad f, imparcialidad f.

detail ['di:teɪl] n detalle m // vt (gen) detallar; (MIL) destacar; **in** ~ en detalle; ~**ed** a detallado.

detain [dɪ'teɪn] vt retener; (in captivity) detener.

detect [dɪ'tɛkt] vt (gen) descubrir; (MED, POLICE) identificar; (MIL, RADAR, TECH) detectar; ~**ion** [dɪ'tɛkʃən] n descubrimiento; identificación f; ~**ive** a detective m; ~**ive story** n novela policíaca; ~**or** n detector m.

détente [deɪ'tɑ:nt] n detente f.

detention [dɪ'tɛnʃən] n detención f, arresto.

deter [dɪ'tɔ:*] vt (discourage) desalentar; (dissuade) disuadir; (prevent) impedir.

detergent [dɪ'tɔ:dʒənt] n detergente m.

deteriorate [dɪ'tɪərɪəreɪt] vi deteriorarse; **deterioration** [-'reɪʃən] n deterioro.

determination [dɪtə:mɪ'neɪʃən] n (gen)

determinación *f*; (*resolve*) resolución *f*.
determine [dı'tə:mın] *vt* (*gen*) determinar; (*limits etc*) definir; (*dispute*) resolver; ~**d** *a* (*person*) resuelto.
deterrent [dı'tɛrənt] *n* fuerza de disuasión.
detest [dı'tɛst] *vt* aborrecer; ~**able** *a* aborrecible.
detonate ['dɛtəneıt] *vi* estallar // *vt* hacer detonar; **detonator** *n* detonador *m*, fulminante *m*.
detour ['di:tuə*] *n* rodeo.
detract [dı'trækt] *vt*: to ~ from quitar mérito a, desvirtuar.
detriment ['dɛtrımənt] *n*: to the ~ of en perjuicio de; ~**al** [dɛtrı'mɛntl] *a* perjudicial (*to* a).
devaluation [dıvælju'eıʃən] *n* devaluación *f*; **devalue** [-'vælju:] *vt* devaluar.
devastate ['dɛvəsteıt] *vt* devastar; **he was** ~**d by the news** las noticias le dejaron desolado; **devastating** *a* devastador(a); (*fig*) arrollador(a).
develop [dı'vɛləp] *vt* (*gen*) desarrollar; (*PHOT*) revelar; (*disease*) coger; (*engine trouble*) empezar a tener // *vi* desarrollarse; (*advance*) progresar; (*appear*) aparecer; ~**ing country** país *m* en desarrollo; ~**ment** *n* desarrollo; (*advance*) progreso; (*of affair*, *case*) desenvolvimiento; (*of land*) urbanización *f*.
deviate ['di:vıeıt] *vi* desviarse; **deviation** [-'eıʃən] *n* desviación *f*.
device [dı'vaıs] *n* (*scheme*) estratagema *f*, recurso; (*apparatus*) aparato, mecanismo.
devil ['dɛvl] *n* diablo, demonio; ~**ish** *a* diabólico.
devious ['di:vıəs] *a* intricado, enrevesado; (*person*) taimado.
devise [dı'vaız] *vt* idear, inventar.
devoid [dı'vɔıd] *a*: ~ of desprovisto de.
devote [dı'vəut] *vt*: to ~ sth to dedicar algo a; ~**d** *a* (*loyal*) leal, fiel; **the book is** ~**d to politics** el libro trata de la política; **devotee** [dɛvəu'ti:] *n* devoto/a.
devotion [dı'vəuʃən] *n* dedicación *f*; (*REL*) devoción *f*.
devour [dı'vauə*] *vt* devorar.
devout [dı'vaut] *a* devoto.
dew [dju:] *n* rocío.
dexterity [dɛks'tɛrıtı] *n* destreza.
diabetes [daıə'bi:ti:z] *n* diabetes *f*; **diabetic** [-'bɛtık] *a*, *n* diabético/a.
diagnose [daıəg'nəuz] *vt* diagnosticar; **diagnosis** [-'nəusıs], *pl* -**ses** [-'nəusi:z] *n* diagnóstico.
diagonal [daı'ægənl] *a* diagonal // *n* diagonal *f*.
diagram ['daıəgræm] *n* diagrama *m*, esquema *m*.
dial ['daıəl] *n* esfera, cuadrante *m* // *vt* (*number*) marcar; ~**ling tone** *n* tono de marcar.
dialect ['daıəlɛkt] *n* dialecto.
dialogue ['daıəlɔg] *n* diálogo.
diameter [daı'æmıtə*] *n* diámetro.

diamond ['daıəmənd] *n* diamante *m*; ~**s** *npl* (*CARDS*) oros *mpl*.
diaper ['daıəpə*] *n* (*US*) pañal *m*.
diaphragm ['daıəfræm] *n* diafragma *m*.
diarrhoea, diarrhea (*US*) [daıə'ri:ə] *n* diarrea.
diary ['daıərı] *n* (*daily account*) diario; (*book*) agenda *m*.
dice [daıs] *n*, *pl inv* dados *mpl* // *vt* (*CULIN*) cortar en cuadritos.
dictate [dık'teıt] *vt* dictar; ~**s** ['dıkteıts] *npl* dictados *mpl*; **dictation** [-'teıʃən] *n* dictado.
dictator [dık'teıtə*] *n* dictador *m*; ~**ship** *n* dictadura.
diction ['dıkʃən] *n* dicción *f*.
dictionary ['dıkʃənrı] *n* diccionario.
did [dıd] *pt of* **do**.
die [daı] *vi* morir; to ~ away *vi* (*sound*, *light*) extinguirse lentamente; to ~ down *vi* (*gen*) apagarse; (*wind*) amainar; to ~ out *vi* desaparecer, extinguirse.
diesel ['di:zəl]: ~ **engine** *n* motor *m* Diesel; ~ (**oil**) *n* gas-oil *m*.
diet ['daıət] *n* dieta; (*restricted food*) régimen *m* // *vi* (*also*: be on a ~) estar a dieta, hacer régimen.
differ ['dıfə*] *vi* (*be different*) ser distinto, diferenciarse; (*disagree*) discrepar; ~**ence** *n* diferencia; (*quarrel*) desacuerdo; ~**ent** *a* diferente, distinto; ~**entiate** [-'rɛnʃıeıt] *vt* distinguir // *vi* diferenciarse; to ~**entiate between** distinguir entre; ~**ently** *ad* de otro modo, en forma distinta.
difficult ['dıfıkəlt] *a* difícil; ~**y** *n* dificultad *f*.
diffidence ['dıfıdəns] *n* timidez *f*; **diffident** [-ənt] *a* tímido.
diffuse [dı'fju:s] *a* difuso // *vt* [dı'fju:z] difundir.
dig [dıg], *pt*, *pp* **dug** *vt* (*hole*) cavar; (*garden*) cultivar; (*coal*) extraer; (*nails etc*) hincar // *n* (*prod*) empujón *m*; (*archaeological*) excavación *f*; (*remark*) indirecta; to ~ **in** *vi* atrincherarse; to ~ **into** *vt* (*savings*) consumir; to ~ **out** *vt* (*hole*) excavar; (*fig*) sacar; to ~ **up** *vt* desenterrar; (*plant*) desarraigar.
digest [daı'dʒɛst] *vt* (*food*) digerir; (*facts*) asimilar // *n* ['daıdʒɛst] resumen *m*; ~**ion** [dı'dʒɛstʃən] *n* digestión *f*.
digital ['dıdʒıtəl] *a* digital.
dignified ['dıgnıfaıd] *a* grave, solemne; (*action*) decoroso.
dignity ['dıgnıtı] *n* dignidad *f*.
digress [daı'grɛs] *vi*: to ~ from apartarse de; ~**ion** [daı'grɛʃən] *n* digresión *f*.
digs [dıgz] *npl* (*Brit: col*) pensión *f*, alojamiento.
dilapidated [dı'læpıdeıtıd] *a* desmoronado, ruinoso.
dilate [daı'leıt] *vt* dilatar // *vi* dilatarse.
dilemma [daı'lɛmə] *n* dilema *m*.
diligent ['dılıdʒənt] *a* diligente.
dilute [daı'lu:t] *vt* diluir // *a* diluido.

dim [dım] a (*light*) débil; (*sight*) turbio; (*outline*) indistinto; (*stupid*) lerdo; (*room*) oscuro // vt (*light*) bajar; (AUT) poner a media luz.

dime [daim] n (US) *moneda de diez centavos.*

dimension [dı'mɛnʃən] n dimensión f.

diminish [dı'mınıʃ] vi disminuirse.

diminutive [dı'mınjutıv] a diminuto // n (LING) diminutivo.

dimly ['dımlı] ad débilmente; (*not clearly*) indistintamente.

dimple ['dımpl] n hoyuelo.

din [dın] n estruendo, estrépito.

dine [daın] vi cenar; **diner** n (*person*) comensal m/f; (RAIL) = **dining car.**

dinghy ['dıŋgı] n bote m; **rubber** ~ lancha (neumática).

dingy ['dındʒı] a (*room*) sombrío; (*dirty*) sucio; (*dull*) deslucido.

dining ['daınıŋ]: ~ **car** n coche-comedor m; ~ **room** n comedor m.

dinner ['dınə*] n (*evening meal*) cena; (*lunch*) comida; (*public*) cena, banquete m; ~ **jacket** n smoking m; ~ **party** n cena; ~ **time** n hora de cenar o comer.

diocese ['daıəsıs] n diócesis f.

dip [dıp] n (*slope*) pendiente m; (*in sea*) baño // vt (*in water*) mojar; (*ladle etc*) meter; (AUT: *lights*) poner a media luz // vi inclinarse hacia abajo.

diphtheria [dıf'θıərıə] n difteria.

diploma [dı'pləumə] n diploma m.

diplomacy [dı'pləuməsı] n diplomacia; **diplomat** ['dıpləmæt] n diplomático; **diplomatic** [dıplə'mætık] a diplomático.

dipstick ['dıpstık] n (AUT) varilla graduada, indicador m de nivel (del aceite).

dire [daıə*] a calamitoso.

direct [daı'rɛkt] a (*gen*) directo // vt dirigir; **can you** ~ **me to...?** ¿puede indicarme dónde está...?

direction [dı'rɛkʃən] n dirección f; ~**s** npl (*advice*) órdenes fpl, instrucciones fpl; ~**s for use** modo de empleo.

directly [dı'rɛktlı] ad (*in straight line*) directamente; (*at once*) en seguida.

director [dı'rɛktə*] n director m; **managing** ~ director gerente.

directory [dı'rɛktərı] n (TEL) guía (telefónica).

dirt [də:t] n suciedad f; ~-**cheap** a tirado, muy barato; ~**y** a sucio; (*joke*) verde // vt ensuciar; (*stain*) manchar; ~**y trick** n juego sucio.

disability [dısə'bılıtı] n incapacidad f; **disabled** [dıs'eıbld] a disminuido, minusválido.

disadvantage [dısəd'va:ntıdʒ] n desventaja, inconveniente m.

disagree [dısə'gri:] vi (*differ*) discrepar; (*be against, think otherwise*): **to** ~ (**with**) no estar de acuerdo (con); ~**able** a desagradable; ~**ment** n (*gen*) desacuerdo; (*quarrel*) riña.

disallow ['dısə'lau] vt (*goal*) anular.

disappear [dısə'pıə*] vi desaparecer; ~**ance** n desaparición f.

disappoint [dısə'pɔınt] vt decepcionar; (*hopes*) defraudar; ~**ing** a decepcionante; ~**ment** n decepción f.

disapproval [dısə'pru:vəl] n desaprobación f.

disapprove [dısə'pru:v] vi: **to** ~ **of** desaprobar.

disarm [dıs'a:m] vt desarmar; ~**ament** n desarme m; ~**ing** a encantador(a).

disaster [dı'za:stə*] n desastre m; **disastrous** a desastroso.

disband [dıs'bænd] vt disolver // vi desbandarse.

disbelief [dısbə'li:f] n incredulidad f.

disc [dısk] n disco.

discard [dıs'ka:d] vt (*old things*) tirar; (*fig*) descartar.

discern [dı'sɔ:n] vt percibir, discernir; ~**ing** a perspicaz.

discharge [dıs'tʃa:dʒ] vt (*duties*) cumplir, desempeñar; (*ship etc*) descargar; (*patient*) dar de alta; (*employee*) despedir; (*soldier*) licenciar; (*defendant*) poner en libertad // n ['dıstʃa:dʒ] (ELEC) descarga; (*dismissal*) despedida; (*of duty*) desempeño; (*of debt*) pago, descargo.

disciple [dı'saıpl] n discípulo.

discipline ['dısıplın] n disciplina // vt disciplinar.

disclaim [dıs'kleım] vt negar.

disclose [dıs'kləuz] vt revelar; **disclosure** [-'kləuʒə*] n revelación f.

disco ['dıskəu] n abbr of **discothèque.**

discoloured [dıs'kʌləd] a descolorado.

discomfort [dıs'kʌmfət] n incomodidad f; (*unease*) inquietud f; (*physical*) malestar m.

disconcert [dıskən'sɔ:t] vt desconcertar.

disconnect [dıskə'nɛkt] vt (*gen*) separar; (ELEC *etc*) desconectar.

discontent [dıskən'tɛnt] n descontento; ~**ed** a descontento.

discontinue [dıskən'tınju:] vt interrumpir; (*payments*) suspender.

discord ['dıskɔ:d] n discordia; (MUS) disonancia; ~**ant** [dıs'kɔ:dənt] a disonante.

discothèque ['dıskəutɛk] n discoteca.

discount ['dıskaunt] n descuento // vt [dıs-'kaunt] descontar.

discourage [dıs'kʌrıdʒ] vt desalentar; (*oppose*) oponerse a; **discouraging** a desalentador(a).

discourteous [dıs'kɔ:tıəs] a descortés.

discover [dıs'kʌvə*] vt descubrir; ~**y** n descubrimiento.

discredit [dıs'krɛdıt] vt desacreditar.

discreet [dı'skri:t] a (*tactful*) discreto; (*careful*) circunspecto, prudente; ~**ly** ad discretamente.

discrepancy [dı'skrɛpənsı] n (*difference*) diferencia; (*disagreement*) discrepancia.

discretion [dı'skrɛʃən] n (*tact*) discreción f; (*care*) prudencia, circunspección f.

discriminate [dɪ'skrɪmɪneɪt] vi: **to ~ between** distinguir entre; **to ~ against** discriminar contra; **discriminating** a perspicaz; **discrimination** [-'neɪʃən] n (discernment) perspicacia; (bias) discriminación f.

discuss [dɪ'skʌs] vt (gen) discutir; (a theme) tratar; **~ion** [dɪ'skʌʃən] n discusión f.

disdain [dɪs'deɪn] n desdén m // vt desdeñar.

disease [dɪ'ziːz] n enfermedad f.

disembark [dɪsɪm'bɑːk] vt, vi desembarcar.

disengage [dɪsɪn'geɪdʒ] vt soltar; (clutch) desembragar.

disentangle [dɪsɪn'tæŋgl] vt desenredar.

disfigure [dɪs'fɪgə*] vt desfigurar.

disgrace [dɪs'greɪs] n ignominia; (downfall) caída; (shame) vergüenza, escándalo // vt deshonrar; **~ful** a vergonzoso; (behaviour) escandaloso.

disgruntled [dɪs'grʌntld] a disgustado, malhumorado.

disguise [dɪs'gaɪz] n disfraz m // vt disfrazar; **in ~** disfrazado.

disgust [dɪs'gʌst] n repugnancia // vt repugnar, dar asco a; **~ing** a repugnante, asqueroso.

dish [dɪʃ] n (gen) plato; **to do** or **wash the ~es** fregar los platos; **to ~ up** vt servir; **to ~ out** vt repartir; **~cloth** n paño de cocina, bayeta.

dishearten [dɪs'hɑːtn] vt desalentar.

dishevelled [dɪ'ʃevəld] a despeinado, desmelenado.

dishonest [dɪs'ɔnɪst] a (person) poco honrado, tramposo; (means) fraudulento; **~y** n falta de honradez.

dishonour [dɪs'ɔnə*] n deshonra; **~able** a deshonroso.

dishwasher ['dɪʃwɔʃə*] n lavaplatos m inv; (person) friegaplatos m/f inv.

disillusion [dɪsɪ'luːʒən] vt desilusionar.

disinfect [dɪsɪn'fɛkt] vt desinfectar; **~ant** n desinfectante m.

disintegrate [dɪs'ɪntɪgreɪt] vi disgregarse, desintegrarse.

disinterested [dɪs'ɪntrəstɪd] a desinteresado.

disjointed [dɪs'dʒɔɪntɪd] a inconexo.

disk [dɪsk] n = **disc.**

dislike [dɪs'laɪk] n antipatía, aversión f // vt tener antipatía a.

dislocate ['dɪsləkeɪt] vt dislocar.

dislodge [dɪs'lɔdʒ] vt sacar; (enemy) desalojar.

disloyal [dɪs'lɔɪəl] a desleal.

dismal ['dɪzml] a (dark) sombrío; (depressing) triste; (depressed) abatido; (very bad) fatal.

dismantle [dɪs'mæntl] vt desmontar, desarmar.

dismay [dɪs'meɪ] n consternación f // vt consternar.

dismiss [dɪs'mɪs] vt (worker) despedir;

(official) destituir; (idea, LAW) rechazar; (possibility) descartar // vi (MIL) romper filas; **~al** n despedida; destitución f.

dismount [dɪs'maunt] vi apearse.

disobedience [dɪsə'biːdɪəns] n desobediencia; **disobedient** [-ənt] a desobediente.

disobey [dɪsə'beɪ] vt desobedecer.

disorder [dɪs'ɔːdə*] n desorden m; (rioting) disturbio; (MED) trastorno; (disease) enfermedad f; **~ly** a (untidy) desordenado; (meeting) alborotado; (conduct) escandaloso.

disorganized [dɪs'ɔːgənaɪzd] a desorganizado.

disorientated [dɪs'ɔːrɪenteɪtəd] a desorientado.

disown [dɪs'əun] vt desconocer.

disparaging [dɪs'pærɪdʒɪŋ] a despreciativo.

disparity [dɪs'pærɪtɪ] n disparidad f.

dispatch [dɪs'pætʃ] vt enviar; (kill) despachar // n (sending) envío; (speed) prontitud f; (PRESS) informe m; (MIL) parte m.

dispel [dɪs'pɛl] vt disipar, dispersar.

dispensary [dɪs'pɛnsərɪ] n dispensario, farmacia.

dispense [dɪs'pɛns] vt dispensar, repartir; **to ~ with** vt fus prescindir de; **dispenser** n (container) distribuidor m automático; **dispensing chemist** n farmacéutico.

dispersal [dɪs'pəːsl] n dispersión f; **disperse** [-'pəːs] vt dispersar // vi dispersarse.

displace [dɪs'pleɪs] vt (shift) sacar de su sitio; **~d person** n (POL) desplazado/a; **~ment** n cambio de sitio.

display [dɪs'pleɪ] n (exhibition) exposición f; (MIL) alarde m; (of feeling) manifestación f; (pej) aparato, pompa // vt exponer; manifestar; (ostentatiously) lucir.

displease [dɪs'pliːz] vt (offend) ofender; (annoy) enojar, enfadar; (be unpleasant to) desagradar; **~d with** disgustado con; **displeasure** [-'plɛʒə*] n disgusto.

disposable [dɪs'pəuzəbl] a para (usar y) tirar.

disposal [dɪs'pəuzl] n (sale) venta; (of house) traspaso; (arrangement) colocación f; (of rubbish) destrucción f; **at one's ~** a disposición de uno.

dispose [dɪs'pəuz] vt: **to ~ of** (time, money) disponer de; (unwanted goods) deshacerse de; (throw away) tirar; **~d to do** dispuesto a hacer; **disposition** [-'zɪʃən] n disposición f.

disproportionate [dɪsprə'pɔːʃənət] a desproporcionado.

disprove [dɪs'pruːv] vt refutar.

dispute [dɪs'pjuːt] n disputa; (verbal) discusión f; (also: **industrial ~**) conflicto (laboral) // vt (argue) disputar; (question) cuestionar.

disqualification [dɪskwɔlɪfɪ'keɪʃən] n

inhabilitación f; (SPORT, from driving) descalificación f.

disqualify [dɪs'kwɔlɪfaɪ] vt (SPORT) descalificar; **to ~ sb for sth/from doing sth** inhabilitar a alguien para algo/hacer algo.

disregard [dɪsrɪ'gɑːd] vt desatender; (ignore) no hacer caso de.

disrepair [dɪsrɪ'pɛə*] n: **to fall into ~** desmoronarse.

disreputable [dɪs'rɛpjutəbl] a (person) de mala fama; (behaviour) vergonzoso.

disrespectful [dɪsrɪ'spɛktful] a irrespetuoso.

disrupt [dɪs'rʌpt] vt (plans) desbaratar; (conversation) interrumpir; **~ion** [-'rʌpʃən] n trastorno; desbaratamiento; interrupción f.

dissatisfaction [dɪssætɪs'fækʃən] n disgusto, descontento; **dissatisfied** [-'sætɪsfaɪd] a insatisfecho.

dissect [dɪ'sɛkt] vt disecar.

dissent [dɪ'sɛnt] n disensión f.

disservice [dɪs'səːvɪs] n: **to do sb a ~** perjudicar a alguien.

dissident ['dɪsɪdnt] a, n disidente m/f.

dissipate ['dɪsɪpeɪt] vt disipar; (waste) desperdiciar.

dissociate [dɪ'səuʃɪeɪt] vt disociar.

dissolute ['dɪsəluːt] a disoluto.

dissolve [dɪ'zɔlv] vt disolver // vi disolverse.

dissuade [dɪ'sweɪd] vt: **to ~ sb (from)** disuadir a alguien (de).

distance ['dɪstns] n distancia; **in the ~** a lo lejos.

distant ['dɪstnt] a lejano; (manner) reservado, frío.

distaste [dɪs'teɪst] n repugnancia; **~ful** a repugnante, desagradable.

distil [dɪs'tɪl] vt destilar; **~lery** n destilería.

distinct [dɪs'tɪŋkt] a (different) distinto; (clear) claro; (unmistakeable) inequívoco; **as ~ from** a diferencia de; **~ion** [dɪs-'tɪŋkʃən] n distinción f; (in exam) sobresaliente m; **~ive** a distintivo; **~ly** ad claramente.

distinguish [dɪs'tɪŋgwɪʃ] vt distinguir; **~ed** a (eminent) distinguido; **~ing** a (feature) distintivo.

distort [dɪs'tɔːt] vt torcer, retorcer; **~ion** [dɪs'tɔːʃən] n deformación f; (of sound) distorsión f.

distract [dɪs'trækt] vt distraer; (attention) apartar; (bewilder) aturdir; **~ed** a distraído; **~ion** [dɪs'trækʃən] n distracción f; (confusion) aturdimiento; (amusement) diversión f.

distraught [dɪs'trɔːt] a turbado, enloquecido.

distress [dɪs'trɛs] n (anguish) angustia; (misfortune) desgracia; (want) miseria; (pain) dolor m; (danger) peligro // vt (cause anguish) apenar, afligir; (pain) doler; **~ing** a doloroso; **~ signal** n señal f de socorro.

distribute [dɪs'trɪbjuːt] vt (gen) distribuir; (share out) repartir; **distribution** [-'bjuːʃən] n distribución f; **distributor** n (AUT) distribuidor m; (COMM) distribuidora.

district ['dɪstrɪkt] n (of country) zona, región f; (of town) barrio; (ADMIN) distrito; **~ attorney** n (US) fiscal m/f; **~ nurse** n (Brit) enfermera que asiste a domicilio.

distrust [dɪs'trʌst] n desconfianza // vt desconfiar de.

disturb [dɪs'təːb] vt (gen) perturbar; (bother) molestar; (interrupt) interrumpir; (upset) trastornar; (disorganize) desordenar; **~ance** n (gen) perturbación f; (political etc) disturbio; (violence) alboroto; (of mind) trastorno; **~ing** a inquietante, perturbador(a).

disuse [dɪs'juːs] n: **to fall into ~** caer en desuso.

disused [dɪs'juːzd] a abandonado.

ditch [dɪtʃ] n zanja; (irrigation ~) acequia // vt (col) deshacerse de.

dither ['dɪðə*] vi vacilar.

ditto ['dɪtəu] ad ídem, lo mismo.

divan [dɪ'væn] n diván m.

dive [daɪv] n (from board) salto; (underwater) buceo; (of submarine) sumersión f; (AVIAT) picada // vi saltar; bucear; sumergirse; picar; **diver** n (SPORT) saltador/a m/f; (underwater) buzo.

diverge [daɪ'vəːdʒ] vi divergir.

diverse [daɪ'vəːs] a diversos(as), varios(as).

diversify [daɪ'vəːsɪfaɪ] vt diversificar.

diversion [daɪ'vəːʃən] n (AUT) desviación f; (distraction, MIL) diversión f.

diversity [daɪ'vəːsɪtɪ] n diversidad f.

divert [daɪ'vəːt] vt (turn aside) desviar; (amuse) divertir.

divest [daɪ'vɛst] vt: **to ~ sb of sth** despojar a alguien de algo.

divide [dɪ'vaɪd] vt dividir; (separate) separar // vi dividirse; (road) bifurcarse.

dividend ['dɪvɪdɛnd] n dividendo; (fig) beneficio.

divine [dɪ'vaɪn] a divino.

diving ['daɪvɪŋ] n (SPORT) salto; (underwater) buceo; **~ board** n trampolín m; **~ suit** n escafandra.

divinity [dɪ'vɪnɪtɪ] n divinidad f; (SCOL) teología.

division [dɪ'vɪʒən] n división f; (sharing out) repartimiento; (disagreement) discordia; (POL) votación f.

divorce [dɪ'vɔːs] n divorcio // vt divorciarse de; **~d** a divorciado; **divorcee** [-'siː] n divorciado/a.

divulge [daɪ'vʌldʒ] vt divulgar, revelar.

D.I.Y. a, n abbr of **do-it-yourself.**

dizziness ['dɪzɪnɪs] n vértigo.

dizzy ['dɪzɪ] a (person) mareado; (height) vertiginoso; **to feel ~** marearse, estar mareado.

DJ n abbr of **disc jockey.**

do [duː] pt **did**, pp **done** vt, vi (gen) hacer; (speed) ir a; (THEATRE) representar // n (*col*) fiesta; **he didn't laugh** no se rió; **she swims better than I** ~ nada mejor que yo; **he laughed, didn't he?** se rió ¿no?; **that will** ~**!** ¡basta!; **to make** ~ **with** contentarse con; ~ **you agree?** ¿está Usted de acuerdo?; **to** ~ **one's hair** (*comb*) peinarse; (*style*) arreglarse el pelo; **will it** ~**?** ¿sirve?, ¿conviene?; **to** ~ **well** prosperar, tener éxito; **to** ~ **without sth** prescindir de algo; **to** ~ **away with** *vt fus* (*kill*) exterminar; (*suppress*) suprimir; **to** ~ **up** *vt* (*laces*) liar, atar; (*room*) renovar.

docile ['dousaıl] *a* dócil.

dock [dɔk] *n* (NAUT) muelle *m*; (LAW) banquillo (de los acusados); ~**s** *npl* muelles *mpl*, puerto // *vi* (*arrive*) llegar; (*enter* ~) atracar el muelle; (*pay etc*) rebajar; ~**er** *n* trabajador *m* portuario, estibador *m*; ~**yard** *n* astillero.

doctor ['dɔktə*] *n* médico; (*Ph.D. etc*) doctor/a *m/f* // *vt* (*fig*) arreglar, falsificar; (*drink etc*) adulterar.

doctrine ['dɔktrın] *n* doctrina.

document ['dɔkjumənt] *n* documento; ~**ary** [-'mɛntərı] *a* documental // *n* documental *m*; ~**ation** [-'teıʃən] *n* documentación *f*.

dodge [dɔdʒ] *n* (*of body*) regate *m*; (*fig*) truco // *vt* (*gen*) evadir; (*blow*) esquivar.

dodgems ['dɔdʒəmz] *npl* coches *mpl* de choque.

dog [dɔg] *n* perro // *vt* seguir los pasos de; ~ **biscuits** *npl* galletas *fpl* de perro; ~ **collar** *n* collar *m* de perro; (*fig*) cuello de cura.

dogged ['dɔgıd] *a* tenaz, obstinado.

dogma ['dɔgmə] *n* dogma *m*; ~**tic** [-'mætık] *a* dogmático.

doings ['duıŋz] *npl* (*events*) sucesos *mpl*; (*acts*) hechos *mpl*.

do-it-yourself [du:ıtjɔ:'sɛlf] *n* bricolaje *m*.

doldrums ['dɔldrəmz] *npl*: **to be in the** ~ (*person*) estar abatido; (*business*) estar encalmado.

dole [dəul] *n* (*Brit*) (*payment*) subsidio de paro; **on the** ~ parado; **to** ~ **out** *vt* repartir.

doleful ['dəulful] *a* triste, lúgubre.

doll [dɔl] *n* muñeca; **to** ~ **o.s. up** ataviarse.

dollar ['dɔlə*] *n* dólar *m*.

dolphin ['dɔlfın] *n* delfín *m*.

domain [də'meın] *n* campo, competencia; (*empire*) dominio.

dome [dəum] *n* (ARCH) cúpula; (*shape*) bóveda.

domestic [də'mɛstık] *a* (*gen*) doméstico; (*national*) nacional; (*home-loving*) hogareño; (*internal: trade*) interior; (: *strife*) interno; ~**ated** *a* domesticado; (*home-loving*) casero, hogareño.

dominant ['dɔmınənt] *a* dominante.

dominate ['dɔmıneıt] *vt* dominar; **domination** [-'neıʃən] *n* dominación *f*.

domineering [dɔmı'nıərıŋ] *a* dominante.

dominion [də'mınıən] *n* dominio.

domino ['dɔmınəu], *pl* ~**es** *n* ficha de dominó; ~**es** *n* (*game*) dominó.

donate [də'neıt] *vt* donar; **donation** [də'neıʃən] *n* donativo.

done [dʌn] *pp of* **do.**

donkey ['dɔŋkı] *n* burro.

donor ['dəunə*] *n* donante *m/f*.

don't [dəunt] = **do not.**

doom [du:m] *n* (*fate*) suerte *f*; (*death*) muerte *f* // *vt*: **to be** ~**ed to failure** ser condenado al fracaso.

door [dɔ:*] *n* puerta; (*entry*) entrada; **next** ~ en la casa de al lado; ~ **handle** *n* tirador *m*; (*of car*) manija; ~ **knocker** *n* aldaba; ~**man** *n* (*in hotel*) portero; ~**mat** *n* felpudo, estera; ~**step** *n* peldaño.

dope [dəup] *n* (*col: person*) imbécil *m/f* // *vt* (*horse etc*) drogar.

dopey ['dəupı] *a* (*dizzy*) mareado.

dormant ['dɔ:mənt] *a* inactivo; (*latent*) latente.

dormitory ['dɔ:mıtrı] *n* dormitorio.

dormouse ['dɔ:maus], *pl* -**mice** [-maıs] *n* lirón *m*.

dosage ['dəusıdʒ] *n* dósis *f inv.*

dose [dəus] *n* dósis *f inv* // *vt*: **to** ~ **o.s.** medicinarse.

doss house ['dɔss-] *n* pensión *f* de mala muerte.

dot [dɔt] *n* punto; ~**ted with** salpicado de; **on the** ~ en punto.

dote [dəut]: **to** ~ **on** *vt fus* adorar, idolatrar.

double ['dʌbl] *a* doble // *ad* (*twice*): **to cost** ~ costar el doble // *n* (*gen*) doble *m* // *vt* doblar; (*efforts*) redoblar // *vi* doblarse; **at the** ~ co₁ riendo; ~**s** *n* (TENNIS) juego de dobles; ~ **bass** *n* contrabajo; ~ **bed** *n* cama matrimonial; ~ **bend** *n* doble curva; ~~**breasted** *a* cruzado; ~~**cross** *vt* (*trick*) engañar; (*betray*) traicionar; ~~**decker** *n* autobús *m* de dos pisos; ~ **room** *n* cuarto para dos; **doubly** *ad* doblemente.

doubt [daut] *n* duda // *vt* dudar; (*suspect*) dudar de; **to** ~ **that** dudar que; **there is no** ~ **that** no cabe duda de que; ~**ful** *a* dudoso; (*person*) sospechoso; ~**less** *ad* sin duda.

dough [dəu] *n* masa, pasta; ~**nut** *n* buñuelo.

dove [dʌv] *n* paloma; ~**tail** *vi* (*fig*) encajar.

dowdy ['daudı] *a* desaliñado; (*inelegant*) poco elegante.

down [daun] *n* (*fluff*) pelusa; (*feathers*) plumón *m*, flojel *m* // *ad* (~**wards**) abajo, hacia abajo; (*on the ground*) por/en tierra // *prep* abajo // *vt* (*col: drink*) beberse; (: *food*) devorar; **the D**~**s** zona de colinas del sur de Inglaterra; ~ **with X!** ¡abajo X!; ~~**at-heel** *a* venido a menos; (*appearance*) desaliñado; ~**cast** *a* abatido; ~**fall** *n* caída, ruina; ~**hearted** *a* desanimado; ~**hill** *ad*: **to go** ~**hill** ir cuesta abajo; ~ **payment** *n* enganche *m*, pago al contado; ~**pour** n aguacero; ~**right** a (clear) manifiesto; (out-and-out) terminante, definitivo; ~**stairs** ad (below) (en la casa) de abajo; (~wards) escaleras abajo; ~**stream** ad aguas o río abajo; ~**-to-earth** a práctico; ~**town** ad en el centro de la ciudad; ~**ward** a, ad, ~**wards** ad hacia abajo.

dowry ['daurɪ] n dote f.

doz. abbr of **dozen.**

doze [dəuz] vi dormitar; **to ~ off** vi quedarse medio dormido.

dozen ['dʌzn] n docena.

Dr. abbr of **doctor; drive.**

drab [dræb] a gris, monótono.

draft [drɑːft] n (first copy) borrador m; (COMM) giro; (US: call-up) quinta // vt (plan) redactar; (send) mandar; (conscript) quintar; (write roughly) hacer un borrador de; see also **draught.**

drag [dræg] vt arrastrar; (river) dragar, rastrear // vi arrastrarse por el suelo // n (col) lata; **to ~ on** vi ser interminable.

dragonfly ['drægənflaɪ] n libélula.

drain [dreɪn] n desaguadero; (in street) sumidero; (source of loss) desagüe m; (loss) pérdida; (on resources) sumidero // vt (land, marshes) desaguar; (MED) drenar; (reservoir) desecar; (fig) agotar // vi escurrirse; ~**age** n (act) desagüe m; (MED, AGR) drenaje m; (sewage) alcantarillado; ~**ing board,** ~**board** (US) n escurridera, escurridor m; ~**pipe** n tubo de desagüe.

dram [dræm] n (drink) trago.

drama ['drɑːmə] n (art) teatro; (play) drama m; ~**tic** [drə'mætɪk] a dramático; ~**tist** ['dræmətɪst] n dramaturgo.

drank [dræŋk] pt of **drink.**

drape [dreɪp] vt cubrir; ~**s** npl (US) cortinas fpl; **draper** n pañero.

drastic ['dræstɪk] a (measure) severo; (change) radical; (forceful) enérgico.

draught [drɑːft] n (of air) corriente f; (drink) trago; (NAUT) calado; ~**s** n juego de damas; **on ~** (beer) de barril; ~**board** n tablero de damas.

draughtsman ['drɑːftsmən] n proyectista m, delineante m.

draw [drɔː] pt **drew,** pp **drawn** vt (pull) tirar; (take out) sacar; (attract) atraer; (picture) dibujar; (money) retirar // vi (SPORT) empatar // n (SPORT) empate m; (lottery) sorteo; (attraction) atracción f; **to ~ near** vi acercarse; **to ~ out** vi (lengthen) alargar; **to ~ up** vi (stop) pararse // vt (document) redactar; ~**back** n inconveniente m, desventaja; ~**bridge** n puente m levadizo.

drawer [drɔː*] n cajón m.

drawing ['drɔːɪŋ] n dibujo; ~ **board** n tablero (de dibujante); ~ **pin** n chinche m; ~ **room** n salón m.

drawl [drɔːl] n habla lenta y cansina.

drawn [drɔːn] pp of **draw.**

dread [drɛd] n pavor m, terror m // vt

temer, tener miedo o pavor a; ~**ful** a espantoso.

dream [driːm] n sueño // vt, vi, pt, pp **dreamed** or **dreamt** [drɛmt] soñar; ~**er** n soñador/a m/f; ~**y** a (distracted) soñador(a), distraído; (music) de sueño.

dreary ['drɪərɪ] a monótono, aburrido.

dredge [drɛdʒ] vt dragar; **dredger** n (ship) draga; (also: **sugar dredger**) espolvoreador m.

dregs [drɛgz] npl heces fpl.

drench [drɛntʃ] vt empapar; **to get** ~**ed** mojarse hasta los huesos.

dress [drɛs] n vestido; (clothing) ropa // vt vestir; (wound) vendar; (CULIN) aliñar // vi vestirse; **to ~ up** vi vestirse de etiqueta; (in fancy dress) disfrazarse; ~ **circle** n principal m; ~**er** n (furniture) aparador m; (: US) cómoda con espejo; ~**ing** n (MED) vendaje m; (CULIN) aliño; ~**ing gown** n bata; ~**ing room** n (THEATRE) camarín m; (SPORT) vestidor m; ~**ing table** n tocador m; ~**maker** n modista, costurera; ~**making** n costura; ~ **rehearsal** n ensayo general; ~ **shirt** n camisa de frac.

drew [druː] pt of **draw.**

dribble ['drɪbl] vi gotear, caer gota a gota; (baby) babear // vt (ball) regatear.

dried [draɪd] a (gen) seco; (fruit) paso; (milk) en polvo.

drift [drɪft] n (of current etc) velocidad f; (of sand etc) montón m; (distance off course) deriva; (meaning) significado // vi (boat) ir a la deriva; (sand, snow) amontonarse; ~**wood** n madera de deriva.

drill [drɪl] n taladro; (bit) broca; (of dentist) fresa; (for mining etc) perforadora, barrena; (MIL) instrucción f // vt perforar, taladrar // vi (for oil) perforar.

drink [drɪŋk] n bebida // vt, vi, pt **drank,** pp **drunk** beber; **to have a ~** tomar; ~**er** n bebedor/a m/f; ~**ing water** n agua potable.

drip [drɪp] n (act) goteo; (one ~) gota; (MED) gota a gota m // vi gotear, caer gota a gota; ~**-dry** a (shirt) de lava y pon; ~**ping** n pringue m; ~**ping wet** a calado.

drive [draɪv] n paseo (en coche); (journey) viaje m; (also: ~**way**) entrada; (energy) energía, vigor m; (PSYCH) impulso; (SPORT) ataque m // (vb: pt **drove,** pp **driven** ['drɪvn]) vt (car) conducir; (urge) hacer trabajar; (by power) mover; (nail) clavar; (push) empujar; (TECH: motor) impulsar // vi (AUT: at controls) conducir; (: travel) pasearse en coche; **left-/right-hand ~** conducción f a la izquierda/derecha.

driver ['draɪvə*] n conductor m; (of taxi, bus) chofer m; ~**'s license** n (US) permiso de conducir.

driving ['draɪvɪŋ] n el conducir, automovilismo; ~ **instructor** n instructor m de conducción; ~ **lesson** n clase f de conducción; ~ **licence** n (Brit) permiso de conducir; ~ **mirror** *n* retrovisor *m*; ~ **school** *n* autoescuela; ~ **test** *n* examen *m* de conducción.

drizzle ['drɪzl] *n* llovizna // *vi* lloviznar.

drone [drəun] *n* zumbido; (*male bee*) zángano.

drool [dru:l] *vi* babear; **to** ~ **over** *sth* extasiarse ante algo.

droop [dru:p] *vi* colgar; (*fig*) decaer, desanimarse.

drop [drɔp] *n* (*of water*) gota; (*lessening*) baja; (*fall*) caída; (*of cliff*) pendiente *m*, declive *m* // *vt* (*allow to fall*) dejar caer; (*voice, eyes, price*) bajar; (*set down from car*) dejar; (*omit*) omitir // *vi* caer; (*price, temperature*) bajar; (*wind*) amainar; **to** ~ **off** *vi* (*sleep*) dormirse // *vt* (*passenger*) bajar; **to** ~ **out** *vi* (*withdraw*) retirarse; ~**-out** *n* marginado; ~**per** *n* cuentagotas *m inv*; ~**pings** *npl* excremento *sg* (de animal).

drought [draut] *n* sequía.

drove [drəuv] *pt of* **drive**.

drown [draun] *vt* ahogar // *vi* ahogarse.

drowsy ['drauzɪ] *a* soñoliento; **to be** ~ tener sueño.

drudgery ['drʌdʒərɪ] *n* trabajo monótono.

drug [drʌg] *n* medicamento; (*narcotic*) droga // *vt* drogar; ~ **addict** *n* drogadicto/a; ~**gist** *n* (*US*) farmacéutico; ~**store** *n* (*US*) farmacia.

drum [drʌm] *n* tambor *m*; (*large*) bombo; (*for oil, petrol*) bidón *m*; ~**s** *npl* batería *sg* // *vi* tocar el tambor; (*with fingers*) tamborilear; ~**mer** *n* tambor *m*; ~**stick** *n* (*MUS*) palillo; (*of chicken*) muslo.

drunk [drʌŋk] *pp of* **drink** // *a* borracho // *n* (*also*: ~**ard**) borracho/a; ~**en** *a* borracho; ~**enness** *n* embriaguez *f*.

dry [draɪ] *a* seco; (*day*) sin lluvia; (*climate*) árido, seco // *vt* secar; (*tears*) enjugarse // *vi* secarse; **to** ~ **up** *vi* agotarse; (*in speech*) atascarse; ~**-cleaner's** *n* tintorería; ~**-cleaning** *n* lavado en seco; ~**er** *n* lavadora; ~**ness** *n* sequedad *f*; ~ **rot** *n* putrefacción *f* fungoide.

dual ['djuəl] *a* doble; ~**-control** *a* de doble mando; ~ **nationality** *n* doble nacionalidad *f*; ~**-purpose** *a* de doble uso.

dubbed [dʌbd] *a* (*CINEMA*) doblado.

dubious ['dju:bɪəs] *a* dudoso; (*reputation, company*) sospechoso.

duchess ['dʌtʃɪs] *n* duquesa.

duck [dʌk] *n* pato // *vi* agacharse; ~**ling** *n* patito.

duct [dʌkt] *n* conducto, canal *m*.

dud [dʌd] *n* (*shell*) obús *m* que no estalla; (*object, tool*): **it's a** ~ es una filfa // *a*: ~ **cheque** cheque *m* sin fondos.

due [dju:] *a* (*proper*) debido; (*expected*) esperado; (*fitting*) conveniente, oportuno // *n* (*debt*) deuda; (*desert*) lo que merece uno // *ad*: ~ **north** derecho al norte; ~**s** *npl* (*for club, union*) cuota *sg*; (*in harbour*) derechos *mpl*; **in** ~ **course** a su debido tiempo; ~ **to** debido a.

duel ['djuəl] *n* duelo.

duet [dju:'ɛt] *n* dúo.

dug [dʌg] *pt, pp of* **dig**.

duke [dju:k] *n* duque *m*.

dull [dʌl] *a* (*light*) apagado; (*slow*) torpe; (*boring*) pesado; (*sound, pain*) sordo; (*weather, day*) gris // *vt* (*pain, grief*) aliviar; (*mind, senses*) entorpecer.

duly ['dju:lɪ] *ad* debidamente; (*on time*) a su debido tiempo.

dumb [dʌm] *a* mudo; (*stupid*) estúpido; ~**founded** [dʌm'faundɪd] *a* pasmado.

dummy ['dʌmɪ] *n* (*tailor's model*) maniquí *m*; (*for baby*) chupete *m* // *a* falso, postizo.

dump [dʌmp] *n* (*heap*) montón *m*; (*place*) basurero, vaciadero; (*col*) casucha; (*MIL*) depósito // *vt* (*put down*) verter, vaciar; (*get rid of*) deshacerse de; (*goods*) inundar el mercado con; ~**ing** *n* (*ECON*) dumping *m*; (*of rubbish*): 'no ~**ing**' 'prohibido verter basura'.

dumpling ['dʌmplɪŋ] *n* bola de masa hervida.

dunce [dʌns] *n* zopenco.

dune [dju:n] *n* duna.

dung [dʌŋ] *n* estiércol *m*.

dungarees [dʌŋgə'ri:z] *npl* mono *sg*.

dungeon ['dʌndʒən] *n* calabozo.

dupe [dju:p] *n* (*victim*) víctima // *vt* engañar.

duplicate ['dju:plɪkət] *n* duplicado // *vt* ['dju:plɪkeɪt] duplicar; (*on machine*) multicopiar; **in** ~ por duplicado; **duplicator** *n* multicopista *m*.

durable ['djuərəbl] *a* duradero.

duration [djuə'reɪʃən] *n* duración *f*.

duress [djuə'rɛs] *n*: **under** ~ por compulsión.

during ['djuərɪŋ] *prep* durante.

dusk [dʌsk] *n* crepúsculo, anochecer *m*.

dust [dʌst] *n* polvo // *vt* (*furniture*) desempolvorar; (*cake etc*): **to** ~ **with** espolvorear de; ~**bin** *n* (*Brit*) cubo de la basura; ~**er** *n* paño, trapo, bayeta; (*feather* ~) plumero; ~ **jacket** *n* sobrecubierta; ~**man** *n* (*Brit*) basurero; ~**y** *a* polvoriento.

Dutch [dʌtʃ] *a* holandés(esa) // *n* (*LING*) holandés *m*; ~**man/woman** *n* holandés/esa *m/f*.

duty ['dju:tɪ] *n* deber *m*; (*tax*) derechos *mpl* de aduana; **on** ~ de servicio; (*at night etc*) de guardia; **off** ~ libre (de servicio); ~**-free** *a* libre de derechos de aduana.

dwarf [dwɔ:f], *pl* **dwarves** [dwɔ:vz] *n* enano // *vt* empequeñecer.

dwell [dwɛl], *pt, pp* **dwelt** [dwɛlt] *vi* morar; **to** ~ **on** *vt fus* explayarse en; ~**ing** *n* vivienda.

dwindle ['dwɪndl] *vi* menguar, disminuir.

dye [daɪ] *n* tinte *m* // *vt* teñir.

dying ['daɪɪŋ] *a* moribundo, agonizante; (*moments*) final; (*words*) último.

dynamic [daɪ'næmɪk] *a* dinámico; ~**s** *n, npl* dinámica *sg*.

dynamite ['daɪnəmaɪt] *n* dinamita.

dynamo ['daɪnəməu] n dinamo f.
dynasty ['dɪnəstɪ] n dinastía.

E

each [i:tʃ] det cada inv // pron cada uno; ~ **other** el uno al otro; **they hate ~ other** se odian (entre ellos o mutuamente); **they have 2 books** ~ tiene 2 libros por persona.

eager ['i:gə*] a (gen) impaciente; (hopeful) ilusionado; (ambitious) ambicioso; **to be ~ to do sth** ansiar hacer algo, impacientarse por hacer algo; **to be ~ for** ansiar, anhelar.

eagle ['i:gl] n águila.

ear [ɪə*] n oreja; (MUS) oído; (of corn) espiga; ~**ache** n dolor m de oídos; ~**drum** n tímpano.

earl [ə:l] n conde m.

early ['ə:lɪ] ad (gen) temprano; (before time) con tiempo, con anticipación // a (gen) temprano; (reply) pronto; (first) primero; (work) juvenil; **have an ~ night** acuéstate temprano; **in the ~ or ~ in the spring/19th century** a principios de primavera/del siglo diez y nueve; **as ~ as possible** cuánto antes, lo más pronto posible.

earmark ['ɪəmɑ:k] vt reservar (for para), destinar (for a).

earn [ə:n] vt (gen) ganar; (salary) percibir; (interest) devengar; (praise) merecerse.

earnest ['ə:nɪst] a serio, formal; **in ~** ad en serio.

earnings ['ə:nɪŋz] npl (personal) sueldo, ingresos mpl; (company) ganancias fpl.

ear: ~phones npl auriculares mpl; ~**ring** n pendiente m, arete m; ~**shot** n: **within ~shot** al alcance del oído.

earth [ə:θ] n (gen) tierra; (ELEC) cable m de toma de tierra // vt (ELEC) conectar a tierra; ~**enware** n loza de barro; ~**quake** n terremoto; ~**y** a (fig: vulgar) grosero; (: sensual) sensual.

earwig ['ɪəwɪg] n tijereta.

ease [i:z] n (gen) facilidad f; (relief) alivio; (calm) tranquilidad f; (relaxed state) comodidad f // vt facilitar; aliviar; tranquilizar; (loosen) soltar; (relieve: pressure) aflojar; (weight) aligerar; (help pass): **to ~ sth in/out** meter/sacar con cuidado; **at ~!** (MIL) ¡descanso!; **to ~ off** or **up** vi (gen) suavizarse; (at work) dejar de trabajar tanto; (wind) amainar; (rain) moderarse.

easel ['i:zl] n caballete m.

east [i:st] n este m, oriente m // a del este, oriental // ad al este, hacia el este; **the E~** el Oriente.

Easter ['i:stə*] n Pascua (de Resurrección).

easterly ['i:stəlɪ] a (to the east) al este; (from the east) del este.

eastern ['i:stən] a del este, oriental.

East Germany n Alemania Oriental.

eastward(s) ['i:stwəd(z)] ad hacia el este.

easy ['i:zɪ] a (gen) fácil; (simple) sencillo; (slow) lento, pausado; (comfortable) holgado, cómodo; (relaxed) natural, llano // ad: **to take it** or **things ~** (not worry) tomarlo con calma; (go slowly) ir despacio; (rest) descansar; ~ **chair** n sillón m; ~ **going** a acomodadizo.

eat [i:t] pt ate, pp eaten ['i:tn] vt (gen) comer; (supper) cenar; **to ~ into, to ~ away at** vt fus corroer; ~**able** a comestible.

eau de Cologne [əudəkə'ləun] n (agua de) Colonia.

eaves [i:vz] npl alero sg.

eavesdrop ['i:vzdrɔp] vi escuchar a escondidas (on sb a uno).

ebb [ɛb] n reflujo // vi bajar; (fig: also: ~ away) decaer; ~ **tide** n marea menguante.

ebony ['ɛbənɪ] n ébano.

eccentric [ɪk'sɛntrɪk] a, n excéntrico/a.

ecclesiastical [ɪkli:zɪ'æstɪkəl] a eclesiástico.

echo ['ɛkəu], pl ~**es** n eco m // vt (sound) repetir // vi resonar, hacer eco.

eclipse [ɪ'klɪps] n eclipse m // vt eclipsar.

ecology [ɪ'kɔlədʒɪ] n ecología.

economic [i:kə'nɔmɪk] a económico; (business etc) rentable; ~**al** a económico; ~**s** n (la) economía; **economist** [ɪ'kɔnəmɪst] n economista m/f.

economize [ɪ'kɔnəmaɪz] vi economizar, ahorrar.

economy [ɪ'kɔnəmɪ] n economía.

ecstasy ['ɛkstəsɪ] n éxtasis m; **ecstatic** [-'tætɪk] a extático.

ecumenical [i:kju'mɛnɪkl] a ecuménico.

eczema ['ɛksɪmə] n eczema m.

edge [ɛdʒ] n (of knife etc) filo; (of object) borde m; (of lake etc) orilla // vt (SEWING) ribetear; **on ~** (fig) = **edgy; to ~ away from** alejarse poco a poco; ~**ways** ad: **he couldn't get a word in** ~**ways** no pudo meter baza; **edging** n (SEWING) ribete m; (of path) borde m.

edgy ['ɛdʒɪ] a nervioso, inquieto.

edible ['ɛdɪbl] a comestible.

edict ['i:dɪkt] n edicto.

edifice ['ɛdɪfɪs] n edificio.

edit ['ɛdɪt] vt (be editor of) dirigir; (cut) cortar; ~**ion** [ɪ'dɪʃən] n (gen) edición f; (number printed) tirada; ~**or** n (of newspaper) director m; (of book) autor m de la edición; ~**orial** [-'tɔ:rɪəl] a editorial, de la dirección // n editorial m.

educate ['ɛdjukeɪt] vt (gen) educar; (instruct) instruir.

education [ɛdju'keɪʃən] n educación f; (schooling) enseñanza; (ESCOL) pedagogía; ~**al** a (policy etc) educacional; (teaching) docente; (instructive) educativo.

EEC n abbr of **European Economic Community** CEE (Comunidad Económica Europea).

eel [i:l] n anguila.

eerie ['ɪərɪ] a (strange) extraño; (mysterious) misterioso.

effect [ɪ'fɛkt] n efecto // vt efectuar, llevar a cabo; ~s npl efectos mpl; **to take** ~ (drug) surtir efecto; **in** ~ en realidad; ~**ive** a (gen) eficaz; (striking) impresionante; (real) efectivo; **to become** ~**ive** entrar en vigor; ~**iveness** n eficacia.
effeminate [ɪ'fɛmɪnɪt] a afeminado.
effervescent [ɛfə'vɛsnt] a efervescente.
efficiency [ɪ'fɪʃənsɪ] n (gen) eficiencia; (of machine) rendimiento.
efficient [ɪ'fɪʃənt] a eficiente.
effigy ['ɛfɪdʒɪ] n efigie f.
effort ['ɛfət] n esfuerzo; **to make an** ~ **to** esforzarse por; ~**less** a sin esfuerzo (alguno).
effrontery [ɪ'frʌntərɪ] n descaro.
effusive [ɪ'fjuːsɪv] a efusivo.
e.g. ad abbr of **exempli gratia** p. ej. (por ejemplo).
egg [ɛg] n huevo; **hard-boiled/poached/soft-boiled** ~ huevo duro/escalfado/pasado por agua; **scrambled** ~**s** huevos revueltos; **to** ~ **on** vt incitar; ~**cup** n huevera; ~**shell** n cáscara de huevo.
ego ['iːgəu] n ego; ~**ism** n egoísmo; ~**ist** n egoísta m/f.
Egypt ['iːdʒɪpt] n Egipto; ~**ian** [ɪ'dʒɪpʃən] a, n egipcio/a.
eiderdown ['aɪdədaun] n edredón m.
eight [eɪt] num ocho; **eighteen** num diez y ocho, dieciocho; **eighth** a, n octavo; ~**y** num ochenta.
Eire ['ɛərə] n Eire m.
either ['aɪðə*] det cualquier ... de los dos; (both, each) uno u otro; **on** ~ **side** en ambos lados // pron: ~ **(of them)** cualquiera (de los dos); **I don't like** ~ no me gusta ni uno ni otro // ad tampoco; **no, I don't** ~ no, yo tampoco // conj: ~ **yes or no** o sí o no.
eject [ɪ'dʒɛkt] vt echar; (tenant) desahuciar; ~**or seat** n asiento proyectable.
eke [iːk]: **to** ~ **out** vt (make last) escatimar; (add to) suplir las deficiencias de.
elaborate [ɪ'læbərɪt] a complicado; (decorated) rebuscado // (vb: [ɪ'læbəreɪt]) vt elaborar // vi explicarse con muchos detalles.
elapse [ɪ'læps] vi transcurrir.
elastic [ɪ'læstɪk] a, n elástico; ~ **band** n gomita.
elated [ɪ'leɪtɪd] a: **to be** ~ regocijarse; **elation** [ɪ'leɪʃən] n regocijo.
elbow ['ɛlbəu] n codo.
elder ['ɛldə*] a mayor // n (tree) saúco; (person) mayor; (of tribe) anciano; ~**ly** a de edad, mayor // n: **the** ~**ly** la gente mayor.
eldest ['ɛldɪst] a, n el/la mayor.
elect [ɪ'lɛkt] vt elegir; **to** ~ **to do** optar por hacer // a: **the president** ~ el presidente electo; ~**ion** [ɪ'lɛkʃən] n elección f; ~**ioneering** [ɪlɛkʃə'nɪərɪŋ] n campaña electoral; ~**or** n elector/a m/f;

~**oral** a electoral; ~**orate** n electorado.
electric [ɪ'lɛktrɪk] a eléctrico; ~**al** a eléctrico; ~ **blanket** n manta eléctrica; ~ **chair** n silla eléctrica; ~ **cooker** n cocina eléctrica; ~ **fire** n estufa eléctrica.
electrician [ɪlɛk'trɪʃən] n electricista m/f.
electricity [ɪlɛk'trɪsɪtɪ] n electricidad f.
electrify [ɪ'lɛktrɪfaɪ] vt (RAIL) electrificar; (audience) electrizar.
electro... [ɪlɛktrəu] pref: ~**cute** [-kjuːt] vt electrocutar; **electrode** [ɪ'lɛktrəud] n electrodo; ~**magnetic** a electromagnético.
electron [ɪ'lɛktrɔn] n electrón m.
electronic [ɪlɛk'trɔnɪk] a electrónico; ~**s** n electrónica.
elegance ['ɛlɪgəns] n elegancia; **elegant** [-gənt] a elegante.
element ['ɛlɪmənt] n (gen) elemento; **to brave the** ~**s** salir a la intemperie; ~**ary** [-'mɛntərɪ] a (gen) elemental; (primitive) rudimentario; (school, education) de primera enseñanza.
elephant ['ɛlɪfənt] n elefante m.
elevate ['ɛlɪveɪt] vt (gen) elevar; (in rank) ascender.
elevation [ɛlɪ'veɪʃən] n elevación f; (rank) ascenso; (height) altura.
elevator ['ɛlɪveɪtə*] n (US) ascensor m.
eleven [ɪ'lɛvn] num once; ~**ses** npl las once; ~**th** a undécimo.
elf [ɛlf], pl **elves** [ɛlvz] n duende m.
elicit [ɪ'lɪsɪt] vt: **to** ~ **(from)** sacar (de).
eligible ['ɛlɪdʒəbl] a elegible; **to be** ~ **for** sth llenar los requisitos para algo.
eliminate [ɪ'lɪmɪneɪt] vt eliminar; (strike out) suprimir; (suspect) descartar; **elimination** [-'neɪʃən] n eliminación f; supresión f.
élite [eɪ'liːt] n élite f.
elm [ɛlm] n olmo.
elocution [ɛlə'kjuːʃən] n elocución f.
elongated ['iːlɔŋgeɪtɪd] a alargado, estirado.
elope [ɪ'ləup] vi fugarse con su amante; ~**ment** n fuga.
eloquence ['ɛləkwəns] n elocuencia; **eloquent** [-wənt] a elocuente.
else [ɛls] ad lo(s) demás; **something** ~ otra cosa; **somewhere** ~ en otra parte; **everywhere** ~ en todas partes (menos aquí); **where** ~? ¿dónde más?, ¿en qué otra parte?; **there was little** ~ **to do** apenas quedaba otra cosa que hacer; **nobody** ~ **spoke** no habló nadie más; ~**where** ad (be) en otra parte; (go) a otra parte.
elucidate [ɪ'luːsɪdeɪt] vt aclarar, elucidar.
elude [ɪ'luːd] vt (gen) eludir; (blow) esquivar; (pursuer) escaparse de, zafarse de.
elusive [ɪ'luːsɪv] a esquivo; (answer) difícil de encontrar.
emaciated [ɪ'meɪsɪeɪtɪd] a demacrado.
emanate ['ɛməneɪt] vi emanar, proceder.

emancipate [ɪ'mænsɪpeɪt] vt emancipar;
~**d** a liberado; **emancipation** [-'peɪʃən] n
emancipación f, liberación f.
embalm [ɪm'bɑːm] vt embalsamar.
embankment [ɪm'bæŋkmənt] n terraplén
m; (riverside) dique m.
embargo [ɪm'bɑːgəu], pl ~**es** n
prohibición f.
embark [ɪm'bɑːk] vi embarcarse // vt
embarcar; **to** ~ **on** (fig) emprender,
lanzarse a; ~**ation** [embɑː'keɪʃən] n
(people) embarco; (goods) embarque m.
embarrass [ɪm'bærəs] vt desconcertar,
azorar; (financially etc) poner en un
aprieto; ~**ing** a embarazoso; ~**ment** n
desconcierto, azoramiento; (financial)
apuros mpl.
embassy ['embəsɪ] n embajada.
embed [ɪm'bed] vt (gen) empotrar; (teeth
etc) clavar.
embellish [ɪm'belɪʃ] vt embellecer; (fig)
adornar.
embers ['embəz] npl rescoldo sg, ascua sg.
embezzle [ɪm'bezl] vt desfalcar,
malversar; ~**ment** n desfalco,
malversación f.
embitter [ɪm'bɪtə*] vt amargar; (fig)
envenenar; ~**ed** a resentido, amargado.
emblem ['embləm] n emblema m.
embody [ɪm'bɒdɪ] vt (features) encarnar;
(ideas) expresar.
embossed [ɪm'bɒst] a realzado; ~ **with**
con grabado en relieve.
embrace [ɪm'breɪs] vt abrazar, dar un
abrazo a; (include) abarcar; (adopt: idea)
adherirse a // vi abrazarse // n abrazo.
embroider [ɪm'brɔɪdə*] vt bordar; (fig:
story) adornar, embellecer; ~**y** n
bordado.
embryo ['embrɪəu] n (also fig) embrión m.
emerald ['emərəld] n esmeralda.
emerge [ɪ'mɜːdʒ] vi (gen) salir, aparecer;
(arise) surgir; **emergence** n salida,
aparición f; surgimiento.
emergency [ɪ'mɜːdʒənsɪ] n (event)
emergencia; (crisis) crisis f; (need)
necesidad f urgente; **in an** ~ en caso de
urgencia; **state of** ~ estado de
emergencia; ~ **exit** n salida de
emergencia; ~ **landing** n aterrizaje m
forzoso; ~ **meeting** n reunión f
extraordinaria.
emery ['emərɪ]: ~ **board** n lima de uñas;
~ **paper** n papel m de esmeril.
emetic [ɪ'metɪk] n emético.
emigrant ['emɪgrənt] n emigrante m/f.
emigrate ['emɪgreɪt] vi emigrarse;
emigration [-'greɪʃən] n emigración f.
eminence ['emɪnəns] n eminencia;
eminent [-ənt] a eminente.
emission [ɪ'mɪʃən] n emisión f.
emit [ɪ'mɪt] vt (gen) emitir; (smoke)
arrojar; (smell) despedir; (sound) producir.
emotion [ɪ'məuʃən] n emoción f; ~**al** a
(person) sentimental; (scene)
conmovedor(a), emocionante; ~**ally** ad
con emoción.

emotive [ɪ'məutɪv] a emotivo.
emperor ['empərə*] n emperador m.
emphasis ['emfəsɪs], pl -**ses** [-siːz] n
énfasis m inv.
emphasize ['emfəsaɪz] vt (word, point)
subrayar, recalcar; (feature) hacer
resaltar.
emphatic [em'fætɪk] a (strong) enérgico;
(unambiguous, clear) enfático; ~**ally** ad
con énfasis.
empire ['empaɪə*] n imperio.
empirical [em'pɪrɪkl] a empírico.
employ [ɪm'plɔɪ] vt emplear; ~**ee** [-'iː]
empleado/a; ~**er** n patrón/ona m/f,
empresario; ~**ment** n (gen) empleo;
(work) trabajo; **full** ~**ment** pleno
empleo; ~**ment agency** n agencia de
colocaciones; ~**ment exchange** n bolsa
de trabajo.
empower [ɪm'pauə*] vt: **to** ~ **sb to do**
sth autorizar a uno a hacer algo.
empress ['emprɪs] n emperatriz f.
emptiness ['emptɪnɪs] n (gen) vacío; (of
life etc) vaciedad f.
empty ['emptɪ] a vacío; (place) desierto;
(house) desocupado; (threat) vano // n
(bottle) envase m // vt vaciar; (place)
dejar vacío // vi vaciarse; (house) quedar
desocupado; (place) quedar desierto;
~-**handed** a con las manos vacías.
emulate ['emjuleɪt] vt emular.
emulsion [ɪ'mʌlʃən] n emulsión f.
enable [ɪ'neɪbl] vt: **to** ~ **sb to do sth**
(allow) permitir a uno hacer algo;
(prepare) capacitar a uno para hacer algo.
enact [ɪn'ækt] vt (law) promulgar; (play)
representar; (role) hacer.
enamel [ɪ'næməl] n esmalte m.
enamoured [ɪ'næməd] a: **to be** ~ **of**
(person) estar enamorado de; (activity etc)
tener gran afición a; (idea) aferrarse a.
encased [ɪn'keɪst] a: ~ **in** (enclosed)
encerrado en; (covered) revestido de.
enchant [ɪn'tʃɑːnt] vt encantar; ~**ing** a
encantador(a).
encircle [ɪn'sɜːkl] vt (gen) rodear; (waist)
ceñir.
encl. abbr of **enclosed** adj. (adjunto).
enclose [ɪn'kləuz] vt (land) cercar; (with
letter etc) adjuntar; (in receptacle)
encerrar; **please find** ~**d** le adjunto.
enclosure [ɪn'kləuʒə*] n cercado, recinto;
(comm) carta adjunta.
encore [ɒŋ'kɔː*] excl ¡otra!, ¡bis! // n bis m.
encounter [ɪn'kauntə*] n encuentro // vt
encontrar, encontrarse con; (difficulty)
tropezar con.
encourage [ɪn'kʌrɪdʒ] vt alentar, animar;
(growth) estimular; ~**ment** n estímulo; (of
industry) fomento.
encroach [ɪn'krəutʃ] vi: **to** ~ (**up)on**
(gen) invadir; (time) ocupar.
encrusted [ɪn'krʌstəd] a: ~ **with**
incrustado de.
encumber [ɪn'kʌmbə*] vt: **to be** ~**ed**
with (carry) tener que cargar con; (debts)
estar gravado de.

encyclop(a)edia [ɛnsaɪklou'piːdɪə] *n* enciclopedia.

end [ɛnd] *n* (*gen, also aim*) fin *m*; (*of table*) extremo; (*of street*) final *m*; (*SPORT*) lado // *vt* terminar, acabar; (*also:* **bring to an** ~, **put an** ~ **to**) acabar con // *vi* terminar, acabar; **in the** ~ al fin, por fin, finalmente; **on** ~ (*object*) de punta, de cabeza; **to stand on** ~ (*hair*) erizarse; **for hours on** ~ horas seguidas; **to** ~ **up** *vi*: **to** ~ **up in** terminar en; (*place*) ir a parar en.

endanger [ɪn'deɪndʒə*] *vt* poner en peligro.

endear [ɪn'dɪə*] *vr*: **to** ~ **o.s. to** hacerse querer de; ~**ing** *a* simpático, atractivo; ~**ment** *n* cariño, palabra cariñosa.

endeavour [ɪn'dɛvə*] *n* esfuerzo; (*attempt*) tentativa; (*striving*) empeño // *vi*: **to** ~ **to do** esforzarse por hacer; (*try*) procurar hacer.

ending ['ɛndɪŋ] *n* fin *m*, conclusión *f*; (*of book*) desenlace *m*; (*LING*) terminación *f*.

endless ['ɛndlɪs] *a* interminable, inacabable.

endorse [ɪn'dɔːs] *vt* (*cheque*) endosar; (*approve*) aprobar; ~**ment** *n* (*on driving licence*) nota de inhabilitación.

endow [ɪn'dau] *vt* (*provide with money*) dotar; (*: institution*) fundar; **to be** ~**ed with** estar dotado de.

endurance [ɪn'djuərəns] *n* resistencia; **endure** *vt* (*bear*) aguantar, soportar; (*resist*) resistir // *vi* (*last*) durar; (*resist*) resistir.

enemy ['ɛnəmɪ] *a*, *n* enemigo/a.

energetic [ɛnə'dʒɛtɪk] *a* enérgico.

energy ['ɛnədʒɪ] *n* energía.

enforce [ɪn'fɔːs] *vt* (*LAW*) hacer cumplir; ~**d** *a* forzoso, forzado.

engage [ɪn'geɪdʒ] *vt* (*attention*) llamar; (*in conversation*) abordar; (*worker*) contratar; (*taxi*) alquilar; (*clutch*) embragar // *vi* (*TECH*) engranar con; **to** ~ **in** dedicarse a, ocuparse en; ~**d** *a* (*busy, in use*) ocupado; (*betrothed*) prometido; **to get** ~**d** prometerse; **he is** ~**d in research** se dedica a la investigación; ~**d tone** *n* señal *f* de comunicando; ~**ment** *n* (*appointment*) compromiso, cita; (*battle*) combate *m*; (*to marry*) compromiso; (*period*) noviazgo; ~**ment ring** *n* alianza, anillo de prometida.

engaging [ɪn'geɪdʒɪŋ] *a* atractivo, simpático.

engender [ɪn'dʒɛndə*] *vt* engendrar.

engine ['ɛndʒɪn] *n* (*AUT*) motor *m*; (*RAIL*) locomotora; ~ **driver** *n* maquinista *m*.

engineer [ɛndʒɪ'nɪə*] *n* ingeniero; (*US: RAIL*) maquinista *m*; ~**ing** *n* ingeniería.

England ['ɪŋglənd] *n* Inglaterra.

English ['ɪŋglɪʃ] *a* inglés(esa) // *n* (*LING*) el inglés; **the** ~ los ingleses; ~**man/woman** *n* inglés/esa *m/f*.

engrave [ɪn'greɪv] *vt* grabar; **engraving** *n* grabado.

engrossed [ɪn'grəust] *a*: ~ **in** absorto en.

engulf [ɪn'gʌlf] *vt* sumergir, hundir.

enhance [ɪn'hɑːns] *vt* (*gen*) intensificar, aumentar; (*beauty*) realzar.

enigma [ɪ'nɪgmə] *n* enigma *m*; ~**tic** [ɛnɪg-'mætɪk] *a* enigmático.

enjoy [ɪn'dʒɔɪ] *vt* (*possess*) poseer; (*have: health, fortune*) disfrutar de, gozar de; (*food*) comer con gusto; **to** ~ **o.s.** divertirse, pasarlo bien; ~**able** *a* (*pleasant*) agradable; (*amusing*) divertido; ~**ment** *n* (*use*) disfrute *m*; (*joy*) placer *m*.

enlarge [ɪn'lɑːdʒ] *vt* aumentar; (*broaden*) extender; (*PHOT*) ampliar // *vi*: **to** ~ **on** (*subject*) tratar con más detalles; ~**ment** *n* (*PHOT*) ampliación *f*.

enlighten [ɪn'laɪtn] *vt* (*inform*) informar, instruir; ~**ed** *a* (*cultured*) culto; (*knowledgeable*) bien informado; (*tolerant*) comprensivo; ~**ment** *n* (*HISTORY*): **the E**~**ment** la Ilustración, el Siglo de las Luces.

enlist [ɪn'lɪst] *vt* alistar; (*support*) conseguir // *vi* alistarse.

enmity ['ɛnmɪtɪ] *n* enemistad *f*.

enormity [ɪ'nɔːmɪtɪ] *n* enormidad *f*; **enormous** [-məs] *a* enorme.

enough [ɪ'nʌf] *a*: ~ **time/books** bastante tiempo/bastantes libros // *n*: **have you got** ~? ¿tiene Usted bastante? // *ad*: **big** ~ bastante grande; **he has not worked** ~ no ha trabajado bastante; ~**!** ¡basta ya!; **that's** ~, **thanks** con eso basta, gracias; **I've had** ~ **of him** estoy harto de él; ... **which, funnily** ~ ... ... lo que, por extraño que parezca... .

enquire [ɪn'kwaɪə*] *vt*, *vi* = **inquire**.

enrage [ɪn'reɪdʒ] *vt* enfurecer, hacer rabiar.

enrich [ɪn'rɪtʃ] *vt* enriquecer.

enrol [ɪn'rəul] *vt* inscribir; (*SCOL*) matricular // *vi* inscribirse; matricularse; ~**ment** *n* inscripción *f*; matriculación *f*.

en route [ɔn'ruːt] *ad* (*on the way to*) camino de; (*on the way*) en camino.

ensign ['ɛnsaɪn] *n* (*flag*) bandera; (*MIL*) alférez *m*.

enslave [ɪn'sleɪv] *vt* esclavizar.

ensue [ɪn'sjuː] *vi* seguirse; (*result*) resultar; (*happen*) sobrevenir.

ensure [ɪn'fuə*] *vt* asegurar.

entail [ɪn'teɪl] *vt* (*imply*) suponer; (*result in*) acarrear.

entangle [ɪn'tæŋgl] *vt* enredar, enmarañar; ~**ment** *n* enredo.

enter ['ɛntə*] *vt* (*room*) entrar en; (*club*) hacerse socio de; (*army*) alistarse en; (*sb for a competition*) inscribir; (*write down*) anotar, apuntar // *vi* entrar; **to** ~ **for** *vt fus* presentarse para; **to** ~ **into** *vt fus* (*relations*) establecer; (*plans*) formar parte de; (*debate*) tomar parte en; (*agreement*) llegar a, firmar; **to** ~ **(up)on** *vt fus* (*career*) emprender.

enteritis [ɛntə'raɪtɪs] *n* enteritis *f*.

enterprise ['ɛntəpraɪz] *n* empresa; (*spirit*) iniciativa; **free** ~ la libre empresa; **private** ~ la iniciativa privada;

enterprising a emprendedor(a).
entertain [ɛntə'teɪn] vt (amuse) divertir; (receive: guest) recibir (en casa); (idea) abrigar; (plan) estudiar; ~er n artista m/f; ~ing a divertido, entretenido; ~ment n (amusement) diversión f; (show) espectáculo; (party) fiesta.
enthralled [ɪn'θrɔːld] a encantado, cautivado.
enthusiasm [ɪn'θuːzɪæzəm] n entusiasmo.
enthusiast [ɪn'θuːzɪæst] n entusiasta m/f; ~ic [-'æstɪk] a entusiasta inv; to be ~ic about entusiasmarse por.
entice [ɪn'taɪs] vt tentar; (seduce) seducir; **enticing** a atractivo, tentador(a).
entire [ɪn'taɪə*] a entero, completo; (in total) total, todo; ~ly ad totalmente; ~ty [ɪn'taɪərətɪ] n: in its ~ty en su totalidad.
entitle [ɪn'taɪtl] vt: to ~ sb to sth dar a uno derecho a algo; ~d a (book) que se titula; to be ~d to do tener derecho a hacer.
entourage [ɔntuː'rɑːʒ] n séquito.
entrails ['ɛntreɪlz] npl entrañas fpl.
entrance ['ɛntrəns] n entrada // vt [ɪn-'trɑːns] encantar, hechizar; to gain ~ to (university etc) ingresar en; ~ examination n examen m de ingreso; ~ fee n cuota.
entrant ['ɛntrənt] n participante m/f.
entreat [ɛn'triːt] vt rogar, suplicar; ~y n ruego, súplica.
entrée ['ɔntreɪ] n (CULIN) entrada.
entrenched [ɛn'trɛntʃd] a atrincherado.
entrepreneur [ɔntrəprə'nəː] n empresario; (of works) contratista m/f.
entrust [ɪn'trʌst] vt: to ~ sth to sb confiar algo a uno.
entry ['ɛntrɪ] n entrada; (permission to enter) acceso; (in register) apunte m; (in account) partida; ~ form n boleto de inscripción; no ~ prohibido el paso; (AUT) dirección prohibida.
enumerate [ɪ'njuːməreɪt] vt enumerar.
enunciate [ɪ'nʌnsɪeɪt] vt pronunciar; (principle etc) enunciar.
envelop [ɪn'vɛləp] vt envolver.
envelope ['ɛnvələup] n sobre m.
envious ['ɛnvɪəs] a envidioso; (look) de envidia.
environment [ɪn'vaɪərnmənt] n medio ambiente; ~al [-'mɛntl] a ambiental.
envisage [ɪn'vɪzɪdʒ] vt (foresee) prever; (imagine) concebir, representarse.
envoy ['ɛnvɔɪ] n enviado.
envy ['ɛnvɪ] n envidia // vt tener envidia a; to ~ sb sth envidiar algo a uno.
enzyme ['ɛnzaɪm] n enzima.
ephemeral [ɪ'fɛmərl] a efímero.
epic ['ɛpɪk] n épica // a épico.
epidemic [ɛpɪ'dɛmɪk] n epidemia.
epilepsy ['ɛpɪlɛpsɪ] n epilepsia; **epileptic** [-'lɛptɪk] a, n epiléptico/a.
episode ['ɛpɪsəud] n episodio.
epistle [ɪ'pɪsl] n epístola.
epitaph ['ɛpɪtɑːf] n epitafio.

epitome [ɪ'pɪtəmɪ] n epítome m; **epitomize** vt epitomar, resumir.
epoch ['iːpɔk] n época.
equable ['ɛkwəbl] a uniforme, igual; (character) tranquilo, afable.
equal ['iːkwl] a (gen) igual; (treatment) equitativo // n igual m/f // vt ser igual a; to be ~ to (task) estar a la altura de; ~ity [iː'kwɔlɪtɪ] n igualdad f; ~ize vt, vi igualar; (SPORT) lograr el empate; ~izer n igualada; ~ly ad igualmente; (share etc) por igual.
equanimity [ɛkwə'nɪmɪtɪ] n ecuanimidad f.
equate [ɪ'kweɪt] vt: to ~ sth with considerar algo equivalente a; **equation** [ɪ'kweɪʃən] n (MATH) ecuación f.
equator [ɪ'kweɪtə*] n ecuador m; ~ial [ɛkwə'tɔːrɪəl] a ecuatorial.
equilibrium [iːkwɪ'lɪbrɪəm] n equilibrio.
equinox ['iːkwɪnɔks] n equinoccio.
equip [ɪ'kwɪp] vt (gen) equipar; (person) proveer; to be well ~ped estar bien dotado; ~ment n equipo; (tools) avíos mpl.
equitable ['ɛkwɪtəbl] a equitativo.
equivalent [ɪ'kwɪvəlnt] a equivalente; to be ~ to equivaler a // n equivalente m.
equivocal [ɪ'kwɪvəkl] a equívoco; (open to suspicion) ambiguo.
era ['ɪərə] n era, época.
eradicate [ɪ'rædɪkeɪt] vt erradicar, extirpar.
erase [ɪ'reɪz] vt borrar; **eraser** n goma de borrar.
erect [ɪ'rɛkt] a erguido // vt erigir, levantar; (assemble) montar.
erection [ɪ'rɛkʃən] n construcción f; (assembly) montaje m; (structure) edificio; (MED) erección f.
ermine ['əːmɪn] n armiño.
erode [ɪ'rəud] vt (GEO) erosionar; (metal) corroer, desgastar; **erosion** [ɪ'rəuʒən] n erosión f; desgaste m.
erotic [ɪ'rɔtɪk] a erótico; ~ism [ɪ'rɔtɪsɪzm] n erotismo.
err [əː*] vi errar, equivocarse; (REL) pecar.
errand ['ɛrnd] n recado, mandado; ~ boy n recadero.
erratic [ɪ'rætɪk] a irregular; (uneven) desigual, poco uniforme.
erroneous [ɪ'rəunɪəs] a erróneo.
error ['ɛrə*] n error m, equivocación f.
erupt [ɪ'rʌpt] vi estar en erupción; (MED) hacer erupción; (fig) estallar; ~ion [ɪ'rʌpʃən] n erupción f; (fig) explosión f.
escalate ['ɛskəleɪt] vi extenderse, intensificarse; **escalation** [-'leɪʃən] n escalamiento, intensificación f.
escalator ['ɛskəleɪtə*] n escalera móvil.
escapade [ɛskə'peɪd] n travesura.
escape [ɪ'skeɪp] n (gen) fuga; (from duties) escapatoria; (from chase) fuga, evasión f // vi (gen) escaparse; (flee) huir, evadirse; (leak) fugarse // vt evitar, eludir; (consequences) escapar a; to ~ from

(*place*) escaparse de; (*person*) escaparse a; (*clutches*) librarse de; **escapism** *n* escapismo.

escort ['ɛskɔːt] *n* acompañante *m/f*; (*MIL*) escolta; (*NAUT*) convoy *m* // *vt* [ɪ'skɔːt] acompañar; (*MIL, NAUT*) escoltar.

Eskimo ['ɛskɪməu] *n* esquimal *m/f*.

especially [ɪ'spɛʃlɪ] *ad* (*gen*) especialmente; (*above all*) sobre todo; (*particularly*) en particular.

espionage ['ɛspɪɔnɑːʒ] *n* espionaje *m*.

esplanade [ɛsplə'neɪd] *n* (*by sea*) paseo marítimo.

espouse [ɪ'spauz] *vt* adherirse a.

Esquire [ɪ'skwaɪə] *n* (*abbr* **Esq.**): J. **Brown, ~** Sr. Don J. Brown.

essay ['ɛseɪ] *n* (*SCOL*) ensayo.

essence ['ɛsns] *n* esencia.

essential [ɪ'sɛnʃl] *a* (*necessary*) imprescindible; (*basic*) esencial; **~ly** *ad* esencialmente.

establish [ɪ'stæblɪʃ] *vt* establecer; (*facts*) verificar; (*proof*) demostrar; (*relations*) entablar; **~ed** *a* (*business*) de buena reputación; (*staff*) de plantilla; **~ment** *n* establecimiento; **the E~ment** la clase dirigente.

estate [ɪ'steɪt] *n* (*land*) finca, hacienda; (*property*) propiedad *f*; (*inheritance*) herencia; (*POL*) estado; **housing ~** urbanización *f*; **industrial ~** polígono industrial; **~ agent** *n* agente *m/f* inmobiliario; **~ car** *n* (*Brit*) furgoneta.

esteem [ɪ'stiːm] *n*: **to hold sb in high ~** estimar en mucho a uno // *vt* estimar.

estimate ['ɛstɪmət] *n* estimación *f*, apreciación *f*; (*assessment*) tasa, cálculo; (*COMM*) presupuesto // *vt* [-meɪt] estimar; tasar, calcular; **estimation** [-'meɪʃən] *n* opinión *f*, juicio; (*esteem*) aprecio.

estrange [ɪ'streɪndʒ] *vt* enajenar.

estuary ['ɛstjuərɪ] *n* estuario, ría.

etching ['ɛtʃɪŋ] *n* aguafuerte *f*.

eternal [ɪ'tɔːnl] *a* eterno.

eternity [ɪ'tɔːnɪtɪ] *n* eternidad *f*.

ether ['iːθə*] *n* éter *m*.

ethical ['ɛθɪkl] *a* ético; (*honest*) honrado; **ethics** ['ɛθɪks] *n* ética // *npl* moralidad *f*.

ethnic ['ɛθnɪk] *a* étnico.

etiquette ['ɛtɪkɛt] *n* etiqueta.

eucalyptus [juːkə'lɪptəs] *n* eucalipto.

euphemism ['juːfəmɪzm] *n* eufemismo.

euphoria [juː'fɔːrɪə] *n* euforia.

Europe ['juərəp] *n* Europa; **European** [-'piːən] *a, n* europeo/a.

euthanasia [juːθə'neɪzɪə] *n* eutanasia.

evacuate [ɪ'vækjueɪt] *vt* desocupar; **evacuation** [-'eɪʃən] *n* evacuación *f*.

evade [ɪ'veɪd] *vt* evadir, eludir.

evaluate [ɪ'væljueɪt] *vt* evaluar; (*value*) tasar; (*evidence*) interpretar.

evangelist [ɪ'vændʒəlɪst] *n* evangelizador *m*, evangelista *m/f*.

evaporate [ɪ'væpəreɪt] *vi* evaporarse, desvanecerse // *vt* evaporar; **~d milk** *n*

leche *f* evaporada; **evaporation** [-'reɪʃən] *n* evaporación *f*.

evasion [ɪ'veɪʒən] *n* evasiva, evasión *f*; **evasive** [-sɪv] *a* evasivo.

eve [iːv] *n*: **on the ~ of** en vísperas de.

even ['iːvn] *a* (*level*) llano; (*smooth*) liso; (*speed, temperature*) uniforme; (*number*) par; (*nature*) ecuánime; (*SPORT*) igual(es) // *ad* hasta, aun, siquiera; **~ more** aun más; **~ so** aun así; **not ~** ni siquiera; **~ he was there** hasta él estuvo allí; **~ on Sundays** incluso los domingos; **to ~ out** *vi* nivelarse; **to get ~ with sb** ajustar cuentas con uno.

evening ['iːvnɪŋ] *n* tarde *f*; (*dusk*) atardecer *m*; (*night*) noche *f*; (*event*) velada; **in the ~** por la tarde; **~ class** *n* clase *f* nocturna; **~ dress** *n* (*man's*) traje *m* de etiqueta; (*woman's*) traje *m* de noche.

event [ɪ'vɛnt] *n* suceso, acontecimiento; (*SPORT*) prueba; **in the ~ of** en caso de (que); **~ful** *a* accidentado; (*game etc*) lleno de emoción.

eventual [ɪ'vɛntʃuəl] *a* (*last*) final; (*resulting*) consiguiente; **~ity** [-'ælɪtɪ] *n* eventualidad *f*; **~ly** *ad* (*finally*) finalmente, al fin y al cabo; (*in time*) a la larga.

ever ['ɛvə*] *ad* nunca, jamás; (*at all times*) alguna vez; **the best ~** el/la mejor que se ha visto jamás; **have you ~ seen it?** ¿lo ha visto Usted jamás?; **better than ~** mejor que nunca; **~ since** *ad* desde entonces // *conj* después de que; **~green** *n* árbol *m* de hoja perenne; **~lasting** *a* eterno, perpetuo.

every ['ɛvrɪ] *det* (*each*) cada; (*all*) todo; **~ day** cada día; **~ other car** cada dos coches; **~ now and then** de vez en cuando; **~body** *pron* todos *pl*, todo el mundo; **~day** *a* (*daily*) diario, cotidiano; (*usual*) corriente; (*common*) vulgar; (*routine*) rutinario; **~one** = **~body**; **~thing** *pron* todo; **~where** *ad* (*be*) en todas partes; (*go*) a *o* por todas partes.

evict [ɪ'vɪkt] *vt* desahuciar; **~ion** [ɪ'vɪkʃən] *n* desahucio.

evidence ['ɛvɪdəns] *n* (*proof*) prueba; (*witness*) testimonio; (*facts*) datos *mpl*, hechos *mpl*; **to give ~** prestar declaración, dar testimonio.

evident ['ɛvɪdənt] *a* evidente, manifiesto; **~ly** *ad* naturalmente.

evil ['iːvl] *a* malo; (*influence*) funesto; (*smell*) horrible // *n* mal *m*, maldad *f*; **~doer** *n* malhechor/a *m/f*.

evocative [ɪ'vɔkətɪv] *a* sugestivo, evocador(a).

evoke [ɪ'vəuk] *vt* evocar.

evolution [iːvə'luːʃən] *n* evolución *f*, desarrollo.

evolve [ɪ'vɔlv] *vt* desarrollar // *vi* evolucionar, desarrollarse.

ewe [juː] *n* oveja.

ex-... [ɛks] *pref* ex.

exact [ɪg'zækt] *a* exacto // *vt*: **to ~ sth**

(from) exigir algo (de); ~**ing** a exigente; (conditions) arduo; ~**itude** n exactitud f; ~**ly** ad exactamente; (time) en punto.

exaggerate [ɪg'zædʒəreɪt] vt, vi exagerar; **exaggeration** [-'reɪʃən] n exageración f.

exalted [ɪg'zɔːltɪd] a exaltado, elevado.

exam [ɪg'zæm] n abbr of **examination**.

examination [ɪgzæmɪ'neɪʃən] n (gen) examen m; (LAW) interrogación f; (inquiry) investigación f.

examine [ɪg'zæmɪn] vt (gen) examinar; (inspect) inspeccionar, escudriñar; (SCOL, LAW: person) interrogar; (at customs: luggage) registrar; **examiner** n inspector m.

example [ɪg'zɑːmpl] n ejemplo; (copy) ejemplar m; **for** ~ por ejemplo.

exasperate [ɪg'zɑːspəreɪt] vt exasperar, irritar; **exasperating** a irritante.

excavate ['ɛkskəveɪt] vt excavar; **excavation** [-'veɪʃən] n excavación f.

exceed [ɪk'siːd] vt exceder; (number) pasar de; (speed limit) sobrepasar; (limits) rebasar; (powers) excederse en; (hopes) superar; ~**ingly** ad sumamente, sobremanera.

excel [ɪk'sɛl] vi sobresalir.

excellence ['ɛksələns] n excelencia.

Excellency ['ɛksələnsɪ] n: **His** ~ Su Excelencia.

excellent ['ɛksələnt] a excelente.

except [ɪk'sɛpt] prep (also: ~ **for**, ~**ing**) excepto, salvo, con excepción de // vt exceptuar, excluir; ~ **if/when** excepto si/cuando; ~ **that** salvo que; ~**ion** [ɪk'sɛpʃən] n excepción f; **to take** ~**ion to** ofenderse por; ~**ional** [ɪk'sɛpʃənl] a excepcional.

excerpt ['ɛksəːpt] n extracto.

excess [ɪk'sɛs] n exceso; (COMM) excedente m; ~ **baggage** n exceso de equipaje; ~ **fare** n suplemento; ~**ive** a excesivo.

exchange [ɪks'tʃeɪndʒ] n cambio; (of goods) canje m; (of ideas) intercambio; (also: **telephone** ~) central f (telefónica) // vt cambiar; canjear.

exchequer [ɪks'tʃekə*] n hacienda.

excise ['ɛksaɪz] n impuestos mpl sobre el comercio exterior // vt [ɛk'saɪz] suprimir.

excite [ɪk'saɪt] vt (stimulate) excitar; (awaken) despertar; (move) entusiasmar; **to get** ~**d** emocionarse; ~**ment** n emoción f; (anticipation) ilusión f; (agitation) agitación f; **exciting** a emocionante.

exclaim [ɪk'skleɪm] vi exclamar; **exclamation** [ɛksklə'meɪʃən] n exclamación f; **exclamation mark** n punto de admiración f.

exclude [ɪk'skluːd] vt excluir; (except) exceptuar; **exclusion** [ɪk'skluːʒən] n exclusión f.

exclusive [ɪk'skluːsɪv] a exclusivo; (club, district) selecto; ~ **of tax** excluyendo impuestos; ~**ly** ad únicamente.

excommunicate [ɛkskə'mjuːnɪkeɪt] vt excomulgar.

excrement ['ɛkskrəmənt] n excremento.

excrete [ɪk'skriːt] vi excretar.

excruciating [ɪk'skruːʃɪeɪtɪŋ] a agudísimo, atroz.

excursion [ɪk'skəːʃən] n excursión f.

excusable [ɪk'skjuːzəbl] a perdonable.

excuse [ɪk'skjuːs] n disculpa, excusa; (evasion) pretexto // vt [ɪk'skjuːz] disculpar, perdonar; **to** ~ **sb from doing sth** dispensar a uno de hacer algo; ~ **me!** ¡perdón!; **if you will** ~ **me** con su permiso.

execute ['ɛksɪkjuːt] vt (plan) realizar; (order) cumplir; (person) ajusticiar, ejecutar; **execution** n realización f; cumplimiento; ejecución f; **executioner** n verdugo.

executive [ɪg'zɛkjutɪv] n (COMM, POL) ejecutivo // a ejecutivo.

executor [ɪg'zɛkjutə*] n albacea m, testamentario.

exemplary [ɪg'zɛmplərɪ] a ejemplar.

exemplify [ɪg'zɛmplɪfaɪ] vt ejemplificar.

exempt [ɪg'zɛmpt] a: ~ **from** exento de // vt: **to** ~ **sb from** eximir a uno de; ~**ion** [ɪg'zɛmpʃən] n exención f; (immunity) inmunidad f.

exercise ['ɛksəsaɪz] n ejercicio // vt ejercer; (right) valerse de; (dog) llevar de paseo // vi hacer ejercicio(s); ~ **book** n cuaderno.

exert [ɪg'zəːt] vt ejercer; **to** ~ **o.s.** esforzarse, afanarse; (overdo things) trabajar demasiado; ~**ion** n esfuerzo.

exhaust [ɪg'zɔːst] n (pipe) escape m; (fumes) gases mpl de escape // vt agotar; ~**ion** [ɪg'zɔːstʃən] n agotamiento; **nervous** ~**ion** postración f nerviosa; ~**ive** a exhaustivo.

exhibit [ɪg'zɪbɪt] n (ART) obra expuesta; (LAW) objeto expuesto // vt (show) manifestar; (emotion) acusar; (film) presentar; (paintings) exponer; ~**ion** [ɛksɪ'bɪʃən] n exposición f; ~**ionist** [ɛksɪ'bɪʃənɪst] n exhibicionista m/f.

exhilarating [ɪg'zɪləreɪtɪŋ] a estimulante, tónico.

exhort [ɪg'zɔːt] vt exhortar.

exile ['ɛksaɪl] n exilio; (person) exiliado/a // vt desterrar, exiliar.

exist [ɪg'zɪst] vi existir; (live) vivir; ~**ence** n existencia; (life) vida; ~**ing** a existente, actual.

exit ['ɛksɪt] n salida.

exonerate [ɪg'zɒnəreɪt] vt: **to** ~ **from** exculpar de.

exorcize ['ɛksɔːsaɪz] vt exorcizar.

exotic [ɪg'zɒtɪk] a exótico.

expand [ɪk'spænd] vt (widen) ensanchar; (number) aumentar // vi (trade etc) expandirse; (gas, metal) dilatarse.

expanse [ɪk'spæns] n extensión f; (of wings) envergadura.

expansion [ɪk'spænʃən] n (of town) ensanche m; (of trade) expansión f.

expatriate [ɛks'pætrɪət] n expatriado/a.

expect [ɪk'spɛkt] vt (gen) esperar; (count

on) contar con; (*suppose*) suponer // *vi*: **to be ~ing** estar encinta; **~ant mother** *n* mujer *f* encinta; **~ation** [ɛkspɛk'teɪʃən] *n* esperanza, expectativa.

expedience [ɛk'spiːdɪəns], **expediency** [ɛk'spiːdɪənsɪ] *n* conveniencia; **expedient** *a* conveniente, oportuno // *n* recurso, expediente *m*.

expedition [ɛkspə'dɪʃən] *n* expedición *f*.

expel [ɪk'spɛl] *vt* arrojar; (*SCOL*) expulsar.

expend [ɪk'spɛnd] *vt* gastar; (*use up*) consumir; **~able** *a* prescindible; **~iture** *n* gastos *mpl*, desembolso.

expense [ɪk'spɛns] *n* gasto, gastos *mpl*; (*high cost*) costa; **~s** *npl* (*COMM*) gastos *mpl*; **at the ~ of** a costa o expensas de; **~ account** *n* cuenta de gastos.

expensive [ɪk'spɛnsɪv] *a* caro, costoso.

experience [ɪk'spɪərɪəns] *n* experiencia // *vt* experimentar; (*suffer*) sufrir; **~d** *a* experimentado.

experiment [ɪk'spɛrɪmənt] *n* experimento // *vi* hacer experimentos; **~al** [-'mɛntl] *a* experimental.

expert ['ɛkspəːt] *a* experto, perito // *n* experto, perito; (*specialist*) especialista *m/f*; **~ise** [-'tiːz] *n* pericia.

expire [ɪk'spaɪə*] *vi* (*gen*) expirar; (*end*) terminar; (*run out*) caducar, vencerse; **expiry** *n* expiración *f*; terminación *f*; vencimiento.

explain [ɪk'spleɪn] *vt* explicar; (*clarify*) aclarar; (*demonstrate*) exponer; **explanation** [ɛksplə'neɪʃən] *n* explicación *f*; aclaración *f*; **explanatory** [ɪk'splænətrɪ] *a* explicativo; aclaratorio.

explicit [ɪk'splɪsɪt] *a* explícito.

explode [ɪk'spləud] *vi* estallar, explotar; (*with anger*) reventar // *vt* volar, explotar.

exploit ['ɛksplɔɪt] *n* hazaña // *vt* [ɪk'splɔɪt] explotar; **~ation** [-'teɪʃən] *n* explotación *f*.

exploration [ɛksplə'reɪʃən] *n* exploración *f*; **exploratory** [ɪk'splɔrətrɪ] *a* (*fig: talks*) exploratorio, de sondaje.

explore [ɪk'splɔ:*] *vt* explorar; (*fig*) examinar, sondar; **explorer** *n* explorador *m*.

explosion [ɪk'spləuʒən] *n* explosión *f*; **explosive** [-sɪv] *a*, *n* explosivo.

exponent [ɪk'spəunənt] *n* exponente *m/f*, intérprete *m/f*.

export [ɛk'spɔ:t] *vt* exportar // *n* ['ɛkspɔ:t] exportación *f* // *cpd* de exportación; **~ation** [-'teɪʃən] *n* exportación *f*; **~er** *n* exportador *m*.

expose [ɪk'spəuz] *vt* exponer; (*unmask*) desenmascarar; **~d** *a* expuesto; (*position*) desabrigado.

exposure [ɪk'spəuʒə*] *n* exposición *f*; (*PHOT*) revelación *f*; (*: shot*) fotografía; **to die from ~** (*MED*) morir de frío; **~ meter** *n* fotómetro.

expound [ɪk'spaund] *vt* exponer, explicar.

express [ɪk'sprɛs] *a* (*definite*) expreso, explícito; (*letter etc*) urgente // *n* (*train*) rápido // *ad* (*send*) por carta urgente // *vt* expresar; (*squeeze*) exprimir; **~ion** [ɪk-**'sprɛʃən**] *n* expresión *f*; **~ive** *a* expresivo; **~ly** *ad* expresamente.

expulsion [ɪk'spʌlʃən] *n* expulsión *f*.

exquisite [ɛk'skwɪzɪt] *a* exquisito.

extend [ɪk'stɛnd] *vt* (*visit, street*) prolongar; (*building*) ensanchar; (*offer*) ofrecer // *vi* (*land*) extenderse.

extension [ɪk'stɛnʃən] *n* extensión *f*; (*building*) ampliación *f*; (*TEL: line*) línea derivada; (*: telephone*) extensión *f*; (*of deadline*) prórroga.

extensive [ɪk'stɛnsɪv] *a* (*gen*) extenso; (*broad*) vasto, ancho; (*frequent*) general, común; **he's travelled ~ly** ha viajado por muchos países.

extent [ɪk'stɛnt] *n* (*breadth*) extensión *f*; (*scope*) alcance *m*; **to some ~** hasta cierto punto; **to the ~ of...** hasta el punto de...; **to such an ~ that...** hasta tal punto que...; **to what ~?** ¿hasta qué punto?

exterior [ɛk'stɪərɪə*] *a* exterior, externo // *n* exterior *m*; (*appearance*) aspecto.

exterminate [ɪk'stə:mɪneɪt] *vt* exterminar; **extermination** [-'neɪʃən] *n* exterminación *f*.

external [ɛk'stə:nl] *a* externo, exterior; **~ly** *ad* por fuera.

extinct [ɪk'stɪŋkt] *a* extinto; **~ion** [ɪk-'stɪŋkʃən] *n* extinción *f*.

extinguish [ɪk'stɪŋgwɪʃ] *vt* extinguir, apagar; **~er** *n* extintor *m*.

extort [ɪk'stɔ:t] *vt* sacar a la fuerza (*from sb* de uno); **~ion** [ɪk'stɔ:ʃən] *n* exacción *f*; **~ionate** [ɪk'stɔ:ʃnət] *a* excesivo, exorbitante.

extra ['ɛkstrə] *a* adicional; (*excessive*) de más, de sobra; (*bonus: payment*) extraordinario // *ad* (*in addition*) especialmente // *n* (*addition*) extra *m*, suplemento; (*THEATRE*) extra *m/f*, comparsa *m/f*; (*newspaper*) edición *f* extraordinaria.

extra... [ɛkstrə] *pref* extra....

extract [ɪk'strækt] *vt* sacar, extraer; (*confession*) arrancar, obtener // *n* ['ɛkstrækt] extracto.

extradite ['ɛkstrədaɪt] *vt* (*from country*) conceder la extradición de; (*to country*) obtener la extradición de; **extradition** [-'dɪʃən] *n* extradición *f*.

extramarital [ɛkstrə'mærɪtl] *a* extra-matrimonial.

extramural [ɛkstrə'mjuərl] *a* de extramuros.

extraordinary [ɪk'strɔ:dnrɪ] *a* extra-ordinario; (*odd*) raro.

extravagant [ɪk'strævəgənt] *a* (*lavish*) pródigo; (*wasteful*) derrochador(a); (*price*) exorbitante; (*praise*) excesivo; (*odd*) raro.

extreme [ɪk'striːm] *a* extremo; (*poverty etc*) extremado; (*case*) excepcional // *n* extremo, extremidad *f*; **~ly** *ad* sumamente, extremadamente; **extremist** *a*, *n* extremista *m/f*.

extremity [ɪk'strɛmətɪ] *n* extremidad *f*, punta; (*need*) apuro, necesidad *f*.

extricate ['ɛkstrɪkeɪt] *vt* librar.

extrovert ['ɛkstrəvɜːt] *n* extrovertido/a.
exuberant [ɪg'zjuːbərnt] *a* (*person*) eufórico; (*style*) exuberante.
exude [ɪg'zjuːd] *vt* rezumar, sudar.
exult [ɪg'zʌlt] *vi* regocijarse.
eye [aɪ] *n* ojo // *vt* mirar de soslayo, ojear; **to keep an ~ on** vigilar, estar pendiente de; **~ball** *n* globo del ojo; **~bath** *n* ojera; **~brow** *n* ceja; **~brow pencil** *n* lápiz *m* de cejas; **~-catching** *a* llamativo; **~drops** *npl* gotas *fpl* para los ojos; **~lash** *n* pestaña; **~lid** *n* párpado; **~-opener** *n* revelación *f*, gran sorpresa; **~shadow** *n* sombreador *m* de ojos; **~sight** *n* vista; **~sore** *n* monstruosidad *f*; **~wash** *n* (*fig*) disparates *mpl*, tonterías *fpl*; **~ witness** *n* testigo *m/f* presencial.
eyrie ['ɪərɪ] *n* aguilera.

F

F. *abbr of* **Fahrenheit.**
fable ['feɪbl] *n* fábula.
fabric ['fæbrɪk] *n* tejido, tela.
fabrication [fæbrɪ'keɪʃən] *n* invención *f*.
fabulous ['fæbjʊləs] *a* fabuloso.
façade [fə'sɑːd] *n* fachada.
face [feɪs] *n* cara, rostro; (*ANAT*) (*of clock*) esfera; (*side, surface*) superficie *f* // *vt* (*person*) encararse con; (*building*) dar a; **to lose ~** desprestigiarse; **in the ~ of** (*difficulties etc*) en vista de; **on the ~ of it** a primera vista; **~ to ~** cara a cara; **to ~ up to** *vt fus* hacer frente a, arrostrar; **~ cloth** *n* paño; **~ cream** *n* crema (de belleza); **~ lift** *n* cirujía estética; **~ powder** *n* polvos *mpl*; **~-saving** *a* para salvar las apariencias.
facet ['fæsɪt] *n* faceta.
facetious [fə'siːʃəs] *a* chistoso.
face value ['feɪs'væljuː] *n* (*of stamp*) valor *m* nominal; **to take sth at ~** (*fig*) tomar algo en sentido literal, aceptar las apariencias de algo.
facial ['feɪʃəl] *a* de la cara.
facile ['fæsaɪl] *a* superficial, ligero.
facilitate [fə'sɪlɪteɪt] *vt* facilitar.
facilities [fə'sɪlɪtɪz] *npl* facilidades *fpl*.
facing ['feɪsɪŋ] *prep* frente a // *a* de enfrente.
fact [fækt] *n* hecho; **in ~** en realidad.
faction ['fækʃən] *n* facción *f*.
factor ['fæktə*] *n* factor *m*.
factory ['fæktərɪ] *n* fábrica.
factual ['fæktjʊəl] *a* objetivo.
faculty ['fækəltɪ] *n* facultad *f*; (*US: teaching staff*) profesorado.
fade [feɪd] *vi* desteñirse; (*sound, hope*) desvanecerse; (*light*) apagarse; (*flower*) marchitarse.
fag [fæg] *n* (*col: cigarette*) pitillo; **~ end** *n* colilla; **~ged out** *a* (*col*) agotado.
fail [feɪl] *vt* (*candidate*) suspender; (*exam*) no aprobar // *vi* acabarse; (*engine*) fallar; (*voice*) desfallecer; (*patient*) debilitarse; **to ~ to do sth** (*neglect*) dejar de hacer algo;

(*be unable*) no poder hacer algo; **without ~** sin falta; **~ing** *n* falta, defecto // *prep* a falta de; **~ure** ['feɪljə*] *n* fracaso; (*person*) fracasado/a; (*mechanical etc*) fallo.
faint [feɪnt] *a* débil; (*recollection*) vago; (*mark*) apenas visible // *n* desmayo // *vi* desmayarse; **to feel ~** estar mareado, marearse; **~-hearted** *a* pusilánime; **~ly** *ad* débilmente; vagamente; **~ness** *n* debilidad *f*.
fair [fɛə*] *a* justo; (*colour*) rubio; (*weather*) bueno; (*good enough*) suficiente; (*sizeable*) considerable // *ad* (*play*) limpio // *n* feria; (*funfair*) parque *m* de atracciones; **~ly** *ad* (*justly*) con justicia; (*equally*) equitativamente; (*quite*) bastante; **~ness** *n* justicia; (*impartiality*) imparcialidad *f*.
fairy ['fɛərɪ] *n* hada; **~ tale** *n* cuento de hadas.
faith [feɪθ] *n* fe *f*; (*trust*) confianza; (*sect*) religión *f*; **~ful** *a* fiel; **~fully** *ad* fielmente; **yours ~fully** le saluda atentamente.
fake [feɪk] *n* (*painting etc*) falsificación *f*; (*person*) impostor *m* // *a* falso // *vt* fingir; (*painting etc*) falsificar; **his illness is a ~** su enfermedad es una invención.
falcon ['fɔːlkən] *n* halcón *m*.
fall [fɔːl] *n* caída; (*US: autumn*) otoño // *vi*, *pt* **fell**, *pp* **fallen** ['fɔːlən] caer, caerse; (*price*) bajar; **~s** *npl* (*waterfall*) cascada, salto de agua; **to ~ flat** *vi* (*on one's face*) caerse (boca abajo); (*plan*) fracasar; **to ~ back** *vi* retroceder; **to ~ back on** *vt fus* (*remedy etc*) recurrir a; **to ~ backwards** *vi* caer de espaldas; **to ~ behind** *vi* quedarse atrás; **to ~ down** *vi* (*person*) caerse; (*building, hopes*) derrumbarse; **to ~ for** *vt fus* (*trick*) dejarse engañar por; (*person*) enamorarse de; **to ~ in** *vi* (*roof*) hundirse; (*MIL*) alinearse; **to ~ off** *vi* caerse; (*diminish*) disminuir; **to ~ out** *vi* (*friends etc*) reñir; (*MIL*) romper filas; **to ~ through** *vi* (*plan, project*) fracasar.
fallacy ['fæləsɪ] *n* (*error*) error *m*; (*lie*) mentira.
fallible ['fæləbl] *a* falible.
fallout ['fɔːlaut] *n* lluvia radioactiva; **~ shelter** *n* refugio contra ataques nucleares.
false [fɔːls] *a* (*gen*) falso; (*hair, teeth etc*) postizo; (*disloyal*) desleal, traidor(a); **under ~ pretences** con engaños; **~hood** *n* (*lie*) mentira; (*falseness*) falsedad *f*; **~ly** *ad* (*accuse*) falsamente; **~ teeth** *npl* dentadura postiza *sg*.
falter ['fɔːltə*] *vi* vacilar.
fame [feɪm] *n* fama.
familiar [fə'mɪlɪə*] *a* familiar; (*well-known*) conocido; (*tone*) de confianza; **to be ~ with** (*subject*) estar enterado de; **~ity** [fəmɪlɪ'ærɪtɪ] *n* familiaridad *f*; **~ize** [fə'mɪlɪəraɪz] *vr*: **to ~ize o.s. with** familiarizarse con.
family ['fæmɪlɪ] *n* familia; **~ business** *n*

negocio familiar; ~ **doctor** n médico de cabecera.

famine ['fæmɪn] n hambre f.

famished ['fæmɪʃt] a hambriento.

famous ['feɪməs] a famoso, célebre; ~**ly** ad (get on) estupendamente.

fan [fæn] n abanico; (ELEC) ventilador m; (person) aficionado/a // vt abanicar; (fire, quarrel) atizar; **to ~ out** vi desparramarse.

fanatic [fə'nætɪk] n fanático/a; ~**al** a fanático.

fan belt ['fænbɛlt] n correa de ventilador.

fanciful ['fænsɪful] a (gen) fantástico; (imaginary) imaginario.

fancy ['fænsɪ] n (whim) capricho, antojo; (taste) afición f, gusto; (imagination) imaginación f; (delusion) quimera // a (decorative) hermoso; (luxury) de lujo; (as decoration) de adorno // vt (feel like, want) tener ganas de; (imagine) imaginarse; (think) creer; **to take a ~ to** encapricharse por, tomar afición a; **it took** or **caught my ~** me cayó en gracia; **to ~ that...** imaginarse que...; **he fancies her** le gusta (ella); ~ **dress** n disfraz m; ~**-dress ball** n baile m de disfraces.

fang [fæŋ] n colmillo.

fantastic [fæn'tæstɪk] a fantástico.

fantasy ['fæntəzɪ] n fantasía.

far [fɑ:*] a (distant) lejano // ad lejos; ~ **away,** ~ **off** (a lo) lejos; ~ **better** mucho mejor; ~ **from** lejos de; **by** ~ con mucho; **go as** ~ **as the farm** vaya hasta la granja; **as** ~ **as I know** que yo sepa; **how** ~? ¿hasta dónde?; (fig) ¿hasta qué punto?; **the F~ East** el Extremo Oriente; ~**away** a remoto.

farce [fɑ:s] n farsa; **farcical** a absurdo.

fare [fɛə*] n (on trains, buses) precio (del billete); (in taxi: cost) tarifa; (: passenger) pasajero; (food) comida.

farewell [fɛə'wɛl] excl, n adiós m.

farm [fɑ:m] n granja, finca, estancia (AM) // vt cultivar; ~**er** n granjero, estanciero (AM); ~**hand** n peón m; ~**house** n casa de labranza; ~**ing** n (gen) agricultura; (tilling) cultivo; ~**land** n tierra de cultivo; ~ **worker** n = ~**hand;** ~**yard** n corral m.

far-sighted ['fɑ:'saɪtɪd] a previsor(a).

fart [fɑ:t] (col!) n pedo // vi tirarse un pedo.

farther ['fɑ:ðə*] ad más lejos, más allá.

farthest ['fɑ:ðɪst] superlative of **far.**

fascinate ['fæsɪneɪt] vt fascinar; **fascination** [-'neɪʃən] n fascinación f.

fascism ['fæʃɪzəm] n fascismo; **fascist** [-ɪst] a, n fascista m/f.

fashion ['fæʃən] n moda; (manner) manera // vt formar; **in** ~ a la moda; **out of** ~ pasado de moda; ~**able** a de moda; ~ **show** n desfile m de modelos.

fast [fɑ:st] a rápido; (dye, colour) sólido; (clock): **to be** ~ estar adelantado // ad rápidamente, de prisa; (stuck, held) firmemente // n ayuno // vi ayunar; ~

asleep profundamente dormido.

fasten ['fɑ:sn] vt asegurar, sujetar; (coat, belt) abrochar // vi cerrarse; ~**er,** ~**ing** n (gen) cierre m; (of door etc) cerrojo; **zip** ~**er** cremallera.

fastidious [fæs'tɪdɪəs] a (fussy) delicado; (demanding) exigente.

fat [fæt] a gordo; (meat) con mucha grasa; (greasy) grasiento // n grasa; (on person) carnes fpl; (lard) manteca.

fatal ['feɪtl] a (gen) fatal; (injury) mortal; (consequence) funesto; ~**ism** n fatalismo; ~**ity** [fə'tælɪtɪ] n (road death etc) víctima m/f; ~**ly** ad: ~**ly injured** herido a muerte.

fate [feɪt] n destino; (of person) suerte f; ~**ful** a fatídico.

father ['fɑ:ðə*] n padre m; ~**hood** n paternidad f; ~**-in-law** n suegro; ~**ly** a. paternal.

fathom ['fæðəm] n braza // vt (NAUT) sondear; (unravel) desentrañar; (understand) lograr comprender.

fatigue [fə'ti:g] n fatiga, cansancio.

fatten ['fætn] vt, vi engordar.

fatty ['fætɪ] a (food) graso // n (fam) gordito/a, gordinflón/ona m/f.

faucet ['fɔ:sɪt] n (US) grifo.

fault [fɔ:lt] n (error) falta; (blame) culpa; (defect: in character) defecto; (in manufacture) desperfecto; (GEO) falla // vt tachar; **it's my** ~ es culpa mía; **to find** ~ **with** criticar, poner peros a; **at** ~ culpable; ~**less** a (action) intachable; (person) sin defectos; ~**y** a defectuoso.

fauna ['fɔ:nə] n fauna.

faux pas ['fou'pɑ:] n paso en falso; (gaffe) plancha.

favour, favor (US) ['feɪvə*] n favor m; (support) apoyo; (approval) aprobación f // vt (proposition) estar a favor de, aprobar; (person etc) favorecer; (assist) ser propicio a; **to ask a** ~ **of** pedir un favor a; **to do sb a** ~ hacer un favor a uno; **to find** ~ **with** caer en gracia de; **in** ~ **of** a favor de; ~**able** a favorable; ~**ite** [-rɪt] a, n favorito, preferido; ~**itism** n favoritismo.

fawn [fɔ:n] n cervato // a (also: ~**-coloured**) color de cervato, leonado.

fear [fɪə*] n miedo, temor m // vt tener miedo a o de, temer; **for** ~ **of** por temor a; ~**ful** a temeroso, miedoso; (cowardly) tímido; (awful) terrible; ~**less** a (gen) sin miedo o temor; (bold) audaz.

feasible ['fi:zəbl] a factible.

feast [fi:st] n banquete m; (REL: also: ~ **day**) fiesta // vt, vi banquetear.

feat [fi:t] n hazaña.

feather ['fɛðə*] n pluma; ~**-weight** n (BOXING) peso pluma.

feature ['fi:tʃə*] n (gen) característica; (ANAT) rasgo; (article) crónica // vt (subj: film) presentar // vi figurar; ~**s** npl (of face) facciones fpl; ~ **film** n película (de largo metraje).

February ['fɛbruərɪ] n febrero.

fed [fɛd] *pt, pp of* **feed.**

federal ['fɛdərəl] *a* federal; **federation** [-'reɪʃən] *n* federación *f.*

fed-up [fɛd'ʌp] *a*: **to be** ~ estar harto.

fee [fi:] *n* derechos *mpl*, honorarios *mpl*; (*of school*) matrícula; (*of club*) cuota.

feeble ['fi:bl] *a* débil; ~**-minded** *a* imbécil.

feed [fi:d] *n* (*gen*) comida; (*of baby*) alimento infantil; (*of animal*) pienso // *vt, pt, pp* **fed** (*gen*) alimentar; (*baby: breastfeed*) dar el pecho a; (*animal*) dar de comer a; (*data, information*): **to** ~ **into** suministrar a; **to** ~ **on** *vt fus* alimentarse de; ~**ing bottle** *n* biberón *m.*

feel [fi:l] *n* (*sensation*) sensación *f*; (*sense of touch*) tacto // *vt, pt, pp* **felt** tocar, palpar; (*cold, pain etc*) sentir; (*think, believe*) creer; **to** ~ **hungry/cold** tener hambre/frío; **to** ~ **lonely/better** sentirse solo/ mejor; **it** ~**s soft** es suave al tacto; **to** ~ **like** (*want*) tener ganas de; **to** ~ **about** *or* **around** tantear; ~**er** *n* (*of insect*) antena; **to put out** ~**ers** (*fig*) sondear; ~**ing** *n* (*gen*) sensación *f*; (*foreboding*) presentimiento; (*opinion*) opinión *f*; (*emotion*) sentimiento.

feet [fi:t] *pl of* **foot.**

feign [feɪn] *vt* fingir.

feline ['fi:laɪn] *a* felino.

fell [fɛl] *pt of* **fall** // *vt* (*tree*) talar.

fellow ['fɛləu] *n* (*gen*) tipo; (*fam*) tío; (*of learned society*) socio; ~ **students** compañeros *mpl* de curso, condiscípulos *mpl*; ~ **citizen** *n* conciudadano; ~**countryman** *n* compatriota *m/f*; ~ **men** *npl* semejantes *mpl*; ~**ship** *n* compañerismo; (*grant*) beca.

felony ['fɛlənɪ] *n* crimen *m.*

felt [fɛlt] *pt, pp of* **feel** // *n* fieltro; ~**-tip pen** *n* rotulador *m.*

female ['fi:meɪl] *n* (*woman*) mujer *f*; (*zool*) hembra // *a* femenino.

feminine ['fɛmɪnɪn] *a* femenino.

feminist ['fɛmɪnɪst] *n* feminista.

fence [fɛns] *n* valla, cerca // *vt* (*also*: ~ **in**) cercar // *vi* hacer esgrima; **fencing** *n* esgrima.

fend [fɛnd] *vi*: **to** ~ **for o.s.** arreglárselas por su cuenta.

fender ['fɛndə*] *n* guardafuego; (*US: AUT*) parachoques *m inv*; (: *RAIL*) trompa.

ferment [fə'mɛnt] *vi* fermentar // *n* ['fɔ:mɛnt] (*fig*) agitación *f*; ~**ation** [-'teɪʃən] *n* fermentación *f.*

fern [fɔ:n] *n* helecho.

ferocious [fə'rəuʃəs] *a* feroz; **ferocity** [-'rɔsɪtɪ] *n* ferocidad *f.*

ferret ['fɛrɪt] *n* hurón *m* // *vt*: **to** ~ **out** descubrir.

ferry ['fɛrɪ] *n* (*small*) barca (de pasaje), balsa; (*large: also*: ~**boat**) transbordador *m* // *vt* transportar.

fertile ['fɔ:taɪl] *a* fértil; (*BIOL*) fecundo; **fertility** [fə'tɪlɪtɪ] *n* fertilidad *f*, fecundidad *f*; **fertilize** ['fɔ:tɪlaɪz] *vt* fertilizar;

fecundar; (*AGR*) abonar; **fertilizer** *n* fertilizante *m.*

fervent ['fɔ:vənt] *a* ardiente, apasionado.

fester ['fɛstə*] *vi* ulcerarse.

festival ['fɛstɪvəl] *n* (*REL*) fiesta; (*ART, MUS*) festival *m.*

festive ['fɛstɪv] *a* festivo; **the** ~ **season** (*Christmas*) las Navidades.

festivities [fɛs'tɪvɪtɪz] *npl* fiestas *fpl.*

fetch [fɛtʃ] *vt* ir a buscar; (*sell for*) venderse por.

fetching ['fɛtʃɪŋ] *a* atractivo.

fête [feɪt] *n* fiesta.

fetish ['fɛtɪʃ] *n* fetiche *m.*

fetters ['fɛtəz] *npl* grillos *mpl.*

feud [fju:d] *n* (*hostility*) enemistad *f*; (*quarrel*) disputa.

feudal ['fju:dl] *a* feudal; ~**ism** *n* feudalismo.

fever ['fi:və*] *n* fiebre *f*; ~**ish** *a* febril.

few [fju:] *a* (*not many*) pocos; (*some*) algunos, unos; **a** ~ a unos pocos // *pron* algunos; ~**er** *a* menos; ~**est** *a* los/las menos.

fiancé [fɪ'ɑ:ŋseɪ] *n* novio, prometido; ~**e** *n* novia, prometida.

fiasco [fɪ'æskəu] *n* fiasco.

fibre, fiber (*US*) ['faɪbə*] *n* fibra; ~**-glass** *n* fibra de vidrio.

fickle ['fɪkl] *a* inconstante.

fiction ['fɪkʃən] *n* (*gen*) ficción *f*; ~**al** *a* novelesco; **fictitious** [fɪk'tɪʃəs] *a* ficticio.

fiddle ['fɪdl] *n* (*MUS*) violín *m*; (*cheating*) trampa; (*swindle*) estafa // *vt* (*accounts*) falsificar; **to** ~ **with** *vt fus* jugar con; **fiddler** *n* violinista *m/f.*

fidelity [fɪ'dɛlɪtɪ] *n* fidelidad *f.*

fidget ['fɪdʒɪt] *vi* moverse nerviosamente; ~**y** *a* nervioso.

field [fi:ld] *n* campo; (*ELEC*) prado; (*fig*) esfera, especialidad *f*; (*competitors*) competidores *mpl*; (*entrants*) concurrentes *mpl*; ~ **glasses** *npl* gemelos *mpl*; ~ **marshal** *n* mariscal *m*; ~**work** *n* trabajo de campo.

fiend [fi:nd] *n* demonio; ~**ish** *a* diabólico.

fierce [fɪəs] *a* feroz; (*wind, attack*) violento; (*heat*) intenso; (*fighting, enemy*) encarnizado.

fiery ['faɪərɪ] *a* (*burning*) ardiente; (*temperament*) apasionado.

fifteen [fɪf'ti:n] *num* quince.

fifth [fɪfθ] *a, n* quinto.

fiftieth ['fɪftɪɪθ] *a* quincuagésimo.

fifty ['fɪftɪ] *num* cincuenta.

fig [fɪg] *n* higo.

fight [faɪt] *n* (*gen*) pelea; (*MIL*) combate *m*; (*struggle*) lucha // (*vb*: *pt, pp* **fought**) *vt* luchar contra; (*cancer, alcoholism*) combatir // *vi* pelear, luchar; ~**er** *n* combatiente *m/f*; (*fig*) luchador/a *m/f*; (*plane*) caza; ~**ing** *n* (*gen*) el luchar; (*battle*) combate *m.*

figment ['fɪgmənt] *n*: **a** ~ **of the imagination** una quimera.

figurative ['fɪgjurətɪv] *a* figurado.

figure 260 **fit**

figure ['fɪgə*] n (DRAWING. GEOM) figura, dibujo; (number. cipher) cifra; (body, outline) talle m, tipo // vt (esp US) imaginar // vi (appear) figurar; **to ~ out** vt (understand) comprender; ~**head** n mascarón m de proa; ~ **skating** n patinaje m de figuras.

file [faɪl] n (tool) lima; (dossier) expediente m; (folder) carpeta; (row) fila // vt limar; (papers) clasificar; (LAW. claim) presentar; (store) archivar; **to ~ in/out** vi entrar/salir en fila; **to ~ past** vt fus desfilar ante; **filing** n el archivar; **filing cabinet** n fichero, archivo.

fill [fɪl] vt llenar // n: **to eat one's ~** llenarse; **to ~ in** vt rellenar; **to ~ up** vt llenar (hasta el borde) // vi (AUT) poner gasolina.

fillet ['fɪlɪt] n filete m.

filling ['fɪlɪŋ] n (CULIN) relleno; (for tooth) empaste m; ~ **station** n estación f de servicio.

film [fɪlm] n película // vt (scene) filmar // vi rodar (una película); ~ **star** n astro, estrella de cine; ~**strip** n tira de película.

filter ['fɪltə*] n filtro // vt filtrar; ~ **tip** n boquilla.

filth [fɪlθ] n suciedad f; ~**y** a sucio; (language) obsceno.

fin [fɪn] n (gen) aleta.

final ['faɪnl] a (last) final, último; (definitive) definitivo, terminante // n (SPORT) final f; ~**s** npl (SCOL) exámenes mpl finales.

finale [fɪ'nɑːlɪ] n final m.

final: ~**ist** n (SPORT) finalista m/f; ~**ize** vt concluir, completar; ~**ly** ad (lastly) por último, finalmente; (eventually) por fin; (irrevocably) de modo definitivo.

finance [faɪ'næns] n (money) fondos mpl; ~**s** npl finanzas fpl // vt financiar; **financial** [-'nænʃəl] a financiero; (economic) económico; **financier** n (gen) financiero; (investor) inversionista m/f.

find [faɪnd], pt, pp **found** vt (gen) encontrar, hallar; (come upon) descubrir // n hallazgo; descubrimiento; **to ~ sb guilty** (LAW) declarar culpable a uno; **to ~ out** vt averiguar; (truth, secret) descubrir; **to ~ out about** (by chance) enterarse de; ~**ings** npl (LAW) veredicto sg, fallo sg; (of report) recomendaciones fpl.

fine [faɪn] a (delicate) fino; (good) bueno; (beautiful) bonito // ad (well) bien; (small) delgado // n (LAW) multa // vt (LAW) multar; **to be ~** (weather) hacer buen tiempo; ~ **arts** npl bellas artes fpl.

finery ['faɪnərɪ] n adornos mpl.

finesse [fɪ'nɛs] n sutileza.

finger ['fɪŋgə*] n dedo // vt (touch) manosear; (MUS) tocar (distraídamente); **little/index ~** dedo meñique/índice; ~**nail** n uña; ~**print** n huella dactilar; ~ **tip** n yema del dedo.

finicky ['fɪnɪkɪ] a (fussy) delicado.

finish ['fɪnɪʃ] n (end) fin m; (goal) meta;

(polish etc) acabado // vt, vi terminar; **to ~ off** vt acabar, terminar; (kill) acabar con; **to ~ third** llegar el tercero; ~**ing line** n línea de llegada o meta.

finite ['faɪnaɪt] a finito.

Finland ['fɪnlənd] n Finlandia.

Finn [fɪn] n finlandés/esa m/f; ~**ish** a finlandés(esa) // n (LING) finlandés m.

fiord [fjɔːd] n fiordo.

fir [fɜː*] n abeto.

fire ['faɪə*] n (gen) fuego; (accidental) incendio // vt (gun) disparar; (set fire to) incendiar; (excite) exaltar; (interest) despertar; (dismiss) despedir // vi encenderse; **on ~** ardiendo, en llamas; ~ **alarm** n alarma de incendios; ~**arm** n arma de fuego; ~ **brigade** n (cuerpo de) bomberos mpl; ~ **engine** n coche m de bomberos; ~ **escape** n escalera de incendios; ~ **extinguisher** n extintor m (de fuego); ~**man** n bombero; ~**place** n chimenea; ~**proof** a a prueba de fuego; ~**side** n hogar m; ~ **station** n parque m de bomberos; ~**wood** n leña; ~**works** npl fuegos mpl artificiales.

firing ['faɪərɪŋ] n (MIL) disparos mpl, tiroteo; ~ **squad** n pelotón m de ejecución.

firm [fɜːm] a firme // n firma; ~**ly** ad firmemente; ~**ness** n firmeza.

first [fɜːst] a primero // ad (before others) primero; (when listing reasons etc) en primer lugar, primeramente // n (person: in race) primero; (AUT) primera; **at ~** al principio; ~ **of all** ante todo; ~**aid kit** n botiquín m; ~-**class** a de primera clase; ~-**hand** a de primera mano; ~**ly** ad en primer lugar; ~ **name** n nombre m de pila; ~-**rate** a de primera clase.

fir tree n abeto.

fiscal ['fɪskəl] a fiscal.

fish [fɪʃ] n, pl inv pez m; (food) pescado // vt, vi pescar; **to go ~ing** ir de pesca; ~**erman** n pescador m; ~**ery** n pesquería; ~ **fingers** npl dedos mpl de pescado; ~**ing boat** n barca de pesca; ~**ing line** n sedal m; ~**ing rod** n caña (de pescar); ~**ing tackle** n aparejo (de pescar); ~ **market** n mercado de pescado; ~**monger** n pescadero; ~**monger's (shop)** n pescadería; ~**y** a (fig) sospechoso.

fission ['fɪʃən] n fisión f.

fissure ['fɪʃə*] n fisura.

fist [fɪst] n puño.

fit [fɪt] a (MED. SPORT) en (buena) forma; (proper) adecuado, apropiado // vt (clothes) sentar bien a; (try on: clothes) probar; (facts) cuadrar o corresponder con; (accommodate) ajustar, adaptar; (correspond exactly) encajar en // vi (clothes) entallar; (in space, gap) caber; (correspond) corresponder // n (MED) ataque m; ~ **to apto para**; ~ **for** apropiado para; **this dress is a good ~** este vestido me sienta bien; **to ~ in** vi (gen) encajarse; (fig: person) llevarse bien

(con todos); **to** ~ **out** (*also:* ~ **up**) *vt*
equipar; ~**ful** *a* espasmódico,
intermitente; ~**ment** *n* mueble *m*;
~**ness** *n* (*MED*) salud *f*; (*of remark*)
conveniencia; ~**ter** *n* ajustador *m*; ~**ting**
a apropiado // *n* (*of dress*) prueba;
~**tings** *npl* instalaciones *fpl*.

five [faiv] *num* cinco; **fiver** *n* (*Brit: col*)
billete *m* de cinco libras.

fix [fiks] *vt* (*secure*) fijar, asegurar; (*mend*)
arreglar // *n*: **to be in a** ~ estar en un
aprieto; ~**ed** [fikst] *a* (*prices etc*) fijo;
~**ture** ['fikstʃə*] *n* cosa fija; (*furniture*)
mueble *m* fijo; (*SPORT*) partido.

fizz [fiz] *vi* hacer efervescencia.

fizzle ['fizl] ~ **out** *vi* apagarse.

fizzy ['fizi] *a* (*drink*) gaseoso; (*gen*)
efervescente.

fjord [fjɔːd] = **fiord.**

flabbergasted ['flæbəgɑːstid] *a* pasmado.

flabby ['flæbi] *a* flojo; (*fat*) gordo.

flag [flæg] *n* bandera; (*stone*) losa // *vi*
acabarse, decaer; **to** ~ **sb down** hacer
signos a uno para que se detenga; ~**pole**
n asta de bandera.

flagrant ['fleigrənt] *a* flagrante.

flair [flɛə*] *n* aptitud *f* especial.

flake [fleik] *n* (*of rust, paint*) escama; (*of
snow, soap powder*) copo // *vi* (*also:* ~ **off**)
desprenderse en escamas.

flamboyant [flæm'bɔiənt] *a* (*dress*)
vistoso; (*person*) extravagante.

flame [fleim] *n* llama.

flamingo [flə'miŋgəu] *n* flamenco.

flammable ['flæməbl] *a* inflamable.

flan [flæn] *n* tarta.

flank [flæŋk] *n* flanco; (*of person*) costado
// *vt* flanquear.

flannel ['flænl] *n* (*also:* **face** ~) paño;
(*fabric*) franela; (*col*) coba; ~**s** *npl*
pantalones *mpl* de franela.

flap [flæp] *n* (*of pocket*) cartera; (*of
envelope*) solapa; (*of table*) hoja
(plegadiza); (*wing movement*) aletazo // *vt*
(*wings*) aletear // *vi* (*sail, flag*) ondear.

flare [flɛə*] *n* llamarada; (*MIL*) bengala; (*in
skirt etc*) vuelo; **to** ~ **up** *vi* encenderse;
(*fig: person*) encolerizarse; (: *revolt*)
estallar.

flash [flæʃ] *n* relámpago; (*also:* **news** ~)
noticias *fpl* de última hora; (*PHOT*) flash *m*
// *vt* (*light, headlights*) encender y apagar
(la luz); (*torch*) encender // *vi* brillar,
relampaguear; **in a** ~ en un instante; **he**
~**ed by** *or* **past** pasó como un rayo;
~**back** *n* flashback *m*; ~ **bulb** *n* bombilla
fusible; ~**er** *n* (*AUT*) intermitente *m*.

flashy ['flæʃi] *a* (*pej*) ostentoso.

flask [flɑːsk] *n* frasco; (*also:* **vacuum** ~)
termo.

flat [flæt] *a* llano; (*smooth*) liso; (*tyre*)
desinflado; (*beer*) muerto; (*MUS*)
desafinado // *n* (*apartment*) piso,
apartamento; (*MUS*) bemol *m*; (*AUT*)
pinchazo; ~**ly** *ad* terminantemente, de
plano; ~**ness** *n* (*of land*) llanura, lo llano;
~**ten** *vt* (*also:* ~**ten out**) allanar;

(*smooth out*) alisar; (*demolish*) aplastar.

flatter ['flætə*] *vt* adular, halagar; ~**er** *n*
adulador/a *m/f*; ~**ing** *a* halagüeño; ~**y** *n*
adulación *f*.

flatulence ['flætjuləns] *n* flatulencia.

flaunt [flɔːnt] *vt* ostentar, lucir.

flavour, flavor (*US*) ['fleivə*] *n* sabor *m*,
gusto // *vt* sazonar, condimentar; ~**ed**
with con sabor a; ~**ing** *n* condimento.

flaw [flɔː] *n* defecto; ~**less** *a* intachable.

flax [flæks] *n* lino; ~**en** *a* rubio.

flea [fliː] *n* pulga; ~**pit** *n* cine *m* de baja
categoría.

flee [fliː], *pt, pp* **fled** [flɛd] *vt* huir de,
abandonar // *vi* huir, fugarse.

fleece [fliːs] *n* vellón *m*; (*wool*) lana // *vt*
(*col*) pelar.

fleet [fliːt] *n* (*gen*) flota; (*of lorries etc*)
escuadra.

fleeting ['fliːtiŋ] *a* fugaz.

Flemish ['flemiʃ] *a* flamenco.

flesh [fleʃ] *n* carne *f*; (*of fruit*) pulpa; **of** ~
and blood de carne y hueso.

flew [fluː] *pt of* **fly.**

flex [fleks] *n* cordón *m* // *vt* (*muscles*)
tensar; ~**ibility** [-ɪ'biliti] *n* flexibilidad *f*;
~**ible** *a* flexible.

flick [flik] *n* golpecito; (*with finger*)
capirotazo; (*with whip*) chasquido // *vt* dar
un golpecito a; **to** ~ **through** *vt fus*
hojear.

flicker ['flikə*] *vi* (*light*) parpadear;
(*flame*) vacilar // *n* parpadeo.

flier ['flaiə*] *n* aviador/a *m/f*.

flight [flait] *n* vuelo; (*escape*) huida, fuga;
(*also:* ~ **of steps**) tramo (de escaleras);
to take ~ huir, darse a la fuga; **to put to**
~ ahuyentar; ~ **deck** *n* (*AVIAT*) cabina.

flimsy ['flimzi] *a* (*thin*) muy ligero; (*weak*)
débil.

flinch [flintʃ] *vi* acobardarse.

fling [fliŋ], *pt, pp* **flung** *vt* arrojar.

flint [flint] *n* pedernal *m*; (*in lighter*)
piedra.

flip [flip] *vt* dar la vuelta a; (*coin*) echar a
cara o cruz.

flippant ['flipənt] *a* poco serio.

flirt [flɜːt] *vi* coquetear, flirtear // *n*
coqueta *m/f*; ~**ation** [-'teiʃən] *n* coqueteo,
flirteo.

flit [flit] *vi* revolotear.

float [fləut] *n* flotador *m*; (*in procession*)
carroza // *vi* flotar; (*swimmer*) hacer la
plancha // *vt* (*gen*) hacer flotar;
(*company*) lanzar.

flock [flɔk] *n* (*of sheep*) rebaño; (*of birds*)
bandada; (*of people*) multitud *f*.

flog [flɔg] *vt* azotar; (*col*) vender.

flood [flʌd] *n* inundación *f*; (*of words, tears
etc*) torrente *m* // *vt* inundar; ~**ing** *n*
inundación *f*; ~**light** *n* foco.

floor [flɔː*] *n* suelo; (*storey*) piso; (*of sea*)
fondo; (*dance* ~) pista // *vt* (*fig*) dejar sin
respuesta; **ground** ~ (*Brit*), **first** ~ (*US*)
planta baja; **first** ~ (*Brit*), **second** ~

(US) primer piso; ~board n tabla; ~ show n cabaret m.

flop [flɔp] n fracaso // vi (fail) fracasar.

floppy ['flɔpɪ] a flojo.

flora ['flɔːrə] n flora; floral ['flɔːrl] a floral.

florid ['flɔrɪd] a (style) florido.

florist ['flɔrɪst] n florista m/f; ~'s (shop) n florería.

flounce [flauns] n volante m; to ~ out vi salir enfadado.

flounder ['flaundə*] vi tropezar.

flour ['flauə*] n harina.

flourish ['flʌrɪʃ] vi florecer; ~ing a floreciente.

flout [flaut] vt burlarse de.

flow [fləu] n (movement) flujo; (direction) curso; (tide) corriente f // vi correr, fluir; (blood) derramarse.

flower ['flauə*] n flor f // vi florecer; ~bed n macizo; ~pot n tiesto; ~y a florido.

flown [fləun] pp of fly.

flu [fluː] n gripe f.

fluctuate ['flʌktjueɪt] vi fluctuar; fluctuation [-'eɪʃən] n fluctuación f.

fluent ['fluːənt] a (speech) elocuente; he speaks ~ French, he's ~ in French domina el francés; ~ly ad con fluidez.

fluff [flʌf] n pelusa; ~y a velloso.

fluid ['fluːɪd] a, n fluido, líquido.

fluke [fluːk] n (col) chiripa.

flung [flʌŋ] pt, pp of fling.

fluorescent [fluə'rɛsnt] a fluorescente.

fluoride ['fluəraɪd] n fluoruro.

flurry ['flʌrɪ] n (of snow) ráfago; (haste) agitación f; ~ of activity frenesí m de actividad.

flush [flʌʃ] n (on face) rubor m; (plenty) plenitud f, abundancia // vt limpiar con agua // vi ruborizarse // a: ~ with a ras de; to ~ the toilet hacer funcionar el WC; ~ed a ruborizado.

flustered ['flʌstəd] a aturdido.

flute [fluːt] n flauta.

flutter ['flʌtə*] n emoción f; (of wings) revoloteo, aleteo; (fam: bet) apuesta // vi revolotear.

flux [flʌks] n flujo; in a state of ~ cambiando continuamente.

fly [flaɪ] n (insect) mosca; (on trousers: also: flies) bragueta // (vb: pt flew, pp flown) vt (gen) hacer volar; (plane) pilot(e)ar; (cargo) transportar (en avión); (distances) recorrer (en avión) // vi volar; (passengers) ir o subir en avión; (escape) evadirse; (flag) ondear; to let ~ desahogarse; ~ing n (activity) (el) volar // a: ~ing visit visita relámpago; with ~ing colours con lucimiento; ~ing saucer n platillo volante; ~over n (Brit: bridge) paso a desnivel o superior; ~past n desfile m aéreo; ~sheet n (for tent) doble techo.

foal [fəul] n potro.

foam [fəum] n espuma // vi echar espuma; ~ rubber n espuma de caucho.

fob [fɔb] vt: to ~ sb off deshacerse de alguien con excusas.

focal ['fəukəl] a focal.

focus ['fəukəs], pl ~es n foco // vt (field glasses etc) enfocar; to ~ on enfocar a; in/out of ~ enfocado/desenfocado.

fodder ['fɔdə*] n pienso.

foe [fəu] n enemigo.

foetus ['fiːtəs] n feto.

fog [fɔg] n niebla; ~gy a: it's ~gy hay niebla, está brumoso.

foil [fɔɪl] vt frustrar // n hoja; (also: kitchen ~) papel m (de) aluminio; (FENCING) florete m.

fold [fəuld] n (bend, crease) pliegue m; (of skin) arruga; (AGR) redil m // vt doblar; to ~ up vi (map etc) plegarse, doblarse; (business) quebrar // vt (map etc) plegar; ~er n (for papers) carpeta; (brochure) folleto; ~ing a (chair, bed) plegable.

foliage ['fəulɪɪdʒ] n follaje m.

folk [fəuk] npl gente f // a popular, folklórico; ~s npl familia, parientes mpl; ~lore ['fəuklɔː*] n folklore m; ~song n canción f popular o folklórica.

follow ['fɔləu] vt seguir // vi seguir; (result) resultar; he ~ed suit hizo lo mismo; to ~ up vt (letter, offer) responder a; (case) investigar; ~er n seguidor/a m/f; (POL) partidario/a; ~ing a siguiente // n afición f, partidarios mpl.

folly ['fɔlɪ] n locura.

fond [fɔnd] a (loving) cariñoso; to be ~ of tener cariño a.

fondle ['fɔndl] vt acariciar.

fondness ['fɔndnɪs] n (for things) gusto; (for people) cariño.

font [fɔnt] n pila bautismal.

food [fuːd] n comida; ~ mixer n batidora; ~ poisoning n botulismo; ~stuffs npl comestibles mpl.

fool [fuːl] n tonto/a; (CULIN) puré m de frutas con nata // vt engañar // vi (gen: ~ around) bromear; (waste time) perder el tiempo; ~hardy a temerario; ~ish a tonto; (stupid) estúpido; (careless) imprudente; ~proof a (plan etc) infalible.

foot [fut], pl feet n pie m; (measure) pie m (= 304 mm); (of animal) pata // vt (bill) pagar; on ~ a pie; ~ball n balón m; (game) fútbol m; ~baller n futbolista m; ~brake n freno de pie; ~bridge n puente m para peatones; ~hills npl estribaciones fpl; ~hold n pie m firme; ~ing n (fig) posición f; to lose one's ~ing perder el pie; on an equal ~ing en pie de igualdad; ~lights npl candilejas fpl; ~man n lacayo; ~note n nota de pie; ~path n sendero; (pavement) acera; ~sore a con los pies adoloridos; ~step n paso; ~wear n calzado.

for [fɔː*] prep (gen) para; (as, in exchange for, because of) por; (during) durante; (in spite of) a pesar de // conj pues, ya que; it was sold ~ 100 pesetas se vendió por 100 pesetas; what ~? ¿para qué?; what's it ~? ¿para qué sirve?; he was away ~

2 years estuvo fuera 2 años; **he went** ~ **the paper** fue a buscar el periódico; ~ **sale** se vende.

forage ['fɔrɪdʒ] n forraje m.

foray ['fɔreɪ] n incursión f.

forbid [fə'bɪd], pt **forbad(e)** [fə'bæd], pp **forbidden** [fə'bɪdn] vt prohibir; ~**ding** a (gloomy) lúgubre; (severe) severo.

force [fɔːs] n fuerza // vt forzar; **to** ~ **o.s.** to hacer un esfuerzo por; **the F**~**s** npl las Fuerzas Armadas; **in** ~ en vigor; ~**d** [fɔːst] a forzado; ~**ful** a enérgico.

forceps ['fɔːsɛps] npl fórceps m inv.

forcibly ['fɔːsəblɪ] ad a la fuerza.

ford [fɔːd] n vado // vt vadear.

forearm ['fɔːrɑːm] n antebrazo.

foreboding [fɔː'bəudɪŋ] n presagio.

forecast ['fɔːkɑːst] n pronóstico // vt (irg: like **cast**) pronosticar.

forefathers ['fɔːfɑːðəz] npl antepasados mpl.

forefinger ['fɔːfɪŋgə*] n (dedo) índice m.

forego = **forgo**.

foregone ['fɔːgɔn] a: **it's a** ~ **conclusion** es una conclusión inevitable.

foreground ['fɔːgraund] n primer plano.

forehead ['fɔrɪd] n frente f.

foreign ['fɔrɪn] a extranjero; (trade) exterior; ~**er** n extranjero; ~ **exchange** n divisas fpl; **F**~ **Minister** n Ministro de Asuntos Exteriores; **F**~ **Office** n Ministerio de Asuntos Exteriores.

foreleg ['fɔːlɛg] n pata delantera.

foreman ['fɔːmən] n capataz m; (in construction) maestro de obras.

foremost ['fɔːməust] a principal.

forensic [fə'rɛnsɪk] a forense.

forerunner ['fɔːrʌnə*] n precursor/a m/f.

foresee [fɔː'siː] (irg: like **see**) vt prever; ~**able** a previsible.

foresight ['fɔːsaɪt] n previsión f.

forest ['fɔrɪst] n bosque m.

forestall [fɔː'stɔːl] vt prevenir.

forestry ['fɔrɪstrɪ] n silvicultura.

foretaste ['fɔːteɪst] n (gen) anticipo; (sample) muestra.

foretell [fɔː'tɛl] (irg: like **tell**) vt predecir, pronosticar.

forever [fə'rɛvə*] ad para siempre.

foreword ['fɔːwəːd] n prefacio.

forfeit ['fɔːfɪt] n pérdida; (fine) multa // vt perder (derecho a).

forgave [fə'geɪv] pt of **forgive**.

forge [fɔːdʒ] n fragua; (smithy) herrería // vt (signature, money) falsificar; (metal) forjar; **to** ~ **ahead** vi avanzar constantemente; **forger** n falsificador/a m/f; ~**ry** n falsificación f.

forget [fə'gɛt], pt **forgot**, pp **forgotten** vt olvidar // vi olvidarse; ~**ful** a olvidadizo; ~**fulness** n (gen) olvido; (thoughtlessness) descuido; (oblivion) falta de memoria.

forgive [fə'gɪv], pt **forgave**, pp **forgiven** vt perdonar; ~ **sb for sth** perdonar algo a uno; ~**ness** n perdón m.

forgo [fɔː'gəu] (irg: like **go**) vt (give up)

renunciar a; (go without) privarse de.

forgot [fə'gɔt] pt of **forget**.

forgotten [fə'gɔtn] pp of **forget**.

fork [fɔːk] n (for eating) tenedor m; (for gardening) horca; (of roads) bifurcación f; (in tree) horcadura // vi (road) bifurcarse; **to** ~ **out** vt (col: pay) desembolsar; ~**ed** [fɔːkt] a (lightning) en zigzag; ~-**lift truck** n elevadora-transportadora de horquilla.

form [fɔːm] n forma; (SCOL) clase f; (questionnaire) formulario // vt formar; **in top** ~ en plena forma.

formal ['fɔːməl] a (offer, receipt) oficial; (person etc) ceremonioso; (occasion, dinner) oficial, protocolario; (dress) de etiqueta; ~**ity** [-'mælɪtɪ] n ceremonia; ~**ities** npl formalidades fpl; ~**ly** ad oficialmente.

format ['fɔːmæt] n formato.

formation [fɔː'meɪʃən] n formación f.

formative ['fɔːmətɪv] a (years) formativo.

former ['fɔːmə*] a anterior; (earlier) antiguo; (ex) ex; **the** ~ ... **the latter** ... aquél ... éste ...; ~**ly** ad antiguamente.

formidable ['fɔːmɪdəbl] a formidable.

formula ['fɔːmjulə] n fórmula.

formulate ['fɔːmjuleɪt] vt formular.

forsake [fə'seɪk], pt **forsook** [fə'suk], pp **forsaken** [fə'seɪkən] vt (gen) abandonar; (plan) renunciar a.

fort [fɔːt] n fuerte m.

forte ['fɔːtɪ] n fuerte m.

forth [fɔːθ] ad en adelante; **back and** ~ de acá para allá; **and so** ~ y así sucesivamente; ~-**coming** a próximo, venidero; (character) comunicativo; ~**right** a franco.

fortieth ['fɔːtɪɪθ] a cuadragésimo.

fortification [fɔːtɪfɪ'keɪʃən] n fortificación f; **fortify** ['fɔːtɪfaɪ] vt fortalecer.

fortitude ['fɔːtɪtjuːd] n fortaleza.

fortnight ['fɔːtnaɪt] n quincena; ~**ly** a quincenal // ad quincenalmente.

fortress ['fɔːtrɪs] n fortaleza.

fortuitous [fɔː'tjuːɪtəs] a fortuito.

fortunate ['fɔːtʃənɪt] a: **to be** ~ tener suerte; **it is** ~ **that...** es afortunado que...; ~**ly** ad afortunadamente.

fortune ['fɔːtʃən] n suerte f; (wealth) fortuna; ~-**teller** n adivina.

forty ['fɔːtɪ] num cuarenta.

forum ['fɔːrəm] n foro.

forward ['fɔːwəd] a (movement, position) avanzado; (front) delantero; (not shy) atrevido // n (SPORT) delantero // vt (letter) remitir; (career) progresar; **to move** ~ avanzar; ~**(s)** ad (hacia) adelante.

fossil ['fɔsl] n fósil m.

foster ['fɔstə*] vt fomentar; ~ **brother** n hermano de leche; ~ **child** n hijo adoptivo; ~ **mother** n madre f adoptiva.

fought [fɔːt] pt, pp of **fight**.

foul [faul] a (gen) sucio, puerco; (weather) horrible; (smell etc) asqueroso // n (FOOTBALL) falta (en contra) // vt (dirty) ensuciar; (*block*) atascar; (*football player*) cometer una falta contra; ~ **play** *n* (*SPORT*) mala jugada; (*LAW*) muerte *f* violenta.

found [faund] *pt, pp of* **find** // *vt* (*establish*) fundar; ~**ation** [-'deɪʃən] *n* (*act*) fundación *f*; (*basis*) base *f*; (*also*: ~**ation cream**) crema base; ~**ations** *npl* (*of building*) cimientos *mpl*.

founder ['faundə*] *n* fundador/a *m/f* // *vi* hundirse.

foundry ['faundrɪ] *n* fundición *f*.

fountain ['fauntɪn] *n* fuente *f*; ~ **pen** *n* pluma-fuente *f*.

four [fɔ:*] *num* cuatro; **on all** ~**s** a gatas; ~**-poster** *n* cama a columnas; ~**some** ['fɔ:səm] *n* grupo de cuatro personas; ~**teen** *num* catorce; ~**teenth** *a* décimocuarto; ~**th** *a* cuarto.

fowl [faul] *n* ave *f* (de corral).

fox [fɔks] *n* zorro // *vt* confundir; ~**trot** *n* fox *m*.

foyer ['fɔɪeɪ] *n* vestíbulo.

fracas ['fræka:] *n* gresca, riña.

fraction ['frækʃən] *n* fracción *f*.

fracture ['fræktʃə*] *n* fractura // *vt* fracturar.

fragile ['frædʒaɪl] *a* frágil.

fragment ['frægmənt] *n* fragmento; ~**ary** *a* fragmentario.

fragrance ['freɪgrəns] *n* fragancia; **fragrant** [-ənt] *a* fragante, oloroso.

frail [freɪl] *a* (*fragile*) frágil, quebradizo; (*weak*) delicado.

frame [freɪm] *n* (*gen*) estructura; (*body*) talle *m*; (*TECH*) armazón *m*; (*of picture, door etc*) marco; (*of spectacles: also*: ~**s**) montura // *vt* encuadrar; (*reply*) formular; (*fam*) incriminar; ~ **of mind** *n* estado de ánimo; ~**work** *n* marco.

France [fra:ns] *n* Francia.

franchise ['fræntʃaɪz] *n* (*POL*) derecho de votar, sufragio.

frank [fræŋk] *a* franco // *vt* (*letter*) franquear; ~**ly** *ad* francamente; ~**ness** *n* franqueza.

frantic ['fræntɪk] *a* frenético.

fraternal [frə'tə:nl] *a* fraterno; **fraternity** [-nɪtɪ] *n* (*club*) fraternidad *f*; (*US*) club *m* de estudiantes; (*guild*) cofradía; **fraternize** ['frætənaɪz] *vi* confraternizar.

fraud [frɔ:d] *n* fraude *m*; (*person*) impostor *m*; ~**ulent** *a* fraudulento.

fraught [frɔ:t] *a*: ~ **with** cargado de.

fray [freɪ] *n* combate *m*, lucha // *vi* deshilacharse; **tempers were** ~**ed** tenían los nervios a punto.

freak [fri:k] *n* (*person*) fenómeno; (*event*) suceso anormal; (*thing*) cosa insólita.

freckle ['frekl] *n* peca.

free [fri:] *a* (*gen*) libre; (*not fixed*) suelto; (*gratis*) gratuito; (*unoccupied*) desocupado; (*liberal*) generoso // *vt* (*prisoner etc*) poner en libertad; (*jammed object*) soltar; ~ **(of charge)** *ad* gratis; ~**dom** ['fri:dəm] *n* libertad *f*; ~**-for-all** *n* riña general; ~ **kick** *n* tiro libre; ~**lance** *a*

independiente; ~**ly** *ad* libremente; generosamente; ~**mason** *n* francmasón *m*; ~ **trade** *n* libre comercio; ~**way** *n* (*US*) autopista; ~**wheel** *vi* ir en punto muerto; ~ **will** *n* libre albedrío; **of one's own** ~ **will** por su propia voluntad.

freeze [fri:z], *pt* **froze**, *pp* **frozen** *vi* helarse, congelarse // *vt* helar; (*prices, food, salaries*) congelar // *n* helada; congelación *f*; **freezer** *n* congelador *m*.

freezing ['fri:zɪŋ] *a* helado; ~ **point** *n* punto de congelación; **3 degrees below** ~ tres grados bajo cero.

freight [freɪt] *n* (*goods*) carga; (*money charged*) flete *m*; ~ **car** *n* (*US*) vagón *m* de mercancías.

French [frentʃ] *a* francés(esa) // *n* (*LING*) francés *m*; **the** ~ los franceses; ~ **fried (potatoes)** *npl* patatas *fpl* fritas; ~**man/woman** *n* francés/esa *m/f*; ~ **window** *n* puertaventana.

frenzy ['frenzɪ] *n* frenesí *m*.

frequency ['fri:kwənsɪ] *n* frecuencia; **frequent** [-ənt] *a* frecuente // *vt* [frɪ'kwent] frecuentar; **frequently** [-əntlɪ] *ad* frecuentemente, a menudo.

fresco ['freskəu] *n* fresco.

fresh [freʃ] *a* (*gen*) fresco; (*new*) nuevo; (*water*) dulce; ~**en** *vi* (*wind, air*) soplar más recio; **to** ~**en up** *vi* (*person*) lavarse, arreglarse; ~**ly** *ad* (*newly*) nuevamente; (*recently*) recientemente; ~**ness** *n* frescura.

fret [fret] *vi* inquietarse.

friar ['fraɪə*] *n* fraile *m*; (*before name*) fray.

friction ['frɪkʃən] *n* fricción *f*.

Friday ['fraɪdɪ] *n* viernes *m*.

fridge [frɪdʒ] *n* nevera *f*.

friend [frend] *n* amigo/a; ~**liness** *n* simpatía; ~**ly** *a* simpático; ~**ship** *n* amistad *f*.

frieze [fri:z] *n* friso.

frigate ['frɪgɪt] *n* fragata *f*.

fright [fraɪt] *n* susto; **to take** ~ asustarse; ~**en** *vt* asustar; ~**ening** *a* espantoso; ~**ful** *a* espantoso, horrible; ~**fully** *ad* terriblemente.

frigid ['frɪdʒɪd] *a* (*MED*) frígido, frío; ~**ity** [frɪ'dʒɪdɪtɪ] *n* frialdad *f*; (*MED*) frigidez *f*.

frill [frɪl] *n* volante *m*.

fringe [frɪndʒ] *n* flequillo; (*edge: of forest etc*) borde *m*, margen *m*; ~ **benefits** *npl* ventajas *fpl* supletorias.

frisky ['frɪskɪ] *a* juguetón(ona), fogoso.

fritter ['frɪtə*] *n* buñuelo; **to** ~ **away** *vt* desperdiciar.

frivolous ['frɪvələs] *a* frívolo.

frizzy ['frɪzɪ] *a* rizado.

fro [frəu] *see* **to**.

frock [frɔk] *n* vestido.

frog [frɔg] *n* rana; ~**man** *n* hombre-rana *m*.

frolic ['frɔlɪk] *vi* juguetear.

from [frɔm] *prep* de; ~ **January (on)** a partir de enero; ~ **what he says** por lo que dice.

front [frʌnt] n (foremost part) parte f delantera; (of house) fachada; (promenade: also: sea ~) paseo marítimo; (MIL, POL, METEOROLOGY) frente m; (fig: appearances) apariencias fpl // a delantero, primero; **in** ~ **(of)** delante (de); ~**al** a frontal; ~ **door** n puerta principal; ~**ier** ['frʌntɪə*] n frontera; ~ **page** n primera plana; ~ **room** n (Brit) salón m, sala; ~**-wheel drive** n tracción f delantera.

frost [frɔst] n (gen) helada; (visible) escarcha; ~**bite** n congelación f; ~**ed** a (glass) deslustrado; ~**y** a (window) cubierto de escarcha; (welcome) glacial.

froth [frɔθ] n espuma.

frown [fraun] n ceño // vi fruncir el ceño.

froze [frəuz] pt of **freeze**.

frozen ['frəuzn] pp of **freeze**.

frugal ['fruːgəl] a frugal.

fruit [fruːt] n, pl inv fruta; ~**erer's** (shop) n frutería; ~**ful** a provechoso; ~**ion** [fruː'ɪʃən] n: **to come to** ~**ion** realizarse; ~ **machine** n máquina tragaperras.

frustrate [frʌs'treɪt] vt frustrar; ~**d** a frustrado; **frustration** [-'treɪʃən] n frustración f.

fry [fraɪ], pt, pp **fried** vt freír; **small** ~ gente f menuda; ~**ing pan** n sartén f.

ft. abbr of **foot, feet.**

fuchsia ['fjuːʃə] n fucsia.

fudge [fʌdʒ] n (CULIN) dulce m de azúcar, manjar m.

fuel [fjuəl] n (for heating) combustible m; (coal) carbón m; (wood) leña; (for propelling) carburante m; ~ **oil** n aceite m combustible; ~ **tank** n depósito de combustible.

fugitive ['fjuːdʒɪtɪv] n fugitivo.

fulfil [ful'fɪl] vt (function) cumplir con; (condition) satisfacer; (wish, desire) realizar; ~**ment** n satisfacción f; realización f.

full [ful] a lleno; (fig) pleno; (complete) completo; (information) detallado // ad: ~ **well** perfectamente; **I'm** ~ estoy lleno; ~ **employment** pleno empleo; ~ **fare** pasaje m completo; **a** ~ **two hours** dos horas completas; **at** ~ **speed** a máxima velocidad; **in** ~ (reproduce, quote) íntegramente; ~**-length** a (portrait) de cuerpo entero; ~ **moon** n luna llena; ~**-sized** a (portrait etc) de tamaño natural; ~ **stop** n punto; ~**-time** a (work) de tiempo completo // n (SPORT) final m; ~**y** ad completamente; ~**y-fledged** a (teacher, barrister) diplomado.

fumble ['fʌmbl]: **to** ~ **with** vt fus revolver, manosear.

fume [fjuːm] vi humear, echar humo; ~**s** npl humo sg, gases mpl.

fumigate ['fjuːmɪgeɪt] vt fumigar.

fun [fʌn] n (amusement) diversión f; (joy) alegría; **to have** ~ divertirse; **for** ~ en broma; **to make** ~ **of** vt fus burlarse de.

function ['fʌŋkʃən] n función f // vi funcionar; ~**al** a funcional.

fund [fʌnd] n fondo; (source, store) fuente f; ~**s** npl fondos mpl.

fundamental [fʌndə'mɛntl] a fundamental.

funeral ['fjuːnərəl] n (burial) entierro; (ceremony) funerales mpl; ~ **service** n misa de difuntos.

funfair ['fʌnfɛə*] n parque m de atracciones.

fungus ['fʌŋgəs], pl **-gi** [-gaɪ] n hongo.

funnel ['fʌnl] n embudo; (of ship) chimenea.

funnily ['fʌnɪlɪ] ad de modo divertido.

funny ['fʌnɪ] a gracioso, divertido; (strange) curioso, raro.

fur [fəː*] n piel f; (in kettle etc) sarro; ~ **coat** n abrigo de pieles.

furious ['fjuərɪəs] a furioso; (effort) violento; ~**ly** ad con furia.

furlong ['fəːlɔŋ] n octava parte de una milla.

furlough ['fəːləu] n (US) licencia.

furnace ['fəːnɪs] n horno.

furnish ['fəːnɪʃ] vt amueblar; (supply) suministrar; ~**ings** npl muebles mpl.

furniture ['fəːnɪtʃə*] n muebles mpl; **piece of** ~ mueble m; ~ **polish** n cera de lustrar.

furrier ['fʌrɪə*] n peletero.

furrow ['fʌrəu] n surco.

furry ['fəːrɪ] a peludo.

further ['fəːðə*] a (new) nuevo, adicional; (place) más lejano // ad más lejos; (more) más; (moreover) además // vt promover, adelantar; ~ **education** n educación f superior; ~**more** [fəːðə'mɔː*] ad además.

furthest ['fəːðɪst] superlative of **far.**

furtive ['fəːtɪv] a furtivo.

fury ['fjuərɪ] n furia.

fuse, fuze (US) [fjuːz] n fusible m; (for bomb etc) mecha // vt (metal) fundir; (fig) fusionar // vi fundirse; fusionarse; (ELEC): **to** ~ **the lights** fundir los plomos; ~ **box** n caja de fusibles.

fuselage ['fjuːzəlɑːʒ] n fuselaje m.

fusion ['fjuːʒən] n fusión f.

fuss [fʌs] n (noise) bulla; (dispute) lío; (complaining) protesta; (ceremony) ceremonias fpl; **to make a** ~ armar un lío o jaleo; ~**y** a (person) exigente.

futile ['fjuːtaɪl] a vano; **futility** [-'tɪlɪtɪ] n inutilidad f.

future ['fjuːtʃə*] a (gen) futuro; (coming) venidero // n futuro; **futuristic** [-'rɪstɪk] a futurístico.

fuzzy ['fʌzɪ] a (PHOT) borroso; (hair) muy rizado.

G

gabble ['gæbl] vi hablar atropelladamente; (gossip) cotorrear.

gable ['geɪbl] n aguilón m.

gadget ['gædʒɪt] n aparato.

Gaelic ['geɪlɪk] n (LING) gaélico.

gag [gæg] n (joke) chiste m // vt amordazar.

gaiety ['geiiti] n alegría.
gaily ['geili] ad alegremente.
gain [gein] n ganancia // vt ganar // vi (watch) adelantarse; **to ~ by sth** sacar provecho de algo; **to ~ on sb** ir ganando terreno a uno.
gait [geit] n modo de andar.
gala ['gɑːlə] n fiesta.
galaxy ['gæləksi] n galaxia.
gale [geil] n (wind) vendaval m.
gallant ['gælənt] a valiente; (towards ladies) atento; **~ry** n valentía; (courtesy) cortesía.
gall-bladder ['gɔːlblædə*] n vesícula biliar.
gallery ['gæləri] n galería; (also: **art ~**) museo.
galley ['gæli] n (ship's kitchen) cocina; (ship) galera.
gallon ['gæln] n galón m (4.543 litros).
gallop ['gæləp] n galope m // vi galopar.
gallows ['gæləuz] n horca.
gallstone ['gɔːlstəun] n cálculo biliario.
gamble ['gæmbl] n (risk) riesgo; (bet) apuesta // vt: **to ~ on** apostar a; (fig) confiar en que // vi jugar; (COMM) especular; **gambler** n jugador/a m/f; **gambling** n el juego.
game [geim] n (gen) juego; (match) partido; (of cards) partida; (HUNTING) caza // a valiente; (ready): **to be ~ for anything** atreverse a todo; **~ bird** n ave f de caza; **~keeper** n guardabosques m inv.
gammon ['gæmən] n (bacon) tocino ahumado; (ham) jamón m ahumado.
gang [gæŋ] n pandilla; (of workmen) brigada // vi: **to ~ up on sb** conspirar contra uno.
gangrene ['gæŋgriːn] n gangrena.
gangster ['gæŋstə*] n gángster m.
gangway ['gæŋwei] n (in theatre etc) pasillo; (on ship) pasarela; (on dock) pasadera.
gaol [dʒeil] = **jail**.
gap [gæp] n vacío, hueco; (in trees, traffic) claro; (in time) intervalo.
gape [geip] vi estar o quedarse boquiabierto; **gaping** a (hole) muy abierto.
garage ['gærɑːʒ] n garaje m.
garbage ['gɑːbidʒ] n basura; **~ can** n (US) cubo de la basura.
garbled ['gɑːbld] a (distorted) falsificado, amañado.
garden ['gɑːdn] n jardín m; **~er** n jardinero; **~ing** n jardinería.
gargle ['gɑːgl] vi hacer gárgaras.
gargoyle ['gɑːgɔil] n gárgola.
garish ['gɛəriʃ] a chillón(ona).
garland ['gɑːlənd] n guirnalda.
garlic ['gɑːlik] n ajo.
garment ['gɑːmənt] n prenda (de vestir).
garnish ['gɑːniʃ] vt adornar; (CULIN) aderezar.

garrison ['gærisn] n guarnición f // vt guarnecer.
garrulous ['gærjuləs] a gárrulo.
garter ['gɑːtə*] n liga; **~ belt** portaligas m inv.
gas [gæs] n gas m; (US: gasoline) gasolina // vt asfixiar con gas; **~ cooker** n cocina de gas; **~ cylinder** n bombona de gas; **~ fire** n estufa de gas.
gash [gæʃ] n raja; (on face) cuchillada // vt (gen) rajar; (with knife) acuchillar.
gasket ['gæskit] n (AUT) junta.
gas: ~mask n careta antigás; **~ meter** n contador m de gas.
gasoline ['gæsəliːn] n (US) gasolina.
gasp [gɑːsp] n grito sofocado // vi (pant) jadear; **to ~ out** vt (say) decir con voz entrecortada.
gas: ~ ring n hornillo de gas; **~ stove** n cocina de gas; **~sy** a gaseoso; **~ tap** n llave f del gas.
gastric ['gæstrik] a gástrico; **~ ulcer** n úlcera gástrica.
gate [geit] n puerta; (RAIL) barrera; **~crash** vt colarse de gorra en; **~way** n puerta.
gather ['gæðə*] vt (flowers, fruit) coger; (assemble) reunir; (pick up) recoger; (SEWING) fruncir; (understand) entender // vi (assemble) reunirse; **~ing** n reunión f, asamblea.
gauche [gəuʃ] a torpe.
gaudy ['gɔːdi] a chillón(ona).
gauge [geidʒ] n medida; (RAIL) entrevía; (instrument) indicador m // vt medir.
gaunt [gɔːnt] a descarnado; (grim, desolate) desolado.
gauntlet ['gɔːntlit] n (fig): **to run the ~** correr baquetas; **to throw down the ~** arrojar el guante.
gauze [gɔːz] n gasa.
gave [geiv] pt of **give**.
gay [gei] a (person) alegre; (colour) vistoso, vivo; (homosexual) gay.
gaze [geiz] n mirada fija; **to ~ at sth** mirar algo con fijeza.
gazelle [gə'zɛl] n gacela.
gazetteer [gæzə'tiə*] n diccionario geográfico.
G.B. abbr of **Great Britain**.
G.C.E. n abbr of **General Certificate of Education**.
gear [giə*] n equipo, herramientas fpl; (TECH) engranaje m; (AUT) velocidad f, marcha; **top/low ~** tercera (o cuarta)/primera velocidad; **in ~** en marcha; **~ box** n caja de cambios; **~ lever, ~ shift** (US) n palanca de velocidades; **~ wheel** n rueda dentada.
geese [giːs] pl of **goose**.
gelatin(e) ['dʒɛlətiːn] n gelatina.
gelignite ['dʒɛlignait] n gelignita.
gem [dʒɛm] n joya.
Gemini ['dʒɛminai] n Géminis m, Gemelos mpl.
gender ['dʒɛndə*] n género.

general ['dʒɛnərl] n general m // a general; **in** ~ en general; ~ **election** n elecciones fpl generales; ~**ization** [-aɪ'zeɪʃən] n generalización f; ~**ize** vi generalizar; ~**ly** ad generalmente, en general; ~ **practitioner (G.P.)** n médico general.
generate ['dʒɛnəreɪt] vt (ELEC) generar; (fig) producir.
generation [dʒɛnə'reɪʃən] n generación f.
generator ['dʒɛnəreɪtə*] n generador m.
generosity [dʒɛnə'rɔsɪtɪ] n generosidad f; **generous** ['dʒɛnərəs] a generoso; (helping etc) abundante.
genetics [dʒɪ'nɛtɪks] n genética.
Geneva [dʒɪ'niːvə] n Ginebra.
genial ['dʒiːnɪəl] a afable, simpático.
genitals ['dʒɛnɪtlz] npl órganos mpl genitales.
genius ['dʒiːnɪəs] n genio.
genocide ['dʒɛnəusaɪd] n genocidio.
gent [dʒɛnt] n abbr of **gentleman**.
genteel [dʒɛn'tiːl] a fino, elegante.
gentle ['dʒɛntl] a (sweet) amable, dulce; (touch etc) ligero, suave; (animal) manso.
gentleman ['dʒɛntlmən] n señor m; (wellbred man) caballero.
gentleness ['dʒɛntlnɪs] n dulzura; (of touch) suavidad f; (of animal) mansedumbre f.
gently ['dʒɛntlɪ] ad suavemente.
gentry ['dʒɛntrɪ] n alta burguesía.
gents [dʒɛnts] n (aseos de) caballeros mpl.
genuine ['dʒɛnjuɪn] a auténtico; (person) sincero.
geographic(al) [dʒɪə'græfɪk(l)] a geográfico; **geography** [dʒɪ'ɔgrəfɪ] n geografía.
geological [dʒɪə'lɔdʒɪkl] a geológico; **geologist** [dʒɪ'ɔlədʒɪst] n geólogo; **geology** [dʒɪ'ɔlədʒɪ] n geología.
geometric(al) [dʒɪə'mɛtrɪk(l)] a geométrico; **geometry** [dʒɪ'ɔmətrɪ] n geometría.
geranium [dʒɪ'reɪnjəm] n geranio.
germ [dʒəːm] n (gen) microbio, bacteria; (BIO, fig) germen m.
German ['dʒəːmən] a alemán(ana) // n alemán/ana m/f; (LING) alemán m; ~ **measles** n rubéola.
Germany ['dʒəːmənɪ] n Alemania.
germination [dʒəːmɪ'neɪʃən] n germinación f.
gesticulate [dʒɛs'tɪkjuleɪt] vi gesticular.
gesture ['dʒɛstjə*] n gesto.
get [gɛt], pt, pp **got**, pp **gotten** (US) vt (obtain) obtener; (receive) recibir; (achieve) conseguir; (find) encontrar; (catch) coger; (fetch) traer, ir a buscar; (understand) entender // vi (become) hacerse, volverse; **to** ~ **old** hacerse viejo, envejecer; **to** ~ **to** (place) llegar a; **he got under the fence** pasó por debajo de la barrera; **to** ~ **ready/washed** prepararse/lavarse; **to** ~ **sb to do sth** hacer que alguien haga algo; **to** ~ **sth**

out of sth sacar algo de algo; **to** ~ **about** vi salir mucho, viajar mucho; (news) divulgarse; **to** ~ **along** vi (agree) entenderse; (depart) marcharse; (manage) = **to get by**; **to** ~ **at** vt fus (attack) atacar; (reach) llegar a; (the truth) descubrir; **to** ~ **away** vi marcharse; (on holiday) irse de vacaciones; (escape) escaparse; **to** ~ **away with** vt fus hacer impunemente; **to** ~ **back** vi (return) volver // vt recobrar; **to** ~ **by** vi (pass) lograr pasar; (manage) arreglárselas; **to** ~ **down** vi bajarse // vt (object) bajar; (depress) deprimir; **to** ~ **down to** vt fus (work) ponerse a (hacer); **to** ~ **in** vi (train) llegar; (arrive home) volver a casa, regresar; **to** ~ **off** vi (from train etc) bajar; (depart: person, car) marcharse // vt fus (train, bus) bajar de; **to** ~ **on** vi (at exam etc) tener éxito; (agree) entenderse // vt (horse) subir; **to** ~ **out** vi salir; (of vehicle) bajar; (news) saberse // vt (take out) sacar; **to** ~ **out of** vt fus (duty etc) escaparse de; **to** ~ **over** vt (illness) recobrarse de; (put across) hacer comprender; **to** ~ **round** vt fus rodear; (fig: person) engatusar a; **to** ~ **through to** vt fus (TEL) comunicar con; **to** ~ **together** vi reunirse // vt (rise) levantarse // vt fus levantar; **to** ~ **up to** vt fus (reach) llegar a; (prank etc) hacer; ~**away** n fuga, escape m.
geyser ['giːzə*] n calentador m de agua; (GEO) géiser m.
Ghana ['gɑːnə] n Ghana.
ghastly ['gɑːstlɪ] a horrible; (pale) pálido.
gherkin ['gəːkɪn] n pepinillo.
ghetto ['gɛtəu] n ghetto.
ghost [gəust] n fantasma m; ~**ly** a fantasmal.
giant ['dʒaɪənt] n gigante m // a gigantesco, gigante.
gibberish ['dʒɪbərɪʃ] n galimatías m.
gibe [dʒaɪb] n pulla.
giblets ['dʒɪblɪts] npl menudillos mpl.
giddiness ['gɪdɪnɪs] n vértigo; **giddy** a (dizzy) mareado; (speed) vertiginoso; (frivolous) atolondrado; **it makes me giddy** me marea.
gift [gɪft] n (gen) regalo; (offering) obsequio; (ability) talento; ~**ed** a dotado.
gigantic [dʒaɪ'gæntɪk] a gigantesco.
giggle ['gɪgl] vi reírse con risa tonta // n risilla tonta.
gill [dʒɪl] n (measure) = 0.14 l // n [gɪl] (of fish) agalla, branquia.
gilt [gɪlt] a, n dorado; ~-**edged** a (COMM) del Estado.
gimmick ['gɪmɪk] n truco.
gin [dʒɪn] n (liquor) ginebra.
ginger ['dʒɪndʒə*] n jengibre m; ~ **ale** n cerveza de jengibre; ~**bread** n pan m de jengibre; ~-**haired** a pelirrojo.
gingerly ['dʒɪndʒəlɪ] ad con pies de plomo.
gipsy ['dʒɪpsɪ] n gitano/a.
giraffe [dʒɪ'rɑːf] n jirafa.
girder ['gəːdə*] n viga.

girdle ['gɔːdl] n (corset) faja // vt ceñir.

girl [gɔːl] n (small) niña; (young woman) chica, joven f, muchacha; **an English ~** una (chica) inglesa; **~friend** n (of girl) amiga; (of boy) novia; **~ish** a de niña.

girth [gɔːθ] n circunferencia; (stoutness) gordura.

· gist [dʒɪst] n lo esencial.

give [gɪv], pt **gave,** pp **given** vt (gen) dar; (deliver) entregar; (as gift) regalar // vi (break) romperse; (stretch: fabric) dar de sí; **to ~ sb sth, ~ sth to sb** dar algo a uno; **to ~ away** vt (give free) regalar; (betray) traicionar; (disclose) revelar; **to ~ back** vt devolver; **to ~ in** vi ceder // vt entregar; **to ~ off** vt despedir; **to ~ out** vt distribuir; **to ~ up** vi renunciar, darse por vencido // vt renunciar a; **to ~ up smoking** dejar de fumar; **to ~ way** vi ceder; (AUT) ceder el paso.

glacier ['glæsɪə*] n glaciar m.

glad [glæd] a contento; **~den** vt alegrar.

gladioli [glædɪ'əulaɪ] npl gladiolos mpl.

gladly ['glædlɪ] ad con mucho gusto.

glamorous ['glæmərəs] a encantador(a), atractivo; **glamour** n encanto, atractivo.

glance [glɑːns] n ojeada, mirada // vi: **to ~ at** echar una ojeada a; **to ~ off** (bullet) rebotar; **glancing** a (blow) oblicuo.

gland [glænd] n glándula.

glare [glɛə*] n luz f deslumbradora, brillo // vi deslumbrar; **to ~ at** mirar ferozmente a; **glaring** a (mistake) notorio.

glass [glɑːs] n vidrio, cristal m; (for drinking) vaso; (: with stem) copa; (also: **looking ~**) espejo; **~es** npl gafas fpl; **~house** n invernadero; **~ware** n cristalería; **~y** a (eyes) vidrioso.

glaze [gleɪz] vt (door) poner cristal a; (pottery) barnizar // n barniz m; **~d** a (eye) vidrioso; (pottery) barnizado.

glazier ['gleɪzɪə*] n vidriero.

gleam [gliːm] n destello // vi brillar; **~ing** a reluciente.

glee [gliː] n alegría, regocijo.

glen [glɛn] n cañada, valle m estrecho.

glib [glɪb] a de mucha labia; **~ness** n labia.

glide [glaɪd] vi deslizarse; (AVIAT, birds) planear // n deslizamiento; (AVIAT) vuelo sin motor; **glider** n (AVIAT) planeador m; **gliding** n (AVIAT) vuelo sin motor.

glimmer ['glɪmə*] n luz f trémula.

glimpse [glɪmps] n vista momentánea, vislumbre m // vt vislumbrar, entrever.

glint [glɪnt] n destello; (in the eye) chispa // vi centellear.

glisten ['glɪsn] vi relucir, brillar.

glitter ['glɪtə*] vi relucir, brillar // n brillo.

gloat [gləut] vi: **to ~ (over)** recrearse en, saborear.

global ['gləubl] a mundial; (sum) global.

globe [gləub] n globo, esfera.

gloom [gluːm] n tinieblas fpl, oscuridad f; (sadness) tristeza, melancolía; **~y** a (dark) oscuro; (sad) triste; (pessimistic) pesimista.

glorify ['glɔːrɪfaɪ] vt glorificar; (praise) alabar.

glorious ['glɔːrɪəs] a glorioso; **glory** n gloria.

gloss [glɔs] n (shine) brillo; (paint) pintura brillante o esmalte; **to ~ over** vt fus encubrir.

glossary ['glɔsərɪ] n glosario.

glossy ['glɔsɪ] a lustroso.

glove [glʌv] n guante m; **~ compartment** n (AUT) guantera.

glow [gləu] vi (shine) brillar; (fire) arder // n brillo.

glower ['glauə*] vi: **to ~ at** mirar con ceño.

glucose ['gluːkəus] n glucosa.

glue [gluː] n goma (de pegar) // vt pegar.

glum [glʌm] a (mood) abatido; (person, tone) melancólico.

glut [glʌt] n superabundancia.

glutton ['glʌtn] n glotón/ona m/f; **a ~ for work** un trabajador incansable; **~y** n gula, glotonería.

glycerin(e) ['glɪsəriːn] n glicerina.

gnarled [nɑːld] a nudoso.

gnat [næt] n mosquito.

gnaw [nɔː] vt roer.

gnome [nəum] n gnomo.

go [gəu], pt **went,** pp **gone** vi ir; (travel) viajar; (depart) irse, marcharse; (work) funcionar, marchar; (be sold) venderse; (time) pasar; (fit, suit): **to ~ with** hacer juego con; (become) ponerse; (break etc) estropearse, romperse // n, pl **~es:** to have a ~ (at) probar suerte (con); **to be on the ~** moverse, estar trabajando; **whose ~ is it?** ¿a quién le toca?; **he's going to do it** va a hacerlo; **to ~ for a walk** ir de paseo; **to ~ dancing** ir a bailar; **how did it ~?** ¿qué tal salió o resultó?, ¿cómo ha ido?; **to ~ about** vi (rumour) propagarse // vt fus: **how do I ~ about this?** ¿cómo me las arreglo para hacer esto?; **to ~ ahead** vi (make progress) avanzar; (get going) seguir; **to ~ along** vi ir // vt fus bordear; **to ~ along with** estar de acuerdo con; **to ~ away** vi irse, marcharse; **to ~ back** vi volver; (fall back) retroceder; **to ~ back on** vt fus (promise) faltar a; **to ~ by** vi (years, time) pasar // vt fus guiarse por; **to ~ down** vi bajar; (ship) hundirse; (sun) ponerse // vt fus bajar por; **to ~ for** vt fus (fetch) ir por; (like) gustar; (attack) atacar; **to ~ in** vi entrar; **to ~ in for** vt fus (competition) presentarse a; **to ~ into** vt fus entrar en; (investigate) investigar; (embark on) embarcarse en; **to ~ off** vi irse, marcharse; (food) pasarse; (explode) estallar; (event) realizarse // vt fus dejar de gustar; **to ~ on** vi seguir, continuar; (happen) pasar, ocurrir; **to ~ on doing sth** seguir haciendo algo; **to ~ out** vi salir; (fire, light) apagarse; **to ~ over** vi (ship) zozobrar // vt fus (check) revisar; **to**

~ **through** vt fus (town etc) atravesar; **to** ~ **up** vi subir; **to** ~ **without** vt fus pasarse sin.

goad [gǝud] vt aguijonear.

go-ahead ['gǝuǝhɛd] a emprendedor(a) // n luz f verde.

goal [gǝul] n meta; (score) gol m; ~**keeper** n portero; ~-**post** n poste m de la portería.

goat [gǝut] n cabrío, cabra m/f.

gobble ['gɔbl] vt (also: ~ **down**, ~ **up**) engullirse (ávidamente).

goblet ['gɔblɪt] n copa.

goblin ['gɔblɪn] n duende m.

go-cart ['gǝukɑːt] n go-cart m.

god [gɔd] n dios m; **G**~ n Dios m; ~**child** n ahijado/a; ~**dess** n diosa; ~**father** n padrino; ~-**forsaken** a dejado de la mano de Dios; ~**mother** n madrina; ~**send** n don m del cielo; ~**son** n ahijado.

goggles ['gɔglz] npl gafas fpl submarinas.

going ['gǝuɪŋ] n (conditions) estado del terreno // a: **the** ~ **rate** la tarifa corriente o en vigor.

gold [gǝuld] n oro // a de oro; ~**en** a (made of ~) de oro; (~ in colour) dorado; ~**fish** n pez m de colores; ~**mine** n mina de oro.

golf [gɔlf] n golf m; ~ **club** n club m de golf; (stick) palo (de golf); ~ **course** n campo de golf; ~**er** n jugador/a m/f de golf.

gondola ['gɔndǝlǝ] n góndola.

gone [gɔn] pp of **go**.

gong [gɔŋ] n gong m.

gonorrhea [gɔnǝ'rɪǝ] n gonorrea.

good [gud] a (gen) bueno; (kind) bueno, amable; (well-behaved) educado; (useful) útil // n bien m, provecho; ~**s** npl bienes mpl; (COMM) mercancías fpl; **to be** ~ **at** tener aptitud para; **to be** ~ **for** servir para; **it's** ~ **for you** te hace bien; **would you be** ~ **enough to...?** ¿podría hacerme el favor de...?, ¿sería tan amable de...?; **a** ~ **deal (of)** mucho; **a** ~ **many** muchos; **to make** ~ reparar; **for** ~ para siempre, definitivamente; ~ **morning/afternoon!** ¡buenos días/buenas tardes!; ~ **evening!** ¡buenas noches!; ~ **night!** ¡buenas noches!; ~**bye!** ¡adiós!; **to say** ~**bye** despedirse; **G**~ **Friday** n Viernes m Santo; ~-**looking** a guapo; ~**ness** n (of person) bondad f; **for** ~**ness sake!** ¡Por Dios!; ~**ness gracious!** ¡Dios mío!; ~**will** n buena voluntad f.

goose [guːs] pl **geese** n ganso, oca.

gooseberry ['guzbǝrɪ] n grosella espinosa.

gooseflesh ['guːsflɛʃ] n, **goose pimples** npl carne f de gallina.

gore [gɔː*] vt cornear // n sangre f.

gorge [gɔːdʒ] n barranco // vr: **to** ~ **o.s. (on)** atracarse (de).

gorgeous ['gɔːdʒǝs] a magnífico, maravilloso.

gorilla [gǝ'rɪlǝ] n gorila m.

gorse [gɔːs] n aulaga.

gory ['gɔːrɪ] a sangriento.

go-slow ['gǝu'slǝu] n huelga de trabajo lento.

gospel ['gɔspl] n evangelio.

gossip ['gɔsɪp] n (scandal) chismorreo, chismes mpl; (chat) charla; (scandalmonger) chismoso/a; (talker) hablador/a m/f // vi cotillear.

got [gɔt] pt, pp of **get**; ~**ten** (US) pp of **get**.

gout [gaut] n gota.

govern ['gʌvǝn] vt (gen) gobernar; (dominate) dominar.

governess ['gʌvǝnɪs] n institutriz f.

government ['gʌvnmǝnt] n gobierno; ~**al** [-'mɛntl] a gubernamental.

governor ['gʌvǝnǝ*] n gobernador m; (of jail) director/a m/f.

gown [gaun] n traje m; (of teacher, judge) toga.

G.P. n abbr of **general practitioner**.

GPO n abbr of **General Post Office**.

grab [græb] vt coger, arrebatar.

grace [greɪs] n (REL) gracia; (gracefulness) elegancia, finura // vt (favour) honrar; (adorn) adornar; **5 days'** ~ un plazo de 5 días; **to say** ~ bendecir la mesa; ~**ful** a elegante, gracioso; **gracious** ['greɪʃǝs] a amable.

grade [greɪd] n (quality) clase f, calidad f; (degree) grado; (US: SCOL) clase f // vt clasificar.

gradient ['greɪdɪǝnt] n pendiente f.

gradual ['grædjuǝl] a paulatino; ~**ly** ad paulatinamente.

graduate ['grædjuɪt] n graduado, licenciado // vi ['grædjueɪt] graduarse, licenciarse; **graduation** [-'eɪʃǝn] n graduación f.

graft [grɑːft] n (AGR, MED) injerto; (bribery) corrupción f // vt injertar.

grain [greɪn] n grano; (corn) granos mpl, cereales mpl; (in wood) fibra.

gram [græm] n gramo.

grammar ['græmǝ*] n gramática; **grammatical** [grǝ'mætɪkl] a gramatical.

gramme [græm] n = **gram**.

gramophone ['græmǝfǝun] n tocadiscos m inv.

granary ['grænǝrɪ] n granero, troj f.

grand [grænd] a magnífico, imponente; ~**children** npl nietos mpl; ~**dad** n yayo, abuelito; ~**daughter** n nieta; ~**eur** ['grændjǝ*] n magnificencia, lo grandioso; ~**father** n abuelo; ~**iose** ['grændɪǝuz] a grandioso; (pej) pomposo; ~**ma** n yaya, abuelita; ~**mother** n abuela; ~**pa** n = ~**dad**; ~ **piano** n piano de cola; ~**son** n nieto; ~**stand** n (SPORT) tribuna.

granite ['grænɪt] n granito.

granny ['grænɪ] n abuelita, yaya.

grant [grɑːnt] vt (concede) conceder; (admit) asentir // n (SCOL) beca; **to take sth for** ~**ed** dar algo por sentado.

granulated sugar ['grænjuleɪtɪd-] n azúcar m granulado.

granule ['grænjuːl] n gránulo.

grape [greɪp] *n* uva; **sour** ~s (*fig*) envidia.

grapefruit ['greɪpfruːt] *n* pomelo, toronja (*AM*).

graph [grɑːf] *n* gráfica; ~ **ic** *a* gráfico.

grapple ['græpl] *vi*: **to** ~ **with sth** esforzarse por resolver algo.

grasp [grɑːsp] *vt* agarrar, asir; (*understand*) comprender // *n* (*grip*) asimiento; (*reach*) alcance *m*; (*understanding*) comprensión *f*; ~**ing** *a* avaro.

grass [grɑːs] *n* hierba; (*lawn*) césped *m*; ~**hopper** *n* saltamontes *m inv*; ~**land** *n* pradera; ~-**roots** *a* popular; ~ **snake** *n* culebra; ~**y** *a* cubierto de hierba.

grate [greɪt] *n* (*fireplace*) chimenea; (*of iron*) parrilla // *vi* rechinar // *vt* (*CULIN*) rallar.

grateful ['greɪtful] *a* agradecido.

grater ['greɪtə*] *n* rallador *m*.

gratify ['grætɪfaɪ] *vt* complacer; (*whim*) satisfacer; ~**ing** *a* grato.

grating ['greɪtɪŋ] *n* (*iron bars*) rejilla // *a* (*noise*) áspero.

gratitude ['grætɪtjuːd] *n* agradecimiento.

gratuity [grə'tjuːɪtɪ] *n* gratificación *f*.

grave [greɪv] *n* tumba // *a* serio, grave; ~**digger** *n* sepulturero.

gravel ['grævl] *n* grava.

grave: ~**stone** *n* lápida; ~**yard** *n* cementerio, camposanto.

gravity ['grævɪtɪ] *n* gravedad *f*; (*seriousness*) seriedad *f*.

gravy ['greɪvɪ] *n* salsa.

gray [greɪ] *a* = **grey**.

graze [greɪz] *vi* pacer // *vt* (*touch lightly*) rozar; (*scrape*) raspar // *n* (*MED*) rasguño.

grease [griːs] *n* (*fat*) grasa; (*lubricant*) lubricante *m* // *vt* engrasar; ~**proof** *a* a prueba de grasa; (*paper*) apergaminado; **greasy** *a* grasiento.

great [greɪt] *a* grande; (*col*) magnífico, estupendo; **G**~ **Britain** *n* Gran Bretaña; ~-**grandfather/mother** *n* bisabuelo/a; ~**ly** *ad* sumamente, mucho, muy; ~**ness** *n* grandeza.

Greece [griːs] *n* Grecia.

greed [griːd] *n* (*also*: ~**iness**) codicia, avaricia; (*for food*) gula; ~**ily** *ad* con avidez; ~**y** *a* avaro; (*for food*) glotón(ona).

Greek [griːk] *a* griego // *n* griego/a; (*LING*) griego.

green [griːn] *a* verde; (*inexperienced*) novato // *n* verde *m*; (*stretch of grass*) césped *m*; ~**s** *npl* verduras *fpl*; ~**gage** *n* claudia; ~**grocer** *n* verdulero; ~**house** *n* invernadero; ~**ish** *a* verdoso.

Greenland ['griːnlənd] *n* Groenlandia.

greet [griːt] *vt* saludar; (*welcome*) dar la bienvenida a; ~**ing** *n* (*gen*) saludo; (*welcome*) bienvenida.

gregarious [grə'gɛərɪəs] *a* gregario.

grenade [grə'neɪd] *n* granada.

grew [gruː] *pt of* **grow**.

grey [greɪ] *a* gris; ~-**haired** *a* canoso; ~**hound** *n* galgo.

grid [grɪd] *n* reja; (*ELEC*) red *f*.

grief [griːf] *n* dolor *m*, pena.

grievance ['griːvəns] *n* motivo de queja, agravio.

grieve [griːv] *vi* afligirse, acongojarse // *vt* dar pena a; **to** ~ **for** llorar por.

grievous ['griːvəs] *a* penoso.

grill [grɪl] *n* (*on cooker*) parrilla // *vt* asar a la parrilla; (*question*) interrogar duramente.

grille [grɪl] *n* reja; (*AUT*) rejilla.

grim [grɪm] *a* siniestro; (*fam*) horrible.

grimace [grɪ'meɪs] *n* mueca // *vi* hacer muecas.

grime [graɪm] *n* mugre *f*; **grimy** *a* mugriento.

grin [grɪn] *n* sonrisa abierta // *vi* sonreír abiertamente.

grind [graɪnd], *pt*, *pp* **ground** *vt* (*coffee, pepper etc*) moler; (*make sharp*) afilar // *n* (*work*) trabajo pesado y aburrido; **to** ~ **one's teeth** rechinar los dientes.

grip [grɪp] *n* (*hold*) asimiento; (*of hands*) apretón *m*; (*handle*) asidero; (*of racquet etc*) mango; (*holdall*) maletín *m*; (*understanding*) comprensión *f* // *vt* agarrar; **to come to** ~s **with** luchar a brazo partido con; ~**ping** *a* absorbente.

grisly ['grɪzlɪ] *a* horripilante, horrible.

gristle ['grɪsl] *n* cartílago.

grit [grɪt] *n* gravilla; (*courage*) valor *m* // *vt* (*road*) poner gravilla en; **to** ~ **one's teeth** apretar los dientes.

groan [grəʊn] *n* gemido, quejido // *vi* gemir, quejarse.

grocer ['grəʊsə*] *n* tendero de ultramarinos; ~**ies** *npl* comestibles *mpl*; ~'**s (shop)** *n* tienda de ultramarinos.

groggy ['grɒgɪ] *a* aturdido; (*BOXING*) grogui.

groin [grɔɪn] *n* ingle *f*.

groom [gruːm] *n* mozo de caballos; (*also*: **bride**~) novio // *vt* (*horse*) cuidar; **well-**~**ed** acicalado.

groove [gruːv] *n* ranura, surco.

grope [grəʊp] *vi* ir a tientas; **to** ~ **for** *vt fus* buscar a tientas.

gross [grəʊs] *a* grueso; (*COMM*) bruto; ~**ly** *ad* (*greatly*) enormemente.

grotesque [grə'tɛsk] *a* grotesco.

grotto ['grɒtəʊ] *n* gruta.

ground [graund] *pt*, *pp of* **grind** // *n* suelo, tierra; (*SPORT*) campo, terreno; (*reason: gen pl*) causa, razón *f* // *vt* (*plane*) mantener en tierra; (*US: ELEC*) conectar con tierra // *vi* (*ship*) varar, encallar; ~**s** *npl* (*of coffee etc*) poso *sg*; (*gardens etc*) jardines *mpl*, parque *m*; **on the** ~ en el suelo; **to the** ~ al suelo; ~ **floor** *n* planta baja; ~**ing** *n* (*in education*) conocimientos *mpl* básicos; ~**less** *a* infundado; ~**sheet** *n* tela impermeable; ~ **staff** *n* personal *m* de tierra; ~**work** *n* preparación *f*.

group [gruːp] *n* grupo; (*musical*) conjunto

// (vb: also: ~ together) vt agrupar // vi agruparse.
grouse [graus] n, pl inv (bird) urogallo // vi (complain) quejarse.
grove [grǝuv] n arboleda.
grovel ['grɔvl] vi (fig) humillarse.
grow [grǝu], pt **grew**, pp **grown** vi (gen) crecer; (plants) cultivarse; (increase) aumentarse; (spread) extenderse, desarrollarse; (become) volverse; **to ~ rich/weak** enriquecerse/debilitarse // vt cultivar, dejar crecer; **to ~ up** vi crecer, hacerse hombre/mujer; **~er** n cultivador/a m/f, productor/a m/f; **~ing** a creciente.
growl [graul] vi gruñir.
grown [grǝun] pp of **grow**; **~-up** n adulto, persona mayor.
growth [grǝuθ] n crecimiento, desarrollo; (what has grown) brote m; (MED) acceso, tumor m.
grub [grʌb] n gusano; (col: food) comida.
grubby ['grʌbɪ] a sucio, mugriento.
grudge [grʌdʒ] n motivo de rencor // vt: **to ~ sb sth** dar algo a uno de mala gana, escatimar algo a uno; **to bear sb a ~** guardar rencor a uno; **he ~s (giving) the money** da el dinero de mala gana.
gruelling ['gruǝlɪŋ] a penoso, duro.
gruesome ['gru:sǝm] a horrible.
gruff [grʌf] a (voice) bronco; (manner) brusco.
grumble ['grʌmbl] vi refunfuñar, quejarse.
grumpy ['grʌmpɪ] a gruñón(ona).
grunt [grʌnt] vi gruñir // n gruñido.
guarantee [gærǝn'ti:] n garantía // vt garantizar.
guarantor [gærǝn'tɔ:*] n garante m/f, fiador/a m/f.
guard [gɑ:d] n guardia; (RAIL) jefe m de tren // vt guardar; **~ed** a (fig) cauteloso; **~ian** n guardián/ana m/f; (of minor) tutor/a m/f; **~'s van** n (RAIL) furgón m.
guerrilla [gǝ'rɪlǝ] n guerrillero; **~ warfare** n guerra de guerrillas.
guess [gɛs] vi, vt (gen) adivinar; (suppose) suponer // n suposición f, conjetura; **to take or have a ~** tratar de adivinar; **~ work** n conjeturas fpl.
guest [gɛst] n invitado/a; (in hotel) huésped/a m/f; **~-house** n casa de huéspedes, pensión f; **~ room** n cuarto de huéspedes.
guffaw [gʌ'fɔ:] n carcajada // vi reírse a carcajadas.
guidance ['gaɪdǝns] n (gen) dirección f; (advice) consejos mpl.
guide [gaɪd] n (person) guía m/f; (book, fig) guía // vt guiar; (girl) **~** n exploradora; **~book** n guía; **~ dog** n perro guía; **~ lines** npl (fig) principios mpl generales.
guild [gɪld] n gremio; **~hall** n (Brit) ayuntamiento.
guile [gaɪl] n astucia; **~less** a cándido.
guillotine ['gɪlǝti:n] n guillotina.
guilt [gɪlt] n culpabilidad f; **~y** a culpable.

guinea pig ['gɪnɪpɪg] n conejillo de Indias.
guise [gaɪz] n: **in or under the ~ of** so capa de.
guitar [gɪ'tɑ:*] n guitarra; **~ist** n guitarrista m/f.
gulf [gʌlf] n golfo; (abyss) abismo.
gull [gʌl] n gaviota.
gullet ['gʌlɪt] n esófago; (fam) garganta.
gullible ['gʌlɪbl] a crédulo.
gully ['gʌlɪ] n barranco.
gulp [gʌlp] vi tragar saliva // vt (also: ~ down) tragarse // n: **at one ~** de un trago.
gum [gʌm] n (ANAT) encía; (glue) goma; (sweet) caramelo de goma; (also: chewing-~) chiclé m // vt engomar, pegar con goma; **~boots** npl botas fpl de goma.
gun [gʌn] n (gen) arma de fuego; (small) pistola; (shotgun) escopeta; (rifle) fusil m; (cannon) cañón m; **~boat** n cañonero; **~fire** n fuego, disparos mpl; **~man** n pistolero; **~ner** n artillero; **at ~point** bajo la amenaza de un arma; **~powder** n pólvora; **~shot** n escopetazo, cañonazo; **~smith** n armero.
gurgle ['gǝ:gl] vi gorgotear.
gush [gʌʃ] vi chorrear; (fig) deshacerse en efusiones.
gusset ['gʌsɪt] n escudete m.
gust [gʌst] n (of wind) ráfaga.
gusto ['gʌstǝu] n entusiasmo.
gut [gʌt] n intestino, tripa; (MUS etc) cuerda de tripa; **~s** npl (courage) valor m.
gutter ['gʌtǝ*] n (of roof) canalón m; (in street) arroyo.
guttural ['gʌtǝrl] a gutural.
guy [gaɪ] n (also: ~rope) cuerda; (col: man) tío, tipo.
guzzle ['gʌzl] vi tragar // vt engullir.
gym [dʒɪm] n (also: **gymnasium**) gimnasio; (also: **gymnastics**) gimnasia; **~nast** n gimnasta m/f; **~nastics** n gimnasia; **~ shoes** npl zapatillas fpl de gimnasia; **~ slip** n túnica de colegiala.
gynaecologist, gynecologist (US) [gaɪnɪ'kɔlǝdʒɪst] n ginecólogo; **gynaecology, gynecology** (US) [-nǝ'kɔlǝdʒɪ] n ginecología.
gypsy ['dʒɪpsɪ] n = **gipsy**.
gyrate [dʒaɪ'reɪt] vi girar.

H

haberdashery ['hæbǝ'dæʃǝrɪ] n mercería.
habit ['hæbɪt] n hábito, costumbre f; (costume) hábito.
habitable ['hæbɪtǝbl] a habitable.
habitual [hǝ'bɪtjuǝl] a acostumbrado, habitual; (drinker, liar) empedernido; **~ly** ad por costumbre.
hack [hæk] vt (cut) cortar; (slice) tajar // n corte m; (axe blow) hachazo.
hackneyed ['hæknɪd] a trillado, gastado.
had [hæd] pt, pp of **have**.

haddock ['hædɔk], *pl* ~ *or* ~**s** *n especie de merluza.*

hadn't ['hædnt] = **had not.**

haemorrhage, hemorrhage (*US*) ['hemɔrɪdʒ] *n* hemorragia.

haemorrhoids, hemorrhoids (*US*) ['hemɔrɔɪdz] *npl* hemorroides *fpl.*

haggard ['hægɔd] *a* ojeroso.

haggle ['hægl] *vi* (*argue*) discutir; (*bargain*) regatear.

Hague [heɪg] *n*: **The** ~ La Haya.

hail [heɪl] *n* (*weather*) granizo // *vt* saludar; (*call*) llamar a // *vi* granizar; ~**stone** *n* (piedra de) granizo.

hair [hɛɔ*] *n* (*gen*) pelo, cabellos *mpl*; (*one* ~) pelo, cabello; (*head of* ~) cabellera; (*on legs*) vello; **grey** ~ canas *fpl*; ~**brush** *n* cepillo (del pelo); ~**cut** *n* corte *m* de pelo; ~**do** *n* peinado; ~**dresser** *n* peluquero; (*dresser's* *n* peluquería; ~**-drier** *n* secador *m* de pelo; ~**net** *n* redecilla; ~**piece** *n* trenza postiza; ~**pin** *n* horquilla; ~**pin bend** *n* curva de horquilla; ~**raising** *a* espeluznante; ~ **remover** *n* depilador *m*; (*cream*) crema depilatoria; ~ **spray** *n* laca; ~**style** *n* peinado; ~**y** *a* peludo; velludo.

half [hɑːf], *pl* **halves** *n* mitad *f* // *a* medio // *ad* medio, a medias; ~**-an-hour** media hora; **two and a** ~ dos y media; ~ **a pound** media libra; **to cut sth in** ~ cortar algo por la mitad; ~ **asleep** medio dormido; ~**-price** a mitad de precio; ~**-back** *n* (*SPORT*) medio; ~**-breed**, ~**-caste** *n* mestizo; ~**-hearted** *a* indiferente, poco entusiasta; ~**-hour** *n* media hora; ~**-penny** ['heɪpnɪ] *n* medio penique; ~**-time** *n* medio tiempo; ~ **way** *ad* a medio camino.

halibut ['hælɪbɔt] *n*, *pl inv* halibut *m.*

hall [hɔːl] *n* (*for concerts*) sala; (*entrance way*) hall *m*, vestíbulo; **town** ~ palacio municipal; ~ **of residence** *n* residencia (universitaria).

hallmark ['hɔːlmɑːk] *n* (*mark*) marca; (*seal*) sello.

hallo [hɔ'lɔu] *excl* = **hello.**

hallucination [hɔluːsɪ'neɪʃɔn] *n* alucinación *f.*

halo ['heɪlɔu] *n* (*of saint*) aureola.

halt [hɔːlt] *n* (*stop*) alto, parada; (*RAIL*) apeadero // *vt* parar // *vi* pararse; (*process*) interrumpirse.

halve [hɑːv] *vt* partir por la mitad.

halves [hɑːvz] *pl of* **half.**

ham [hæm] *n* jamón *m* (cocido); (*actor*) comicastro.

hamburger ['hæmbɔːgɔ*] *n* hamburguesa.

hamlet ['hæmlɪt] *n* aldea.

hammer ['hæmɔ*] *n* martillo // *vt* amartillar // *vi* (*on door*) golpear.

hammock ['hæmɔk] *n* hamaca.

hamper ['hæmpɔ*] *vt* estorbar // *n* cesto.

hand [hænd] *n* mano *f*; (*of clock*) manecilla; (*writing*) letra; (*applause*) aplausos *mpl*; (*worker*) obrero; (*measure*) palmo // *vt* (*give*) dar, pasar; (*deliver*) entregar; **to give sb a** ~ dar una mano a uno, ayudar a uno; **at** ~ a la mano; **in** ~ entre manos; **on the one** ~ ..., **on the other** ~ ... por una parte ... por otra (parte) ...; **to** ~ **in** *vt* entregar; **to** ~ **out** *vt* distribuir; **to** ~ **over** *vt* (*deliver*) entregar; (*surrender*) ceder; ~**bag** *n* bolso; ~**basin** *n* lavabo; ~**book** *n* manual *m*; ~**brake** *n* freno de mano; ~**cuffs** *npl* esposas *fpl*; ~**ful** *n* puñado.

handicap ['hændɪkæp] *n* handicap *m*, desventaja // *vt* estorbar; **mentally/physically** ~**ped** incapacitado mentalmente/físicamente.

handicraft ['hændɪkrɑːft] *n* artesanía.

handkerchief ['hæŋkɔtʃɪf] *n* pañuelo.

handle ['hændl] *n* (*of door etc*) tirador *m*, manija; (*of cup etc*) asa; (*of knife etc*) mango; (*for winding*) manivela; (*fam: name*) título // *vt* (*touch*) tocar; (*deal with*) encargarse de; (*treat: people*) manejar; '~ **with care'** 'tratar con cuidado'; **to fly off the** ~ perder los estribos; ~**bar(s)** *n*(*pl*) manillar *m.*

hand-luggage ['hændlʌgɪdʒ] *n* equipaje *m* de mano.

handmade ['hændmeɪd] *a* hecho a mano.

handout ['hændaut] *n* (*distribution*) repartición *f*; (*charity*) limosna; (*leaflet*) folleto.

handshake ['hændʃeɪk] *n* apretón *m* de manos.

handsome ['hænsɔm] *a* guapo.

handwriting ['hændraɪtɪŋ] *n* letra.

handy ['hændɪ] *a* (*close at hand*) a mano; (*convenient*) práctico; (*skilful*) hábil, diestro; ~**man** *n* (hombre) mañoso.

hang [hæŋ], *pt*, *pp* **hung** *vt* colgar; (*criminal: pt*, *pp* **hanged**) ahorcar; (*head*) bajar // *vi* colgar; **to** ~ **about** *vi* haraganear; **to** ~ **on** *vi* (*wait*) esperar; **to** ~ **up** *vi* (*TEL*) colgar.

hangar ['hæŋɔ*] *n* hangar *m.*

hanger ['hæŋɔ*] *n* percha; ~**-on** *n* parásito.

hangover ['hæŋɔuvɔ*] *n* (*after drinking*) resaca.

hang-up ['hæŋʌp] *n* complejo.

hanker ['hæŋkɔ*] *vi*: **to** ~ **after** (*miss*) echar de menos; (*long for*) añorar.

hankie, hanky ['hæŋkɪ] *n abbr of* **handkerchief.**

haphazard [hæp'hæzɔd] *a* fortuito.

happen ['hæpɔn] *vi* suceder, ocurrir; (*take place*) tener lugar, realizarse; **to** ~ **upon** tropezar con; ~**ing** *n* suceso, acontecimiento.

happily ['hæpɪlɪ] *ad* (*luckily*) afortunadamente; (*cheerfully*) alegremente.

happiness ['hæpɪnɪs] *n* (*gen*) felicidad *f*; (*joy*) alegría.

happy ['hæpɪ] *a* feliz, alegre; **to be** ~ (**with**) estar contento (con); **to be** ~ ser feliz.

harass ['hærɔs] *vt* acosar, hostigar;

~**ment** *n* persecución *f*; (*worry*) preocupación *f*.

harbour, harbor (*US*) ['hɑ:bə*] *n* puerto // *vt* (*hope etc*) abrigar; (*hide*) esconder.

hard [hɑ:d] *a* (*gen*) duro; (*difficult*) difícil; (*work*) arduo; (*person*) severo // *ad* (*work*) mucho, duro, duramente; (*think*, *try*) seriamente; **to look** ~ mirar fijo *o* fijamente; **no** ~ **feelings!** sin rencor; **to be** ~ **of hearing** ser duro de oído; **to be** ~ **done by** ser tratado injustamente; ~**back** *n* libro encuadernado; ~**board** *n* chapa de madera; ~**en** *vt* endurecer; (*fig*) curtir // *vi* endurecerse; ~-**headed** *a* poco sentimental, práctico; ~ **labour** *n* trabajos *mpl* forzados.

hardly ['hɑ:dlɪ] *ad* (*scarcely*) apenas; **that can** ~ **be true** difícilmente puede ser cierto; ~ **ever** casi nunca.

hardness ['hɑ:dnɪs] *n* dureza.

hardship ['hɑ:dʃɪp] *n* (*troubles*) penas *fpl*; (*financial*) apuro.

hard-up [hɑ:d'ʌp] *a* (*col*) pelado.

hardware ['hɑ:dwɛə*] *n* ferretería; (*COMPUTERS*) material *m*; ~ **shop** *n* ferretería.

hard-wearing [hɑ:d'wɛərɪŋ] *a* resistente, duradero.

hard-working [hɑ:d'wə:kɪŋ] *a* trabajador(a).

hardy ['hɑ:dɪ] *a* fuerte; (*plant*) resistente.

hare [hɛə*] *n* liebre *f*; ~-**brained** *a* casquivano.

harem [hɑ:'ri:m] *n* harén *m*.

haricot (bean) ['hærɪkəu] *n* alubia.

harm [hɑ:m] *n* daño, mal *m* // *vt* (*person*) hacer daño a, perjudicar; (*thing*) dañar; **out of** ~'**s way** a salvo; ~**ful** *a* perjudicial; (*pest*) dañino; ~**less** *a* inofensivo.

harmonica [hɑ:'mɔnɪkə] *n* armónica.

harmonious [hɑ:'məunɪəs] *a* armonioso; **harmonize** ['hɑ:mənaɪz] *vt*, *vi* armonizar; **harmony** ['hɑ:mənɪ] *n* armonía.

harness ['hɑ:nɪs] *n* arreos *mpl* // *vt* (*horse*) enjaezar; (*resources*) aprovechar.

harp [hɑ:p] *n* arpa // *vi*: **to** ~ **on about** hablar constantemente de; ~**ist** *n* arpista *m/f*.

harpoon [hɑ:'pu:n] *n* arpón *m*.

harrowing ['hærəuɪŋ] *a* horroroso.

harsh [hɑ:ʃ] *a* (*hard*) duro, cruel; (*severe*) severo; (*unpleasant*) desagradable; (: *colour*) chillón(ona); (*contrast*) violento; ~**ness** *n* dureza.

harvest ['hɑ:vɪst] *n* cosecha; (*of grapes*) vendimia // *vt*, *vi* cosechar; ~**er** *n* (*machine*) cosechadora.

has [hæz] *vb see* **have**.

hash [hæʃ] *n* (*CULIN*) picadillo; (*fig*: *mess*) lío.

hashish ['hæʃɪʃ] *n* hachís *m*, hachich *m*.

hasn't ['hæznt] = **has not**.

hassle ['hæsl] *n* pelea // *vt* molestar a.

haste [heɪst] *n* prisa; **hasten** ['heɪsn] *vt* acelerar // *vi* darse prisa; **hastily** *ad* de prisa; **hasty** *a* apresurado.

hat [hæt] *n* sombrero.

hatch [hætʃ] *n* (*NAUT. also*: ~**way**) escotilla // *vi* salir del cascarón // *vt* incubar; (*plot*) tramar.

hatchback ['hætʃbæk] *n* (*AUT*) coche *m* con puerta trasera.

hatchet ['hætʃɪt] *n* hacha.

hate [heɪt] *vt* odiar, aborrecer // *n* odio; ~**ful** *a* odioso; **hatred** *n* odio.

hat trick ['hættrɪk] *n* (*SPORT, also fig*) tres triunfos seguidos.

haughty ['hɔ:tɪ] *a* altanero, arrogante.

haul [hɔ:l] *vt* tirar; (*by lorry*) transportar // *n* (*of fish*) redada; (*of stolen goods etc*) botín *m*; ~**age** *n* transporte *m*; (*costs*) gastos *mpl* de transporte; ~**ier** *n* contratista *m* de transportes.

haunch [hɔ:ntʃ] *n* anca; (*of meat*) pierna.

haunt [hɔ:nt] *vt* (*subj: ghost*) aparecer en; (*frequent*) frecuentar; (*obsess*) obsesionar // *n* guarida; ~**ed house** casa de fantasmas.

have [hæv], *pt*, *pp* **had** *vt* (*gen*) tener; (*possess*) poseer; (*meal*, *shower*) tomar; **to** ~ **sth done** hacer hacer algo; **she has to do it** tiene que hacerlo; **I had better leave** más vale que me marche; **I won't** ~ **it** no lo tolero; **he has gone** se ha ido; **to** ~ **it out with sb** ajustar cuentas con alguien; **to** ~ **a baby** parir, dar a luz.

haven ['heɪvn] *n* puerto; (*fig*) refugio.

haven't ['hævnt] = **have not**.

haversack ['hævəsæk] *n* mochila.

havoc ['hævək] *n* estragos *mpl*.

hawk [hɔ:k] *n* halcón *m*.

hay [heɪ] *n* heno; ~ **fever** *n* fiebre *f* del heno; ~**stack** *n* almiar *m*.

haywire ['heɪwaɪə*] *a* (*col*): **to go** ~ (*person*) volverse loco; (*plan*) embarullarse.

hazard ['hæzəd] *n* riesgo // *vt* aventurar; ~**ous** *a* (*dangerous*) peligroso; (*risky*) arriesgado.

haze [heɪz] *n* neblina.

hazelnut ['heɪzlnʌt] *n* avellana.

hazy ['heɪzɪ] *a* brumoso; (*idea*) vago.

he [hi:] *pron* él; ~ **who...** él que..., quien...; ~-**man** *n* macho.

head [hɛd] *n* cabeza; (*leader*) jefe/a *m/f* // *vt* (*list*) encabezar; (*group*) capitanear; ~**s (or tails)** cara (o cruz); ~ **first** de cabeza; ~ **over heels** patas arriba; **to** ~ **the ball** cabecear (la pelota); **to** ~ **for** *vt fus* dirigirse a; ~**ache** *n* dolor *m* de cabeza; ~**ing** *n* título; ~**lamp** *n* faro; ~**land** *n* promontorio; ~**light** = ~**lamp**; ~**line** *n* titular *m*; ~**long** *ad* (*fall*) de cabeza; (*rush*) precipitadamente; ~**master/ mistress** *n* director/a *m/f* (de escuela); ~ **office** *n* oficina central, central *f*; ~-**on** *a* (*collision*) de frente; ~**phones** *npl* auriculares *mpl*; ~**quarters (HQ)** *npl* sede *f* central; (*MIL*) cuartel *m* general; ~-**room** *n* (*in car*) espacio para la cabeza; (*under bridge*) luz *f*; ~**scarf** *n* pañuelo (de cabeza); ~**stone** *n* lápida mortuoria; ~**strong** *a* voluntarioso; ~ **waiter** *n* jefe *m* de camareros; ~**way** *n* progreso; **to make** ~**way** avanzar; ~**wind** *n* viento contrario.

heal [hi:l] *vt* curar // *vi* cicatrizarse.

health [hɛlθ] *n* salud *f*; **good** ~! ¡salud y pesetas!; ~ **food** *n* comida natural; **H**~ **Service** *n* Seguro de Enfermedad; ~**y** *a* (*gen*) sano.

heap [hi:p] *n* montón *m* // *vt* amontonar; (*plate*) colmar.

hear [hɪə*], *pt, pp* **heard** [hə:d] *vt* oír; (*perceive*) sentir; (*listen to*) escuchar; (*lecture*) asistir a // *vi* oír; **to** ~ **about** oír hablar de; **to** ~ **from sb** tener noticias de alguien; ~**ing** *n* (*sense*) oído; (*LAW*) vista; ~**ing aid** *n* audífono; ~**say** *n* rumores *mpl*, hablillas *fpl*.

hearse [hə:s] *n* coche *m* fúnebre.

heart [ha:t] *n* corazón *m*; ~**s** *npl* (*CARDS*) corazones *mpl*; **at** ~ en el fondo; **by** ~ (*learn, know*) de memoria; ~ **attack** *n* ataque *m* cardíaco; ~**beat** *n* latido (del corazón); ~**breaking** *a* desgarrador(a); **to be** ~**broken** estar angustiado; ~**burn** *n* acedía; ~ **failure** *n* fallo cardíaco; ~**felt** *a* (*cordial*) cordial; (*deeply felt*) más sentido.

hearth [ha:θ] *n* (*gen*) hogar *m*; (*fireplace*) chimenea.

heartily ['ha:tɪlɪ] *ad* sinceramente, cordialmente; (*laugh*) a carcajadas; (*eat*) con buen apetito.

heartless ['ha:tlɪs] *a* cruel.

hearty ['ha:tɪ] *a* cordial.

heat [hi:t] *n* (*gen*) calor *m*; (*ardour*) ardor *m*; (*SPORT. also*: **qualifying** ~) prueba eliminatoria // *vt* calentar; (*fig*) acalorar; **to** ~ **up** *vi* (*gen*) calentarse; ~**ed** *a* caliente; (*fig*) acalorado; ~**er** *n* calentador *m*.

heath [hi:θ] *n* (*Brit*) brezal *m*.

heathen ['hi:ðn] *a, n* pagano/a.

heather ['hɛðə*] *n* brezo.

heating ['hi:tɪŋ] *n* calefacción *f*.

heatstroke ['hi:tstrəuk] *n* insolación *f*.

heatwave ['hi:tweɪv] *n* ola de calor.

heave [hi:v] *vt* (*pull*) tirar de; (*push*) empujar con esfuerzo; (*lift*) levantar (con esfuerzo) // *vi* (*water*) agitarse // *n* tirón *m*; empujón *m*; (*effort*) esfuerzo; (*throw*) echada.

heaven ['hɛvn] *n* cielo; (*REL*) paraíso; ~**ly** *a* celestial; (*REL*) divino.

heavily ['hɛvɪlɪ] *ad* pesadamente; (*drink, smoke*) con exceso; (*sleep, sigh*) profundamente.

heavy ['hɛvɪ] *a* pesado; (*work*) duro; (*sea, rain, meal*) fuerte; (*drinker, smoker*) gran; (*eater*) comilón(ona); ~**weight** *n* (*SPORT*) peso pesado.

Hebrew ['hi:bru:] *a* hebreo.

heckle ['hɛkl] *vt* interrumpir.

hectic ['hɛktɪk] *a* febril, agitado.

he'd [hi:d] = **he would; he had.**

hedge [hɛdʒ] *n* seto // *vt* cercar (con un

seto) // *vi* contestar con evasivas; **to** ~ **one's bets** (*fig*) cubrirse.

hedgehog ['hɛdʒhɔg] *n* erizo.

heed [hi:d] *vt* (*also*: **take** ~ **of**) (*attend to*) hacer caso de; (*bear in mind*) tener en cuenta; ~**less** *a* desatento.

heel [hi:l] *n* talón *m* // *vt* (*shoe*) poner tacón a.

hefty ['hɛftɪ] *a* (*person*) fornido; (*piece*) grande; (*price*) gordo.

heifer ['hɛfə*] *n* novilla, ternera.

height [haɪt] *n* (*of person*) talle *m*; (*of building*) altura; (*high ground*) cerro; (*altitude*) altitud *f*; ~**en** *vt* elevar; (*fig*) aumentar.

heir [ɛə*] *n* heredero; ~**ess** *n* heredera; ~**loom** *n* reliquia de familia.

held [hɛld] *pt, pp of* **hold.**

helicopter ['hɛlɪkɔptə*] *n* helicóptero.

hell [hɛl] *n* infierno; ~! ¡demonios!

he'll [hi:l] = **he will, he shall.**

hellish ['hɛlɪʃ] *a* infernal; (*fam*) horrible.

hello [hə'ləu] *excl* ¡hola!; (*surprise*) ¡caramba!

helm [hɛlm] *n* (*NAUT*) timón *m*.

helmet ['hɛlmɪt] *n* casco.

help [hɛlp] *n* ayuda; (*charwoman*) criada, asistenta; (*assistant etc*) empleado // *vt* ayudar; ~! ¡socorro!; ~ **yourself** sírvete; **he can't** ~ **it** no es culpa suya; ~**er** *n* ayudante *m/f*; ~**ful** *a* útil, servicial; ~**ing** *n* ración *f*; ~**less** *a* (*incapable*) incapaz; (*defenceless*) indefenso.

hem [hɛm] *n* dobladillo; **to** ~ **in** *vt* cercar.

hemisphere ['hɛmɪsfɪə*] *n* hemisferio.

hen [hɛn] *n* gallina.

hence [hɛns] *ad* (*therefore*) por lo tanto; **2 years** ~ de aquí a 2 años; ~**forth** *ad* de hoy en adelante.

henchman ['hɛntʃmən] *n* (*pej*) secuaz *m*.

henpecked ['hɛnpɛkt] *a* dominado por su mujer.

her [hə:*] *pron* (*direct*) la; (*indirect*) le; (*stressed, after prep*) ella *// a* su.

herald ['hɛrəld] *n* (*forerunner*) precursor/a *m/f* // *vt* anunciar.

heraldry ['hɛrəldrɪ] *n* heráldica.

herb [hə:b] *n* hierba.

herd [hə:d] *n* rebaño.

here [hɪə*] *ad* aquí; ~! (*present*) presente; ~ **she is** aquí está; ~**after** *ad* en el futuro // *n*: **the** ~**after** (la vida de) ultratumba; ~**by** *ad* (*in letter*) por la presente.

hereditary [hɪ'rɛdɪtrɪ] *a* hereditario; **heredity** [-tɪ] *n* herencia.

heresy ['hɛrəsɪ] *n* herejía.

heretic ['hɛrətɪk] *n* hereje *m/f*; ~**al** [hɪ'rɛtɪkl] *a* herético.

heritage ['hɛrɪtɪdʒ] *n* (*gen*) herencia; (*fig*) patrimonio.

hermit ['hə:mɪt] *n* ermitaño.

hernia ['hə:nɪə] *n* hernia.

hero ['hɪərəu], *pl* ~**es** *n* héroe *m*; (*in book, film*) protagonista *m*; ~**ic** [hɪ'rəuɪk] *a* heroico.

heroin ['hɛrəuɪn] *n* heroína.
heroine ['hɛrəuɪn] *n* heroína; (*in book, film*) protagonista.
heroism ['hɛrəuɪzm] *n* heroísmo.
heron ['hɛrən] *n* garza.
herring ['hɛrɪŋ] *n* arenque *m.*
hers [hɔːz] *pron* (el) suyo/(la) suya *etc.*
herself [hɔː'sɛlf] *pron* (*reflexive*) se; (*emphatic*) ella misma; (*after prep*) sí (misma).
he's [hiːz] = **he is; he has.**
hesitant ['hɛzɪtənt] *a* vacilante, dudoso.
hesitate ['hɛzɪteɪt] *vi* dudar, vacilar; **hesitation** ['-teɪʃən] *n* indecisión *f.*
hew [hjuː] *vt* cortar con hacha.
hexagon ['hɛksəgən] *n* hexágono; ~al [-'sægənl] *a* hexagonal.
hi [haɪ] *excl* ¡oye!, ¡hola!
hibernate ['haɪbəneɪt] *vi* invernar.
hiccough, hiccup ['hɪkʌp] *vi* hipar; ~s *npl* hipo *sg.*
hid [hɪd] *pt of* **hide.**
hidden ['hɪdn] *pp of* **hide.**
hide [haɪd] *n* (*skin*) piel *f* // (*vb: pt* **hid,** *pp* **hidden**) *vt* esconder, ocultar // *vi:* **to** ~ **(from sb)** esconderse *o* ocultarse (de alguien); ~**-and-seek** *n* escondite *m;* ~**away** *n* escondite *m.*
hideous ['hɪdɪəs] *a* horrible.
hiding ['haɪdɪŋ] *n* (*beating*) paliza; **to be in** ~ (*concealed*) estar escondido; ~ **place** *n* escondrijo.
hierarchy ['haɪərɑːkɪ] *n* jerarquía.
high [haɪ] *a* (*gen*) alto; (*speed, number*) grande; (*price*) elevado; (*wind*) fuerte; (*voice*) agudo // *ad* alto, a gran altura; **it is 20 m** ~ tiene 20 m de altura; ~ **in the air** en las alturas; ~**brow** *a* culto; ~**chair** *n* silla alta; ~**-handed** *a* despótico; ~**-heeled** *a* de tacón alto; ~**jack** = **hijack;** ~ **jump** *n* (*SPORT*) salto de altura; ~**light** *n* (*fig: of event*) punto culminante // *vt* subrayar; ~**ly** *ad* sumamente; ~**ly strung** *a* hipertenso; **H**~ **Mass** *n* misa mayor; ~**ness** *n* altura; **Her H**~**ness** Su Alteza; ~**-pitched** *a* agudo; ~**-rise block** *n* torre *f* de pisos; ~ **school** *n* colegio de segunda enseñanza, Instituto; ~ **street** *n* calle *f* mayor; ~**way** *n* carretera.
hijack ['haɪdʒæk] *vt* secuestrar; ~**er** *n* secuestrador/a *m/f.*
hike [haɪk] *vi* (*go walking*) ir de excursión; (*tramp*) caminar // *n* caminata; **hiker** *n* excursionista *m/f.*
hilarious [hɪ'lɛərɪəs] *a* (*behaviour, event*) regocijante.
hill [hɪl] *n* colina; (*high*) montaña; (*slope*) cuesta; ~**side** *n* ladera; ~**y** *a* montañoso; (*uneven*) accidentado.
hilt [hɪlt] *n* (*of sword*) empuñadura; **to the** ~ completamente.
him [hɪm] *pron* (*direct*) le, lo; (*indirect*) le; (*stressed, after prep*) él; ~**self** *pron* (*reflexive*) se; (*emphatic*) él mismo; (*after prep*) sí (mismo).
hind [haɪnd] *a* posterior // *n* cierva.

hinder ['hɪndə*] *vt* estorbar, impedir; **hindrance** ['hɪndrəns] *n* estorbo, obstáculo.
Hindu ['hɪnduː] *n* hindú *m/f.*
hinge [hɪndʒ] *n* bisagra, gozne *m* // *vi* (*fig*): **to** ~ **on** depender de.
hint [hɪnt] *n* indirecta; (*advice*) consejo // *vt:* **to** ~ **that** insinuar que // *vi* soltar indirectas; **to** ~ **at** hacer una alusión a.
hip [hɪp] *n* cadera; ~ **pocket** *n* bolsillo de atrás.
hippopotamus [hɪpə'pɔtəməs], *pl* ~**es** or **-mi** [-maɪ] *n* hipopótamo.
hire ['haɪə*] *vt* (*car, equipment*) alquilar; (*worker*) contratar // *n* alquiler *m;* (*of person*) salario; **for** ~ se alquila; (*taxi*) libre; ~ **purchase (H.P.)** *n* compra a plazos.
his [hɪz] *pron* (el) suyo/(la) suya *etc* // *a* su.
Hispanic [hɪs'pænɪk] *a* hispánico.
hiss [hɪs] *vi* silbar, sisear // *n* silbido, siseo.
historian [hɪ'stɔːrɪən] *n* historiador/a *m/f.*
historic(al) [hɪ'stɔrɪk(l)] *a* histórico.
history ['hɪstərɪ] *n* historia.
hit [hɪt], *pt, pp* **hit** *vt* (*strike*) golpear, pegar; (*reach: target*) alcanzar; (*collide with: car*) chocar contra // *n* golpe *m;* (*success*) éxito, sensación *f;* **to** ~ **it off with sb** hacer buenas migas con alguien.
hitch [hɪtʃ] *vt* (*fasten*) atar, amarrar; (*also:* ~ **up**) alzar // *n* (*difficulty*) dificultad *f;* **to** ~ **a lift** hacer autostop.
hitch-hike ['hɪtʃhaɪk] *vi* hacer autostop; **hitch-hiker** *n* autostopista *m/f.*
hive [haɪv] *n* colmena.
hoard [hɔːd] *n* acumulación *f* // *vt* acumular; ~**ing** *n* acumulación *f;* (*for posters*) cartelera.
hoarfrost ['hɔːfrɔst] *n* escarcha.
hoarse [hɔːs] *a* ronco.
hoax [həuks] *n* trampa.
hobble ['hɔbl] *vi* cojear // *vt* (*horse*) manear.
hobby ['hɔbɪ] *n* pasatiempo, afición *f;* ~**-horse** *n* (*fig*) tema, manía.
hobo ['həubəu] *n* (*US*) vagabundo.
hockey ['hɔkɪ] *n* hockey *m.*
hoe [həu] *n* azadón *m* // *vt* azadonar.
hog [hɔg] *n* cerdo, puerco // *vt* (*fig*) acaparar; **to go the whole** ~ liarse la manta a la cabeza.
hoist [hɔɪst] *n* (*lift*) montacargas *m inv;* (*crane*) grúa.
hold [həuld], *pt, pp* **held** *vt* tener; (*contain*) contener; (*keep back*) retener; (*believe*) sostener; (*take* ~ *of*) coger; (*take weight*) soportar; (*meeting*) celebrar // *vi* (*withstand pressure*) resistir; (*be valid*) valer; (*stick*) pegarse // *n* (*handle*) asidero; (*grasp*) asimiento; (*fig*) dominio; (*WRESTLING*) presa; (*NAUT*) bodega; ~ **the line!** (*TEL*) no cuelgue; **to** ~ **one's own** (*fig*) defenderse; **to catch** *or* **get (a)** ~ **of** agarrarse, asirse de; **to** ~ **back** *vt* retenerse; (*secret*) guardarse; **to** ~ **down** *vt* (*person*) sujetar; (*job*) conservar; **to** ~ **off** *vt* (*enemy*) rechazar; **to** ~ **on** *vi*

agarrarse bien; (*wait*) esperar; ~ **on!**
(*TEL*) no cuelgue; **to ~ on to** *vt fus*
agarrarse a; (*keep*) guardar; **to ~ out** *vt*
alargar // *vi* (*resist*) resistir; **to ~ up** *vt*
(*raise*) levantar; (*support*) apoyar; (*delay*)
atrasar; (*rob*) asaltar; ~**all** *n* funda,
neceser *m*; ~**er** *n* (*of ticket, record*)
poseedor/a *m/f*; (*of office, title etc*) titular
m/f; ~**ing** *n* (*share*) interés *m*; ~**up** *n*
(*robbery*) atraco; (*delay*) parada; (*in
traffic*) embotellamiento.

hole [həul] *n* agujero // *vt* agujerear.

holiday ['hɔlədɪ] *n* vacaciones *fpl*; (*day off*)
(día de) fiesta, feriado; ~-**maker** *n*
veraneante *m/f*; ~ **resort** *n* punto de
veraneo.

holiness ['həulɪnɪs] *n* santidad *f*.

Holland ['hɔlənd] *n* Holanda.

hollow ['hɔləu] *a* hueco, vacío; (*eyes*)
hundido; (*sound*) sordo; (*doctrine*) falso //
n (*gen*) hueco; (*in ground*) hoyo // *vt*: **to
~ out** ahuecar.

holly ['hɔlɪ] *n* acebo; ~**hock** *n* malva loca.

holster ['həulstə*] *n* pistolera.

holy ['həulɪ] *a* (*gen*) santo, sagrado;
(*water*) bendito; **H~ Ghost** or **Spirit** *n*
Espíritu *m* Santo.

homage ['hɔmɪdʒ] *n* homenaje *m*; **to pay
~ to** rendir homenaje a.

home [həum] *n* casa; (*country*) patria;
(*institution*) asilo // *a* (*domestic*) casero, de
casa; (*ECON, POL*) nacional // *ad* (*direction*)
a casa; **at ~** en casa; **to go/come ~**
ir/volver a casa; **make yourself at ~**
¡estás en tu casa!; ~ **address** *n* señas *fpl*;
~**land** *n* tierra natal; ~**less** *a* sin hogar,
sin casa; ~**ly** *a* (*domestic*) casero;
(*simple*) sencillo; ~-**made** *a* hecho en
casa; ~ **rule** *n* autonomía; **H~
Secretary** *n* (*Brit*) Ministro del Interior;
~ **sick** *a*: **to be ~sick** tener morriña,
tener nostalgia; ~ **town** *n* ciudad *f* natal;
~**ward** ['həumwəd] *a* (*journey*) hacia
casa; ~ **work** *n* tarea.

homicide ['hɔmɪsaɪd] *n* (*US*) homicidio.

homosexual [hɔməu'sɛksjuəl] *a*, *n*
homosexual *m*.

honest ['ɔnɪst] *a* honrado; (*sincere*) franco,
sincero; ~**ly** *ad* honradamente;
francamente; ~**y** *n* honradez *f*.

honey ['hʌnɪ] *n* miel *f*; ~**comb** *n* panal *m*;
(*pattern*) nido de abejas; ~**moon** *n* luna
de miel; (*trip*) viaje *m* de novios.

honk [hɔŋk] *vi* (*AUT*) tocar la bocina.

honorary ['ɔnərərɪ] *a* no remunerado;
(*duty, title*) honorario.

honour, honor (*US*) ['ɔnə*] *vt* honrar // *n*
honor *m*, honra; ~**able** *a* honorable; ~**s
degree** *n* (*SCOL*) título universitario.

hood [hud] *n* capucha; (*Brit*: *AUT*) capota;
(*US*: *AUT*) capó *m*.

hoodlum ['hu:dləm] *n* matón *m*.

hoof [hu:f], *pl* **hooves** *n* pezuña.

hook [huk] *n* gancho; (*on dress*) corchete
m, broche *m*; (*for fishing*) anzuelo // *vt*
enganchar.

hooligan ['hu:lɪgən] *n* gamberro.

hoop [hu:p] *n* aro.

hoot [hu:t] *vi* (*AUT*) tocar la bocina; (*siren*)
tocar la sirena // *n* bocinazo; toque *m* de
sirena; **to ~ with laughter** morirse de
risa; ~**er** *n* (*AUT*) bocina; (*NAUT*) sirena.

hooves [hu:vz] *pl of* **hoof**.

hop [hɔp] *vi* saltar, brincar; (*on one foot*)
saltar con un pie // *n* salto, brinco.

hope [həup] *vt*, *vi* esperar // *n* esperanza; **I
~ so/not** espero que sí/no; ~**ful** *a*
(*person*) optimista, lleno de esperanzas;
(*situation*) prometedor(a); ~**fully** *ad* con
optimismo, con esperanza; ~**less** *a*
desesperado.

hops [hɔps] *npl* lúpulo *sg*.

horde [hɔːd] *n* horda.

horizon [hə'raɪzn] *n* horizonte *m*; ~**tal**
[hɔrɪ'zɔntl] *a* horizontal.

hormone ['hɔːməun] *n* hormona.

horn [hɔːn] *n* cuerno; (*MUS*) trompa; (*AUT*)
bocina; ~-**rimmed** de concha; ~**ed** *a*
(*animal*) con cuernos.

hornet ['hɔːnɪt] *n* avispón *m*.

horny ['hɔːnɪ] *a* (*material*) córneo; (*hands*)
calloso.

horoscope ['hɔrəskəup] *n* horóscopo.

horrible ['hɔrɪbl] *a* horrible.

horrid ['hɔrɪd] *a* horrible, horroroso.

horrify ['hɔrɪfaɪ] *vt* horrorizar.

horror ['hɔrə*] *n* horror *m*; ~ **film** *n*
película de horror.

hors d'œuvre [ɔː'dəːvrə] *n* entremeses
mpl.

horse [hɔːs] *n* caballo; **on ~back** *a*
caballo; ~**man/woman** *n* jinete
m/amazona; ~**power (h.p.)** *n* caballo (de
fuerza); ~-**racing** *n* carreras *fpl* de
caballos; ~**radish** *n* rábano picante;
~**shoe** *n* herradura.

horticulture ['hɔːtɪkʌltʃə*] *n* horticultura.

hose [həuz] *n* (*also*: ~**pipe**) manga.

hosiery ['həuzɪərɪ] *n* calcetería.

hospitable ['hɔspɪtəbl] *a* hospitalario.

hospital ['hɔspɪtl] *n* hospital *m*.

hospitality [hɔspɪ'tælɪtɪ] *n* hospitalidad *f*.

host [həust] *n* anfitrión *m*; (*in hotel etc*)
huésped *m*; (*large number*): **a ~ of**
multitud de; (*REL*) hostia.

hostage ['hɔstɪdʒ] *n* rehén *m*.

hostel ['hɔstl] *n* hostal *m*; **youth ~** *n*
albergue *m* de juventud.

hostess ['həustɪs] *n* anfitriona; (*air ~*)
azafata; (*in night-club*) cabaretera.

hostile ['hɔstaɪl] *a* hostil; **hostility** [-'stɪlɪtɪ]
n hostilidad *f*.

hot [hɔt] *a* caliente; (*weather*) caluroso, de
calor; (*as opposed to only warm*) muy
caliente; (*spicy*) picante; (*fig*) ardiente,
acalorado; ~ **dog** *n* perro caliente.

hotel [həu'tɛl] *n* hotel *m*; ~**ier** *n* hotelero.

hot: ~**headed** *a* exaltado; ~**house** *n*
invernadero; ~**ly** *ad* con pasión,
apasionadamente; ~-**water bottle** *n*
bolsa de agua caliente.

hound [haund] *vt* acosar // *n* perro de
caza.

hour ['auə*] *n* hora; ~**ly** *ad* cada hora.

house [haus, *pl*: 'hauzɪz] *n* (*also*: *firm*) casa; (*POL*) cámara; (*THEATRE*) sala // *vt* [hauz] (*person*) alojar; **on the** ~ (*fig*) la casa invita; ~ **arrest** *n* arresto domiciliario; ~**boat** *n* casa flotante; ~**breaking** *n* robo (en una casa); ~**coat** *n* bata; ~**hold** *n* familia; ~**keeper** *n* ama de llaves; ~**keeping** *n* (*work*) trabajos domésticos *mpl*; ~**keeping (money)** dinero para gastos domésticos; ~-**warming party** *n* fiesta de estreno de casa; ~**wife** *n* ama de casa; ~**work** *n* faenas *fpl* (de la casa).

housing ['hauzɪŋ] *n* (*act*) alojamiento; (*houses*) viviendas *fpl*; ~ **estate** *n* bloque *m* de viviendas.

hovel ['hɒvl] *n* pocilga.

hover ['hɒvə*] *vi* flotar (en el aire); ~**craft** *n* hidroala *m*, aerodeslizador *m*.

how [hau] *ad* cómo; ~ **are you?** ¿cómo está Vd?, ¿cómo estás?; ~ **long have you been here?** ¿cuánto tiempo hace que estás aquí?; ~ **lovely!** ¡qué bonito!; ~ **many/much?** ¿cuántos/cuánto?; ~ **old are you?** ¿cuántos años tienes?; ~**ever** *ad* de cualquier manera; (+ *adjective*) por muy ... que; (*in questions*) cómo // *conj* sin embargo, no obstante.

howl [haul] *n* aullido // *vi* aullar.

h.p., H.P. *abbr of* **hire purchase; horse power.**

HQ *abbr of* **headquarters.**

hub [hʌb] *n* (*of wheel*) centro.

hubbub ['hʌbʌb] *n* barahúnda, barullo.

hubcap ['hʌbkæp] *n* tapacubo.

huddle ['hʌdl] *vi*: **to** ~ **together** amontonarse.

hue [hju:] *n* color *m*, matiz *m*; ~ **and cry** *n* alarma.

huff [hʌf] *n*: **in a** ~ con rabieta.

hug [hʌg] *vt* abrazar // *n* abrazo.

huge [hju:dʒ] *a* enorme.

hulk [hʌlk] *n* (*wreck*) barco viejo; (*hull*) casco.

hull [hʌl] *n* (*of ship*) casco.

hullo [hə'ləu] *excl* = **hello.**

hum [hʌm] *vt* tararear, canturrear // *vi* tararear, canturrear; (*insect*) zumbar // *n* zumbido.

human ['hju:mən] *a, n* humano.

humane [hju:'meɪn] *a* humano, humanitario.

humanity [hju:'mænɪtɪ] *n* humanidad *f*.

humble ['hʌmbl] *a* humilde // *vt* humillar; **humbly** *ad* humildemente.

humbug ['hʌmbʌg] *n* embustes *mpl*; (*sweet*) caramelo de menta.

humdrum ['hʌmdrʌm] *a* (*boring*) monótono, aburrido; (*routine*) rutinario.

humid ['hju:mɪd] *a* húmedo; ~**ity** [-'mɪdɪtɪ] *n* humedad *f*.

humiliate [hju:'mɪlɪeɪt] *vt* humillar; **humiliation** [-'eɪʃən] *n* humillación *f*.

humility [hju:'mɪlɪtɪ] *n* humildad *f*.

humorist ['hju:mərɪst] *n* humorista *m/f*.

humorous ['hju:mərəs] *a* gracioso, divertido.

humour, humor (*US*) ['hju:mə*] *n* humorismo, sentido del humor; (*mood*) humor *m* // *vt* (*person*) complacer.

hump [hʌmp] *n* (*in ground*) montículo; (*camel's*) giba.

hunch [hʌntʃ] *n* (*premonition*) presentimiento; ~**back** *n* joroba; ~**ed** *a* jorobado.

hundred ['hʌndrəd] *num* ciento; (*before n*) cien; ~**weight** *n* (*Brit*) = 50.8 *kg*; 112 *lb*; (*US*) = 45.3 *kg*; 100 *lb*.

hung [hʌŋ] *pt, pp of* **hang.**

Hungarian [hʌŋ'gɛərɪən] *a, n* húngaro/a.

Hungary ['hʌŋgərɪ] *n* Hungría.

hunger ['hʌŋgə*] *n* hambre *f* // *vi*: **to** ~ **for** (*gen*) tener hambre de; (*desire*) anhelar; ~ **strike** *n* huelga de hambre; **hungrily** [-grəlɪ] *ad* ávidamente, con ganas; **hungry** [-grɪ] *a* hambriento; **to be hungry** tener hambre.

hunt [hʌnt] *vt* (*seek*) buscar; (*SPORT*) cazar // *vi* cazar // *n* caza, cacería; ~**er** *n* cazador *m*; ~**ing** *n* caza.

hurdle ['hɜ:dl] *n* (*SPORT*) valla; (*fig*) obstáculo.

hurl [hɜ:l] *vt* lanzar, arrojar.

hurrah [hu'rɑ:], **hurray** [hu'reɪ] *n* ¡viva!, ¡vítor!

hurricane ['hʌrɪkən] *n* huracán *m*.

hurried ['hʌrɪd] *a* (*fast*) apresurado; (*rushed*) hecho de prisa; ~**ly** *ad* con prisa, apresuradamente.

hurry ['hʌrɪ] *n* prisa // *vi* apresurarse, darse prisa // *vt* (*person*) dar prisa a; (*work*) apresurar; **to be in a** ~ tener prisa.

hurt [hɜ:t], *pt, pp* **hurt** *vt* hacer daño a // *vi* doler // *a* lastimado; ~**ful** *a* (*gen*) dañoso; (*remark*) hiriente.

hurtle ['hɜ:tl] *vi*: **to** ~ **past** pasar como un rayo; **to** ~ **down** caer con violencia.

husband ['hʌzbənd] *n* marido.

hush [hʌʃ] *n* silencio // *vt* hacer callar; (*cover up*) encubrir; ~**!** ¡chitón!, ¡cállate!

husk [hʌsk] *n* (*of wheat*) cáscara.

husky ['hʌskɪ] *a* ronco; (*burly*) fornido // *n* perro esquimal.

hustle ['hʌsl] *vt* (*push*) empujar; (*hurry*) dar prisa a // *n* bullicio, actividad *f* febril; ~ **and bustle** *n* vaivén *m*.

hut [hʌt] *n* cabaña; (*shed*) cobertizo.

hutch [hʌtʃ] *n* conejera.

hyacinth ['haɪəsɪnθ] *n* jacinto.

hybrid ['haɪbrɪd] *a, n* híbrido.

hydrant ['haɪdrənt] *n* (*also*: **fire** ~) boca de incendios.

hydraulic [haɪ'drɔ:lɪk] *a* hidráulico.

hydroelectric [haɪdrəu'lektrɪk] *a* hidroeléctrico.

hydrogen ['haɪdrədʒən] *n* hidrógeno.

hyena [haɪ'i:nə] *n* hiena.

hygiene ['haɪdʒi:n] *n* higiene *f*; **hygienic** [-'dʒi:nɪk] *a* higiénico.

hymn [hɪm] *n* himno.

hyphen ['haɪfn] *n* guión *m*.
hypnosis [hɪp'nəʊsɪs] *n* hipnosis *f*; **hypnotic** [-'nɒtɪk] *a* hipnótico; **hypnotism** ['hɪpnətɪzm] *n* hipnotismo; **hypnotist** ['hɪpnətɪst] *n* hipnotista *m/f*; **hypnotize** ['hɪpnətaɪz] *vt* hipnotizar.
hypocrisy [hɪ'pɒkrɪsɪ] *n* hipocresía; **hypocrite** ['hɪpəkrɪt] *n* hipócrita *m/f*; **hypocritical** [hɪpə'krɪtɪkl] *a* hipócrita.
hypothesis [haɪ'pɒθɪsɪs], *pl* -**ses** [-siːz] *n* hipótesis *f*; **hypothetic(al)** [-pəʊ'θɛtɪk(l)] *a* hipotético.
hysteria [hɪ'stɪərɪə] *n* histeria; **hysterical** [-'stɛrɪkl] *a* histérico; **hysterics** [-'stɛrɪks] *npl* histeria *sg*, histerismo *sg*.

I

I [aɪ] *pron* yo.
ice [aɪs] *n* hielo // *vt* (*cake*) alcorzar; (*drink*) helar // *vi* (*also*: ~ **over**, ~ **up**) helarse; ~ **age** *n* período glacial; ~ **axe** *n* piolet *m*; ~**berg** *n* iceberg *m*; ~**box** *n* (*US*) nevera; ~**-cold** *a* helado; ~ **cream** *n* helado; ~ **cube** *n* cubito de hielo; ~ **hockey** *n* hockey *m* sobre hielo.
Iceland ['aɪslənd] *n* Islandia; ~**er** *n* islandés/esa *m/f*; ~**ic** [-'lændɪk] *a* islandés(esa).
ice: ~ **rink** *n* pista de hielo; ~ **skating** *n* patinaje *m* sobre hielo.
icicle ['aɪsɪkl] *n* carámbano.
icing ['aɪsɪŋ] *n* (*CULIN*) alcorza, garapiña; (*AVIAT etc*) formación *f* de hielo; ~ **sugar** *n* azúcar *m* de alcorza.
icon ['aɪkɒn] *n* ícono.
icy ['aɪsɪ] *a* (*road*) helado; (*fig*) glacial.
I'd [aɪd] = **I would**; **I had**.
idea [aɪ'dɪə] *n* idea.
ideal [aɪ'dɪəl] *n* ideal *m* // *a* ideal; ~**ist** *n* idealista *m/f*.
identical [aɪ'dɛntɪkl] *a* idéntico.
identification [aɪdɛntɪfɪ'keɪʃən] *n* identificación *f*; **means of** ~ documentos *mpl* personales.
identify [aɪ'dɛntɪfaɪ] *vt* identificar.
identikit picture [aɪ'dɛntɪkɪt-] *n* retrato-robot *m*.
identity [aɪ'dɛntɪtɪ] *n* identidad *f*.
ideological [aɪdɪə'lɒdʒɪkəl] *a* ideológico; **ideology** [-dɪ'ɒlədʒɪ] *n* ideología.
idiocy ['ɪdɪəsɪ] *n* idiotez *f*; (*stupid act*) estupidez *f*.
idiom ['ɪdɪəm] *n* modismo; (*style of speaking*) lenguaje *m*.
idiosyncrasy [ɪdɪəʊ'sɪŋkrəsɪ] *n* idiosincrasia.
idiot ['ɪdɪət] *n* (*gen*) idiota *m/f*; (*fool*) tonto/a; ~**ic** [-'ɒtɪk] *a* idiota; tonto.
idle ['aɪdl] *a* (*gen*) ocioso; (*lazy*) holgazán(ana); (*unemployed*) desocupado; (*pointless*) inútil // *vi* (*machine*) marchar en vacío // *vt*: **to** ~ **away the time** malgastar el tiempo; ~**ness** *n* ociosidad *f*; holgazanería; desocupación *f*.
idol ['aɪdl] *n* ídolo; ~**ize** *vt* idolatrar.

if [ɪf] *conj* si.
igloo ['ɪgluː] *n* iglú *m*.
ignite [ɪg'naɪt] *vt* encender; (*set fire to*) incendiar // *vi* encenderse.
ignition [ɪg'nɪʃən] *n* (*AUT*) encendido; **to switch on/off the** ~ encender/apagar el motor; ~ **key** *n* (*AUT*) llave *f* de contacto.
ignorance ['ɪgnərəns] *n* ignorancia; **ignorant** [-ənt] *a* ignorante; **to be ignorant of** ignorar.
ignore [ɪg'nɔː*] *vt* (*person*) no hacer caso de; (*fact*) pasar por alto.
I'll [aɪl] = **I will**, **I shall**.
ill [ɪl] *a* enfermo, malo; (*bad*) malo // *n* mal *m*; (*fig*) infortunio // *ad* mal; **to take** *or* **be taken** ~ ponerse enfermo, enfermar; ~**-advised** *a* poco recomendable; (*misled*) mal aconsejado; ~**-at-ease** *a* incómodo.
illegal [ɪ'liːgl] *a* ilegal.
illegible [ɪ'lɛdʒɪbl] *a* ilegible.
illegitimate [ɪlɪ'dʒɪtɪmət] *a* ilegítimo.
ill: ~**-fated** *a* malogrado; ~ **feeling** *n* rencor *m*.
illicit [ɪ'lɪsɪt] *a* ilícito.
illiterate [ɪ'lɪtərət] *a* analfabeto.
ill-mannered [ɪl'mænəd] *a* mal educado.
illness ['ɪlnɪs] *n* enfermedad *f*.
illogical [ɪ'lɒdʒɪkl] *a* ilógico.
ill-treat [ɪl'triːt] *vt* maltratar.
illuminate [ɪ'luːmɪneɪt] *vt* (*room, street*) iluminar, alumbrar; (*subject*) aclarar; **illumination** [-'neɪʃən] *n* alumbrado; **illuminations** *npl* luminarias *fpl*.
illusion [ɪ'luːʒən] *n* ilusión *f*; **to be under the** ~ **that...** estar bajo la ilusión de que...; **illusory** [-sərɪ] *a* ilusorio.
illustrate ['ɪləstreɪt] *vt* (*gen*) ilustrar; (*subject*) aclarar; (*point*) poner ejemplos a; **illustration** [-'streɪʃən] *n* (*example*) ejemplo; (*explanation*) aclaración *f*; (*in book*) lámina.
illustrious [ɪ'lʌstrɪəs] *a* ilustre.
ill will [ɪl'wɪl] *n* rencor *m*.
I'm [aɪm] = **I am**.
image ['ɪmɪdʒ] *n* imagen *f*.
imaginary [ɪ'mædʒɪnərɪ] *a* imaginario; **imagination** [-'neɪʃən] *n* imaginación *f*; (*inventiveness*) inventiva; (*illusion*) fantasía; **imaginative** [-nətɪv] *a* imaginativo; **imagine** *vt* imaginarse; (*delude o.s.*) hacerse la ilusión (de que).
imbalance [ɪm'bæləns] *n* (*gen*) desequilibrio; (*inequality*) falta de correspondencia.
imbecile ['ɪmbəsiːl] *n* imbécil *m/f*.
imbue [ɪm'bjuː] *vt*: **to** ~ **sth with** imbuir algo de.
imitate ['ɪmɪteɪt] *vt* imitar; **imitation** [-'teɪʃən] *n* imitación *f*; (*copy*) copia; (*mimicry*) mímica.
immaculate [ɪ'mækjulət] *a* perfectamente limpio; (*REL*) inmaculado.
immaterial [ɪmə'tɪərɪəl] *a* incorpóreo; **it is** ~ **whether...** no importa si... .

immature [ɪmə'tjuə*] *a* (*person*) poco maduro; (*of one's youth*) juvenil.
immediate [ɪ'miːdɪət] *a* inmediato; (*pressing*) urgente, apremiante; ~ly *ad* (*at once*) en seguida; ~ly next to muy junto a.
immense [ɪ'mɛns] *a* inmenso, enorme.
immerse [ɪ'məːs] *vt* (*submerge*) sumergir; (*sink*) hundir; to be ~d in (*fig*) estar absorto en.
immersion heater [ɪ'məːʃn-] *n* calentador *m* de inmersión.
immigrant ['ɪmɪgrənt] *n* inmigrante *m/f*; **immigrate** [-greɪt] *vi* inmigrar; **immigration** [-'greɪʃən] *n* inmigración *f.*
imminent ['ɪmɪnənt] *a* inminente.
immobile [ɪ'məubaɪl] *a* inmóvil; **immobilize** [-bɪlaɪz] *vt* inmovilizar.
immoral [ɪ'mɔrl] *a* inmoral; ~ity [-'rælɪtɪ] *n* inmoralidad *f.*
immortal [ɪ'mɔːtl] *a* inmortal; ~ize *vt* inmortalizar.
immune [ɪ'mjuːn] *a*: ~ (to) inmune (contra); **immunity** *n* (*MED*) inmunidad *f*; (*COMM*) exención *f.*
immunization [ɪmjunaɪ'zeɪʃən] *n* inmunización *f*; **immunize** ['ɪmjunaɪz] *vt* inmunizar.
imp [ɪmp] *n* diablillo.
impact ['ɪmpækt] *n* (*gen*) impacto.
impair [ɪm'pɛə*] *vt* perjudicar.
impale [ɪm'peɪl] *vt* atravesar.
impart [ɪm'pɑːt] *vt* comunicar.
impartial [ɪm'pɑːʃl] *a* imparcial; ~ity [ɪmpɑːʃɪ'ælɪtɪ] *n* imparcialidad *f.*
impassable [ɪm'pɑːsəbl] *a* (*barrier*) infranqueable; (*river*) invadeable; (*road*) intransitable.
impatience [ɪm'peɪʃəns] *n* impaciencia; **impatient** [-ənt] *a* impaciente; to get *or* grow impatient impacientarse.
impeccable [ɪm'pɛkəbl] *a* impecable.
impede [ɪm'piːd] *vt* estorbar, dificultar.
impediment [ɪm'pɛdɪmənt] *n* obstáculo, estorbo; (*also*: **speech** ~) defecto (del habla).
impending [ɪm'pɛndɪŋ] *a* (*near*) próximo.
impenetrable [ɪm'pɛnɪtrəbl] *a* (*gen*) impenetrable; (*unfathomable*) insondable.
imperative [ɪm'pɛrətɪv] *a* (*tone*) imperioso; (*necessary*) indispensable; (*pressing*) urgente // *n* (*LING*) imperativo.
imperceptible [ɪmpə'sɛptɪbl] *a* imperceptible, insensible.
imperfect [ɪm'pəːfɪkt] *a* imperfecto; (*goods etc*) defectuoso; ~ion [-'fɛkʃən] *n* (*blemish*) desperfecto; (*state*) imperfección *f.*
imperial [ɪm'pɪərɪəl] *a* imperial; ~ism *n* imperialismo.
imperil [ɪm'pɛrɪl] *vt* arriesgar, poner en peligro.
impersonal [ɪm'pəːsənl] *a* impersonal.
impersonate [ɪm'pəːsəneɪt] *vt* hacerse pasar por; (*THEATRE*) imitar.

impertinent [ɪm'pəːtɪnənt] *a* impertinente, insolente.
impervious [ɪm'pəːvɪəs] *a* impermeable; (*fig*): ~ to insensible a.
impetuous [ɪm'pɛtjuəs] *a* impetuoso, irreflexivo.
impetus ['ɪmpətəs] *n* ímpetu *m*; (*fig*) impulso.
impinge [ɪm'pɪndʒ]: to ~ on *vt fus* invadir, abusar de; (*affect*) afectar a.
implausible [ɪm'plɔːzɪbl] *a* inverosímil.
implement ['ɪmplɪmənt] *n* instrumento, herramienta // *vt* ['ɪmplɪmɛnt] hacer efectivo; (*carry out*) realizar.
implicate ['ɪmplɪkeɪt] *vt* (*compromise*) comprometer; (*involve*) enredar; **implication** [-'keɪʃən] *n* consecuencia, implicancia (*AM*).
implicit [ɪm'plɪsɪt] *a* (*gen*) implícito; (*complete*) absoluto.
implore [ɪm'plɔː*] *vt* (*person*) suplicar.
imply [ɪm'plaɪ] *vt* (*involve*) implicar; (*mean*) significar; (*hint*) dar a entender que; it is implied se sobreentiende.
impolite [ɪmpə'laɪt] *a* mal educado.
import [ɪm'pɔːt] *vt* importar // *n* ['ɪmpɔːt] (*COMM*) importación *f*; (: *article*) artículo importado; (*meaning*) significado, sentido.
importance [ɪm'pɔːtəns] *n* importancia; **important** [-ənt] *a* importante; it's not important no importa, no tiene importancia.
importer [ɪm'pɔːtə*] *n* importador/a *m/f.*
impose [ɪm'pəuz] *vt* imponer // *vi*: to ~ on sb abusar de uno; **imposing** *a* imponente, impresionante.
impossible [ɪm'pɔsɪbl] *a* imposible; (*person*) insoportable.
impostor [ɪm'pɔstə*] *n* impostor/a *m/f.*
impotence ['ɪmpətəns] *n* impotencia; **impotent** [-ənt] *a* impotente.
impound [ɪm'paund] *vt* embargar.
impoverished [ɪm'pɔvərɪʃt] *a* necesitado; (*land*) agotado.
impracticable [ɪm'præktɪkəbl] *a* no factible, irrealizable.
impractical [ɪm'præktɪkl] *a* (*person*) poco práctico.
imprecise [ɪmprɪ'saɪs] *a* impreciso.
impregnable [ɪm'prɛgnəbl] *a* invulnerable; (*castle*) inexpugnable.
impregnate ['ɪmprɛgneɪt] *vt* (*gen*) impregnar; (*soak*) empapar; (*fertilize*) fecundar.
impresario [ɪmprɪ'sɑːrɪəu] *n* empresario.
impress [ɪm'prɛs] *vt* impresionar; (*mark*) estampar // *vi* hacer buena impresión; to ~ sth on sb convencer a uno de algo; it ~ed itself on me se me grabó (en la memoria).
impression [ɪm'prɛʃən] *n* impresión *f*; (*footprint etc*) huella; (*print run*) edición *f*; to be under the ~ that tener la impresión de que; ~able *a* influenciable; (*sensitive*) sensible; ~ist *n* impresionista *m/f.*
impressive [ɪm'prɛsɪv] *a* impresionante.

imprint ['ımprınt] n impresión f, huella.
imprison [ım'prızn] vt encarcelar; ~**ment** n encarcelamiento, cárcel f.
improbable [ım'prɔbəbl] a improbable, inverosímil.
impromptu [ım'prɔmptjuː] a improvisado // ad de improviso.
improper [ım'prɔpə*] a (incorrect) impropio; (unseemly) indecoroso; (indecent) indecente.
impropriety [ımprə'praıətı] n falta de decoro; (indecency) indecencia; (of language) impropiedad f.
improve [ım'pruːv] vt mejorar // vi mejorarse; (become perfect) perfeccionarse; (pupils) hacer progresos; ~**ment** n mejoramiento; perfección f; progreso.
improvise ['ımprəvaız] vt, vi improvisar.
imprudent [ım'pruːdnt] a imprudente.
impudent ['ımpjudnt] a descarado, insolente.
impulse ['ımpʌls] n impulso; to act on ~ obrar sin reflexión; **impulsive** [-'pʌlsıv] a irreflexivo.
impunity [ım'pjuːnıtı] n: with ~ impunemente.
impure [ım'pjuə*] a (adulterated) adulterado; (not pure) impuro; **impurity** n (gen) impureza.
in [ın] prep en; (within) dentro de; (with time: during, within): ~ 2 days en 2 días; (: after): ~ 2 weeks dentro de 2 semanas; (with town, country): it's ~ France está en Francia // ad dentro, adentro; (fashionable) de moda; is he ~? ¿está en casa?; ~ the country en el campo; ~ the distance a lo lejos; ~ town en el centro (de la ciudad); ~ the sun al sol, bajo el sol; ~ the rain bajo la lluvia; ~ French en francés; 1 ~ 10 uno sobre 10, uno de cada 10; ~ hundreds por centenares; the best pupil ~ the class el mejor alumno de la clase; written ~ pencil escrito con lápiz; ~ saying this al decir esto; their party is ~ su partido ha llegado al poder; to ask sb ~ invitar a uno a entrar; to run/limp ~ entrar corriendo/cojeando; the ~s and outs los recovecos.
in., ins abbr of **inch(es)**.
inability [ınə'bılıtı] n incapacidad f.
inaccessible [ınək'sɛsıbl] a inaccesible.
inaccuracy [ın'ækjurəsı] n inexactitud f; **inaccurate** [-rət] a inexacto, incorrecto.
inactivity [ınæk'tıvıtı] n inactividad f.
inadequate [ın'ædıkwət] a (insufficient) insuficiente; (unsuitable) inadecuado; (person) incapaz.
inadvertently [ınəd'vɔːtntlı] ad por equivocación o descuido.
inadvisable [ınəd'vaızəbl] a no aconsejable.
inane [ı'neın] a necio, fatuo.
inanimate [ın'ænımət] a inanimado.
inapplicable [ın'æplıkəbl] a inaplicable.
inappropriate [ınə'prəuprıət] a

inoportuno, inconveniente; (word, expression) impropio.
inapt [ın'æpt] a impropio; ~**itude** n incapacidad f.
inarticulate [ınɑː'tıkjulət] a (person) incapaz de expresarse; (speech) inarticulado.
inasmuch as [ınəz'mʌtʃæz] ad (given that) puesto que; (since) ya que.
inattentive [ınə'tɛntıv] a distraído.
inaudible [ın'ɔːdıbl] a inaudible.
inaugural [ı'nɔːgjurəl] a (speech) de apertura; **inaugurate** [-reıt] vt inaugurar; **inauguration** [-'reıʃən] n ceremonia de apertura.
in-between [ınbı'twiːn] a intermedio, de entre medio.
inborn [ın'bɔːn] a (feeling) innato.
inbred [ın'brɛd] a innato; (family) engendrado por endogamia.
incalculable [ın'kælkjuləbl] a incalculable.
incapable [ın'keıpəbl] a incapaz.
incapacitate [ınkə'pæsıteıt] vt: to ~ sb incapacitar a uno.
incapacity [ınkə'pæsıtı] n (inability) incapacidad f.
incarcerate [ın'kɑːsəreıt] vt encarcelar.
incarnate [ın'kɑːnıt] a en persona // vt ['ınkɑːneıt] encarnar; **incarnation** [-'neıʃən] n encarnación f.
incendiary [ın'sɛndıərı] a incendiario.
incense ['ınsɛns] n incienso // vt [ın'sɛns] (anger) indignar, encolerizar.
incentive [ın'sɛntıv] n incentivo, estímulo.
incessant [ın'sɛsnt] a incesante, contínuo; ~**ly** ad constantemente.
incest ['ınsɛst] n incesto.
inch [ıntʃ] n pulgada; to be within an ~ of estar a dos dedos de; he didn't give an ~ no dio concesión alguna; to ~ forward avanzar palmo a palmo.
incidence ['ınsıdns] n (of crime, disease) frecuencia.
incident ['ınsıdnt] n incidente m, suceso; (in book) episodio.
incidental [ınsı'dɛntl] a no esencial, accesorio; (unplanned) fortuito; ~ to al margen de; ~**ly** [-'dɛntəlı] ad (by the way) a propósito.
incinerator [ın'sınəreıtə*] n incinerador m.
incipient [ın'sıpıənt] a incipiente.
incision [ın'sıʒən] n corte m.
incisive [ın'saısıv] a (mind) penetrante; (tone) mordaz; (remark etc) tajante.
incite [ın'saıt] vt provocar.
inclination [ınklı'neıʃən] n (tendency) tendencia, inclinación f.
incline ['ınklaın] n pendiente m, cuesta // (vb: [ın'klaın]) vt (slope) inclinar; (head) poner de lado // vi inclinarse; to be ~d to (tend) ser propenso a; (be willing) estar dispuesto a.
include [ın'kluːd] vt incluir, comprender;

(*in letter*) adjuntar; **including** *prep* incluso, inclusive.

inclusion [ɪnˈkluːʒən] *n* inclusión *f*; **inclusive** [-sɪv] *a* inclusivo // *ad* inclusive.

incognito [ɪnkɔgˈniːtəu] *ad* de incógnito.

incoherent [ɪnkəuˈhɪərənt] *a* incoherente.

income [ˈɪŋkʌm] *n* (*personal*) ingresos *mpl*; (*from property etc*) renta; (*profit*) rédito; ~ **tax** *n* impuesto sobre la renta; ~ **tax inspector** *n* inspector/a *m/f* fiscal; ~ **tax return** *n* registro fiscal.

incoming [ˈɪnkʌmɪŋ] *a*: ~ **flight** vuelo entrante.

incomparable [ɪnˈkɔmpərəbl] *a* incomparable, sin par.

incompatible [ɪnkəmˈpætɪbl] *a* incompatible.

incompetence [ɪnˈkɔmpɪtəns] *n* incompetencia; **incompetent** [-ənt] *a* incompetente.

incomplete [ɪnkəmˈpliːt] *a* incompleto; (*unfinished*) sin terminar.

incomprehensible [ɪnkɔmprɪˈhɛnsɪbl] *a* incomprensible.

inconceivable [ɪnkənˈsiːvəbl] *a* inconcebible.

inconclusive [ɪnkənˈkluːsɪv] *a* sin resultado (definitivo); (*argument*) poco convincente.

incongruous [ɪnˈkɔŋgruəs] *a* (*foolish*) absurdo, estrafalario; (*remark, act*) disonante, nada lógico.

inconsiderate [ɪnkənˈsɪdərət] *a* desconsiderado; **how** ~ **of him!** ¡qué falta de consideración (de su parte)!

inconsistent [ɪnkənˈsɪstnt] *a* inconsecuente; ~ **with** (que) no concuerda con.

inconspicuous [ɪnkənˈspɪkjuəs] *a* poco llamativo, modesto; **to make o.s.** ~ no llamar la atención.

inconstant [ɪnˈkɔnstnt] *a* inconstante.

incontinent [ɪnˈkɔntɪnənt] *a* incontinente.

inconvenience [ɪnkənˈviːnjəns] *n* (*gen*) inconvenientes *mpl*; (*trouble*) molestia, incomodidad *f* // *vt* incomodar; **inconvenient** [-ənt] *a* incómodo, poco práctico; (*time, place*) inoportuno.

incorporate [ɪnˈkɔːpəreɪt] *vt* incorporar; (*contain*) comprender; (*add*) agregar; ~**d** *a*: ~**d company** (*US: abbr* **Inc.**) Sociedad Anónima (S.A.).

incorrect [ɪnkəˈrɛkt] *a* incorrecto.

incorruptible [ɪnkəˈrʌptɪbl] *a* (*gen*) incorruptible; (*not open to bribes*) insobornable.

increase [ˈɪnkriːs] *n* aumento // *vi* [ɪnˈkriːs] aumentarse; (*grow*) crecer; (*price*) subir; **increasing** *a* (*number*) creciente, en aumento; **increasingly** *ad* de más en más, cada vez más.

incredible [ɪnˈkrɛdɪbl] *a* increíble.

incredulous [ɪnˈkrɛdjuləs] *a* incrédulo.

increment [ˈɪnkrɪmənt] *n* aumento, incremento.

incriminate [ɪnˈkrɪmɪneɪt] *vt* incriminar.

incubation [ɪnkjuˈbeɪʃən] *n* incubación *f*;

incubator [ˈɪnkjubeɪtə*] *n* incubadora.

incumbent [ɪnˈkʌmbənt] *n* ocupante *m/f* // *a*: **it is** ~ **on him to...** le incumbe... .

incur [ɪnˈkə:*] *vt* (*expenses*) contraer; (*gen*) incurrir en.

incurable [ɪnˈkjuərəbl] *a* incurable; (*fig*) irremediable.

incursion [ɪnˈkə:ʃən] *n* incursión *f*.

indebted [ɪnˈdɛtɪd] *a*: **to be** ~ **to sb** estar en deuda con uno.

indecent [ɪnˈdiːsnt] *a* indecente; ~ **assault** *n* atentado contra el pudor; ~ **exposure** *n* exhibicionismo.

indecisive [ɪndɪˈsaɪsɪv] *a* indeciso; (*discussion*) no resuelto, inconcluyente.

indeed [ɪnˈdiːd] *ad* de hecho, realmente; **yes** ~! claro que sí.

indefinite [ɪnˈdɛfɪnɪt] *a* indefinido; (*uncertain*) incierto; ~**ly** *ad* (*wait*) indefinidamente.

indelible [ɪnˈdɛlɪbl] *a* imborrable.

indemnify [ɪnˈdɛmnɪfaɪ] *vt* indemnizar, resarcir.

indentation [ɪndɛnˈteɪʃən] *n* mella; (*TYP*) sangría.

independence [ɪndɪˈpɛndns] *n* independencia; **independent** [-ənt] *a* independiente; **to become independent** independizarse.

index [ˈɪndɛks] *n* (*pl*: ~**es**: *in book*) índice *m*; (: *in library etc*) catálogo; (*pl*: **indices** [ˈɪndɪsiːz]: *ratio, sign*) exponente *m*; ~ **card** *n* ficha; ~ **finger** *n* índice *m*; ~**-linked** *a* vinculado al índice del coste de la vida.

India [ˈɪndɪə] *n* la India; ~**n** *a*, *n* indio/a; **Red** ~**n** piel roja *m/f*.

indicate [ˈɪndɪkeɪt] *vt* indicar; **indication** [-ˈkeɪʃən] *n* indicio, señal *f*; **indicator** *n* (*gen*) indicador *m*.

indices [ˈɪndɪsiːz] *pl of* **index**.

indict [ɪnˈdaɪt] *vt* acusar; ~**ment** *n* acusación *f*.

indifference [ɪnˈdɪfrəns] *n* indiferencia; **indifferent** [-ənt] *a* indiferente; (*poor*) regular.

indigenous [ɪnˈdɪdʒɪnəs] *a* indígena *inv*.

indigestion [ɪndɪˈdʒɛstʃən] *n* indigestión *f*, empacho.

indignant [ɪnˈdɪgnənt] *a*: **to be** ~ **about sth** indignarse por algo; **indignation** [-ˈneɪʃən] *n* indignación *f*.

indignity [ɪnˈdɪgnɪtɪ] *n* indignidad *f*; (*insult*) ultraje *m*, afrenta.

indigo [ˈɪndɪgəu] *a* color de añil // *n* añil *m*.

indirect [ɪndɪˈrɛkt] *a* indirecto; ~**ly** *ad* indirectamente.

indiscreet [ɪndɪˈskriːt] *a* indiscreto; (*rash*) imprudente; **indiscretion** [-ˈskrɛʃən] *n* indiscreción *f*; imprudencia.

indiscriminate [ɪndɪˈskrɪmɪnət] *a* indistinto.

indispensable [ɪndɪˈspɛnsəbl] *a* indispensable, imprescindible.

indisposed [ɪndɪˈspəuzd] *a* (*unwell*) indispuesto.

indisputable [ˌɪndɪ'spjuːtəbl] *a* incontestable.

indistinct [ˌɪndɪ'stɪŋkt] *a* indistinto; (*memory, noise*) confuso.

individual [ˌɪndɪ'vɪdjuəl] *n* individuo // *a* individual; (*personal*) personal; (*for/of one only*) particular; ~ **ist** *n* individualista *m/f*; ~ **ity** [-'ælɪtɪ] *n* individualidad *f*; ~ **ly** *ad* individualmente; particularmente.

indoctrinate [ɪn'dɔktrɪneɪt] *vt* adoctrinar; **indoctrination** [-'neɪʃən] *n* adoctrinamiento.

indolent ['ɪndələnt] *a* indolente, perezoso.

indoor ['ɪndɔː*] *a* (*inner*) interior; (*household*) de casa; (*inside*) de puertas adentro; (*swimming-pool*) cubierto; (*games*) de salón; (*sport*) bajo cubierta; ~**s** [ɪn'dɔːz] *ad* dentro; (*at home*) en casa.

induce [ɪn'djuːs] *vt* inducir; (*bring about*) producir; (*provoke*) provocar; ~**ment** *n* (*incentive*) incentivo, aliciente *m*.

induction [ɪn'dʌkʃən] *n* (*MED. of birth*) inducción *f*; ~ **course** *n* curso de inducción.

indulge [ɪn'dʌldʒ] *vt* (*desire*) dar rienda suelta a; (*whim*) condescender con; (*person*) complacer; (*child*) consentir // *vi*: **to** ~ **in** darse el lujo de; **indulgence** *n* (*of desire*) gratificación *f*; (*leniency*) complacencia; **indulgent** *a* indulgente.

industrial [ɪn'dʌstrɪəl] *a* industrial; ~ **action** *n* huelga; ~ **estate** *n* zona industrial; ~ **ist** *n* industrial *m/f*; ~ **ize** *vt* industrializar.

industrious [ɪn'dʌstrɪəs] *a* (*gen*) trabajador(a); (*student*) aplicado.

industry ['ɪndəstrɪ] *n* industria; (*diligence*) aplicación *f*.

inebriated [ɪ'niːbrɪeɪtɪd] *a* borracho.

inedible [ɪn'ɛdɪbl] *a* incomible; (*plant etc*) no comestible.

ineffective [ˌɪnɪ'fɛktɪv] *a* ineficaz, inútil.

inefficiency [ˌɪnɪ'fɪʃənsɪ] *n* ineficacia; **inefficient** [-ənt] *a* ineficaz, ineficiente.

ineligible [ɪn'ɛlɪdʒɪbl] *a* (*candidate*) inelegible; **to be** ~ **for sth** no tener derecho a algo.

inept [ɪ'nɛpt] *a* incompetente, incapaz.

inequality [ˌɪnɪ'kwɔlɪtɪ] *n* desigualdad *f*.

inert [ɪ'nɜːt] *a* inerte, inactivo; (*immobile*) inmóvil; ~ **ia** [ɪ'nɜːʃə] *n* inercia; (*laziness*) pereza.

inescapable [ˌɪnɪ'skeɪpəbl] *a* ineludible.

inestimable [ɪn'ɛstɪməbl] *a* inestimable.

inevitable [ɪn'ɛvɪtəbl] *a* inevitable; (*necessary*) forzoso.

inexcusable [ˌɪnɪks'kjuːzəbl] *a* imperdonable.

inexhaustible [ˌɪnɪg'zɔːstɪbl] *a* inagotable.

inexorable [ɪn'ɛksɔrəbl] *a* inexorable, implacable.

inexpensive [ˌɪnɪk'spɛnsɪv] *a* económico.

inexperience [ˌɪnɪk'spɪərɪəns] *n* falta de experiencia; ~**d** *a* inexperto.

inexplicable [ˌɪnɪk'splɪkəbl] *a* inexplicable.

inextricable [ˌɪnɪk'strɪkəbl] *a* inextricable.

infallible [ɪn'fælɪbl] *a* infalible.

infamous ['ɪnfəməs] *a* infame; **infamy** [-mɪ] *n* infamia.

infancy ['ɪnfənsɪ] *n* infancia.

infant ['ɪnfənt] *n* (*baby*) criatura; (*young child*) niño/a; ~ **ile** *a* infantil; (*pej*) aniñado; ~ **school** *n* escuela de párvulos.

infantry ['ɪnfəntrɪ] *n* infantería; ~**man** *n* soldado (de infantería).

infatuated [ɪn'fætjueɪtɪd] *a*: ~ **with** (*gen*) encaprichado por; (*in love*) enamorado de; **infatuation** [-'eɪʃən] *n* encaprichamiento; enamoramiento.

infect [ɪn'fɛkt] *vt* (*wound*) infectar; (*person*) contagiar; (*fig: pej*) corromper; ~**ed with** (*illness*) contagiado de; ~**ion** [ɪn'fɛkʃən] *n* infección *f*; (*fig*) contagio; ~**ious** [ɪn'fɛkʃəs] *a* contagioso; (*also: fig*) infeccioso.

infer [ɪn'fɜː*] *vt* deducir, inferir; ~**ence** ['ɪnfərəns] *n* deducción *f*, inferencia.

inferior [ɪn'fɪərɪə*] *a, n* inferior *m/f*; ~**ity** [-rɪ'ɔrətɪ] *n* inferioridad *f*; ~**ity complex** *n* complejo de inferioridad.

infernal [ɪn'fɜːnl] *a* infernal.

inferno [ɪn'fɜːnəu] *n* infierno; (*fig*) hoguera.

infertile [ɪn'fɜːtaɪl] *a* estéril, infecundo; **infertility** [-'tɪlɪtɪ] *n* esterilidad *f*, infecundidad *f*.

infested [ɪn'fɛstɪd] *a*: ~ **(with)** plagado (de).

infidelity [ˌɪnfɪ'dɛlɪtɪ] *n* infidelidad *f*.

in-fighting ['ɪnfaɪtɪŋ] *n* (*fig*) luchas *fpl* internas.

infiltrate ['ɪnfɪltreɪt] *vt* (*troops etc*) infiltrarse en // *vi* infiltrarse.

infinite ['ɪnfɪnɪt] *a* infinito.

infinitive [ɪn'fɪnɪtɪv] *n* infinitivo.

infinity [ɪn'fɪnɪtɪ] *n* (*also MATH*) infinito; (*an* ~) infinidad *f*.

infirm [ɪn'fɜːm] *a* enfermo, débil; ~**ary** *n* hospital *m*; ~**ity** *n* debilidad *f*; (*illness*) enfermedad *f*, achaque *m*.

inflame [ɪn'fleɪm] *vt* inflamar.

inflammable [ɪn'flæməbl] *a* inflamable; (*explosive*) explosivo.

inflammation [ˌɪnflə'meɪʃən] *n* inflamación *f*.

inflate [ɪn'fleɪt] *vt* (*tyre, balloon*) inflar; (*fig*) hinchar; ~**d** *a* (*style*) exagerado; (*value*) excesivo; **inflation** [ɪn'fleɪʃən] *n* (*ECON*) inflación *f*; **inflationary** [ɪn-'fleɪʃnərɪ] *a* inflacionario.

inflexible [ɪn'flɛksɪbl] *a* inflexible.

inflict [ɪn'flɪkt] *vt*: **to** ~ **on** infligir en; (*tax etc*) imponer a; ~**ion** [ɪn'flɪkʃən] *n* imposición *f*.

inflow ['ɪnfləu] *n* afluencia.

influence ['ɪnfluəns] *n* influencia // *vt* influir en, influenciar; (*persuade*) sugestionar; **under the** ~ **of alcohol** en estado de embriaguez; **influential** [-'ɛnʃl] *a* influyente.

influenza [ˌɪnflu'ɛnzə] *n* gripe *f*.

influx ['ɪnflʌks] *n* afluencia.

inform [ɪn'fɔːm] vt: **to ~ sb of sth** informar a uno sobre o de algo; (warn) avisar a uno de algo; (communicate) comunicar algo a uno // vi soplar; **to ~ on sb** delatar a uno.

informal [ɪn'fɔːml] a (person, manner) desenvuelto; (tone) familiar; (visit, discussion) extraoficial; (intimate) de confianza; **~ity** [-'mælɪtɪ] n falta de ceremonia; (intimacy) intimidad f; (familiarity) familiaridad f; (ease) afabilidad f.

information [ɪnfə'meɪʃən] n información f, informes mpl; (news) noticias fpl; (knowledge) conocimientos mpl; (LAW) delatación f; **a piece of ~** un dato.

informative [ɪn'fɔːmətɪv] a informativo.

informer [ɪn'fɔːmə*] n delator/a m/f; (also: **police ~**) soplón/ona m/f.

infra-red [ɪnfrə'rɛd] a infrarrojo.

infrequent [ɪn'friːkwənt] a infrecuente.

infringe [ɪn'frɪndʒ] vt infringir, violar // vi: **to ~ on** invadir, abusar de; **~ment** n infracción f; (of rights) invasión f; (SPORT) falta.

infuriate [ɪn'fjuərɪeɪt] vt enfurecer; **infuriating** a enloquecedor(a).

ingenious [ɪn'dʒiːnjəs] a ingenioso; **ingenuity** [-dʒɪ'njuːɪtɪ] n ingeniosidad f.

ingenuous [ɪn'dʒɛnjuəs] a ingenuo.

ingot ['ɪŋgət] n lingote m, barra f.

ingrained [ɪn'greɪnd] a arraigado.

ingratiate [ɪn'greɪʃɪeɪt] vt: **to ~ o.s. with** congraciarse con.

ingratitude [ɪn'grætɪtjuːd] n ingratitud f.

ingredient [ɪn'griːdɪənt] n ingrediente m.

inhabit [ɪn'hæbɪt] vt habitar, vivir en; (occupy) ocupar; **~ant** n habitante m/f.

inhale [ɪn'heɪl] vt inhalar // vi (in smoking) aspirar.

inherent [ɪn'hɪərənt] a: **~ in** or **to** inherente a.

inherit [ɪn'hɛrɪt] vt heredar; **~ance** n herencia f; (fig) patrimonio.

inhibit [ɪn'hɪbɪt] vt inhibir, impedir; **to ~ sb from doing sth** impedir a uno hacer algo; **~ion** [-'bɪʃən] n inhibición f.

inhospitable [ɪnhɔs'pɪtəbl] a (person) inhospitalario; (place) inhóspito.

inhuman [ɪn'hjuːmən] a inhumano.

inimitable [ɪ'nɪmɪtəbl] a inimitable.

iniquity [ɪ'nɪkwɪtɪ] n inicuidad f; (injustice) injusticia.

initial [ɪ'nɪʃl] a inicial; (first) primero // n inicial f // vt firmar con las iniciales; **~s** npl iniciales fpl; (abbreviation) siglas fpl; **~ly** ad al principio, en primer lugar.

initiate [ɪ'nɪʃɪeɪt] vt (start) iniciar, dar comienzo a; **to ~ sb into a secret** iniciar a uno en un secreto; **to ~ proceedings against sb** (LAW) entablar proceso contra uno; **initiation** [-'eɪʃən] n (into secret etc) iniciación f; (beginning) comienzo.

initiative [ɪ'nɪʃətɪv] n iniciativa.

inject [ɪn'dʒɛkt] vt (liquid) inyectar; (fig) injertar; **~ion** [ɪn'dʒɛkʃən] n inyección f.

injunction [ɪn'dʒʌŋkʃən] n interdicto.

injure ['ɪndʒə*] vt herir, lastimar; (fig) perjudicar; (offend) ofender; **injury** n herida, lesión f; (wrong) perjuicio, daño; **injury time** n (SPORT) descuento.

injustice [ɪn'dʒʌstɪs] n injusticia.

ink [ɪŋk] n tinta.

inkling ['ɪŋklɪŋ] n sospecha; (idea) idea, atisbo.

inlaid ['ɪnleɪd] a taraceado, entarimado.

inland ['ɪnlənd] a interior, del interior // ad [ɪn'lænd] tierra adentro; **I~ Revenue** n (Brit) el fisco.

in-laws ['ɪnlɔːz] npl parientes mpl políticos.

inlet ['ɪnlɛt] n (GEO) ensenada, cala; (TECH) admisión f, entrada.

inmate ['ɪnmeɪt] n (in prison) presidiario; (in asylum) internado/a.

inn [ɪn] n posada, mesón m.

innate [ɪ'neɪt] a innato.

inner ['ɪnə*] a interior, interno; **~ city** n centro de la ciudad; **~ tube** n (of tyre) cámara.

innocence ['ɪnəsns] n inocencia; **innocent** [-nt] a inocente.

innocuous [ɪ'nɔkjuəs] a innocuo.

innovation [ɪnəʊ'veɪʃən] n novedad f.

innuendo [ɪnju'ɛndəʊ], pl **~es** n indirecta.

innumerable [ɪ'njuːmrəbl] a innumerable.

inoculation [ɪnɔkju'leɪʃən] n inoculación f.

inopportune [ɪn'ɔpətjuːn] a inoportuno.

inordinately [ɪ'nɔːdɪnətlɪ] ad desmesuradamente.

inorganic [ɪnɔː'gænɪk] a inorgánico.

in-patient ['ɪnpeɪʃənt] n paciente m/f interno/a.

input ['ɪnput] n (ELEC) entrada; (COMM) inversión f.

inquest ['ɪnkwɛst] n pesquisa judicial; (coroner's) encuesta judicial.

inquire [ɪn'kwaɪə*] vi pedir informes // vt (ask) preguntar; (seek information about) pedir informes sobre; **to ~ about** vt fus (person) preguntar por; (fact) informarse de; **to ~ into** vt fus investigar, indagar; **inquiring** a (mind) penetrante; (look) interrogativo; **inquiry** n pregunta; (LAW) investigación f, pesquisa; (commission) comisión f investigadora; **inquiry office** n oficina de informaciones.

inquisitive [ɪn'kwɪzɪtɪv] a (curious) activo, inquiridor(a); (prying) preguntón(ona), fisgón(ona).

inroad ['ɪnrəʊd] n incursión f; (fig) invasión f.

insane [ɪn'seɪn] a loco; (MED) demente.

insanitary [ɪn'sænɪtərɪ] a insalubre.

insanity [ɪn'sænɪtɪ] n demencia, locura.

insatiable [ɪn'seɪʃəbl] a insaciable.

inscribe [ɪn'skraɪb] vt inscribir; (book etc): **to ~ (to sb)** dedicar (a uno).

inscription [ɪn'skrɪpʃən] n (gen) inscripción f; (in book) dedicatoria.

inscrutable [ɪn'skruːtəbl] a inescrutable, insondable.

insect ['ɪnsɛkt] n insecto; ~icide [ɪn-'sɛktɪsaɪd] n insecticida m.
insecure [ɪnsɪ'kjuə*] a inseguro;
insecurity n inseguridad f.
insensible [ɪn'sɛnsɪbl] a impasible,
insensible; (unconscious) inconsciente.
insensitive [ɪn'sɛnsɪtɪv] a insensible.
inseparable [ɪn'sɛprəbl] a inseparable;
they were ~ friends les unía una
estrecha amistad.
insert [ɪn'sɜːt] vt (between things)
intercalar; (into sth) introducir; (in paper)
publicar; (: advert) poner // n ['ɪnsɜːt] hoja
suelta (intercalada); ~ion [ɪn'sɜːʃən] n
inserción f; (publication) publicación f; (of
pages) materia añadida.
inshore [ɪn'ʃɔː*] a cercano a la orilla o
costa // ad (be) cerca de la orilla; (move)
hacia la orilla.
inside ['ɪn'saɪd] n interior m; (lining) forro
// a interior, interno; (secret) secreto //
ad (within) (por) dentro; (with movement)
hacia dentro; (fam: in prison) en la cárcel
// prep dentro de; (of time): ~ 10
minutes en menos de 10 minutos; ~s npl
(col) tripas fpl; ~ forward n (SPORT)
delantero interior; ~ lane n (AUT: in
Britain) el lado o carril izquierdo; ~ out
ad (turn) al revés; (know) a fondo.
insidious [ɪn'sɪdɪəs] a insidioso;
(underground) clandestino.
insight ['ɪnsaɪt] n perspicacia.
insignificant [ɪnsɪg'nɪfɪknt] a insignificante.
insincere [ɪnsɪn'sɪə*] a poco sincero;
insincerity [-'sɛrɪtɪ] n falta de sinceridad,
doblez f.
insinuate [ɪn'sɪnjueɪt] vt insinuar;
insinuation [-'eɪʃən] n insinuación f; (hint)
indirecta.
insipid [ɪn'sɪpɪd] a soso, insulso.
insist [ɪn'sɪst] vi insistir; to ~ on doing
empeñarse en hacer; to ~ that insistir en
que; (claim) exigir que; ~ence n
insistencia; (stubbornness) empeño; ~ent
a insistente; empeñado.
insole ['ɪnsəul] n plantilla.
insolence ['ɪnsələns] n insolencia,
descaro; insolent [-ənt] a insolente,
descarado.
insoluble [ɪn'sɔljubl] a insoluble.
insolvent [ɪn'sɔlvənt] a insolvente.
insomnia [ɪn'sɔmnɪə] n insomnio.
inspect [ɪn'spɛkt] vt inspeccionar,
examinar; (troops) pasar revista a; ~ion
[ɪn'spɛkʃən] n inspección f, examen m;
~or n inspector/a m/f; (RAIL) revisor m.
inspiration [ɪnspə'reɪʃən] n inspiración f;
inspire [ɪn'spaɪə*] vt inspirar.
instability [ɪnstə'bɪlɪtɪ] n inestabilidad f.
install [ɪn'stɔːl] vt instalar; ~ation
[ɪnstə'leɪʃən] n instalación f.
instalment, installment (US) [ɪn-
'stɔːlmənt] n plazo; (of story) entrega; (of
TV serial etc) episodio.
instance ['ɪnstəns] n ejemplo, caso; for ~

por ejemplo; in the first ~ en primer
lugar.
instant ['ɪnstənt] n instante m, momento
// a instantáneo, inmediato; (coffee) en
polvo; ~ly ad en seguida.
instead [ɪn'stɛd] ad en cambio; ~ of en
lugar de, en vez de.
instep ['ɪnstɛp] n empeine m.
instigation [ɪnstɪ'geɪʃən] n instigación f.
instil [ɪn'stɪl] vt: to ~ into infundir a,
inculcar en.
instinct ['ɪnstɪŋkt] n instinto; ~ive
[-'stɪŋktɪv] a instintivo; ~ively
[-'stɪŋktɪvlɪ] ad por instinto.
institute ['ɪnstɪtjuːt] n instituto;
(professional body) colegio // vt (inquiry)
iniciar, empezar; (proceedings) entablar.
institution [ɪnstɪ'tjuːʃən] n (gen)
institución f; (beginning) iniciación f;
(organization) instituto; (MED: home) asilo;
(asylum) manicomio; (custom) costumbre
f.
instruct [ɪn'strʌkt] vt: to ~ sb in sth
instruir a uno en o sobre algo; to ~ sb to
do sth dar instrucciones a uno de hacer
algo; ~ion [ɪn'strʌkʃən] n (teaching)
instrucción f; ~ions npl órdenes fpl;
~ions (for use) modo sg de empleo;
~ive a aleccionador(a); ~or n
instructor/a m/f.
instrument ['ɪnstrumənt] n instrumento;
~al [-'mɛntl] a (MUS) instrumental; to be
~al in contribuir materialmente a; ~
panel n tablero (de instrumentos).
insubordinate [ɪnsə'bɔːdənɪt] a
insubordinado; insubordination [-'neɪʃən]
n insubordinación f; (disobedience)
desobediencia.
insufferable [ɪn'sʌfrəbl] a insufrible.
insufficient [ɪnsə'fɪʃənt] a insuficiente.
insular ['ɪnsjulə*] a insular; (outlook) de
miras estrechas.
insulate ['ɪnsjuleɪt] vt aislar; insulating
tape n cinta aislante; insulation [-'leɪʃən]
n aislamiento.
insulin ['ɪnsjulɪn] n insulina.
insult ['ɪnsʌlt] n insulto; (offence) ofensa //
vt [ɪn'sʌlt] insultar, injuriar; ofender;
~ing a insultante; ofensivo.
insuperable [ɪn'sjuːprəbl] a insuperable.
insurance [ɪn'ʃuərəns] n seguro; fire/life
~ seguro sobre la vida/contra incendios;
~ agent n agente m/f de seguros; ~
policy n póliza (de seguros).
insure [ɪn'ʃuə*] vt asegurar.
insurrection [ɪnsə'rɛkʃən] n insurrección
f.
intact [ɪn'tækt] a íntegro; (unharmed)
ileso, sano.
intake ['ɪnteɪk] n (TECH) entrada, toma; (:
pipe) tubo de admisión; (of food) cantidad
admitida; (SCOL): an ~ of 200 a year 200
matriculados al año.
intangible [ɪn'tændʒɪbl] a intangible.
integral ['ɪntɪgrəl] a (whole) íntegro;
(part) integrante.

integrate ['ɪntɪgreɪt] vt integrar // vi integrarse.

integrity [ɪn'tɛgrɪtɪ] n honradez f, rectitud f.

intellect ['ɪntəlɛkt] n intelecto; ~ual [-'lɛktjuəl] a, n intelectual m/f.

intelligence [ɪn'tɛlɪdʒəns] n inteligencia; (MIL etc) informes mpl; I~ Service n Servicio de Inteligencia; **intelligent** [-ənt] a inteligente.

intelligible [ɪn'tɛlɪdʒɪbl] a inteligible, comprensible.

intend [ɪn'tɛnd] vt (gift etc): **to** ~ **sth for** destinar algo a; **to** ~ **to do sth** tener intención de o proponerse hacer algo; ~**ed** a (effect) deseado // n prometido/a.

intense [ɪn'tɛns] a intenso; (person) nervioso; ~**ly** ad intensamente; (very) sumamente.

intensify [ɪn'tɛnsɪfaɪ] vt intensificar; (increase) aumentar.

intensity [ɪn'tɛnsɪtɪ] n intensidad f; (strength) fuerza.

intensive [ɪn'tɛnsɪv] a intensivo; ~ **care unit** n centro de cuidados intensivos.

intent [ɪn'tɛnt] n propósito // a (absorbed) absorto; (attentive) atento; **to all** ~**s and purposes** prácticamente; **to be** ~ **on doing sth** estar resuelto a hacer algo.

intention [ɪn'tɛnʃən] n intento, propósito; (plan) proyecto; ~**al** a intencional, deliberado; ~**ally** ad a propósito.

intently [ɪn'tɛntlɪ] ad atentamente, fijamente.

inter [ɪn'tə:*] vt enterrar.

interact [ɪntər'ækt] vi influirse mutuamente; ~**ion** [-'ækʃən] n influencia mútua, acción f recíproca.

intercede [ɪntə'si:d] vi: **to** ~ (**with**) interceder (con).

intercept [ɪntə'sɛpt] vt interceptar; (stop) detener; ~**ion** [-'sɛpʃən] n interceptación f; detención f.

interchange ['ɪntətʃeɪndʒ] n intercambio; (exchange) canje m; (on motorway) paso a desnivel // vt [ɪntə'tʃeɪndʒ] intercambiar; canjear; ~**able** a intercambiable.

intercom ['ɪntəkɔm] n sistema m de intercomunicación.

interconnect [ɪntəkə'nɛkt] vi (rooms) conectarse.

intercourse ['ɪntəkɔ:s] n (sexual) relaciones fpl; (social) trato.

interest ['ɪntrɪst] n (also COMM) interés m; (profit) ventaja, provecho // vt interesar; **to be** ~**ed in** interesarse por; ~**ing** a interesante.

interfere [ɪntə'fɪə*] vi: **to** ~ **in** (quarrel, other people's business) entrometerse. o mezclarse en; **to** ~ **with** (hinder) estorbar; (damage) estropear; (radio) interferir con.

interference [ɪntə'fɪərəns] n (gen) intromisión f; (RADIO, TV) interferencia.

interim ['ɪntərɪm] n: **in the** ~ entretanto, en el interino.

interior [ɪn'tɪərɪə*] n interior m // a interior.

interject [ɪntə'dʒɛkt] vt interponerse; ~**ion** [-'dʒɛkʃən] n interyección f.

interlock [ɪntə'lɔk] vi entrelazarse; (wheels etc) endentarse.

interloper ['ɪntələupə*] n intruso.

interlude ['ɪntəlu:d] n intérvalo; (rest) descanso; (THEATRE) intermedio.

intermarry [ɪntə'mærɪ] vi casarse (parientes).

intermediary [ɪntə'mi:dɪərɪ] n intermediario.

intermediate [ɪntə'mi:dɪət] a intermedio, medio.

intermission [ɪntə'mɪʃən] n (THEATRE) descanso.

intermittent [ɪntə'mɪtnt] a intermitente.

intern [ɪn'tə:n] vt internar; (enclose) encerrar // n ['ɪntə:n] (US) interno.

internal [ɪn'tə:nl] a interno, interior; ~**ly** ad interiormente; **'not to be taken** ~**ly'** 'uso externo'; ~ **revenue** n (US) rentas fpl públicas.

international [ɪntə'næʃənl] a internacional; ~ **game** partido internacional; ~ **player** jugador/a m/f internacional.

interplay ['ɪntəpleɪ] n interacción f.

interpret [ɪn'tə:prɪt] vt interpretar; (translate) traducir; (understand) entender // vi hacer de intérprete; ~**ation** [-'teɪʃən] n interpretación f; traducción f; entendimiento; ~**er** n intérprete m/f.

interrelated [ɪntərɪ'leɪtɪd] a interrelacionado.

interrogate [ɪn'tɛrəugeɪt] vt interrogar; **interrogation** [-'geɪʃən] n interrogatorio; **interrogative** [ɪntə'rɔgətɪv] a interrogativo.

interrupt [ɪntə'rʌpt] vt, vi interrumpir; ~**ion** [-'rʌpʃən] n interrupción f.

intersect [ɪntə'sɛkt] vt cruzar // vi (roads) cruzarse; ~**ion** [-'sɛkʃən] n intersección f; (of roads) cruce m.

intersperse [ɪntə'spə:s] vt esparcir, entremezclar.

intertwine [ɪntə'twaɪn] vt entrelazar // vi entrelazarse.

interval ['ɪntəvl] n intérvalo; (SCOL) recreo; (THEATRE, SPORT) descanso; **at** ~**s** a ratos, de vez en cuando.

intervene [ɪntə'vi:n] vi (gen) intervenir; (take part) participar; (occur) sobrevenir; **intervention** [-'vɛnʃən] n intervención f.

interview ['ɪntəvju:] n (RADIO, TV etc) entrevista // vt entrevistarse con; ~**ee** [-'i:] n entrevistado/a; ~**er** n entrevistador/a m/f.

intestine [ɪn'tɛstɪn] n: **large/small** ~ intestino grueso/delgado.

intimacy ['ɪntɪməsɪ] n intimidad f; (relations) relaciones fpl íntimas.

intimate ['ɪntɪmət] a íntimo; (friendship) estrecho; (knowledge) profundo // vt ['ɪntɪmeɪt] (announce) dar a entender.

intimidate [ɪn'tɪmɪdeɪt] vt intimidar,

amedrentar; **intimidation** [-'deɪʃən] *n* intimidación *f.*

into ['ɪntu] *prep* (*gen*) en; (*towards*) a; (*inside*) hacia el interior de; ~ **3 pieces/French** en 3 pedazos/ francés.

intolerable [ɪn'tɔlərəbl] *a* intolerable, insufrible; **intolerance** [-rəns] *n* intolerancia; **intolerant** [-rənt] *a*: **intolerant of** intolerante con *o* para.

intonation [ɪntəu'neɪʃən] *n* entonación *f.*

intoxicate [ɪn'tɔksɪkeɪt] *vt* embriagar; ~**d** *a* embriagado; **intoxication** [-'keɪʃən] *n* embriaguez *f.*

intractable [ɪn'træktəbl] *a* (*child*) intratable; (*material*) difícil de trabajar; (*problem*) espinoso.

intransigent [ɪn'trænsɪdʒənt] *a* intransigente.

intransitive [ɪn'trænsɪtɪv] *a* intransitivo.

intravenous [ɪntrə'viːnəs] *a* intravenoso.

intrepid [ɪn'trepɪd] *a* intrépido.

intricate ['ɪntrɪkət] *a* intrincado; (*complex*) complejo.

intrigue [ɪn'triːg] *n* intriga // *vt* interesar, fascinar // *vi* andar en intrigas; **intriguing** *a* intrigante.

intrinsic [ɪn'trɪnsɪk] *a* intrínseco.

introduce [ɪntrə'djuːs] *vt* introducir, meter; **to** ~ **sb (to sb)** presentar uno (a otro); **to** ~ **sb to** (*pastime, technique*) introducir a uno a; **introduction** [-'dʌkʃən] *n* introducción *f*; (*of person*) presentación *f*; **introductory** [-'dʌktərɪ] *a* preliminar.

introspective [ɪntrəu'spektɪv] *a* introspectivo.

introvert ['ɪntrəuvəːt] *a, n* introvertido/a.

intrude [ɪn'truːd] *vi* (*person*) entrometerse; **to** ~ **on** *or* **into** estorbar; **intruder** *n* intruso/a; **intrusion** [-ʒən] *n* invasión *f*; **intrusive** [-sɪv] *a* intruso.

intuition [ɪntjuː'ɪʃən] *n* intuición *f*; **intuitive** [-'tjuːɪtɪv] *a* intuitivo.

inundate ['ɪnʌndeɪt] *vt*: **to** ~ **with** inundar de.

invade [ɪn'veɪd] *vt* invadir; **invader** *n* invasor/a *m/f.*

invalid ['ɪnvəlɪd] *n* inválido/a // *a* [ɪn'vælɪd] (*not valid*) inválido, nulo; ~**ate** [ɪn'vælɪdeɪt] *vt* invalidar, anular.

invaluable [ɪn'væljuəbl] *a* inestimable.

invariable [ɪn'vɛərɪəbl] *a* invariable.

invasion [ɪn'veɪʒən] *n* invasión *f.*

invent [ɪn'vent] *vt* inventar; ~**ion** [ɪn'venʃən] *n* invento; (*inventiveness*) inventiva; (*lie*) ficción *f*, mentira; ~**ive** *a* ingenioso; ~**iveness** *n* ingenio, inventiva; ~**or** *n* inventor/a *m/f.*

inventory ['ɪnvəntrɪ] *n* inventario.

inverse [ɪn'vəːs] *a, n* inverso; ~**ly** *ad* a la inversa.

invert [ɪn'vəːt] *vt* invertir, volver al revés; ~**ed commas** *npl* comillas *fpl.*

invertebrate [ɪn'vəːtɪbrət] *n* invertebrado.

invest [ɪn'vest] *vt, vi* invertir.

investigate [ɪn'vestɪgeɪt] *vt* investigar; (*study*) estudiar, examinar; **investigation** [-'geɪʃən] *n* investigación *f*, pesquisa; examen *m*; **investigator** *n* investigador/a *m/f.*

investiture [ɪn'vestɪtʃə*] *n* investidura.

investment [ɪn'vestmənt] *n* inversión *f.*

investor [ɪn'vestə*] *n* inversionista *m/f.*

inveterate [ɪn'vetərət] *a* empedernido.

invigorating [ɪn'vɪgəreɪtɪŋ] *a* vigorizante.

invincible [ɪn'vɪnsɪbl] *a* invencible.

inviolate [ɪn'vaɪələt] *a* inviolado.

invisible [ɪn'vɪzɪbl] *a* invisible; ~ **ink** *n* tinta simpática.

invitation [ɪnvɪ'teɪʃən] *n* invitación *f.*

invite [ɪn'vaɪt] *vt* (*gen*) invitar; (*to drink, food*) convidar; (*opinions etc*) solicitar, pedir; (*trouble*) buscarse; **inviting** *a* atractivo; (*look*) incitante; (*food*) apetitoso.

invoice ['ɪnvɔɪs] *n* factura // *vt* facturar.

invoke [ɪn'vəuk] *vt* invocar; (*aid*) implorar; (*law*) recurrir a.

involuntary [ɪn'vɔləntrɪ] *a* involuntario.

involve [ɪn'vɔlv] *vt* (*entail*) suponer, implicar; **to** ~ **sb (in)** comprometer a uno (con); ~**d** *a* complicado; ~**ment** *n* (*gen*) enredo; (*obligation*) compromiso; (*difficulty*) apuro.

invulnerable [ɪn'vʌlnərəbl] *a* invulnerable.

inward ['ɪnwəd] *a* (*movement*) interior, interno; (*thought, feeling*) íntimo; ~**ly** *ad* (*feel, think etc*) para sí, para dentro; ~(**s**) *ad* hacia dentro.

iodine ['aɪəudiːn] *n* yodo.

iota [aɪ'əutə] *n* (*fig*) jota, ápice *m.*

IOU *n abbr of* **I owe you** pagaré *m.*

IQ *n abbr of* **intelligence quotient** cociente *m* intelectual.

Iran [ɪ'rɑːn] *n* Irán *m*; ~**ian** [ɪ'reɪnɪən] *a, n* iraní *m/f.*

Iraq [ɪ'rɑːk] *n* El Irak; ~**i** *a, n* irakí *m/f.*

irascible [ɪ'ræsɪbl] *a* irascible.

irate [aɪ'reɪt] *a* enojado, indignado.

Ireland ['aɪələnd] *n* Irlanda.

iris ['aɪrɪs], *pl* ~**es** *n* (*ANAT*) iris *m*; (*BOT*) lirio.

Irish ['aɪrɪʃ] *a* irlandés(esa) // *npl*: **the** ~ los irlandeses; ~**man/ woman** *n* irlandés/esa *m/f.*

irk [əːk] *vt* fastidiar; ~**some** *a* fastidioso.

iron ['aɪən] *n* hierro; (*for clothes*) plancha // *a* de hierro // *vt* (*clothes*) planchar; ~**s** *npl* (*chains*) grillos *mpl*; **to** ~ **out** *vt* (*crease*) quitar; (*fig*) allanar.

ironic(al) [aɪ'rɔnɪk(l)] *a* irónico.

ironing ['aɪənɪŋ] *n* (*act*) planchado; (*ironed clothes*) ropa planchada; (*to be ironed*) ropa por planchar; ~ **board** *n* tabla de planchar.

ironmonger ['aɪənmʌŋgə*] *n* ferretero; ~'**s (shop)** *n* ferretería, quincallería.

iron ore ['aɪən'ɔː*] *n* mineral *m* de hierro.

irony ['aɪrənɪ] *n* ironía; **the** ~ **of it is that...** lo irónico es que...

irrational [ɪ'ræʃənl] *a* irracional.

irreconcilable [ɪrekən'saɪləbl] *a*

inconciliable, irreconciliable.
irrefutable [ɪrɪ'fjuːtəbl] *a* irrefutable.
irregular [ɪ'rɛgjulə*] *a* irregular; (*surface*) desigual; (*illegal*) ilegal; ~**ity** [-'lærɪtɪ] *n* irregularidad *f*; desigualdad *f*.
irrelevant [ɪ'rɛləvənt] *a* fuera de lugar, inoportuno.
irreparable [ɪ'rɛprəbl] *a* irreparable.
irreplaceable [ɪrɪ'pleɪsəbl] *a* irremplazable.
irrepressible [ɪrɪ'prɛsəbl] *a* irrefrenable.
irreproachable [ɪrɪ'prəʊtʃəbl] *a* irreprochable.
irresistible [ɪrɪ'zɪstɪbl] *a* irresistible.
irresolute [ɪ'rɛzəluːt] *a* indeciso.
irrespective [ɪrɪ'spɛktɪv]: ~ **of** *prep* sin tener en cuenta, no importa.
irresponsible [ɪrɪ'spɔnsɪbl] *a* (*act*) irresponsable; (*person*) poco serio.
irreverent [ɪ'rɛvərnt] *a* irreverente, irrespetuoso.
irrevocable [ɪ'rɛvəkəbl] *a* irrevocable.
irrigate ['ɪrɪgeɪt] *vt* regar; **irrigation** [-'geɪʃən] *n* riego.
irritable ['ɪrɪtəbl] *a* irritable; (*mood*) de mal humor.
irritate ['ɪrɪteɪt] *vt* irritar; (MED) picar; **irritation** [-'teɪʃən] *n* irritación *f*, enojo; picazón *m*, picor *m*.
is [ɪz] *vb see* be.
Islam ['ɪzlɑːm] *n* Islam *m*.
island ['aɪlənd] *n* isla; (*also*: **traffic** ~) refugio; ~**er** *n* isleño/a.
isle [aɪl] *n* isla.
isn't ['ɪznt] = **is not**.
isolate ['aɪsəleɪt] *vt* aislar; ~**d** *a* aislado; **isolation** [-'leɪʃən] *n* aislamiento.
isotope ['aɪsəʊtəʊp] *n* isótopo.
Israel ['ɪzreɪl] *n* Israel *m*; ~**i** [ɪz'reɪlɪ] *a*, *n* israelí *m/f*.
issue ['ɪsjuː] *n* cuestión *f*, asunto; (*outcome*) resultado; (*of banknotes etc*) emisión *f*; (*of newspaper etc*) número; (*offspring*) sucesión *f*, descendencia // *vt* (*rations, equipment*) distribuir, repartir; (*orders*) dar; (*certificate*) expedir; (*decree*) promulgar; (*book*) publicar; (*cheques*) extender; (*banknotes, stamps*) emitir.
isthmus ['ɪsməs] *n* istmo.
it [ɪt] *pron* (*subject*) él/ella; (*direct object*) lo/la; (*indirect object*) le; (*impersonal*) ello; (*after prep*) él/ella/ello; ~'**s raining** llueve, está lloviendo; **where is** ~? ¿dónde está?; **he's proud of** ~ le enorgullece; **he agreed to** ~ está de acuerdo (con ello).
Italian [ɪ'tæljən] *a* italiano // *n* italiano/a; (LING) el italiano.
italic [ɪ'tælɪk] *a* cursivo; ~**s** *npl* cursiva *sg*.
Italy ['ɪtəlɪ] *n* Italia.
itch [ɪtʃ] *n* comezón *m*; (*fig*) prurito // *vi* (*person*) sentir o tener comezón; (*part of body*) picar; **I'm** ~**ing to do sth** rabio por hacer algo; ~**ing** *n* comezón *m*; ~**y** *a*: **to be** ~**y** picar.
it'd ['ɪtd] = **it would**; **it had**.

item ['aɪtəm] *n* (*gen*) artículo; (*detail*) detalle *m*; (*on agenda*) asunto a tratar; (*in programme*) número; (*also*: **news** ~) noticia; ~**ize** *vt* detallar.
itinerant [ɪ'tɪnərənt] *a* ambulante.
itinerary [aɪ'tɪnərərɪ] *n* itinerario.
it'll ['ɪtl] = **it will, it shall**.
its [ɪts] *a* su // *pron* (el) suyo/(la) suya.
it's [ɪts] = **it is; it has**.
itself [ɪt'sɛlf] *pron* (*reflexive*) sí mismo/a; (*emphatic*) él mismo/ella misma.
ITV *n abbr of* **Independent Television**.
I.U.D. *n abbr of* **intra-uterine device** DIU.
I've [aɪv] = **I have**.
ivory ['aɪvərɪ] *n* marfil *m*; ~ **tower** *n* (*fig*) torre *f* de marfil.
ivy ['aɪvɪ] *n* hiedra.

J

jab [dʒæb] *vt* (*elbow*) dar un codazo a; (*punch*) dar un golpe rápido a; **to** ~ **sth into sth** clavar algo en algo // *n* codazo; golpe *m* (rápido); (MED: *col*) pinchazo.
jabber ['dʒæbə*] *vt, vi* farfullar.
jack [dʒæk] *n* (AUT) gato; (BOWLS) boliche *m*; (CARDS) sota; **to** ~ **up** *vt* (AUT) alzar con gato.
jackdaw ['dʒækdɔː] *n* grajilla.
jacket ['dʒækɪt] *n* chaqueta, americana; (*of boiler etc*) camisa; (*of book*) sobrecubierta; **potatoes in their** ~**s** patatas con su piel.
jack-knife ['dʒæknaɪf] *n* navaja.
jackpot ['dʒækpɔt] *n* premio gordo.
jade [dʒeɪd] *n* (*stone*) jade *m*.
jaded ['dʒeɪdɪd] *a* (*tired*) cansado; (*fed-up*) hastiado.
jagged ['dʒægɪd] *a* dentado.
jail [dʒeɪl] *n* cárcel *f*; ~**break** *n* fuga o evasión *f* (de la cárcel); ~**er** *n* carcelero.
jam [dʒæm] *n* mermelada; (*also*: **traffic** ~) embotellamiento; (*difficulty*) apuro // *vt* (*passage etc*) obstruir, cerrar; (*mechanism, drawer etc*) atascar; (RADIO) interferir // *vi* atascarse, trabarse; **to** ~ **sth into sth** meter algo por la fuerza en algo.
Jamaica [dʒə'meɪkə] *n* Jamaica.
jangle ['dʒæŋgl] *vi* sonar (de manera) discordante.
janitor ['dʒænɪtə*] *n* (*caretaker*) portero, conserje *m*.
January ['dʒænjuərɪ] *n* enero.
Japan [dʒə'pæn] *n* (el) Japón; ~**ese** [dʒæpə'niːz] *a* japonés(esa) // *n, pl inv* japonés/esa *m/f*; (LING) japonés *m*.
jar [dʒɑː*] *n* (*glass: large*) jarra; (: *small*) tarro // *vi* (*sound*) chirriar; (*colours*) desentonar.
jargon ['dʒɑːgən] *n* jerga.
jasmin(e) ['dʒæzmɪn] *n* jazmín *m*.
jaundice ['dʒɔːndɪs] *n* ictericia; ~**d** *a* (*fig: embittered*) amargado; (: *disillusioned*) desilusionado.

jaunt [dʒɔ:nt] *n* excursión *f*; ~y *a* alegre.
javelin ['dʒævlɪn] *n* jabalina.
jaw [dʒɔ:] *n* mandíbula.
jaywalker ['dʒeɪwɔ:kə*] *n* peatón *m* imprudente.
jazz [dʒæz] *n* jazz *m*; **to ~ up** *vt* (*liven up*) animar, avivar; ~y *a* de colores llamativos.
jealous ['dʒɛləs] *a* (*gen*) celoso; (*envious*) envidioso; **to be ~** tener celos; ~y *n* celos *mpl*; envidia.
jeans [dʒi:nz] *npl* (*pantalones*) vaqueros *o* tejanos *mpl*.
jeep [dʒi:p] *n* jeep *m*.
jeer [dʒɪə*] *vi*: **to ~** (**at**) (*boo*) abuchear; (*mock*) mofarse (de).
jelly ['dʒɛlɪ] *n* jalea, gelatina; ~**fish** *n* medusa.
jeopardize ['dʒɛpədaɪz] *vt* arriesgar, poner en peligro; **jeopardy** [-dɪ] *n*: **to be in jeopardy** estar en peligro *o* a riesgo.
jerk [dʒə:k] *n* (*jolt*) sacudida; (*wrench*) tirón *m* // *vt* dar una sacudida a // *vi* (*vehicle*) traquetear.
jerkin ['dʒə:kɪn] *n* cazadora.
jerky ['dʒə:kɪ] *a* espasmódico.
jersey ['dʒə:zɪ] *n* jersey *m*.
jest [dʒɛst] *n* broma.
jet [dʒɛt] *n* (*of gas, liquid*) chorro; (*AVIAT*) avión *m* a reacción; ~-**black** *a* de azabache; ~ **engine** *n* motor *m* a reacción.
jettison ['dʒɛtɪsn] *vt* desechar.
jetty ['dʒɛtɪ] *n* muelle *m*, embarcadero.
Jew [dʒu:] *n* judío; ~**ess** *n* judía.
jewel ['dʒu:əl] *n* joya; (*in watch*) rubí *m*; ~**ler** *n* joyero; ~**ler's** (**shop**) *n* joyería; ~**lery** *n* joyas *fpl*, alhajas *fpl*.
Jewish ['dʒu:ɪʃ] *a* judío.
jibe [dʒaɪb] *n* pulla.
jiffy ['dʒɪfɪ] *n* (*col*): **in a ~** en un instante.
jig [dʒɪg] *n* jiga.
jigsaw ['dʒɪgsɔ:] *n* (*also*: ~ **puzzle**) rompecabezas *m inv*.
jilt [dʒɪlt] *vt* dar calabazas a.
jingle ['dʒɪŋgl] *n* (*advert*) estribillo // *vi* tintinear.
jinx [dʒɪŋks] *n* (*col*) gafe *m*, maldición *f*.
jitters ['dʒɪtəz] *npl* (*col*): **to get the ~** ponerse nervioso.
job [dʒɔb] *n* (*gen*) trabajo; (*task*) tarea; (*duty*) deber *m*; (*post*) empleo; (*fam: difficulty*) dificultad *f*; **it's a good ~ that...** menos mal que...; **just the ~!** ¡estupendo!; ~**less** *a* sin trabajo.
jockey ['dʒɔkɪ] *n* jockey *m* // *vi*: **to ~ for position** maniobrar para conseguir una posición.
jocular ['dʒɔkjulə*] *a* (*humorous*) jocoso; (*merry*) alegre.
jog [dʒɔg] *vt* empujar (ligeramente) // *vi* (*run*) hacer footing; **to ~ along** ir tirando; **to ~ sb's memory** refrescar la memoria a uno; ~**ging** *n* footing *m*.
join [dʒɔɪn] *vt* (*things*) juntar, unir; (*become member of*) inscribirse en, afiliarse a;

(*meet: people*) reunirse *o* encontrarse con // *vi* (*roads, rivers*) confluir // *n* juntura; **to ~ up** *vi* unirse; (*MIL*) alistarse.
joiner ['dʒɔɪnə*] *n* carpintero; ~y *n* carpintería.
joint [dʒɔɪnt] *n* (*TECH*) junta, unión *f*; (*wood*) ensambladura; (*ANAT*) articulación *f*; (*CULIN*) asado; (*col: place*) garito // *a* (*common*) común; (*combined*) combinado; (*committee*) mixto; **by ~ agreement** por común acuerdo; ~**ly** *ad* (*gen*) mutuamente, en común; (*collectively*) colectivamente; (*together*) conjuntamente.
joke [dʒəuk] *n* chiste *m*; (*also*: **practical ~**) broma // *vi* bromear; **to play a ~ on** gastar una broma a; **joker** *n* chistoso/a, bromista *m/f*; (*CARDS*) comodín *m*.
jolly ['dʒɔlɪ] *a* (*merry*) alegre; (*enjoyable*) divertido // *ad* (*col*) muy, terriblemente.
jolt [dʒəult] *n* (*shake*) sacudida; (*blow*) golpe *m*; (*shock*) susto // *vt* sacudir; asustar.
Jordan ['dʒɔ:dən] *n* Jordania.
jostle ['dʒɔsl] *vt* dar empellones a, codear.
jot [dʒɔt] *n*: **not one ~** ni jota, ni pizca; **to ~ down** *vt* apuntar; ~**ter** *n* bloc *m*; (*SCOL*) cuaderno.
journal ['dʒə:nl] *n* (*paper*) periódico; (*magazine*) revista; (*diary*) diario; ~**ese** [-'li:z] *n* (*pej*) lenguaje *m* periodístico; ~**ism** *n* periodismo; ~**ist** *n* periodista *m/f*.
journey ['dʒə:nɪ] *n* viaje *m*; (*distance covered*) trayecto // *vi* viajar; **return ~** viaje de regreso.
joy [dʒɔɪ] *n* alegría; ~**ful**, ~**ous** *a* alegre; ~ **ride** *n* paseo en coche; (*illegal*) paseo en coche robado.
J.P. *n abbr of* **Justice of the Peace.**
Jr, Jun., Junr *abbr of* **junior.**
jubilant ['dʒu:bɪlnt] *a* jubiloso; **jubilation** [-'leɪʃən] *n* júbilo.
jubilee ['dʒu:bɪli:] *n* aniversario.
judge [dʒʌdʒ] *n* juez *m* // *vt* (*gen*) juzgar; (*estimate*) considerar; **judg(e)ment** *n* juicio; (*punishment*) sentencia, fallo.
judicial [dʒu:'dɪʃl] *a* judicial.
judicious [dʒu:'dɪʃəs] *a* juicioso.
judo ['dʒu:dəu] *n* judo.
jug [dʒʌg] *n* jarro.
juggernaut ['dʒʌgənɔ:t] *n* (*huge truck*) mastodonte *m*.
juggle ['dʒʌgl] *vi* hacer juegos malabares; **juggler** *n* malabarista *m/f*.
Jugoslav ['ju:gəu'slɑ:v] *a*, *n* = **Yugoslav.**
juice [dʒu:s] *n* zumo, jugo; **juicy** *a* jugoso.
jukebox ['dʒu:kbɔks] *n* rocola.
July [dʒu:'laɪ] *n* julio.
jumble ['dʒʌmbl] *n* revoltijo // *vt* (*also*: ~ **up**: *mix up*) revolver; (: *disarrange*) mezclar; ~ **sale** *n* (*Brit*) venta de objetos usados.
jumbo (jet) ['dʒʌmbəu] *n* jumbo-jet *m*.
jump [dʒʌmp] *vi* saltar, dar saltos; (*start*) asustarse, sobresaltarse; (*increase*) aumentar // *vt* saltar // *n* salto; aumento; **to ~ the queue** colarse.

jumper ['dʒʌmpə*] n suéter m, jersey m.
jumpy ['dʒʌmpı] a nervioso.
junction ['dʒʌŋkʃən] n (of roads) cruce m; (RAIL) empalme m.
juncture ['dʒʌŋktʃə*] n: **at this ~** en este momento, en esta coyuntura.
June [dʒu:n] n junio.
jungle ['dʒʌŋgl] n selva, jungla.
junior ['dʒu:nıə*] a (in age) menor, más joven; (competition) juvenil; (position) subalterno // n menor m/f, joven m/f; **~ school** n escuela primaria.
junk [dʒʌŋk] n (cheap goods) baratijas fpl; (lumber) trastos viejos mpl; (rubbish) basura; (ship) junco; **~shop** n tienda de objetos usados.
jurisdiction [dʒuərıs'dıkʃən] n jurisdicción f.
jurisprudence [dʒuərıs'pru:dəns] n jurisprudencia.
jury ['dʒuərı] n jurado.
just [dʒʌst] a justo // ad (exactly) exactamente; (only) sólo, solamente; **he's ~ done it/left** acaba de hacerlo/irse; **~ right** perfecto, perfectamente; **~ two o'clock** las dos en punto; **~ as well that...** menos mal que...; **~ as he was leaving** en el momento en que se marchaba; **~ before/enough** justo antes/lo suficiente; **~ here** aquí mismo; **he ~ missed** ha fallado por poco; **~ listen** escucha (solamente).
justice ['dʒʌstıs] n justicia; **J~ of the Peace (J.P.)** n juez m de paz.
justifiable [dʒʌstı'faıəbl] a justificable; **justifiably** ad justificadamente.
justification [dʒʌstıfı'keıʃən] n justificación f; **justify** ['dʒʌstıfaı] vt justificar.
justly ['dʒʌstlı] ad (gen) justamente; (with reason) con razón.
justness ['dʒʌstnıs] n justicia.
jut [dʒʌt] vi (also: **~ out**) sobresalir.
juvenile ['dʒu:vənaıl] a juvenil; (court) de menores; (books) para jóvenes // n joven m/f, menor m/f de edad.
juxtapose ['dʒʌkstəpəuz] vt yuxtaponer.

K

kaleidoscope [kə'laıdəskəup] n calidoscopio.
kangaroo [kæŋgə'ru:] n canguro.
keel [ki:l] n quilla; **on an even ~** (fig) en equilibrio.
keen [ki:n] a (interest, desire) grande, vivo; (eye, intelligence) agudo; (competition) intenso; (edge) afilado; (eager) entusiasta inv; **to be ~ to do** or **on doing sth** tener muchas ganas de hacer algo; **to be ~ on sth/sb** interesarse por algo/alguien; **~ness** n (eagerness) entusiasmo, interés m.
keep [ki:p], pt, pp **kept** vt (retain, preserve) guardar; (hold back) quedarse con; (shop, diary) llevar; (feed: family etc) mantener; (promise) cumplir; (chickens, bees etc)

criar // vi (food) conservarse; (remain) seguir, continuar // n (of castle) torreón m; (food etc) comida, subsistencia; **to ~ doing sth** seguir haciendo algo; **to ~ sb from doing sth** impedir a alguien hacer algo; **to ~ sth from happening** impedir que algo ocurra; **to ~ sb happy** hacer a alguien feliz; **to ~ a place tidy** mantener un lugar limpio; **to ~ sth to o.s.** guardar algo para sí mismo; **to ~ sth (back) from sb** ocultar algo a alguien; **to ~ time** (clock) mantener la hora exacta; **to ~ on** vi seguir, continuar; **to ~ out** vi (stay out) permanecer fuera; **'~ out'** prohibida la entrada; **to ~ up** vt mantener, conservar // vi no retrasarse; **to ~ up with** (pace) ir al paso de; (level) mantenerse a la altura de; **~er** n guardián m; **~ing** n (care) cuidado; **in ~ing with** de acuerdo con; **~sake** n recuerdo.
keg [kɛg] n barrilete m, barril m.
kennel ['kɛnl] n perrera; **~s** npl criadero sg de perros.
Kenya ['kɛnjə] n Kenia.
kept [kɛpt] pt, pp of **keep.**
kerb [kə:b] n bordillo.
kernel ['kə:nl] n almendra.
kerosene ['kɛrəsi:n] n keroseno.
ketchup ['kɛtʃəp] n salsa de tomate, catsup m.
kettle ['kɛtl] n hervidor m, olla.
key [ki:] n (gen) llave f; (MUS) tono; (of piano, typewriter) tecla; **~board** n teclado; **~hole** n ojo (de la cerradura); **~note** n (MUS) tónica; **~ring** n llavero; **~stone** n piedra clave.
khaki ['kɑ:kı] n caqui.
kick [kık] vt (person) dar una patada a; (ball) dar un puntapié a // vi (horse) dar coces // n patada; puntapié m; (of rifle) culetazo; (thrill): **he does it for ~s** lo hace para divertirse; **to ~ off** vi (SPORT) hacer el saque inicial; **~-off** n (SPORT) saque m inicial.
kid [kıd] n (child) chiquillo; (animal) cabrito; (leather) cabritilla // vi (col) bromear.
kidnap ['kıdnæp] vt secuestrar; **~per** n secuestrador/a m/f; **~ping** n secuestro.
kidney ['kıdnı] n riñón m.
kill [kıl] vt (gen) matar; (murder) asesinar; (destroy) destruir; (finish off) acabar con // n acto de matar; **~er** n asesino; **~ing** n (one) asesinato; (several) matanza // a (funny) divertido.
kiln [kıln] n horno.
kilo ['ki:ləu] n kilo; **~gram(me)** ['kıləugræm] n kilo, kilogramo; **~metre, ~meter** (US) ['kıləmi:tə*] n kilómetro; **~watt** ['kıləuwɔt] n kilovatio.
kilt [kılt] n falda escocesa.
kimono [kı'məunəu] n quimono.
kin [kın] n parientes mpl.
kind [kaınd] a (generous) bondadoso; (good) bueno, amable // n clase f, especie f; (species) género; **in ~** (COMM) en

especie; **a ~ of** una especie de; **two of a ~** dos de la misma especie.

kindergarten ['kɪndəgɑ:tn] *n* jardín *m* de infancia.

kind-hearted [kaɪnd'hɑ:tɪd] *a* bondadoso, de buen corazón.

kindle ['kɪndl] *vt* encender.

kindly ['kaɪndlɪ] *a* (*gen*) bondadoso; (*good*) bueno; (*gentle*) cariñoso // *ad* bondadosamente, amablemente; **will you ~...** sea Usted tan amable de... .

kindness ['kaɪndnɪs] *n* bondad *f*, amabilidad *f*.

kindred ['kɪndrɪd] *n* familia, parientes *mpl* // *a*: **~ spirit** espíritu *m* afín.

king [kɪŋ] *n* rey *m*; **~dom** *n* reino; **~fisher** *n* martín *m* pescador; **~-size** *a* de tamaño extra.

kink [kɪŋk] *n* (*of rope*) enroscadura.

kinky ['kɪŋkɪ] *a* (*odd*) excéntrico; (*pej*) pervertido.

kiosk ['ki:ɔsk] *n* quiosco; (*TEL*) cabina.

kipper ['kɪpə*] *n* arenque *m* ahumado.

kiss [kɪs] *n* beso // *vt* besar; **to ~ (each other)** besarse.

kit [kɪt] *n* (*gen*) avíos *mpl*; (*equipment*) equipo; (*set of tools etc*) (caja de) herramientas *fpl*; (*for assembly*) mecano.

kitchen ['kɪtʃɪn] *n* cocina; **~ garden** *n* huerto; **~ sink** *n* fregadero; **~ware** *n* batería de cocina.

kite [kaɪt] *n* (*toy*) cometa.

kitten ['kɪtn] *n* gatito.

kitty ['kɪtɪ] *n* (*pool of money*) fondo común; (*CARDS*) polla.

kleptomaniac [klɛptəu'meɪnɪæk] *n* cleptómano/a.

knack [næk] *n*: **to have the ~ of doing sth** tener el don de hacer algo.

knapsack ['næpsæk] *n* mochila.

knead [ni:d] *vt* amasar.

knee [ni:] *n* rodilla; **~cap** *n* rótula.

kneel [ni:l], *pt, pp* **knelt** *vi* arrodillarse.

knell [nɛl] *n* toque *m* de difuntos.

knelt [nɛlt] *pt, pp of* **kneel.**

knew [nju:] *pt of* **know.**

knickers ['nɪkəz] *npl* bragas *fpl*.

knife [naɪf], *pl* **knives** *n* cuchillo // *vt* acuchillar.

knight [naɪt] *n* caballero; (*CHESS*) caballo; **~hood** *n* caballería; (*title*): **to get a ~hood** recibir el título de sir.

knit [nɪt] *vt* hacer a punto; (*brows*) fruncir // *vi* hacer punto; (*bones*) soldarse; **to ~ together** (*fig*) unir, juntar; **~ting** *n* labor *f* de punto; **~ting machine** *n* máquina de tricotar; **~ting needle** *n* aguja de hacer punto; **~wear** *n* géneros *mpl* de punto.

knives [naɪvz] *pl of* **knife.**

knob [nɔb] *n* (*of door*) tirador *m*; (*of stick*) puño; (*lump*) bulto; (*fig*): **a ~ of butter** una porción de mantequilla.

knock [nɔk] *vt* (*strike*) golpear; (*bump into*) chocar contra; (*fig: col*) denigrar // *n* golpe *m*; (*on door*) llamada; **to ~ at** *or* **on the door** llamar a la puerta; **to ~ down**

vt atropellar; **to ~ off** *vi* (*col: finish*) despachar // *vt* (*col: steal*) birlar; **to ~ out** *vt* dejar sin sentido; (*BOXING*) poner fuera de combate, dejar K.O.; **~er** *n* (*on door*) aldaba; **~-kneed** *a* patizambo; **~out** *n* (*BOXING*) K.O. *m*, knockout *m*.

knot [nɔt] *n* (*gen*) nudo // *vt* anudar; **~ty** *a* (*fig*) complicado.

know [nəu], *pt* **knew**, *pp* **known** *vt* (*gen*) saber; (*person, author, place*) conocer; **to ~ that...** saber que...; **to ~ how to swim** saber nadar; **~-all** *n* sabelotodo *m/f*; **~-how** *n* habilidad *f*; **~ing** *a* (*look: of complicity*) de complicidad; (*: spiteful*) malicioso; **~ingly** *ad* (*purposely*) adrede; (*spitefully*) maliciosamente.

knowledge ['nɔlɪdʒ] *n* (*gen*) conocimiento; (*range of learning*) saber *m*, conocimientos *mpl*; (*learning*) erudición *f*, ciencia; **~able** *a* entendido, erudito.

known [nəun] *pp of* **know.**

knuckle ['nʌkl] *n* nudillo.

K.O. *n abbr of* **knockout.**

Koran [kɔ'rɑ:n] *n* Corán *m*.

L

l. *abbr of* **litre.**

lab [læb] *n abbr of* **laboratory.**

label ['leɪbl] *n* etiqueta; (*brand: of record*) marca // *vt* poner etiqueta a.

laboratory [lə'bɔrətərɪ] *n* laboratorio.

laborious [lə'bɔ:rɪəs] *a* penoso.

labour, labor (*US*) ['leɪbə*] *n* (*task*) trabajo; (**~ force**) mano *f* de obra; (*workers*) trabajadores *mpl*; (*MED*) (dolores *mpl* del) parto // *vi*: **to ~ (at)** trabajar (en) // *vt* insistir en; **in ~** (*MED*) de parto; **L~, the L~ party** el partido laborista; **hard ~** trabajos *mpl* forzados; **~ed** *a* (*movement*) penoso; (*style*) pesado; **~er** *n* peón *m*; (*on farm*) peón *m*, bracero; (*day ~er*) jornalero.

labyrinth ['læbɪrɪnθ] *n* laberinto.

lace [leɪs] *n* encaje *m*; (*of shoe etc*) cordón *m* // *vt* (*shoe*) atar.

lack [læk] *n* (*absence*) falta; (*scarcity*) escasez *f* // *vt* no tener, carecer de; **through** *or* **for ~ of** por falta de; **to be ~ing** faltar, no haber.

lackadaisical [lækə'deɪzɪkl] *a* (*careless*) descuidado; (*indifferent*) indiferente.

laconic [lə'kɔnɪk] *a* lacónico.

lacquer ['lækə*] *n* laca.

lad [læd] *n* muchacho, chico; (*in stable etc*) mozo.

ladder ['lædə*] *n* escalera (de mano); (*in tights*) carrera // *vt* (*tights*) hacer una carrera en.

laden ['leɪdn] *a*: **~ (with)** cargado (de).

ladle ['leɪdl] *n* cucharón *m*.

lady ['leɪdɪ] *n* señora; (*distinguished, noble*) dama; **young ~** señorita; **'ladies' (toilets)'** 'señoras'; **~bird, ~bug** (*US*) *n* mariquita; **~-in-waiting** *n* dama de honor; **~like** *a* fino.

lag [læg] *vi* (*also*: **~ behind**) retrasarse,

quedarse atrás // vt (*pipes*) calorifugar.
lager ['lɑ:gə*] n cerveza (rubia).
lagging ['lægɪŋ] n revestimiento.
lagoon [lə'gu:n] n laguna.
laid [leɪd] pt, pp of **lay.**
lain [leɪn] pp of **lie.**
lair [lɛə*] n guarida.
lake [leɪk] n lago.
lamb [læm] n cordero; (*meat*) carne f de cordero; ~ **chop** n chuleta de cordero; **lambswool** n lana de cordero.
lame [leɪm] a cojo; (*weak*) débil, poco convincente.
lament [lə'mɛnt] n lamento // vt lamentarse de; ~**able** ['læmɔntəbl] a lamentable.
laminated ['læmɪneɪtɪd] a laminado.
lamp [læmp] n lámpara.
lampoon [læm'pu:n] vt satirizar.
lamp: ~**post** n farol m; ~**shade** n pantalla.
lance [lɑ:ns] n lanza // vt (MED) abrir con lanzeta; ~ **corporal** n soldado de primera clase.
lancet ['lɑ:nsɪt] n lanceta.
land [lænd] n (*gen*) tierra; (*country*) país m; (*piece of* ~) terreno; (*estate*) tierras fpl, finca; (AGR) campo // vi (*from ship*) desembarcar; (AVIAT) aterrizar; (*fig: fall*) caer, terminar // vt (*obtain*) conseguir; (*passengers, goods*) desembarcar; **to** ~ **up in/at** ir a parar a/en; ~**ing** n desembarco; aterrizaje m; (*of staircase*) rellano; ~**ing craft** n barca de desembarco; ~**ing gear** n tren m de aterrizaje; ~**ing stage** n desembarcadero; ~**ing strip** n pista de aterrizaje; ~**lady** n (*of boarding house*) patrona; (*owner*) dueña; ~**locked** a cercado de tierra; ~**lord** n propietario; (*of pub etc*) patrón m; ~**lubber** n hombre m de tierra; ~**mark** n lugar m conocido; **to be a** ~**mark** (*fig*) hacer época; ~**owner** n terrateniente m/f.
landscape ['lænskeɪp] n paisaje m; ~**d** a reformado artísticamente.
landslide ['lændslaɪd] n (GEO) corrimiento de tierras; (*fig: POL*) victoria arrolladora.
lane [leɪn] n (*in country*) vereda; (*in town*) callejón m; (AUT) carril m; (*in race*) calle f; (*for air or sea traffic*) ruta.
language ['læŋgwɪdʒ] n lenguaje m; (*national tongue*) idioma m, lengua; **bad** ~ lenguaje indecente.
languid ['læŋgwɪd] a lánguido.
languish ['læŋgwɪʃ] vi languidecer.
lank [læŋk] a (*hair*) lacio.
lanky ['læŋkɪ] a larguirucho.
lantern ['læntn] n linterna; (NAUT) farol m.
lap [læp] n (*of track*) vuelta; (*of body*): **to sit on sb's** ~ sentarse en las rodillas de uno // vt (*also:* ~ **up**) lamer // vi (*waves*) chapotear; ~**dog** n perro faldero.
lapel [lə'pɛl] n solapa.
Lapland ['læplænd] n Laponia; **Lapp** [læp] a, n lapón/ona m/f.
lapse [læps] n error m, equivocación f;

(*moral*) desliz m // vi (*expire*) caducar; (LAW) equivocarse; (*morally*) caer en un desliz; (*time*) pasar, transcurrir; **to** ~ **into bad habits** volver a las andadas; ~ **of time** lapso, período.
larceny ['lɑ:sənɪ] n latrocinio; **petty** ~ robo de menor cuantía.
lard [lɑ:d] n manteca (de cerdo).
larder ['lɑ:də*] n despensa.
large [lɑ:dʒ] a (*gen*) grande; (*fat*) gordo; **at** ~ (*free*) en libertad; (*generally*) en general; ~**ly** ad en gran parte; ~-**scale** a (*map*) en gran escala; (*fig*) importante.
lark [lɑ:k] n (*bird*) alondra; (*joke*) travesura, broma; **to** ~ **about** vi bromear, divertirse tontamente
larva ['lɑ:və], pl -**vae** [-vi:] n larva.
laryngitis [lærɪn'dʒaɪtɪs] n laringitis f.
larynx ['lærɪŋks] n laringe f.
lascivious [lə'sɪvɪəs] a lascivo.
laser ['leɪzə*] n laser m.
lash [læʃ] n latigazo; (*punishment*) azote m; (*gen: eyelash*) pestaña // vt azotar; (*tie*) atar; **to** ~ **out** vi: **to** ~ **out at** or **against sb** atacar violentamente a alguien; **to** ~ **out** (*col: spend*) gastar generosamente.
lass [læs] n chica.
lasso [læ'su:] n lazo // vt coger con lazo.
last [lɑ:st] a (*gen*) último; (*final*) último, final // ad por último // vi (*endure*) durar; (*continue*) continuar, seguir; ~ **week** la semana pasada; ~ **night** anoche; **at** ~ por fin; ~ **but one** penúltimo; ~**ing** a duradero; ~-**minute** a de última hora.
latch [lætʃ] n picaporte m, pestillo; ~**key** n llavín m.
late [leɪt] a (*not on time*) tarde, atrasado; (*far on in day etc*) tardío; (*hour*) avanzado; (*recent*) reciente; (*former*) antiguo, ex; (*dead*) fallecido // ad tarde; (*behind time, schedule*) con retraso; **of** ~ últimamente; **in** ~ **May** hacia fines de mayo; **the** ~ **Mr X** el difunto Sr X; ~**comer** n recién llegado; ~**ly** ad últimamente; ~**ness** n (*of person*) retraso; (*of event*) lo tardío.
latent ['leɪtnt] a latente.
later ['leɪtə*] a (*date etc*) posterior; (*version etc*) más reciente // ad más tarde, después.
lateral ['lætərl] a lateral.
latest ['leɪtɪst] a último; **at the** ~ a más tardar.
lathe [leɪð] n torno.
lather ['lɑ:ðə*] n espuma (de jabón) // vt enjabonar // vi hacer espuma.
Latin ['lætɪn] n latín m // a latino; ~ **America** n América latina; ~-**American** a latinoamericano.
latitude ['lætɪtju:d] n latitud f.
latrine [lə'tri:n] n letrina.
latter ['lætə*] a último; (*of two*) segundo // n: **the** ~ el último, éste; ~**ly** ad últimamente.
lattice ['lætɪs] n enrejado; (*on window*) reja.
laudable ['lɔ:dəbl] a loable.
laugh [lɑ:f] n risa; (*loud*) carcajada // vi

reírse, reír; reírse a carcajadas; **to ~ at** *vt fus* reírse de; **to ~ off** *vt* tomar algo a risa; **~able** *a* risible, ridículo; **to be the ~ing stock of the town** ser el hazmerreír de la ciudad; **~ter** *n* risa.

launch [lɔ:ntʃ] *n* (*boat*) lancha; *see also* **~ing** // *vt* (*ship, rocket, plan*) lanzar; **~ing** *n* (*of rocket etc*) lanzamiento; (*inauguration*) estreno; **~(ing) pad** *n* plataforma de lanzamiento.

launder ['lɔ:ndə*] *vt* lavar.

launderette [lɔ:n'drɛt] *n* lavandería (automática).

laundry ['lɔ:ndrɪ] *n* lavandería; (*clothes*) ropa sucia; **to do the ~** hacer la colada.

laureate ['lɔ:rɪət] *a see* **poet.**

laurel ['lɔrl] *n* laurel *m*.

lava ['lɑ:və] *n* lava.

lavatory ['lævətərɪ] *n* lavabo; **lavatories** *npl* servicios *mpl*, aseos *mpl*.

lavender ['lævəndə*] *n* lavanda.

lavish ['lævɪʃ] *a* abundante; (*giving freely*): **~ with** pródigo en // *vt*: **to ~ sth on sb** colmar a uno de algo.

law [lɔ:] *n* ley *f*; (*study*) derecho; (*of game*) regla; **~-abiding** *a* que cumple la ley; **~ and order** *n* órden *m* público; **~breaker** *n* infractor *m* (de la ley); **~ court** *n* tribunal *m* (de justicia); **~ful** *a* legítimo, lícito; **~fully** *ad* legalmente; **~less** *a* (*act*) ilegal; (*person*) rebelde; (*country*) desordenado.

lawn [lɔ:n] *n* césped *m*; **~mower** *n* cortacésped *m*; **~ tennis** [-'tɛnɪs] *n* tenis *m*.

law: ~ school *n* facultad *f* de derecho; **~ student** *n* estudiante *m/f* de derecho.

lawsuit ['lɔ:su:t] *n* pleito.

lawyer ['lɔ:jə*] *n* abogado; (*for sales, wills etc*) notario.

lax [læks] *a* flojo; (*negligent*) negligente.

laxative ['læksətɪv] *n* laxante *m*.

laxity ['læksɪtɪ] *n* flojedad *f*; (*moral*) relajamiento; (*negligence*) negligencia.

lay [leɪ] *pt of* **lie** // *a* laico; (*not expert*) profano // *vt, pt, pp* **laid** (*place*) colocar; (*eggs, table*) poner; (*trap*) tender; **to ~ aside** *or* **by** *vt* dejar a un lado; **to ~ down** *vt* (*pen etc*) dejar; (**~ flat**) acostar; (*arms*) rendir; (*policy*) asentar; **to ~ down the law** imponer la ley; **to ~ off** *vt* (*workers*) despedir, poner en paro; **to ~ on** *vt* (*water, gas*) instalar; (*provide*) proveer; **to ~ out** *vt* (*design*) diseñar; (*display*) disponer; (*spend*) gastar; **to ~ up** *vt* (*store*) guardar; (*ship*) desarmar; (*subj: illness*) obligar a guardar cama; **~about** *n* vago/a; **~-by** *n* apartadero.

layer ['leɪə*] *n* capa.

layette [leɪ'ɛt] *n* canastilla, ajuar *m* (de niño).

layman ['leɪmən] *n* persona no experta; (*REL*) lego.

layout ['leɪaʊt] *n* (*design*) plan *m*, trazado; (*disposition*) disposición *f*; (*PRESS*) composición *f*.

laze [leɪz] *vi* no hacer nada; (*pej*)

holgazanear; **laziness** *n* pereza; **lazy** *a* perezoso, vago.

lb. *abbr of* **pound** (*weight*).

lead [li:d] *n* (*front position*) delantera; (*SPORT*) liderato; (*distance, time ahead*) ventaja; (*clue*) pista; (*ELEC*) cable *m*; (*for dog*) correa; (*THEATRE*) papel *m* principal // *n* [lɛd] plomo; (*in pencil*) mina // (*vb: pt, pp* **led**) *vt* conducir; (*induce*) llevar; (*be leader of*) dirigir; (*SPORT*) ir en cabeza de // *vi* ir primero; **to ~ to** llevar a, salir a; **to ~ astray** *vt* llevar por mal camino; **to ~ away** *vt* llevar; **to ~ back** *vt* hacer volver; **to ~ on** *vt* (*tease*) coquetear con; **to ~ on to** *vt* (*induce*) incitar a; **to ~ up to** conducir a.

leader ['li:də*] *n* (*gen*) jefe *m*, líder *m*; (*of union etc*) dirigente *m/f*; (*of gang*) cabecilla *m*; (*guide*) guía *m/f*; (*of newspaper*) artículo de fondo; **~ship** *n* dirección *f*; (*quality*) dotes *fpl* de mando.

leading ['li:dɪŋ] *a* (*main*) principal; (*outstanding*) destacado; (*first*) primero; (*front*) delantero; **~ lady** *n* (*THEATRE*) primera actriz *f*; **~ light** *n* (*person*) figura principal.

leaf [li:f], *pl* **leaves** *n* hoja // *vi*: **to ~ through** hojear; **to turn over a new ~** reformarse.

leaflet ['li:flɪt] *n* folleto.

league [li:g] *n* sociedad *f*; (*FOOTBALL*) liga; **to be in ~ with** estar de manga con.

leak [li:k] *n* (*of liquid, gas*) escape *m*, fuga; (*hole*) agujero; (*in roof*) gotera; (*of money*) filtración *f* // *vi* (*shoes, ship*) hacer agua; (*pipe*) tener (un) escape; (*roof*) gotear; (*container*) salirse; (*gas*) escaparse; (*fig: news*) filtrarse // *vt* (*gen*) dejar escapar; (*exude*) rezumar; **the information was ~ed to the enemy** las informaciones se pasaron al enemigo; **the news ~ed out** trascendió la noticia.

lean [li:n] *a* (*thin*) flaco; (*meat*) magro // (*vb: pt, pp* **leaned** *or* **leant** [lɛnt]) *vt*: **to ~ sth on** apoyar algo en // *vi* (*slope*) inclinarse; (*rest*): **to ~ against** apoyarse contra; **to ~ on** apoyarse en; (*fig: rely on*) contar con (el apoyo de); **to ~ back/forward** *vi* inclinarse hacia atrás/hacia adelante; **to ~ over** *vi* ladearse; **~ing** *a* inclinado // *n*: **~ing (towards)** inclinación *f* (hacia); **~-to** *n* colgadizo.

leap [li:p] *n* salto // *vi, pt, pp* **leaped** *or* **leapt** [lɛpt] saltar; **~frog** *n* pídola; **~ year** *n* año bisiesto.

learn [lɔ:n], *pt, pp* **learned** *or* **learnt** *vt* (*gen*) aprender; (*come to know of*) enterarse de // *vi* aprender; **to ~ how to do sth** aprender a hacer algo; **~ed** ['lɔ:nɪd] *a* erudito; **~er** *n* principiante *m/f*; **~ing** *n* el saber *m*, conocimientos *mpl*.

lease [li:s] *n* arriendo // *vt* arrendar.

leash [li:ʃ] *n* cuerda.

least [li:st] *a* (*slightest*) menor; (*smallest*) más pequeño; (*smallest amount of*) mínimo // *ad* menos // *n*: **the ~** lo menos; **the ~**

possible **effort** el mínimo de esfuerzo posible; **at** ~ por lo menos, al menos; **not in the** ~ en absoluto.

leather ['lɛðə*] n cuero.

leave [li:v], pt, pp **left** vt dejar; (go away from) abandonar // vi irse; (train) salir // n permiso; **to be left** quedar, sobrar; **there's some milk left over** sobra o queda algo de leche; **on** ~ de permiso; **to take one's** ~ **of** despedirse de; **to** ~ **out** vt omitir.

leaves [li:vz] pl of **leaf**.

Lebanon ['lɛbənən] n Líbano.

lecherous ['lɛtʃərəs] a lascivo.

lecture ['lɛktʃə*] n conferencia; (SCOL) clase f // vi dar una clase // vt (scold) sermonear; **to give a** ~ **on** dar una conferencia sobre; **lecturer** n conferenciante m/f; (at university) profesor adjunto/profesora adjunta m/f.

led [lɛd] pt, pp of **lead**.

ledge [lɛdʒ] n (of window, on wall) repisa, reborde m; (of mountain) plataforma.

ledger ['lɛdʒə*] n libro mayor.

lee [li:] n sotavento.

leek [li:k] n puerro.

leer [lɪə*] vi: **to** ~ **at sb** mirar impúdicamente a alguien.

leeway ['li:weɪ] n (fig): **to have some** ~ tener cierta libertad de acción.

left [lɛft] pt, pp of **leave** // a izquierdo; (POL) de izquierda // n izquierda // ad a la izquierda; **the L** ~ (POL) la izquierda; ~-**handed** a zurdo; **the** ~-**hand side** n la izquierda; ~-**luggage (office)** n consigna; ~-**overs** npl sobras fpl; ~-**wing** a (POL) de izquierdas, izquierdista.

leg [lɛg] n pierna; (of animal) pata; (of chair) pie m; (CULIN. of meat) pierna; (of journey) etapa; **lst/2nd** ~ (SPORT) partido de ida/de vuelta; **to pull sb's** ~ bromear con uno.

legacy ['lɛgəsɪ] n legado.

legal ['li:gl] a (gen) lícito; (of law) legal; (enquiry etc) jurídico; ~**ize** vt legalizar; ~**ly** ad legalmente; ~ **tender** n moneda corriente.

legend ['lɛdʒənd] n leyenda; ~**ary** a legendario.

legible ['lɛdʒəbl] a legible.

legion ['li:dʒən] n legión f.

legislate ['lɛdʒɪsleɪt] vi legislar; **legislation** [-'leɪʃən] n legislación f; **legislative** ['-lətɪv] a legislativo; **legislature** [-lətʃə*] n cuerpo legislativo.

legitimacy [lɪ'dʒɪtɪməsɪ] n legitimidad f; **legitimate** [-mət] a legítimo.

leg-room ['lɛgru:m] n espacio para las piernas.

leisure ['lɛʒə*] n ocio, tiempo libre; **at** ~ con tranquilidad; ~ **centre** n centro de diversiones; ~**ly** a pausado, lento.

lemon ['lɛmən] n limón m; ~**ade** [-'neɪd] n (fruit juice) limonada; (fizzy) gaseosa.

lend [lɛnd], pt, pp **lent** vt: **to** ~ **sth to sb** prestar algo a alguien; ~**er** n prestador/a

m/f; ~**ing library** n biblioteca circulante.

length [lɛŋθ] n largo, longitud f; (section: of road, pipe etc) tramo; **at** ~ (at last) por fin, finalmente; (lengthily) largamente; ~**en** vt alargar // vi alargarse; ~**ways** ad de largo; ~**y** a largo, extenso; (meeting) prolongado.

leniency ['li:nɪənsɪ] n indulgencia; **lenient** [-ənt] a indulgente.

lens [lɛnz] n (of spectacles) lente f; (of camera) objetivo.

lent [lɛnt] pt, pp of **lend**.

Lent [lɛnt] n Cuaresma.

lentil ['lɛntl] n lenteja.

Leo ['li:əu] n Leo.

leopard ['lɛpəd] n leopardo.

leotard ['li:əta:d] n leotardo.

leper ['lɛpə*] n leproso/a; **leprosy** [-prəsɪ] n lepra.

lesbian ['lɛzbɪən] n lesbiana.

less [lɛs] det a (in size, degree etc) menor; (in quantity) menos // pron, ad menos; ~ **than half** menos de la mitad; ~ **and** ~ cada vez menos; **the** ~ **he works...** cuanto menos trabaja... .

lessen ['lɛsn] vi disminuir, menguar // vt disminuir, reducir.

lesson ['lɛsn] n lección f; **a maths** ~ una clase o una lección de matemáticas.

lest [lɛst] conj: ~ **it happen** para que no pase.

let [lɛt], pt, pp **let** vt (allow) dejar, permitir; (lease) alquilar; ~**'s go** ¡vamos!; ~ **him come** que venga; 'to ~' 'se alquila'; **to** ~ **down** vt (lower) bajar; (dress) alargar; (tyre) desinflar; (hair) soltar; (disappoint) defraudar; **to** ~ **go** vi soltar; (fig) dejarse ir // vt abandonar; **to** ~ **in** vt dejar entrar; (visitor etc) hacer pasar; **to** ~ **off** vt dejar libre; (firework etc) disparar; (smell etc) despedir; **to** ~ **on** vt (col) divulgar (that que); **to** ~ **out** vt dejar salir; (dress) ensanchar; **to** ~ **up** vi amainar, disminuir.

lethal ['li:θl] a mortífero; (wound) mortal.

lethargic [lɛ'θɑ:dʒɪk] a letárgico; **lethargy** ['lɛθədʒɪ] n letargo.

letter ['lɛtə*] n (of alphabet) letra; (correspondence) carta; ~ **bomb** n carta con bomba explosiva; ~**box** n buzón m; ~**ing** n letras fpl.

lettuce ['lɛtɪs] n lechuga.

let-up ['lɛtʌp] n descanso, tregua.

leukaemia, leukemia (US) [lu:'ki:mɪə] n leucemia.

level ['lɛvl] a (flat) llano; (flattened) nivelado; (uniform) igual // ad a nivel // n nivel m; (flat place) llano // vt nivelar, allanar; **to be** ~ **with** estar a nivel de; 'A' ~**s** npl Bachillerato Superior, B.U.P.; 'O' ~**s** npl bachillerato elemental, octavo de básica; **on the** ~ (fig: honest) en serio; **to** ~ **off** or **out** vi (prices etc) estabilizarse; ~ **crossing** n paso a nivel; ~-**headed** a sensato.

lever ['li:və*] n palanca // vt: **to** ~ **up**

alzar con palanca; ~**age** n (fig: influence) influencia.
levity ['lɛvɪtɪ] n frivolidad f, informalidad f.
levy ['lɛvɪ] n impuesto // vt exigir, recaudar.
lewd [luːd] a impúdico, obsceno.
liability [laɪə'bɪlɪtɪ] n responsabilidad f; (handicap) desventaja; (risk) riesgo; **liabilities** npl obligaciones fpl; (COMM) deudas fpl, pasivo sg.
liable ['laɪəbl] a (subject): ~ **to** sujeto a; **to be** ~ **for** ser responsable de; **to be** ~ **to** (likely) tener tendencia a.
liaison [liː'eɪzɔn] n (coordination) enlace m; (affair) relaciones fpl amorosas.
liar ['laɪə*] n mentiroso/a.
libel ['laɪbl] n calumnia // vt calumniar.
liberal ['lɪbərl] a (gen) liberal; (generous): ~ **with** generoso con.
liberate ['lɪbəreɪt] vt liberar; **liberation** [-'reɪʃɔn] n liberación f.
liberty ['lɪbətɪ] n libertad f; **to be at** ~ **to** tener permiso para; **to take the** ~ **of doing sth** tomarse la libertad de hacer algo.
Libra ['liːbrə] n Libra.
librarian [laɪ'brɛərɪən] n bibliotecario/a; **library** ['laɪbrərɪ] n biblioteca.
libretto [lɪ'brɛtəu] n libreto.
Libya ['lɪbɪə] n Libia; ~**n** a, n libio/a.
lice [laɪs] pl of **louse.**
licence, license (US) ['laɪsns] n (gen) licencia; (permit) permiso; (also: **driving** ~) carnet m de conducir; (excessive freedom) libertinaje m; ~ **number** n matrícula; ~ **plate** n placa (de matrícula).
license ['laɪsns] n (US) = **licence** // vt autorizar, licenciar; ~**d** a (for alcohol) autorizado para la venta de bebidas alcohólicas.
licensee [laɪsən'siː] n (in a pub) patrón/ona m/f.
licentious [laɪ'sɛnʃəs] a licencioso.
lichen ['laɪkən] n liquen m.
lick [lɪk] vt lamer // n lamedura; **a** ~ **of paint** una mano de pintura.
licorice ['lɪkərɪs] n = **liquorice.**
lid [lɪd] n (of box, case) tapa; (of pan) cobertera.
lido ['laɪdəu] n piscina.
lie [laɪ] n mentira // vi mentir // vi, pt **lay**, pp **lain** (act) echarse; (state) estar echado, estar acostado; (of object: be situated) estar, encontrarse; **to** ~ **low** (fig) esconderse; **to** ~ **about** vi (things) estar en desorden; (people) gandulear; **to have a** ~**-down** echarse una siesta); **to have a** ~**-in** quedarse pegado a las sábanas.
lieu [luː]: **in** ~ **of** prep en lugar de.
lieutenant [lɛf'tɛnənt] n lugarteniente m; (MIL) teniente m.
life [laɪf], pl **lives** n (gen) vida; (way of ~) modo de vivir; (of licence etc) vigencia; ~ **assurance** n seguro de vida; ~**belt** n cinturón m salvavidas; ~**boat** n bote m salvavidas; ~**guard** n vigilante m; ~

jacket n chaleco salvavidas; ~**less** a sin vida; (dull) soso; ~**like** a natural; ~**line** n cuerda salvavidas; ~**long** a de toda la vida; ~**-saver** n bañero, socorrista m/f; ~ **sentence** n condena perpetua; ~**-sized** a de tamaño natural; ~ **span** n vida; ~ **support system** n (MED) respirador m artificial; ~**time** n: **in his** ~**time** durante su vida; **once in a** ~**time** una vez en la vida.
lift [lɪft] vt levantar; (steal) robar // vi (fog) levantarse, disiparse // n (elevator) ascensor m; **to give sb a** ~ llevar a uno en el coche; ~**-off** n despegue m.
ligament ['lɪgəmənt] n ligamento.
light [laɪt] n (gen) luz f; (flame) lumbre f; (lamp) luz f, lámpara; (daylight) luz del día; (headlight) faro; (rear ~) luz trasera; (for cigarette etc): **have you got a** ~? ¿tiene fuego? // vt, pt, pp **lighted** or **lit** (candle, cigarette, fire) encender; (room) alumbrar // a (colour) claro; (not heavy, also fig) ligero; (room) alumbrado; **to** ~ **up** vi (smoke) encender un cigarrillo; (face) iluminarse // vt (illuminate) iluminar, alumbrar; ~ **bulb** n bombilla; ~**en** vi (grow ~) clarear // vt (give light to) iluminar; (make lighter) aclarar; (make less heavy) aligerar; ~**er** n (also: **cigarette** ~**er**) encendedor m, mechero; ~**-headed** a (dizzy) mareado; (excited) exaltado; (by nature) casquivano; ~**-hearted** a alegre; ~**house** n faro; ~**ing** n (act) iluminación f; (system) alumbrado; ~**ly** ad (touch) ligeramente; (thoughtlessly) a la ligera; (slightly) levemente; **to get off** ~**ly** ser castigado con poca severidad; ~ **meter** n (PHOT) fotómetro; ~**ness** n claridad f; (in weight) ligereza.
lightning ['laɪtnɪŋ] n relámpago, rayo; ~ **conductor** n pararrayos m inv.
light: ~**weight** a (suit) ligero // n (BOXING) peso ligero; ~ **year** n año luz.
like [laɪk] vt (person) querer, tener cariño a; (things) gustarle a uno // prep como // a parecido, semejante // n: **the** ~ semejante m/f; **his** ~**s and dislikes** sus gustos y aversiones; **I would** ~, **I'd** ~ me gustaría; (for purchase) quisiera; **would you** ~ **a coffee?** ¿te apetece un café?; **to be** or **look** ~ **sb/sth** parecerse a alguien/algo; **that's just** ~ **him** es muy de él, es característico de él; **it is nothing** ~**...** no tiene parecido alguno con...; ~**able** a simpático, agradable.
likelihood ['laɪklɪhud] n probabilidad f; **likely** [-lɪ] a probable; **he's likely to leave** es probable que se vaya.
like-minded [laɪk'maɪndɪd] a de la misma opinión.
liken ['laɪkən] vt: **to** ~ **sth to sth** comparar algo con algo.
likewise ['laɪkwaɪz] ad igualmente.
liking ['laɪkɪŋ] n: **to his** ~ para su gusto.

lilac ['laɪlək] n lila // a (colour) de color lila.

lily ['lɪlɪ] n lirio, azucena; ~ **of the valley** n lirio de los valles.

limb [lɪm] n miembro.

limber ['lɪmbə*]: **to** ~ **up** vi (fig) entrenarse; (SPORT) desentumecerse.

limbo ['lɪmbəʊ] n: **to be in** ~ (fig) caer en el olvido.

lime [laɪm] n (tree) limero; (fruit) lima; (GEO) cal f.

limelight ['laɪmlaɪt] n: **to be in the** ~ (fig) ser el centro de atención.

limerick ['lɪmərɪk] n quintilla humorística.

limestone ['laɪmstəʊn] n piedra caliza.

limit ['lɪmɪt] n límite m // vt limitar; ~**ation** [-'teɪʃən] n limitación f; ~**ed** a limitado; **to be** ~**ed to** limitarse a; ~**ed (liability) company (Ltd)** n sociedad f anónima; ~**less** a sin límites.

limousine ['lɪməzɪːn] n limusina.

limp [lɪmp] n: **to have a** ~ tener cojera // vi cojear // a flojo.

limpet ['lɪmpɪt] n lapa.

limpid ['lɪmpɪd] a límpido, cristalino.

line [laɪn] n (gen) línea; (straight ~) raya; (rope) cuerda; (for fishing) sedal m; (wire) hilo; (row, series) fila, hilera; (of writing) renglón m; (on face) arruga; (specialty) rama // vt (SEWING) forrar (with de); **to** ~ **the streets** ocupar las aceras; **in** ~ **with** de acuerdo con; **to** ~ **up** vi hacer cola // vt alinear, poner en fila; ~**d** a (face) arrugado; (paper) rayado.

linear ['lɪnɪə*] a lineal.

linen ['lɪnɪn] n ropa blanca; (cloth) lino.

liner ['laɪnə*] n vapor m de línea, transatlántico.

linesman ['laɪnzmən] n (SPORT) juez m de línea.

line-up ['laɪnʌp] n alineación f.

linger ['lɪŋgə*] vi retrasarse, tardar en marcharse; (smell, tradition) persistir.

lingerie ['læŋʒəriː] n ropa interior (de mujer).

lingering ['lɪŋgərɪŋ] a persistente; (death) lento.

lingo ['lɪŋgəʊ], pl ~**es** n (pej) jerga.

linguist ['lɪŋgwɪst] n lingüista m/f; ~**ic** a lingüístico; ~**ics** n lingüística.

lining ['laɪnɪŋ] n forro.

link [lɪŋk] n (of a chain) eslabón m; (connection) conexión f; (bond) vínculo, lazo // vt vincular, unir; ~**s** npl campo sg de golf; **to** ~ **up** vt acoplar // vi unirse; ~-**up** n (gen) unión f; (in space) acoplamiento.

lino ['laɪnəʊ], **linoleum** [lɪ'nəʊlɪəm] n linóleo.

lintel ['lɪntl] n dintel m.

lion ['laɪən] n león m; ~**ess** n leona.

lip [lɪp] n labio; (of jug) pico; (of cup etc) borde m; ~**read** vi leer los labios; ~ **service** n: **to pay** ~ **service to sth** alabar algo pero sin hacer nada; ~**stick**

n lápiz m labial, barra de labios.

liquefy ['lɪkwɪfaɪ] vt liquidar.

liqueur [lɪ'kjʊə*] n licor m.

liquid ['lɪkwɪd] a, n líquido.

liquidate ['lɪkwɪdeɪt] vt liquidar; **liquidation** [-'deɪʃən] n liquidación f; **liquidator** n liquidador/a m/f.

liquidize ['lɪkwɪdaɪz] vt (CULIN) licuar.

liquor ['lɪkə*] n licor m, bebidas alcohólicas fpl.

liquorice ['lɪkərɪs] n regaliz m.

lisp [lɪsp] n ceceo.

list [lɪst] n lista; (of ship) inclinación f // vt (write down) hacer una lista de; (enumerate) catalogar // vi (ship) inclinarse.

listen ['lɪsn] vi escuchar, oír; (pay attention) atender; ~**er** n oyente m/f.

listless ['lɪstlɪs] a apático, indiferente.

lit [lɪt] pt, pp of **light**.

litany ['lɪtənɪ] n letanía.

literacy ['lɪtərəsɪ] n capacidad f de leer y escribir; ~ **campaign** campaña de alfabetización.

literal ['lɪtərl] a literal; ~**ly** ad literalmente.

literary ['lɪtərərɪ] a literario.

literate ['lɪtərət] a que sabe leer y escribir; (fig) culto.

literature ['lɪtərɪtʃə*] n literatura; (brochures etc) folletos mpl.

lithe [laɪð] a ágil.

litigation [lɪtɪ'geɪʃən] n litigio.

litre, liter (US) ['lɪːtə*] n litro.

litter ['lɪtə*] n (rubbish) basura; (paper) papel m tirado; (young animals) camada, cría; (stretcher) camilla; ~ **bin** n papelera; ~**ed** a: ~**ed with** (scattered) esparcido con; (covered with) lleno de.

little ['lɪtl] a (small) pequeño; (not much) poco; often translated by suffix: eg ~ **house** casita // ad poco; **a** ~ un poco (de); ~ **by** ~ poco a poco.

liturgy ['lɪtədʒɪ] n liturgia.

live [lɪv] vi vivir // vt (a life) llevar; (experience) vivir // a [laɪv] (animal) vivo; (wire) conectado; (broadcast) en directo; (shell) cargado; **to** ~ **down** vt hacer olvidar; **to** ~ **on** vt fus (food) vivirse de, alimentarse de; **to** ~ **up to** vt fus (fulfil) cumplir con; (justify) justificar.

livelihood ['laɪvlɪhud] n sustento.

lively ['laɪvlɪ] a (gen) vivo; (talk) animado; (pace) rápido; (party, tune) alegre.

liver ['lɪvə*] n (ANAT) hígado; ~**ish** a (fig) rezongón(ona).

livery ['lɪvərɪ] n librea.

lives [laɪvz] pl of **life**.

livestock ['laɪvstɔk] n ganado.

livid ['lɪvɪd] a lívido; (furious) furioso.

living ['lɪvɪŋ] a (alive) vivo // n: **to earn** or **make a** ~ ganarse la vida; ~ **conditions** npl condiciones fpl de vida; ~ **room** n sala (de estar); ~ **standards** npl nivel m de vida; ~ **wage** n sueldo suficiente para vivir.

lizard ['lızəd] *n* lagartija.
llama ['lɑ:mə] *n* llama.
load [ləud] *n* (*gen*) carga; (*weight*) peso // *vt*: **to ~ (with)** cargar (con); (*fig*) colmar (de); **a ~ of, ~s of** (*fig*) (gran) cantidad de, montones de; **~ed** *a* (*dice*) cargado; (*question, word*) intencionado; (*col: rich*) forrado (de dinero); (: *drunk*) trompa.
loaf [ləuf], *pl* **loaves** *n* (barra de) pan *m* // *vi* (*also*: **~ about, ~ around**) holgazanear.
loan [ləun] *n* préstamo; (*COMM*) empréstito // *vt* prestar; **on ~** prestado.
loath [ləuθ] *a*: **to be ~ to do sth** estar poco dispuesto a hacer algo.
loathe [ləuð] *vt* aborrecer; (*person*) odiar; **loathing** *n* aversión *f*; odio; **it fills me with loathing** me da asco.
loaves [ləuvz] *pl of* **loaf.**
lobby ['lɔbı] *n* vestíbulo, sala de espera; (*POL: pressure group*) grupo de presión // *vt* presionar.
lobe [ləub] *n* lóbulo.
lobster ['lɔbstə*] *n* langosta; (*large*) bogavante *m*.
local ['ləukl] *a* local // *n* (*pub*) bar *m*; **the ~s** *npl* los vecinos, los del lugar; **~ity** [-'kælıtı] *n* localidad *f*; **~ly** [-kəlı] *ad* en la vecindad.
locate [ləu'keıt] *vt* (*find*) localizar; (*situate*) colocar.
location [ləu'keıʃən] *n* situación *f*; **on ~** (*CINEMA*) en exteriores, fuera del estudio.
loch [lɔx] *n* lago.
lock [lɔk] *n* (*of door, box*) cerradura; (*of canal*) esclusa; (*stop*) tope *m*; (*of hair*) mechón *m* // *vt* (*with key*) cerrar con llave; (*immobilize*) inmovilizar // *vi* (*door etc*) cerrarse con llave; (*wheels*) bloquearse, trabarse.
locker ['lɔkə*] *n* casillero.
locket ['lɔkıt] *n* medallón *m*.
lockout ['lɔkaut] *n* paro patronal, lockout *m*.
locomotive [ləukə'məutıv] *n* locomotora.
locum ['ləukəm] *n* (*MED*) (médico) interino.
locust ['ləukəst] *n* langosta.
lodge [lɔdʒ] *n* casa del guarda; (*porter's*) portería; (*FREEMASONRY*) logia // *vi* (*person*): **to ~ (with)** alojarse (en casa de) // *vt* (*complaint*) presentar; **lodger** *n* huésped/a *m/f*.
lodgings ['lɔdʒıŋz] *npl* alojamiento *sg*; (*house*) casa *sg* de huéspedes.
loft [lɔft] *n* desván *m*.
lofty ['lɔftı] *a* alto; (*haughty*) orgulloso.
log [lɔg] *n* (*of wood*) leño, tronco; (*book*) = **logbook.**
logarithm ['lɔgərıðəm] *n* logaritmo.
logbook ['lɔgbuk] *n* (*NAUT*) diario de a bordo; (*AVIAT*) libro de vuelo; (*of car*) documentación *f* (del coche).
loggerheads ['lɔgəhɛdz] *npl*: **at ~ (with)** de pique (con).
logic ['lɔdʒık] *n* lógica; **~al** *a* lógico.

logistics [lɔ'dʒıstıks] *n* logística.
loin [lɔın] *n* (*CULIN*) lomo, solomillo; **~s** *npl* lomos *mpl*; **~ cloth** *n* taparrobo.
loiter ['lɔıtə*] *vi* perder el tiempo; (*pej*) merodear.
loll [lɔl] *vi* (*also*: **~ about**) repantigarse.
lollipop ['lɔlıpɔp] *n* pirulí *m*; (*iced*) polo; **~ man/lady** *n* persona encargada de ayudar a los niños a cruzar la calle.
London ['lʌndən] *n* Londres; **~er** *n* londinense *m/f*.
lone [ləun] *a* solitario.
loneliness ['ləunlınıs] *n* soledad *f*, aislamiento; **lonely** [-lı] *a* solitario, solo.
loner ['ləunə*] *n* solitario.
long [lɔŋ] *a* largo // *ad* mucho tiempo, largamente // *vi*: **to ~ for sth** anhelar *o* suspirar por algo; **in the ~ run** a la larga; **so** *or* **as ~ as** mientras, con tal que; **don't be ~!** ¡no tardes!, ¡vuelve pronto!; **how ~ is the street?** ¿cuánto tiene la calle de largo?; **how ~ is the lesson?** ¿cuánto dura la lección?; **6 metres ~** que mide 6 metros, de 6 metros de largo; **6 months ~** que dura 6 meses, de 6 meses de duración; **all night ~** toda la noche; **~ before** mucho antes; **before ~** (+ *future*) dentro de poco; (+ *past*) poco tiempo después; **at ~ last** al fin, por fin; **~-distance** *a* (*race*) de larga distancia; (*call*) interurbano; **~-haired** *a* de pelo largo; **~hand** *n* escritura (corriente); **~ing** *n* anhelo, ansia; (*nostalgia*) nostalgia // *a* anhelante.
longitude ['lɔŋgıtju:d] *n* longitud *f*.
long: **~ jump** *n* salto de longitud; **~-lost** *a* desaparecido hace mucho tiempo; **~-playing record (L.P.)** *n* elepé *m*, disco de larga duración; **~-range** *a* de gran alcance; **~-sighted** *a* (*fig*) previsor(a); **~-standing** *a* de mucho tiempo; **~-suffering** *a* sufrido; **~-term** *a* a largo plazo; **~ wave** *a* de onda larga; **~-winded** *a* prolijo.
loo [lu:] *n* (*col*) wáter *m*.
loofah ['lu:fə] *n* esponja de lufa.
look [luk] *vi* mirar; (*seem*) parecer; (*building etc*): **to ~ south/on to the sea** dar al sur/al mar // *n* mirada; (*glance*) vistazo; (*appearance*) aire *m*, aspecto; **~s** *npl* físico, apariencia; **to ~ like sb** parecerse a alguien; **to ~ after** *vt fus* cuidar a; **to ~ at** *vt fus* mirar; (*consider*) considerar; **to ~ back** *vi* mirar hacia atrás; **to ~ down on** *vt fus* (*fig*) despreciar, mirar con desprecio; **to ~ for** *vt fus* buscar; **to ~ forward to** *vt fus* esperar con ilusión; **to ~ into** *vt* investigar; **to ~ on** *vi* mirar (como espectador); **to ~ out** *vi* (*beware*): **to ~ out (for)** tener cuidado (de); **to ~ out for sb** *vt fus* (*seek*) buscar; (*await*) esperar; **to ~ round** *vi* volver la cabeza; **to ~ to** *vt fus* ocuparse de; (*rely on*) contar con; **to ~ up** *vi* mirar hacia arriba; (*improve*) mejorar // *vt* (*word*) buscar; (*friend*) visitar; **to ~ up to** *vt fus* admirar; **~-out**

n (*tower etc*) puesto de observación; (*person*) vigía *m*; **to be on the ~-out for sth** estar al acecho de algo.
loom [luːm] *n* telar *m* // *vi* asomarse; (*threaten*) amenazar.
loony ['luːnɪ] *n* (*col*) loco/a; ~ **bin** *n* (*col*) manicomio.
loop [luːp] *n* lazo; (*bend*) vuelta, recodo; (*contraceptive*) espiral *f*; ~**hole** *n* escapatoria.
loose [luːs] *a* (*gen*) suelto; (*not tight*) flojo; (*wobbly etc*) movedizo; (*clothes*) ancho; (*morals, discipline*) relajado; **to be at a ~ end** no saber qué hacer; ~**ly** *ad* libremente, aproximadamente; **loosen** *vt* (*free*) soltar; (*untie*) desatar; (*slacken*) aflojar.
loot [luːt] *n* botín *m* // *vt* saquear; ~**ing** *n* pillaje *m*.
lop [lɔp]: **to ~ off** *vt* cortar; (*branches*) podar.
lop-sided ['lɔp'saɪdɪd] *a* desequilibrado.
lord [lɔːd] *n* señor *m*; **L~ Smith** Lord Smith; **the L~** el Señor; **the (House of) L~s** la Cámara de los Lores; ~**ly** *a* señorial; (*arrogant*) arrogante; ~**ship** *n*: **your L~ship** su señoría.
lore [lɔː*] *n* saber *m* popular, tradiciones *fpl*.
lorry ['lɔrɪ] *n* camión *m*; ~ **driver** *n* camionero.
lose [luːz], *pt, pp* **lost** *vt* perder // *vi* perder, ser vencido; **to ~ (time)** (*clock*) atrasarse; **loser** *n* perdedor/a *m/f*.
loss [lɔs] *n* pérdida; **to be at a ~** no saber qué hacer; **to be a dead ~** ser completamente inútil.
lost [lɔst] *pt, pp of* **lose** // *a* perdido; ~ **property** *n* objetos *mpl* perdidos.
lot [lɔt] *n* (*at auctions*) lote *m*; (*destiny*) suerte *f*; **the ~** el todo, todos; **a ~ mucho, bastante; a ~ of, ~s of** mucho(s) (*pl*); **to draw ~s (for sth)** echar suertes (para decidir algo); **I read a ~** leo bastante.
lotion ['ləʊʃən] *n* loción *f*.
lottery ['lɔtərɪ] *n* lotería.
loud [laud] *a* (*voice*) alto; (*shout*) fuerte; (*noisy*) estrepitoso; (*gaudy*) chillón(ona) // *ad* (*speak etc*) en alta voz; ~**hailer** *n* megáfono; ~**ly** *ad* (*noisily*) ruidosamente; (*aloud*) en alta voz; ~**speaker** *n* altavoz *m*.
lounge [laundʒ] *n* salón *m*, sala (de estar) // *vi* reposar, holgazanear; ~ **suit** *n* traje *m* de calle.
louse [laus], *pl* **lice** *n* piojo.
lousy ['lauzɪ] *a* (*fig*) vil, asqueroso.
lout [laut] *n* gamberro.
lovable ['lʌvəbl] *a* amable, simpático.
love [lʌv] *n* amor *m* // *vt* amar, querer; **to ~ to do** gustar(le a uno) mucho hacer; **to be in ~ with** estar enamorado de; **to make ~** hacer el amor; **for the ~ of** por amor de; **'15 ~'** (*TENNIS*) 15 a cero; **I ~ paella** me gusta mucho la paella; **'with ~'** con cariño; ~ **affair** *n* aventura

sentimental; ~ **letter** *n* carta de amor; ~ **life** *n* vida sentimental.
lovely ['lʌvlɪ] *a* (*delightful*) precioso, encantador(a); (*beautiful*) hermoso.
lover ['lʌvə*] *n* amante *m/f*; (*amateur*): **a ~ of** un aficionado a *o* un amante de.
lovesong ['lʌvsɔŋ] *n* canción *f* de amor.
loving ['lʌvɪŋ] *a* amoroso, cariñoso.
low [ləu] *a, ad* bajo // *n* (*METEOROLOGY*) área de baja presión // *vi* (*cow*) mugir; **to feel ~** sentirse deprimido; **to turn (down)** ~ *vt* bajar; ~**-cut** *a* (*dress*) escotado.
lower ['ləuə*] *vt* bajar; (*reduce*) reducir // *vr*: **to ~ o.s. to** (*fig*) rebajarse a.
low: ~**-grade** *a* de baja calidad; ~**ly** *a* humilde; ~**-lying** *a* de bajo nivel.
loyal ['lɔɪəl] *a* leal; ~**ty** *n* lealtad *f*.
lozenge ['lɔzɪndʒ] *n* (*MED*) pastilla.
L.P. *n abbr of* **long-playing record.**
L-plates ['ɛlpleɪts] *npl* placa de aprendiz de conductor.
Ltd *abbr of* **limited company** S.A.
lubricant ['luːbrɪkənt] *n* lubricante *m*; **lubricate** [-keɪt] *vt* lubricar, engrasar.
lucid ['luːsɪd] *a* lúcido; ~**ity** [-'sɪdɪtɪ] *n* lucidez *f*.
luck [lʌk] *n* suerte *f*; **bad ~** mala suerte; **good ~!** ¡que tengas suerte!, ¡suerte!; ~**ily** *ad* afortunadamente; ~**y** *a* afortunado.
lucrative ['luːkrətɪv] *a* lucrativo.
ludicrous ['luːdɪkrəs] *a* absurdo.
ludo ['luːdəu] *n* parchís *m*.
lug [lʌg] *vt* (*drag*) arrastrar; (*pull*) tirar de.
luggage ['lʌgɪdʒ] *n* equipaje *m*; ~ **rack** *n* (*in train*) rejilla, redecilla; (*on car*) vaca, portaequipajes *m inv*.
lukewarm ['luːkwɔːm] *a* tibio, templado.
lull [lʌl] *n* tregua // *vt* (*child*) acunar; (*person, fear*) calmar.
lullaby ['lʌləbaɪ] *n* canción *f* de cuna.
lumbago [lʌm'beɪgəu] *n* lumbago.
lumber ['lʌmbə*] *n* (*junk*) trastos viejos *mpl*; (*wood*) maderos *mpl*; ~**jack** *n* maderero.
luminous ['luːmɪnəs] *a* luminoso.
lump [lʌmp] *n* terrón *m*; (*fragment*) trozo; (*in sauce*) grumo; (*in throat*) nudo; (*swelling*) bulto // *vt* (*also*: ~ **together**) amontonar; **a ~ sum** suma global; ~**y** *a* (*sauce*) lleno de grumos.
lunacy ['luːnəsɪ] *n* locura.
lunar ['luːnə*] *a* lunar.
lunatic ['luːnətɪk] *a, n* loco/a; ~ **asylum** *n* manicomio.
lunch [lʌntʃ] *n* almuerzo, comida // *vi* almorzar; ~ **time** *n* hora del almuerzo *o* de comer.
luncheon ['lʌntʃən] *n* almuerzo; ~ **meat** *n* pastel *m* de carne.
lung [lʌŋ] *n* pulmón *m*; ~ **cancer** *n* cáncer *m* de pulmón.
lunge [lʌndʒ] *vi* (*also*: ~ **forward**) abalanzarse; **to ~ at** arremeter contra.
lurch [ləːtʃ] *vi* dar sacudidas // *n* sacudida;

to leave sb in the ~ dejar a uno plantado.

lure [luǝ*] n (*bait*) cebo; (*decoy*) señuelo // vt atraer, seducir.

lurid ['luǝrɪd] a (*light*) misterioso; (*dress*) chillón(ona); (*account*) sensacional; (*detail*) horrible.

lurk [lɔːk] vi (*hide*) esconderse; (*wait*) estar al acecho.

luscious ['lʌʃǝs] a delicioso.

lush [lʌʃ] a exuberante.

lust [lʌst] n lujuria; (*greed*) codicia; **to** ~ **after** vt fus codiciar; ~**ful** a lascivo, lujurioso.

lustre, luster (*US*) ['lʌstǝ*] n lustre m, brillo.

lusty ['lʌstɪ] a robusto, fuerte.

lute [luːt] n laúd m.

Luxembourg ['lʌksǝmbɔːg] n Luxemburgo.

luxuriant [lʌg'zjuǝrɪǝnt] a exuberante.

luxurious [lʌg'zjuǝrɪǝs] a lujoso; **luxury** ['lʌkʃǝrɪ] n lujo // cpd de lujo.

lying ['laɪɪŋ] n mentiras fpl // a mentiroso.

lynch [lɪntʃ] vt linchar; ~**ing** n linchamiento.

lynx [lɪŋks] n lince m.

lyre ['laɪǝ*] n lira.

lyric ['lɪrɪk] a lírico; ~**s** npl (*of song*) letra sg; ~**al** a lírico.

M

m. abbr of **metre; mile; million.**

M.A. abbr of **Master of Arts** licenciado en letras.

mac [mæk] n impermeable m.

macaroni [mækǝ'rǝunɪ] n macarrones mpl.

mace [meɪs] n (*BOT*) macis f.

machine [mǝ'ʃiːn] n máquina // vt (*dress etc*) coser a máquina; ~ **gun** n ametralladora; ~**ry** n maquinaria; (*fig*) mecanismo; **machinist** n operario (de máquina).

mackerel ['mækrl] n, pl inv caballa.

mackintosh ['mækɪntɔʃ] n impermeable m.

mad [mæd] a (*gen*) loco; (*crazed*) demente; (*angry*) furioso.

madam ['mædǝm] n señora.

madden ['mædn] vt volver loco.

made [meɪd] pt, pp of **make;** ~**-to-measure** a hecho a la medida.

madly ['mædlɪ] ad locamente.

madman ['mædmǝn] n loco.

madness ['mædnɪs] n locura.

magazine [mægǝ'ziːn] n revista; (*MIL: store*) almacén m; (*of firearm*) recámara.

maggot ['mægǝt] n gusano.

magic ['mædʒɪk] n magia // a mágico; ~**al** a mágico; ~**ian** [mǝ'dʒɪʃǝn] n mago; (*conjurer*) prestidigitador m.

magistrate ['mædʒɪstreɪt] n juez m/f (municipal).

magnanimous [mæg'nænɪmǝs] a magnánimo.

magnate ['mægneɪt] n magnate m.

magnet ['mægnɪt] n imán m; ~**ic** [-'nɛtɪk] a magnético; ~**ism** n magnetismo.

magnification [mægnɪfɪ'keɪʃǝn] n aumento.

magnificence [mæg'nɪfɪsns] n magnificencia; **magnificent** [-nt] a magnífico.

magnify ['mægnɪfaɪ] vt aumentar; (*fig*) exagerar; ~**ing glass** n lupa.

magnitude ['mægnɪtjuːd] n magnitud f.

magnolia [mæg'nǝulɪǝ] n magnolia.

magpie ['mægpaɪ] n urraca.

mahogany [mǝ'hɔgǝnɪ] n caoba // cpd de caoba.

maid [meɪd] n criada; **old** ~ (*pej*) solterona.

maiden ['meɪdn] n doncella // a (*aunt etc*) solterona; (*speech, voyage*) inaugural; ~ **name** n nombre m de soltera.

mail [meɪl] n correo; (*letters*) cartas fpl // vt (*post*) echar al correo; (*send*) mandar por correo; ~**box** n (*US*) buzón m; ~**-order** n pedido postal; (*business*) venta por correo.

maim [meɪm] vt mutilar, lisiar.

main [meɪn] a principal, mayor // n (*pipe*) cañería maestra; **the** ~**s** (*ELEC*) la red eléctrica; **in the** ~ en general; ~**land** n continente m; ~**stay** n (*fig*) pilar m; ~**stream** n corriente f principal.

maintain [meɪn'teɪn] vt mantener; (*keep up*) conservar (en buen estado); (*affirm*) sostener; **maintenance** ['meɪntǝnǝns] n mantenimiento.

maisonette [meɪzǝ'nɛt] n apartamento de dos pisos.

maize [meɪz] n maíz m.

majestic [mǝ'dʒɛstɪk] a majestuoso; **majesty** ['mædʒɪstɪ] n majestad f.

major ['meɪdʒǝ*] n (*MIL*) comandante m // a principal; (*MUS*) mayor.

Majorca [mǝ'jɔːkǝ] n Mallorca.

majority [mǝ'dʒɔrɪtɪ] n mayoría.

make [meɪk] pt, pp **made** vt hacer; (*manufacture*) hacer, fabricar; (*cause to be*): **to** ~ **sb sad** hacer o poner triste a alguien; (*force*): **to** ~ **sb do sth** obligar a uno a hacer algo; (*equal*): **2 and 2** ~ **4** 2 y 2 son 4 // n marca; **to** ~ **do with** contentarse con; **to** ~ **for** vt fus (*place*) dirigirse a; **to** ~ **out** vt (*decipher*) descifrar; (*understand*) entender; (*see*) distinguir; **to** ~ **up** vt (*invent*) inventar; (*parcel*) envolver // vi reconciliarse; (*with cosmetics*) maquillarse; **to** ~ **up for** vt fus compensar; ~**-believe** a fingido; **maker** n fabricante m/f; ~**shift** a improvisado; ~**-up** n maquillaje m.

making ['meɪkɪŋ] n (*fig*): **in the** ~ en vías de formación.

malaise [mæ'leɪz] n malestar m.

malaria [mǝ'lɛǝrɪǝ] n malaria.

Malay [mǝ'leɪ] a, n malayo/a.

Malaysia [mǝ'leɪzɪǝ] n Malaysia.

male [meɪl] *n* (*BIOL*, *ELEC*) macho // *a* (*sex*, *attitude*) masculino; (*child etc*) varón.
malevolent [mə'levələnt] *a* malévolo.
malfunction [mæl'fʌŋkʃən] *n* funcionamiento defectuoso.
malice ['mælɪs] *n* (*ill will*) malevolencia; (*rancour*) rencor *m*; **malicious** [mə'lɪʃəs] *a* malévolo; rencoroso.
malign [mə'laɪn] *vt* difamar, calumniar // *a* maligno.
malignant [mə'lɪgnənt] *a* (*MED*) maligno.
malingerer [mə'lɪŋgərə*] *n* enfermo fingido.
malleable ['mælɪəbl] *a* maleable.
mallet ['mælɪt] *n* mazo.
malnutrition [mælnju:'trɪʃən] *n* desnutrición *f.*
malpractice [mæl'præktɪs] *n* falta profesional.
malt [mɔ:lt] *n* malta.
Malta ['mɔ:ltə] *n* Malta; **Maltese** [-'ti:z] *a*, *n*, *pl inv* maltés/esa *m/f.*
maltreat [mæl'tri:t] *vt* maltratar.
mammal ['mæml] *n* mamífero.
mammoth ['mæməθ] *n* mamut *m* // *a* gigantesco.
man [mæn], *pl* **men** *n* hombre *m*; (*CHESS*) pieza // *vt* (*NAUT*) tripular; (*MIL*) guarnecer; **an old** ~ un viejo; ~ **and wife** marido y mujer.
manacle ['mænəkl] *n* manilla; ~**s** *npl* grillos *mpl.*
manage ['mænɪdʒ] *vi* arreglárselas, ir tirando // *vt* (*be in charge of*) dirigir; (*person etc*) manejar; ~**able** *a* manejable; ~**ment** *n* dirección *f*, administración *f*; **manager/ess** *n* director/a *m/f*; (*SPORT*) entrenador/a *m/f*; **managerial** [-ə'dʒɪərɪəl] *a* directivo; **managing director** *n* director *m* general.
mandarin ['mændərɪn] *n* (*also*: ~ **orange**) mandarina; (*person*) mandarín *m.*
mandate ['mændeɪt] *n* mandato.
mandatory ['mændətərɪ] *a* obligatorio.
mandolin(e) ['mændəlɪn] *n* mandolina.
mane [meɪn] *n* (*of horse*) crin *f*; (*of lion*) melena.
manfully ['mænfəlɪ] *ad* violentemente.
mangle ['mæŋgl] *vt* mutilar, magullar // *n* rodillo.
mango ['mæŋgəu], *pl* ~**es** *n* mango.
mangy ['meɪndʒɪ] *a* roñoso, sarnoso.
manhandle ['mænhændl] *vt* maltratar.
manhole ['mænhəul] *n* pozo de visita.
manhood ['mænhud] *n* edad *f* viril.
man-hour ['mæn'auə*] *n* hora-hombre *f.*
manhunt ['mænhʌnt] *n* caza de hombre.
mania ['meɪnɪə] *n* manía; **maniac** ['meɪnɪæk] *n* maníaco; (*fig*) maniático.
manicure ['mænɪkjuə*] *n* manicura // *vt* (*person*) hacer la manicura a; ~ **set** *n* estuche *m* de manicura.
manifest ['mænɪfest] *vt* manifestar, mostrar // *a* manifiesto; ~**ation** [-'teɪʃən] *n* manifestación *f.*

manifesto [mænɪ'festəu] *n* manifiesto.
manipulate [mə'nɪpjuleɪt] *vt* manipular, manejar.
mankind [mæn'kaɪnd] *n* la humanidad, el género humano.
manly ['mænlɪ] *a* varonil.
man-made ['mæn'meɪd] *a* artificial.
manner ['mænə*] *n* manera, modo; (*behaviour*) conducta, manera de ser; (*type*) clase *f*; ~**s** *npl* modales *mpl*, educación *f*; **bad** ~**s** mala educación; ~**ism** *n* hábito, peculiaridad *f.*
manoeuvre, maneuver (*US*) [mə'nu:və*] *vt*, *vi* maniobrar // *n* maniobra.
manor ['mænə*] *n* (*also*: ~ **house**) casa solariega.
manpower ['mænpauə*] *n* mano *f* de obra.
mansion ['mænʃən] *n* palacio, casa grande.
manslaughter ['mænslɔːtə*] *n* homicidio no premeditado.
mantelpiece ['mæntlpiːs] *n* repisa, chimenea.
mantle ['mæntl] *n* manto; (*fig*) capa.
manual ['mænjuəl] *a* manual // *n* manual *m*; (*MUS*) teclado.
manufacture [mænju'fæktʃə*] *vt* fabricar // *n* fabricación *f*; **manufacturer** *n* fabricante *m/f.*
manure [mə'njuə*] *n* estiércol *m*, abono.
manuscript ['mænjuskrɪpt] *n* manuscrito.
Manx [mæŋks] *a* de la Isla de Man.
many ['menɪ] *det* muchos(as) // *pron* muchos/as; **a great** ~ muchísimos, buen número de; ~ **a time** muchas veces.
map [mæp] *n* mapa *m* // *vt* trazar el mapa de; **to** ~ **out** *vt* proyectar.
maple ['meɪpl] *n* arce *m.*
mar [mɑ:*] *vt* estropear.
marathon ['mærəθən] *n* maratón *m.*
marauder [mə'rɔːdə*] *n* merodeador *m*; (*intruder*) intruso.
marble ['mɑːbl] *n* mármol *m*; (*toy*) canica.
March [mɑːtʃ] *n* marzo.
march [mɑːtʃ] *vi* (*MIL*) marchar; (*fig*) caminar con resolución // *n* marcha; (*demonstration*) manifestación *f*, marcha; ~**-past** *n* desfile *m.*
mare [mɛə*] *n* yegua.
margarine [mɑːdʒə'riːn] *n* margarina.
margin ['mɑːdʒɪn] *n* margen *m*; ~**al** *a* marginal.
marigold ['mærɪgəuld] *n* caléndula.
marijuana [mærɪ'wɑːnə] *n* marijuana.
marina [mə'riːnə] *n* marina.
marine [mə'riːn] *a* marino // *n* soldado de marina.
marital ['mærɪtl] *a* matrimonial; ~ **status** estado civil.
maritime ['mærɪtaɪm] *a* marítimo.
marjoram ['mɑːdʒərəm] *n* orégano.
mark [mɑːk] *n* marca, señal *f*; (*imprint*) huella; (*stain*) mancha; (*SCOL*) puntuación *f*, nota; (*currency*) marco // *vt* marcar;

manchar; (SCOL) calificar; **to** ~ **time** marcar el paso; **to** ~ **out** vt trazar; ~**ed** a marcado, acusado; ~**er** n (sign) marcador m; (bookmark) registro.

market ['mɑːkɪt] n mercado // vt (COMM) vender; **black** ~ mercado negro; **Common M** ~ Mercado Común; ~ **day** n día de mercado; ~ **garden** n (Brit) huerto; ~**ing** n márketing m, mercadotecnia; ~-**place** n mercado; ~ **research** n análisis m inv de mercados.

marksman ['mɑːksmən] n tirador m; ~**ship** n puntería.

marmalade ['mɑːməleɪd] n mermelada (de naranjas).

maroon [mə'ruːn] vt (fig): **to be** ~**ed** (shipwrecked) naufragarse; (fig) quedar abandonado // a marrón.

marquee [mɑː'kiː] n entoldado.

marquess, marquis ['mɑːkwɪs] n marqués m.

marriage ['mærɪdʒ] n (state) matrimonio; (wedding) boda; (act) casamiento; ~ **bureau** n agencia matrimonial; ~ **certificate** n partida de casamiento.

married ['mærɪd] a casado; (life, love) conyugal.

marrow ['mærəu] n médula; (vegetable) calabacín m.

marry ['mærɪ] vt casarse con; (subj: father, priest etc) casar // vi (also: **get married**) casarse.

marsh [mɑːʃ] n pantano; (salt ~) marisma.

marshal ['mɑːʃl] n (MIL) mariscal m; (at sports meeting etc) oficial m // vt (facts) ordenar; (soldiers) formar.

marshmallow [mɑːʃ'mæləu] n malvavisco.

marshy ['mɑːʃɪ] a pantanoso.

martial ['mɑːʃl] a marcial; ~ **law** n ley f marcial.

martyr ['mɑːtə*] n mártir m/f // vt martirizar; ~**dom** n martirio.

marvel ['mɑːvl] n maravilla, prodigio // vi: **to** ~ **(at)** maravillarse (de); ~**lous**, ~**ous** (US) a maravilloso.

Marxism ['mɑːksɪzəm] n marxismo; **Marxist** [-sɪst] a, n marxista m/f.

marzipan ['mɑːzɪpæn] n mazapán m.

mascara [mæs'kɑːrə] n rimel m.

mascot ['mæskət] n mascota.

masculine ['mæskjulɪn] a masculino; **masculinity** [-'lɪnɪtɪ] n masculinidad f.

mash [mæʃ] n (mix) mezcla; (pulp) amasijo; ~**ed potatoes** puré m de patatas.

mask [mɑːsk] n máscara // vt enmascarar.

masochist ['mæsəukɪst] n masoquista m/f.

mason ['meɪsn] n (also: **stone** ~) albañil m; (also: **free** ~) masón m; ~**ic** [mə'sɔnɪk] a masónico; ~**ry** n masonería; (building) mampostería.

masquerade [mæskə'reɪd] n baile m de máscaras; (fig) farsa // vi: **to** ~ **as** disfrazarse de, hacerse pasar por.

mass [mæs] n (people) muchedumbre f; (PHYSICS) masa; (REL) misa; (great quantity)

montón m // vi reunirse; (MIL) concentrarse; **the** ~**es** las masas.

massacre ['mæsəkə*] n masacre f // vt masacrar.

massage ['mæsɑːʒ] n masaje m // vt dar masaje a.

masseur [mæ'sɔː*] n masajista m; **masseuse** [-'sɔːz] n masajista f.

massive ['mæsɪv] a (solid) sólido; (head etc) grande; (support, intervention) masivo.

mass media ['mæs'miːdɪə] npl medios mpl de comunicación masiva.

mass-production ['mæsprə'dʌkʃən] n fabricación f en serie.

mast [mɑːst] n (NAUT) mástil m; (RADIO etc) torre f.

master ['mɑːstə*] n maestro; (landowner) señor m, amo; (in secondary school) profesor m; (title for boys): **M** ~ **X** Señorito X // vt dominar; (learn) aprender a fondo; ~ **key** n llave f maestra; ~**ly** a magistral; ~**mind** n inteligencia superior // vt dirigir, planear; **M** ~ **of Arts** n Licenciado en Letras; ~**piece** n obra maestra; ~ **plan** n plan m rector; ~ **stroke** n golpe m maestro; ~**y** n maestría.

masturbate ['mæstəbeɪt] vi masturbarse; **masturbation** [-'beɪʃən] n masturbación f.

mat [mæt] n estera; (also: **door** ~) felpudo // a = **matt**.

match [mætʃ] n cerilla; (game) partido; (fig) igual m/f // vt emparejar; (go well with) hacer juego con; (equal) igualar, ser igual a // vi hacer juego; **to be a good** ~ hacer una buena pareja; ~**box** n caja de cerillas; ~**ing** a que hace juego; ~**less** a sin par, incomparable.

mate [meɪt] n compañero; (assistant) ayudante m/f; (CHESS) mate m; (in merchant navy) segundo de a bordo // vi acoplarse, parearse // vt acoplar, parear.

material [mə'tɪərɪəl] n (substance) materia; (equipment) material m; (cloth) tela, tejido; (data) datos mpl // a material; (important) importante; ~**s** npl materiales mpl; ~**istic** [-ə'lɪstɪk] a materialista; ~**ize** vi materializarse.

maternal [mə'tɜːnl] a maternal.

maternity [mə'tɜːnɪtɪ] n maternidad f; ~ **dress** n vestido premamá; ~ **hospital** n hospital m de maternidad.

mathematical [mæθə'mætɪkl] a matemático; **mathematician** [-mə'tɪʃən] n matemático; **mathematics** [-tɪks], **maths** [mæθs] n matemáticas fpl.

matinée ['mætɪneɪ] n función f de tarde.

mating ['meɪtɪŋ] n apareamiento; ~ **call** n llamada del macho; ~ **season** n época de celo.

matriarchal [meɪtrɪ'ɑːkl] a matriarcal.

matrices ['meɪtrɪsiːz] pl of **matrix**.

matrimonial [mætrɪ'məunɪəl] a matrimonial.

matrimony ['mætrɪmənɪ] n matrimonio.

matrix ['meɪtrɪks], pl **matrices** n matriz f.

matron ['meɪtrən] *n* (*in hospital*) enfermera jefe; (*in school*) ama de llaves; ~**ly** *a* de matrona; (*fig*: *figure*) corpulento.
matt [mæt] *a* mate.
matted ['mætɪd] *a* enmarañado.
matter ['mætə*] *n* cuestión *f*, asunto; (*PHYSICS*) sustancia, materia; (*content*) contenido; (*MED*: *pus*) pus *m* // *vi* importar; **it doesn't** ~ no importa; **what's the** ~? ¿qué pasa?; **no** ~ **what** pase lo que pase; **as a** ~ **of course** por rutina; **as a** ~ **of fact** de hecho; ~**-of-fact** *a* prosaico, práctico.
mattress ['mætrɪs] *n* colchón *m*.
mature [mə'tjuə*] *a* maduro // *vi* madurar; **maturity** *n* madurez *f*.
maudlin ['mɔːdlɪn] *a* llorón(ona).
maul [mɔːl] *vt* magullar.
mausoleum [mɔːsə'liəm] *n* mausoleo.
mauve [məuv] *a* de color malva.
maxim ['mæksɪm] *n* máxima.
maxima ['mæksɪmə] *pl of* **maximum.**
maximum ['mæksɪməm] *a* máximo // *n*, *pl* **maxima** máximo.
May [meɪ] *n* mayo.
may [meɪ] *vi* (*conditional*: **might**) (*indicating possibility*): **he** ~ **come** puede que venga; (*be allowed to*): ~ **I smoke?** ¿puedo fumar?; (*wishes*): ~ **God bless you!** que Dios le bendiga.
maybe ['meɪbiː] *ad* quizá(s).
mayday ['meɪdeɪ] *n* S.O.S. *m* (*llamada de socorro internacional*).
mayhem ['meɪhɛm] *n* mutilación *f* criminal.
mayonnaise [meɪə'neɪz] *n* mayonesa.
mayor [mɛə*] *n* alcalde *m*; ~**ess** *n* alcaldesa.
maypole ['meɪpəul] *n* mayo.
maze [meɪz] *n* laberinto.
M.D. *abbr of* **Doctor of Medicine.**
me [miː] *pron* me; (*stressed, after prep*) mí; **with** ~ conmigo; **it's** ~ soy yo.
meadow ['mɛdəu] *n* prado, pradera.
meagre, meager (*US*) ['miːgə*] *a* escaso, pobre.
meal [miːl] *n* comida; (*flour*) harina; ~**time** *n* hora de comer.
mean [miːn] *a* (*with money*) tacaño; (*unkind*) mezquino, malo; (*shabby*) humilde, vil; (*of poor quality*) inferior; (*average*) medio // *vt*, *pt*, *pp* **meant** (*signify*) querer decir, significar; (*intend*): **to** ~ **to do sth** pensar *o* pretender hacer algo // *n* medio, término medio; ~**s** *npl* medio *sg*, manera *sg*; (*resource*) recursos *mpl*, medios *mpl*; **by** ~**s of** mediante, por medio de; **by all** ~**s!** ¡naturalmente!, ¡claro que sí!; **do you** ~ **it?** ¿lo dices en serio?; **what do you** ~? ¿qué quiere decir?
meander [mɪ'ændə*] *vi* (*river*) serpentear; (*person*) vagar.
meaning ['miːnɪŋ] *n* significado, sentido; ~**ful** *a* significativo; ~**less** *a* sin sentido.
meanness ['miːnnɪs] *n* (*with money*)

tacañería; (*shabbiness*) vileza, bajeza; (*unkindness*) maldad *f*, mezquindad *f*.
meant [mɛnt] *pt*, *pp of* **mean.**
meantime ['miːntaɪm], **meanwhile** ['miːnwaɪl] *ad* (*also*: **in the** ~) mientras tanto.
measles ['miːzlz] *n* sarampión *m*; **German** ~ rubéola.
measly ['miːzlɪ] *a* (*col*) miserable.
measure ['mɛʒə*] *vt* medir; (*for clothes etc*) tomar las medidas a; (*consider*) pesar // *vi* medir // *n* medida; (*ruler*) regla; ~**d** *a* moderado; (*tone*) mesurado; ~**ments** *npl* medidas *fpl*.
meat [miːt] *n* carne *f*; **cold** ~ fiambre *m*; ~**ball** *n* albóndiga; ~ **pie** *n* pastel *m* de carne; ~**y** *a* carnoso; (*fig*) sustancioso.
mechanic [mɪ'kænɪk] *n* mecánico; ~**s** *n* mecánica // *npl* mecanismo *sg*; ~**al** *a* mecánico.
mechanism ['mɛkənɪzəm] *n* mecanismo.
mechanization [mɛkənaɪ'zeɪʃən] *n* mecanización *f*.
medal ['mɛdl] *n* medalla; ~**lion** [mɪ'dælɪən] *n* medallón *m*; ~**list**, ~**ist** (*US*) *n* (*SPORT*) ganador/a *m/f*.
meddle ['mɛdl] *vi*: **to** ~ **in** entrometerse en; **to** ~ **with sth** manosear algo; ~**some** *a* entrometido.
media ['miːdɪə] *npl* medios *mpl* de comunicación.
mediaeval [mɛdɪ'iːvl] *a* = **medieval.**
mediate ['miːdɪeɪt] *vi* mediar; **mediation** [-'eɪʃən] *n* mediación *f*; **mediator** *n* intermediario, mediador/a *m/f*.
medical ['mɛdɪkl] *a* médico // *n* reconocimiento médico.
medicated ['mɛdɪkeɪtɪd] *a* medicinal.
medicinal [mɛ'dɪsɪnl] *a* medicinal.
medicine ['mɛdsɪn] *n* medicina; (*drug*) medicamento; ~ **chest** *n* botiquín *m*.
medieval [mɛdɪ'iːvl] *a* medieval.
mediocre [miːdɪ'əukə*] *a* mediocre; **mediocrity** [-'ɔkrɪtɪ] *n* mediocridad *f*.
meditate ['mɛdɪteɪt] *vi* meditar; **meditation** [-'teɪʃən] *n* meditación *f*.
Mediterranean [mɛdɪtə'reɪnɪən] *a* mediterráneo; **the** ~ (**Sea**) el (Mar) Mediterráneo.
medium ['miːdɪəm] *a* mediano, regular // *n* (*pl* **media**: *means*) medio; (*pl* **mediums**: *person*) médium *m/f*.
medley ['mɛdlɪ] *n* mezcla; (*MUS*) popurrí *m*.
meek [miːk] *a* manso, dócil.
meet [miːt] *pt*, *pp* **met** *vt* (*gen*) encontrar; (*accidentally*) encontrarse con, tropezar con; (*by arrangement*) reunirse con; (*for the first time*) conocer; (*go and fetch*) ir a buscar; (*opponent*) enfrentarse con; (*obligations*) cumplir // *vi* encontrarse; (*in session*) reunirse; (*join*: *objects*) unirse; (*get to know*) conocerse; **to** ~ **with** *vt fus* reunirse con; (*face*: *difficulty*) tropezar con; ~**ing** *n* encuentro; (*session*: *of club etc*) reunión *f*; (*interview*) entrevista; (*COMM*) junta, sesión *f*; (*POL*) mítin *m*.

megalomaniac [mɛgələu'meɪnɪæk] a, n megalómano/a.
megaphone ['mɛgəfəun] n megáfono.
melancholy ['mɛlənkəlɪ] n melancolía // a melancólico.
melee ['mɛleɪ] n refriega.
mellow ['mɛləu] a (sound) dulce; (colour) suave; (fruit) maduro // vi (person) madurar.
melodious [mɪ'ləudɪəs] a melodioso.
melodrama ['mɛləudrɑːmə] n melodrama m.
melody ['mɛlədɪ] n melodía.
melon ['mɛlən] n melón m.
melt [mɛlt] vi (metal) fundirse; (snow) derretirse; (fig) ablandarse // vt (also: ~ down) fundir; **to ~ away** vi desvanecerse; ~**ing point** n punto de fusión; ~**ing pot** n (fig) crisol m.
member ['mɛmbə*] n (gen) miembro; (of club) socio; **M~ of Parliament (M.P.)** diputado; ~**ship** n (members) número de miembros; **to seek** ~**ship of** pedir el ingreso a; ~**ship card** carnet m de socio.
membrane ['mɛmbreɪn] n membrana.
memento [mə'mɛntəu] n recuerdo.
memo ['mɛməu] n apunte m, nota.
memoirs ['mɛmwɑːz] npl memorias fpl.
memorable ['mɛmərəbl] a memorable.
memorandum [mɛmə'rændəm], pl **-da** [-də] n apunte m, nota; (POL) memorándum m.
memorial [mɪ'mɔːrɪəl] n monumento conmemorativo // a conmemorativo.
memorize ['mɛməraɪz] vt aprender de memoria.
memory ['mɛmərɪ] n memoria; (recollection) recuerdo.
men [mɛn] pl of **man.**
menace ['mɛnəs] n amenaza // vt amenazar; **menacing** a amenazador(a).
menagerie [mɪ'nædʒərɪ] n casa de fieras.
mend [mɛnd] vt reparar, arreglar; (darn) zurcir // vi reponerse // n (gen) remiendo; (darn) zurcido; **to be on the ~** ir mejorando; ~**ing** n reparación f; (clothes) ropa por remendar.
menial ['miːnɪəl] a doméstico; (pej) bajo // n criado.
meningitis [mɛnɪn'dʒaɪtɪs] n meningitis f.
menopause ['mɛnəupɔːz] n menopausia.
menstruate ['mɛnstrueɪt] vi menstruar; **menstruation** [-'eɪʃən] n menstruación f.
mental ['mɛntl] a mental; ~**ity** [-'tælɪtɪ] n mentalidad f.
mention ['mɛnʃən] n mención f // vt mencionar; (speak of) hablar de; **don't ~ it!** ¡de nada!
menu ['mɛnjuː] n (set ~) menú m; (printed) carta.
mercenary ['mɜːsɪnərɪ] a, n mercenario.
merchandise ['mɜːtʃəndaɪz] n mercancías fpl.
merchant ['mɜːtʃənt] n comerciante m/f; ~ **bank** n banco comercial; ~ **navy** n marina mercante.

merciful ['mɜːsɪful] a compasivo; (fortunate) afortunado.
merciless ['mɜːsɪlɪs] a despiadado.
mercury ['mɜːkjurɪ] n mercurio.
mercy ['mɜːsɪ] n compasión f; (REL) misericordia; **at the ~ of** a la merced de.
mere [mɪə*] a simple, mero; ~**ly** ad simplemente, sólo.
merge [mɜːdʒ] vt (join) unir; (mix) mezclar; (fuse) fundir // vi unirse; (COMM) fusionarse; **merger** n (COMM) fusión f.
meridian [mə'rɪdɪən] n meridiano.
meringue [mə'ræŋ] n merengue m.
merit ['mɛrɪt] n mérito // vt merecer.
mermaid ['mɜːmeɪd] n sirena.
merriment ['mɛrɪmənt] n alegría.
merry ['mɛrɪ]38 a alegre; ~**-go-round** n tiovivo.
mesh [mɛʃ] n malla; (TECH) engranaje m // vi (gears) engranar.
mesmerize ['mɛzməraɪz] vt hipnotizar.
mess [mɛs] n (gen) confusión f; (of objects) revoltijo; (tangle) lío; (MIL) comedor m; **to ~ about** vi (col) perder el tiempo; (pass the time) entretenerse; **to ~ about with** vt fus (col) (play with) divertirse con; (handle) manosear; **to ~ up** vt (disarrange) desordenar; (spoil) estropear; (dirty) ensuciar.
message ['mɛsɪdʒ] n recado, mensaje m.
messenger ['mɛsɪndʒə*] n mensajero/a.
messy ['mɛsɪ] a (dirty) sucio; (untidy) desordenado.
met [mɛt] pt, pp of **meet.**
metabolism [mɛ'tæbəlɪzəm] n metabolismo.
metal ['mɛtl] n metal m; ~**lic** [-'tælɪk] a metálico; ~**lurgy** [-'tælədʒɪ] n metalurgia.
metamorphosis [mɛtə'mɔːfəsɪs], pl **-ses** [-siːz] n metamorfosis f inv.
metaphor ['mɛtəfə*] n metáfora.
metaphysics [mɛtə'fɪzɪks] n metafísica.
mete [miːt]: **to ~ out** vt fus (gen) repartir; (punishment) imponer.
meteor ['miːtɪə*] n meteoro.
meteorological [miːtɪərə'lɔdʒɪkl] a meteorológico; **meteorology** [-'rɔlədʒɪ] n meteorología.
meter ['miːtə*] n (instrument) contador m; (US) = **metre.**
method ['mɛθəd] n método; ~**ical** [mɪ'θɔdɪkl] a metódico.
Methodist ['mɛθədɪst] a, n metodista m/f.
meths [mɛθs], **methylated spirit** ['mɛθɪleɪtɪd-] n alcohol m metilado o desnaturalizado.
meticulous [mɛ'tɪkjuləs] a meticuloso.
metre, meter (US) ['miːtə*] n metro.
metric ['mɛtrɪk] a métrico.
metronome ['mɛtrənəum] n metrónomo.
metropolis [mɪ'trɔpəlɪs] n metrópoli f.
mettle ['mɛtl] n (spirit) valor m, ánimo; (tone) temple m.
mew [mjuː] vi (cat) maullar.
mews [mjuːz] n: ~ **cottage** casa

acondicionada en antiguos establos o cocheras.

Mexican ['mɛksɪkən] a, n mejicano/a, mexicano/a (AM).

Mexico ['mɛksɪkəʊ] n Méjico, México (AM).

mezzanine ['mɛtsəni:n] n entresuelo.

miaow [mi:'aʊ] vi maullar.

mice [maɪs] pl of mouse.

microbe ['maɪkrəʊb] n microbio.

micro... [maɪkrəʊ] pref micro...; ~**film** n microfilm m; ~**phone** n micrófono; ~**processor** n microprocesador m; ~**scope** n microscopio; ~**scopic** [-'skɔpɪk] a microscópico; ~**wave** a de microonda.

mid [mɪd] a: **in** ~ **May** a mediados de mayo; **in** ~ **afternoon** a media tarde; **in** ~ **air** en el aire; ~**day** n mediodía m.

middle ['mɪdl] n medio, centro; (half) mitad f; (waist) cintura f; a medio; (quantity, size) mediano; ~-**aged** a de mediana edad; **the M**~ **Ages** npl la Edad Media; ~-**class** a de clase media; **M**~ **East** n Oriente m Medio; ~**man** n intermediario; ~ **name** n segundo nombre.

middling ['mɪdlɪŋ] a mediano.

midge [mɪdʒ] n mosca.

midget ['mɪdʒɪt] n enano // a minúsculo.

Midlands ['mɪdləndz] npl la región central de Inglaterra.

midnight ['mɪdnaɪt] n medianoche f.

midriff ['mɪdrɪf] n diafragma m.

midst [mɪdst] n: **in the** ~ **of** entre, en medio de.

midsummer [mɪd'sʌmə*] n: **a** ~ **day** un día de pleno verano.

midway [mɪd'weɪ] a, ad: ~ (**between**) a mitad de camino, a medio camino (entre).

midweek [mɪd'wi:k] ad entre semana.

midwife ['mɪdwaɪf], pl -**wives** [-waɪvz] n comadrona, partera; ~**ry** [-wɪfərɪ] n partería.

midwinter [mɪd'wɪntə*] n: **in** ~ en pleno invierno.

might [maɪt] vb: **he** ~ **be there** podría estar allí, puede que está allí; **I** ~ **as well go** más vale que vaya; **you** ~ **like to try** podría intentar // n fuerza, poder m; ~**y** a fuerte, poderoso.

migraine ['mi:greɪn] n jaqueca.

migrant ['maɪgrənt] n (bird) ave f migratoria; (person) emigrante m/f; (fig) nómada m/f // a migratorio; (worker) emigrante.

migrate [maɪ'greɪt] vi emigrar; **migration** [-'greɪʃən] n emigración f.

mike [maɪk] n abbr of **microphone** micro.

mild [maɪld] a (character) pacífico; (climate) templado; (slight) ligero; (taste) suave; (illness) benigno, leve.

mildew ['mɪldju:] n moho.

mildness ['maɪldnɪs] n (softness) suavidad f; (gentleness) dulzura; (quiet character) apacibilidad f.

mile [maɪl] n milla; ~**age** n número de millas; (AUT) kilometraje m; ~**stone** n mojón m.

milieu ['mi:ljə:] n medio, medio ambiente.

militant ['mɪlɪtnt] a, n militante m/f.

military ['mɪlɪtərɪ] a militar.

militate ['mɪlɪteɪt] vi: **to** ~ **against** militar contra.

militia [mɪ'lɪʃə] n milicia.

milk [mɪlk] n leche f // vt (cow) ordeñar; (fig) chupar; ~**man** n lechero; ~ **shake** n batido de leche; ~**y** a lechoso; **M**~**y Way** n Vía Láctea.

mill [mɪl] n (windmill etc) molino; (coffee ~) molinillo; (factory) fábrica; (spinning ~) hilandería // vt moler // vi (also: ~ **about**) moverse por todas partes, apiñarse.

millennium [mɪ'lɛnɪəm], pl ~**s** or -**ia** [-nɪə] n milenio, milenario.

miller ['mɪlə*] n molinero.

millet ['mɪlɪt] n mijo.

milli... ['mɪlɪ] pref: ~**gram(me)** n miligramo; ~**litre** n mililitro; ~**metre** n milímetro.

milliner ['mɪlɪnə*] n modista de sombreros; ~**y** n sombrerería.

million ['mɪljən] n millón m; **a** ~ **times** un millón de veces; ~**aire** n millonario.

millstone ['mɪlstəʊn] n piedra de molino.

milometer [maɪ'lɔmɪtə*] n cuenta-kilómetros m inv.

mime [maɪm] n mímica; (actor) mimo // vt remedar // vi actuar de mimo.

mimic ['mɪmɪk] n imitador/a m/f // a mímico // vt remedar, imitar; ~**ry** n imitación f.

min. abbr of **minute(s)**; **minimum.**

minaret [mɪnə'rɛt] n alminar m.

mince [mɪns] vt picar // vi (in walking) andar con pasos menudos // n (CULIN) carne f picada, picadillo; ~**meat** n conserva de fruta picada; ~ **pie** n empanadilla rellena de fruta picada; **mincer** n máquina de picar carne.

mind [maɪnd] n (gen) mente f; (intellect) inteligencia; (contrasted with matter) espíritu // vt (attend to, look after) ocuparse de, cuidar; (be careful of) tener cuidado con; (object to): **I don't** ~ **the noise** no me importa el ruido; **it is on my** ~ me preocupa; **to my** ~ en mi opinión; **to be out of one's** ~ estar fuera de juicio; **never** ~! ¡es igual!, ¡no importa!; (don't worry) ¡no se preocupe!; **to bear sth in** ~ tomar o tener algo en cuenta; **to make up one's** ~ decidirse; '~ **the step'** cuidado con el escalón; ~**ful** a: ~**ful of** consciente de; ~**less** a estúpido.

mine [maɪn] pron (el) mío/(la) mía etc // a: **this book is** ~ este libro es mío // n mina // vt (coal) extraer, explotar; (ship, beach) minar; ~**field** n campo de minas; **miner** n minero.

mineral ['mɪnərəl] a mineral // n mineral m; ~**s** npl (soft drinks) aguas fpl minerales, gaseosa sg.

minesweeper [ˈmaɪnswiːpə*] n dragaminas m inv.

mingle [ˈmɪŋgl] vi: to ~ with mezclarse con.

mingy [ˈmɪndʒɪ] a (col) tacaño.

miniature [ˈmɪnətʃə*] a (en) miniatura // n miniatura.

minibus [ˈmɪnɪbʌs] n microbús m.

minicab [ˈmɪnɪkæb] n microtaxi m.

minim [ˈmɪnɪm] n (MUS) blanca.

minimal [ˈmɪnɪml] a mínimo.

minimize [ˈmɪnɪmaɪz] vt minimizar.

minimum [ˈmɪnɪməm] n, pl **minima** [ˈmɪnɪmə] mínimo // a mínimo.

mining [ˈmaɪnɪŋ] n explotación f minera // a minero.

miniskirt [ˈmɪnɪskəːt] n minifalda.

minister [ˈmɪnɪstə*] n (POL) ministro; (REL) pastor m // vi atender; ~ial [-ˈtɪərɪəl] a (POL) ministerial.

ministry [ˈmɪnɪstrɪ] n ministerio.

mink [mɪŋk] n visón m; ~ coat n abrigo de visón.

minnow [ˈmɪnəu] n pececillo (de agua dulce).

minor [ˈmaɪnə*] a menor; (unimportant) sin importancia; (inferior) secundario; (MUS) menor // n (LAW) menor m/f de edad.

minority [maɪˈnɔrɪtɪ] n minoría; (age) minoridad f.

minster [ˈmɪnstə*] n catedral f.

minstrel [ˈmɪnstrəl] n juglar m.

mint [mɪnt] n (plant) menta, herbabuena; (sweet) caramelo de menta // vt (coins) acuñar; **the (Royal) M**~ la (Real) Casa de la Moneda; **in** ~ **condition** en perfecto estado.

minuet [mɪnjuˈɛt] n minué m.

minus [ˈmaɪnəs] n (also: ~ **sign**) signo de menos // prep menos.

minute [ˈmɪnɪt] n minuto; (fig) momento; ~s npl actas fpl // a [maɪˈnjuːt] diminuto; (search) minucioso; **at the last** ~ a última hora.

miracle [ˈmɪrəkl] n milagro; **miraculous** [mɪˈrækjuləs] a milagroso.

mirage [ˈmɪrɑːʒ] n espejismo.

mirror [ˈmɪrə*] n espejo; (in car) retrovisor m // vt reflejar.

mirth [məːθ] n alegría; (laughter) risa, risas fpl.

misadventure [mɪsədˈvɛntʃə*] n desgracia, accidente m.

misanthropist [mɪˈzænθrəpɪst] n misántropo.

misapprehension [ˈmɪsæprɪˈhɛnʃən] n equivocación f.

misbehave [mɪsbɪˈheɪv] vi portarse mal; **misbehaviour** n mala conducta.

miscalculate [mɪsˈkælkjuleɪt] vt calcular mal; **miscalculation** [-ˈleɪʃən] n error m (de cálculo).

miscarriage [ˈmɪskærɪdʒ] n (MED) aborto; (failure) fracaso; ~ **of justice** error m judicial.

miscellaneous [mɪsɪˈleɪnɪəs] a vario(s), diverso(s).

mischance [mɪsˈtʃɑːns] n desgracia, mala suerte f.

mischief [ˈmɪstʃɪf] n (naughtiness) travesura; (harm) mal m, daño; (maliciousness) malicia; **mischievous** [-ʃɪvəs] a travieso; dañoso; (playful) malicioso.

misconception [ˈmɪskənˈsɛpʃən] n concepto erróneo, equivocación f.

misconduct [mɪsˈkɔndʌkt] n mala conducta; **professional** ~ falta profesional.

miscount [mɪsˈkaunt] vt, vi contar mal.

misdeed [mɪsˈdiːd] n delito.

misdemeanour, misdemeanor (US) [mɪsdɪˈmiːnə*] n delito, ofensa.

misdirect [mɪsdɪˈrɛkt] vt (person) informar mal; (letter) poner señas incorrectas en.

miser [ˈmaɪzə*] n avaro/a.

miserable [ˈmɪzərəbl] a (unhappy) triste, desgraciado; (wretched) miserable; (despicable) despreciable.

miserly [ˈmaɪzəlɪ] a avariento, tacaño.

misery [ˈmɪzərɪ] n (unhappiness) tristeza, sufrimiento; (wretchedness) miseria, desdicha.

misfire [mɪsˈfaɪə*] vi fallar.

misfit [ˈmɪsfɪt] n (person) inadaptado/a, desplazado/a.

misfortune [mɪsˈfɔːtʃən] n desgracia.

misgiving(s) [mɪsˈgɪvɪŋ(z)] n(pl) (mistrust) recelo; (apprehension) presentimiento.

misguided [mɪsˈgaɪdɪd] a equivocado.

mishandle [mɪsˈhændl] vt (treat roughly) maltratar; (mismanage) manejar mal.

mishap [ˈmɪshæp] n desgracia, contratiempo.

mishear [mɪsˈhɪə*] (irg: like hear) vt oír mal.

misinform [mɪsɪnˈfɔːm] vt informar mal.

misinterpret [mɪsɪnˈtəːprɪt] vt interpretar mal.

misjudge [mɪsˈdʒʌdʒ] vt juzgar mal.

mislay [mɪsˈleɪ] (irg: like lay) vt extraviar, perder.

mislead [mɪsˈliːd] (irg: like lead) vt llevar a conclusiones erróneas; ~ing a engañoso, erróneo.

mismanage [mɪsˈmænɪdʒ] vt administrar mal; ~ment n mala administración f.

misnomer [mɪsˈnəumə*] n nombre m inapropiado o equivocado.

misogynist [mɪˈsɔdʒɪnɪst] n misógino.

misplace [mɪsˈpleɪs] vt (lose) extraviar, perder.

misprint [ˈmɪsprɪnt] n errata, error m de imprenta.

mispronounce [mɪsprəˈnauns] vt pronunciar mal.

misread [mɪsˈriːd] (irg: like read) vt leer mal.

misrepresent [mɪsrɛprɪ'zɛnt] *vt* falsificar.

miss [mɪs] *vt* (*train etc*) perder; (*fail to hit*) errar, fallar; (*regret the absence of*): **I ~ him** (yo) le echo de menos *o* a faltar // *vi* fallar // *n* (*shot*) tiro fallido *o* perdido; (*fig*): **that was a near ~** (*near accident*) faltó poco para que chocáramos; **to ~ out** *vt* omitir.

Miss [mɪs] *n* Señorita.

missal ['mɪsl] *n* misal *m*.

misshapen [mɪs'ʃeɪpən] *a* deforme.

missile ['mɪsaɪl] *n* (*AVIAT*) mísil *m*; (*object thrown*) proyectil *m*.

missing ['mɪsɪŋ] *a* (*pupil*) ausente; (*thing*) perdido; (*MIL*) desaparecido; **to go ~** desaparecer.

mission ['mɪʃən] *n* misión *f*; **~ary** *n* misionero.

misspent ['mɪs'spɛnt] *a*: **his ~ youth** su juventud disipada.

mist [mɪst] *n* (*light*) neblina; (*heavy*) niebla; (*at sea*) bruma // *vi* (*also*: **~ over, ~ up**) empañarse.

mistake [mɪs'teɪk] *n* error *m* // *vt* (*irg*: *like* **take**) entender mal, equivocarse sobre; **to ~ A for B** confundir A con B; **mistaken** *a* (*idea etc*) equivocado; **to be mistaken** equivocarse, engañarse.

mister ['mɪstə*] *n* (*col*) señor *m*; *see* **Mr**.

mistletoe ['mɪsltəu] *n* muérdago.

mistook [mɪs'tuk] *pt of* **mistake**.

mistreat [mɪs'triːt] *vt* maltratar; **~ment** *n* maltrato.

mistress ['mɪstrɪs] *n* (*lover*) amante *f*; (*of house*) señora (de la casa); (*in primary school*) maestra; (*in secondary school*) profesora; *see* **Mrs**.

mistrust [mɪs'trʌst] *vt* desconfiar de, dudar de.

misty ['mɪstɪ] *a* nebuloso, brumoso; (*day*) de niebla; (*glasses*) empañado.

misunderstand [mɪsʌndə'stænd] (*irg*: *like* **understand**) *vt*, *vi* entender mal; **~ing** *n* malentendido.

misuse [mɪs'juːs] *n* mal uso; (*of power*) abuso // *vt* [mɪs'juːz] abusar de; (*funds*) malversar.

mitigate ['mɪtɪgeɪt] *vt* mitigar.

mitre, miter (*US*) ['maɪtə*] *n* mitra; (*CARPENTRY*) inglete *m*.

mitt(en) ['mɪt(n)] *n* mitón *m*.

mix [mɪks] *vt* (*gen*) mezclar; (*combine*) unir // *vi* mezclarse; (*people*) llevarse bien // *n* mezcla; **to ~ up** *vt* mezclar; (*confuse*) confundir; **~ed** *a* (*assorted*) variado, surtido; (*school etc*) mixto; **~ed-up** *a* (*confused*) confuso, revuelto; **~er** *n* (*for food*) licuadora; (*person*) persona sociable; **~ture** *n* mezcla; **~-up** *n* confusión *f*.

moan [məun] *n* gemido // *vi* gemir; (*col*: *complain*): **to ~ (about)** quejarse (de).

moat [məut] *n* foso.

mob [mɔb] *n* multitud *f*; (*pej*): **the ~** el populacho // *vt* acosar.

mobile ['məubaɪl] *a* móvil // *n* móvil *m*; **~ home** *n* caravana.

mobility [məu'bɪlɪtɪ] *n* movilidad *f*.

mobilize ['məubɪlaɪz] *vt* movilizar.

moccasin ['mɔkəsɪn] *n* mocasín *m*.

mock [mɔk] *vt* (*make ridiculous*) ridiculizar; (*laugh at*) burlarse de // *a* fingido; **~ery** *n* burla; **~ing** *a* burlón(ona); **~-up** *n* maqueta.

mode [məud] *n* modo; (*fashion*) moda.

model ['mɔdl] *n* (*gen*) modelo; (*ARCH*) maqueta; (*person: for fashion, ART*) modelo *m/f* // *a* modelo // *vt* modelar // *vi* servir de modelo; **~ railway** ferrocarril *m* de juguete; **to ~ clothes** pasar modelos, ser modelo.

moderate ['mɔdərət] *a*, *n* moderado/a // (*vb*: [-reɪt]) *vi* moderarse, calmarse // *vt* moderar; **moderation** [-'reɪʃən] *n* moderación *f*.

modern ['mɔdən] *a* moderno; **~ize** *vt* modernizar.

modest ['mɔdɪst] *a* modesto; **~y** *n* modestia.

modicum ['mɔdɪkəm] *n*: **a ~ of** un mínimo de.

modification [mɔdɪfɪ'keɪʃən] *n* modificación *f*; **modify** ['mɔdɪfaɪ] *vt* modificar.

modulation [mɔdju'leɪʃən] *n* modulación *f*.

mohair ['məuhɛə*] *n* moer *m*.

moist [mɔɪst] *a* húmedo; **~en** ['mɔɪsn] *vt* humedecer; **~ure** ['mɔɪstʃə*] *n* humedad *f*; **~urizer** ['mɔɪstʃəraɪzə*] *n* crema hidratante.

molar ['məulə*] *n* muela.

molasses [məu'læsɪz] *n* melaza.

mole [məul] *n* (*animal*) topo; (*spot*) lunar *m*.

molecule ['mɔlɪkjuːl] *n* molécula.

molehill ['məulhɪl] *n* topera.

molest [məu'lɛst] *vt* importunar.

mollusc ['mɔləsk] *n* molusco.

mollycoddle ['mɔlɪkɔdl] *vt* mimar.

molten ['məultən] *a* fundido; (*lava*) líquido.

moment ['məumənt] *n* momento; **~ary** *a* momentáneo; **~ous** [-'mɛntəs] *a* trascendental, importante.

momentum [məu'mɛntəm] *n* momento; (*fig*) ímpetu *m*; **to gather ~** cobrar velocidad.

monarch ['mɔnək] *n* monarca *m/f*; **~y** *n* monarquía.

monastery ['mɔnəstərɪ] *n* monasterio.

monastic [mə'næstɪk] *a* monástico.

Monday ['mʌndɪ] *n* lunes *m*.

monetary ['mʌnɪtərɪ] *a* monetario.

money ['mʌnɪ] *n* dinero; **to make ~** ganar dinero; **~lender** *n* prestamista *m/f*; **~ order** *n* giro.

mongol ['mɔŋgəl] *a*, *n* (*MED*) mongólico.

mongrel ['mʌŋgrəl] *n* (*dog*) perro cruzado.

monitor ['mɔnɪtə*] *n* (*SCOL*) monitor *m*; (*also*: **television ~**) receptor *m* de control // *vt* controlar.

monk [mʌŋk] *n* monje *m*.

monkey ['mʌŋkɪ] *n* mono; **~ nut** *n*

cacahuete m; ~ **wrench** n llave f inglesa.
mono... [mɔnəu] pref: ~**chrome** a monocromo.
monocle ['mɔnəkl] n monóculo.
monogram ['mɔnəgræm] n monograma m.
monologue ['mɔnəlɔg] n monólogo.
monopoly [mə'nɔpəlı] n monopolio.
monorail ['mɔnəureıl] n monorriel m.
monosyllabic [mɔnəusı'læbık] a monosilábico.
monotone ['mɔnətəun] n monotonía; **to speak in a** ~ hablar en un solo tono.
monotonous [mə'nɔtənəs] a monótono; **monotony** [-nı] n monotonía.
monsoon [mɔn'suːn] n monzón m/f.
monster ['mɔnstə*] n monstruo.
monstrosity [mɔns'trɔsıtı] n monstruosidad f.
monstrous ['mɔnstrəs] a (huge) enorme; (atrocious) monstruoso.
montage [mɔn'tɑːʒ] n montaje m.
month [mʌnθ] n mes m; ~**ly** a mensual // ad mensualmente // n (magazine) revista mensual.
monument ['mɔnjumənt] n monumento; ~**al** [-'mɛntl] a monumental.
moo [muː] vi mugir.
mood [muːd] n humor m; **to be in a good/bad** ~ estar de buen/mal humor; ~**y** a (variable) de humor variable; (sullen) melancólico.
moon [muːn] n luna; ~**beam** n rayo de luna; ~**light** n luz f de la luna; ~**lit** a: **a** ~**lit night** una noche de luna.
moor [muə*] n páramo // vt (ship) amarrar // vi echar las amarras.
Moor [muə*] n moro/a.
moorings ['muərıŋz] npl (chains) amarras fpl; (place) amarradero sg.
Moorish ['muərıʃ] a moro; (architecture) árabe, morisco.
moorland ['muələnd] n páramo, brezal m.
moose [muːs] n, pl inv alce m.
mop [mɔp] n fregona; (of hair) greña, melena // vt fregar; **to** ~ **up** vt limpiar.
mope [məup] vi estar o andar deprimido.
moped ['məupɛd] n (Brit) ciclomotor m.
moral ['mɔrl] a moral // n moraleja; ~**s** npl moralidad f, moral f.
morale [mɔ'rɑːl] n moral f.
morality [mə'rælıtı] n moralidad f.
morass [mə'ræs] n pantano.
morbid ['mɔːbıd] a (depressed) melancólico; (MED) mórbido; **don't be** ~! ¡no seas morboso!
more [mɔː*] det, ad más; **once** ~ otra vez, una vez más; **I want** ~ quiero más; ~ **dangerous than** más peligroso que; ~ **or less** más o menos; ~ **than ever** más que nunca.
moreover [mɔː'rəuvə*] ad además, por otra parte.
morgue [mɔːg] n depósito de cadáveres.
moribund ['mɔrıbʌnd] a moribundo.
Mormon ['mɔːmən] n mormón/ona m/f.

morning ['mɔːnıŋ] n (gen) mañana; (early ~) madrugada; **good** ~ buenas días; **in the** ~ por la mañana; **7 o'clock in the** ~ las 7 de la mañana; **tomorrow** ~ mañana por la mañana.
Moroccan [mə'rɔkən] a, n marroquí m/f.
Morocco [mə'rɔkəu] n Marruecos m.
moron ['mɔːrɔn] n imbécil m/f; ~**ic** [mə'rɔnık] a imbécil.
morose [mə'rəus] a hosco, malhumorado.
morphine ['mɔːfiːn] n morfina.
Morse [mɔːs] n (also: ~ **code**) (alfabeto) morse.
morsel ['mɔːsl] n (of food) bocado.
mortal ['mɔːtl] a, n mortal m/f; ~**ity** [-'tælıtı] n mortalidad f.
mortar ['mɔːtə*] n argamasa; (dish) mortero.
mortgage ['mɔːgıdʒ] n hipoteca // vt hipotecar.
mortify ['mɔːtıfaı] vt mortificar, humillar.
mortuary ['mɔːtjuərı] n depósito de cadáveres.
mosaic [məu'zeıık] n mosaico.
Moscow ['mɔskəu] n Moscú m.
Moslem ['mɔzləm] a, n = **Muslim.**
mosque [mɔsk] n mezquita.
mosquito [mɔs'kiːtəu] pl ~**es** n mosquito.
moss [mɔs] n musgo.
most [məust] det la mayor parte de, la mayoría de // pron la mayor parte, la mayoría // ad el más; (very) muy; **the** ~ (also: + adjective) el más; ~ **of them** la mayor parte de ellos; **I saw the** ~ yo vi el que más; **at the (very)** ~ a lo sumo, todo lo más; **to make the** ~ **of** aprovechar (al máximo); ~**ly** ad en su mayor parte, principalmente; **a** ~ **interesting book** un libro interesantísimo.
MOT n abbr of **Ministry of Transport: the** ~ **(test)** inspección (anual) obligatoria de coches y camiones.
motel [məu'tɛl] n motel m.
moth [mɔθ] n mariposa nocturna; (clothes ~) polilla; ~**ball** n bola de naftalina; ~**-eaten** a apolillado.
mother ['mʌðə*] n madre f // a materno // vt (care for) cuidar (como una madre); ~**hood** n maternidad f; ~**-in-law** n suegra; ~**ly** a maternal; ~**-of-pearl** n nácar m; ~**-to-be** n futura madre; ~ **tongue** n lengua materna.
motif [məu'tiːf] n motivo; (theme) tema m.
motion ['məuʃən] n movimiento; (gesture) ademán m, señal f; (at meeting) moción f // vt, vi: **to** ~ **(to) sb to do sth** hacer señas a uno para que haga algo; ~**less** a inmóvil; ~ **picture** n película.
motivated ['məutıveıtıd] a motivado; **motivation** [-'veıʃən] n motivación f.
motive ['məutıv] n motivo a motor (f: motora, motriz).
motley ['mɔtlı] a variado.
motor ['məutə*] n motor m; (col: vehicle) coche m, automóvil m // a motor (f:

motora, motriz); ~**bike** n moto f; ~**boat** n lancha motora; ~**car** n coche m, automóvil m; ~**cycle** n motocicleta; ~**cyclist** n motorista m/f; ~**ing** n automovilismo; ~**ist** n conductor/a m/f, automovilista m/f; ~ **oil** n aceite m de coche; ~ **racing** n carreras fpl de coches, automovilismo; ~ **scooter** n moto f; ~ **vehicle** n automóvil m; ~**way** n (Brit) autopista.

mottled ['mɔtld] a abigarrado, multicolor.

motto ['mɔtəu] pl ~**es** n lema m; (watchword) consigna.

mould, mold (US) [məuld] n molde m; (mildew) moho // vt moldear; (fig) formar; ~**er** vi (decay) decaer; ~**ing** n moldura; ~**y** a enmohecido.

moult, molt (US) [məult] vi mudar (la piel/la pluma).

mound [maund] n montón m, montículo.

mount [maunt] n monte m; (horse) montura; (for jewel etc) engaste m; (for picture) marco // vt montar, subir a // vi (also: ~ **up**) subirse, montarse.

mountain ['mauntin] n montaña // cpd de montaña; ~**eer** [-'niə*] n alpinista m/f, montañero/a; ~**eering** [-'niəriŋ] n alpinismo, montañismo; **to go** ~**eering** hacer alpinismo; ~**ous** a montañoso; ~**side** n ladera de la montaña.

mourn [mɔ:n] vt llorar, lamentar // vi: **to** ~ **for** llorar la muerte de, lamentarse por; ~**er** n pariente m/f/amigo del difunto; ~**ful** a triste, lúgubre; ~**ing** n luto // cpd (dress) de luto; **in** ~**ing** de luto.

mouse [maus] pl **mice** n ratón m; ~**trap** n ratonera.

moustache [məs'tɑ:ʃ] n bigote m.

mousy ['mausi] a (person) tímido; (hair) pardusco.

mouth [mauθ] pl ~**s** [-ðz] n boca; (of river) desembocadura; ~**ful** n bocado; ~**organ** n armónica; ~**piece** n (of musical instrument) boquilla; (spokesman) portavoz m; ~**wash** n enjuague m; ~-**watering** a apetitoso.

movable ['mu:vəbl] a movible.

move [mu:v] n (movement) movimiento; (in game) jugada; (: turn to play) turno; (change of house) mudanza // vt mover; (emotionally) conmover; (POL: resolution etc) proponer // vi (gen) moverse; (traffic) circular; (also: ~ **house**) trasladarse, mudarse; **to** ~ **sb to do sth** mover a uno a hacer algo; **to get a** ~ **on** darse prisa; **to** ~ **about** vi ir de acá para allá; (travel) viajar; **to** ~ **along** vi avanzar, adelantarse; **to** ~ **away** vi alejarse; **to** ~ **back** vi retroceder; **to** ~ **forward** vi avanzar // vt adelantar; **to** ~ **in** vi (to a house) instalarse (en una casa); **to** ~ **on** vi ponerse en camino; **to** ~ **out** vi (of house) abandonar (una casa); **to** ~ **up** vi subir; (employee) ser ascendido.

movement ['mu:vmənt] n movimiento; (TECH) mecanismo.

movie ['mu:vi] n película; **to go to the** ~**s** ir al cine; ~ **camera** n cámara cinematográfica.

moving ['mu:viŋ] a (emotional) conmovedor(a); (that moves) móvil.

mow [məu], pt **mowed**, pp **mowed** or **mown** vt (grass) cortar; (corn: also: ~ **down**) segar; ~**er** n segadora; (for lawn) cortacéspedes m inv.

M.P. n abbr of **Member of Parliament.**

m.p.h. abbr of **miles per hour.**

Mr ['mistə*] n: ~ **Smith** (el) Sr. Smith.

Mrs ['misiz] n: ~ **Smith** (la) Sra. Smith.

Ms [miz] n = **Miss** or **Mrs**: ~ **Smith** (la) Sa. Smith.

M.Sc. abbr of **Master of Science.**

much [mʌtʃ] det mucho // ad, n or pron mucho; (before pp) muy; **how** ~ **is it?** ¿cuánto es?, ¿cuánto cuesta?; **too** ~ demasiado; **it's not** ~ no es mucho; **as** ~ **as** tanto como; **however** ~ **he tries** por mucho que se esfuerce.

muck [mʌk] n (dirt) suciedad f; (fig) porquería; **to** ~ **about** vi (col) perder el tiempo; (enjoy o.s.) entretenerse; **to** ~ **up** vt (col: ruin) arruinar, estropear; ~**y** a (dirty) sucio.

mucus ['mju:kəs] n moco.

mud [mʌd] n barro, lodo.

muddle ['mʌdl] n desorden m, confusión f; (mix-up) embrollo, lío // vt (also: ~ **up**) embrollar, confundir; **to** ~ **through** vi salir del paso sin saber cómo.

mud: ~**dy** a fangoso, cubierto de lodo; ~**guard** n guardabarros m inv; ~**pack** n mascarilla (de belleza); ~-**slinging** n injurias fpl, difamación f.

muff [mʌf] n manguito // vt (chance) desperdiciar; (lines) estropear.

muffin ['mʌfin] n mollete m.

muffle ['mʌfl] vt (sound) amortiguar; (against cold) embozar; ~**d** a sordo, apagado.

mufti ['mʌfti] n: **in** ~ vestido de paisano.

mug [mʌg] n (cup) taza (alta, sin platillo); (: for beer) jarra; (col: face) jeta; (: fool) bobo // vt (assault) asaltar; ~**ging** n asalto.

muggy ['mʌgi] a bochornoso.

mule [mju:l] n mula.

mull [mʌl]: **to** ~ **over** vt meditar sobre.

mulled [mʌld] a: ~ **wine** vino calentado y con especias.

multi... [mʌlti] pref multi...; ~**coloured**, ~**colored** (US) a multicolor.

multifarious [mʌlti'fɛəriəs] a múltiple.

multiple ['mʌltipl] a, n múltiplo; ~ **sclerosis** n esclerósis f múltiple; ~ **store** n (cadena de) grandes almacenes.

multiplication [mʌltipli'keiʃən] n multiplicación f; **multiply** ['mʌltiplai] vt multiplicar // vi multiplicarse.

multitude ['mʌltitju:d] n multitud f.

mum [mʌm] n mamá // a: **to keep** ~ callarse.

mumble ['mʌmbl] vt, vi hablar entre dientes, refunfuñar.
mummy ['mʌmɪ] n (mother) mamá; (embalmed) momia.
mumps [mʌmps] n paperas fpl.
munch [mʌntʃ] vt, vi mascar.
mundane [mʌn'deɪn] a mundano.
municipal [mju:'nɪsɪpl] a municipal; ~ity [-'pælɪtɪ] n municipio.
munitions [mju:'nɪʃənz] npl municiones fpl.
mural ['mjuərl] n (pintura) mural m.
murder ['mɔ:də*] n asesinato; (in law) homicidio // vt asesinar, matar; (spoil) estropear; ~er n asesino; ~ess n asesina; ~ous a homicida.
murky ['mɔ:kɪ] a oscuro; (fig) tenebroso.
murmur ['mɔ:mə*] n murmullo // vt, vi murmurar.
muscle ['mʌsl] n músculo; (fig: strength) fuerza (muscular); to ~ in vi introducirse por fuerza; **muscular** ['muskjulə*] a muscular; (person) musculoso.
muse [mju:z] vi meditar // n musa.
museum [mju:'zɪəm] n museo.
mushroom ['mʌʃrum] n (gen) seta, hongo; (food) champiñón m // vi (fig) crecer de la noche a la mañana.
mushy ['mʌʃɪ] a triturado; (pej) sensiblero.
music ['mju:zɪk] n música; ~al a melodioso; (person) musical // n (show) (comedia) musical; ~al instrument n instrumento musical; ~ hall n teatro de variedades; ~ian [-'zɪʃən] n músico/a.
musket ['mʌskɪt] n mosquete m.
Muslim ['mʌzlɪm] a, n musulmán/ana m/f.
muslin ['mʌzlɪn] n muselina.
mussel ['mʌsl] n mejillón m.
must [mʌst] auxiliary vb (obligation): I ~ do it debo hacerlo, tengo que hacerlo; (probability): he ~ be there by now ya debe estar allí // n necesidad f; it's a ~ es imprescindible.
mustard ['mʌstəd] n mostaza.
muster ['mʌstə*] vt juntar, reunir.
mustn't ['mʌsnt] = must not.
musty ['mʌstɪ] a mohoso, que huele a humedad.
mute [mju:t] a, n mudo/a.
muted ['mju:tɪd] a callado; (MUS) apagado.
mutilate ['mju:tɪleɪt] vt mutilar; **mutilation** [-'leɪʃən] n mutilación f.
mutinous ['mju:tɪnəs] a (troops) amotinado; (attitude) rebelde.
mutiny ['mju:tɪnɪ] n motín m // vi amotinarse.
mutter ['mʌtə*] vt, vi murmurar, hablar entre dientes.
mutton ['mʌtn] n carne f de cordero.
mutual ['mju:tʃuəl] a mutuo; (gen: shared) común; ~ly ad mutuamente.
muzzle ['mʌzl] n hocico; (protective device) bozal m; (of gun) boca // vt amordazar; (dog) poner un bozal a.
my [maɪ] a mi // interj: ~! ¡caramba!
mynah bird ['maɪnə] n mainat m.

myopic [maɪ'ɔpɪk] a miope.
myself [maɪ'sɛlf] pron (reflexive) me; (emphatic) yo mismo; (after prep) mí (mismo).
mysterious [mɪs'tɪərɪəs] a misterioso; **mystery** ['mɪstərɪ] n misterio.
mystic ['mɪs·ɪk] a, n místico/a; ~al a místico.
mystify ['mɪstɪfaɪ] vt (perplex) dejar perplejo; (disconcert) desconcertar.
myth [mɪθ] n mito; ~ical a mítico; ~ological [mɪθə'lɔdʒɪkl] a mitológico; ~ology [mɪ'θɔlədʒɪ] n mitología.

N

nab [næb] vt (col: grab) coger; (: catch out) pillar.
nag [næg] n (pej: horse) rocín m // vt (scold) regañar; (annoy) fastidiar; ~ging a (doubt) persistente; (pain) continuo // n quejas fpl.
nail [neɪl] n (human) uña; (metal) clavo // vt clavar; (fig: catch) coger, pillar; to ~ sb down to doing sth comprometer a uno a que haga algo; ~brush n cepillo para las uñas; ~file n lima para las uñas; ~ polish n esmalte m o laca para las uñas; ~ scissors npl tijeras fpl para las uñas.
naïve [naɪ'i:v] a ingenuo; (simple) sencillo.
naked ['neɪkɪd] a (nude) desnudo; (fig) inerme, indefenso; (flame) expuesto al aire; ~ness n desnudez f.
name [neɪm] n (gen) nombre m; (surname) apellido; (reputation) fama, renombre m // vt (child) poner nombre a; (criminal) dar el nombre de; (appoint) nombrar; by ~ de nombre; **maiden** ~ nombre de soltera; in the ~ of en nombre de; what's your ~? ¿cómo se llama?; to give one's ~ and address dar las señas; ~less a anónimo, sin nombre; ~ly ad a saber; ~sake n tocayo/a.
nanny ['nænɪ] n niñera; ~ goat n cabra.
nap [næp] n (sleep) sueñecito, siesta.
napalm ['neɪpɑ:m] n nápalm m.
nape [neɪp] n: the ~ of the neck la nuca, el cogote.
napkin ['næpkɪn] n (also: table ~) servilleta; (Brit: for baby) pañal m.
nappy ['næpɪ] n pañal m; ~ liner n gasa; ~ rash n prurito.
narcissus [nɑ:'sɪsəs], pl -si [-saɪ] n narciso.
narcotic [nɑ:'kɔtɪk] a, n narcótico.
narrate [nə'reɪt] vt narrar, contar; **narrative** ['nærətɪv] n narrativa // a narrativo; **narrator** n narrador/a m/f.
narrow ['nærəʊ] a estrecho, angosto; (fig) de miras estrechas, intolerante // vi estrecharse, angostarse; (diminish) reducirse; to ~ down the possibilities to reducir las posibilidades a; ~ly ad (miss) por poco; ~-minded a de miras estrechas.
nasal ['neɪzl] a nasal.
nastiness ['nɑ:stɪnɪs] n (malice)

malevolencia; (*rudeness*) grosería.

nasty ['nɑːstɪ] *a* (*unpleasant: remark*) feo, horrible; (: *person*) antipático; (*malicious*) rencoroso; (*rude*) grosero; (*revolting: taste, smell*) asqueroso, repugnante; (*wound, disease etc*) peligroso, grave.

nation ['neɪʃən] *n* nación *f*.

national ['næʃənl] *a, n* nacional *m/f*; ~**ism** *n* nacionalismo; ~**ist** *a, n* nacionalista *m/f*; ~**ity** [-'nælɪtɪ] *n* nacionalidad *f*; ~**ization** [-aɪ'zeɪʃən] *n* nacionalización *f*; ~**ize** *vt* nacionalizar; ~**ly** *ad* (*nationwide*) en escala nacional; (*as a nation*) nacionalmente, como nación.

nationwide ['neɪʃənwaɪd] *a* en escala *o* a nivel nacional.

native ['neɪtɪv] *n* (*local inhabitant*) natural *m/f*, nacional *m/f*; (*in colonies*) indígena *m/f*, nativo/a // *a* (*indigenous*) indígena; (*of one's birth*) natal; (*innate*) natural, innato.

NATO ['neɪtəu] *n abbr of* **North Atlantic Treaty Organization** OTAN (Organización del Tratado del Atlántico del Norte).

natter ['nætə*] *vi* charlar.

natural ['nætʃrəl] *a* natural; (*unaffected: manner*) inafectado, sin afectación; ~**ist** *n* naturalista *m/f*; ~**ize** *vt*: **to become** ~**ized** (*person*) naturalizarse; (*plant*) aclimatarse; ~**ly** *ad* naturalmente; (*of course*) desde luego, por supuesto; (*instinctively*) por instinto, por naturaleza; ~**ness** *n* naturalidad *f*.

nature ['neɪtʃə*] *n* naturaleza; (*group, sort*) género, clase *f*; (*character*) carácter *m*, genio; **by** ~ por *o* de naturaleza.

naughty ['nɔːtɪ] *a* (*child*) travieso; (*story, film*) verde, escabroso.

nausea ['nɔːsɪə] *n* náusea; **nauseate** [-sɪeɪt] *vt* dar náuseas a; (*fig*) dar asco a; **nauseating** [-sɪeɪtɪŋ] *a* nauseabundo; (*fig*) asqueroso.

nautical ['nɔːtɪkl] *a* náutico, marítimo; (*mile*) marino.

naval ['neɪvl] *a* naval, de marina; ~ **officer** *n* oficial *m/f* de marina.

nave [neɪv] *n* nave *f*.

navel ['neɪvl] *n* ombligo.

navigable ['nævɪgəbl] *a* navegable.

navigate ['nævɪgeɪt] *vt* (*guide*) gobernar; (*sail along*) navegar por; (*fig*) guiar // *vi* navegar; **navigation** [-'geɪʃən] *n* (*action*) navegación *f*; (*science*) náutica; **navigator** *n* navegador/a *m/f*, navegante *m/f*.

navvy ['nævɪ] *n* peón *m* caminero.

navy ['neɪvɪ] *n* marina de guerra; (*ships*) armada, flota; ~**(-blue)** *a* azul marino.

Nazi ['nɑːtsɪ] *n* nazi *m/f*; **nazism** *n* nazismo.

neap tide [niːp-] *n* marea muerta.

near [nɪə*] *a* (*place*) cercano, vecino; (*time*) próximo; (*relation*) estrecho, íntimo // *ad* cerca // *prep* (*also:* ~ **to**) (*space*) cerca de, junto a; (*time*) cerca de, casi // *vt* acercarse a, aproximarse a; ~**by**

[nɪə'baɪ] *a* cercano, próximo // *ad* cerca; **N**~ **East** *n* Cercano Oriente *m*; ~**ly** *ad* casi, por poco; **I** ~**ly fell** por poco me caigo; ~ **miss** *n* tiro cercano; ~**ness** *n* proximidad *f*, cercanía; (*relationship*) intimidad *f*; ~**side** *n* (AUT: *in Britain*) lado izquierdo; (: *in Spain*) lado derecho; ~**-sighted** *a* miope, corto de vista.

neat [niːt] *a* (*place*) bien arreglado *o* cuidado; (*person*) pulcro, esmerado; (*skilful*) diestro; (: *plan*) hábil, ingenioso; (*spirits*) solo.

nebulous ['nɛbjuləs] *a* nebuloso; (*fig*) vago, confuso.

necessarily ['nɛsɪsrɪlɪ] *ad* necesariamente.

necessary ['nɛsɪsrɪ] *a* necesario, preciso; **he did all that was** ~ hizo todo lo necesario.

necessitate [nɪ'sɛsɪteɪt] *vt* necesitar, exigir.

necessity [nɪ'sɛsɪtɪ] *n* (*thing needed*) necesidad *f*, requisito; (*compelling circumstances*) la necesidad; **necessities** *npl* artículos *mpl* de primera necesidad.

neck [nɛk] *n* (ANAT) cuello; (*of animal*) pescuezo // *vi* besuquearse, abrazarse; ~ **and** ~ parejos; **to stick one's** ~ **out** arriesgarse.

necklace ['nɛklɪs] *n* collar *m*.

neckline ['nɛklaɪn] *n* escote *m*.

necktie ['nɛktaɪ] *n* corbata.

née [neɪ] *a*: ~ **Scott** de soltera Scott.

need [niːd] *n* (*lack*) escasez *f*, falta; (*necessity*) necesidad *f*; (*thing needed*) requisito, necesidad *f* // *vt* (*require*) necesitar; **I** ~ **to do it** tengo que *o* debo hacerlo, hay que hacerlo; **you don't** ~ **to go** no hace falta que vayas.

needle ['niːdl] *n* aguja // *vt* (*fig: fam*) picar, fastidiar.

needless ['niːdlɪs] *a* innecesario, inútil; ~ **to say** huelga decir que.

needlework ['niːdlwəːk] *n* (*activity*) costura, labor *f* de aguja.

needy ['niːdɪ] *a* necesitado.

negation [nɪ'geɪʃən] *n* negación *f*.

negative ['nɛgətɪv] *n* (PHOT) negativo; (*answer*) negativa // *a* negativo.

neglect [nɪ'glɛkt] *vt* (*one's duty*) faltar a, no cumplir con; (*child*) descuidar, desatender // *n* (*gen*) negligencia, abandono; (*personal*) dejadez *f*; (*of duty*) incumplimiento.

negligee ['nɛglɪʒeɪ] *n* (*nightdress*) salto de cama; (*housecoat*) bata.

negligence ['nɛglɪdʒəns] *n* negligencia, descuido; **negligent** [-ənt] *a* (*careless*) descuidado, negligente; (*forgetful*) olvidadizo.

negligible ['nɛglɪdʒɪbl] *a* insignificante, despreciable.

negotiable [nɪ'gəuʃɪəbl] *a* (*cheque*) negociable; (*road*) transitable.

negotiate [nɪ'gəuʃɪeɪt] *vi* negociar // *vt* (*treaty*) negociar; (*transaction*) gestionar, tramitar; (*obstacle*) franquear;

negotiation [-'eɪʃən] *n* negociación *f*, gestión *f*; **negotiator** *n* negociador/a *m/f*.
Negress [' niːgrɪs] *n* negra.
Negro ['niːgrəu] *a, n* negro.
neigh [neɪ] *n* relincho // *vi* relinchar.
neighbour, neighbor (*US*) ['neɪbə*] *n* vecino/a; ~**hood** *n* (*place*) vecindad *f*, barrio; (*people*) vecindario; ~**ing** *a* vecino; ~**ly** *a* amistoso, de buen vecino.
neither ['naɪðə*] *a* ni // *conj*: **I didn't move and** ~ **did John** no me he movido, ni Juan tampoco // *pron* ninguno // *ad*: ~ **good nor bad** ni bueno ni malo.
neo... [niːəu] *pref* neo-.
neon ['niːɔn] *n* neón *m*; ~ **light** *n* lámpara de neón.
nephew ['nɛvjuː] *n* sobrino.
nerve [nɔːv] *n* (*ANAT*) nervio; (*courage*) valor *m*; (*impudence*) descaro, frescura; ~-**racking** *a* que crispa los nervios; ~**s** *npl* (*fig*: *anxiety*) nerviosidad *f*, nerviosismo.
nervous ['nɔːvəs] *a* (*anxious, ANAT*) nervioso; (*timid*) tímido, miedoso; ~ **breakdown** *n* crisis *f* nerviosa; ~**ly** *ad* nerviosamente; tímidamente; ~**ness** *n* nerviosidad *f*, nerviosismo; timidez *f*.
nest [nɛst] *n* (*of bird*) nido; (*of wasp*) avispero // *vi* anidar.
nestle ['nɛsl] *vi*: **to** ~ **up to sb** arrimarse a uno.
net [nɛt] *n* (*gen*) red *f*; (*fig*) trampa // *a* (*COMM*) neto, líquido // *vt* coger con red; (*SPORT*) marcar; ~**ball** *n* básquet *m*.
Netherlands ['nɛðələndz] *npl*: **the** ~ los Países Bajos.
nett [nɛt] *a* = **net.**
netting ['nɛtɪŋ] *n* red *f*, redes *fpl*.
nettle ['nɛtl] *n* ortiga.
network ['nɛtwɔːk] *n* red *f*.
neurosis [njuə'rəusɪs] *pl* -**ses** [-siːz] *n* neurosis *f*; **neurotic** [-'rɔtɪk] *a, n* neurótico/a.
neuter ['njuːtə*] *a* (*sexless*) castrado, sin sexo; (*LING*) neutro // *vt* castrar, capar.
neutral ['njuːtrəl] *a* (*person*) neutral; (*colour etc, ELEC*) neutro // *n* (*AUT*) punto muerto; ~**ity** [-'trælɪtɪ] *n* neutralidad *f*.
neutron ['njuːtrɔn] *n* neutrón *m*; ~ **bomb** *n* bomba de neutrones.
never ['nɛvə*] *ad* nunca, jamás; **I** ~ **went** no fui nunca; ~ **in my life** jamás en la vida; ~-**ending** *a* interminable, sin fin; ~**theless** [nɛvəðə'lɛs] *ad* sin embargo, no obstante.
new [njuː] *a* (*brand* ~) nuevo; (*recent*) reciente; (*different*) nuevo, distinto; (*inexperienced*) tierno, nuevo; ~**born** *a* recién nacido; ~**comer** ['njuːkʌmə*] *n* recién venido *o* llegado; ~**ly** *ad* nuevamente, recién; ~**moon** *n* luna nueva; ~**ness** *n* novedad *f*; (*fig*) inexperiencia.
news [njuːz] *n* noticias *fpl*; **a piece of** ~ una noticia; **the** ~ (*RADIO, TV*) las noticias *fpl*, telediario; ~ **agency** *n* agencia de noticias; ~**agent** *n* vendedor/a *m/f* de periódicos; ~**caster** *n* presentador/a *m/f*

de noticias; ~ **flash** *n* noticia de última hora; ~**letter** *n* hoja informativa, boletín *m*; ~**paper** *n* periódico, diario; ~**reel** *n* noticiario; ~ **stand** *n* quiosco *o* puesto de periódicos.
New Year ['njuː'jɪə*] *n* Año Nuevo; ~**'s Day** *n* Día *m* de Año Nuevo; ~**'s Eve** *n* Nochevieja.
New York ['njuː'jɔːk] *n* Nueva York.
New Zealand [njuː'ziːlənd] *n* Nueva Zelanda.
next [nɛkst] *a* (*in space*) próximo, vecino; (*in time*) próximo, siguiente // *ad* (*place*) después; (*time*) después, luego; ~ **time** la próxima vez; ~ **year** el año próximo *o* que viene; ~ **door** *ad* en la casa de al lado // *a* vecino, de al lado; ~-**of-kin** *n* pariente(s) *m(pl)* cercano(s); ~ **to** *prep* junto a, al lado de.
N.H.S. *n abbr of* **National Health Service.**
nib [nɪb] *n* plumilla.
nibble ['nɪbl] *vt* mordisquear, mordiscar; (*ZOOL*) roer.
nice [naɪs] *a* (*likeable*) simpático, majo; (*kind*) amable; (*pleasant*) agradable; (*attractive*) bonito, mono; (*subtle*) fino, preciso; ~-**looking** *a* atractivo, guapo; ~**ly** *ad* amablemente, bien.
niche [niːʃ] *n* nicho.
nick [nɪk] *n* (*wound*) rasguño; (*cut, indentation*) mella, muesca // *vt* (*col*) birlar, robar; **in the** ~ **of time** a última hora.
nickel ['nɪkl] *n* níquel *m*.
nickname ['nɪkneɪm] *n* apodo, mote *m* // *vt* apodar.
nicotine ['nɪkətiːn] *n* nicotina.
niece [niːs] *n* sobrina.
Nigeria [naɪ'dʒɪərɪə] *n* Nigeria; ~**n** *a, n* nigeriano/a.
niggardly ['nɪgədlɪ] *a* (*person*) avaro, tacaño; (*amount*) miserable.
niggling ['nɪglɪŋ] *a* (*trifling*) nimio, insignificante; (*annoying*) molesto.
night [naɪt] *n* (*gen*) noche *f*; (*evening*) tarde *f*; **last** ~ anoche; **the** ~ **before last** anteanoche; **good** ~! ¡buenas noches!; **at** *or* **by** ~ de noche, por la noche; ~**cap** *n* (*drink*) resopón *m*; ~ **club** *n* cabaret *m*; ~**dress** *n* camisón *m*; ~**fall** *n* anochecer *m*; ~**ie** ['naɪtɪ] *n* camisón *m*.
nightingale ['naɪtɪŋgeɪl] *n* ruiseñor *m*.
nightly ['naɪtlɪ] *a* de noche, nocturno // *ad* todas las noches, cada noche.
night: ~**mare** *n* pesadilla; ~ **school** *n* clase(s) *f(pl)* nocturna(s); ~ **shift** *n* turno nocturno *o* de noche; ~-**time** *n* noche *f*; ~ **watchman** *n* sereno.
nil [nɪl] *n* cero, nada.
nimble ['nɪmbl] *a* (*agile*) ágil, ligero; (*skilful*) diestro.
nine [naɪn] *num* nueve; ~**teen** *num* diecinueve, diez y nueve; ~**ty** *num* noventa.
ninth [naɪnθ] *a* noveno.

nip [nɪp] vt (*pinch*) pellizcar; (*bite*) morder // n (*drink*) trago, gota.

nipple ['nɪpl] n (ANAT) pezón m; (*of bottle*) tetilla; (TECH) boquilla, manguito.

nippy ['nɪpɪ] a (*person*) ágil, rápido; (*taste*) picante.

nitrate ['naɪtreɪt] n nitrato.

nitrogen ['naɪtrədʒən] n nitrógeno.

no [nəu] ad no // a ninguno, no ... alguno // n no.

nobility [nəu'bɪlɪtɪ] n nobleza.

noble ['nəubl] a (*person*) noble; (*title*) de nobleza; (*generous*) noble; ~**man** n noble m, aristócrata m.

nobody ['nəubədɪ] pron nadie.

nod [nɔd] vi saludar con la cabeza; (*in agreement*) decir que sí con la cabeza; (*doze*) cabecear // vt inclinar // n inclinación f de cabeza; **to** ~ **off** vi cabecear.

noise [nɔɪz] n ruido; (*din*) escándalo, estrépito; **noisily** ad ruidosamente; **noisy** a (*gen*) ruidoso; (*child*) escandaloso.

nomad ['nəumæd] n nómada m/f; ~**ic** [-'mædɪk] a nómada.

nominal ['nɔmɪnl] a nominal.

nominate ['nɔmɪneɪt] vt (*propose*) proponer; (*appoint*) nombrar; **nomination** [-'neɪʃən] n propuesta; nombramiento.

nominee [nɔmɪ'niː] n candidato/a.

non... [nɔn] pref no, des..., in...; ~-**alcoholic** a no alcohólico; ~-**aligned** a no alineado; ~-**committal** ['nɔnkə'mɪtl] a (*reserved*) reservado; (*uncommitted*) evasivo; ~**conformist** a no conformista; ~**descript** ['nɔndɪskrɪpt] a indeterminado; (*pej*) mediocre.

none [nʌn] pron (*person*) nadie; (*thing*) ninguno, nada // ad de ninguna manera.

nonentity [nɔ'nentɪtɪ] n cero a la izquierda, nulidad f.

nonetheless [nʌnðə'lɛs] ad sin embargo, no obstante.

non: ~-**fiction** n literatura no novelesca; ~**plussed** a perplejo.

nonsense ['nɔnsəns] n tonterías fpl, disparates fpl.

non-stop ['nɔn'stɔp] a continuo; (RAIL) directo // ad sin parar.

noodles ['nuːdlz] npl tallarines mpl.

nook [nuk] n rincón m; ~**s and crannies** escondrijos mpl.

noon [nuːn] n mediodía m.

no-one ['nəuwʌn] pron = **nobody.**

noose [nuːs] n lazo corredizo; (*hangman's*) dogal m.

nor [nɔː*] conj = **neither** // ad see **neither.**

norm [nɔːm] n norma.

normal ['nɔːml] a (*usual*) normal; (*ordinary*) corriente, regular; ~**ly** ad normalmente.

north [nɔːθ] n norte m // a del norte, norteño // ad al o hacia el norte; **N~ America** n América del Norte; ~-**east** n nor(d)este m; ~**ern** ['nɔːðən] a norteño,

del norte; **N~ern Ireland** n Irlanda del Norte; **N~ Pole** n Polo Norte; **N~ Sea** n Mar m del Norte; ~**ward(s)** ['nɔːθwəd(z)] ad hacia el norte; ~-**west** n nor(d)oeste m.

Norway ['nɔːweɪ] n Noruega; **Norwegian** [-'wiːdʒən] a, n noruego/a.

nose [nəuz] n (ANAT) nariz f; (ZOOL) hocico; (*sense of smell*) olfato // vi: **to** ~ **about** curiosear; ~**bleed** n hemorragia nasal; ~-**dive** n (*deliberate*) picado vertical; (*involuntary*) caída de narices; ~**y** a curioso, fisgón(ona).

nostalgia [nɔs'tældʒɪə] n nostalgia; **nostalgic** a nostálgico.

nostril ['nɔstrɪl] n ventana de la nariz; ~**s** npl narices fpl.

nosy ['nəuzɪ] a = **nosey.**

not [nɔt] ad no; ~ **at all** no ... en absoluto; ~ **that...** no es que...; ~ **yet** todavía no; ~ **now** ahora no; **why** ~? ¿por qué no?

notable ['nəutəbl] a notable.

notary ['nəutərɪ] n notario.

notch [nɔtʃ] n muesca, corte m.

note [nəut] n (MUS) nota; (*banknote*) billete m; (*letter*) nota, carta; (*record*) nota, apunte m; (*fame*) importancia, renombre m; (*tone*) tono // vt (*observe*) notar, observar; (*write down*) apuntar, anotar; ~**book** n libreta, cuaderno; ~-**case** n cartera, billetero; ~**d** ['nəutɪd] a célebre, conocido; ~**paper** n papel m para cartas.

nothing ['nʌθɪŋ] n nada; (*zero*) cero; **for** ~ (*free*) gratis, sin pago; (*in vain*) en balde.

notice ['nəutɪs] n (*announcement*) anuncio; (*attention*) atención f, interés m; (*warning*) aviso; (*dismissal*) despido; (*resignation*) dimisión f; (*period of time*) plazo // vt (*observe*) notar, observar; **to take** ~ **of** tomar nota de, prestar atención a; **at short** ~ a corto plazo, con poco anticipación; **until further** ~ hasta nuevo aviso; ~**able** a evidente, obvio; ~**board** n (*Brit*) tablón m de anuncios.

notification [nəutɪfɪ'keɪʃən] n aviso; **notify** ['nəutɪfaɪ] vt avisar, notificar.

notion ['nəuʃən] n noción f, concepto; (*opinion*) opinión f.

notorious [nəu'tɔːrɪəs] a notorio, célebre.

notwithstanding [nɔtwɪθ'stændɪŋ] ad no obstante, sin embargo; ~ **this** a pesar de esto.

nougat ['nuːgɑː] n turrón m.

nought [nɔːt] n cero.

noun [naun] n nombre m, sustantivo.

nourish ['nʌrɪʃ] vt nutrir, alimentar; (*fig*) fomentar, nutrir; ~**ing** a nutritivo, rico; ~**ment** n alimento, sustento.

novel ['nɔvl] n novela // a (*new*) nuevo, original; (*unexpected*) insólito; ~**ist** n novelista m/f; ~**ty** n novedad f.

November [nəu'vembə*] n noviembre m.

novice ['nɔvɪs] n principiante m/f, novato/a; (REL) novicio/a.

now [nau] ad (*at the present time*) ahora; (*these days*) actualmente, hoy día; **right**

~ ahora mismo; ~ **and then,** ~ **and
again** de vez en cuando; **from** ~ **on** de
ahora en adelante; ~**adays** ['nauɔdeɪz] ad
hoy (en) día, actualmente.

nowhere ['nɔuwɛɔ*] ad (direction) a
ninguna parte; (location) en ninguna
parte.

nozzle ['nɔzl] n (gen) boquilla; (TECH)
tobera, inyector m.

nuance ['njuːɑːns] n matiz m.

nuclear ['njuːklɪɔ*] a nuclear.

nucleus ['njuːklɪɔs], pl -**lei** [-lɪaɪ] n núcleo.

nude [njuːd] a, n desnudo/a; **in the** ~
desnudo.

nudge [nʌdʒ] vt dar un codazo a.

nudist ['njuːdɪst] n nudista m/f.

nudity ['njuːdɪtɪ] n desnudez f.

nuisance ['njuːsns] n molestia, fastidio;
(person) pesado, latoso; **what a** ~! ¡qué
lata!

null [nʌl] a: ~ **and void** nulo y sin efecto;
~**ify** ['nʌlɪfaɪ] vt anular, invalidar.

numb [nʌm] a entumecido; (fig) insensible
// vt entumecer, entorpecer.

number ['nʌmbɔ*] n número; (numeral)
número, cifra // vt (pages etc) numerar,
poner número a; (amount to) sumar,
ascender a; **to be** ~**ed among** figurar
entre; **a** ~ **of** varios, algunos; **they were
ten in** ~ eran diez; ~ **plate** n placa de
matrícula.

numbness ['nʌmnɪs] n entumecimiento;
(fig) insensibilidad f.

numeral ['njuːmɔrɔl] n número, cifra.

numerical ['njuːˈmɛrɪkl] a numérico.

numerous ['njuːmɔrɔs] a numeroso,
muchos.

nun [nʌn] n monja, religiosa.

nurse [nɔːs] n enfermero/a; (nanny) niñera
// vt (patient) cuidar, atender; (baby)
criar, amamantar; (fig) guardar; **wet** ~
nodriza.

nursery ['nɔːsɔrɪ] n (institution) guardería
infantil; (room) cuarto de los niños; (for
plants) criadero, semillero; ~ **rhyme** n
canción f infantil; ~ **school** n parvulario,
escuela de párvulos; ~ **slope** n (SKI)
cuesta para principiantes.

nursing ['nɔːsɪŋ] n (profession) profesión f
de enfermera; (care) asistencia, cuidado;
~ **home** n clínica de reposo.

nut [nʌt] n (TECH) tuerca; (BOT) nuez f; ~**s**
a (col) loco; ~**case** n (col) loco/a,
chalado/a; ~**crackers** npl cascanueces
m inv; ~**meg** ['nʌtmɛg] n nuez f moscada.

nutrient ['njuːtrɪɔnt] n nutrimento.

nutrition [njuːˈtrɪʃɔn] n nutrición f,
alimentación f; **nutritious** [-ʃɔs] a
nutritivo, rico.

nutshell ['nʌtʃɛl] n cáscara de nuez; **in a**
~ en resumidas cuentas.

nylon ['naɪlɔn] n nilón m // a de nilón; ~**s**
npl medias fpl (de nilón).

nymph [nɪmf] n ninfa.

O

oaf [ɔuf] n zoquete m.

oak [ɔuk] n roble m // a de roble.

O.A.P. abbr of **old-age pensioner.**

oar [ɔː*] n remo; **oarsman** n remero.

oasis [ɔuˈeɪsɪs], pl -**ses** [-siːz] n oasis m.

oath [ɔuθ] n juramento; (swear word)
palabrota; **on** ~ bajo juramento.

oatmeal ['ɔutmiːl] n harina de avena.

oats [ɔuts] n avena.

obedience [ɔˈbiːdɪɔns] n obediencia; **in** ~
to de acuerdo con; **obedient** [-ɔnt] a
obediente.

obesity [ɔuˈbiːsɪtɪ] n obesidad f.

obey [ɔˈbeɪ] vt obedecer; (instructions,
regulations) cumplir.

obituary [ɔˈbɪtjuɔrɪ] n necrología.

object ['ɔbdʒɪkt] n (gen) objeto; (purpose)
objeto, propósito; (LING) complemento //
vi [ɔbˈdʒɛkt]: **to** ~ **to** (attitude) protestar
contra; (proposal) oponerse a; **I** ~! ¡yo
protesto!; ~**ion** [ɔbˈdʒɛkʃɔn] n protesta; **I
have no** ~**ion to...** no tengo
inconveniente en que...; ~**ionable** [ɔb-
ˈdʒɛkʃɔnɔbl] a (gen) desagradable;
(conduct) censurable; ~**ive** a, n objetivo;
~**ivity** [ɔbdʒɪkˈtɪvɪtɪ] n objetividad f; ~**or**
n objetor/a m/f.

obligation [ɔblɪˈgeɪʃɔn] n obligación f;
(debt) deber m; **without** ~ sin
compromiso.

obligatory [ɔˈblɪgɔtɔrɪ] a obligatorio.

oblige [ɔˈblaɪdʒ] vt (force): **to** ~ **sb to do
sth** forzar o obligar a uno a hacer algo;
(do a favour for) complacer, hacer un
favor a; **I should be** ~**d if...** le
agradecería que...; **obliging** a servicial,
atento.

oblique [ɔˈbliːk] a oblicuo; (allusion)
indirecto.

obliterate [ɔˈblɪtɔreɪt] vt borrar.

oblivion [ɔˈblɪvɪɔn] n olvido; **oblivious**
[-ɪɔs] a: **oblivious of** inconsciente de.

oblong ['ɔblɔŋ] a rectangular // n
rectángulo.

obnoxious [ɔbˈnɔkʃɔs] a odioso, detestable;
(smell) nauseabundo.

oboe ['ɔubɔu] n oboe m.

obscene [ɔbˈsiːn] a obsceno; **obscenity**
[-ˈsɛnɪtɪ] n obscenidad f.

obscure [ɔbˈskjuɔ*] a oscuro // vt
oscurecer; (hide: sun) esconder; **obscurity** n oscuridad f.

obsequious [ɔbˈsiːkwɪɔs] a obsequioso.

observance [ɔbˈzɔːvns] n observancia,
cumplimiento; (ritual) práctica.

observant [ɔbˈzɔːvnt] a observador(a).

observation [ɔbzɔˈveɪʃɔn] n observación f;
(by police etc) vigilancia; (MED) examen m.

observatory [ɔbˈzɔːvɔtrɪ] n observatorio.

observe [ɔbˈzɔːv] vt (gen) observar; (rule)
cumplir; **observer** n observador/a m/f.

obsess [ɔbˈsɛs] vt obsesionar; ~**ion** [ɔb-

'sɛʃən] *n* obsesión *f*, idea fija; ~**ive** *a* obsesivo, obsesionante.

obsolescence [ɔbsə'lɛsns] *n* caída en desuso; **obsolete** ['ɔbsəli:t] *a* (que está) en desuso.

obstacle ['ɔbstəkl] *n* obstáculo; (*nuisance*) estorbo; ~ **race** *n* carrera de obstáculos.

obstetrician [ɔbstə'trɪʃən] *n* obstétrico; **obstetrics** [-'stɛtrɪks] *n* obstetricia.

obstinate ['ɔbstɪnɪt] *a* terco, porfiado; (*determined*) tenaz.

obstruct [əb'strʌkt] *vt* (*block*) obstruir; (*hinder*) estorbar, obstaculizar; ~**ion** [əb-'strʌkʃən] *n* obstrucción *f*; estorbo, obstáculo.

obtain [əb'teɪn] *vt* (*get*) obtener; (*achieve*) conseguir; ~**able** *a* asequible.

obtrusive [əb'truːsɪv] *a* (*person*) importuno, entrometido; (*building etc*) demasiado visible.

obvious ['ɔbvɪəs] *a* (*clear*) obvio, evidente; (*unsubtle*) poco sutil; ~**ly** *ad* evidentemente, naturalmente.

occasion [ə'keɪʒən] *n* (*gen*) oportunidad *f*, ocasión *f*; (*reason*) motivo; (*time*) ocasión *f*, vez *f*; (*event*) acontecimiento // *vt* ocasionar, causar; ~**ally** *ad* de vez en cuando.

occult [ɔ'kʌlt] *a* (*gen*) oculto.

occupant ['ɔkjupənt] *n* (*of house*) inquilino/a; (*of car*) ocupante *m/f*.

occupation [ɔkju'peɪʃən] *n* (*of house*) tenencia; (*job*) trabajo; (: *calling*) oficio; **unfit for** ~ (*house*) inhabitable; ~**al hazard** *n* riesgo profesional.

occupier ['ɔkjupaɪə*] *n* inquilino/a.

occupy ['ɔkjupaɪ] *vt* (*gen*) ocupar; (*house*) habitar, vivir en; (*time*) emplear, pasar; (*attention*) entretener; **to** ~ **o.s. with** *or* **by doing** (*as job*) dedicarse a hacer; (*to pass time*) pasar el tiempo haciendo.

occur [ə'kə:*] *vi* pasar, suceder; **to** ~ **to sb** ocurrírsele a uno; **it** ~**s to me that...** se me ocurre que...; ~**rence** *n* (*event*) acontecimiento; (*existence*) existencia.

ocean ['əuʃən] *n* océano; ~**-going** *a* de alta mar; ~ **liner** *n* transatlántico.

o'clock [ə'klɔk] *ad*: **it is 5** ~ son las 5.

octagonal [ɔk'tægənl] *a* octagonal.

octane ['ɔkteɪn] *n* octano.

octave ['ɔktɪv] *n* octava.

October [ɔk'təubə*] *n* octubre *m*.

octopus ['ɔktəpəs] *n* pulpo.

odd [ɔd] *a* (*strange*) extraño, raro; (*number*) impar; (*left over*) sobrante, suelto; **60-**~ 60 y pico; **at** ~ **times** de vez en cuando; **to be the** ~ **one out** estar de más; ~**ity** *n* rareza; (*person*) excéntrico; ~**-job man** *n* hombre *m* que hace de todo; ~ **jobs** *npl* bricolaje *m*; ~**ly** *ad* curiosamente, extrañamente; ~**ments** *npl* (*COMM*) retales *mpl*; ~**s** *npl* (*in betting*) puntos *mpl* de ventaja; **it makes no** ~**s** no importa, lo mismo da; **at** ~**s** reñidos(as).

ode [əud] *n* oda.

odious ['əudɪəs] *a* odioso.

odour, odor (*US*) ['əudə*] *n* olor *m*; (*perfume*) perfume *m*; ~**less** *a* inodoro.

of [ɔv, əv] *prep* de; **a friend** ~ **ours** un amigo nuestro; **3** ~ **them** 3 de ellos; **the 5th** ~ **July** el 5 de julio; **a boy** ~ **10** un niño de 10 años; **made** ~ **wood** hecho de madera.

off [ɔf] *a, ad* (*engine*) desconectado; (*light*) apagado; (*tap*) cerrado; (*food: bad*) pasado, malo; (*milk*) cortado; (*cancelled*) anulado // *prep* de; **to be** ~ (*to leave*) irse, marcharse; **to be 5 km** ~ estar a 5 kilómetros; **a day** ~ un día libre *o* sin trabajar; **to have an** ~ **day** tener un día malo; **he had his coat** ~ se había quitado el abrigo; **10%** ~ (*COMM*) (con el) 10% de descuento; **5 km** ~ **(the road)** a 5 km (de la carretera); ~ **the coast** frente a la costa; **on the** ~ **chance** por si acaso.

offal ['ɔfl] *n* (*CULIN*) menudencias *fpl*.

off-colour ['ɔf'kʌlə*] *a* (*ill*) indispuesto.

offence, offense (*US*) [ə'fɛns] *n* (*crime*) delito; (*insult*) ofensa; **to take** ~ **at** ofenderse por.

offend [ə'fɛnd] *vt* (*person*) ofender; ~**er** *n* delincuente *m/f*; (*against regulations*) infractor/a *m/f*.

offensive [ə'fɛnsɪv] *a* ofensivo; (*smell etc*) repugnante // *n* (*MIL*) ofensiva.

offer ['ɔfə*] *n* (*gen*) oferta, ofrecimiento; (*proposal*) propuesta // *vt* ofrecer; (*opportunity*) facilitar; **'on** ~' (*COMM*) 'en oferta'; ~**ing** *n* ofrenda; ~**tory** *n* (*REL*) ofertorio.

offhand [ɔf'hænd] *a* informal // *ad* de improviso.

office ['ɔfɪs] *n* (*place*) oficina; (*room*) despacho; (*position*) carga, oficio; **to take** ~ entrar en funciones; ~ **block** *n* bloque *m* de oficinas; ~ **boy** *n* mozo (de oficina); **officer** *n* (*MIL etc*) oficial *m*; (*of organization*) director *m*; (*also*: **police officer**) agente *m/f* de policía; ~ **worker** *n* oficinista *m/f*.

official [ə'fɪʃl] *a* (*authorized*) oficial, autorizado // *n* funcionario, oficial *m*; ~**dom** *n* burocracia.

officious [ə'fɪʃəs] *a* oficioso.

offing ['ɔfɪŋ] *n*: **in the** ~ (*fig*) en perspectiva.

off: ~**-licence** *n* (*Brit*: *shop*) bodega, tienda de vinos y bebidas alcohólicas; ~**-peak** *a* de temporada de poca actividad; ~**-putting** *a* que desanima; ~**-season** *a, ad* fuera de temporada.

offset ['ɔfsɛt] (*irg*: *like* **set**) *vt* (*counteract*) contrarrestar, compensar // *n* (*also*: ~ **printing**) offset *m*.

offshore [ɔf'ɔ:*] *a* (que está) cerca de la costa.

offside ['ɔf'saɪd] *a* (*SPORT*) fuera de juego.

offspring ['ɔfsprɪŋ] *n* descendencia, descendientes *mpl or fpl*.

off: ~**-stage** *ad* entre bastidores; ~**-the-peg** *ad* confeccionado; ~**-white** *a* blanco grisáceo.

often ['ɔfn] *ad* a menudo, con frecuencia.

ogle ['ǝugl] *vt* echar miradas a.

oil [ɔil] *n* aceite *m*; (*petroleum*) petróleo // *vt* (*machine*) engrasar; ~**can** *n* lata de aceite; ~**field** *n* campo petrolífero; ~**-fired** *a* que quema aceite combustible; ~ **painting** *n* pintura de óleo; ~ **refinery** *n* refinería de petróleo; ~ **rig** *n* torre *f* de perforación; ~**skins** *npl* impermeables *mpl* de hule, chubasquero *sg*; ~ **tanker** *n* petrolero; ~ **well** *n* pozo (de petróleo); ~**y** *a* aceitoso; (*food*) grasiento.

ointment ['ɔintmǝnt] *n* ungüento.

O.K., okay ['ǝu'kei] *excl* O.K., ¡está bien!, ¡vale! // *a* bien // *vt* dar el visto bueno a.

old [ǝuld] *a* viejo; (*former*) antiguo; **how ~ are you?** ¿cuántos años tienes?, ¿qué edad tienes?; **he's 10 years ~** tiene 10 años; ~**er brother** hermano mayor; ~ **age** *n* la vejez; ~**-age pensioner (O.A.P.)** *n* jubilado/a; ~**-fashioned** *a* anticuado, pasado de moda.

olive ['ɔliv] *n* (*fruit*) aceituna; (*tree*) olivo // *a* (*also:* ~**-green**) verde oliva; ~ **oil** *n* aceite *m* de oliva.

Olympic [ǝu'limpik] *a* olímpico; **the ~ Games, the** ~**s** los Juegos Olímpicos.

omelet(te) ['ɔmlit] *n* tortilla (de huevo).

omen ['ǝumǝn] *n* presagio.

ominous ['ɔminǝs] *a* de mal agüero, amenazador(a).

omission [ǝu'miʃǝn] *n* omisión *f*; (*error*) descuido.

omit [ǝu'mit] *vt* omitir; (*by mistake*) olvidar, descuidar.

on [ɔn] *prep* en, sobre // *ad* (*machine*) conectado; (*light, radio*) encendido; (*tap*) abierto; **is the meeting still ~?** ¿todavía hay reunión?; **when is this film ~?** ¿cuándo van a poner esta película?; ~ **the wall** en la pared, colgado de la pared; ~ **television** en la televisión; ~ **horseback** a caballo; ~ **seeing this** al ver esto; ~ **arrival** al llegar; ~ **the left** a la izquierda; ~ **Friday** el viernes; **a week ~ Friday** el viernes en ocho días; **to have one's coat ~** tener el abrigo puesto; **to go ~** seguir adelante; **it's not ~!** ¡eso no se hace!

once [wʌns] *ad* una vez; (*formerly*) antiguamente // *conj* una vez que; **at ~** en seguida, inmediatamente; (*simultaneously*) a la vez; ~ **a week** una vez por semana; ~ **more** otra vez; ~ **and for all** de una vez por todas; ~ **upon a time** érase una vez.

oncoming ['ɔnkʌmiŋ] *a* (*traffic*) que viene de frente.

one [wʌn] *det, num* un, uno, una // *pron* uno; (*impersonal*) se // *a* (*sole*) único; (*same*) mismo; **this ~** éste/a; **that ~** ése/a, aquél/aquella; ~ **by ~** uno por uno; ~ **never knows** nunca se sabe; ~ **another** el uno al otro; ~**-man** *a* (*business*) individual; ~**-man band** *n* un hombre-orquesta; ~**self** *pron* uno mismo; (*after*

prep, also emphatic) sí (mismo/a); **'~-way'** 'dirección única'.

ongoing ['ɔngǝuiŋ] *a* continuo.

onion ['ʌnjǝn] *n* cebolla.

onlooker ['ɔnlukǝ*] *n* espectador/a *m/f*.

only ['ǝunli] *ad* solamente, sólo // *a* único, solo // *conj* solamente que, pero; **an ~ child** un hijo único; **not ~ ... but also...** no sólo ... sino también... .

onset ['ɔnsɛt] *n* (*beginning*) comienzo; (*attack*) ataque *m*.

onslaught ['ɔnslɔ:t] *n* ataque *m*, embestida.

onto ['ɔntu] *prep* = **on to**.

onus ['ǝunǝs] *n* responsabilidad *f*.

onward(s) ['ɔnwǝd(z)] *ad* (*move*) (hacia) adelante; **from this time ~** de ahora en adelante.

onyx ['ɔniks] *n* ónice *m*, onyx *m*.

ooze [u:z] *vi* rezumar.

opal ['ǝupl] *n* ópalo.

opaque [ǝu'peik] *a* opaco.

open ['ǝupn] *a* abierto; (*car*) descubierto; (*road, view*) despejado; (*meeting*) público; (*admiration*) manifiesto // *vt* abrir // *vi* (*flower, eyes, door, debate*) abrirse; (*book etc: commence*) comenzar; **to ~ on to** *vt fus* (*subj: room, door*) dar a; **to ~ up** *vt* abrir; (*blocked road*) despejar // *vi* abrirse, empezar; **in the ~ (air)** al aire libre; ~**ing** *n* abertura, comienzo; (*opportunity*) oportunidad *f*; (*job*) puesto vacante, vacante *f*; ~**ly** *ad* abiertamente; ~**-minded** *a* imparcial; ~**-necked** *a* sin corbata.

opera ['ɔpǝrǝ] *n* ópera; ~ **glasses** *npl* gemelos *mpl*; ~ **house** *n* teatro de la ópera.

operate ['ɔpǝreit] *vt* (*machine*) hacer funcionar; (*company*) dirigir // *vi* funcionar; (*drug*) hacer efecto; **to ~ on sb** (*MED*) operar a uno.

operatic [ɔpǝ'rætik] *a* de ópera.

operating ['ɔpǝreitiŋ]: ~ **table** *n* mesa de operaciones; ~ **theatre** *n* sala de operaciones.

operation [ɔpǝ'reiʃǝn] *n* (*gen*) operación *f*; (*of machine*) funcionamiento; **to be in ~** estar en funcionamiento *o* funcionando; ~**al** *a* operacional, en buen estado.

operative ['ɔpǝrǝtiv] *a* (*measure*) en vigor.

operator ['ɔpǝreitǝ*] *n* (*of machine*) maquinista *m/f*, operario; (*TEL*) operador/a *m/f*, telefonista *m/f*.

operetta [ɔpǝ'retǝ] *n* opereta; (*in Spain*) zarzuela.

ophthalmic [ɔf'θælmik] *a* oftálmico.

opinion [ǝ'piniǝn] *n* (*gen*) opinión *f*; (*point of view*) parecer *m*, juicio; ~**ated** *a* testarudo; ~ **poll** *n* encuesta, sondeo.

opium ['ǝupiǝm] *n* opio.

opponent [ǝ'pǝunǝnt] *n* adversario/a, contrincante *m/f*.

opportune ['ɔpǝtju:n] *a* oportuno; **opportunist** [-'tju:nist] *a* oportunista *m/f*.

opportunity [ɔpǝ'tju:niti] *n* oportunidad *f*.

oppose [ə'pəuz] *vt* oponerse a; **to be** ~**d to sth** oponerse a algo, resistirse a aceptar algo; **opposing** *a (side)* opuesto, contrario.

opposite ['ɔpəzɪt] *a* opuesto; *(house etc)* de enfrente // *ad* en frente // *prep* en frente de, frente a // *n* lo contrario.

opposition [ɔpə'zɪʃən] *n* oposición *f.*

oppress [ə'prɛs] *vt* oprimir; ~**ion** [ə'prɛʃən] *n* opresión *f*; ~**ive** *a* opresivo.

opt [ɔpt] *vi*: **to** ~ **for** elegir; **to** ~ **to do** optar por hacer; **to** ~ **out of** optar por no hacer.

optical ['ɔptɪkl] *a* óptico.

optician [ɔp'tɪʃən] *n* óptico.

optimism ['ɔptɪmɪzəm] *n* optimismo.

optimist ['ɔptɪmɪst] *n* optimista *m/f*; ~**ic** [-'mɪstɪk] *a* optimista.

optimum ['ɔptɪməm] *a* óptimo.

option ['ɔpʃən] *n* opción *f*; **to keep one's** ~**s open** *(fig)* mantener las opciones abiertas; ~**al** *a* facultativo, discrecional.

opulent ['ɔpjulənt] *a* opulento.

or [ɔ:*] *conj* o; *(before o, ho)* u; *(with negative)*: **he hasn't seen** ~ **heard anything** no ha visto ni oído nada; ~ **else** si no.

oracle ['ɔrəkl] *n* oráculo.

oral ['ɔ:rəl] *a* oral // *n* examen *m* oral.

orange ['ɔrɪndʒ] *n (fruit)* naranja // *a* color naranja.

oration [ɔ:'reɪʃən] *n* oración *f*; **orator** ['ɔrətə*] *n* orador/a *m/f.*

orbit ['ɔ:bɪt] *n* órbita // *vt, vi* orbitar.

orchard ['ɔ:tʃəd] *n* huerto.

orchestra ['ɔ:kɪstrə] *n* orquesta; **orchestral** [-'kɛstrəl] *a* orquestal.

orchid ['ɔ:kɪd] *n* orquídea.

ordain [ɔ:'deɪn] *vt (REL)* ordenar, decretar; *(decide)* mandar.

ordeal [ɔ:'di:l] *n* experiencia penosa.

order ['ɔ:də*] *n* orden *m*; *(command)* orden *f*; *(type, kind)* clase *f*; *(state)* estado; *(COMM)* pedido, encargo // *vt (also:* **put in** ~*)* arreglar, poner en orden; *(COMM)* encargar, pedir; *(command)* mandar, ordenar; **in** ~ *(of document)* en regla; **in** ~ **to do** para hacer; **to** ~ **sb to do sth** mandar a uno hacer algo; ~**ly** *n (MIL)* ordenanza *m*; *(MED)* enfermero (auxiliar) // *a (room)* en orden, ordenado; *(person)* ordenado.

ordinary ['ɔ:dnrɪ] *a* corriente, normal; *(pej)* ordinario, vulgar; **out of the** ~ fuera de lo común.

ordnance ['ɔ:dnəns] *n (MIL: unit)* artillería; **O**~ **Survey** *n servicio oficial de topografía y cartografía.*

ore [ɔ:*] *n* mineral *m.*

organ ['ɔ:gən] *n* órgano; ~**ic** [ɔ:'gænɪk] *a* orgánico.

organism ['ɔ:gənɪzəm] *n* organismo.

organist ['ɔ:gənɪst] *n* organista *m/f.*

organization [ɔ:gənaɪ'zeɪʃən] *n* organización *f*; **organize** ['ɔ:gənaɪz] *vt* organizar; **organizer** ['ɔ:gənaɪzə*] *n* organizador/a *m/f.*

orgasm ['ɔ:gæzəm] *n* orgasmo.

orgy ['ɔ:dʒɪ] *n* orgía.

Orient ['ɔ:rɪənt] *n* Oriente *m*; **oriental** [-'ɛntl] *a* oriental.

orientate ['ɔ:rɪənteɪt] *vt* orientar.

origin ['ɔrɪdʒɪn] *n* origen *m*; *(point of departure)* procedencia.

original [ə'rɪdʒɪnl] *a* original; *(first)* primero; *(earlier)* primitivo // *n* original *m*; ~**ity** [-'nælɪtɪ] *n* originalidad *f*; ~**ly** *ad (at first)* al principio; *(with originality)* con originalidad.

originate [ə'rɪdʒɪneɪt] *vi*: **to** ~ **from** *or* **in** surgir de, tener su origen en.

ornament ['ɔ:nəmənt] *n* adorno; *(trinket)* chuchería; ~**al** [-'mɛntl] *a* decorativo, de adorno.

ornate [ɔ:'neɪt] *a* muy ornado, vistoso.

ornithologist [ɔ:nɪ'θɔlədʒɪst] *n* ornitólogo; **ornithology** [-dʒɪ] *n* ornitología.

orphan ['ɔ:fn] *n* huérfano // *vt*: **to be** ~**ed** quedar huérfano; ~**age** *n* orfelinato.

orthodox ['ɔ:θədɔks] *a* ortodoxo; ~**y** *n* ortodoxia.

orthopaedic, orthopedic *(US)* [ɔ:θə'pi:dɪk] *a* ortopédico; ~**s** *n* ortopedia.

oscillate ['ɔsɪleɪt] *vi* oscilar; *(person)* vacilar.

ostensibly [ɔs'tɛnsɪblɪ] *ad* aparentemente.

ostentatious [ɔstɛn'teɪʃəs] *a* pretencioso, aparatoso; *(person)* ostentativo.

osteopath ['ɔstɪəpæθ] *n* osteópata *m/f.*

ostracize ['ɔstrəsaɪz] *vt* condenar al ostracismo.

ostrich ['ɔstrɪtʃ] *n* avestruz *m.*

other ['ʌðə*] *a* otro; ~ **than** *(in another way)* de otra manera que; *(apart from)* aparte de; ~**wise** *ad, conj* de otra manera; *(if not)* si no.

otter ['ɔtə*] *n* nutria.

ought [ɔ:t], *pt* **ought** *auxiliary vb*: **I** ~ **to do it** debería hacerlo; **this** ~ **to have been corrected** esto debiera de haberse corregido; **he** ~ **to win** *(probability)* debe *o* debiera ganar.

ounce [auns] *n* onza *(28.35g).*

our ['auə*] *a* nuestro; ~**s** *pron* (el) nuestro/(la) nuestra *etc*; ~**selves** *pron pl (reflexive, after prep)* nosotros; *(emphatic)* nosotros mismos.

oust [aust] *vt* desalojar.

out [aut] *ad* fuera, afuera; *(not at home)* fuera (de casa); *(light, fire)* apagado; ~ **there** allí, allí fuera; **he's** ~ *(absent)* no está, ha salido; **to be** ~ **in one's calculations** equivocarse (en sus cálculos); **to run** ~ salir corriendo; ~ **loud** en alta voz; ~ **of** *(outside)* fuera de; *(because of: anger etc)* por; ~ **of petrol** sin gasolina; **"**~ **of order"** "no funciona"; ~**-of-the-way** *(fig)* insólito.

outback ['autbæk] *n* interior *m.*

outboard ['autbɔ:d] *a*: ~ **motor** motor *m* de fuera de borda.

outbreak ['autbreɪk] *n (of war)* comienzo;

(*of disease*) epidemia; (*of violence etc*) arranque *m.*

outburst ['autbɔːst] *n* explosión *f,* arranque *m.*

outcast ['autkɑːst] *n* paria *m/f.*

outcome ['autkʌm] *n* resultado.

outcry ['autkraɪ] *n* protesta ruidosa.

outdated [aut'deɪtɪd] *a* anticuado, fuera de moda.

outdo [aut'duː] (*irg: like do*) *vt* exceder.

outdoor [aut'dɔː*] *a,* ~**s** *ad* al aire libre.

outer ['autə*] *a* exterior, externo; ~ **space** *n* el espacio.

outfit ['autfɪt] *n* equipo; (*clothes*) traje *m;* ~**ter's** *n* camisería.

outgoing ['autgəuɪŋ] *a* (*character*) extrovertido; ~**s** *npl* gastos *mpl.*

outgrow [aut'grəu] (*irg: like grow*) *vt:* **he has** ~**n his clothes** su ropa le queda pequeña ya.

outing ['autɪŋ] *n* excursión *f,* paseo.

outlandish [aut'lændɪʃ] *a* estrafalario.

outlaw ['autlɔː] *n* proscrito // *vt* (*person*) declarar fuera de la ley; (*practice*) declarar ilegal.

outlay ['autleɪ] *n* inversión *f.*

outlet ['autlɛt] *n* salida; (*of pipe*) desagüe *m;* (*for emotion*) desahogo; (*also:* **retail** ~) lugar *m* de venta.

outline ['autlaɪn] *n* (*shape*) contorno, perfil *m;* (*of plan*) trazado; (*sketch*) esbozo, idea general.

outlive [aut'lɪv] *vt* sobrevivir.

outlook ['autluk] *n* perspectiva; (*opinion*) punto de vista.

outlying ['autlaɪŋ] *a* remoto, aislado.

outmoded [aut'məudɪd] *a* anticuado, pasado de moda.

outnumber [aut'nʌmbə*] *vt* exceder en número.

outpatient ['autpeɪʃənt] *n* paciente *m/f* de consulta externa.

outpost ['autpəust] *n* puesto avanzado.

output ['autput] *n* (*volumen m de*) producción *f,* rendimiento.

outrage ['autreɪdʒ] *n* (*scandal*) escándalo; (*atrocity*) atrocidad *f* // *vt* ultrajar; ~**ous** [-'reɪdʒəs] *a* monstruoso.

outright [aut'raɪt] *ad* completamente // *a* ['autraɪt] completo.

outset ['autsɛt] *n* principio.

outside [aut'saɪd] *n* exterior *m;* (*surface*) superficie *f;* (*aspect*) aspecto // *a* exterior, externo // *ad* fuera // *prep* fuera de; (*beyond*) más allá de; **at the** ~ (*fig*) a lo sumo; ~ **lane** *n* (*AUT. in Britain*) carril *m* de la derecha; ~-**left** *n* (*FOOTBALL*) extremo izquierdo; **outsider** *n* (*stranger*) extraño, forastero.

outsize ['autsaɪz] *a* (*clothes*) de talla grande.

outskirts ['autskɜːts] *npl* alrededores *mpl,* afueras *fpl.*

outspoken [aut'spəukən] *a* muy franco.

outstanding [aut'stændɪŋ] *a* excepcional, destacado; (*unfinished*) pendiente.

outstay [aut'steɪ] *vt:* **to** ~ **one's welcome** quedarse más tiempo de lo indicado.

outstretched [aut'strɛtʃt] *a* (*hand*) extendido.

outward ['autwəd] *a* (*sign, appearances*) externo; (*journey*) de ida; ~**ly** *ad* por fuera.

outweigh [aut'weɪ] *vt* pesar más que.

outwit [aut'wɪt] *vt* ser más listo que, burlar.

oval ['əuvl] *a* ovalado // *n* óvalo.

ovary ['əuvərɪ] *n* ovario.

ovation [əu'veɪʃən] *n* ovación *f.*

oven ['ʌvn] *n* horno; ~**proof** *a* refractario.

over ['əuvə*] *ad* encima, por encima // *a* (*or ad*) (*finished*) terminado // *prep* (por) encima de; (*above*) sobre; (*on the other side of*) al otro lado de; (*more than*) más de; (*during*) durante; ~ **here** (por) aquí; ~ **there** (por) allí *o* allá; **all** ~ (*everywhere*) por todas partes; ~ **and** ~ (**again**) una y otra vez; ~ **and above** más de; **to ask sb** ~ invitar a uno; **to bend** ~ inclinarse.

over... [əuvə*] *pref* sobre..., super...; ~**abundant** *a* superabundante.

overall ['əuvərɔːl] *a* (*length*) total; (*study*) de conjunto // *ad* [əuvər'ɔːl] en conjunto; ~**s** *npl* mono *sg o* bata *sg* (de trabajo).

overbalance [əuvə'bæləns] *vi* perder el equilibrio.

overbearing [əuvə'bɛərɪŋ] *a* autoritario, imperioso.

overboard ['əuvəbɔːd] *ad* (*NAUT*) por la borda; **man** ~! ¡hombre al agua!

overcast ['əuvəkɑːst] *a* encapotado.

overcharge [əuvə'tʃɑːdʒ] *vt:* **to** ~ **sb** cobrar un precio excesivo a uno.

overcoat ['əuvəkəut] *n* abrigo, sobretodo.

overcome [əuvə'kʌm] (*irg: like come*) *vt* (*gen*) vencer; (*difficulty*) superar.

overcrowded [əuvə'kraudɪd] *a* atestado de gente; (*country*) superpoblado.

overdo [əuvə'duː] (*irg: like do*) *vt* exagerar; (*overcook*) cocer demasiado.

overdose ['əuvədəus] *n* dosis *f* excesiva.

overdraft ['əuvədrɑːft] *n* saldo deudor.

overdrawn [əuvə'drɔːn] *a* (*account*) en descubierto.

overdue [əuvə'djuː] *a* retrasado; (*recognition*) tardío.

overestimate [əuvər'ɛstɪmeɪt] *vt* sobreestimar.

overexcited [əuvərɪk'saɪtɪd] *a* sobreexcitado.

overexpose [əuvərɪk'spəuz] *vt* (*PHOT*) sobreexponer.

overflow [əuvə'fləu] *vi* desbordarse // *n* ['əuvəfləu] (*excess*) exceso; (*of river*) desbordamiento; (*also:* ~ **pipe**) (cañería de) desagüe *m.*

overgrown [əuvə'grəun] *a* (*garden*) cubierto de hierba.

overhaul [əuvə'hɔːl] *vt* revisar, repasar // *n* ['əuvəhɔːl] revisión *f.*

overhead [əuvə'hɛd] *ad* por lo alto // *a*

['ɔuvəhɛd] de arriba; (*railway*) elevado, aéreo; ~s *npl* gastos *mpl* generales.

overhear [əuvə'hɪə*] (*irg: like* **hear**) *vt* oír por casualidad.

overjoyed [əuvə'dʒɔɪd] *a* encantado, lleno de alegría.

overland ['əuvəlænd] *a, ad* por tierra.

overlap [əuvə'læp] *vi* traslaparse // *n* ['əuvəlæp] traslapo.

overleaf [əuvə'li:f] *ad* al dorso.

overload [əuvə'ləud] *vt* sobrecargar.

overlook [əuvə'luk] *vt* (*have view on*) dar a, tener vistas a; (*miss: by mistake*) pasar por alto; (: *deliberately*) no hacerse caso de; (*forgive*) perdonar.

overnight [əuvə'naɪt] *ad* durante la noche; (*fig*) de la noche a la mañana // *a* de noche; **to stay** ~ pasar la noche.

overpass ['əuvəpɑːs] *n* paso superior.

overpower [əuvə'pauə*] *vt* dominar; ~**ing** *a* (*heat, stench*) abrumador(a).

overrate [əuvə'reɪt] *vt* sobreestimar.

override [əuvə'raɪd] (*irg: like* **ride**) *vt* (*order, objection*) no hacer caso de; **overriding** *a* predominante.

overrule [əuvə'ru:l] *vt* (*decision*) anular; (*claim*) denegar.

overseas [əuvə'si:z] *ad* en ultramar; (*abroad*) en el extranjero // *a* (*trade*) exterior; (*visitor*) extranjero.

overseer ['əuvəsɪə*] *n* (*in factory*) superintendente *m/f*; (*foreman*) capataz *m*.

overshadow [əuvə'ʃædəu] *vt* (*fig*) eclipsar.

overshoot [əuvə'ʃu:t] (*irg: like* **shoot**) *vt* excederse.

oversight ['əuvəsaɪt] *n* descuido.

oversleep [əuvə'sli:p] (*irg: like* **sleep**) *vi* despertarse (muy) tarde.

overspend [əuvə'spɛnd] (*irg: like* **spend**) *vi* gastar demasiado.

overspill ['əuvəspɪl] *n* exceso de población.

overstate [əuvə'steɪt] *vt* exagerar; ~**ment** *n* exageración *f*.

overt [əu'və:t] *a* abierto.

overtake [əuvə'teɪk] (*irg: like* **take**) *vt* sobrepasar; (AUT) adelantar; **overtaking** *n* (AUT) adelantamiento.

overthrow [əuvə'θrəu] (*irg: like* **throw**) *vt* (*government*) derrocar.

overtime ['əuvətaɪm] *n* horas *fpl* extraordinarias.

overtone ['əuvətəun] *n* (*fig*) sugestión *f*, alusión *f*.

overture ['əuvətʃuə*] *n* (MUS) obertura; (*fig*) propuesta.

overturn [əuvə'tə:n] *vt, vi* volcar.

overweight [əuvə'weɪt] *a* demasiado gordo *o* pesado.

overwhelm [əuvə'wɛlm] *vt* aplastar; ~**ing** *a* (*victory, defeat*) arrollador(a); (*desire*) irresistible.

overwork [əuvə'wə:k] *n* trabajo excesivo // *vt* hacer trabajar demasiado // *vi* trabajar demasiado.

overwrought [əuvə'rɔ:t] *a* sobreexcitado.

owe [əu] *vt* deber; **to** ~ **sb sth, to** ~ **sth to sb** deber algo a uno; **owing to** *prep* debido a, por causa de.

owl [aul] *n* búho, lechuza.

own [əun] *vt* tener, poseer // *a* propio; **a room of my** ~ una habitación propia; **to get one's** ~ **back** tomar revancha; **on one's** ~ solo, a solas; **to** ~ **up** *vi* confesar; ~**er** *n* dueño; ~**ership** *n* posesión *f*.

ox [ɔks], *pl* ~**en** ['ɔksn] *n* buey *m*.

oxide ['ɔksaɪd] *n* óxido.

oxtail ['ɔksteɪl] *n*: ~ **soup** sopa de rabo de buey.

oxygen ['ɔksɪdʒən] *n* oxígeno; ~ **mask/tent** máscara/tienda de oxígeno.

oyster ['ɔɪstə*] *n* ostra.

oz. *abbr of* **ounce(s)**.

ozone ['əuzəun] *n* ozono.

P

p [pi:] *abbr of* **penny, pence**.

p.a. *abbr of* **per annum**.

pa [pɑ:] *n* (*col*) papá *m*.

pace [peɪs] *n* paso; (*rhythm*) ritmo // *vi*: **to** ~ **up and down** pasarse de un lado a otro; **to keep** ~ **with** llevar el mismo paso que; (*events*) mantenerse a la altura de *o* al corriente de; ~**maker** *n* (MED) regulador *m* cardíaco, marcapasos *m inv*.

pacific [pə'sɪfɪk] *a* pacífico // *n*: **the P**~ **(Ocean)** el (Océano) Pacífico.

pacifist ['pæsɪfɪst] *n* pacifista *m/f*.

pacify ['pæsɪfaɪ] *vt* (*soothe*) apaciguar; (*country*) pacificar.

pack [pæk] *n* (*gen*) paquete *m*; (*of hounds*) jauría; (*of thieves etc*) manada, bando; (*of cards*) baraja; (*bundle*) fardo; (*back* ~) mochila // *vt* (*wrap*) empaquetar; (*fill*) llenar; (*in suitcase etc*) meter *o* poner (en maleta); (*cram*) llenar, atestar; (*fig: meeting etc*) llenar de partidarios; **to** ~ **sb off** despachar a uno; ~ **it in!** (*col*) ¡déjalo!; **to** ~ **one's case** hacerse la maleta.

package ['pækɪdʒ] *n* paquete *m*; (*bulky*) bulto; (*also*: ~ **deal**) acuerdo global; ~ **tour** *n* viaje *m* todo incluido.

packet ['pækɪt] *n* paquete *m*; (NAUT) paquebote *m*.

packing ['pækɪŋ] *n* embalaje *m*; (*external*) envase *m*; (*internal*) relleno; ~ **case** *n* cajón *m* de embalaje.

pact [pækt] *n* pacto.

pad [pæd] *n* (*of paper*) bloc *m*; (*cushion*) cojinete *m*; (*launching* ~) plataforma (de lanzamiento); (*foot*) pata; (*col: flat*) casa // *vi* andar (sin hacer ruido); ~**ding** *n* relleno; (*fig*) paja.

paddle ['pædl] *n* (*oar*) canalete *m* // *vt* impulsar con canalete // *vi* (*with feet*) chapotear; ~ **steamer** *n* vapor *m* de ruedas; **paddling pool** *n* estanque *m* de juegos.

paddock ['pædək] *n* corral *m*.

paddy field ['pædɪ-] n arrozal m.
padlock ['pædlɔk] n candado // vt cerrar con candado.
padre ['pɑːdrɪ] n capellán m.
paediatrics, pediatrics (US) [piːdɪ'ætrɪks] n pediatría.
pagan ['peɪgən] a, n pagano/a.
page [peɪdʒ] n (of book) página; (of newspaper) plana; (also: ~ **boy**) paje m // vt (in hotel etc) buscar (a uno) llamando su nombre.
pageant ['pædʒənt] n (procession) desfile m; (show) espectáculo; ~**ry** n pompa.
pagoda [pə'gəudə] n pagoda.
paid [peɪd] pt, pp of **pay** // a (work) remunerado; (official) asalariado; **to put** ~ **to** acabar con.
pail [peɪl] n cubo, balde m.
pain [peɪn] n dolor m; **to be in** ~ sufrir; **on** ~ **of death** so pena de muerte; **to take** ~**s to do sth** tomarse trabajo en hacer algo; ~**ed** a (expression) afligido; ~**ful** a doloroso; (difficult) penoso; (disagreeable) desagradable; ~**fully** ad (fig: very) terriblemente; ~**killer** n calmante m; ~**less** a que no causa dolor; **painstaking** ['peɪnzteɪkɪŋ] a (person) concienzudo, esmerado.
paint [peɪnt] n pintura // vt pintar; **to** ~ **one's face** pintarse (la cara); **to** ~ **the door blue** pintar la puerta de azul; ~**brush** n (artist's) pincel m; (decorator's) brocha; ~**er** n pintor/a m/f; ~**ing** n pintura.
pair [pɛə*] n (of shoes, gloves etc) par m; (of people) pareja; **a** ~ **of scissors** unas tijeras; **a** ~ **of trousers** unos pantalones, un pantalón.
pajamas [pɪ'dʒɑːməz] npl (US) pijama m.
Pakistan [pɑːkɪ'stɑːn] n Paquistán m; ~**i** a, n paquistaní.
pal [pæl] n (col) compinche m/f, compañero/a.
palace ['pæləs] n palacio.
palatable ['pælɪtəbl] a sabroso; (acceptable) aceptable.
palate ['pælɪt] n paladar m.
palaver [pə'lɑːvə*] n (fuss) lío; (hindrances) molestias fpl.
pale [peɪl] a (gen) pálido; (colour) claro; **to grow** ~ palidecer; **to be beyond the** ~ estar excluido; ~**ness** n palidez f.
Palestine ['pælɪstaɪn] n Palestina; **Palestinian** [-'tɪnɪən] a, n palestino/a.
palette ['pælɪt] n paleta.
paling ['peɪlɪŋ] n (stake) estaca; (fence) valla.
palisade [pælɪ'seɪd] n palizada.
pall [pɔːl] n (of smoke) capa (de humo) // vi perder el sabor.
pallid ['pælɪd] a pálido.
palm [pɑːm] n (gen) palma; (also: ~ **tree**) palmera, palma // vt: **to** ~ **sth off on sb** (col) encajar algo a uno; ~**ist** n quiromántico/a; **P**~ **Sunday** n Domingo de Ramos.
palpable ['pælpəbl] a palpable.

palpitation [pælpɪ'teɪʃən] n palpitación f; **to have** ~**s** tener vahídos.
paltry ['pɔːltrɪ] a (insignificant) baladí; (miserable) vil.
pamper ['pæmpə*] vt mimar.
pamphlet ['pæmflət] n folleto.
pan [pæn] n (also: **sauce**~) cacerola, cazuela; (also: **frying** ~) sartén m; (of lavatory) taza // vi (CINEMA) tomar una vista panorámica.
panacea [pænə'sɪə] n panacea.
Panama ['pænəmɑː] n Panamá m.
pancake ['pænkeɪk] n canapé m.
panda ['pændə] n panda m/f; ~ **car** n coche m de la policía.
pandemonium [pændɪ'məunɪəm] n (noise) estruendo; (mess) caos m.
pander ['pændə*] vi: **to** ~ **to** complacer a.
pane [peɪn] n cristal m.
panel ['pænl] n (of wood) panel m; (of cloth) paño; (RADIO, TV) tablero; ~**ing**, ~**ing** (US) n paneles mpl, entrepaños mpl.
pang [pæŋ] n: ~**s of conscience** remordimiento sg; ~**s of hunger** dolores mpl del hambre.
panic ['pænɪk] n (terror) pánico // vi aterrarse; ~**ky** a (person) asustadizo; ~-**stricken** a preso de pánico.
pannier ['pænɪə*] n (on bicycle) cartera; (on mule etc) alforja.
panorama [pænə'rɑːmə] n panorama m.
pansy ['pænzɪ] n (BOT) pensamiento; (col) maricón m.
pant [pænt] vi jadear.
panther ['pænθə*] n pantera.
panties ['pæntɪz] npl bragas fpl, pantis mpl.
pantomime ['pæntəmaɪm] n revista musical representada en Navidad, basada en cuentos de hadas.
pantry ['pæntrɪ] n despensa.
pants [pænts] n (woman's) bragas fpl; (man's) calzoncillos mpl; (US: trousers) pantalones mpl.
papal ['peɪpəl] a papal.
paper ['peɪpə*] n papel m; (also: **news**~) periódico, diario; (study, article) artículo; (exam) examen m // a de papel // vt empapelar; (identity) ~**s** npl papeles mpl, documentos mpl; ~**back** n libro de bolsillo; ~ **bag** n saco de papel; ~ **clip** n grapa; ~ **hankie** n pañuelo de papel; ~ **money** n papel moneda; ~**weight** n pisapapeles m inv; ~**work** n trabajo administrativo; (pej) papeleo.
papier-mâché ['pæpɪeɪ'mæʃeɪ] n cartón m piedra.
paprika ['pæprɪkə] n pimienta húngara o roja.
par [pɑː*] n par f; (GOLF) par m; **to be on a** ~ **with** correr parejas con.
parable ['pærəbl] n parábola.
parachute ['pærəʃuːt] n paracaídas m inv // vi lanzarse en paracaídas; ~ **jump** n salto en paracaídas.
parade [pə'reɪd] n desfile m // vt (gen)

recorrer, desfilar por; (*show off*) hacer alarde de // *vi* desfilar; (*MIL*) pasar revista.

paradise ['pærədaıs] *n* paraíso.

paradox ['pærədɔks] *n* paradoja; ~**ical** [-'dɔksıkl] *a* paradójico.

paraffin ['pærəfın] *n*: ~ (**oil**) petróleo.

paragraph ['pærəgrɑːf] *n* párrafo.

parallel ['pærəlɛl] *a* en paralelo; (*fig*) semejante // *n* (*line*) paralela; (*fig, GEO*) paralelo.

paralysis [pə'rælısıs] *n* parálisis *f*; **paralyze** ['pærəlaız] *vt* paralizar.

paramount ['pærəmaunt] *a*: **of** ~ **importance** de la mayor importancia, primordial.

paranoia [pærə'nɔıə] *n* paranoia; **paranoiac** *a* paranoico.

paraphernalia [pærəfə'neılıə] *n* (*gear*) avíos *mpl*.

paraplegic [pærə'pliːdʒık] *n* parapléjico.

parasite ['pærəsaıt] *n* parásito.

parasol [pærə'sɔl] *n* sombrilla, quitasol *m*.

paratrooper ['pærətruːpə*] *n* paracaidista *m/f*.

parcel ['pɑːsl] *n* paquete *m* // *vt* (*also*: ~ **up**) empaquetar, embalar.

parch [pɑːtʃ] *vt* secar, resecar; ~**ed** *a* (*person*) muerto de sed.

parchment ['pɑːtʃmənt] *n* pergamino.

pardon ['pɑːdn] *n* perdón *m*; (*LAW*) indulto // *vt* perdonar; indultar; ~! ¡perdone!; ~ **me!, I beg your** ~! ¡perdone Usted!; (**I beg your**) ~? ¿cómo?

parent ['pɛərənt] *n* padre *m*/madre *f*; ~**s** *npl* padres *mpl*; ~**al** [pə'rɛntl] *a* paternal/maternal.

parenthesis [pə'rɛnθısıs], *pl* -**theses** [-θısiːz] *n* paréntesis *m inv*.

Paris ['pærıs] *n* París.

parish ['pærıʃ] *n* parroquia; ~**ioner** [pə'rıʃənə*] *n* feligrés/esa *m/f*.

Parisian [pə'rızıən] *a*, *n* parisino/a, parisiense *m/f*.

parity ['pærıtı] *n* paridad *f*, igualdad *f*.

park [pɑːk] *n* parque *m* // *vt* estacionar // *vi* aparcar, estacionarse; ~**ing** *n* aparcamiento, estacionamiento; '**no** ~**ing**' 'prohibido estacionarse'; ~**ing lot** *n* (*US*) parking *m*; ~**ing meter** *n* parquímetro.

parliament ['pɑːləmənt] *n* parlamento; (*Spanish*) Cortes *mpl*; ~**ary** [-'mɛntərı] *a* parlamentario.

parlour, parlor (*US*) ['pɑːlə*] *n* sala de recibo, salón *m*.

parochial [pə'rəukıəl] *a* parroquial; (*pej*) de miras estrechas.

parody ['pærədı] *n* parodia // *vt* parodiar.

parole [pə'rəul] *n*: **on** ~ libre bajo palabra.

parquet ['pɑːkeı] *n*: ~ **floor(ing)** parquet *m*.

parrot ['pærət] *n* loro, papagayo; ~ **fashion** *ad* mecánicamente.

parry ['pærı] *vt* parar.

parsimonious [pɑːsı'məunıəs] *a* parco.

parsley ['pɑːslı] *n* perejil *m*.

parsnip ['pɑːsnıp] *n* chirivía.

parson ['pɑːsn] *n* (*parish*) párroco; (*gen*) cura *m*.

part [pɑːt] *n* (*gen, MUS*) parte *f*; (*bit*) trozo; (*of machine*) pieza; (*THEATRE etc*) papel *m*; (*of serial*) entrega // *ad* = **partly** // *vt* dividir; (*break*) partir // *vi* (*people*) separarse; (*roads*) bifurcarse; (*crowd*) apartarse; (*break*) romperse; **to take** ~ **in** participar *o* tomar parte en; **to take sth in good** ~ tomar algo en buena parte; **to take sb's** ~ defender a uno; **for my** ~ por mi parte; **for the most** ~ en la mayor parte; **to** ~ **with** *vt fus* ceder, entregar; (*money*) pagar; (*get rid of*) deshacerse de; **in** ~ **exchange** como parte del pago; **spare** ~ pieza de recambio.

partial ['pɑːʃl] *a* parcial; **to be** ~ **to** ser aficionado a; ~**ly** *ad* en parte.

participant [pɑː'tısıpənt] *n* (*in competition*) concursante *m/f*; **participate** [-peıt] *vi*: **to participate in** participar en; **participation** [-'peıʃən] *n* participación *f*.

participle ['pɑːtısıpl] *n* participio.

particle ['pɑːtıkl] *n* partícula; (*of dust*) grano; (*fig*) pizca.

particular [pə'tıkjulə*] *a* (*special*) particular; (*concrete*) concreto; (*given*) determinado; (*detailed*) detallado, minucioso; (*fussy*) quisquilloso, exigente; ~**s** *npl* (*information*) datos *mpl*, detalles *mpl*; (*details*) pormenores *mpl*; ~**ly** *ad* especialmente, en particular.

parting ['pɑːtıŋ] *n* (*act of*) separación *f*; (*farewell*) despedida; (*in hair*) raya // *a* de despedida.

partisan [pɑːtı'zæn] *a*, *n* partidario/a.

partition [pɑː'tıʃən] *n* (*POL*) división *f*; (*wall*) tabique *m* // *vt* dividir; dividir con tabique.

partly ['pɑːtlı] *ad* en parte.

partner ['pɑːtnə*] *n* (*COMM*) socio/a; (*SPORT, at dance*) pareja; (*spouse*) cónyuge *m/f*; (*friend etc*) compañero/a // *vt* acompañar; ~**ship** *n* (*gen*) asociación *f*; (*COMM*) sociedad *f*.

partridge ['pɑːtrıdʒ] *n* perdiz *f*.

part-time ['pɑːt'taım] *a*, *ad* de medio tiempo *o* media jornada.

party ['pɑːtı] *n* (*POL*) partido; (*celebration*) fiesta; (*group*) grupo; (*LAW*) parte *f*, interesado // *a* (*POL*) de partido; (*dress etc*) de fiesta, de gala.

pass [pɑːs] *vt* (*time, object*) pasar; (*place*) pasar por; (*exam*) aprobar; (*overtake, surpass*) rebasar; (*approve*) aprobar // *vi* pasar; (*SCOL*) aprobar, ser aprobado // *n* (*permit*) permiso; (*membership card*) carnet *m*; (*in mountains*) puerto, desfiladero; (*SPORT*) pase *m*; (*SCOL: also*: ~ **mark**): **to get a** ~ **in** aprobar en; **to** ~ **sth through sth** pasar algo por algo; **to** ~ **away** *vi* fallecer; **to** ~ **by** *vi* pasar //

vt (*ignore*) pasar por alto; **to ~ for** pasar por; **to ~ out** *vi* desmayarse; **to ~ up** *vt* renunciar a; **~able** *a* (*road*) transitable; (*work*) pasable.

passage ['pæsɪdʒ] *n* (*also:* **~way**) pasillo; (*act of passing*) tránsito; (*fare, in book*) pasaje *m*; (*by boat*) travesía; (MECH, MED) tubo.

passenger ['pæsɪndʒə*] *n* pasajero, viajero.

passer-by [pɑːsə'baɪ] *n* transeúnte *m/f*.

passing ['pɑːsɪŋ] *a* (*fleeting*) pasajero; **in ~** de paso.

passion ['pæʃən] *n* pasión *f*; (*anger*) cólera; **~ate** *a* apasionado; colérico.

passive ['pæsɪv] *a* (*also* LING) pasivo.

Passover ['pɑːsəuvə*] *n* Pascua (de los judíos).

passport ['pɑːspɔːt] *n* pasaporte *m*.

password ['pɑːswɜːd] *n* santo y seña.

past [pɑːst] *prep* (*further than*) más allá de; (*later than*) después de // *a* pasado; (*president etc*) ex, antiguo // *n* el pasado; (*antecedents*) antecedentes *mpl*; **he's ~ forty** tiene más de cuarenta años; **for the ~ few/3 days** durante los últimos/3 días; **to run ~** pasar a la carrera por.

pasta ['pæstə] *n* pastas *fpl*.

paste [peɪst] *n* (*gen*) pasta; (*glue*) engrudo // *vt* (*stick*) pegar; (*glue*) engomar.

pastel ['pæstl] *a* pastel; (*painting*) al pastel.

pasteurized ['pæstəraɪzd] *a* pasteurizado.

pastille ['pæstl] *n* pastilla.

pastime ['pɑːstaɪm] *n* pasatiempo.

pastor ['pɑːstə*] *n* pastor *m*.

pastoral ['pɑːstərl] *a* pastoral.

pastry ['peɪstrɪ] *n* pasta; (*cakes*) pastas *fpl*, pasteles *mpl*.

pasture ['pɑːstʃə*] *n* (*grass*) pasto; (*land*) prado, pasto.

pasty ['pæstɪ] *n* empanada // *a* ['peɪstɪ] pastoso; (*complexion*) pálido.

pat [pæt] *vt* dar una palmadita a; (*dog etc*) acariciar // *n* (*of butter*) pastelillo; **to give sb a ~ on the back** felicitar a uno.

patch [pætʃ] *n* (*of material*) parche *m*; (*piece*) pedazo; (*mend*) remiendo; (*of land*) terreno // *vt* (*clothes*) remendar; **to ~ up** *vt* (*mend temporarily*) componer de modo provisional; (*quarrel*) hacer las paces con; **~work** *n* labor *m* de retazos; **~y** *a* desigual.

pâté ['pæteɪ] *n* pastel *m* de carne.

patent ['peɪtnt] *n* patente *f* // *vt* patentar // *a* patente, evidente; **~ leather** *n* charol *m*.

paternal [pə'tɜːnl] *a* paternal; (*relation*) paterno; **paternity** [-nɪtɪ] *n* paternidad *f*.

path [pɑːθ] *n* senda, sendero; (*trail, track*) pista; (*of missile*) trayectoria.

pathetic [pə'θetɪk] *a* (*pitiful*) patético, lastimoso; (*very bad*) malísimo; (*moving*) conmovedor(a).

pathologist [pə'θɒlədʒɪst] *n* patólogo; **pathology** [-dʒɪ] *n* patología.

pathos ['peɪθɒs] *n* patetismo, lo patético.

pathway ['pɑːθweɪ] *n* sendero, vereda.

patience ['peɪʃns] *n* paciencia; (CARDS) solitario.

patient ['peɪʃnt] *n* paciente *m/f* // *a* paciente, sufrido.

patio ['pætɪəu] *n* patio.

patriot ['peɪtrɪət] *n* patriota *m/f*; **~ic** [pætrɪ'ɔtɪk] *a* patriótico.

patrol [pə'trəul] *n* patrulla // *vt* patrullar por; **~ car** *n* coche *m* patrulla; **~man** *n* (US) policía *m*.

patron ['peɪtrən] *n* (*in shop*) cliente *m/f*; (*of charity*) patrocinador/a *m/f*; **~ of the arts** mecenas *m*; **~age** ['pætrənɪdʒ] *n* mecenazgo, protección *f*; **~ize** ['pætrənaɪz] *vt* (*shop*) ser cliente de; (*business*) patrocinar; (*look down on*) tratar con condescendencia; **~ saint** *n* patrono.

patter ['pætə*] *n* golpeteo; (*of feet*) pasos *mpl* ligeros; (*sales talk*) jerga // *vi* andar con pasos ligeros; (*rain*) tamborilear.

pattern ['pætən] *n* modelo; (SEWING) patrón *m*; (*design*) dibujo; (*sample*) muestra.

paunch [pɔːntʃ] *n* panza, barriga.

pauper ['pɔːpə*] *n* pobre *m/f*.

pause [pɔːz] *n* pausa; (*interval*) intérvalo // *vi* hacer una pausa.

pave [peɪv] *vt* pavimentar; **to ~ the way for** preparar el terreno para.

pavement ['peɪvmənt] *n* (*Brit*) acera.

pavilion [pə'vɪlɪən] *n* pabellón *m*; (*for band etc*) quiosco; (SPORT) caseta.

paving ['peɪvɪŋ] *n* pavimento, enlosado; **~ stone** *n* losa.

paw [pɔː] *n* pata; (*of cat*) garra // *vt* tocar con la pata; (*touch*) tocar, manosear; (*amorously*) sobar.

pawn [pɔːn] *n* (CHESS) peón *m*; (*fig*) instrumento // *vt* empeñar; **~broker** *n* prestamista *m/f*; **~shop** *n* monte *m* de piedad.

pay [peɪ] *n* paga; (*wage etc*) sueldo // (*vb: pt, pp* **paid**) *vt* pagar; (*debt*) liquidar; (*visit*) hacer; (*respect*) ofrecer // *vi* pagar; (*be profitable*) rendir; **to ~ attention (to)** prestar atención (a); **to ~ back** *vt* (*money*) devolver; (*person*) pagar; **to ~ for** *vt* pagar por; **to ~ in** *vt* ingresar; **to ~ off** *vt* liquidar; **to ~ up** *vt* pagar (de mala gana); **~able** *a* pagadero; **~ day** *n* día *m* de paga; **~ee** *n* portador/a *m/f*; **~ing** *a* provechoso; **~ment** *n* pago; **advance ~ment** anticipo; **monthly ~ment** mensualidad *f*; **~ packet** *n* sobre *m* de paga; **~roll** *n* nómina; **~ slip** *n* hoja de paga.

p.c. *abbr of* **per cent.**

pea [piː] *n* guisante *m*; **sweet ~** guisante de olor.

peace [piːs] *n* paz *f*; (*calm*) paz *f*, tranquilidad *f*; **~able** *a* pacífico; **~ful** *a* (*gentle*) pacífico; (*calm*) tranquilo, sosegado; **~-keeping** *n* pacificación *f*; **~ offering** *n* prenda de paz.

peach [piːtʃ] *n* melocotón *m*, durazno (AM).

peacock ['piːkɔk] *n* pavo real.

peak [pi:k] n (of mountain: top) cumbre f, cima; (: point) pico; (of cap) visera; (fig) cumbre f; ~ **hours** npl horas fpl punta.

peal [pi:l] n (of bells) repique m, toque m de campanas; ~ **of laughter** carcajada.

peanut ['pi:nʌt] n cacahuete m, maní m (AM); ~ **butter** n manteca de cacahuete.

pear [pɛə*] n pera; ~ **tree** n peral m.

pearl [pɜ:l] n perla; **mother-of-~** n nácar m.

peasant ['pɛznt] n campesino/a.

peat [pi:t] n turba.

pebble ['pɛbl] n guijarro.

peck [pɛk] vt (also: ~ **at**) picotear; (food) comer sin ganas // n picotazo; (kiss) beso ligero; ~**ing order** n orden m de jerarquía; ~**ish** a (col) con hambre.

peculiar [pɪ'kju:lɪə*] a (odd) extraño, raro; (typical) propio, característico; (marked) especial; ~ **to** propio de; ~**ity** [pɪkju:lɪ'ærɪtɪ] n peculiaridad f; (feature) característica; (oddity) rareza, singularidad f.

pedal ['pɛdl] n pedal m // vi pedalear.

pedantic [pɪ'dæntɪk] a pedante.

peddle ['pɛdl] vt vender (de puerta en puerta); **peddler** n vendedor/a m/f ambulante.

pedestal ['pɛdəstl] n pedestal m.

pedestrian [pɪ'dɛstrɪən] n peatón m // a pedestre; ~ **crossing** n paso de peatones.

pedigree ['pɛdɪgri:] n genealogía; (of animal) raza // cpd (animal) de raza, de casta.

peek [pi:k] vi mirar a hurtadillas.

peel [pi:l] n piel f; (of orange, lemon) peladuras fpl // vt pelar // vi (paint etc) desconcharse; (wallpaper) despegarse, desprenderse.

peep [pi:p] n (look) mirada furtiva; (sound) pío // vi piar; **to** ~ **out** vi asomar la cabeza; ~**hole** n mirilla.

peer [pɪə*] vi: **to** ~ **at** mirar con ojos de miope // n (noble) par m; (equal) igual m; ~**age** n nobleza; ~**less** a sin par.

peeved [pi:vd] a enojado.

peevish ['pi:vɪʃ] a malhumorado.

peg [pɛg] n clavija; (for coat etc) gancho, colgadero; (also: **clothes** ~) pinza; (tent ~) estaca // vt (prices) fijar; **off the** ~ ad de confección.

pejorative [pɪ'dʒɔrətɪv] a peyorativo.

pekingese [pi:kɪ'ni:z] n pequinés/esa m/f.

pelican ['pɛlɪkən] n pelícano.

pellet ['pɛlɪt] n bolita; (bullet) perdigón m.

pelmet ['pɛlmɪt] n galería.

pelt [pɛlt] vt: **to** ~ **sb with sth** tirar algo a uno // vi (rain) llover a cántaros // n pellejo.

pelvis ['pɛlvɪs] n pelvis f.

pen [pɛn] n pluma; (for sheep) redil m; **play**~ parque m de niño; ~ **name** n seudónimo.

penal ['pi:nl] a penal; ~**ize** vt penar; (SPORT) castigar.

penalty ['pɛnltɪ] n (gen) pena; (fine) multa; (SPORT) castigo; ~ **(kick)** n (FOOTBALL) penalty m.

penance ['pɛnəns] n penitencia.

pence [pɛns] pl of **penny.**

pencil ['pɛnsl] n lápiz m; (for eyebrows) lapiz de cejas; **propelling** ~ lapicero; ~ **sharpener** n sacapuntas m inv.

pendant ['pɛndnt] n pendiente m.

pending ['pɛndɪŋ] prep antes de // a pendiente.

pendulum ['pɛndjuləm] n péndulo.

penetrate ['pɛnɪtreɪt] vt penetrar; **penetrating** a penetrante; **penetration** [-'treɪʃən] n penetración f.

penfriend ['pɛnfrɛnd] n amigo/a por correspondencia.

penguin ['pɛŋgwɪn] n pingüino.

penicillin [pɛnɪ'sɪlɪn] n penicilina.

peninsula [pə'nɪnsjulə] n península.

penis ['pi:nɪs] n pene m.

penitence ['pɛnɪtns] n penitencia; **penitent** [-nt] a (gen) arrepentido; (REL) penitente.

penitentiary [pɛnɪ'tɛnʃərɪ] n (US) cárcel f, presidio.

penknife ['pɛnnaɪf] n navaja.

pennant ['pɛnənt] n banderola.

penniless ['pɛnɪlɪs] a sin dinero.

penny ['pɛnɪ], pl **pennies** ['pɛnɪz] or **pence** [pɛns] n penique m.

pension ['pɛnʃən] n (gen) pensión f; (old-age) jubilación f; (MIL) retiro; ~**er** n jubilado; ~ **fund** n caja de jubilaciones.

pensive ['pɛnsɪv] a pensativo; (withdrawn) preocupado.

pentagon ['pɛntəgən] n pentágono.

Pentecost ['pɛntɪkɔst] n Pentecostés m.

penthouse ['pɛnthaus] n ático.

pent-up ['pɛntʌp] a (feelings) reprimido.

penultimate [pɛ'nʌltɪmət] a penúltimo.

people ['pi:pl] npl gente f; (citizens) pueblo sg, ciudadanos mpl // n (nation, race) pueblo, nación f // vt poblar; **several** ~ **came** vinieron varias personas; ~ **say that...** dice la gente que... .

pep [pɛp] n (col) energía; **to** ~ **up** vt animar.

pepper ['pɛpə*] n pimienta; (vegetable) pimiento // vt (fig) salpicar; ~**mint** n menta; (sweet) pastilla de menta.

peptalk ['pɛptɔ:k] n (col) palabras fpl para levantar los ánimos.

per [pɜ:*] prep por; ~ **day/person** por día/persona; ~ **cent** por ciento; ~ **annum** al año.

perceive [pə'si:v] vt percibir; (realize) darse cuenta de.

percentage [pə'sɛntɪdʒ] n porcentaje m.

perception [pə'sɛpʃən] n percepción f; (insight) perspicacia; **perceptive** [-'sɛptɪv] a perspicaz.

perch [pɜ:tʃ] n (fish) perca; (for bird) percha // vi posarse.

percolator ['pɜ:kəleɪtə*] n cafetera filtradora.

percussion [pə'kʌʃən] n percusión f.

peremptory [pə'rɛmptərɪ] a perentorio; (*person*: *imperious*) imperioso.
perennial [pə'rɛnɪəl] a perenne.
perfect ['pə:fɪkt] a perfecto // n (*also*: ~ **tense**) perfecto // vt [pə'fɛkt] perfeccionar; ~**ion** [-'fɛkʃən] n perfección f; ~**ionist** n perfeccionista m/f.
perforate ['pə:fəreit] vt perforar; ~**d** a (*stamp*) dentado; **perforation** [-'reiʃən] n perforación f.
perform [pə'fɔ:m] vt (*carry out*) realizar, cumplir; (*concert etc*) representar; (*piece of music*) interpretar // vi (*animal*) hacer trucos; (*THEATRE*) actuar; (*TECH*) funcionar; ~**ance** n (*of task*) cumplimiento, realización f; (*of an artist*) representación f; (*of player etc*) actuación f; (*of car, engine*) funcionamiento; (*of function*) desempeño; ~**er** n (*actor*) actor/actriz m/f; (*MUS*) interprete m/f; ~**ing** a (*animal*) amaestrado.
perfume ['pə:fju:m] n perfume m // vt perfumar.
perhaps [pə'hæps] ad quizá(s), tal vez.
peril ['pɛrɪl] n peligro, riesgo.
perimeter [pə'rɪmɪtə*] n perímetro.
period ['pɪərɪəd] n período; (*HISTORY*) época; (*time limit*) plazo; (*SCOL*) clase f; (*full stop*) punto; (*MED*) regla, reglas fpl // a (*costume, furniture*) de época; ~**ic** [-'ɔdɪk] a periódico; ~**ical** [-'ɔdɪkl] n periódico; ~**ically** [-'ɔdɪklɪ] ad de vez en cuando, cada cierto tiempo.
peripheral [pə'rɪfərəl] a periférico; **periphery** [-rɪ] n periferia.
periscope ['pərɪskəup] n periscopio.
perish ['pɛrɪʃ] vi perecer; (*decay*) echarse a perder, deteriorar(se); ~**able** a perecedero; ~**ing** a (*col*: *cold*) helado, glacial.
perjure ['pə:dʒə*] vt: to ~ o.s. perjurarse; **perjury** n (*LAW*) perjurio.
perk [pə:k] n pago encima del sueldo; to ~ up vi (*cheer up*) animarse; (*in health*) sentirse mejor; ~**y** a (*cheerful*) alegre, despabilado.
perm [pə:m] n permanente f.
permanent ['pə:mənənt] a permanente.
permissible [pə'mɪsɪbl] a permisible, lícito.
permission [pə'mɪʃən] n permiso; (*authorization*) licencia.
permissive [pə'mɪsɪv] a permisivo.
permit ['pə:mɪt] n permiso, licencia // vt [pə'mɪt] permitir; (*authorize*) autorizar; (*accept*) tolerar.
permutation [pə:mju'teiʃən] n permutación f.
pernicious [pə:'nɪʃəs] a nocivo; (*MED*) pernicioso.
perpendicular [pə:pən'dɪkjulə*] a perpendicular.
perpetrate ['pə:pɪtreit] vt cometer.
perpetual [pə'pɛtjuəl] a perpetuo.
perpetuate [pə'pɛtjueit] vt perpetuar.
perplex [pə'plɛks] vt dejar perplejo.
persecute ['pə:sɪkju:t] vt (*pursue*)

perseguir; (*harass*) acosar; **persecution** [-'kju:ʃən] n persecución f.
persevere [pə:sɪ'vɪə*] vi persistir.
Persian ['pə:ʃən] a, n persa m/f.
persist [pə'sɪst] vi: to ~ (in doing sth) persistir (en hacer algo); ~**ence** n empeño; (*of disease*) pertinacia; ~**ent** a persistente; (*determined*) porfiado; (*disease*) pertinaz.
person ['pə:sn] n persona; ~**able** a atractivo; ~**al** a personal; (*private*) particular; (*visit*) en persona; (*TEL*) persona a persona; (*column*) de anuncios personales; ~**ality** [-'nælɪtɪ] n personalidad f; ~**ally** ad personalmente; ~**ify** [-'sɔnɪfaɪ] vt encarnar.
personnel [pə:sə'nɛl] n personal m.
perspective [pə'spɛktɪv] n perspectiva.
perspex ['pə:spɛks] n plexiglás m.
perspiration [pə:spɪ'reiʃən] n transpiración f, sudor m; **perspire** [-'spaɪə*] vi transpirar, sudar.
persuade [pə'sweid] vt persuadir; **persuasion** [-'sweiʒən] n persuasión f; (*persuasiveness*) persuasiva; (*creed*) creencia; **persuasive** [-'sweisɪv] a persuasivo.
pert [pə:t] a impertinente, fresco.
pertaining [pə:'teinɪŋ]: ~ to prep relacionado con.
pertinent ['pə:tɪnənt] a pertinente, a propósito.
perturb [pə'tə:b] vt perturbar.
Peru [pə'ru:] n el Perú.
peruse [pə'ru:z] vt leer con detención, examinar.
Peruvian [pə'ru:vjən] a, n peruano/a.
pervade [pə'veid] vt impregnar, saturar.
perverse [pə'və:s] a perverso; (*stubborn*) terco; (*wayward*) travieso; **perversion** [-'və:ʃən] n perversión f.
pervert ['pə:və:t] n pervertido/a // vt [pə'və:t] pervertir.
pessary ['pɛsərɪ] n pesario.
pessimism ['pɛsɪmɪzəm] n pesimismo; **pessimist** [-mɪst] n pesimista m/f; **pessimistic** [-'mɪstɪk] a pesimista.
pest [pɛst] n plaga; (*insect*) insecto nocivo; (*fig*) lata, molestia.
pester ['pɛstə*] vt molestar, acosar.
pesticide ['pɛstɪsaɪd] n pesticida m.
pet [pɛt] n animal doméstico; (*favourite*) favorito // vt acariciar // vi (*col*) besuquearse, sobarse.
petal ['pɛtl] n pétalo.
peter ['pi:tə*]: to ~ out vi agotarse, acabarse.
petite [pə'ti:t] a chiquita.
petition [pə'tɪʃən] n petición f.
petrified ['pɛtrɪfaɪd] a (*fig*) pasmado, horrorizado; **petrify** vt petrificar; (*frighten*) pasmar.
petrol ['pɛtrəl] n (*Brit*) gasolina; (*for lighter*) bencina.
petroleum [pə'trəulɪəm] n petróleo.
petrol: ~ **pump** n (*in car*) bomba de

gasolina; (*in garage*) surtidor *m* de gasolina; ~ **station** *n* gasolinera; ~ **tank** *n* depósito de gasolina.

petticoat ['pɛtɪkəut] *n* enagua; (*slip*) combinación *f*.

pettiness ['pɛtɪnɪs] *n* mezquindad *f*.

petty ['pɛtɪ] *a* (*mean*) mezquino; (*unimportant*) nimio; ~ **cash** *n* dinero suelto; ~ **officer** *n* contramaestre *m*.

petulant ['pɛtjulənt] *a* malhumorado.

pew [pju:] *n* banco.

pewter ['pju:tə*] *n* peltre *m*.

phallic ['fælɪk] *a* fálico.

phantom ['fæntəm] *n* fantasma *m*.

Pharaoh ['fɛərəu] *n* Faraón *m*.

pharmacist ['fɑːməsɪst] *n* farmacéutico; **pharmacy** [-sɪ] *n* farmacia.

phase [feɪz] *n* fase *f* // *vt*: to ~ sth in/out introducir/reducir algo por etapas.

Ph.D. *abbr of* **Doctor of Philosophy**.

pheasant ['fɛznt] *n* faisán *m*.

phenomenon [fə'nɔmɪnən], *pl* **-mena** [-mɪnə] *n* fenómeno.

phial ['faɪəl] *n* ampolla.

philanthropist [fɪ'lænθrəpɪst] *n* filántropo/a.

philately [fɪ'lætəlɪ] *n* filatelia.

Philippines ['fɪlɪpi:nz] *npl* (*also:* **Philippine Islands**) (Islas) Filipinas *fpl*.

philosopher [fɪ'lɔsəfə*] *n* filósofo; **philosophical** [fɪlə'sɔfɪkl] *a* filosófico; **philosophy** [-fɪ] *n* filosofía.

phlegm [flɛm] *n* flema; ~**atic** [flɛg-'mætɪk] *a* flemático.

phobia ['fəubjə] *n* fobia.

phone [fəun] *n* teléfono // *vt* telefonear, llamar (por teléfono); **to be on the** ~ tener teléfono; (*be calling*) estar llamando; **to ~ back** *vt, vi* devolver la llamada.

phonetics [fə'nɛtɪks] *n* fonética.

phoney ['fəunɪ] *a* falso; (*person*) insincero // *n* (*person*) farsante *m/f*.

phosphate ['fɔsfeɪt] *n* fosfato.

phosphorus ['fɔsfərəs] *n* fósforo.

photo ['fəutəu] *n* fotografía.

photo... [fəutəu] *pref*: ~**copier** *n* fotocopiador *m*; ~**copy** *n* fotocopia // *vt* fotocopiar; ~**genic** [-'dʒɛnɪk] *a* fotogénico; ~**graph** *n* fotografía // *vt* fotografiar; ~**grapher** [fə'tɔgrəfə*] *n* fotógrafo; ~**graphic** [-'græfɪk] *a* fotográfico; ~**graphy** [fə'tɔgrəfɪ] *n* fotografía; ~**stat** ['fəutəustæt] *n* fotóstato.

phrase [freɪz] *n* frase *f* // *vt* expresar; ~**book** *n* libro de frases.

physical ['fɪzɪkl] *a* físico.

physician [fɪ'zɪʃən] *n* médico.

physicist ['fɪzɪsɪst] *n* físico.

physics ['fɪzɪks] *n* física.

physiology [fɪzɪ'ɔlədʒɪ] *n* fisiología.

physiotherapy [fɪzɪəu'θɛrəpɪ] *n* fisioterapia.

physique [fɪ'zi:k] *n* físico.

pianist ['pi:ənɪst] *n* pianista *m/f*.

piano [pɪ'ænəu] *n* piano; **grand** ~ piano de cola.

pick [pɪk] *n* (*tool: also:* ~**-axe**) pico, piqueta // *vt* (*select*) elegir, escoger; (*gather*) recoger; (*lock*) forzar; **take your** ~ escoja lo que quiera; **the** ~ **of** lo mejor de; **to** ~ **one's teeth** limpiarse los dientes; **to** ~ **pockets** ratear, ser carterista; **to** ~ **off** *vt* (*kill*) matar de un tiro; **to** ~ **on** *vt fus* (*person*) meterse con; **to** ~ **out** *vt* escoger; (*distinguish*) lograr ver; **to** ~ **up** *vi* (*improve*) reponerse // *vt* (*from floor*) recoger; (*telephone*) descolgar; (*buy*) comprar; (*find*) encontrar; (*learn*) aprender; **to** ~ **up speed** acelerarse; **to** ~ **o.s. up** levantarse.

picket ['pɪkɪt] *n* (*in strike*) guardia, piquete *m* // *vt* piquetear; ~ **line** *n* línea de huelgistas.

pickle ['pɪkl] *n* (*also:* ~**s**: *as condiment*) escabeche *m*; (*fig: mess*) apuro // *vt* encurtir; (*in vinegar*) conservar en vinagre.

pickpocket ['pɪkpɔkɪt] *n* carterista *m/f*.

pickup ['pɪkʌp] *n* (*on record player*) pickup *m*; (*small truck*) furgoneta.

picnic ['pɪknɪk] *n* picnic *m*, merienda de campo // *vi* merendar en el campo.

pictorial [pɪk'tɔːrɪəl] *a* pictórico; (*magazine etc*) ilustrado.

picture ['pɪktʃə*] *n* cuadro; (*painting*) pintura; (*photograph*) fotografía; (*film*) película // *vt* pintar; **the** ~**s** el cine; ~**book** *n* libro de imágenes.

picturesque [pɪktʃə'rɛsk] *a* pintoresco.

pidgin ['pɪdʒɪn] *a*: ~ **English** el inglés macarrónico.

pie [paɪ] *n* pastel *m*; (*open*) tarta; (*of meat*) empanada.

piebald ['paɪbɔːld] *a* pío.

piece [pi:s] *n* pedazo, trozo; (*of land*) terreno; (*of cake*) porción *f*; (*item*): **a** ~ **of furniture/advice** un mueble/un consejo // *vt*: **to** ~ **together** juntar; (*TECH*) montar; **to take to** ~**s** desmontar; ~**meal** *ad* poco a poco; ~**work** *n* trabajo a destajo.

pier [pɪə*] *n* muelle *m*; (*jetty*) embarcadero, malecón *m*.

pierce [pɪəs] *vt* penetrar, atravesar; (*puncture*) pinchar.

piercing ['pɪəsɪŋ] *a* (*cry*) penetrante.

piety ['paɪətɪ] *n* piedad *f*.

pig [pɪg] *n* cerdo, puerco; (*fig*) cochino.

pigeon ['pɪdʒən] *n* paloma; (*as food*) pichón *m*; ~**hole** *n* casilla.

piggy bank ['pɪgɪbæŋk] *n* hucha en forma de cerdito.

pigheaded ['pɪg'hɛdɪd] *a* terco, testarudo.

pigment ['pɪgmənt] *n* pigmento; ~**ation** [-'teɪʃən] *n* pigmentación *f*.

pigmy ['pɪgmɪ] *n* = **pygmy**.

pigsty ['pɪgstaɪ] *n* pocilga.

pigtail ['pɪgteɪl] *n* (*girl's*) trenza; (*Chinese*) coleta.

pike [paɪk] *n* (*spear*) pica; (*fish*) lucio.

pilchard ['pɪltʃəd] *n* sardina arenque.

pile [paɪl] *n* (*heap*) montón *m*; (*of carpet*)

pelo; *(of cloth)* pelillo // *(vb: also:* ~ **up)** *vt* amontonar; *(fig)* acumular // *vi* amontonarse.

piles [paɪlz] *npl* (MED) almorranas *fpl.* hemorroides *mpl.*

pile-up [ˈpaɪlʌp] *n* (AUT) accidente *m* múltiple.

pilfer [ˈpɪlfə*] *vt* ratear; ~**ing** *n* ratería.

pilgrim [ˈpɪlgrɪm] *n* peregrino/a; ~**age** *n* peregrinaje *m.* romería.

pill [pɪl] *n* píldora; **the** ~ la píldora.

pillage [ˈpɪlɪdʒ] *n* saqueo, pillaje *m.*

pillar [ˈpɪlə*] *n* (gen) pilar *m;* (concrete) columna; ~ **box** *n* (Brit) buzón *m.*

pillion [ˈpɪljən] *n* (of motor cycle) asiento de atrás.

pillory [ˈpɪlərɪ] *vt* poner en ridículo.

pillow [ˈpɪləu] *n* almohada; ~**case** *n* funda.

pilot [ˈpaɪlət] *n* piloto // *a* (scheme etc) piloto // *vt* pilotar; *(fig)* guiar, conducir; ~ **light** *n* piloto.

pimp [pɪmp] *n* alcahuete *m,* chulo.

pimple [ˈpɪmpl] *n* grano.

pin [pɪn] *n* alfiler *m;* (TECH) perno; (: wooden) clavija // *vt* prender (con alfiler); sujetar con perno; ~**s and needles** hormigueo *sg;* **rolling/ safety** ~ rodillo/imperdible *m;* **to** ~ **sb down** (fig) hacer que uno concrete; **to** ~ **sth on sb** (fig) acusar (falsamente) a uno de algo.

pinafore [ˈpɪnəfɔ:*] *n* delantal *m;* ~ **dress** *n* mandil *m.*

pinball [ˈpɪnbɔ:l] *n* billar *m* automático.

pincers [ˈpɪnsəz] *npl* pinzas *fpl,* tenazas *fpl.*

pinch [pɪntʃ] *n* pellizco; (of salt etc) pizca // *vt* pellizcar; (col: steal) birlar; (: arrest) coger, pescar // *vi* (shoe) apretar; **to feel the** ~ pasar apuros.

pincushion [ˈpɪnkuʃən] *n* acerico.

pine [paɪn] *n* (also: ~ **tree**) pino // *vi:* **to** ~ **for** suspirar por; **to** ~ **away** languidecer.

pineapple [ˈpaɪnæpl] *n* piña, ananás *m.*

ping [pɪŋ] *n* (noise) tintineo; (of bullet through air) subido; ~-**pong** *n* pingpong *m.*

pink [pɪŋk] *a* rosado, color de rosa // *n* (colour) color *m* de rosa; (BOT) clavel *m,* clavellina.

pinnacle [ˈpɪnəkl] *n* cumbre *f.*

pinpoint [ˈpɪnpɔɪnt] *vt* poner el dedo en.

pint [paɪnt] *n* pinta (0.57 litros); **to go for a** ~ ir a tomar una cerveza.

pin-up [ˈpɪnʌp] *n* fotografía de mujer bonita.

pioneer [paɪəˈnɪə*] *n* pionero.

pious [ˈpaɪəs] *a* piadoso, devoto.

pip [pɪp] *n* (seed) pepita; (time signal on radio) señal *f.*

pipe [paɪp] *n* tubo, caño; (for smoking) pipa // *vt* conducir en cañerías; ~**s** *npl* (gen) cañería *sg;* (also: **bag**~**s)** gaita *sg;* **to** ~ **down** *vi* (col) callarse; ~ **dream** *n* sueño imposible; ~ **line** *n* tubería, cañería; (for oil) oleoducto; (for gas) gasoducto; **piper** *n*

(gen) flautista *m/f;* (with bagpipes) gaitero.

piping [ˈpaɪpɪŋ] *ad:* ~ **hot** bien caliente.

piquant [ˈpi:kənt] *a* picante.

pique [pi:k] *n* pique *m.* resentimiento.

pirate [ˈpaɪərət] *n* pirata *m;* ~ **radio** *n* emisora ilegal.

pirouette [pɪruˈɛt] *n* pirueta // *vi* piruetear.

Pisces [ˈpaɪsi:z] *n* Piscis *m.*

piss [pɪs] *vi* (col) mear; ~**ed** *a* (col: drunk) trompa.

pistol [ˈpɪstl] *n* pistola.

piston [ˈpɪstən] *n* pistón *m,* émbolo.

pit [pɪt] *n* hoyo; (also: **coal** ~) mina; (in garage) foso de inspección; (also: **orchestra** ~) platea; (quarry) cantera // *vt:* **to** ~ **A against B** oponer A a B; ~**s** *npl* (AUT) box *m.*

pitch [pɪtʃ] *n* (throw) lanzamiento; (MUS) tono; (SPORT) campo, terreno; (tar) brea; (in market etc) puesto // *vt* (throw) arrojar, lanzar // *vi* (fall) caer(se); (NAUT) cabecear; **to** ~ **a tent** armar una tienda (de campaña); ~-**black** *a* negro como boca de lobo; ~**ed battle** *n* batalla campal.

pitcher [ˈpɪtʃə*] *n* cántaro, jarro.

pitchfork [ˈpɪtʃfɔ:k] *n* horca.

piteous [ˈpɪtɪəs] *a* lastimoso.

pitfall [ˈpɪtfɔ:l] *n* escollo, peligro.

pith [pɪθ] *n* (of orange) médula; (fig) meollo.

pithy [ˈpɪθɪ] *a* jugoso.

pitiable [ˈpɪtɪəbl] *a* lastimoso.

pitiful [ˈpɪtɪful] *a* (touching) lastimoso, conmovedor(a); (contemptible) lamentable, miserable.

pitiless [ˈpɪtɪlɪs] *a* despiadado.

pittance [ˈpɪtns] *n* miseria.

pity [ˈpɪtɪ] *n* (compassion) compasión *f,* piedad *f;* (shame) lástima // *vt* tener lástima a, compadecer(se de); **what a** ~! ¡qué lástima!

pivot [ˈpɪvət] *n* eje *m* // *vi:* **to** ~ **on** girar sobre; (fig) depender de.

pixie [ˈpɪksɪ] *n* duende *m.*

placard [ˈplækɑ:d] *n* (sign) letrero; (in march etc) pancarta.

placate [pləˈkeɪt] *vt* apaciguar.

place [pleɪs] *n* lugar *m,* sitio; (rank) rango; (seat) plaza, asiento; (post) puesto; (home): **at/to his** ~ en/a su casa // *vt* (object) poner, colocar; (identify) reconocer, ubicar; (find a post for) dar un puesto a, colocar; **to take** ~ tener lugar; **to be** ~**d** (in race, exam) colocarse; **out of** ~ (not suitable) fuera de lugar; **in the first** ~ en primer lugar; **to change** ~**s with sb** trocarse con uno.

placid [ˈplæsɪd] *a* apacible.

plagiarism [ˈpleɪdʒjərɪzm] *n* plagio.

plague [pleɪg] *n* plaga; (MED) peste *f* // *vt* (fig) acosar, atormentar; **to** ~ **sb** fastidiar a uno.

plaice [pleɪs] *n, pl inv* platija.

plaid [plæd] n (material) tela a cuadros; (pattern) plaid m.

plain [pleɪn] a (clear) claro, evidente; (simple) sencillo, llano; (frank) franco, abierto; (not handsome) sin atractivo; (pure) natural, puro // ad claro, claramente // n llano, llanura; **in ~ clothes** (police) de paisano; **~ly** ad claramente, evidentemente; (frankly) francamente, con franqueza; **~ness** n claridad f; sencillez f; franqueza.

plaintiff ['pleɪntɪf] n demandante m/f.

plait [plæt] n trenza // vt trenzar.

plan [plæn] n (drawing) plano; (scheme) plan m, proyecto; (schedule) programa m // vt (think in advance) proyectar; (prepare) planear, planificar // vi hacer proyectos; **to ~ to do** proponerse hacer.

plane [pleɪn] n (AVIAT) avión m; (tree) plátano; (tool) cepillo; (MATH) plano.

planet ['plænɪt] n planeta m; **~arium** [-'tɛərɪəm] n planetario.

plank [plæŋk] n tabla; (POL) punto.

planner ['plænə*] n planificador/a m/f.

planning ['plænɪŋ] n planificación f; **family ~** planificación familiar.

plant [plɑːnt] n planta; (machinery) maquinaria; (factory) fábrica // vt plantar; (field) sembrar; (bomb) colocar; (fam) colocar a escondidas.

plantation [plæn'teɪʃən] n plantación f; (estate) hacienda.

plaque [plæk] n placa.

plasma ['plæzmə] n plasma m.

plaster ['plɑːstə*] n (for walls) yeso; (also: **sticking ~**) curitas m inv, parche m // vt enyesar; (cover): **to ~ with** llenar o cubrir de; **~ed** a (col) trompa; **~er** n yesero.

plastic ['plæstɪk] n plástico // a de plástico.

plasticine ['plæstɪsiːn] n plasticina.

plastic surgery ['plæstɪk'sɜːdʒərɪ] n cirujía plástica.

plate [pleɪt] n (dish) plato; (metal, in book) lámina; (PHOT, dental) placa.

plateau ['plætəu], pl **~s** or **~x** [-z] n meseta, altiplanicie f.

plateful ['pleɪtful] n plato.

plate glass [pleɪt'glɑːs] n vidrio cilindrado.

platform ['plætfɔːm] n (RAIL) andén m; (stage) plataforma; (at meeting) tribuna; (POL) programa m electoral; **~ ticket** n billete m de andén.

platinum ['plætɪnəm] n platino.

platitude ['plætɪtjuːd] n lugar m común, tópico.

platoon [plə'tuːn] n pelotón m.

platter ['plætə*] n fuente f, platón m.

plausible ['plɔːzɪbl] a verosímil, admisible; (person) convincente.

play [pleɪ] n (gen) juego; (also: **~time**) recreo; (THEATRE) obra, comedia // vt (game) jugar; (instrument) tocar; (THEATRE) representar; (: part) hacer (el papel de); (fig) desempeñar // vi jugar; (amuse o.s.) divertirse; (frolic) juguetear; **to ~ down** vt quitar importancia a; **to ~ up** vt (cause trouble to) fastidiar a; **~-acting** n teatro; **~er** n jugador/a m/f; (THEATRE) actor/actriz m/f; (MUS) músico/a; **~ful** a juguetón(ona); **~ground** n (in park) parque m de juegos; (in school) patio de recreo; **~group** n jardín m de niños; **~ing card** n naipe m, carta; **~ing field** n campo de deportes; **~mate** n compañero de juego; **~-off** n (SPORT) partido de desempate; **~pen** n corral m; **~thing** n juguete m; **~wright** n dramaturgo.

plea [pliː] n (request) súplica, petición f; (excuse) pretexto, disculpa; (LAW) alegato, defensa.

plead [pliːd] vt (LAW) interceder; (give as excuse) poner como pretexto // vi (LAW) declarar; (beg): **to ~ with sb** suplicar o rogar a uno.

pleasant ['plɛznt] a agradable; (surprise) grato; (person) simpático; **~ness** n (of person) simpatía, amabilidad f; (of place) lo agradable; **~ries** npl (polite remarks) cortesías fpl.

please [pliːz] vt (give pleasure to) dar gusto a, agradar; (get on well with) caer en gracia a // vi (think fit): **do as you ~** haga lo que quiera o lo que le da la gana; **~!** ¡por favor!; **~ yourself!** ¡como Usted guste!, ¡como quiera!; **~d** a (happy) alegre, contento; **~d (with)** satisfecho (de); **pleasing** a (gen) agradable; (surprise) grato; (flattering) halagüeño.

pleasure ['plɛʒə*] n placer m, gusto; (will) voluntad f // cpd de recreo; **'it's a ~'** el gusto es mío; **it's a ~ to see him** da gusto verle.

pleat [pliːt] n pliegue m.

plebs [plɛbz] npl (pej) la plebe.

plectrum ['plɛktrəm] n plectro.

pledge [plɛdʒ] n (object) prenda; (promise) promesa, voto // vt (pawn) empeñar; (promise) prometer.

plentiful ['plɛntɪful] a copioso, abundante.

plenty ['plɛntɪ] n abundancia; **~ of** (enough) bastante; (many) muchos.

pleurisy ['pluərɪsɪ] n pleuresía.

pliable ['plaɪəbl] a flexible; (fig) manejable.

pliers ['plaɪəz] npl alicates mpl, tenazas fpl.

plight [plaɪt] n condición f, situación f difícil.

plimsolls ['plɪmsəlz] npl zapatos mpl de tenis.

plod [plɔd] vi caminar penosamente; (fig) trabajar laboriosamente; **~der** n empollón/ona m/f; **~ding** a laborioso.

plonk [plɔŋk] (col) n (wine) vino corriente // vt: **to ~ sth down** dejar caer algo (pesadamente).

plot [plɔt] n (scheme) complot m, conjura; (of story, play) argumento; (of land) terreno // vt (mark out) trazar; (conspire) tramar, urdir // vi conspirar; **~ter** n conspirador/a m/f.

plough, plow (*US*) [plau] *n* arado // *vt* (*earth*) arar; **to ~ back** *vt* (*COMM*) reinvertir; **to ~ through** *vt fus* (*crowd*) abrirse paso por la fuerza.

ploy [plɔi] *n* truco, estratagema.

pluck [plʌk] *vt* (*fruit*) coger; (*musical instrument*) puntear; (*bird*) desplumar // *n* valor *m*, ánimo; **to ~ up courage** hacer de tripas corazón; **~y** *a* valiente, valeroso.

plug [plʌg] *n* tapón *m*; (*ELEC*) enchufe *m*, clavija; (*AUT: also*: **sparking ~**) bujía // *vt* (*hole*) tapar; (*col: advertise*) dar publicidad a.

plum [plʌm] *n* (*fruit*) ciruela // *a* (*col: job*) breva, chollo.

plumage ['plu:mɪdʒ] *n* plumaje *m*.

plumb [plʌm] *ad* (*exactly*) exactamente, en punto // *vt* sondar, sondear.

plumber ['plʌmə*] *n* fontanero; **plumbing** [-mɪŋ] *n* (*trade*) fontanería; (*piping*) instalación *f* de cañerías.

plume [plu:m] *n* (*gen*) pluma; (*on helmet*) penacho.

plummet ['plʌmɪt] *vi*: **to ~ (down)** caer a plomo.

plump [plʌmp] *a* rechoncho, rollizo // *vt*: **to ~ sth (down) on** dejar caer algo en; **to ~ for** (*col: choose*) optar por.

plunder ['plʌndə*] *n* pillaje *m*; (*loot*) botín *m* // *vt* pillar, saquear; (*tomb*) robar.

plunge [plʌndʒ] *n* (*dive*) salto; (*submersion*) zambullida; (*bath*) baño // *vt* sumergir, hundir // *vi* (*fall*) caer; (*dive*) saltar; (*person*) arrojarse; (*sink*) hundirse; **to take the ~** resolverse; **plunger** *n* émbolo; **plunging** *a* (*neckline*) escotado.

pluperfect [plu:'pə:fɪkt] *n* pluscuamperfecto.

plural ['pluərl] *n* plural *m*.

plus [plʌs] *n* (*also*: **~ sign**) signo más // *prep* más, y, además de; **ten/twenty ~** diez/veinte y pico.

plush [plʌʃ] *a* de felpa.

ply [plaɪ] *vt* (*a trade*) ejercer // *vi* (*ship*) ir y venir; (*for hire*) ofrecerse (para alquilar); **three ~** (*wool*) de tres cordones; **to ~ sb with drink** ofrecer bebidas a alguien muchas veces; **~wood** *n* madera contrachapada.

P.M. *abbr of* **Prime Minister.**

p.m. *ad abbr of* **post meridiem** de la tarde *o* noche.

pneumatic [nju:'mætɪk] *a* neumático.

pneumonia [nju:'məunɪə] *n* pulmonía.

poach [pəutʃ] *vt* (*cook*) escalfar; (*steal*) cazar en vedado // *vi* cazar/pescar en finca ajena; **~ed** *a* (*egg*) escalfado; **~er** *n* cazador *m* furtivo; **~ing** *n* caza/pesca furtiva.

pocket ['pɔkɪt] *n* bolsillo; (*of air, GEO, fig*) bolsa; (*BILLIARDS*) tronera // *vt* meter en el bolsillo; (*steal*) embolsar; (*BILLIARDS*) entronerar; **to be out of ~** salir perdiendo; **~book** *n* (*us: wallet*) cartera; **~ knife** *n* navaja; **~ money** *n* dinero para gastos personales.

pod [pɔd] *n* vaina.

podgy ['pɔdʒɪ] *a* gordinflón(ona).

poem ['pəuɪm] *n* poema *m*.

poet ['pəuɪt] *n* poeta *m/f*; **~ess** *n* poetisa; **~ic** [-'ɛtɪk] *a* poético; **~ laureate** *n* poeta laureado; **~ry** *n* poesía.

poignant ['pɔɪnjənt] *a* conmovedor(a); (*sharp*) agudo.

point [pɔɪnt] *n* (*gen*) punto; (*tip*) punta; (*purpose*) fin *m*, finalidad *f*; (*use*) utilidad *f*; (*significant part*) lo significativo; (*characteristic*) rasgo; (*also*: **decimal ~**): **2 ~ 3 (2.3)** dos punto tres // *vt* (*show*) subrayar; (*gun etc*): **to ~ sth at sb** apuntar algo a uno // *vi* señalar con el dedo; **~s** *npl* (*AUT*) contactos *mpl*; (*RAIL*) agujas *fpl*; **to make a ~ of** no dejar de; **to get the ~** comprender; **to come to the ~** ir al grano; **there's no ~ (in doing)** no hay para qué (hacer); **to ~ out** *vt* señalar; **to ~ to** indicar con el dedo; (*fig*) indicar, señalar; **~-blank** *ad* (*also*: **at ~-blank range**) a quemarropa; **~ed** *a* (*shape*) puntiagudo, afilado; (*remark*) directo, enfático; **~edly** *ad* directamente, con énfasis; **~er** *n* (*stick*) puntero; (*needle*) aguja, indicador *m*; **~less** *a* (*useless*) inútil; (*senseless*) sin sentido; (*motiveless*) sin motivo; **~ of view** *n* punto de vista.

poise [pɔɪz] *n* (*balance*) equilibrio; (*of head, body*) aire *m*, porte *m*; (*calmness*) confianza.

poison ['pɔɪzn] *n* veneno // *vt* envenenar; **~ing** *n* envenenamiento; **~ous** *a* venenoso; (*fumes etc*) tóxico; (*fig*) pernicioso.

poke [pəuk] *vt* (*fire*) hurgar, atizar; (*jab with finger, stick etc*) empujar; (*put*): **to ~ sth in(to)** introducir algo en // *n* (*to fire*) hurgonada; (*push*) empujón *m*; (*with elbow*) codazo; **to ~ about** *vi* fisgar.

poker ['pəukə*] *n* badila, atizador *m*; (*CARDS*) póker *m*; **~-faced** *a* de cara impasible.

poky ['pəukɪ] *a* estrecho.

Poland ['pəulənd] *n* Polonia.

polar ['pəulə*] *a* polar; **~ bear** *n* oso polar.

polarize ['pəuləraɪz] *vt* polarizar.

pole [pəul] *n* palo; (*GEO*) polo; (*TEL*) poste *m*; (*flag ~*) asta; (*tent ~*) mástil *m*.

Pole [pəul] *n* polaco/a.

pole vault ['pəulvɔ:lt] *n* salto con pértiga.

police [pə'li:s] *n* policía // *vt* mantener el orden en; **~ car** *n* coche-patrulla *m*; **~ man** *n* policía *m*, guardia *m*; **~ state** *n* estado policíaco; **~ station** *n* comisaría; **~woman** *n* mujer *f* policía.

policy ['pɔlɪsɪ] *n* política; (*also*: **insurance ~**) póliza.

polio ['pəulɪəu] *n* polio *f*.

Polish ['pəulɪʃ] *a, n* polaco.

polish ['pɔlɪʃ] *n* (*for shoes*) betún *m*; (*for floor*) cera (de lustrar); (*for nails*) esmalte *m*; (*shine*) brillo, lustre *m*; (*fig: refinement*) cultura, urbanidad *f* // *vt* (*shoes*) limpiar;

(*make shiny*) pulir, sacar brillo a; (*fig: improve*) refinar, repasar; **to ~ off** *vt* (*work*) terminar; (*food*) despachar; **~ed** *a* (*fig: person*) culto; (: *manners*) fino.

polite [pə'laɪt] *a* cortés, atento; (*formal*) correcto; **~ness** *n* cortesía.

politic ['pɒlɪtɪk] *a* prudente; **~al** [pə'lɪtɪkl] *a* político; **~ian** [-'tɪʃən] *n* político; **~s** *npl* política *sg*.

polka ['pɒlkə] *n* polca; **~ dot** *n* punto.

poll [pəul] *n* (*votes*) votación *f*, votos *mpl*; (*also:* **opinion ~**) sondeo, encuesta // *vt* (*votes*) recibir, obtener.

pollen ['pɒlən] *n* polen *m*.

pollination [pɒlɪ'neɪʃən] *n* polinización *f*.

polling ['pəulɪŋ]: **~ booth** *n* cabina de votar; **~ day** *n* día *m* de elecciones; **~ station** *n* centro electoral.

pollute [pə'luːt] *vt* contaminar; **pollution** [-'luːʃən] *n* polución *f*, contaminación *f*.

polo ['pəuləu] *n* (*sport*) polo; **~-neck** *a* de cuello vuelto.

polyester [pɒlɪ'ɛstə*] *n* poliéster *m*.

polygamy [pə'lɪgəmɪ] *n* poligamia.

Polynesia [pɒlɪ'niːzɪə] *n* Polinesia.

polytechnic [pɒlɪ'tɛknɪk] *n* politécnico, escuela de formación profesional.

polythene ['pɒlɪθiːn] *n* politeno.

pomegranate ['pɒmɪgrænɪt] *n* granada.

pommel ['pɒml] *n* pomo // *vt* dar de puñetazos.

pomp [pɒmp] *n* pompa.

pompous ['pɒmpəs] *a* pomposo.

pond [pɒnd] *n* (*natural*) charca; (*artificial*) estanque *m*.

ponder ['pɒndə*] *vt* meditar; **~ous** *a* pesado.

pontiff ['pɒntɪf] *n* pontífice *m*.

pontificate [pɒn'tɪfɪkeɪt] *vi* (*fig*): **to ~ (about)** pontificar (sobre).

pontoon [pɒn'tuːn] *n* pontón *m*; (*card game*) veintiuna.

pony ['pəunɪ] *n* poney *m*, jaca; **~tail** *n* cola de caballo; **~ trekking** *n* excursión *f* a caballo.

poodle ['puːdl] *n* perro de lanas.

pool [puːl] *n* (*of rain*) charca; (*pond*) estanque *m*; (*also:* **swimming ~**) piscina; (*billiards*) trucos *mpl* // *vt* juntar; (**football**) **~s** quinielas *fpl*.

poor [puə*] *a* pobre; (*bad*) de baja calidad // *npl*: **the ~** los pobres; **~ly** *a* mal, enfermo.

pop [pɒp] *n* ¡pum!; (*sound*) ruido seco; (*MUS*) pop *m*; (*US: col: father*) papá *m*; (*lemonade*) gaseosa // *vt* (*put*) poner // *vi* reventar; (*cork*) saltar; **to ~ in** *vi* entrar de sopetón; **to ~ out** *vi* salir un momento; **to ~ up** *vi* aparecer inesperadamente; **~ concert** *n* concierto pop; **~corn** *n* palomitas *fpl*.

pope [pəup] *n* papa *m*.

poplar ['pɒplə*] *n* álamo.

poplin ['pɒplɪn] *n* popelina.

poppy ['pɒpɪ] *n* amapola.

populace ['pɒpjuləs] *n* pueblo, plebe *f*.

popular ['pɒpjulə*] *a* popular; (*fashionable*) de moda; **~ity** [-'lærɪtɪ] *n* popularidad *f*; **~ize** *vt* popularizar; (*disseminate*) vulgarizar.

populate ['pɒpjuleɪt] *vt* poblar; **population** [-'leɪʃən] *n* población *f*.

populous ['pɒpjuləs] *a* populoso.

porcelain ['pɔːslɪn] *n* porcelana.

porch [pɔːtʃ] *n* pórtico, entrada.

porcupine ['pɔːkjupaɪn] *n* puerco espín.

pore [pɔː*] *n* poro // *vi*: **to ~ over** estar absorto en.

pork [pɔːk] *n* carne *f* de cerdo.

pornographic [pɔːnə'græfɪk] *a* pornográfico; **pornography** [-'nɒgrəfɪ] *n* pornografía.

porous ['pɔːrəs] *a* poroso.

porpoise ['pɔːpəs] *n* marsopa.

porridge ['pɒrɪdʒ] *n* avena.

port [pɔːt] *n* (*harbour*) puerto; (*NAUT: left side*) babor *m*; (*wine*) (vino de) oporto.

portable ['pɔːtəbl] *a* portátil.

portend [pɔː'tɛnd] *vt* presagiar, anunciar; **portent** ['pɔːtɛnt] *n* presagio, augurio.

porter ['pɔːtə*] *n* (*for luggage*) mozo; (*doorkeeper*) portero, conserje *m*.

porthole ['pɔːthəul] *n* portilla.

portion ['pɔːʃən] *n* porción *f*; (*helping*) ración *f*.

portly ['pɔːtlɪ] *a* corpulento.

portrait ['pɔːtreɪt] *n* retrato.

portray [pɔː'treɪ] *vt* retratar; (*in writing*) describir, representar; **~al** *n* representación *f*.

Portugal ['pɔːtjugl] *n* Portugal *m*.

Portuguese [pɔːtju'giːz] *a* portugués(esa) // *n, pl inv* portugués/esa *m/f*; (*LING*) portugués *m*.

pose [pəuz] *n* postura, actitud *f*; (*pej*) afectación *f*, pose *f* // *vi* posar; (*pretend*): **to ~ as** darse tono de // *vt* (*question*) plantear.

posh [pɒʃ] *a* (*col*) elegante, de lujo.

position [pə'zɪʃən] *n* posición *f*; (*job*) puesto // *vt* colocar.

positive ['pɒzɪtɪv] *a* positivo; (*certain*) seguro; (*definite*) definitivo.

posse ['pɒsɪ] *n* (*US*) pelotón *m*.

possess [pə'zɛs] *vt* poseer; **~ion** [pə'zɛʃən] *n* posesión *f*; **~ive** *a* posesivo.

possibility [pɒsɪ'bɪlɪtɪ] *n* posibilidad *f*; **possible** ['pɒsɪbl] *a* posible; **as big as possible** lo más grande posible; **possibly** ['pɒsɪblɪ] *ad* (*perhaps*) posiblemente, tal vez; **I cannot possibly come** me es imposible venir.

post [pəust] *n* (*letters, delivery*) correo; (*job, situation*) puesto; (*pole*) poste *m* // *vt* (*send by post*) echar al correo; (*MIL*) apostar; (*bills*) fijar, pegar; (*appoint*): **to ~ to** enviar a; **~age** *n* porte *m*, franqueo; **~al** *a* postal, de correos; **~al order** *n* giro postal; **~ box** *n* buzón *m*; **~card** *n* tarjeta postal.

postdate [pəust'deɪt] *vt* (*cheque*) poner fecha adelantada a.

poster ['pɔustə*] n cartel m.
posterior [pɔs'tɪərɪə*] n (col) culo, trasero.
posterity [pɔs'tɛrɪtɪ] n posteridad f.
postgraduate ['pɔust'grædjuət] n postgraduado.
posthumous ['pɔstjuməs] a póstumo.
post: ~**man** n cartero; ~**mark** n matasellos m inv; ~**master** n administrador/a m/f de correos.
post-mortem [pɔust'mɔːtəm] n autopsia.
post office ['pɔustɔfɪs] n (building) correos f; (organization) Administración General de Correos; ~ **box (P.O. box)** n apartado postal.
postpone [pɔs'pɔun] vt aplazar; ~**ment** n aplazamiento.
postscript ['pɔustskrɪpt] n posdata.
postulate ['pɔstjuleɪt] vt postular.
posture ['pɔstʃə*] n postura, actitud f.
postwar [pɔust'wɔː*] a de posguerra.
posy ['pɔuzɪ] n ramillete m (de flores).
pot [pɔt] n (for cooking) olla; (for flowers) maceta; (for jam) tarro, pote m; (col: marijuana) mota // vt (plant) poner en tiesto; (conserve) conservar.
potato [pə'teɪtəu], pl ~**es** n patata, papa (AM).
potent ['pɔutnt] a potente, poderoso; (drink) fuerte.
potential [pə'tɛnʃl] a potencial, en potencial // n potencial m, potencialidad f.
pothole ['pɔthəul] n (in road) bache m; (underground) caverna; **potholer** n espeleólogo; **potholing** n: **to go potholing** dedicarse a la espeleología.
potion ['pɔuʃən] n poción f, pócima.
potluck [pɔt'lʌk] n: **to take** ~ contentarse con lo que haya.
potshot ['pɔtʃɔt] n: **to take a** ~ **at sth** tirar a algo sin apuntar.
potted ['pɔtɪd] a (food) en conserva; (plant) en tiesto o maceta.
potter ['pɔtə*] n (artistic) ceramista m/f; (artisan) alfarero // vi: **to** ~ **around,** ~ **about** ocuparse en fruslerías; ~**y** n cerámica; alfarería.
potty ['pɔtɪ] a (col: mad) chiflado // n orinal m de niño.
pouch [pautʃ] n (ZOOL) bolsa; (for tobacco) petaca.
pouf(fe) [puːf] n pouf m.
poultice ['pɔultɪs] n cataplasma, emplasto.
poultry ['pɔultrɪ] n aves fpl de corral; (dead) pollos mpl; ~ **farm** n granja avícola.
pounce [pauns] vi: **to** ~ **on** precipitarse sobre // n salto, ataque m.
pound [paund] n (gen) libra; (for dogs) corral m; (for cars) depósito // vt (beat) golpear; (crush) machacar // vi (beat) dar golpes; ~ **sterling** n (libra) esterlina.
pour [pɔː*] vt echar; (tea) servir // vi correr, fluir; (rain) llover a cántaros; **to** ~ **away or off** vt vaciar, verter; **to** ~ **in** vi (people) entrar en tropel; **to** ~ **out** vi

(people) salir en tropel // vt (drink) echar, servir; ~**ing** a: ~**ing rain** lluvia torrencial.
pout [paut] vi hacer pucheros.
poverty ['pɔvətɪ] n pobreza, miseria; (fig) falta, escasez f; ~-**stricken** a necesitado.
powder ['paudə*] n polvo; (face ~) polvos mpl; (gun ~) pólvora // vt polvorear; **to** ~ **one's face** empolvarse; ~ **compact** n polvera; ~ **room** n aseos mpl; ~**y** a polvoriento.
power ['pauə*] n (gen) poder m; (strength) fuerza; (nation) potencia; (ability, POL: of party, leader) poder m, poderío; (drive) empuje m; (TECH) potencia; (ELEC) fuerza, energía // vt impulsar; ~ **cut** n apagón m; ~**ed** a: ~**ed** by impulsado por; ~**ful** a poderoso; (engine) potente; (build) fuerte; (emotion) intenso; ~**less** a impotente, ineficaz; ~ **line** n línea de conducción eléctrica; ~ **point** n enchufe m; ~ **station** n central f eléctrica.
p.p. abbr of **per procurationem:** ~ **J. Smith** p.p. (por poder de) J. Smith.
practicable ['præktɪkəbl] a (scheme) factible.
practical ['præktɪkl] a práctico; ~ **joke** n broma pesada; ~**ly** ad (almost) prácticamente.
practice ['præktɪs] n (habit) costumbre f; (exercise) práctica, ejercicio; (training) adiestramiento; (MED) clientela // vt, vi (US) = **practise; in** ~ (in reality) en la práctica; **out of** ~ desentrenado.
practise, practice (US) ['præktɪs] vt (carry out) practicar; (be in the habit of) tener por costumbre; (profession) ejercer; (train at) hacer ejercicios de // vi ejercer (profesión); (train) entrenar, adiestrarse; **practising** a (Christian etc) practicante; (lawyer) que ejerce.
practitioner [præk'tɪʃənə*] n practicante m/f; (MED) médico/a.
pragmatic [præg'mætɪk] a pragmático.
prairie ['prɛərɪ] n pradera, pampa.
praise [preɪz] n alabanza, elogio, alabanzas fpl, elogios mpl; ~**worthy** a loable, digno de elogios.
pram [præm] n cochecito de niño.
prance [prɑːns] vi (horse) hacer cabriolas.
prank [præŋk] n travesura.
prattle ['prætl] vi parlotear; (child) balbucear.
prawn [prɔːn] n gamba; (small) quisquilla.
pray [preɪ] vi rezar; ~**er** n oración f, rezo; (entreaty) ruego, súplica; ~**er book** n devocionario, misal m.
preach [priːtʃ] vi predicar; ~**er** n predicador/a m/f; (US) pastor m.
preamble [prɪ'æmbl] n preámbulo.
prearranged [priːə'reɪndʒd] a arreglado de antemano.
precarious [prɪ'kɛərɪəs] a precario.
precaution [prɪ'kɔːʃən] n precaución f.
precede [prɪ'siːd] vt, vi preceder.
precedence ['prɛsɪdəns] n precedencia;

preceding (*priority*) prioridad *f*; **precedent** [-ɔnt] *n* precedente *m*.
preceding [prɪ'siːdɪŋ] *a* precedente.
precept ['priːsɛpt] *n* precepto.
precinct ['priːsɪŋkt] *n* recinto; ~s *npl* contornos *mpl*; **pedestrian** ~ zona reservada para peatones; **shopping** ~ zona comercial.
precious ['prɛʃəs] *a* precioso; (*stylized*) afectado.
precipice ['prɛsɪpɪs] *n* precipicio, despeñadero.
precipitate [prɪ'sɪpɪtɪt] *a* (*hasty*) precipitado, apresurado // *vt* [prɪ'sɪpɪteɪt] (*hasten*) acelerar; (*bring about*) causar; **precipitation** [-'teɪʃən] *n* precipitación *f*.
precipitous [prɪ'sɪpɪtəs] *a* (*steep*) escarpado.
precise [prɪ'saɪs] *a* preciso, exacto; (*person*) escrupuloso; ~**ly** *ad* exactamente, precisamente; **precision** [-'sɪʒən] *n* precisión *f*.
preclude [prɪ'kluːd] *vt* excluir.
precocious [prɪ'kəʊʃəs] *a* precoz.
preconceived [priːkən'siːvd] *a* (*idea*) preconcebido.
precursor [priː'kɜːsə*] *n* precursor/a *m/f*.
predator ['prɛdətə*] *n* animal *m* de rapiña; ~**y** *a* rapaz, de rapiña.
predecessor ['priːdɪsɛsə*] *n* antecesor/a *m/f*.
predestination [priːdɛstɪ'neɪʃən] *n* predestinación *f*.
predetermine [priːdɪ'tɜːmɪn] *vt* predeterminar.
predicament [prɪ'dɪkəmənt] *n* apuro.
predict [prɪ'dɪkt] *vt* pronosticar; ~**ion** [-'dɪkʃən] *n* pronóstico.
predominant [prɪ'dɒmɪnənt] *a* predominante; **predominate** [-neɪt] *vi* predominar.
pre-eminent [priː'ɛmɪnənt] *a* preeminente.
pre-empt [priː'ɛmt] *vt* apropiarse de antemano.
preen [priːn] *vt*: **to** ~ **itself** (*bird*) limpiarse (las plumas); **to** ~ **o.s.** pavonearse.
prefab ['priːfæb] *n* casa prefabricada.
prefabricated [priː'fæbrɪkeɪtɪd] *a* prefabricado.
preface ['prɛfəs] *n* prefacio.
prefect ['priːfɛkt] *n* (*Brit: in school*) tutor *m*, monitor *m*.
prefer [prɪ'fɜː*] *vt* preferir; ~**able** ['prɛfrəbl] *a* preferible; ~**ably** ['prɛfrəblɪ] *ad* de preferencia; ~**ence** ['prɛfrəns] *n* preferencia, prioridad *f*; ~**ential** [prɛfə'rɛnʃəl] *a* preferente.
prefix ['priːfɪks] *n* prefijo.
pregnancy ['prɛgnənsɪ] *n* embarazo; **pregnant** [-ɔnt] *a* embarazada; **to be pregnant** estar encinta; **pregnant with** preñado de.
prehistoric ['priːhɪs'tɒrɪk] *a* prehistórico.
prejudge [priː'dʒʌdʒ] *vt* prejuzgar.

prejudice ['prɛdʒʊdɪs] *n* (*bias*) prejuicio; (*harm*) perjuicio // *vt* (*predispose*) predisponer; (*harm*) perjudicar; ~**d** *a* (*person*) predispuesto, con prejuicios; (*view*) parcial, interesado.
prelate ['prɛlət] *n* prelado.
preliminary [prɪ'lɪmɪnərɪ] *a* preliminar.
prelude ['prɛljuːd] *n* preludio.
premarital ['priː'mærɪtl] *a* premarital.
premature ['prɛmətʃuə*] *a* prematuro.
premeditated [priː'mɛdɪteɪtɪd] *a* premeditado.
premier ['prɛmɪə*] *a* primero, principal // *n* (*POL*) primer ministro.
première ['prɛmɪɛə*] *n* estreno.
premise ['prɛmɪs] *n* premisa; ~**s** *npl* local *m*; (*house*) casa *sg*; (*shop*) tienda *sg*; **on the** ~**s** en el local.
premium ['priːmɪəm] *n* premio; (*COMM*) prima; **to be at a** ~ ser muy solicitado.
premonition [prɛmə'nɪʃən] *n* presentimiento.
preoccupation [priːɒkju'peɪʃən] *n* preocupación *f*; **preoccupied** [-'ɒkjupaɪd] *a* (*worried*) preocupado; (*absorbed*) absorto.
prep [prɛp] *n* (*SCOL: study*) deberes *mpl*; ~ **school** *n* = **preparatory school**.
prepaid [priː'peɪd] *a* con porte pagado.
preparation [prɛpə'reɪʃən] *n* preparación *f*; ~**s** *npl* preparativos *mpl*.
preparatory [prɪ'pærətərɪ] *a* preparatorio, preliminar; ~ **to** con miras a; ~ **school** *n* escuela preparatoria.
prepare [prɪ'pɛə*] *vt* preparar, disponer // *vi*: **to** ~ **for** prepararse o disponerse para; (*make preparations*) hacer preparativos para; ~**d to** dispuesto a.
preponderance [prɪ'pɒndərns] *n* preponderancia, predominio.
preposition [prɛpə'zɪʃən] *n* preposición *f*.
preposterous [prɪ'pɒstərəs] *a* absurdo, ridículo.
prerequisite [priː'rɛkwɪzɪt] *n* requisito (previo).
prerogative [prɪ'rɒgətɪv] *n* prerrogativa.
presbyterian [prɛzbɪ'tɪərɪən] *a*, *n* presbiteriano/a.
preschool ['priː'skuːl] *a* preescolar.
prescribe [prɪ'skraɪb] *vt* prescribir; (*MED*) recetar.
prescription [prɪ'skrɪpʃən] *n* prescripción *f*; (*MED*) receta.
presence ['prɛzns] *n* presencia; (*attendance*) asistencia; ~ **of mind** *n* presencia de ánimo.
present ['prɛznt] *a* (*in attendance*) presente; (*current*) actual // *n* (*gift*) regalo; (*actuality*) actualidad *f*, presente *m* // *vt* [prɪ'zɛnt] (*introduce*) presentar; (*expound*) exponer; (*give*) presentar, dar, ofrecer; (*THEATRE*) representar; **at** ~ actualmente; ~**able** [prɪ'zɛntəbl] *a* presentable; ~**ation** [-'teɪʃən] *n* presentación *f*; (*gift*) obsequio; (*of case*) exposición *f*; (*THEATRE*) representación *f*;

~-**day** a actual; ~**ly** ad (soon) dentro de poco.
preservation [prɛzə'veiʃən] n conservación f.
preservative [pri'zɔ:vətiv] n preservativo.
preserve [pri'zɔ:v] vt (keep safe) preservar, proteger; (maintain) conservar; (food) hacer una conserva de; (in salt) salar // n (for game) coto, vedado; (often pl: jam) conserva, confitura.
preside [pri'zaid] vi presidir.
presidency ['prɛzidənsı] n presidencia; **president** [-ənt] n presidente m/f; **presidential** [-'dɛnʃl] a presidencial.
press [prɛs] n (tool, machine, newspapers) prensa; (printer's) imprenta; (crowd) apiñamiento, agolpamiento; (of hand) apretón m // vt (push) empujar; (squeeze) apretar; (clothes: iron) planchar; (TECH) prensar; (harry) acosar; (insist): **to ~ sth on sb** insistir en que uno acepte algo // vi (squeeze) apretar; (pressurize) ejercer presión; **we are ~ed for time** tenemos poco tiempo; **to ~ on** vi avanzar; (hurry) apretar el paso; ~ **agency** n agencia de prensa; ~ **conference** n conferencia de prensa; ~ **cutting** n recorte m (de periódico); ~**ing** a apremiante; ~ **stud** n botón m de presión.
pressure ['prɛʃə*] n presión f; (urgency) apremio, urgencia; (influence) influencia; (MED) tensión f nerviosa; ~ **cooker** n olla a presión; ~ **gauge** n manómetro; ~ **group** n grupo de presión; **pressurized** a a presión.
prestige [prɛs'ti:ʒ] n prestigio; **prestigious** [-'tidʒəs] a prestigioso.
presumably [pri'zju:məbli] ad se supone que, cabe presumir que.
presume [pri'zju:m] vt presumir, suponer; **to ~ to do** (dare) atreverse a; (set out to) pretender.
presumption [pri'zʌmpʃən] n suposición f; (pretension) pretensión f; (boldness) atrevimiento.
presuppose [pri:sə'pəuz] vt presuponer.
pretence, pretense (US) [pri'tɛns] n (claim) pretensión f; (display) ostentación f; (pretext) pretexto; (make-believe) fingimiento; **on the ~ of** so pretexto de.
pretend [pri'tɛnd] vt (feign) fingir // vi (feign) fingir; (claim): **to ~ to sth** pretender a algo.
pretension [pri'tɛnʃən] n (presumption) presunción f; (claim) pretensión f.
pretentious [pri'tɛnʃəs] a presumido; (ostentacious) ostenso, aparatoso.
pretext ['pri:tɛkst] n pretexto.
pretty ['priti] a (gen) hermoso; (person) guapo; (dress) bonito; (sum) importante // ad (quite) bastante; (nearly) casi.
prevail [pri'veil] vi (win) imponerse; (be current) imperar; (be in fashion) estar de moda; (be usual) prevalecer; (persuade): **to ~ (up)on sb to do sth** persuadir a uno a hacer algo; ~**ing** a (dominant)

imperante; (usual) corriente.
prevalent ['prɛvələnt] a (dominant) predominante; (usual) corriente; (fashionable) en boga; (present-day) actual.
prevent [pri'vɛnt] vt: **to ~ (sb) from doing sth** impedir (a uno) hacer algo; ~**able** a evitable; ~**ative** a preventivo; ~**ion** [-'vɛnʃən] n prevención f; ~**ive** a preventivo.
preview ['pri:vju:] n (of film) preestreno; (fig) anticipo.
previous ['pri:vjəs] a previo, anterior; (hasty) prematuro; ~**ly** ad previamente, con anticipación; (in earlier times) antes.
prewar [pri:'wɔ:*] a de preguerra, prebélico.
prey [prei] n presa // vi: **to ~ on** vivir a costa de; (feed on) alimentarse de; (plunder) robar, pillar; **it was ~ing on his mind** le agobiaba, le preocupaba.
price [prais] n precio // vt (goods) fijar el precio de; ~**less** a inapreciable.
prick [prik] n pinchazo; (with pin) alfilerazo; (sting) picadura // vt pinchar; picar; **to ~ up one's ears** aguzar el oído.
prickle ['prikl] n (sensation) escozor m; (BOT) espina; (ZOOL) púa; **prickly** a espinoso; (fig: person) malhumorado; (: touchy) quisquilloso.
pride [praid] n orgullo; (pej) soberbia // vt: **to ~ o.s. on** enorgullecerse de, ufanarse de.
priest [pri:st] n sacerdote m; ~**ess** n sacerdotisa; ~**hood** n (practice) sacerdocio; (priests) clero.
prig [prig] n presumido/a, pedante m/f.
prim [prim] a (formal) estirado; (affected) remilgado; (prudish) gazmoño.
primarily ['praimərili] ad (above all) ante todo; (firstly) en primer lugar.
primary ['praiməri] a primario; (first in importance) principal; ~ **school** n escuela primaria.
primate ['praimit] n (REL) primado // n ['praimeit] (ZOOL) primate m.
prime [praim] a primero, principal; (basic) fundamental; (excellent) selecto, de primera clase // vt (gun, pump) cebar; (fig) preparar, aprestar; **in the ~ of life** en la flor de la vida; ~ **minister** n primer ministro; **primer** (book) libro de texto; (paint) pintura de base.
primitive ['primitiv] a primitivo; (crude) rudimentario; (uncivilized) inculto.
primrose ['primrəuz] n primavera, prímula.
primus (stove) ['praiməs] n hornillo de campaña a presión.
prince [prins] n príncipe m.
princess [prin'sɛs] n princesa.
principal ['prinsipl] a principal, mayor // n director/a m/f.
principality [prinsi'pæliti] n principado.
principle ['prinsipl] n principio.
print [print] n (impression) marca, impresión f; (letters) letra de molde; (fabric) estampado; (ART) estampa,

grabado; (*PHOT*) positiva // *vt* (*gen*) imprimir; (*on mind*) grabar; (*write in capitals*) escribir en letras de molde; **out of** ~ agotado; ~**ed matter** *n* impresos *mpl*; ~**er** *n* impresor/a *m/f*; ~**ing** *n* (*art*) imprenta; (*act*) impresión *f*; (*quantity*) tirada; ~**ing press** *n* (prensa de) imprenta.

prior ['praɪə*] *a* anterior, previo // *n* prior *m*; ~ **to doing** antes de *o* hasta hacer.

priority [praɪ'ɔrɪtɪ] *n* prioridad *f*.

prise [praɪz] *vt*: **to** ~ **open** abrir con palanca.

prism ['prɪzəm] *n* prisma *m*.

prison ['prɪzn] *n* cárcel *f*, prisión *f* // *a* carcelario; ~**er** *n* (*in prison*) preso; (*under arrest*) detenido; (*in dock*) acusado.

privacy ['prɪvəsɪ] *n* (*seclusion*) aislamiento, soledad *f*; (*intimacy*) intimidad *f*.

private ['praɪvɪt] *a* (*personal*) particular; (*confidential*) secreto, reservado; (*intimate*) privado, íntimo; (*sitting etc*) a puertas cerradas // *n* soldado raso; '~' (*on envelope*) 'privado'; (*on door*) 'uso particular *o* privado'; **in** ~ en privado; ~ **enterprise** *n* la empresa privada; ~ **eye** *n* detective *m* privado; ~**ly** *ad* en privado; (*in o.s.*) en el fondo.

privet ['prɪvɪt] *n* alheña.

privilege ['prɪvɪlɪdʒ] *n* privilegio; (*prerogative*) prerrogativa; ~**d** *a* privilegiado.

privy ['prɪvɪ] *a*: **to be** ~ **to** estar enterado de; **P** ~ **Council** *n* Consejo Privado.

prize [praɪz] *n* premio // *a* premiado; (*first class*) de primera clase // *vt* apreciar, estimar; ~**-giving** *n* distribución *f* de premios; ~**winner** *n* premiado/a.

pro [prəu] *n* (*SPORT*) profesional *m/f*; **the** ~**s and cons** los pros y los contras.

probability [prɔbə'bɪlɪtɪ] *n* probabilidad *f*; **probable** ['prɔbəbl] *a* probable; (*plausible*) verosímil; **probably** ['prɔbəblɪ] *ad* probablemente.

probation [prə'beɪʃən] *n*: **on** ~ (*employee*) de prueba; (*LAW*) en libertad condicional.

probe [prəub] *n* (*MED, SPACE*) sonda; (*enquiry*) encuesta, sondeo // *vt* sondar; (*investigate*) indagar.

problem ['prɔbləm] *n* problema *m*; ~**atic** [-'mætɪk] *a* problemático.

procedure [prə'siːdʒə*] *n* (*ADMIN, LAW*) procedimiento; (*method*) proceder *m*; (*bureaucratic*) trámites *mpl*.

proceed [prə'siːd] *vi* proceder; (*continue*): **to** ~ (**with**) continuar *o* seguir (con); ~**ings** *npl* acto *sg*, actos *mpl*; (*LAW*) medidas *fpl*; (*meeting*) función *f*; (*records*) actas *fpl*; ~**s** ['prəusiːdz] *npl* ganancias *fpl*, ingresos *mpl*.

process ['prəusɛs] *n* proceso; (*method*) método, sistema *m*; (*proceeding*) procedimiento // *vt* tratar, elaborar; **in** ~ en curso; ~**ing** *n* elaboración *f*.

procession [prə'sɛʃən] *n* desfile *m*; **funeral** ~ cortejo fúnebre.

proclaim [prə'kleɪm] *vt* proclamar; (*announce*) anunciar; **proclamation** [prɔklə'meɪʃən] *n* proclamación *f*; (*written*) proclama.

procreation [prəukrɪ'eɪʃən] *n* procreación *f*.

procure [prə'kjuə*] *vt* conseguir, obtener.

prod [prɔd] *vt* (*push*) empujar; (*with elbow*) dar un codazo a; (*jab*) pinchar // *n* empuje *m*; codazo; pinchazo.

prodigal ['prɔdɪgl] *a* pródigo.

prodigious [prə'dɪdʒəs] *a* prodigioso.

prodigy ['prɔdɪdʒɪ] *n* prodigio.

produce ['prɔdjuːs] *n* (*AGR*) productos *mpl* agrícolas // *vt* [prə'djuːs] (*gen*) producir; (*profit*) rendir; (*show*) presentar, mostrar; (*THEATRE*) presentar, poner en escena; (*offspring*) dar a luz; **producer** *n* (*THEATRE*) director/a *m/f*; (*AGR, CINEMA*) productor/a *m/f*.

product ['prɔdʌkt] *n* (*thing*) producto; (*result*) fruto, resultado.

production [prə'dʌkʃən] *n* (*act*) producción *f*; (*thing*) producto; (*THEATRE*) representación *f*, obra; ~ **line** *n* línea *o* cadena de montaje.

productive [prə'dʌktɪv] *a* productivo; **productivity** [prɔdʌk'tɪvɪtɪ] *n* productividad *f*.

profane [prə'feɪn] *a* profano; (*language etc*) fuerte.

profess [prə'fɛs] *vt* profesar; (*regret*) manifestar.

profession [prə'fɛʃən] *n* profesión *f*; ~**al** *n* profesional *m/f*; (*expert*) perito // *a* profesional; perito, experto; (*by profession*) de oficio.

professor [prə'fɛsə*] *n* catedrático/a.

proficiency [prə'fɪʃənsɪ] *n* pericia, habilidad *f*; **proficient** [-ənt] *a* perito, hábil.

profile ['prəufaɪl] *n* perfil *m*.

profit ['prɔfɪt] *n* (*COMM*) ganancia; (*fig*) provecho // *vi*: **to** ~ **by** *or* **from** aprovechar *o* sacar provecho de; ~**ability** [-ə'bɪlɪtɪ] *n* rentabilidad *f*; ~**able** *a* (*ECON*) rentable; (*useful*) provechoso; ~**eering** [-'tɪərɪŋ] *n* (*pej*) ganancias *fpl* excesivas.

profound [prə'faund] *a* profundo.

profuse [prə'fjuːs] *a* profuso, pródigo; ~**ly** *ad* profusamente, pródigamente; **profusion** [-'fjuːʒən] *n* profusión *f*, abundancia.

progeny ['prɔdʒɪnɪ] *n* progenie *f*, prole *f*.

programme, program (*US*) ['prəugræm] *n* programa *m* // *vt* programar; **programming, programing** (*US*) *n* programación *f*.

progress ['prəugrɛs] *n* progreso; (*development*) desarrollo // *vi* [prə'grɛs] progresar, avanzar; desarrollarse; **in** ~ en marcha; ~**ion** [-'grɛʃən] *n* progresión *f*; ~**ive** [-'grɛsɪv] *a* progresivo; (*person*) progresista *m/f*.

prohibit [prə'hıbıt] *vt* prohibir; **to ~ sb from doing sth** prohibir a uno hacer algo; **~ion** [prəuı'bıʃən] *n* (*US*) prohibicionismo; **~ive** *a* (*price etc*) excesivo.

project ['prɔdʒɛkt] *n* proyecto // (*vb*: [prə'dʒɛkt]) *vt* proyectar // *vi* (*stick out*) salir, sobresalir.

projectile [prə'dʒɛktaıl] *n* proyectil *m*.

projection [prə'dʒɛkʃən] *n* proyección *f*; (*overhang*) saliente *m*.

projector [prə'dʒɛktə*] *n* proyector *m*.

proletarian [prəulı'tɛərıən] *a, n* proletario/a; **proletariat** [-rıət] *n* proletariado.

proliferate [prə'lıfəreıt] *vi* proliferar, multiplicarse; **proliferation** [-'reıʃən] *n* proliferación *f*.

prolific [prə'lıfık] *a* prolífico.

prologue ['prəulɔg] *n* prólogo.

prolong [prə'lɔŋ] *vt* prolongar, extender.

prom [prɔm] *n abbr of* **promenade** baile *m* de gala.

promenade [prɔmə'nɑːd] *n* (*by sea*) paseo marítimo; **~ concert** *n* concierto (en que parte del público permanece de pie).

prominence ['prɔmınəns] *n* (*fig*) eminencia, importancia; **prominent** [-ənt] *a* (*standing out*) saliente; (*important*) eminente, importante.

promiscuous [prə'mıskjuəs] *a* (*sexually*) libertino.

promise ['prɔmıs] *n* promesa // *vt, vi* prometer; **promising** *a* prometedor(a).

promontory ['prɔməntrı] *n* promontorio.

promote [prə'məut] *vt* (*gen*) promover; (*new product*) hacer propaganda por; (*MIL*) ascender; **promoter** *n* (*of sporting event*) promotor/a *m/f*; **promotion** [-'məuʃən] *n* (*gen*) promoción *f*; (*MIL*) ascenso.

prompt [prɔmpt] *a* pronto // *ad* (*punctually*) puntualmente // *vt* (*urge*) mover, incitar; (*THEATRE*) apuntar; **to ~ sb to do sth** mover a uno a hacer algo; **~er** *n* (*THEATRE*) apuntador/a *m/f*; **~ly** *ad* (*punctually*) puntualmente; (*rapidly*) rápidamente; **~ness** *n* puntualidad *f*; rapidez *f*.

prone [prəun] *a* (*lying*) postrado; **~ to** propenso a.

prong [prɔŋ] *n* diente *m*, púa.

pronoun ['prəunaun] *n* pronombre *m*.

pronounce [prə'nauns] *vt* pronunciar; (*declare*) declarar // *vi*: **to ~ (up)on** pronunciarse sobre; **~d** *a* (*marked*) marcado; **~ment** *n* declaración *f*.

pronunciation [prənʌnsı'eıʃən] *n* pronunciación *f*.

proof [pruːf] *n* prueba; (*of alcohol*) graduación *f* normal // *a*: **~ against** a prueba de; **~reader** *n* corrector/a *m/f* de pruebas.

prop [prɔp] *n* apoyo, (*fig*) sostén *m* // *vt* (*also*: **~ up**) apoyar; (*lean*): **to ~ sth against** apoyar algo contra.

propaganda [prɔpə'gændə] *n* propaganda.

propagate ['prɔpəgeıt] *vt* propagar.

propel [prə'pɛl] *vt* impulsar, propulsar; **~ler** *n* hélice *f*; **~ling pencil** *n* lapicero.

proper ['prɔpə*] *a* (*suited, right*) propio; (*exact*) justo; (*apt*) apropiado, conveniente; (*timely*) oportuno; (*seemly*) correcto, decente; (*authentic*) verdadero; (*col: real*) auténtico.

property ['prɔpətı] *n* (*gen*) propiedad *f*; (*goods*) bienes *mpl*; (*estate*) hacienda; **it's their ~** es suyo, les pertenece.

prophecy ['prɔfısı] *n* profecía; **prophesy** [-saı] *vt* profetizar; (*fig*) predecir.

prophet ['prɔfıt] *n* profeta *m/f*; **~ic** [prə'fɛtık] *a* profético.

proportion [prə'pɔːʃən] *n* proporción *f*; (*share*) parte *f*, porción *f*; **~al** *a* proporcional; **~ate** *a* proporcionado.

proposal [prə'pəuzl] *n* propuesta; (*offer*) oferta; (*plan*) proyecto; (*of marriage*) declaración *f*; (*suggestion*) sugerencia.

propose [prə'pəuz] *vt* proponer; (*offer*) ofrecer // *vi* declararse; **to ~ to do** proponerse hacer.

proposition [prɔpə'zıʃən] *n* propuesta, proposición *f*.

proprietor [prə'praıətə*] *n* propietario, dueño.

propulsion [prə'pʌlʃən] *n* propulsión *f*.

pro rata [prəu'rɑːtə] *ad* a prorrateo.

prosaic [prəu'zeıık] *a* prosaico.

prose [prəuz] *n* prosa.

prosecute ['prɔsıkjuːt] *vt* (*LAW*) procesar; **prosecution** [-'kjuːʃən] *n* procesa, causa; (*accusing side*) parte *f* actora; **prosecutor** *n* acusador/a *m/f*; (*also*: **public prosecutor**) fiscal *m*.

prospect ['prɔspekt] *n* (*view*) vista; (*chance*) posibilidad *f*; (*outlook*) perspectiva; (*hope*) esperanza // (*vb*: [prə'spekt]) *vt* explorar // *vi* buscar; **~s** *npl* (*for work etc*) perspectivas *fpl*; **~ing** *n* prospección *f*; **~ive** *a* (*possible*) probable, esperado; (*certain*) futuro; (*heir*) presunto; (*legislation*) en perspectiva; **~or** *n* explorador/a *m/f*.

prospectus [prə'spektəs] *n* prospecto.

prosper ['prɔspə*] *vi* prosperar; **~ity** [-'spɛrıtı] *n* prosperidad *f*; **~ous** *a* próspero.

prostitute ['prɔstıtjuːt] *n* prostituta.

prostrate ['prɔstreıt] *a* postrado; (*fig*) abatido.

protagonist [prə'tægənıst] *n* protagonista *m/f*.

protect [prə'tɛkt] *vt* proteger; **~ion** *n* protección *f*; **~ive** *a* protector(a); **~or** *n* protector/a *m/f*.

protégé ['prəutɛʒeı] *n* protegido.

protein ['prəutiːn] *n* proteína.

protest ['prəutɛst] *n* protesta // (*vb*: [prə'tɛst]) *vi* protestar // *vt* (*affirm*) afirmar, declarar.

Protestant ['prɔtıstənt] *a, n* protestante *m/f*.

protocol ['prəutəkɔl] *n* protocolo.

prototype ['prəutətaıp] *n* prototipo.

protracted [prə'træktıd] *a* prolongado.

protrude [prə'tru:d] *vi* salir fuera, sobresalir.

proud [praud] *a* orgulloso; (*pej*) soberbio, altanero; (*imposing*) imponente.

prove [pru:v] *vt* probar; (*verify*) comprobar; (*show*) demostrar // *vi*: **to ~ correct** resultar correcto; **to ~ o.s.** ponerse a prueba.

proverb ['prɔvɔ:b] *n* refrán *m*; **~ial** [prə'vɔ:biɔl] *a* proverbial.

provide [prə'vaid] *vt* proporcionar, dar; **to ~ sb with sth** proveer a uno de algo; **to ~ for** *vt* (*person*) mantener a; (*emergency*) prevenir; **~d (that)** *conj* con tal que, siempre que.

providing [prə'vaidiŋ] *conj* a condición de que, siempre que.

province ['prɔvins] *n* provincia; (*fig*) esfera; **provincial** [prə'vinʃəl] *a* de provincia; (*pej*) provinciano.

provision [prə'viʒən] *n* (*gen*) provisión *f*; (*supply*) suministro; (*supplying*) abastecimiento; **~s** *npl* (*food*) comestibles *mpl*; **~al** *a* provisional; (*temporary*) interino.

proviso [prə'vaizəu] *n* condición *f*, estipulación *f*.

provocation [prɔvə'keiʃən] *n* provocación *f*.

provocative [prə'vɔkətiv] *a* provocativo; (*stimulating*) sugestivo.

provoke [prə'vəuk] *vt* (*arouse*) provocar, incitar; (*cause*) causar, producir; (*anger*) irritar.

prow [prau] *n* proa.

prowess ['prauis] *n* (*skill*) destreza, habilidad *f*; (*courage*) valor *m*.

prowl [praul] *vi* (*also*: **~ about, ~ around**) rondar // *n*: **on the ~** de ronda; **~er** *n* rondador/a *m/f*; (*thief*) ladrón/ona *m/f*.

proximity [prɔk'simiti] *n* proximidad *f*.

proxy ['prɔksi] *n* poder *m*; (*person*) apoderado/a; **by ~** por poder *o* poderes.

prudence ['pru:dns] *n* prudencia; **prudent** [-ɔnt] *a* prudente.

prudish ['pru:diʃ] *a* gazmoño.

prune [pru:n] *n* ciruela pasa // *vt* podar.

pry [prai] *vi*: **to ~ into** entrometerse en.

psalm [sɑ:m] *n* salmo.

pseudo- [sju:dəu] *pref* seudo...; **~nym** *n* seudónimo.

psychiatric [saiki'ætrik] *a* psiquiátrico; **psychiatrist** [-'kaiətrist] *n* psiquiatra *m/f*; **psychiatry** [-'kaiətri] *n* psiquiatría.

psychic ['saikik] *a* (*also*: **~al**) psíquico // *n* medium *m/f*.

psychoanalyse [saikəu'ænəlaiz] *vt* psicoanalizar; **psychoanalysis** [-kəuə'nælisis] *n* psicoanálisis *m inv*; **psychoanalyst** [-'ænəlist] *n* psicoanalista *m/f*.

psychological [saikə'lɔdʒikl] *a* psicológico.

psychologist [sai'kɔlədʒist] *n* psicólogo; **psychology** [-dʒi] *n* psicología.

psychopath ['saikəupæθ] *n* psicópata *m/f*.

psychosomatic ['saikəusə'mætik] *a* psicosomático.

psychotic [sai'kɔtik] *a, n* psicótico.

pub [pʌb] *n abbr of* **public house** pub *m*, taberna.

puberty ['pju:bəti] *n* pubertad *f*.

public ['pʌblik] *a, n* público.

publican ['pʌblikən] *n* tabernero.

publication [pʌbli'keiʃən] *n* publicación *f*.

public: **~ convenience** *n* aseos *mpl* públicos; **~ house** *n* bar *m*, pub *m*.

publicity [pʌb'lisiti] *n* publicidad *f*.

publicly ['pʌblikli] *ad* públicamente, en público.

public: **~ opinion** *n* opinión *f* pública; **~ relations** *n* relaciones *fpl* públicas; **~ school** *n* (*Brit*) escuela privada; **~-spirited** *a* de buen ciudadano.

publish ['pʌbliʃ] *vt* publicar; **~er** *n* editor/a *m/f*; **~ing** *n* (*industry*) la industria editorial.

puce [pju:s] *a* de color pardo rojizo.

pucker ['pʌkə*] *vt* (*pleat*) arrugar; (*brow etc*) fruncir.

pudding ['pudiŋ] *n* pudín *m*; (*sweet*) postre *m*; **black ~** morcilla.

puddle ['pʌdl] *n* charco.

puff [pʌf] *n* soplo; (*from mouth*) bocanada; (*sound*) resoplido; (*also*: **powder ~**) borla // *vt*: **to ~ one's pipe** chupar la pipa // *vi* (*gen*) soplar; (*pant*) jadear; **to ~ out smoke** echar humo; **to ~ up** *vt* hinchar, inflar; **~ed** *a* (*col*: *out of breath*) sin aliento.

puffin ['pʌfin] *n* frailecillo.

puffy ['pʌfi] *a* hinchado.

pull [pul] *n* (*tug*): **to give sth a ~** dar un tirón a algo; (*fig*: *advantage*) ventaja; (: *influence*) influencia // *vt* tirar de; (*tug*) jalar; (*muscle*) torcerse; (*haul*) tirar, arrastrar // *vi* tirar, dar un tirón; **to ~ a face** hacer muecas; **to ~ to pieces** hacer pedazos; **to ~ one's punches** no emplear toda la fuerza; **to ~ one's weight** hacer su parte; **to ~ o.s. together** serenarse; **to ~ sb's leg** tomarle el pelo a uno; **to ~ apart** *vt* (*break*) romper (en dos); **to ~ down** *vt* (*house*) derribar; **to ~ in** *vi* (*AUT*: *at the kerb*) parar (junto a la acera); (*RAIL*) llegar (al andén); **to ~ off** *vt* (*deal etc*) cerrar, concluir con éxito; **to ~ out** *vi* irse, marcharse; (*AUT*: *from kerb*) salir // *vt* sacar, arrancar; **to ~ through** *vi* salir (de un apuro); (*MED*) recobrar la salud; **to ~ up** *vi* (*stop*) parar // *vt* (*uproot*) arrancar, desarraigar; (*stop*) parar.

pulley ['puli] *n* polea.

pullover ['puləuvə*] *n* jersey *m*.

pulp [pʌlp] *n* (*of fruit*) pulpa; (*for paper*) pasta.

pulpit ['pulpit] *n* púlpito.

pulsate [pʌl'seit] *vi* pulsar, latir.

pulse [pʌls] *n* (*ANAT*) pulso; (*of music, engine*) pulsación *f*; (*BOT*) legumbre *f*.

pulverize ['pʌlvəraiz] *vt* pulverizar; (*fig*) hacer polvo.

puma ['pjuːmə] *n* puma.

pummel ['pʌml] *vt* dar de puñetazos.

pump [pʌmp] *n* bomba; (*shoe*) zapato de tenis // *vt* sacar con una bomba; (*fig: col*) sonsacar; **to ~ up** *vt* inflar.

pumpkin ['pʌmpkin] *n* calabaza.

pun [pʌn] *n* juego de palabras.

punch [pʌntʃ] *n* (*blow*) golpe *m*, puñetazo; (*tool*) punzón *m*; (*for tickets*) taladro; (*drink*) ponche *m* // *vt* (*hit*): **to ~ sb/sth** dar un puñetazo *o* golpear a uno/algo; (*make a hole in*) punzar; **~card** *n* tarjeta perforada; **~line** *n* palabras que rematan un chiste; **~-up** *n* (*col*) riña.

punctual ['pʌŋktjuəl] *a* puntual; **~ity** [-'ælıtı] *n* puntualidad *f*.

punctuate ['pʌŋktjueit] *vt* interrumpir; **punctuation** [-'eiʃən] *n* puntuación *f*.

puncture ['pʌŋktʃə*] *n* pinchazo // *vt* pinchar.

pundit ['pʌndit] *n* sabio.

pungent ['pʌndʒənt] *a* acre.

punish ['pʌnıʃ] *vt* castigar; **~ment** *n* castigo.

punt [pʌnt] *n* (*boat*) batea.

punter ['pʌntə*] *n* (*gambler*) jugador/a *m/f*.

puny ['pjuːnı] *a* débil.

pup [pʌp] *n* cachorro.

pupil ['pjuːpl] *n* alumno/a.

puppet ['pʌpit] *n* títere *m*.

puppy ['pʌpı] *n* cachorro, perrito.

purchase ['pəːtʃis] *n* compra; (*grip*) pie *m* firme // *vt* comprar; **purchaser** *n* comprador/a *m/f*.

pure [pjuə*] *a* puro.

purée ['pjuərei] *n* puré *m*.

purge [pəːdʒ] *n* (*MED*) purgante *m*; (*POL*) purga // *vt* purgar.

purification [pjuərıfı'keiʃən] *n* purificación *f*, depuración *f*; **purify** ['pjuərıfai] *vt* purificar, depurar.

purist ['pjuərist] *n* purista *m/f*.

puritan ['pjuəritən] *n* puritano/a; **~ical** [-'tænıkl] *a* puritano.

purity ['pjuərıtı] *n* pureza.

purl [pəːl] *n* punto del revés.

purple ['pəːpl] *a* purpúreo; (*bruise*) morado.

purport [pəː'pəːt] *vi*: **to ~ to be/do** dar a entender que es/hace.

purpose ['pəːpəs] *n* propósito; **on ~** a propósito, adrede; **~ful** *a* resuelto, determinado.

purr [pəː*] *n* ronroneo // *vi* ronronear.

purse [pəːs] *n* monedero; (*bag*) bolsa // *vt* fruncir.

purser ['pəːsə*] *n* (*NAUT*) contador *m* de navío.

pursue [pə'sjuː] *vt* seguir, perseguir; (*profession*) ejercer; **pursuer** *n* perseguidor/a *m/f*.

pursuit [pə'sjuːt] *n* (*chase*) caza; (*persecution*) persecución *f*; (*occupation*) carrera; (*pastime*) pasatiempo.

purveyor [pə'veiə*] *n* proveedor/a *m/f*.

pus [pʌs] *n* pus *m*.

push [puʃ] *n* (*gen*) empuje *m*; (*shove*) empujón *m*; (*attack*) ataque *m*; (*advance*) avance *m* // *vt* empujar; (*button*) apretar; (*promote*) promover; (*thrust*): **to ~ sth (into)** meter algo a la fuerza (en) // *vi* empujar; (*fig*) hacer esfuerzos; **to ~ aside** *vt* apartar con la mano; **to ~ off** *vi* (*col*) largarse; **to ~ on** *vi* (*continue*) seguir adelante; **to ~ through** *vt* (*measure*) despachar; **to ~ up** *vt* (*total, prices*) hacer subir; **~chair** *n* sillita de ruedas; **~ing** *a* emprendedor(a), enérgico; **~over** *n* (*col*): **it's a ~over** está tirado; **~y** *a* (*pej*) agresivo.

puss [pus], **pussy(-cat)** ['pusı(kæt)] *n* minino.

put [put], *pt, pp* **put** *vt* (*place*) poner, colocar; (*~ into*) meter; (*say*) declarar, expresar; (*a question*) hacer; (*estimate*) calcular; **to ~ about** *vi* (*NAUT*) virar // *vt* (*rumour*) diseminar; **to ~ across** *vt* (*ideas etc*) comunicar; **to ~ away** *vt* (*store*) guardar; **to ~ back** *vt* (*replace*) devolver a su lugar; (*postpone*) posponer; **to ~ by** *vt* (*money*) guardar; **to ~ down** *vt* (*on ground*) poner en el suelo; (*animal*) sacrificar; (*in writing*) apuntar; (*suppress: revolt etc*) sofocar; (*attribute*) atribuir; **to ~ forward** *vt* (*ideas*) presentar, proponer; (*date*) adelantar; **to ~ in** *vt* (*application, complaint*) presentar; **to ~ off** *vt* (*postpone*) aplazar; (*discourage*) desanimar; **to ~ on** *vt* (*clothes, lipstick etc*) ponerse; (*light etc*) encender; (*play etc*) presentar; (*weight*) ganar; (*brake*) echar; (*attitude*) adoptar postura de; **to ~ out** *vt* (*fire, light*) apagar; (*one's hand*) alargar; (*news, rumour*) sacar a luz, diseminar; (*tongue etc*) sacar; (*person: inconvenience*) molestar, fastidiar; **to ~ up** *vt* (*raise*) levantar, alzar; (*hang*) colgar; (*build*) construir; (*increase*) aumentar; (*accommodate*) alojar; **to ~ up with** *vt fus* aguantar.

putrid ['pjuːtrid] *a* podrido.

putt [pʌt] *vt* golpear con poca fuerza // *n* put *m*, golpe *m* corto; **~er** *n* (*GOLF*) putter *m*; **~ing green** *n* campo de golf en miniatura.

putty ['pʌtı] *n* masilla.

puzzle ['pʌzl] *n* (*riddle*) acertijo; (*jigsaw*) rompecabezas *m inv*; (*crossword*) crucigrama *m*; (*mystery*) misterio, problema *m* // *vt* dejar perplejo, confundir // *vi* devanarse los sesos; **puzzling** *a* misterioso, enigmático.

pygmy ['pigmi] *n* pigmeo.

pyjamas [pı'dʒɑːməz] *npl* pijama *m*.

pylon ['pailən] *n* pilón *m*, poste *m*.

pyramid ['pirəmid] *n* pirámide *m*.

python ['paiθən] *n* pitón *m*.

Q

quack [kwæk] n (of duck) graznido; (pej: doctor) curandero // vi graznar.
quad [kwɔd] abbr of **quadrangle; quadruplet.**
quadrangle ['kwɔdræŋgl] n (courtyard: abbr: **quad**) patio.
quadruple [kwɔ'drupl] a cuádruple // n cuádruplo // vt, vi cuadruplicar.
quadruplets [kwɔ:'dru:plɪts] npl cuatrillizos mpl.
quagmire ['kwægmaɪɔ*] n lodazal m, cenegal m.
quail [kweɪl] n (bird) codorniz f // vi amedrentarse.
quaint [kweɪnt] a curioso; (picturesque) pintoresco.
quake [kweɪk] vi temblar // n abbr of **earthquake.**
Quaker ['kweɪkɔ*] n cuáquero/a.
qualification [kwɔlɪfɪ'keɪʃən] n (reservation) reserva; (modification) modificación f; (act) calificación f; (degree) título; **qualified** ['kwɔlɪfaɪd] a (trained) cualificado; (fit) apto, competente; (limited) limitado; (professionally) con título.
qualify ['kwɔlɪfaɪ] vt calificar; (capacitate) capacitar; (modify) modificar; (limit) moderar // vi (SPORT) clasificarse; **to ~ (as)** calificarse (de), graduarse (en); **to ~ (for)** reunir los requisitos (para).
quality ['kwɔlɪtɪ] n calidad f; (moral) cualidad f.
qualm [kwɑ:m] n escrúpulo.
quandary ['kwɔndrɪ] n: **to be in a ~** estar en un dilema.
quantity ['kwɔntɪtɪ] n cantidad f.
quarantine ['kwɔrntiːn] n cuarentena.
quarrel ['kwɔrl] n (argument) riña; (fight) pelea // vi reñir; pelearse; **~some** a pendenciero.
quarry ['kwɔrɪ] n (for stone) cantera; (animal) presa.
quart [kwɔ:t] n cuarto de galón = 1.136 litros.
quarter ['kwɔ:tɔ*] n cuarto, cuarta parte f; (of year) trimestre m; (district) barrio // vt dividir en cuartos; (MIL: lodge) alojar; **~s** npl (barracks) cuartel m; (living ~s) alojamiento sg; **a ~ of an hour** un cuarto de hora; **~ final** n cuarto de final; **~ly** a trimestral // ad cada 3 meses, trimestralmente; **~master** n (MIL) comisario, intendente m militar.
quartet(te) [kwɔ:'tɛt] n cuarteto.
quartz [kwɔ:ts] n cuarzo.
quash [kwɔʃ] vt (verdict) anular.
quasi- ['kweɪzaɪ] pref cuasi.
quaver ['kweɪvɔ*] n (MUS) corchea // vi temblar.
quay [ki:] n (also: **~side**) muelle m.
queasy ['kwi:zɪ] a (sickly) delicado.
queen [kwi:n] n (gen) reina; (CARDS etc)

dama; **~ mother** n reina madre.
queer [kwɪɔ*] a (odd) raro, extraño; (suspect) sospechoso // n (col) maricón m.
quell [kwɛl] vt calmar; (put down) sofocar.
quench [kwɛntʃ] vt apagar.
query ['kwɪɔrɪ] n (question) pregunta; (doubt) duda; (fig) interrogante f // vt preguntar; poner en duda.
quest [kwɛst] n busca, búsqueda.
question ['kwɛstʃən] n pregunta; (matter) asunto, cuestión f // vt (gen) preguntar; (doubt) dudar de; (interrogate) interrogar, hacer preguntas a; **beyond ~** fuera de toda duda; **out of the ~** imposible, ni hablar; **~able** a discutible; (doubtful) dudoso; **~ mark** n punto de interrogación; **~naire** [-'nɛɔ*] n cuestionario.
queue [kju:] n cola // vi hacer cola.
quibble ['kwɪbl] vi sutilizar.
quick [kwɪk] a rápido; (temper) vivo; (agile) ágil; (mind) listo; (eye) agudo; (ear) fino; **be ~!** ¡date prisa!; **~en** vt apresurar // vi apresurarse, darse prisa; **~ly** ad rápidamente, de prisa; **~ness** n rapidez f; agilidad f; (liveliness) viveza; **~sand** n arenas fpl movedizas; **~step** n (dance) fox-trot m, quickstep m; **~-witted** a perspicaz.
quid [kwɪd] n, pl inv (Brit: col) libra.
quiet ['kwaɪɔt] a tranquilo; (silent) callado; (ceremony) discreto // n silencio, tranquilidad f; **keep ~!** ¡cállate!, ¡silencio!; **~en** (also: **~en down**) vi (grow calm) calmarse; (grow silent) callarse // vt calmar; hacer callar; **~ly** ad (gen) tranquilamente; (silently) silenciosamente; **~ness** n (silence) silencio; (calm) tranquilidad f.
quilt [kwɪlt] n edredón m; (continental) **~** n edredón m.
quin [kwɪn] abbr of **quintuplet.**
quinine [kwɪ'ni:n] n quinina.
quintet(te) [kwɪn'tɛt] n quinteto.
quintuplets [kwɪn'tju:plɪts] npl quintillizos mpl.
quip [kwɪp] n pulla.
quirk [kwɔ:k] n peculiaridad f.
quit [kwɪt] pt, pp **quit** or **quitted** vt dejar, abandonar; (premises) desocupar // vi (give up) retirarse; (go away) irse; (resign) dimitir; (stop work) abandonar (una empresa).
quite [kwaɪt] ad (rather) bastante; (entirely) completamente; **~ a few of them** un buen número de ellos; **~ (so)!** ¡así es!, ¡exactamente!
quits [kwɪts] a: **~ (with)** en paz (con).
quiver ['kwɪvɔ*] vi estremecerse // n (for arrows) carcaj m.
quiz [kwɪz] n (game) concurso; (questioning) interrogatorio // vt interrogar; **~zical** a burlón(ona).
quoits [kwɔɪts] npl juego de aros.
quorum ['kwɔ:rəm] n quórum m.
quota ['kwɔutɔ] n cuota.
quotation [kwɔu'teɪʃən] n cita; (estimate)

presupuesto; ~ **marks** *npl* comillas *fpl.*

quote [kwǝut] *n* cita // *vt* (*sentence*) citar; (*price*) fijar // *vi*: **to ~ from** citar de.

quotient ['kwǝuʃǝnt] *n* cociente *m.*

R

rabbi ['ræbaɪ] *n* rabino.

rabbit ['ræbɪt] *n* conejo; ~ **hole** *n* hura (de conejos); ~ **hutch** *n* conejera.

rabble ['ræbl] *n* (*pej*) chusma, populacho.

rabies ['reɪbiːz] *n* rabia.

RAC *n abbr of* **Royal Automobile Club.**

raccoon [rǝ'kuːn] *n* mapache *m.*

race [reɪs] *n* (*gen*) carrera; (*species*) raza, estirpe *f* // *vt* (*horse*) presentar (en carrera); (*engine*) acelerar // *vi* (*compete*) competir; (*run*) correr; (*pulse*) latir a ritmo acelerado; ~ **course** *n* hipódromo; ~ **horse** *n* caballo de carreras; ~ **track** *n* hipódromo; (*for cars*) autódromo.

racial ['reɪʃl] *a* racial; ~ **ism** *n* racismo; ~ **ist** *a, n* racista *m/f.*

racing ['reɪsɪŋ] *n* carreras *fpl*; ~ **car** *n* coche *m* de carreras; ~ **driver** *n* corredor/a *m/f* de coches.

racist ['reɪsɪst] *a, n* (*pej*) racista *m/f.*

rack [ræk] *n* (*also*: **luggage ~**) rejilla; (*shelf*) estante *m*; (*also*: **roof ~**) baca, portaequipajes *m inv*; (*clothes ~*) percha // *vt* (*cause pain to*) atormentar.

racket ['rækɪt] *n* (*for tennis*) raqueta; (*noise*) ruido, estrépito; (*swindle*) estafa, timo.

racoon [rǝ'kuːn] *n* = **raccoon.**

racquet ['rækɪt] *n* raqueta.

racy ['reɪsɪ] *a* picante, salado.

radar ['reɪdɑː*] *n* radar *m.*

radiance ['reɪdɪǝns] *n* brillantez *f,* resplandor *m*; **radiant** [-ǝnt] *a* brillante, resplandeciente.

radiate ['reɪdɪeɪt] *vt* (*heat*) radiar, irradiar // *vi* (*lines*) extenderse.

radiation [reɪdɪ'eɪʃǝn] *n* radiación *f.*

radiator ['reɪdɪeɪtǝ*] *n* radiador *m*; ~ **cap** *n* tapón *m* de radiador.

radical ['rædɪkl] *a* radical.

radio ['reɪdɪǝu] *n* radio *f*; **on the ~** por radio; ~ **station** *n* emisora.

radio... [reɪdɪǝu] *pref*: ~ **active** *a* radioactivo; ~ **activity** *n* radioactividad *f*; ~ **-controlled** *a* teledirigido; ~ **graphy** [-'ɔgrǝfɪ] *n* radiografía; ~ **logy** [-'ɔlǝdʒɪ] *n* radiología; ~ **telephone** *n* radioteléfono; ~ **therapy** *n* radioterapia.

radish ['rædɪʃ] *n* rábano.

radius ['reɪdɪǝs], *pl* **radii** [-ɪaɪ] *n* radio.

raffia ['ræfɪǝ] *n* rafia.

raffle ['ræfl] *n* rifa, sorteo // *vt* rifar.

raft [rɑːft] *n* (*also*: **life ~**) balsa.

rafter ['rɑːftǝ*] *n* viga.

rag [ræg] *n* (*piece of cloth*) trapo; (*torn cloth*) harapo; (*pej*: *newspaper*) periodicucho; (*for charity*) actividades estudiantiles benéficas // *vt* tomar el pelo a; ~ **s** *npl* harapos *mpl*; ~ **-and-bone man**

n trapero; ~ **doll** *n* muñeca de trapo.

rage [reɪdʒ] *n* (*fury*) rabia, furor *m*; (*fashion*) boga // *vi* (*person*) rabiar, estar furioso; (*storm*) bramar.

ragged ['rægɪd] *a* (*edge*) desigual, mellado; (*cuff*) roto; (*appearance*) andrajoso, harapiento; (*coastline*) accidentado.

raid [reɪd] *n* (MIL) incursión *f*; (*criminal*) asalto; (*attack*) ataque *m*; (*by police*) redada // *vt* invadir, atacar; asaltar; ~ **er** *n* invasor/a *m/f*; (*criminal*) asaltante *m/f.*

rail [reɪl] *n* (*on stair*) barandilla, pasamanos *m inv*; (*on bridge, balcony*) pretil *m*; (*of ship*) borda; (*for train*) riel *m,* carril *m*; ~ **s** *npl* vía *sg*; **by** ~ por ferrocarril; ~ **ing(s)** *n(pl)* verja *sg,* enrejado *sg*; ~ **road** (US), ~ **way** *n* ferrocarril *m*, vía férrea; ~ **wayman** *n* ferroviario; ~ **way station** *n* estación *f* de ferrocarril.

rain [reɪn] *n* lluvia // *vi* llover; **in the ~** bajo la lluvia; **it's ~ ing** llueve, está lloviendo; ~ **bow** *n* arco iris; ~ **coat** *n* impermeable *m*; ~ **drop** *n* gota de lluvia; ~ **fall** *n* lluvia; ~ **y** *a* lluvioso.

raise [reɪz] *n* aumento // *vt* (*lift*) levantar; (*build*) erigir, edificar; (*increase*) aumentar; (*doubts*) suscitar; (*a question*) plantear; (*cattle, family*) criar; (*crop*) cultivar; (*army*) reclutar; (*funds*) reunir; (*loan*) obtener; **to ~ one's voice** alzar la voz.

raisin ['reɪzn] *n* paso de Corinto.

rake [reɪk] *n* (*tool*) rastrillo; (*person*) libertino // *vt* (*garden*) rastrillar; (*fire*) hurgar; (*with machine gun*) barrer.

rakish ['reɪkɪʃ] *a* (*suave*) gallardo; **at a ~ angle** echado al lado.

rally ['rælɪ] *n* (POL *etc*) reunión *f,* mitin *m*; (AUT) rallye *m*; (TENNIS) peloteo // *vt* reunir; (*encourage*) reanimar // *vi* reunirse; (*sick person, Stock Exchange*) recuperarse; **to ~ round** *vt fus* (*fig*) dar apoyo a.

ram [ræm] *n* carnero; (TECH) pisón *m* // *vt* (*crash into*) dar contra, chocar con; (*tread down*) apisonar.

ramble ['ræmbl] *n* caminata, excursión *f* en el campo // *vi* (*pej*: *also*: ~ **on**) divagar; **rambler** *n* excursionista *m/f*; (BOT) trepadora; **rambling** *a* (*speech*) divagador(a); (BOT) trepador(a) // *n* excursionismo.

ramp [ræmp] *n* rampa.

rampage [ræm'peɪdʒ] *n*: **to be on the ~** desbocarse // *vi*: **they went rampaging through the town** corrieron como locos por la ciudad.

rampant ['ræmpǝnt] *a* (*disease etc*) violento.

rampart ['ræmpɑːt] *n* terraplén *m*; (*wall*) muralla.

ramshackle ['ræmʃækl] *a* destartalado.

ran [ræn] *pt of* **run.**

ranch [rɑːntʃ] *n* hacienda, estancia; ~ **er** *n* ganadero.

rancid ['rænsıd] a rancio.
rancour, rancor (US) ['ræŋkə*] n rencor m.
random ['rændəm] a fortuito, sin orden // n: **at** ~ al azar.
randy ['rændı] a (col) cachondo.
rang [ræŋ] pt of **ring.**
range [reındʒ] n (of mountains) cadena, cordillera; (of missile) alcance m; (of voice) extensión f; (series) serie f; (of products) surtido; (MIL: also: **shooting** ~) campo de tiro; (also: **kitchen** ~) fogón m // vt (place) colocar; (arrange) arreglar // vi: **to** ~ **over** (wander) recorrer; (extend) extenderse por; **to** ~ **from ... to...** oscilar entre ... y...; **ranger** n guardabosques m inv.
rank [ræŋk] n (row) fila; (MIL) rango; (status) categoría; (also: **taxi** ~) parada // vi: **to** ~ **among** figurar entre // a (stinking) fétido, rancio; **the** ~ **and file** (fig) la base.
rankle ['ræŋkl] vi (insult) doler.
ransack ['rænsæk] vt (search) registrar; (plunder) saquear.
ransom ['rænsəm] n rescate m; **to hold sb to** ~ (fig) poner a uno entre la espada y la pared.
rant [rænt] vi divagar, desvariar; ~**ing** n lenguaje m declamatorio.
rap [ræp] n golpecito, golpe m seco // vt tocar, dar un golpecito en.
rape [reıp] n violación f // vt violar.
rapid ['ræpıd] a rápido; ~**s** npl (GEO) rápidos mpl; ~**ity** [rə'pıdıtı] n rapidez f.
rapist ['reıpıst] n violador m.
rapport [ræ'pɔ:*] n armonía, relación f amistosa.
rapture ['ræptʃə*] n éxtasis m, rapto; **rapturous** a extático; (applause) entusiasta.
rare [rɛə*] a raro, poco común; (CULIN: steak) poco hecho.
rarely ['rɛəlı] ad rara vez.
rarity ['rɛərıtı] n rareza.
rascal ['rɑ:skl] n pillo, pícaro.
rash [ræʃ] a imprudente, precipitado // n (MED) salpullido, erupción f (cutánea).
rasher ['ræʃə*] n lonja.
rasp [rɑ:sp] n (tool) escofina.
raspberry ['rɑ:zbərı] n frambuesa; ~ **bush** n frambueso.
rasping ['rɑ:spıŋ] a: **a** ~ **noise** un ruido áspero.
rat [ræt] n rata.
ratchet ['rætʃıt] n (TECH) trinquete m.
rate [reıt] n (ratio) razón f; (percentage) tanto por ciento; (price) precio; (: of hotel) tarifa; (of interest) tipo; (speed) velocidad f // vt (value) tasar; (estimate) estimar; **to** ~ **as** ser considerado como; ~**s** npl (Brit) impuesto sg municipal; (fees) tarifa sg; ~**able value** n valor m impuesto; ~**payer** n contribuyente m/f.
rather ['rɑ:ðə*] ad antes, más bien; (in speech) mejor dicho; **it's** ~ **expensive** es algo caro; (too much) es demasiado caro;

there's ~ **a lot** hay bastante; **I would** or **I'd** ~ **go** preferiría ir.
ratify ['rætıfaı] vt ratificar.
rating ['reıtıŋ] n (valuation) tasación f; (value) valor m; (standing) posición f; (NAUT. category) clase f; (: sailor) marinero.
ratio ['reıʃıəu] n razón f; **in the** ~ **of 100 to 1** a razón de 100 a 1.
ration ['ræʃən] n ración f; ~**s** npl víveres mpl // vt racionar.
rational ['ræʃənl] a racional; (solution, reasoning) lógico, razonable; (person) cuerdo, sensato; **rationale** [-'nɑ:l] n razón f fundamental; ~**ize** vt organizar lógicamente, racionalizar; ~**ly** ad racionalmente; (logically) lógicamente.
rationing ['ræʃnıŋ] n racionamiento.
rattle ['rætl] n golpeteo; (of train etc) traqueteo; (of hail) tamborileo; (object: of baby) sonaja, sonajero; (: of sports fan) matraca; (of snake) cascabel m // vi sonar, golpear; traquetear; tamborilear; (small objects) castañetear // vt agitar, sacudir; ~**snake** n serpiente f de cascabel.
raucous ['rɔ:kəs] a estridente, ronco.
ravage ['rævıdʒ] vt hacer estragos, destrozar; ~**s** npl estragos mpl.
rave [reıv] vi (in anger) encolerizarse; (with enthusiasm) entusiasmarse; (MED) delirar, desvariar.
raven ['reıvən] n cuervo.
ravenous ['rævənəs] a hambriento, famélico.
ravine [rə'vi:n] n barranco.
raving ['reıvıŋ] a: ~ **lunatic** loco de atar.
ravioli [rævı'əulı] n raviolis mpl.
ravish ['rævıʃ] vt encantar; ~**ing** a encantador(a).
raw [rɔ:] a (uncooked) crudo; (not processed) bruto; (sore) vivo; (inexperienced) novato, inexperto; ~ **material** n materia prima.
ray [reı] n rayo; ~ **of hope** (rayo de) esperanza.
rayon ['reıɔn] n rayón m.
raze [reız] vt arrasar.
razor ['reızə*] n (open) navaja; (safety ~) máquina de afeitar; ~ **blade** n hoja de afeitar.
Rd abbr of **road.**
re [ri:] prep con referencia a.
reach [ri:tʃ] n alcance m; (BOXING) envergadura; (of river etc) extensión f entre dos recodos // vt alcanzar, llegar a; (achieve) lograr; (stretch out) alargar, extender // vi alcanzar, extenderse; **within** ~ (object) al alcance (de la mano); **out of** ~ fuera del alcance; **to** ~ **out for sth** alargar o tender la mano para tomar algo.
react [ri:'ækt] vi reaccionar; ~**ion** [-'ækʃən] n reacción f; ~**ionary** [-'ækʃənrı] a, n reaccionario/a.
reactor [ri:'æktə*] n reactor m.
read [ri:d], pt, pp **read** [rɛd] vi leer // vt

leer; (*understand*) entender; (*study*) estudiar; **to ~ out** *vt* leer en alta voz; **~able** *a* (*writing*) legible; (*book*) que merece leerse; **~er** *n* lector/a *m/f*; (*book*) libro de lecturas; (*at university*) profesor/a *m/f*; **~ership** *n* (*of paper etc*) número de lectores.

readily ['rɛdɪlɪ] *ad* (*willingly*) de buena gana; (*easily*) fácilmente; (*quickly*) en seguida.

readiness ['rɛdɪnɪs] *n* buena voluntad; (*preparedness*) preparación *f*; **in ~** (*prepared*) listo, preparado.

reading ['riːdɪŋ] *n* lectura; (*understanding*) comprensión *f*; (*on instrument*) indicación *f*.

readjust [riːə'dʒʌst] *vt* reajustar // *vi* (*person*): **to ~ to** reorientarse a.

ready ['rɛdɪ] *a* listo, preparado; (*willing*) dispuesto; (*available*) disponible // *ad*: **~-cooked** listo para comer // *n*: **at the ~** (*MIL*) listo para tirar; **~-made** *a* confeccionado; **~ reckoner** *n* libro de cálculos hechos.

reaffirm [riːə'fɜːm] *vt* reafirmar.

real [rɪəl] *a* verdadero, auténtico; **in ~ terms** en términos reales; **~ estate** *n* bienes *mpl* raíces; **~ism** *n* (*also ART*) realismo; **~ist** *n* realista *m/f*; **~istic** [-'lɪstɪk] *a* realista.

reality [riː'ælɪtɪ] *n* realidad *f*; **in ~** en realidad.

realization [rɪəlaɪ'zeɪʃən] *n* comprensión *f*; (*COMM*) realización *f*.

realize ['rɪəlaɪz] *vt* (*understand*) darse cuenta de; (*a project, COMM: asset*) realizar.

really ['rɪəlɪ] *ad* verdaderamente, realmente; **~?** ¿de veras?

realm [rɛlm] *n* reino; (*fig*) esfera.

reap [riːp] *vt* segar; (*fig*) cosechar, recoger; **~er** *n* segadora.

reappear [riːə'pɪə*] *vi* reaparecer; **~ance** *n* reaparición *f*.

reapply [riːə'plaɪ] *vi*: **to ~ for** aplicar de nuevo.

rear [rɪə*] *a* trasero // *n* parte *f* trasera // *vt* (*cattle, family*) criar // *vi* (*also: ~ up*) (*animal*) encabritarse; **~-engined** *a* (*AUT*) con motor trasero; **~guard** *n* retaguardia.

rearm [riː'ɑːm] *vt, vi* rearmar; **~ament** *n* rearme *m*.

rearrange [riːə'reɪndʒ] *vt* ordenar o arreglar de nuevo.

rear-view ['rɪəvjuː] *a*: **~ mirror** (*AUT*) espejo retrovisor.

reason ['riːzn] *n* (*gen*) razón *f*; (*cause*) motivo, causa; (*sense*) sensatez *f* // *vi*: **to ~ with sb** alegar razones para convencer a uno; **it stands to ~ that** es lógico que; **~able** *a* razonable; (*sensible*) sensato; **~ably** *ad* razonablemente; **~ed** *a* (*argument*) razonado; **~ing** *n* razonamiento, argumentos *mpl*.

reassemble [riːə'sɛmbl] *vt* (*machine*) montar de nuevo // *vi* reunirse de nuevo.

reassure [riːə'ʃuə*] *vt* tranquilizar,

alentar; **to ~ sb of** tranquilizar a uno diciendo que; **reassuring** *a* alentador(a).

rebate ['riːbeɪt] *n* (*on product*) rebaja; (*on tax etc*) descuento.

rebel ['rɛbl] *n* rebelde *m/f* // *vi* [rɪ'bɛl] rebelarse, sublevarse; **~lion** *n* rebelión *f*, sublevación *f*; **~lious** *a* rebelde; (*child*) revoltoso.

rebirth [riː'bɜːθ] *n* renacimiento.

rebound [rɪ'baund] *vi* (*ball*) rebotar // *n* ['riːbaund] rebote *m*.

rebuff [rɪ'bʌf] *n* desaire *m*, rechazo // *vt* rechazar.

rebuild [riː'bɪld] (*irg: like* **build**) *vt* reconstruir.

rebuke [rɪ'bjuːk] *n* reprimenda // *vt* reprender.

recalcitrant [rɪ'kælsɪtrənt] *a* reacio.

recall [rɪ'kɔːl] *vt* (*remember*) recordar; (*ambassador etc*) retirar // *n* aviso, llamada.

recant [rɪ'kænt] *vi* retractarse.

recap ['riːkæp] *vt, vi* recapitular.

recapture [riː'kæptʃə*] *vt* (*town*) reconquistar; (*atmosphere*) hacer revivir.

recede [rɪ'siːd] *vi* retroceder; **receding** *a* (*forehead, chin*) huidizo.

receipt [rɪ'siːt] *n* (*document*) recibo; (*act of receiving*) recepción *f*; **~s** *npl* (*COMM*) ingresos *mpl*.

receive [rɪ'siːv] *vt* recibir; (*guest*) acoger; (*wound*) sufrir; **receiver** *n* (*TEL*) auricular *m*; (*of stolen goods*) receptador/a *m/f*; (*COMM*) recibidor/a *m/f*.

recent ['riːsnt] *a* reciente; **~ly** *ad* recién, recientemente.

receptacle [rɪ'sɛptɪkl] *n* receptáculo.

reception [rɪ'sɛpʃən] *n* (*gen*) recepción *f*; (*welcome*) acogida; **~ desk** *n* recepción *f*; **~ist** *n* recepcionista *m/f*.

receptive [rɪ'sɛptɪv] *a* receptivo.

recess [rɪ'sɛs] *n* (*in room*) hueco; (*for bed*) nicho; (*secret place*) escondrijo; (*POL etc: holiday*) vacaciones *fpl*; **~ion** *n* recesión *f*.

recharge [riː'tʃɑːdʒ] *vt* (*battery*) recargar.

recipe ['rɛsɪpɪ] *n* receta.

recipient [rɪ'sɪpɪənt] *n* recibidor/a *m/f*; (*of letter*) destinatario/a.

reciprocal [rɪ'sɪprəkl] *a* recíproco.

recital [rɪ'saɪtl] *n* recital *m*.

recite [rɪ'saɪt] *vt* (*poem*) recitar; (*complaints etc*) enumerar.

reckless ['rɛkləs] *a* temerario, imprudente; (*speed*) excesivo, peligroso; **~ly** *ad* imprudentemente; de modo peligroso.

reckon ['rɛkən] *vt* (*count*) contar; (*consider*) considerar; (*think*): **I ~ that...** me parece que...; **~ing** *n* (*calculation*) cálculo; **the day of ~ing** el día del juicio (final).

reclaim [rɪ'kleɪm] *vt* (*land*) recuperar; (: *from sea*) rescatar; (*demand back*) reclamar; **reclamation** [rɛklə'meɪʃən] *n* recuperación *f*; rescate *m*.

recline [rɪ'klaɪn] *vi* reclinarse; (*lean*) apoyarse; **reclining** *a* (*seat*) reclinable.

recluse [rɪ'kluːs] n recluso.
recognition [rɛkəg'nɪʃən] n reconocimiento; **transformed beyond** ~ tan transformado que resulta irreconocible.
recognizable ['rɛkəgnaɪzəbl] a: ~ **(by)** reconocible (por).
recognize ['rɛkəgnaɪz] vt reconocer, conocer; **to** ~ **by/as** reconocer de/por.
recoil [rɪ'kɔɪl] vi (gun) retroceder; (person): **to** ~ **from doing sth** sentir repugnancia por hacer algo.
recollect [rɛkə'lɛkt] vt recordar, acordarse de; ~**ion** [-'lɛkʃən] n recuerdo.
recommend [rɛkə'mɛnd] vt recomendar; ~**ation** [-'deɪʃən] n recomendación f.
recompense ['rɛkəmpɛns] vt recompensar // n recompensa.
reconcile ['rɛkənsaɪl] vt (two people) reconciliar; (two facts) conciliar; **to** ~ **o.s. to sth** resignarse a algo, conformarse a algo; **reconciliation** [-sɪlɪ'eɪʃən] n reconciliación f.
reconnaissance [rɪ'kɒnɪsns] n (MIL) reconocimiento.
reconnoitre, reconnoiter (US) [rɛkə'nɔɪtə*] vt, vi (MIL) reconocer.
reconsider [riːkən'sɪdə*] vt repensar.
reconstitute [riː'kɒnstɪtjuːt] vt reconstituir.
reconstruct [riːkən'strʌkt] vt reconstruir; ~**ion** [-kʃən] n reconstrucción f.
record ['rɛkɔːd] n (MUS) disco; (of meeting etc) relación f; (register) registro, partida; (file) archivo; (also: **police** ~) antecedentes mpl; (written) expediente m; (SPORT) récord m // vt [rɪ'kɔːd] (set down) registrar; (relate) hacer constar; (MUS: song etc) grabar; **in** ~ **time** en un tiempo récord; **off the** ~ a no oficial // ad confidencialmente; ~ **card** n (in file) ficha; ~**er** n (MUS) flauta de pico; (TECH) contador m; ~ **holder** n (SPORT) recordman m; ~ **-ing** n (MUS) grabación f; ~ **player** n tocadiscos m inv.
recount [rɪ'kaunt] vt contar.
re-count ['riːkaunt] n (POL: of votes) segundo escrutinio // vt [riː'kaunt] volver a contar.
recoup [rɪ'kuːp] vt: **to** ~ **one's losses** recuperar las pérdidas.
recourse [rɪ'kɔːs] n recurso; **to have** ~ **to** recurrir a.
recover [rɪ'kʌvə*] vt recobrar, recuperar; (rescue) rescatar // vi (from illness) reponerse; (from shock) sobreponerse; ~**y** n recuperación f; rescate m; (MED) mejora.
recreate [riːkrɪ'eɪt] vt recrear.
recreation [rɛkrɪ'eɪʃən] n recreación f; (play) recreo; ~**al** a de recreo.
recrimination [rɪkrɪmɪ'neɪʃən] n recriminación f.
recruit [rɪ'kruːt] n recluta m/f // vt reclutar; ~**ment** n reclutamiento.
rectangle ['rɛktæŋgl] n rectángulo; **rectangular** [-'tæŋgjulə*] a rectangular.
rectify ['rɛktɪfaɪ] vt rectificar.

rector ['rɛktə*] n (REL) párroco; (SCOL) rector/a m/f; ~**y** n casa del párroco.
recuperate [rɪ'kuːpəreɪt] vi reponerse, restablecerse.
recur [rɪ'kəː*] vi repetirse; (opportunity) producirse de nuevo; ~**rence** n repetición f; ~**rent** a repetido.
red [rɛd] n rojo // a rojo; **to be in the** ~ deber dinero; **R** ~ **Cross** n Cruz f Roja; ~**currant** n grosella; ~**den** vt enrojecer // vi enrojecerse; ~**dish** a (hair) rojizo.
redecorate [riː'dɛkəreɪt] vt decorar de nuevo; **redecoration** [-'reɪʃən] n renovación f.
redeem [rɪ'diːm] vt (gen) redimir; (sth in pawn) desempeñar; (fig, also REL) rescatar; ~**ing** a: ~**ing feature** rasgo bueno o favorable.
redeploy [riːdɪ'plɔɪ] vt (resources) disponer de nuevo.
red: ~**-haired** a pelirrojo; ~**-handed** a: **to be caught** ~**-handed** cogerse con las manos en la masa; ~**head** n pelirrojo/a; ~**-hot** a candente.
redirect [riːdaɪ'rɛkt] vt (mail) reexpedir.
redness ['rɛdnɪs] n lo rojo; (of hair) rojez f.
redo [riː'duː] (irg: like **do**) vt rehacer.
redouble [riː'dʌbl] vt: **to** ~ **one's efforts** intensificar los esfuerzos.
redress [rɪ'drɛs] n reparación f // vt reajustar.
red tape n (fig) trámites mpl, papeleo.
reduce [rɪ'djuːs] vt reducir; (lower) rebajar; '~ **speed now'** (AUT) 'reduzca la velocidad'; **at a** ~**d price** (of goods) (a precio) rebajado; **reduction** [rɪ'dʌkʃən] n reducción f; (of price) rebaja; (discount) descuento.
redundancy [rɪ'dʌndənsɪ] n desempleo.
redundant [rɪ'dʌndnt] a (worker) parado, sin trabajo; (detail, object) superfluo; **to be made** ~ quedarse sin trabajo.
reed [riːd] n (BOT) junco, caña; (MUS: of clarinet etc) lengüeta.
reef [riːf] n (at sea) arrecife m.
reek [riːk] vi: **to** ~ **(of)** oler o heder a.
reel [riːl] n (gen) carrete m, bobina; (of film) rollo, película // vt (TECH) devanar; (also: ~ **in**) cobrar // vi (sway) tambalear.
re-election [riːɪ'lɛkʃən] n reelección f.
re-enter [riː'ɛntə*] vt reingresar en; **re-entry** n reingreso.
ref [rɛf] n (col) abbr of **referee**.
refectory [rɪ'fɛktərɪ] n refectorio, comedor m.
refer [rɪ'fəː*] vt (send) remitir; (ascribe) referir a, relacionar con // vi: **to** ~ **to** (allude to) referirse a, aludir a; (apply to) relacionarse con; (consult) remitirse a.
referee [rɛfə'riː] n árbitro; (for job application) persona que recomienda a otro // vt arbitrar.
reference ['rɛfrəns] n (mention) referencia; (sending) remisión f; (relevance) relación f; (for job application: letter) referencia, carta de

recomendación; **with** ~ **to** con referencia a; (COMM: in letter) me remito a; ~ **book** n libro de consulta.

referendum [rɛfə'rɛndəm], pl -da [-də] n referéndum m.

refill [ri:'fil] vt rellenar // n ['ri:fil] repuesto, recambio.

refine [ri'fain] vt (sugar, oil) refinar; ~**d** a (person, taste) refinado, culto; ~**ment** n (of person) cultura, educación f; ~**ry** n refinería.

reflect [ri'flɛkt] vt (light, image) reflejar // vi (think) reflexionar, pensar; **it** ~**s badly/well on him** le perjudica/le hace honor; ~**ion** [-'flɛkʃən] n (act) reflexión f; (image) reflejo; (criticism) reproche m, crítica; **on** ~**ion** pensándolo bien; ~**or** n (also AUT) captáfaros m inv, reflector m.

reflex ['ri:flɛks] a, n reflejo; ~**ive** [ri'flɛksiv] a (LING) reflexivo.

reform [ri'fɔ:m] n reforma // vt reformar; **the R**~**ation** [rɛfə'meiʃən] n la Reforma; ~**er** n reformador/a m/f; ~**ist** n reformista m/f.

refrain [ri'frein] vi: **to** ~ **from doing** abstenerse de hacer // n estribillo.

refresh [ri'frɛʃ] vt refrescar; ~**er course** n curso de repaso; ~**ments** npl (drinks) refrescos mpl.

refrigeration [rifridʒə'reiʃən] n refrigeración f; **refrigerator** [-'fridʒəreitə*] n refrigeradora, nevera.

refuel [ri:'fjuəl] vi repostar combustible.

refuge ['rɛfju:dʒ] n refugio, asilo; **to take** ~ **in** refugiarse en.

refugee [rɛfju'dʒi:] n refugiado/a.

refund ['ri:fʌnd] n reembolso // vt [ri'fʌnd] devolver, reembolsar.

refurbish [ri:'bɜ:biʃ] vt restaurar, renovar.

refusal [ri'fju:zəl] n negativa; **first** ~ primera opción.

refuse ['rɛfju:s] n basura // (vb: [ri'fju:z]) vt (reject) rehusar; (say no to) negarse a // vi negarse; (horse) rehusar; ~ **bin** n cubo de la basura; ~ **tip** n vertedero.

refute [ri'fju:t] vt refutar, rebatir.

regain [ri'gein] vt recobrar, recuperar.

regal ['ri:gl] a regio, real.

regalia [ri'geiliə] n, npl insignias fpl reales.

regard [ri'gɑ:d] n (gaze) mirada; (aspect) respecto; (attention) atención f; (esteem) respeto, consideración f // vt (consider) considerar; (look at) mirar; '**with kindest** ~**s**' con muchos recuerdos; ~**ing, as** ~**s, with** ~ **to** con respecto a, en cuanto a; ~**less** ad a pesar de todo.

regatta [ri'gætə] n regata.

regent ['ri:dʒənt] n regente m/f.

régime [rei'ʒi:m] n régimen m.

regiment ['rɛdʒimənt] n regimiento // vt reglamentar; ~**al** [-'mɛntl] a militar; ~**ation** [-'teiʃən] n regimentación f.

region ['ri:dʒən] n región f; **in the** ~ **of** (fig) alrededor de; ~**al** a regional.

register ['rɛdʒistə*] n (gen) registro; (list) lista // vt registrar; (birth) declarar; (letter) certificar; (subj: instrument)

marcar, indicar // vi (at hotel) registrarse; (sign on) inscribirse; (make impression) producir impresión; ~**ed** a (design) registrado; (letter) certificado.

registrar ['rɛdʒistrɑ:*] n secretario (del registro civil).

registration [rɛdʒis'treiʃən] n (act) inscripción f; (AUT: also: ~ **number**) matrícula.

registry ['rɛdʒistri] n registro, archivo; ~ **office** n registro civil; **to get married in a** ~ **office** casarse por lo civil.

regret [ri'grɛt] n sentimiento, pesar m; (remorse) remordimiento // vt sentir, lamentar; (repent of) arrepentirse de; ~**fully** ad con pesar, sentidamente; ~**table** a lamentable; (loss) sensible.

regroup [ri:'gru:p] vt reagrupar // vi reagruparse.

regular ['rɛgjulə*] a (gen) regular; (usual) corriente, normal; (soldier) de línea; (intensive) verdadero // n (client etc) cliente m/f habitual; ~**ity** [-'læriti] n regularidad f; ~**ly** ad con regularidad.

regulate ['rɛgjuleit] vt regular; (TECH) arreglar, ajustar; **regulation** [-'leiʃən] n (rule) regla, reglamento; (adjustment) ajuste m.

rehabilitation ['ri:həbili'teiʃən] n rehabilitación f.

rehearsal [ri'hɜ:səl] n ensayo; **rehearse** vt ensayar.

reign [rein] n reinado; (fig) dominio // vi reinar; (fig) imperar; ~**ing** a (monarch) reinante, actual; (predominant) imperante.

reimburse [ri:im'bɜ:s] vt reembolsar; ~**ment** n reembolso.

rein [rein] n (for horse) rienda; **to give** ~ **to** dar rienda suelta a.

reincarnation [ri:inkɑ:'neiʃən] n reencarnación f.

reindeer ['reindiə*] n, pl inv reno.

reinforce [ri:in'fɔ:s] vt reforzar; ~**d** a (concrete) armado; ~**ment** n (action) reforzamiento; ~**ments** npl (MIL) refuerzos mpl.

reinstate [ri:in'steit] vt (worker) reintegrar a su puesto.

reiterate [ri:'itəreit] vt reiterar, repetir.

reject ['ri:dʒɛkt] n (COMM) artículo defectuoso // vt [ri'dʒɛkt] rechazar; (plan) desechar; (solution) descartar; ~**ion** [ri'dʒɛkʃən] n rechazo.

rejoice [ri'dʒɔis] vi: **to** ~ **at** or **over** regocijarse o alegrarse de.

rejuvenate [ri'dʒu:vəneit] vt rejuvenecer.

rekindle [ri:'kindl] vt reencender; (fig) despertar.

relapse [ri'læps] n (MED) recaída; (into crime) reincidencia.

relate [ri'leit] vt (tell) contar, relatar; (connect) relacionar // vi relacionarse; ~**d** a afín, conexo; (person) emparentado; ~**d to** con referencia a, relacionado con; **relating to** prep acerca de.

relation [ri'leiʃən] n (person) pariente m/f; (link) relación f; ~**ship** n relación f;

(*personal ties*) relaciones *fpl*; (*also*: **family ~ship**) parentesco.

relative ['rɛlətɪv] *n* pariente *m/f*, familiar *m/f* // *a* relativo.

relax [rɪ'læks] *vi* descansar; (*person: unwind*) relajarse // *vt* relajar; (*mind, person*) descansar; **~ation** [riːlæk'seɪʃən] *n* (*rest*) descanso; (*ease*) relajación *f*, relax *m*; (*amusement*) recreo; (*entertainment*) diversión *f*; **~ed** *a* relajado; (*tranquil*) tranquilo; **~ing** *a* enervante.

relay ['riːleɪ] *n* (*race*) carrera de relevos // *vt* (*message*) retransmitir.

release [rɪ'liːs] *n* (*from prison, obligation*) liberación *f*, libertad *f*; (*of shot*) disparo; (*of gas etc*) escape *m*; (*of film etc*) estreno // *vt* (*prisoner*) poner en libertad; (*book, film*) estrenar; (*report, news*) publicar; (*gas etc*) despedir, arrojar; (*free: from wreckage etc*) soltar; (*TECH. catch, spring etc*) desenganchar; (*let go*) soltar, aflojar.

relegate ['rɛlɛgeɪt] *vt* relegar; (*SPORT*): **to be ~d** descender.

relent [rɪ'lɛnt] *vi* ablandarse, ceder; **~less** *a* implacable.

relevance ['rɛləvəns] *n* relación *f*; **relevant** [-ənt] *a* relacionado; (*fact*) pertinente; (*apt*) oportuno.

reliable [rɪ'laɪəbl] *a* (*person, firm*) de confianza, de fiar; (*method, machine*) seguro; (*news*) fidedigno; **reliably** *ad*: **to be reliably informed that...** saber de fuente fidedigna que... .

reliance [rɪ'laɪəns] *n*: **~ (on)** dependencia (de).

relic ['rɛlɪk] *n* (*REL*) reliquia; (*of the past*) vestigio.

relief [rɪ'liːf] *n* (*from pain, anxiety*) alivio, desahogo; (*help, supplies*) socorro, ayuda; (*ART, GEO*) relieve *m*.

relieve [rɪ'liːv] *vt* (*pain, patient*) aliviar; (*bring help to*) ayudar, socorrer; (*burden*) aligerar; (*take over from: gen*) sustituir a; (: *guard*) relevar; **to ~ sb of sth** quitar algo a uno; **to ~ o.s.** hacer sus necesidades.

religion [rɪ'lɪdʒən] *n* religión *f*; **religious** *a* religioso.

relinquish [rɪ'lɪŋkwɪʃ] *vt* abandonar; (*plan, habit*) renunciar a.

relish ['rɛlɪʃ] *n* (*CULIN*) salsa, condimento; (*enjoyment*) entusiasmo; (*flavour*) sabor *m*, gusto // *vt* (*food etc*) saborear; **to ~ doing** gustar de hacer.

reload [riː'ləud] *vt* recargar.

reluctance [rɪ'lʌktəns] *n* renuencia; **reluctant** [-ənt] *a* renuente; **reluctantly** [-əntlɪ] *ad* con renuencia.

rely [rɪ'laɪ]: **to ~ on** *vt fus* confiar en, fiarse de; (*be dependent on*) depender de.

remain [rɪ'meɪn] *vi* (*survive*) quedar; (*be left*) sobrar; (*continue*) quedar(se), permanecer; **~der** *n* resto; **~ing** *a* sobrante; **~s** *npl* restos *mpl*; (*leftovers*) desperdicios *mpl*.

remand [rɪ'mɑːnd] *n*: **on ~** detenido (en espera del juicio) // *vt*: **to ~ in custody**

reencarcelar, mantener bajo custodia; **~ home** *n* reformatorio.

remark [rɪ'mɑːk] *n* comentario // *vt* comentar; (*notice*) observar, notar; **~able** *a* notable; (*outstanding*) extraordinario.

remarry [riː'mærɪ] *vi* casarse por segunda vez.

remedial [rɪ'miːdɪəl] *a* (*tuition, classes*) de niños atrasados.

remedy ['rɛmədɪ] *n* remedio // *vt* remediar, curar.

remember [rɪ'mɛmbə*] *vt* recordar, acordarse de; (*bear in mind*) tener presente; **remembrance** *n* (*memory*) memoria; (*souvenir*) recuerdo.

remind [rɪ'maɪnd] *vt*: **to ~ sb to do sth** recordar a uno que haga algo; **to ~ sb of sth** recordar algo a uno; **she ~s me of her mother** me recuerda a su madre; **~er** *n* advertencia; (*souvenir*) recuerdo.

reminisce [rɛmɪ'nɪs] *vi* recordar viejas historias; **reminiscent** *a*: **to be reminiscent of sth** recordar algo.

remiss [rɪ'mɪs] *a* descuidado; **it was ~ of him** fue un descuido suyo.

remission [rɪ'mɪʃən] *n* remisión *f*; (*of debt, sentence*) perdón *m*.

remit [rɪ'mɪt] *vt* (*send: money*) remitir, enviar; **~tance** *n* remesa, envío.

remnant ['rɛmnənt] *n* resto; (*of cloth*) retazo.

remorse [rɪ'mɔːs] *n* remordimientos *mpl*; **~ful** *a* arrepentido; **~less** *a* (*fig*) implacable, despiadado.

remote [rɪ'məut] *a* (*distant*) lejano; (*person*) distante; **~ control** *n* telecontrol *m*; **~ly** *ad* remotamente; (*slightly*) levemente; **~ness** *n* alejamiento; distancia.

remould ['riːməuld] *vt* (*tyre*) recauchutar.

removable [rɪ'muːvəbl] *a* (*detachable*) amovible, separable.

removal [rɪ'muːvəl] *n* (*taking away*) el quitar; (*from house*) mudanza; (*from office: sacking*) destitución *f*; (*MED*) extirpación *f*; **~ van** *n* camión *m* de mudanzas.

remove [rɪ'muːv] *vt* quitar; (*employee*) destituir; (*name: from list*) tachar, borrar; (*doubt, abuse*) disipar; (*TECH*) retirar, separar; (*MED*) extirpar; **removers** *npl* (*company*) agencia de mudanzas.

remuneration [rɪmjuːnə'reɪʃən] *n* remuneración *f*.

rend [rɛnd], *pt*, *pp* **rent** *vt* rasgar, desgarrar.

render ['rɛndə*] *vt* (*give*) dar, prestar; (*hand over*) entregar; (*reproduce*) reproducir; (*make*) hacer, volver; (*return*) devolver; **~ing** *n* (*MUS etc*) interpretación *f*.

rendez-vous ['rɒndɪvuː] *n* cita.

renegade ['rɛnɪgeɪd] *n* renegado.

renew [rɪ'njuː] *vt* renovar; (*resume*) reanudar; (*loan etc*) prorrogar; (*negotiations*) volver a; (*acquaintance*) entablar de nuevo; ~**al** n renovación f; reanudación f; prórroga.

renounce [rɪ'nauns] vt renunciar a; (*disown*) renunciar.

renovate ['rɛnəveɪt] vt renovar; **renovation** [-'veɪʃən] n renovación f.

renown [rɪ'naun] n renombre m; ~**ed** a renombrado.

rent [rɛnt] pt, pp of **rend** // n alquiler m, arriendo // vt alquilar; ~**al** n (for television, car) alquiler m.

renunciation [rɪnʌnsɪ'eɪʃən] n renuncia.

reorganize [riː'ɔːgənaɪz] vt reorganizar.

rep [rɛp] n abbr of **representative; repertory.**

repair [rɪ'pɛə*] n reparación f, compostura; (*patch*) remiendo // vt reparar, componer; (*shoes*) remendar; **in good/bad** ~ en buen/mal estado; ~ **kit** n caja de herramientas para reparaciones.

repartee [rɛpɑː'tiː] n dimes y diretes.

repay [riː'peɪ] (*irg: like* **pay**) vt (*money*) devolver, reembolsar; (*person*) pagar; (*debt*) liquidar; (*sb's efforts*) devolver, corresponder a; ~**ment** n reembolso, devolución f; (*of debt*) pago.

repeal [rɪ'piːl] n (*of law*) abrogación f; (*of sentence*) anulación f // vt abrogar, revocar.

repeat [rɪ'piːt] n (RADIO, TV) retransmisión f // vt repetir // vi repetirse; ~**edly** ad repetidas veces.

repel [rɪ'pɛl] vt (*lit, fig*) repugnar; ~**lent** a repugnante // n: **insect** ~**lent** crema/loción f anti-insectos.

repent [rɪ'pɛnt] vi: **to** ~ (**of**) arrepentirse (de); ~**ance** n arrepentimiento.

repercussion [riːpə'kʌʃən] n (*consequence*) repercusión f; **to have** ~**s** repercutir.

repertoire ['rɛpətwɑː*] n repertorio.

repertory ['rɛpətərɪ] n (*also:* ~ **theatre**) teatro de repertorio.

repetition [rɛpɪ'tɪʃən] n repetición f.

repetitive [rɪ'pɛtɪtɪv] a (*movement, work*) reiterativo; (*speech*) lleno de repeticiones.

replace [rɪ'pleɪs] vt (*put back*) devolver a su sitio; (*take the place of*) reemplazar, sustituir; ~**ment** n (*gen*) reemplazo; (*act*) reposición f; (*person*) suplente m/f.

replenish [rɪ'plɛnɪʃ] vt (*glass*) rellenar; (*stock etc*) reponer; (*with fuel*) repostar.

replete [rɪ'pliːt] a repleto; (*well-fed*) lleno.

replica ['rɛplɪkə] n copia, reproducción f.

reply [rɪ'plaɪ] n respuesta, contestación f // vi contestar, responder.

report [rɪ'pɔːt] n informe m; (PRESS etc) reportaje m; (*also:* **school** ~) nota; (*of gun*) estallido // vt informar sobre; (PRESS etc) hacer un reportaje sobre; (*bring to notice: occurrence*) dar cuenta de // vi (*make a report*) presentar un informe; (*present o.s.:* **to** ~ (**to sb**) presentarse (ante uno); ~**er** n periodista m/f.

reprehensible [rɛprɪ'hɛnsɪbl] a reprensible, censurable.

represent [rɛprɪ'zɛnt] vt representar; (*fig*) hablar en nombre de; (COMM) ser agente de; ~**ation** [-'teɪʃən] n representación f; (*petition*) petición f; ~**ations** npl (*protest*) quejas fpl; ~**ative** n representante m/f // a representativo.

repress [rɪ'prɛs] vt reprimir; ~**ion** [-'prɛʃən] n represión f; ~**ive** a represivo.

reprieve [rɪ'priːv] n (LAW) indulto; (*fig*) alivio // vt indultar, suspender la pena de.

reprimand ['rɛprɪmɑːnd] n reprimenda // vt reprender.

reprint ['riːprɪnt] n reimpresión f // vt [riː'prɪnt] reimprimir.

reprisal [rɪ'praɪzl] n represalia.

reproach [rɪ'prəutʃ] n reproche m // vt: **to** ~ **sb with sth** reprochar algo a uno; **beyond** ~ intachable; ~**ful** a lleno de reproches.

reproduce [riːprə'djuːs] vt reproducir // vi reproducirse; **reproduction** [-'dʌkʃən] n reproducción f; **reproductive** [-'dʌktɪv] a reproductor(a).

reprove [rɪ'pruːv] vt: **to** ~ **sb for sth** reprender algo a uno.

reptile ['rɛptaɪl] n reptil m.

republic [rɪ'pʌblɪk] n república; ~**an** a, n republicano/a.

repudiate [rɪ'pjuːdɪeɪt] vt (*accusation*) rechazar; (*friend*) repudiar; (*obligation*) desconocer.

repugnant [rɪ'pʌgnənt] a repugnante.

repulse [rɪ'pʌls] vt rechazar, repulsar; **repulsive** a repulsivo.

reputable ['rɛpjutəbl] a (*make etc*) de toda confianza; (*person*) formal.

reputation [rɛpju'teɪʃən] n reputación f.

repute [rɪ'pjuːt] n reputación f, fama; ~**d** a supuesto; ~**dly** ad según dicen o se dice.

request [rɪ'kwɛst] n petición f; (*formal*) solicitud f // vt: **to** ~ **sth of** or **from sb** pedir algo a uno; (*formally*) solicitar algo a uno.

requiem ['rɛkwɪəm] n réquiem m.

require [rɪ'kwaɪə*] vt (*need: subj: person*) necesitar, tener necesidad de; (: *thing, situation*) exigir; (*want*) pedir; (*order*) insistir en que; ~**ment** n requisito; (*need*) necesidad f.

requisite ['rɛkwɪzɪt] n requisito // a preciso, imprescindible; **toilet** ~**s** artículos mpl de aseo personal.

requisition [rɛkwɪ'zɪʃən] n: ~ (**for**) solicitud f (de) // vt (MIL) requisar.

reroute [riː'ruːt] vt (*train etc*) desviar.

resale ['riː'seɪl] n reventa.

rescue ['rɛskjuː] n rescate m // vt rescatar; **to** ~ **from** librar de; ~ **party** n expedición f de salvamento; **rescuer** n salvador/a m/f.

research [rɪ'səːtʃ] n investigaciones fpl // vt investigar; ~**er** n investigador/a m/f; ~ **work** n investigación f.

resell [riː'sɛl] vt revender.

resemblance [rɪ'zɛmbləns] n parecido; **to**

bear a ~ to parecerse a; **resemble** vt parecerse a.
resent [rɪˈzɛnt] vt resentirse de; ~**ful** a resentido; ~**ment** n resentimiento.
reservation [rɛzəˈveɪʃən] n (gen) reserva; (on road: also: **central** ~) faja intermedia.
reserve [rɪˈzɜːv] n reserva; (SPORT) suplente m/f; (game ~) coto // vt (seats etc) reservar; ~**s** npl (MIL) reserva sg; **in** ~ **de** reserva; ~**d** a reservado.
reservoir [ˈrɛzəvwɑː*] n (large) embalse m; (small) depósito.
reshape [riːˈʃeɪp] vt (policy) reformar, rehacer.
reshuffle [riːˈʃʌfl] n: **Cabinet** ~ (POL) reconstrucción f del gabinete.
reside [rɪˈzaɪd] vi residir, vivir.
residence [ˈrɛzɪdəns] n residencia; (formal: home) domicilio; (length of stay) permanencia; **resident** [-ənt] n vecino; (in hotel) huésped/a m/f // a (population) permanente; (doctor) interno; **residential** [-ˈdɛnʃəl] a residencial.
residue [ˈrɛzɪdjuː] n resto, residuo; (COMM) saldo.
resign [rɪˈzaɪn] vt (one's post) renunciar a // vi dimitir; **to** ~ **o.s. to** (endure) resignarse a; ~**ation** [rɛzɪgˈneɪʃən] n renuncia; (state of mind) resignación f; ~**ed** a resignado.
resilience [rɪˈzɪlɪəns] n (of material) elasticidad f; (of person) resistencia; **resilient** [-ənt] a (person) resistente.
resin [ˈrɛzɪn] n resina.
resist [rɪˈzɪst] vt resistir, oponerse a; ~**ance** n resistencia.
resolute [ˈrɛzəluːt] a resuelto.
resolution [rɛzəˈluːʃən] n (gen) resolución f; (purpose) propósito.
resolve [rɪˈzɔlv] n resolución f; (purpose) propósito // vt resolver // vi resolverse; **to** ~ **to do** resolver hacer; ~**d** a resuelto.
resonant [ˈrɛzənənt] a resonante.
resort [rɪˈzɔːt] n (town) centro de turismo; (recourse) recurso // vi: **to** ~ **to** recurrir a; **in the last** ~ en último caso.
resound [rɪˈzaʊnd] vi resonar, retumbar; **the room** ~**ed with shouts** los gritos resonaron en el cuarto; ~**ing** a sonoro; (fig) clamoroso.
resource [rɪˈsɔːs] n recurso; ~**s** npl recursos mpl; ~**ful** a inventivo, ingenioso.
respect [rɪsˈpɛkt] n (consideration) respeto; (relation) respecto; ~**s** npl recuerdos mpl, saludos mpl // vt respetar; **with** ~ **to** con respecto a; **in this** ~ en cuanto a eso; ~**ability** [-əˈbɪlɪtɪ] n respetabilidad f; ~**able** a respetable; (large) apreciable; (passable) tolerable; ~**ful** a respetuoso.
respective [rɪsˈpɛktɪv] a respectivo; ~**ly** ad respectivamente.
respiration [rɛspɪˈreɪʃən] n respiración f.
respiratory [rɛsˈpɪrətərɪ] a respiratorio.
respite [ˈrɛspaɪt] n respiro; (LAW) prórroga.

resplendent [rɪsˈplɛndənt] a resplandeciente.
respond [rɪsˈpɔnd] vi responder; (react) reaccionar; **response** [-ˈpɔns] n respuesta; reacción f.
responsibility [rɪspɔnsɪˈbɪlɪtɪ] n responsabilidad f.
responsible [rɪsˈpɔnsɪbl] a (liable): ~ (**for**) responsable (de); (character) serio, formal; (job) de confianza.
responsive [rɪsˈpɔnsɪv] a sensible.
rest [rɛst] n descanso, reposo; (MUS) pausa, silencio; (support) apoyo; (remainder) resto // vi descansar; (be supported): **to** ~ **on** posar(se) en // vt (lean): **to** ~ **sth on/against** apoyar algo en o sobre/contra.
restart [riːˈstɑːt] vt (engine) volver a arrancar; (work) volver a empezar.
restaurant [ˈrɛstərɔŋ] n restorán m, restaurante m; ~ **car** n coche-comedor m.
restful [ˈrɛstful] a descansado, reposado.
rest home n residencia para jubilados.
restitution [rɛstɪˈtjuːʃən] n: **to make** ~ **to sb for sth** indemnizar a uno por algo.
restive [ˈrɛstɪv] a inquieto; (horse) rebelón(ona).
restless [ˈrɛstlɪs] a inquieto; ~**ly** ad inquietamente.
restoration [rɛstəˈreɪʃən] n restauración f; **restore** [rɪsˈtɔː*] vt (building) restaurar; (sth stolen) devolver; (health) restablecer.
restrain [rɪsˈtreɪn] vt (feeling) contenar, refrenar; (person): **to** ~ (**from doing**) disuadir (de hacer); ~**ed** a (style) moderado; ~**t** n (restriction) freno, control m; (moderation) moderación f; (of style) reserva.
restrict [rɪsˈtrɪkt] vt restringir, limitar; ~**ion** [-kʃən] n restricción f, limitación f; ~**ive** a restrictivo.
rest room n (US) aseos mpl.
result [rɪˈzʌlt] n resultado // vi: **to** ~ **in** terminar en, dar por resultado; **as a** ~ **of** a consecuencia de.
resume [rɪˈzjuːm] vt, vi (work, journey) reanudar.
résumé [ˈreɪzjuːmeɪ] n resumen m.
resumption [rɪˈzʌmpʃən] n reanudación f.
resurgence [rɪˈsɜːdʒəns] n resurgimiento.
resurrection [rɛzəˈrɛkʃən] n resurrección f.
resuscitate [rɪˈsʌsɪteɪt] vt (MED) resucitar; **resuscitation** [-ˈteɪʃn] n resucitación f.
retail [ˈriːteɪl] n venta al por menor // cpd al por menor // vt vender al por menor o al detalle; ~**er** n detallista m/f.
retain [rɪˈteɪn] vt (keep) retener, conservar; (employ) contratar; ~**er** n (servant) criado; (fee) anticipo.
retaliate [rɪˈtælɪeɪt] vi: **to** ~ (**against**) tomar represalias (contra); **retaliation** [-ˈeɪʃən] n represalias fpl.
retarded [rɪˈtɑːdɪd] a retrasado.
retch [rɛtʃ] vi dar arcadas.

retentive [rɪ'tɛntɪv] a (*memory*) retentivo.
reticent ['rɛtɪsnt] a reservado.
retina ['rɛtɪnə] n retina.
retinue ['rɛtɪnju:] n séquito, comitiva.
retire [rɪ'taɪə*] vi (*give up work*) jubilarse; (*withdraw*) retirarse; (*go to bed*) ir a) acostarse; ~**d** a (*person*) jubilado; ~**ment** n (*state*) retiro; (*act*) jubilación f; **retiring** a (*leaving*) saliente; (*shy*) retraído.
retort [rɪ'tɔ:t] n (*reply*) réplica // vi contestar.
retrace [ri:'treɪs] vt: **to** ~ **one's steps** volver sobre sus pasos, desandar lo andado.
retract [rɪ'trækt] vt (*statement*) retirar; (*claws*) retraer; (*undercarriage, aerial*) replegar // vi retractarse; ~**able** a replegable.
retrain [ri:'treɪn] vt reeducar; ~**ing** n readaptación f profesional.
retreat [rɪ'tri:t] n (*place*) retiro; (*act*) retraimiento; (*MIL*) retirada // vi retirarse; (*flood*) bajar.
retribution [rɛtrɪ'bju:ʃən] n desquite m.
retrieve [rɪ'tri:v] vt (*gen*) recobrar; (*situation, honour*) salvar; (*error, loss*) recuperar; **retriever** n perro cobrador, perdiguero.
retrospect ['rɛtrəspɛkt] n: **in** ~ retrospectivamente, mirando hacia atrás; ~**ive** [-'spɛktɪv] a (*law*) retroactivo.
return [rɪ'tə:n] n (*going or coming back*) vuelta, regreso; (*of sth stolen etc*) devolución f; (*recompense*) recompensa; (*FINANCE: from land, shares*) ganancia, ingresos mpl; (*report*) informe m // cpd (*journey*) de regreso; (*ticket*) de ida y vuelta; (*match*) de vuelta // vi (*person etc: come or go back*) volver, regresar; (*symptoms etc*) reaparecer // vt devolver; (*favour, love etc*) corresponder a; (*verdict*) declarar; (*POL: candidate*) elegir; ~**s** npl (*COMM*) ingresos mpl; **in** ~ en cambio; **many happy** ~**s (of the day)!** ¡muchas felicidades!, ¡feliz cumpleaños!
reunion [ri:'ju:nɪən] n reunión f.
reunite [ri:ju:'naɪt] vt reunir; (*reconcile*) reconciliar.
rev [rɛv] n abbr of **revolution** (*AUT*) // (*vb: also:* ~ **up**) vt girar (el motor de) // vi acelerarse.
reveal [rɪ'vi:l] vt (*make known*) revelar; ~**ing** a revelador(a).
reveille [rɪ'vælɪ] n (*MIL*) diana.
revel ['rɛvl] vi: **to** ~ **in sth/in doing sth** deleitarse en algo/en hacer algo.
revelation [rɛvə'leɪʃən] n revelación f.
reveller ['rɛvlə*] n jaranero, juergista m/f; **revelry** [-rɪ] n jarana, juerga.
revenge [rɪ'vɛndʒ] n venganza; (*in sport*) revancha; **to take** ~ **on** vengarse de.
revenue ['rɛvənju:] n ingresos mpl, renta; (*on investment*) rédito; (*profit*) ganancia.
reverberate [rɪ'və:bəreɪt] vi (*sound*) resonar, retumbar; **reverberation** [-'reɪʃən] n retumbo, eco.
revere [rɪ'vɪə*] vt reverenciar, venerar;

reverence ['rɛvərəns] n reverencia; **reverent** ['rɛvərənt] a reverente.
reverie ['rɛvərɪ] n ensueño.
reversal [rɪ'və:sl] n (*of order*) inversión f; (*of direction*) cambio completo; (*of decision*) revocación f.
reverse [rɪ'və:s] n (*opposite*) contrario; (*back: of cloth*) revés m; (: *of coin*) reverso, (: *of paper*) dorso; (*AUT: also:* ~ **gear**) marcha atrás, contramarcha // a (*order*) inverso; (*direction*) contrario // vt (*turn over*) volver al revés; (*invert*) invertir; (*change: opinion*) cambiar (completamente) de // vi (*AUT*) poner en marcha atrás.
revert [rɪ'və:t] vi: **to** ~ **to** volver a.
review [rɪ'vju:] n (*magazine, MIL*) revista; (*of book, film*) reseña; (*examination*) repaso, examen m // vt repasar, examinar; (*MIL*) pasar revista a; (*book, film*) reseñar; ~**er** n crítico/a.
revile [rɪ'vaɪl] vt injuriar, vilipendiar.
revise [rɪ'vaɪz] vt (*manuscript*) corregir; (*opinion*) modificar; (*study: subject*) repasar; (*look over*) revisar; **revision** [rɪ'vɪʒən] n corrección f; modificación f; repaso; revisión f.
revitalize [ri:'vaɪtəlaɪz] vt revivificar.
revival [rɪ'vaɪvəl] n (*recovery*) restablecimiento; (*of interest*) renacimiento; (*THEATRE*) reestreno; (*of faith*) despertar m.
revive [rɪ'vaɪv] vt (*gen*) resucitar; (*custom*) restablecer; (*hope, courage*) reanimar; (*play*) reestrenar // vi (*person*) volver en sí, restablecerse; (*from faint*) revivir; (*activity*) recobrarse.
revoke [rɪ'vəuk] vt revocar.
revolt [rɪ'vəult] n rebelión f, sublevación f // vi rebelarse, sublevarse // vt dar asco a, repugnar; ~**ing** a asqueroso, repugnante.
revolution [rɛvə'lu:ʃən] n revolución f; ~**ary** a, n revolucionario/a; ~**ize** vt revolucionar.
revolve [rɪ'vɔlv] vi dar vueltas, girar.
revolver [rɪ'vɔlvə*] n revólver m.
revolving [rɪ'vɔlvɪŋ] a (*chair etc*) giratorio; ~ **door** n puerta giratoria.
revue [rɪ'vju:] n (*THEATRE*) revista.
revulsion [rɪ'vʌlʃən] n asco, repugnancia.
reward [rɪ'wɔ:d] n premio, recompensa // vt: **to** ~ (**for**) recompensar o premiar (por); ~**ing** a (*fig*) provechoso, valioso.
rewire [ri:'waɪə*] vt (*house*) renovar el alambrado de.
reword [ri:'wə:d] vt expresar en otras palabras.
rewrite [ri:'raɪt] (*irg: like* **write**) vt volver a escribir o redactar.
rhapsody ['ræpsədɪ] n (*MUS*) rapsodia; (*fig*) transporte m (de admiración).
rhetoric ['rɛtərɪk] n retórica; ~**al** [rɪ'tɔrɪkl] a retórico.
rheumatic [ru:'mætɪk] a reumático; **rheumatism** ['ru:mətɪzəm] n reumatismo, reúma.

Rhine [raɪn] *n*: **the** ~ el (río) Rin.
rhinoceros [raɪˈnɔsərəs] *n* rinoceronte *m*.
rhododendron   [rəudəˈdɛndrn]   *n* rododendro.
Rhone [rəun] *n*: **the** ~ el (río) Ródano.
rhubarb [ˈruːbɑːb] *n* ruibarbo.
rhyme [raɪm] *n* rima; (*verse*) poesía.
rhythm [ˈrɪðm] *n* ritmo; ~ **method** método de Ojino; ~**ic(al)** *a* rítmico.
rib [rɪb] *n* (ANAT) costilla // *vt* (*mock*) tomar el pelo a.
ribald [ˈrɪbəld] *a* escabroso.
ribbon [ˈrɪbən] *n* cinta; **in** ~**s** (*torn*) hecho trizas.
rice [raɪs] *n* arroz *m*; ~**field** *n* arrozal *m*; ~ **pudding** *n* arroz *m* con leche.
rich [rɪtʃ] *a* rico; (*banquet*) suntuoso; (*soil*) fértil; (*food*) fuerte; (: *sweet*) empalagoso; **the** ~ los ricos; ~**es** *npl* riqueza *sg*; ~**ness** *n* riqueza; suntuosidad *f*; fertilidad *f*.
rickets [ˈrɪkɪts] *n* raquitismo.
rickety [ˈrɪkɪtɪ] *a* desvencijado; (*shaky*) tambaleante.
rickshaw [ˈrɪkʃɔː] *n* rikisha.
ricochet [ˈrɪkəʃeɪ] *n* rebote *m* // *vi* rebotar.
rid [rɪd], *pt, pp* **rid** *vt*: **to** ~ **sb of sth** librar a uno de algo; **to get** ~ **of** deshacerse o desembarazarse de.
ridden [ˈrɪdn] *pp of* **ride.**
riddle [ˈrɪdl] *n* (*conundrum*) acertijo; (*mystery*) enigma *m*, misterio; (*sieve*) criba // *vt*: **to be** ~**d with** ser lleno o plagado de.
ride [raɪd] *n* (*gen*) paseo; (*on horse*) cabalgata; (*distance covered*) viaje *m*, recorrido // (*vb*: *pt* **rode,** *pp* **ridden**) *vi* (*as sport*) montar; (*go somewhere: on horse, bicycle*) dar un paseo, pasearse; (*journey: on bicycle, motor cycle, bus*) viajar // *vt* (*a horse*) montar a; (*distance*) viajar; **to** ~ **a bicycle** ir en bicicleta; **to** ~ **at anchor** (NAUT) estar al ancla; **to take sb for a** ~ (*fig*) engañar a uno; **rider** *n* (*on horse*) jinete *m*; (*on bicycle*) ciclista *m/f*; (*on motorcycle*) motociclista *m/f*.
ridge [rɪdʒ] *n* (*of hill*) cresta; (*of roof*) caballete *m*; (*wrinkle*) arruga.
ridicule [ˈrɪdɪkjuːl] *n* irrisión *f*, mofa // *vt* poner en ridículo, mofarse de; **ridiculous** [-ˈdɪkjuləs] *a* ridículo.
riding [ˈraɪdɪŋ] *n* montar *m* a caballo; ~ **school** *n* escuela de equitación.
rife [raɪf] *a*: **to be** ~ ser muy común; **to be** ~ **with** abundar en.
riffraff [ˈrɪfræf] *n* gentuza.
rifle [ˈraɪfl] *n* rifle *m*, fusil *m* // *vt* saquear; ~ **range** *n* campo de tiro; (*at fair*) tiro al blanco.
rift [rɪft] *n* (*fig: disagreement: between friends*) desavenencia; (: *in party*) escisión *f*.
rig [rɪg] *n* (*also:* **oil** ~) torre *f* de perforación // *vt* (*election etc*) falsificar los resultados de; **to** ~ **out** *vt* ataviar de;

to ~ **up** *vt* armar; ~**ging** *n* (NAUT) aparejo.
right [raɪt] *a* (*true, correct*) correcto, exacto; (*suitable*) indicado, debido; (*proper*) apropiado, propio; (*just*) justo; (*morally good*) bueno; (*not left*) derecho // *n* (*title, claim*) derecho; (*not left*) derecha // *a* (*correctly*) bien, correctamente; (*straight*) derecho, directamente; (*not on the left*) a la derecha; (*to the* ~) hacia la derecha // *vt* enderezar // *excl* ¡bueno!, ¡está bien!; **to be** ~ (*person*) tener razón; **all** ~! ¡está bien!; (*enough*) ¡basta!; ~ **now** ahora mismo; ~ **in the middle** justo en medio, en pleno centro; ~ **away** en seguida; **by** ~**s** en justicia; **on the** ~ a la derecha; ~ **angle** *n* ángulo recto; ~**eous** [ˈraɪtʃəs] *a* justado, honrado; (*anger*) justificado; ~**eousness** [ˈraɪtʃəsnɪs] *n* justicia; ~**ful** *a* (*heir*) legítimo; ~-**hand** *a* por la derecha; ~-**handed** *a* (*person*) que usa la mano derecha; ~**ly** *ad* correctamente, debidamente; (*with reason*) con razón; ~-**wing** *a* (POL) derechista.
rigid [ˈrɪdʒɪd] *a* rígido; (*principle*) inflexible; ~**ity** [rɪˈdʒɪdɪtɪ] *n* rigidez *f*, inflexibilidad *f*.
rigmarole [ˈrɪgmərəul] *n* galimatías *m*.
rigorous [ˈrɪgərəs] *a* riguroso.
rigour, rigor (US) [ˈrɪgə*] *n* rigor *m*, severidad *f*.
rig-out [ˈrɪgaut] *n* (*col*) atuendo.
rile [raɪl] *vt* irritar.
rim [rɪm] *n* borde *m*; (*of spectacles*) aro; (*of wheel*) aro, llanta.
rind [raɪnd] *n* (*of bacon*) piel *f*; (*of lemon etc*) cáscara; (*of cheese*) costra.
ring [rɪŋ] *n* (*of metal*) aro; (*on finger*) anillo; (*of people, objects*) círculo, grupo; (*of spies*) camarilla; (*for boxing*) cuadrilátero; (*of circus*) pista; (*bull*~) ruedo, plaza; (*sound of bell*) toque *m*; (*telephone call*) llamada // (*vb*: *pt* **rang,** *pp* **rung**) *vi* (*on telephone*) llamar por teléfono; (*large bell*) repicar; (*also:* ~ **out:** *voice, words*) sonar; (*ears*) zumbar // *vt* (TEL: *also:* ~ **up**) llamar; (*bell etc*) hacer sonar; (*doorbell*) tocar; **to** ~ **back** *vt, vi* (TEL) devolver la llamada; **to** ~ **off** *vi* (TEL) colgar, cortar la comunicación; ~**ing** *n* (*of large bell*) repique *m*; (*in ears*) zumbido; ~**leader** *n* (*of gang*) cabecilla *m/f*.
ringlets [ˈrɪŋlɪts] *npl* rizos *mpl*, tirabuzones *mpl*.
ring road *n* carretera periférica o de circunvalación.
rink [rɪŋk] *n* (*also:* **ice** ~) pista.
rinse [rɪns] *n* (*of dishes*) enjuague *m*; (*of hair*) reflejo // *vt* enjuagar; dar reflejos a.
riot [ˈraɪət] *n* motín *m*, disturbio // *vi* amotinarse; **to run** ~ desmandarse; ~**er** *n* amotinado/a; ~**ous** *a* (*gen*) alborotado; (*party*) bullicioso; (*uncontrolled*) desenfrenado.
rip [rɪp] *n* rasgón *m*, rasgadura // *vt*

rasgar, desgarrar // vi correr; ~cord n cabo de desgarre.

ripe [raip] a (fruit) maduro; (ready) listo; ~n vt madurar // vi madurarse; ~ness n madurez f.

ripple ['ripl] n onda, rizo; (sound) murmullo // vi rizarse // vt rizar.

rise [raiz] n (slope) cuesta, pendiente m; (hill) altura; (increase: in wages) aumento; (: in prices, temperature) subida, alza; (fig: to power etc) ascenso // vi, pt **rose**, pp **risen** ['rizn] (gen) elevarse; (prices) subir; (waters) crecer; (river) nacer; (sun) salir; (person: from bed etc) levantarse; (also: ~ up: rebel) sublevarse; (in rank) ascender; **to give ~ to** dar lugar o origen a; **to ~ to the occasion** ponerse a la altura de las circunstancias.

risk [risk] n riesgo, peligro // vt (gen) arriesgar; (dare) atreverse a; **to take or run the ~ of doing** correr el riesgo de hacer; **at ~** en peligro; **at one's own ~** bajo su propia responsabilidad; ~**y** a arriesgado, peligroso.

risqué ['ri:skei] a (joke) subido de color.

rissole ['risoul] n croqueta.

rite [rait] n rito; **funeral ~s** exequias fpl.

ritual ['ritjuəl] a ritual // n ritual m, rito.

rival ['raivl] n rival m/f; (in business) competidor/a m/f // a rival, opuesto // vt competir con; ~**ry** n rivalidad f, competencia.

river ['rivə*] n río; **up/down ~** río arriba/abajo; ~**bank** n orilla (del río); ~**bed** n lecho, cauce m; ~**side** n ribera, orilla // cpd (port, traffic) de río, del río.

rivet ['rivit] n roblón m, remache m // vt remachar; (fig) clavar.

Riviera [rivi'ɛərə] n: **the (French) ~** la Costa Azul (Francesa).

road [roud] n (gen) camino; (motorway etc) carretera; (in town) calle f; ~**block** n barricada; ~**hog** n loco del volante; ~**map** n mapa m de carreteras; ~**side** n borde m (del camino) // cpd al lado de la carretera; ~**sign** n señal f (de carretera o calle); ~ **user** n usuario de la vía pública; ~**way** n calzada; ~**worthy** a (car) listo para conducir.

roam [roum] vi vagar // vt vagar por.

roar [ro:*] n (of animal) rugido, bramido; (of crowd) rugido; (of vehicle, storm) estruendo; (of laughter) carcajada // vi rugir, bramar; hacer estruendo; **to ~ with laughter** reírse a carcajadas; **to do a ~ing trade** hacer buen negocio.

roast [roust] n carne f asada, asado // vt (meat) asar; (coffee) tostar.

rob [rob] vt robar; **to ~ sb of sth** robar algo a uno; (fig: deprive) quitarle algo a uno; ~**ber** n ladrón/ona m/f; ~**bery** n robo.

robe [roub] n (for ceremony etc) toga; (also: **bath~**) bata.

robin ['rɔbin] n petirrojo.

robot ['rɔubɔt] n robot m.

robust [rou'bʌst] a robusto, fuerte.

rock [rɔk] n (gen) roca; (boulder) peña, peñasco; (sweet) pirulí // vt (swing gently: cradle) balancear, mecer; (: child) arrullar; (shake) sacudir // vi mecerse, balancearse; sacudirse; **on the ~s** (drink) sobre las rocas; (marriage etc) en ruinas; **to ~ the boat** (fig) causar perturbaciones; ~ **and roll** n rocanrol m; ~-**bottom** a (fig) por los suelos; ~**ery** n cuadro alpino.

rocket ['rɔkit] n cohete m.

rocking ['rɔkiŋ]: ~ **chair** n mecedora; ~ **horse** n caballo de balancín.

rocky ['rɔki] a (gen) rocoso; (unsteady: table) débil.

rod [rɔd] n vara, varilla; (TECH) barra; (also: **fishing ~**) caña.

rode [roud] pt of **ride.**

rodent ['roudnt] n roedor m.

rodeo ['roudiəu] n rodeo.

roe [rou] n (species: also: ~ **deer**) corzo; (of fish): **hard/soft ~** hueva/lecha.

rogue [roug] n pícaro, pillo; **roguish** a pícaro.

role [roul] n papel m, rol m.

roll [roul] n rollo; (of banknotes) fajo; (also: **bread ~**) panecillo, bollo; (register) lista, nómina; (sound: of drums etc) redoble m; (movement: of ship) balanceo // vt hacer rodar; (also: ~ **up**: string) enrollar; (: sleeves) arremangar; (cigarettes) liar; (also: ~ **out**: pastry) aplanar // vi (gen) rodar; (drum) redoblar; (in walking) bambolearse; (ship) balancearse; **to ~ by** vi (time) pasar; **to ~ in** vi (mail, cash) entrar a raudales; **to ~ over** vi dar una vuelta; **to ~ up** vi (col: arrive) presentarse, aparecer // vt (carpet) arrollar; ~ **call** n acto de pasar lista; ~**er** n rodillo; (wheel) rueda; ~**er skates** npl patines mpl de rueda.

rollicking ['rɔlikiŋ] a alegre, divertido.

rolling ['rouliŋ] a (landscape) ondulado; ~ **pin** n rodillo (de cocina); ~ **stock** n (RAIL) material m rodante.

Roman ['roumən] a, n romano/a; ~ **Catholic** a, n católico (romano).

romance [rə'mæns] n (love affair) amoríos mpl, aventura sentimental; (charm) lo romántico.

Romanesque [roumə'nɛsk] a románico.

Romania [rou'meiniə] n = **Rumania.**

romantic [rə'mæntik] a romántico; ~**ism** [-tisizəm] n romanticismo.

romp [rɔmp] n retozo, juego // vi (also: ~ **about**) jugar, brincar.

rompers ['rɔmpəz] npl pelele m.

roof [ru:f], pl ~**s** n (gen) techo; (of house) techo, tejado; (of car) baca // vt techar, poner techo a; **the ~ of the mouth** el paladar, el cielo de la boca; ~**ing** n techumbre f; ~ **rack** n (AUT) baca, portaequipajes m inv.

rook [ruk] n (bird) graja; (CHESS) torre f.

room [ru:m] n (in house) cuarto, habitación f, pieza; (also: **bed~**) dormitorio; (in school etc) sala; (space) sitio, cabida; ~**s**

npl (lodging) alojamiento *sg;* '~s **to let'** 'se alquilan pisos *o* cuartos'; **single/double** ~ habitación individual/doble *o* para dos personas; ~**mate** *n* compañero/a de cuarto; ~ **service** *n* servicio de habitaciones; ~**y** *a* espacioso.

roost [ru:st] *n* percha // *vi* pasar la noche.

rooster ['ru:stə*] ʊ gallo.

root [ru:t] *n (BOT, MATH)* raíz *f* // *vi (plant, belief)* arriesgarse; **to** ~ **about** *vi (fig)* andar buscando; **to** ~ **for** *vt fus* apoyar a; **to** ~ **out** *vt* desarraigar.

rope [rəup] *n* cuerda; *(NAUT)* cable *m* // *vt (box)* atar *o* amarrar con (una) cuerda; *(climbers: also:* ~ **together)** encordarse; **to** ~ **sb in** *(fig)* persuadir a uno a tomar parte; **to know the** ~**s** *(fig)* conocer un negocio a fondo; ~ **ladder** *n* escala de cuerda.

rosary ['rəuzəri] *n* rosario.

rose [rəuz] *pt of* **rise** // *n* rosa; *(also:* ~**bush)** rosal *m*; *(on watering can)* roseta // *a* color de rosa.

rosé ['rəuzei] *n* vino rosado, clarete *m*.

rose: ~**bed** *n* rosaleda; ~**bud** *n* capullo de rosa; ~**bush** *n* rosal *m*.

rosemary ['rəuzməri] *n* romero.

rosette [rəu'zɛt] *n* rosetón *m*.

roster ['rɔstə*] *n*: **duty** ~ lista de deberes.

rostrum ['rɔstrəm] *n* tribuna.

rosy ['rəuzi] *a* rosado, sonrosado; **a** ~ **future** un futuro prometedor.

rot [rɔt] *n (decay)* putrefacción *f*, podredumbre *f*; *(fig: pej)* decadencia // *vt, vi* pudrirse, corromperse.

rota ['rəutə] *n* lista (de tandas).

rotary ['rəutəri] *a* rotativo.

rotate [rəu'teit] *vt (revolve)* hacer girar, dar vueltas a; *(change round: crops)* cultivar en rotación; (: *jobs)* alternar // *vi (revolve)* girar, dar vueltas; **rotating** *a (movement)* rotativo; **rotation** [-'teiʃən] *n* rotación *f*; **in rotation** por turno.

rotor ['rəutə*] *n* rotor *m*.

rotten ['rɔtn] *a (decayed)* podrido; (: *wood)* carcomido; *(fig)* corrompido; *(col: bad)* vil, miserable; **to feel** ~ *(ill)* sentirse muy mal.

rotting ['rɔtiŋ] *a* podrido.

rotund [rəu'tʌnd] *a* rotundo.

rouble, ruble *(US)* ['ru:bl] *n* rublo.

rouge [ru:ʒ] *n* colorete *m*.

rough [rʌf] *a (skin, surface)* áspero; *(terrain)* quebrado; *(road)* desigual; *(voice)* bronco; *(person, manner: coarse)* tosco, grosero; *(weather)* borrascoso; *(treatment)* brutal; *(sea)* bravo; *(cloth)* basto; *(plan)* preliminar; *(guess)* aproximado; *(violent)* violento // *n (person)* matón *m*; *(GOLF)*: **in the** ~ en las hierbas altas; **to** ~ **it** vivir sin comodidades; **to sleep** ~ pasar la noche al raso; ~-**and-ready** *a* improvisado; ~**en** *vt (a surface)* poner áspero; ~**ly** *ad (handle)* torpemente; *(make)* toscamente; *(approximately)* aproximadamente; ~**ness** *n* aspereza; tosquedad *f*; brutalidad *f*.

roulette [ru:'lɛt] *n* ruleta.

Roumania [ru:'meiniə] *n* = **Rumania.**

round [raund] *a* redondo // *n* círculo; *(of toast)* rodaja; *(of policeman)* ronda; *(of milkman)* recorrido; *(of doctor)* visitas *fpl*; *(game: of cards, in competition)* partida; *(of ammunition)* cartucho; *(BOXING)* asalto; *(of talks)* ronda // *vt (corner)* doblar // *prep* alrededor de // *ad*: **all** ~ por todos lados; **the long way** ~ el camino menos directo; **all the year** ~ durante todo el año; **it's just** ~ **the corner** *(fig)* está a la vuelta de la esquina; **to go** ~ **to sb's (house)** ir a casa de uno; **to go** ~ **the back** pasar por atrás; **to go** ~ **a house** visitar una casa; **to go the** ~**s** *(story)* divulgarse; **to** ~ **off** *vt (speech etc)* acabar, poner término a; **to** ~ **up** *vt (cattle)* acorralar; *(people)* reunir; *(prices)* redondear; ~**about** *n (AUT)* glorieta, redondel *m*; *(at fair)* tiovivo // *a (route, means)* indirecto; **a** ~ **of applause** una salva de aplausos; **a** ~ **of drinks** una ronda de bebidas; ~**ed** *a* redondeado; *(style)* expresivo; ~**ly** *ad (fig)* rotundamente; ~- **shouldered** *a* cargado de espaldas; ~ **trip** *n* viaje *m* de ida y vuelta; ~**up** *n* rodeo; *(of criminals)* redada.

rouse [rauz] *vt (wake up)* despertar; *(stir up)* suscitar; **rousing** *a* emocionado, entusiasta.

rout [raut] *n (MIL)* derrota; *(flight)* fuga // *vt* derrotar.

route [ru:t] *n* ruta, camino; *(of bus)* recorrido; *(of shipping)* rumba, derrota; ~ **map** *n (for journey)* mapa *m* de carreteras.

routine [ru:'ti:n] *a (work)* rutinario // *n* rutina; *(THEATRE)* número.

roving ['rəuviŋ] *a (wandering)* errante; *(salesman)* ambulante.

row [rəu] *n (line)* fila, hilera; *(KNITTING)* pasada // *n* [rau] *(noise)* estrépito, estruendo; *(racket)* escándalo; *(dispute)* bronca, pelea; *(fuss)* jaleo, follón *m*; *(scolding)* regaño // *vi (in boat)* remar // *vi* [rau] reñir(se) // *vt (boat)* conducir remando.

rowdy ['raudi] *a (person: noisy)* ruidoso; (: *quarrelsome)* pendenciero; *(occasion)* alborotado // *n* pendenciero.

rowing ['rəuiŋ] *n* remo; ~ **boat** *n* bote *m* de remos.

royal ['rɔiəl] *a* real; ~**ist** *a*, *n* monárquico/a; ~**ty** *n (*~ *persons)* familia real; *(payment to author)* derechos *mpl* de autor.

R.S.V.P. *abbr of* **répondez s'il vous plaît** SRC (Se Ruega Contestación).

rub [rʌb] *vt (gen)* frotar; *(hard)* restregar; *(polish)* sacar brillo a // *n (gen)* frotamiento; *(touch)* roce *m*; **to** ~ **sb up the wrong way** coger a uno a contrapelo;

to ~ off vi borrarse; **to ~ off on** influir en; **to ~ out** vt borrar.

rubber ['rʌbə*] n caucho, goma; (Brit: eraser) goma de borrar; **~ band** n goma, gomita; **~ plant** n árbol m del caucho, gomero; **~y** a elástico.

rubbish ['rʌbɪʃ] n (from household) basura; (waste) desperdicios mpl; (fig: pej) tonterías fpl; (trash) pacotilla; **~ bin** n cubo de la basura; **~ dump** n (in town) vertedero, basurero.

rubble ['rʌbl] n escombros mpl.

ruby ['ru:bɪ] n rubí m.

rucksack ['rʌksæk] n mochila.

ructions ['rʌkʃənz] npl lío sg, jaleo sg.

rudder ['rʌdə*] n timón m.

ruddy ['rʌdɪ] a (face) rubicundo, frescote; (col: damned) condenado.

rude [ru:d] a (impolite: person) grosero; (: word, manners) rudo, grosero; (sudden) repentino; (shocking) verde, indecente; **~ly** ad groseramente, toscamente; repentinamente; **~ness** n grosería, tosquedad f.

rudiment ['ru:dɪmənt] n rudimento; **~ary** [-'mɛntərɪ] a rudimentario.

rue [ru:] vt arrepentirse de; **~ful** a arrepentido.

ruffian ['rʌfɪən] n matón m, criminal m.

ruffle ['rʌfl] vt (hair) despeinar; (clothes) arrugar; (fig: person) agitar.

rug [rʌg] n alfombra; (for knees) manta.

rugby ['rʌgbɪ] n (also: **~ football**) rugby m.

rugged ['rʌgɪd] a (landscape) accidentado; (features, character) fuerte.

rugger ['rʌgə*] n (col) rugby m.

ruin ['ru:ɪn] n ruina // vt arruinar; (spoil) estropear; **~s** npl ruinas fpl, restos mpl; **~ous** a ruinoso.

rule [ru:l] n (norm) norma, costumbre f; (regulation) regla; (government) dominio; (ruler) metro // vt (country, person) gobernar; (decide) disponer; (draw: lines) trazar // vi regir; (LAW) fallar; **to ~ out** excluir; **as a ~** por regla general; **~d** a (paper) rayado; **ruler** n (sovereign) soberano; (for measuring) regla; **ruling** a (party) gobernante; (class) dirigente // n (LAW) fallo, decisión f.

rum [rʌm] n ron m.

Rumania [ru:'meɪnɪə] n Rumanía; **~n** a, n rumano/a.

rumble ['rʌmbl] n retumbo, ruido sordo; (of thunder) redoble m // vi retumbar, hacer un ruido sordo; (stomach, pipe) sonar.

rummage ['rʌmɪdʒ] vi revolverlo todo.

rumour, rumor (US) ['ru:mə*] n rumor m // vt: **it is ~ed that...** se rumorea que... .

rump [rʌmp] n (of animal) ancas fpl, grupa; **~ steak** n filete m de lomo.

rumpus ['rʌmpəs] n (col) lío, jaleo; (quarrel) pelea, riña.

run [rʌn] n carrera; (outing) paseo, excursión f; (distance travelled) trayecto; (series) serie f; (THEATRE) temporada; (SKI) pista // (vb: pt **ran**, pp **run**) vi

(operate: business) dirigir; (: competition, course) organizar; (: hotel, house) administrar, llevar; (to pass: hand) pasar; (water, bath) abrir el grifo (del baño) // vi (gen) correr; (work: machine) funcionar, marchar; (bus, train: operate) circular, ir; (: travel) ir; (continue: play) seguir; (: contract) ser válido; (flow: river, bath) fluir; (colours, washing) desteñirse; (in election) ser candidato; **there was a ~ on** (meat, tickets) hubo mucha demanda de; **in the long ~** a la larga, a largo plazo; **on the ~** en fuga; **I'll ~ you to the station** te llevaré a la estación en coche; **to ~ a risk** correr un riesgo; **to ~ about** vi (children) correr por todos lados; **to ~ across** vt fus (find) dar con, toparse con; **to ~ away** vi huir; **to ~ down** vi (clock) parar // vt (AUT) atropellar; (criticize) criticar; **to be ~ down** estar debilitado; **to ~ off** vt (water) dejar correr // vi huir corriendo; **to ~ out** vi (person) salir corriendo; (liquid) irse; (lease) caducar, vencer; (money) acabarse; **to ~ out of** vt fus quedar sin; **to ~ over** vt sep (AUT) atropellar // vt fus (revise) repasar; **to ~ through** vt fus (instructions) repasar; **to ~ up** vt (debt) incurrir en; **to ~ up against** (difficulties) tropezar con; **~away** a (horse) desbocado; (truck) sin frenos; (person) fugitivo.

rung [rʌŋ] pp of **ring** // n (of ladder) escalón m, peldaño.

runner ['rʌnə*] n (in race: person) corredor/a m/f; (: horse) caballo; (on sledge) patín m; (on curtain) anillo; (wheel) ruedecilla; **~ bean** n (BOT) judía escarlata; **~-up** n subcampeón/ona m/f.

running ['rʌnɪŋ] n (sport) atletismo; (race) carrera // a (water) corriente; (commentary) continuo; **6 days ~** 6 días seguidos; **~ board** n estribo.

runny ['rʌnɪ] a derretido.

run-of-the-mill ['rʌnəvðə'mɪl] a común y corriente.

runt [rʌnt] n (also: pej) redrojo, enano.

runway ['rʌnweɪ] n (AVIAT) pista de aterrizaje.

rupee [ru:'pi:] n rupia.

rupture ['rʌptʃə*] n (MED) hernia // vt: **to ~ o.s.** causarse una hernia, quebrarse.

rural ['ruərl] a rural.

ruse [ru:z] n ardid m.

rush [rʌʃ] n ímpetu m; (hurry) prisa; (COMM) demanda repentina; (BOT) junco; (current) corriente f fuerte, ráfaga // vt apresurar; (work) hacer de prisa; (attack: town etc) asaltar // vi correr, precipitarse; **~ hour** n horas fpl punta.

rusk [rʌsk] n bizcocho tostado.

Russia ['rʌʃə] n Rusia; **~n** a, n ruso/a.

rust [rʌst] n herrumbre f, moho // vi oxidarse.

rustic ['rʌstɪk] a rústico.

rustle ['rʌsl] vi susurrar // vt (paper) hacer crujir; (US: cattle) hurtar, robar.

rustproof ['rʌstpruːf] *a* inoxidable, a prueba de herrumbre.

rusty ['rʌstɪ] *a* oxidado, mohoso.

rut [rʌt] *n* rodera, carril *m*; (*zool*) celo; **to be in a** ~ ir encarrilado.

ruthless ['ruːθlɪs] *a* despiadado; ~**ness** *n* crueldad *f*, implacabilidad *f*.

rye [raɪ] *n* centeno; ~ **bread** *n* pan de centeno.

S

sabbath ['sæbəθ] *n* domingo; (*Jewish*) sábado.

sabbatical [sə'bætɪkl] *a*: ~ **year** año de licencia.

sabotage ['sæbətɑːʒ] *n* sabotaje *m* // *vt* sabotear.

saccharin(e) ['sækərɪn] *n* sacarina.

sack [sæk] *n* (*bag*) saco, costal *m* // *vt* (*dismiss*) despedir; (*plunder*) saquear; **to get the** ~ ser despedido; ~**ing** *n* (*material*) harpillera.

sacrament ['sækrəmənt] *n* sacramento.

sacred ['seɪkrɪd] *a* sagrado, santo.

sacrifice ['sækrɪfaɪs] *n* sacrificio // *vt* sacrificar.

sacrilege ['sækrɪlɪdʒ] *n* sacrilegio.

sacrosanct ['sækrəʊsæŋkt] *a* sacrosanto.

sad [sæd] *a* (*unhappy*) triste; (*deplorable*) lamentable; ~**den** *vt* entristecer.

saddle ['sædl] *n* silla (de montar); (*of cycle*) sillín *m* // *vt* (*horse*) ensillar; **to be** ~**d with sth** (*col*) quedar cargado con algo; ~**bag** *n* alforja.

sadism ['seɪdɪzm] *n* sadismo; **sadist** *n* sadista *m/f*; **sadistic** [sə'dɪstɪk] *a* sádico.

sadly ['sædlɪ] *ad* tristemente; ~ **lacking (in)** muy deficiente (en).

sadness ['sædnɪs] *n* tristeza.

safari [sə'fɑːrɪ] *n* safari *m*.

safe [seɪf] *a* (*out of danger*) fuera de peligro; (*not dangerous, sure*) seguro; (*unharmed*) a salvo, ileso; (*trustworthy*) digno de confianza // *n* caja de caudales, caja fuerte; ~ **and sound** sano y salvo; **(just) to be on the** ~ **side** por mayor seguridad; ~**guard** *n* protección *f*, garantía // *vt* proteger, defender; ~**keeping** *n* custodia; ~**ly** *ad* seguramente, con seguridad; (*without mishap*) sin peligro.

safety ['seɪftɪ] *n* seguridad *f* // *a* de seguridad; ~ **first!** ¡precaución!; ~ **belt** *n* cinturón *m* (de seguridad); ~ **pin** *n* imperdible *m*.

saffron ['sæfrən] *n* azafrán *m*.

sag [sæg] *vi* aflojarse.

sage [seɪdʒ] *n* (*herb*) salvia; (*man*) sabio.

Sagittarius [sædʒɪ'tɛərɪəs] *n* Sagitario.

sago ['seɪgəʊ] *n* sagú *m*.

said [sɛd] *pt, pp of* **say.**

sail [seɪl] *n* (*on boat*) vela; (*trip*): **to go for a** ~ tomar un paseo en barco // *vt* (*boat*) gobernar // *vi* (*travel: ship*) navegar; (: *passenger*) pasear en barco; (*set off*)

zarpar; **they** ~**ed into Copenhagen** llegaron a Copenhague; **to** ~ **through** *vi, vt fus* (*fig*) hacer con facilidad; ~**boat** *n* (*US*) velero, barco de vela; ~**ing** *n* (*sport*) balandrismo; **to go** ~**ing** salir en balandro; ~**ing ship** *n* barco de vela; ~**or** *n* marinero, marino.

saint [seɪnt] *n* santo; **S**~ **John** San Juan; ~**ly** *a* santo.

sake [seɪk] *n*: **for the** ~ **of** por (motivo de).

salad ['sæləd] *n* ensalada; ~ **bowl** *n* ensaladera; ~ **cream** *n* mayonesa; ~ **dressing** *n* aliño; ~ **oil** *n* aceite *m* para ensaladas.

salami [sə'lɑːmɪ] *n* salami *m*.

salary ['sælərɪ] *n* sueldo.

sale [seɪl] *n* venta; (*at reduced prices*) liquidación *f*, saldo; **"grand** ~**"** grandes rebajas; **"for** ~**"** "se vende"; **on** ~ en venta; ~**room** *n* sala de subastas; **salesman/woman** *n* vendedor/a *m/f*; (*in shop*) dependiente/a *m/f*; (*representative*) viajante *m/f*; **salesmanship** *n* arte *m* de vender.

saliva [sə'laɪvə] *n* saliva.

sallow ['sæləʊ] *a* cetrino.

salmon ['sæmən] *n, pl inv* salmón *m*.

saloon [sə'luːn] *n* (*US*) bar *m*, taberna; (*aut*) (coche *m* de) turismo; (*ship's lounge*) cámara, salón *m*.

salt [sɔlt] *n* sal *f* // *vt* salar; (*put* ~ *on*) poner sal en; ~ **cellar** *n* salero; ~**water** *a* de agua salada; ~**y** *a* salado.

salutary ['sæljutərɪ] *a* saludable.

salute [sə'luːt] *n* saludo; (*of guns*) salva // *vt* saludar.

salvage ['sælvɪdʒ] *n* (*saving*) salvamento, recuperación *f*; (*things saved*) objetos *mpl* salvados // *vt* salvar.

salvation [sæl'veɪʃən] *n* salvación *f*; **S**~ **Army** *n* Ejército de Salvación.

salve [sælv] *n* (*cream etc*) ungüento, bálsamo.

salver ['sælvə*] *n* bandeja.

same [seɪm] *a* mismo // *ad* de la misma forma, igual // *pron*: **the** ~ el mismo/la misma; **the** ~ **book as** el mismo libro que; **all** *or* **just the** ~ sin embargo, aun así; **to do the** ~ **(as sb)** hacer lo mismo (que otro); **the** ~ **to you!** ¡igualmente!

sample ['sɑːmpl] *n* muestra // *vt* (*food, wine*) probar.

sanatorium [sænə'tɔːrɪəm] *, pl* **-ria** [-rɪə] *n* sanatorio.

sanctify ['sæŋktɪfaɪ] *vt* santificar.

sanctimonious [sæŋktɪ'məʊnɪəs] *a* santurrón(ona).

sanction ['sæŋkʃən] *n* sanción *f* // *vt* sancionar.

sanctity ['sæŋktɪtɪ] *n* (*gen*) santidad *f*; (*inviolability*) inviolabilidad *f*.

sanctuary ['sæŋktjʊərɪ] *n* (*gen*) santuario; (*refuge*) asilo, refugio.

sand [sænd] *n* arena; (*beach*) playa // *vt* enarenar.

sandal ['sændl] *n* sandalia; (*wood*) sándalo.

sand: ~**bag** *n* saco de arena; ~**bank** *n* banco de arena; ~**castle** *n* castillo de arena; ~ **dune** *n* duna; ~**paper** *n* papel *m* de lija; ~**pit** *n* (*for children*) cajón *m* de arena; ~**stone** *n* piedra arenisca.

sandwich ['sændwıtʃ] *n* bocadillo, sándwich *m* // *vt* (*also:* ~ **in**) intercalar; ~**ed between** apretujado entre; **cheese/ham** ~ sándwich de queso/jamón; ~ **board** *n* cartelón *m*; ~ **course** *n* curso de medio tiempo.

sandy ['sændı] *a* arenoso; (*colour*) rojizo.

sane [seın] *a* cuerdo, sensato; (*sensible*) prudente.

sang [sæŋ] *pt of* **sing.**

sanitarium [sænı'tɛərıəm] (*US*) = **sanatorium.**

sanitary ['sænıtərı] *a* (*system, arrangements*) sanitario; (*clean*) higiénico; ~ **towel**, ~ **napkin** (*US*) *n* paño higiénico, compresa higiénica.

sanitation [sænı'teıʃən] *n* (*in house*) saneamiento; (*in town*) sanidad *f*, higiene *f*.

sanity ['sænıtı] *n* cordura; (*common sense*) juicio, sentido común.

sank [sæŋk] *pt of* **sink.**

Santa Claus [sæntə'klɔːz] *n* San Nicolás, Papá Noel.

sap [sæp] *n* (*of plants*) savia // *vt* (*strength*) minar, agotar.

sapling ['sæplıŋ] *n* árbol nuevo *o* joven.

sapphire ['sæfaıə*] *n* zafiro.

sarcasm ['sɑːkæzm] *n* sarcasmo; **sarcastic** [-'kæstık] *a* sarcástico.

sardine [sɑː'diːn] *n* sardina.

Sardinia [sɑː'dınıə] *n* Cerdeña.

sari ['sɑːrı] *n* sari *m*.

sash [sæʃ] *n* faja.

sat [sæt] *pt, pp of* **sit.**

Satan ['seıtn] *n* Satanás *m*.

satchel ['sætʃl] *n* bolsa; (*child's*) cartera.

satellite ['sætəlaıt] *n* satélite *m*.

satin ['sætın] *n* raso // *a* de raso.

satire ['sætaıə*] *n* sátira; **satirical** [sə'tırıkl] *a* satírico; **satirize** ['sætıraız] *vt* satirizar.

satisfaction [sætıs'fækʃən] *n* satisfacción *f*; (*of debt*) liquidación *f*; **satisfactory** [-'fæktərı] *a* satisfactorio.

satisfy ['sætısfaı] *vt* satisfacer; (*pay*) liquidar; (*convince*) convencer; ~**ing** *a* satisfactorio.

saturate ['sætʃəreıt] *vt*: **to** ~ **(with)** empapar *o* saturar (de); **saturation** [-'reıʃən] *n* saturación *f*.

Saturday ['sætədı] *n* sábado.

sauce [sɔːs] *n* salsa; (*sweet*) crema; (*fig: cheek*) frescura; ~**pan** *n* perola.

saucer ['sɔːsə*] *n* platillo.

saucy ['sɔːsı] *a* fresco, descarado; (*flirtatious*) coqueta.

sauna ['sɔːnə] *n* sauna.

saunter ['sɔːntə*] *vi* deambular.

sausage ['sɔsıdʒ] *n* salchicha; (*cold meat*) embutido; ~ **roll** *n* empanadita.

sauté ['sɔuteı] *a* salteado.

savage ['sævıdʒ] *a* (*cruel, fierce*) feroz, furioso; (*primitive*) salvaje // *n* salvaje *m/f* // *vt* (*attack*) embestir; ~**ry** *n* ferocidad *f*; salvajismo.

save [seıv] *vt* (*rescue*) salvar, rescatar; (*money, time*) ahorrar; (*put by*) guardar; (*avoid: trouble*) evitar // *vi* (*also:* ~ **up**) ahorrar // *n* (*SPORT*) parada // *prep* salvo, excepto.

saving ['seıvıŋ] *n* (*on price etc*) economía // *a*: **the** ~ **grace of** el único mérito de; ~**s** *npl* ahorros *mpl*; ~**s bank** *n* caja de ahorros.

saviour ['seıvjə*] *n* salvador/a *m/f*.

savour, savor (*US*) ['seıvə*] *n* sabor *m*, gusto // *vt* saborear; ~**y** *a* sabroso; (*dish: not sweet*) no dulce; (: *salted*) salado.

saw [sɔː] *pt of* **see** // *n* (*tool*) sierra // *vt*, *pt* **sawed**, *pp* **sawed** *or* **sawn** serrar; ~**dust** *n* (a)serrín *m*; ~**mill** *n* aserradero.

saxophone ['sæksəfəun] *n* saxófono.

say [seı] *n*: **to have one's** ~ expresar su opinión; **to have a** *or* **some** ~ **in sth** tener voz *o* tener que ver en algo // *vt*, *pt*, *pp* **said** decir; **to** ~ **yes/no** decir que sí/no; **that is to** ~ es decir; **that goes without** ~**ing** eso va sin decir; ~**ing** *n* dicho, refrán *m*.

scab [skæb] *n* costra; (*pej*) esquirol/a *m/f*; ~**by** *a* costroso, lleno de costras.

scaffold ['skæfəuld] *n* (*for execution*) cadalso, patíbulo; ~**ing** *n* andamios *mpl*, andamiaje *m*.

scald [skɔːld] *n* escaldadura // *vt* escaldar; ~**ing** *a* (*hot*) hirviendo.

scale [skeıl] *n* (*gen, MUS*) escala; (*of fish*) escama; (*of salaries, fees etc*) escalafón *m*; (*of map, also size, extent*) escala // *vt* (*mountain*) escalar; (*tree*) trepar; ~**s** *npl* (*small*) balanza *sg*; (*large*) báscula *sg*; **on a large** ~ a gran escala; ~ **of charges** tarifa, lista de precios; **social** ~ escala social; ~ **drawing** *n* dibujo a escala; ~ **model** *n* modelo a escala.

scallop ['skɔləp] *n* (*ZOOL*) venera; (*SEWING*) festón *m*.

scalp [skælp] *n* cabellera // *vt* escalpar.

scalpel ['skælpl] *n* escalpelo.

scamp [skæmp] *n* diablillo, travieso.

scamper ['skæmpə*] *vi*: **to** ~ **away,** ~ **off** irse corriendo.

scan [skæn] *vt* (*examine*) escudriñar; (*glance at quickly*) dar un vistazo a; (*TV, RADAR*) explorar, registrar.

scandal ['skændl] *n* escándalo; (*gossip*) chismes *mpl*; ~**ize** *vt* escandalizar; ~**ous** *a* escandaloso; (*libellous*) calumnioso.

Scandinavia [skændı'neıvıə] *n* Escandinavia; ~**n** *a* escandinavo.

scant [skænt] *a* escaso; ~**y** *a* escaso.

scapegoat ['skeıpgəut] *n* cabeza de turco, chivo expiatorio.

scar [skɑː] *n* cicatriz *f* // *vt* marcar con una cicatriz // *vi* cicatrizarse.

scarce [skɛəs] *a* escaso; ~**ly** *ad* apenas; **scarcity** *n* escasez *f*; (*shortage*) carestía.

scare [skɛə*] *n* susto, sobresalto; (*panic*)

pánico // vt asustar, espantar; to ~ sb
stiff dejar muerto de miedo a uno; bomb
~ amenaza de bomba; ~crow n
espantapájaros m inv; ~d a: to be ~d
asustarse, estar asustado.
scarf [skɑːf], pl scarves n (long) bufanda;
(square) pañuelo.
scarlet ['skɑːlɪt] a escarlata; ~ fever n
escarlatina.
scarves [skɑːvz] pl of scarf.
scary ['skɛərɪ] a (col) de miedo.
scathing ['skeɪðɪŋ] a mordaz.
scatter ['skætə*] vt (spread) esparcir,
desparramar; (put to flight) dispersar // vi
desparramarse; dispersarse; ~brained a
ligero de cascos; (forgetful) olvidadizo.
scavenger ['skævəndʒə*] n (refuse
collector) basurero; (zool) animal m/ave f
que se alimenta de la carroña.
scene [siːn] n (theatre, fig etc) escena; (of
crime, accident) escenario; (sight, view)
vista, perspectiva; (fuss) escándalo; ~ry
n (theatre) decorado; (landscape) paisaje
m; scenic a (picturesque) pintoresco.
scent [sɛnt] n perfume m, olor m; (fig:
track) rastro, pista; (sense of smell) olfato
// vt perfumar; (smell) oler; (sniff out)
husmear; (suspect) sospechar.
sceptic, skeptic (US) ['skɛptɪk] n
escéptico/a; ~al a escéptico; ~ism
['skɛptɪsɪzm] n escepticismo.
sceptre, scepter (US) ['sɛptə*] n cetro.
schedule ['ʃɛdjuːl] n (of trains) horario; (of
events) programa m; (plan) plan m; (list)
lista // vt (timetable) establecer el horario
de; (list) catalogar; (visit) fijar la hora de;
on ~ a la hora, sin retraso; to be ahead
of/behind ~ estar adelantado/en
retraso.
scheme [skiːm] n (plan) plan m, proyecto;
(method) esquema m; (plot) intriga; (trick)
ardid m; (arrangement) disposición f // vt
proyectar // vi (plan) hacer proyectos;
(intrigue) intrigar; scheming a intrigante.
schism ['skɪzəm] n cisma m.
schizophrenia [skɪtsəu'friːnɪə] n
esquizofrenia; schizophrenic [-ə'frɛnɪk]
a esquizofrénico.
scholar ['skɔlə*] n (pupil) alumno/a,
estudiante m/f; (learned person) sabio,
erudito; ~ly a erudito; ~ship n erudición
f; (grant) beca.
school [skuːl] n (gen) escuela, colegio; (in
university) facultad f // vt (animal)
amaestrar; ~ age n edad f escolar;
~book n libro de texto; ~boy n alumno;
~days npl años mpl del colegio; ~girl n
alumna; ~ing n enseñanza;
~master/mistress n (primary)
maestro/a; (secondary) profesor/a m/f;
~room n clase f; ~teacher n
maestro/a.
schooner ['skuːnə*] n (ship) goleta; (glass)
jarra.
sciatica [saɪ'ætɪkə] n ciática.
science ['saɪəns] n ciencia; ~ fiction n
ciencia-ficción f; scientific [-'tɪfɪk] a

científico; scientist n científico.
scimitar ['sɪmɪtə*] n cimitarra.
scintillating ['sɪntɪleɪtɪŋ] a brillante,
ingenioso.
scissors ['sɪzəz] npl tijeras fpl; a pair of
~ unas tijeras.
scoff [skɔf] vt (col: eat) engullir // vi: to ~
(at) (mock) mofarse (de).
scold [skəuld] vt regañar.
scone [skɔn] n panecillo.
scoop [skuːp] n cucharón m; (for flour etc)
pala; (press) exclusiva; to ~ out vt
excavar; to ~ up vt recoger.
scooter ['skuːtə*] n (motor cycle) moto f;
(toy) patinete m.
scope [skəup] n (of plan, undertaking)
ámbito; (reach) alcance m; (of person)
competencia; (opportunity) campo (de
acción).
scorch [skɔːtʃ] vt (clothes) chamuscar;
(earth, grass) quemar, secar; ~er n (col:
hot day) día m abrasador; ~ing a
abrasador(a).
score [skɔː*] n (points etc) puntuación f;
(mus) partitura; (reckoning) cuenta;
(twenty) veinte m, veintena // vt (goal,
point) ganar; (mark) rayar // vi marcar un
tanto; (football) marcar (un) gol; (keep
score) llevar el tanteo; on that ~ en lo
que se refiere a eso; to ~ 6 out of 10
obtener una puntuación de 6 sobre 10;
~board n marcador m; ~card n (sport)
tanteador m; scorer n marcador m; (keeping score) tanteador m.
scorn [skɔːn] n desprecio // vt despreciar;
~ful a desdeñoso, despreciativo.
Scorpio ['skɔːpɪəu] n Escorpión m.
scorpion ['skɔːpɪən] n escorpión m.
Scot [skɔt] n escocés/esa m/f.
scotch [skɔtʃ] vt (rumour) desmentir;
(plan) abandonar; S~ n whisky m
escocés.
Scotland ['skɔtlənd] n Escocia.
Scots [skɔts] a escocés(esa);
~man/woman n escocés/esa m/f;
Scottish ['skɔtɪʃ] a escocés(esa).
scoundrel ['skaundrl] n canalla m/f,
sinvergüenza m/f.
scour ['skauə*] vt (clean) fregar, estregar;
(search) recorrer, registrar; ~er n
estropajo.
scourge [skɔːdʒ] n azote m.
scout [skaut] n (mil, also: boy ~)
explorador m; to ~ around reconocer el
terreno.
scowl [skaul] vi fruncir el ceño; to ~ at
sb mirar con ceño a uno.
scraggy ['skrægɪ] a flaco, descarnado.
scram [skræm] vi (col) largarse.
scramble ['skræmbl] n (climb) subida
(difícil); (struggle) pelea // vi: to ~
out/through salir/abrirse paso con
dificultad; to ~ for pelear por; ~d eggs
npl huevos mpl revueltos.
scrap [skræp] n (bit) pedacito; (fig) pizca;
(fight) riña, bronca; (also: ~ iron)
chatarra, hierro viejo // vt reducir a

chatarra; (*discard*) desechar, descartar // *vi* reñir, armar (una) bronca; ~**s** *npl* (*waste*) sobras *fpl*, desperdicios *mpl*; ~**book** *n* álbum *m* de recortes.

scrape [skreip] *n* (*fig*) lío, apuro // *vt* raspar; (*skin etc*) rasguñar; (~ *against*) rozar // *vi*: **to** ~ **through** pasar con dificultad; **scraper** *n* raspador *m*.

scrap: ~ **heap** *n* (*fig*): **on the** ~ **heap** desperdiciado; ~ **merchant** *n* chatarrero; ~ **paper** *n* pedazos *mpl* de papel; ~**py** *a* (*poor*) pobre; (*speech*) inconexo; (*bitty*) fragmentario.

scratch [skrætʃ] *n* rasguño; (*from claw*) arañazo // *a*: ~ **team** equipo improvisado // *vt* (*record*) rayar; (*with claw, nail*) rasguñar, arañar // *vi* rascarse; **to start from** ~ partir de cero, empezar desde el principio; **to be up to** ~ estar a la altura (de las circunstancias).

scrawl [skrɔ:l] *n* garabatos *mpl* // *vi* hacer garabatos.

scream [skri:m] *n* chillido // *vi* chillar.

screech [skri:tʃ] *vi* chirriar.

screen [skri:n] *n* (CINEMA, TV) pantalla; (*movable*) biombo; (*wall*) tabique *m*; (*also*: **wind**~) parabrisas *m inv*; (*fig*) cortina // *vt* (*conceal*) tapar; (*from the wind etc*) proteger; (*film*) proyectar; (*candidates etc*) investigar a; ~**ing** *n* (MED) investigación *f* médica; ~ **test** *n* prueba de pantalla.

screw [skru:] *n* tornillo; (*propeller*) hélice *f* // *vt* atornillar; (*also*: ~ **in**) apretar; ~**driver** *n* destornillador *m*; ~**y** *a* (*col*) chiflado.

scribble ['skrɪbl] *n* garabatos *mpl* // *vt* escribir con prisa.

script [skrɪpt] *n* (CINEMA *etc*) guión *m*; (*writing*) escritura, letra.

Scripture ['skrɪptʃə*] *n* Sagrada Escritura.

scriptwriter ['skrɪptraitə*] *n* guionista *m/f*.

scroll [skrəul] *n* rollo.

scrounge [skraundʒ] *vt* (*col*): **to** ~ **sth off** *or* **from sb** obtener algo de otro por gorronería // *vi*: **to** ~ **on sb** vivir a costa de uno; **scrounger** *n* gorrón/ona *m/f*.

scrub [skrʌb] *n* (*clean*) fregado; (*land*) maleza // *vt* fregar, restregar; (*reject*) cancelar, anular.

scruff [skrʌf] *n*: **by the** ~ **of the neck** por el pescuezo.

scruffy ['skrʌfɪ] *a* desaliñado, piojoso.

scruple ['skru:pl] *n* escrúpulo; **scrupulous** *a* escrupuloso.

scrutinize ['skru:tɪnaɪz] *vt* escudriñar; (*votes*) escrutar; **scrutiny** [-nɪ] *n* escrutinio, examen *m*.

scuff [skʌf] *vt* desgastar, restregar.

scuffle ['skʌfl] *n* refriega.

scullery ['skʌlərɪ] *n* fregadero, trascocina.

sculptor ['skʌlptə*] *n* escultor *m*; **sculpture** [-tʃə*] *n* escultura.

scum [skʌm] *n* (*on liquid*) nata; (*pej*: *people*) canalla; (*fig*) heces *fpl*.

scurry ['skʌrɪ] *vi*: **to** ~ **off** escabullirse.

scurvy ['skə:vɪ] *n* escorbuto.

scuttle ['skʌtl] *n* (*also*: **coal** ~) cubo, carbonera // *vt* (*ship*) barrenar // *vi* (*scamper*): **to** ~ **away,** ~ **off** escabullirse.

scythe [saɪð] *n* guadaña.

sea [si:] *n* mar *m or f*; **on the** ~ (*boat*) en el mar; (*town*) junto al mar; **to be all at** ~ (*fig*) estar despistado; **out to** *or* **at** ~ en alta mar; ~**board** *n* litoral *m*; ~ **breeze** *n* brisa de mar; ~**farer** *n* marinero; ~**food** *n* mariscos *mpl*; ~ **front** *n* (*beach*) playa; (*prom*) paseo marítimo; ~**going** *a* (*ship*) de alta mar; ~**gull** *n* gaviota.

seal [si:l] *n* (*animal*) foca; (*stamp*) sello // *vt* (*close*) cerrar; (: *with* ~) sellar; **to** ~ **off** obturar; **it** ~**ed his fate** decidió su destino.

sea level ['si:lɛvl] *n* nivel *m* del mar.

sealing wax ['si:lɪŋwæks] *n* lacre *m*.

sea lion ['si:laɪən] *n* león *m* marino.

seam [si:m] *n* costura; (*of metal*) juntura; (*of coal*) veta, filón *m*.

seaman ['si:mən] *n* marinero.

seamless ['si:mlɪs] *a* sin costura.

seamstress ['sɛmstrɪs] *n* costurera.

seance ['seɪɔns] *n* sesión *f* de espiritismo.

sea: ~**plane** *n* hidroavión *m*; ~**port** *n* puerto de mar.

search [sə:tʃ] *n* (*for person, thing*) busca, búsqueda; (*of drawer, pockets*) registro; (*inspection*) reconocimiento // *vt* (*look in*) buscar en; (*examine*) examinar; (*person, place*) registrar // *vi*: **to** ~ **for** buscar; **to** ~ **through** *vt fus* registrar; **in** ~ **of** en busca de; ~**ing** *a* penetrante; ~**light** *n* reflector *m*; ~ **party** *n* pelotón *m* de salvamento; ~ **warrant** *n* mandamiento (judicial).

sea: ~**shore** *n* playa, orilla del mar; ~**sick** *a* mareado; ~**side** *n* playa, orilla del mar; ~**side resort** *n* playa.

season ['si:zn] *n* (*of year*) estación *f*; (*sporting etc*) temporada; (*gen*) época, período // *vt* (*food*) sazonar; ~**al** *a* estacional; ~**ing** *n* condimento, aderezo; ~ **ticket** *n* billete *m* de abono.

seat [si:t] *n* (*in bus, train: place*) asiento; (*chair*) silla; (PARLIAMENT) escaño; (*buttocks*) culo, trasero; (*of government*) sede *f* // *vt* sentar; (*have room for*) tener asientos para; **to be** ~**ed** sentarse; ~ **belt** *n* cinturón *m* de seguridad.

sea: ~ **water** *n* agua *m* del mar; ~**weed** *n* alga marina; ~ **worthy** *a* marinero, en condiciones de navegar.

sec. *abbr of* **second(s)**.

secede [sɪ'si:d] *vi* separarse.

secluded [sɪ'klu:dɪd] *a* retirado; **seclusion** [-'klu:ʒən] *n* retiro.

second ['sɛkənd] *a* segundo // *ad* (*in race etc*) en segundo lugar // *n* (*gen*) segundo; (AUT: *also*: ~ **gear**) segunda; (COMM) artículo con algún desperfecto // *vt* (*motion*) apoyar; ~**ary** *a* secundario; ~**ary school** *n* escuela secundaria; ~**class** *a* de segunda clase; ~**hand** *a* de segunda

mano, usado; ~ **hand** n (on clock) segundero; ~**ly** ad en segundo lugar; ~**ment** [sɪ'kɔndmənt] n traslado temporal; ~**rate** a de segunda categoría.
secrecy ['siːkrəsɪ] n secreto; **secret** [-krɪt] a, n secreto.
secretarial [sɛkrɪ'tɛərɪəl] a de secretario/a.
secretariat [sɛkrɪ'tɛərɪət] n secretaría.
secretary ['sɛkrətərɪ] n secretario/a; S ~ **of State** (Brit: POL) Ministro (con cartera).
secretive ['siːkrətɪv] a reservado, sigiloso.
sect [sɛkt] n secta; ~**arian** [-'tɛərɪən] a sectario.
section ['sɛkʃən] n sección f; (part) parte f; (of document) artículo; (of opinion) sector m; ~**al** a (drawing) en corte.
sector ['sɛktə*] n sector m.
secular ['sɛkjulə*] a secular, seglar.
secure [sɪ'kjuə*] a (free from anxiety) seguro; (firmly fixed) firme, fijo // vt (fix) asegurar, afianzar; (get) conseguir.
security [sɪ'kjurɪtɪ] n seguridad f; (for loan) fianza; (: object) prenda.
sedate [sɪ'deɪt] a (calm) tranquilo; (formal) serio, formal // vt tratar con calmantes.
sedation [sɪ'deɪʃən] n (MED) sedación f; **sedative** ['sɛdɪtɪv] n sedante m, sedativo.
sedentary ['sɛdntrɪ] a sedentario.
sediment ['sɛdɪmənt] n sedimento.
seduce [sɪ'djuːs] vt (gen) seducir; **seduction** [-'dʌkʃən] n seducción f; **seductive** [-'dʌktɪv] a seductor(a).
see [siː], pt **saw**, pp **seen** vt (gen) ver; (accompany): **to ~ sb to the door** acompañar a uno a la puerta; (understand) ver, comprender; (look at) mirar // vi ver // n sede f; **to ~ that** (ensure) asegurar que; **to ~ about** vi atender a, encargarse de; **to ~ off** vt despedirse de; **to ~ through** vt penetrar (con la vista) // vt fus llevar a cabo; **to ~ to** vt fus atender a, encargarse de.
seed [siːd] n semilla; (in fruit) pepita; (sperm) semen m, simiente f; (fig) germen m; (TENNIS) preseleccionado/a; ~**ling** n planta de semillero; ~**y** a (shabby) desaseado, raído.
seeing ['siːɪŋ] conj: ~ **(that)** visto que, en vista de que.
seek [siːk], pt, pp **sought** vt (gen) buscar; (post) solicitar.
seem [siːm] vi parecer; ~**ingly** ad aparentemente, según parece.
seen [siːn] pp of **see.**
seep [siːp] vi filtrarse.
seesaw ['siːsɔː] n balancín m, columpio.
seethe [siːð] vi hervir; **to ~ with anger** enfurecerse.
segment ['sɛgmənt] n segmento.
segregate ['sɛgrɪgeɪt] vt segregar; **segregation** [-'geɪʃən] n segregación f.
seismic ['saɪzmɪk] a sísmico.
seize [siːz] vt (grasp) agarrar, asir; (take possession of) secuestrar; (: territory) apoderarse de; (opportunity) aprovecharse

de; **to ~ (up)on** vt fus valerse de; **to ~ up** vi (TECH) agarrotarse.
seizure ['siːʒə*] n (MED) ataque m; (LAW) incautación f.
seldom ['sɛldəm] ad rara vez.
select [sɪ'lɛkt] a selecto, escogido // vt escoger, elegir; (SPORT) seleccionar; ~**ion** [-'lɛkʃən] n selección f, elección f; (COMM) surtido; ~**ive** a selectivo; ~**or** n (person) seleccionador/a m/f.
self [sɛlf] pron se; (after prep) sí mismo // n, pl **selves** uno mismo; **him~/her~** él mismo/ella misma; **the ~** el yo.
self... pref auto...; ~**-appointed** a autonombrado; ~**-assured** a seguro de sí mismo; ~**-catering** a sin pensión; ~**-centred** a egocéntrico; ~**-coloured** a de color natural; (of one colour) de un color; ~**-confidence** n confianza en sí mismo; ~**-conscious** a cohibido; ~**-contained** a (gen) independiente; (flat) con entrada particular; ~**-control** n autodominio; ~**-defence** n defensa propia; ~**-discipline** n autodisciplina; ~**-employed** a que trabaja por cuenta propia; ~**-evident** a patente; ~**-governing** a autónomo; ~**-important** a presumido; ~**-indulgent** a inmoderado; ~**-interest** n egoísmo; ~**-ish** a egoísta; ~**-ishness** n egoísmo; ~**-lessly** ad desinteresadamente; ~**-pity** n autocompasión f; ~**-portrait** n autorretrato; ~**-possessed** a sereno, dueño de sí mismo; ~**-preservation** n propia conservación f; ~**-reliant** a independiente, seguro de sí mismo; ~**-respect** n amor m propio; ~**-righteous** a santurrón(ona); ~**-sacrifice** n abnegación f; ~**-satisfied** a satisfecho de sí mismo; ~**-service** a de autoservicio; ~**-sufficient** a autosuficiente; ~**-taught** a autodidacta.
sell [sɛl], pt, pp **sold** vt vender // vi venderse; **to ~ at or for £10** vender a 10 libros; **to ~ off** vt liquidar; **to ~ out** vi transigir, transar (AM); ~**er** n vendedor/a m/f; ~**ing price** n precio de venta.
sellotape ['sɛləuteɪp] n celo.
sellout ['sɛlaut] n traición f; (of tickets): **it was a ~** fue un éxito de taquilla.
selves [sɛlvz] pl of **self.**
semaphore ['sɛməfɔː*] n semáforo.
semen ['siːmən] n semen m.
semi... [sɛmɪ] pref semi..., medio...; ~**circle** n semicírculo; ~**colon** n punto y coma; ~**conscious** a semiconsciente; ~**detached (house)** n (casa) semiseparada; ~**-final** n semi-final m.
seminar ['sɛmɪnɑː*] n seminario.
semitone ['sɛmɪtəun] n (MUS) semitono.
semolina [sɛmə'liːnə] n sémola.
senate ['sɛnɪt] n senado; **senator** n senador/a m/f.
send [sɛnd], pt, pp **sent** vt mandar, enviar; (dispatch) despachar; (telegram) poner; **to ~ away** vt (letter, goods) despachar; **to ~ away for** vt fus despachar por; **to ~**

back vt devolver; **to** ~ **for** vt fus mandar traer; **to** ~ **off** vt (goods) despachar; (SPORT: player) expulsar; **to** ~ **out** vt (invitation) mandar; (signal) emitir; **to** ~ **up** vt (person, price) hacer subir; (parody) parodiar; ~**er** n remitente m/f; ~**-off** n: **a good** ~**-off** una buena despedida.

senile ['si:naɪl] a senil; **senility** [sɪ'nɪlɪtɪ] n senilidad f.

senior ['si:nɪə*] a (older) mayor, más viejo; (: on staff) más antiguo; (of higher rank) superior // n mayor m; (in service) miembro más antiguo; ~**ity** [-'ɔrɪtɪ] n antigüedad f.

sensation [sɛn'seɪʃən] n sensación f; ~**al** a sensacional; ~**alism** n sensacionalismo.

sense [sɛns] n sentido; (feeling) sensación f; (good ~) sentido común, juicio; (sentiment) opinión f // vt sentir, percibir; **it makes** ~ tiene sentido; ~**less** a estúpido, insensato; (unconscious) sin sentido.

sensibility [sɛnsɪ'bɪlɪtɪ] n sensibilidad f; **sensibilities** npl delicadeza sg.

sensible ['sɛnsɪbl] a sensato, juicio; (cautious) prudente; (reasonable) razonable, lógico; (perceptible) apreciable.

sensitive ['sɛnsɪtɪv] a sensible; (touchy) susceptible; **sensitivity** [-'tɪvɪtɪ] n sensibilidad f; susceptibilidad f.

sensual ['sɛnsjuəl] a sensual.

sensuous ['sɛnsjuəs] a sensual.

sent [sɛnt] pt, pp of **send.**

sentence ['sɛntns] n (LING) frase f, oración f; (LAW) sentencia, fallo // vt: **to** ~ **sb to death/to 5 years** condenar a uno a muerte/a 5 años de cárcel.

sentiment ['sɛntɪmənt] n sentimiento; (opinion) opinión f; ~**al** [-'mɛntl] a sentimental; ~**ality** [-'tælɪtɪ] n sentimentalismo.

sentry ['sɛntrɪ] n centinela m.

separate ['sɛprɪt] a separado; (distinct) distinto // (vb: ['sɛpəreɪt]) vt separar; (part) dividir // vi separarse; ~**ly** ad por separado; ~**s** npl (clothes) coordinados mpl; **separation** [-'reɪʃən] n separación f.

September [sɛp'tɛmbə*] n se(p)tiembre m.

septic ['sɛptɪk] a séptico.

sequel ['si:kwl] n consecuencia, resultado; (of story) continuación f.

sequence ['si:kwəns] n sucesión f, serie f; (CINEMA) secuencia.

sequin ['si:kwɪn] n lentejuela.

serenade [sɛrə'neɪd] n serenata // vt dar serenata a.

serene [sɪ'ri:n] a sereno, tranquilo; **serenity** [sə'rɛnɪtɪ] n serenidad f, tranquilidad f.

sergeant ['sɑ:dʒənt] n sargento.

serial ['sɪərɪəl] n novela por entregas; ~**ize** vt publicar por entregas; ~ **number** n número de serie.

series ['sɪəri:s] n serie f.

serious ['sɪərɪəs] a serio; (grave) grave;

~**ly** ad en serio; gravemente; ~**ness** n seriedad f; gravedad f.

sermon ['sɔ:mən] n sermón m.

serrated [sɪ'reɪtɪd] a serrado, dentellado.

serum ['sɪərəm] n suero.

servant ['sɔ:vənt] n (gen) servidor/a m/f; (house ~) criado/a; **civil** ~ funcionario.

serve [sɔ:v] vt (gen) servir; (in shop: goods) servir, despachar; (: customer) atender; (subj: train) pasar por; (treat) tratar; (apprenticeship) hacer; (prison term) cumplir // vi (also TENNIS) sacar; (be useful): **to** ~ **as/for/to do** servir de/para/para hacer // n (TENNIS) saque m; **to** ~ **out,** ~ **up** vt (food) servir.

service ['sɔ:vɪs] n (gen) servicio; (REL) misa; (AUT) mantenimiento; (of dishes) vajilla, juego // vt (car, washing machine) mantener; (: repair) reparar; **the S**~**s** las fuerzas armadas; **to be of** ~ **to sb** ser útil a uno; ~**able** a servible, utilizable; ~ **area** n (on motorway) servicios mpl; ~**man** n militar m; ~ **station** n estación f de servicio.

serviette [sɔ:vɪ'ɛt] n servilleta.

servile ['sɔ:vaɪl] a servil.

session ['sɛʃən] n (sitting) sesión f; **to be in** ~ estar celebrando sesión.

set [sɛt] n juego; (RADIO) aparato; (TV) televisor m; (of utensils) batería; (of cutlery) cubierto; (of books) colección f; (TENNIS) set m; (group of people) grupo; (CINEMA) plató m; (THEATRE) decorado; (HAIRDRESSING) marcado // a (fixed) fijo; (ready) listo; (resolved) resuelto, decidido // (vb: pt, pp set) vt (place) poner, colocar; (fix) fijar; (: a time) señalar; (adjust) ajustar, arreglar; (decide: rules etc) establecer, decidir // vi (sun) ponerse; (jam, jelly) cuajarse; (concrete) fraguar; **to be** ~ **on doing sth** estar empeñado en hacer algo; **to** ~ **to music** poner música a; **to** ~ **on fire** incendiar, poner fuego a; **to** ~ **free** poner en libertad; **to** ~ **sth going** poner algo en marcha; **to** ~ **sail** zarpar, hacerse a la vela; **to** ~ **about** vt fus (task) ponerse a; **to** ~ **aside** vt poner aparte, dejar de lado; **to** ~ **back** vt (in time): **to** ~ **back (by)** retrasar (por); **to** ~ **off** vi partir // vt (bomb) hacer estallar; (cause to start) poner en marcha; (show up well) hacer resaltar; **to** ~ **out** vi: **to** ~ **out to do sth** ponerse a hacer algo // vt (arrange) disponer; (state) exponer; **to** ~ **up** vt (organization, record) establecer; **to** ~ **up shop** (fig) establecerse; ~**back** n (hitch) revés m, contratiempo.

settee [sɛ'ti:] n sofá m.

setting ['sɛtɪŋ] n (frame) marco; (placing) colocación f; (of sun) puesta; (of jewel) engaste m, montadura.

settle ['sɛtl] vt (argument, matter) componer; (accounts) ajustar, liquidar; (land) colonizar; (MED: calm) calmar, sosegar // vi (dust etc) depositarse; (weather) serenarse; (also: ~ **down**) instalarse, establecerse; **to** ~ **for sth** convenir en aceptar algo; **to** ~ **in** vi instalarse; **to** ~ **on sth** quedar en algo; **to** ~ **up with sb** ajustar cuentas con uno; ~**ment** n (payment) liquidación f; (agreement) acuerdo, convenio; (village etc) pueblo; **settler** n colono/a, colonizador/a m/f.

setup ['sɛtʌp] n (arrangement) plan m; (situation) situación f.

seven ['sɛvn] num siete; ~**teen** num diez y siete, dieciséis; ~**th** a séptimo; ~**ty** num setenta.

sever ['sɛvə*] vt cortar; (relations) romper.

several ['sɛvərl] a, pron varios mpl, algunos mpl; ~ **of us** varios de nosotros.

severance ['sɛvərəns] n (of relations) ruptura; ~ **pay** n pago de despedida.

severe [sɪ'vɪə*] a severo; (serious) grave; (hard) duro; (pain) intenso; **severity** [sɪ'vɛrɪtɪ] n severidad f; gravedad f; intensidad f.

sew [səu], pt **sewed**, pp **sewn** vt, vi coser; **to** ~ **up** vt coser, zurcir.

sewage ['su:ɪdʒ] n (effluence) aguas fpl residuales; (system) alcantarillado.

sewer ['su:ə*] n alcantarilla, cloaca.

sewing ['səuɪŋ] n costura; ~ **machine** n máquina de coser.

sewn [səun] pp of **sew**.

sex [sɛks] n sexo; **to have** ~ **with sb** tener sexo con alguien; ~ **act** n acto sexual.

sextet [sɛks'tɛt] n sexteto.

sexual ['sɛksjuəl] a sexual.

sexy ['sɛksɪ] a sexy.

shabby ['ʃæbɪ] a (person) desharrapado; (clothes) raído, gastado.

shack [ʃæk] n choza, chabola.

shackles ['ʃæklz] npl grillos mpl, grilletes mpl.

shade [ʃeɪd] n sombra; (for lamp) pantalla; (for eyes) visera; (of colour) matiz m, tonalidad f // vt dar sombra a; **in the** ~ en la sombra.

shadow ['ʃædəu] n sombra // vt (follow) seguir y vigilar; ~ **cabinet** n (POL) gabinete paralelo formado por el partido de oposición; ~**y** a oscuro; (dim) indistinto.

shady ['ʃeɪdɪ] a sombreado; (fig: dishonest) sospechoso; (: deal) turbio.

shaft [ʃɑ:ft] n (of arrow, spear) astil m; (AUT, TECH) eje m, árbol m; (of mine) pozo; (of lift) hueco, caja; (of light) rayo.

shaggy ['ʃægɪ] a peludo.

shake [ʃeɪk], pt **shook**, pp **shaken** vt sacudir; (building) hacer temblar; (perturb) inquietar, perturbar; (weaken) debilitar; (surprise) sorprender, pasmar // vi estremecerse; (tremble) temblar // n (movement) sacudida; **to** ~ **hands with sb** estrechar la mano con uno; **to** ~ **off** vt sacudirse; (fig) deshacerse de; **to** ~ **up** vt agitar; **shaky** a (hand, voice) trémulo; (building) inestable.

shall [ʃæl] auxiliary vb: **I** ~ **go** iré.

shallot [ʃə'lɔt] n chalote m.

shallow ['ʃæləu] a poco profundo; (fig) superficial.

sham [ʃæm] n fraude m, engaño // a falso, fingido // vt fingir, simular.

shambles ['ʃæmblz] n confusión f.

shame [ʃeɪm] n vergüenza; (pity) lástima // vt avergonzar; **it is a** ~ **that/to do** es una lástima que/hacer; **what a** ~! ¡qué lástima!; ~**faced** a avergonzado; ~**ful** a vergonzoso; ~**less** a descarado; (immodest) impúdico.

shampoo [ʃæm'pu:] n champú m // vt lavar el pelo (con champú).

shamrock ['ʃæmrɔk] n trébol m.

shandy ['ʃændɪ] n mezcla de cerveza con gaseosa.

shan't [ʃɑ:nt] = **shall not**.

shanty town ['ʃæntɪ-] n barrio de chabolas.

shape [ʃeɪp] n forma // vt formar, dar forma a; (sb's ideas) formar; (sb's life) determinar // vi (also: ~ **up**) (events) desarrollarse; (person) formarse; **to take** ~ tomar forma, **-shaped** suff: **heart-shaped** en forma de corazón; ~**less** a informe, sin forma definida; ~**ly** a bien formado o proporcionado.

share [ʃɛə*] n (part) parte f, porción f; (contribution) cuota; (COMM) acción f // vt dividir; (have in common) compartir; **to** ~ **out** (among or between) repartir (entre); ~**holder** n accionista m/f.

shark [ʃɑ:k] n tiburón m.

sharp [ʃɑ:p] a (razor, knife) afilado; (point) puntiagudo; (outline) definido; (pain) intenso; (MUS) desafinado; (contrast) marcado; (voice) agudo; (person: quick-witted) astuto; (dishonest) poco escrupuloso // n (MUS) sostenido // ad: **at 2 o'clock** ~ a las 2 en punto; ~**en** vt afilar; (pencil) sacar punta a; (fig) agudizar; ~**ener** n (also: **pencil** ~**ener**) afilador m; ~**-eyed** a de vista aguda; ~**-witted** a listo, perspicaz.

shatter ['ʃætə*] vt hacer añicos o pedazos; (fig: ruin) destruir, acabar con // vi hacerse añicos.

shave [ʃeɪv] vt afeitar, rasurar // vi afeitarse // n: **to have a** ~ afeitarse; **shaver** n (also: **electric shaver**) máquina de afeitar (eléctrica).

shaving ['ʃeɪvɪŋ] n (action) el afeitarse, rasurado; ~**s** npl (of wood etc) virutas fpl; ~ **brush** n brocha (de afeitar); ~ **cream** n crema (de afeitar).

shawl [ʃɔ:l] n chal m.

she [ʃi:] pron ella; ~**-cat** n gata; NB: for ships, countries follow the gender of your translation.

sheaf [ʃi:f], pl **sheaves** n (of corn) gavilla; (of arrows) haz m; (of papers) fajo.

shear [ʃɪə*], pt **sheared**, pp **sheared** or **shorn** vt (sheep) esquilar, trasquilar; **to** ~ **off** vt cercenar; ~**s** npl (for hedge) tijeras fpl de jardín.

sheath [ʃi:θ] n vaina; (contraceptive) preservativo.

sheaves [ʃiːvz] *pl of* **sheaf.**

shed [ʃɛd] *n* cobertizo // *vt, pt, pp* **shed** (*gen*) desprenderse de; (*skin*) mudar; (*tears*) derramar.

she'd [ʃiːd] = **she had; she would.**

sheep [ʃiːp] *n, pl inv* oveja; ~**dog** *n* perro pastor; ~**ish** *a* tímido, vergonzoso; ~**skin** *n* piel *f* de carnero.

sheer [ʃɪə*] *a* (*utter*) puro, completo; (*steep*) escarpado; (*almost transparent*) diáfano // *ad* verticalmente.

sheet [ʃiːt] *n* (*on bed*) sábana; (*of paper*) hoja; (*of glass, metal*) lámina.

sheik(h) [ʃeɪk] *n* jeque *m*.

shelf [ʃelf], *pl* **shelves** *n* estante *m*.

shell [ʃel] *n* (*on beach*) concha; (*of egg, nut etc*) cáscara; (*explosive*) proyectil *m*, obús *m*; (*of building*) armazón *m* // *vt* (*peas*) desenvainar; (*MIL*) bombardear.

she'll [ʃiːl] = **she will; she shall.**

shellfish ['ʃelfɪʃ] *n, pl inv* crustáceo; (*pl: as food*) mariscos *mpl*.

shelter ['ʃeltə*] *n* abrigo, refugio // *vt* (*aid*) amparar, proteger; (*give lodging to*) abrigar; (*hide*) esconder // *vi* abrigarse, refugiarse; ~**ed** *a* (*life*) protegido; (*spot*) abrigado.

shelve [ʃelv] *vt* (*fig*) aplazar; ~**s** *pl of* **shelf.**

shepherd ['ʃepəd] *n* pastor *m* // *vt* (*guide*) guiar, conducir; ~**ess** *n* pastora *f*; ~**'s pie** *n* pastel *m* de carne y patatas.

sheriff ['ʃerɪf] *n* sheriff *m*.

sherry ['ʃerɪ] *n* jerez *m*.

she's [ʃiːz] = **she is; she has.**

shield [ʃiːld] *n* escudo; (*TECH*) blindaje *m* // *vt*: **to** ~ (**from**) proteger (contra).

shift [ʃɪft] *n* (*change*) cambio; (*of place*) traslado; (*of workers*) turno // *vt* trasladar; (*remove*) quitar // *vi* moverse; (*change place*) cambiar de sitio; ~ **work** *n* trabajo por turno; ~**y** *a* tramposo; (*eyes*) furtivo.

shilling ['ʃɪlɪŋ] *n* chelín *m*.

shimmer ['ʃɪmə*] *n* reflejo trémulo // *vi* relucir.

shin [ʃɪn] *n* espinilla.

shine [ʃaɪn] *n* brillo, lustre *m* // (*vb: pt, pp* **shone**) *vi* brillar, relucir // *vt* (*shoes*) lustrar, sacar brillo a; **to** ~ **a torch on sth** dirigir una linterna hacia algo.

shingle ['ʃɪŋgl] *n* (*on beach*) guijarras *fpl*; ~**s** *n* (*MED*) herpes *mpl or fpl*.

shiny ['ʃaɪnɪ] *a* brillante, lustroso.

ship [ʃɪp] *n* buque *m*, barco // *vt* (*goods*) embarcar; (*oars*) desarmar; (*send*) transportar *o* enviar (por vía marítima); ~**building** *n* construcción *f* de barcos; ~**ment** *n* (*act*) embarque *m*; (*goods*) envío; ~**per** *n* exportador/a *m/f*; ~**ping** *n* (*act*) embarque *m*; (*traffic*) buques *mpl*; ~**shape** *a* en regla; ~**wreck** *n* naufragio; ~**yard** *n* astillero.

shire ['ʃaɪə*] *n* condado.

shirk [ʃɔːk] *vt* eludir, esquivar; (*obligations*) faltar a.

shirt [ʃɔːt] *n* camisa; **in** ~ **sleeves** en mangas de camisa.

shiver ['ʃɪvə*] *n* temblor *m*, estremecimiento // *vi* temblar, estremecerse.

shoal [ʃəul] *n* (*of fish*) banco.

shock [ʃɔk] *n* (*impact*) choque *m*; (*ELEC*) descarga (eléctrica); (*emotional*) conmoción *f*; (*start*) sobresalto, susto; (*MED*) postración *f* nerviosa // *vt* dar un susto a; (*offend*) escandalizar; ~**absorber** *n* amortiguador *m*; ~**ing** *a* (*awful*) espantoso; (*improper*) escandaloso; ~**proof** *a* a prueba de choques.

shod [ʃɔd] *pt, pp of* **shoe** // *a* calzado.

shoddy ['ʃɔdɪ] *a* de pacotilla, de bajísima calidad.

shoe [ʃuː] *n* zapato; (*for horse*) herradura; (*brake* ~) zapata // *vt, pt, pp* **shod** (*horse*) herrar; ~**brush** *n* cepillo para zapatos; ~**horn** *n* calzador *m*; ~ **lace** *n* cordón *m*; ~**maker** *n* zapatero; ~ **polish** *n* betún *m*; ~**shop** *n* zapatería.

shone [ʃɔn] *pt, pp of* **shine.**

shook [ʃuk] *pt of* **shake.**

shoot [ʃuːt] *n* (*on branch, seedling*) retoño, vástago // (*vb: pt, pp* **shot**) *vt* disparar; (*kill*) matar (con arma de fuego); (*wound*) herir (con arma de fuego); (*execute*) fusilar; (*film*) rodear, filmar // *vi* (*with gun, bow*): **to** ~ (**at**) tirar (a); (*FOOTBALL*) chutar; **to** ~ **down** *vt* (*plane*) derribar; **to** ~ **in/out** *vi* entrar corriendo/salir disparado; **to** ~ **up** *vi* (*fig*) subir (vertiginosamente); ~**ing** *n* (*shots*) tiros *mpl*; (*HUNTING*) caza con escopeta; ~**ing star** *n* estrella fugaz.

shop [ʃɔp] *n* tienda; (*workshop*) taller *m* // *vi* (*also*: **go** ~**ping**) ir de compras; ~ **assistant** *n* dependiente/a *m/f*; ~ **floor** *a* (*fig*) de la base; ~**keeper** *n* tendero/a; ~**lifter** *n* mechero/a; ~**lifting** *n* mechería; ~**per** *n* comprador/a *m/f*; ~**ping** *n* (*goods*) compras *fpl*; ~**ping bag** *n* bolsa (de compras); ~**ping centre**, ~**ping center** (*US*) *n* zona comercial *o* de tiendas; ~-**soiled** *a* usado; ~ **steward** *n* (*INDUSTRY*) enlace *m/f*; ~ **window** *n* escaparate *m*.

shore [ʃɔː*] *n* (*of sea, lake*) orilla // *vt*: **to** ~ (**up**) reforzar.

shorn [ʃɔːn] *pp of* **shear.**

short [ʃɔːt] *a* (*not long*) corto; (*in time*) breve, de corta duración; (*person*) bajo; (*curt*) brusco, seco; (*insufficient*) insuficiente // *vi* (*ELEC*) ponerse en cortocircuito // *n* (*also*: ~ **film**) cortometraje *m*; (**a pair of**) ~**s** (*unos*) pantalones *mpl* cortos; **to be** ~ **of sth** estar falto de algo; **in** ~ en pocas palabras; **it is** ~ **for** es la forma abreviada de; **to cut** ~ (*speech, visit*) interrumpir, terminar inesperadamente; **to fall** ~ **of** resultar (ser) insuficiente; **to stop** ~ parar en seco; **to stop** ~ **of** detenerse antes de; ~**age** *n* escasez *f*, falta; ~**bread** *n* torta seca y quebradiza; ~-**circuit** *n* cortocircuito // *vt* poner en cortocircuito // *vi* ponerse en cortocircuito; ~**coming** n defecto, deficiencia; ~**(crust) pastry** n pasta quebradiza; ~**cut** n atajo; ~**en** vt acortar; (visit) interrumpir; ~**hand** n taquigrafía; ~**hand typist** n taquimecanógrafo/a; ~ **list** n (for job) lista de candidatos escogidos; ~**-lived** a efímero; ~**ly** ad en breve, dentro de poco; ~ **ness** n (of distance) cortedad f; (of time) brevedad f; (manner) brusquedad f; ~**-sighted** a corto de vista, miope; (fig) imprudente; ~ **story** n cuento; ~**-tempered** a enojadizo; ~**-term** a (effect) a corto plazo; ~ **wave** n (RADIO) onda corta.

shot [ʃɔt] pt, pp of **shoot** // n (sound) tiro, disparo; (person) tirador/a m/f; (try) tentativa; (injection) inyección f; (PHOT) toma, fotografía; ~**gun** n escopeta.

should [ʃud] auxiliary vb: **I** ~ **go now** debo irme ahora; **he** ~ **be there now** debe de haber llegado (ya); **I** ~ **go if I were you** yo en tu lugar me iría; **I** ~ **like to me** gustaría.

shoulder ['ʃəuldə*] n hombro; (of road): **hard** ~ andén m // vt (fig) cargar con; ~ **blade** n omóplato.

shouldn't ['ʃudnt] = **should not.**

shout [ʃaut] n grito // vt gritar // vi gritar, dar voces; **to** ~ **down** vt hundir a gritos; ~**ing** n gritería.

shove [ʃʌv] n empujón m // vt empujar; (col: put): **to** ~ **sth in** meter algo; **to** ~ **off** vi (NAUT) alejarse del muelle; (fig: col) largarse.

shovel ['ʃʌvl] n pala; (mechanical) excavadora // vt mover con pala.

show [ʃəu] n (of emotion) demostración f; (semblance) apariencia; (exhibition) exposición f; (THEATRE) función f, espectáculo // (vb: pt showed, pp shown) vt mostrar, enseñar; (courage etc) mostrar, manifestar; (exhibit) exponer; (film) proyectar // vi mostrarse; (appear) aparecer; **to** ~ **sb in** hacer pasar a uno; **to** ~ **off** vi (pej) presumir // vt (display) lucir; (pej) hacer gala de; **to** ~ **sb out** acompañar a uno a la puerta; **to** ~ **up** vi (stand out) destacar; (col: turn up) presentarse // vt descubrir; (unmask) desenmascarar; ~ **business** n el mundo del espectáculo; ~**down** n crisis f, momento decisivo.

shower ['ʃauə*] n (rain) chaparrón m, chubasco; (of stones etc) lluvia; (also: ~bath) ducha // vi llover // vt: **to** ~ **sb with sth** colmar a uno de algo; ~**proof** a impermeable; ~**y** a (weather) lluvioso.

showing ['ʃəuiŋ] n (of film) proyección f.

show jumping ['ʃəudʒʌmpiŋ] n hipismo.

shown [ʃəun] pp of **show.**

show: ~**-off** n (col: person) presumido; ~**piece** n (of exhibition etc) obra más importante o central; ~**room** n sala de muestras.

shrank [ʃræŋk] pt of **shrink.**

shrapnel ['ʃræpnl] n metralla.

shred [ʃrɛd] n (gen pl) triza, jirón m // vt hacer trizas; (CULIN) desmenuzar.

shrewd [ʃru:d] a astuto; ~**ness** n astucia.

shriek [ʃri:k] n chillido // vt, vi chillar.

shrill [ʃril] a agudo, estridente.

shrimp [ʃrimp] n camarón m.

shrine [ʃrain] n santuario, sepulcro.

shrink [ʃriŋk], pt **shrank**, pp **shrunk** vi encogerse; (be reduced) reducirse // vt encoger; **to** ~ **from doing sth** no atreverse a hacer algo; ~**age** n encogimiento; reducción f.

shrivel ['ʃrivl] (also: ~ **up**) vt (dry) secar; (crease) arrugar // vi secarse; arrugarse.

shroud [ʃraud] n sudario // vt: ~**ed in mystery** envuelto en el misterio.

Shrove Tuesday ['ʃrəuv'tju:zdi] n martes m de carnaval.

shrub [ʃrʌb] n arbusto; ~**bery** n arbustos mpl.

shrug [ʃrʌg] n encogimiento de hombros // vt, vi: **to** ~ **(one's shoulders)** encogerse de hombros; **to** ~ **off** vt negar importancia a.

shrunk [ʃrʌŋk] pp of **shrink.**

shudder ['ʃʌdə*] n estremecimiento, escalofrío // vi estremecerse.

shuffle ['ʃʌfl] vt (cards) barajar; **to** ~ **(one's feet)** arrastrar los pies.

shun [ʃʌn] vt rehuir, esquivar.

shunt [ʃʌnt] vt (RAIL) maniobrar // vi: **to** ~ **to and fro** mandar de aquí para allá.

shut [ʃʌt], pt, pp **shut** vt cerrar // vi cerrarse; **to** ~ **down** vt, vi cerrarse, parar; **to** ~ **off** vt (supply etc) interrumpir, cortar; **to** ~ **up** vi (col: keep quiet) callarse // vt (close) cerrar; (silence) callar; ~**ter** n contraventana; (PHOT) obturador m.

shuttle ['ʃʌtl] n lanzadera; (also: ~ **service**) servicio de transporte entre dos estaciones.

shuttlecock ['ʃʌtlkɔk] n volante m.

shy [ʃai] a tímido; (reserved) reservado, cohibido; (unsociable) huraño; ~**ness** n timidez f; reserva; lo huraño.

Siamese [saiə'mi:z] a: ~ **cat** gato siamés.

Sicily ['sisili] n Sicilia.

sick [sik] a (ill) enfermo; (nauseated) mareado; (humour) negro; (vomiting): **to be** ~ vomitar; **to feel** ~ estar mareado; **to be** ~ **of** (fig) estar harto de; ~ **bay** n enfermería; ~**en** vt dar asco a // vi enfermar; ~**ening** a (fig) asqueroso.

sickle ['sikl] n hoz f.

sick: ~ **leave** n baja por enfermedad; ~**ly** a enfermizo; (causing nausea) nauseabundo; ~**ness** n enfermedad f, mal m; (vomiting) náuseas fpl; ~ **pay** n subsidio de enfermedad.

side [said] n (gen) lado; (of body) costado; (of lake) orilla; (aspect) aspecto; (team) equipo; (of hill) ladera // a (door, entrance) accesorio // vi: **to** ~ **with sb** tomar el partido de uno; **by the** ~ **of** al lado de; ~ **by** ~ juntos(as), lado a lado; **from all** ~**s** de todos lados; **to take** ~**s (with)**

tomar partido (con); ~**board** n aparador
m; ~**boards, ~burns** npl patillas fpl; ~
effect n efecto secundario; ~**light** n
(AUT) luz f lateral; ~**line** n (SPORT) línea
lateral; (fig) empleo suplementario;
~**long** a de soslayo; ~ **road** n calle f
lateral; ~**saddle** ad a mujeriegas, a la
inglesa; ~ **show** n (stall) caseta; (fig)
atracción f secundaria; ~**step** vt (fig)
esquivar; ~**track** vt (fig) desviar (de su
propósito); ~**walk** n (US) acera; ~**ways**
ad de lado.
siding ['saidiŋ] n (RAIL) apartadero, vía
muerta.
sidle ['saidl] vi: **to ~ up (to)** acercarse
furtivamente (a).
siege [si:dʒ] n cerco, sitio.
sieve [siv] n coladera // vt cribar.
sift [sift] vt cribar; (fig: information)
escudriñar.
sigh [sai] n suspiro // vi suspirar.
sight [sait] n (faculty) vista, visión f;
(spectacle) espectáculo; (on gun) mira,
alza // vt ver, divisar; **in ~** a la vista; **out
of ~** fuera de (la) vista; ~**seeing** n
excursionismo, turismo; **to go ~seeing**
visitar monumentos.
sign [sain] n (with hand) señal f, seña;
(indication) indicio; (trace) huella, rastro;
(notice) letrero; (written) signo // vt
firmar; **to ~ sth over to sb** firmar el
traspaso de algo a uno; **to ~ up** vi (MIL)
alistarse // vt (contract) contratar.
signal ['signl] n señal f // vi (AUT)
señalizar // vt (person) hacer señas a uno;
(message) transmitir.
signature ['signətʃə*] n firma.
signet ring ['signətriŋ] n anillo de sello.
significance [sig'nifikəns] n significado;
(importance) trascendencia; **significant**
[-ənt] a significativo; trascendente.
signify ['signifai] vt significar.
sign: ~ language n la mímica, lenguaje
m por señas o de señas; ~**post** n
indicador m.
silence ['sailns] n silencio // vt hacer
callar; (guns) reducir al silencio; **silencer**
n (on gun, AUT) silenciador m.
silent ['sailnt] a (gen) silencioso; (not
speaking) callado; (film) mudo; **to remain
~** guardar silencio.
silhouette [silu:'ɛt] n silueta; ~**d against**
destacado sobre o contra.
silicon chip ['silikən'tʃip] n plata de
silicio, astilla de silicona.
silk [silk] n seda // a de seda; ~**y** a sedoso.
silly ['sili] a (person) tonto; (idea) absurdo.
silt [silt] n sedimento.
silver ['silvə*] n plata; (money) moneda
suelta // a de plata, plateado; ~ **paper** n
papel m de plata; ~**-plated** a plateado;
~**smith** n platero; ~**y** a plateado.
similar ['similə*] a: ~ **to** parecido o
semejante a; ~**ity** [-'læriti] n parecido,
semejanza; ~**ly** ad del mismo modo.
simmer ['simə*] vi hervir a fuego lento.

simpering ['simpəriŋ] a afectado;
(foolish) bobo.
simple ['simpl] a (easy) sencillo; (foolish,
COMM) simple; ~**ton** n inocentón/ona m/f;
simplicity [-'plisiti] n sencillez f;
(foolishness) ingenuidad f; **simplify**
['simplifai] vt simplificar.
simulate ['simjuleit] vt simular;
simulation [-'leiʃən] n simulación f.
simultaneous [siməl'teiniəs] a
simultáneo; ~**ly** ad simultáneamente.
sin [sin] n pecado // vi pecar.
since [sins] ad desde entonces, después //
prep desde // conj (time) desde que;
(because) ya que, puesto que; ~ **then**
desde entonces.
sincere [sin'siə*] a sincero; **yours ~ly** le
saluda (afectuosamente); **sincerity**
[-'sɛriti] n sinceridad f.
sinful ['sinful] a (thought) pecaminoso;
(person) pecador/a.
sing [siŋ], pt **sang**, pp **sung** vt cantar // vi
(gen) cantar; (bird) trinar; (ears) zumbar.
singe [sindʒ] vt chamuscar.
singer ['siŋə*] n cantante m/f.
singing ['siŋiŋ] n (gen) canto; (songs)
canciones fpl; (in the ears) zumbido.
single ['siŋgl] a único, solo; (unmarried)
soltero; (not double) simple, sencillo; (bed,
room) individual // n (also: ~ **ticket**)
billete m sencillo; (record) single m; ~**s**
npl (TENNIS) individual m; **to ~ out** vt
(choose) escoger; (point out) singularizar;
~ **bed** n cama individual; **in ~ file** en
fila de uno; ~**-handed** ad sin ayuda;
~**-minded** a resuelto, firme; ~ **room** n
cuarto individual.
singular ['siŋgjulə*] a (odd) raro, extraño;
(LING) singular // n (LING) singular m.
sinister ['sinistə*] a siniestro.
sink [siŋk] n fregadero // (vb: pt **sank**, pp
sunk) vt (ship) hundir, echar a pique;
(foundations) excavar; (piles etc): **to ~ sth**
fijar algo bajo tierra // vi (gen) hundirse;
to ~ in vi (fig) penetrar, calar; **a ~ing
feeling** un sentimiento de que toda se
acaba.
sinner ['sinə*] n pecador/a m/f.
sinus ['sainəs] n (ANAT) seno.
sip [sip] n sorbo // vt sorber, beber a
sorbitos.
siphon ['saifən] n sifón m; **to ~ off** vt
quitar poco a poco.
sir [sə*] n señor m; **S~ John Smith** el
Señor John Smith; **yes ~** sí, señor.
siren ['saiərn] n sirena.
sirloin ['sə:lɔin] n solomillo.
sister ['sistə*] n hermana; (nurse)
enfermera jefe; ~**-in-law** n cuñada.
sit [sit], pt, pp **sat** vi sentarse; (be sitting)
estar sentado; (assembly) reunirse // vt
(exam) presentarse a; **to ~ down** vi
sentarse; **to ~ in on** asistir a; **to ~ up** vi
incorporarse; (not go to bed) velar.
site [sait] n sitio; (also: **building ~**) solar
m // vt situar.
sit-in ['sitin] n (demonstration)

manifestación *f* de brazos caídos.
sitting ['sɪtɪŋ] *n* (*of assembly etc*) sesión *f*; (*in canteen*) turno; ～ **room** *n* sala de estar.
✗ **situated** ['sɪtjueɪtɪd] *a* situado.
situation [sɪtju'eɪʃən] *n* situación *f.*
six [sɪks] *num* seis; ～ **teen** *num* diez y seis, dieciséis; ～ **th** *a* sexto; ～ **ty** *num* sesenta.
size [saɪz] *n* (*gen*) tamaño; (*extent*) extensión *f*; (*of clothing*) talla; (*of shoes*) número; (*glue*) cola, apresto; **to** ～ **up** *vt* formarse una idea de; ～ **able** *a* importante, considerable.
sizzle ['sɪzl] *vi* crepitar.
skate [skeɪt] *n* patín *m*; (*fish: pl inv*) raya // *vi* patinar; ～ **board** *n* skateboard *m*; **skater** *n* patinador/a *m/f*; **skating** *n* patinaje *m*; **skating rink** *n* pista de patinaje.
skeleton ['skɛlɪtn] *n* esqueleto; (*TECH*) armazón *m*; (*outline*) esquema *m*; ～ **key** *n* llave *f* maestra; ～ **staff** *n* personal *m* reducido.
sketch [skɛtʃ] *n* (*drawing*) dibujo; (*outline*) esbozo, bosquejo; (*THEATRE*) pieza corta // *vt* dibujar; esbozar; ～ **book** *n* libro de dibujos; ～ **pad** *n* bloc *m* de dibujo; ～ **y** *a* incompleto.
skewer ['skju:ə*] *n* broqueta.
ski [ski:] *n* esquí *m* // *vi* esquiar; ～ **boot** *n* bota de esquí.
skid [skɪd] *n* patinazo // *vi* patinar; ～ **mark** *n* huella de patinazo.
ski: ～ **er** *n* esquiador/a *m/f*; ～ **ing** *n* esquí *m*; ～ **jump** *n* pista para salto de esquí.
skilful ['skɪlful] *a* diestro, experto.
ski lift *n* telesilla.
skill [skɪl] *n* destreza, pericia; ～ **ed** *a* hábil, diestro; (*worker*) cualificado.
skim [skɪm] *vt* (*milk*) desnatar; (*glide over*) rozar, rasar // *vi*: **to** ～ **through** (*book*) hojear.
skimp [skɪmp] *vt* (*work*) chapucear; (*cloth etc*) escatimar; ～ **y** *a* (*meagre*) escaso; (*skirt*) muy corto.
skin [skɪn] *n* (*gen*) piel *f*; (*complexion*) cutis *m* // *vt* (*fruit etc*) pelar; (*animal*) despellejar; ～ **deep** *a* superficial; ～ **diving** *n* natación *f* submarina; ～ **ny** *a* flaco, magro; ～ **tight** *a* (*dress etc*) muy ajustado.
skip [skɪp] *n* brinco, salto; (*container*) cuba // *vi* brincar; (*with rope*) saltar a la comba // *vt* (*pass over*) omitir, saltar.
ski pants *npl* pantalones *mpl* de esquí.
skipper ['skɪpə*] *n* (*NAUT, SPORT*) capitán *m.*
skipping rope ['skɪpɪŋ-] *n* cuerda (de saltar).
skirmish ['skə:mɪʃ] *n* escaramuza.
skirt [skə:t] *n* falda // *vt* (*surround*) ceñir, rodear; (*go round*) ladear; ～ **ing board** *n* rodapié *m.*
skit [skɪt] *n* sátira, parodia.
skittle ['skɪtl] *n* bolo; ～ **s** *n* (*game*) boliche *m.*
skive [skaɪv] *vi* (*Brit: col*) gandulear.

skull [skʌl] *n* calavera; (*ANAT*) cráneo.
skunk [skʌŋk] *n* mofeta; (*fig: person*) canalla *m/f.*
sky [skaɪ] *n* cielo; ～ **blue** *a* azul celeste; ～ **light** *n* tragaluz *m*, claraboya; ～ **scraper** *n* rascacielos *m inv.*
slab [slæb] *n* (*stone*) bloque *m*; (*flat*) losa; (*of cake*) porción *f* gruesa.
slack [slæk] *a* (*loose*) flojo; (*slow*) de poca actividad; (*careless*) descuidado; ～ **s** *npl* pantalones *mpl*; ～ **en** (*also*: ～ **en off**) *vi* aflojarse // *vt* aflojar; (*speed*) disminuir.
slag [slæg] *n* escoria, escombros *mpl*; ～ **heap** *n* escorial *m*, escombrera.
slalom ['slɑːləm] *n* slalom *m.*
slam [slæm] *vt* (*door*) cerrar de golpe; (*throw*) arrojar (violentamente); (*criticize*) hablar mal de // *vi* cerrarse de golpe.
slander ['slɑːndə*] *n* calumnia, difamación *f* // *vt* calumniar, difamar; ～ **ous** *a* calumnioso, difamatorio.
slang [slæŋ] *n* argot *m*; (*jargon*) jerga; (*private language*) caló.
slant [slɑːnt] *n* sesgo, inclinación *f*; (*fig*) punto de vista; ～ **ed**, ～ **ing** *a* inclinado.
slap [slæp] *n* palmada; (*in face*) bofetada; (*fig*) palmetazo // *vt* dar una palmada/bofetada a // *ad* (*directly*) exactamente, directamente; ～ **dash** *a* descuidado; ～ **stick** *n* (*comedy*) payasadas *fpl.*
slash [slæʃ] *vt* acuchillar; (*fig: prices*) quemar.
slate [sleɪt] *n* pizarra // *vt* (*fig: criticize*) criticar duramente.
slaughter ['slɔːtə*] *n* (*of animals*) matanza; (*of people*) carnicería // *vt* matar; ～ **house** *n* matadero.
Slav [slɑːv] *a* eslavo.
slave [sleɪv] *n* esclavo // *vi* (*also*: ～ **away**) sudar tinta; ～ **ry** *n* esclavitud *f*; **slavish** *a* servil.
Slavonic [slə'vɒnɪk] *a* eslavo.
slay [sleɪ] *vt* matar.
sleazy ['sliːzɪ] *a* (*fig: place*) de mala fama.
sledge [slɛdʒ] *n* trineo; ～ **hammer** *n* mazo.
sleek [sliːk] *a* (*gen*) lustroso; (*neat*) pulcro.
sleep [sliːp] *n* sueño // *vi, pt, pp* **slept** dormir; **to go to** ～ dormirse; **to** ～ **in** *vi* (*oversleep*) dormir tarde; ～ **er** *n* (*person*) durmiente *m/f*; (*RAIL: on track*) traviesa; (: *train*) coche-cama *m*; ～ **ily** *ad* soñolientamente; ～ **ing bag** *n* saco de dormir; ～ **ing car** *n* coche-cama *m*; ～ **ing pill** *n* somnífero; ～ **lessness** *n* insomnio; ～ **walker** *n* sonámbulo/a; ～ **y** *a* soñoliento.
sleet [sliːt] *n* nevisca.
sleeve [sliːv] *n* manga; (*TECH*) manguito; ～ **less** *a* (*garment*) sin mangas.
sleigh [sleɪ] *n* trineo.
sleight [slaɪt] *n*: ～ **of hand** escamoteo.
slender ['slɛndə*] *a* delgado; (*means*) escaso.
slept [slɛpt] *pt, pp of* **sleep.**
slice [slaɪs] *n* (*of meat*) tajada; (*of bread*)

rebanada; (*of lemon*) rodaja; (*utensil*) pala // *vt* cortar, tajar; rebanar.

slick [slık] *a* (*skilful*) hábil, diestro; (*quick*) rápido; (*astute*) astuto // *n* (*also*: **oil** ~) masa flotante.

slid [slıd] *pt, pp of* **slide.**

slide [slaıd] *n* (*in playground*) tobogán *m*; (PHOT) diapositiva; (*also*: **hair** ~) pasador *m* // (*vb*: *pt, pp* **slid**) *vt* correr, deslizar // *vi* (*slip*) resbalarse; (*glide*) deslizarse; **sliding** *a* (*door*) corredizo.

slight [slaıt] *a* (*slim*) delgado; (*frail*) delicado; (*pain etc*) leve; (*trifling*) sin importancia; (*small*) pequeño // *n* desaire *m* // *vt* (*offend*) ofender, desairar; **not in the** ~**est** (ni) en lo más mínimo, en absoluto; ~**ly** *ad* ligeramente, un poco.

slim [slım] *a* delgado, esbelto // *vi* adelgazar.

slime [slaım] *n* limo, cieno; **slimy** *a* limoso.

slimming ['slımıŋ] *n* adelgazamiento; **a** ~ **diet** un régimen.

sling [slıŋ] *n* (MED) cabestrillo; (*weapon*) honda // *vt, pt, pp* **slung** tirar, arrojar.

slip [slıp] *n* (*slide*) resbalón *m*; (*fall*) tropezón *m*; (*mistake*) descuido; (*underskirt*) combinación *f*; (*of paper*) trozo // *vt* (*slide*) deslizar // *vi* (*slide*) deslizarse; (*stumble*) resbalar(se); (*decline*) decaer; **to give sb the** ~ eludir *o* escaparse de uno; **to** ~ **away** *vi* escabullirse; **to** ~ **in** *vt* meter // *vi* meterse; **to** ~ **out** *vi* (*go out*) salir (un momento).

slipper ['slıpə*] *n* zapatilla.

slippery ['slıpərı] *a* resbaladizo.

slip: ~ **road** *n* carretera de acceso; ~**shod** *a* descuidado; ~-**up** *n* (*error*) equivocación *f*; (*by neglect*) descuido; ~**way** *n* grada, gradas *fpl*.

slit [slıt] *n* raja; (*cut*) corte *m* // *vt, pt, pp* **slit** rajar, cortar.

slither ['slıðə*] *vi* deslizarse.

slob [slɔb] *n* (*col*) patán *m*.

slog [slɔg] *vi* sudar tinta; **it was a** ~ costó trabajo (hacerlo).

slogan ['sləugən] *n* slogan *m*, lema *m*.

slop [slɔp] *vi* (*also*: ~ **over**) derramarse, desbordarse // *vt* derramar, verter.

slope [sləup] *n* (*up*) cuesta, pendiente *m*; (*down*) declive *m*; (*side of mountain*) falda, vertiente *m* // *vi*: **to** ~ **down** estar en declive; **to** ~ **up** inclinarse; **sloping** *a* en pendiente; en declive.

sloppy ['slɔpı] *a* (*work*) descuidado; (*appearance*) desaliñado.

slot [slɔt] *n* ranura // *vt*: **to** ~ **into** encajar en; ~ **machine** *n* máquina tragaperras.

slouch [slautʃ] *vi*: **to** ~ **about** (*laze*) gandulear.

slovenly ['slʌvənlı] *a* (*dirty*) desaliñado, desaseado; (*careless*) descuidado.

slow [sləu] *a* lento; (*watch*): **to be** ~ atrasarse // *ad* lentamente, despacio // *vt, vi* (*also*: ~ **down**, ~ **up**) retardar; '~' (*road sign*) 'disminuir velocidad'; ~**ly** *ad*

lentamente, despacio; **in** ~ **motion** a cámara lenta; ~**ness** *n* lentitud *f*.

sludge [slʌdʒ] *n* lodo, fango.

slug [slʌg] *n* babosa; (*bullet*) posta; ~**gish** *a* (*slow*) lento; (*lazy*) perezoso.

sluice [slu:s] *n* (*gate*) esclusa; (*channel*) canal *m*.

slum [slʌm] *n* (*area*) tugurios *mpl*; (*house*) casucha.

slumber ['slʌmbə*] *n* sueño.

slump [slʌmp] *n* (*economic*) depresión *f* // *vi* hundirse.

slung [slʌŋ] *pt, pp of* **sling.**

slur [slə:*] *n* calumnia // *vt* calumniar, difamar; (*word*) pronunciar indistintamente.

slush [slʌʃ] *n* nieve *f* a medio derretir; ~**y** *a* (*snow*) a medio derretir; (*street*) fangoso; (*fig*) sentimental, sensiblero.

slut [slʌt] *n* marrana.

sly [slaı] *a* (*clever*) astuto; (*nasty*) malicioso.

smack [smæk] *n* (*slap*) manotada; (*blow*) golpe *m* // *vt* dar una manotada a, golpear con la mano // *vi*: **to** ~ **of** saber a, oler a.

small [smɔ:l] *a* pequeño; ~**holder** *n* granjero, parcelero; ~**ish** *a* más bien pequeño; ~**pox** *n* viruela; ~ **talk** *n* cháchara.

smart [smɑ:t] *a* elegante; (*clever*) listo, inteligente; (*quick*) rápido, vivo // *vi* escocer, picar; **to** ~**en up** *vi* arreglarse // *vt* arreglar.

smash [smæʃ] *n* (*also*: ~-**up**) choque *m* // *vt* (*break*) hacer pedazos; (*car etc*) estrellar; (SPORT: *record*) romper // *vi* (*collide*) chocar; (*against wall etc*) estrellarse; ~**ing** *a* (*col*) cojonudo.

smattering ['smætərıŋ] *n*: **a** ~ **of** ligeros conocimientos *mpl* de.

smear [smıə*] *n* mancha; (MED) citología // *vt* untar; (*fig*) calumniar, difamar.

smell [smɛl] *n* olor *m*; (*sense*) olfato // (*vb*: *pt, pp* **smelt** *or* **smelled**) *vt, vi* oler; **it** ~**s good/of garlic** huele bien/a ajo; ~**y** *a* que huele mal.

smile [smaıl] *n* sonrisa // *vi* sonreír; **smiling** *a* sonriente.

smirk [smə:k] *n* sonrisa falsa *o* afectada.

smith [smıθ] *n* herrero; ~**y** ['smıðı] *n* herrería.

smock [smɔk] *n* blusa; (*children's*) delantal *m*.

smoke [sməuk] *n* humo // *vi* fumar; (*chimney*) echar humo // *vt* (*cigarettes*) fumar; ~**d** *a* (*bacon, glass*) ahumado; **smoker** *n* (*person*) fumador/a *m/f*; (RAIL) coche *m* fumador; ~ **screen** *n* cortina de humo; **smoking** *n*: 'no **smoking**' (*sign*) 'prohibido fumar'; **smoky** *a* (*gen*) humeante; (*room*) lleno de humo.

smooth [smu:ð] *a* (*gen*) liso; (*sea*) tranquilo; (*flat*) llano; (*flavour, movement*) suave; (*person*) culto, refinado; (: *pej*) meloso // *vt* alisar; (*also*: ~ **out**) (*creases, difficulties*) allanar.

smother ['smʌðə*] vt sofocar; (repress) ahogar.
smoulder ['sməuldə*] vi arder sin llama.
smudge [smʌdʒ] n mancha // vt manchar.
smug [smʌg] a presumido.
smuggle ['smʌgl] vt pasar de contrabando; **smuggler** n contrabandista m/f; **smuggling** n contrabando.
smutty ['smʌtɪ] a (fig) verde, obsceno.
snack [snæk] n bocado; ~ **bar** n cafetería.
snag [snæg] n dificultad f, pero.
snail [sneɪl] n caracol m.
snake [sneɪk] n (gen) serpiente f; (harmless) culebra; (poisonous) víbora.
snap [snæp] n (sound) castañetazo; (of whip) chasquido; (click) golpe m seco; (photograph) foto f // a repentino // vt (fingers etc) castañetear; (whip) chasquear; (break) quebrar; (photograph) tomar una foto de // vi (break) quebrarse; (fig: person) contestar bruscamente; (sound) hacer un ruido seco; to ~ **shut** cerrarse de golpe; **to** ~ **at** vt fus (subj: dog) intentar morder; **to** ~ **off** vi (break) romperse (y separarse); **to** ~ **up** vt aprovecharse de, agarrar; ~ **shot** foto f (instantánea).
snare [snɛə*] n trampa // vt cazar con trampa; (fig) engañar.
snarl [snɑːl] n gruñido // vi gruñir.
snatch [snætʃ] n (fig) robo; (small amount): ~**es of** trocitos mpl de // vt (~ away) arrebatar; (grasp) coger, agarrar.
sneak [sniːk] vi: **to** ~ **in/out** entrar/salir a hurtadillas // n (fam) soplón/ona m/f; ~**y** a furtivo.
sneer [snɪə*] n sonrisa de desprecio // vi sonreír con desprecio; (mock) mofarse.
sneeze [sniːz] n estornudo // vi estornudar.
sniff [snɪf] n (of dog) husmeo; (of person) sorbo (por las narices) // vi sorber (por la nariz) // vt husmear, oler.
snigger ['snɪgə*] n risa disimulada // vi reírse con disimulo.
snip [snɪp] n tijeretazo; (piece) recorte m; (bargain) ganga // vt tijeretear.
sniper ['snaɪpə*] n francotirador/a m/f.
snippet ['snɪpɪt] n retazo.
snivelling ['snɪvlɪŋ] a (whimpering) llorón(ona).
snob [snɔb] n snob m/f; ~**bery** n snobismo; ~**bish** a snob.
snooker ['snuːkə*] n especie de billar.
snoop [snuːp] vi: **to** ~ **about** fisgonear; ~**er** n fisgón/ona m/f.
snooty ['snuːtɪ] a presumido.
snooze [snuːz] n siesta // vi echar una siesta.
snore [snɔː*] vi roncar // n ronquido.
snorkel ['snɔːkl] n tubo snorkel.
snort [snɔːt] n bufido // vi bufar.
snout [snaut] n hocico, morro.
snow [snəu] n nieve f // vi nevar; ~**ball** n bola de nieve // vi acumularse; ~**bound** a bloqueado por la nieve; ~**drift** n ventisquero; ~**drop** n campanilla; ~**fall**

n nevada; ~**flake** n copo de nieve; ~**man** n figura de nieve; ~**plough**, ~**plow** (US) n quitanieves m inv; ~**storm** n nevada, nevasca; S~ **White** n Blanca Nieves.
snub [snʌb] vt rechazar con desdén // n desaire m, repulsa.
snuff [snʌf] n rapé m.
snug [snʌg] a (sheltered) abrigado; (fitted) ajustado.
snuggle ['snʌgl] vi: **to** ~ **up to sb** arrimarse a uno.
so [səu] ad (degree) tan; (manner: thus) así, de este modo // conj así que, por tanto; ~ **that** (purpose) para que, a fin de que; (result) de modo que; ~ **do I** yo también; **if** ~ de ser así, si es así; **I hope** ~ espero que sí; **10 or** ~ 10 más o menos; ~ **far** hasta aquí; ~ **long!** ¡hasta luego!; ~ **many** tantos(as); ~ **much** ad, det tanto; ~ **and** ~ n Fulano.
soak [səuk] vt (drench) empapar; (put in water) remojar // vi remojarse, estar a remojo; **to** ~ **in** vi penetrar; **to** ~ **up** vt absorber.
soap [səup] n jabón m; ~**flakes** npl escamas fpl de jabón; ~ **powder** n jabón en polvo; ~**y** a jabonoso.
soar [sɔː*] vi (on wings) remontarse; (building etc) elevarse.
sob [sɔb] n sollozo // vi sollozar.
sober ['səubə*] a (serious) serio; (sensible) sensato; (moderate) moderado; (not drunk) sobrio; (colour, style) discreto; **to** ~ **up** vi pasársele a uno la borrachera.
Soc. abbr of **society**.
so-called ['səu'kɔːld] a llamado.
soccer ['sɔkə*] n fútbol m.
sociable ['səuʃəbl] a sociable.
social ['səuʃl] a (gen) social; (sociable) sociable // n velada, fiesta; ~ **climber** n arribista m/f; ~ **club** n club m; ~**ism** n socialismo; ~**ist** a, n socialista m/f; ~**ly** ad socialmente; ~ **science** n ciencias fpl sociales; ~ **security** n seguridad f social; ~ **work** n asistencia social; ~ **worker** n asistente/a m/f social.
society [sə'saɪətɪ] n sociedad f; (club) asociación f; (also: **high** ~) buena sociedad.
sociologist [səusɪ'ɔlədʒɪst] n sociólogo.
sociology [-dʒɪ] n sociología.
sock [sɔk] n calcetín m.
socket ['sɔkɪt] n (ELEC) enchufe m.
sod [sɔd] n (of earth) césped m; (col!) cabrón/ona m/f.
soda ['səudə] n (CHEM) sosa; (also: ~ **water**) sifón m.
sodden ['sɔdn] a empapado.
sodium ['səudɪəm] n sodio.
sofa ['səufə] n sofá m.
soft [sɔft] a (gen) blando; (gentle, not loud) suave; (kind) tierno, compasivo; (weak) débil; (stupid) tonto; ~ **drink** n bebida no alcohólica; ~**en** ['sɔfn] vt ablandar; suavizar; debilitar // vi ablandarse; suavizarse; debilitarse; ~**-hearted** a

compasivo, bondadoso; ~**ly** *ad* suavemente; (*gently*) delicadamente, con delicadeza; ~**ness** *n* blandura; suavidad *f*; (*sweetness*) dulzura; (*tenderness*) ternura.

soggy ['sɔgɪ] *a* empapado.

soil [sɔɪl] *n* (*earth*) tierra, suelo // *vt* ensuciar; ~**ed** *a* sucio.

solace ['sɔlɪs] *n* consuelo.

solar ['sɔulə*] *a* solar.

sold [sɔuld] *pt, pp of* **sell**; ~ **out** (*COMM*) agotado.

solder ['sɔuldə*] *vt* soldar // *n* soldadura.

soldier ['sɔuldʒə*] *n* (*gen*) soldado; (*army man*) militar *m*.

sole [sɔul] *n* (*of foot*) planta; (*of shoe*) suela; (*fish: pl inv*) lenguado // *a* único; ~**ly** *ad* únicamente, sólo, solamente.

solemn ['sɔləm] *a* solemne.

solicitor [sə'lɪsɪtə*] *n* (*for wills etc*) notario; (*in court*) abogado.

solid ['sɔlɪd] *a* (*not hollow*) sólido; (*gold etc*) macizo; (*person*) serio // *n* sólido.

solidarity [sɔlɪ'dærɪtɪ] *n* solidaridad *f*.

solidify [sə'lɪdɪfaɪ] *vi* solidificarse.

solitaire [sɔlɪ'tɛə*] *n* (*game, gem*) solitario.

solitary ['sɔlɪtərɪ] *a* solitario, solo; (*isolated*) apartado, aislado; (*only*) único; ~ **confinement** *n* incomunicación *f*.

solitude ['sɔlɪtjuːd] *n* soledad *f*.

solo ['sɔuləu] *n* solo; ~**ist** *n* solista *m/f*.

soluble ['sɔljubl] *a* soluble.

solution [sə'luːʃən] *n* solución *f*.

solve [sɔlv] *vt* resolver, solucionar.

solvent ['sɔlvənt] *a* (*COMM*) solvente // *n* (*CHEM*) solvente *m*.

sombre, somber (*US*) ['sɔmbə*] *a* sombrío.

some [sʌm] *det* (*a few*) algunos(as); (*certain*) algún/una; (*a certain number or amount*) *see phrases below*; (*unspecified*) algo de // *pron* algunos/as; (*a bit*) algo // *ad*: ~ **10 people** unas 10 personas; ~ **children came** vinieron algunos niños; **have** ~ **tea** tome té; **there's** ~ **milk in the fridge** hay leche en la refrigeradora; ~ **was left** quedaba algo; **I've got** ~ (*books etc*) tengo algunos; (*milk, money etc*) tengo algo; ~**body** *pron* alguien; ~**day** *ad* algún día; ~**how** *ad* de alguna manera; (*for some reason*) por una u otra razón; ~**one** *pron* = ~**body**.

somersault ['sʌməsɔːlt] *n* (*deliberate*) salto mortal; (*accidental*) vuelco // *vi* dar un salto mortal; dar vuelcos.

something ['sʌmθɪŋ] *pron* algo.

sometime ['sʌmtaɪm] *ad* (*in future*) algún día, en algún momento; (*in past*): ~ **last month** durante el mes pasado.

sometimes ['sʌmtaɪmz] *ad* a veces.

somewhat ['sʌmwɔt] *ad* algo.

somewhere ['sʌmwɛə*] *ad* (*be*) en alguna parte; (*go*) a alguna parte; ~ **else** (*be*) en otra parte; (*go*) a otra parte.

son [sʌn] *n* hijo.

song [sɔŋ] *n* canción *f*; ~**writer** *n*

compositor/a *m/f* de canciones.

sonic ['sɔnɪk] *a* (*boom*) sónico.

son-in-law ['sʌnɪnlɔ:] *n* yerno.

sonnet ['sɔnɪt] *n* soneto.

soon [suːn] *ad* pronto, dentro de poco; (*early*) temprano; ~ **afterwards** poco después; *see also* **as**; ~**er** *ad* (*time*) antes, más temprano; (*preference*): **I would** ~**er do that** preferiría hacer eso; ~**er or later** tarde o temprano.

soot [sut] *n* hollín *m*.

soothe [suːð] *vt* tranquilizar; (*pain*) aliviar.

sophisticated [sə'fɪstɪkeɪtɪd] *a* sofisticado.

soporific [sɔpə'rɪfɪk] *a* soporífero.

sopping ['sɔpɪŋ] *a*: ~ **wet** totalmente empapado.

soppy ['sɔpɪ] *a* (*pej*) bobo, tonto.

soprano [sə'prɑːnəu] *n* soprano *f*.

sorcerer ['sɔːsərə*] *n* hechicero.

sordid ['sɔːdɪd] *a* (*dirty*) sucio, asqueroso; (*wretched*) miserable.

sore [sɔ:*] *a* (*painful*) doloroso, que duele; (*offended*) resentido // *n* llaga; ~**ly** *ad*: **I am** ~**ly tempted** casi estoy por.

sorrow ['sɔrəu] *n* pena, dolor *m*; ~**ful** *a* afligido, triste.

sorry ['sɔrɪ] *a* (*regretful*) arrepentido; (*condition, excuse*) lastimoso; ~! ¡lo siento!, ¡perdón!, ¡perdone!; **to feel** ~ **for sb** sentir lástima por uno; **I feel** ~ **for him** me da lástima.

sort [sɔːt] *n* clase *f*, género, tipo // *vt* (*also*: ~ **out**: *papers*) clasificar; (: *problems*) arreglar, solucionar; ~**ing office** *n* oficina de distribución de correos.

SOS *n abbr of* **save our souls**.

so-so ['səusəu] *ad* regular, así-así.

soufflé ['suːfleɪ] *n* suflé *m*.

sought [sɔːt] *pt, pp of* **seek**.

soul [sɔul] *n* alma *m*; ~**-destroying** *a* embrutecedor(a); ~**ful** *a* lleno de sentimiento; ~**less** *a* desalmado.

sound [saund] *a* (*healthy*) sano; (*safe, not damaged*) firme, sólido; (*secure*) seguro; (*reliable, not superficial*) formal, digno de confianza; (*sensible*) sensato, razonable // *ad*: ~ **asleep** profundamente dormido // *n* (*noise*) sonido, ruido; (*GEO*) estrecho // *vt* (*alarm*) sonar; (*also*: ~ **out**: *opinions*) consultar, sondear // *vi* sonar, resonar; (*fig: seem*) parecer; **to** ~ **like** sonar a; ~ **barrier** *n* barrera del sonido; ~ **effects** *npl* efectos *mpl* sonoros; ~**ing** *n* (*NAUT etc*) sondeo; ~**ly** *ad* (*sleep*) profundamente; (*beat*) completamente; ~**proof** *a* a prueba de sonidos; ~**track** *n* (*of film*) banda sonora.

soup [suːp] *n* (*thick*) sopa; (*thin*) caldo; **in the** ~ (*fig*) en apuros; ~**spoon** *n* cuchara sopera.

sour ['sauə*] *a* agrio; (*milk*) cortado; (*fig*) desabrido, acre.

source [sɔːs] *n* fuente *f*.

south [sauθ] *n* sur *m* // *a* del sur // *ad* al sur, hacia el sur; **S~ Africa** *n* África del Sur; **S~ African**, *a* sudafricano/a; **S~ America** *n* América (del Sur); **S~**

American a, n sudamericano/a; ~-**east** n sudeste m; ~**erly** ['sʌðǝlı] a sur; (from the ~) del sur; ~**ern** ['sʌðǝn] a del sur, meridional; **S**~ **Pole** n Polo Sur; ~**ward(s)** ad hacia el sur; ~-**west** n suroeste m.
souvenir [suːvǝ'nıǝ*] n recuerdo.
sovereign ['sɔvrın] a, n soberano; ~**ty** n soberanía.
soviet ['sɔuvıǝt] a soviético; **the S**~ **Union** la Unión Soviética.
sow [sau] n cerda, puerca // vt [sǝu], pt **sowed**, pp **sown** [sǝun] (gen) sembrar; (spread) esparcir.
soy [sɔı] n: ~ **sauce** salsa de soja.
soya bean ['sɔıbiːn] n semilla de soja.
spa [spaː] n (spring) baños mpl térmicos; (town) balneario.
space [speıs] n (gen) espacio; (room) sitio // vt (also: ~ **out**) espaciar; ~**craft** n nave f espacial; ~**man/woman** n astronauta m/f, cosmonauta m/f; **spacing** n espaciamiento.
spacious ['speıʃǝs] a amplio.
spade [speıd] n (tool) pala, laya; ~**s** npl (CARDS: British) picos mpl; (: Spanish) espadas fpl.
spaghetti [spǝ'gɛtı] n espaguetis mpl, fideos mpl.
Spain [speın] n España.
span [spæn] n (of bird, plane) envergadura; (of hand) palmo; (of arch) luz f; (in time) lapso // vt extenderse sobre, cruzar; (fig) abarcar.
Spaniard ['spænjǝd] n español/a m/f.
spaniel ['spænjǝl] n perro de aguas.
Spanish ['spænıʃ] a español(a) // n (LING) español m, castellano.
spank [spæŋk] vt zurrar.
spanner ['spænǝ*] n llave f (inglesa).
spar [spaː*] n palo, verga // vi (BOXING) entrenarse.
spare [spɛǝ*] a (free) desocupado; (surplus) sobrante, de más; (available) disponible // n (part) pieza de repuesto // vt (do without) pasarse sin; (afford to give) tener de sobra; (refrain from hurting) perdonar; (be grudging with) escatimar; ~ **part** n pieza de repuesto; ~ **time** n ratos mpl de ocio, tiempo libre.
sparing ['spɛǝrıŋ] a: **to be** ~ **with** ser parco en; ~**ly** ad escasamente.
spark [spaːk] n chispa; (fig) chispazo; ~(**ing**) **plug** n bujía.
sparkle ['spaːkl] n centelleo, destello // vi centellear; (shine) relucir, brillar; **sparkling** a centelleante; (wine) espumoso.
sparrow ['spærǝu] n gorrión m.
sparse [spaːs] a esparcido, escaso.
spasm ['spæzǝm] n (MED) espasmo; (fig) arranque m, acceso; ~**odic** [-'mɔdık] a espasmódico.
spastic ['spæstık] n espástico/a.
spat [spæt] pt, pp of **spit**.
spate [speıt] n (fig): ~ **of** torrente m de; **in** ~ (river) crecido.

spatter ['spætǝ*] vt salpicar, rociar.
spatula ['spætjulǝ] n espátula.
spawn [spɔːn] vi desovar, frezar // n huevas fpl.
speak [spiːk], pt **spoke**, pp **spoken** vt (language) hablar; (truth) decir // vi hablar; (make a speech) intervenir; **to** ~ **to sb/of** or **about sth** hablar con uno/de o sobre algo; ~ **up!** ¡habla fuerte!; ~**er** n (in public) orador/a m/f; (also: **loud**~**er**) altavoz m, parlante m; (POL): **the S**~**er** el Presidente del Congreso.
spear [spıǝ*] n lanza; (for fishing) arpón m // vt alancear; arponear; ~**head** n punta de lanza.
special ['spɛʃl] a especial; (edition etc) extraordinario; (delivery) urgente; **take** ~ **care** ponga un cuidado especial; ~**ist** n especialista m/f; ~**ity** [spɛʃı'ælıtı] n especialidad f; ~**ize** vi: **to** ~**ize (in)** especializarse en; ~**ly** ad sobre todo, en particular.
species ['spiːʃiːz] n especie f.
specific [spǝ'sıfık] a específico; ~**ally** ad específicamente.
specification [spɛsıfı'keıʃǝn] n especificación f; ~**s** npl presupuesto; **specify** ['spɛsıfaı] vt, vi especificar, precisar.
specimen ['spɛsımǝn] n ejemplar m, espécimen m.
speck [spɛk] n grano, mota.
speckled ['spɛkld] a moteado.
specs [spɛks] npl (col) gafas fpl.
spectacle ['spɛktǝkl] n espectáculo; ~**s** npl gafas fpl, anteojos mpl; **spectacular** [-'tækjulǝ*] a espectacular; (success) impresionante.
spectator [spɛk'teıtǝ*] n espectador/a m/f.
spectre, specter (US) ['spɛktǝ*] n espectro, fantasma m.
spectrum ['spɛktrǝm], pl **-tra** [-trǝ] n espectro.
speculate ['spɛkjuleıt] vi especular; (try to guess): **to** ~ **about** especular sobre; **speculation** [-'leıʃǝn] n especulación f.
speech [spiːtʃ] n (faculty) habla, palabra; (formal talk) discurso; (talk) palabras fpl; (language) idioma m, lenguaje m; ~**less** a mudo, estupefacto.
speed [spiːd] n velocidad f, rapidez f; (haste) prisa; (promptness) prontitud f; **at full** or **top** ~ a máxima velocidad; **to** ~ **up** vi acelerarse // vt acelerar; ~**boat** n lancha motora; ~**ily** ad rápido, rápidamente; ~**ing** n (AUT) exceso de velocidad; ~ **limit** n límite m de velocidad, velocidad f máxima; ~**ometer** [spı'dɔmıtǝ*] n velocímetro; ~**way** n (SPORT) carreras fpl de moto; ~**y** a (fast) veloz, rápido; (prompt) pronto.
spell [spɛl] n (also: **magic** ~) encanto, hechizo; (period of time) rato, período; (turn) turno // vt, pt, pp **spelt** or **spelled** (also: ~ **out**) deletrear; (fig) anunciar, presagiar; **to cast a** ~ **on sb** hechizar a

uno; **he can't** ~ no sabe escribir bien, sabe poco de ortografía; ~**bound** *a* embelesado, hechizado; ~**ing** *n* ortografía.

spend [spɛnd], *pt, pp* **spent** [spɛnt] *vt* (*money*) gastar; (*time*) pasar; (*life*) dedicar; ~**thrift** *n* derrochador/a *m/f*, pródigo/a.

sperm [spɔːm] *n* esperma; ~ **whale** *n* cachalote *m*.

spew [spjuː] *vt* vomitar, arrojar.

sphere [sfɪə*] *n* esfera; **spherical** ['sfɛrɪkl] *a* esférico.

sphinx [sfɪŋks] *n* esfinge *f*.

spice [spaɪs] *n* especia // *vt* especiar; **spicy** *a* especiado; (*fig*) picante.

spider ['spaɪdə*] *n* araña.

spike [spaɪk] *n* (*point*) punta; (*ZOOL*) pincho, púa; (*BOT*) espiga.

spill [spɪl], *pt, pp* **spilt** *or* **spilled** *vt* derramar, verter // *vi* derramarse; **to** ~ **over** desbordarse.

spin [spɪn] *n* (*revolution of wheel*) vuelta, revolución *f*; (*AVIAT*) barrena; (*trip in car*) paseo (en coche) // (*vb*: *pt, pp* **spun**) *vt* (*wool etc*) hilar; (*wheel*) girar // *vi* girar, dar vueltas; **to** ~ **out** *vt* alargar, prolongar.

spinach ['spɪnɪtʃ] *n* espinaca; (*as food*) espinacas *fpl*.

spinal ['spaɪnl] *a* espinal; ~ **cord** *n* columna vertebral.

spindly ['spɪndlɪ] *a* zanquivano.

spin-drier [spɪn'draɪə*] *n* secador *m* centrífugo.

spine [spaɪn] *n* espinazo, columna vertebral; (*thorn*) espina; ~**less** *a* (*fig*) débil, flojo.

spinning ['spɪnɪŋ] *n* (*of thread*) hilado; (*art*) hilandería; ~ **top** *n* peonza; ~ **wheel** *n* rueca, torno de hilar.

spinster ['spɪnstə*] *n* soltera; (*pej*) solterona.

spiral ['spaɪərl] *n* espiral *m* // *a* en espiral; ~ **staircase** *n* escalera de caracol.

spire ['spaɪə*] *n* aguja, chapitel *m*.

spirit ['spɪrɪt] *n* (*gen*) espíritu *m*; (*soul*) alma *m*; (*ghost*) fantasma *m*; (*humour*) humor *m*; (*courage*) valor *m*, ánimo; ~**s** *npl* (*drink*) alcohol *m*, bebidas *fpl* alcohólicas; **in good** ~**s** alegre, de buen ánimo; ~**ed** *a* enérgico, vigoroso; ~ **level** *n* nivel *m* de aire.

spiritual ['spɪrɪtjuəl] *a* espiritual // *n* (*also*: **Negro** ~) canción *f* religiosa, espiritual *m*; ~**ism** *n* espiritualismo.

spit [spɪt] *n* (*for roasting*) asador *m*, espetón *m* // *vi*, *pt, pp* **spat** escupir; (*sound*) chisporrotear.

spite [spaɪt] *n* rencor *m*, ojeriza // *vt* causar pena a, mortificar; **in** ~ **of** *a* pesar de, pese a; ~**ful** *a* rencoroso, malévolo.

spittle ['spɪtl] *n* saliva, baba.

splash [splæʃ] *n* (*sound*) chapoteo; (*of colour*) mancha // *vt* salpicar de // *vi* (*also*: ~ **about**) chapotear.

spleen [spliːn] *n* (*ANAT*) bazo.

splendid ['splendɪd] *a* espléndido; **splendour, splendor** (*US*) [-də*] *n* esplendor *m*; (*of achievement*) brillo, gloria.

splint [splɪnt] *n* tablilla.

splinter ['splɪntə*] *n* (*of wood*) astilla; (*in finger*) espigón *m* // *vi* astillarse, hacer astillas.

split [splɪt] *n* hendedura, raja; (*fig*) división *f*; (*POL*) escisión *f* // (*vb*: *pt, pp* **split**) *vt* partir, rajar; (*party*) dividir; (*work, profits*) repartir // *vi* (*divide*) dividirse, escindirse; **to** ~ **up** *vi* (*couple*) separarse; (*meeting*) acabarse.

splutter ['splʌtə*] *vi* chisporrotear; (*person*) balbucear.

spoil [spɔɪl], *pt, pp* **spoilt** *or* **spoiled** *vt* (*damage*) dañar; (*mar*) estropear, echar a perder; (*child*) mimar, consentir; ~**s** *npl* despojo *sg*, botín *m*; ~**sport** *n* aguafiestas *m inv*.

spoke [spəuk] *pt of* speak // *n* rayo, radio.

spoken ['spəukn] *pp of* **speak**.

spokesman ['spəuksmən] *n* vocero, portavoz *m*.

sponge [spʌndʒ] *n* esponja; (*cake*) pastel *m* // *vt* (*wash*) lavar con esponja // *vi*: **to** ~ **on sb** vivir a costa de uno; ~ **bag** *n* esponjera; ~ **cake** *n* bizcocho, pastel *m*; **spongy** *a* esponjoso.

sponsor ['spɔnsə*] *n* (*RADIO, TV*) patrocinador/a *m/f*; (*for membership*) padrino; (*COMM*) fiador/a *m/f* // *vt* patrocinar; apadrinar; (*idea etc*) presentar, promover; ~**ship** *n* patrocinio.

spontaneous [spɔn'teɪnɪəs] *a* espontáneo.

spool [spuːl] *n* carrete *m*; (*of sewing machine*) canilla.

spoon [spuːn] *n* cuchara; ~-**feed** *vt* dar de comer con cuchara; (*fig*) tratar como un niño; ~**ful** *n* cucharada.

sporadic [spə'rædɪk] *a* esporádico.

sport [spɔːt] *n* deporte *m*; (*person*) buen perdedor *m*; ~**ing** *a* deportivo; ~**s car** *n* coche *m* sport; ~**s jacket** *n* chaqueta sport; **sportsman** *n* deportista *m*; **sportsmanship** *n* deportividad *f*; **sportswear** *n* trajes *mpl* de deporte *o* sport; **sportswoman** *n* deportista; ~**y** *a* deportivo.

spot [spɔt] *n* sitio, lugar *m*; (*dot: on pattern*) punto, mancha; (*pimple*) grano; (*freckle*) peca; (*small amount*): **a** ~ **of** un poquito de // *vt* (*notice*) notar, observar; **on the** ~ en el acto, acto seguido; (*in difficulty*) en un aprieto; ~ **check** *n* reconocimiento rápido; ~**less** *a* nítido, perfectamente limpio; ~**light** *n* foco, reflector *m*; ~**ted** *a* (*pattern*) de puntos; ~**ty** *a* (*face*) con granos.

spouse [spauz] *n* cónyuge *m/f*.

spout [spaut] *n* (*of jug*) pico; (*pipe*) caño // *vi* chorrear.

sprain [spreɪn] *n* torcedura // *vt*: **to** ~ **one's ankle** torcerse el tobillo.

sprang [spræŋ] *pt of* **spring**.

sprawl [sprɔːl] *vi* tumbarse.
spray [spreɪ] *n* rociada; (*of sea*) espuma; (*container*) atomizador *m*; (*of paint*) pistola rociadora; (*of flowers*) ramita // *vt* rociar; (*crops*) regar.
spread [sprɛd] *n* extensión *f*; (*distribution*) diseminación *f*, propagación *f*; (*col: food*) comilona // (*vb: pt, pp* **spread**) *vt* extender; diseminar; (*butter*) untar; (*wings, sails*) desplegar; (*scatter*) esparcir // *vi* extenderse; diseminarse; untarse; desplegarse; esparcirse.
spree [spriː] *n*: **to go on a ~** ir de juerga.
sprightly ['spraɪtlɪ] *a* vivo, enérgico.
spring [sprɪŋ] *n* (*leap*) salto, brinco; (*coiled metal*) resorte *m*; (*season*) primavera; (*of water*) fuente *f*, manantial *f* // *vi, pt* **sprang**, *pp* **sprung** (*arise*) brotar, nacer; (*leap*) saltar, brincar; **to ~ up** *vi* nacer de repente, aparecer repentinamente; **~board** *n* trampolín *m*; **~-clean** *n* (*also*: **~-cleaning**) limpieza general; **~time** *n* primavera; **~y** *a* elástico; (*grass*) muelle.
sprinkle ['sprɪŋkl] *vt* (*pour*) rociar; **to ~ water on, ~ with water** rociar *o* salpicar de agua; **~d with** (*fig*) sembrado *o* salpicado de.
sprint [sprɪnt] *n* sprint *m* // *vi* (*gen*) correr a toda velocidad; (*sport*) sprintar; **~er** *n* sprinter *m/f*, corredor/a *m/f*.
sprite [spraɪt] *n* duende *m*.
sprout [spraut] *vi* brotar, retoñar; **(Brussels) ~s** *npl* colecillos *mpl* de Bruselas.
spruce [spruːs] *n* (*bot*) pícea // *a* aseado, pulcro.
sprung [sprʌŋ] *pp of* **spring.**
spry [spraɪ] *a* ágil, activo.
spun [spʌn] *pt, pp of* **spin.**
spur [spɔː*] *n* espuela; (*fig*) estímulo, aguijón *m* // *vt* (*also*: **~ on**) estimular, incitar; **on the ~ of the moment** de improviso.
spurn [spɔːn] *vt* desdeñar, rechazar.
spurt [spɔːt] *n* esfuerzo supremo; (*of energy*) arrebato // *vi* hacer un esfuerzo supremo.
spy [spaɪ] *n* espía *m/f* // *vi*: **to ~ on** espiar a // *vt* (*see*) divisar, lograr ver; **~ing** *n* espionaje *m*.
sq. *abbr of* **square.**
squabble ['skwɔbl] *n* riña, pelea // *vi* reñir, pelear.
squad [skwɔd] *n* (*mil, police*) pelotón *m*, escuadra.
squadron ['skwɔdrn] *n* (*mil*) escuadrón *m*; (*aviat, naut*) escuadra.
squalid ['skwɔlɪd] *a* vil, miserable, escuálido.
squall [skwɔːl] *n* (*storm*) chubasco; (*wind*) ráfaga.
squalor ['skwɔlə*] *n* miseria.
squander ['skwɔndə*] *vt* (*money*) derrochar, despilfarrar; (*chances*) desperdiciar.
square [skwɛə*] *n* cuadro; (*in town*) plaza // *a* cuadrado; (*col: ideas, tastes*) pasota //

vt (*arrange*) arreglar; (*math*) cuadrar; **all ~** igual(es); **a ~ meal** una comida abundante; **2 metres ~** 2 metros en cuadro; **1 ~ metre** un metro cuadrado; **~ly** *ad* en cuadro; (*fully*) de lleno.
squash [skwɔʃ] *n* (*drink*): **lemon/orange ~** zumo de limón/naranja; (*sport*) squash *m*, frontenis *m* // *vt* aplastar; **to ~ together** apiñar.
squat [skwɔt] *a* achaparrado // *vi* agacharse, sentarse en cuclillas; **~ter** *n* persona que ocupa ilegalmente una casa.
squawk [skwɔːk] *vi* graznar.
squeak [skwiːk] *n* chirrido, rechinamiento; (*of shoe*) crujido; (*of mouse*) chillido // *vi* chirriar, rechinar; crujir; chillar.
squeal [skwiːl] *vi* chillar, dar gritos agudos.
squeamish ['skwiːmɪʃ] *a* delicado, remilgado.
squeeze [skwiːz] *n* (*gen*) estrujón *m*; (*of hand*) apretón *m*; (*in bus etc*) apiñamiento // *vt* estrujar, apretar; (*hand, arm*) apretar; **to ~ out** *vt* exprimir; (*fig*) excluir; **to ~ through** abrirse paso con esfuerzos.
squelch [skwɛltʃ] *vi* aplastar, despachurrar.
squid [skwɪd] *n* calamar *m*.
squint [skwɪnt] *vi* bizquear, ser bizco // *n* (*med*) estrabismo; **to ~ at sth** mirar algo de soslayo.
squirm [skwɜːm] *vi* retorcerse, revolverse.
squirrel ['skwɪrəl] *n* ardilla.
squirt [skwɜːt] *vi* salir a chorros.
Sr *abbr of* **senior.**
St *abbr of* **saint; street.**
stab [stæb] *n* (*with knife etc*) puñalada; (*of pain*) pinchazo; (*col: try*): **to have a ~ at (doing) sth** intentar (hacer) algo // *vt* apuñalar.
stability [stə'bɪlɪtɪ] *n* estabilidad *f*;
stabilize ['steɪbəlaɪz] *vt* estabilizar // *vi* estabilizarse; **stable** ['steɪbl] *a* estable // *n* cuadra, caballeriza.
stack [stæk] *n* montón *m*, pila // *vt* amontonar, apilar.
stadium ['steɪdɪəm] *n* estadio.
staff [stɑːf] *n* (*work force*) personal *m*, plantilla; (*stick*) bastón *m* // *vt* proveer de personal.
stag [stæg] *n* ciervo, venado.
stage [steɪdʒ] *n* escena; (*profession*): **the ~** el escenario, el teatro; (*point*) etapa; (*platform*) plataforma // *vt* (*play*) poner en escena, representar; (*demonstration*) montar, organizar; (*fig: perform: recovery etc*) llevar a cabo; **~coach** *n* diligencia; **~ door** *n* entrada de artistas; **~ manager** *n* director/a *m/f* de escena.
stagger ['stægə*] *vi* tambalear // *vt* (*amaze*) asombrar; (*hours, holidays*) escalonar; **~ing** *a* (*amazing*) asombroso, pasmoso.
stagnant ['stægnənt] *a* estancado;
stagnate [-'neɪt] *vi* estancarse.
stag party *n* fiesta de solteros.

staid [steɪd] *a* serio, formal.
stain [steɪn] *n* mancha; (*colouring*) tintura // *vt* manchar; (*wood*) teñir; ~**ed glass window** *n* vidriera de colores; ~**less** *a* (*steel*) inoxidable.
stair [stɛə*] *n* (*step*) peldaño, escalón *m*; ~**s** *npl* escaleras *fpl*; ~**case**, ~**way** *n* escalera.
stake [steɪk] *n* estaca, poste *m*; (*BETTING*) apuesta // *vt* apostar; **to be at** ~ estar en juego.
stalactite ['stæləktaɪt] *n* estalactita.
stalagmite ['stæləgmaɪt] *n* estalagmita.
stale [steɪl] *a* (*bread*) duro; (*food*) no fresco, pasado.
stalemate ['steɪlmeɪt] *n* tablas *fpl* (por ahogado); (*fig*) estancamiento.
stalk [stɔ:k] *n* tallo, caña // *vt* acechar, cazar al acecho; **to** ~ **off** irse con paso airado.
stall [stɔ:l] *n* (*in market*) puesto; (*in stable*) casilla (de establo) // *vt* (*AUT*) parar // *vi* (*AUT*) pararse; (*fig*) buscar evasivas; ~**s** *npl* (*in cinema, theatre*) butacas *fpl*.
stallion ['stælɪən] *n* caballo padre, semental *m*.
stalwart ['stɔ:lwət] *n* (*in build*) fornido; (*in spirit*) valiente.
stamina ['stæmɪnə] *n* resistencia.
stammer ['stæmə*] *n* tartamudeo, balbuceo // *vi* tartamudear, balbucir.
stamp [stæmp] *n* sello, estampilla; (*mark, also fig*) marca, huella; (*on document*) timbre *m* // *vi* patear // *vt* patear, golpear con el pie; (*in dance*) zapatear; (*letter*) poner sellos en; (*with rubber* ~) marcar con estampilla; ~ **album** *n* álbum *m* para sellos; ~ **collecting** *n* filatelia.
stampede [stæm'pi:d] *n* estampida.
stance [stæns] *n* postura.
stand [stænd] *n* (*position*) posición *f*, postura; (*for taxis*) parada; (*hall* ~) perchero; (*music* ~) atril *m*; (*SPORT*) tribuna; (*news* ~) quiosco // (*vb: pt, pp* **stood**) *vi* (*be*) estar, encontrarse; (*be on foot*) estar de pie; (*rise*) levantarse; (*remain*) quedar en pie // *vt* (*place*) poner, colocar; (*tolerate, withstand*) aguantar, soportar; (*cost*) pagar; (*invite*) invitar; **to make a** ~ resistir; (*fig*) aferrarse a un principio; **to** ~ **for parliament** presentarse como candidato al parlamento; **to** ~ **by** *vi* (*be ready*) estar listo // *vt fus* (*opinion*) aferrarse a; **to** ~ **for** *vt fus* (*defend*) apoyar; (*signify*) significar; (*tolerate*) aguantar, permitir; **to** ~ **in for** *vt fus* suplir a; **to** ~ **out** *vi* (*be prominent*) destacarse; **to** ~ **up** *vi* (*rise*) levantarse, ponerse de pie; **to** ~ **up for** *vt fus* defender; **to** ~ **up to** *vt fus* hacer frente a.
standard ['stændəd] *n* patrón *m*, norma; (*flag*) estandarte *m*; (*degree*) grado // *a* (*size etc*) normal, corriente, stándard; ~**s** *npl* (*morals*) valores *mpl* morales; ~**ize** *vt* estandarizar; ~ **lamp** *n* lámpara de pie; ~ **of living** *n* nivel *m* de vida.
stand-by ['stændbaɪ] *n* (*alert*) alerta, aviso; **to be on** ~ estar sobre aviso; ~ **ticket** *n* (*AVIAT*) billete *m* standby.
stand-in ['stændɪn] *n* suplente *m/f*; (*CINEMA*) doble *m/f*.
standing ['stændɪŋ] *a* (*upright*) derecho; (*on foot*) de pie, en pie // *n* reputación *f*; **of many years'** ~ que lleva muchos años; ~ **order** *n* (*at bank*) giro bancario; ~ **orders** *npl* (*MIL*) reglamento *sg* general; ~ **room** *n* sitio para estar de pie.
stand: ~**-offish** *a* reservado, poco afable; ~**point** *n* punto de vista; ~**still** *n*: **at a** ~**still** paralizado, en paro; **to come to a** ~**still** pararse, quedar paralizado.
stank [stæŋk] *pt of* **stink**.
staple ['steɪpl] *n* (*for papers*) grapa // *a* (*food etc*) corriente // *vt* unir con grapa, engrapar; **stapler** *n* grapadora.
star [sta:*] *n* estrella; (*celebrity*) estrella, astro // *vi*: **to** ~ **in** ser la estrella *o* el astro de.
starboard ['sta:bəd] *n* estribor *m*.
starch [sta:tʃ] *n* almidón *m*; ~**ed** *a* (*collar*) almidonado; ~**y** *a* feculento.
stardom ['sta:dəm] *n* estrellato, calidad *f* de estrella.
stare [stɛə*] *n* mirada fija // *vt*: **to** ~ **at** mirar fijo.
starfish ['sta:fɪʃ] *n* estrella de mar.
stark [sta:k] *a* (*bleak*) severo, escueto // *ad*: ~ **naked** en cueros, en pelota.
starlight ['sta:laɪt] *n*: **by** ~ a la luz de las estrellas.
starling ['sta:lɪŋ] *n* estornino.
starry ['sta:rɪ] *a* estrellado; ~**-eyed** *a* (*innocent*) inocentón(ona), ingenuo.
start [sta:t] *n* (*beginning*) principio, comienzo; (*departure*) salida; (*sudden movement*) salto, sobresalto; (*advantage*) ventaja // *vt* empezar, comenzar; (*cause*) causar; (*found*) fundar; (*engine*) poner en marcha // *vi* (*begin*) comenzar, empezar; (*with fright*) asustarse, sobresaltarse; (*train etc*) salir; **to** ~ **off** *vi* empezar, comenzar; (*leave*) salir, ponerse en camino; **to** ~ **up** *vi* comenzar; (*car*) ponerse en marcha // *vt* comenzar; (*car*) poner en marcha; ~**er** *n* (*AUT*) botón *m* de arranque; (*SPORT: official*) juez *m/f* de salida; (: *runner*) corredor/a *m/f*; (*CULIN*) entrada; ~**ing point** *n* punto de partida.
startle ['sta:tl] *vt* asustar, sobrecoger; **startling** *a* alarmante.
starvation [sta:'veɪʃən] *n* hambre *f*; (*MED*) inanición *f*; **starve** *vi* pasar hambre; (*to death*) morir de hambre // *vt* hacer pasar hambre; (*fig*) privar; **I'm starving** estoy muerto de hambre.
state [steɪt] *n* estado // *vt* (*say, declare*) afirmar; (*a case*) presentar, exponer; **the S~s** los Estados Unidos; **to be in a** ~ estar agitado; ~**ly** *a* majestuoso, imponente; ~**ment** *n* afirmación *f*; (*LAW*) declaración *f*; **statesman** *n* estadista *m*.
static ['stætɪk] *n* (*RADIO*) parásitos *mpl* // *a* estático; ~ **electricity** *n* estática.

station ['steɪʃən] *n* (*gen*) estación *f*; (*place*) puesto, sitio; (*RADIO*) emisora; (*rank*) posición *f* social // *vt* colocar, situar; (*MIL*) apostar.

stationary ['steɪʃnərɪ] *a* estacionario, fijo.

stationer's (**shop**) ['steɪʃənəz] *n* papelería; **stationery** [-nərɪ] *n* papel *m* de escribir.

station master *n* (*RAIL*) jefe *m* de estación.

station wagon *n* (*US*) break *m*.

statistic [stə'tɪstɪk] *n* estadística; ~**s** *npl* (*science*) estadística *sg*; ~**al** *a* estadístico.

statue ['stætjuː] *n* estatua.

stature ['stætʃə*] *n* estatura; (*fig*) talla.

status ['steɪtəs] *n* condición *f*, estado; (*reputation*) reputación *f*, státus *m*; **the** ~ **quo** el statu quo; ~ **symbol** *n* símbolo de prestigio.

statute ['stætjuːt] *n* estatuto, ley *f*; **statutory** *a* estatutario.

staunch [stɔːntʃ] *a* firme, incondicional.

stave [steɪv] *vt*: **to** ~ **off** (*attack*) rechazar; (*threat*) evitar.

stay [steɪ] *n* (*period of time*) estancia // *vi* (*remain*) quedar, quedarse; (*as guest*) hospedarse; (*spend some time*) pasar (un) tiempo; **to** ~ **put** seguir en el mismo sitio; **to** ~ **the night** pasar la noche; **to** ~ **behind** *vi* quedar atrás; **to** ~ **in** *vi* (*at home*) quedarse en casa; **to** ~ **on** *vi* quedarse; **to** ~ **out** *vi* (*of house*) no volver a casa; **to** ~ **up** *vi* (*at night*) velar, no acostarse; ~**ing power** *n* resistencia.

steadfast ['stɛdfɑːst] *a* firme, resuelto.

steadily ['stɛdɪlɪ] *ad* (*firmly*) firmemente; (*unceasingly*) sin parar; (*fixedly*) fijamente; (*walk*) normalmente; (*drive*) a velocidad constante.

steady ['stɛdɪ] *a* (*constant*) constante, fijo; (*unswerving*) firme; (*regular*) regular; (*person, character*) sensato, juicioso; (*diligent*) trabajador; (*calm*) sereno // *vt* (*hold*) mantener firme; (*stabilize*) estabilizar; (*nerves*) calmar; **to** ~ **o.s. on** *or* **against sth** afirmarse en algo.

steak [steɪk] *n* (*gen*) filete *m*; (*beef*) bistec *m*.

steal [stiːl], *pt* **stole**, *pp* **stolen** *vt*, *vi* robar.

stealth [stɛlθ] *n*: **by** ~ a escondidas, sigilosamente; ~**y** *a* cauteloso, sigiloso.

steam [stiːm] *n* vapor *m*; (*mist*) vaho, humo // *vt* empañar; (*CULIN*) cocer al vapor // *vi* echar vapor; (*ship*): **to** ~ **along** avanzar, ir avanzando; ~ **engine** *n* máquina de vapor; ~**er** *n* vapor *m*; ~**roller** *n* apisonadora; ~**y** *a* vaporoso; (*room*) lleno de vapor; (*window*) empañado.

steel [stiːl] *n* acero // *a* de acero; ~**works** *n* (fábrica) siderúrgica.

steep [stiːp] *a* escarpado, abrupto; (*stair*) empinado; (*price*) exorbitante, excesivo // *vt* empapar, remojar.

steeple ['stiːpl] *n* aguja, campanario; ~**chase** *n* carrera de obstáculos; ~**jack**

n reparador *m* de chimeneas.

steer [stɪə*] *vt* conducir, dirigir // *vi* conducir; ~**ing** *n* (*AUT*) dirección *f*; ~**ing wheel** *n* volante *m*.

stellar ['stɛlə*] *a* estelar.

stem [stɛm] *n* (*of plant*) tallo; (*of glass*) pie *m*; (*of pipe*) cañón *m* // *vt* detener; (*blood*) restañar; **to** ~ **from** *vt fus* proceder de.

stench [stɛntʃ] *n* hedor *m*.

stencil ['stɛnsl] *n* (*typed*) cliché *m*, clisé *m*; (*lettering*) plantilla // *vt* hacer un cliché de.

step [stɛp] *n* paso; (*sound*) paso, pisada; (*stair*) peldaño, escalón *m* // *vi*: **to** ~ **forward** dar un paso adelante; ~**s** *npl* = ~**ladder**; **to** ~ **down** *vi* (*fig*) retirarse; **to** ~ **off** *vt fus* bajar de; **to** ~ **on** *vt fus* pisar; **to** ~ **over** *vt fus* pasar por encima de; **to** ~ **up** *vt* (*increase*) aumentar; ~**brother** *n* hermanastro; ~**daughter** *n* hijastra; ~**father** *n* padrastro; ~**ladder** *n* escalera de tijera *o* doble; ~**mother** *n* madrastra; ~**ping stone** *n* pasadera; ~**sister** *n* hermanastra; ~**son** *n* hijastro.

stereo ['stɛrɪəu] *n* estereo // *a* (*also*: ~**phonic**) estereo(fónico).

stereotype ['stɪərɪətaɪp] *n* estereotipo // *vt* estereotipar.

sterile ['stɛraɪl] *a* estéril; **sterility** [-'rɪlɪtɪ] *n* esterilidad *f*; **sterilization** [-'zeɪʃən] *n* esterilización *f*; **sterilize** ['stɛrɪlaɪz] *vt* esterilizar.

sterling ['stɜːlɪŋ] *a* esterlina; (*silver*) de ley; (*fig*) auténtico.

stern [stɜːn] *a* severo, austero // *n* (*NAUT*) popa.

stethoscope ['stɛθəskəup] *n* estetoscopio.

stew [stjuː] *n* cocido, estofado; (*fig*: *mess*) apuro // *vt*, *vi* estofar, guisar; (*fruit*) cocer.

steward ['stjuːəd] *n* (*gen*) camarero; ~**ess** *n* azafata.

stick [stɪk] *n* palo; (*as weapon*) porra; (*walking* ~) bastón *m* // (*vb*: *pt*, *pp* **stuck**) *vt* (*glue*) pegar; (*thrust*): **to** ~ **sth into** clavar *o* hincar algo en; (*col*: *put*) meter; (*col*: *tolerate*) aguantar, soportar // *vi* pegar, pegarse; (*come to a stop*) quedarse parado; (*in mind etc*) atascarse; (*pin etc*) clavarse; **to** ~ **out**, ~ **up** *vi* sobresalir; **to** ~ **up for** *vt fus* defender; ~**er** *n* etiqueta engomada.

stickler ['stɪklə*] *n*: **to be a** ~ **for** dar mucha importancia a.

stick-up ['stɪkʌp] *n* asalto, atraco.

sticky ['stɪkɪ] *a* pegajoso; (*label*) engomado; (*fig*) difícil.

stiff [stɪf] *a* rígido, tieso; (*hard*) duro; (*difficult*) difícil; (*person*) inflexible; (*price*) exorbitante; ~**en** *vt* hacer más rígido; (*limb*) entumecer // *vi* endurecerse; (*grow stronger*) fortalecerse; ~**ness** *n* rigidez *f*, tiesura; dificultad *f*; (*character*) frialdad *f*.

stifle ['staɪfl] *vt* ahogar, sofocar; **stifling** *a* (*heat*) sofocante, bochornoso.

stigma ['stɪgmə], *pl* (*BOT, MED, REL*) ~**ta** [-tə], (*fig*) ~**s** *n* estigma *m*.

stile [staɪl] *n* escalera para pasar una cerca.

stiletto [stɪ'letəu] *n* (*also:* ~ **heel**) tacón *m* de aguja.

still [stɪl] *a* inmóvil, quieto // *ad* (*up to this time*) todavía; (*even*) aún; (*nonetheless*) sin embargo, aun así; ~**born** *a* nacido muerto; ~ **life** *n* naturaleza muerta.

stilt [stɪlt] *n* zanco; (*pile*) pilar *m*, soporte *m*.

stilted ['stɪltɪd] *a* afectado.

stimulant ['stɪmjulənt] *n* estimulante *m*.

stimulate ['stɪmjuleɪt] *vt* estimular; **stimulating** *a* estimulante; **stimulation** [-'leɪʃən] *n* estímulo.

stimulus ['stɪmjuləs], *pl* **-li** [-laɪ] *n* estímulo, incentivo.

sting [stɪŋ] *n* (*wound*) picadura; (*pain*) escozor *m*, picazón *m*; (*organ*) aguijón *m* // (*vb: pt, pp* **stung**) *vt* picar // *vi* picar, escocer.

stingy ['stɪndʒɪ] *a* tacaño.

stink [stɪŋk] *n* hedor *m*, tufo // *vi, pt* **stank**, *pp* **stunk** heder, apestar; ~**ing** *a* hediondo, fétido.

stint [stɪnt] *n* tarea, destajo; **to do one's** ~ hacer su parte // *vi:* **to** ~ **on** escatimar.

stipend ['staɪpɛnd] *n* (*of vicar etc*) estipendio, sueldo.

stipulate ['stɪpjuleɪt] *vt* estipular, poner como condición; **stipulation** [-'leɪʃən] *n* estipulación *f*, condición *f*.

stir [stə:*] *n* (*fig: agitation*) conmoción *f* // *vt* (*tea etc*) remover; (*fire*) atizar; (*move*) mover; (*fig: emotions*) conmover // *vi* moverse, menearse; **to** ~ **up** *vt* excitar; (*trouble*) fomentar; ~**ring** *a* conmovedor(a).

stirrup ['stɪrəp] *n* estribo.

stitch [stɪtʃ] *n* (*SEWING*) puntada; (*KNITTING*) punto; (*MED*) punto (de sutura); (*pain*) punzada // *vt* coser; (*MED*) suturar.

stoat [stəut] *n* armiño.

stock [stɔk] *n* (*COMM: reserves*) existencias *fpl*, stock *m*; (*: selection*) surtido; (*AGR*) ganado, ganadería; (*CULIN*) caldo; (*fig: lineage*) estirpe *f*; (*FINANCE*) capital *m*; (*: shares*) acciones *fpl* // *a* (*fig: reply etc*) clásico, acostumbrado // *vt* (*have in* ~) tener (en existencia o almacén); (*supply*) proveer, abastecer; **to take** ~ **of** (*fig*) asesorar, examinar; **to** ~ **up with** *vt* abastecerse de; ~**s** *npl* cepo *sg*; ~**s and shares** acciones y valores.

stockade [stɔ'keɪd] *n* estacada.

stockbroker ['stɔkbrəukə*] *n* agente *m/f* o corredor/a *m/f* de bolsa.

stock exchange *n* bolsa.

stocking ['stɔkɪŋ] *n* media.

stock market *n* bolsa (de valores).

stockpile ['stɔkpaɪl] *n* reserva // *vt* acumular, almacenar.

stocktaking ['stɔkteɪkɪŋ] *n* (*COMM*) inventario, balance *m*.

stocky ['stɔkɪ] *a* (*strong*) robusto; (*short*) achaparrado.

stodgy ['stɔdʒɪ] *a* indigesto, pesado.

stoical ['stəuɪkəl] *a* estoico.

stoke [stəuk] *vt* cargar, cebar.

stole [stəul] *pt of* **steal** // *n* estola.

stolen ['stəuln] *pp of* **steal.**

stomach ['stʌmək] *n* (*ANAT*) estómago; (*belly*) vientre *m*; (*appetite*) apetito // *vt* tragar, aguantar; ~ **ache** *n* dolor *m* de estómago.

stone [stəun] *n* piedra; (*in fruit*) hueso; (*weight*) medida de peso (*6.348kg*) // *a* de piedra // *vt* apedrear; ~-**cold** *a* helado; ~-**deaf** *a* totalmente sordo; ~**work** *n* (*art*) cantería; (*stones*) piedras *fpl*; **stony** *a* pedregoso; (*glance*) glacial.

stood [stud] *pt, pp of* **stand.**

stool [stu:l] *n* taburete *m*.

stoop [stu:p] *vi* (*also:* **have a** ~) ser cargado de espaldas; (*bend*) inclinarse, encorvarse.

stop [stɔp] *n* parada, alto; (*in punctuation*) punto // *vt* parar, detener; (*break off*) suspender; (*block*) tapar, cerrar; (*also:* **put a** ~ **to**) terminar, poner término a // *vi* pararse, detenerse; (*end*) acabarse; **to** ~ **doing sth** dejar de hacer algo; **to** ~ **dead** *vi* pararse en seco; **to** ~ **off** *vi* interrumpir el viaje; **to** ~ **up** *vt* (*hole*) tapar; ~**gap** *n* recurso (temporal); ~**lights** *npl* (*AUT*) luces *fpl* de detención; ~**over** *n* parada intermedia.

stoppage ['stɔpɪdʒ] *n* (*strike*) paro; (*temporary stop*) interrupción *f*; (*of pay*) suspensión *f*; (*blockage*) obstrucción *f*.

stopper ['stɔpə*] *n* tapón *m*.

stopwatch ['stɔpwɔtʃ] *n* cronómetro.

storage ['stɔ:rɪdʒ] *n* almacenaje *m*.

store [stɔ:*] *n* (*stock*) provisión *f*; (*depot, large shop*) almacén *m*; (*reserve*) reserva, repuesto; ~**s** *npl* víveres *mpl* // *vt* almacenar; (*keep*) guardar; **to** ~ **up** *vt* acumular; ~**room** *n* despensa.

storey, story (*US*) ['stɔ:rɪ] *n* piso.

stork [stɔ:k] *n* cigüeña.

storm [stɔ:m] *n* tormenta; (*wind*) vendaval *m*; (*fig*) tempestad *f* // *vi* (*fig*) rabiar // *vt* tomar por asalto, asaltar; ~ **cloud** *n* nubarrón *m*; ~**y** *a* tempestuoso.

story ['stɔ:rɪ] *n* historia, relato; (*joke*) cuento, chiste *m*; (*plot*) argumento; (*lie*) cuento, embuste *m*; (*US*) = **storey**; ~**book** *n* libro de cuentos; ~**teller** *n* cuentista *m/f*.

stout [staut] *a* (*strong*) sólido, macizo; (*fat*) gordo, corpulento // *n* cerveza negra.

stove [stəuv] *n* (*for cooking*) cocina; (*for heating*) estufa.

stow [stəu] *vt* meter, poner; (*NAUT*) estibar; ~**away** *n* polizón/ona *m/f*.

straddle ['strædl] *vt* montar a horcajadas.

straggle ['strægl] *vi* (*wander*) vagar en desorden; (*lag behind*) rezagarse; **straggler** *n* rezagado; **straggling, straggly** *a* (*hair*) desordenado.

straight [streɪt] *a* recto, derecho; (*honest*) honrado; (*frank*) franco, directo; (*simple*) sencillo; (*in order*) en orden // *ad* derecho, directamente; (*drink*) sin mezcla; **to put**

or **get sth** ~ dejar algo en claro; ~ **away,** ~ **off** (*at once*) en seguida; ~**en** *vt* (*also*: ~**en out**) enderezar, poner derecho; ~**-faced** *a* solemne, sin expresión; ~**forward** *a* (*simple*) sencillo; (*honest*) honrado, franco.

strain [streɪn] *n* (*gen*) tensión *f*; (*TECH*) esfuerzo; (*MED*) torcedura; (*breed*) raza // *vt* (*back etc*) torcerse; (*tire*) cansar; (*stretch*) estirar; (*filter*) filtrar // *vi* esforzarse; ~**s** *npl* (*MUS*) son *m*; ~**ed** *a* (*muscle*) torcido; (*laugh*) forzado; (*relations*) tenso; ~**er** *n* colador *m*.

strait [streɪt] *n* (*GEO*) estrecho; ~**-jacket** *n* camisa de fuerza; ~**-laced** *a* mojigato, gazmoño.

strand [strænd] *n* (*of thread*) hebra; (*of hair*) trenza; (*of rope*) ramal *m*; ~**ed** *a* abandonado (sin recursos), desamparado.

strange [streɪndʒ] *a* (*not known*) desconocido; (*odd*) extraño, raro; **stranger** *n* desconocido/a; (*from another area*) forastero/a.

strangle [ˈstræŋgl] *vt* estrangular; (*sobs etc*) ahogar; ~**hold** *n* (*fig*) dominio completo; **strangulation** [-ˈleɪʃən] *n* estrangulación *f*.

strap [stræp] *n* correa; (*of slip, dress*) tirante *m* // *vt* atar con correa; (*punish*) azotar.

strapping [ˈstræpɪŋ] *a* robusto, fornido.

strata [ˈstrɑːtə] *pl of* **stratum.**

stratagem [ˈstrætɪdʒəm] *n* estratagema.

strategic [strəˈtiːdʒɪk] *a* estratégico.

strategy [ˈstrætɪdʒɪ] *n* estrategia.

stratum [ˈstrɑːtəm], *pl* **-ta** *n* estrato.

straw [strɔː] *n* paja; (*drinking* ~) caña, pajita.

strawberry [ˈstrɔːbərɪ] *n* fresa.

stray [streɪ] *a* (*animal*) extraviado; (*bullet*) perdido; (*scattered*) disperso // *vi* extraviarse, perderse.

streak [striːk] *n* raya; (*fig: of madness etc*) vena // *vt* rayar // *vi*: **to** ~ **past** pasar como un rayo; ~**y** *a* rayado.

stream [striːm] *n* riachuelo, arroyo; (*jet*) chorro; (*current*) corriente *f*; (*of people*) oleada // *vt* (*SCOL*) dividir en grupos por habilidad // *vi* correr, fluir; **to** ~ **in/out** (*people*) entrar/salir en tropel.

streamer [ˈstriːmə*] *n* serpentina.

streamlined [ˈstriːmlaɪnd] *a* aerodinámico.

street [striːt] *n* calle *f* // *a* callejero; ~**car** *n* (*US*) tranvía; ~ **lamp** *n* farol *m*.

strength [streŋθ] *n* fuerza; (*of girder, knot etc*) resistencia; ~**en** *vt* fortalecer, reforzar.

strenuous [ˈstrenjuəs] *a* (*tough*) arduo; (*energetic*) enérgico; (*determined*) tenaz.

stress [stres] *n* (*force, pressure*) presión *f*; (*mental strain*) tensión *f*; (*accent*) énfasis *m*, acento; (*TECH*) tensión *f*, carga // *vt* subrayar, recalcar.

stretch [stretʃ] *n* (*of sand etc*) trecho, tramo // *vi* estirarse; (*extend*): **to** ~ **to** *or* **as far as** extenderse hasta // *vt* extender,

estirar; (*make demands of*) exigir el máximo esfuerzo a; **to** ~ **out** *vi* tenderse // *vt* (*arm etc*) extender; (*spread*) estirar.

stretcher [ˈstretʃə*] *n* camilla.

strewn [struːn] *a*: ~ **with** cubierto *o* sembrado de.

stricken [ˈstrɪkən] *a* (*wounded*) herido; (*ill*) enfermo.

strict [strɪkt] *a* (*person*) severo, riguroso; (*precise*) estricto, exacto; ~**ly** *ad* (*exactly*) estrictamente; (*totally*) terminantemente; (*severely*) rigurosamente; ~**ness** *n* exactitud *f*; rigor *m*, severidad *f*.

stride [straɪd] *n* zancada, tranco // *vi, pt* **strode,** *pp* **stridden** [ˈstrɪdn] dar zancadas, andar a trancos.

strident [ˈstraɪdnt] *a* estridente; (*colour*) chillón(ona).

strife [straɪf] *n* lucha.

strike [straɪk] *n* huelga; (*of oil etc*) descubrimiento; (*attack*) ataque *m*; (*SPORT*) golpe *m* // (*vb: pt, pp* **struck**) *vt* golpear, pegar; (*oil etc*) descubrir; (*obstacle*) topar con // *vi* declarar la huelga; (*attack*) atacar; (*clock*) dar la hora; **to** ~ **a match** encender un fósforo; **to** ~ **down** *vt* derribar; **to** ~ **out** *vt* borrar, tachar; **to** ~ **up** *vt* (*MUS*) empezar a tocar; (*conversation*) entablar; (*friendship*) trabar; ~**breaker** *n* rompehuelgas *m/f inv*; **striker** *n* huelgista *m/f*; (*SPORT*) delantero; **striking** *a* impresionante; (*nasty*) chocante; (*colour*) llamativo.

string [strɪŋ] *n* (*gen*) cuerda; (*row*) hilera // *vt, pt, pp* **strung: to** ~ **together** ensartar // *vi*: **to** ~ **out** extenderse; **the** ~**s** *npl* (*MUS*) los instrumentos de cuerda; **to pull** ~**s** (*fig*) mover palancas; ~ **bean** *n* judía verde, habichuela; ~**(ed) instrument** *n* (*MUS*) instrumento de cuerda.

stringent [ˈstrɪndʒənt] *a* riguroso, severo.

strip [strɪp] *n* tira; (*of land*) franja; (*of metal*) cinta, lámina // *vt* desnudar; (*also*: ~ **down**: *machine*) desmontar // *vi* desnudarse; ~ **cartoon** *n* tira cómica.

stripe [straɪp] *n* raya; (*MIL*) galón *m*; ~**d** *a* a rayas, rayado.

stripper [ˈstrɪpə*] *n* artista de striptease.

striptease [ˈstrɪptiːz] *n* striptease *m*.

strive [straɪv], *pt* **strove,** *pp* **striven** [ˈstrɪvn] *vi*: **to** ~ **to do sth** esforzarse *o* luchar por hacer algo.

strode [strəud] *pt of* **stride.**

stroke [strəuk] *n* (*blow*) golpe *m*; (*MED*) ataque *m* fulminante; (*caress*) caricia; (*of pen*) trazo // *vt* acariciar, frotar suavemente; **at a** ~ de golpe.

stroll [strəul] *n* paseo, vuelta // *vi* dar un paseo *o* una vuelta.

strong [strɔŋ] *a* fuerte; **they are 50** ~ son 50; ~**box** *n* caja fuerte; ~**hold** *n* fortaleza; (*fig*) baluarte *m*; ~**ly** *ad* fuertemente, con fuerza; (*believe*)

firmemente; ~**room** *n* cámara acorazada.
strove [strəuv] *pt of* **strive.**
struck [strʌk] *pt, pp of* **strike.**
structural ['strʌktʃərəl] *a* estructural; **structure** *n* estructura; (*building*) construcción *f.*
struggle ['strʌgl] *n* lucha // *vi* luchar.
strum [strʌm] *vt* (*guitar*) rasguear.
strung [strʌŋ] *pt, pp of* **string.**
strut [strʌt] *n* puntal *m* // *vi* pavonearse.
stub [stʌb] *n* (*of ticket etc*) talón *m*; (*of cigarette*) colilla; **to ~ out** *vt* apagar; **to ~ one's toe** dar con el dedo contra algo.
stubble ['stʌbl] *n* rastrojo; (*on chin*) barba (de pocos días).
stubborn ['stʌbən] *a* terco, testarudo.
stuck [stʌk] *pt, pp of* **stick** // *a* (*jammed*) atascado; ~**-up** *a* engreído, presumido.
stud [stʌd] *n* (*shirt* ~) botón *m*; (*of boot*) taco; (*of horses*) caballeriza; (*also:* ~ **horse**) caballo padre *o* semental // *vt* (*fig*): ~**ded with** sembrado de.
student ['stju:dənt] *n* estudiante *m/f* // *a* estudiantil.
studio ['stju:diəu] *n* estudio; (*sculptor's*) taller *m.*
studious ['stju:diəs] *a* aplicado; (*studied*) calculado; ~**ly** *ad* (*carefully*) con esmero.
study ['stʌdi] *n* (*gen*) estudio // *vt* estudiar; (*examine*) examinar, escudriñar // *vi* estudiar.
stuff [stʌf] *n* materia; (*cloth*) tela; (*substance*) material *m*, sustancia // *vt* llenar; (*CULIN*) rellenar; (*animals*) disecar; ~**ing** *n* relleno; ~**y** *a* (*room*) mal ventilado; (*person*) de miras estrechas.
stumble ['stʌmbl] *vi* tropezar, dar un traspié; **to ~ across** (*fig*) tropezar con; **stumbling block** *n* tropiezo, obstáculo.
stump [stʌmp] *n* (*of tree*) tocón *m*; (*of limb*) muñón *m* // *vt*: **to be ~ed** quedar perplejo.
stun [stʌn] *vt* dejar sin sentido.
stung [stʌŋ] *pt, pp of* **sting.**
stunk [stʌŋk] *pp of* **stink.**
stunning ['stʌnɪŋ] *a* (*fig*) pasmoso.
stunt [stʌnt] *n* proeza excepcional; (*AVIAT*) vuelo acrobático; (*publicity* ~) truco publicitario; ~**ed** *a* enano, achaparrado; ~**man** *n* doble *m.*
stupefy ['stju:pɪfaɪ] *vt* dejar estupefacto.
stupendous [stju:'pɛndəs] *a* estupendo, asombroso.
stupid ['stju:pɪd] *a* estúpido, tonto; ~**ity** [-'pɪdɪtɪ] *n* estupidez *f*; ~**ly** *ad* estúpidamente.
stupor ['stju:pə*] *n* estupor *m.*
sturdy ['stə:dɪ] *a* robusto, fuerte.
stutter ['stʌtə*] *n* tartamudeo // *vi* tartamudear.
sty [staɪ] *n* (*for pigs*) pocilga.
stye [staɪ] *n* (*MED*) orzuelo.
style [staɪl] *n* estilo; **stylish** *a* elegante, a la moda.
stylus ['staɪləs] *n* (*of record player*) aguja.

suave [swɑ:v] *a* cortés, fino.
sub... [sʌb] *pref* sub...; ~**conscious** *a* subconsciente // *n* subconsciente *m*; ~**divide** *vt* subdividir; ~**division** *n* subdivisión *f.*
subdue [səb'dju:] *vt* sojuzgar; (*passions*) dominar; ~**d** *a* (*light*) tenue; (*person*) sumiso, manso.
subject ['sʌbdʒɪkt] *n* súbdito; (*SCOL*) tema *m*, materia // *vt* [səb'dʒɛkt]: **to ~ sb to sth** someter a uno a algo; **to be ~ to** (*law*) estar sujeto a; ~**ion** [-'dʒɛkʃən] *n* sometimiento, sujeción *f*; ~**ive** *a* subjetivo; ~ **matter** *n* materia; (*content*) contenido.
subjugate ['sʌbdʒugeɪt] *vt* subyugar.
sublet [sʌb'lɛt] *vt* subarrendar.
sublime [sə'blaɪm] *a* sublime.
submachine gun ['sʌbməʼʃi:n-] *n* metralleta.
submarine [sʌbməʼri:n] *n* submarino.
submerge [səb'mə:dʒ] *vt* sumergir; (*flood*) inundar // *vi* sumergirse.
submission [səb'mɪʃən] *n* sumisión *f*; **submissive** [-'mɪsɪv] *a* sumiso.
submit [səb'mɪt] *vt* someter // *vi* someterse.
subnormal [sʌb'nɔ:məl] *a* anormal; (*backward*) retrasado.
subordinate [sə'bɔ:dɪnət] *a, n* subordinado.
subpoena [səb'pi:nə] (*LAW*) *n* comparendo, citación *f* // *vt* mandar comparecer.
subscribe [səb'skraɪb] *vi* suscribir; **to ~ to** (*opinion, fund*) suscribir, aprobar; (*newspaper*) suscribirse a; **subscriber** *n* (*to periodical, telephone*) abonado/a.
subscription [səb'skrɪpʃən] *n* abono, suscripción *f.*
subsequent ['sʌbsɪkwənt] *a* subsiguiente, posterior; ~**ly** *ad* después, más tarde.
subside [səb'saɪd] *vi* hundirse; (*flood*) bajar; (*wind*) amainar; **subsidence** [-'saɪdns] *n* hundimiento; (*in road*) socavón *m.*
subsidiary [səb'sɪdɪərɪ] *n* sucursal *f*, filial *f.*
subsidize ['sʌbsɪdaɪz] *vt* subvencionar; **subsidy** [-dɪ] *n* subvención *f.*
subsistence [səb'sɪstəns] *n* subsistencia; (*allowance*) dietas *fpl.*
substance ['sʌbstəns] *n* sustancia; (*fig*) esencia.
substandard [sʌb'stændəd] *a* inferior.
substantial [səb'stænʃl] *a* sustancial, sustancioso; (*fig*) importante; ~**ly** *ad* sustancialmente.
substantiate [səb'stænʃɪeɪt] *vt* comprobar.
substitute ['sʌbstɪtju:t] *n* (*person*) suplente *m/f*; (*thing*) sustituto // *vt*: **to ~ A for B** sustituir B por A, reemplazar A por B; **substitution** [-'tju:ʃən] *n* sustitución *f*, reemplazo.
subterfuge ['sʌbtəfju:dʒ] *n* subterfugio.
subterranean [sʌbtə'reɪnɪən] *a* subterráneo.

subtitle ['sʌbtaɪtl] *n* subtítulo.
subtle ['sʌtl] *a* sutil; ~ **ty** *n* sutileza.
subtract [səb'trækt] *vt* sustraer, restar;
~ **ion** [-'trækʃən] *n* sustracción *f*, resta.
suburb ['sʌbəːb] *n* arrabal *m*, suburbio;
~ **an** [sə'bəːbən] *a* suburbano; (*train etc*)
de cercanías.
subversive [səb'vəːsɪv] *a* subversivo.
subway ['sʌbweɪ] *n* (*Brit*) paso
subterráneo *o* inferior; (*US*) metro.
succeed [sək'siːd] *vi* (*person*) tener éxito;
(*plan*) salir bien // *vt* suceder a; **to** ~ **in**
doing lograr hacer; ~ **ing** *a* (*following*)
sucesivo, seguido.
success [sək'sɛs] *n* éxito; (*gain*) triunfo;
~ **ful** *a* (*venture*) de éxito; **to be** ~ **ful** (**in**
doing) lograr (hacer); ~ **fully** *ad* con
éxito.
succession [sək'sɛʃən] *n* (*series*) sucesión
f, serie *f*; (*descendants*) descendencia;
successive [-'sɛsɪv] *a* sucesivo,
consecutivo; **successor** [-'sɛsə*] *n*
sucesor/a *m/f*.
succinct [sək'sɪŋkt] *a* sucinto.
succulent ['sʌkjulənt] *a* suculento.
succumb [sə'kʌm] *vi* sucumbir.
such [sʌtʃ] *a, det* tal, semejante; (*of that
kind*): ~ **a book** un libro parecido; ~
books tales libros; (*so much*): ~ **courage**
tanto valor; ~ **a long trip** un viaje tan
largo; ~ **a lot of** tanto; ~ **as** (*like*) tal
como; **a noise** ~ **as** to un ruido tal que;
as ~ *ad* como tal // *pron* los/las que;
~ **-and-** ~ *det* tal o cual; **until** ~ **time as**
hasta que.
suck [sʌk] *vt* chupar; (*bottle*) sorber;
(*breast*) mamar; ~ **er** *n* (*BOT*) serpollo;
(*ZOOL*) ventosa; (*col*) bobo, primo.
suckle ['sʌkl] *vt* amamantar.
suction ['sʌkʃən] *n* succión *f*.
sudden ['sʌdn] *a* (*rapid*) repentino, súbito;
(*unexpected*) imprevisto; **all of a** ~, ~ **ly**
ad de repente; (*unexpectedly*)
inesperadamente.
suds [sʌdz] *npl* jabonaduras *fpl*.
sue [suː] *vt* demandar.
suede [sweɪd] *n* ante *m*.
suet ['suɪt] *n* sebo.
suffer ['sʌfə*] *vt* sufrir, padecer; (*bear*)
aguantar; (*allow*) permitir, tolerar // *vi*
sufrir, padecer; ~ **er** *n* víctima *m/f*; (*MED*)
enfermo; ~ **ing** *n* sufrimiento,
padecimiento; (*pain*) dolor *m*.
suffice [sə'faɪs] *vi* bastar, ser suficiente.
sufficient [sə'fɪʃənt] *a* suficiente, bastante.
suffix ['sʌfɪks] *n* sufijo.
suffocate ['sʌfəkeɪt] *vi* ahogarse,
asfixiarse; **suffocation** [-'keɪʃən] *n*
sofocación *f*, asfixia.
suffrage ['sʌfrɪdʒ] *n* sufragio; (*vote*)
derecho de votar.
sugar ['ʃugə*] *n* azúcar *m* // *vt* echar
azúcar a; ~ **beet** *n* remolacha; ~ **cane** *n*
caña de azúcar; ~ **y** *a* azucarado.
suggest [sə'dʒɛst] *vt* sugerir; (*advise*)
aconsejar; ~ **ion** [-'dʒɛstʃən] *n* sugerencia;

(*hypnotic*) sugestión *f*; ~ **ive** *a* sugestivo;
(*pej*) indecente.
suicidal [suɪ'saɪdl] *a* suicida; **suicide**
['suɪsaɪd] *n* suicidio; (*person*) suicida *m/f*.
suit [suːt] *n* (*man's*) traje *m*; (*woman's*)
conjunto; (*LAW*) litigio, pleito; (*CARDS*) palo
// *vt* (*gen*) convenir; (*clothes*) sentar a, ir
bien a; (*adapt*): **to** ~ **sth to** adaptar *o*
ajustar algo a; ~ **able** *a* conveniente; (*apt*)
indicado; ~ **ably** *ad* convenientemente, en
forma debida.
suitcase ['suːtkeɪs] *n* maleta.
suite [swiːt] *n* (*of rooms*) grupo de
habitaciones; (*MUS*) suite *f*; (*furniture*):
bedroom/dining room ~ (juego de)
dormitorio/comedor *m*.
suitor ['suːtə*] *n* pretendiente *m*.
sulk [sʌlk] *vi* tener mohíno; ~ **y** *a* con
mohíno.
sullen ['sʌlən] *a* hosco, malhumorado.
sulphur, sulfur (*US*) ['sʌlfə*] *n* azufre *m*.
sultan ['sʌltən] *n* sultán *m*.
sultana [sʌl'tɑːnə] *n* (*fruit*) pasa de
Esmirna.
sultry ['sʌltrɪ] *a* (*weather*) bochornoso;
(*seductive*) seductor(a).
sum [sʌm] *n* (*gen*) suma; (*total*) total *m*; **to**
~ **up** *vt* recapitular // *vi* hacer un
resumen.
summarize ['sʌməraɪz] *vt* resumir.
summary ['sʌmərɪ] *n* resumen *m* // *a*
(*justice*) sumario.
summer ['sʌmə*] *n* verano // *a* de verano;
~ **house** *n* (*in garden*) cenador *m*,
glorieta; ~ **time** *n* (*season*) verano; ~
time *n* (*by clock*) hora de verano.
summit ['sʌmɪt] *n* cima, cumbre *f*; ~
(**conference**) *n* conferencia cumbre.
summon ['sʌmən] *vt* (*person*) llamar;
(*meeting*) convocar; (*LAW*) citar; **to** ~ **up**
vt cobrar; ~ **s** *n* llamamiento, llamada //
vt citar, emplazar.
sump [sʌmp] *n* (*AUT*) cárter *m*.
sumptuous ['sʌmptjuəs] *a* suntuoso.
sun [sʌn] *n* sol *m*; ~ **bathe** *vi* tomar el sol;
~ **burn** *n* (*painful*) quemadura; (*tan*)
bronceado; ~ **burnt** *a* (*tanned*)
bronceado; (*painfully*) quemado por el sol.
Sunday ['sʌndɪ] *n* domingo.
sundial ['sʌndaɪəl] *n* reloj *m* de sol.
sundry ['sʌndrɪ] *a* varios, diversos; **all and**
~ todos y cada uno; **sundries** *npl* géneros
mpl diversos.
sunflower ['sʌnflauə*] *n* girasol *m*.
sung [sʌŋ] *pp of* **sing.**
sunglasses ['sʌnglɑːsɪz] *npl* gafas *fpl* de
sol.
sunk [sʌŋk] *pp of* **sink.**
sun: ~ **light** *n* luz *f* del sol; ~ **lit** *a*
iluminado por el sol; ~ **ny** *a* soleado; (*day*)
de sol; (*fig*) alegre; ~ **rise** *n* salida del sol;
~ **set** *n* puesta del sol; ~ **shade** *n* (*over
table*) sombrilla; ~ **shine** *n* sol *m*; ~ **spot**
n mancha solar; ~ **stroke** *n* insolación *f*,
~ **tan** *n* bronceado; ~ **tan oil** *n* broncea-
dor *m*, crema bronceadora.
super ['suːpə*] *a* (*col*) bárbaro.

superannuation [su:pərænju'eɪʃən] *n* jubilación *f*.

superb [su:'pə:b] *a* magnífico, espléndido.

supercilious [su:pə'sɪlɪəs] *a* (*disdainful*) desdeñoso; (*haughty*) altanero.

superficial [su:pə'fɪʃəl] *a* superficial.

superfluous [su'pə:fluəs] *a* superfluo, de sobra.

superhuman [su:pə'hju:mən] *a* sobrehumano.

superimpose ['su:pərɪm'pəuz] *vt* sobreponer.

superintendent [su:pərɪn'tɛndənt] *n* superintendente *m/f*; (*POLICE*) subjefe *m*.

superior [su'pɪərɪə*] *a* superior; (*smug*) desdeñoso // *n* superior *m*; ~**ity** [-'ɔrɪtɪ] *n* superioridad *f*; desdén *m*.

superlative [su'pə:lətɪv] *a, n* superlativo.

superman ['su:pəmæn] *n* superhombre *m*.

supermarket ['su:pəmɑ:kɪt] *n* supermercado.

supernatural [su:pə'nætʃərəl] *a* sobrenatural.

superpower ['su:pəpauə*] *n* (*POL*) superpotencia.

supersede [su:pə'si:d] *vt* suplantar.

supersonic ['su:pə'sɔnɪk] *a* supersónico.

superstition [su:pə'stɪʃən] *n* superstición *f*; **superstitious** [-ʃəs] *a* supersticioso.

supertanker ['su:pətæŋkə*] *n* superpetrolero.

supervise ['su:pəvaɪz] *vt* supervisar; **supervision** [-'vɪʒən] *n* supervisión *f*; **supervisor** *n* supervisor/a *m/f*.

supper ['sʌpə*] *n* cena; **to have** ~ cenar.

supple ['sʌpl] *a* flexible.

supplement ['sʌplɪmənt] *n* suplemento // *vt* [sʌplɪ'mɛnt] suplir; ~**ary** [-'mɛntərɪ] *a* suplementario.

supplier [sə'plaɪə*] *n* suministrador/a *m/f*; (*COMM*) distribuidor/a *m/f*.

supply [sə'plaɪ] *vt* (*provide*) suministrar, facilitar; (*equip*): **to** ~ (**with**) abastecer (de) // *n* suministro, provisión *f*; (*supplying*) abastecimiento // *a* (*teacher etc*) suplente; **supplies** *npl* (*food*) víveres *npl*; (*MIL*) pertrechos *mpl*; ~ **and demand** la oferta y la demanda.

support [sə'pɔ:t] *n* (*moral, financial etc*) apoyo; (*TECH*) soporte *m* // *vt* apoyar; (*financially*) mantener; (*uphold*) sostener; ~**er** *n* (*POL etc*) partidario; (*SPORT*) aficionado.

suppose [sə'pəuz] *vt, vi* (*gen*) suponer; (*imagine*) imaginar; **to be** ~**d to do sth** deber hacer algo; ~**dly** [sə'pəuzɪdlɪ] *ad* que se supone, según cabe suponer; **supposing** *conj* en caso de que; **supposition** [sʌpə'zɪʃən] *n* suposición *f*.

suppository [sə'pɔzɪtərɪ] *n* supositorio.

suppress [sə'prɛs] *vt* suprimir; (*yawn*) ahogar; ~**ion** [sə'prɛʃən] *n* represión *f*.

supremacy [su'prɛməsɪ] *n* supremacía; **supreme** [-'pri:m] *a* supremo.

surcharge ['sə:tʃɑ:dʒ] *n* sobrecarga; (*extra tax*) recargo.

sure [ʃuə*] *a* (*gen*) seguro; (*definite, convinced*) cierto; (*aim*) certero; ~**!** (*of course*) ¡claro!, ¡por supuesto!; ~-**footed** *a* de pie firme; ~**ly** *ad* (*certainly*) seguramente.

surety ['ʃuərətɪ] *n* garantía, fianza; (*person*) fiador/a *m/f*.

surf [sə:f] *n* olas *fpl*.

surface ['sə:fɪs] *n* superficie *f* // *vt* (*road*) revestir // *vi* salir a la superficie.

surfboard ['sə:fbɔ:d] *n* plancha (de surfing), acuaplano.

surfeit ['sə:fɪt] *n*: **a** ~ **of** exceso de.

surfing ['sə:fɪŋ] *n* surfing *m*.

surge [sə:dʒ] *n* oleada, oleaje *m* // *vi* avanzar a tropel.

surgeon ['sə:dʒən] *n* cirujano; **dental** ~ odontólogo.

surgery ['sə:dʒərɪ] *n* cirugía; (*room*) consultorio; **to undergo** ~ operarse; ~ **hours** *npl* horas *fpl* de consulta.

surgical ['sə:dʒɪkl] *a* quirúrgico; ~ **spirit** *n* alcohol *m*.

surly ['sə:lɪ] *a* hosco, malhumorado.

surmount [sə:'maunt] *vt* superar, sobreponerse a.

surname ['sə:neɪm] *n* apellido.

surpass [sə:'pɑ:s] *vt* superar, exceder.

surplus ['sə:pləs] *n* (*gen*) excedente *m*; (*COMM*) superávit *m* // *a* excedente, sobrante.

surprise [sə'praɪz] *n* (*gen*) sorpresa; (*astonishment*) asombro // *vt* sorprender; asombrar; **surprising** *a* sorprendente; asombroso.

surrealist [sə'rɪəlɪst] *a* surrealista.

surrender [sə'rɛndə*] *n* rendición *f*, entrega // *vi* rendirse, entregarse.

surreptitious [sʌrəp'tɪʃəs] *a* subrepticio.

surround [sə'raund] *vt* rodar, circundar; (*MIL etc*) cercar; ~**ing** *a* circundante; ~**ings** *npl* alrededores *mpl*, cercanías *fpl*.

surveillance [sə:'veɪləns] *n* vigilancia.

survey ['sə:veɪ] *n* inspección *f*, examen *m*; (*inquiry*) encuesta // *vt* [sə:'veɪ] (*gen*) examinar, inspeccionar; (*look at*) mirar, contemplar; (*make inquiries about*) hacer una encuesta sobre; ~**or** *n* agrimensor *m*.

survival [sə'vaɪvl] *n* supervivencia; **survive** *vi* sobrevivir; (*custom etc*) perdurar // *vt* sobrevivir a; **survivor** *n* superviviente *m/f*.

susceptible [sə'sɛptəbl] *a*: ~ (**to**) susceptible *o* sensible (a).

suspect ['sʌspɛkt] *a, n* sospechoso // *vt* [səs'pɛkt] sospechar.

suspend [səs'pɛnd] *vt* suspender; ~**er belt** *n* portaligas *m inv*; ~**ers** *npl* ligas *fpl*; (*US*) tirantes *mpl*.

suspense [səs'pɛns] *n* incertidumbre *f*, duda; (*in film etc*) suspense *m*.

suspension [səs'pɛnʃən] *n* (*gen, AUT*) suspensión *f*; (*of driving licence*) privación *f*; ~ **bridge** *n* puente *m* colgante.

suspicion [səs'pɪʃən] *n* (*gen*) sospecha; (*distrust*) recelo; (*trace*) traza; **suspicious**

[-ʃəs] a (*suspecting*) receloso; (*causing* ~) sospechoso.

sustain [səs'teɪn] vt sostener, apoyar; (*suffer*) sufrir, padecer; ~ed a (*effort*) sostenido.

sustenance ['sʌstɪnəns] n sustento.

swab [swɔb] n (*MED*) algodón m, torunda.

swagger ['swægə*] vi pavonearse.

swallow ['swɔləu] n (*bird*) golondrina; (*of food etc*) trago // vt tragar; **to** ~ **up** vt (*savings etc*) consumir.

swam [swæm] pt of **swim**.

swamp [swɔmp] n pantano, ciénaga // vt abrumar, agobiar; ~y a pantanoso.

swan [swɔn] n cisne m.

swap [swɔp] n canje m, intercambio // vt: **to** ~ (**for**) canjear (por).

swarm [swɔ:m] n (*of bees*) enjambre m; (*gen*) multitud f // vi hormiguear, pulular.

swarthy ['swɔ:ðɪ] a moreno.

swastika ['swɔstɪkə] n suástika, cruz f gamada.

swat [swɔt] vt aplastar.

sway [sweɪ] vi mecerse, balancearse // vt (*influence*) mover, influir en.

swear [sweə*], pt **swore**, pp **sworn** vi jurar; **to** ~ **to sth** declarar algo bajo juramento; ~word n taco, palabrota.

sweat [swɛt] n sudor m // vi sudar.

sweater ['swɛtə*] n suéter m.

sweaty ['swɛtɪ] a sudoroso.

swede [swi:d] n nabo.

Swede [swi:d] n sueco/a; **Sweden** n Suecia; **Swedish** a, n (*LING*) sueco.

sweep [swi:p] n (*act*) barredura; (*of arm*) golpe m; (*range*) extensión f, alcance m; (*also*: **chimney** ~) deshollinador m // (*vb*: pt, pp **swept**) vt barrer; (*mines*) rastrear // vi barrer; **to** ~ **away** vt barrer; (*rub out*) borrar; **to** ~ **past** vi pasar rápidamente; (*brush by*) rozar; **to** ~ **up** vi recoger la basura; ~**ing** a (*gesture*) dramático; (*generalized*) generalizado.

sweet [swi:t] n (*candy*) dulce m, caramelo; (*pudding*) postre m // a dulce; (*sugary*) azucarado; (*fresh*) fresco, nuevo; (*fig*) dulce, amable; ~**corn** n maíz m; ~**en** vt endulzar; (*add sugar to*) poner azúcar a; ~**heart** n novio/a; (*in speech*) amor; ~**ly** ad dulcemente; (*gently*) suavemente; ~**ness** n (*gen*) dulzura; (*amount of sugar*) lo dulce, lo azucarado; ~ **pea** n guisante m de olor.

swell [swɛl] n (*of sea*) marejada, oleaje m // a (*col*: *excellent*) estupendo, excelente // (*vb*: pt **swelled**, pp **swollen** or **swelled**) vt hinchar, inflar // vi hincharse, inflarse; ~**ing** n (*MED*) hinchazón m.

sweltering ['swɛltərɪŋ] a sofocante, de mucho calor.

swept [swɛpt] pt, pp of **sweep**.

swerve [swə:v] vi desviarse bruscamente.

swift [swɪft] n (*bird*) vencejo // a rápido, veloz; ~**ness** n rapidez f, velocidad f.

swig [swɪg] n (*col*: *drink*) trago.

swill [swɪl] n bazofia // vt (*also*: ~ **out**, ~

down) lavar, limpiar con agua.

swim [swɪm] n: **to go for a** ~ ir a nadar // (*vb*: pt **swam**, pp **swum**) vi nadar; (*head, room*) dar vueltas // vt pasar a nado; ~**mer** n nadador/a m/f; ~**ming** n natación f; ~**ming baths** npl piscina sg; ~**ming cap** n gorro de baño; ~**ming costume** n bañador m, traje m de baño; ~**ming pool** n piscina; ~**suit** n bañador m, traje m de baño.

swindle ['swɪndl] n estafa // vt estafar; **swindler** n estafador/a m/f.

swine [swaɪn] n, pl inv cerdos mpl, puercos mpl, (*col!*) canalla sg.

swing [swɪŋ] n (*in playground*) columpio; (*movement*) balanceo, vaivén m; (*change of direction*) viraje m; (*rhythm*) ritmo // (*vb*: pt, pp **swung**) vt balancear; (*on a* ~) columpiar; (*also*: ~ **round**) voltear bruscamente // vi balancearse, columpiarse; (*also*: ~ **round**) volver bruscamente; **to be in full** ~ estar en plena marcha; ~ **bridge** n puente m giratorio; ~ **door** n puerta giratoria.

swipe [swaɪp] n golpe m fuerte // vt (*hit*) golpear fuerte; (*col*: *steal*) guindar.

swirl [swə:l] vi arremolinarse.

Swiss [swɪs] a, n, pl inv suizo/a.

switch [swɪtʃ] n (*for light, radio etc*) interruptor m; (*change*) cambio; (*of hair*) trenza postiza // vt (*change*) cambiar de; **to** ~ **off** vt apagar; (*engine*) parar; **to** ~ **on** vt encender, prender; (*engine, machine*) arrancar; ~**board** n (*TEL*) central f de teléfonos.

Switzerland ['swɪtsələnd] n Suiza.

swivel ['swɪvl] vi (*also*: ~ **round**) girar.

swollen ['swəulən] pp of **swell**.

swoon [swu:n] vi desmayarse, desvanecerse.

swoop [swu:p] n (*by police etc*) redada // vi (*also*: ~ **down**) calarse, precipitarse.

swop [swɔp] = **swap**.

sword [sɔ:d] n espada; ~**fish** n pez m espada.

swore [swɔ:*] pt of **swear**.

sworn [swɔ:n] pp of **swear**.

swot [swɔt] vt, vi empollar.

swum [swʌm] pp of **swim**.

swung [swʌŋ] pt, pp of **swing**.

sycamore ['sɪkəmɔ:*] n sicomoro.

syllable ['sɪləbl] n sílaba.

syllabus ['sɪləbəs] n programa m de estudios.

symbol ['sɪmbl] n símbolo; ~**ic(al)** [-'bɔlɪk(l)] a simbólico; ~**ism** n simbolismo; ~**ize** vt simbolizar.

symmetrical [sɪ'mɛtrɪkl] a simétrico; **symmetry** ['sɪmɪtrɪ] n simetría.

sympathetic [sɪmpə'θɛtɪk] a compasivo; (*pleasant*) simpático; ~**ally** ad con compasión.

sympathize ['sɪmpəθaɪz] vi: **to** ~ **with** sb compadecerse de uno; **sympathizer** n (*POL*) simpatizante m/f.

sympathy ['sɪmpəθɪ] n (*pity*) compasión f; (*liking*) simpatía; **with our deepest** ~

nuestro más sentido pésame; ~ strike *n* huelga por solidaridad.

symphony ['sɪmfənɪ] *n* sinfonía; ~ **orchestra** *n* orquesta sinfónica.

symposium [sɪm'pəuzɪəm] *n* simposio.

symptom ['sɪmptəm] *n* síntoma *m*, indicio; ~**atic** [-'mætɪk] *a* sintomático.

synagogue ['sɪnəgɔg] *n* sinagoga.

synchronize ['sɪŋkrənaɪz] *vt* sincronizar // *vi*: **to** ~ **with** sincronizarse con.

syndicate ['sɪndɪkɪt] *n* (*gen*) sindicato; (*of newspapers*) cadena.

syndrome ['sɪndrəum] *n* síndrome *m*.

synonym ['sɪnənɪm] *n* sinónimo; ~**ous** [sɪ'nɔnɪməs] *a*: ~**ous (with)** sinónimo (con).

synopsis [sɪ'nɔpsɪs], *pl* -**ses** [-siːz] *n* sinopsis *f inv*.

syntax ['sɪntæks] *n* sintáxis *f*.

synthesis ['sɪnθəsɪs], *pl* -**ses** [-siːz] *n* síntesis *f inv*.

synthetic [sɪn'θɛtɪk] *a* sintético.

syphilis ['sɪfɪlɪs] *n* sífilis *f*.

syphon ['saɪfən] = **siphon.**

Syria ['sɪrɪə] *n* Siria; ~**n** *a*, *n* sirio/a.

syringe [sɪ'rɪndʒ] *n* jeringa.

syrup ['sɪrəp] *n* jarabe *m*, almíbar *m*.

system ['sɪstəm] *n* (*gen*) sistema; (*method*) método; (*ANAT*) organismo; ~**atic** [-'mætɪk] *a* sistemático; metódico; ~**s analyst** *n* analista *m/f* de sistemas.

T

ta [tɑː] *excl* (*Brit: col*) gracias.

tab [tæb] *n* (*gen*) lengüeta; (*label*) etiqueta; **to keep** ~**s on** (*fig*) vigilar.

tabby ['tæbɪ] *n* (*also*: ~ **cat**) gato atigrado.

table ['teɪbl] *n* mesa; (*of statistics etc*) cuadro, tabla // *vt* (*motion etc*) presentar; **to lay** *or* **set the** ~ poner la mesa; ~**cloth** *n* mantel *m*; ~ **d'hôte** [tɑːbl'dəut] *n* menú *m*; ~**mat** *n* mantel *m* individual; ~**spoon** *n* cuchara grande; (*also*: ~**spoonful**: *as measurement*) cucharada.

tablet ['tæblɪt] *n* (*MED*) tableta, pastilla; (*for writing*) bloc *m*; (*of stone*) lápida.

table: ~ **tennis** *n* ping-pong *m*, tenis *m* de mesa; ~ **wine** *n* vino de mesa.

taboo [tə'buː] *n* tabú *m* // *a* tabú.

tacit ['tæsɪt] *a* tácito.

taciturn ['tæsɪtəːn] *a* taciturno.

tack [tæk] *n* (*nail*) tachuela, chincheta; (*stitch*) hilván *m*; (*NAUT*) bordada // *vt* (*nail*) clavar con chinchetas; (*stitch*) hilvanar // *vi* virar.

tackle ['tækl] *n* (*gear*) equipo; (*also*: **fishing** ~) aparejo; (*for lifting*) polea; (*RUGBY*) atajo // *vt* (*difficulty*) enfrentar; (*grapple with*) agarrar; (*RUGBY*) atajar.

tacky ['tækɪ] *a* pegajoso.

tact [tækt] *n* tacto, discreción *f*; ~**ful** *a* discreto, diplomático; ~**fully** *ad* discretamente.

tactical ['tæktɪkl] *a* táctico; **tactics** [-tɪks] *n*, *npl* táctica *sg*.

tactless ['tæktlɪs] *a* indiscreto, falto de tacto; ~**ly** *ad* indiscretamente.

tadpole ['tædpəul] *n* renacuajo.

tag [tæg] *n* (*label*) etiqueta; (*loose end*) cabo; **to** ~ **along with sb** acompañar a uno.

tail [teɪl] *n* (*gen*) cola; (*ZOOL*) rabo; (*of shirt, coat*) faldón *m* // *vt* (*follow*) seguir los talones a; **to** ~ **away**, ~ **off** *vi* (*in size, quality etc*) ir disminuyendo; ~ **coat** *n* frac *m*; ~ **end** *n* cola, parte *f* final; ~**gate** *n* puerta trasera.

tailor ['teɪlə*] *n* sastre *m*; ~**ing** *n* (*cut*) corte *m*; (*craft*) sastrería; ~-**made** *a* hecho a la medida; (*fig*) especial.

tailwind ['teɪlwɪnd] *n* viento de cola.

tainted ['teɪntɪd] *a* (*food*) pasado; (*water, air*) contaminado; (*fig*) manchado.

take [teɪk], *pt* **took**, *pp* **taken** *vt* (*gen*) tomar; (*grab*) coger; (*gain: prize*) ganar; (*require: effort, courage*) exigir, hacer falta; (*tolerate*) aguantar; (*hold: passengers etc*) tener cabida para; (*accompany, bring, carry*) llevar; (*exam*) presentarse a; **to** ~ **sth from** (*drawer etc*) sacar algo de; (*person*) coger algo a; **I** ~ **it that...** supongo que...; **to** ~ **after** *vt fus* parecerse a; **to** ~ **apart** *vt* desmontar; **to** ~ **away** *vt* (*remove*) quitar; (*carry off*) llevar; **to** ~ **back** *vt* (*return*) devolver; (*one's words*) retractar; **to** ~ **down** *vt* (*building*) demoler; (*letter etc*) poner por escrito; **to** ~ **in** *vt* (*deceive*) engañar; (*understand*) entender; (*include*) abarcar; (*lodger*) acoger, recibir; **to** ~ **off** *vi* (*AVIAT*) despegar // *vt* (*remove*) quitar; (*imitate*) imitar; **to** ~ **on** *vt* (*work*) emprender; (*employee*) contratar; (*opponent*) desafiar; **to** ~ **out** *vt* sacar; (*remove*) quitar; **to** ~ **over** *vt* (*business*) tomar posesión de // *vi*: **to** ~ **over from sb** relevar a uno; **to** ~ **to** *vt fus* (*person*) coger simpatía a; (*activity*) aficionarse a; **to** ~ **up** *vt* (*a dress*) acortar; (*occupy: time, space*) ocupar; (*engage in: hobby etc*) dedicarse a; ~**away** *a* (*food*) para llevar; ~-**home pay** *n* salario neto; ~**off** *n* (*AVIAT*) despegue *m*; ~**over** *n* (*COMM*) absorción *f*; ~**over bid** *n* oferta de compra.

takings ['teɪkɪŋz] *npl* (*COMM*) ingresos *mpl*.

talc [tælk] *n* (*also*: ~**um powder**) talco.

tale [teɪl] *n* (*story*) cuento; (*account*) relación *f*; **to tell** ~**s** (*fig: lie*) chismear.

talent ['tælnt] *n* talento; ~**ed** *a* talentoso, de talento.

talk [tɔːk] *n* (*gen*) charla; (*gossip*) habladurías *fpl*, chismes *mpl*; (*conversation*) conversación *f* // *vi* (*speak*) hablar; (*chatter*) charlar; **to** ~ **about** hablar de; **to** ~ **sb into doing sth** convencer a uno de que debe hacer algo; **to** ~ **sb out of doing sth** disuadir a uno de algo; **to** ~ **shop** hablar de asuntos profesionales; **to ~ over** vt hablar de; **~ative** a hablador(a).

tall [tɔ:l] a (gen) alto; (tree) grande; **to be 6 feet ~** medir 6 pies, tener 6 pies de alto; **~boy** n cómoda alta; **~ness** n altura; **~ story** n historia inverosímil.

tally ['tælɪ] n cuenta // vi: **to ~ (with)** corresponder (con).

talon ['tælən] n garra.

tambourine [tæmbə'ri:n] n pandereta.

tame [teɪm] a (mild) manso; (tamed) domesticado; (fig: story, style) soso.

tamper ['tæmpə*] vi: **to ~ with** entrometerse en.

tampon ['tæmpɔn] n tampón m.

tan [tæn] n (also: **sun~**) bronceado // vt broncear // vi ponerse moreno // a (colour) marrón.

tandem ['tændəm] n tándem m.

tang [tæŋ] n sabor m fuerte.

tangerine [tændʒə'ri:n] n mandarina.

tangible ['tændʒəbl] a tangible.

tangle ['tæŋgl] n enredo; **to get in(to) a ~** enredarse.

tango ['tæŋgou] n tango.

tank [tæŋk] n (water ~) depósito, tanque m; (for fish) acuario; (MIL) tanque m.

tanker ['tæŋkə*] n (ship) petrolero; (truck) camión m cisterna o tanque.

tanned [tænd] a (skin) moreno, bronceado.

tantalizing ['tæntəlaɪzɪŋ] a tentador(a).

tantamount ['tæntəmaunt] a: **~ to** equivalente a.

tantrum ['tæntrəm] n rabieta.

tap [tæp] n (on sink etc) grifo; (gentle blow) golpecito; (gas ~) llave f // vt dar golpecitos; (resources) utilizar, explotar; **~-dancing** n zapateado.

tape [teɪp] n cinta; (also: **magnetic ~**) cinta magnética; (sticky ~) cinta adhesiva // vt (record) grabar (en cinta); **~ measure** n cinta métrica, metro.

taper ['teɪpə*] n cirio // vi afilarse.

tape recorder ['teɪprɪkɔ:də*] n grabadora.

tapered ['teɪpəd], **tapering** ['teɪpərɪŋ] a afilado.

tapestry ['tæpɪstrɪ] n (object) tapiz m; (art) tapicería.

tapioca [tæpɪ'ɔukə] n tapioca.

tar [tɑ:] n alquitrán m, brea.

tarantula [tə'ræntjulə] n tarántula.

target ['tɑ:gɪt] n (gen) blanco; **~ practice** tiro al blanco.

tariff ['tærɪf] n tarifa.

tarmac ['tɑ:mæk] n (on road) alquitranado; (AVIAT) pista de aterrizaje.

tarnish ['tɑ:nɪʃ] vt quitar el brillo a.

tarpaulin [tɑ:'pɔ:lɪn] n alquitranado.

tarragon ['tærəgən] n estragón m.

tart [tɑ:t] n (CULIN) tarta; (col: pej: woman) fulana // a (flavour) agrio, ácido.

tartan ['tɑ:tn] n tartán m, escocés m // a de tartán.

tartar ['tɑ:tə*] n (on teeth) sarro; **~(e) sauce** n salsa tártara.

task [tɑ:sk] n tarea; **to take to ~** reprender; **~ force** n (MIL, POLICE) destacamento especial.

tassel ['tæsl] n borla.

taste [teɪst] n sabor m, gusto; (also: **after~**) dejo; (sip) sorbo; (fig: glimpse, idea) muestra, idea // vt probar // vi: **to ~ of** or **like** (fish etc) saber a; **you can ~ the garlic (in it)** se nota el sabor a ajo; **can I have a ~ of this wine?** ¿puedo probar el vino?; **to have a ~ for sth** ser aficionado a algo; **in good/bad ~** de buen/mal gusto; **~ful** a de buen gusto; **~fully** ad con buen gusto; **~less** a (food) insípido; (remark) de mal gusto; **tasty** a sabroso, rico.

tattered ['tætəd] a see **tatters**.

tatters ['tætəz] npl: **in ~** (also: **tattered**) hecho jirones.

tattoo [tə'tu:] n tatuaje m; (spectacle) espectáculo militar // vt tatuar.

tatty ['tætɪ] a (col) raído.

taught [tɔ:t] pt, pp of **teach**.

taunt [tɔ:nt] n burla // vt burlarse de.

Taurus ['tɔ:rəs] n Tauro.

taut [tɔ:t] a tirante, tenso.

tawdry ['tɔ:drɪ] a cursi, de mal gusto.

tawny ['tɔ:nɪ] a leonado.

tax [tæks] n impuesto // vt gravar (con un impuesto); (fig: test) abrumar; (: patience) agotar; **direct ~** contribución directa; **~ation** [-'seɪʃən] n impuestos mpl; **~ collector** n recaudador/a m/f; **~-free** a libre de impuestos.

taxi ['tæksɪ] n taxi m // vi (AVIAT) rodar de suelo.

taxidermist ['tæksɪdə:mɪst] n taxidermista m/f.

taxi: ~ driver n taxista m/f; **~ rank, ~ stand** n parada de taxis.

tax: ~ payer n contribuyente m/f; **~ return** n declaración f de ingresos.

TB abbr of **tuberculosis**.

tea [ti:] n té m; (snack) merienda; **high ~** merienda-cena; **~ bag** n bolsa de té; **~ break** n descanso para el té; **~cake** n bollo.

teach [ti:tʃ], pt, pp **taught** vt: **to ~ sb sth, ~ sth to sb** enseñar algo a uno // vi enseñar; (be a teacher) ser profesor/a; **~er** n (in secondary school) profesor/a m/f; (in primary school) maestro/a; **~ing** n enseñanza.

tea: ~ cosy n cubretetera; **~cup** n taza para el té.

teak [ti:k] n (madera de) teca.

tea leaves npl hojas fpl de té.

team [ti:m] n equipo; (of animals) pareja; **~work** n trabajo de equipo.

teapot ['ti:pɔt] n tetera.

tear [tɛə*] n rasgón m, desgarrón m // n [tɪə*] lágrima // (vb: pt **tore**, pp **torn**) vt romper, rasgar // vi rasgarse; **in ~s** llorando; **to burst into ~s** deshacerse en lágrimas; **to ~ along** vi (rush) precipitarse; **~ful** a lloroso; **~ gas** n gas m lacrimógeno.

tearoom ['tiːruːm] n salón m de té, cafetería.

tease [tiːz] n bromista m/f // vt bromear, tomar el pelo a.

tea: ~ **set** n juego de té; ~**spoon** n cucharilla; (also: ~**spoonful:** as measurement) cucharadita.

teat [tiːt] n (of bottle) tetina.

tea: ~**time** n hora del té; ~ **towel** n trapo de cocina.

technical ['tɛknɪkl] a técnico; ~**ity** [-'kælɪtɪ] n detalle m técnico; ~**ly** ad técnicamente.

technician [tɛk'nɪʃn] n técnico.

technique [tɛk'niːk] n técnica.

technological [tɛknə'lɔdʒɪkl] a tecnológico; **technology** [-'nɔlədʒɪ] n tecnología.

teddy (bear) ['tɛdɪ] n osito de felpa.

tedious ['tiːdɪəs] a pesado, aburrido.

tee [tiː] n (GOLF) tee m.

teem [tiːm] vi abundar, pulular; **to** ~ **with** rebosar de; **it is** ~**ing (with rain)** llueve a mares.

teenage ['tiːneɪdʒ] a (fashions etc) de o para los jóvenes; **teenager** n joven m/f (de 13 a 19 años).

teens [tiːnz] npl: **to be in one's** ~ ser un adolescente, no haber cumplido los 20.

tee-shirt ['tiːʃɔːt] n = **T-shirt.**

teeter ['tiːtə*] vi balancearse.

teeth [tiːθ] pl of **tooth.**

teethe [tiːð] vi echar los dientes.

teething ['tiːðɪŋ]: ~ **ring** n mordedor m; ~ **troubles** npl (fig) dificultades fpl iniciales.

teetotal ['tiː'təutl] a (person) abstemio.

telecommunications ['tɛlɪkəmjuːnɪ'keɪʃənz] n telecomunicaciones fpl.

telegram ['tɛlɪgræm] n telegrama m.

telegraph ['tɛlɪgrɑːf] n telégrafo; ~**ic** [-'græfɪk] a telegráfico; ~ **pole** n poste m de telégrafos.

telepathic [tɛlɪ'pæθɪk] a telepático; **telepathy** [tə'lɛpəθɪ] n telepatía.

telephone ['tɛlɪfəun] n teléfono // vt (person) llamar por teléfono; (message) telefonear; ~ **booth,** ~ **box** n cabina telefónica; ~ **call** n llamada (telefónica); ~ **directory** n guía (telefónica); ~ **exchange** n central f telefónica; ~ **number** n número de teléfono; **telephonist** [tə'lɛfənɪst] n telefonista m/f.

telephoto ['tɛlɪ'fəutəu] a: ~ **lens** teleobjetivo.

teleprinter ['tɛlɪprɪntə*] n teletipo.

telescope ['tɛlɪskəup] n telescopio; **telescopic** [-'skɔpɪk] a telescópico.

televise ['tɛlɪvaɪz] vt televisar.

television ['tɛlɪvɪʒən] n televisión f; ~ **set** n televisor m.

telex ['tɛlɛks] n telex m.

tell [tɛl], pt, pp **told** vt decir; (relate: story) contar; (distinguish): **to** ~ **sth from** distinguir algo de // vi (have effect) tener efecto; **to** ~ **sb to do sth** mandar a uno que haga algo; **to** ~ **sb off** reñir o regañar a uno; ~**er** n (in bank) cajero; ~**ing** a (remark, detail) revelador(a); ~**tale** a (sign) indicador(a).

telly ['tɛlɪ] n (col) abbr of **television.**

temerity [tə'mɛrɪtɪ] n temeridad f.

temper ['tɛmpə*] n (nature) carácter m; (mood) humor m; (bad ~) genio, mal genio; (fit of anger) cólera; (of child) rabieta // vt (moderate) moderar; **to be in a** ~ estar de mal humor; **to lose one's** ~ perder la paciencia.

temperament ['tɛmprəmənt] n (nature) temperamento; ~**al** [-'mɛntl] a temperamental.

temperance ['tɛmpərns] n moderación f; (in drinking) sobriedad f.

temperate ['tɛmprət] a moderado; (climate) templado.

temperature ['tɛmprətʃə*] n temperatura; **to have** or **run a** ~ tener fiebre.

tempered ['tɛmpəd] a (steel) templado.

tempest ['tɛmpɪst] n tempestad f.

temple ['tɛmpl] n (building) templo; (ANAT) sien f.

tempo ['tɛmpəu], pl ~**s** or **tempi** [-piː] n tempo; (fig: of life etc) ritmo.

temporal ['tɛmpərl] a temporal.

temporarily ['tɛmpərərɪlɪ] ad temporalmente.

temporary ['tɛmpərərɪ] a provisional, temporal; (passing) transitorio; (worker) temporero.

tempt [tɛmpt] vt tentar; **to** ~ **sb into doing sth** tentar o inducir a uno a hacer algo; ~**ation** [-'teɪʃən] n tentación f; ~**ing** a tentador(a).

ten [tɛn] num diez.

tenable ['tɛnəbl] a sostenible.

tenacious [tə'neɪʃəs] a tenaz; **tenacity** [-'næsɪtɪ] n tenacidad f.

tenancy ['tɛnənsɪ] n alquiler m; (of house) inquilinato; **tenant** n (rent-payer) inquilino; (occupant) habitante m/f.

tend [tɛnd] vt cuidar // vi: **to** ~ **to do sth** tener tendencia a hacer algo.

tendency ['tɛndənsɪ] n tendencia.

tender ['tɛndə*] a tierno, blando; (delicate) delicado; (sore) sensible, dolorido; (affectionate) tierno, cariñoso // n (COMM: offer) oferta; (money): **legal** ~ moneda de curso legal // vt ofrecer; ~**ize** vt (CULIN) ablandar; ~**ness** n ternura; (of meat) blandura.

tendon ['tɛndən] n tendón m.

tenement ['tɛnəmənt] n casa de pisos.

tennis ['tɛnɪs] n tenis m; ~ **ball** n pelota de tenis; ~ **court** n pista de tenis; ~ **racket** n raqueta de tenis.

tenor ['tɛnə*] n (MUS) tenor m.

tenpin bowling ['tɛnpɪn-] n los bolos mpl.

tense [tɛns] a tenso; (stretched) tirante; (stiff) rígido, tieso // n (LING) tiempo; ~**ness** n tensión f.

tension ['tɛnʃən] n tensión f.

tent [tɛnt] *n* tienda (de campaña).
tentacle ['tɛntəkl] *n* tentáculo.
tentative ['tɛntətɪv] *a* experimental; (*conclusion*) provisional.
tenterhooks ['tɛntəhuks] *npl*: **on ~** sobre ascuas.
tenth [tɛnθ] *a* décimo.
tent: ~ peg *n* clavija, estaquilla; **~ pole** *n* mástil *m*.
tenuous ['tɛnjuəs] *a* tenue.
tenure ['tɛnjuə*] *n* posesión *f*, tenencia.
tepid ['tɛpɪd] *a* tibio.
term [tɔ:m] *n* (*limit*) límite *m*; (*COMM*) plazo; (*word*) término; (*period*) período; (*SCOL*) trimestre *m* // *vt* llamar; **~s** *npl* (*conditions*) condiciones *fpl*; (*COMM*) precio, tarifa; **in the short/long ~** a corto/largo plazo; **to be on good ~s with sb** llevarse bien con uno; **to come to ~s with** (*person*) llegar a un acuerdo con; (*problem*) adaptarse a.
terminal ['tɔ:mɪnl] *a* terminal; (*disease*) mortal // *n* (*ELEC*) borne *m*; (*also:* **air ~**) terminal *f*; (*also:* **coach ~**) estación *f* terminal.
terminate ['tɔ:mɪneɪt] *vt* terminar // *vi*: **to ~ in** acabar por; **termination** [-'neɪʃən] *n* terminación *f*; (*of contract*) conclusión *f*.
terminology [tɔ:mɪ'nɔlədʒɪ] *n* terminología.
terminus ['tɔ:mɪnəs], *pl* **-mini** [-mɪnaɪ] *n* término, estación *f* terminal.
termite ['tɔ:maɪt] *n* termita.
terrace ['tɛrəs] *n* terraza; (*row of houses*) hilera de casas adosadas; **the ~s** (*SPORT*) gradas *fpl*; **~d** *a* (*garden*) escalonado; (*house*) adosado.
terrain [tɛ'reɪn] *n* terreno.
terrible ['tɛrɪbl] *a* terrible, horrible; (*fam*) malísimo; **terribly** *ad* terriblemente; (*very badly*) malísimamente.
terrier ['tɛrɪə*] *n* terrier *m*.
terrific [tə'rɪfɪk] *a* fantástico, fenomenal; (*wonderful*) maravilloso.
terrify ['tɛrɪfaɪ] *vt* aterrorizar.
territorial [tɛrɪ'tɔ:rɪəl] *a* territorial.
territory ['tɛrɪtərɪ] *n* territorio.
terror ['tɛrə*] *n* terror *m*; **~ism** *n* terrorismo; **~ist** *n* terrorista *m/f*; **~ize** *vt* aterrorizar.
terse [tɔ:s] *a* (*style*) conciso; (*reply*) brusco.
test [tɛst] *n* (*trial, check*) prueba, ensayo; (: *of goods in factory*) control *m*; (*of courage etc, CHEM*) prueba; (*MED*) examen *m*; (*exam*) examen *m*, test *m*; (*also:* **driving ~**) examen *m* de conducir // *vt* probar, poner a prueba.
testament ['tɛstəmənt] *n* testamento; **the Old/New T~** el Antiguo/Nuevo Testamento.
testicle ['tɛstɪkl] *n* testículo.
testify ['tɛstɪfaɪ] *vi* (*LAW*) prestar declaración; **to ~ to sth** atestiguar algo.
testimonial [tɛstɪ'məunɪəl] *n* (*reference*) recomendación *f*; (*gift*) obsequio.

testimony ['tɛstɪmənɪ] *n* (*LAW*) testimonio, declaración *f*.
test: ~ match *n* (*CRICKET, RUGBY*) partido internacional; **~ pilot** *n* piloto de pruebas; **~ tube** *n* probeta.
testy ['tɛstɪ] *a* irritable.
tetanus ['tɛtənəs] *n* tétano.
tether ['tɛðə*] *vt* atar (con una cuerda) // *n*: **at the end of one's ~** a punto de perder la paciencia.
text [tɛkst] *n* texto; **~book** *n* libro de texto.
textiles ['tɛkstaɪlz] *npl* textiles *mpl*, tejidos *mpl*.
texture ['tɛkstʃə*] *n* textura.
Thai [taɪ] *a*, *n* tailandés/esa *m/f*; **~land** *n* Tailandia.
Thames [tɛmz] *n*: **the ~** el (río) Támesis.
than [ðæn, ðən] *conj* que; (*with numerals*): **more ~ 10/once** más de 10/una vez; **I have more/less ~ you** tengo más/menos que tú.
thank [θæŋk] *vt* dar las gracias a, agradecer; **~ you (very much)** muchas gracias; **~s** *npl* gracias *fpl*; **~s to** *prep* gracias a; **~ful** *a*: **~ful (for)** agradecido por; **~less** *a* ingrato; **Thanksgiving (Day)** *n* día *m* de acción de gracias.
that [ðæt, ðət] *conj* que // *det* ese/esa; (*more remote*) aquel/ aquella // *pron* ése/ésa; aquél/ aquélla; (*neuter*) eso; aquello; (*relative: subject*) que; (: *object*) que, el cual/la cual *etc*; (*with time*): **on the day ~ he came** el día que vino // *ad*: **~ high** tan alto, así de alto; **it's about ~ high** es más o menos así de alto; **~ one** ése/ésa; aquél/aquélla; **what's ~?** ¿qué es eso?; **who's ~?** ¿quién es?; **is ~ you?** ¿eres tú?; (*formal*) ¿es Usted?; **~'s what he said** eso es lo que dijo; **all ~** todo eso; **I can't work ~ much** no puedo trabajar tanto.
thatched [θætʃt] *a* (*roof*) de paja; **~ cottage** casita con tejado de paja.
thaw [θɔ:] *n* deshielo // *vi* (*ice*) derretirse; (*food*) descongelarse // *vt* (*food*) descongelar.
the [ðiː, ðə] *def art* el/la; (*pl*) los/las; (*neuter*) lo; **~ sooner ~ better** cuanto antes mejor.
theatre, theater (*US*) ['θɪətə*] *n* teatro; **~-goer** *n* aficionado al teatro.
theatrical [θɪ'ætrɪkl] *a* teatral.
theft [θɛft] *n* robo.
their [ðɛə*] *a* su; **~s** *pron* (el) suyo/(la) suya *etc*; **a friend of ~s** un amigo suyo.
them [ðɛm, ðəm] *pron* (*direct*) los/las; (*indirect*) les; (*stressed, after prep*) ellos/ellas; **I see ~** los veo; **give ~ the book** dales el libro.
theme [θiːm] *n* tema *m*; **~ song** tema (musical).
themselves [ðəm'sɛlvz] *pl pron* (*subject*) ellos mismos/ellas mismas; (*complement*) se; (*after prep*) sí (mismos/as).
then [ðɛn] *ad* (*at that time*) entonces; (*next*) pues; (*later*) luego, después; (*and also*)

además // conj (therefore) en ese caso, entonces // a: the ~ president el entonces presidente; from ~ on desde entonces.

theological [θɪə'lɔdʒɪkl] a teológico; **theology** [θɪ'ɔlədʒɪ] n teología.

theorem ['θɪərəm] n teorema m.

theoretical [θɪə'rɛtɪkl] a teórico; **theorize** ['θɪəraɪz] vi elaborar una teoría; **theory** ['θɪərɪ] n teoría.

therapeutic(al) [θɛrə'pju:tɪk(l)] a terapéutico.

therapist ['θɛrəpɪst] n terapeuta m/f; **therapy** n terapia.

there [ðɛə*] ad allí, allá, ahí; ~, ~! ¡cálmate!; it's ~ está ahí; ~ is, ~ are hay; ~ he is ahí está; on/in ~ allí encima/dentro; ~abouts ad por ahí; ~after ad después; ~fore ad por lo tanto; ~'s = ~ is; ~ has.

thermal ['θə:ml] a termal.

thermometer [θə'mɔmɪtə*] n termómetro.

Thermos ['θə:məs] n termo.

thermostat ['θə:məustæt] n termostato.

thesaurus [θɪ'sɔ:rəs] n tesoro.

these [ði:z] pl det estos/as // pl pron éstos/as.

thesis ['θi:sɪs], pl -ses [-si:z] n tesis f.

they [ðeɪ] pl pron ellos/ellas; (stressed) ellos (mismos)/ellas (mismas); ~ say that... (it is said that) se dice que...; ~'d = they had; they would; ~'ll = they shall, they will; ~'re = they are; ~'ve = they have.

thick [θɪk] a espeso; (fat) grueso; (dense) denso, espeso; (stupid) torpe // n: in the ~ of the battle en plena batalla; it's 20 cm ~ tiene 20 cm de espesor; ~en vi espesarse // vt (sauce etc) espesar; ~ness n espesor m, grueso; ~set a rechoncho; ~skinned a (fig) insensible.

thief [θi:f], pl **thieves** [θi:vz] n ladrón/ona m/f.

thieving ['θi:vɪŋ] n robo.

thigh [θaɪ] n muslo.

thimble ['θɪmbl] n dedal m.

thin [θɪn] a (gen) delgado; (watery) aguado; (light) tenue; (hair, crowd) escaso; (fog) poco denso // vt: to ~ (down) (sauce, paint) diluir.

thing [θɪŋ] n (gen) cosa; (object) objeto, artículo; (matter) asunto; (mania) manía; ~s npl (belongings) efectos mpl (personales); the best ~ would be to... lo mejor sería...; how are ~s? ¿qué tal?

think [θɪŋk], pt, pp **thought** vi pensar // vt pensar, creer; (imagine) imaginar; what did you ~ of them? ¿qué te parecieron?; to ~ about sth/sb pensar en algo/alguien; I'll ~ about it lo pensaré; to ~ of doing sth pensar en hacer algo; I ~ so/not creo que sí/no; to ~ well of sb tener buen concepto de alguien; to ~ over vt reflexionar sobre, meditar; to ~ up vt imaginar; ~ing a pensante.

thinly ['θɪnlɪ] ad (cut) en lonchas finas; (spread) con una capa fina.

thinness ['θɪnnɪs] n delgadez f.

third [θə:d] a tercer(a) // n tercero; (fraction) tercio; (SCOL: degree) de tercera clase; ~ly ad en tercer lugar; ~ party insurance n seguro contra terceras personas; ~-rate a (de calidad) mediocre; the T~ World n el Tercer Mundo.

thirst [θə:st] n sed f; ~y a (person) sediento; to be ~y tener sed.

thirteen ['θə:'ti:n] num trece.

thirty ['θə:tɪ] num treinta.

this [ðɪs] det este/esta // pron éste/ésta; (neuter) esto; ~ is what he said esto es lo que dijo; ~ high así de alto.

thistle ['θɪsl] n cardo.

thong [θɔŋ] n correa.

thorn [θɔ:n] n espina; ~y a espinoso.

thorough ['θʌrə] a (search) minucioso; (knowledge, research) profundo; ~bred a (horse) de pura sangre; ~fare n calle f; 'no ~fare' "prohibido el paso"; ~ly ad minuciosamente; profundamente, a fondo.

those [ðəuz] pl pron esos/esas; (more remote) aquellos/as // pl det ésos/ésas; aquéllos/as.

though [ðəu] conj aunque // ad sin embargo.

thought [θɔ:t] pt, pp of **think** // n pensamiento; (opinion) opinión f; (intention) intención f; ~ful a pensativo; (considerate) considerado; ~less a desconsiderado.

thousand ['θauzənd] num mil; two ~ dos mil; ~s of miles de; ~th a milésimo.

thrash [θræʃ] vt apalear; (defeat) derrotar; to ~ about vi revolcarse; to ~ out vt discutir largamente.

thread [θrɛd] n hilo; (of screw) rosca // vt (needle) enhebrar; ~bare a raído.

threat [θrɛt] n amenaza; ~en vi amenazar // vt: to ~en sb with sth/to do amenazar a uno con algo/ con hacer.

three [θri:] num tres; ~-dimensional a tridimensional; ~fold ad: to increase ~fold triplicar; ~-piece suit n traje m de tres piezas; ~-piece suite n tresillo; ~-ply a (wool) triple; ~-wheeler n (car) coche m de tres ruedas.

thresh [θrɛʃ] vt (AGR) trillar.

threshold ['θrɛʃhəuld] n umbral m.

threw [θru:] pt of **throw.**

thrift [θrɪft] n economía; ~y a económico.

thrill [θrɪl] n (excitement) emoción f; (shudder) estremecimiento // vt emocionar; estremecer; to be ~ed (with gift etc) estar encantado; ~er n película/novela de suspense.

thrive [θraɪv], pt **thrived** or **throve** [θrəuv], pp **thrived** or **thriven** ['θrɪvn] vi (grow) crecer; (do well) prosperar; **thriving** a próspero.

throat [θrəut] n garganta; to have a sore ~ tener dolor de garganta.

throb [θrɔb] n (of heart) latido; (of engine)

vibración f // vi latir; vibrar; (pain) dar punzadas.

throes [θrɔuz] npl: **in the ~ of** en medio de.

thrombosis [θrɔm'bɔusıs] n trombosis f.

throne [θrɔun] n trono.

throttle ['θrɔtl] n (AUT) acelerador m // vt ahogar.

through [θruː] prep por, a través de; (time) durante; (by means of) por medio de, mediante; (owing to) gracias a // a (ticket, train) directo // ad completamente, de parte a parte; **to put sb ~ to sb** (TEL) poner a alguien (en comunicación) con alguien; **to be ~** (TEL) tener comunicación; (have finished) haber terminado; **"no ~ way"** "calle sin salida"; **~out** prep (place) por todas partes de, por todo; (time) durante todo, en todo // ad por o en todas partes.

throw [θrɔu] n tirada, tiro; (SPORT) lanzamiento // vt, pt **threw**, pp **thrown** tirar, echar; (SPORT) lanzar; (rider) derribar; (fig) desconcertar; **to ~ a party** dar una fiesta; **to ~ away** vt tirar; **to ~ off** vt deshacerse de; **to ~ out** vt tirar; **to ~ up** vi vomitar; **~away** a para tirar, desechable; **~-in** n (SPORT) saque m.

thru [θruː] (US) = **through.**

thrush [θrʌʃ] n zorzal m, tordo.

thrust [θrʌst] n (TECH) empuje m // vt, pt, pp **thrust** empujar; (push in) introducir.

thud [θʌd] n golpe m sordo.

thug [θʌg] n (criminal) criminal m/f; (pej) bruto.

thumb [θʌm] n (ANAT) pulgar m, dedo gordo (col) // vt (book) hojear; **to ~ a lift** hacer dedo o autostop; **~tack** n (US) chinche m.

thump [θʌmp] n golpe m; (sound) porrazo // vt, vi golpear.

thunder ['θʌndə*] n (gen) trueno; (sudden noise) tronido; (of applause etc) estruendo // vi tronar; (train etc): **to ~ past** pasar como un trueno; **~bolt** n rayo; **~clap** n trueno; **~storm** n tormenta; **~struck** a pasmado; **~y** a tormentoso.

Thursday ['θɔːzdı] n jueves m.

thus [ðʌs] ad así, de este modo.

thwart [θwɔːt] vt frustrar.

thyme [taım] n tomillo.

thyroid ['θaırɔıd] n tiroides m.

tiara [tı'ɑːrə] n tiara, diadema.

tic [tık] n tic m.

tick [tık] n (sound: of clock) tictac m; (mark) palomita; (ZOOL) garrapata; (col): **in a ~** en un instante // vi hacer tictac // vt marcar; **to ~ off** vt marcar; (person) poner como un trapo.

ticket ['tıkıt] n billete m, tíquet m; (for cinema) entrada; (in shop: on goods) etiqueta; (for library) tarjeta; **~ collector** n revisor m; **~ office** n taquilla.

tickle ['tıkl] n cosquillas fpl // vt hacer cosquillas a; **ticklish** a que tiene cosquillas.

tidal ['taıdl] a de marea; **~ wave** n maremoto.

tiddlywinks ['tıdlıwıŋks] n juego de la pulga.

tide [taıd] n marea; (fig: of events) curso, marcha.

tidiness ['taıdınıs] n (good order) buen orden m; (neatness) limpieza, aseo.

tidy ['taıdı] a (room) ordenado; (dress, work) limpio; (person) (bien) arreglado // vt (also: **~ up**) poner en orden.

tie [taı] n (string etc) atadura; (also: **neck~**) corbata; (fig: link) vínculo, lazo; (SPORT: draw) empate m // vt (gen) atar // vi (SPORT) empatar; **to ~ in a bow** hacer un lazo; **to ~ a knot in sth** hacer un nudo a algo; **to ~ down** vt atar; (fig): **~ sb down** to obligar a uno a; **to ~ up** vt (parcel) envolver; (dog) atar; (boat) amarrar; (arrangements) concluir, despachar; **to be ~d up** (busy) estar ocupado.

tier [tıə*] n grada; (of cake) piso.

tiger ['taıgə*] n tigre m/f.

tight [taıt] a (rope) tirante; (money) escaso; (clothes) ajustado; (budget, programme) apretado; (col: drunk) borracho // ad (squeeze) muy fuerte; (shut) herméticamente; **~s** npl pantimedias fpl; (for gym) malla sg; **~en** vt (rope) estirar; (screw) apretar // vi apretarse, estirarse; **~-fisted** a tacaño; **~ly** ad (grasp) muy fuerte; **~-rope** n cuerda floja.

tile [taıl] n (on roof) teja; (on floor) baldosa; (on wall) azulejo, baldosín m; **~d** a embaldosado.

till [tıl] n caja (registradora) // vt (land) cultivar // prep, conj = **until.**

tiller ['tılə*] n (NAUT) caña del timón.

tilt [tılt] vt inclinar // vi inclinarse.

timber ['tımbə*] n (material) madera; (trees) árboles mpl.

time [taım] n tiempo; (epoch: often pl) época; (by clock) hora; (moment) momento; (occasion) vez f; (MUS) compás m // vt (gen) calcular o medir el tiempo de; (race) cronometrar; (remark etc) elegir el momento para; **a long ~** mucho tiempo; **for the ~ being** de momento, por ahora; **from ~ to ~** de vez en cuando; **in ~** (soon enough) a tiempo; (after some time) con el tiempo; (MUS) al compás; **in a week's ~** dentro de una semana; **on ~** a la hora; **5 ~s 5** 5 por 5; **what ~ is it?** ¿qué hora es?; **to have a good ~** pasarlo bien, divertirse; **~ bomb** n bomba de efecto retardado; **~keeper** n (SPORT) cronómetro; **~less** a eterno; **~ limit** n (gen) limitación f de tiempo; (COMM) plazo; **~ly** a oportuno; **~ off** n tiempo libre; **timer** n (in kitchen) reloj m programador; **~ switch** n interruptor m; **~table** n horario; **~ zone** n huso horario.

timid ['tımıd] a tímido.

timing ['taımıŋ] n (SPORT) cronometraje

m; (gen) elección f del momento; the ~ of his resignation el momento que eligió para dimitir.
timpani ['tɪmpənɪ] npl tímpanos mpl.
tin [tɪn] n estaño; (also: ~ plate) hojalata; (can) lata; ~ foil n papel m de estaño.
tinge [tɪndʒ] n matiz m // vt: ~d with teñido de.
tingle ['tɪŋgl] n picotazo // vi sentir picazón.
tinker ['tɪŋkə*] n calderero; (gipsy) gitano; to ~ with vt manosear.
tinkle ['tɪŋkl] vi tintinear // n (col): to give sb a ~ dar un telefonazo a alguien.
tinned [tɪnd] a (food) en lata, en conserva.
tin opener ['tɪnəupnə*] n abrelatas m inv.
tinsel ['tɪnsl] n oropel m.
tint [tɪnt] n matiz m; (for hair) tinte m.
tiny ['taɪnɪ] a minúsculo, pequeñito.
tip [tɪp] n (end) punta; (gratuity) propina; (for rubbish) basurero; (advice) aviso // vt (waiter) dar una propina a; (tilt) inclinar; (overturn: also: ~ over) dar la vuelta a, volcar; (empty: also: ~ out) vaciar, echar; ~-off n (hint) aviso, advertencia; ~ped a (cigarette) con filtro.
tipsy ['tɪpsɪ] a algo borracho, mareado.
tiptoe ['tɪptəu] n: on ~ de puntillas.
tiptop ['tɪp'tɔp] a: in ~ condition en perfectas condiciones.
tire ['taɪə*] n (US) = tyre // vt cansar // vi (gen) cansarse; (become bored) aburrirse; ~d a cansado; to be ~d of sth estar cansado o harto de algo; tiredness n cansancio; ~less a incansable; ~some a aburrido; tiring a cansado.
tissue ['tɪʃu:] n tejido; (paper handkerchief) pañuelo de papel, kleenex m; ~ paper n papel m de seda.
tit [tɪt] n (bird) herrerillo común; to give ~ for tat dar ojo por ojo.
titbit ['tɪtbɪt] n (food) golosina; (news) suceso.
titillate ['tɪtɪleɪt] vt estimular, excitar.
titivate ['tɪtɪveɪt] vt emperejillar.
title ['taɪtl] n título; ~ deed n (LAW) título de propiedad; ~ role n papel m principal.
titter ['tɪtə*] vi reírse entre dientes.
titular ['tɪtjulə*] a (in name only) nominal.
to [tu:, tə] prep a; (towards) hacia; (of time) a, hasta; (of) de; give it ~ me dámelo; the key ~ the front door la llave de la puerta; the main thing is ~... lo importante es...; to go ~ France/school ir a Francia/al colegio; a quarter ~ 5 las 5 menos cuarto; pull/push the door ~ tirar/empujar la puerta; to go ~ and fro ir y venir.
toad [təud] n sapo; ~stool n hongo venenoso.
toast [təust] n (CULIN. also: piece of ~) tostada; (drink, speech) brindis m // vt (CULIN) tostar; (drink to) brindar; ~er n tostador m.
tobacco [tə'bækəu] n tabaco; ~nist n estanquero; ~nist's (shop) n estanco.
toboggan [tə'bɔgən] n tobogán m.

today [tə'deɪ] ad, n (also fig) hoy m.
toddler ['tɔdlə*] n niño que empieza a andar.
toddy ['tɔdɪ] n ponche m.
toe [təu] n dedo (del pie); (of shoe) punta; to ~ the line (fig) obedecer, conformarse; ~nail n uña del pie.
toffee ['tɔfɪ] n caramelo; ~ apple n pirulí m.
toga ['təugə] n toga.
together [tə'gɛðə*] ad juntos; (at same time) al mismo tiempo, a la vez; ~ with prep junto con; ~ness n compañerismo.
toil [tɔɪl] n trabajo duro, labor f // vi esforzarse.
toilet ['tɔɪlət] n (lavatory) servicios mpl, wáter m // cpd (bag, soap etc) de aseo; ~ bowl n palangana; ~ paper n papel m higiénico; ~ries npl artículos mpl de aseo; (make-up etc) artículos mpl de tocador; ~ roll n rollo de papel higiénico; ~ water n agua de tocador.
token ['təukən] n (sign) señal f, muestra; (souvenir) recuerdo; (voucher) cupón m; book/record ~ vale m para comprar libros/discos.
told [təuld] pt, pp of tell.
tolerable ['tɔlərəbl] a (bearable) soportable; (fairly good) pasable.
tolerance ['tɔləns] n (also: TECH) tolerancia; tolerant a: tolerant of tolerante con.
tolerate ['tɔləreɪt] vt tolerar; toleration [-'reɪʃən] n tolerancia.
toll [təul] n (of casualties) número de víctimas; (tax, charge) peaje m // vi (bell) doblar; ~bridge n puente m de peaje.
tomato [tə'mɑ:təu], pl ~es n tomate m.
tomb [tu:m] n tumba.
tombola [tɔm'bəulə] n tómbola.
tomboy ['tɔmbɔɪ] n marimacho.
tombstone ['tu:mstəun] n lápida.
tomcat ['tɔmkæt] n gato.
tomorrow [tə'mɔrəu] ad, n (also fig) mañana; the day after ~ pasado mañana; ~ morning mañana por la mañana.
ton [tʌn] n tonelada; ~s of (col) montones mpl de.
tone [təun] n tono // vi armonizar; to ~ down vt (colour, criticism) suavizar; (sound) bajar; (MUS) entonar; to ~ up vt (muscles) tonificar; ~-deaf a que no tiene oído.
tongs [tɔŋz] npl (for coal) tenazas fpl; (for hair) tenacillas fpl.
tongue [tʌŋ] n lengua; ~ in cheek ad irónicamente; ~-tied a (fig) mudo; ~-twister n trabalenguas m inv.
tonic ['tɔnɪk] n (MED) tónico; (MUS) tónica; (also: ~ water) (agua) tónica.
tonight [tə'naɪt] ad, n esta noche.
tonnage ['tʌnɪdʒ] n (NAUT) tonelaje m.
tonsil ['tɔnsl] n amígdala, anginas fpl (col); ~litis [-'laɪtɪs] n amigdalitis f, (inflamación f de las) anginas.

too [tu:] ad (*excessively*) demasiado; (*very*) muy; (*also*) también; ~ **much** ad demasiado; ~ **many** det demasiados/as.

took [tuk] pt of **take.**

tool [tu:l] n herramienta; ~ **box** n caja de herramientas.

toot [tu:t] n (*of horn*) bocinazo; (*of whistle*) silbido // vi (*with car-horn*) tocar la bocina.

tooth [tu:θ], pl **teeth** n (ANAT, TECH) diente m; (*molar*) muela; ~**ache** n dolor m de muelas; ~**brush** n cepillo de dientes; ~**paste** n pasta de dientes; ~**pick** n palillo.

top [tɔp] n (*of mountain*) cumbre f, cima; (*of head*) coronilla; (*of ladder*) lo alto; (*of cupboard, table*) superficie f; (*lid: of box, jar*) tapa, tapadera; (: *of bottle*) tapón m; (*of list etc*) cabeza; (*toy*) peonza // a más alto; (*in rank*) principal, primero; (*best*) mejor // vt (*exceed*) exceder; (*be first in*) ir a la cabeza de; **on** ~ **of** sobre, encima de; **from** ~ **to toe** de pies a cabeza; **to** ~ **up** vt llenar; ~**coat** n sobretodo; ~ **hat** n sombrero de copa; ~-**heavy** a (*object*) desequilibrado.

topic ['tɔpɪk] n tema m, tópico; ~**al** a actual.

top: ~**less** a (*bather etc*) con el pecho al descubierto, topless; ~-**level** a (*talks*) al más alto nivel; ~**most** a más alto.

topple ['tɔpl] vt volcar, derribar // vi caerse.

topsy-turvy ['tɔpsi'tə:vi] a, ad patas arriba.

torch [tɔ:tʃ] n antorcha; (*electric*) linterna.

tore [tɔ:*] pt of **tear.**

torment ['tɔ:mɛnt] n tormento // vt [tɔ:'mɛnt] atormentar; (*fig: annoy*) fastidiar.

torn [tɔ:n] pp of **tear.**

tornado [tɔ:'neɪdəu], pl ~**es** n tornado.

torpedo [tɔ:'pi:dəu], pl ~**es** n torpedo.

torrent ['tɔrnt] n torrente m; ~**ial** [-'rɛnʃl] a torrencial.

torso ['tɔ:səu] n torso.

tortoise ['tɔ:təs] n tortuga; ~**shell** ['tɔ:təʃɛl] a de carey.

tortuous ['tɔ:tjuəs] a tortuoso.

torture ['tɔ:tʃə*] n tortura // vt torturar; (*fig*) atormentar.

Tory ['tɔ:ri] a, n conservador/a m/f.

toss [tɔs] vt tirar, echar; (*head*) sacudir (la cabeza); **to** ~ **a coin** echar a cara o cruz; **to** ~ **up for sth** jugar a cara o cruz algo; **to** ~ **and turn in bed** dar vueltas en la cama.

tot [tɔt] n (*drink*) copita; (*child*) nene/a m/f.

total ['təutl] a total, entero // n total m, suma // vt (*add up*) sumar; (*amount to*) ascender a.

totalitarian [təutælɪ'tɛərɪən] a totalitario.

totem pole ['təutəm-] n poste m totémico.

totter ['tɔtə*] vi tambalearse.

touch [tʌtʃ] n (*gen*) tacto; (*contact*) contacto; (FOOTBALL) fuera de juego // vt (*gen*) tocar; (*emotionally*) conmover; **a** ~ **of** (*fig*) una pizca o un poquito de; **to get** **in** ~ **with sb** ponerse en contacto con uno; **to lose** ~ (*friends*) perder contacto; **to** ~ **on** vt fus (*topic*) aludir (brevemente) a; **to** ~ **up** vt (*paint*) retocar; ~-**and-go** a arriesgado; ~**down** n aterrizaje m; (*on sea*) amerizaje m; ~**ed** a conmovido; (*col*) chiflado; ~**ing** a conmovedor(a); ~**line** n (SPORT) línea de banda; ~**y** a (*person*) susceptible.

tough [tʌf] a (*gen*) duro; (*difficult*) difícil; (*resistant*) resistente; (*person*) fuerte; (: *pej*) bruto // n (*gangster etc*) gorila m; ~**en** vt endurecer; ~**ness** n dureza; dificultad f; resistencia; fuerza.

toupee ['tu:peɪ] n peluca.

tour ['tuə*] n viaje m, vuelta; (*also: package* ~) viaje m organizado; (*of town, museum*) visita // vt viajar por; ~**ing** n viajes mpl turísticos, turismo.

tourism ['tuərɪzm] n turismo.

tourist ['tuərɪst] n turista m/f // cpd turístico; ~ **office** n oficina de turismo.

tournament ['tuənəmənt] n torneo.

tousled ['tauzld] a (*hair*) despeinado.

tout [taut] vi: **to** ~ **for** solicitar clientes para // n: **ticket** ~ revendedor/a m/f.

tow [təu] vt remolcar; **'on** ~' (AUT) "a remolque".

toward(s) [tə'wɔ:d(z)] prep hacia; (*of attitude*) respecto a, con; (*of purpose*) para.

towel ['tauəl] n toalla; ~**ling** n (*fabric*) felpa; ~ **rail** n toallero.

tower ['tauə*] n torre f; ~ **block** n rascacielos m inv; ~**ing** a muy alto, imponente.

town [taun] n ciudad f; **to go to** ~ ir a la ciudad; (*fig*) hacer con entusiasmo; ~ **clerk** n secretario del Ayuntamiento; ~ **council** n consejo municipal; ~ **hall** n ayuntamiento; ~ **planning** n urbanismo.

towrope ['təurəup] n cable m de remolque.

toxic ['tɔksɪk] a tóxico.

toy [tɔɪ] n juguete m; **to** ~ **with** vt fus jugar con; (*idea*) acariciar; ~**shop** n juguetería.

trace [treɪs] n rastro // vt (*draw*) trazar, delinear; (*follow*) seguir la pista de; (*locate*) encontrar.

track [træk] n (*mark*) huella, pista; (*path: gen*) camino, senda; (: *of bullet etc*) trayectoria; (: *of suspect, animal*) pista, rastro; (RAIL) vía; (*on tape, SPORT*) pista // vt seguir la pista de; **to keep** ~ **of** mantenerse al tanto de, seguir; **to** ~ **down** vt (*prey*) averiguar el paradero de; (*sth lost*) buscar y encontrar; ~ **suit** n chandal m.

tract [trækt] n (GEO) región f; (*pamphlet*) folleto.

tractor ['træktə*] n tractor m.

trade [treɪd] n comercio, negocio; (*skill, job*) oficio, empleo // vi negociar, comerciar; **to** ~ **in** vt (*old car etc*) ofrecer como parte del pago; ~-**in price** n valor m de un objeto usado que se descuenta del precio de otro nuevo; ~**mark** n marca de fábrica; ~ **name** n marca registrada;

trader n comerciante m/f; **tradesman** n (*shopkeeper*) tendero; ~ **union** n sindicato; ~ **unionism** n sindicalismo; **trading** n comercio; **trading estate** n zona comercial.

tradition [trə'dıʃən] n tradición f; ~**al** a tradicional.

traffic ['træfık] n (*gen*, AUT) tráfico, circulación f; (*air* ~ *etc*) tránsito // vi: **to** ~ **in** (*pej: liquor, drugs*) traficar en; ~ **circle** n (US) cruce m giratorio; ~ **jam** n embotellamiento; ~ **lights** npl semáforo sg; ~ **warden** n guardia m/f de tráfico.

tragedy ['trædʒədı] n tragedia.

tragic ['trædʒık] a trágico.

trail [treıl] n (*tracks*) rastro, pista; (*path*) camino, sendero; (*wake*) estela // vt (*drag*) arrastrar; (*follow*) seguir la pista de; (*follow closely*) vigilar // vi arrastrarse; **to** ~ **behind** vi quedar a la zaga; ~**er** n (AUT) remolque m; (US) caravana; (CINEMA) trailer m, ávance m.

train [treın] n tren m; (*of dress*) cola; (*series*) serie f; (*followers*) séquito // vt (*educate*) formar; (*teach skills to*) adiestrar; (*sportsman*) entrenar; (*dog*) amaestrar; (*point: gun etc*): **to** ~ **on** apuntar a // vi (SPORT) entrenarse; (*be educated*) recibir una formación; ~**ed** a (*worker*) cualificado, adiestrado; (*teacher*) diplomado; (*animal*) amaestrado; ~**ee** [treı'niː] n persona que está aprendiendo; (*in trade*) aprendiz a m/f; ~**er** n (SPORT) entrenador/a m/f; (*of animals*) domador/a m/f; ~**ing** n formación f; adiestramiento; entrenamiento; **in** ~**ing** (SPORT) en forma; ~**ing college** n (*for teachers*) escuela normal; (*gen*) colegio de formación profesional.

traipse [treıps] vi andar con desgana.

trait [treıt] n rasgo.

traitor ['treıtə*] n traidor/a m/f.

tram [træm] n (*also*: ~**car**) tranvía m.

tramp [træmp] n (*person*) vagabundo // vi andar con pasos pesados.

trample ['træmpl] vt: **to** ~ (**underfoot**) pisotear.

trampoline ['træmpəliːn] n trampolín m.

trance [trɑːns] n trance m; (MED) catalepsia.

tranquil ['træŋkwıl] a tranquilo; ~**lity** n tranquilidad f; ~**lizer** n (MED) tranquilizante m.

transact [træn'zækt] vt (*business*) tramitar; ~**ion** [-'zækʃən] n transacción f, negocio.

transatlantic ['trænzət'læntık] a transatlántico.

transcend [træn'send] vt trascender.

transcript ['trænskrıpt] n copia; ~**ion** [-'skrıpʃən] n transcripción f.

transept ['trænsept] n crucero.

transfer ['trænsfə*] n (*gen*) transferencia; (SPORT) traspaso; (*picture, design*) calcomanía // vt [træns'fə:*] trasladar, pasar; **to** ~ **the charges** (TEL) llamar a cobro revertido; ~**able** [-'fɔːrəbl] a trans-

ferible; '**not** ~**able**' "intransferible".

transform [træns'fɔːm] vt transformar; ~**ation** [-'meıʃən] n transformación f; ~**er** n (ELEC) transformador m.

transfusion [træns'fjuːʒən] n transfusión f.

transient ['trænzıənt] a transitorio.

transistor [træn'zıstə*] n (ELEC) transistor m; ~ **radio** n radio f a transistores.

transit ['trænzıt] n: **in** ~ de tránsito, de paso.

transition [træn'zıʃən] n transición f; ~**al** a transitorio.

transitive ['trænzıtıv] a (LING) transitivo.

transitory ['trænzıtərı] a transitorio.

translate [trænz'leıt] vt traducir; **translation** [-'leıʃən] n traducción f; **translator** n traductor/a m/f.

transmission [trænz'mıʃən] n transmisión f.

transmit [trænz'mıt] vt transmitir; ~**ter** n transmisor m; (*station*) emisora.

transparency [træns'pɛərnsı] n (PHOT) diapositiva.

transparent [træns'pærnt] a transparente.

transplant [træns'plɑːnt] vt transplantar // n ['trænsplɑːnt] (MED) transplante m.

transport ['trænspɔːt] n (*gen*) transporte m; (*also*: **road/rail** ~) transportes mpl // vt [-'pɔːt] transportar; (*carry*) acarrear; ~**ation** [-'teıʃən] n transporte m; ~ **café** n cafetería de carretera.

transverse ['trænzvɔːs] a transversal.

transvestite [trænz'vestaıt] n travesti m/f.

trap [træp] n (*snare, trick*) trampa; (*carriage*) cabriolé m // vt coger en una trampa; (*immobilize*) bloquear; (*jam*) atascar; ~ **door** n escotilla.

trapeze [trə'piːz] n trapecio.

trappings ['træpıŋz] npl adornos mpl.

trash [træʃ] n (*pej: goods*) pacotilla; (: *nonsense*) basura; ~ **can** n (US) cubo de la basura.

trauma ['trɔːmə] n trauma m; ~**tic** [-'mætık] a traumático.

travel ['trævl] n viaje m // vi viajar // vt (*distance*) recorrer; ~ **agency** n agencia de viajes; ~**ler**, ~**er** (US) n viajero/a; ~**ler's cheque** n cheque m de viajero; ~**ling**, ~**ing** (US) n los viajes mpl, el viajar; ~ **sickness** n mareo.

traverse ['trævəs] vt atravesar, cruzar.

travesty ['trævəstı] n parodia.

trawler ['trɔːlə*] n barco rastreador o de rastra.

tray [treı] n (*for carrying*) bandeja; (*on desk*) cajón m.

treacherous ['tretʃərəs] a traidor(a); **treachery** n traición f.

treacle ['triːkl] n melaza.

tread [tred] n (*step*) paso, pisada; (*sound*) ruido de pasos; (*of tyre*) banda de rodadura // vi, pt **trod**, pp **trodden** pisar; **to** ~ **on** vt fus pisar sobre.

treason ['triːzn] n traición f.

treasure ['trɛʒɔ*] n tesoro // vt (value) apreciar, valorar; ~ **hunt** n caza del tesoro.

treasurer ['trɛʒɔrɔ*] n tesorero.

treasury ['trɛʒɔrı] n: **the T**~ (POL) el Ministerio de Hacienda.

treat [tri:t] n (present) regalo; (pleasure) placer m // vt tratar; **to** ~ **sb to sth** invitar a uno a algo.

treatise ['tri:tız] n tratado.

treatment ['tri:tmənt] n tratamiento.

treaty ['tri:tı] n tratado.

treble ['trɛbl] a triple // n (MUS) triple m // vt triplicar // vi triplicarse.

tree [tri:] n árbol m; ~ **trunk** n tronco de árbol.

trek [trɛk] n (long journey) viaje m largo y peligroso; (tiring walk) caminata; (as holiday) excursión f.

trellis ['trɛlıs] n enrejado.

tremble ['trɛmbl] vi temblar; **trembling** n temblor m // a tembloroso.

tremendous [trı'mɛndəs] a tremendo; (enormous) enorme; (excellent) estupendo.

tremor ['trɛmə*] n temblor m; (also: **earth** ~) temblor m de tierra.

trench [trɛntʃ] n trinchera.

trend [trɛnd] n (tendency) tendencia; (of events) curso; (fashion) moda; ~**y** a (idea) según las tendencias actuales; (clothes) a la última moda.

trepidation [trɛpı'deıʃən] n agitación f; (fear) ansia.

trespass ['trɛspəs] vi: **to** ~ **on** entrar sin permiso en; **"no** ~**ing"** "prohibido el paso".

tress [trɛs] n trenza.

trestle ['trɛsl] n caballete m; ~ **table** n mesa de caballete.

trial ['traıəl] n (LAW) juicio, proceso; (test: of machine etc) prueba; (hardship) desgracia; **by** ~ **and error** por tanteo.

triangle ['traıæŋgl] n (MATH, MUS) triángulo; **triangular** [-'æŋgjulə*] a triangular.

tribal ['traıbəl] a tribal.

tribe [traıb] n tribu f; **tribesman** n miembro de una tribu.

tribulation [trıbju'leıʃən] n tribulación f, sufrimiento.

tribunal [traı'bju:nl] n tribunal m.

tributary ['trıbju:tərı] n (river) afluente m.

tribute ['trıbju:t] n homenaje m; (payment) tributo; **to pay** ~ **to** rendir homenaje a.

trice [traıs] n: **in a** ~ en un santiamén.

trick [trık] n trampa; (deceit) truco; (joke) broma; (CARDS) baza // vt engañar; **to play a** ~ **on sb** gastar una broma a uno; ~**ery** n astucia.

trickle ['trıkl] n (of water etc) hililillo // vi gotear.

tricky ['trıkı] a difícil, delicado.

tricycle ['traısıkl] n triciclo.

trifle ['traıfl] n bagatela; (CULIN) dulce m de bizcocho, fruta y natillas // ad: **a** ~ **long** un poquito largo; **trifling** a insignificante.

trigger ['trıgə*] n (of gun) gatillo; **to** ~ **off** vt desencadenar.

trigonometry [trıgə'nɔmətrı] n trigonometría.

trill [trıl] n (of bird) trino.

trim [trım] a (elegant) aseado; (house, garden) en buen estado; (figure) con buen tipo // n (haircut etc) recorte m; (on car) tapicería // vt arreglar; (cut) recortar; (decorate) adornar; (NAUT: a sail) orientar; ~**mings** npl decoraciones fpl; (cuttings) recortes mpl.

Trinity ['trınıtı] n: **the** ~ la Trinidad.

trinket ['trınkıt] n chuchería; (piece of jewellery) baratija.

trio ['tri:əu] n trío.

trip [trıp] n viaje m; (excursion) excursión f; (stumble) traspié m // vi (also: ~ **up**) tropezar; (go lightly) andar a paso ligero // vt poner la zancadilla a.

tripe [traıp] n (CULIN) callos mpl; (pej: rubbish) bobadas fpl.

triple ['trıpl] a triple.

triplets ['trıplıts] npl trillizos/as m/fpl.

triplicate ['trıplıkət] n: **in** ~ por triplicado.

tripod ['traıpɔd] n trípode m.

trite [traıt] a gastado, trillado.

triumph ['traıʌmf] n triunfo // vi: **to** ~ **(over)** vencer; ~**ant** [-'ʌmfənt] a triunfante.

trivia ['trıvıə] npl trivialidades fpl.

trivial ['trıvıəl] a insignificante; (commonplace) trivial; ~**ity** [-'ælıtı] n trivialidad f.

trod [trɔd], **trodden** ['trɔdn] pt, pp of **tread**.

trolley ['trɔlı] n carrito; ~ **bus** n trolebús m.

trombone [trɔm'bəun] n trombón m.

troop [tru:p] n grupo, banda; ~**s** npl (MIL) tropas fpl; **to** ~ **in/out** vi entrar/salir en grupo; ~**er** n (MIL) soldado de caballería.

trophy ['trəufı] n trofeo.

tropic ['trɔpık] n trópico; ~**al** a tropical.

trot [trɔt] n trote m // vi trotar; **on the** ~ (fig: col) de corrido.

trouble ['trʌbl] n problema m, dificultad f; (worry) preocupación f; (bother, effort) molestia, esfuerzo; (unrest) inquietud f; (MED): **stomach** ~ problemas mpl gástricos // vt molestar; (worry) preocupar, inquietar // vi: **to** ~ **to do sth** molestarse en hacer algo; ~**s** npl (POL etc) conflictos mpl; **to be in** ~ estar en un apuro; **to go to the** ~ **of doing sth** tomarse la molestia de hacer algo; **what's the** ~? ¿qué pasa?; ~**d** a (person) preocupado; (epoch, life) agitado; ~**maker** n elemento perturbador; (child) niño alborotado; ~**shooter** n (in conflict) conciliador m; ~**some** a molesto, inoportuno.

trough [trɔf] n (also: **drinking** ~)

abrevadero; (*also:* **feeding** ~) comedero; (*channel*) canal *m*.

troupe [tru:p] *n* grupo.

trousers ['trauzəz] *npl* pantalones *mpl*.

trousseau ['tru:səu], *pl* ~**x** *or* ~**s** [-z] *n* ajuar *m*.

trout [traut] *n, pl inv* trucha.

trowel ['trauəl] *n* paleta.

truant ['truənt] *n*: **to play** ~ hacer novillos.

truce [tru:s] *n* tregua.

truck [trʌk] *n* camión *m*; (*RAIL*) vagón *m*; ~ **driver** *n* camionero; ~ **farm** *n* (*US*) huerto de hortalizas.

truculent ['trʌkjulənt] *a* agresivo.

trudge [trʌdʒ] *vi* andar con dificultad *o* pesadamente.

true [tru:] *a* verdadero; (*accurate*) exacto; (*genuine*) auténtico; (*faithful*) fiel.

truffle ['trʌfl] *n* trufa.

truly ['tru:lı] *ad* auténticamente; (*truthfully*) verdaderamente; (*faithfully*) fielmente; **yours** ~ (*in letter*) (le saluda) atentamente.

trump [trʌmp] *n* triunfo; ~**ed-up** *a* inventado.

trumpet ['trʌmpıt] *n* trompeta.

truncheon ['trʌntʃən] *n* porra.

trundle ['trʌndl] *vt, vi*: **to** ~ **along** rodar haciendo ruido.

trunk [trʌŋk] *n* (*of tree, person*) tronco; (*of elephant*) trompa; (*case*) baúl *m*; ~**s** *npl* (*also:* **swimming** ~**s**) bañador *m*; ~ **call** *n* (*TEL*) llamada interurbana.

truss [trʌs] *n* (*MED*) braguero; **to** ~ (**up**) *vt* atar.

trust [trʌst] *n* confianza *f*; (*COMM*) trust *m*, cartel *m*; (*obligation*) responsabilidad *f*; (*LAW*) fideicomiso // *vt* (*rely on*) tener confianza en; (*entrust*): **to** ~ **sth to sb** confiar algo a uno; ~**ed** *a* de confianza; ~**ee** [trʌs'ti:] *n* (*LAW*) depositario, fideicomisario; (*of school etc*) administrador/a *m/f*; ~**ful**, ~**ing** *a* confiado; ~**worthy** *a* digno de confianza; ~**y** *a* fiel.

truth [tru:θ], *pl* ~**s** [tru:ðz] *n* verdad *f*; ~**ful** *a* (*person*) que dice la verdad; ~**fully** *ad* sinceramente; ~**fulness** *n* veracidad *f*.

try [traı] *n* tentativa, intento; (*RUGBY*) ensayo // *vt* (*LAW*) juzgar, procesar; (*test: sth new*) probar, someter a prueba; (*attempt*) intentar; (*strain*) hacer sufrir // *vi* probar; **to** ~ **to do sth** intentar hacer algo; **to** ~ **on** *vt* (*clothes*) probarse; **to** ~ **out** *vt* probar, poner a prueba; ~**ing** *a* penoso, cansado.

tsar [zɑ:*] *n* zar *m*.

T-shirt ['ti:ʃə:t] *n* camiseta.

tub [tʌb] *n* cubo; (*bath*) tina, bañera.

tuba ['tju:bə] *n* tuba.

tubby ['tʌbı] *a* regordete.

tube [tju:b] *n* tubo; (*underground*) metro; (*for tyre*) cámara de aire; ~**less** *a* sin cámara.

tuberculosis [tjubə:kju'ləusıs] *n* tuberculosis *f*.

tube station *n* estación *f* de metro.

tubing ['tju:bıŋ] *n* tubería; **a piece of** ~ un trozo de tubo.

tubular ['tju:bjulə*] *a* tubular; (*furniture*) de tubo.

TUC *n abbr of* **Trades Union Congress.**

tuck [tʌk] *n* (*SEWING*) pliegue *m* // *vt* (*put*) poner; **to** ~ **away** *vt* esconder; **to** ~ **in** *vt* meter; (*child*) arropar // *vi* (*eat*) comer con mucho apetito; **to** ~ **up** *vt* (*child*) arropar; ~ **shop** *n* tienda de golosinas.

Tuesday ['tju:zdı] *n* martes *m*.

tuft [tʌft] *n* mechón *m*; (*of grass etc*) manojo.

tug [tʌg] *n* (*ship*) remolcador *m* // *vt* remolcar; ~**-of-war** *n* lucha de la cuerda.

tuition [tju:'ıʃən] *n* enseñanza; (*private* ~) clases *fpl* particulares.

tulip ['tju:lıp] *n* tulipán *m*.

tumble ['tʌmbl] *n* (*fall*) caída // *vi* caerse, tropezar // *vt* tirar; ~**down** *a* destartalado; ~ **dryer** *n* secador *m* de ropa automático.

tumbler ['tʌmblə*] *n* vaso.

tummy ['tʌmı] *n* (*col: belly*) barriga; (: *stomach*) vientre *m*.

tumour ['tju:mə*] *n* tumor *m*.

tumult ['tju:mʌlt] *n* tumulto; ~**uous** [-'mʌltjuəs] *a* tumultuoso.

tuna ['tju:nə] *n, pl inv* (*also:* ~ **fish**) atún *m*.

tune [tju:n] *n* (*melody*) melodía // *vt* (*MUS*) afinar; (*RADIO, TV, AUT*) sintonizar; **to be in/out of** ~ (*instrument*) estar afinado/ desafinado; (*singer*) cantar bien/ mal; **to be in/out of** ~ **with** (*fig*) armonizar/desentonar con; **to** ~ **up** *vi* (*musician*) afinar (su instrumento); ~**ful** *a* melodioso; **tuner** *n* (*radio set*) sintonizador *m*; **piano tuner** afinador *m* de pianos.

tunic ['tju:nık] *n* túnica.

tuning ['tju:nıŋ] *n* sintonización *f*; (*MUS*) afinación *f*; ~ **fork** *n* diapasón *m*.

Tunisia [tju:'nızıə] *n* Tunez *m*.

tunnel ['tʌnl] *n* túnel *m*; (*in mine*) galería // *vi* construir un túnel/una galería.

tunny ['tʌnı] *n* atún *m*.

turban ['tə:bən] *n* turbante *m*.

turbine ['tə:baın] *n* turbina.

turbulence ['tə:bjuləns] *n* (*AVIAT*) turbulencia; **turbulent** *a* turbulento.

tureen [tə'ri:n] *n* sopera.

turf [tə:f] *n* turba; (*clod*) césped *m* // *vt* poner césped; **to** ~ **out** *vt* (*col*) echar a la calle.

turgid ['tə:dʒıd] *a* (*speech*) pesado.

Turk [tə:k] *n* turco/a.

turkey ['tə:kı] *n* pavo.

Turkey ['tə:kı] *n* Turquía; **Turkish** *a, n* turco; **Turkish bath** *n* baño turco.

turmoil ['tə:mɔıl] *n* desorden *m*, alboroto.

turn [tə:n] *n* turno; (*in road*) curva; (*tendency: of mind, events*) disposición *f*, propensión *f*; (*THEATRE*) número; (*MED*) desmayo // *vt* girar, volver; (*collar, steak*) dar la vuelta a; (*change*): **to ~ sth into** convertir algo en // *vi* volver; (*person: look back*) volverse; (*reverse direction*) dar la vuelta; (*milk*) cortarse; (*change*) cambiar; (*become*) convertirse en; **a good ~** un favor; **it gave me quite a ~** me dio un susto (bastante grande); **'no left ~'** (*AUT*) 'prohibido girar a la izquierda'; **it's your ~** te toca a ti; **in ~** por turnos; **to take ~s** turnarse; **to ~ about** *vi* dar una vuelta completa; **to ~ away** *vi* volver la cabeza; **to ~ back** *vi* volverse atrás; **to ~ down** (*refuse*) rechazar; (*reduce*) bajar; (*fold*) doblar (hacia abajo); **to ~ in** *vi* (*col: go to bed*) acostarse // *vt* (*fold*) doblar hacia dentro; **to ~ off** *vi* (*from road*) desviarse // *vt* (*light, radio etc*) apagar; (*engine*) parar; **to ~ on** *vt* (*light, radio etc*) encender; (*engine*) poner en marcha; **to ~ out** *vt* (*light, gas*) apagar // *vi*: **to ~ out to be...** resultar ser...; **to ~ up** *vi* (*person*) llegar, presentarse; (*lost object*) aparecer // *vt* (*gen*) subir; **~ing** *n* (*in road*) vuelta; **~ing point** *n* (*fig*) momento decisivo.

turnip ['tɔːnɪp] *n* nabo.
turnout ['tɔːnaut] *n* asistencia, número de asistentes.
turnover ['tɔːnəuvə*] *n* (*COMM: amount of money*) cifra de negocios; (*: of goods*) movimiento.
turnpike ['tɔːnpaɪk] *n* (*US*) autopista de peaje.
turnstile ['tɔːnstaɪl] *n* torniquete *m*.
turntable ['tɔːnteɪbl] *n* (*on record player*) plato.
turn-up ['tɔːnʌp] *n* (*on trousers*) vuelta.
turpentine ['tɔːpəntaɪn] *n* (*also*: **turps**) trementina.
turquoise ['tɔːkwɔɪz] *n* (*stone*) turquesa // *a* color turquesa.
turret ['tʌrɪt] *n* torrecilla.
turtle ['tɔːtl] *n* tortuga marina.
tusk [tʌsk] *n* colmillo.
tussle ['tʌsl] *n* (*fight*) lucha; (*scuffle*) pelea.
tutor ['tjuːtə*] *n* (*gen*) profesor/a *m/f*; **~ial** [-'tɔːrɪəl] *n* (*SCOL*) seminario.
T.V. [tiː'viː] *n abbr of* **television.**
twaddle ['twɔdl] *n* tonterías *fpl*, bobadas *fpl*.
twang [twæŋ] *n* (*of instrument*) punteado; (*of voice*) timbre *m* nasal // *vi* vibrar // *vt* (*guitar*) puntear.
tweed [twiːd] *n* tweed *m*.
tweezers ['twiːzəz] *npl* pinzas *fpl* de depilar.
twelfth [twɛlfθ] *a* duodécimo; **T~ Night** *n* Día de Reyes.
twelve [twɛlv] *num* doce.
twentieth ['twɛntɪɪθ] *a* vigésimo.
twenty ['twɛntɪ] *num* veinte.
twerp [twɔːp] *n* (*col*) imbécil *m/f*.
twice [twaɪs] *ad* dos veces; **~ as much** dos veces más.

twig [twɪg] *n* ramita // *vi* (*col*) caer en la cuenta.
twilight ['twaɪlaɪt] *n* crepúsculo, ocaso.
twin [twɪn] *a, n* gemelo/a // *vt* tener como gemelo.
twine [twaɪn] *n* bramante *m* // *vi* (*plant*) enroscarse.
twinge [twɪndʒ] *n* (*of pain*) punzada; (*of conscience*) remordimiento.
twinkle ['twɪŋkl] *n* centelleo // *vi* centellear; (*eyes*) parpadear.
twirl [twɔːl] *n* giro // *vt* dar vueltas a // *vi* girar rápidamente.
twist [twɪst] *n* (*action*) torsión *f*; (*in road, coil*) vuelta; (*in wire, flex*) enroscadura; (*in story*) cambio imprevisto // *vt* torcer, retorcer; (*weave*) entrelazar; (*roll around*) enrollar; (*fig*) deformar // *vi* serpentear.
twit [twɪt] *n* (*col*) tonto.
twitch [twɪtʃ] *n* sacudida; (*nervous*) tic *m* nervioso // *vi* moverse nerviosamente.
two [tuː] *num* dos; **to put ~ and ~ together** (*fig*) atar cabos; **~-door** *a* (*AUT*) de dos puertas; **~-faced** *a* (*pej: person*) falso; **~-fold** *ad*: **to increase ~fold** duplicar; **~-piece (suit)** *n* traje *m* de dos piezas; **~-piece (swimsuit)** *n* dos piezas *m inv*, bikini *m*; **~-seater** *n* (*plane*) avión *m* biplaza; (*car*) coche *m* de dos plazas; **~some** *n* (*people*) pareja; **~-way** *a*: **~-way traffic** circulación *f* en ambas direcciones.
tycoon [taɪ'kuːn] *n*: **(business) ~** magnate *m*.
type [taɪp] *n* (*category*) tipo, género; (*model*) modelo; (*TYP*) tipo, letra // *vt* (*letter etc*) escribir a máquina; **~-cast** *a* (*actor*) encasillado; **~script** *n* texto mecanografiado; **~writer** *n* máquina de escribir; **~written** *a* mecanografiado.
typhoid ['taɪfɔɪd] *n* tifoidea.
typhoon [taɪ'fuːn] *n* tifón *m*.
typhus ['taɪfəs] *n* tifus *m*.
typical ['tɪpɪkl] *a* típico; **typify** [-faɪ] *vt* ser típico de.
typing ['taɪpɪŋ] *n* mecanografía; **typist** *n* mecanógrafa.
tyranny ['tɪrənɪ] *n* tiranía.
tyrant ['taɪərnt] *n* tirano/a.
tyre, tire (*US*) ['taɪə*] *n* neumático, llanta.
tzar [zɑː*] *n* = **tsar.**

U

U-bend ['juːbɛnd] *n* (*in pipe*) recodo.
ubiquitous [juː'bɪkwɪtəs] *a* ubicuo, omnipresente.
udder ['ʌdə*] *n* ubre *f*.
UFO ['juːfəu] *n abbr of* **unidentified flying object** O.V.N.I. *m* (objeto volante no identificado).
ugliness ['ʌglɪnɪs] *n* fealdad *f*; **ugly** *a* feo; (*dangerous*) peligroso.
U.K. *n abbr of* **United Kingdom.**
ulcer ['ʌlsə*] *n* úlcera.

Ulster ['ʌlstə*] n Úlster m, Irlanda del Norte.

ulterior [ʌl'tɪərɪə*] a ulterior; ~ **motive** motivo oculto.

ultimate ['ʌltɪmət] a último, final; (authority) supremo; ~**ly** ad (in the end) por último, al final; (fundamentally) en el fondo.

ultimatum [ʌltɪ'meɪtəm] n ultimátum m.

ultraviolet ['ʌltrə'vaɪəlɪt] a ultravioleta.

umbilical cord [ʌmbɪ'laɪkl-] n cordón m umbilical.

umbrella [ʌm'brelə] n paraguas m inv.

umpire ['ʌmpaɪə*] n árbitro // vt arbitrar.

umpteen [ʌmp'ti:n] a tantísimos; **for the** ~**th time** por enésima vez.

UN, UNO abbr of **United Nations (Organization).**

unable [ʌn'eɪbl] a: **to be** ~ **to do sth** ser incapaz o no poder hacer algo.

unabridged [ʌnə'brɪdʒd] a íntegro.

unaccompanied [ʌnə'kʌmpənɪd] a no acompañado.

unaccountably [ʌnə'kauntəblɪ] ad inexplicablemente.

unaccustomed [ʌnə'kʌstəmd] a: **to be** ~ **to** no tener costumbre de.

unaided [ʌn'eɪdɪd] a sin ayuda, por sí solo.

unanimous [ju:'nænɪməs] a unánime; ~**ly** ad unánimamente.

unarmed [ʌn'ɑ:md] a (without a weapon) desarmado; (defenceless) inerme.

unassuming [ʌnə'sju:mɪŋ] a modesto, sin pretensiones.

unattached [ʌnə'tætʃt] a (person) libre; (part etc) suelto, separable.

unattended [ʌnə'tendɪd] a (car, luggage) sin vigilancia.

unattractive [ʌnə'træktɪv] a poco atractivo.

unauthorized [ʌn'ɔ:θəraɪzd] a desautorizado.

unavoidable [ʌnə'vɔɪdəbl] a inevitable.

unaware [ʌnə'wɛə*] a: **to be** ~ **of** ignorar, no darse cuenta de; ~**s** ad de improviso.

unbalanced [ʌn'bælənst] a desequilibrado; (mentally) trastornado.

unbearable [ʌn'bɛərəbl] a insoportable.

unbeatable [ʌn'bi:təbl] a (team) imbatible; (price) inmejorable.

unbeaten [ʌn'bi:tn] a imbatido.

unbeknown(st) [ʌnbɪ'nəun(st)] ad: ~ **to me** sin saberlo (yo).

unbelievable [ʌnbɪ'li:vəbl] a increíble.

unbend [ʌn'bend] (irg: like bend) vi suavizarse // vt (wire) enderezar.

unblock [ʌn'blɔk] vt (pipe) desatascar.

unborn [ʌn'bɔ:n] a sin nacer.

unbounded [ʌn'baundɪd] a ilimitado, sin límite.

unbreakable [ʌn'breɪkəbl] a irrompible.

unbridled [ʌn'braɪdld] a (fig) desenfrenado.

unbroken [ʌn'brəukən] a (seal) intacto;

(series) continuo; (record) imbatido; (spirit) indómito.

unburden [ʌn'bə:dn] vr: **to** ~ **o.s.** desahogarse.

unbutton [ʌn'bʌtn] vt desabrochar.

uncalled-for [ʌn'kɔ:ldfɔ:*] a gratuito, inmerecido.

uncanny [ʌn'kænɪ] a extraño, extraordinario.

unceasing [ʌn'si:sɪŋ] a incesante.

uncertain [ʌn'sə:tn] a incierto; (character) indeciso; ~**ty** n incertidumbre f.

unchanged [ʌn'tʃeɪndʒd] a sin cambiar o alterar.

uncharitable [ʌn'tʃærɪtəbl] a poco caritativo.

uncharted [ʌn'tʃɑ:tɪd] a inexplorado.

unchecked [ʌn'tʃekt] a desenfrenado.

uncivil [ʌn'sɪvɪl] a grosero.

uncle ['ʌŋkl] n tío.

uncomfortable [ʌn'kʌmfətəbl] a incómodo; (uneasy) molesto.

uncommon [ʌn'kɔmən] a poco común, raro.

unconcerned [ʌnkən'sə:nd] a indiferente, despreocupado.

unconditional [ʌnkən'dɪʃənl] a incondicional.

unconscious [ʌn'kɔnʃəs] a sin sentido; (unaware) inconsciente // n: **the** ~ el inconsciente; ~**ly** ad inconscientemente.

uncontrollable [ʌnkən'trəuləbl] a (temper) ingobernable; (laughter) incontenible.

uncouth [ʌn'ku:θ] a grosero, inculto.

uncover [ʌn'kʌvə*] vt (gen) descubrir; (take lid off) destapar.

undecided [ʌndɪ'saɪdɪd] a (character) indeciso; (question) no resuelto, pendiente.

undeniable [ʌndɪ'naɪəbl] a innegable.

under ['ʌndə*] prep debajo de; (less than) menos de; (according to) según, de acuerdo con // ad debajo, abajo; ~ **there** allí abajo; ~ **repair** en reparación.

under... [ʌndə*] pref sub; ~-**age** a menor de edad; ~**carriage** n tren m de aterrizaje; ~**clothes** npl ropa sg interior; ~**coat** n (paint) primera mano; ~**cover** a clandestino; ~**current** n corriente f submarina; (fig) tendencia oculta; ~**cut** vt irg rebajar los precios para competir con; ~**developed** a subdesarrollado; ~**dog** n desvalido; ~**done** a (CULIN) poco hecho; ~**estimate** vt subestimar; ~**exposed** a (PHOT) subexpuesto; ~**fed** a subalimentado; ~**foot** ad bajo los pies; ~**go** vt irg sufrir; (treatment) recibir; ~**graduate** n estudiante m/f; ~**ground** n (railway) metro; (POL) movimiento clandestino // a subterráneo; ~**growth** n maleza; ~**hand(ed)** a (fig) turbio; ~**lie** vt irg estar debajo de; (fig) ser la razón fundamental de; ~**line** vt subrayar; ~**ling** ['ʌndəlɪŋ] n (pej) subalterno; ~**mine** vt socavar, minar; ~**neath** [ʌndə'ni:θ] ad debajo // prep debajo de, bajo; ~**paid** a mal pagado; ~**pants** npl

(Brit) calzoncillos mpl; ~**pass** n paso
subterráneo; ~**price** vt vender
demasiado barato; ~**privileged** a
desamparado; ~**rate** vt menospreciar,
subestimar; ~**side** n parte f inferior,
revés m; ~**skirt** n enaguas fpl.
understand [ʌndə'stænd] (irg: like **stand**)
vt, vi entender, comprender; (assume)
sobreentender; ~**able** a comprensible;
~**ing** a comprensivo // n comprensión f,
entendimiento; (agreement) acuerdo.
understatement [ʌndə'steɪtmənt] n
descripción f insuficiente; (quality)
modestia (excesiva).
understood [ʌndə'stud] pt, pp of **understand** // a entendido; (implied)
sobreentendido.
understudy ['ʌndəstʌdɪ] n suplente m/f.
undertake [ʌndə'teɪk] (irg: like **take**) vt
acometer; **to** ~ **to do** sth
comprometerse a hacer algo.
undertaker ['ʌndəteɪkə*] n director m de
pompas fúnebres, sepulturero.
undertaking [ʌndə'teɪkɪŋ] n empresa;
(promise) promesa.
underwater [ʌndə'wɔ:tə*] ad bajo el agua
// a submarino.
underwear ['ʌndəwɛə*] n ropa interior.
underweight [ʌndə'weɪt] a de peso
insuficiente; (person) demasiado delgado.
underworld ['ʌndəwɔ:ld] n (of crime)
hampa, inframundo.
underwriter ['ʌndəraɪtə*] n (INSURANCE)
(re)asegurador/a m/f.
undesirable [ʌndɪ'zaɪərəbl] a indeseable.
undies ['ʌndɪz] npl (col) paños mpl
menores.
undignified [ʌn'dɪgnɪfaɪd] a indecoroso.
undisputed [ʌndɪ'spju:tɪd] a incontestable.
undo [ʌn'du:] (irg: like **do**) vt deshacer;
~**ing** n ruina, perdición f.
undoubted [ʌn'dautɪd] a indudable; ~**ly**
ad indudablemente, sin duda.
undress [ʌn'drɛs] vi desnudarse.
undue [ʌn'dju:] a indebido, excesivo.
undulating ['ʌndjuleɪtɪŋ] a ondulante.
unduly [ʌn'dju:lɪ] ad excesivamente,
demasiado.
unearth [ʌn'ə:θ] vt desenterrar.
unearthly [ʌn'ə:θlɪ] a (hour) inverosímil.
uneasy [ʌn'i:zɪ] a intranquilo; (worried)
preocupado.
uneconomic(al) ['ʌni:kə'nɔmɪk(l)] a
antieconómico.
uneducated [ʌn'ɛdjukeɪtɪd] a sin
educación, inculto.
unemployed [ʌnɪm'plɔɪd] a parado, sin
trabajo // n: **the** ~ los parados;
unemployment [-'plɔɪmənt] n paro,
desempleo.
unending [ʌn'ɛndɪŋ] a interminable.
unenthusiastic [ʌnɪnθu:zɪ'æstɪk] a poco
entusiasta.
unerring [ʌn'ə:rɪŋ] a infalible.
uneven [ʌn'i:vn] a desigual; (road etc)
quebrado, accidentado.

unexpected [ʌnɪk'spɛktɪd] a inesperado.
unfair [ʌn'fɛə*] a: ~ **(to)** injusto (con);
~**ly** ad injustamente.
unfaithful [ʌn'feɪθful] a infiel.
unfamiliar [ʌnfə'mɪlɪə*] a nuevo,
desconocido.
unfashionable [ʌn'fæʃnəbl] a pasado o
fuera de moda.
unfasten [ʌn'fɑ:sn] vt desatar.
unfavourable, unfavorable (US) [ʌn-
'feɪvərəbl] a desfavorable.
unfeeling [ʌn'fi:lɪŋ] a insensible.
unfinished [ʌn'fɪnɪʃt] a incompleto, sin
terminar.
unfit [ʌn'fɪt] a con mala salud, enfermo;
(incompetent) incompetente, incapaz; ~
for work no apto para trabajar.
unflagging [ʌn'flægɪŋ] a incansable.
unfold [ʌn'fould] vt desdoblar; (fig) revelar
// vi abrirse; revelarse.
unforeseen ['ʌnfɔ:'si:n] a imprevisto.
unforgettable [ʌnfə'gɛtəbl] a inolvidable.
unforgivable [ʌnfə'gɪvəbl] a imperdonable.
unfortunate [ʌn'fɔ:tʃnət] a desgraciado;
(event, remark) inoportuno; ~**ly** ad des-
graciadamente.
unfounded [ʌn'faundɪd] a infundado.
unfriendly [ʌn'frɛndlɪ] a antipático.
unfurnished [ʌn'fə:nɪʃt] a desamueblado.
ungainly [ʌn'geɪnlɪ] a desgarbado.
unhappiness [ʌn'hæpɪnɪs] n tristeza;
unhappy a (sad) triste; (unfortunate)
desgraciado; (childhood) infeliz; **unhappy**
with (arrangements etc) poco contento
con, descontento de.
unharmed [ʌn'hɑ:md] a ileso; (col) sano y
salvo.
unhealthy [ʌn'hɛlθɪ] a (gen) malsano;
(person) enfermizo, con poca salud.
unheard-of [ʌn'hə:dɔv] a inaudito, sin
precedente.
unhook [ʌn'huk] vt desenganchar; (from
wall) descolgar; (dress) desabrochar.
unhurt [ʌn'hə:t] a ileso.
unidentified [ʌnaɪ'dɛntɪfaɪd] a no
identificado.
uniform ['ju:nɪfɔ:m] n uniforme m // a
uniforme; ~**ity** [-'fɔ:mɪtɪ] n uniformidad f.
unify ['ju:nɪfaɪ] vt unificar, unir.
unilateral [ju:nɪ'lætərəl] a unilateral.
unintentional [ʌnɪn'tɛnʃənəl] a
involuntario.
union ['ju:njən] n unión f; (also: **trade** ~)
sindicato // a sindical; **U**~ **Jack** n
bandera del Reino Unido.
unique [ju:'ni:k] a único.
unison ['ju:nɪsn] n: **in** ~ en armonía.
unit ['ju:nɪt] n unidad f; (team, squad)
grupo; **kitchen** ~ mueble m de cocina.
unite [ju:'naɪt] vt unir // vi unirse; ~**d** a
unido; **U**~**d Kingdom (U.K.)** n Reino
Unido; **U**~**d Nations (Organization)**
(UN, UNO) n (Las) Naciones Unidas fpl
(O.N.U.); **U**~**d States (of America)**

(US, USA) *n* (Los) Estados Unidos *mpl* (EE.UU.).

unity ['juːnɪtɪ] *n* unidad *f*.

universal [juːnɪ'vɜːsl] *a* universal.

universe ['juːnɪvɜːs] *n* universo.

university [juːnɪ'vɜːsɪtɪ] *n* universidad *f*.

unjust [ʌn'dʒʌst] *a* injusto.

unkempt [ʌn'kempt] *a* descuidado; (*hair*) despeinado.

unkind [ʌn'kaɪnd] *a* poco amable; (*comment etc*) cruel.

unknown [ʌn'nəun] *a* desconocido.

unladen [ʌn'leɪdn] *a* (*ship, weight*) vacío.

unleash [ʌn'liːʃ] *vt* soltar; (*fig*) desencadenar.

unless [ʌn'les] *conj* a menos que, a no ser que; ~ **he comes** a menos que venga; ~ **otherwise stated** salvo indicación contraria.

unlike [ʌn'laɪk] *a* distinto // *prep* a diferencia de.

unlikely [ʌn'laɪklɪ] *a* improbable.

unlimited [ʌn'lɪmɪtɪd] *a* ilimitado.

unload [ʌn'ləud] *vt* descargar.

unlock [ʌn'lɔk] *vt* abrir (con llave).

unlucky [ʌn'lʌkɪ] *a* desgraciado; (*object, number*) que da mala suerte; **to be** ~ tener mala suerte.

unmarried [ʌn'mærɪd] *a* soltero.

unmask [ʌn'mɑːsk] *vt* desenmascarar.

unmistakable [ʌnmɪs'teɪkəbl] *a* inconfundible.

unmitigated [ʌn'mɪtɪgeɪtɪd] *a* no mitigado, absoluto.

unnatural [ʌn'nætʃrəl] *a* (*gen*) antinatural; (*manner*) afectado; (*habit*) perverso.

unnecessary [ʌn'nesəsərɪ] *a* innecesario, inútil.

unnoticed [ʌn'nəutɪst] *a*: **to go** ~ pasar desapercibido.

unobtainable [ʌnəb'teɪnəbl] *a* inconseguible.

unoccupied [ʌn'ɔkjupaɪd] *a* (*seat etc*) libre.

unofficial [ʌnə'fɪʃl] *a* no oficial; (*strike*) espontáneo, sin la aprobación de la central.

unorthodox [ʌn'ɔːθədɔks] *a* poco ortodoxo.

unpack [ʌn'pæk] *vi* deshacer las maletas.

unpalatable [ʌn'pælətəbl] *a* (*truth*) desagradable.

unparalleled [ʌn'pærəleld] *a* (*unequalled*) sin par; (*unique*) sin precedentes.

unpleasant [ʌn'pleznt] *a* (*disagreeable*) desagradable; (*person, manner*) antipático.

unplug [ʌn'plʌg] *vt* desenchufar, desconectar.

unpopular [ʌn'pɔpjulə*] *a* poco popular.

unprecedented [ʌn'presɪdəntɪd] *a* sin precedentes.

unpredictable [ʌnprɪ'dɪktəbl] *a* imprevisible.

unproductive [ʌnprə'dʌktɪv] *a* improductivo.

unqualified [ʌn'kwɔlɪfaɪd] *a* (*teacher*) sin

título, no cualificado; (*success*) total, incondicional.

unravel [ʌn'rævl] *vt* desenmarañar.

unreal [ʌn'rɪəl] *a* irreal.

unrealistic [ʌnrɪə'lɪstɪk] *a* poco realista.

unreasonable [ʌn'riːznəbl] *a* poco razonable; (*demand*) excesivo.

unrelated [ʌnrɪ'leɪtɪd] *a* sin relación; (*family*) sin parentesco.

unrelenting [ʌnrɪ'lentɪŋ] *a* implacable.

unreliable [ʌnrɪ'laɪəbl] *a* (*person*) informal; (*machine*) de poca confianza.

unrelieved [ʌnrɪ'liːvd] *a* (*monotony*) monótono.

unrepeatable [ʌnrɪ'piːtəbl] *a* (*offer*) irrepetible.

unrepresentative [ʌnreprɪ'zentətɪv] *a* poco representativo o característico.

unrest [ʌn'rest] *n* inquietud *f*, malestar *m*; (*POL*) disturbios *mpl*.

unroll [ʌn'rəul] *vt* desenrollar.

unruly [ʌn'ruːlɪ] *a* indisciplinado.

unsafe [ʌn'seɪf] *a* (*journey*) peligroso; (*car etc*) inseguro.

unsaid [ʌn'sed] *a*: **to leave sth** ~ dejar algo sin decir.

unsatisfactory ['ʌnsætɪs'fæktərɪ] *a* insatisfactorio.

unsavoury, unsavory (*US*) [ʌn'seɪvərɪ] *a* (*fig*) repugnante.

unscathed [ʌn'skeɪðd] *a* ileso.

unscrew [ʌn'skruː] *vt* destornillar.

unscrupulous [ʌn'skruːpjuləs] *a* sin escrúpulos.

unsettled [ʌn'setld] *a* inquieto, inestable; (*weather*) variable.

unshaven [ʌn'ʃeɪvn] *a* sin afeitar.

unsightly [ʌn'saɪtlɪ] *a* feo.

unskilled [ʌn'skɪld] *a*: ~ **worker** obrero no cualificado.

unspeakable [ʌn'spiːkəbl] *a* indecible; (*bad*) horrible.

unsteady [ʌn'stedɪ] *a* inestable.

unstuck [ʌn'stʌk] *a*: **to come** ~ despegarse; (*fig*) fracasar.

unsuccessful [ʌnsək'sesful] *a* (*attempt*) infructuoso; (*writer, proposal*) sin éxito; **to be** ~ (*in attempting sth*) no tener éxito, fracasar; ~**ly** *ad* en vano, sin éxito.

unsuitable [ʌn'suːtəbl] *a* inconveniente, inapropiado.

unsure [ʌn'ʃuə*] *a* inseguro, poco seguro.

unsuspecting [ʌnsə'spektɪŋ] *a* confiado.

unswerving [ʌn'swɜːvɪŋ] *a* inquebrantable.

untangle [ʌn'tæŋgl] *vt* desenredar.

untapped [ʌn'tæpt] *a* (*resources*) sin explotar.

unthinkable [ʌn'θɪŋkəbl] *a* inconcebible, impensable.

untidy [ʌn'taɪdɪ] *a* (*room*) desordenado, en desorden; (*appearance*) descuidado.

untie [ʌn'taɪ] *vt* desatar.

until [ən'tɪl] *prep* hasta // *conj* hasta que; ~ **he comes** hasta que venga; ~ **then** hasta entonces.

untimely [ʌn'taɪmlɪ] *a* inoportuno; (*death*) prematuro.

untold [ʌn'təʊld] *a* (*story*) inédito; (*suffering*) indecible; (*wealth*) incalculable.

untoward [ʌntə'wɔːd] *a* desfavorable.

unused [ʌn'juːzd] *a* sin usar, nuevo.

unusual [ʌn'juːʒʊəl] *a* insólito, poco común.

unveil [ʌn'veɪl] *vt* (*statue*) descubrir.

unwavering [ʌn'weɪvərɪŋ] *a* inquebrantable.

unwelcome [ʌn'wɛlkəm] *a* (*at a bad time*) inoportuno; (*unpleasant*) desagradable.

unwell [ʌn'wɛl] *a*: **to feel ~** estar indispuesto; **to be ~** estar enfermo.

unwieldy [ʌn'wiːldɪ] *a* difícil de manejar.

unwilling [ʌn'wɪlɪŋ] *a*: **to be ~ to do sth** estar poco dispuesto a hacer algo; **~ly** *ad* de mala gana.

unwind [ʌn'waɪnd] (*irg: like* **wind**) *vt* desenvolver // *vi* (*relax*) relajarse.

unwitting [ʌn'wɪtɪŋ] *a* inconsciente.

unworthy [ʌn'wɔːðɪ] *a* indigno.

unwrap [ʌn'ræp] *vt* desenvolver.

up [ʌp] *prep*: **to go/be ~ sth** subir/estar encima de algo // *ad* hacia arriba, arriba; **~ there** allí arriba; **~ above** encima, allí arriba; **to be ~** (*out of bed*) estar levantado; **it is ~ to you** Ud. decide/tú decides; **what is he ~ to?** ¿qué es lo que quiere?, ¿qué está tramando?; **he is not ~ to it** no es capaz de hacerlo; **~-and-coming** *a* prometedor(a); **~s and downs** *npl* (*fig*) altibajos *mpl*.

upbringing ['ʌpbrɪŋɪŋ] *n* educación *f*.

update [ʌp'deɪt] *vt* poner al día, modernizar; (*contract etc*) actualizar.

upgrade [ʌp'greɪd] *vt* ascender; (*job*) revalorizar.

upheaval [ʌp'hiːvl] *n* trastorno, conmoción *f*.

uphill [ʌp'hɪl] *a* cuesta arriba; (*fig: task*) penoso, difícil // *ad*: **to go ~** ir cuesta arriba.

uphold [ʌp'həʊld] (*irg: like* **hold**) *vt* sostener.

upholstery [ʌp'həʊlstərɪ] *n* tapicería.

upkeep ['ʌpkiːp] *n* mantenimiento.

upon [ə'pɒn] *prep* sobre.

upper ['ʌpə*] *a* superior, de arriba // *n* (*of shoe*) pala; **~-class** *a* de clase alta; **~most** *a* el más alto; **what was ~most in my mind** lo que me preocupaba más.

upright ['ʌpraɪt] *a* vertical; (*fig*) honrado.

uprising ['ʌpraɪzɪŋ] *n* sublevación *f*.

uproar ['ʌprɔː*] *n* tumulto, escándalo.

uproot [ʌp'ruːt] *vt* desarraigar.

upset ['ʌpsɛt] *n* (*to plan etc*) revés *m*, contratiempo; (*MED*) trastorno // *vt* [ʌp'sɛt] (*irg: like* **set**) (*glass etc*) volcar; (*spill*) derramar; (*plan*) alterar; (*person*) molestar, perturbar // *a* [ʌp'sɛt] preocupado, perturbado; (*stomach*) trastornado.

upshot ['ʌpʃɒt] *n* resultado.

upside-down ['ʌpsaɪddaʊn] *ad* al revés.

upstairs [ʌp'stɛəz] *ad* arriba // *a* (*room*) de arriba // *n* el piso superior.

upstart ['ʌpstɑːt] *n* advenedizo.

upstream [ʌp'striːm] *ad* río arriba.

uptake ['ʌpteɪk] *n*: **he is quick/slow on the ~** es muy listo/ algo torpe.

up-to-date ['ʌptə'deɪt] *a* moderno, actual.

upturn ['ʌptəːn] *n* (*in luck*) mejora.

upward ['ʌpwəd] *a* ascendente; **~(s)** *ad* hacia arriba.

uranium [jʊə'reɪnɪəm] *n* uranio.

urban ['əːbən] *a* urbano.

urbane [əː'beɪn] *a* cortés.

urchin ['əːtʃɪn] *n* pilluelo, golfillo.

urge [əːdʒ] *n* (*force*) impulso; (*desire*) deseo // *vt*: **to ~ sb to do sth** incitar a uno a hacer algo.

urgency ['əːdʒənsɪ] *n* urgencia; (*of tone*) insistencia; **urgent** *a* urgente.

urinal ['jʊərɪnl] *n* urinario.

urinate ['jʊərɪneɪt] *vi* orinar; **urine** *n* orina, orines *mpl*.

urn [əːn] *n* urna; (*also:* **tea ~**) tetera.

us [ʌs] *pron* nos; (*after prep*) nosotros/as.

US, USA *n abbr of* **United States (of America)**.

usage ['juːzɪdʒ] *n* uso, costumbre *f*.

use [juːs] *n* uso, empleo; (*usefulness*) utilidad *f* // *vt* [juːz] usar, emplear; **she ~d to do it** (ella) solía hacerlo; **in ~** en uso; **out of ~** anticuado, que ya no se usa; **to be of ~** servir; **it's no ~** (*pointless*) es inútil; (*not useful*) no sirve; **to be ~d to** estar acostumbrado a; **to ~ up** *vt* agotar, consumir; **~d** *a* (*car*) usado; **~ful** *a* útil; **to be ~ful** servir; **~less** *a* inútil; **user** *n* usuario/a.

usher ['ʌʃə*] *n* ujier *m*, portero; **~ette** [-'rɛt] *n* (*in cinema*) acomodadora.

USSR *n*: **the ~** la U.R.S.S.

usual ['juːʒʊəl] *a* normal, corriente; **~ly** *ad* normalmente.

usurp [juː'zəːp] *vt* usurpar.

utensil [juː'tɛnsl] *n* utensilio; **kitchen ~s** batería *sg* de cocina.

uterus ['juːtərəs] *n* útero.

utilitarian [juːtɪlɪ'tɛərɪən] *a* utilitario.

utility [juː'tɪlɪtɪ] *n* utilidad *f*; **~ room** *n* trascocina.

utilize ['juːtɪlaɪz] *vt* utilizar.

utmost ['ʌtməʊst] *a* mayor // *n*: **to do one's ~** hacer todo lo posible.

utter ['ʌtə*] *a* total, completo // *vt* pronunciar, proferir; **~ance** *n* palabras *fpl*, declaración *f*; **~ly** *ad* completamente, totalmente.

U-turn ['juː'təːn] *n* viraje *m* en U.

V

v. *abbr of* **verse; versus; volt; vide** véase.

vacancy ['veɪkənsɪ] *n* (*job*) vacante *f*; (*room*) cuarto libro; **vacant** *a* desocupado, libre; (*expression*) distraído; **vacate**

[və'keɪt] *vt* (*house*) desocupar; (*job*) salir de; (*throne*) renunciar a.
vacation [və'keɪʃən] *n* vacaciones *fpl*.
vaccinate ['væksɪneɪt] *vt* vacunar; **vaccination** [-'neɪʃən] *n* vacunación *f*.
vaccine ['væksiːn] *n* vacuna.
vacuum ['vækjum] *n* vacío; ~ **cleaner** *n* aspiradora; ~ **flask** *n* termo.
vagabond ['vægəbɔnd] *n* vagabundo.
vagina [və'dʒaɪnə] *n* vagina.
vagrant ['veɪgrnt] *n* vagabundo.
vague [veɪg] *a* vago; (*blurred: memory*) borroso; (*uncertain*) incierto, impreciso; (*person*) distraído; ~**ly** *ad* vagamente.
vain [veɪn] *a* (*conceited*) vanidoso; (*useless*) vano, inútil; **in** ~ en vano.
vale [veɪl] *n* valle *m*.
valentine ['væləntaɪn] *n*: **V**~'**s Day** Día *m* de los Enamorados.
valid ['vælɪd] *a* válido; (*ticket*) valedero; (*law*) vigente; ~**ity** [-'lɪdɪtɪ] *n* validez *f*; vigencia.
valley ['vælɪ] *n* valle *m*.
valour, valor (*US*) ['vælə*] *n* valor *m*, valentía.
valuable ['væljuəbl] *a* (*jewel*) de valor; (*time*) valioso; ~**s** *npl* objetos *mpl* de valor.
valuation [vælju'eɪʃən] *n* tasación *f*, valuación *f*.
value ['væljuː] *n* valor *m*; (*importance*) importancia // *vt* (*fix price of*) tasar, valorar; (*esteem*) apreciar; (*cherish*) tener en mucho; ~ **added tax (VAT)** *n* tasa al valor añadido *o* agregado; ~**d** *a* (*appreciated*) apreciado.
valve [vælv] *n* (*gen*) válvula; (*MED*) valva.
vampire ['væmpaɪə*] *n* vampiro/vampiresa.
van [væn] *n* (*AUT*) furgoneta; (*RAIL*) furgón *m* (de equipajes).
vandal ['vændl] *n* vándalo; ~**ism** *n* vandalismo; ~**ize** *vt* dañar, destruir.
vanilla [və'nɪlə] *n* vainilla.
vanish ['vænɪʃ] *vi* desvanecerse, esfumarse.
vanity ['vænɪtɪ] *n* vanidad *f*; ~ **case** *n* neceser *m*.
vantage point ['vɑːntɪdʒ-] *n* posición *f* ventajosa.
vapour, vapor (*US*) ['veɪpə*] *n* vapor *m*; (*steam*) vaho.
variable ['vɛərɪəbl] *a* variable.
variance ['vɛərɪəns] *n*: **to be at** ~ **(with)** desentonar (con), estar en desacuerdo (con).
variation [vɛərɪ'eɪʃən] *n* variedad *f*; (*in opinion*) variación *f*.
varicose ['værɪkəus] *a*: ~ **veins** varices *fpl*.
varied ['vɛərɪd] *a* variado.
variety [və'raɪətɪ] *n* variedad *f*, diversidad *f*; (*quantity*) surtido; ~ **show** *n* variedades *fpl*.
various ['vɛərɪəs] *a* varios(as), diversos(as).

varnish ['vɑːnɪʃ] *n* (*gen*) barniz *m*; (*nail* ~) esmalte *m* // *vt* (*gen*) barnizar; (*nails*) pintar (con esmalte).
vary ['vɛərɪ] *vt* variar; (*change*) cambiar // *vi* variar; (*disagree*) discrepar; (*deviate*) desviarse; ~**ing** *a* diversos(as).
vase [vɑːz] *n* florero.
vaseline ['væsɪliːn] *n* vaselina.
vast [vɑːst] *a* enorme; (*success*) abrumador(a); ~**ness** *n* inmensidad *f*.
vat [væt] *n* tina, tinaja.
VAT [væt] *n abbr of* **Value Added Tax.**
Vatican ['vætɪkən] *n*: **the** ~ el Vaticano.
vault [vɔːlt] *n* (*of roof*) bóveda; (*tomb*) tumba; (*in bank*) sótano // *vt* (*also*: ~ **over**) saltar (por encima de).
veal [viːl] *n* ternera.
veer [vɪə*] *vi* virar.
vegetable ['vɛdʒtəbl] *n* (*BOT*) vegetal *m*; (*edible plant*) legumbre *f*, hortaliza; ~**s** *npl* (*cooked*) verduras *fpl* // *a* vegetal; ~ **garden** *n* huerto.
vegetarian [vɛdʒɪ'tɛərɪən] *a*, *n* vegetariano/a.
vegetate ['vɛdʒɪteɪt] *vi* vegetar.
vegetation [vɛdʒɪ'teɪʃən] *n* vegetación *f*.
vehement ['viːɪmənt] *a* vehemente; (*impassioned*) apasionado.
vehicle ['viːɪkl] *n* vehículo.
veil [veɪl] *n* velo // *vt* velar.
vein [veɪn] *n* vena; (*of ore etc*) veta.
velocity [vɪ'lɔsɪtɪ] *n* velocidad *f*.
velvet ['vɛlvɪt] *n* terciopelo // *a* aterciopelado.
vendetta [vɛn'dɛtə] *n* vendetta.
vending machine ['vɛndɪŋ-] *n* distribuidor *m* automático.
vendor ['vɛndə*] *n* vendedor/a *m/f*.
veneer [və'nɪə*] *n* chapa, enchapado; (*fig*) barniz *m*, apariencia.
venereal [vɪ'nɪərɪəl] *a*: ~ **disease (VD)** enfermedad *f* venérea.
Venetian blind [vɪ'niːʃən-] *n* persiana.
Venezuela [vɛnɛ'zweɪlə] *n* Venezuela; ~**n** *a*, *n* venezolano/a.
vengeance ['vɛndʒəns] *n* venganza; **with** **a** ~ (*fig*) con creces.
venison ['vɛnɪsn] *n* carne *f* de venado.
venom ['vɛnəm] *n* veneno; ~**ous** *a* venenoso.
vent [vɛnt] *n* (*opening*) abertura; (*air-hole*) respiradero; (*in wall*) rejilla (de ventilación) // *vt* (*fig: feelings*) desahogar.
ventilate ['vɛntɪleɪt] *vt* ventilar; **ventilation** [-'leɪʃən] *n* ventilación *f*; **ventilator** *n* ventilador *m*.
ventriloquist [vɛn'trɪləkwɪst] *n* ventrílocuo.
venture ['vɛntʃə*] *n* empresa // *vt* aventurar; (*opinion*) ofrecer // *vi* arriesgarse, lanzarse.
venue ['vɛnjuː] *n* lugar *m*; (*meeting place*) lugar *m* de reunión.
veranda(h) [və'rændə] *n* terraza; (*with glass*) galería.
verb [vɜːb] *n* verbo; ~**al** *a* verbal.

verbatim [vəˈbeɪtɪm] *a, ad* palabra por palabra.

verbose [vəˈbəus] *a* prolijo.

verdict [ˈvɜːdɪkt] *n* veredicto, fallo; (*fig*) opinión *f*, juicio.

verge [vɜːdʒ] *n* borde *m*, margen *m*; **to be on the ~ of doing sth** estar a punto de hacer algo; **to ~ on** *vt fus* rayar en.

verify [ˈvɛrɪfaɪ] *vt* comprobar, verificar.

vermin [ˈvɜːmɪn] *npl* (*animals*) bichos *mpl*; (*insects, fig*) sabandijas *fpl*.

vermouth [ˈvɜːməθ] *n* vermut *m*.

vernacular [vəˈnækjulə*] *n* vernáculo.

versatile [ˈvɜːsətaɪl] *a* (*person*) de talentos variados; (*machine, tool etc*) que tiene muchos usos; (*mind*) ágil, flexible.

verse [vɜːs] *n* versos *mpl*, poesía; (*stanza*) estrofa; (*in bible*) versículo.

versed [vɜːst] *a*: (**well-**)**~ in** versado en, conocedor de.

version [ˈvɜːʃən] *n* versión *f*.

versus [ˈvɜːsəs] *prep* contra.

vertebra [ˈvɜːtɪbrə], *pl* **~e** [-briː] *n* vértebra; **vertebrate** [-brɪt] *n* vertebrado.

vertical [ˈvɜːtɪkl] *a* vertical.

vertigo [ˈvɜːtɪgəu] *n* vértigo.

very [ˈvɛrɪ] *ad* muy // *a*: **the ~ book which** el mismo libro que; **the ~ last** el último (de todos); **at the ~ least** al menos; **~ much** muchísimo.

vespers [ˈvɛspəz] *npl* vísperas *fpl*.

vessel [ˈvɛsl] *n* (ANAT, NAUT) vaso; (*container*) vasija.

vest [vɛst] *n* camiseta; (*US*: waistcoat) chaleco; **~ed interests** *npl* (COMM) intereses *mpl* creados.

vestibule [ˈvɛstɪbjuːl] *n* vestíbulo.

vestige [ˈvɛstɪdʒ] *n* vestigio, rastro.

vestry [ˈvɛstrɪ] *n* sacristía.

vet [vɛt] *n abbr of* **veterinary surgeon** // *vt* repasar, revisar.

veteran [ˈvɛtərn] *n* veterano; **~ car** *n* coche *m* antiguo.

veterinary [ˈvɛtrɪnərɪ] *a* veterinario; **~ surgeon** *n* veterinario.

veto [ˈviːtəu], *pl* **~es** *n* veto // *vt* vetar, vedar.

vex [vɛks] *vt* (*irritate*) fastidiar; (*make impatient*) impacientar; **~ed** *a* (*question*) batallón(ona), controvertido.

via [ˈvaɪə] *prep* por, por vía de.

viable [ˈvaɪəbl] *a* viable.

viaduct [ˈvaɪədʌkt] *n* viaducto.

vibrate [vaɪˈbreɪt] *vi* vibrar; **vibration** [-ˈbreɪʃən] *n* vibración *f*.

vicar [ˈvɪkə*] *n* párroco; **~age** *n* parroquia.

vice [vaɪs] *n* (*evil*) vicio; (TECH) torno de banco.

vice- [vaɪs] *pref* vice; **~chairman** *n* vicepresidente *m*.

vice versa [ˈvaɪsɪˈvɜːsə] *ad* viceversa.

vicinity [vɪˈsɪnɪtɪ] *n* (*area*) vecindad *f*; (*nearness*) proximidad *f*.

vicious [ˈvɪʃəs] *a* (*violent*) violento; (*depraved*) depravado; (*cruel*) cruel;

(*bitter*) rencoroso; **~ness** *n* violencia; depravación *f*; crueldad *f*; rencor *m*.

victim [ˈvɪktɪm] *n* víctima *m/f*; **~ization** [-ˈzeɪʃən] *n* (*gen*) persecución *f*; (*in strike*) represalias *fpl*; **~ize** *vt* (*strikers etc*) tomar represalias contra.

victor [ˈvɪktə*] *n* vencedor/a *m/f*.

Victorian [vɪkˈtɔːrɪən] *a* victoriano.

victorious [vɪkˈtɔːrɪəs] *a* vencedor(a).

victory [ˈvɪktərɪ] *n* victoria.

video [ˈvɪdɪəu] *cpd* video; **~(-tape) recorder** *n* video-grabadora.

vie [vaɪ] *vi*: **to ~ with** competir con.

Vienna [vɪˈɛnə] *n* Viena.

view [vjuː] *n* vista, perspectiva; (*landscape*) paisaje *m*; (*opinion*) opinión *f*, criterio // *vt* (*look at*) mirar; (*examine*) examinar; **on ~** (*in museum etc*) expuesto; **in full ~ (of)** en plena vista (de); **in ~ of the fact that** en vista del hecho de que; **~er** *n* (*small projector*) visionadora; (TV) televidente *m/f*; **~finder** *n* visor *m* de imagen; **~point** *n* punto de vista.

vigil [ˈvɪdʒɪl] *n* vigilia; **to keep ~** velar; **~ance** *n* vigilancia; **~ant** *a* vigilante.

vigorous [ˈvɪgərəs] *a* enérgico, vigoroso; **vigour, vigor** (*US*) *n* energía, vigor *m*.

vile [vaɪl] *a* (*action*) vil, infame; (*smell*) asqueroso.

vilify [ˈvɪlɪfaɪ] *vt* vilipendiar.

villa [ˈvɪlə] *n* (*country house*) casa de campo; (*suburban house*) chalet *m*.

village [ˈvɪlɪdʒ] *n* aldea; **villager** *n* aldeano/a.

villain [ˈvɪlən] *n* (*scoundrel*) malvado; (*criminal*) maleante *m/f*.

vindicate [ˈvɪndɪkeɪt] *vt* vindicar, justificar.

vindictive [vɪnˈdɪktɪv] *a* vengativo.

vine [vaɪn] *n* vid *f*.

vinegar [ˈvɪnɪgə*] *n* vinagre *m*.

vineyard [ˈvɪnjɑːd] *n* viña, viñedo.

vintage [ˈvɪntɪdʒ] *n* (*year*) vendimia, cosecha; **~ wine** *n* vino añejo.

vinyl [ˈvaɪnl] *n* vinilo.

violate [ˈvaɪəleɪt] *vt* violar; **violation** [-ˈleɪʃən] *n* violación *f*.

violence [ˈvaɪələns] *n* violencia; **violent** *a* (*gen*) violento; (*intense*) intenso.

violet [ˈvaɪələt] *a* violado, violeta // *n* (*plant*) violeta.

violin [vaɪəˈlɪn] *n* violín *m*; **~ist** *n* violinista *m/f*.

VIP *n abbr of* **very important person**.

viper [ˈvaɪpə*] *n* víbora.

virgin [ˈvɜːdʒɪn] *n* virgen *m/f* // *a* virgen; **the Blessed V~** la Santísima Virgen; **~ity** [-ˈdʒɪnɪtɪ] *n* virginidad *f*.

Virgo [ˈvɜːgəu] *n* Virgo.

virile [ˈvɪraɪl] *a* viril; **virility** [vɪˈrɪlɪtɪ] *n* virilidad *f*; (*fig*) machismo.

virtually [ˈvɜːtjuəlɪ] *ad* (*almost*) virtualmente.

virtue [ˈvɜːtjuː] *n* virtud *f*; **by ~ of** en virtud de.

virtuoso [vɜːtjuˈəuzəu] *n* virtuoso.

virtuous ['vɜːtjuəs] *a* virtuoso.
virulent ['vɪrulənt] *a* virulento.
virus ['vaɪərəs] *n* virus *m*.
visa ['viːzə] *n* visado, visa (*AM*).
vis-à-vis [viːzə'viː] *prep* respecto de.
visibility [vɪzɪ'bɪlɪtɪ] *n* visibilidad *f*.
visible ['vɪzəbl] *a* visible; **visibly** *ad* visiblemente.
vision ['vɪʒən] *n* (*sight*) vista; (*foresight, in dream*) visión *f*; ~**ary** *n* visionario.
visit ['vɪzɪt] *n* visita // *vt* (*person*) visitar, hacer una visita a; (*place*) ir a, (ir a) conocer; ~**or** *n* (*gen*) visitante *m/f*; (*to one's house*) visita; (*tourist*) turista *m/f*; (*tripper*) excursionista *m/f*; ~ **ors' book** *n* libro de visitas.
visor ['vaɪzə*] *n* visera.
vista ['vɪstə] *n* vista, panorama.
visual ['vɪzjuəl] *a* visual; ~**ize** *vt* imaginarse; (*foresee*) prever.
vital ['vaɪtl] *a* (*essential*) esencial, imprescindible; (*important*) de suma importancia; (*crucial*) crítico; (*person*) enérgico, vivo; (*of life*) vital; ~**ity** [-'tælɪtɪ] *n* energía, vitalidad *f*; ~**ly** *ad*: ~**ly important** de primera importancia.
vitamin ['vɪtəmɪn] *n* vitamina.
vivacious [vɪ'veɪʃəs] *a* vivaz, alegre.
vivid ['vɪvɪd] *a* (*account*) gráfico; (*light*) intenso; (*imagination*) vivo.
vivisection [vɪvɪ'sekʃən] *n* vivisección *f*.
V-neck ['viːnek] *n* cuello de pico.
vocabulary [vəu'kæbjulərɪ] *n* vocabulario.
vocal ['vəukl] *a* vocal; (*noisy*) ruidoso; ~ **chords** *npl* cuerdas *fpl* vocales; ~**ist** *n* cantante *m/f*.
vocation [vəu'keɪʃən] *n* vocación *f*; ~**al** *a* vocacional.
vociferous [və'sɪfərəs] *a* vocinglero.
vodka ['vɔdkə] *n* vodka.
vogue [vəug] *n* boga, moda.
voice [vɔɪs] *n* voz *f* // *vt* (*opinion*) expresar.
void [vɔɪd] *n* vacío; (*hole*) hueco // *a* (*gen*) vacío; (*vacant*) vacante; (*null*) nulo, inválido.
volatile ['vɔlətaɪl] *a* volátil.
volcanic [vɔl'kænɪk] *a* volcánico; **volcano** [-'keɪnəu], *pl* -es *n* volcán *m*.
volley ['vɔlɪ] *n* (*of gunfire*) descarga; (*of stones etc*) lluvia; (*TENNIS etc*) voleo; ~**ball** *n* balonvolea, vol(e)ibol *m* (*AM*).
volt [vəult] *n* voltio; ~**age** *n* voltaje *m*.
voluble ['vɔljubl] *a* locuaz, hablador(a).
volume ['vɔljuːm] *n* (*gen*) volumen *m*; (*book*) tomo.
voluntarily ['vɔləntrɪlɪ] *ad* libremente, de su propia voluntad.
voluntary ['vɔləntərɪ] *a* voluntario, espontáneo; (*unpaid*) (a título) gratuito.
volunteer [vɔlən'tɪə*] *n* voluntario // *vi* ofrecerse (de voluntario).
voluptuous [və'lʌptjuəs] *a* voluptuoso.
vomit ['vɔmɪt] *n* vómito // *vt, vi* vomitar.
vote [vəut] *n* voto; (*votes cast*) votación *f*; (*right to* ~) derecho de votar; (*franchise*) sufragio // *vt* (*chairman*) elegir // *vi* votar,

ir a votar; **voter** *n* votante *m/f*; **voting** *n* votación *f*.
vouch [vautʃ]: **to** ~ **for** *vt* garantizar, responder de.
voucher ['vautʃə*] *n* (*for meal, petrol*) vale *m*.
vow [vau] *n* voto // *vi* hacer voto.
vowel ['vauəl] *n* vocal *f*.
voyage ['vɔɪdʒ] *n* (*journey*) viaje *m*; (*crossing*) travesía.
vulgar ['vʌlgə*] *a* (*rude*) ordinario, grosero; (*in bad taste*) de mal gusto; ~**ity** [-'gærɪtɪ] *n* grosería; mal gusto.
vulnerable ['vʌlnərəbl] *a* vulnerable.
vulture ['vʌltʃə*] *n* buitre *m*.

W

wad [wɔd] *n* (*of cotton wool, paper*) bolita; (*of banknotes etc*) fajo.
waddle ['wɔdl] *vi* anadear.
wade [weɪd] *vi*: **to** ~ **through** caminar por el agua; (*fig: a book*) leer con dificultad.
wafer ['weɪfə*] *n* (*biscuit*) galleta, barquillo; (*REL*) oblea.
waffle ['wɔfl] *n* (*CULIN*) buñuelo, panqueque *m* // *vi* meter paja.
waft [wɔft] *vt* hacer flotar // *vi* flotar.
wag [wæg] *vt* menear, agitar // *vi* moverse, menearse.
wage [weɪdʒ] *n* (*also*: ~**s**) sueldo, salario // *vt*: **to** ~ **war** hacer la guerra; ~ **claim** *n* demanda de aumento de sueldo; ~ **earner** *n* asalariado/a; ~ **freeze** *n* congelación *f* de salarios.
wager ['weɪdʒə*] *n* apuesta // *vt* apostar.
waggle ['wægl] *vt* menear, mover.
wag(g)on ['wægən] *n* (*horse-drawn*) carro; (*truck*) camión *m*; (*RAIL*) vagón *m*.
wail [weɪl] *n* gemido // *vi* gemir.
waist [weɪst] *n* cintura, talle *m*; ~**coat** *n* chaleco; ~**line** *n* talle *m*.
wait [weɪt] *n* espera; (*interval*) pausa // *vi* esperar; **to lie in** ~ **for** acechar a; **I can't** ~ **to** (*fig*) estoy deseando; **to** ~ **for** esperar (a); **to** ~ **on** *vt fus* servir a; **'no** ~**ing'** (*AUT*) 'prohibido aparcar'; ~**er** *n* camarero; ~**ing list** *n* lista de espera; ~**ing room** *n* sala de espera; ~**ress** *n* camarera.
waive [weɪv] *vt* renunciar a.
wake [weɪk], *pt* **woke** or **waked**, *pp* **woken** or **waked** *vt* (*also*: ~ **up**) despertar // *vi* (*also*: ~ **up**) despertarse // *n* (*for dead person*) vela, velatorio; (*NAUT*) estela; **waken** *vt, vi* = **wake**.
Wales [weɪlz] *n* País *m* de Gales.
walk [wɔːk] *n* paseo; (*hike*) excursión *f* a pie, caminata; (*gait*) paso, andar *m*; (*in park etc*) paseo, alameda // *vi* andar; (*for pleasure, exercise*) pasearse // *vt* (*distance*) recorrer a pie, andar; (*dog*) sacar de paseo, pasear; **10 minutes'** ~ **from here** desde aquí hay 10 minutos a pie; **people from all** ~**s of life** gente de todas las esferas; ~**er** *n* (*person*)

paseante *m/f*, caminante *m/f*; ~**ie-talkie** ['wɔːkɪ'tɔːkɪ] *n* walkie-talkie *m*, transmisor-receptor *m* (portátil); ~**ing** *n* el andar; ~**ing shoes** *npl* zapatos *mpl* para andar; ~**ing stick** *n* bastón *m*; ~**out** *n* (*of workers*) huelga sorpresa; ~**over** *n* (*col*) triunfo fácil; ~**way** *n* paseo.

wall [wɔːl] *n* pared *f*; (*exterior*) muro; (*city* ~ *etc*) muralla; ~**ed** *a* (*city*) amurallado; (*garden*) con tapia.

wallet ['wɔlɪt] *n* cartera.

wallflower ['wɔːlflauə*] *n* alhelí *m*; **to be a** ~ (*fig*) comer pavo.

wallop ['wɔləp] *vt* (*col*) zurrar.

wallow ['wɔləu] *vi* revolcarse.

wallpaper ['wɔːlpeɪpə*] *n* papel *m* pintado.

walnut ['wɔːlnʌt] *n* nuez *f*; (*tree*) nogal *m*.

walrus ['wɔːlrəs], *pl* ~ *or* ~**es** *n* morsa.

waltz [wɔːlts] *n* vals *m* // *vi* bailar el vals.

wand [wɔnd] *n* (*also*: **magic** ~) varita (mágica).

wander ['wɔndə*] *vi* (*person*) vagar, deambular; (*thoughts*) divagar; (*get lost*) extraviarse // *vt* recorrer, vagar por; ~**er** *n* vagabundo; ~**ing** *a* errante; (*thoughts*) distraído.

wane [weɪn] *vi* menguar.

wangle ['wæŋgl] *vt* (*col*): **to** ~ **sth** agenciarse algo.

want [wɔnt] *vt* (*wish for*) querer, desear; (*demand*) exigir; (*need*) necesitar; (*lack*) carecer de // *n*: **for** ~ **of** por falta de; ~**s** *npl* (*needs*) necesidades *fpl*; **to** ~ **to do** querer hacer; **to** ~ **sb to do sth** querer que uno haga algo; ~**ing** *a* falto, deficiente; **to be found** ~**ing** no estar a la altura de las circunstancias.

wanton ['wɔntn] *a* (*playful*) juguetón(ona); (*licentious*) lascivo.

war [wɔː*] *n* guerra; **to make** ~ hacer la guerra.

ward [wɔːd] *n* (*in hospital*) sala; (*POL*) distrito electoral; (*LAW: child*) pupilo; **to** ~ **off** *vt* desviar, parar; (*attack*) rechazar.

warden ['wɔːdn] *n* (*of institution*) director *m*; (*of park, game reserve*) guardián *m*; (*also*: **traffic** ~) guardia *m/f*.

warder ['wɔːdə*] *n* guardián *m*, carcelero.

wardrobe ['wɔːdrəub] *n* (*cupboard*) armario; (*clothes*) guardarropa.

warehouse ['wɛəhaus] *n* almacén *m*, depósito.

wares [wɛəz] *npl* mercancías *fpl*.

war: ~**fare** *n* guerra; ~**head** *n* cabeza armada.

warily ['wɛərɪlɪ] *ad* con cautela, cautelosamente.

warlike ['wɔːlaɪk] *a* guerrero.

warm [wɔːm] *a* caliente; (*thanks*) efusivo; (*clothes etc*) cálido; (*welcome, day*) caluroso; **it's** ~ hace calor; **I'm** ~ tengo calor; **to** ~ **up** *vi* (*person, room*) calentarse; (*athlete*) hacer ejercicios de calentamiento; (*discussion*) acalorarse // *vt* calentar; ~**hearted** *a* afectuoso; ~**ly** *ad* afectuosamente; ~**th** *n* calor *m*.

warn [wɔːn] *vt* avisar, prevenir; ~**ing** *n* aviso, advertencia; ~**ing light** *n* luz *f* de advertencia.

warp [wɔːp] *vi* diformarse.

warrant ['wɔrnt] *n* (*guarantee*) garantía; (*LAW*) mandato judicial.

warranty ['wɔrəntɪ] *n* garantía.

warren ['wɔrən] *n* (*of rabbits*) madriguera; (*house*) conejera.

warrior ['wɔrɪə*] *n* guerrero.

warship ['wɔːʃɪp] *n* buque *m* o barco de guerra.

wart [wɔːt] *n* verruga.

wartime ['wɔːtaɪm] *n*: **in** ~ en tiempos de guerra, en la guerra.

wary ['wɛərɪ] *a* cauteloso, cauto.

was [wɔz] *pt of* **be**.

wash [wɔʃ] *vt* lavar // *vi* lavarse // *n* (*clothes etc*) lavado; (*bath*) baño; (*of ship*) estela; **to have a** ~ lavarse; **to** ~ **away** *vt* (*stain*) quitar lavando; (*subj: river etc*) llevarse; (*fig*) regar; **to** ~ **off** *vt* quitar lavando; **to** ~ **up** *vi* fregar los platos; ~**able** *a* lavable; ~**basin** *n* lavabo; ~**er** *n* (*TECH*) arandela; ~**ing** *n* (*dirty*) ropa sucia; (*clean*) colada; ~**ing machine** *n* lavadora; ~**ing powder** *n* jabón *m* en polvo; ~**ing-up** *n* fregado, platos *mpl* (para fregar); ~**-out** *n* (*col*) fracaso; ~**room** *n* servicios *mpl*.

wasn't ['wɔznt] = **was not**.

wasp [wɔsp] *n* avispa.

wastage ['weɪstɪdʒ] *n* desgaste *m*; (*loss*) pérdida; **natural** ~ desgaste natural.

waste [weɪst] *n* derroche *m*, despilfarro; (*wastage*) desgaste *m*; (*of time*) pérdida; (*food*) sobras *fpl*; (*rubbish*) basura, desperdicios *mpl* // *a* (*material*) de desecho; (*left over*) sobrante; (*land*) baldío // *vt* (*squander*) malgastar, derrochar; (*time*) perder; (*opportunity*) desperdiciar; (*use up*) consumir; **to** ~ **away** *vi* consumirse; ~**bin** *n* cubo de la basura; ~**disposal unit** *n* triturador *m* de basura; ~**ful** *a* derrochador(a); (*process*) antieconómico; ~ **ground** *n* terreno baldío; ~**paper basket** *n* papelera; ~ **pipe** *n* tubo de desagüe.

watch [wɔtʃ] *n* reloj *m*; (*act of watching*) vigilia; (*vigilance*) vigilancia; (*guard*: MIL) centinela *m*; (NAUT: *spell of duty*) guardia // *vt* (*look at*) mirar, observar; (: *match, programme*) ver; (*spy on, guard*) vigilar; (*be careful of*) cuidarse de, tener cuidado de // *vi* ver, mirar; (*keep guard*) montar guardia; **to** ~ **out** *vi* cuidarse, tener cuidado; ~**dog** *n* perro guardián; ~**ful** *a* vigilante, observador(a); ~**maker** *n* relojero; ~**man** *n* guardián *m*; (*also*: **night** ~**man**) sereno; (*in factory*) vigilante *m* nocturno; ~**strap** *n* pulsera (de reloj); ~**word** *n* lema *m*.

water ['wɔːtə*] *n* agua // *vt* (*plant*) regar; **to** ~ **down** *vt* (*milk*) aguar; ~ **closet** *n* wáter *m*; ~**colour** *n* acuarela; ~**cress** *n* berro; ~**fall** *n* cascada, salto de agua; ~ **hole** *n* charco; ~**ing can** *n* regadera; ~

level n nivel m del agua; ~ lily n nenúfar m; ~line n (NAUT) línea de flotación; ~logged a empapado; ~ main n cañería del agua; ~mark n (on paper) filigrana; ~melon n sandía; ~ polo n polo acuático; ~proof a impermeable; ~shed n (GEO) cuenca; (fig) momento crítico; ~-skiing n esquí m acuático; ~ tank n depósito de agua; ~tight a hermético; ~works npl central f depuradora; ~y a (colour) desvaído; (coffee) aguado; (eyes) lloroso.

watt [wɔt] n vatio.

wave [weɪv] n ola; (of hand) ademán m, señal f; (RADIO) onda; (in hair) ondulación f; (fig) oleada // vi agitar la mano; (flag) ondear // vt (handkerchief) agitar; (weapon) blandir; (hair) ondular; ~length n longitud f de onda.

waver ['weɪvə*] vi oscilar; (person) vacilar.

wavy ['weɪvɪ] a ondulado.

wax [wæks] n cera // vt encerar // vi (moon) crecer; ~works npl museo sg de cera.

way [weɪ] n (gen) camino; (distance) trayecto, recorrido; (direction) dirección f, sentido; (manner) modo, manera; (habit) costumbre f; (condition) estado; which ~? ¿por dónde?, ¿en qué dirección?; to be on one's ~ estar en camino; to be in the ~ bloquear el camino; to go out of one's ~ to do sth desvivirse por hacer algo; to lose one's ~ extraviarse; in a ~ en cierto modo o sentido; by the ~ a propósito; '~ out' 'salida'; the ~ back el camino de vuelta; 'give ~' (AUT) 'ceda el paso'.

waylay [weɪ'leɪ] (irg: like lay) vt acechar.

wayward ['weɪwəd] a (wilful) voluntarioso; (capricious) caprichoso; (naughty) travieso.

W.C. ['dʌblju'si:] n wáter m.

we [wi:] pl pron nosotros/as.

weak [wi:k] a (gen) débil, flojo; (tea) claro; ~en vi debilitarse; (give way) ceder // vt debilitar; (lessen) disminuir; ~ling n persona débil o delicada; ~ness n debilidad f; (fault) punto débil.

wealth [wɛlθ] n (money, resources) riqueza; (of details) abundancia; ~y a rico.

wean [wi:n] vt destetar.

weapon ['wɛpən] n arma.

wear [wɛə*] n (use) uso; (deterioration through use) desgaste m; (clothing): sports/baby~ ropa de deportes/para niños // (vb: pt wore, pp worn) vt (clothes) llevar; (shoes) calzar; (put on) ponerse; (damage: through use) gastar, usar // vi (last) durar; (rub through etc) desgastarse; ~ and tear n desgaste m; to ~ away vt gastar // vi desgastarse; to ~ down vt gastar; (strength) agotar; to ~ off vi (pain etc) pasar, desaparecer; to ~ out vt desgastar; (person, strength) agotar.

weariness ['wɪərɪnɪs] n cansancio; (boredom) aburrimiento, hastío.

weary ['wɪərɪ] a (tired) cansado; (dispirited) abatido // vt cansar // vi: to ~ of cansarse de, aburrirse de.

weasel ['wi:zl] n (ZOOL) comadreja.

weather ['wɛðə*] n tiempo // vt (storm, crisis) hacer frente a; ~-beaten a curtido; ~ cock n veleta; ~ forecast n boletín m meteorológico; ~ vane n = ~ cock.

weave [wi:v], pt wove, pp woven vt (cloth) tejer; (fig) entretejer; weaver n tejedor/a m/f; weaving n tejeduría.

web [wɛb] n (of spider) telaraña; (on foot) membrana; (network) red f; ~bed a (foot) palmeado; ~bing n (on chair) cinchas fpl.

wed [wɛd], pt, pp wedded vt casar // vi casarse // n: the newly-~s los recién casados.

we'd [wi:d] = we had; we would.

wedded ['wɛdɪd] pt, pp of wed.

wedding ['wɛdɪŋ] n boda, casamiento; silver/golden ~ bodas fpl de plata/de oro; ~ day n día m de la boda; ~ dress n traje m de novia; ~ present n regalo de boda; ~ ring n anillo de boda.

wedge [wɛdʒ] n (of wood etc) cuña; (of cake) porción f // vt acuñar; (pack tightly) apretar.

wedlock ['wɛdlɔk] n matrimonio.

Wednesday ['wɛdnzdɪ] n miércoles m.

wee [wi:] a (Scottish) pequeñito.

weed [wi:d] n mala hierba, maleza // vt escardar, desherbar; ~-killer n herbicida m.

week [wi:k] n semana; ~day n día m laborable; ~end n fin m de semana; ~ly ad semanalmente, cada semana // a semanal // n semanario.

weep [wi:p], pt, pp wept vi, vt llorar; ~ing willow n sauce m llorón.

weigh [weɪ] vt, vi pesar; to ~ down vt sobrecargar; (fig: with worry) agobiar; to ~ up vt pesar; ~bridge n báscula-puente f.

weight [weɪt] n peso; (on scale) pesa; to lose/put on ~ adelgazarse/engordarse; ~lessness n ingravidez f; ~ lifter n levantador m de pesos; ~y a pesado.

weir [wɪə*] n presa.

weird [wɪəd] a raro, extraño.

welcome ['wɛlkəm] a bienvenido // n bienvenida // vt dar la bienvenida a; (be glad of) alegrarse de; welcoming a acogedor(a); (speech) de bienvenida.

weld [wɛld] n soldadura // vt soldar; ~er n (person) soldador m; ~ing n soldadura.

welfare ['wɛlfɛə*] n bienestar m; (social aid) asistencia social; ~ state n estado de bienestar.

well [wɛl] n fuente f, pozo // ad bien // a: to be ~ estar bien (de salud) // excl ¡vaya!, ¡bueno!; as ~ también; as ~ as igual que; ~ done! ¡bien hecho!; get ~ soon! ¡que te mejores pronto!; to do ~ ir o salir bien; to ~ up vi brotar.

we'll [wi:l] = we will, we shall.

well: ~**-behaved** a bien educado, formal; ~**-being** n bienestar m; ~**-built** a (person) fornido; ~**-deserved** a merecido; ~**-developed** a bien desarrollado; ~**-dressed** a bien vestido; ~**-heeled** a (col: wealthy) rico; ~**-informed** a enterado.

wellingtons ['wɛlɪŋtənz] n (also: **wellington boots**) botas fpl de goma.

well: ~**-known** a (person) conocido; ~**-mannered** a educado; ~**-meaning** a bienintencionado; ~**-off** a pudiente, con dinero; ~**-read** a culto; ~**-to-do** a acomodado; ~**-wisher** n admirador/a m/f, amigo.

Welsh [wɛlʃ] a galés(esa) // n (LING) galés m; ~ **man/woman** n galés/esa m/f.

went [wɛnt] pt of **go.**

wept [wɛpt] pt, pp of **weep.**

were [wɔː*] pt of **be.**

we're [wɪə*] = **we are.**

weren't [wɔːnt] = **were not.**

west [wɛst] n oeste m // a occidental, del oeste // ad hacia el o al oeste; **the W~** n el Oeste, el Occidente; **the W~ Country** n el suroeste de Inglaterra; ~**erly** a (situation) oeste; (wind) del oeste; ~**ern** a occidental // n (CINEMA) película del oeste; **W~ Germany** n Alemania Occidental; **W~ Indies** npl Antillas fpl; ~**ward(s)** ad hacia el oeste.

wet [wɛt] a (damp) húmedo; (~ through) mojado; (rainy) lluvioso; **to get** ~ mojarse; '~ **paint** 'recién pintado'; **to be a** ~ **blanket** (fig) ser un/una aguafiestas; ~**ness** n humedad f; ~ **suit** n traje m de buzo.

we've [wiːv] = **we have.**

whack [wæk] vt dar un buen golpe a; ~**ed** a (col: tired) reventado.

whale [weɪl] n (ZOOL) ballena.

wharf [wɔːf], pl **wharves** [wɔːvz] n muelle m.

what [wɔt] excl ¡qué!, ¡cómo! // det que // pron (interrogative) ¿qué?, ¿cómo?; (relative, indirect: object) lo que; (: subject) el/la que; ~ **are you doing?** ¿qué haces?; **I saw** ~ **you did** he visto lo que hiciste; ~ **a mess!** ¡qué lío!; ~ **is it called?** ¿cómo se llama?; ~ **about me?** ¿y yo?; ~**ever** det: ~**ever book you choose** cualquier libro que elijas // pron: **do** ~**ever is necessary** haga lo que sea necesario; **no reason** ~**ever** or ~**soever** ninguna razón sea la que sea; **nothing** ~**ever** nada en absoluto.

wheat [wiːt] n trigo.

wheel [wiːl] n rueda; (AUT. also: **steering** ~) volante m; (NAUT) timón m // vt (pram etc) empujar // vi (also: ~ **round**) dar la vuelta, girar; ~**barrow** n carretilla; ~**chair** n silla de ruedas; ~**house** n timonera.

wheeze [wiːz] n respiración f ruidosa // vi resollar.

when [wɛn] ad cuándo // conj cuando; (whereas) mientras; **on the day** ~ **I met**

him el día que le conocí; ~**ever** conj cuando, todas las veces que; (every time that) siempre que.

where [wɛə*] ad dónde // conj donde; **this is** ~ aquí es donde; ~**abouts** ad ¿dónde? // n: **nobody knows his** ~**abouts** nadie conoce su paradero; ~**as** conj visto que, mientras; **wherever** [-'ɛvə*] ad dondequiera que; (interrogative) ¿dónde?; ~**withal** n recursos mpl.

whet [wɛt] vt estimular.

whether ['wɛðə*] conj si; **I don't know** ~ **to accept or not** no sé si aceptar o no; ~ **you go or not** vayas o no vayas.

which [wɪtʃ] det (interrogative) ¿qué?, ¿cuál?; ~ **one of you?** ¿cuál de vosotros?; ~ **picture do you want?** ¿qué cuadro quieres? // pron (interrogative) ¿cuál?; (relative: subject) que, lo que; (: object) el que etc, el cual etc, lo cual; **I don't mind** ~ no me importa cuál; **the apple** ~ **is on the table** la manzana que está sobre la mesa; **the chair on** ~ **you are sitting** la silla sobre la que estás sentado; **he said he knew,** ~ **is true** el dijo que sabía, lo cual es cierto; **in** ~ **case** en cuyo caso; ~**ever** det: **take** ~**ever book you prefer** coja el libro que prefiera; ~**ever book you take** cualquier libro que coja.

whiff [wɪf] n bocanada.

while [waɪl] n rato, momento // conj durante; (as long as) mientras; (although) aunque; **for a** ~ durante algún tiempo.

whim [wɪm] n capricho.

whimper ['wɪmpə*] n (weeping) lloriqueo; (moan) quejido // vi lloriquear; quejarse.

whimsical ['wɪmzɪkl] a (person) caprichoso; (look) extraño.

whine [waɪn] n (of pain) gemido; (of engine) zumbido // vi gemir; zumbar.

whip [wɪp] n látigo; (for riding) fusta; (Brit: POL) oficial disciplinario del partido // vt azotar; (snatch) arrebatar; ~**ped cream** n crema batida; ~**-round** n colecta.

whirl [wɔːl] n remolino // vt hacer girar, dar vueltas a // vi girar, dar vueltas; (leaves, water etc) arremolinarse; ~**pool** n remolino; ~**wind** n torbellino.

whirr [wɔː*] vi rechinar, zumbar.

whisk [wɪsk] n (CULIN) batidor m // vt batir; **to** ~ **sth away from sb** arrebatarle algo a uno; **to** ~ **sb away** or **off** llevar rápidamente a uno.

whisker [wɪskə*] n: ~**s** (of animal) bigotes mpl; (of man) patillas fpl.

whisk(e)y ['wɪskɪ] n whisky m.

whisper ['wɪspə*] n cuchicheo; (rumour) rumor m; (fig) susurro, murmullo // vi cuchichear, hablar bajo; (fig) susurrar.

whist [wɪst] n whist m.

whistle ['wɪsl] n (sound) silbido; (object) silbato // vi silbar.

white [waɪt] a blanco; (pale) pálido // n blanco; (of egg) clara; ~**-collar worker** n oficinista m/f; ~ **elephant** n (fig) maula; ~ **lie** n mentira piadosa; ~**ness** n blancura; ~ **paper** n (POL) libro rojo; ~**wash** n (paint) jalbegue m, cal f // vt enjalbegar; (fig) encubrir.

whiting ['waɪtɪŋ] n, pl inv (fish) pescadilla.

Whitsun ['wɪtsn] n pentecostés m.

whittle ['wɪtl] vt: **to** ~ **away,** ~ **down** reducir poco a poco.

whizz [wɪz] vi: **to** ~ **past** or **by** pasar a toda velocidad; ~ **kid** n (col) prodigio, portento.

who [huː] pron (relative) que, el que etc, quien; (interrogative) ¿quién?; (pl) ¿quiénes?; ~**ever** pron: ~**ever finds it** cualquiera o quienquiera que lo encuentre; **ask** ~**ever you like** pregunta a quien quieras; ~**ever be marries** no importa con quién se case.

whole [həʊl] a (complete) todo, entero; (not broken) intacto // n (total) total m; (sum) conjunto; **the** ~ **of the town** toda la ciudad, la ciudad entera; **on the** ~, **as a** ~ en general; ~**hearted** a sincero, cordial; ~**sale** n venta al por mayor // a al por mayor; (destruction) sistemático; ~**saler** n mayorista m/f; ~**some** a sano; **wholly** ad totalmente, enteramente.

whom [huːm] pron que, a quien; (interrogative) ¿a quién?

whooping cough ['huːpɪŋkɔf] n tos f ferina.

whopper ['wɔpə*] n cosa muy grande; (lie) bola; **whopping** a (col: big) enorme.

whore [hɔː*] n (col: pej) puta.

whose [huːz] det: ~ **book is this?** ¿de quién es este libro?; **the man** ~ **son you rescued** el hombre cuyo hijo salvaste; **the girl** ~ **sister you were speaking to** la chica con cuya hermana estabas hablando // pron: ~ **is this?** ¿de quién es esto?; **I know** ~ **it is** yo sé de quien es.

why [waɪ] ad por qué; (interrogative) ¿por qué?, ¿para qué? // excl ¡toma!, ¡cómo!; **tell me** ~ dime por qué, dime la razón; ~**ever** ad por qué.

wick [wɪk] n mecha.

wicked ['wɪkɪd] a malvado, cruel.

wicker ['wɪkə*] n (also: ~**work**) artículos mpl de mimbre.

wicket ['wɪkɪt] n (CRICKET) palos mpl.

wide [waɪd] a ancho; (region, knowledge) vasto, grande; (choice) grande // ad: **to open** ~ abrir de par en par; **to shoot** ~ errar el tiro; ~-**awake** a bien despierto; (fig) despabilado; ~**ly** ad (different) muy; **it is** ~**ly believed that...** hay una convicción general de que...; **widen** vt ensanchar; ~**ness** n anchura; ~ **open** a abierto de par en par; ~**spread** a (belief etc) extendido, general.

widow ['wɪdəʊ] n viuda; ~**ed** a viudo; ~**er** n viudo.

width [wɪdθ] n anchura; (of cloth) ancho.

wield [wiːld] vt (sword) manejar; (power) ejercer.

wife [waɪf], pl **wives** [waɪvz] n mujer f, esposa.

wig [wɪg] n peluca.

wiggle ['wɪgl] vt menear (rápidamente) // vi menearse.

wild [waɪld] a (animal) salvaje; (plant) silvestre; (rough) furioso, violento; (idea) disparatado, descabellado; (person) loco; ~**s** npl regiones fpl salvajes, tierras fpl vírgenes; ~**erness** ['wɪldənɪs] n desierto; ~**life** n fauna; ~**ly** ad (roughly) violentamente; (foolishly) locamente; (rashly) descabelladamente.

wilful ['wɪlful] a (person) voluntarioso; (action) deliberado; (obstinate) testarudo; (child) travieso.

will [wɪl] auxiliary vb: **he** ~ **come** vendrá // vt, pt, pp **willed**: **to** ~ **sb to do sth** desear que alguien haga algo; **he** ~**ed himself to go on** con gran fuerza de voluntad, continuó // n voluntad f; (testament) testamento; ~**ing** a (with goodwill) de buena voluntad; (submissive) complaciente; ~**ingly** ad con mucho gusto; ~**ingness** n buena voluntad.

willow ['wɪləʊ] n sauce m.

will power n fuerza de voluntad.

wilt [wɪlt] vi marchitarse.

wily ['waɪlɪ] a astuto.

win [wɪn] n (in sports etc) victoria, triunfo // (vb: pt, pp **won**) vt ganar; (obtain) conseguir, lograr // vi ganar, tener éxito; **to** ~ **over,** ~ **round** vt atraerse.

wince [wɪns] vi estremecerse.

winch [wɪntʃ] n torno.

wind [wɪnd] n viento; (MED) flatulencia; (breath) aliento // (vb: [waɪnd], pt, pp **wound**) vt enrollar; (wrap) envolver; (clock, toy) dar cuerda a // vi (road, river) serpentear // vt [wɪnd] (take breath away from) dejar sin aliento a; **to** ~ **up** vt (clock) dar cuerda a; (debate) concluir, terminar; ~**break** n abrigada; ~**fall** n golpe m de suerte; ~**ing** a (road) tortuoso; ~ **instrument** n (MUS) instrumento de viento; ~**mill** n molino de viento.

window ['wɪndəʊ] n ventana; (in car, train) ventanilla; (in shop etc) escaparate m; ~ **box** n jardinera (de ventana); ~ **cleaner** n (person) limpiacristales m inv; ~ **ledge** n alféizar m; ~ **pane** n cristal m; ~**sill** n alféizar m.

windpipe ['wɪndpaɪp] n tráquea.

windscreen ['wɪndskriːn], **windshield** ['wɪndʃiːld] (US) n parabrisas m inv; ~ **washer** n lavaparabrisas m inv; ~ **wiper** n limpiaparabrisas m inv.

windswept ['wɪndswɛpt] a azotado por el viento.

windy ['wɪndɪ] a de mucho viento; **it's** ~ hace viento.

wine [waɪn] n vino; ~ **cellar** n bodega; ~ **glass** n copa (para vino); ~ **list** n lista de vinos; ~ **merchant** n vinatero; ~ **tasting** n degustación f de vinos.

wing [wɪŋ] n (gen) ala; (AUT) aleta, guardabarros m inv; ~**s** npl (THEATRE) bastidores mpl; ~**er** n (SPORT) extremo.

wink [wɪŋk] n guiño, pestañeo // vi guiñar,

pestañear; (*light etc*) parpadear.

winner ['wɪnə*] *n* ganador/a *m/f*.

winning ['wɪnɪŋ] *a* (*team*) ganador(a); (*goal*) decisivo; ~s *npl* ganancias *fpl*; ~ **post** *n* meta.

winter ['wɪntə*] *n* invierno // *vi* invernar; ~ **sports** *npl* deportes *mpl* de invierno.

wintry ['wɪntrɪ] *a* invernal.

wipe [waɪp] *n*: **to give sth a** ~ pasar un trapo sobre algo // *vt* limpiar; **to** ~ **off** *vt* limpiar con un trapo; **to** ~ **out** *vt* (*debt*) liquidar; (*memory*) borrar; (*destroy*) destruir.

wire ['waɪə*] *n* alambre *m*; (ELEC) cable *m* (eléctrico); (TEL) telegrama *m* // *vt* (*house*) instalar el alambrado de; (*also*: ~ **up**) conectar // *vi* poner un telegrama.

wireless ['waɪəlɪs] *n* radio *f*.

wiring ['waɪərɪŋ] *n* instalación *f* eléctrica, alambrado.

wiry ['waɪərɪ] *a* nervioso, nervudo.

wisdom ['wɪzdəm] *n* sabiduría, saber *m*; (*good sense*) cordura; (*care*) prudencia; ~ **tooth** *n* muela del juicio.

wise [waɪz] *a* sabio; (*sensible*) cuerdo; (*careful*) prudente.

...wise [waɪz] *suff*: **time**~ en cuanto a *o* respecto al tiempo.

wisecrack ['waɪzkræk] *n* broma.

wish [wɪʃ] *n* (*desire*) deseo // *vt* desear; (*want*) querer; **best** ~**es** (*on birthday etc*) felicidades *fpl*; **with best** ~**es** (*in letter*) saludos *mpl*, recuerdos *mpl*; **to** ~ **sb goodbye** despedirse de uno; **he** ~**ed me well** me deseó mucha suerte; **to** ~ **to do/sb to do sth** querer hacer/que alguien haga algo; **to** ~ **for** desear; **it's** ~**ful thinking** es un espejismo.

wisp [wɪsp] *n* mechón *m*; (*of smoke*) voluta.

wistful ['wɪstful] *a* pensativo.

wit [wɪt] *n* (*wittiness*) ingenio, gracia; (*intelligence*) entendimiento; (*person*) chistoso/a.

witch [wɪtʃ] *n* bruja; ~**craft** *n* brujería.

with [wɪð, wɪθ] *prep* con; **red** ~ **anger** rojo de cólera; **the man** ~ **the grey hat** el hombre del sombrero gris; **to be** ~ **it** (*fig*) estar al tanto *o* a la moda; **I am** ~ **you** (*I understand*) te entiendo.

withdraw [wɪθ'drɔː] (*irg: like draw*) *vt* retirar, sacar // *vi* retirarse; (*go back on promise*) retractarse; **to** ~ **money (from the bank)** retirar fondos (del banco); ~**al** *n* retirada; ~**n** *a* (*person*) reservado, introvertido.

wither ['wɪðə*] *vi* marchitarse; ~**ed** *a* marchito.

withhold [wɪθ'həuld] (*irg: like hold*) *vt* (*money*) retener; (*decision*) aplazar; (*permission*) negar; (*information*) ocultar.

within [wɪð'ɪn] *prep* dentro de // *ad* dentro; ~ **reach** al alcance de la mano; ~ **sight of** a la vista de; ~ **the week** antes de acabar la semana.

without [wɪð'aut] *prep* sin.

withstand [wɪθ'stænd] (*irg: like stand*) *vt* resistir a.

witness ['wɪtnɪs] *n* (*person*) testigo; (*evidence*) testimonio // *vt* (*event*) presenciar; (*document*) atestiguar la veracidad de; ~ **box**, ~ **stand** (US) *n* tribuna de los testigos.

witticism ['wɪtɪsɪzm] *n* dicho ingenioso.

witty ['wɪtɪ] *a* ingenioso, salado.

wives [waɪvz] *pl of* **wife**.

wizard ['wɪzəd] *n* hechicero.

wk *abbr of* **week**.

wobble ['wɔbl] *vi* tambalearse; (*chair*) ser poco firme.

woe [wəu] *n* desgracia.

woke [wəuk], **woken** ['wəukən] *pt, pp of* **wake**.

wolf [wulf], *pl* **wolves** [wulvz] *n* lobo.

woman ['wumən], *pl* **women** *n* mujer *f*; ~**ly** *a* femenino.

womb [wuːm] *n* (ANAT) matriz *f*, útero.

women ['wɪmɪn] *pl of* **woman**.

won [wʌn] *pt, pp of* **win**.

wonder ['wʌndə*] *n* maravilla, prodigio; (*feeling*) asombro // *vi*: **to** ~ **whether** preguntarse si; **to** ~ **at** asombrarse de; ~ **about** pensar sobre *o* en; **it's no** ~ **that** no es de extrañarse que; ~**ful** *a* maravilloso; ~**fully** *ad* maravillosamente, estupendamente.

won't [wəunt] = **will not.**

woo [wuː] *vt* (*woman*) cortejar.

wood [wud] *n* (*timber*) madera; (*forest*) bosque *m*; ~ **carving** *n* escultura de madera; ~**ed** *a* arbolado; ~**en** *a* de madera; (*fig*) inexpresivo; ~**pecker** *n* pájaro carpintero; ~**wind** *n* (MUS) instrumentos *mpl* de viento de madera; ~**work** *n* carpintería; ~**worm** *n* carcoma.

wool [wul] *n* lana; **to pull the** ~ **over sb's eyes** (*fig*) dar a uno gato por liebre; ~**len**, ~**en** (US) *a* de lana; ~**lens** *npl* géneros *mpl* de lana; ~**ly**, ~**y** (US) *a* lanudo, de lana; (*fig: ideas*) confuso.

word [wəːd] *n* palabra; (*news*) noticia; (*message*) aviso // *vt* redactar; **in other** ~**s** en otras palabras; **to break/keep one's** ~ faltar a la palabra/cumplir la promesa; ~**ing** *n* redacción *f*.

wore [wɔː*] *pt of* **wear.**

work [wəːk] *n* (*gen*) trabajo; (*job*) empleo, trabajo; (ART, LITERATURE) obra // *vi* trabajar; (*mechanism*) funcionar, marchar; (*medicine*) ser eficaz, surtir efecto // *vt* (*clay, wood etc*) tallar; (*mine etc*) explotar; (*machine*) manejar, hacer funcionar; (*cause*) producir; **to be out of** ~ estar parado, no tener trabajo; ~**s** *n* (*factory*) fábrica // *npl* (*of clock, machine*) mecanismo *sg*; **to** ~ **loose** *vi* (*part*) desprenderse; (*knot*) aflojarse; **to** ~ **on** *vt fus* trabajar en, dedicarse a; (*principle*) basarse en; **to** ~ **out** *vi* (*plans etc*) salir bien, funcionar // *vt* (*problem*) resolver; (*plan*) elaborar; **does it** ~ **out?** ¿da resultado?; **it** ~**s out at £100** suma 100 libras; **to get** ~**ed up** exaltarse; ~**able** *a* (*solution*) práctico, factible; ~**er** *n* trabajador/a, obrero; ~**ing class** *n* clase

f obrera; ~**ing-class** *a* de clase obrera; **in** ~**ing order** en funcionamiento; ~**man** *n* obrero; ~**manship** *n* (*art*) hechura, arte *m*; (*skill*) habilidad *f*, trabajo; ~**shop** *n* taller *m*; ~**-to-rule** *n* huelga de celo.
world [wɔːld] *n* mundo // *cpd* (*champion*) del mundo; (*power, war*) mundial; **to think the** ~ **of sb** (*fig*) tener un concepto muy alto de uno; ~**ly** *a* mundano; ~**-wide** *a* mundial, universal.
worm [wɔːm] *n* gusano; (*earth*~) lombriz *f*.
worn [wɔːn] *pp of* **wear** // *a* usado; ~**-out** *a* (*object*) gastado; (*person*) rendido, agotado.
worried ['wʌrɪd] *a* preocupado.
worry ['wʌrɪ] *n* preocupación *f* // *vt* preocupar, inquietar // *vi* preocuparse; ~**ing** *a* inquietante.
worse [wɔːs] *a, ad* peor, inferior // *n* el peor, lo peor; **a change for the** ~ un empeoramiento; **worsen** *vt, vi* empeorar; ~ **off** *a* (*fig*): **you'll be** ~ **off this way** de esta forma estarás peor que nunca.
worship ['wɔːʃɪp] *n* culto; (*act*) adoración *f* // *vt* adorar; **Your W**~ (*to mayor*) señor alcalde; (*to judge*) señor juez; ~**per** *n* devoto/a.
worst [wɔːst] *a* (el/la) peor // *ad* peor // *n* lo peor; **at** ~ en lo peor de los casos.
worth [wɔːθ] *n* valor *m* // *a*: **to be** ~ valer; **it's** ~ **it** vale *o* merece la pena; ~**less** *a* sin valor; (*useless*) inútil; ~**while** *a* (*activity*) que merece la pena; (*cause*) loable.
worthy [wɔːðɪ] *a* (*person*) respetable; (*motive*) honesto; ~ **of** digno de.
would [wud] *auxiliary vb*: **she** ~ **come** ella vendría; **he** ~ **have come** él hubiera venido; ~ **you like a biscuit?** ¿quieres una galleta?; **he** ~ **go on Mondays** solía ir los lunes; ~**-be** *a* (*pej*) presunto, aspirante.
wound [waund] *pt, pp of* **wind** // *n* [wuːnd] herida // *vt* [wuːnd] herir.
wove [wəuv], **woven** ['wəuvən] *pt, pp of* **weave**.
wrangle ['ræŋgl] *n* riña // *vi* reñir.
wrap [ræp] *n* (*stole*) chal *m*; (*cape*) capa // *vt* (*also*: ~ **up**) envolver; ~**per** *n* (*of book*) cubierta, tapa; ~**ping paper** *n* papel *m* de envolver.
wrath [rɔθ] *n* cólera.
wreath [riːθ], *pl* ~**s** [riːðz] *n* (*funeral* ~) corona; (*of flowers*) guirnalda.
wreathe [riːð] *vt* ceñir.
wreck [rɛk] *n* naufragio; (*ship*) restos *mpl* del barco; (*pej: person*) ruina // *vt* destruir, hundir; (*fig*) arruinar; ~**age** *n* restos *mpl*; (*of building*) escombros *mpl*.
wren [rɛn] *n* (*ZOOL*) reyezuelo.
wrench [rɛntʃ] *n* (*TECH*) llave *f* inglesa; (*tug*) tirón *m* // *vt* arrancar; **to** ~ **sth from sb** arrebatar algo violentamente a uno.
wrestle ['rɛsl] *vi*: **to** ~ (**with sb**) luchar (con *o* contra uno); **wrestler** *n* luchador *m*

(de lucha libre); **wrestling** *n* lucha libre; **wrestling match** *n* partido de lucha libre.
wretched ['rɛtʃɪd] *a* miserable.
wriggle ['rɪgl] *n* (*gen*) culebreo // *vi* (*gen*) serpentear.
wring [rɪŋ], *pt, pp* **wrung** *vt* torcer, retorcer; (*wet clothes*) escurrir; (*fig*): **to** ~ **sth out of sb** sacar algo por la fuerza a uno.
wrinkle ['rɪŋkl] *n* arruga // *vt* arrugar // *vi* arrugarse.
wrist [rɪst] *n* muñeca; ~ **watch** *n* reloj *m* de pulsera.
writ [rɪt] *n* mandato judicial; **to issue a** ~ **against sb** demandar a uno (en juicio).
write [raɪt], *pt* **wrote**, *pp* **written** *vt, vi* escribir; **to** ~ **down** *vt* escribir; (*note*) apuntar; **to** ~ **off** *vt* (*debt*) borrar (como incobrable); (*depreciate*) depreciar; **to** ~ **out** *vt* escribir; **to** ~ **up** *vt* redactar; ~**-off** *n* pérdida total; **the car is a** ~**-off** el coche es pura chatarra; **writer** *n* escritor/a *m/f*.
writhe [raɪð] *vi* retorcerse.
writing ['raɪtɪŋ] *n* escritura; (*hand*-~) letra; (*of author*) obra; **in** ~ por escrito; ~ **paper** *n* papel *m* de escribir.
written ['rɪtn] *pp of* **write**.
wrong [rɔŋ] *a* (*bad*) malo; (*unfair*) injusto; (*incorrect*) equivocado, incorrecto; (*not suitable*) inoportuno, inconveniente // *ad* mal; equivocadamente // *n* mal *m*; (*injustice*) injusticia // *vt* ser injusto con; (*hurt*) agraviar; **you are** ~ **to do it** estás equivocado en hacerlo, cometes un error al hacerlo; **you are** ~ **about that, you've got it** ~ en eso, estás equivocado; **to be in the** ~ no tener razón, tener la culpa; **what's** ~? ¿qué pasa?; **to go** ~ (*person*) equivocarse; (*plan*) salir mal; (*machine*) tener una avería; ~**ful** *a* injusto; ~**ly** *ad* injustamente.
wrote [rəut] *pt of* **write**.
wrought [rɔːt] *a*: ~ **iron** hierro forjado.
wrung [rʌŋ] *pt, pp of* **wring**.
wry [raɪ] *a* irónico.
wt. *abbr of* **weight**.

X

Xmas ['ɛksməs] *n abbr of* **Christmas**.
X-ray [ɛks'reɪ] *n* radiografía; ~**s** *npl* rayos *mpl* X // *vt* hacer una radiografía a.
xylophone ['zaɪləfəun] *n* xilófono.

Y

yacht [jɔt] *n* yate *m*; ~**ing** *n* (*sport*) balandrismo; **yachtsman** *n* balandrista *m*.
Yank [jæŋk] *n* (*pej*) yanqui *m/f*.
yap [jæp] *vi* (*dog*) aullar.
yard [jɑːd] *n* patio; (*measure*) yarda; ~**stick** *n* (*fig*) criterio, norma.
yarn [jɑːn] *n* hilo; (*tale*) cuento, historia.
yawn [jɔːn] *n* bostezo // *vi* bostezar.

yd. *abbr of* **yard(s).**

year [jɪə*] *n* año; **to be 8 ~s old** tener 8 años; **~ly** *a* anual // *ad* anualmente, cada año.

yearn [jɔːn] *vi*: **to ~ for sth** añorar *o* suspirar por algo; **~ing** *n* ansia, añoranza.

yeast [jiːst] *n* levadura.

yell [jɛl] *n* grito, alarido // *vi* gritar.

yellow ['jɛləu] *a, n* amarillo.

yelp [jɛlp] *n* aullido // *vi* aullar.

yeoman ['jəumən] *n*: **Y~ of the Guard** alabardero de la Casa Real.

yes [jɛs] *ad, n* sí *m*.

yesterday ['jɛstədɪ] *ad, n* ayer *m*.

yet [jɛt] *ad* todavía // *conj* sin embargo, a pesar de todo; **it is not finished ~** todavía no está acabado; **the best ~** el mejor hasta ahora; **as ~** hasta ahora, todavía.

yew [juː] *n* tejo.

Yiddish ['jɪdɪʃ] *n* judío.

yield [jiːld] *n* producción *f*; (*AGR*) cosecha; (*COMM*) rendimiento // *vt* (*gen*) producir; (*profit*) rendir // *vi* rendirse, ceder.

yoga ['jəugə] *n* yoga.

yog(h)ourt, yog(h)urt ['jəugət] *n* yogur *m*.

yoke [jəuk] *n* (*of oxen*) yunta; (*on shoulders*) balancín *m*; (*fig*) yugo // *vt* acoplar.

yolk [jəuk] *n* yema (de huevo).

yonder ['jɔndə*] *ad* allá (a lo lejos).

you [juː] *pron* tú; (*pl*) vosotros; (*polite form*) usted; (: *pl*) ustedes; (*complement*) te; (: *pl*) os; (*after prep*) tí; (: *pl*) vosotros; (: *formal*) le/la; (: *pl*) les; (*after prep*) usted; (: *pl*) ustedes; (*one*): **~ never know** uno nunca sabe; (*impersonal*): **~ can't do that** eso no se hace.

you'd [juːd] = **you had; you would.**

you'll [juːl] = **you will, you shall.**

young [jʌŋ] *a* joven // *npl* (*of animal*) la cría *sg*; (*people*): **the ~** los jóvenes, la juventud *sg*; **~er** *a* (*brother etc*) menor; **~ish** *a* bastante joven; **~ster** *n* joven *m/f*.

your [jɔː*] *a* tu; (*pl*) vuestro; (*formal*) su.

you're [juə*] = **you are.**

yours [jɔːz] *pron* tuyo; (: *pl*) vuestro; (*formal*) suyo; **is it ~?** ¿es tuyo *etc*?; **~ sincerely** *or* **faithfully** le saluda atentamente.

yourself [jɔː'sɛlf] *pron* (*reflexive*) tú mismo; (*complement*) te; (*after prep*) tí (mismo); (*formal*) usted mismo; (: *complement*) se; (: *after prep*) sí (mismo); **yourselves** *pl pron* vosotros mismos; (*after prep*) vosotros (mismos); (*formal*) ustedes (mismos); (: *complement*) se; (: *after prep*) sí mismos.

youth [juːθ] *n* juventud *f*; (*young man: pl* **~s** [juːðz]) joven *m*; **~ful** *a* juvenil; **~ hostel** *n* albergue *m* de juventud.

you've [juːv] = **you have.**

Yugoslav ['juːgəu'slɑːv] *a, n* yugoeslavo/a; **~ia** *n* Yugoeslavia.

Yuletide ['juːltaɪd] *n* Navidad *f*.

Z

zany ['zeɪnɪ] *a* tonto.

zeal [ziːl] *n* celo, entusiasmo; **~ous** ['zɛləs] *a* celoso, entusiasta.

zebra ['ziːbrə] *n* cebra; **~ crossing** *n* paso de peatones.

zenith ['zɛnɪθ] *n* cénit *m*.

zero ['zɪərəu] *n* cero.

zest [zɛst] *n* ánimo, vivacidad *f*.

zigzag ['zɪgzæg] *n* zigzag *m* // *vi* zigzaguear.

zinc [zɪŋk] *n* cinc *m*, zinc *m*.

Zionism ['zaɪənɪzm] *n* sionismo; **Zionist** *n* sionista *m/f*.

zip [zɪp] *n* (*also*: **~ fastener, ~per**) cremallera // *vt* (*also*: **~ up**) cerrar la cremallera de.

zodiac ['zəudɪæk] *n* zodíaco.

zombie ['zɔmbɪ] *n* (*fig*): **like a ~** como un sonámbulo.

zone [zəun] *n* zona.

zoo [zuː] *n* (*jardín m*) zoológico.

zoological [zuə'lɔdʒɪkl] *a* zoológico.

zoologist [zuː'ɔlədʒɪst] *n* zoólogo.

zoology [zuː'ɔlədʒɪ] *n* zoología.

zoom [zuːm] *vi*: **to ~ past** pasar zumbando; **~ lens** *n* zoom *m*.

SPANISH VERB TABLES

1 Gerund. *2* Imperative. *3* Present. *4* Preterite. *5* Future. *6* Present subjunctive. *7* Imperfect subjunctive. *8* Past participle. *9* Imperfect.
Etc indicates that the irregular root is used for all persons of the tense, e.g. **oír**: *6* oiga, oigas, oigamos, oigáis, oigan.

acertar *2* acierta *3* acierto, aciertas, acierta, aciertan *6* acierte, aciertes, acierte, acierten

acordar *2* acuerda *3* acuerdo, acuerdas, acuerda, acuerdan *6* acuerde, acuerdes, acuerde, acuerden

advertir *1* advirtiendo *2* advierte *3* advierto, adviertes, advierte, advierten *4* advirtió, advirtieron *6* advierta, adviertas, advierta, advirtamos, advirtáis, adviertan *7* advirtiera *etc*

agradecer *3* agradezco *6* agradezca *etc*

aparecer *3* aparezco *6* aparezca *etc*

aprobar *2* aprueba *3* apruebo, apruebas, aprueba, aprueban *6* apruebe, apruebes, apruebe, aprueben

atravesar *2* atraviesa *3* atravieso, atraviesas, atraviesa, atraviesan *6* atraviese, atravieses, atraviese, atraviesen

caber *3* quepo *4* cupe, cupiste, cupo, cupimos, cupisteis, cupieron *5* cabré *etc* *6* quepa *etc* *7* cupiera *etc*

caer *1* cayendo *3* caigo *4* cayó, cayeron *6* caiga *etc* *7* cayera *etc*

calentar *2* calienta *3* caliento, calientas, calienta, calientan *6* caliente, calientes, caliente, calienten

cerrar *2* cierra *3* cierro, cierras, cierra, cierran *6* cierre, cierres, cierre, cierren

COMER *1* comiendo *2* come, comed *3* como, comes, come, comemos, coméis, comen *4* comí, comiste, comió, comimos, comisteis, comieron *5* comeré, comerás, comerá, comeremos, comeréis, comerán *6* coma, comas, coma, comamos, comáis, coman *7* comiera, comieras, comiera, comiéramos, comierais, comieran *8* comido *9* comía, comías, comía, comíamos comíais, comian

conocer *3* conozco *6* conozca *etc*

contar *2* cuenta *3* cuento, cuentas, cuenta, cuentan *6* cuente, cuentes, cuente, cuenten

costar *2* cuesta *3* cuesto, cuestas, cuesta, cuestan *6* cueste, cuestes, cueste, cuesten

dar *3* doy *4* di, diste, dio, dimos, disteis, dieron *7* diera *etc*

decir *2* di *3* digo *4* dije, dijiste, dijo, dijimos, dijisteis, dijeron *5* diré *etc* *6* diga *etc* *7* dijera *etc* *8* dicho

despertar *2* despierta *3* despierto, despiertas, despierta, despiertan *6* despierte, despiertes, despierte, despierten

divertir *1* divirtiendo *2* divierte *3* divierto, diviertes, divierte, divierten *4* divirtió, divirtieron *6* divierta, diviertas, divierta, divirtamos, divirtáis, diviertan *7* divirtiera *etc*

dormir *1* durmiendo *2* duerme *3* duermo, duermes, duerme, duermen *4* durmió, durmieron *6* duerma, duermas, duerma, durmamos, durmáis, duerman *7* durmiera *etc*

empezar *2* empieza *3* empiezo, empiezas, empieza, empiezan *4* empecé *6* empiece, empieces, empiece, empecemos, empecéis, empiecen

entender *2* entiende *3* entiendo, entiendes, entiende, entienden *6* entienda, entiendas, entienda, entiendan

ESTAR *2* está *3* estoy, estás, está, están *4* estuve, estuviste, estuvo, estuvimos, estuvisteis, estuvieron *6* esté, estés, esté, estén *7* estuviera *etc*

HABER *3* he, has, ha, hemos, han *4* hube, hubiste, hubo, hubimos,

hubisteis, hubieron *5* habré *etc 6*
haya *etc 7* hubiera *etc*

HABLAR *1* hablando *2* habla,
hablad *3* hablo, hablas, habla,
hablamos, habláis, hablan *4* hablé
hablaste, habló, hablamos,
hablasteis, hablaron *5* hablaré,
hablarás, hablará, hablaremos,
hablaréis, hablarán *6* hable, hables,
hable, hablemos, habléis, hablen *7*
hablara, hablaras, hablara,
habláramos, hablarais, hablaran *8*
hablado *9* hablaba, hablabas,
hablaba, hablábamos, hablabais,
hablaban

hacer *2* haz *3* hago *4* hice, hiciste,
hizo, hicimos, hicisteis, hicieron *5*
haré *etc 6* haga *etc 7* hiciera *etc 8*
hecho

instruir *1* instruyendo *2* instruye *3*
instruyo, instruyes, instruye,
instruyen *4* instruyó, instruyeron *6*
instruya *etc 7* instruyera *etc*

ir *1* yendo *2* ve *3* voy, vas, va, vamos,
vais, van *4* fui, fuiste, fue, fuimos,
fuisteis, fueron *6* vaya, vayas, vaya,
vayamos, vayáis, vayan *7* fuera *etc*
8 iba, ibas, iba, íbamos, ibais, iban

jugar *2* juega *3* juego, juegas, juega,
juegan *4* jugué *6* juegue *etc*

leer *1* leyendo *4* leyó, leyeron *7* leyera
etc

morir *1* muriendo *2* muere *3* muero,
mueres, muere, mueren *4* murió,
murieron *6* muera, mueras, muera,
muramos, muráis, mueran *7*
muriera *etc 8* muerto

mostrar *2* muestra *3* muestro,
muestras, muestra, muestran *6*
muestre, muestres, muestre,
muestren

mover *2* mueve *3* muevo, mueves,
mueve, mueven *6* mueva, muevas,
mueva, muevan

negar *2* niega *3* niego, niegas, niega,
niegan *4* negué *6* niegue, niegues,
niegue, neguemos, neguéis,
nieguen

ofrecer *3* ofrezco *6* ofrezca *etc*

oír *1* oyendo *2* oye *3* oigo, oyes, oye,
oyen *4* oyó, oyeron *6* oiga *etc 7*
oyera *etc*

oler *2* huele *3* huelo, hueles, huele,

huelen *6* huela, huelas, huela,
huelan

parecer *3* parezco *6* parezca *etc*

pedir *1* pidiendo *2* pide *3* pido,
pides, pide, piden *4* pidió, pidieron
6 pida *etc 7* pidiera *etc*

pensar *2* piensa *3* pienso, piensas,
piensa, piensan *6* piense, pienses,
piense, piensen

perder *2* pierde *3* pierdo, pierdes,
pierde, pierden *6* pierda, pierdas,
pierda, pierdan

poder *1* pudiendo *2* puede *3* puedo,
puedes, puede, pueden *4* pude,
pudiste, pudo, pudimos, pudisteis,
pudieron *5* podré *etc 6* pueda,
puedas, pueda, puedan *7* pudiera
etc

poner *2* pon *3* pongo *4* puse, pusiste,
puso, pusimos, pusisteis, pusieron
5 pondré *etc 6* ponga *etc 7* pusiera
etc 8 puesto

preferir *1* prefiriendo *2* prefiere *3*
prefiero, prefieres, prefiere,
prefieren *4* prefirió, prefirieron *6*
prefiera, prefieras, prefiera,
prefiramos, prefiráis, prefieran *7*
prefiriera *etc*

querer *2* quiere *3* quiero, quieres,
quiere, quieren *4* quise, quisiste,
quiso, quisimos, quisisteis,
quisieron *5* querré *etc 6* quiera,
quieras, quiera, quieran *7* quisiera
etc

reír *2* ríe *3* río, ríes, ríe, ríen *4* rió,
rieron *6* ría, rías, ría, riamos, riáis,
rían *7* riera *etc*

repetir *1* repitiendo *2* repite *3* repito,
repites, repite, repiten *4* repitió,
repitieron *6* repita *etc 7* repitiera *etc*

rogar *2* ruega *3* ruego, ruegas, ruega,
ruegan *4* rogué *6* ruegue, ruegues,
ruegue, roguemos, roguéis,
rueguen

saber *3* sé *4* supe, supiste, supo,
supimos, supisteis, supieron *5*
sabré *etc 6* sepa *etc 7* supiera *etc*

salir *2* sal *3* salgo *5* saldré *etc 6* salga
etc

seguir *1* siguiendo *2* sigue *3* sigo,
sigues, sigue, siguen *4* siguió,
siguieron *6* siga *etc 7* siguiera *etc*

sentar *2* sienta *3* siento, sientas,

sienta, sientan *6* siente, sientes, siente, sienten

sentir *1* sintiendo *2* siente *3* siento, sientes, siente, sienten *4* sintió, sintieron *6* sienta, sientas, sienta, sintamos, sintáis, sientan *7* sintiera *etc*

SER *2* sé *3* soy, eres, es, somos, sois, son *4* fui, fuiste, fue, fuimos, fuisteis, fueron *6* sea *etc* *7* fuera *etc* *9* era, eras, era, éramos, erais, eran

servir *1* sirviendo *2* sirve *3* sirvo, sirves, sirve, sirven *4* sirvió, sirvieron *6* sirva *etc* *7* sirviera *etc*

soñar *2* sueña *3* sueño, sueñas, sueña, sueñan *6* sueñe, sueñes, sueñe, sueñen

tener *2* ten *3* tengo, tienes, tiene, tienen *4* tuve, tuviste, tuvo, tuvimos, tuvisteis, tuvieron *5* tendré *etc* *6* tenga *etc* *7* tuviera *etc*

traer *1* trayendo *3* traigo *4* traje, trajiste, trajo, trajimos, trajisteis, trajeron *6* traiga *etc* *7* trajera *etc*

valer *2* val *3* valgo *5* valdré *etc* *6* valga *etc*

venir *2* ven *3* vengo, vienes, viene, vienen *4* vine, viniste, vino, vinimos, vinisteis, vinieron *5* vendré *etc* *6* venga *etc* *7* viniera *etc*

ver *3* veo *6* vea *etc* *8* visto *9* veía *etc*

vestir *1* vistiendo *2* viste *3* visto, vistes, viste, visten *4* vistió, vistieron *6* vista *etc* *7* vistiera *etc*

VIVIR *1* viviendo *2* vive, vivid *3* vivo, vives, vive, vivimos, vivís, viven *4* viví, viviste, vivió, vivimos, vivisteis, vivieron *5* viviré, vivirás, vivirá, viviremos, viviréis, vivirán *6* viva, vivas, viva, vivamos, viváis, vivan *7* viviera, vivieras, viviera, viviéramos, vivierais, vivieran *8* vivido *9* vivía, vivías, vivía, vivíamos, vivíais, vivían

volver *2* vuelve *3* vuelvo, vuelves, vuelve, vuelven *6* vuelva, vuelvas, vuela, vuelvan *8* vuelto.

VERBOS IRREGULARES EN INGLÉS

present	pt	pp	present	pt	pp
arise	arose	arisen	eat	ate	eaten
awake	awoke	awaked	fall	fell	fallen
be (am, is, are; being)	was, were	been	feed	fed	fed
			feel	felt	felt
			fight	fought	fought
bear	bore	born(e)	find	found	found
beat	beat	beaten	flee	fled	fled
become	became	become	fling	flung	flung
befall	befell	befallen	fly	flew	flown
begin	began	begun	forbid	forbade	forbidden
behold	beheld	beheld	forecast	forecast	forecast
bend	bent	bent	forget	forgot	forgotten
beset	beset	beset	forgive	forgave	forgiven
bet	bet, betted	bet, betted	forsake	forsook	forsaken
			freeze	froze	frozen
bid	bid	bid	get	got	got, (US) gotten
bind	bound	bound			
bite	bit	bitten	give	gave	given
bleed	bled	bled	go (goes)	went	gone
blow	blew	blown			
break	broke	broken	grind	ground	ground
breed	bred	bred	grow	grew	grown
bring	brought	brought	hang	hung, hanged	hung, hanged
build	built	built			
burn	burnt, burned	burnt, burned	have	had	had
			hear	heard	heard
burst	burst	burst	hide	hid	hidden
buy	bought	bought	hit	hit	hit
can	could	(been able)	hold	held	held
cast	cast	cast	hurt	hurt	hurt
catch	caught	caught	keep	kept	kept
choose	chose	chosen	kneel	knelt, kneeled	knelt, kneeled
cling	clung	clung			
come	came	come	know	knew	known
cost	cost	cost	lay	laid	laid
creep	crept	crept	lead	led	led
cut	cut	cut	lean	leant, leaned	leant, leaned
deal	dealt	dealt			
dig	dug	dug	leap	leapt, leaped	leapt, leaped
do (3rd person; he/she/it/does)	did	done			
			learn	learnt, learned	learnt, learned
			leave	left	left
draw	drew	drawn	lend	lent	lent
dream	dreamed, dreamt	dreamed, dreamt	let	let	let
			lie (lying)	lay	lain
drink	drank	drunk	light	lit, lighted	lit, lighted
drive	drove	driven			
dwell	dwelt	dwelt			

present	pt	pp	present	pt	pp
lose	lost	lost	speed	sped,	sped,
make	made	made		speeded	speeded
may	might	—	spell	spelt,	spelt,
mean	meant	meant		spelled	spelled
meet	met	met	spend	spent	spent
mistake	mistook	mistaken	spill	spilt,	spilt,
mow	mowed	mown,		spilled	spilled
		mowed	spin	spun	spun
must	(had to)	(had to)	spit	spat	spat
pay	paid	paid	split	split	split
put	put	put	spoil	spoiled,	spoiled,
quit	quit,	quit,		spoilt	spoilt
	quitted	quitted	spread	spread	spread
read	read	read	spring	sprang	sprung
rend	rent	rent	stand	stood	stood
rid	rid	rid	steal	stole	stolen
ride	rode	ridden	stick	stuck	stuck
ring	rang	rung	sting	stung	stung
rise	rose	risen	stink	stank	stunk
run	ran	run	stride	strode	strode
saw	sawed	sawn	strike	struck	struck,
say	said	said			stricken
see	saw	seen	strive	strove	striven
seek	sought	sought	swear	swore	sworn
sell	sold	sold	sweep	swept	swept
send	sent	sent	swell	swelled	swollen,
set	set	set			swelled
shake	shook	shaken	swim	swam	swum
shall	should	—	swing	swung	swung
shear	sheared	shorn,	take	took	taken
		sheared	teach	taught	taught
shed	shed	shed			
shine	shone	shone	tear	tore	torn
shoot	shot	shot	tell	told	told
show	showed	shown	think	thought	thought
shrink	shrank	shrunk	throw	threw	thrown
shut	shut	shut	thrust	thrust	thrust
sing	sang	sung	tread	trod	trodden
sink	sank	sunk	wake	woke,	woken,
sit	sat	sat		waked	waked
slay	slew	slain	wear	wore	worn
sleep	slept	slept	weave	wove,	woven,
slide	slid	slid		weaved	weaved
sling	slung	slung	wed	wedded,	wedded,
slit	slit	slit		wed	wed
smell	smelt,	smelt,	weep	wept	wept
	smelled	smelled	win	won	won
sow	sowed	sown,	wind	wound	wound
		sowed	wring	wrung	wrung
speak	spoke	spoken	write	wrote	written

NOTES TO THE USER OF THIS DICTIONARY

I Using the dictionary

II Notes on Spanish grammar

III Spanish verb conjugations

IV The sounds of Spanish

V The time, dates and numbers

I. Using the dictionary

In using this book, you will either want to check the meaning of a Spanish word you don't know, or find the Spanish for an English word. These two operations are quite different, and so are the problems you may face when using one side of the dictionary or the other. In order to help you, we have tried to explain below the main features of this book.

The 'wordlist' is the alphabetical list of all the items in large bold type, i.e. all the 'headwords'. Each 'entry', or article, is introduced by a headword, and may contain additional 'references' in smaller bold type, such as phrases, derivatives, and compound words. Section 1. below deals with the way references are listed.

The typography distinguishes between three broad categories of text within the dictionary. All items in bold type, large or small, are 'source language' references, for which an equivalent in the other language is provided. All items in standard type are translations. Items in italics are information about the words being translated, i.e. either labels, or 'signposts' pinpointing the appropriate translation, or explanations.

1. *Where to look for a word*

1.1 Derivatives

In order to save space, a number of derivatives have been listed within entries, provided this does not break alphabetical order. Thus, **laborar**, **laborioso**, and **laborista** are listed under the entry for **labor**, and **caller** and **calling** under **call**. You must remember this when looking for a word you don't find listed as a headword. These derivatives are always listed last within an entry (see also I.2 on entry layout).

1.2 Homographs

Homographs are words which are spelt in exactly the same way, like **pago** (payment) and **pago** (district), or **hacha** (axe) and **hacha** (torch). As a rule, in order to save space, such words have been treated under one headword only. In the very few cases where this was not possible, the presence of a feminine form helps distinguish between two consecutive homograph entries (e.g. **rapaz** and **rapaz, -a**).

1.3 Phrases

Because of the constraints of space, there can be only a limited number of idiomatic phrases in a pocket dictionary like this one. Particular emphasis is given to verbal phrases like **sacar a luz, dar a luz, dar una vuelta, dar vueltas, estar de vuelta,** etc, and also to basic constructions (see the entries for **apply, agree, ponerse, deber, dar**). Verbal phrases with the ten or so basic verbs (ser, estar, poner etc.) are listed under the noun. Other phrases and idioms are listed under the first key word, for instance **de antemano** under **antemano, no obstante** under **obstante**.

1.4 Abbreviations and proper names

For easier reference, abbreviations, acronyms and proper names have been listed alphabetically in the wordlist, as opposed to being relegated to the appendices. **M.O.T.** is used in every way like **certificate** or **permit, OVNI** like **objeto**, and these words are treated like other nouns.

1.5 Compounds

Housewife, smoke screen, caja fuerte and **lámpara de pie** are all compounds. One-word compounds like 'housewife' are not a problem when consulting the dictionary, since they can appear only in one place and in strict alphabetical order. When it comes to other compounds, however – hyphenated compounds and compounds made up of separate words – each language presents its own peculiar problems.

1.5.1 Spanish compounds

There are many compounds made up of two or more 'words'. When checking a Spanish compound, you might not be aware that you are dealing with a compound and not a string of autonomous words, and there may inevitably be some toing and froing between entries.

As spelling is regular in Spanish, we have listed Spanish compounds under the first word, and grouped them alphabetically within that entry. For instance, **cama de matrimonio** is within the entry for **cama** and comes before the headword **camada. Tos ferina** comes before the headword **tosco**, in the entry for **tos**. Remember that the meaning of a phrase or of a compound can be quite different from that of its elements taken separately, so be prepared to check through an entry thoroughly before giving up.

1.5.2   English compounds

Here there is a problem of where to find a compound because of less predictable spelling than is the case with Spanish : is it **airgun, air-gun** or **air gun**? This is why we choose to list them according to strict alphabetical order. Thus **coal field** and **coalman** are separated by **coalition.** The entries between **tax** and **technical** will provide a good illustration of the system of listing. It has drawbacks, for instance in that **tax-free** and **tax-payer** are separated by **taxi, taxidermist** and three 'taxi' compounds. However, in a short dictionary used by beginners, it has the merit of simplicity and consistency.

1.5.3   English 'phrasal verbs'

'Phrasal verbs' are verbs like **go off, blow up, cut down** etc. Here you have the advantage of knowing that these words belong together, whereas it will take the foreign user some time before he can identify these verbs immediately. They have been listed under the entry for the basic verb (e.g. **go, blow, cut**), grouped alphabetically before any other derivative or compound – for instance, **pull up** comes before **pulley.** (See also **to back out, to look up** (a word), **to look out.**)

1.6   Irregular forms

When looking up a Spanish word, you may not immediately find the form you are looking for, although the word in question has been duly entered in the dictionary. This is possibly because you are looking up an irregular noun or verb form, and these are not always given as entries in their own right.

We have assumed that you know basic Spanish grammar. Thus you will be expected to know that 'cantan' is a form of the verb **cantar,** 'luces' the plural of **luz** and so on. However, in order to help you, we have included the main irregular forms as entries in their own right, with a cross-reference to the basic form. Thus, if you come across the word 'fui' and attempt to look up a verb 'fuir', you won't find it, but what you will find between **fuga** and **fulano,** is the entry **fui** *vb ver* **ser, ir.** Similarly **hizo, hecho** etc.

With past participles, it sometimes happens that in addition to the purely verbal form there is an adjectival or noun use, for instance **herido** or **bendito.** These usages are translated as autonomous words, but they are also cross-referred to the verb whenever appropriate (see for instance entries for **abierto** or **muerto**).

2. Entry layout

All entries, however long or complex, are arranged systematically. But it may be a little difficult at first to find one's way through an entry like Spanish **parte,** or English **back, round** or **run** because homographs are grouped under the same entry (see 1.2) and the text is run on without any breakdown into paragraphs, in order to save space. Ease of reference comes with practice, but the guidelines below will make it easier for you.

2.1 'Signposting'

If you look up a Spanish word and find a string of quite different English translations, you are unlikely to have much trouble finding out which is the relevant one for the context, because you know what the English words mean, and the context will almost automatically rule out unsuitable translations. It is quite a different matter when you want to find the Spanish for, say, **lock,** in the context 'we got to the lock around lunchtime', and are faced with an entry that reads 'lock: cerradura; esclusa; mechón *m.*' You can of course go to the other side and check what each translation means. But this is time-consuming, and it doesn't always work. This is why we have provided the user with signposts which pinpoint the relevant translation. For instance with **lock,** the entry reads: ... (*of door, box*) cerradura; (*of canal*) esclusa; (*of hair*) mechón *m* ... For the context suggested above, it is now clear that 'esclusa' is the right word.

2.2 Grammatical categories and meaning categories

Complex entries are first broken down into grammatical categories, e.g.: **lock** *m // vt // vi.* Be prepared to go through entries like **run** or **back** carefully, and you will find how useful all these 'signposts' are. Each grammatical category is then split where appropriate into the various meanings, e.g.:

> **lock** *n* (*of door, box*) cerradura; (*of canal*) esclusa; (*of hair*) mechón *m // vt* (*with key*) cerrar con llave; (*immobilize*) inmovilizar *// vi* (*door etc*) cerrarse con llave; (*wheels*) bloquearse, trabarse.

3. Using the translations

3.1 Gender

Feminine endings for Spanish adjectives ending in -o have not been given on the English-Spanish side, but endings for other adjectives are shown: 'charming *a* encantador(a)'; 'Danish *a* danés(esa)'; 'German *a* alemán(ana)'. This may appear to duplicate information given in the Spanish-English side of the dictionary, but we feel it is a useful reminder where and when it matters. The feminine form is also given for words like **teacher, researcher** etc.

3.2   Plurals

Information on the formation of plurals in Spanish, including the plural of compounds is given in section II. Most plural forms in Spanish are regular and are not shown, but where a problem could arise, the plural is shown beside the headword on the Spanish side, e.g. **carácter,** *pl* **caracteres.** We have shown when the translation of a word used in the singular is plural; see for instance **hair, jealousy, offal.**

3.3   Verb forms

Irregular Spanish verbs appearing as translations have not been marked as such, and the user should refer to the Spanish verb tables when in doubt (pp. 400–402).

3.4   Colloquial language

You should as a rule proceed with great caution when handling foreign language which has a degree of informality. When an English word or phrase has been labelled *(col)*, i.e. colloquial, you must assume that the translation belongs to a similar level of informality. If the translation is followed by (!) you should use it with extreme care, or better still avoid it unless you are with close friends!

3.5   'Grammatical words'

It is exceedingly difficult to give adequate treatment for words like **for, away, whose, which, out, off** etc. in a short dictionary such as this one. We have tried to go some way towards providing as much relevant information as possible about the most frequent uses of these words. However, for further information use a good monolingual dictionary of Spanish, and a good modern Spanish grammar.

3.6   'Approximate' translations and cultural equivalents

It is not always possible to give a genuine translation, when for instance an English word denotes a thing or institution which either doesn't exist in Spain, or is quite different. Therefore, only an approximate equivalent can be given, or else an explanation. See for instance **whip, shadow cabinet,** and on the Spanish-English side **gazpacho, doña.**

3.7   Alternative translations

As a rule, translations separated by commas can be regarded as broadly interchangeable for the meaning indicated. Translations separated by a semi-colon are not interchangeable and when in doubt you should consult either a larger bilingual dictionary such as the Collins Spanish Dictionary, or a good monolingual Spanish dictionary. You will find however that there are very few cases of translations separated by a semi-colon without an intervening 'signpost'.

II. Notes on Spanish grammar

Although a relatively easy language to learn, Spanish may seem very different from English when you first meet it in school or hear a Spanish speaker talk. Certainly the order of words and the way a Spaniard says certain things will be strange (in fact a general feeling might be that everything is the wrong way round), but if you were to compare it to languages like Arabic, Swahili or Chinese, you would soon recognize that the basic structure and pattern of Spanish is quite close to English.

We have tried here to show some of these differences, especially with the beginner and the dictionary user in mind, without dwelling on subtleties or the aspects of Spanish which are broadly similar to English. Among the greatest obstacles for the beginner are gender, verb forms and tenses, the position of adjectives, the uses of prepositions and of course, in a few cases, the sounds of Spanish (although once you have mastered each sound it is arguably one of the easiest languages to speak and understand). There are of course many more differences, some of which take us into the realm of style etc., but this is beyond the scope of this introduction.

1. *Nouns and 'satellite' words (i.e. articles, adjectives etc.)*

1.1   Gender

Note the basic difference: 'the table and the knife', but '*la* mesa y *el* cuchill*o*'. Gender can usually be determined by the ending of the word: 'mesa' ends in *a* and is feminine; 'cuchillo' ends in *o* and is masculine. Certain endings are always one gender, e.g. -ción is always feminine and -tor masculine. Otherwise you just have to learn the genders in each case. What *is* important, however, is that you get the article right and also the agreement of adjectives and past participles: '*un* hombre alt*o* con *la* nariz torcid*a*'. See also 1.4 (possessive adjectives).

1.2   Articles: *'el, la, lo; un; del'* etc.

Apart from the problem of gender, there is the question of whether the article is used or not, and Spanish does not always follow the English pattern. For instance, you say 'I like wine', but the Spanish say 'me gusta **el** vino'. Conversely, 'my father is **a** mechanic', but 'mi padre es mecánico'.

1.2.1   *'el, la, lo; los, las'*

(a)   In almost all cases where 'the' is not used in English, the article must be used in Spanish. For instance:

apples are good for you   **las** manzanas son buenas para la salud
salmon is expensive   **el** salmón es caro

patience is a virtue   **la** paciencia es una virtud
I don't like fighting   no me gustan **las** peleas

N.B.   With names of countries, Spanish is gradually losing the habit of using the article, but you may still find a few cases where it persists:

e.g.   **el** Canadá, **el** Japón, **la** China.

(b)   Use of *'el/la'* with parts of the body

Where the possessive is used in English, *'el/la'* tends to be used in Spanish (often in conjunction with a pronoun):

I've twisted **my** ankle   **me** he torcido **el** tobillo
Put up **your** hand   levante **la** mano
My nose is bleeding   **me** está sangrando **la** nariz

(c)   *'a + el; de + el'*

Remember the contracted forms (shown in the dictionary under **a** and **de**):
voy **al** cine; vengo **del** huerto

(d)   'lo'

Spanish also has a neuter gender: 'lo' is often used with an adjective to express general or abstract ideas, e.g. 'eso es **lo** bueno' (that's **the** good **thing** about it)

414

1.2.2 'un, una, uno; unos, unas'

(a) In structures like 'my father is a postman' (i.e. expressing occupation, nationality or rank), Spanish does not use the indefinite article:

my brother is a mechanic   mi hermano es mecánico
he's a Frenchman   es francés

(b) After negatives, the article 'un/una' is not used with unspecified nouns:

I don't have a car   no tengo coche
she went out without saying a word   ella salió sin decir palabra

(c) The form 'uno' is used either to express the number 'one' when a masculine noun is understood, or to express the neuter idea of 'one' (i.e. we, people)

how many cats have you? **One**   ¿cuántos gatos tiene? **Uno**
(whereas: he has only **one cat**   tiene sólo **un gato**)

when **one** thinks about it   cuando **uno** lo piensa

(d) 'unos/unas'

Remember to use the plural of the article, even though there may be no article in English:

friends from Madrid have arrived   **unos** amigos de Madrid han llegado

1.2.3 'some/any'

Unless 'some/any' expresses something specific, it is normally not translated in Spanish, especially after a negative:

me quedan **unas** pesetas   I have **some** pesetas left

BUT: ¿quiere usted patatas?   do you want *some/any* potatoes?
        quiero pan   I want *some* bread
        no tengo cigarillos   I haven't *any* cigarettes

1.3   Adjectives

Apart from the question of gender, the main difficulty is the position of adjectives. As a general rule, they follow the noun (las leyes físicas, una comida sabrosísima, unos guantes rojos). Some adjectives or types of adjectives will *always* go after the noun, especially if their meaning can only be literal (una casa desmoronada, las leyes físicas, un vestido rojo). Others can also go before the noun in a figurative sense or for stylistic effect (una sabrosísima comida).

Adjectives, however, which 'limit' rather than 'describe' (mucho, poco, demasiado, tanto, primero, último) always come in front of the noun.

Finally, many common adjectives like 'bueno, malo; grande, pequeño; viejo, joven; nuevo, antiguo; pobre, rico' and others like 'mismo, cierto' will be found before or after, but with different meanings: before the meaning is usually figurative, after it is literal (the dictionary makes these differences clear).

1.3.1   Remember that certain adjectives have a shortened masculine form before nouns: bueno, BUT: un buen hombre

1.4   Possessives:

1.4.1   *'su/sus'*

Since this form can be ambiguous (his, hers, its; yours, theirs), Spanish often substitutes 'el ... de él, de ella; de usted, de ellos':

e.g. their father   su padre: **el** padre **de ellos**

1.4.2   *'el mío/la mía; los míos/las mías'* etc.

The possessive pronouns vary according to the gender of the noun they qualify as well as the number:

¿de quién es este **coche**?   es mío   whose is this car?   it's mine.
aquí están las entra**das**; las tu**yas** costaron más   here are the tickets; yours cost more

1.5   Demonstratives: *'este, ese, aquel; esta, esa, aquella; esto'* etc.

1.5.1

Demonstrative adjectives agree in gender and number with the noun they qualify. Spanish also has a neuter form for the pronouns 'this' and 'that'.

¿qué es **eso**? what's that? ¿qué es **esto**? what's this?

The main problem, however, is choosing between the three forms of demonstrative: the 'este' forms are straightforward and mean 'this'; the 'ese' forms mean 'that' in the sense of 'that nearby or near you'; the 'aquel' forms mean 'that yonder':

este libro **this** book
¿qué es **eso** que tienes en la mano? what is **that** you have (*there*) in your hand?
¿cómo se llaman **aquellas** montañas? what are **those** mountains called (*yonder*)?

1.6 Comparative and superlative: '*más ... que*' etc.

1.6.1

Generally you use 'más' + *adjective* or *adverb* to form the comparative; the superlative is slightly more complicated because you use the definite article with the 'más' and the article must agree in gender and number with the adjective. The superlative adverb is formed with 'lo' + 'más' + *adverb*.

más bonito/más frecuentemente prettier/more frequently
esa casa es la *más* bonita that is the pretti*est house*
lo *más* frecuentemente the *most* frequent*ly*

2. *Verbs*

This is one of the main areas of difficulty for English-speaking learners. There are four major problems. First, the variety of endings (hablo, hablamos etc.) and the number of irregular or 'semi-irregular' forms. Second, the difference in the formation of negative or interrogative phrases (no equivalent of 'do', 'did' etc., as in 'I didn't go; did you?'). Third, the difference in the use of tenses (e.g. two past tenses, imperfect and preterite). Fourth, the use of two verbs meaning 'to be' (ser, estar).

2.1 Verb forms

The verb tables on pp. 424 and 425 will give you the patterns for the main verb groups; irregular verb forms are shown on page 400. There is no substitute for practice on this, but try not to look upon these forms as a vast array of separate items to be learnt: there are two basic combining patterns, one relating to the person doing the action ('*I* speak vs *you* speak: habl*o*/habl*as*) and one relating to the tense (I *speak*/I *spoke*:

hablo/hablé). The present, perfect, imperfect, future and conditional will cater for most of your needs at first.

2.2 Negatives and questions

Although the simple negative 'no' is the same as English, most other negative words also need a 'no' in front when they follow the verb, but their meaning is not a 'double' negative:

no lo sé   I do *not* know
nunca lo sé   I *never* know
BUT: **no** lo sabía **nunca**   I *never* knew
ALSO: **no** lo sabe **nunca nadie**   *nobody ever* knows

The way Spanish forms questions is really a matter of the tone of voice in which the sentence is said and presents no real problem because we often use the same tone in English. When Spanish questions are written therefore, they need a special question mark at the beginning to warn you that it is a question:

es loco   he is mad
¿es loco?   is he mad?

2.3 Tenses

2.3.1

The Spanish equivalent to our continuous '-ing' form is just the same but you must remember to use the 'estar' verb 'to be' and not 'ser':

estoy ley*endo*   I am read*ing*
estaré ley*endo*   I shall be read*ing*

2.3.2

The perfect tense in English (I have done it) corresponds fairly closely to the Spanish (lo he hecho); but what seems to be a preterite in English (I did it) can in certain circumstances be translated by any of the three past tenses in Spanish (lo hice, lo he hecho, lo hacía). Basically it is a question of 'when' and 'how often'.

2.3.2.1 The imperfect

The 'imperfect' describes an action done repeatedly in the past or which went on for some time (often being a replacement for the continuous tense), e.g. lo hacían means 'they *used to* do it' or 'they *were doing* it', which is what the English preterite implies in a sentence such as 'they *did* it *all the time*'.

2.3.2.2. The perfect

The perfect in Spanish describes an action which has been carried out recently, usually that day. Because it expresses recent time, it can therefore translate English 'preterites': such as 'they *did* it this morning' lo *han hecho* esta mañana.

2.3.2.3 The preterite

The preterite denotes completed actions in the more distant past and is more a tense of written Spanish, e.g. 'he *did* it yesterday/the day before lo *hizo* ayer/el día anterior.

2.3.3

Don't be surprised to see Spanish use a present tense instead of the future in phrases like 'I *shall go* tomorrow': me *voy* mañana.

2.3.4 The subjunctive: 'quiero que lo haga' *vs* 'sé que lo hace' etc.

Good command of both the present and imperfect subjunctive is necessary in order to speak good Spanish, but you can probably cover a lot of situations with just the present. Even without the subjunctive you would probably be understood, except that is with verbs like 'decir' where misunderstandings might arise, e.g. dígale que **venga** means 'tell him *to come*', but dígale que **viene** means 'tell him he *is coming*'.

It is not possible to give you all the rules governing the use of the subjunctive but here are a few basic ideas explaining its use:

(a) The subjunctive is used to express a command when the polite form 'usted' is implied:
hágalo usted   you do it
lea esto   read this

(b) The subjunctive is used in subordinate clauses when doubt, hypothesis and denial are expressed (i.e. it is not a fact):

dudo que lo tenga   I doubt if he has it
no creo que lo tenga   I don't believe he has it

(c) The best guide perhaps is to see whether the subjects of the clauses change: if they do, then there will probably be a subjunctive.

I want *him* to do it   quiero que lo **haga** él
it is good for *him* to do it   es bueno que él lo **haga**

(d) It is also used for actions which are not yet facts.
until he comes   hasta que *venga*.

2.4 Spanish has two verbs 'to be': ser, estar.

2.4.1 *ser*

Ser means 'to exist' but it also covers the meanings of 'to be' which express qualities or permanent states: 'es bueno'   he is good (always); 'es profesor'   he is a teacher. It is also used to form the passive tense: 'fui herido'   I was wounded.

2.4.2 *estar*

Estar means 'to be situated' or 'to be in a state of ...': ' ¿dónde está el banco?'   where is the bank (situated)?; 'estaba herido'   I was (in a) wounded (state); 'está sentado'   he is (in a) sitting down (state); 'está bueno'   he is well.

3. *Prepositions*

Most prepositions present no problems. The main confusion will be about when to use 'por' and when to use 'para' when translating English 'for'. Essentially, 'por' expresses *cause* or *reason* and 'para' expresses *purpose*:

lo hizo *por* mí   he did it *for* me (because of me, for my sake)
¿*para* qué lo quieres?   what do you want it *for*?

'por' also expresses exchange: ¿cuánto me da *por* esto?   how much will you give me *for* this?

3.1 Don't forget that many verbs in English are followed by prepositions but they are usually contained in the Spanish verb: to go *up* 'subir'; to sit *down* 'sentarse' etc.

4. *Adverbs*

Adverbs can be formed from most adjectives by taking the feminine form and adding '-mente': quick-ly rápida-mente; easi-ly fácil-mente. Spanish often uses idiomatic constructions, such as 'por lo general' (generally).

5. *Pronouns*: yo, te, le, sí etc.

5.1 Subject pronouns are not normally used in Spanish except for emphasis since the verb form tells you who is doing the action: hablo *I* speak; *él* lo tiene, *yo* no *he* has it, not *me*.

5.2 Pronoun table

	SUBJECT	REFLEX.	INDIRECT OBJECT	OBJECT	PREPOSITIONAL
I	yo	me	me	me	para mí/conmigo
you	tu	te	te	te	para ti/contigo
he	él	se	le (se)	le, lo	para él
she	ella	se	le (se)	le, la	para ella
it	(ello)	se		lo, la	para (ello)
you	usted	se	le (se)	le	para usted
we	nosotros/as	nos	nos	nos	para nosotros/as
you	vosotros/as	os	os	os	para vosotros/as
they	ellos	se	les (se)	les, los	para ellos
they	ellas	se	les (se)	les, las	para ellas

III. Spanish verb conjugations

1. The table of irregular verbs on p. 400 is self-explanatory. Unless stated otherwise, if one form only is given it is the first person singular; if two forms are given, they are the third person singular and plural; if four forms are shown, they are the first, second and third person singular plus the third person plural. Any forms not shown are regular and can be found by consulting the model verb tables below: table A for an infinitive ending in '-ar' and table B for infinitives ending in '-er' or '-ir'.

2. Do not forget to use the appropriate pronoun with reflexive verbs: *me* lavo, *te* lavaste, *se* había cortado.

3. 'Semi-irregular' verbs.
   Some verbs appear to be irregular but they are in fact predictable with reference to the following guidelines:

   3.1 Because a 'c' or a 'g' in Spanish is pronounced differently depending on the vowel which follows, these letters will change in certain cases in order to maintain the original root sound:
        Roots ending in 'c': sac-ar, saqu-é; venc-er, venz-o; zurc-ir, zurz-o
        Roots ending in 'g': pag-ar, pagu-é; proteg-er, protej-o; fing-ir, finj-o
        Roots ending in 'qu' and 'gu': delinqu-ir, delinc-o; averigu-ar, averigü-é; distingu-ir, disting-o
        Roots ending in 'z': cazar, cac-é

   3.2 A root ending in 'i' or 'u' has to be strengthened by an accent when it takes the stress:
        'i' – confiar: confío, confías, confía, confiamos, confiais, confían
        'u' – situar: sitúo, sitúas, sitúa, situamos, situais, sitúan
        (N.B. there are exceptions, e.g. cambiar: cambio, cambias, cambia, etc.)

3.3.1 When a root ends in 'ñ', 'll' and 'ch' it will 'absorb' any unstressed 'i' which follows: thus 'gruñ + iendo' becomes 'gruñendo', 'gruñ + ió' 'gruñó'.

3.3.2 The opposite happens when the root is a vowel itself: when an unstressed 'i' follows, it is strengthened into a 'y', e.g. 'o + iendo' becomes 'oyendo', 'argü + iendo' 'arguyendo'.

3.4 Spanish also has what are called 'root-changing' verbs, where the vowel within the root becomes a diphthong when stressed: e > ie; o > ue. The common verbs like 'acertar' and 'acordar' are already in the verb tables, but be prepared for other verbs to follow this model, e.g. fregar friego; doler duele.

4. The 'compound tenses' are formed as follows:
Indicative:
(a) 'perfect': *present* of 'haber' + *past participle* (he hablado/comido)
(b) 'pluperfect': *imperfect* of 'haber' + *past participle* (había hablado/comido)
(c) 'future perfect': *future* of 'haber' + *past participle* (habré hablado/comido)
(d) 'conditional perfect': *conditional* of 'haber' + *past participle* (habría hablado/comido)

Subjunctive:
(a) 'perfect': *present subjunctive* of 'haber' + *past participle* (haya hablado/comido)
(b) 'pluperfect': *imperfect subjunctive* of 'haber' + *past participle* (hubiera/hubiese hablado)

5. The passive is formed by using the verb 'ser' + *past participle*. The past participle agrees in number and gender with the subject: la televisión *fue* inventada en el año… television was invented in… (Note that Spanish often avoids the passive by using a reflexive construction: la televisión *se inventó* en el año…)

6. Irregular past participles not appearing in the verb tables are formed as follows:
abrir *abierto*; cubrir *cubierto*; escribir *escrito*; imprimir *impreso*; freír *frito*; romper *roto*.

7. Imperative forms·
The familiar imperative forms are found in the verb tables (tú, vosotros). The formal imperative (usted, ustedes) adopts the form of the subjunctive: hable (usted); hablen (ustedes).

A. A regular '-ar' verb: 'hablar'

PRESENT: Indicative		Subjunctive	
habl	o	habl	e
	as		es
	a		e
	amos		emos
	áis		éis
	an		en

IMPERFECT: Indicative		Subjunctive	
habl	aba	habl	ara/ase
	abas		aras/ases
	aba		ara/ase
	ábamos		áramos/ásemos
	ábais		arais/aseis
	aban		aran/asen

PRETERITE	
habl	é
	aste
	ó
	amos
	asteis
	aron

FUTURE		CONDITIONAL	
hablar	é	hablar	ía
	ás		ías
	á		ía
	emos		íamos
	éis		íais
	án		ían

IMPERATIVE: habla, hablad

PAST PARTICIPLE: hablado

GERUND: hablando

B. Regular '-er' and '-ir' verbs: 'comer' and 'partir'

PRESENT: Indicative		Subjunctive	
com/part	o es e emos/imos éis/is en	com/part	a as a amos áis an

IMPERFECT: Indicative		Subjunctive	
com/part	ía ías ía íamos íais ían	com/part	iera/iese ieras/ieses iera/iese iéramos/iésemos ierais/ieseis ieran/iesen

PRETERITE	
com/part	í iste ió imos isteis ieron

FUTURE		CONDITIONAL	
comer/partir	é ás á emos éis án	comer/partir	ía ías ía íamos íais ían

IMPERATIVE: come/parte, comed/partid

PAST PARTICIPLE: comido/partido

GERUND: comiendo/partiendo

IV. The sounds of Spanish

Learning to pronounce Spanish well is, as with all foreign languages, largely a matter of adopting different 'speech habits' from those used in speaking English.

A 'foreign accent' results from using the sounds of one's own language to approximate the sounds of the foreign language. This is particularly tempting when the same letter or letters represent similar sounds in each language. For instance the letter 'i' is used in both Spanish and English, but to represent slightly different sounds in each, and many Spanish speakers are unable to pronounce it in the English manner. It is possible that many do not even realise that the English speaker uses a different sound from the Spanish – hence the typical Spanish pronunciation of 'it is' which to the English speaker sounds as if it were written 'eet eess'.

These are the main ways in which Spanish 'speech habits' differ from the English:

1. *Activity of the lips, tongue etc.*

When you first hear (or even just see) a Spaniard talking, your immediate impression will probably be one of great activity and speed. However the truth is that he/she is not necessarily talking any quicker, but merely using all the 'instruments' of speech (lips, tongue, cheeks, jaw, throat, etc.) to their fullest extent.

English-speakers, on the other hand, tend to be 'lazy' in the use of these instruments – lip position, especially, is fairly unimportant and as a result vowel sounds tend to merge together, whereas in Spanish the activity of the lips etc. means that every vowel sound is clearly distinct from every other.

2. *Fewer diphthongs*

A diphthong is a glide between two vowel sounds in the same syllable. In English there are few 'pure' vowel sounds and a great many diphthongs instead. Although speakers of English may think they produce one vowel sound in the word 'day', in fact they use a diphthong, which in this instance is a glide between the vowels [e] and [ɪ] : [deɪ]. In Spanish the tension maintained in the lips, tongue and the mouth in general prevents diphthongs occurring, as the vowel sound is kept constant throughout. Hence the Spanish word corresponding to the above example, 'de', is pronounced with no final [ɪ] sound, but is phonetically represented thus: [de]. Spanish does have diphthongs, of course, but they are always a combination of two 'pure' vowel sounds.

3. *Consonants*

Consonants in Spanish are always given their full value (except in regional dialects). In English, consonants are often pronounced with a degree of laxness that can result in their becoming 'muted' but not entirely silent. In a relaxed pronunciation of a word such as 'hat', the 't' is often scarcely heard, or may even be replaced by a 'glottal stop' (a sort of 'stutter' in the throat, as in Cockney: bottle = bo'le). Hence a Spaniard sounds unmistakeably foreign to an English speaker if he 'over'-pronounces the 't' and 'l' in 'bottle' as if it were Spanish.

4. *Stress*

In English, each word has its own particular stress pattern – for instance, the two different stress patterns for the word 'escort' produces two different words, one a noun and one a verb (*an escort bureau*; *may I escort you*). This does not happen in Spanish because each word can only be stressed in one way, the rules for which are as follows:

(a) When a word ends in a *vowel* or in 'n' or 's', the *next to last* syllable is stressed: pat*a*ta, pat*a*tas, com*e*dia, c*o*me, c*o*men.

(b) When a word ends in a consonant *other* than 'n' or 's', the stress falls on the last syllable: par*e*d, habl*a*r, aud*a*z.

(c) Whenever these rules (a,b) are not applied, then an acute accent appears over the stressed vowel: hablar*á*, comi*ó*, geograf*í*a.

(d) Normally the same syllable is stressed in the plural as in the singular, so that accents may appear or disappear accordingly: c*a*rmen, c*á*rmenes; ingl*é*s, ingl*e*ses. There are two exceptions to this rule: car*á*cter, caract*e*res; r*é*gimen, reg*í*menes.

428

Pronunciation of the sounds of Spanish

I. Vowel

symbol	as in	hints on pronunciation
[a]	*a*mo	not as long as 'a' in English f*a*r
[æ]	am*a*nte	in a closed syllable (ending in a consonant) the 'a' is short, as in English 'bat'
[e]	c*e*lo	like 'e' in the 'they' (or even 'a' in 'pay') but without the 'y' sound
[ɛ]	g*e*nte	in a closed syllable the 'e' is short, as in English 'p*e*t'
[i]	m*i*na	as in English 'm*ea*n', 'mach*i*ne', but without slight 'y' sound
[o]	l*o*c*o*	as in English 'l*o*cal', but without slight 'w' sound
[ɔ]	c*o*ntr*o*l	in a closed syllable the 'o' is short as in English 'c*o*t'
[u]	m*u*la	as in English 'r*u*le', 'r*u*e', but without slight 'w' sound. It is silent after 'q' and in the groups 'gue', 'gui' unless marked with a diaeresis (argüir, averigüe).

II. Diphthongs

[ai]	b*ai*le, car*ay*	like the 'i' in English 'r*i*de'
[au]	fr*au*de	like the 'ou' in English 'shout'
[ei]	p*ei*ne, r*ey*	like the 'ey' in English 'gr*ey*'
[eu]	d*eu*da	like 'ay' as in 'bay' plus 'oo' as in 'too', in rapid succession
[oi]	*oi*go, h*oy*	like the 'oy' in English 't*oy*'

III. Semiconsonants

[j]	b*i*en, *y*ugo	both '*i*' and '*y*' can stand for the sound 'y' in English 'yacht'
[w]	ag*u*a, f*u*era	the Spanish 'u' can also convey the 'w' sound of English

IV. Consonants

[b]	*v*oy, en*v*iar, *b*ola	'*b*' and '*v*' are pronounced the same in Spanish. Here at the beginning of a phrase, or after 'm' or 'n', they are pronounced like English 'b' in '*b*oy', em*b*er'
[ß]	hu*b*o, de *v*eras	in any other position they are pronounced like an English 'v' but with *both lips* and not lip and teeth together
[k]	*c*o*c*o, *c*al*c*ulo	'c' before 'a', 'o' or 'u' is pronounced as in English '*c*at'
[θ]	*c*ero, *c*inco	before 'e' or 'i' it is pronounced like 'th' in English '*th*ink'
[d]	*d*oy, bal*d*e	at the beginning of a phrase, or after 'l' or 'n', 'd' is pronounced as in English
[ð]	mo*d*o, Ma*d*ri(*d*)	in any other position it is pronounced something like the 'th' in English '*th*e'; at the end of words it almost disappears
[g]	*g*ano, pon*g*o	'g' before 'a', 'o' or 'u' is pronounced as in English 'gap' if at the beginning of a phrase or after 'n'
[ɤ]	ha*g*a	'g' before 'a', 'o', 'u' but in median position and not after 'n' is pronounced more softly
[x]	*g*iro, *g*ente	before 'e' or 'i' it is pronounced as the Spanish 'j' below
[x]	*j*oven	'j' (and 'ge', 'gi') is similar to the 'ch' sound of Scottish 'lo*ch*' or Welsh 'ba*ch*'

[ʎ]	ca*ll*e, *ll*uvia	'll' is like the 'lli' in English 'mi*lli*on', but is being pronounced more and more like 'y' in '*ye*t'
[n]-[m]	e*n*viar	when followed by a 'v', an 'n' changes to 'm'
[ñ]	ca*ñ*a	something like the 'ni' in English 'o*ni*on
[k]	*qu*ien, *qu*ince	'q' is always followed by a silent 'u' and pronounced as 'k' in English '*k*ing'
[rr]	*r*ápido, co*rr*e	('r' is *always* pronounced in Spanish, unlike the often silent 'r' in English 'dance*r*'); after 'l', 'n' or 's', at the beginning of a phrase or when the 'r' is doubled, it is trilled something like a Scottish or Welsh 'r'
[s]	pa*s*a, ca*s*tillo	's' is usually pronounced as in English 'pa*ss*'
[z]	mi*s*mo, de*s*de	before 'b', 'd', 'g', 'l', 'm' or 'n' it sounds like the 's' in English 'ro*s*e'
[ks]	pró*x*imo	as in English 'pro*x*y'
[gs]	e*x*amen	like the 'gs' in 'pi*gs*kin
[s]	se*x*ta	before a consonant (and even in the other cases above) the 'x' is more and more being pronounced as an English 's' as in 'pe*s*t'
[i]	*y*	by itself the 'y' is pronounced as the Spanish 'i'
[θ]	*z*ona, lu*z*	like the 'th' in English '*th*ink' (but in many regions it will be pronounced as an 's')

Note that the 'h' is always silent in Spanish: 'haya'[ˈaja], 'ahora' [aˈɔra]

From Spelling to Sounds

1. Spanish is an *almost* 'phonetic' language, by which we mean that every vowel and consonant has a fixed sound value. As you will have seen from the previous list, this value changes for only a few letters, and even

then in only one alternative position: pon*go*; *c*acé etc. Some letters also duplicate the same sound (i/y; b/v) or are not even pronounced (h).

If you look at the language in this manner, you will soon appreciate how simple it is to pronounce. There are only two important factors, therefore, which hinder this: first, the temptation (as with any foreign language) to see the language as if it were written in English, e.g. Spanish 'lee' [lee] might be seen as English 'lee' [liː]; and secondly, the related problem of knowing when two or more vowels *do* form a diphthong or are pronounced separately.

1.2.1 The solution to the first is always to look upon Spanish vowels as clearly distinct, individual sounds which are *always* pronounced.

1.2.2 The second is solved according to the following rules:

(a) to start with, vowels are either *weak* or *strong*: 'i' and 'u' are weak, whereas 'a', 'e' and 'o' are strong.

(b) a *weak* and *strong* combination forms a diphthong in which the stress falls on the *strong* vowel: ba*i*le, vu*e*stro, si*e*rra, p*e*ine, p*a*usa.

(c) a *weak* and *weak* combination forms a diphthong and the stress falls on the *second* vowel: fu*i*, ru*i*do, vi*u*da.

(d) a *strong* and *strong* combination remains as two separate vowels, and stress follows the normal rules (4a,b): ca-*e*r; cre-*e*r; cr*e*-e; c*a*-os.

(e) any word which is to be pronounced otherwise will carry an accent on the stressed vowel: ca*í*do, r*í*o, cre*í*, ba*ú*l.

2. The letters of the Spanish alphabet

When a Spaniard wishes to spell out a word he pronounces the letters like this:

a [a]	b [be]	c [θe]	ch [tʃe]	d [de]	e [e]
f [efe]	g [xe]	h [atʃe]	i [i]	j [xota]	k [ka]
l [ele]	ll [eʎe]	m [eme]	n [ene]	o [o]	p [pe]
q [ku]	r [ere]	rr [erre]	s [ese]	t [te]	u [u]
v [uße]	x [ekis]	y [iɣrjeɣa]	z [θeta]		

The letters are feminine and you therefore talk of 'una a' or 'la a'. 'Miguel se escribe con una *m* mayúscula'.

3. It is virtually impossible for a Spaniard to pronounce an 's' at the beginning of a word without an 'e' in front: this explains why English loan-words which are established in the language already are spelled with an 'e' (*e*snob), or why you will hear new additions *pronounced* with an 'e' though not written with one (slip = 'eslip').

V. The time

what is the time?   ¿qué hora es?

it's...   es... (*midnight, noon, 1 o'clock*), son... (*other times*)

00.00	*es* medianoche; *son* las doce (de la noche)
01.00	*es* la una (de la noche)
01.10	la una y diez
01.15	la una y cuarto
	la una y quince
01.30	la una y media
01.45	*son* las dos menos quarto
01.50	las dos menos diez
	la una cincuenta
02.00	*son* las dos
12.00	mediodía
	las doce (de la tarde)
13.00	la una
	las trece (horas)
18.00	las seis
	las dieciocho
22.30	las diez y media
	las veintidós horas y media

at what time?   ¿a qué hora?

at one   a la una

at 2.15   a las dos y cuarto

just after 3.00   a las tres y pico

about 4.30   hacia las cuatro y media

from 6.00 to 8.00   de seis a ocho

it's nearly 9.00   son casi las nueve

at 4.00 sharp   a las cuatro en punto

Dates and numbers

1. The date

what is the date today? ¿qué día es hoy?

the first of May   el primero de mayo

the 2nd of March   el dos de marzo (*cardinals are used from 2nd to 31st*)

today is the 14th   hoy es catorce; estamos a catorce

on the 10th of June   el diez de junio

on Tuesday   el martes

on Tuesdays   los martes

from the 1st to the 3rd desde el día uno hasta el día tres

Letter headings: dates on Spanish letters are usually written thus:

22nd October, 1949   22 de octubre de 1949

Years: **1981**   mil novecientos ochenta y uno

       2000 B.C.   2000 a. de J.C. (= antes de Jesucristo)

       70 A.D.   70 d. de J.C. (= después de Jesucristo)

       in the 12th century en el siglo doce

       in the 1940s   durante los años cuarenta

2. Notes on numbers

Cardinals

(a) 'uno' (+ 'veintiuno' etc.) agrees in gender (but not number) with its noun: treinta y un*a* person*as*; the masculine form is shortened to 'un' unless it stands alone: veinti*un* caballos, veinti*uno*

(b) 'cien' is the commonest form; 'ciento' is mainly used for the compound numbers (except when it multiplies: 'cien mil')

434

(c) large numbers are divided by a full stop in Spanish:
3.461.203 = English 3,461,203

Ordinals

(a) they are adjectives and therefore agree in number and gender.

(b) 'primero' and 'tercero' lose the final 'o' in front of masculine nouns: 'el primer año', 'en tercer lugar'.

(c) they are not commonly used above 21, except for 100th and 1,000th.

(d) in the case of centuries and titles, the ordinals are only used up to 9th, and from then on the cardinals are used: 'en el siglo *quinto*' BUT 'en el siglo *diecinueve*'; 'Alfonso *primero*' BUT 'Alfonso *doce*'.

(e) the ordinals are also used for fractions:
a third   un tercio
a quarter of a kilo   un cuarto de kilo

(f) Spanish abbreviations for 1st, 2nd, 3rd etc. depend on gender and are written thus:
1st   1º (masculine), 1ª (feminine)
4th   4º, 4ª etc.

Decimals
Where English uses a point, Spanish uses a comma:

101.7   101,7 (ciento uno coma siete)
0.031   0,031 (cero coma cero tres uno)

Calculations
4 + 7 = 11   cuatro *más* siete *son* once
12 − 3 = 9   doce *menos* tres *resta* nueve
3 × 7 = 21   tres *por* siete *son* veintiuno
16 ÷ 4 = 4   dieciséis *divido por* cuatro *es* cuatro

Telephone numbers
Spaniards normally read telephone numbers by dividing them into two-figure numbers:

019567   01-95-67 (cero uno, noventa y cinco, sesenta y siete)

Numbers

1	uno(un, una)*	1st	primero(primer, primera)*
2	dos	2nd	segundo(a)
3	tres	3rd	tercero(tercer, tercera)*
4	cuatro	4th	cuarto(a)
5	cinco	5th	quinto(a)
6	seis	6th	sexto(a)
7	siete	7th	séptimo(a)
8	ocho	8th	octavo(a)
9	nueve	9th	noveno(a); nono(a)
10	diez	10th	décimo(a)
11	once	11th	undécimo(a)
12	doce	12th	duodécimo(a)
13	trece	13th	decimotercero(a)***
14	catorce	14th	decimocuarto(a)
15	quince	15th	decimoquinto(a)
16	dieciséis	16th	decimosexto(a)
17	diecisiete	17th	decimoséptimo(a)
18	dieciocho	18th	decimoctavo(a)
19	diecinueve	19th	decimonono(a)
20	veinte	20th	vigésimo(a)
21	veintiuno(-ún, -una)*	21st	vigésimo primero(a)**
22	veintidós	22nd	vigésimo segundo(a)
30	treinta	30th	trigésimo(a)
31	treinta y uno(un, una)*	31st	trigésimo primero(a)**
32	treinta y dos	32nd	trigésimo segundo(a)
40	cuarenta	40th	cuadragésimo(a)
50	cincuenta	50th	quincuagésimo(a)
60	sesenta	60th	sexagésimo(a)
70	setenta	70th	septuagésimo(a)
80	ochenta	80th	octogésimo(a)
90	noventa	90th	nonogésimo(a)
100	cien(ciento)*	100th	centésimo(a)
101	ciento uno(un, una)*		
102	ciento dos	5 1/2	cinco y medio
156	ciento cincuenta y seis	0.31	cero coma tres uno (0,31)
200	doscientos(as)	10%	diez por ciento
500	quinientos(as)		
1,000	mil	1000th	milésimo(a)
1,003	mil tres		
2,000	dos mil	2^2	dos al cuadrado
1,000,000	un millón	2^4	dos a la cuarta potencia

*, **, ***: *see notes on pages 434, 435*